# THE LAYMAN'S BIBLE STUDY NOTEBOOK

*An Inductive Bible Study*

Irving Jensen

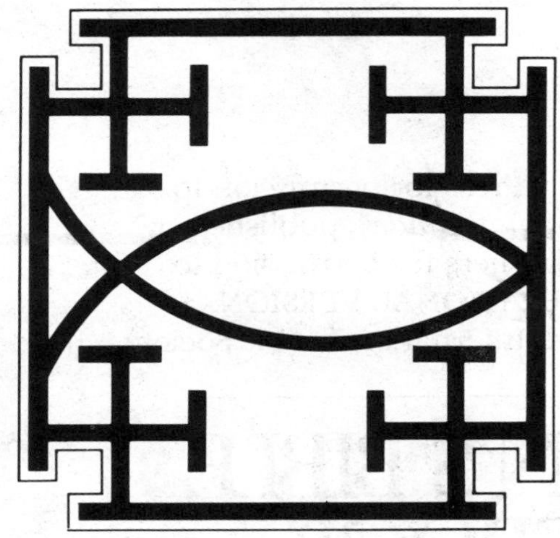

Eugene, Oregon 97402

Acknowledgments:

This author wishes to thank Moody Press for permission to quote from his series of *Bible Self-Study Guides*, published by Moody Press; Zondervan Bible Publishers for permission to use the HOLY BIBLE: NEW INTERNATIONAL VERSION.


# THE LAYMAN'S BIBLE STUDY NOTEBOOK


Eugene, Oregon 97402
Library of Congress Catalog Card Number: 77-93518
ISBN # 0-89081-116-4



Printed in the United States of America.

# CONTENTS

# PREFACE

The Bible will always be the Book of books, simply because its author, God, wrote no other book like it. It is God's communication to man recorded and transmitted through human instruments. It reveals eternal truths about life and death, about the way to God and the walk with God. Over the centuries men have tried to destroy this Bible, deny its truth or twist its meaning, but it remains invincible. And as long as there are souls seeking the Truth, the Bible will be an open book, waiting to transform lives.

## The Bible Is for Everyone

The Bible was written not just for certain groups of people—it was written for *Everyone.* Laymen need it, and the clergy need it. It is for young and old, rich and poor, educated and uneducated. This is because every soul needs the salvation of God which is the theme of the Bible, and all His saved ones need the Bible's instruction for their daily walk. "The holy Scriptures, which are able to make you wise for salvation through faith in Christ Jesus" (2 Timothy 3:15, *New International Version*). "All scripture is given by inspiration of God, and is profitable for doctrine, for reproof, for correction, for instruction in righteousness: that the man of God may be perfect, thoroughly furnished unto all good works" (2 Timothy 3:16-17, *King James Version*). No one can afford to evade or neglect the voice of God as recorded in His Book.

## Bible Study Can be Enjoyable and Exciting

The reading and study of the New Testament can be your most fruitful daily exercise. The purpose of this *Layman's Bible Study Notebook* is to help you experience such a joy. The suggestions given below show you how to use this notebook.

1. Study the Bible the Way God Wrote It

Someone has aptly said, "Study the Bible the way God wrote it: book by book." From this it follows that we should study each individual *book* of the Bible thought by thought, for this is how God wrote it. Actually the original autographs of the books of the Bible did not visibly show any thought pattern through the mechanics of chapter, paragraph or verse divisions. In fact, there was not even a space between words and sentences. But we know from studying the Bible book that the human authors did write with an organized pattern in mind, thought by thought, from beginning to end.

The format of published Bibles today tries to show this progression by providing chapter and verse divisions (and sometimes paragraph divisions). However, for practical Bible study with workable units in mind, the chapter-division format is not consistently the best, partly because of misplaced divisions and also because many chapter units are too long. A better study format breaks down the Bible book into shorter workable segments (thought units), which are then divided into paragraphs. This is how *The Layman's Bible Study Notebook* is organized.

2. Make Your Bible Study Workable and Practical

The purpose of *The Layman's Bible Study Notebook* is to make Bible study both workable and practical. You will find the study units are workable lengths and are not so long as to be cumbersome. You should determine what *pace* of study is best for you. If you are interested in studying the New Testament in the span of one year, you could do this by completing ten units each week.

Always keep application in mind. Recall the classic passage of the Scripture's purpose, 2 Timothy 3:16-17 (quoted earlier).

The stages of Bible study are listed in order below and are known as the inductive approach to Bible study:

1. OBSERVATION—What does the text say?
2. INTERPRETATION—What does the text mean?
3. APPLICATION—How does this apply to me, and to others?

3. Study the Bible Text Yourself

You can never spend too much time examining the Bible text yourself. As you do, keep doing two things:

1. *looking* at the text
2. *recording* things you see (suggestions on recording are given below). This is very helpful, because "the pencil is one of the best eyes." One of the main purposes of *The Layman's Bible Study Notebook* is to encourage you to mark the Bible text and make various notations in the marginal spaces.

One of the many good features of *group* Bible study is

that it encourages each member of the group to study the Bible text himself and *then* share with other members what he has found.

## Features of The Layman's Bible Study Notebook

1. *Organized segment by segment.* The New Testament is organized and printed so that your study of the text is always focused on *one complete unit of thought.* Each pair of pages presents one such unit, called a segment. There are 500 segments in this notebook.

   The segment is a group of paragraphs. It varies in length, from page to page, depending on how much the Bible author wrote on that particular theme (thought unit).
2. *Paragraph divisions.* Each segment (thought unit) is divided into paragraphs (shorter thought units). The paragraph units show up very clearly, to aid in surveying the general theme of each paragraph. Draw a horizontal line at each •.
3. *One-column format.* This format enhances analysis of words and phrases, for the eye can concentrate more easily on the text of the one column.
4. *Two parallel versions.* Each study unit is represented by two parallel versions: *King James* on the right page, and *The New International Version* on the left page.

   The *King James Version* is especially helpful for *analyzing* the Bible text, since it makes you conscious of the strength of words and phrases. On this page, your study will concentrate on OBSERVATION.

   *The New International Version* is very useful to clarify obscure readings of the *King James Version* and retains the accuracy of the Bible text. It also emphasizes things to be emphasized, and interprets difficult passages. Your study on this page will concentrate on INTERPRETATION and APPLICATION.
5. *Study questions.* Questions and suggestions for study appear on both pages of each study unit. On the right page specific questions concern each of the paragraphs. They are not intended to be exhaustive, but to direct your eyes to some of the most important parts of the paragraphs.

   On the left page you are asked to record lists of truths (such as doctrines) taught by the segment, and lists of practical applications which can be made of the passage. If you are studying the Bible with a group you will find the discussion of this part of your study to be very interesting.

   This workbook can supplement other study aids used in Sunday School classes and similar group sessions.
6. Margins enclose the Bible text. Use these to record such things as isolated observations or extended outlines which you arrive at in the course of your study.
7. *Segment outlines.* A simple outline of the segment, paragraph by paragraph, appears in the margin to the left of the King James text. A two-point outline is usually printed to the right of the text, comparing the beginning and end of a segment (e.g. A TROUBLED KING; JOYFUL WISE MEN, page 13). Try looking for other comparisons, and record these in the blank spaces of the margin.

   When an Old Testament passage is quoted by the text of the segment, the location of the Old Testament passage is given in the right-hand margin.
8. *Topical headings.* A main subject of each study unit is printed at the top of the King James text (e.g. VISITORS FROM THE EAST, page 13). You may want to compare your own studies with these headings.

   A key sentence appears at the top of *The New International Version* page, suggesting an important subject in the text (e.g. "When they saw the star, they were overjoyed." Matthew 2:10).
9. *Introduction to each book.* An introduction to each of the 27 New Testament books appears at the beginning of each book. Included here are such things as background, author, date written, and purpose of the New Testament book. An outline of the book follows the introduction.

## How to Use The Layman's Bible Study Notebook

There are various ways *The Layman's Bible Study Notebook* may be used. Below is a suggested pattern of study which will use all the benefits of the notebook.

Remember that the pencil is one of the best eyes, so make it a regular habit to jot down things you see in the Bible text. (Note: Use a pencil, not a pen or marker, for all of your recording on the pages of this notebook.)

*RIGHT PAGE*-Begin your studies on the right page, since the first stage of OBSERVATION is emphasized here.

1. Read the title at the top of the page.
2. Keep in mind where the segment is located in

the structure of the whole New Testament book. To learn this, check with the outline of the book.

3. Observe how many paragraphs the segment is divided into. (The column of the Bible text shows this clearly.) Always be paragraph-conscious while you are studying the Bible text.
4. Read the segment outline (in the left-hand margin).
5. Read the Bible text, paragraph by paragraph. Underline key words and phrases of the Bible text as you read. In fact, always keep a pencil in your hand, and make notations on the page. You can never overdo this learning activity.
6. Relate the segment outline to the text as you read. The blank spaces below each point of the segment outline may be used for recording observations which you make of the paragraph. For example, on the study unit of Matthew 1:1-25 (page 11): Under point 2, ANGEL'S WORD, you may want to list the things the angel said.
7. Now work with the questions to the right of the segment outline. Record answers to all the questions. Refer to *The New International Version* text (opposite page) for help in understanding the *King James* reading.
8. Don't hesitate to re-read the paragraphs during the course of your study. You can never read the Bible text too much.

*LEFT PAGE* - Now concentrate on the left page, where *The New International Version* appears.

1. Read the paraphrase slowly, without relating it to the *King James* text which you have been studying thus far.
2. Then read *The New International Version* text a second time, this time comparing the paraphrase lines with the parallel *King James* text. Underline words and phrases which strike you as significant or especially interesting.
3. Spend the remainder of your time answering questions and compiling the lists of Bible truths and applications which are called for in the designated area of this page. For each subject heading shown (e.g. DEMONISM, page 172) you will have to move through the text of the whole segment (both versions), recording truths as they come to you. For example, in the passage of Mark 9:14-32 under DEMONISM you might include truths like these:
   a. Demons sometimes work alone (Mark 9:17).
   b. Demons violently affect the subject (Mark 9:18).
   Keep in mind that truths are taught in scripture in different ways, such as the following:
   a. directly (e.g. Casting out a demon comes through prayer and fasting. Mark 9:29)
   b. indirectly (e.g. The disciples needed more faith. Mark 9:28-29)
   c. by types or symbols (e.g. "lifted him up" illustrates spiritual lifting up. Mark 9:27)
   d. by implication (e.g. Jesus is very compassionate. Mark 9:25)
   e. by illustration (e.g. Jesus is omnipotent. Mark 9:26)
   f. by figure of speech (e.g. Evil spirits can be forced to leave a person—learned from "drive out" Mark 9:18).
4. When recording applications, use wording that is simple and direct. Example:
   (1) I should exercise more faith in my daily life.
   (2) I should be compassionate, as Jesus was.
5. When you have completed the activities called for, review all the work you have done with the study unit before moving to the next passage.

Don't think that you have seen all there is to see in the Bible passage you have just completed. Return to the study unit at a later time to discover more truths. Keep recording new studies in your notebook, which will become a valuable, permanent record of the hours spent in your personal Bible study.

## Using The Layman's Bible Study Notebook for Devotions

Since each page of *The Layman's Bible Study Notebook* contains one segment of practical length, daily devotions can follow the simple pattern of one page per day (that is, reading either *The New International Version* or the *King James Version* or including both in the reading) or one segment per day.

Bible reading and study is a key to fulfilling the command to "grow in the grace and knowledge of our Lord and Savior Jesus Christ" (2 Peter 3:18, *NIV*). Beginners in the faith, like newborn babes, should "grow up in (their) salvation," and they should "like newborn babies, crave pure spiritual milk" (1 Peter 2:2, *NIV*). Then as they grow and mature spiritually, they discover new and deeper truths in the Book, described by the writer of Hebrews as "solid food" (Hebrews 5:12-14).

May you experience this daily spiritual growth which comes by studying God's precious Word.

Irving L. Jensen

## About The Author

Irving Jensen is professor of Bible and Chairman of the Bible Department at Bryan College, Dayton, Tennessee. He has been a college Bible Teacher for 26 years and is the author of 50 Bible study books, including *Bible Self-Study Guides* (Moody Press). Mr. Jensen's main objective in teaching and writing is to inspire and guide laymen in independent, inductive Bible study.

Irving Jensen holds degrees from: Wagner College (B.A.), The Biblical Seminary in New York (S.T.B.), Northwestern Theological Seminary (Th.D.), and Massachusetts Institute of Technology (Diploma in Meteorology). He is a member of the Evangelical Theological Society and the Ministerial Association of Evangelical Free Church of America.

Irving and his wife, Charlotte, have three children Donna, Karen and Robert.

Recommended books related to the purposes of this workbook:

Irving L. Jensen, *Independent Bible Study*. Chicago: Moody Press, 1963. Gives help on observing and recording stages of Bible study.

———, *Jensen Bible Study Charts*, revised edition. Chicago: Moody Press, 1981. Includes a complete survey chart of all 27 New Testament books, with overhead transparencies for teachers. Valuable for checking the context of a segment being analyzed.

———, *Jensen's Survey of the New Testament*, Chicago: Moody Press, 1981.

# MATTHEW

## AUTHORSHIP

Tradition is unanimous in ascribing the writing of this gospel to Matthew, son of Alphaeus, whose Jewish name was Levi. Matthew was the tax collector whom Jesus called to be His disciple (Matthew 9:9-13).

## DATE

Matthew wrote his account of the gospel before the destruction of Jerusalem (A.D. 70). If this was the first of the four gospels to be written, the date was in the 50's (e.g. A.D. 58). If not it was in the 60's.

## PURPOSE AND THEME

Matthew's reporting of the gospel is the historical connecting link between the Old and New Testaments. It is the gospel of fulfillment—the fulfillment of the Old Testament prophecies about the Messiah of the Jew.

The book was written for the immediate audience of Jews. But it is not exclusively oriented to Israel. Throughout the account Jesus' ministry is related to all the people of the world, such as in the Great Commission of 28:19-20, and in Jesus' identification of Himself as the Son of man (e.g. 16:13).

## MATTHEW: Jesus and His Promised Kingdom

| | |
|---|---|
| PRESENTATION | 1:1-4:11 |
| Birth and Infancy Narratives | 1:1-2:23 |
| Preparation of the King | 3:1-4:11 |
| PROCLAMATION | 4:12-16:20 |
| First Ministries | 4:12-25 |
| Discourse: Sermon on the Mount | 5:1-7:29 |
| Power of the King | 8:1-9:34 |
| Discourse: Charge of the Twelve | 9:35-11:1 |
| Rejection of the King | 11:2-12:50 |
| Discourse: Parables | 13:1-53 |
| Mission of the King | 13:54-16:20 |
| PASSION | 16:21-28:20 |
| Death Foretold | 16:21-17:27 |
| Discourse: Relationships | 18:1-19:1a |
| Final Ministries of the King | 19:1b-23:39 |
| Discourse: Second Coming | 24:1-25:46 |
| Death and Resurrection of the King | 26:1-28:20 |

# MATTHEW

NEW INTERNATIONAL VERSION

What reasons would there be for a gospel writer to record the names of Jesus' ancestors?

Rahab (v.5) was a harlot, according to Hebrews 11:31. David was a king (v.6), but he committed sins of murder and adultery. Both were ancestors of Jesus. What does this teach you?

What does the name "Jesus" mean (v.21)?

How does the name "Immanuel" relate to the trust of salvation taught by the name "Jesus"?

What spiritual lessons does this passage teach you?

1 A record of the genealogy of Jesus
Christ the son of David, the son of
Abraham:

[2]Abraham was the father of Isaac,
Isaac the father of Jacob,
Jacob the father of Judah and his brothers,
[3]Judah the father of Perez and Zerah, whose mother was Tamar,
Perez the father of Hezron,
Hezron the father of Ram,
[4]Ram the father of Amminadab,
Amminadab the father of Nahshon,
Nahshon the father of Salmon,
[5]Salmon the father of Boaz, whose mother was Rahab,
Boaz the father of Obed, whose mother was Ruth,
Obed the father of Jesse,
[6]and Jesse the father of King David.

David was the father of Solomon, whose mother had been Uriah's wife,
[7]Solomon the father of Rehoboam,
Rehoboam the father of Abijah,
Abijah the father of Asa,
[8]Asa the father of Jehoshaphat,
Jehoshaphat the father of Joram,
Joram the father of Uzziah,
[9]Uzziah the father of Jotham,
Jotham the father of Ahaz,
Ahaz the father of Hezekiah,
[10]Hezekiah the father of Manasseh,
Manasseh the father of Amon,
Amon the father of Josiah,
[11]and Josiah the father of Jeconiah[a] and his brothers at the time of the exile to Babylon.

[12]After the exile to Babylon:
Jeconiah was the father of Shealtiel,
Shealtiel the father of Zerubbabel,
[13]Zerubbabel the father of Abiud,
Abiud the father of Eliakim,
Eliakim the father of Azor,
[14]Azor the father of Zadok,
Zadok the father of Akim,
Akim the father of Eliud,
[15]Eliud the father of Eleazar,
Eleazar the father of Matthan,
Matthan the father of Jacob,
[16]and Jacob the father of Joseph, the husband of Mary, of whom was born Jesus, who is called Christ.

[17]Thus there were fourteen generations
in all from Abraham to David, fourteen
from David to the exile to Babylon, and
fourteen from the exile to the Christ.[b] ●

*The Birth of Jesus Christ*

[18]This is how the birth of Jesus Christ
came about. His mother Mary was pledged
to be married to Joseph, but before they
came together, she was found to be with
child through the Holy Spirit. [19]Because
Joseph her husband was a righteous man
and did not want to expose her to public
disgrace, he had in mind to divorce her
quietly. ●

[20]But after he had considered this, an
angel of the Lord appeared to him in a
dream and said, "Joseph son of David, do
not be afraid to take Mary home as your
wife, because what is conceived in her is
from the Holy Spirit. [21]She will give birth
to a son, and you are to give him the name
Jesus,[c] because he will save his people
from their sins." ●

[22]All this took place to fulfill what the
Lord had said through the prophet: [23]"The
virgin will be with child and will give birth
to a son, and they will call him Immanuel"[d]—which means, "God with us." ●

[24]When Joseph woke up, he did what the
angel of the Lord had commanded him and
took Mary home as his wife. [25]But he had
no union with her until she gave birth to a
son. And he gave him the name Jesus. ●

[a] *11* That is, Jehoiachin; also in verse 12
[b] *17* Or *Messiah*. "The Christ" (Greek) and "the Messiah" (Hebrew) both mean "the Anointed One."
[c] *21* *Jesus* is the Greek form of *Joshua*, which means *the LORD saves*.
[d] *23* Isaiah 7:14

KING JAMES

# MATTHEW

**1. ANCESTORS**

**Abraham to David**

1 The book of the generation of Jesus
Christ, the son of David, the son of
Abraham.
2 Abraham begat Isaac; and Isaac be- ABRAHAM
gat Jacob; and Jacob begat Judah and his
brethren; 3 and Judah begat Pharez and
Zerah of Tamar; and Pharez begat Hezron; and Hezron begat Ram; 4 and Ram
begat Ammin'adab; and Ammin'adab begat Nahshon; and Nahshon begat Salmon; 5 and Salmon begat Boaz of Ra-
chab; and Boaz begat Obed of Ruth; and
Obed begat Jesse; 6 and Jesse begat
David the king.●

**David to Babylon**

And David the king begat Solomon of
her *that had been the wife* of Uri'ah; 7 and
Solomon begat Rehobo'am; and Reho-
bo'am begat Abi'jah; and Abi'jah begat
Asa; 8 and Asa begat Jehosh'aphat; and
Jehosh'aphat begat Jeho'ram; and Jeho'-
ram begat Uzzi'ah; 9 and Uzzi'ah begat
Jotham; and Jotham begat Ahaz; and
Ahaz begat Hezeki'ah; 10 and Hezeki'ah
begat Manas'seh; and Manas'seh begat
Amon; and Amon begat Josi'ah; 11 and
Josi'ah begat Jeconi'ah and his brethren,
about the time they were carried away to
Babylon.●

**Babylon to Christ**

12 And after they were brought to
Babylon, Jeconi'ah begat She-al'ti-el; and
She-al'ti-el begat Zerub'babel; 13 and Zerub'babel begat Abi'ud; and Abi'ud begat
Eli'akim; and Eli'akim begat Azor;
14 and Azor begat Zadok; and Zadok
begat Achim; and Achim begat Eli'ud;
15 and Eli'ud begat Ele-a'zar; and Ele-
a'zar begat Matthan; and Matthan begat
Jacob; 16 and Jacob begat Joseph the
husband of Mary, of whom was born
Jesus, who is called Christ.●

**summary**

17 So all the generations from Abraham
to David *are* fourteen generations; and
from David until the carrying away into
Babylon *are* fourteen generations; and
from the carrying away into Babylon unto
Christ *are* fourteen generations.●

**2. ANGEL'S WORD**

18 Now the birth of Jesus Christ was on
this wise: When as his mother Mary was
espoused to Joseph, before they came together, she was found with child of the
Holy Ghost. 19 Then Joseph her husband, being a just *man*, and not willing to
make her a public example, was minded
to put her away privily. 20 But while he
thought on these things, behold, the angel
of the Lord appeared unto him in a
dream, saying, Joseph, thou son of David,
fear not to take unto thee Mary thy wife:
for that which is conceived in her is of the
Holy Ghost. 21 And she shall bring forth
a son, and thou shalt call his name JESUS:
for he shall save his people from their

**3. PROPHECY**

sins.● 22 Now all this was done, that it Isa. 7:14
might be fulfilled which was spoken of the
Lord by the prophet, saying,
23 Behold, a virgin shall be with child,
and shall bring forth a son,
and they shall call his name Im-
man'u-el,
which being interpreted is, God with us.●

**4. FULFILLMENT**

24 Then Joseph being raised from sleep
did as the angel of the Lord had bidden
him, and took unto him his wife: 25 and
knew her not till she had brought forth
her firstborn son: and he called his name JESUS
JESUS.●

---

*1:1-17* How far back in ancestry does this list go?

Why would this be of special interest to a Jewish reader?

Deportation to Babylon (vv.11,12,17) was God's judgment for Israel's sin. Why does Matthew even emphasize this era?

*1:18-21* What part did each play in Jesus' birth:

Mary

Holy Spirit

Joseph

How was Joseph related to David?

By whom had Jesus been conceived?

*1:22* What name was to be given the virgin's child?

What did this name mean, literally?

*1:24-25* How do these verses emphasize Joseph's obedience?

NEW INTERNATIONAL VERSION

What part of this story illustrates the great truth of Matthew 7:8, "He that seeketh findeth"?

Compare the two intentions of worship: verse 2 and verse 8.

What spiritual lessons do you learn from

THE ASTROLOGERS (wise men)

JOSEPH AND MARY

What does the passage teach about:

DISHONESTY

JOY

DIRECTIONS FROM GOD

2 After Jesus was born in Bethlehem in
Judea, during the time of King Herod,
Magi[e] from the east came to Jerusalem
2 and asked, "Where is the one who has
been born king of the Jews? We saw his
star in the east[a] and have come to worship
him."
3 When King Herod heard this he was
disturbed, and all Jerusalem with him.
4 When he had called together all the
people's chief priests and teachers of the
law, he asked them where the Christ[b] was
to be born. 5 "In Bethlehem in Judea," they
replied, "for this is what the prophet has
written:

6 " 'But you, Bethlehem, in the land
of Judah,
are by no means least among the
rulers of Judah;
for out of you will come a ruler
who will be the shepherd of my
people Israel.'[c]" ●

7 Then Herod called the Magi secretly
and found out from them the exact time the
star had appeared. 8 He sent them to Bethlehem and said, "Go and make a careful
search for the child. As soon as you find
him, report to me, so that I too may go and
worship him."
9 After they had heard the king, they went
on their way, and the star they had seen in
the east[d] went ahead of them until it
stopped over the place where the child
was. 10 When they saw the star, they were
overjoyed. 11 On coming to the house, they
saw the child with his mother Mary, and
they bowed down and worshiped him.
Then they opened their treasures and
presented him with gifts of gold and of incense and of myrrh. 12 And having been
warned in a dream not to go back to Herod,
they returned to their country by another
route. ●

e1 Traditionally *Wise Men*
a2 Or *star when it rose*
b4 Or *Messiah*
c6 Micah 5:2
d9 Or *seen when it rose*

KING JAMES

1.SEEKING JESUS

**2** Now when Jesus was born in Bethlehem of Judea in the days of Herod the
king, behold, there came wise men from
the east to Jerusalem, 2 saying, Where is
he that is born King of the Jews? for we
have seen his star in the east, and are
come to worship him. 3 When Herod the
king had heard *these things*, he was
troubled, and all Jerusalem with him.
4 And when he had gathered all the chief
priests and scribes of the people together,
he demanded of them where Christ should
be born. 5 And they said unto him, In
Bethlehem of Judea: for thus it is written
by the prophet,
6 And thou Bethlehem, *in* the land of
Judah,
art not the least among the princes
of Judah:
for out of thee shall come a Governor,
that shall rule my people Israel.●

A TROUBLED KING

Mic. 5:2

2.FINDING HIM

7 Then Herod, when he had privily
called the wise men, inquired of them diligently what time the star appeared.
8 And he sent them to Bethlehem, and
said, Go and search diligently for the
young child; and when ye have found
*him*, bring me word again, that I may
come and worship him also. 9 When they
had heard the king, they departed; and,
lo, the star, which they saw in the east,
went before them, till it came and stood
over where the young child was. 10 When
they saw the star, they rejoiced with exceeding great joy. 11 And when they were
come into the house, they saw the young
child with Mary his mother, and fell
down, and worshipped him: and when
they had opened their treasures, they presented unto him gifts; gold, and frankincense, and myrrh. 12 And being warned
of God in a dream that they should not
return to Herod, they departed into their
own country another way.●

JOYFUL WISE MEN

NOTES

Compare Herod and the wise men, according to this segment.

*2:1-6* What do you learn here about a miracle star and a miracle book?

List the different parts of the prophecy of verse 6.

*2:7-12* Was Herod honest in stating his desire to worship Jesus (v.8)?

What led the wise men to the exact place where Jesus was?

How did the wise men worship Jesus?

NEW INTERNATIONAL VERSION

[13]When they had gone, an angel of the
Lord appeared to Joseph in a dream. "Get
up," he said, "take the child and his
mother and escape to Egypt. Stay there
until I tell you, for Herod is going to search
for the child to kill him."
[14]So he got up, took the child and his
mother during the night and left for Egypt,
[15]where he stayed until the death of Herod.
And so was fulfilled what the Lord had said
through the prophet: "Out of Egypt I
called my son."[e] ●
[16]When Herod realized that he had been
outwitted by the Magi, he was furious, and
he gave orders to kill all the boys in Bethlehem and its vicinity who were two years
old and under, in accordance with the time
he had learned from the Magi. [17]Then what
was said through the prophet Jeremiah was
fulfilled:

[18]"A voice is heard in Ramah,
weeping and great mourning,
Rachel weeping for her children
and refusing to be comforted,
because they are no more."[f] ●

[19]After Herod died, an angel of the Lord
appeared in a dream to Joseph in Egypt
[20]and said, "Get up, take the child and his
mother and go to the land of Israel, for
those who were trying to take the child's
life are dead."
[21]So he got up, took the child and his
mother and went to the land of Israel. [22]But
when he heard that Archelaus was reigning
in Judea in place of his father Herod, he
was afraid to go there. Having been
warned in a dream, he withdrew to the
district of Galilee, [23]and he went and lived
in a town called Nazareth. So was fulfilled
what was said through the prophets: "He
will be called a Nazarene." ●

*e15* Hosea 11:1 *f18* Jer. 31:15

What spiritual lessons do you learn here about:

PROVIDENCE OF GOD ______

WICKEDNESS OF MAN ______

OBEDIENCE TO GOD'S INSTRUCTIONS ______

Record other applications of the passage to everyday living.

## KING JAMES

EGYPT
13 And when they were departed, be- FLIGHT
hold, the angel of the Lord appeareth to
Joseph in a dream, saying, Arise, and take
the young child and his mother, and flee
into Egypt, and be thou there until I bring
thee word: for Herod will seek the young
child to destroy him. 14 When he arose,
he took the young child and his mother by
night, and departed into Egypt: 15 and
was there until the death of Herod: that
it might be fulfilled which was spoken of
the Lord by the prophet, saying, Out of Hos. 11:1
Egypt have I called my son.●

BETHLEHEM
16 Then Herod, when he saw that he
was mocked of the wise men, was exceeding wroth, and sent forth, and slew all the
children that were in Bethlehem, and in
all the coasts thereof, from two years old
and under, according to the time which
he had diligently inquired of the wise men.
17 Then was fulfilled that which was
spoken by Jeremiah the prophet, saying,
18 In Ramah was there a voice heard, Jer. 31:15
lamentation, and weeping, and great
mourning,
Rachel weeping *for* her children,
and would not be comforted,
because they are not.●

NAZARETH
19 But when Herod was dead, behold,
an angel of the Lord appeareth in a
dream to Joseph in Egypt, 20 saying,
Arise, and take the young child and his
mother, and go into the land of Israel: for
they are dead which sought the young
child's life. 21 And he arose, and took the
young child and his mother, and came
into the land of Israel. 22 But when he
heard that Archela'us did reign in Judea
in the room of his father Herod, he was
afraid to go thither: notwithstanding,
being warned of God in a dream, he
turned aside into the parts of Galilee:
23 and he came and dwelt in a city called
Nazareth: that it might be fulfilled Isa. 11:1
which was spoken by the prophets, He
shall be called a Nazarene.●

RESIDENCE

*2:13-15* What do you learn about Joseph here?

What did the angel prophesy in verse 13?

Where in the segment is the fulfillment of that prophecy reported?

*2:16-18* How is Herod described here?

Compare his heart with the hearts of the mothers (v.18).

*2:19-23* What are the three geographical areas of this paragraph?

How did God reveal His instructions to Joseph?

What was Jesus to be called in later life?

NEW INTERNATIONAL VERSION

What does this passage teach about:

REPENTANCE

SALVATION

RELIGIOUS HYPOCRISY

FAITH AND WORKS

GOD THE FATHER

JESUS THE SON

3 In those days John the Baptist came,
preaching in the Desert of Judea 2and
saying, "Repent, for the kingdom of
heaven is near." 3This is he who was
spoken of through the prophet Isaiah:

"A voice of one calling in the
desert,
'Prepare the way for the Lord,
make straight paths for him.' "[g]

4John's clothes were made of camel's
hair, and he had a leather belt around his
waist. His food was locusts and wild
honey. 5People went out to him from
Jerusalem and all Judea and the whole region of the Jordan. 6Confessing their sins,
they were baptized by him in the Jordan
River.●
7But when he saw many of the Pharisees
and Sadducees coming to where he was
baptizing, he said to them: "You brood of
vipers! Who warned you to flee from the
coming wrath? 8Produce fruit in keeping
with repentance. 9And do not think you
can say to yourselves, 'We have Abraham
as our father.' I tell you that out of these
stones God can raise up children for Abraham. 10The ax is already at the root of the
trees, and every tree that does not produce
good fruit will be cut down and thrown into
the fire.
11"I baptize you with[h] water for repentance. But after me will come one who is
more powerful than I, whose sandals I am
not fit to carry. He will baptize you with
the Holy Spirit and with fire. 12His win-
nowing fork is in his hand, and he will clear
his threshing floor, gathering the wheat
into his barn and burning up the chaff with
unquenchable fire."●
13Then Jesus came from Galilee to the
Jordan to be baptized by John. 14But John
tried to deter him, saying, "I need to be
baptized by you, and do you come to me?"
15Jesus replied, "Let it be so now; it is
proper for us to do this to fulfill all righteousness." Then John consented.
16As soon as Jesus was baptized, he went
up out of the water. At that moment
heaven was opened, and he saw the Spirit
of God descending like a dove and lighting
on him. 17And a voice from heaven said,
"This is my Son, whom I love; with him I
am well pleased."●

KING JAMES

1. JOHN THE BAPTIST CAME

3 In those days came John the Baptist,
preaching in the wilderness of Judea,
2 and saying, Repent ye: for the kingdom
of heaven is at hand. 3 For this is he
that was spoken of by the prophet Isaiah,
saying,

The voice of one crying in the wilderness,
Prepare ye the way of the Lord,
make his paths straight.

4 And the same John had his raiment of
camel's hair, and a leathern girdle about
his loins; and his meat was locusts and
wild honey. 5 Then went out to him
Jerusalem, and all Judea, and all the
region round about Jordan, 6 and were
baptized of him in Jordan, confessing
their sins.●

7 But when he saw many of the Pharisees and Sadducees come to his baptism,
he said unto them, O generation of vipers,[j]
who hath warned you to flee from the
wrath to come? 8 Bring forth therefore
fruits meet for repentance: 9 and think
not to say within yourselves, We have
Abraham to *our* father: for I say unto
you, that God is able of these stones to
raise up children unto Abraham. 10 And
now also the axe is laid unto the root of
the trees: therefore every tree which
bringeth not forth good fruit is hewn
down, and cast into the fire.

11 I indeed baptize you with water unto
repentance: but he that cometh after me
is mightier than I, whose shoes I am not
worthy to bear: he shall baptize you with
the Holy Ghost, and *with* fire: 12 whose
fan *is* in his hand, and he will thoroughly
purge his floor, and gather his wheat into
the garner; but he will burn up the chaff
with unquenchable fire.●

2. THEN JESUS ARRIVES

13 Then cometh Jesus from Galilee to
Jordan unto John, to be baptized of him.
14 But John forbade him, saying, I have
need to be baptized of thee, and comest
thou to me? 15 And Jesus answering said
unto him, Suffer *it to be so* now: for thus
it becometh us to fulfil all righteousness.
Then he suffered him. 16 And Jesus,
when he was baptized, went up straightway out of the water: and, lo, the heavens
were opened unto him, and he saw the
Spirit of God descending like a dove, and
lighting upon him: 17 and lo a voice from
heaven, saying, This is my beloved Son,
in whom I am well pleased.●

JOHN PREACHED

Isa. 40:3

FATHER COMMENDED

*3:1-6* What were the three strong points of John's sermons (v.2)?

What verse records that the multitudes heeded John's command to repent?

*3:7-12* What religious people were among the multitudes coming to John for baptism?

Why did John object to their coming for baptism?

How are John's and Jesus' baptizing ministries compared (v.11)?

*3:13-17* Baptism is a public testimony. Of what was Jesus testifying by His baptism?

NEW INTERNATIONAL VERSION

Many truths and spiritual applications may be made from this passage. Record your findings:

SATAN

TEMPTATION

SPIRITUAL FOOD

DIVINE HELP

TRUE RICHES

TRUE WORSHIP

WORD OF GOD

4 Then Jesus was led by the Spirit into
the desert to be tempted by the devil.
2After fasting forty days and forty nights,
he was hungry. 3The tempter came to him
and said, "If you are the Son of God, tell
these stones to become bread."
4Jesus answered, "It is written: 'Man
does not live on bread alone, but on every
word that comes from the mouth of
God.'[a]" ●
5Then the devil took him to the holy city
and had him stand on the highest point of
the temple. 6"If you are the Son of God,"
he said, "throw yourself down. For it is
written:

" 'He will command his angels
concerning you,
and they will lift you up in their
hands,
so that you will not strike your foot
against a stone.'[b]"

7Jesus answered him, "It is also written:
'Do not put the Lord your God to the
test.'[c]" ●
8Again, the devil took him to a very high
mountain and showed him all the kingdoms
of the world and their splendor. 9"All this
I will give you," he said, "if you will bow
down and worship me."
10Jesus said to him, "Away from me,
Satan! For it is written: 'Worship the Lord
your God, and serve him only.'[d]"
11Then the devil left him, and angels
came and attended him. ●

[a]4 Deut. 8:3 [b]6 Psalm 91:11,12 [c]7 Deut. 6:16 [d]10 Deut. 6:13

## KING JAMES

Three Temptations

1.FOOD

**4** Then was Jesus led up of the Spirit
into the wilderness to be tempted of
the devil. 2 And when he had fasted
forty days and forty nights, he was afterward ahungered. 3 And when the tempter came to him, he said, If thou be the
Son of God, command that these stones
be made bread. 4 But he answered and
said, It is written,
Man shall not live by bread alone,
but by every word that proceedeth
out of the mouth of God.●

2.PROTECTION

5 Then the devil taketh him up into the
holy city, and setteth him on a pinnacle
of the temple, 6 and saith unto him, If
thou be the Son of God, cast thyself
down: for it is written,
He shall give his angels charge concerning thee:
and in *their* hands they shall bear
thee up,
lest at any time thou dash thy foot
against a stone.
7 Jesus said unto him, It is written again,
Thou shalt not tempt the Lord thy God.●

3.POSSESSIONS

8 Again, the devil taketh him up into an
exceeding high mountain, and showeth
him all the kingdoms of the world, and the
glory of them; 9 and saith unto him, All
these things will I give thee, if thou wilt
fall down and worship me. 10 Then saith
Jesus unto him, Get thee hence, Satan:
for it is written,
Thou shalt worship the Lord thy
God,
and him only shalt thou serve.
11 Then the devil leaveth him, and, behold, angels came and ministered unto
him.●

LED BY THE SPIRIT

Deu. 8:3

Ps. 91:11,12

Deu. 6:16

ATTENDED BY ANGELS

First read 3:17 of the preceding segment. Compare that verse with the opening verse of this segment.

____________________

____________________

*4:1-4* Record the different parts of the setting (vv.1,2):

____________________

____________________

____________________

Record:

SATAN'S TEMPTATION ____________________

____________________

____________________

JESUS' ANSWER ____________________

____________________

____________________

*4:5-7*

TEMPTATION ____________________

____________________

____________________

JESUS' ANSWER ____________________

____________________

____________________

*4:8-11*

TEMPTATION ____________________

____________________

____________________

JESUS' ANSWER ____________________

____________________

____________________

NEW INTERNATIONAL VERSION

What does this passage teach about:

DARKNESS OF SIN

LIGHT OF GOSPEL

REPENTANCE

KINGDOM OF HEAVEN

PERSONAL EVANGELISM

FOLLOWING CHRIST

OTHER

Why do you think Jesus included physical healing as one of His ministries?

12When Jesus heard that John had been
put in prison, he returned to Galilee.
13Leaving Nazareth, he went and lived in
Capernaum, which was by the lake in the
area of Zebulun and Naphtali— 14to fulfill
what was said through the prophet Isaiah:

15"Land of Zebulun and land of
Naphtali,
the way to the sea, along the
Jordan,
Galilee of the Gentiles—
16the people living in darkness
have seen a great light;
on those living in the land of the
shadow of death
a light has dawned."[e]

17From that time on Jesus began to
preach, "Repent, for the kingdom of
heaven is near."●

*The Calling of the First Disciples*

18As Jesus was walking beside the Sea of
Galilee, he saw two brothers, Simon called
Peter and his brother Andrew. They were
casting a net into the lake, for they were
fishermen. 19"Come, follow me," Jesus
said, "and I will make you fishers of men."
20At once they left their nets and followed
him.

21Going on from there, he saw two other
brothers, James son of Zebedee and his
brother John. They were in a boat with
their father Zebedee, preparing their nets.
Jesus called them, 22and immediately they
left the boat and their father and followed
him.●

*Jesus Heals the Sick*

23Jesus went throughout Galilee, teaching in their synagogues, preaching the good
news of the kingdom, and healing every
disease and sickness among the people.
24News about him spread all over Syria,
and people brought to him all who were ill
with various diseases, those suffering
severe pain, the demon-possessed, the epi-
leptics and the paralytics, and he healed
them. 25Large crowds from Galilee, the
Decapolis,[f] Jerusalem, Judea and the region across the Jordan followed him.●

[e]16 Isaiah 9:1,2 [f]25 That is, the Ten Cities

## KING JAMES

**1. LIGHT**

12 Now when Jesus had heard that
John was cast into prison, he departed
into Galilee; 13 and leaving Nazareth,
he came and dwelt in Caper'na-um,
which is upon the seacoast, in the borders
of Zeb'ulun and Naph'tali: 14 that it
might be fulfilled which was spoken by
Isaiah the prophet, saying,
15 The land of Zeb'ulun, and the land
of Naph'tali,
*by* the way of the sea, beyond
Jordan,
Galilee of the Gentiles;
16 the people which sat in darkness saw
great light;
and to them which sat in the region
and shadow of death
light is sprung up.
17 From that time Jesus began to preach,
and to say, Repent: for the kingdom of
heaven is at hand.●

**2. ETERNAL PURPOSE**

18 And Jesus, walking by the sea of
Galilee, saw two brethren, Simon called
Peter, and Andrew his brother, casting a
net into the sea: for they were fishers.
19 And he saith unto them, Follow me,
and I will make you fishers of men.
20 And they straightway left *their* nets,
and followed him. 21 And going on from
thence, he saw other two brethren, James
*the son* of Zeb'edee, and John his brother,
in a ship with Zeb'edee their father, mending their nets; and he called them. 22 And
they immediately left the ship and their
father, and followed him.●

**3. POWER**

23 And Jesus went about all Galilee,
teaching in their synagogues, and preaching the gospel of the kingdom, and healing
all manner of sickness and all manner of
disease among the people. 24 And his
fame went throughout all Syria: and they
brought unto him all sick people that were
taken with divers diseases and torments,
and those which were possessed with
devils, and those which were lunatic, and
those that had the palsy; and he healed
them. 25 And there followed him great
multitudes of people from Galilee, and
*from* Decap'olis, and *from* Jerusalem,
and *from* Judea, and *from* beyond Jordan.●

JOHN IMPRISONED

Isa. 9:1,2

"Repent"

"Follow me"

JESUS ACTIVE

At 4:12 Matthew begins to record the long section called PROCLAMATION (4:12—16:20).

Read verse 17, which points back to 4:12 as the beginning of a new period in Jesus' ministry. Compare 16:21.

In your own words, what is each paragraph about?

4:12-17 ______________________

4:18-22 ______________________

4:23-25 ______________________

What words of Jesus are quoted in the first paragraph?

What words of Jesus are quoted in the second paragraph?

What different ministries of Jesus are reported in this passage?

List all the names of people recorded in the passage.

NEW INTERNATIONAL VERSION

The beatitudes describe how Christians ought to be living, as children of God. Read verses 3-12, and try to think of times in your own experience when such qualities are tested. Record these.

Go through the list of beatitudes again and observe how the reward matches the behavior. Record practical lessons which can be learned from this.

How can a believer be happy when he is persecuted? Support your answer.

Why is it so important for Christians to let their influence be felt in the world?

5 Now when he saw the crowds, he went
up on a mountainside and sat down.
His disciples came to him, [2]and he began to
teach them, saying:

[3]"Blessed are the poor in spirit,
for theirs is the kingdom of
heaven.
[4]Blessed are those who mourn,
for they will be comforted.
[5]Blessed are the meek,
for they will inherit the earth.
[6]Blessed are those who hunger and
thirst for righteousness,
for they will be filled.
[7]Blessed are the merciful,
for they will be shown mercy.
[8]Blessed are the pure in heart,
for they will see God.
[9]Blessed are the peacemakers,
for they will be called sons of
God. ●
[10]Blessed are those who are
persecuted because of
righteousness,
for theirs is the kingdom of
heaven.

[11]"Blessed are you when people insult
you, persecute you and falsely say all kinds
of evil against you because of me. [12]Re-
joice and be glad, because great is your
reward in heaven, for in the same way they
persecuted the prophets who were before
you. ●

*Salt and Light*

[13]"You are the salt of the earth. But if the
salt loses its saltiness, how can it be made
salty again? It is no longer good for anything, except to be thrown out and trampled by men.
[14]"You are the light of the world. A city
on a hill cannot be hidden. [15]Neither do
people light a lamp and put it under a bowl.
Instead they put it on its stand, and it gives
light to everyone in the house. [16]In the
same way, let your light shine before men,
that they may see your good deeds and
praise your Father in heaven. ●

KING JAMES

1.CHRISTIAN CHARACTER

5 And seeing the multitudes, he went
up into a mountain: and when he was
set, his disciples came unto him: 2 and he
opened his mouth, and taught them,
saying,
3 Blessed *are* the poor in spirit: for
theirs is the kingdom of heaven.
4 Blessed *are* they that mourn: for they
shall be comforted.
5 Blessed *are* the meek: for they shall
inherit the earth.
6 Blessed *are* they which do hunger and
thirst after righteousness: for they shall
be filled.
7 Blessed *are* the merciful: for they
shall obtain mercy.
8 Blessed *are* the pure in heart: for they
shall see God.
9 Blessed *are* the peacemakers: for
they shall be called the children of
God.●
10 Blessed *are* they which are persecuted for righteousness' sake: for theirs
is the kingdom of heaven.
11 Blessed are ye, when *men* shall revile
you, and persecute *you*, and shall say all
manner of evil against you falsely, for my
sake. 12 Rejoice, and be exceeding glad:
for great *is* your reward in heaven: for so
persecuted they the prophets which were
before you.●

2.CHRISTIAN INFLUENCE

13 Ye are the salt of the earth: but if the
salt have lost his savor, wherewith shall it
be salted? it is thenceforth good for nothing, but to be cast out, and to be trodden
under foot of men.
14 Ye are the light of the world. A
city that is set on a hill cannot be hid.
15 Neither do men light a candle, and put
it under a bushel, but on a candlestick;
and it giveth light unto all that are in the
house. 16 Let your light so shine before
men, that they may see your good works,
and glorify your Father which is in
heaven.●

KINGDOM OF HEAVEN

FATHER IN HEAVEN

The words of Jesus beginning with the word "Blessed" are called The Beatitudes. The word "blessed" means "happy" in the deepest sense of life—joy regardless of outward conditions.

*5:1-9* Record the beatitudes of verses 3-9:

| BLESSED ARE THE | FOR THEY SHALL |
|---|---|
| | |
| | |
| | |
| | |
| | |
| | |
| | |
| | |
| | |

*5:10-12* How are verses 10-12 different from the preceding verses?

*5:13-16* What pictures are drawn in the last paragraph to teach about Christian influence?

NEW INTERNATIONAL VERSION

According to Jesus, are the Old Testament commandments outdated and out of force?

What did Jesus say He came to do, with respect to the laws of Moses?

What did He mean by this?

Record what this passage teaches about:

KINGDOM OF HEAVEN

ANGER

RECONCILIATION OF TWO PEOPLE

THE THOUGHT LIFE

DIVORCE

ADULTERY

### *The Fulfillment of the Law*

17"Do not think that I have come to abolish the Law or the Prophets; I have not
come to abolish them but to fulfill them. 18I
tell you the truth, until heaven and earth
disappear, not the smallest letter, not the
least stroke of a pen, will by any means
disappear from the Law until everything is
accomplished. 19Anyone who breaks one
of the least of these commandments and
teaches others to do the same will be called
least in the kingdom of heaven, but whoever practices and teaches these commands will be called great in the kingdom
of heaven. 20For I tell you that unless your
righteousness surpasses that of the Pharisees and the teachers of the law, you will
certainly not enter the kingdom of heaven. ●

### *Murder*

21"You have heard that it was said to the
people long ago, 'Do not murder,[a] and anyone who murders will be subject to judgment.' 22But I tell you that anyone who is
angry with his brother[b] will be subject to
judgment. Again, anyone who says to his
brother, 'Raca,[c]' is answerable to the Sanhedrin. But anyone who says, 'You fool!'
will be in danger of the fire of hell.
23"Therefore, if you are offering your
gift at the altar and there remember that
your brother has something against you,
24leave your gift there in front of the altar.
First go and be reconciled to your brother;
then come and offer your gift.
25"Settle matters quickly with your adversary who is taking you to court. Do it
while you are still with him on the way, or
he may hand you over to the judge, and the
judge may hand you over to the officer, and
you may be thrown into prison. 26I tell you
the truth, you will not get out until you
have paid the last penny.[d] ●

### *Adultery*

27"You have heard that it was said, 'Do
not commit adultery.'[e] 28But I tell you that
anyone who looks at a woman lustfully has
already committed adultery with her in his
heart. 29If your right eye causes you to sin,
gouge it out and throw it away. It is better
for you to lose one part of your body than
for your whole body to be thrown into hell.
30And if your right hand causes you to sin,
cut it off and throw it away. It is better for
you to lose one part of your body than for
your whole body to go into hell.

### *Divorce*

31"It has been said, 'Anyone who divorces his wife must give her a certificate
of divorce.'[f] 32But I tell you that anyone
who divorces his wife, except for marital
unfaithfulness, causes her to commit adultery, and anyone who marries a woman so
divorced commits adultery. ●

[a]*21* Exodus 20:13 [b]*22* Some manuscripts *brother without cause* [c]*22* An Aramaic term of contempt [d]*26* Greek *kodrantes* [e]*27* Exodus 20:14 [f]*31* Deut. 24:1

## KING JAMES

**1. OLD TESTAMENT LAW**

THE WRITTEN LAW

17 Think not that I am come to destroy
the law, or the prophets: I am not come to
destroy, but to fulfil. 18 For verily I say
unto you, Till heaven and earth pass, one
jot or one tittle shall in no wise pass from
the law, till all be fulfilled. 19 Whosoever
therefore shall break one of these least
commandments, and shall teach men so,
he shall be called the least in the kingdom
of heaven: but whosoever shall do and
teach *them*, the same shall be called great
in the kingdom of heaven. 20 For I say
unto you, That except your righteousness
shall exceed *the righteousness* of the
scribes and Pharisees, ye shall in no case
enter into the kingdom of heaven.●

**2. CHRIST'S LAW**

—murder

Deu. 5:17

21 Ye have heard that it was said by
them of old time, Thou shalt not kill;
and whosoever shall kill shall be in danger
of the judgment: 22 but I say unto you,
That whosoever is angry with his brother
without a cause shall be in danger of the
judgment: and whosoever shall say to his
brother, Raca, shall be in danger of the
council: but whosoever shall say, Thou
fool, shall be in danger of hell fire.
23 Therefore if thou bring thy gift to the
altar, and there rememberest that thy
brother hath aught against thee; 24 leave
there thy gift before the altar, and go thy
way; first be reconciled to thy brother,
and then come and offer thy gift. 25 Agree
with thine adversary quickly, while thou
art in the way with him; lest at any time
the adversary deliver thee to the judge,
and the judge deliver thee to the officer,
and thou be cast into prison. 26 Verily I
say unto thee, Thou shalt by no means
come out thence, till thou hast paid the
uttermost farthing.●

—adultery and divorce

Deu. 5:18

27 Ye have heard that it was said by
them of old time, Thou shalt not commit
adultery: 28 but I say unto you, That
whosoever looketh on a woman to lust
after her hath committed adultery with
her already in his heart. 29 And if thy
right eye offend thee, pluck it out, and
cast *it* from thee: for it is profitable for
thee that one of thy members should
perish, and not *that* thy whole body
should be cast into hell. 30 And if thy
right hand offend thee, cut it off, and cast
*it* from thee: for it is profitable for thee
that one of thy members should perish,
and not *that* thy whole body should be
cast into hell.

Deu. 24:1,3

31 It hath been said, Whosoever shall
put away his wife, let him give her a writing of divorcement: 32 but I say unto
you, That whosoever shall put away his
wife, saving for the cause of fornication,
causeth her to commit adultery: and whosoever shall marry her that is divorced
committeth adultery.●

JESUS' WORD

---

*5:17-20* The first paragraph teaches various truths about God's law. List these.

*5:21-26* From 5:21 to 5:48 Christ applies the principles of 5:17-20 to various life situations. What sin is discussed here?

In your own words, what does the paragraph say?

*5:27-32* What different things are discussed in this paragraph?

What does the eye and the hand have to do with the discussion?

NEW INTERNATIONAL VERSION

If a person's word is not reliable, then his making an oath will not add any credibility. What are your reflections about verse 37?

Record applications of the passage in these areas:

NON-RESISTANCE

GOING THE EXTRA MILE

GENUINE CHRISTIAN LOVE

INTERCESSORY PRAYER

CHRISTIAN PERFECTION

*Oaths*

33 "Again, you have heard that it was said to the people long ago, 'Do not break your oath, but keep the oaths you have made to the Lord.' 34 But I tell you, Do not swear at all: either by heaven, for it is God's throne; 35 or by the earth, for it is his footstool; or by Jerusalem, for it is the city of the Great King. 36 And do not swear by your head, for you cannot make even one hair white or black. 37 Simply let your 'Yes' be 'Yes,' and your 'No,' 'No'; anything beyond this comes from the evil one. ●

*An Eye for an Eye*

38 "You have heard that it was said, 'Eye for eye, and tooth for tooth.'[a] 39 But I tell you, Do not resist an evil person. If someone strikes you on the right cheek, turn to him the other also. 40 And if someone wants to sue you and take your tunic, let him have your cloak as well. 41 If someone forces you to go one mile, go with him two miles. 42 Give to the one who asks you, and do not turn away from the one who wants to borrow from you. ●

*Love for Enemies*

43 "You have heard that it was said, 'Love your neighbor[b] and hate your enemy.' 44 But I tell you: Love your enemies[c] and pray for those who persecute you, 45 that you may be sons of your Father in heaven. He causes his sun to rise on the evil and the good, and sends rain on the righteous and the unrighteous. 46 If you love those who love you, what reward will you get? Are not even the tax collectors doing that? 47 And if you greet only your brothers, what are you doing more than others? Do not even pagans do that? 48 Be perfect, therefore, as your heavenly Father is perfect. ●

[a] *38* Exodus 21:24; Lev. 24:20; Deut. 19:21 [b] *43* Lev. 19:18
[c] *44* Some late manuscripts *enemies, bless those who curse you, do good to those who hate you*

## KING JAMES

1. OATHS

33 Again, ye have heard that it hath
been said by them of old time, Thou shalt
not forswear thyself, but shalt perform
unto the Lord thine oaths: 34 but I say
unto you, Swear not at all; neither by
heaven; for it is God's throne: 35 nor
by the earth; for it is his footstool: neither by Jerusalem; for it is the city of the
great King. 36 Neither shalt thou swear
by thy head, because thou canst not make
one hair white or black. 37 But let your
communication be, Yea, yea; Nay, nay:
for whatsoever is more than these cometh
of evil.●

Lev. 19:12

NO OATHS

2. RESISTANCE

38 Ye have heard that it hath been said,
An eye for an eye, and a tooth for a tooth:
39 but I say unto you, That ye resist not
evil: but whosoever shall smite thee on
thy right cheek, turn to him the other also.
40 And if any man will sue thee at the
law, and take away thy coat, let him have
*thy* cloak also. 41 And whosoever shall
compel thee to go a mile, go with him
twain. 42 Give to him that asketh thee,
and from him that would borrow of thee
turn not thou away.●

Ex. 21:24

3. LOVE

43 Ye have heard that it hath been said,
Thou shalt love thy neighbor, and hate
thine enemy. 44 But I say unto you, Love
your enemies, bless them that curse you,
do good to them that hate you, and pray
for them which despitefully use you, and
persecute you; 45 that ye may be the
children of your Father which is in
heaven: for he maketh his sun to rise on
the evil and on the good, and sendeth rain
on the just and on the unjust. 46 For if
ye love them which love you, what reward
have ye? do not even the publicans the
same? 47 And if ye salute your brethren
only, what do ye more *than others?* do not
even the publicans so? 48 Be ye therefore
perfect, even as your Father which is in
heaven is perfect.●

Lev. 19:18

MUCH LOVE

Attitudes are vitally important in every area of life. Christ talks here about three attitudes for Christian living. See if you can identify each one in each paragraph.

______________________

______________________

______________________

*5:33-37* In your own words, what is the situation described here?

______________________

______________________

______________________

What is the command? ______________________

______________________

______________________

*5:38-42* What is the basic appeal here?

______________________

______________________

______________________

______________________

*5:43-48* What is the basic appeal here?

______________________

______________________

______________________

______________________

What should motivate the Christian to maintain this love relationship?

______________________

______________________

______________________

______________________

______________________

______________________

______________________

______________________

______________________

______________________

NEW INTERNATIONAL VERSION

Good deeds are defiled by wrong motives. What basic evil motive is common to the three subjects of this passage?

GIVING GIFTS
List ways to give gifts today to needy persons, following Jesus' instructions.

PRAYER
There are many important practical truths taught about prayer here. List as many as you can.

FASTING
What is the purpose of fasting?

What is the ever-present danger of fasting?

Who rewards genuine fasting?

6 "Be careful not to do your 'acts of
righteousness' before men, to be seen
by them. If you do, you will have no reward from your Father in heaven.
2 "So when you give to the needy, do not
announce it with trumpets, as the hypocrites do in the synagogues and on the
streets, to be honored by men. I tell you
the truth, they have received their reward
in full. 3 But when you give to the needy, do
not let your left hand know what your right
hand is doing, 4 so that your giving may be
in secret. Then your Father, who sees what
is done in secret, will reward you. ●

*Prayer*

5 "But when you pray, do not be like the
hypocrites, for they love to pray standing
in the synagogues and on the street corners
to be seen by men. I tell you the truth, they
have received their reward in full. 6 When
you pray, go into your room, close the door
and pray to your Father, who is unseen.
Then your Father, who sees what is done
in secret, will reward you. 7 And when you
pray, do not keep on babbling like pagans,
for they think they will be heard because of
their many words. 8 Do not be like them, for
your Father knows what you need before
you ask him.
9 "This is how you should pray:

" 'Our Father in heaven,
hallowed be your name,
10 your kingdom come,
your will be done
on earth as it is in heaven.
11 Give us today our daily bread.
12 Forgive us our debts,
as we also have forgiven our
debtors.
13 And lead us not into temptation,
but deliver us from the evil one.[d]'

14 For if you forgive men when they sin
against you, your heavenly Father will also
forgive you. 15 But if you do not forgive
men their sins, your Father will not forgive
your sins. ●

*Fasting*

16 "When you fast, do not look somber as
the hypocrites do, for they disfigure their
faces to show men they are fasting. I tell
you the truth, they have received their reward in full. 17 But when you fast, put oil on
your head and wash your face, 18 so that it
will not be obvious to men that you are
fasting, but only to your Father, who is
unseen; and your Father, who sees what is
done in secret, will reward you. ●

[d]13 Or *from evil;* some late manuscripts *one, / for yours is the kingdom and the power and the glory forever. Amen.*

KING JAMES

**1. GIVING**

—outward look

6 Take heed that ye do not your alms
before men, to be seen of them:
otherwise ye have no reward of your
Father which is in heaven.
2 Therefore when thou doest *thine* alms,
do not sound a trumpet before thee, as the
hypocrites do in the synagogues and in the
streets, that they may have glory of men.
Verily I say unto you, They have their reward. 3 But when thou doest alms, let
not thy left hand know what thy right
hand doeth: 4 that thine alms may be in
secret: and thy Father which seeth in
secret himself shall reward thee openly.●

**2. PRAYING**

—upward look

5 And when thou prayest, thou shalt
not be as the hypocrites *are:* for they love
to pray standing in the synagogues and in
the corners of the streets, that they may be
seen of men. Verily I say unto you, They
have their reward. 6 But thou, when thou
prayest, enter into thy closet, and when
thou hast shut thy door, pray to thy
Father which is in secret; and thy Father
which seeth in secret shall reward thee
openly.
7 But when ye pray, use not vain repetitions, as the heathen *do:* for they think
that they shall be heard for their much
speaking. 8 Be not ye therefore like unto
them: for your Father knoweth what
things ye have need of, before ye ask him.
9 After this manner therefore pray ye:
Our Father which art in heaven,
Hallowed be thy name.
10 Thy kingdom come.
Thy will be done
in earth, as *it is* in heaven.
11 Give us this day our daily bread.
12 And forgive us our debts,
as we forgive our debtors.
13 And lead us not into temptation,
but deliver us from evil:
For thine is the kingdom, and the
power, and the glory, for ever.
Amen.
14 For if ye forgive men their trespasses,
your heavenly Father will also forgive
you: 15 but if ye forgive not men their
trespasses, neither will your Father forgive your trespasses.●

**3. FASTING**

—inward look

16 Moreover when ye fast, be not, as
the hypocrites, of a sad countenance: for
they disfigure their faces, that they may
appear unto men to fast. Verily I say unto
you, They have their reward. 17 But
thou, when thou fastest, anoint thine
head, and wash thy face; 18 that thou
appear not unto men to fast, but unto thy
Father which is in secret: and thy Father
which seeth in secret shall reward thee
openly.●

Father who is in heaven

Father who sees in secret

The opening verse of this passage identifies the two ways of practicing righteousness. One way is to want to be noticed by other people. What is the other way?

*6:1-4* How is God identified in this paragraph?

How is He referred to in the other paragraphs?

What evil motive is rebuked here?

Does this motive appear in the other paragraphs?

*6:5-15* Study carefully the model of prayer given by Jesus. For example, try to account for the *order* in which the statements appear.

*6:16-18* Fasting should be as *unto* God. Is this true also of giving and praying?

NEW INTERNATIONAL VERSION

What does this passage teach about:

A MAN'S TREASURE ______

HEART DESIRE ______

LOVE OF MONEY ______

WORRY ______

FAITH ______

GOD ______

How is the faith life strengthened by knowing more *who God is?* ______

19"Do not store up for yourselves treasures on earth, where moth and rust destroy, and where thieves break in and
steal. 20But store up for yourselves treasures in heaven, where moth and rust do
not destroy, and where thieves do not
break in and steal. 21For where your treasure is, there your heart will be also.●
22"The eye is the lamp of the body. If
your eyes are good, your whole body will
be full of light. 23But if your eyes are bad,
your whole body will be full of darkness. If
then the light within you is darkness, how
great is that darkness! ●
24"No one can serve two masters. Either
he will hate the one and love the other, or
he will be devoted to the one and despise
the other. You cannot serve both God and
Money.●

*Do Not Worry*

25"Therefore I tell you, do not worry
about your life, what you will eat or drink;
or about your body, what you will wear. Is
not life more important than food, and the
body more important than clothes? 26Look
at the birds of the air; they do not sow or
reap or store away in barns, and yet your
heavenly Father feeds them. Are you not
much more valuable than they? 27Who of
you by worrying can add a single hour to
his life[a]?●
28"And why do you worry about
clothes? See how the lilies of the field
grow. They do not labor or spin. 29Yet I tell
you that not even Solomon in all his splendor was dressed like one of these. 30If that
is how God clothes the grass of the field,
which is here today and tomorrow is
thrown into the fire, will he not much more
clothe you, O you of little faith? 31So do not
worry, saying, 'What shall we eat?' or
'What shall we drink?' or 'What shall we
wear?' 32For the pagans run after all these
things, and your heavenly Father knows
that you need them. 33But seek first his
kingdom and his righteousness, and all
these things will be given to you as well.
34Therefore do not worry about tomorrow,
for tomorrow will worry about itself. Each
day has enough trouble of its own.●

[a]27 Or *single cubit to his height*

## KING JAMES

**1. TREASURES AND HEAVEN**

19 Lay not up for yourselves treasures
upon earth, where moth and rust doth
corrupt, and where thieves break through
and steal: 20 but lay up for yourselves
treasures in heaven, where neither moth
nor rust doth corrupt, and where thieves
do not break through nor steal: 21 for
where your treasure is, there will your
heart be also.●

**2. EYE AND BODY**

22 The light of the body is the eye: if
therefore thine eye be single, thy whole
body shall be full of light. 23 But if thine
eye be evil, thy whole body shall be full of
darkness. If therefore the light that is in
thee be darkness, how great *is* that darkness!●

**3. GOD AND POSSESSIONS**

24 No man can serve two masters: for
either he will hate the one, and love the
other; or else he will hold to the one, and
despise the other. Ye cannot serve God
and mammon.●
25 Therefore I say unto you, Take no
thought for your life, what ye shall eat, or
what ye shall drink; nor yet for your
body, what ye shall put on. Is not the life
more than meat, and the body than raiment? 26 Behold the fowls of the air: for
they sow not, neither do they reap, nor
gather into barns; yet your heavenly
Father feedeth them. Are ye not much
better than they? 27 Which of you by
taking thought can add one cubit unto his
stature?● 28 And why take ye thought for
raiment? Consider the lilies of the field,
how they grow; they toil not, neither do
they spin: 29 and yet I say unto you,
That even Solomon in all his glory was
not arrayed like one of these. 30 Wherefore, if God so clothe the grass of the
field, which today is, and tomorrow is
cast into the oven, *shall he* not much more
*clothe* you, O ye of little faith? 31 Therefore take no thought, saying, What shall
we eat? or, What shall we drink? or,
Wherewithal shall we be clothed? 32 (For
after all these things do the Gentiles seek:)
for your heavenly Father knoweth that ye
have need of all these things. 33 But seek
ye first the kingdom of God, and his
righteousness; and all these things shall
be added unto you.
34 Take therefore no thought for the
morrow: for the morrow shall take
thought for the things of itself. Sufficient
unto the day *is* the evil thereof.●

**TREASURES**

Priorities in a Christian's heart determine his actions. What priorities are cited at the beginning and end of this passage?

Verse 19 ______________________

______________________

Verse 33 ______________________

______________________

In the body, what organ determines how much light is let in (vv.22-23)?

______________________

*6:24*
What is exclusive about the servant-master relationship (v.24)?

______________________

______________________

______________________

*6:25-27* What three material necessities are referred to here?

______________________

______________________

______________________

*6:28-34* This paragraph expands on what is taught in the preceding one.

How is God brought into the picture?

______________________

______________________

______________________

**ALL THESE THINGS**

What are the "all these things" in verse 33?

______________________

______________________

______________________

What is the command of verse 33?

______________________

______________________

______________________

______________________

______________________

NEW INTERNATIONAL VERSION

Criticism and judging of others can mar the witness of a Christian and bring much grief to his heart. Record the spiritual lessons you learn about this from verse 1-5.

To interpret verse 6, you have to decide what is meant by "holy things" and "depraved men" ("dogs"). What do you think?

The truths of verses 7-11 are priceless in the Christian's prayer life. Record practical truths you learn here.

Why is the command of verse 12 both fair and sound?

*Judging Others*

7 "Do not judge, or you too will be
judged. 2For in the same way you judge
others, you will be judged, and with the
measure you use, it will be measured to
you.
3"Why do you look at the speck of saw-
dust in your brother's eye and pay no attention to the plank in your own eye? 4How
can you say to your brother, 'Let me take
the speck out of your eye,' when all the
time there is a plank in your own eye? 5You
hypocrite, first take the plank out of your
own eye, and then you will see clearly to
remove the speck from your brother's eye.●
6"Do not give dogs what is sacred; do
not throw your pearls to pigs. If you do,
they may trample them under their feet,
and then turn and tear you to pieces.●

*Ask, Seek, Knock*

7"Ask and it will be given to you; seek
and you will find; knock and the door will
be opened to you. 8For everyone who asks
receives; he who seeks finds; and to him
who knocks, the door will be opened.
9"Which of you, if his son asks for
bread, will give him a stone? 10Or if he asks
for a fish, will give him a snake? 11If you,
then, though you are evil, know how to
give good gifts to your children, how much
more will your Father in heaven give good
gifts to those who ask him! 12In everything,
do to others what you would have them do
to you, for this sums up the Law and the
Prophets.●

KING JAMES

1.JUDGING

7 Judge not, that ye be not judged.
2 For with what judgment ye judge,
ye shall be judged: and with what measure
ye mete, it shall be measured to you
again. 3 And why beholdest thou the
mote that is in thy brother's eye, but con-
siderest not the beam that is in thine own
eye? 4 Or how wilt thou say to thy
brother, Let me pull out the mote out of
thine eye; and, behold, a beam *is* in thine
own eye? 5 Thou hypocrite, first cast out
the beam out of thine own eye; and then
shalt thou see clearly to cast out the mote
out of thy brother's eye.●

2.GIVING

6 Give not that which is holy unto the
dogs, neither cast ye your pearls before
swine, lest they trample them under their
feet, and turn again and rend you.●

3.ASKING

7 Ask, and it shall be given you; seek,
and ye shall find; knock, and it shall be
opened unto you: 8 for every one that
asketh receiveth; and he that seeketh
findeth; and to him that knocketh it shall
be opened. 9 Or what man is there of you,
whom if his son ask bread, will he give
him a stone? 10 Or if he ask a fish, will he
give him a serpent? 11 If ye then, being
evil, know how to give good gifts unto
your children, how much more shall your
Father which is in heaven give good things
to them that ask him? 12 Therefore all
things whatsoever ye would that
men should do to you, do ye even so to
them:[b] for this is the law and the prophets.●

YOUR STANDARD

THE LAW AND THE PROPHETS

Read the three paragraphs. Which give instructions on *what not* to do, and on *what* to do?

_______________

*7:1-5* Record what Jesus taught about:

SPECKS _______________

LOGS _______________

*7:6* What are holy things likened to? _______________

Why should holy things be withheld in such a case?

_______________

COMMAND: _______________

PROMISE: _______________

ILLUSTRATION: _______________

PROMISE: _______________

NEW INTERNATIONAL VERSION

This passage says much about heaven. Record what you learn about these related subjects:

DESCRIPTION OF HEAVEN

WAY TO HEAVEN

FALSE TEACHERS

THOSE WHO WON'T ENTER HEAVEN

THE TRUE PROPHET JESUS

*The Narrow and Wide Gates*

13"Enter through the narrow gate. For
wide is the gate and broad is the road that
leads to destruction, and many enter
through it. 14But small is the gate and narrow the road that leads to life, and only a
few find it.●

*A Tree and Its Fruit*

15"Watch out for false prophets. They
come to you in sheep's clothing, but inwardly they are ferocious wolves. 16By
their fruit you will recognize them. Do
people pick grapes from thornbushes, or
figs from thistles? 17Likewise every good
tree bears good fruit, but a bad tree bears
bad fruit. 18A good tree cannot bear bad
fruit, and a bad tree cannot bear good fruit.
19Every tree that does not bear good fruit
is cut down and thrown into the fire.
20Thus, by their fruit you will recognize
them.●

21"Not everyone who says to me, 'Lord
Lord,' will enter the kingdom of heaven,
but only he who does the will of my Father
who is in heaven. 22Many will say to me on
that day, 'Lord, Lord, did we not prophesy
in your name, and in your name drive out
demons and perform many miracles?'
23Then I will tell them plainly, 'I never
knew you. Away from me, you evildoers!'●

*The Wise and Foolish Builders*

24"Therefore everyone who hears these
words of mine and puts them into practice
is like a wise man who built his house on
the rock. 25The rain came down, the
streams rose, and the winds blew and beat
against that house; yet it did not fall, because it had its foundation on the rock.
26But everyone who hears these words of
mine and does not put them into practice is
like a foolish man who built his house on
sand. 27The rain came down, the streams
rose, and the winds blew and beat against
that house, and it fell with a great crash."●

28When Jesus had finished saying these
things, the crowds were amazed at his
teaching, 29because he taught as one who
had authority, and not as their teachers of
the law.●

## KING JAMES

**1. GATE** — narrow and wide

13 Enter ye in at the strait gate: for
wide *is* the gate, and broad *is* the way,
that leadeth to destruction, and many
there be which go in thereat: 14 because
strait *is* the gate, and narrow *is* the way,
which leadeth unto life, and few there be
that find it. ●

**2. FRUIT** — true and false

15 Beware of false prophets, which
come to you in sheep's clothing, but inwardly they are ravening wolves. 16 Ye
shall know them by their fruits. Do men
gather grapes of thorns, or figs of thistles?
17 Even so every good tree bringeth forth
good fruit; but a corrupt tree bringeth
forth evil fruit. 18 A good tree cannot
bring forth evil fruit, neither *can* a corrupt tree bring forth good fruit. 19 Every
tree that bringeth not forth good fruit is
hewn down, and cast into the fire.[c]
20 Wherefore by their fruits ye shall
know them.●

21 Not every one that saith unto me,
Lord, Lord, shall enter into the kingdom
of heaven; but he that doeth the will of
my Father which is in heaven. 22 Many
will say to me in that day, Lord, Lord,
have we not prophesied in thy name? and
in thy name have cast out devils? and in
thy name done many wonderful works?
23 And then will I profess unto them, I
never knew you: depart from me, ye that
work iniquity.●

**3. FOUNDATION** — wise and foolish

24 Therefore whosoever heareth these
sayings of mine, and doeth them, I will
liken him unto a wise man, which built his
house upon a rock: 25 and the rain descended, and the floods came, and the
winds blew, and beat upon that house;
and it fell not: for it was founded upon a
rock. 26 And every one that heareth these
sayings of mine, and doeth them not, shall
be likened unto a foolish man, which
built his house upon the sand: 27 and the
rain descended, and the floods came, and
the winds blew, and beat upon that house;
and it fell: and great was the fall of
it.●

**—effect of Jesus' sermon**

28 And it came to pass, when Jesus had
ended these sayings, the people were astonished at his doctrine: 29 for he taught
them as *one* having authority, and not as
the scribes.●

---

The first two paragraphs begin with commands. What are they?

______________________________

______________________________

______________________________

______________________________

This is a segment of many contrasts. Underline in the Bible text the ones recorded in the margin. Look for others. Jesus' Sermon on the Mount concludes with verse 27. How is 7:24-27 a very fitting conclusion to the sermon?

______________________________

______________________________

______________________________

What was the effect of the sermon? ______________

______________________________

______________________________

How does Matthew account for such an effect?

______________________________

______________________________

______________________________

*7:13-14* What do these verses teach about the kingdom?

______________________________

______________________________

______________________________

*7:15-20* What is the test of a true prophet?

______________________________

______________________________

______________________________

*7:21-23* Who will enter the kingdom of heaven?

______________________________

______________________________

______________________________

Who will be excluded? ______________

______________________________

______________________________

NEW INTERNATIONAL VERSION

Faith is a basic ingredient of Christian living, just as one's salvation comes through faith. These stories of Jesus' miracles teach many truths about faith which God honors. List as many of these as you can find in the stories.

What do verses 11-12 teach about who will inhabit heaven?

What does it *really* mean to follow Jesus, according to 8:18-22?

### *The Man With Leprosy*

8 When he came down from the mountainside, large crowds followed him.
2A man with leprosy[a] came and knelt before him and said, "Lord, if you are willing, you can make me clean."
3Jesus reached out his hand and touched
the man. "I am willing," he said. "Be
clean!" Immediately he was cured[b] of his
leprosy. 4Then Jesus said to him, "See that
you don't tell anyone. But go, show yourself to the priest and offer the gift Moses
commanded, as a testimony to them."●

### *The Faith of the Centurion*

5When Jesus had entered Capernaum, a
centurion came to him, asking for help.
6"Lord," he said, "my servant lies at
home paralyzed and in terrible suffering."
7Jesus said to him, "I will go and heal
him."
8The centurion replied, "Lord, I do not
deserve to have you come under my roof.
But just say the word, and my servant will
be healed. 9For I myself am a man under
authority, with soldiers under me. I tell this
one, 'Go,' and he goes; and that one,
'Come,' and he comes. I say to my servant,
'Do this,' and he does it."
10When Jesus heard this, he was astonished and said to those following him, "I
tell you the truth, I have not found anyone
in Israel with such great faith. 11I say to you
that many will come from the east and the
west, and will take their places at the feast
with Abraham, Isaac and Jacob in the kingdom of heaven. 12But the subjects of the
kingdom will be thrown outside, into the
darkness, where there will be weeping and
gnashing of teeth."
13Then Jesus said to the centurion, "Go!
It will be done just as you believed it
would." And his servant was healed at that
very hour.●

### *Jesus Heals Many*

14When Jesus came into Peter's house,
he saw Peter's mother-in-law lying in bed
with a fever. 15He touched her hand and
the fever left her, and she got up and began
to wait on him.
16When evening came, many who were
demon-possessed were brought to him,
and he drove out the spirits with a word
and healed all the sick. 17This was to fulfill
what was spoken through the prophet
Isaiah:

"He took up our infirmities
and carried our diseases."[c]●

### *The Cost of Following Jesus*

18When Jesus saw the crowd around
him, he gave orders to cross to the other
side of the lake. 19Then a teacher of the law
came to him and said, "Teacher, I will
follow you wherever you go."
20Jesus replied, "Foxes have holes and
birds of the air have nests, but the Son of
Man has no place to lay his head."
21Another man, one of his disciples, said
to him, "Lord, first let me go and bury my
father."
22But Jesus told him, "Follow me, and
let the dead bury their own dead."●

[a]2 The Greek word was used for various diseases affecting the skin—not necessarily leprosy.
[b]3 Greek *made clean* [c]17 Isaiah 53:4

KING JAMES

1.LEPER

Following: Curiosity

8 When he was come down from the
mountain, great multitudes followed
him. 2 And, behold, there came a leper
and worshipped him, saying, Lord, if thou
wilt, thou canst make me clean. 3 And
Jesus put forth *his* hand, and touched him,
saying, I will; be thou clean. And immediately his leprosy was cleansed.
4 And Jesus saith unto him, See thou tell
no man; but go thy way, show thyself to
the priest, and offer the gift that Moses
commanded, for a testimony unto
them.●

2.PARA-LYTIC

5 And when Jesus was entered into
Caper'na-um, there came unto him a centurion, beseeching him, 6 and saying,
Lord, my servant lieth at home sick of the
palsy, grievously tormented. 7 And Jesus
saith unto him, I will come and heal him.
8 The centurion answered and said, Lord,
I am not worthy that thou shouldest
come under my roof: but speak the word
only, and my servant shall be healed.
9 For I am a man under authority, having
soldiers under me: and I say to this *man*,
Go, and he goeth; and to another, Come,
and he cometh; and to my servant, Do
this, and he doeth *it*. 10 When Jesus
heard *it*, he marveled, and said to them
that followed, Verily I say unto you, I
have not found so great faith, no, not in
Israel. 11 And I say unto you, That many
shall come from the east and west, and
shall sit down with Abraham, and Isaac,
and Jacob, in the kingdom of heaven:
12 but the children of the kingdom shall
be cast out into outer darkness: there shall
be weeping and gnashing of teeth.
13 And Jesus said unto the centurion, Go
thy way; and as thou hast believed, *so* be
it done unto thee. And his servant was
healed in the selfsame hour.●

3.FEVER

14 And when Jesus was come into
Peter's house, he saw his wife's mother
laid, and sick of a fever. 15 And he
touched her hand, and the fever left her:
and she arose, and ministered unto them.
16 When the even was come, they brought
unto him many that were possessed with
devils: and he cast out the spirits with *his*
word, and healed all that were sick:
17 that it might be fulfilled which was
spoken by Isaiah the prophet, saying,
Himself took our infirmities, and bare *our*
sicknesses.●

Isa. 53:4

—Disciple-ship

18 Now when Jesus saw great multitudes about him, he gave commandment
to depart unto the other side. 19 And a
certain scribe came, and said unto him,
Master, I will follow thee whithersoever
thou goest. 20 And Jesus saith unto him,
The foxes have holes, and the birds of the
air *have* nests; but the Son of man hath
not where to lay *his* head. 21 And another
of his disciples said unto him, Lord, suffer
me first to go and bury my father. 22 But
Jesus said unto him, Follow me; and let
the dead bury their dead.●

Following: Reservation

At this point in his gospel Matthew reports three groups of Jesus' miracles. Each group is followed in the text by a short section on discipleship:

| | |
|---|---|
| 8:1-17 | MIRACLES |
| 8:18-22 | DISCIPLESHIP |
| 8:23-9:8 | MIRACLES |
| 9:9-17 | DISCIPLESHIP |
| 9:18-34 | MIRACLES |
| 9:35-10:15 | DISCIPLESHIP |

Look for the following in each of the miracles of this passage:

THE FAITH INVOLVED

8:1-4 ______

8:5-13 ______

8:14-17 ______

JESUS' METHOD OF HEALING

8:1-4 ______

8:5-13 ______

8:14-17 ______

SPIRITUAL INSTRUCTION

8:1-4 ______

8:5-13 ______

8:14-17 ______

NEW INTERNATIONAL VERSION

There are spiritual storms in everyone's life. How can the story of 8:23-27 be applied to those experiences?

Read 8:28-34 again.
Record what is said about each of the participants:

TWO MEN

DEMONS

JESUS

PIGS

HERDSMEN

MULTITUDES

What does this story teach you about the demon-world?

Record everything you learn from 9:1-8 about SIN.

### *Jesus Calms the Storm*

23 Then he got into the boat and his disciples followed him. 24 Without warning, a
furious storm came up on the lake, so that
the waves swept over the boat. But Jesus
was sleeping. 25 The disciples went and
woke him, saying, "Lord, save us! We're
going to drown!"
26 He replied, "You of little faith, why
are you so afraid?" Then he got up and
rebuked the winds and the waves, and it
was completely calm.
27 The men were amazed and asked,
"What kind of man is this? Even the winds
and the waves obey him!" ●

### *The Healing of Two Demon-possessed Men*

28 When he arrived at the other side in the
region of the Gadarenes,[d] two demon-possessed men coming from the tombs met
him. They were so violent that no one
could pass that way. 29 "What do you want
with us, Son of God?" they shouted.
"Have you come here to torture us before
the appointed time?"
30 Some distance from them a large herd
of pigs was feeding. 31 The demons begged
Jesus, "If you drive us out, send us into the
herd of pigs."
32 He said to them, "Go!" So they came
out and went into the pigs, and the whole
herd rushed down the steep bank into the
lake and died in the water. 33 Those tending
the pigs ran off, went into the town and
reported all this, including what had happened to the demon-possessed men.
34 Then the whole town went out to meet
Jesus. And when they saw him, they pleaded with him to leave their region. ●

### *Jesus Heals a Paralytic*

9 Jesus stepped into a boat, crossed over
and came to his own town. 2 Some men
brought to him a paralytic, lying on a mat.
When Jesus saw their faith, he said to the
paralytic, "Take heart, son; your sins are
forgiven."
3 At this, some of the teachers of the law
said to themselves, "This fellow is blas-
pheming!"
4 Knowing their thoughts, Jesus said,
"Why do you entertain evil thoughts in
your hearts? 5 Which is easier: to say, 'Your
sins are forgiven,' or to say, 'Get up and
walk'? 6 But so that you may know that the
Son of Man has authority on earth to forgive sins. . . ." Then he said to the paralytic, "Get up, take your mat and go home."
7 And the man got up and went home.
8 When the crowd saw this, they were filled
with awe; and they praised God, who had
given such authority to men. ●

[d] 28 Some manuscripts *Gergesenes;* others *Gerasenes*

KING JAMES

POWER OVER

1. NATURE

23 And when he was entered into a ship,
his disciples followed him. 24 And, behold, there arose a great tempest in the
sea, insomuch that the ship was covered
with the waves: but he was asleep. 25 And
his disciples came to *him*, and awoke him,
saying, Lord, save us: we perish. 26 And
he saith unto them, Why are ye fearful,
O ye of little faith? Then he arose, and
rebuked the winds and the sea; and there
was a great calm. 27 But the men marveled, saying, What manner of man is
this, that even the winds and the sea obey
him! ●

MEN OF LITTLE FAITH

2. SPIRITS

28 And when he was come to the other
side into the country of the Ger'gesenes,
there met him two possessed with devils,
coming out of the tombs, exceeding fierce,
so that no man might pass by that way.
29 And, behold, they cried out, saying,
What have we to do with thee, Jesus, thou
Son of God? art thou come hither to torment us before the time? 30 And there
was a good way off from them a herd of
many swine feeding. 31 So the devils besought him, saying, If thou cast us out,
suffer us to go away into the herd of swine.
32 And he said unto them, Go. And
when they were come out, they went into
the herd of swine: and, behold, the whole
herd of swine ran violently down a steep
place into the sea, and perished in the
waters. 33 And they that kept them fled,
and went their ways into the city, and told
every thing, and what was befallen to the
possessed of the devils. 34 And, behold,
the whole city came out to meet Jesus: and
when they saw him, they besought *him*
that he would depart out of their coasts. ●

3. BODY

9 And he entered into a ship, and passed
over, and came into his own city.
2 And, behold, they brought to him a man
sick of the palsy, lying on a bed: and
Jesus seeing their faith said unto the sick
of the palsy; Son, be of good cheer; thy
sins be forgiven thee. 3 And, behold, certain of the scribes said within themselves,
This *man* blasphemeth. 4 And Jesus
knowing their thoughts said, Wherefore
think ye evil in your hearts? 5 For
whether is easier, to say, *Thy* sins be forgiven thee; or to say, Arise, and walk?
6 But that ye may know that the Son of
man hath power on earth to forgive sins,
(then saith he to the sick of the palsy,)
Arise, take up thy bed, and go unto thine
house. 7 And he arose, and departed to
his house. 8 But when the multitudes
saw *it*, they marveled, and glorified
God, which had given such power unto
men. ●

SON OF MAN WITH AUTHORITY

Study this passage like you studied 8:1-22. Record your observations for all three paragraphs wherever applicable.

THE FAITH INVOLVED

8:23-27 ____________

8:28-34 ____________

9:1-8 ____________

JESUS' METHOD OF HEALING

8:23-27 ____________

8:28-34 ____________

9:1-8 ____________

SPIRITUAL INSTRUCTION

8:23-27 ____________

8:28-34 ____________

9:1-8 ____________

NEW INTERNATIONAL VERSION

What do you like about the story of Jesus' calling of Matthew (v.9)?

Record ways to apply the truths and examples of verses 10-13.

What does paragraph 9:14-17 teach about mourning and rejoicing?

List other spiritual lessons taught by this passage.

*The Calling of Matthew*

9As Jesus went on from there, he saw a
man named Matthew sitting at the tax collector's booth. "Follow me," he told him,
and Matthew got up and followed him.●
10While Jesus was having dinner at Matthew's house, many tax collectors and
"sinners" came and ate with him and his
disciples. 11When the Pharisees saw this,
they asked his disciples, "Why does your
teacher eat with tax collectors and 'sinners'?"
12On hearing this, Jesus said, "It is not
the healthy who need a doctor, but the
sick. 13But go and learn what this means: 'I
desire mercy, not sacrifice.'[a] For I have
not come to call the righteous, but sinners."●

*Jesus Questioned About Fasting*

14Then John's disciples came and asked
him, "How is it that we and the Pharisees
fast, but your disciples do not fast?"
15Jesus answered, "How can the guests
of the bridegroom mourn while he is with
them? The time will come when the bridegroom will be taken from them; then they
will fast.
16"No one sews a patch of unshrunk
cloth on an old garment, for the patch will
pull away from the garment, making the
tear worse. 17Neither do men pour new
wine into old wineskins. If they do, the
skins will burst, the wine will run out and
the wineskins will be ruined. No, they pour
new wine into new wineskins, and both are
preserved."●

[a]13 Hosea 6:6

KING JAMES

1.CALLING OF MATTHEW

FOLLOWING

9 And as Jesus passed forth from
thence, he saw a man, named Matthew,
sitting at the receipt of custom: and he
saith unto him, Follow me. And he arose,
and followed him.●

2.GOSPEL FOR SINNERS

10 And it came to pass, as Jesus sat at
meat in the house, behold, many publicans and sinners came and sat down with
him and his disciples. 11 And when the
Pharisees saw *it*, they said unto his disciples, Why eateth your master with publicans and sinners? 12 But when Jesus
heard *that*, he said unto them, They that
be whole need not a physician, but they
that are sick. 13 But go ye and learn
what *that* meaneth, I will have mercy, and
not sacrifice: for I am not come to call
the righteous, but sinners to repentance.●

3.FASTING

NOT MOURNING

14 Then came to him the disciples of
John, saying, Why do we and the Pharisees fast oft, but thy disciples fast not?
15 And Jesus said unto them, Can the
children of the bridechamber mourn, as
long as the bridegroom is with them? but
the days will come, when the bridegroom
shall be taken from them, and then shall
they fast. 16 No man putteth a piece of
new cloth unto an old garment; for that
which is put in to fill it up taketh from the
garment, and the rent is made worse.
17 Neither do men put new wine into old
bottles: else the bottles break, and the
wine runneth out, and the bottles perish:
but they put new wine into new bottles,
and both are preserved.●

This section 9:9-17 is another passage on discipleship, before Matthew records other miracles of Jesus demonstrating His power.

*9:9* What does this verse teach about discipleship?

*9:10-17* Two "WHY" questions appear in the two paragraphs. Summarize the questions and replies, in your own words.

"WHY

REPLY:

"WHY

REPLY:

NEW INTERNATIONAL VERSION

List various spiritual lessons taught here.

### *A Dead Girl and a Sick Woman*

18While he was saying this, a ruler came
and knelt before him and said, "My daughter has just died.[b] But come and put your
hand on her, and she will live." 19Jesus got
up and went with him, and so did his disciples.
20Just then a woman who had been subject to bleeding for twelve years came up
behind him and touched the edge of his
cloak. 21She said to herself, "If I only
touch his cloak, I will be healed."
22Jesus turned and saw her. "Take heart,
daughter," he said, "your faith has healed
you." And the woman was healed from
that moment.
23When Jesus entered the ruler's house
and saw the flute players and the noisy
crowd, 24he said, "Go away. The girl is not
dead but asleep." But they laughed at him.
25After the crowd had been put outside, he
went in and took the girl by the hand, and
she got up. 26News of this spread through
all that region.●

### *Jesus Heals the Blind and Dumb*

27As Jesus went on from there, two blind
men followed him, calling out, "Have
mercy on us, Son of David!"
28When he had gone indoors, the blind
men came to him, and he asked them, "Do
you believe that I am able to do this?"
"Yes, Lord," they replied.
29Then he touched their eyes and said,
"According to your faith will it be done to
you"; 30and their sight was restored. Jesus
warned them sternly, "See that no one
knows about this." 31But they went out
and spread the news about him all over that
region.●
32While they were going out, a man who
was demon-possessed and could not talk
was brought to Jesus. 33And when the demon was driven out, the man who had been
dumb spoke. The crowd was amazed and
said, "Nothing like this has ever been seen
in Israel."
34But the Pharisees said, "It is by the
prince of demons that he drives out demons."●

[b]18 Or *daughter is now dying*

KING JAMES

1. DISEASE AND DEATH

18 While he spake these things unto
them, behold, there came a certain ruler,
and worshipped him, saying, My daughter is even now dead: but come and lay
thy hand upon her, and she shall live.
19 And Jesus arose, and followed him,
and *so did* his disciples. 20 And, behold,
a woman, which was diseased with an
issue of blood twelve years, came behind
*him*, and touched the hem of his garment:
21 for she said within herself, If I may but
touch his garment, I shall be whole.
22 But Jesus turned him about, and when
he saw her, he said, Daughter, be of good
comfort; thy faith hath made thee whole.
And the woman was made whole from
that hour. 23 And when Jesus came into
the ruler's house, and saw the minstrels
and the people making a noise, 24 he said
unto them, Give place: for the maid is not
dead, but sleepeth. And they laughed him
to scorn. 25 But when the people were
put forth, he went in, and took her by the
hand, and the maid arose. 26 And the
fame hereof went abroad into all that
land.●

DEATH

2. BLINDNESS

27 And when Jesus departed thence,
two blind men followed him, crying, and
saying, *Thou* Son of David, have mercy
on us. 28 And when he was come into the
house, the blind men came to him: and
Jesus saith unto them, Believe ye that I am
able to do this? They said unto him, Yea,
Lord. 29 Then touched he their eyes,
saying, According to your faith be it unto
you. 30 And their eyes were opened; and
Jesus straitly charged them, saying, See
*that* no man know *it*. 31 But they, when
they were departed, spread abroad his
fame in all that country.●

3. DEMON POSSESSION

32 As they went out, behold, they
brought to him a dumb man possessed
with a devil. 33 And when the devil was
cast out, the dumb spake: and the multitudes marveled, saying, It was never so
seen in Israel. 34 But the Pharisees said,
He casteth out devils through the prince
of the devils. ●

SATAN

Record truths in each paragraph which have not appeared in Matthew's gospel before this, concerning Jesus' ministry of miracles.

*9:18-26* ____________________

*9:27-31* ____________________

*9:32-34* ____________________

NEW INTERNATIONAL VERSION

List the various things which went through Jesus' mind as He ministered to the multitudes.

In view of the needy harvest field, what was Jesus' command?

Why do you think He said this?

What three things did Jesus do, involving His twelve disciples (10:1,5)?

List spiritual applications to be made from 10:1-15.

*The Workers Are Few*

35Jesus went through all the towns and
villages, teaching in their synagogues,
preaching the good news of the kingdom
and healing every disease and sickness.
36When he saw the crowds, he had compassion on them, because they were
harassed and helpless, like sheep without a
shepherd. 37Then he said to his disciples,
"The harvest is plentiful but the workers
are few. 38Ask the Lord of the harvest,
therefore, to send out workers into his harvest field."●

*Jesus Sends Out the Twelve*

10 He called his twelve disciples to him
and gave them authority to drive out
evil[a] spirits and to heal every disease and
sickness.
2These are the names of the twelve apostles: first, Simon (who is called Peter) and
his brother Andrew; James son of Zebedee, and his brother John; 3Philip and Bartholomew; Thomas and Matthew the tax
collector; James son of Alphaeus, and
Thaddaeus; 4Simon the Zealot and Judas
Iscariot, who betrayed him.●
5These twelve Jesus sent out with the
following instructions: "Do not go among
the Gentiles or enter any town of the
Samaritans. 6Go rather to the lost sheep of
Israel. 7As you go, preach this message:
'The kingdom of heaven is near.' 8Heal the
sick, raise the dead, cleanse those who
have leprosy,[b] drive out demons. Freely
you have received, freely give. 9Do not
take along any gold or silver or copper in
your belts; 10take no bag for the journey, or
extra tunic, or sandals or a staff; for the
worker is worth his keep.
11"Whatever town or village you enter,
search for some worthy person there and
stay at his house until you leave. 12As you
enter the home, give it your greeting. 13If
the home is deserving, let your peace rest
on it; if it is not, let your peace return to
you. 14If anyone will not welcome you or
listen to your words, shake the dust off
your feet when you leave that home or
town. 15I tell you the truth, it will be more
bearable for Sodom and Gomorrah on the
day of judgment than for that town.●

[a]1 Greek *unclean*
[b]8 The Greek word was used for various diseases affecting the skin—not necessarily leprosy.

KING JAMES

1.HARVEST

COMPASSION FOR ALL

35 And Jesus went about all the cities
and villages, teaching in their synagogues, and preaching the gospel of the
kingdom, and healing every sickness and
every disease among the people. 36 But
when he saw the multitudes, he was
moved with compassion on them, because they fainted, and were scattered
abroad, as sheep having no shepherd.
37 Then saith he unto his disciples, The
harvest truly *is* plenteous, but the laborers

—pray

*are* few; 38 pray ye therefore the Lord of
the harvest, that he will send forth laborers into his harvest.●

2.WORKERS

10 And when he had called unto *him*
his twelve disciples, he gave them
power *against* unclean spirits, to cast
them out, and to heal all manner of sickness and all manner of disease. 2 Now the
names of the twelve apostles are these;
The first, Simon, who is called Peter, and
Andrew his brother; James *the son* of
Zeb'edee, and John his brother; 3 Philip,
and Bartholomew; Thomas, and Matthew the publican; James *the son* of
Al'pheus, and Lebbe'us, whose surname
was Thad'deus; 4 Simon the Canaanite,
and Judas Iscar'i-ot, who also betrayed
him.●

3.MISSION

5 These twelve Jesus sent forth, and
commanded them, saying, Go not into the
way of the Gentiles, and into *any* city of
the Samaritans enter ye not: 6 but go
rather to the lost sheep of the house of

—go

Israel. 7 And as ye go, preach, saying,
The kingdom of heaven is at hand.
8 Heal the sick, cleanse the lepers, raise
the dead, cast out devils: freely ye have

—give

received, freely give. 9 Provide neither
gold, nor silver, nor brass in your purses;
10 nor scrip for *your* journey, neither two
coats, neither shoes, nor yet staves: for the
workman is worthy of his meat. 11 And
into whatsoever city or town ye shall
enter, inquire who in it is worthy; and
there abide till ye go thence. 12 And
when ye come into a house, salute it.
13 And if the house be worthy, let your
peace come upon it: but if it be not
worthy, let your peace return to you.
14 And whosoever shall not receive you,
nor hear your words, when ye depart out
of that house or city, shake off the dust
of your feet. 15 Verily I say unto you, It
shall be more tolerable for the land of
Sodom and Gomor'rah in the day of
judgment, than for that city.●

NOT ALL RESPOND

Study the segment carefully, then record observations from all three paragraphs.

ATTRIBUTES OF JESUS

THE HARVEST FIELD

DISCIPLES AND THEIR WORK

OPPOSITION

—Disciple

—Demons

—House

—City

NEW INTERNATIONAL VERSION

This passage teaches many important practical lessons for Christians today. Record in your own words lessons for these selected verses:

10:16

10:19-20

10:22

10:24

10:29-31

List other practical lessons which you see in the passage.

16"I am sending you out like sheep
among wolves. Therefore be as shrewd as
snakes and as innocent as doves. 17But be
on your guard against men; they will hand
you over to the local councils and flog you
in their synagogues. 18On my account you
will be brought before governors and kings
as witnesses to them and to the Gentiles.
19But when they arrest you, do not worry
about what to say or how to say it. At that
time you will be given what to say, 20for it
will not be you speaking, but the Spirit of
your Father speaking through you.
21"Brother will betray brother to death,
and a father his child; children will rebel
against their parents and have them put to
death. 22All men will hate you because of
me, but he who stands firm to the end will
be saved. 23When you are persecuted in
one place, flee to another. I tell you the
truth, you will not finish going through the
cities of Israel before the Son of Man
comes.●
24"A student is not above his teacher,
nor a servant above his master. 25It is
enough for the student to be like his
teacher, and the servant like his master. If
the head of the house has been called Beelzebub,[c] how much more the members of
his household!
26"So do not be afraid of them. There is
nothing concealed that will not be disclosed, or hidden that will not be made
known. 27What I tell you in the dark, speak
in the daylight; what is whispered in your
ear, proclaim from the housetops. 28Do not
be afraid of those who kill the body but
cannot kill the soul. Rather, be afraid of the
one who can destroy both soul and body in
hell. 29Are not two sparrows sold for a penny[d]? Yet not one of them will fall to the
ground apart from the will of your Father.
30And even the very hairs of your head are
all numbered. 31So don't be afraid; you are
worth more than many sparrows.
32"Whoever acknowledges me before
men, I will also acknowledge him before
my Father in heaven. 33But whoever disowns me before men, I will disown him
before my Father in heaven.●

[c]25 Greek *Beezeboul* or *Beelzeboul*
[d]29 Greek *an assarion*

KING JAMES

1.PERSECUTION

16 Behold, I send you forth as sheep in
the midst of wolves: be ye therefore wise
as serpents, and harmless as doves.
17 But beware of men: for they will deliver you up to the councils, and they will
scourge you in their synagogues; 18 and
ye shall be brought before governors and
kings for my sake, for a testimony against
them and the Gentiles. 19 But when they
deliver you up, take no thought how or
what ye shall speak: for it shall be given
you in that same hour what ye shall speak.
20 For it is not ye that speak, but the
Spirit of your Father which speaketh in
you. 21 And the brother shall deliver up
the brother to death, and the father the
child: and the children shall rise up
against *their* parents, and cause them to
be put to death. 22 And ye shall be hated
of all *men* for my name's sake: but he
that endureth to the end shall be saved.
23 But when they persecute you in this
city, flee ye into another: for verily I say
unto you, Ye shall not have gone over the
cities of Israel, till the Son of man be
come.●

2.EXHORTATION

24 The disciple is not above *his* master,
nor the servant above his lord. 25 It is
enough for the disciple that he be as his
master, and the servant as his lord. If they
have called the master of the house Beel'zebub, how much more *shall they call*
them of his household?

26 Fear them not therefore: for there is
nothing covered, that shall not be revealed; and hid, that shall not be known.
27 What I tell you in darkness, *that* speak
ye in light: and what ye hear in the ear,
*that* preach ye upon the housetops.
28 And fear not them which kill the body,
but are not able to kill the soul: but rather
fear him which is able to destroy both soul
and body in hell. 29 Are not two sparrows sold for a farthing? and one of them
shall not fall on the ground without your
Father. 30 But the very hairs of your
head are all numbered. 31 Fear ye not
therefore, ye are of more value than many
sparrows. 32 Whosoever therefore shall
confess me before men, him will I confess
also before my Father which is in heaven.
33 But whosoever shall deny me before
men, him will I also deny before my
Father which is in heaven.●

"I send you out"

"I will confess"

This passage continues Jesus' instructions to His disciples, begun at 9:37. Read 11:1, observing how Matthew concludes this section.

Note Jesus' words in the center column. How are the two statements related?

Record what each paragraph teaches about DISCIPLES and DISCIPLESHIP:

*10:16-23* ______________________

*10:24-33* ______________________

NEW INTERNATIONAL VERSION

Record practical lessons taught by this passage. Be sure to relate the lessons to your own experience, whenever possible:

In your own words, what did Jesus mean by these verses:

v.35

v.37

34 "Do not suppose that I have come to
bring peace to the earth. I did not come to
bring peace, but a sword. 35 For I have
come to turn

"'a man against his father,
a daughter against her mother,
a daughter-in-law against her
mother-in-law—
36 a man's enemies will be the
members of his own
household.'[e]

37 "Anyone who loves his father or
mother more than me is not worthy of me;
anyone who loves his son or daughter more
than me is not worthy of me; 38 and anyone
who does not take his cross and follow me
is not worthy of me. 39 Whoever finds his
life will lose it, and whoever loses his life
for my sake will find it.●

40 "He who receives you receives me,
and he who receives me receives the one
who sent me. 41 Anyone who receives a
prophet because he is a prophet will receive a prophet's reward, and anyone who
receives a righteous man because he is a
righteous man will receive a righteous
man's reward. 42 And if anyone gives a cup
of cold water to one of these little ones
because he is my disciple, I tell you the
truth, he will certainly not lose his reward."●

*Jesus and John the Baptist*

11 After Jesus had finished instructing
his twelve disciples, he went on
from there to teach and preach in the towns
of Galilee.[a]●

[e] 36 Micah 7:6

[a] 1 Greek *in their towns*

KING JAMES

1.CONFLICT

34 Think not that I am come to send
peace on earth: I came not to send peace,
but a sword. 35 For I am come to set a
man at variance against his father, and the
daughter against her mother, and the
daughter-in-law against her mother-in-
law. 36 And a man's foes *shall be* they of
his own household. 37 He that loveth
father or mother more than me is not
worthy of me: and he that loveth son or
daughter more than me is not worthy of
me. 38 And he that taketh not his cross,
and followeth after me, is not worthy of
me. 39 He that findeth his life shall lose
it: and he that loseth his life for my sake
shall find it. ●

SWORD

2.RECEPTION

40 He that receiveth you receiveth me;
and he that receiveth me receiveth him
that sent me. 41 He that receiveth a
prophet in the name of a prophet shall
receive a prophet's reward; and he that
receiveth a righteous man in the name of
a righteous man shall receive a righteous
man's reward. 42 And whosoever shall
give to drink unto one of these little ones
a cup of cold *water* only in the name of a
disciple, verily I say unto you, he shall in
no wise lose his reward.●

WATER

—conclusion

11 And it came to pass, when Jesus had made an end of commanding his twelve disciples, he departed thence to teach and to preach in their cities.●

This segment continues the instructional ministry of Jesus recorded in the preceding segment. Both should be studied together.

Record the different instructions of each of the first two paragraphs:

*10:34-39* ______________________

*10:40-42* ______________________

*11:1* Record the ministries of Jesus: ______________________

NEW INTERNATIONAL VERSION

There are many interesting practical truths in the verses about John the Baptist and Jesus (verses 2-19). Record what you learn about these subjects:

DOUBT ____________________

HUMILITY ____________________

SERVANT OF CHRIST ____________________

GREATNESS ____________________

RESPONDING TO GOD'S LIGHT ____________________

APATHY ____________________

UNBELIEF ____________________

What does verse 20 suggest about a major purpose of Jesus' miracles?

What do verses 22-24 teach about Judgment Day? ____________________

2 When John heard in prison what Christ was doing, he sent his disciples 3 to ask him, "Are you the one who was to come, or should we expect someone else?"

4 Jesus replied, "Go back and report to John what you hear and see: 5 The blind receive sight, the lame walk, those who have leprosy[b] are cured, the deaf hear, the dead are raised, and the good news is preached to the poor. 6 Blessed is the man who does not fall away on account of me." ●

7 As John's disciples were leaving, Jesus began to speak to the crowd about John: "What did you go out into the desert to see? A reed swayed by the wind? 8 If not, what did you go out to see? A man dressed in fine clothes? No, those who wear fine clothes are in kings' palaces. 9 Then what did you go out to see? A prophet? Yes, I tell you, and more than a prophet. 10 This is the one about whom it is written:

"'I will send my messenger ahead of you,
who will prepare your way before you.'[c]

11 I tell you the truth: Among those born of women there has not risen anyone greater than John the Baptist; yet he who is least in the kingdom of heaven is greater than he. 12 From the days of John the Baptist until now, the kingdom of heaven has been forcefully advancing, and forceful men lay hold of it. 13 For all the Prophets and the Law prophesied until John. 14 And if you are willing to accept it, he is the Elijah who was to come. 15 He who has ears, let him hear.

16 "To what can I compare this generation? They are like children sitting in the marketplaces and calling out to others:

17 "'We played the flute for you,
and you did not dance;
we sang a dirge,
and you did not mourn.'

18 For John came neither eating nor drinking, and they say, 'He has a demon.' 19 The Son of Man came eating and drinking, and they say, 'Here is a glutton and a drunkard, a friend of tax collectors and "sinners."' But wisdom is proved right by her actions." ●

*Woe on Unrepentant Cities*

20 Then Jesus began to denounce the cities in which most of his miracles had been performed, because they did not repent. 21 "Woe to you, Korazin! Woe to you, Bethsaida! If the miracles that were performed in you had been performed in Tyre and Sidon, they would have repented long ago in sackcloth and ashes. 22 But I tell you, it will be more bearable for Tyre and Sidon on the day of judgment than for you. 23 And you, Capernaum, will you be lifted up to the skies? No, you will go down to the depths.[d] If the miracles that were performed in you had been performed in Sodom, it would have remained to this day. 24 But I tell you that it will be more bearable for Sodom on the day of judgment than for you." ●

[b] *5* The Greek word was used for various diseases affecting the skin—not necessarily leprosy.
[c] *10* Mal. 3:1 [d] *23* Greek *Hades*

KING JAMES

**1. JOHN'S DOUBTS ABOUT JESUS**

PROPHET IN PRISON

2 Now when John had heard in the
prison the works of Christ, he sent two of
his disciples, 3 and said unto him, Art
thou he that should come, or do we look
for another? 4 Jesus answered and said
unto them, Go and show John again those
things which ye do hear and see: 5 the
blind receive their sight, and the lame
walk, the lepers are cleansed, and the deaf
hear, the dead are raised up, and the
poor have the gospel preached to them.
6 And blessed is *he*, whosoever shall not
be offended in me.●

**2. JESUS' PRAISE OF JOHN**

7 And as they departed, Jesus began to
say unto the multitudes concerning John,
What went ye out into the wilderness to
see? A reed shaken with the wind?
8 But what went ye out for to see? A
man clothed in soft raiment? behold, they
that wear soft *clothing* are in kings'
houses. 9 But what went ye out for to
see? A prophet? yea, I say unto you, and
more than a prophet. 10 For this is *he*,
of whom it is written,

> Behold, I send my messenger before thy face,
> which shall prepare thy way before thee.

Mal. 3:1

11 Verily I say unto you, Among them
that are born of women there hath not
risen a greater than John the Baptist:
notwithstanding, he that is least in the
kingdom of heaven is greater than he.
12 And from the days of John the Baptist
until now the kingdom of heaven suffereth violence, and the violent take it by
force. 13 For all the prophets and the
law prophesied until John. 14 And if ye
will receive *it*, this is Eli'jah, which was for
to come. 15 He that hath ears to hear,
let him hear.
16 But whereunto shall I liken this generation? It is like unto children sitting in
the markets, and calling unto their fellows,
17 and saying,

> We have piped unto you, and ye have not danced;
> we have mourned unto you, and ye have not lamented.

18 For John came neither eating nor
drinking, and they say, He hath a devil.
19 The Son of man came eating and
drinking, and they say, Behold a man
gluttonous, and a winebibber, a friend of
publicans and sinners. But wisdom is justified of her children.●

**3. JESUS' REPROACH OF CITIES**

20 Then began he to upbraid the cities
wherein most of his mighty works were
done, because they repented not: 21 Woe
unto thee, Chora'zin! woe unto thee,
Bethsai'da! for if the mighty works,
which were done in you, had been done
in Tyre and Sidon, they would have repented long ago in sackcloth and ashes.
22 But I say unto you, It shall be more
tolerable for Tyre and Sidon at the day of
judgment, than for you. 23 And thou,
Caper'na-um, which art exalted unto
heaven, shalt be brought down to hell:
for if the mighty works, which have been
done in thee, had been done in Sodom,
it would have remained until this day.
24 But I say unto you, That it shall be
more tolerable for the land of Sodom in
the day of judgment, than for thee.●

CITY IN JUDGMENT

---

At this point in his gospel Matthew begins to write about a growing rejection of Jesus as King. The narrative section 8:1—9:34 was about POWER OF THE KING. The discourse of 9:35—11:1 was Jesus' charge to the twelve disciples. Now the narrative section 11:2—12:50 is about REJECTION OF THE KING. Compare the beginning and end of this segment: for example, a prophet, and a city.

*11:2-6* Analyze John's question and Jesus' reply.

*11:7-19* Record the different things Jesus said about John and about Himself.

JOHN ______

JESUS ______

*11:20-24* Why did Jesus reproach the cities?

NEW INTERNATIONAL VERSION

Do verses 25-26 imply that God does not love haughty people who think they are wise? If not, what do the verses teach?

Why are verses 28-30 such beloved verses?

Read *Exodus 20:10*. The Pharisees applied this law to the disciples' "work" and Jesus' healing, and accused them of breaking the law. Study Jesus' answers to the accusations.

What things were greater than or more superior to the law of the Sabbath? Apply your answers to situations you find yourself in, today.

### *Rest for the Weary*

25At that time Jesus said, "I praise you,
Father, Lord of heaven and earth, because
you have hidden these things from the wise
and learned, and revealed them to little
children. 26Yes, Father, for this was your
good pleasure.●
27"All things have been committed to me
by my Father. No one knows the Son except the Father, and no one knows the Father except the Son and those to whom the
Son chooses to reveal him.
28"Come to me, all you who are weary
and burdened, and I will give you rest.
29Take my yoke upon you and learn from
me, for I am gentle and humble in heart,
and you will find rest for your souls. 30For
my yoke is easy and my burden is light."●

### *Lord of the Sabbath*

12 At that time Jesus went through the
grainfields on the Sabbath. His disciples were hungry and began to pick some
heads of grain and eat them. 2When the
Pharisees saw this, they said to him,
"Look! Your disciples are doing what is
unlawful on the Sabbath."
3He answered, "Haven't you read what
David did when he and his companions
were hungry? 4He entered the house of
God, and he and his companions ate the
consecrated bread—which was not lawful
for them to do, but only for the priests. 5Or
haven't you read in the Law that on the
Sabbath the priests in the temple desecrate
the day and yet are innocent? 6I tell you
that one[a] greater than the temple is here.
7If you had known what these words mean,
'I desire mercy, not sacrifice,'[b] you would
not have condemned the innocent. 8For the
Son of Man is Lord of the Sabbath."●
9Going on from that place, he went into
their synagogue, 10and a man with a shriveled hand was there. Looking for a reason
to accuse Jesus, they asked him, "Is it
lawful to heal on the Sabbath?"
11He said to them, "If any of you has a
sheep and it falls into a pit on the Sabbath,
will you not take hold of it and lift it out?
12How much more valuable is a man than
a sheep! Therefore it is lawful to do good
on the Sabbath."
13Then he said to the man, "Stretch out
your hand." So he stretched it out and it
was completely restored, just as sound as
the other. 14But the Pharisees went out and
plotted how they might kill Jesus.●

[a]6 Or *something;* also in verses 41 and 42
[b]7 Hosea 6:6

## KING JAMES

1. PRAYER

PRAISE OF THE FATHER

**25 At that time Jesus answered and
said, I thank thee, O Father, Lord of
heaven and earth, because thou hast hid
these things from the wise and prudent,
and hast revealed them unto babes.
26 Even so, Father; for so it seemed good
in thy sight.● 27 All things are delivered**

2. TEACHING

**unto me of my Father: and no man
knoweth the Son, but the Father; neither
knoweth any man the Father, save the
Son, and *he* to whomsoever the Son will
reveal *him*. 28 Come unto me, all *ye* that
labor and are heavy laden, and I will give
you rest. 29 Take my yoke upon you, and
learn of me; for I am meek and lowly in
heart: and ye shall find rest unto your
souls. 30 For my yoke *is* easy, and my
burden is light.●**

—true rest

3. OPPOSITION

**12 At that time Jesus went on the sab-
bath day through the corn; and his
disciples were ahungered, and began to
pluck the ears of corn, and to eat. 2 But
when the Pharisees saw *it*, they said unto
him, Behold, thy disciples do that which
is not lawful to do upon the sabbath day.
3 But he said unto them, Have ye not read
what David did, when he was ahungered,
and they that were with him; 4 how he
entered into the house of God, and did
eat the showbread, which was not lawful
for him to eat, neither for them which
were with him, but only for the priests ?
5 Or have ye not read in the law, how that
on the sabbath days the priests in the
temple profane the sabbath, and are
blameless ? 6 But I say unto you, That
in this place is *one* greater than the temple.
7 But if ye had known what *this* meaneth,
I will have mercy, and not sacrifice, ye
would not have condemned the guiltless.
8 For the Son of man is Lord even of the
sabbath day. ●**

—legal Sabbath

—Lord of the Sabbath

**9 And when he was departed thence, he
went into their synagogue: 10 and, behold, there was a man which had *his* hand
withered. And they asked him, saying,
Is it lawful to heal on the sabbath days?
that they might accuse him. 11 And he
said unto them, What man shall there be
among you, that shall have one sheep, and
if it fall into a pit on the sabbath day, will
he not lay hold on it, and lift *it* out?
12 How much then is a man better than a
sheep? Wherefore it is lawful to do well
on the sabbath days. 13 Then saith he to
the man, Stretch forth thine hand. And
he stretched *it* forth; and it was restored
whole, like as the other. 14 Then the
Pharisees went out, and held a council
against him, how they might destroy him.●**

—good on the Sabbath

PLOT AGAINST THE SON

*11:25-26* What did Jesus praise His Father for?

What do you think "these things" refer to?

*11:27-30* What do you learn from verse 27 about the Father and the Son?

In a person's salvation, relate the *Son's will* (v.27) to the *sinner's coming* (v.28).

*12:1-8* How does Jesus defend His disciples here?

What do you think is the key sentence of the paragraph?

*12:9-14* Choose a key sentence of verses 9-13. Record it here.

What does verse 14 tell as to how intense the opposition against Jesus had become?

NEW INTERNATIONAL VERSION

Record what you learn from this passage about these four subjects:

JESUS

SATAN

HOLY SPIRIT

SPEECH

*God's Chosen Servant*

[15]Aware of this, Jesus withdrew from
that place. Many followed him, and he
healed all their sick, [16]warning them not to
tell who he was. [17]This was to fulfill what
was spoken through the prophet Isaiah:

[18]"Here is my servant whom I have
chosen,
the one I love, in whom I delight;
I will put my Spirit on him,
and he will proclaim justice to the
nations.
[19]He will not quarrel or cry out;
no one will hear his voice in the
streets.
[20]A bruised reed he will not break,
and a smoldering wick he will not
snuff out,
till he leads justice to victory.
[21] In his name the nations will put
their hope."[c] ●

*Jesus and Beelzebub*

[22]Then they brought him a demon-possessed man who was blind and mute, and
Jesus healed him, so that he could both talk
and see. [23]All the people were astonished
and said, "Could this be the Son of David?"
[24]But when the Pharisees heard this,
they said, "It is only by Beelzebub,[d] the
prince of demons, that this fellow drives
out demons."
[25]Jesus knew their thoughts and said to
them, "Every kingdom divided against itself will be ruined, and every city or
household divided against itself will not
stand. [26]If Satan drives out Satan, he is
divided against himself. How then can his
kingdom stand? [27]And if I drive out demons by Beelzebub, by whom do your
people drive them out? So then, they will
be your judges. [28]But if I drive out demons
by the Spirit of God, then the kingdom of
God has come upon you.
[29]"Or again, how can anyone enter a
strong man's house and carry off his
possessions unless he first ties up the
strong man? Then he can rob his house.
[30]"He who is not with me is against me,
and he who does not gather with me scatters. [31]And so I tell you, every sin and
blasphemy will be forgiven men, but the
blasphemy against the Spirit will not be
forgiven. [32]Anyone who speaks a word
against the Son of Man will be forgiven, but
anyone who speaks against the Holy Spirit
will not be forgiven, either in this age or in
the age to come. ●
[33]"Make a tree good and its fruit will be
good, or make a tree bad and its fruit will
be bad, for a tree is recognized by its fruit.
[34]You brood of vipers, how can you who
are evil say anything good? For out of the
overflow of the heart the mouth speaks.
[35]The good man brings good things out of
the good stored up in him, and the evil man
brings evil things out of the evil stored up
in him. [36]But I tell you that men will have
to give account on the day of judgment for
every careless word they have spoken.
[37]For by your words you will be acquitted,
and by your words you will be condemned." ●

c*21* Isaiah 42:1-4
d*24* Greek *Beezeboul* or *Beelzeboul*; also in verse 27

KING JAMES

1. COMMEN-DATION BY GOD

15 But when Jesus knew *it*, he withdrew
himself from thence: and great multitudes
followed him, and he healed them all;
16 and charged them that they should not
make him known: 17 that it might be
fulfilled which was spoken by Isaiah the
prophet, saying,
18 Behold my servant, whom I have
chosen;
my beloved, in whom my soul is well
pleased:
I will put my Spirit upon him,
and he shall show judgment to the
Gentiles.
19 He shall not strive, nor cry;
neither shall any man hear his voice
in the streets.
20 A bruised reed shall he not break,
and smoking flax shall he not quench,
till he send forth judgment unto
victory.
21 And in his name shall the Gentiles
trust.●

BELOVED SERVANT

Isa. 42:1-4

2. ACCUSATION BY ENEMY

22 Then was brought unto him one
possessed with a devil, blind, and dumb:
and he healed him, insomuch that the
blind and dumb both spake and saw.
23 And all the people were amazed, and
said, Is not this the Son of David? 24 But
when the Pharisees heard *it*, they said,
This *fellow* doth not cast out devils, but by
Beel′zebub the prince of the devils.
25 And Jesus knew their thoughts, and
said unto them, Every kingdom divided
against itself is brought to desolation; and
every city or house divided against itself
shall not stand: 26 and if Satan cast out
Satan, he is divided against himself; how
shall then his kingdom stand? 27 And if
I by Beel′zebub cast out devils, by whom
do your children cast *them* out? therefore
they shall be your judges. 28 But if I cast
out devils by the Spirit of God, then the
kingdom of God is come unto you. 29 Or
else, how can one enter into a strong man's
house, and spoil his goods, except he first
bind the strong man? and then he will
spoil his house. 30 He that is not with me
is against me; and he that gathereth not
with me scattereth abroad. 31 Wherefore
I say unto you, All manner of sin and
blasphemy shall be forgiven unto men:
but the blasphemy *against* the *Holy* Ghost
shall not be forgiven unto men. 32 And
whosoever speaketh a word against the
Son of man, it shall be forgiven him: but
whosoever speaketh against the Holy
Ghost, it shall not be forgiven him, neither in this world, neither in the *world* to
come.●

3. TEST BY FRUIT

33 Either make the tree good, and his
fruit good; or else make the tree corrupt,
and his fruit corrupt: for the tree is known
by *his* fruit. 34 O generation of vipers,
how can ye, being evil, speak good things?
for out of the abundance of the heart the
mouth speaketh. 35 A good man out of
the good treasure of the heart bringeth
forth good things: and an evil man out of
the evil treasure bringeth forth evil things.
36 But I say unto you, That every idle
word that men shall speak, they shall give
account thereof in the day of judgment.
37 For by thy words thou shalt be justified, and by thy words thou shalt be condemned.●

GOOD FRUIT

Read the first sentence of verse 15. The phrase "knew it" refers back to 12:14. Read that verse.

List the different things prophesied about Jesus in verses 18-21:

*12:22-32* This paragraph is about the two spirit worlds: good and evil. Record truths taught:

| EVIL | GOOD |
| --- | --- |
| | |

*12:33-37* Is this paragraph about words or deeds?

Relate the paragraph to the preceding one.

NEW INTERNATIONAL VERSION

What is a miracle?

Why did Jesus perform miracles during His earthly ministry?

What was Jesus' reply to those who wanted to see more miracles?

What great sign was yet to be given to the world?

Write different thoughts that come to mind as you meditate on these two statements:

"YOU REFUSE TO BELIEVE HIM"

"HE IS WORSE OFF THAN BEFORE"

How does one get close to the heart of Jesus?

*The Sign of Jonah*

38 Then some of the Pharisees and teachers of the law said to him, "Teacher, we want to see a miraculous sign from you."

39 He answered, "A wicked and adulterous generation asks for a miraculous sign! But none will be given it except the sign of the prophet Jonah. 40 For as Jonah was three days and three nights in the belly of a huge fish, so the Son of Man will be three days and three nights in the heart of the earth. 41 The men of Nineveh will stand up at the judgment with this generation and condemn it; for they repented at the preaching of Jonah, and now one greater than Jonah is here. 42 The Queen of the South will rise at the judgment with this generation and condemn it; for she came from the ends of the earth to listen to Solomon's wisdom, and now one greater than Solomon is here.●

43 "When an evil[a] spirit comes out of a man, it goes through arid places seeking rest and does not find it. 44 Then it says, 'I will return to the house I left.' When it arrives, it finds the house unoccupied, swept clean and put in order. 45 Then it goes and takes with it seven other spirits more wicked than itself, and they go in and live there. And the final condition of that man is worse than the first. That is how it will be with this wicked generation."●

*Jesus' Mother and Brothers*

46 While Jesus was still talking to the crowd, his mother and brothers stood outside, wanting to speak to him. 47 Someone told him, "Your mother and brothers are standing outside, wanting to speak to you."[b]

48 He replied, "Who is my mother, and who are my brothers?" 49 Pointing to his disciples, he said, "Here are my mother and my brothers. 50 For whoever does the will of my Father in heaven is my brother and sister and mother."●

[a] 43 Greek *unclean*

[b] 47 Some manuscripts do not have verse 47.

KING JAMES

1. REJECTORS OF JESUS

EVIL GENERATION

38 Then certain of the scribes and of the
Pharisees answered, saying, Master, we
would see a sign from thee. 39 But he
answered and said unto them, An evil and
adulterous generation seeketh after a
sign; and there shall no sign be given to
it, but the sign of the prophet Jonah:
40 for as Jonah was three days and three
nights in the whale's belly; so shall the
Son of man be three days and three nights
in the heart of the earth. 41 The men of
Nin'eveh shall rise in judgment with this
generation, and shall condemn it: because they repented at the preaching of
Jonah; and, behold, a greater than Jonah
*is* here. 42 The queen of the south shall
rise up in the judgment with this generation, and shall condemn it: for she came
from the uttermost parts of the earth to
hear the wisdom of Solomon; and, behold, a greater than Solomon *is* here.●

43 When the unclean spirit is gone out
of a man, he walketh through dry places,
seeking rest, and findeth none. 44 Then
he saith, I will return into my house from
whence I came out; and when he is come,
he findeth *it* empty, swept, and garnished.
45 Then goeth he, and taketh with himself seven other spirits more wicked than
himself, and they enter in and dwell there:
and the last *state* of that man is worse
than the first. Even so shall it be also
unto this wicked generation.●

2. FAMILY OF JESUS

46 While he yet talked to the people,
behold, *his* mother and his brethren stood
without, desiring to speak with him.
47 Then one said unto him, Behold, thy
mother and thy brethren stand without,
desiring to speak with thee. 48 But he
answered and said unto him that told him,
Who is my mother? and who are my
brethren? 49 And he stretched forth his
hand toward his disciples, and said, Behold my mother and my brethren! 50 For
whosoever shall do the will of my Father
which is in heaven, the same is my brother,
and sister, and mother.●

INTIMATE FAMILY

This is the last passage in the narrative section about REJECTION OF THE KING.

Compare the persons at the beginning of the segment with those at the end.

_______________

_______________

_______________

_______________

_______________

_______________

Where in the passage does Jesus prophesy His coming death and burial?

_______________

_______________

*12:38-42* Jesus exposed the unbelief of His rejectors by two Old Testament examples. Record these.

1) _______________

_______________

_______________

2) _______________

_______________

_______________

*12:43-45* What is the main point of this paragraph? (Let the phrase "worse than the first" be a guide to your answer.)

_______________

_______________

_______________

_______________

_______________

*12:46-50* What is Jesus' main reason for saying what He says?

_______________

_______________

_______________

_______________

NEW INTERNATIONAL VERSION

What is a parable?

Apply the parable of the four soils to today. Think of particular situations, for your listings.

THE SOILS

THE YIELDS

THE CAUSES

*The Parable of the Sower*

13 That same day Jesus went out of the
house and sat by the lake. 2Such
large crowds gathered around him that he
got into a boat and sat in it, while all the
people stood on the shore. 3Then he told
them many things in parables, saying: "A
farmer went out to sow his seed. 4As he
was scattering the seed, some fell along the
path, and the birds came and ate it up.
5Some fell on rocky places, where it did not
have much soil. It sprang up quickly, because the soil was shallow. 6But when the
sun came up, the plants were scorched,
and they withered because they had no
root. 7Other seed fell among thorns, which
grew up and choked the plants. 8Still other
seed fell on good soil, where it produced a
crop—a hundred, sixty or thirty times
what was sown. 9He who has ears, let him
hear."●

10The disciples came to him and asked,
"Why do you speak to the people in parables?"

11He replied, "The knowledge of the secrets of the kingdom of heaven has been
given to you, but not to them. 12Whoever
has will be given more, and he will have an
abundance. Whoever does not have, even
what he has will be taken from him. 13This
is why I speak to them in parables:

"Though seeing, they do not see;
though hearing, they do not hear
or understand.

14In them is fulfilled the prophecy of Isaiah:

" 'You will be ever hearing but
never understanding;
you will be ever seeing but never
perceiving.
15For this people's heart has become
calloused;
they hardly hear with their ears,
and they have closed their eyes.
Otherwise they might see with their
eyes,
hear with their ears,
understand with their hearts
and turn, and I would heal them.'[c]

16But blessed are your eyes because they
see, and your ears because they hear. 17For
I tell you the truth, many prophets and
righteous men longed to see what you see
but did not see it, and to hear what you
hear but did not hear it.●

18"Listen then to what the parable of the
sower means: 19When anyone hears the
message about the kingdom and does not
understand it, the evil one comes and
snatches away what was sown in his heart.
This is the seed sown along the path.
20What was sown on rocky places is the
man who hears the word and at once receives it with joy. 21But since he has no
root, he lasts only a short time. When trouble or persecution comes because of the
word, he quickly falls away. 22What was
sown among the thorns is the man who
hears the word, but the worries of this life
and the deceitfulness of wealth choke it,
making it unfruitful. 23But what was sown
on good soil is the man who hears the word
and understands it. He produces a crop,
yielding a hundred, sixty or thirty times
what was sown."●

[c]15 Isaiah 6:9,10

KING JAMES

1.PARABLE

MULTITUDES HEAR THE PARABLE

**13** The same day went Jesus out of the
house, and sat by the sea side.
2 And great multitudes were gathered together unto him, so that he went into a
ship, and sat; and the whole multitude
stood on the shore. 3 And he spake many
things unto them in parables, saying, Behold, a sower went forth to sow; 4 and
when he sowed, some *seeds* fell by the
wayside, and the fowls came and devoured them up: 5 some fell upon stony
places, where they had not much earth:
and forthwith they sprung up, because
they had no deepness of earth: 6 and
when the sun was up, they were scorched;
and because they had no root, they withered away. 7 And some fell among thorns;
and the thorns sprung up, and choked
them: 8 but other fell into good ground,
and brought forth fruit, some a hundredfold, some sixtyfold, some thirtyfold.
9 Who hath ears to hear, let him hear.●

2.REASON FOR PARABLES

10 And the disciples came, and said unto him, Why speakest thou unto them in
parables? 11 He answered and said unto
them, Because it is given unto you to
know the mysteries of the kingdom of
heaven, but to them it is not given. 12 For
whosoever hath, to him shall be given,
and he shall have more abundance: but
whosoever hath not, from him shall be
taken away even that he hath. 13 Therefore speak I to them in parables: because
they seeing see not; and hearing they hear
not, neither do they understand. 14 And
in them is fulfilled the prophecy of Isaiah,
which saith,

Isa. 6:9-10

> By hearing ye shall hear, and shall not understand;
> and seeing ye shall see, and shall not perceive:
> 15 for this people's heart is waxed gross,
> and *their* ears are dull of hearing,
> and their eyes they have closed;
> lest at any time they should see with *their* eyes,
> and hear with *their* ears,
> and should understand with *their* heart,
> and should be converted, and I should heal them.

16 But blessed *are* your eyes, for they see:
and your ears, for they hear. 17 For verily
I say unto you, That many prophets and
righteous *men* have desired to see *those
things* which ye see, and have not seen
*them;* and to hear *those things* which ye
hear, and have not heard *them*.●

3.INTERPRETATION

ONE MAN HEARING THE WORD

18 Hear ye therefore the parable of the
sower. 19 When any one heareth the
word of the kingdom, and understandeth
*it* not, then cometh the wicked one, and
catcheth away that which was sown in his
heart. This is he which received seed by
the wayside. 20 But he that received the
seed into stony places, the same is he that
heareth the word, and anon with joy receiveth it; 21 yet hath he not root in
himself, but dureth for a while: for when
tribulation or persecution ariseth because
of the word, by and by he is offended.
22 He also that received seed among the
thorns is he that heareth the word; and
the care of this world, and the deceitfulness of riches, choke the word, and he becometh unfruitful. 23 But he that received
seed into the good ground is he that heareth the word, and understandeth *it;* which
also beareth fruit, and bringeth forth,
some a hundredfold, some sixty, some
thirty.●

The PROCLAMATION section of Matthew (4:12—16:20) emphasizes especially the discourses of Jesus. The discourse of parables is 13:1-53. This first part (13:1-23) was spoken to the crowds by the sea (Cf. 13:1,2,3,4).

*13:1-9*

List the four kinds of soil, and what the seed plantings brought forth in each:

v.4 ______________________

______________________

vv.5-6 ______________________

______________________

v.7 ______________________

______________________

v.8 ______________________

______________________

*13:10-17* What was the disciples' question?

______________________

______________________

______________________

______________________

In your own words, what was Jesus' answer?

______________________

______________________

______________________

*13:18-23* Record the three hindrances to fruit for the first three plantings:

______________________

______________________

______________________

______________________

______________________

______________________

NEW INTERNATIONAL VERSION

Record spiritual lessons taught by the three parables of this passage:

GOOD SEED AND TARES

MUSTARD SEED

LEAVEN

*The Parable of the Weeds*

[24]Jesus told them another parable: "The
kingdom of heaven is like a man who
sowed good seed in his field. [25]But while
everyone was sleeping, his enemy came
and sowed weeds among the wheat, and
went away. [26]When the wheat sprouted
and formed heads, then the weeds also appeared.
[27]"The owner's servants came to him
and said, 'Sir, didn't you sow good seed in
your field? Where then did the weeds come
from?'
[28]" 'An enemy did this,' he replied.
"The servants asked him, 'Do you want
us to go and pull them up?'
[29]" 'No,' he answered, 'because while
you are pulling the weeds, you may root up
the wheat with them. [30]Let both grow together until the harvest. At that time I will
tell the harvesters: First collect the weeds
and tie them in bundles to be burned, then
gather the wheat and bring it into my
barn.' " ●

*The Parables of the Mustard Seed and the Yeast*

[31]He told them another parable: "The
kingdom of heaven is like a mustard seed,
which a man took and planted in his field.
[32]Though it is the smallest of all your seeds,
yet when it grows, it is the largest of garden
plants and becomes a tree, so that the birds
of the air come and perch in its branches." ●
[33]He told them still another parable:
"The kingdom of heaven is like yeast that
a woman took and mixed into a large
amount[a] of flour until it worked all through
the dough." ●
[34]Jesus spoke all these things to the
crowd in parables; he did not say anything
to them without using a parable. [35]So was
fulfilled what was spoken through the
prophet:

"I will open my mouth in parables,
I will utter things hidden since the
creation of the world."[b]

*The Parable of the Weeds Explained*

[36]Then he left the crowd and went into
the house. ●

[a]33 Greek *three satas* (probably about 1/2 bushel or 22 liters) [b]35 Psalm 78:2

## KING JAMES

**1. GOOD SEED AND TARES**

SEASIDE

**24 Another parable put he forth unto
them, saying, The kingdom of heaven is
likened unto a man which sowed good
seed in his field: 25 but while men slept,
his enemy came and sowed tares among
the wheat, and went his way. 26 But
when the blade was sprung up, and
brought forth fruit, then appeared the
tares also. 27 So the servants of the
householder came and said unto him, Sir,
didst not thou sow good seed in thy field?
from whence then hath it tares? 28 He
said unto them, An enemy hath done
this. The servants said unto him, Wilt
thou then that we go and gather them up?
29 But he said, Nay; lest while ye gather
up the tares, ye root up also the wheat
with them. 30 Let both grow together
until the harvest: and in the time of harvest I will say to the reapers, Gather ye
together first the tares, and bind them in
bundles to burn them: but gather the
wheat into my barn.●**

**2. MUSTARD SEED**

**31 Another parable put he forth unto
them, saying, The kingdom of heaven is
like to a grain of mustard seed, which a
man took, and sowed in his field: 32 which
indeed is the least of all seeds: but when
it is grown, it is the greatest among herbs,
and becometh a tree, so that the birds of
the air come and lodge in the branches
thereof.●**

**3. LEAVEN**

**33 Another parable spake he unto
them; The kingdom of heaven is like unto
leaven, which a woman took, and hid in
three measures of meal, till the whole was
leavened.●**

**34 All these things spake Jesus unto the
multitude in parables; and without a
parable spake he not unto them: 35 that
it might be fulfilled which was spoken by
the prophet, saying,**

> **I will open my mouth in parables;** Ps. 78:2
> **I will utter things which have been kept secret from the foundation of the world.**

HOUSE

**36 Then Jesus sent the multitude away,
and went into the house: ●**

---

Record the main parts of each of the parables of this segment.

*13:24-30* ______________________

*13:31-32* ______________________

*13:33* ______________________

*13:34-36* What is the main point of this paragraph?

______________________

NEW INTERNATIONAL VERSION

Most of Jesus' parables are introduced with the phrase, "The kingdom of heaven is like." What do you think Jesus means by this?

Record important practical truths taught by the parable of the good seed and tares (verses 37-43).

Interpret each of the other parables, and apply the truths to people today.

HID TREASURE (v.44)

PEARL (vv.45-46)

DRAGNET (vv.47-50)

HOUSEHOLDER (vv.51-52)

His disciples came to him and
said, "Explain to us the parable of the
weeds in the field."
37He answered, "The one who sowed
the good seed is the Son of Man. 38The field
is the world, and the good seed stands for
the sons of the kingdom. The weeds are the
sons of the evil one, 39and the enemy who
sows them is the devil. The harvest is the
end of the age, and the harvesters are angels.
40"As the weeds are pulled up and
burned in the fire, so it will be at the end
of the age. 41The Son of Man will send out
his angels, and they will weed out of his
kingdom everything that causes sin and all
who do evil. 42They will throw them into
the fiery furnace, where there will be
weeping and gnashing of teeth. 43Then the
righteous will shine like the sun in the kingdom of their Father. He who has ears, let
him hear.●

*The Parables of the Hidden Treasure and the Pearl*

44"The kingdom of heaven is like treasure hidden in a field. When a man found
it, he hid it again, and then in his joy went
and sold all he had and bought that field.●
45"Again, the kingdom of heaven is like
a merchant looking for fine pearls. 46When
he found one of great value, he went away
and sold everything he had and bought it.●

*The Parable of the Net*

47"Once again, the kingdom of heaven is
like a net that was let down into the lake
and caught all kinds of fish. 48When it was
full, the fishermen pulled it up on the
shore. Then they sat down and collected
the good fish in baskets, but threw the bad
away. 49This is how it will be at the end of
the age. The angels will come and separate
the wicked from the righteous 50and throw
them into the fiery furnace, where there
will be weeping and gnashing of teeth."●
51"Have you understood all these
things?" Jesus asked.
"Yes," they replied.
52He said to them, "Therefore every
teacher of the law who has been instructed
about the kingdom of heaven is like the
owner of a house who brings out of his
storeroom new treasures as well as old."●

*A Prophet Without Honor*

53When Jesus had finished these parables, he moved on from there.●

KING JAMES

—interpretation

and his disciples
came unto him, saying, Declare unto us
the parable of the tares of the field. 37 He
answered and said unto them, He that
soweth the good seed is the Son of man;
38 the field is the world; the good seed
are the children of the kingdom; but the
tares are the children of the wicked one;
39 the enemy that sowed them is the devil;
the harvest is the end of the world; and
the reapers are the angels. 40 As therefore the tares are gathered and burned in
the fire; so shall it be in the end of this
world. 41 The Son of man shall send
forth his angels, and they shall gather out
of his kingdom all things that offend, and
them which do iniquity; 42 and shall cast
them into a furnace of fire: there shall be
wailing and gnashing of teeth. 43 Then
shall the righteous shine forth as the sun
in the kingdom of their Father. Who
hath ears to hear, let him hear.●

1. HID TREASURE

44 Again, the kingdom of heaven is like
unto treasure hid in a field; the which
when a man hath found, he hideth, and
for joy thereof goeth and selleth all that
he hath, and buyeth that field.●

2. PEARL

45 Again, the kingdom of heaven is like
unto a merchantman, seeking goodly
pearls: 46 who, when he had found one
pearl of great price, went and sold all that
he had, and bought it.●

3. DRAGNET

47 Again, the kingdom of heaven is like
unto a net, that was cast into the sea, and
gathered of every kind: 48 which, when
it was full, they drew to shore, and sat
down, and gathered the good into vessels,
but cast the bad away. 49 So shall it be
at the end of the world: the angels shall
come forth, and sever the wicked from
among the just, 50 and shall cast them
into the furnace of fire: there shall be
wailing and gnashing of teeth.●

4. HOUSEHOLDER

51 Jesus saith unto them, Have ye
understood all these things? They say
unto him, Yea, Lord. 52 Then said he
unto them, Therefore every scribe *which
is* instructed unto the kingdom of heaven,
is like unto a man *that is* a householder,
which bringeth forth out of his treasure
*things* new and old.●

CONCLUSION

53 And it came to pass, *that* when Jesus
had finished these parables, he departed
thence.●

EXPLANATION

This segment continues the discourse of parables which began at 13:1. Read verse 53. How does this conclude the discourse? Recall 13:36a, where it is reported that Jesus left the multitude. Now He is talking just with His disciples.

*13:36b-43* Record the different interpreted parts of this parable.

_______________

_______________

_______________

_______________

_______________

_______________

_______________

*13:44-52*

Record the main parts of these parables:

HID TREASURE _______________

_______________

_______________

_______________

_______________

PEARL _______________

_______________

_______________

_______________

_______________

DRAGNET _______________

_______________

_______________

_______________

HOUSEHOLDER

_______________

_______________

_______________

_______________

NEW INTERNATIONAL VERSION

Why is it that a Christian worker is usually honored more away from his hometown than in his hometown?

What was the people's spiritual problem which brought on their disowning Jesus as a genuine miracle-worker?

How can you account for their anger?

Did King Herod believe that the miracles were genuine?

How did he try to explain them?

What was his spiritual problem?

List some important practical truths taught by this passage.

54Coming to
his home town, he began teaching the
people in their synagogue, and they were
amazed. "Where did this man get this wisdom and these miraculous powers?" they
asked. 55"Isn't this the carpenter's son?
Isn't his mother's name Mary, and aren't
his brothers James, Joseph, Simon and
Judas? 56Aren't all his sisters with us?
Where then did this man get all these
things?" 57And they took offense at him.
But Jesus said to them, "Only in his
home town and in his own house is a
prophet without honor."
58And he did not do many miracles there
because of their lack of faith.●

*John the Baptist Beheaded*

14 At that time Herod the tetrarch
heard the reports about Jesus, 2and
he said to his attendants, "This is John the
Baptist; he has risen from the dead! That is
why miraculous powers are at work in
him."
3Now Herod had arrested John and
bound him and put him in prison because
of Herodias, his brother Philip's wife, 4for
John had been saying to him: "It is not
lawful for you to have her." 5Herod wanted to kill John, but he was afraid of the
people, because they considered him a
prophet.
6On Herod's birthday the daughter of
Herodias danced for them and pleased
Herod so much 7that he promised with an
oath to give her whatever she asked.
8Prompted by her mother, she said, "Give
me here on a platter the head of John the
Baptist." 9The king was distressed, but because of his oaths and his dinner guests, he
ordered that her request be granted 10and
had John beheaded in the prison. 11His
head was brought in on a platter and given
to the girl, who carried it to her mother.
12John's disciples came and took his body
and buried it. Then they went and told
Jesus.●

KING JAMES

1. PROPHET JESUS DISHONORED

54 And when he was come into
his own country, he taught them in their
synagogue, insomuch that they were astonished, and said, Whence hath this *man*
this wisdom, and *these* mighty works?
55 Is not this the carpenter's son? is not
his mother called Mary? and his brethren, James, and Joses, and Simon, and
Judas? 56 And his sisters, are they not all
with us? Whence then hath this *man* all
these things? 57 And they were offended
in him. But Jesus said unto them, A
prophet is not without honor, save in his
own country, and in his own house.
58 And he did not many mighty works
there because of their unbelief.●

2. PROPHET JOHN BEHEADED

14 At that time Herod the tetrarch
heard of the fame of Jesus, 2 and
said unto his servants, This is John the
Baptist; he is risen from the dead; and
therefore mighty works do show forth
themselves in him. 3 For Herod had laid
hold on John, and bound him, and put
*him* in prison for Hero′di-as' sake, his
brother Philip's wife. 4 For John said unto him, It is not lawful for thee to have
her. 5 And when he would have put
him to death, he feared the multitude, because they counted him as a prophet.
6 But when Herod's birthday was kept,
the daughter of Hero′di-as danced before
them, and pleased Herod. 7 Whereupon
he promised with an oath to give her
whatsoever she would ask. 8 And she,
being before instructed of her mother,
said, Give me here John Baptist's head in
a charger. 9 And the king was sorry:
nevertheless for the oath's sake, and them
which sat with him at meat, he commanded *it* to be given *her*. 10 And he
sent, and beheaded John in the prison.
11 And his head was brought in a charger,
and given to the damsel: and she brought
*it* to her mother. 12 And his disciples
came, and took up the body, and buried
it, and went and told Jesus.●

—report to Herod

—report to Jesus

This is a study of two different kinds of opposition against the prophets Jesus and John the Baptist.

The action of verses 3-12 is parenthetical, for it refers back to an earlier time when Herod had beheaded John. (Cf. the first three words of 14:3.) Study the two paragraphs, and record all the different things related to the opposition being reported. (E.g., who, where, when, what, why, etc.)

*AGAINST JESUS* ____________________

*AGAINST JOHN THE BAPTIST* ____________________

NEW INTERNATIONAL VERSION

List the practical truths taught by the passage on these subjects:

COMPASSION

PRAYER

FEAR

FAITH

*Jesus Feeds the Five Thousand*

13 When Jesus heard what had happened,
he withdrew by boat privately to a solitary
place. Hearing of this, the crowds followed
him on foot from the towns. 14 When Jesus
landed and saw a large crowd, he had compassion on them and healed their sick.●
15 As evening approached, the disciples
came to him and said, "This is a remote
place, and it's already getting late. Send
the crowds away, so they can go to the
villages and buy themselves some food."
16 Jesus replied, "They do not need to go
away. You give them something to eat."
17 "We have here only five loaves of
bread and two fish," they answered.
18 "Bring them here to me," he said.
19 And he directed the people to sit down on
the grass. Taking the five loaves and the
two fish and looking up to heaven, he gave
thanks and broke the loaves. Then he gave
them to the disciples, and the disciples
gave them to the people. 20 They all ate and
were satisfied, and the disciples picked up
twelve basketfuls of broken pieces that
were left over. 21 The number of those who
ate was about five thousand men, besides
women and children.●

*Jesus Walks on the Water*

22 Immediately Jesus made the disciples
get into the boat and go on ahead of him to
the other side, while he dismissed the
crowd. 23 After he had dismissed them, he
went up into the hills by himself to pray.
When evening came, he was there alone,
24 but the boat was already a considerable
distance[a] from land, buffeted by the waves
because the wind was against it.
25 During the fourth watch of the night
Jesus went out to them, walking on the
lake. 26 When the disciples saw him walking
on the lake, they were terrified. "It's a
ghost," they said, and cried out in fear.
27 But Jesus immediately said to them:
"Take courage! It is I. Don't be afraid."
28 "Lord, if it's you," Peter replied, "tell
me to come to you on the water."
29 "Come," he said.
Then Peter got down out of the boat and
walked on the water to Jesus. 30 But when
he saw the wind, he was afraid and, beginning to sink, cried out, "Lord, save me!"
31 Immediately Jesus reached out his
hand and caught him. "You of little faith,"
he said, "why did you doubt?"
32 And when they climbed into the boat,
the wind died down. 33 Then those who
were in the boat worshiped him, saying,
"Truly you are the Son of God."●
34 When they had crossed over, they
landed at Gennesaret. 35 And when the men
of that place recognized Jesus, they sent
word to all the surrounding country.
People brought all their sick to him 36 and
begged him to let the sick just touch the
edge of his cloak, and all who touched him
were healed.●

[a]24 Greek *many stadia*

## KING JAMES

—Jesus seeks solitude

MANY HEALED

13 When Jesus heard *of it*, he departed
thence by ship into a desert place apart:
and when the people had heard *thereof*,
they followed him on foot out of the cities.
14 And Jesus went forth, and saw a great
multitude, and was moved with compassion toward them, and he healed their
sick.● 15 And when it was evening, his

1.FOOD MULTIPLIED

disciples came to him, saying, This is a
desert place, and the time is now past;
send the multitude away, that they may
go into the villages, and buy themselves
victuals. 16 But Jesus said unto them,
They need not depart; give ye them to
eat. 17 And they say unto him, We have
here but five loaves, and two fishes. 18 He
said, Bring them hither to me. 19 And he
commanded the multitude to sit down on
the grass, and took the five loaves, and the
two fishes, and looking up to heaven, he
blessed, and brake, and gave the loaves to
*his* disciples, and the disciples to the multitude. 20 And they did all eat, and were
filled: and they took up of the fragments
that remained twelve baskets full. 21 And
they that had eaten were about five thousand men, beside women and children.●

2.GRAVITY OVER-POWERED

22 And straightway Jesus constrained
his disciples to get into a ship, and to go
before him unto the other side, while he
sent the multitudes away. 23 And when
he had sent the multitudes away, he went
up into a mountain apart to pray: and
when the evening was come, he was there
alone. 24 But the ship was now in the
midst of the sea, tossed with waves: for
the wind was contrary. 25 And in the
fourth watch of the night Jesus went unto
them, walking on the sea. 26 And when
the disciples saw him walking on the sea,
they were troubled, saying, It is a spirit;
and they cried out for fear. 27 But
straightway Jesus spake unto them, saying, Be of good cheer; it is I; be not
afraid.
28 And Peter answered him and said,
Lord, if it be thou, bid me come unto thee
on the water. 29 And he said, Come.
And when Peter was come down out of
the ship, he walked on the water, to go to
Jesus. 30 But when he saw the wind
boisterous, he was afraid; and beginning
to sink, he cried, saying, Lord, save me.
31 And immediately Jesus stretched forth
*his* hand, and caught him, and said unto
him, O thou of little faith, wherefore didst

3.STORM STILLED

thou doubt? 32 And when they were
come into the ship, the wind ceased.
33 Then they that were in the ship came
and worshipped him, saying, Of a truth
thou art the Son of God.●

—multitudes seek Jesus

34 And when they were gone over, they
came into the land of Gennes'aret.
35 And when the men of that place had
knowledge of him, they sent out into all
that country round about, and brought
unto him all that were diseased; 36 and
besought him that they might only touch
the hem of his garment: and as many as
touched were made perfectly whole.●

MANY HEALED

What does the introductory paragraph teach about Jesus and the multitudes?

*14:15-21* What does this paragraph teach about Jesus'

POWER

METHODS

*14:22-33* What does this paragraph teach about

JESUS' METHODS

DISCIPLES' FAITH

What does the concluding paragraph (14:34-36) add to the entire passage?

NEW INTERNATIONAL VERSION

Tradition has a lot to do with the ways and habits of people. Try to think of traditions which are observed today with a religious background or setting. How might it be interpreted if such traditions were broken?

Also, think of Bible passages which would teach higher and greater principles of behavior than what those traditions support. Record your studies below.

Jesus correctly. As who?

In your own words, what is real spiritual defilement?

*Clean and Unclean*

15 Then some Pharisees and teachers
of the law came to Jesus from
Jerusalem and asked, 2"Why do your disciples break the tradition of the elders?
They don't wash their hands before they
eat!"
3Jesus replied, "And why do you break
the command of God for the sake of your
tradition? 4For God said, 'Honor your father and mother'[b] and 'Anyone who curses
his father or mother must be put to death.'[c]
5But you say that if a man says to his father
or mother, 'Whatever help you might otherwise have received from me is a gift devoted to God,' 6he is not to 'honor his father[d]' with it. Thus you nullify the word of
God for the sake of your tradition. 7You
hypocrites! Isaiah was right when he
prophesied about you:

8" 'These people honor me with their lips,
but their hearts are far from me.
9They worship me in vain;
their teachings are but rules taught by men.'[a]"

10Jesus called the crowd to him and said,
"Listen and understand. 11What goes into
a man's mouth does not make him 'unclean,' but what comes out of his mouth,
that is what makes him 'unclean.' "●
12Then the disciples came to him and
asked, "Do you know that the Pharisees
were offended when they heard this?"
13He replied, "Every plant that my heavenly Father has not planted will be pulled
up by the roots. 14Leave them; they are
blind guides.[b] If a blind man leads a blind
man, both will fall into a pit."●
15Peter said, "Explain the parable to
us."
16"Are you still so dull?" Jesus asked
them. 17"Don't you see that whatever enters the mouth goes into the stomach and
then out of the body? 18But the things that
come out of the mouth come from the
heart, and these make a man 'unclean.'
19For out of the heart come evil thoughts,
murder, adultery, sexual immorality, theft,
false testimony, slander. 20These are what
make a man 'unclean'; but eating with unwashed hands does not make him 'unclean.' "●

c4 Exodus 21:17; Lev. 20:9
b4 Exodus 20:12; Deut. 5:16
d6 Some manuscripts *father or his mother*
a9 Isaiah 29:13 b14 Some manuscripts *guides of the blind*

## KING JAMES

1. ACCUSATION OF DEFILEMENT

—Pharisees and scribes

15 Then came to Jesus scribes and
Pharisees, which were of Jerusalem, saying, 2 Why do thy disciples
transgress the tradition of the elders? for
they wash not their hands when they eat
bread. 3 But he answered and said unto
them, Why do ye also transgress the commandment of God by your tradition?
4 For God commanded, saying,
Honor thy father and mother: Ex. 20:12
and,
He that curseth father or mother, Ex. 21:17
let him die the death.
5 But ye say, Whosoever shall say to *his*
father or *his* mother, *It is* a gift, by whatsoever thou mightest be profited by me;
6 and honor not his father or his mother,
*he shall be free.* Thus have ye made the
commandment of God of none effect by
your tradition. 7 *Ye* hypocrites, well did
Isaiah prophesy of you, saying,
8 This people draweth nigh unto me Isa. 29:13
with their mouth,
and honoreth me with *their* lips;
but their heart is far from me.
9 But in vain they do worship me,
teaching *for* doctrines the commandments of men.
10 And he called the multitude, and
said unto them, Hear, and understand:
11 Not that which goeth into the mouth
defileth a man; but that which cometh out
of the mouth, this defileth a man.● 12 Then
came his disciples, and said unto him,
Knowest thou that the Pharisees were
offended, after they heard this saying?
13 But he answered and said, Every plant,
which my heavenly Father hath not
planted, shall be rooted up. 14 Let them
alone: they be blind leaders of the blind.
And if the blind lead the blind, both shall
fall into the ditch.● 15 Then answered
Peter and said unto him, Declare unto us
this parable. 16 And Jesus said, Are ye
also yet without understanding? 17 Do
not ye yet understand, that whatsoever
entereth in at the mouth goeth into the
belly, and is cast out into the draught?
18 But those things which proceed out of
the mouth come forth from the heart;
and they defile the man. 19 For out of the
heart proceed evil thoughts, murders,
adulteries, fornications, thefts, false witness, blasphemies: 20 these are *the things*
which defile a man: but to eat with unwashen hands defileth not a man.●

—disciples

OUT OF THE MOUTH

—Peter

2. EXPOSURE OF REAL DEFILEMENT

OUT OF THE HEART

*15:1-11* Underline every reference to the Word of God. (Include such phrases as "did Isaiah prophesy.")

Then underline the repeated word "tradition." Study all that is written about each, and record below.

TRADITION (of men) __________

COMMANDMENT (of God) __________

*15:12-14* What truths does Jesus teach here?

*15:15-20* What parable does Peter refer to in verse 15?

What is Jesus' interpretation of the parable?

NEW INTERNATIONAL VERSION

What does this passage teach about:

MERCY

FAITH

JESUS' MISSION

JESUS' COMPASSION

Read verses 29-39 again, and record various spiritual applications which can be made.

### *The Faith of the Canaanite Woman*

[21]Leaving that place, Jesus withdrew to
the region of Tyre and Sidon. [22]A Canaanite woman from that vicinity came to him,
crying out, "Lord, Son of David, have
mercy on me! My daughter is suffering ter-
ribly from demon-possession."
[23]Jesus did not answer a word. So his
disciples came to him and urged him,
"Send her away, for she keeps crying out
after us."
[24]He answered, "I was sent only to the
lost sheep of Israel."
[25]The woman came and knelt before him.
"Lord, help me!" she said.
[26]He replied, "It is not right to take the
children's bread and toss it to their dogs."
[27]"Yes, Lord," she said, "but even the
dogs eat the crumbs that fall from their
masters' table."
[28]Then Jesus answered, "Woman, you
have great faith! Your request is granted."
And her daughter was healed from that
very hour.●

### *Jesus Feeds the Four Thousand*

[29]Jesus left there and went along the Sea
of Galilee. Then he went up into the hills
and sat down. [30]Great crowds came to him,
bringing the lame, the blind, the crippled,
the dumb and many others, and laid them
at his feet; and he healed them. [31]The
people were amazed when they saw the
dumb speaking, the crippled made well,
the lame walking and the blind seeing. And
they praised the God of Israel.●
[32]Jesus called his disciples to him and
said, "I have compassion for these people;
they have already been with me three days
and have nothing to eat. I do not want to
send them away hungry, or they may collapse on the way."
[33]His disciples answered, "Where could
we get enough bread in this remote place to
feed such a crowd?"
[34]"How many loaves do you have?"
Jesus asked.
"Seven," they replied, "and a few small
fish."
[35]He told the crowd to sit down on the
ground. [36]Then he took the seven loaves
and the fish, and when he had given
thanks, he broke them and gave them to
the disciples, and they in turn to the
people. [37]They all ate and were satisfied.
Afterward the disciples picked up seven
basketfuls of broken pieces that were left
over. [38]The number of those who ate was
four thousand, besides women and children. [39]After Jesus had sent the crowd
away, he got into the boat and went to the
vicinity of Magadan.●

KING JAMES

**1. DEMON POSSESSION** — ONE WOMAN

21 Then Jesus went thence, and departed into the coasts of Tyre and Sidon.
22 And, behold, a woman of Canaan
came out of the same coasts, and cried
unto him, saying, Have mercy on me, O
Lord, *thou* Son of David; my daughter is
grievously vexed with a devil. 23 But he
answered her not a word. And his disciples came and besought him, saying,
Send her away; for she crieth after us.
24 But he answered and said, I am not
sent but unto the lost sheep of the house
of Israel. 25 Then came she and worshipped him, saying, Lord, help me.
26 But he answered and said, It is not
meet to take the children's bread, and to
cast *it* to dogs. 27 And she said, Truth,
Lord: yet the dogs eat of the crumbs
which fall from their masters' table.
28 Then Jesus answered and said unto
her, O woman, great *is* thy faith: be it unto thee even as thou wilt. And her daughter was made whole from that very hour. ●

**2. VARIOUS HEALINGS**

29 And Jesus departed from thence, and
came nigh unto the sea of Galilee; and
went up into a mountain, and sat down
there. 30 And great multitudes came unto
him, having with them *those that were*
lame, blind, dumb, maimed, and many
others, and cast them down at Jesus' feet;
and he healed them: 31 insomuch that the
multitude wondered, when they saw the
dumb to speak, the maimed to be whole,
the lame to walk, and the blind to see: and
they glorified the God of Israel. ●

**3. FEEDING THE MULTITUDES** — MULTITUDES

32 Then Jesus called his disciples *unto*
*him*, and said, I have compassion on the
multitude, because they continue with me
now three days, and have nothing to eat:
and I will not send them away fasting,
lest they faint in the way. 33 And his
disciples say unto him, Whence should we
have so much bread in the wilderness, as
to fill so great a multitude? 34 And Jesus
saith unto them, How many loaves have
ye? And they said, Seven, and a few little
fishes. 35 And he commanded the multitude to sit down on the ground. 36 And
he took the seven loaves and the fishes,
and gave thanks, and brake *them*, and
gave to his disciples, and the disciples to
the multitude. 37 And they did all eat,
and were filled: and they took up of the
broken *meat* that was left seven baskets
full. 38 And they that did eat were four
thousand men, beside women and children. 39 And he sent away the multitude, and took ship, and came into the
coasts of Mag'dala. ●

This is another passage recording miracles of Jesus. Always keep in mind, while you are studying passages like this, *WHY* Jesus performed miracles, and *WHAT* the effects were.

*15:21-28* What does this passage teach about:

JESUS ______

______

______

______

THE CANAANITE WOMAN ______

______

______

______

*15:29-31* What kinds of miracles did Jesus perform here?

______

______

What was the effect? ______

______

______

______

______

______

*15:32-39* What does this paragraph reveal about the *heart* of Jesus?

______

______

______

Record what you observe about Jesus' methods of performing this miracle.

______

______

______

______

______

______

______

______

NEW INTERNATIONAL VERSION

The false religious teachers were demanding to see more signs of Jesus' Messiahship. In your own words, what was Jesus' response to that (vv.2-4)?

Jesus likened the teaching of the Pharisees and Sadducees to yeast. And He warned His disciples to beware that yeast. Why do you think He used the figure of yeast?

Account for the wrong identifications of Jesus by some people (v.14).

Simon Peter identified Jesus correctly. As who?

What accounted for the correct identification?

Christ would build His church upon a rock foundation, of which Peter was a witness. Did Christ give Peter authority independent of divine authority? To answer this, observe the verb tense in the *New American Standard Bible* reading (v.19): "whatever you shall bind on earth *shall have been bound* in heaven...."

*The Demand for a Sign*

16 The Pharisees and Sadducees came
to Jesus and tested him by asking
him to show them a sign from heaven.
2He replied,[c] "When evening comes,
you say, 'It will be fair weather, for the sky
is red,' 3and in the morning, 'Today it will
be stormy, for the sky is red and overcast.'
You know how to interpret the appearance
of the sky, but you cannot interpret the
signs of the times. 4A wicked and adulterous generation looks for a miraculous sign,
but none will be given it except the sign of
Jonah." Jesus then left them and went
away.●

*The Yeast of the Pharisees and Sadducees*

5When they went across the lake, the
disciples forgot to take bread. 6"Be careful," Jesus said to them. "Be on your
guard against the yeast of the Pharisees
and Sadducees."
7They discussed this among themselves
and said, "It is because we didn't bring any
bread."
8Aware of their discussion, Jesus asked,
"You of little faith, why are you talking
among yourselves about having no bread?
9Do you still not understand? Don't you
remember the five loaves for the five thousand, and how many basketfuls you gathered? 10Or the seven loaves for the four
thousand, and how many basketfuls you
gathered? 11How is it you don't understand
that I was not talking to you about bread?
But be on your guard against the yeast of
the Pharisees and Sadducees." 12Then
they understood that he was not telling
them to guard against the yeast used in
bread, but against the teaching of the
Pharisees and Sadducees.●

*Peter's Confession of Christ*

13When Jesus came to the region of Caesarea Philippi, he asked his disciples,
"Who do people say the Son of Man is?"
14They replied, "Some say John the Baptist; others say Elijah; and still others, Jeremiah or one of the prophets."
15"But what about you?" he asked.
"Who do you say I am?"
16Simon Peter answered, "You are the
Christ,[a] the Son of the living God."
17Jesus replied, "Blessed are you, Simon
son of Jonah, for this was not revealed to
you by man, but by my Father in heaven.
18And I tell you that you are Peter,[b] and on
this rock I will build my church, and the
gates of Hades[c] will not overcome it.[d] 19I
will give you the keys of the kingdom of
heaven; whatever you bind on earth will be
bound in heaven, and whatever you loose
on earth will be loosed in heaven." 20Then
he warned his disciples not to tell anyone
that he was the Christ.●

[c]2 Some early manuscripts do not have the rest of verse 2 and all of verse 3.
[a]16 Or *Messiah*; also in verse 20 [b]18 *Peter* means *rock*.
[c]18 Or *hell* [d]18 Or *not prove stronger than it*

KING JAMES

1. JESUS AND THE ENEMIES

**16** The Pharisees also with the Sadducees came, and tempting desired him that he would show them a sign from heaven. 2 He answered and said unto them, When it is evening, ye say, *It will be* fair weather: for the sky is red. 3 And in the morning, *It will be* foul weather today: for the sky is red and lowering. O *ye* hypocrites, ye can discern the face of the sky; but can ye not *discern* the signs of the times? 4 A wicked and adulterous generation seeketh after a sign; and there shall no sign be given unto it, but the sign of the prophet Jonah. And he left them, and departed. ●

2. JESUS AND HIS DISCIPLES

5 And when his disciples were come to the other side, they had forgotten to take bread. 6 Then Jesus said unto them, Take heed and beware of the leaven of the Pharisees and of the Sadducees. 7 And they reasoned among themselves, saying, *It is* because we have taken no bread. 8 *Which* when Jesus perceived, he said unto them, O ye of little faith, why reason ye among yourselves, because ye have brought no bread? 9 Do ye not yet understand, neither remember the five loaves of the five thousand, and how many baskets ye took up? 10 neither the seven loaves of the four thousand, and how many baskets ye took up? 11 How is it that ye do not understand that I spake *it* not to you concerning bread, that ye should beware of the leaven of the Pharisees and of the Sadducees? 12 Then understood they how that he bade *them* not beware of the leaven of bread, but of the doctrine of the Pharisees and of the Sadducees. ●

3. "WHO AM I?"

13 When Jesus came into the coasts of Caesare'a Phil'ippi, he asked his disciples, saying, Whom do men say that I, the Son of man, am? 14 And they said, Some *say that thou art* John the Baptist; some, Eli'jah; and others, Jeremiah, or one of the prophets. 15 He saith unto them, But whom say ye that I am? 16 And Simon Peter answered and said, Thou art the Christ, the Son of the living God. 17 And Jesus answered and said unto him, Blessed art thou, Simon Bar–jona: for flesh and blood hath not revealed *it* unto thee, but my Father which is in heaven. 18 And I say also unto thee, That thou art Peter, and upon this rock I will build my church; and the gates of hell shall not prevail against it. 19 And I will give unto thee the keys of the kingdom of heaven: and whatsoever thou shalt bind on earth shall be bound in heaven; and whatsoever thou shalt loose on earth shall be loosed in heaven. 20 Then charged he his disciples that they should tell no man that he was Jesus the Christ. ●

FALSE TEACHERS

TRUE MESSIAH

This is the concluding passage of the long section of Matthew's gospel called PROCLAMATION (4:12—16:20). In these chapters Matthew has recorded the words and works which Jesus had spoken and performed to show the people that He was the promised Messiah. Now he takes inventory of the effectiveness of His ministry, and asks His disciples, "Who do people say that the Son of Man is?" (v.13). The third paragraph is a key point in Matthew's gospel.

*16:1-4* How did Jesus deal with the false religious leaders?

______________________________

*16:5-12* What did Jesus teach the disciples about the false religious leaders?

______________________________

______________________________

______________________________

______________________________

______________________________

*16:13-20* Record Jesus' two questions, and the answers:

"WHO ______________________________

______________________________

______________________________

ANSWER: ______________________________

______________________________

______________________________

"WHO ______________________________

______________________________

______________________________

ANSWER: ______________________________

______________________________

______________________________

Jesus' response: ______________________________

______________________________

______________________________

______________________________

______________________________

NEW INTERNATIONAL VERSION

Anyone who follows Jesus is His disciple. It is important for Christians today to know what true discipleship is. Record here what Jesus taught about this.

Some very important spiritual lessons can be learned from the transfiguration story of 17:1-8. Record your conclusions.

What spiritual applications can be made from John the Baptist's ministry?

### *Jesus Predicts His Death*

21From that time on Jesus began to explain to his disciples that he must go to
Jerusalem and suffer many things at the
hands of the elders, chief priests and
teachers of the law, and that he must be
killed and on the third day be raised to life.
22Peter took him aside and began to
rebuke him. "Never, Lord!" he said.
"This shall never happen to you!"
23Jesus turned and said to Peter, "Out of
my sight, Satan! You are a stumbling block
to me; you do not have in mind the things
of God, but the things of men."●
24Then Jesus said to his disciples, "If
anyone would come after me, he must
deny himself and take up his cross and
follow me. 25For whoever wants to save his
life[e] will lose it, but whoever loses his life
for me will find it. 26What good will it be for
a man if he gains the whole world, yet for-
feits his soul? Or what can a man give in
exchange for his soul? 27For the Son of
Man is going to come in his Father's glory
with his angels, and then he will reward
each person according to what he has
done. 28I tell you the truth, some who are
standing here will not taste death before
they see the Son of Man coming in his
kingdom."●

### *The Transfiguration*

17 After six days Jesus took with him
Peter, James and John the brother
of James, and led them up a high mountain
by themselves. 2There he was transfigured
before them. His face shone like the sun,
and his clothes became as white as the
light. 3Just then there appeared before
them Moses and Elijah, talking with Jesus.
4Peter said to Jesus, "Lord, it is good for
us to be here. If you wish, I will put up
three shelters—one for you, one for Moses
and one for Elijah."
5While he was still speaking, a bright
cloud enveloped them, and a voice from
the cloud said, "This is my Son, whom I
love; with him I am well pleased. Listen to
him!"
6When the disciples heard this, they fell
facedown to the ground, terrified. 7But
Jesus came and touched them. "Get up,"
he said. "Don't be afraid." 8When they
looked up, they saw no one except Jesus.●
9As they were coming down the mountain, Jesus instructed them, "Don't tell
anyone what you have seen, until the Son
of Man has been raised from the dead."
10The disciples asked him, "Why then do
the teachers of the law say that Elijah must
come first?"
11Jesus replied, "To be sure, Elijah
comes and will restore all things. 12But I
tell you, Elijah has already come, and they
did not recognize him, but have done to
him everything they wished. In the same
way the Son of Man is going to suffer at
their hands." 13Then the disciples understood that he was talking to them about
John the Baptist.●

[e]25 The Greek word means either *life* or *soul;* also in verse 26.

KING JAMES

**1. CHRIST'S CROSS**

**JESUS CHRIST MUST SUFFER**

21 From that time forth began Jesus to
show unto his disciples, how that he must
go unto Jerusalem, and suffer many things
of the elders and chief priests and scribes,
and be killed, and be raised again the
third day. 22 Then Peter took him, and
began to rebuke him, saying, Be it far
from thee, Lord: this shall not be unto
thee. 23 But he turned, and said unto
Peter, Get thee behind me, Satan: thou
art an offense unto me: for thou savorest
not the things that be of God, but those
that be of men. ●

**2. DISCIPLES' CROSS**

24 Then said Jesus unto his disciples,
If any *man* will come after me, let him
deny himself, and take up his cross, and
follow me. 25 For whosoever will save
his life shall lose it: and whosoever will
lose his life for my sake shall find it.
26 For what is a man profited, if he shall
gain the whole world, and lose his own
soul? or what shall a man give in exchange for his soul? 27 For the Son of
man shall come in the glory of his Father
with his angels; and then he shall reward
every man according to his works.
28 Verily I say unto you, There be some
standing here, which shall not taste of
death, till they see the Son of man coming
in his kingdom. ●

**3. FATHER COMMENDS HIS SON**

17 And after six days Jesus taketh
Peter, James, and John his brother,
and bringeth them up into a high mountain apart, 2 and was transfigured before
them: and his face did shine as the sun,
and his raiment was white as the light.
3 And, behold, there appeared unto them
Moses and Eli'jah talking with him.
4 Then answered Peter, and said unto
Jesus, Lord, it is good for us to be here:
if thou wilt, let us make here three tabernacles; one for thee, and one for Moses,
and one for Eli'jah. 5 While he yet spake,
behold, a bright cloud overshadowed
them: and behold a voice out of the cloud,
which said, This is my beloved Son, in
whom I am well pleased; hear ye him.
6 And when the disciples heard *it*, they
fell on their face, and were sore afraid.
7 And Jesus came and touched them, and
said, Arise, and be not afraid. 8 And
when they had lifted up their eyes, they
saw no man, save Jesus only. ●

**4. JOHN THE BAPTIST ANNOUNCES THE SON OF MAN**

9 And as they came down from the
mountain, Jesus charged them, saying,
Tell the vision to no man, until the Son of
man be risen again from the dead. 10 And
his disciples asked him, saying, Why then
say the scribes that Eli'jah must first
come? 11 And Jesus answered and said
unto them, Eli'jah truly shall first come,
and restore all things. 12 But I say unto
you, That Eli'jah is come already, and
they knew him not, but have done unto
him whatsoever they listed. Likewise shall
also the Son of man suffer of them.
13 Then the disciples understood that
he spake unto them of John the Baptist. ●

**SON OF MAN IS GOING TO SUFFER**

At 16:21 Matthew begins to record the final and crucial era of Jesus' public ministry, called PASSION. What is the opening phrase of this passage?

Compare this with the similar phrase at 4:12.

Relate the first three words of 16:21 to the previous paragraph.

*16:21-23* What did Jesus foretell would happen soon?

*16:24-28* List some important truths taught here.

*17:1-8* What phrases or statements of this paragraph stand out as key ones?

*17:9-13* Why do you think Jesus gave the direction of verse 9?

NEW INTERNATIONAL VERSION

What does this passage reveal about the hearts of these people:

*Father of a deranged son* (vv.14-17)

*Disciples* (vv.19-21;23)

Faith is always an important subject in the Bible. Record everything you learn about faith in this passage.

*The Healing of an Epileptic Boy*

[14]When they came to the crowd, a man
approached Jesus and knelt before him.
[15]"Lord, have mercy on my son," he said.
"He is an epileptic and is suffering greatly.
He often falls into the fire or into the water.
[16]I brought him to your disciples, but they
could not heal him."
[17]"O unbelieving and perverse generation," Jesus replied, "how long shall I stay
with you? How long shall I put up with
you? Bring the boy here to me." [18]Jesus
rebuked the demon, and it came out of the
boy, and he was healed from that moment.●
[19]Then the disciples came to Jesus in private and asked, "Why couldn't we drive it
out?"
[20]He replied, "Because you have so little
faith. I tell you the truth, if you have faith
as small as a mustard seed, you can say to
this mountain, 'Move from here to there'
and it will move. Nothing will be impossible for you.[a]"●
[22]When they came together in Galilee, he
said to them, "The Son of Man is going to
be betrayed into the hands of men. [23]They
will kill him, and on the third day he will be
raised to life." And the disciples were
filled with grief.●

*The Temple Tax*

[24]After Jesus and his disciples arrived in
Capernaum, the collectors of the two-
drachma tax came to Peter and asked,
"Doesn't your teacher pay the temple
tax[b]?"
[25]"Yes, he does," he replied.
When Peter came into the house, Jesus
was the first to speak. "What do you think,
Simon?" he asked. "From whom do the
kings of the earth collect duty and taxes—
from their own sons or from others?"
[26]"From others," Peter answered.
"Then the sons are exempt," Jesus said
to him. [27]"But so that we may not offend
them, go to the lake and throw out your
line. Take the first fish you catch; open its
mouth and you will find a four-drachma
coin. Take it and give it to them for my tax
and yours."●

[a]20 Some manuscripts *you.* [21]*But this kind does not go out except by prayer and fasting.*
[b]24 Greek *the two drachmas*

KING JAMES

**1.NO CURE**

**SON NEEDS HEALING**

14 And when they were come to the
multitude, there came to him a *certain*
man, kneeling down to him, and saying,
15 Lord, have mercy on my son; for he is
lunatic, and sore vexed: for ofttimes he
falleth into the fire, and oft into the water.
16 And I brought him to thy disciples, and
they could not cure him. 17 Then Jesus
answered and said, O faithless and perverse generation, how long shall I be with
you? how long shall I suffer you? bring
him hither to me. 18 And Jesus rebuked
the devil; and he departed out of him: and
the child was cured from that very hour.●

**2.LITTLE FAITH**

19 Then came the disciples to Jesus apart,
and said, Why could not we cast him out?
20 And Jesus said unto them, Because of
your unbelief: for verily I say unto you,
If ye have faith as a grain of mustard seed,
ye shall say unto this mountain, Remove
hence to yonder place; and it shall remove: and nothing shall be impossible
unto you. 21 Howbeit this kind goeth not
out but by prayer and fasting.●

**3.DEEP GRIEF**

22 And while they abode in Galilee,
Jesus said unto them, The Son of man
shall be betrayed into the hands of men:
23 and they shall kill him, and the third
day he shall be raised again. And they
were exceeding sorry.●

**4.NO OFFENSE**

24 And when they were come to Caper'-
na-um, they that received tribute *money*
came to Peter, and said, Doth not your
master pay tribute? 25 He saith, Yes.
And when he was come into the house,
Jesus prevented him, saying, What thinkest thou, Simon? of whom do the kings of
the earth take custom or tribute? of their
own children, or of strangers? 26 Peter
saith unto him, Of strangers. Jesus saith
unto him, Then are the children free.

**JESUS NEEDS TAX MONEY**

27 Notwithstanding, lest we should offend
them, go thou to the sea, and cast a hook,
and take up the fish that first cometh up;
and when thou hast opened his mouth,
thou shalt find a piece of money: that take,
and give unto them for me and thee.●

During the last months and days of Jesus' public ministry, He was concerned to train His disciples to continue the gospel ministry after He left this earth. This passage reports some of His contact with the disciples at this time.

*17:14-18* The key verse of this passage is verse 16. What does it reveal?

*17:19-21* What was the disciples' problem and Jesus' solution?

*17:22-23* Recall that Matthew reported this prediction by Jesus at an earlier time (16:21). Note the words "began to" in that verse. Why would Jesus want to repeat the prediction?

*17:24-27* A key phrase of the paragraph is "lest we should offend them" (17:27). Study the paragraph in light of this.

NEW INTERNATIONAL VERSION

What is there about the human heart that makes it desire greatness?

What are Jesus' teachings about greatness in this passage?

Does it take humble hearts to bring about the restoration described in verses 15-17? Explain.

What important truths does this passage teach about children?

Record spiritual lessons taught by verses 19-20.

### *The Greatest in the Kingdom of Heaven*

**18** At that time the disciples came to Jesus and asked, "Who is the greatest in the kingdom of heaven?"

[2]He called a little child and had him stand among them. [3]And he said: "I tell you the truth, unless you change and become like little children, you will never enter the kingdom of heaven. [4]Therefore, whoever humbles himself like this child is the greatest in the kingdom of heaven. [5]And whoever welcomes a little child like this in my name welcomes me.

[6]"But if anyone causes one of these little ones who believe in me to sin, it would be better for him to have a large millstone hung around his neck and to be drowned in the depths of the sea. [7]Woe to the world because of the things that cause people to sin! Such things must come, but woe to the man through whom they come! [8]If your hand or your foot causes you to sin, cut it off and throw it away. It is better for you to enter life maimed or crippled than to have two hands or two feet and be thrown into eternal fire. [9]And if your eye causes you to sin, gouge it out and throw it away. It is better for you to enter life with one eye than to have two eyes and be thrown into the fire of hell.●

### *The Parable of the Lost Sheep*

[10]"See that you do not look down on one of these little ones. For I tell you that their angels in heaven always see the face of my Father in heaven.[c]

[12]"What do you think? If a man owns a hundred sheep, and one of them wanders away, will he not leave the ninety-nine on the hills and go to look for the one that wandered off? [13]And if he finds it, I tell you the truth, he is happier about that one sheep than about the ninety-nine that did not wander off. [14]In the same way your Father in heaven is not willing that any of these little ones should be lost.●

### *A Brother Who Sins Against You*

[15]"If your brother sins against you,[d] go and show him his fault, just between the two of you. If he listens to you, you have won your brother over. [16]But if he will not listen, take one or two others along, so that 'every matter may be established by the testimony of two or three witnesses.'[a] [17]If he refuses to listen to them, tell it to the church; and if he refuses to listen even to the church, treat him as you would a pagan or a tax collector.

[18]"I tell you the truth, whatever you bind on earth will be bound in heaven, and whatever you loose on earth will be loosed in heaven.

[19]"Again, I tell you that if two of you on earth agree about anything you ask for, it will be done for you by my Father in heaven. [20]For where two or three come together in my name, there am I with them."●

[c]10 Some manuscripts *heaven. [11]The Son of Man came to save what was lost.*

[d]15 Some manuscripts do not have *against you.*

[a]16 Deut. 19:15

KING JAMES

1. TRUE GREATNESS

CHILDREN

**18** At the same time came the disciples unto Jesus, saying, Who is the greatest in the kingdom of heaven? 2 And Jesus called a little child unto him, and set him in the midst of them, 3 and said, Verily I say unto you, Except ye be converted, and become as little children, ye shall not enter into the kingdom of heaven. 4 Whosoever therefore shall humble himself as this little child, the same is greatest in the kingdom of heaven. 5 And whoso shall receive one such little child in my name receiveth me.

6 But whoso shall offend one of these little ones which believe in me, it were better for him that a millstone were hanged about his neck, and *that* he were drowned in the depth of the sea.●

2. FATAL STUMBLING BLOCKS

7 Woe unto the world because of offenses! for it must needs be that offenses come; but woe to that man by whom the offense cometh! 8 Wherefore if thy hand or thy foot offend thee, cut them off, and cast *them* from thee: it is better for thee to enter into life halt or maimed, rather than having two hands or two feet to be cast into everlasting fire. 9 And if thine eye offend thee, pluck it out, and cast *it* from thee: it is better for thee to enter into life with one eye, rather than having two eyes to be cast into hell fire.●

3. PRECIOUS CHILDREN

10 Take heed that ye despise not one of these little ones; for I say unto you, That in heaven their angels do always behold the face of my Father which is in heaven. 11 For the Son of man is come to save that which was lost. 12 How think ye? if a man have a hundred sheep, and one of them be gone astray, doth he not leave the ninety and nine, and goeth into the mountains, and seeketh that which is gone astray? 13 And if so be that he find it, verily I say unto you, he rejoiceth more of that *sheep*, than of the ninety and nine which went not astray. 14 Even so it is not the will of your Father which is in heaven, that one of these little ones should perish.●

4. RESTORED BROTHERS

BROTHERS

15 Moreover if thy brother shall trespass against thee, go and tell him his fault between thee and him alone: if he shall hear thee, thou hast gained thy brother. 16 But if he will not hear *thee*, *then* take with thee one or two more, that in the mouth of two or three witnesses every word may be established. 17 And if he shall neglect to hear them, tell *it* unto the church: but if he neglect to hear the church, let him be unto thee as a heathen man and a publican. 18 Verily I say unto you, Whatsoever ye shall bind on earth shall be bound in heaven; and whatsoever ye shall loose on earth shall be loosed in heaven. 19 Again I say unto you, That if two of you shall agree on earth as touching any thing that they shall ask, it shall be done for them of my Father which is in heaven. 20 For where two or three are gathered together in my name, there am I in the midst of them.●

Jesus had much more to teach His disciples. One thing was an attitude of humility. The disciples brought up the subject by asking a question. What was it? (v.1).

______________________________

______________________________

______________________________

*18:1-6* What is Jesus' answer to the question of verse 1?

______________________________

______________________________

What else does Jesus teach in the paragraph? (vv.5-6)

______________________________

______________________________

*18:7-9* What is the key repeated word of the paragraph?

______________________________

Who are the objects of stumbling blocks in verse 7?

______________________________

In verses 8-9? ______________________________

*18:10-14* What is the main point of this paragraph?

______________________________

*18:15-20* Record the teaching of these parts:

v.15-17 ______________________________

______________________________

______________________________

v.18 ______________________________

______________________________

______________________________

______________________________

vv.19-20 ______________________________

______________________________

______________________________

______________________________

NEW INTERNATIONAL VERSION

Derive as many applications as you can from this passage on the following important subjects:

FORGIVENESS ____________________

JUSTICE ____________________

CONCERN ____________________

COMPASSION ____________________

GRATITUDE ____________________

EQUITY ____________________

*The Parable of the Unmerciful Servant*

21Then Peter came to Jesus and asked,
"Lord, how many times shall I forgive my
brother when he sins against me? Up to
seven times?"
22Jesus answered, "I tell you, not seven
times, but seventy-seven times.[b]●
23"Therefore, the kingdom of heaven is
like a king who wanted to settle accounts
with his servants. 24As he began the settle-
ment, a man who owed him ten thousand
talents[c] was brought to him. 25Since he was
not able to pay, the master ordered that he
and his wife and his children and all that he
had be sold to repay the debt.
26"The servant fell on his knees before
him. 'Be patient with me,' he begged, 'and
I will pay back everything.' 27The servant's
master took pity on him, canceled the debt
and let him go.●
28"But when that servant went out, he
found one of his fellow servants who owed
him a hundred denarii.[d] He grabbed him
and began to choke him. 'Pay back what
you owe me!' he demanded.
29"His fellow servant fell to his knees
and begged him, 'Be patient with me, and
I will pay you back.'
30"But he refused. Instead, he went off
and had the man thrown into prison until he
could pay the debt. 31When the other servants saw what had happened, they were
greatly distressed and went and told their
master everything that had happened.
32"Then the master called the servant in.
'You wicked servant,' he said, 'I canceled
all that debt of yours because you begged
me to. 33Shouldn't you have had mercy on
your fellow servant just as I had on you?'
34In anger his master turned him over to the
jailers until he should pay back all he owed.
35"This is how my heavenly Father will
treat each of you unless you forgive your
brother from your heart."●

*Divorce*

19 When Jesus had finished saying
these things, he left Galilee●

[b]22 Or *seventy times seven*
[c]24 That is, several million dollars
[d]28 That is, a few dollars

KING JAMES

1. QUESTION AND ANSWER

21 Then came Peter to him, and said,
Lord, how oft shall my brother sin against
me, and I forgive him? till seven times?
22 Jesus saith unto him, I say not unto
thee, Until seven times: but, Until seventy
times seven.●

2. ILLUSTRATIONS

—king

23 Therefore is the kingdom of heaven
likened unto a certain king, which would
take account of his servants. 24 And
when he had begun to reckon, one was
brought unto him, which owed him ten
thousand talents. 25 But forasmuch as he
had not to pay, his lord commanded him
to be sold, and his wife, and children, and
all that he had, and payment to be made.
26 The servant therefore fell down, and
worshipped him, saying, Lord, have patience with me, and I will pay thee all.
27 Then the lord of that servant was
moved with compassion, and loosed him,

—slave

and forgave him the debt.● 28 But the
same servant went out, and found one of
his fellow servants, which owed him a
hundred pence: and he laid hands on him,
and took *him* by the throat, saying, Pay
me that thou owest. 29 And his fellow
servant fell down at his feet, and besought
him, saying, Have patience with me, and
I will pay thee all. 30 And he would not:
but went and cast him into prison, till he
should pay the debt. 31 So when his
fellow servants saw what was done, they
were very sorry, and came and told unto
their lord all that was done. 32 Then his
lord, after that he had called him, said
unto him, O thou wicked servant, I forgave thee all that debt, because thou de-
siredst me: 33 shouldest not thou also
have had compassion on thy fellow servant, even as I had pity on thee? 34 And
his lord was wroth, and delivered him to
the tormentors, till he should pay all that
was due unto him. 35 So likewise shall
my heavenly Father do also unto you, if
ye from your hearts forgive not every one
his brother their trespasses.●

—departure

19 And it came to pass, *that* when
Jesus had finished these sayings, he
departed from Galilee,●

10,000 talents

100 pence

This passage continues the discourses which Jesus had with His disciples at this time. Read 19:1a, which concludes the discourse.

*18:21-22* What was on Peter's mind?

Whom did Jesus mean by his answer?

*18:23-27* What parts of the paragraph illustrate these:

JUSTICE

SUPPLICATION

MERCY

*18:28-35* Contrast this paragraph with the preceding one. For example, compare the money amounts (see TLB).

What truth does 18:31-34 add to the parable?

NEW INTERNATIONAL VERSION

Record what this passage teaches about the important subjects listed below:

DIVORCE ______________________

MARRIAGE ______________________

Record some practical applications not included in the above lists.

and
went into the region of Judea to the other
side of the Jordan. 2Large crowds followed
him, and he healed them there.●
3Some Pharisees came to him to test him.
They asked, "Is it lawful for a man to divorce his wife for any and every reason?"
4"Haven't you read," he replied, "that
at the beginning the Creator 'made them
male and female,'[e] 5and said, 'For this reason a man will leave his father and mother
and be united to his wife, and the two will
become one flesh'[f]? 6So they are no longer
two, but one. Therefore what God has
joined together, let man not separate."
7"Why then," they asked, "did Moses
command that a man give his wife a certificate of divorce and send her away?"
8Jesus replied, "Moses permitted you to
divorce your wives because your hearts
were hard. But it was not this way from the
beginning. 9I tell you that anyone who divorces his wife, except for marital unfaithfulness, and marries another woman commits adultery."●
10The disciples said to him, "If this is the
situation between a husband and wife, it is
better not to marry."
11Jesus replied, "Not everyone can accept this teaching, but only those to whom
it has been given. 12For some are eunuchs
because they were born that way; others
were made that way by men; and others
have renounced marriage[g] because of the
kingdom of heaven. The one who can accept this should accept it."●

[e]4 Gen. 1:27
[f]5 Gen. 2:24
[g]12 Or *have made themselves eunuchs*

KING JAMES

and came into the
coasts of Judea beyond Jordan; 2 and
great multitudes followed him; and he
healed them there.●

1. DIVORCE

3 The Pharisees also came unto him,
tempting him, and saying unto him, Is it
lawful for a man to put away his wife for
every cause? 4 And he answered and said
unto them, Have ye not read, that he
which made *them* at the beginning made
them male and female, 5 and said,

PHARISEES' QUESTION

For this cause shall a man leave
father and mother,
and shall cleave to his wife:
and they twain shall be one flesh ?

Gen. 2:24

6 Wherefore they are no more twain, but
one flesh. What therefore God hath
joined together, let not man put asunder.
7 They say unto him, Why did Moses then
command to give a writing of divorcement, and to put her away? 8 He saith
unto them, Moses because of the hardness of your hearts suffered you to put
away your wives: but from the beginning
it was not so. 9 And I say unto you,
Whosoever shall put away his wife, except
*it be* for fornication, and shall marry
another, committeth adultery: and whoso
marrieth her which is put away doth
commit adultery.●

2. MARRIAGE

10 His disciples say unto him, If the
case of the man be so with *his* wife, it is
not good to marry. 11 But he said unto
them, All *men* cannot receive this saying,
save *they* to whom it is given. 12 For
there are some eunuchs, which were so
born from *their* mother's womb: and
there are some eunuchs, which were made
eunuchs of men: and there be eunuchs,
which have made themselves eunuchs for
the kingdom of heaven's sake. He that is
able to receive *it*, let him receive *it*.●

DISCIPLES' QUESTION

The final ministries of Jesus before His death are recorded in this and the next few chapters. What ministry is reported in 19:2?

What ministry is the subject of the remainder of the segment?

This ministry continues into the next segment.

*19:1b-2* What does Matthew report here?

Record the question and Jesus' answer in each paragraph:

*19:3-9*

QUESTION

ANSWER

*19:10-12*

QUESTION

ANSWER

NEW INTERNATIONAL VERSION

Record truths taught by this passage about the grand subject of SALVATION. State in your own words the truths suggested by the outline:

1. Foundation of salvation: Sovereignty of God (19:13-15)

2. Standard of salvation: Word of God (19:16-22)

3. Possibility of salvation: Omnipotence of God (19:23-26)

4. Reward of salvation: Abundant graces of God (19:27-30)

Record practical lessons of this passage:

*The Little Children and Jesus*

13Then little children were brought to
Jesus for him to place his hands on them
and pray for them. But the disciples
rebuked those who brought them.
14Jesus said, "Let the little children
come to me, and do not hinder them, for
the kingdom of heaven belongs to such as
these." 15When he had placed his hands on
them, he went on from there.●

*The Rich Young Man*

16Now a man came up to Jesus and
asked, "Teacher, what good thing must I
do to get eternal life?"
17"Why do you ask me about what is
good?" Jesus replied. "There is only One
who is good. If you want to enter life, obey
the commandments."
18"Which ones?" the man inquired.
Jesus replied, " 'Do not murder, do not
commit adultery, do not steal, do not give
false testimony, 19honor your father and
mother,'[a] and 'love your neighbor as yourself.'[b]"
20"All these I have kept," the young
man said. "What do I still lack?"
21Jesus answered, "If you want to be
perfect, go, sell your possessions and give
to the poor, and you will have treasure in
heaven. Then come, follow me."
22When the young man heard this, he
went away sad, because he had great
wealth.●
23Then Jesus said to his disciples, "I tell
you the truth, it is hard for a rich man to
enter the kingdom of heaven. 24Again I tell
you, it is easier for a camel to go through
the eye of a needle than for a rich man to
enter the kingdom of God."
25When the disciples heard this, they
were greatly astonished and asked, "Who
then can be saved?"
26Jesus looked at them and said, "With
man this is impossible, but with God all
things are possible."●
27Peter answered him, "We have left
everything to follow you! What then will
there be for us?"
28Jesus said to them, "I tell you the
truth, at the renewal of all things, when the
Son of Man sits on his glorious throne, you
who have followed me will also sit on
twelve thrones, judging the twelve tribes of
Israel. 29And everyone who has left houses
or brothers or sisters or father or mother or
children or fields for my sake will receive
a hundred times as much and will inherit
eternal life. 30But many who are first will
be last, and many who are last will be first.●

[a]*19* Exodus 20:12-16; Deut. 5:16-20 [b]*19* Lev. 19:18

KING JAMES

1.CHILDREN

SALVATION:

—foundation

13 Then were there brought unto him
little children, that he should put *his* hands
on them, and pray: and the disciples rebuked them. 14 But Jesus said, Suffer
little children, and forbid them not, to
come unto me; for of such is the kingdom
of heaven. 15 And he laid *his* hands on
them, and departed thence.●

2.ETERNAL LIFE

—standard

16 And, behold, one came and said unto him, Good Master, what good thing
shall I do, that I may have eternal life?
17 And he said unto him, Why callest
thou me good? *there is* none good but
one, *that is*, God: but if thou wilt enter
into life, keep the commandments. 18 He
saith unto him, Which? Jesus said, Thou
shalt do no murder, Thou shalt not commit adultery, Thou shalt not steal, Thou
shalt not bear false witness, 19 Honor
thy father and *thy* mother: and, Thou
shalt love thy neighbor as thyself. 20 The
young man saith unto him, All these
things have I kept from my youth up:
what lack I yet? 21 Jesus said unto him,
If thou wilt be perfect, go *and* sell that
thou hast, and give to the poor, and thou
shalt have treasure in heaven: and come
*and* follow me. 22 But when the young
man heard that saying, he went away
sorrowful: for he had great possessions.●

Ex. 20:12-16

3.WEALTH

—possibility

23 Then said Jesus unto his disciples,
Verily I say unto you, That a rich man
shall hardly enter into the kingdom of
heaven. 24 And again I say unto you, It
is easier for a camel to go through the eye
of a needle, than for a rich man to enter
into the kingdom of God. 25 When his
disciples heard *it*, they were exceedingly
amazed, saying, Who then can be saved?
26 But Jesus beheld *them*, and said unto
them, With men this is impossible; but

4.DISCIPLESHIP

—reward

with God all things are possible.●27 Then
answered Peter and said unto him, Behold, we have forsaken all, and followed
thee; what shall we have therefore?
28 And Jesus said unto them, Verily I say
unto you, That ye which have followed
me, in the regeneration when the Son of
man shall sit in the throne of his glory,
ye also shall sit upon twelve thrones,
judging the twelve tribes of Israel.
29 And every one that hath forsaken
houses, or brethren, or sisters, or father,
or mother, or wife, or children, or lands,
for my name's sake, shall receive a hundredfold, and shall inherit everlasting life.
30 But many *that are* first shall be last;
and the last *shall be* first.●

Record the main truths of each paragraph. When a question is asked, record the question and answer.

*19:13-15* ______________________

*19:16-22*

QUESTION (v.16) ______________________

ANSWER ______________________

QUESTION (v.20) ______________________

ANSWER ______________________

*19:23-26*

QUESTION ______________________

ANSWER ______________________

*19:27-30*

QUESTION ______________________

ANSWER ______________________

NEW INTERNATIONAL VERSION

This parable is another illustration of the Kingdom of Heaven.

Who is represented by the landowner, and who is represented by the laborers?

Should it be a joy and privilege for Christians to work in Christ's kingdom? If so, would those working for a longer time have more times of such joy?

Is that a reward for service?

The same wages were given to all the workers. In what sense are the same wages given to all born again believers in Christ's kingdom?

Is this fair and just? Why?

What spiritual lessons do you especially learn from this parable?

Read verses 17-19 carefully. What do you learn about Jews here?

### *The Parable of the Workers in the Vineyard*

20 "For the kingdom of heaven is like a landowner who went out early in the morning to hire men to work in his vineyard. [2]He agreed to pay them a denarius for the day and sent them into his vineyard.

[3]"About the third hour he went out and saw others standing in the marketplace doing nothing. [4]He told them, 'You also go and work in my vineyard, and I will pay you whatever is right.' [5]So they went.

"He went out again about the sixth hour and the ninth hour and did the same thing. [6]About the eleventh hour he went out and found still others standing around. He asked them, 'Why have you been standing here all day long doing nothing?'

[7]" 'Because no one has hired us,' they answered.

"He said to them, 'You also go and work in my vineyard.'

[8]"When evening came, the owner of the vineyard said to his foreman, 'Call the workers and pay them their wages, beginning with the last ones hired and going on to the first.'

[9]"The workers who were hired about the eleventh hour came and each received a denarius. [10]So when those came who were hired first, they expected to receive more. But each one of them also received a denarius. [11]When they received it, they began to grumble against the landowner. [12]'These men who were hired last worked only one hour,' they said, 'and you have made them equal to us who have borne the burden of the work and the heat of the day.'

[13]"But he answered one of them, 'Friend, I am not being unfair to you. Didn't you agree to work for a denarius? [14]Take your pay and go. I want to give the man who was hired last the same as I gave you. [15]Don't I have the right to do what I want with my own money? Or are you envious because I am generous?'

[16]"So the last will be first, and the first will be last."●

### *Jesus Again Predicts His Death*

[17]Now as Jesus was going up to Jerusalem, he took the twelve disciples aside and said to them, [18]"We are going up to Jerusalem, and the Son of Man will be betrayed to the chief priests and the teachers of the law. They will condemn him to death [19]and will turn him over to the Gentiles to be mocked and flogged and crucified. On the third day he will be raised to life!"●

KING JAMES

1.WAGES

LAND-OWNER HIRING

**20** For the kingdom of heaven is like
unto a man *that is* a householder,
which went out early in the morning to
hire laborers into his vineyard. 2 And
when he had agreed with the laborers for
a penny a day, he sent them into his vineyard. 3 And he went out about the third
hour, and saw others standing idle in the
market place, 4 and said unto them; Go
ye also into the vineyard, and whatsoever
is right I will give you. And they went
their way. 5 Again he went out about the
sixth and ninth hour, and did likewise.
6 And about the eleventh hour he went
out, and found others standing idle, and
saith unto them, Why stand ye here all the
day idle? 7 They say unto him, Because
no man hath hired us. He saith unto
them, Go ye also into the vineyard; and
whatsoever is right, *that* shall ye receive.
8 So when even was come, the lord of the
vineyard saith unto his steward, Call the
laborers, and give them *their* hire, beginning from the last unto the first. 9 And
when they came that *were hired* about the
eleventh hour, they received every man a
penny. 10 But when the first came, they
supposed that they should have received
more; and they likewise received every
man a penny. 11 And when they had received *it*, they murmured against the
goodman of the house, 12 saying, These
last have wrought *but* one hour, and thou
hast made them equal unto us, which
have borne the burden and heat of the
day. 13 But he answered one of them, and
said, Friend, I do thee no wrong: didst
not thou agree with me for a penny?
14 Take *that* thine *is*, and go thy way: I
will give unto this last, even as unto thee.
15 Is it not lawful for me to do what I will
with mine own? Is thine eye evil, because
I am good? 16 So the last shall be first,
and the first last: for many be called, but
few chosen.●

2.PREDIC-TIONS

SON OF MAN DE-LIVERED UP

17 And Jesus going up to Jerusalem
took the twelve disciples apart in the way,
and said unto them, 18 Behold, we go up
to Jerusalem; and the Son of man shall be
betrayed unto the chief priests and unto
the scribes, and they shall condemn him
to death, 19 and shall deliver him to the
Gentiles to mock, and to scourge, and to
crucify *him*: and the third day he shall
rise again.●

*20:1-16* Before you try to interpret this parable, record the main parts:

persons: ____________

setting: ____________

wages: ____________

principle of wages: ____________

What is the main point Jesus intended by the parable?

____________

*20:17-19* This is the third time Matthew records Jesus' prediction of His death and resurrection. Why did Jesus keep repeating this?

____________

NEW INTERNATIONAL VERSION

The life of Jesus is the supreme example of thought, word and deed in a Christian's walk. Record practical truths taught by this passage on these three subjects:

HUMILITY

SERVICE

COMPASSION

*A Mother's Request*

[20]Then the mother of Zebedee's sons
came to Jesus with her sons and, kneeling
down, asked a favor of him.
[21]"What is it you want?" he asked.
She said, "Grant that one of these two
sons of mine may sit at your right and the
other at your left in your kingdom."
[22]"You don't know what you are asking," Jesus said to them. "Can you drink
the cup I am going to drink?"
"We can," they answered.
[23]Jesus said to them, "You will indeed
drink from my cup, but to sit at my right or
left is not for me to grant. These places
belong to those for whom they have been
prepared by my Father."
[24]When the ten heard about this, they
were indignant with the two brothers.●
[25]Jesus called them together and said,
"You know that the rulers of the Gentiles
lord it over them, and their high officials
exercise authority over them. [26]Not so
with you. Instead, whoever wants to
become great among you must be your servant, [27]and whoever wants to be first must
be your slave— [28]just as the Son of Man did
not come to be served, but to serve, and to
give his life as a ransom for many."●

*Two Blind Men Receive Sight*

[29]As Jesus and his disciples were leaving
Jericho, a large crowd followed him. [30]Two
blind men were sitting by the roadside, and
when they heard that Jesus was going by,
they shouted, "Lord, Son of David, have
mercy on us!"
[31]The crowd rebuked them and told them
to be quiet, but they shouted all the louder,
"Lord, Son of David, have mercy on us!"
[32]Jesus stopped and called them. "What
do you want me to do for you?" he asked.
[33]"Lord," they answered, "we want our
sight."
[34]Jesus had compassion on them and
touched their eyes. Immediately they received their sight and followed him.●

## KING JAMES

1. HUMILITY

20 Then came to him the mother of
Zeb'edee's children with her sons, worshipping *him*, and desiring a certain thing
of him. 21 And he said unto her, What
wilt thou? She saith unto him, Grant
that these my two sons may sit, the one
on thy right hand, and the other on the
left, in thy kingdom. 22 But Jesus answered and said, Ye know not what ye
ask. Are ye able to drink of the cup that
I shall drink of, and to be baptized with
the baptism that I am baptized with?
They say unto him, We are able. 23 And
he saith unto them, Ye shall drink indeed
of my cup, and be baptized with the baptism that I am baptized with: but to sit on
my right hand, and on my left, is not mine
to give, but *it shall be given to them* for
whom it is prepared of my Father.
24 And when the ten heard *it*, they were
moved with indignation against the two
brethren.●

"What do you wish?"

—request for honor

2. SERVICE

25 But Jesus called them *unto*
*him*, and said, Ye know that the princes of
the Gentiles exercise dominion over them,
and they that are great exercise authority
upon them. 26 But it shall not be so
among you: but whosoever will be great
among you, let him be your minister;
27 and whosoever will be chief among
you, let him be your servant: 28 even as
the Son of man came not to be ministered
unto, but to minister, and to give his life
a ransom for many.●

—necessity or service

3. COMPASSION

29 And as they departed from Jericho, a
great multitude followed him. 30 And,
behold, two blind men sitting by the wayside, when they heard that Jesus passed
by, cried out, saying, Have mercy on us,
O Lord, *thou* Son of David. 31 And the
multitude rebuked them, because they
should hold their peace: but they cried the
more, saying, Have mercy on us, O Lord,
*thou* Son of David. 32 And Jesus stood
still, and called them, and said, What will
ye that I shall do unto you? 33 They say
unto him, Lord, that our eyes may be
opened. 34 So Jesus had compassion *on*
*them*, and touched their eyes: and immediately their eyes received sight, and
they followed him.●

"What do you wish?"

*20:20-24* Who has the authority to bestow honor in Christ's kingdom?

What was the mother's request?

Was it vain?

*20:25-28* What is the way to greatness according to this paragraph?

*20:29-34* List the many things taught about Jesus in this paragraph.

NEW INTERNATIONAL VERSION

This passage teaches much about Jesus. Record what you see of Him:

Omniscience (knowledge of all things) ____________________

Acquaintance with Scripture ____________________

Humility ____________________

Lordship ____________________

Messiahship ____________________

Attraction ____________________

Authority ____________________

Anger ____________________

Perception ____________________

Tenderness ____________________

### *The Triumphal Entry*

21 As they approached Jerusalem and
came to Bethphage on the Mount of
Olives, Jesus sent two disciples, 2saying to
them, "Go to the village ahead of you, and
at once you will find a donkey tied there,
with her colt by her. Untie them and bring
them to me. 3If anyone says anything to
you, tell him that the Lord needs them, and
he will send them right away."
4This took place to fulfill what was
spoken through the prophet:

5"Say to the Daughter of Zion,
'See, your king comes to you,
gentle and riding on a donkey,
on a colt, the foal of a
donkey.' "[a]

6The disciples went and did as Jesus had
instructed them. 7They brought the donkey
and the colt, placed their cloaks on them,
and Jesus sat on them. 8A very large crowd
spread their cloaks on the road, while
others cut branches from the trees and
spread them on the road. 9The crowds that
went ahead of him and those that followed
shouted,

"Hosanna[b] to the Son of David!"

"Blessed is he who comes in the
name of the Lord!"[c]

"Hosanna[b] in the highest!"

10When Jesus entered Jerusalem, the
whole city was stirred and asked, "Who is
this?"
11The crowds answered, "This is Jesus,
the prophet from Nazareth in Galilee."

### *Jesus at the Temple*

12Jesus entered the temple area and
drove out all who were buying and selling
there. He overturned the tables of the
money changers and the benches of those
selling doves. 13"It is written," he said to
them, " 'My house will be called a house
of prayer,'[d] but you are making it a 'den of
robbers.'[e]"
14The blind and the lame came to him at
the temple, and he healed them. 15But
when the chief priests and the teachers of
the law saw the wonderful things he did
and the children shouting in the temple
area, "Hosanna to the Son of David," they
were indignant.
16"Do you hear what these children are
saying?" they asked him.
"Yes," replied Jesus, "have you never
read,

" 'From the lips of children and
infants
you have ordained praise'[f]?"

17And he left them and went out of the
city to Bethany, where he spent the night.

[a]5 Zech. 9:9
[b]9 A Hebrew expression meaning "Save!" which became an exclamation of praise; also in verse 15
[c]9 Psalm 118:26 [d]13 Isaiah 56:7 [e]13 Jer. 7:11
[f]16 Psalm 8:2

KING JAMES

1.ROAD

21 And when they drew nigh unto
Jerusalem, and were come to Bethphage, unto the mount of Olives, then
sent Jesus two disciples, 2 saying unto
them, Go into the village over against
you, and straightway ye shall find an ass
tied, and a colt with her: loose *them*, and
bring *them* unto me. 3 And if any *man*
say aught unto you, ye shall say, The
Lord hath need of them; and straightway
he will send them. 4 All this was done,
that it might be fulfilled which was spoken
by the prophet, saying,
5 Tell ye the daughter of Zion,
Behold, thy King cometh unto thee,
meek, and sitting upon an ass,
and a colt the foal of an ass.
6 And the disciples went, and did as Jesus
commanded them, 7 and brought the ass,
and the colt, and put on them their clothes,
and they set *him* thereon.● 8 And a very
great multitude spread their garments in
the way; others cut down branches from
the trees, and strewed *them* in the way.
9 And the multitudes that went before,
and that followed, cried, saying,
Hosanna to the Son of David:
Blessed *is* he that cometh in the
name of the Lord;
Hosanna in the highest.
10 And when he was come into Jerusalem, all the city was moved, saying,
Who is this? 11 And the multitude said,
This is Jesus the prophet of Nazareth of
Galilee.●

2.TEMPLE

12 And Jesus went into the temple of
God, and cast out all them that sold and
bought in the temple, and overthrew the
tables of the money changers, and the
seats of them that sold doves, 13 and said
unto them, It is written, My house shall
be called the house of prayer; but ye
have made it a den of thieves.●
14 And the blind and the lame came to
him in the temple; and he healed them.
15 And when the chief priests and scribes
saw the wonderful things that he did, and
the children crying in the temple, and
saying, Hosanna to the Son of David;
they were sore displeased, 16 and said
unto him, Hearest thou what these say?
And Jesus saith unto them, Yea; have ye
never read,
Out of the mouth of babes and
sucklings
thou hast perfected praise ?
17 And he left them, and went out of the
city into Bethany; and he lodged there.●

—disciples

Zech. 9:9

—multi-
tudes

Ps. 118:26f.

—temple
traders

Isa. 56:7
Jer. 7:11

—children

Ps. 8:2

Now begins the last week of Jesus' earthly career before His death. Where does the action take place?

*21:1-7* What does this paragraph teach about:

JESUS

DISCIPLES

*21:8-11* The word "hosanna" means "save, now" or "save, Lord." How were the words of the multitudes both plea and praise?

What is the key question of verse 11?

How is it answered?

*21:12-13* What is the prominent point of this paragraph?

*21:14-17* Look for contrasts here.

NEW INTERNATIONAL VERSION

Record practical truths taught by this passage about the following:

PRETENSION AND FALSE PROFESSION

DIVINE JUDGMENT

DOUBTING PRAYER

REPENTANCE

OBEDIENCE

FAITH

*The Fig Tree Withers*

18Early in the morning, as he was on his
way back to the city, he was hungry. 19See-
ing a fig tree by the road, he went up to it
but found nothing on it except leaves. Then
he said to it, "May you never bear fruit
again!" Immediately the tree withered.
20When the disciples saw this, they were
amazed. "How did the fig tree wither so
quickly?" they asked.
21Jesus replied, "I tell you the truth, if
you have faith and do not doubt, not only
can you do what was done to the fig tree,
but also you can say to this mountain, 'Go,
throw yourself into the sea,' and it will be
done. 22If you believe, you will receive
whatever you ask for in prayer."●

*The Authority of Jesus Questioned*

23Jesus entered the temple courts, and,
while he was teaching, the chief priests and
the elders of the people came to him. "By
what authority are you doing these
things?" they asked. "And who gave you
this authority?"
24Jesus replied, "I will also ask you one
question. If you answer me, I will tell you
by what authority I am doing these things.
25John's baptism—where did it come from?
Was it from heaven, or from men?"
They discussed it among themselves and
said, "If we say, 'From heaven,' he will
ask, 'Then why didn't you believe him?'
26But if we say, 'From men'—we are afraid
of the people, for they all hold that John
was a prophet."
27So they answered Jesus, "We don't
know."
Then he said, "Neither will I tell you by
what authority I am doing these things.●

*The Parable of the Two Sons*

28"What do you think? There was a man
who had two sons. He went to the first and
said, 'Son, go and work today in the vineyard.'
29" 'I will not,' he answered, but later he
changed his mind and went.
30"Then the father went to the other son
and said the same thing. He answered, 'I
will, sir,' but he did not go.
31"Which of the two did what his father
wanted?"
"The first," they answered.
Jesus said to them, "I tell you the truth,
the tax collectors and the prostitutes are
entering the kingdom of God ahead of you.
32For John came to you to show you the
way of righteousness, and you did not believe him, but the tax collectors and the
prostitutes did. And even after you saw
this, you did not repent and believe him.●

## KING JAMES

1.FAITH

18 Now in the morning, as he returned
into the city, he hungered. 19 And when
he saw a fig tree in the way, he came to it,
and found nothing thereon, but leaves
only, and said unto it, Let no fruit grow
on thee henceforward for ever. And
presently the fig tree withered away.
20 And when the disciples saw *it*, they
marveled, saying, How soon is the fig tree
withered away! 21 Jesus answered and
said unto them, Verily I say unto you, If
ye have faith, and doubt not, ye shall not
only do this *which is done* to the fig tree,
but also if ye shall say unto this mountain, Be thou removed, and be thou cast
into the sea; it shall be done. 22 And all
things, whatsoever ye shall ask in prayer,
believing, ye shall receive.●

DISCIPLES DOUBT

*21:18-22* This was a parable in action. There should have been figs on the tree with the crop of leaves, since the early figs in the spring began appearing before the leaves. Do you see how Jesus was rebuking false profession here?

What else was Jesus teaching the disciples?

______

______

______

2.AUTHORITY

23 And when he was come into the
temple, the chief priests and the elders of
the people came unto him as he was
teaching, and said, By what authority
doest thou these things? and who gave
thee this authority? 24 And Jesus answered and said unto them, I also will ask
you one thing, which if ye tell me, I in like
wise will tell you by what authority I do
these things. 25 The baptism of John,
whence was it? from heaven, or of men?
And they reasoned with themselves, saying, If we shall say, From heaven; he will
say unto us, Why did ye not then believe
him? 26 But if we shall say, Of men; we
fear the people; for all hold John as a
prophet. 27 And they answered Jesus,
and said, We cannot tell. And he said
unto them, Neither tell I you by what
authority I do these things.●

*21:23-27* What is the key repeated word of the paragraph?

______

Did the religious leaders really know the source of Jesus' authority? Relate this to the parable of the fig tree.

______

______

______

______

______

3.OBEDIENCE

28 But what think ye? A *certain* man
had two sons; and he came to the first,
and said, Son, go work today in my vineyard. 29 He answered and said, I will
not; but afterward he repented, and went.
30 And he came to the second, and said
likewise. And he answered and said, I *go*,
sir; and went not. 31 Whether of them
twain did the will of *his* father? They say
unto him, The first. Jesus saith unto
them, Verily I say unto you, That the publicans and the harlots go into the kingdom
of God before you. 32 For John came
unto you in the way of righteousness, and
ye believed him not; but the publicans
and the harlots believed him: and ye,
when ye had seen *it*, repented not afterward, that ye might believe him.●

RELIGIOUS LEADERS REJECT

*21:28-32* Compare the two sons. ______

______

______

______

______

Which response did Jesus commend? ______

______

Why? ______

______

______

______

______

______

______

______

______

______

NEW INTERNATIONAL VERSION

Read Hebrews 1:1-2. Observe that God spoke to people in Old Testament times in various ways. You may recall from Old Testament Scripture that many of God's prophets to the people were rejected and even slain. How is this rejection of God's servants illustrated in this parable?

Then Jesus, God's Son, came. Who rejected Him?

Is this parable being fulfilled even today? If so, in what ways?

Why do people reject what God wants them to have?

Why is obedience to Christ so important for a Christian?

Is it possible that Christ would take away something which He has given a Christian, such as opportunities to witness, if the Christian is living in disobedience?

*The Parable of the Tenants*

33 "Listen to another parable: There was
a landowner who planted a vineyard. He
put a wall around it, dug a winepress in it
and built a watchtower. Then he rented the
vineyard to some farmers and went away
on a journey. 34 When the harvest time approached, he sent his servants to the tenants to collect his fruit.
35 "The tenants seized his servants; they
beat one, killed another, and stoned a
third. 36 Then he sent other servants to
them, more than the first time, and the
tenants treated them the same way. 37 Last
of all, he sent his son to them. 'They will
respect my son,' he said.
38 "But when the tenants saw the son,
they said to each other, 'This is the heir.
Come, let's kill him and take his inheritance.' 39 So they took him and threw him
out of the vineyard and killed him.
40 "Therefore, when the owner of the
vineyard comes, what will he do to those
tenants?"
41 "He will bring those wretches to a
wretched end," they replied, "and he will
rent the vineyard to other tenants, who will
give him his share of the crop at harvest
time." ●
42 Jesus said to them, "Have you never
read in the Scriptures:

" 'The stone the builders rejected
has become the capstone[a];
the Lord has done this,
and it is marvelous in our eyes'[b]?

43 "Therefore I tell you that the kingdom
of God will be taken away from you and
given to a people who will produce its fruit.
44 He who falls on this stone will be broken
to pieces, but he on whom it falls will be
crushed."[c] ●
45 When the chief priests and the Pharisees heard Jesus' parables, they knew he
was talking about them. 46 They looked for
a way to arrest him, but they were afraid of
the crowd because the people held that he
was a prophet. ●

[a]42 Or *cornerstone* [b]42 Psalm 118:22,23
[c]44 Some manuscripts do not have verse 44.

KING JAMES

1.SON

PARABLE SPOKEN

33 Hear another parable: There was a
certain householder, which planted a vineyard, and hedged it round about, and
digged a winepress in it, and built a tower,
and let it out to husbandmen, and went
into a far country: 34 and when the time
of the fruit drew near, he sent his servants
to the husbandmen, that they might receive the fruits of it. 35 And the husbandmen took his servants, and beat one,
and killed another, and stoned another.
36 Again, he sent other servants more
than the first: and they did unto them
likewise. 37 But last of all he sent unto
them his son, saying, They will reverence
my son. 38 But when the husbandmen
saw the son, they said among themselves,
This is the heir; come, let us kill him, and
let us seize on his inheritance. 39 And
they caught him, and cast *him* out of the
vineyard, and slew *him*. 40 When the lord
therefore of the vineyard cometh, what
will he do unto those husbandmen?
41 They say unto him, He will miserably
destroy those wicked men, and will let out
*his* vineyard unto other husbandmen,
which shall render him the fruits in their
seasons.●

2.STONE

42 Jesus saith unto them, Did ye never
read in the Scriptures,

Ps. 118:22

The stone which the builders rejected,
the same is become the head of the
corner:
this is the Lord's doing,
and it is marvelous in our eyes[c]?
43 Therefore say I unto you, The kingdom
of God shall be taken from you, and given
to a nation bringing forth the fruits thereof. 44 And whosoever shall fall on this
stone shall be broken: but on whomsoever it shall fall, it will grind him to
powder.●

3.PROPHET

PARABLE BEING FULFILLED

45 And when the chief priests and
Pharisees had heard his parables, they
perceived that he spake of them. 46 But
when they sought to lay hands on him,
they feared the multitude, because they
took him for a prophet.●

*21:33-41* Record the main stages of the action of this parable.

Whom does the landowner's son represent?

*21:42-44* Record what each of the four lines of the Old Testament passage teaches:

a)

b)

c)

d)

The nation of Israel, following their false leaders, rejected Christ, and the Church, after Christ's ascension, owned Him as Lord. Is this predicted in verse 43? If so, how?

*21:45-46* Compare the religious leaders and the multitudes.

NEW INTERNATIONAL VERSION

Try to interpret the main parts of the parable of verses 1-14. Record your conclusions:

king: ______________________________

son: ______________________________

first guests to be invited (cf. Matt. 10:5,6; Rom.1:16): ______________

messengers beaten: ______________________________

"invite everyone" (v.9): ______________________________

wedding robe: ______________________________

What do you think is Jesus' main purpose in teaching the parable?

A key statement of the last paragraph is "Give it to Caesar if it is his, and give God everything that belongs to God." (v.21)

Apply this to your own life:

*The Parable of the Wedding Banquet*

22 Jesus spoke to them again in parables, saying: 2"The kingdom of
heaven is like a king who prepared a wedding banquet for his son. 3He sent his servants to those who had been invited to the
banquet to tell them to come, but they
refused to come.
4"Then he sent some more servants and
said, 'Tell those who have been invited
that I have prepared my dinner: My oxen
and fattened cattle have been butchered,
and everything is ready. Come to the wedding banquet.'
5"But they paid no attention and went
off—one to his field, another to his
business. 6The rest seized his servants,
mistreated them and killed them. 7The king
was enraged. He sent his army and destroyed those murderers and burned their
city.
8"Then he said to his servants, 'The
wedding banquet is ready, but those I invited did not deserve to come. 9Go to the
street corners and invite to the banquet
anyone you find.' 10So the servants went
out into the streets and gathered all the
people they could find, both good and bad,
and the wedding hall was filled with guests.●
11"But when the king came in to see the
guests, he noticed a man there who was not
wearing wedding clothes. 12'Friend,' he
asked, 'how did you get in here without
wedding clothes?' The man was speechless.
13"Then the king told the attendants,
'Tie him hand and foot, and throw him
outside, into the darkness, where there will
be weeping and gnashing of teeth.'
14"For many are invited, but few are
chosen."●

*Paying Taxes to Caesar*

15Then the Pharisees went out and laid
plans to trap him in his words. 16They sent
their disciples to him along with the
Herodians. "Teacher," they said, "we
know you are a man of integrity and that
you teach the way of God in accordance
with the truth. You aren't swayed by men,
because you pay no attention to who they
are. 17Tell us then, what is your opinion? Is
it right to pay taxes to Caesar or not?"
18But Jesus, knowing their evil intent,
said, "You hypocrites, why are you trying
to trap me? 19Show me the coin used for
paying the tax." They brought him a
denarius, 20and he asked them, "Whose
portrait is this? And whose inscription?"
21"Caesar's," they replied.
Then he said to them, "Give to Caesar
what is Caesar's, and to God what is
God's."
22When they heard this, they were
amazed. So they left him and went away.●

## KING JAMES

**1. WEDDING FEAST READY**

22 And Jesus answered and spake unto
them again by parables, and said,
2 The kingdom of heaven is like unto a
certain king, which made a marriage for
his son, 3 and sent forth his servants to
call them that were bidden to the wedding: and they would not come. 4 Again,
he sent forth other servants, saying, Tell
them which are bidden, Behold, I have
prepared my dinner: my oxen and *my*
fatlings *are* killed, and all things *are*
ready: come unto the marriage. 5 But
they made light of *it*, and went their ways,
one to his farm, another to his merchandise: 6 and the remnant took his servants, and entreated *them* spitefully, and
slew *them*. 7 But when the king heard
*thereof*, he was wroth: and he sent forth
his armies, and destroyed those murderers, and burned up their city. 8 Then saith
he to his servants, The wedding is ready,
but they which were bidden were not
worthy. 9 Go ye therefore into the highways, and as many as ye shall find, bid to
the marriage. 10 So those servants went
out into the highways, and gathered together all as many as they found, both
bad and good: and the wedding was furnished with guests.●

**2. NO WEDDING CLOTHES**

11 And when the king came in to see the
guests, he saw there a man which had not
on a wedding garment: 12 and he saith
unto him, Friend, how camest thou in
hither not having a wedding garment?
And he was speechless. 13 Then said the
king to the servants, Bind him hand and
foot, and take him away, and cast *him*
into outer darkness; there shall be weeping and gnashing of teeth. 14 For many
are called, but few *are* chosen.●

**3. TRIBUTE**

15 Then went the Pharisees, and took
counsel how they might entangle him in
*his* talk. 16 And they sent out unto him
their disciples with the Hero'di-ans, saying, Master, we know that thou art true,
and teachest the way of God in truth,
neither carest thou for any *man*: for thou
regardest not the person of men. 17 Tell
us therefore, What thinkest thou? Is it
lawful to give tribute unto Caesar, or not?
18 But Jesus perceived their wickedness,
and said, Why tempt ye me, *ye* hypocrites?
19 Show me the tribute money. And they
brought unto him a penny. 20 And he
saith unto them, Whose *is* this image and
superscription? 21 They say unto him,
Caesar's. Then saith he unto them,
Render therefore unto Caesar the things
which are Caesar's; and unto God the
things that are God's. 22 When they had
heard *these words*, they marveled, and
left him, and went their way.●

**INVITATION**

During this last week of Jesus' public ministry (Passion Week) He wanted to make very clear to the people that He wanted everyone to come into His kingdom, and also that each one must personally respond to His gracious invitation to come.
This passage says more about this.

*22:1-10* Record these parts of the parable:

Who gave the wedding feast? ______________________

In whose honor? ______________________

What problem arose? ______________________

What was the solution? ______________________

*22:11-14* Wedding clothes were provided by the host, according to customs of that day. Why was the king so severe in his treatment of the guests?

______________________

**OBLIGATION**

*22:15-22* The domain of Christ's kingdom is not political. Yet a Christian has a relationship to human government. What is a key statement of the paragraph?

______________________

NEW INTERNATIONAL VERSION

Why is the doctrine of resurrection a key doctrine of the Christian faith?

List all the truths taught about the resurrection in verses 23-33.

How does verse 40 explain why the two commandments of verses 37-39 are the most important?

Apply these two commandments to life today.

Jesus is the Son of God. Why is this a crucial doctrine of the Christian faith?

*Marriage at the Resurrection*
23That same day the Sadducees, who say
there is no resurrection, came to him with
a question. 24"Teacher," they said,
"Moses told us that if a man dies without
having children, his brother must marry
the widow and have children for him.
25Now there were seven brothers among
us. The first one married and died, and
since he had no children, he left his wife to
his brother. 26The same thing happened to
the second and third brother, right on
down to the seventh. 27Finally, the woman
died. 28Now then, at the resurrection,
whose wife will she be of the seven, since
all of them were married to her?"
29Jesus replied, "You are in error because you do not know the Scriptures or
the power of God. 30At the resurrection
people will neither marry nor be given in
marriage; they will be like the angels in
heaven. 31But about the resurrection of the
dead—have you not read what God said to
you, 32'I am the God of Abraham, the God
of Isaac, and the God of Jacob'[a]? He is not
the God of the dead but of the living."
33When the crowds heard this, they were
astonished at his teaching.●

*The Greatest Commandment*
34Hearing that Jesus had silenced the
Sadducees, the Pharisees got together.
35One of them, an expert in the law, tested
him with this question: 36"Teacher, which
is the greatest commandment in the Law?"
37Jesus replied: " 'Love the Lord your
God with all your heart and with all your
soul and with all your mind.'[b] 38This is the
first and greatest commandment. 39And the
second is like it: 'Love your neighbor as
yourself.'[c] 40All the Law and the Prophets
hang on these two commandments."●

*Whose Son Is the Christ?*
41While the Pharisees were gathered together, Jesus asked them, 42"What do you
think about the Christ[d]? Whose son is he?"
"The son of David," they replied.
43He said to them, "How is it then that
David, speaking by the Spirit, calls him
'Lord'? For he says,

44" 'The Lord said to my Lord:
"Sit at my right hand
until I put your enemies
under your feet." '[e]

45If then David calls him 'Lord,' how can
he be his son?" 46No one could say a word
in reply, and from that day on no one dared
to ask him any more questions.●

[a]32 Exodus 3:6 [b]37 Deut. 6:5 [c]39 Lev. 19:18
[d]42 Or *Messiah* [e]44 Psalm 110:1

KING JAMES

1. RESURRECTION

QUESTIONS

23 The same day came to him the Sadducees, which say that there is no resurrection, and asked him, 24 saying,
Master, Moses said, If a man die, having
no children, his brother shall marry his
wife, and raise up seed unto his brother. —Deu. 25:5
25 Now there were with us seven breth-
ren: and the first, when he had married a
wife, deceased, and, having no issue, left
his wife unto his brother: 26 likewise the
second also, and the third, unto the
seventh. 27 And last of all the woman
died also. 28 Therefore in the resurrection, whose wife shall she be of the seven?
for they all had her.
29 Jesus answered and said unto them,
Ye do err, not knowing the Scriptures,
nor the power of God. 30 For in the resurrection they neither marry, nor are
given in marriage, but are as the angels of
God in heaven. 31 But as touching the
resurrection of the dead, have ye not read
that which was spoken unto you by God,
saying, 32 I am the God of Abraham, and Ex. 3:6
the God of Isaac, and the God of Jacob?
God is not the God of the dead, but of the
living. 33 And when the multitude heard
*this*, they were astonished at his doctrine.●

2. COMMANDMENTS

34 But when the Pharisees had heard
that he had put the Sadducees to silence,
they were gathered together. 35 Then one
of them, *which was* a lawyer, asked *him a
question*, tempting him, and saying,
36 Master, which *is* the great commandment in the law? 37 Jesus said unto him,
Thou shalt love the Lord thy God
with all thy heart,
and with all thy soul, and with all Deu. 6:5
thy mind.
38 This is the first and great command-
ment. 39 And the second *is* like unto it, Lev. 19:18
Thou shalt love thy neighbor as
thyself.
40 On these two commandments hang all
the law and the prophets.●

3. MESSIAH

41 While the Pharisees were gathered
together, Jesus asked them, 42 saying,
What think ye of Christ? whose son is he?
They say unto him, *The son* of David.
43 He saith unto them, How then doth
David in spirit call him Lord, saying,
44 The LORD said unto my Lord,
Sit thou on my right hand, Ps. 110:1
till I make thine enemies thy footstool?
45 If David then call him Lord, how is he
his son? 46 And no man was able to
answer him a word, neither durst any
*man* from that day forth ask him any
more *questions*.●

NO MORE QUESTIONS

As you study this passage keep in mind these false doctrines of Jesus' opponents:

Sadducees:
—denied the resurrection

Pharisees:
—salvation by works
—Jesus just a teacher, not the Son of God.

*22:23-33* Note Jesus' answer (v.29) to the Sadducees' trick question. What two things did the Sadducees not understand?

1. ____________________

____________________

2. ____________________

____________________

How did Jesus expound on this in verses 30-33?

____________________

____________________

____________________

*22:34-40* Did Jesus answer more than what was asked? If so, why?

____________________

____________________

____________________

____________________

____________________

*22:41-46* Now Jesus does the questioning. Why does He ask *this* question? (The name "Christ" is the same as "Messiah.")

____________________

____________________

____________________

____________________

____________________

____________________

____________________

____________________

____________________

NEW INTERNATIONAL VERSION

A common saying heard often is "Practice what you preach." What do verses 1-4 teach about:

RULES AND REGULATIONS

IMPOSING RULES ON OTHERS

What are different ways in which people today "show off" their religion? Compare your list with that of verses 5-7.

Reflect on each of the following three titles, and record some spiritual applications to be derived from each, concerning a believer's relation to God:

Teacher (Christ)

Father (God)

Leader (Christ)

*Seven Woes*

23 Then Jesus said to the crowds and to
his disciples: 2"The teachers of the
law and the Pharisees sit in Moses' seat.
3So you must obey them and do everything
they tell you. But do not do what they do,
for they do not practice what they preach.
4They tie up heavy loads and put them on
men's shoulders, but they themselves are
not willing to lift a finger to move them.●
5"Everything they do is done for men to
see: They make their phylacteries[f] wide
and the tassels of their prayer shawls long;
6they love the place of honor at banquets
and the most important seats in the synagogues;
7they love to be greeted in the
marketplaces and to have men call them
'Rabbi.'●
8"But you are not to be called 'Rabbi,'
for you have only one Master and you are
all brothers. 9And do not call anyone on
earth 'father,' for you have one Father,
and he is in heaven. 10Nor are you to be
called 'teacher,' for you have one Teacher,
the Christ.[a] 11The greatest among you will
be your servant. 12For whoever exalts himself
will be humbled, and whoever humbles
himself will be exalted.●

*f5* That is, boxes containing Scripture verses, which were worn on the forehead and arms

*a10* Or *Messiah*

KING JAMES

1.HYPOCRISY

23 Then spake Jesus to the multitude,
and to his disciples, 2 saying, The
scribes and the Pharisees sit in Moses'
seat: 3 all therefore whatsoever they bid
you observe, *that* observe and do; but do
not ye after their works: for they say, and
do not. 4 For they bind heavy burdens
and grievous to be borne, and lay *them* on
men's shoulders; but they *themselves* will
not move them with one of their fingers.●

2.VANITY

5 But all their works they do for to be
seen of men: they make broad their
phylacteries, and enlarge the borders of
their garments, 6 and love the uppermost
rooms at feasts, and the chief seats in the
synagogues, 7 and greetings in the markets,
and to be called of men, Rabbi,

3.TRUE HONOR

Rabbi.● 8 But be not ye called Rabbi: for
one is your Master, *even* Christ; and all
ye are brethren. 9 And call no *man* your
father upon the earth: for one is your
Father, which is in heaven. 10 Neither be
ye called masters: for one is your Master,
*even* Christ. 11 But he that is greatest
among you shall be your servant.
12 And whosoever shall exalt himself shall
be abased; and he that shall humble himself
shall be exalted.●

MOSES

CHRIST

Here Matthew reports more of Jesus' exposure of the sins of His religious opponents. So much of the gospel story is devoted to Jesus' confrontations with these opponents that it is clear that this conflict will bring on all the events leading up to His crucifixion.

*23:1-4* What basic sin is exposed here?

*23:5-7* List the vain ways cited.

*23:8-12* What are the three titles mentioned?

Relate verses 11-12 to verses 5-7.

NEW INTERNATIONAL VERSION

What do you learn about Jesus from this long series of "woes"? ______________

The same kind of sins exposed here are being committed today. Human nature is that changeless. Record some of the sins below.

13"Woe to you, teachers of the law and
Pharisees, you hypocrites! You shut the
kingdom of heaven in men's faces. You
yourselves do not enter, nor will you let
those enter who are trying to.[b]●
15"Woe to you, teachers of the law and
Pharisees, you hypocrites! You travel over
land and sea to win a single convert, and
when he becomes one, you make him twice
as much a son of hell as you are.●
16"Woe to you, blind guides! You say,
'If anyone swears by the temple, it means
nothing; but if anyone swears by the gold
of the temple, he is bound by his oath.'
17You blind fools! Which is greater: the
gold, or the temple that makes the gold
sacred? 18You also say, 'If anyone swears
by the altar, it means nothing; but if anyone
swears by the gift on it, he is bound by his
oath.' 19You blind men! Which is greater:
the gift, or the altar that makes the gift
sacred? 20Therefore, he who swears by the
altar swears by it and by everything on it.
21And he who swears by the temple swears
by it and by the one who dwells in it. 22And
he who swears by heaven swears by God's
throne and by the one who sits on it.●
23"Woe to you, teachers of the law and
Pharisees, you hypocrites! You give a
tenth of your spices—mint, dill and cummin. But you have neglected the more important matters of the law—justice, mercy
and faithfulness. You should have practiced the latter, without neglecting the former. 24You blind guides! You strain out a
gnat but swallow a camel.●
25"Woe to you, teachers of the law and
Pharisees, you hypocrites! You clean the
outside of the cup and dish, but inside they
are full of greed and self-indulgence.
26Blind Pharisee! First clean the inside of
the cup and dish, and then the outside also
will be clean.●
27"Woe to you, teachers of the law and
Pharisees, you hypocrites! You are like
whitewashed tombs, which look beautiful
on the outside but on the inside are full of
dead men's bones and everything unclean.
28In the same way, on the outside you appear to people as righteous but on the inside you are full of hypocrisy and wickedness.●

*b13 Some manuscripts to. 14Woe to you, teachers of the law and Pharisees, you hypocrites! You devour widows' houses and for a show make lengthy prayers. Therefore you will be punished more severely.*

KING JAMES

CONDEMNING FALSE TEACHERS

13 But woe unto you, scribes and
Pharisees, hypocrites! for ye shut up the
kingdom of heaven against men: for ye
neither go in *yourselves*, neither suffer ye
them that are entering to go in. 14 Woe
1. unto you, scribes and Pharisees, hypocrites! for ye devour widows' houses, and
for a pretense make long prayer: therefore ye shall receive the greater damna-
2. tion.● 15 Woe unto you, scribes and Pharisees, hypocrites! for ye compass sea and
land to make one proselyte; and when he
is made, ye make him twofold more the
child of hell than yourselves.●
3. 16 Woe unto you, *ye* blind guides,
which say, Whosoever shall swear by the
temple, it is nothing; but whosoever shall
swear by the gold of the temple, he is a
debtor! 17 *Ye* fools and blind: for
whether is greater, the gold, or the temple
that sanctifieth the gold? 18 And, Whosoever shall swear by the altar, it is nothing; but whosoever sweareth by the gift
that is upon it, he is guilty. 19 *Ye* fools
and blind: for whether *is* greater, the gift,
or the altar that sanctifieth the gift?
20 Whoso therefore shall swear by the
altar, sweareth by it, and by all things
thereon. 21 And whoso shall swear by the
temple, sweareth by it, and by him that
dwelleth therein. 22 And he that shall
swear by heaven, sweareth by the throne
of God, and by him that sitteth thereon.●
4. 23 Woe unto you, scribes and Pharisees, hypocrites! for ye pay tithe of mint
and anise and cummin, and have omitted
the weightier *matters* of the law, judgment,
mercy, and faith: these ought ye to have
done, and not to leave the other undone.
24 *Ye* blind guides, which strain at a gnat,
and swallow a camel.●
5. 25 Woe unto you, scribes and Pharisees, hypocrites! for ye make clean the
outside of the cup and of the platter, but
within they are full of extortion and excess.
26 *Thou* blind Pharisee, cleanse first that
*which is* within the cup and platter,
that the outside of them may be clean
also.●
6. 27 Woe unto you, scribes and Pharisees, hypocrites! for ye are like unto
whited sepulchres, which indeed appear
beautiful outward, but are within full of
dead *men's* bones, and of all uncleanness.
28 Even so ye also outwardly appear
righteous unto men, but within ye are full
of hypocrisy and iniquity.●

LONG PRAYERS

WHITE-WASHED TOMBS

Jesus here exposes many sins of the false teachers. List these below.

*23:13-14* ____________________

____________________

____________________

____________________

*23:15* ____________________

____________________

____________________

____________________

*23:16-22* ____________________

____________________

____________________

____________________

*23:23-24* ____________________

____________________

____________________

____________________

*23:25-26* ____________________

____________________

____________________

____________________

*23:27-28* ____________________

____________________

____________________

____________________

____________________

____________________

NEW INTERNATIONAL VERSION

What does this passage teach about:

SELF-CONDEMNATION

JUDGMENT FOR SIN

PERSECUTION OF GOD'S SERVANTS

LONGSUFFERING AND PATIENCE OF CHRIST

CHRIST REIGNING AS KING

29 "Woe to you, teachers of the law and
Pharisees, you hypocrites! You build
tombs for the prophets and decorate the
graves of the righteous. 30 And you say, 'If
we had lived in the days of our forefathers,
we would not have taken part with them in
shedding the blood of the prophets.' 31 So
you testify against yourselves that you are
the descendants of those who murdered
the prophets. 32 Fill up, then, the measure
of the sin of your forefathers!
33 "You snakes! You brood of vipers!
How will you escape being condemned to
hell? 34 Therefore I am sending you prophets and wise men and teachers. Some of
them you will kill and crucify; others you
will flog in your synagogues and pursue
from town to town. 35 And so upon you will
come all the righteous blood that has been
shed on earth, from the blood of righteous
Abel to the blood of Zechariah son of Bera-
kiah, whom you murdered between the
temple and the altar. 36 I tell you the truth,
all this will come upon this generation.
37 "O Jerusalem, Jerusalem, you who kill
the prophets and stone those sent to you,
how often I have longed to gather your
children together, as a hen gathers her
chicks under her wings, but you were not
willing. 38 Look, your house is left to you
desolate. 39 For I tell you, you will not see
me again until you say, 'Blessed is he who
comes in the name of the Lord.'[c]"

[c]39 Psalm 118:26

KING JAMES

1.CONDEMNATION

"Woe!"

29 Woe unto you, scribes and Pharisees, hypocrites! because ye build the
tombs of the prophets, and garnish the
sepulchres of the righteous, 30 and say,
If we had been in the days of our fathers,
we would not have been partakers with
them in the blood of the prophets.
31 Wherefore ye be witnesses unto yourselves, that ye are the children of them
which killed the prophets. 32 Fill ye up
then the measure of your fathers. 33 *Ye*
serpents, *ye* generation of vipers, how
can ye escape the damnation of hell?●
34 Wherefore, behold, I send unto you
prophets, and wise men, and scribes: and
*some* of them ye shall kill and crucify;
and *some* of them shall ye scourge in your
synagogues, and persecute *them* from city
to city: 35 that upon you may come all
the righteous blood shed upon the earth,
from the blood of righteous Abel unto
the blood of Zechari'ah son of Berechi'ah, whom ye slew between the temple
and the altar. 36 Verily I say unto you,
All these things shall come upon this
generation.●

2.INVITATION

37 O Jerusalem, Jerusalem, *thou* that
killest the prophets, and stonest them
which are sent unto thee, how often
would I have gathered thy children together, even as a hen gathereth her
chickens under *her* wings, and ye would
not! 38 Behold, your house is left unto
you desolate. 39 For I say unto you, Ye
shall not see me henceforth, till ye shall
say, Blessed *is* he that cometh in the name
of the Lord.●

"Blessed!"

The previous segment mainly described the hypocrisy of the scribes and Pharisees. In this segment there is more description, but Jesus also predicts the punishments which would fall.

Record the sins and the punishments for each paragraph.

*23:29-33*

SINS ____________________

____________________

____________________

PUNISHMENT ____________________

____________________

____________________

*23:34-36*

SINS ____________________

____________________

____________________

PUNISHMENT ____________________

____________________

____________________

*23:37-39*

SINS ____________________

____________________

____________________

PUNISHMENT ____________________

NEW INTERNATIONAL VERSION

There are various interpretations as to the particular events and times which Jesus was referring to in this discourse. You will probably want help from commentaries in the interpretation stage. For example, some hold that verses 4-14 describe the first half of the tribulation in end times, and verses 15-28 deal with the last half. The end times are involved, and just a study of the prophecies, warnings and exhortations is very profitable for all Bible students. Record these, for this passage.

*24:4-14*

PROPHECIES

EXHORTATIONS AND WARNINGS

*24:15-28*

PROPHECIES

EXHORTATIONS AND WARNINGS

*Signs of the End of the Age*

24 Jesus left the temple and was walking away when his disciples came up
to him to call his attention to its buildings.
2"Do you see all these things?" he asked.
"I tell you the truth, not one stone here will
be left on another; every one will be thrown
down."●
3As Jesus was sitting on the Mount of
Olives, the disciples came to him privately.
"Tell us," they said, "when will this happen, and what will be the sign of your coming and of the end of the age?"
4Jesus answered: "Watch out that no
one deceives you. 5For many will come in
my name, claiming, 'I am the Christ,[d]' and
will deceive many. 6You will hear of wars
and rumors of wars, but see to it that you
are not alarmed. Such things must happen,
but the end is still to come. 7Nation will rise
against nation, and kingdom against kingdom. There will be famines and earthquakes in various places. 8All these are the
beginning of birth pains.
9"Then you will be handed over to be
persecuted and put to death, and you will
be hated by all nations because of me. 10At
that time many will turn away from the
faith and will betray and hate each other,
11and many false prophets will appear and
deceive many people. 12Because of the increase of wickedness, the love of most will
grow cold, 13but he who stands firm to the
end will be saved. 14And this gospel of the
kingdom will be preached in the whole
world as a testimony to all nations, and
then the end will come.●
15"So when you see standing in the holy
place 'the abomination that causes desolation,'[a] spoken of through the prophet Daniel—let the reader understand— 16then let
those who are in Judea flee to the mountains. 17Let no one on the roof of his house
go down to take anything out of the house.
18Let no one in the field go back to get his
cloak. 19How dreadful it will be in those
days for pregnant women and nursing
mothers! 20Pray that your flight will not
take place in winter or on the Sabbath.
21For then there will be great distress, unequaled from the beginning of the world
until now—and never to be equaled again.
22If those days had not been cut short, no
one would survive, but for the sake of the
elect those days will be shortened. 23At
that time if anyone says to you, 'Look,
here is the Christ!' or, 'There he is!' do not
believe it. 24For false Christs and false
prophets will appear and perform great
signs and miracles to deceive even the
elect—if that were possible. 25See, I have
told you ahead of time.●
26"So if anyone tells you, 'There he is,
out in the desert,' do not go out; or, 'Here
he is, in the inner rooms,' do not believe it.
27For as the lightning comes from the east
and flashes to the west, so will be the coming of the Son of Man. 28Wherever there is
a carcass, there the vultures will gather.●

*d5* Or *Messiah*; also in verse 23
*a15* Daniel 9:27; 11:31; 12:11

KING JAMES

1.SETTING

STONES TORN DOWN

24 And Jesus went out, and departed
from the temple: and his disciples
came to *him* for to show him the buildings
of the temple. 2 And Jesus said unto
them, See ye not all these things? verily I
say unto you, There shall not be left here
one stone upon another, that shall not be
thrown down.●

2.TRIBULATION DAYS

3 And as he sat upon the mount of
Olives, the disciples came unto him privately, saying, Tell us, when shall these
things be? and what *shall be* the sign of
thy coming, and of the end of the world?
4 And Jesus answered and said unto
them, Take heed that no man deceive you.
5 For many shall come in my name, saying, I am Christ; and shall deceive many.
6 And ye shall hear of wars and rumors
of wars: see that ye be not troubled: for all
*these things* must come to pass, but the
end is not yet. 7 For nation shall rise
against nation, and kingdom against
kingdom: and there shall be famines, and
pestilences, and earthquakes, in divers
places. 8 All these *are* the beginning of
sorrows.
9 Then shall they deliver you up to be
afflicted, and shall kill you: and ye shall
be hated of all nations for my name's
sake. 10 And then shall many be offended, and shall betray one another, and
shall hate one another. 11 And many
false prophets shall rise, and shall deceive
many. 12 And because iniquity shall
abound, the love of many shall wax cold.
13 But he that shall endure unto the
end, the same shall be saved. 14 And
this gospel of the kingdom shall be
preached in all the world for a witness
unto all nations; and then shall the end
come.●

3.GREAT TRIBULATION DAYS

15 When ye therefore shall see the
abomination of desolation, spoken of by
Daniel the prophet, stand in the holy
place, (whoso readeth, let him understand,) 16 then let them which be in
Judea flee into the mountains: 17 let him
which is on the housetop not come down
to take any thing out of his house:
18 neither let him which is in the field
return back to take his clothes. 19 And
woe unto them that are with child, and to
them that give suck in those days! 20 But
pray ye that your flight be not in the winter, neither on the sabbath day: 21 for
then shall be great tribulation, such as
was not since the beginning of the world
to this time, no, nor ever shall be. 22 And
except those days should be shortened,
there should no flesh be saved: but for the
elect's sake those days shall be shortened.
23 Then if any man shall say unto you,
Lo, here *is* Christ, or there; believe *it* not.
24 For there shall arise false Christs, and
false prophets, and shall show great signs
and wonders; insomuch that, if *it were*
possible, they shall deceive the very elect.●

4.CAUTION

VULTURES WILL GATHER

25 Behold, I have told you before.
26 Wherefore if they shall say unto you,
Behold, he is in the desert; go not forth:
behold, *he is* in the secret chambers; believe *it* not. 27 For as the lightning cometh out of the east, and shineth even unto
the west; so shall also the coming of the
Son of man be. 28 For wheresoever the
carcass is, there will the eagles be gathered together.●

Chapters 24 and 25 report the last discourse of Jesus before His death. The discourse is about the end of the age and His second coming to the earth.

*24:1-2* What is Jesus' general prophecy here?

*24:3-14* What were the disciples' questions?

The "end shall come" (v.14) after the signs. Record the signs (vv.4-14):

*24:15-24* The "abomination of desolation" may be a reference to Antichrist (2 Thess. 2:4). Record the main signs which will follow those of verses 4-14:

*24:25-28* What is Jesus cautioning here?

NEW INTERNATIONAL VERSION

After prophesying the event of His second coming (24:29-31), Jesus said, "Now learn a lesson from the fig tree" (v.32). All that He says from this point to the end of chapter 25 is intended to instruct the hearers and readers to apply the truths effectively.

Record below the practical lessons which Jesus teaches by His illustrations.

*FIG TREE* __________

*DAYS OF NOAH* __________

*HOUSEHOLDER* __________

*WISE SERVANT* __________

29 "Immediately after the distress of
those days

" 'the sun will be darkened,
and the moon will not give its
light;
the stars will fall from the sky,
and the heavenly bodies will be
shaken.'[b]

30 "At that time the sign of the Son of
Man will appear in the sky, and all the
nations of the earth will mourn. They will
see the Son of Man coming on the clouds
of the sky, with power and great glory.
31 And he will send his angels with a loud
trumpet call, and they will gather his elect
from the four winds, from one end of the
heavens to the other.●
32 "Now learn this lesson from the fig
tree: As soon as its twigs get tender and its
leaves come out, you know that summer is
near. 33 Even so, when you see all these
things, you know that it[c] is near, right at
the door. 34 I tell you the truth, this generation[d] will certainly not pass away until all
these things have happened. 35 Heaven and
earth will pass away, but my words will
never pass away.●

### *The Day and Hour Unknown*

36 "No one knows about that day or hour,
not even the angels in heaven, nor the
Son,[e] but only the Father. 37 As it was in the
days of Noah, so it will be at the coming of
the Son of Man. 38 For in the days before
the flood, people were eating and drinking,
marrying and giving in marriage, up to the
day Noah entered the ark; 39 and they knew
nothing about what would happen until the
flood came and took them all away. That is
how it will be at the coming of the Son of
Man. 40 Two men will be in the field; one
will be taken and the other left. 41 Two
women will be grinding with a hand mill;
one will be taken and the other left.●
42 "Therefore keep watch, because you
do not know on what day your Lord will
come. 43 But understand this: If the owner
of the house had known at what time of
night the thief was coming, he would have
kept watch and would not have let his
house be broken into. 44 So you also must
be ready, because the Son of Man will
come at an hour when you do not expect
him.●
45 "Who then is the faithful and wise servant, whom the master has put in charge of
the servants in his household to give them
their food at the proper time? 46 It will be
good for that servant whose master finds
him doing so when he returns. 47 I tell you
the truth, he will put him in charge of all his
possessions. 48 But suppose that servant is
wicked and says to himself, 'My master is
staying away a long time,' 49 and he then
begins to beat his fellow servants and to eat
and drink with drunkards. 50 The master of
that servant will come on a day when he
does not expect him and at an hour he is
not aware of. 51 He will cut him to pieces
and assign him a place with the hypocrites,
where there will be weeping and gnashing
of teeth.●

*b29* Isaiah 13:10; 34:4 *c33* Or *he* *d34* Or *race*
*e36* Some manuscripts do not have *nor the Son.*

KING JAMES

JESUS' SECOND COMING

1. THE EVENT

29 Immediately after the tribulation of
those days shall the sun be darkened, and
the moon shall not give her light, and the
stars shall fall from heaven, and the
powers of the heavens shall be shaken:
30 and then shall appear the sign of the
Son of man in heaven: and then shall all
the tribes of the earth mourn, and they
shall see the Son of man coming in the
clouds of heaven with power and great
glory. 31 And he shall send his angels
with a great sound of a trumpet, and they
shall gather together his elect from the
four winds, from one end of heaven to the
other.●

HIS ELECT

2. ILLUSTRATIONS

a. fig tree

32 Now learn a parable of the fig tree;
When his branch is yet tender, and putteth forth leaves, ye know that summer *is*
nigh: 33 so likewise ye, when ye shall
see all these things, know that it is
near, *even* at the doors. 34 Verily I
say unto you, This generation shall
not pass, till all these things be fulfilled. 35 Heaven and earth shall pass
away, but my words shall not pass
away.●

b. days of Noah

36 But of that day and hour knoweth
no *man*, no, not the angels of heaven, but
my Father only. 37 But as the days of
Noah *were*, so shall also the coming of
the Son of man be. 38 For as in the days
that were before the flood they were eating
and drinking, marrying and giving in marriage, until the day that Noah entered into
the ark, 39 and knew not until the flood
came, and took them all away; so shall
also the coming of the Son of man be.
40 Then shall two be in the field; the one
shall be taken, and the other left. 41 Two
*women shall be* grinding at the mill; the
one shall be taken, and the other left.●

c. householder

42 Watch therefore; for ye know not
what hour your Lord doth come. 43 But
know this, that if the goodman of the
house had known in what watch the thief
would come, he would have watched, and
would not have suffered his house to be
broken up. 44 Therefore be ye also ready:
for in such an hour as ye think not the
Son of man cometh.●

d. wise servant

45 Who then is a faithful and wise servant, whom his lord hath made ruler over
his household, to give them meat in due
season? 46 Blessed *is* that servant, whom
his lord when he cometh shall find so
doing. 47 Verily I say unto you, That he
shall make him ruler over all his goods.
48 But and if that evil servant shall say in
his heart, My lord delayeth his coming;
49 and shall begin to smite *his* fellow
servants, and to eat and drink with the
drunken; 50 the lord of that servant shall
come in a day when he looketh not for
*him*, and in an hour that he is not aware
of, 51 and shall cut him asunder, and appoint *him* his portion with the hypocrites:
there shall be weeping and gnashing of
teeth.●

HIS SLAVES

Now Jesus speaks about His second coming. Verses 29-31 prophesy the event itself, and 24:32—25:46 reports the illustrations and exhortations which Jesus gave in connection with this coming.

*24:29-31* What signs will attend Jesus' coming?

*24:32-51* Record the main point of each of the illustrations.

Fig tree (32-35)

Days of Noah (36-41)

Householder (42-44)

Wise servant (45-51)

NEW INTERNATIONAL VERSION

Record different practical lessons taught by Jesus in this parable.

What event of Jesus' ministry do you think verse 13 refers to?

*The Parable of the Ten Virgins*

25 "At that time the kingdom of
heaven will be like ten virgins who
took their lamps and went out to meet the
bridegroom. 2Five of them were foolish
and five were wise. 3The foolish ones took
their lamps but did not take any oil with
them. 4The wise, however, took oil in jars
along with their lamps. 5The bridegroom
was a long time in coming, and they all
became drowsy and fell asleep.
6"At midnight the cry rang out: 'Here's
the bridegroom! Come out to meet him!'
7"Then all the virgins woke up and
trimmed their lamps. 8The foolish ones
said to the wise, 'Give us some of your oil;
our lamps are going out.'
9"'No,' they replied, 'there may not be
enough for both us and you. Instead, go to
those who sell oil and buy some for yourselves.'
10"But while they were on their way to
buy the oil, the bridegroom arrived. The
virgins who were ready went in with him to
the wedding banquet. And the door was
shut.
11"Later the others also came. 'Sir! Sir!'
they said. 'Open the door for us!'
12"But he replied, 'I tell you the truth, I
don't know you.'
13"Therefore keep watch, because you
do not know the day or the hour.

KING JAMES

1. PREPARATIONS

2. PLIGHT OF FIVE

3. BRIDEGROOM COMES

**25** Then shall the kingdom of heaven
be likened unto ten virgins, which
took their lamps, and went forth to meet
the bridegroom. 2 And five of them were
wise, and five *were* foolish. 3 They that
*were* foolish took their lamps, and took
no oil with them: 4 but the wise took oil
in their vessels with their lamps. ● 5 While
the bridegroom tarried, they all slumbered
and slept. 6 And at midnight there was a
cry made, Behold, the bridegroom cometh; go ye out to meet him. 7 Then all
those virgins arose, and trimmed their
lamps. 8 And the foolish said unto the
wise, Give us of your oil; for our lamps
are gone out. 9 But the wise answered,
saying, *Not so;* lest there be not enough
for us and you: but go ye rather to them
that sell, and buy for yourselves. ● 10 And
while they went to buy, the bridegroom
came; and they that were ready went in
with him to the marriage: and the door
was shut. 11 Afterward came also the
other virgins, saying, Lord, Lord, open to
us. 12 But he answered and said, Verily I
say unto you, I know you not. 13 Watch
therefore; for ye know neither the day nor
the hour wherein the Son of man cometh. ●

PRUDENT

ALERT

This passage continues Jesus' using illustrations to teach about His second coming.

*25:1-13* What verse applies this parable to Jesus' coming, in a concluding way?

Record the main parts of the parable:

*25:1-4*

*25:5-9*

*25:10-13*

NEW INTERNATIONAL VERSION

*The Parable of the Talents*

14“Again, it will be like a man going on
a journey, who called his servants and entrusted his property to them. 15To one he
gave five talents[a] of money, to another two
talents, and to another one talent, each according to his ability. Then he went on his
journey. 16The man who had received the
five talents went at once and put his money
to work and gained five more. 17So also,
the one with the two talents gained two
more. 18But the man who had received the
one talent went off, dug a hole in the
ground and hid his master's money.●
19“After a long time the master of those
servants returned and settled accounts
with them. 20The man who had received
the five talents brought the other five.
‘Master,’ he said, ‘you entrusted me with
five talents. See, I have gained five more.’
21“His master replied, ‘Well done, good
and faithful servant! You have been faithful with a few things; I will put you in
charge of many things. Come and share
your master's happiness!’
22“The man with the two talents also
came. ‘Master,’ he said, ‘you entrusted me
with two talents; see, I have gained two
more.’
23“His master replied, ‘Well done, good
and faithful servant! You have been faithful with a few things; I will put you in
charge of many things. Come and share
your master's happiness!’●
24“Then the man who had received the
one talent came. ‘Master,’ he said, ‘I knew
that you are a hard man, harvesting where
you have not sown and gathering where
you have not scattered seed. 25So I was
afraid and went out and hid your talent in
the ground. See, here is what belongs to
you.’
26“His master replied, ‘You wicked,
lazy servant! So you knew that I harvest
where I have not sown and gather where I
have not scattered seed? 27Well then, you
should have put my money on deposit with
the bankers, so that when I returned I
would have received it back with interest.
28“ ‘Take the talent from him and give it
to the one who has the ten talents. 29For
everyone who has will be given more, and
he will have an abundance. Whoever does
not have, even what he has will be taken
from him. 30And throw that worthless servant outside, into the darkness, where
there will be weeping and gnashing of
teeth.’●

Record different things this passage teaches about Jesus, represented by the master in the parable:

Record various applications of the parable to today.

[a]15 A talent was worth more than a thousand dollars.

KING JAMES

1. ASSIGNMENTS

GIVING

14 For *the kingdom of heaven is* as a
man traveling into a far country, *who*
called his own servants, and delivered unto them his goods. 15 And unto one he
gave five talents, to another two, and to
another one; to every man according to
his several ability; and straightway took
his journey. 16 Then he that had received
the five talents went and traded with the
same, and made *them* other five talents.
17 And likewise he that *had received* two,
he also gained other two. 18 But he that
had received one went and digged in the
earth, and hid his lord's money.● 19 After

2. TWO GOOD ACCOUNTINGS

a long time the lord of those servants
cometh, and reckoneth with them. 20 And
so he that had received five talents came
and brought other five talents, saying,
Lord, thou deliveredst unto me five
talents: behold, I have gained beside them
five talents more. 21 His lord said unto
him, Well done, *thou* good and faithful
servant: thou hast been faithful over a few
things, I will make thee ruler over many
things: enter thou into the joy of thy lord.
22 He also that had received two talents
came and said, Lord, thou deliveredst unto me two talents: behold, I have gained
two other talents beside them. 23 His lord
said unto him, Well done, good and faithful servant; thou hast been faithful over a
few things, I will make thee ruler over
many things: enter thou into the joy of thy
lord.● 24 Then he which had received the

3. ONE BAD ACCOUNTING

one talent came and said, Lord, I knew
thee that thou art a hard man, reaping
where thou hast not sown, and gathering
where thou hast not strewed: 25 and I
was afraid, and went and hid thy talent in
the earth: lo, *there* thou hast *that is* thine.
26 His lord answered and said unto him,
*Thou* wicked and slothful servant, thou
knewest that I reap where I sowed not,
and gather where I have not strewed:
27 thou oughtest therefore to have put my
money to the exchangers, and *then* at my
coming I should have received mine own
with usury. 28 Take therefore the talent
from him, and give *it* unto him which
hath ten talents. 29 For unto every one
that hath shall be given, and he shall have
abundance: but from him that hath not
shall be taken away even that which
he hath. 30 And cast ye the unprofitable servant into outer darkness:
there shall be weeping and gnashing of
teeth.●

PUNISHING

Jesus teaches more about the kingdom of heaven by another parable—this one a long parable.

Record for each paragraph the main point of the parable:

*25:14-18* __________

*25:19-23* __________

*25:24-30* __________

NEW INTERNATIONAL VERSION

Record what you learn from this passage about the following:

*CHRIST*

*JUSTICE*

*REWARDS*

*GOOD DEEDS*

Read verse 46 again. Some think that heaven will be everlasting (without end) but that hell will not be endless. The two appearances of the word "eternal" (*New American Standard Bible*) is the same Greek word in the originals. If heaven is eternal, so also is hell.

*The Sheep and the Goats*

31 "When the Son of Man comes in his
glory, and all the angels with him, he will
sit on his throne in heavenly glory. 32 All the
nations will be gathered before him, and he
will separate the people one from another
as a shepherd separates the sheep from the
goats. 33 He will put the sheep on his right
and the goats on his left.●
34 "Then the King will say to those on his
right, 'Come, you who are blessed by my
Father; take your inheritance, the kingdom
prepared for you since the creation of the
world. 35 For I was hungry and you gave me
something to eat, I was thirsty and you
gave me something to drink, I was a
stranger and you invited me in, 36 I needed
clothes and you clothed me, I was sick and
you looked after me, I was in prison and
you came to visit me.'
37 "Then the righteous will answer him,
'Lord, when did we see you hungry and
feed you, or thirsty and give you something
to drink? 38 When did we see you a stranger
and invite you in, or needing clothes and
clothe you? 39 When did we see you sick or
in prison and go to visit you?'
40 "The King will reply, 'I tell you the
truth, whatever you did for one of the least
of these brothers of mine, you did for me.'●
41 "Then he will say to those on his left,
'Depart from me, you who are cursed, into
the eternal fire prepared for the devil and
his angels. 42 For I was hungry and you
gave me nothing to eat, I was thirsty and
you gave me nothing to drink, 43 I was a
stranger and you did not invite me in, I
needed clothes and you did not clothe me,
I was sick and in prison and you did not
look after me.'
44 "They also will answer, 'Lord, when
did we see you hungry or thirsty or a
stranger or needing clothes or sick or in
prison, and did not help you?'
45 "He will reply, 'I tell you the truth,
whatever you did not do for one of the least
of these, you did not do for me.'
46 "Then they will go away to eternal
punishment, but the righteous to eternal
life."●

KING JAMES

1. THRONE — GLORY

31 When the Son of man shall come in
his glory, and all the holy angels with him,
then shall he sit upon the throne of his
glory: 32 and before him shall be gathered all nations: and he shall separate
them one from another, as a shepherd
divideth *his* sheep from the goats: 33 and
he shall set the sheep on his right hand,
but the goats on the left.● 34 Then shall

2. JUDGMENTS

a. sheep

the King say unto them on his right hand,
Come, ye blessed of my Father, inherit
the kingdom prepared for you from the
foundation of the world: 35 for I was
ahungered, and ye gave me meat: I was
thirsty, and ye gave me drink: I was a
stranger, and ye took me in: 36 naked,
and ye clothed me: I was sick, and ye
visited me: I was in prison, and ye came
unto me. 37 Then shall the righteous answer him, saying, Lord, when saw we thee
ahungered, and fed *thee?* or thirsty, and
gave *thee* drink? 38 When saw we thee a
stranger, and took *thee* in? or naked, and
clothed *thee?* 39 Or when saw we thee
sick, or in prison, and came unto thee?
40 And the King shall answer and say unto them, Verily I say unto you, Inasmuch
as ye have done *it* unto one of the least of
these my brethren, ye have done *it* unto
me.● 41 Then shall he say also unto them

b. goats

on the left hand, Depart from me, ye
cursed, into everlasting fire, prepared for
the devil and his angels: 42 for I was
ahungered, and ye gave me no meat: I was
thirsty, and ye gave me no drink: 43 I
was a stranger, and ye took me not in:
naked, and ye clothed me not: sick, and
in prison, and ye visited me not. 44 Then
shall they also answer him, saying, Lord,
when saw we thee ahungered, or athirst,
or a stranger, or naked, or sick, or in
prison, and did not minister unto thee?
45 Then shall he answer them, saying,
Verily I say unto you, Inasmuch as ye did
*it* not to one of the least of these, ye did *it*
not to me. 46 And these shall go away
into everlasting punishment: but the
righteous into life eternal.●

ETERNAL LIFE

This passage is the concluding part of Jesus' discourse. The opening verse (v.31) is a key to its interpretation. What does it teach?

________________________

*25:31-33* A literal interpretation of verse 31 sees Christ coming *to this earth,* to sit on His throne *on this earth*. Thus begins His *earthly* millennial reign.

What will happen then, according to verse 32?

________________________

(Note: the phrase "all nations" refers to individuals which make up Gentile nations.)

*25:34-40* What inheritance is given to this group?

________________________

What determines the inheritance? ____________

(Note: Some interpret "these my brethren," v.40, as Jews.)

*25:41-46* What judgment falls upon this group?

________________________

Why? ____________

NEW INTERNATIONAL VERSION

Record what you learn about these:

ENEMIES OF JESUS

JESUS

FRIENDS AND DISCIPLES OF JESUS

What things impress you most about this passage?

*The Plot Against Jesus*

26 When Jesus had finished saying all
these things, he said to his disciples,
2 "As you know, the Passover is two days
away—and the Son of Man will be handed
over to be crucified."
3 Then the chief priests and the elders of
the people assembled in the palace of the
high priest, whose name was Caiaphas,
4 and they plotted to arrest Jesus in some
sly way and kill him. 5 "But not during the
Feast," they said, "or there may be a riot
among the people."●

*Jesus Anointed at Bethany*

6 While Jesus was in Bethany in the home
of a man known as Simon the Leper, 7 a
woman came to him with an alabaster jar
of very expensive perfume, which she
poured on his head as he was reclining at
the table.
8 When the disciples saw this, they were
indignant. "Why this waste?" they asked.
9 "This perfume could have been sold at a
high price and the money given to the
poor."
10 Aware of this, Jesus said to them,
"Why are you bothering this woman? She
has done a beautiful thing to me. 11 The
poor you will always have with you, but
you will not always have me. 12 When she
poured this perfume on my body, she did
it to prepare me for burial. 13 I tell you the
truth, wherever this gospel is preached
throughout the world, what she has done
will also be told, in memory of her."●

*Judas Agrees to Betray Jesus*

14 Then one of the Twelve—the one
called Judas Iscariot—went to the chief
priests 15 and asked, "What are you willing
to give me if I hand him over to you?" So
they counted out for him thirty silver
coins. 16 From then on Judas watched for
an opportunity to hand him over.●

*The Lord's Supper*

17 On the first day of the Feast of Unleavened Bread, the disciples came to Jesus
and asked, "Where do you want us to
make preparations for you to eat the Passover?"
18 He replied, "Go into the city to a certain man and tell him, 'The Teacher says:
My appointed time is near. I am going to
celebrate the Passover with my disciples at
your house.'" 19 So the disciples did as
Jesus had directed them and prepared the
Passover.●
20 When evening came, Jesus was reclining at the table with the Twelve. 21 And
while they were eating, he said, "I tell you
the truth, one of you will betray me."
22 They were very sad and began to say to
him one after the other, "Surely not I,
Lord?"
23 Jesus replied, "The one who has
dipped his hand into the bowl with me will
betray me. 24 The Son of Man will go just as
it is written about him. But woe to that man
who betrays the Son of Man! It would be
better for him if he had not been born."
25 Then Judas, the one who would betray
him, said, "Surely not I, Rabbi?"
Jesus answered, "Yes, it is you."[a]●

[a]25 Or *"You yourself have said it"*

KING JAMES

1. PLOT TO KILL

**26** And it came to pass, when Jesus had finished all these sayings, he said unto his disciples, 2 Ye know that after two days is *the feast of* the passover, and the Son of man is betrayed to be crucified.

3 Then assembled together the chief priests, and the scribes, and the elders of the people, unto the palace of the high priest, who was called Cai'aphas, 4 and consulted that they might take Jesus by subtilty, and kill *him.* 5 But they said, Not on the feast *day*, lest there be an uproar among the people.●

CHIEF PRIESTS AND ELDERS

2. ANOINTING

6 Now when Jesus was in Bethany, in the house of Simon the leper, 7 there came unto him a woman having an alabaster box of very precious ointment, and poured it on his head, as he sat at meat. 8 But when his disciples saw *it*, they had indignation, saying, To what purpose *is* this waste? 9 For this ointment might have been sold for much, and given to the poor. 10 When Jesus understood *it*, he said unto them, Why trouble ye the woman? for she hath wrought a good work upon me. 11 For ye have the poor always with you; but me ye have not always. 12 For in that she hath poured this ointment on my body, she did *it* for my burial. 13 Verily I say unto you, Wheresoever this gospel shall be preached in the whole world, *there* shall also this, that this woman hath done, be told for a memorial of her.●

PARENTHESIS

3. CONSPIRACY TO BETRAY

14 Then one of the twelve, called Judas Iscar'i-ot, went unto the chief priests, 15 and said *unto them*, What will ye give me, and I will deliver him unto you? And they covenanted with him for thirty pieces of silver. 16 And from that time he sought opportunity to betray him.●

4. PASSOVER PREPARATION

17 Now the first *day* of the *feast of* unleavened bread the disciples came to Jesus, saying unto him, Where wilt thou that we prepare for thee to eat the passover? 18 And he said, Go into the city to such a man, and say unto him, The Master saith, My time is at hand; I will keep the passover at thy house with my disciples. 19 And the disciples did as Jesus had appointed them; and they made ready the passover.●

5. BETRAYER REVEALED

20 Now when the even was come, he sat down with the twelve. 21 And as they did eat, he said, Verily I say unto you, that one of you shall betray me. 22 And they were exceeding sorrowful, and began every one of them to say unto him, Lord, is it I? 23 And he answered and said, He that dippeth *his* hand with me in the dish, the same shall betray me. 24 The Son of man goeth as it is written of him: but woe unto that man by whom the Son of man is betrayed! it had been good for that man if he had not been born. 25 Then Judas, which betrayed him, answered and said, Master, is it I? He said unto him, Thou hast said.●

A DISCIPLE

From this point to the end of the gospel the events of Jesus' Passion Week take place in quick succession.

*26:1-5* How is the paragraph an introduction to the passage?

Compare Jesus' prophecy about time (26:2) and the rulers' preference (16:5).

*26:6-13* This anointing had happened earlier (read John 12:1-8). Contrast it with the paragraph that follows.

*26:14-16* Compare the fee with the evaluation of a slave according to Exodus 21:32.

*26:17-19* Record the key phrases: ____

*26:20-25* What do you learn about Judas here?

NEW INTERNATIONAL VERSION

The closer Jesus moved toward Calvary the more He talked about it. Go through the entire passage and record the different things Jesus said about His coming death.

What do you learn about the disciples from this passage?

What does the passage teach about prayer?

26While they were eating, Jesus took
bread, gave thanks and broke it, and gave
it to his disciples, saying, "Take and eat;
this is my body."
27Then he took the cup, gave thanks and
offered it to them, saying, "Drink from it,
all of you. 28This is my blood of the[b] covenant, which is poured out for many for the
forgiveness of sins. 29I tell you, I will not
drink of this fruit of the vine from now on
until that day when I drink it anew with you
in my Father's kingdom."
30When they had sung a hymn, they went
out to the Mount of Olives.●

*Jesus Predicts Peter's Denial*

31Then Jesus told them, "This very night
you will all fall away on account of me, for
it is written:

" 'I will strike the shepherd,
and the sheep of the flock will be
scattered.'[a]

32But after I have risen, I will go ahead of
you into Galilee."
33Peter replied, "Even if all fall away on
account of you, I never will."
34"I tell you the truth," Jesus answered,
"this very night, before the rooster crows,
you will disown me three times."
35But Peter declared, "Even if I have to
die with you, I will never disown you."
And all the other disciples said the same.●

*Gethsemane*

36Then Jesus went with his disciples to a
place called Gethsemane, and he said to
them, "Sit here while I go over there and
pray." 37He took Peter and the two sons of
Zebedee along with him, and he began to
be sorrowful and troubled. 38Then he said
to them, "My soul is overwhelmed with
sorrow to the point of death. Stay here and
keep watch with me."
39Going a little farther, he fell with his
face to the ground and prayed, "My Father, if it is possible, may this cup be taken
from me. Yet not as I will, but as you will."
40Then he returned to his disciples and
found them sleeping. "Could you men not
keep watch with me for one hour?" he
asked Peter. 41"Watch and pray so that
you will not fall into temptation. The spirit
is willing, but the body is weak."
42He went away a second time and
prayed, "My Father, if it is not possible for
this cup to be taken away unless I drink it,
may your will be done."
43When he came back, he again found
them sleeping, because their eyes were
heavy. 44So he left them and went away
once more and prayed the third time, saying the same thing.
45Then he returned to the disciples and
said to them, "Are you still sleeping and
resting? Look, the hour is near, and the
Son of Man is betrayed into the hands of
sinners. 46Rise, let us go! Here comes my
betrayer!"●

[b]28 Some manuscripts *the new* [a]31 Zech. 13:7

KING JAMES

## 1. LORD'S SUPPER

26 And as they were eating, Jesus took EATING
bread, and blessed *it*, and brake *it*, and
gave *it* to the disciples, and said, Take,
eat; this is my body. 27 And he took the
cup, and gave thanks, and gave *it* to them,
saying, Drink ye all of it; 28 for this is
my blood of the new testament, which
is shed for many for the remission of sins.
29 But I say unto you, I will not drink
henceforth of this fruit of the vine, until
that day when I drink it new with you in
my Father's kingdom.
30 And when they had sung a hymn, SINGING
they went out into the mount of Olives.●

## 2. DENIAL PREDICTED

31 Then saith Jesus unto them, All ye shall
be offended because of me this night: for
it is written,
I will smite the shepherd, Zech. 13:7
and the sheep of the flock shall be
scattered abroad.
32 But after I am risen again, I will go
before you into Galilee. 33 Peter answered and said unto him, Though all
*men* shall be offended because of thee, *yet*
will I never be offended. 34 Jesus said
unto him, Verily I say unto thee, That this
night, before the cock crow, thou shalt
deny me thrice. 35 Peter said unto him,
Though I should die with thee, yet will I VOWING
not deny thee. Likewise also said all the
disciples.●

## 3. GETHSEMANE

36 Then cometh Jesus with them unto
a place called Gethsem'ane, and saith unto the disciples, Sit ye here, while I go and
pray yonder. 37 And he took with him
Peter and the two sons of Zeb'edee, and
began to be sorrowful and very heavy.
38 Then saith he unto them, My soul is
exceeding sorrowful, even unto death:
tarry ye here, and watch with me. 39 And
he went a little further, and fell on his
face, and prayed, saying, O my Father, if
it be possible, let this cup pass from me:
nevertheless, not as I will, but as thou
*wilt*. 40 And he cometh unto the disciples,
and findeth them asleep, and saith unto
Peter, What, could ye not watch with me
one hour? 41 Watch and pray, that ye
enter not into temptation: the spirit indeed
*is* willing, but the flesh *is* weak. 42 He
went away again the second time, and
prayed, saying, O my Father, if this cup
may not pass away from me, except I
drink it, thy will be done. 43 And he
came and found them asleep again: for
their eyes were heavy. 44 And he left
them, and went away again, and prayed
the third time, saying the same words.
45 Then cometh he to his disciples, and
saith unto them, Sleep on now, and take SLEEPING
*your* rest: behold, the hour is at hand, and
the Son of man is betrayed into the hands
of sinners. 46 Rise, let us be going:
behold, he is at hand that doth betray
me.●

Observe and study the various activities of the disciples.

*26:26-30* List the elements and actions of this original communion service.

*26:31-35* Is Peter the only one to make the vow?

*26:36-46* What were Jesus' prayers to His Father?

v.39

v.42

v.44

What different things did He say to the disciples?

v.37

vv.40-41

v.44

NEW INTERNATIONAL VERSION

This is one of the saddest portions of Scripture. Meditate on it much. Think of all that it teaches about Christ and sinful man. Record your reflections.

Why do you think all the disciples desert Jesus at this time?

*Jesus Arrested*

47While he was still speaking, Judas, one of the Twelve, arrived. With him was a large crowd armed with swords and clubs, sent from the chief priests and the elders of the people. 48Now the betrayer had arranged a signal with them: "The one I kiss is the man; arrest him." 49Going at once to Jesus, Judas said, "Greetings, Rabbi!" and kissed him.

50Jesus replied, "Friend, do what you came for."[b]

Then the men stepped forward, seized Jesus and arrested him. 51With that, one of Jesus' companions reached for his sword, drew it out and struck the servant of the high priest, cutting off his ear.

52"Put your sword back in its place," Jesus said to him, "for all who draw the sword will die by the sword. 53Do you think I cannot call on my Father, and he will at once put at my disposal more than twelve legions of angels? 54But how then would the Scriptures be fulfilled that say it must happen in this way?"

55At that time Jesus said to the crowd, "Am I leading a rebellion, that you have come out with swords and clubs to capture me? Every day I sat in the temple courts teaching, and you did not arrest me. 56But this has all taken place that the writings of the prophets might be fulfilled." Then all the disciples deserted him and fled.

[b]50 Or *"Friend, why have you come?"*

KING JAMES

1.ARREST

47 And while he yet spake, lo, Judas,
one of the twelve, came, and with him a
great multitude with swords and staves,
from the chief priests and elders of the
people. 48 Now he that betrayed him
gave them a sign, saying, Whomsoever I
shall kiss, that same is he; hold him fast.
49 And forthwith he came to Jesus, and
said, Hail, Master; and kissed him.
50 And Jesus said unto him, Friend,
wherefore art thou come? Then came
they, and laid hands on Jesus, and took
him.●

2.REBUKE

51 And, behold, one of them which
were with Jesus stretched out *his* hand,
and drew his sword, and struck a servant
of the high priest, and smote off his ear.
52 Then said Jesus unto him, Put up
again thy sword into his place: for all they
that take the sword shall perish with the
sword. 53 Thinkest thou that I cannot
now pray to my Father, and he shall presently give me more than twelve legions
of angels? 54 But how then shall the
Scriptures be fulfilled, that thus it must
be?●

3.QUESTION

55 In that same hour said Jesus to the
multitudes, Are ye come out as against a
thief with swords and staves for to take
me? I sat daily with you teaching in the
temple, and ye laid no hold on me.
56 But all this was done, that the Scriptures of the prophets might be fulfilled.
Then all the disciples forsook him, and
fled.●

JUDAS BETRAYS JESUS

DISCIPLES LEAVE JESUS

Compare Judas' betrayal of Jesus (vv.47-49) and the disciples' leaving Him. (v.56).

*26:47-50* Record what you think were the different feelings in the hearts of the different persons of this scene.

*26:51-54* Record what Jesus teaches in these verses:

v.52

v.53

v.54

*26:55-56* What is revealed here about:

JESUS

MULTITUDES

DISCIPLES

NEW INTERNATIONAL VERSION

What does this passage teach about:

HATE

FALSEHOOD

VIOLENCE

JESUS AS MESSIAH

PETER

LYING

BETRAYING CHRIST

*Before the Sanhedrin*

57Those who had arrested Jesus took him
to Caiaphas, the high priest, where the
teachers of the law and the elders had assembled. 58But Peter followed him at a distance, right up to the courtyard of the high
priest. He entered and sat down with the
guards to see the outcome.
59The chief priests and the whole Sanhedrin were looking for false evidence
against Jesus so that they could put him to
death. 60But they did not find any, though
many false witnesses came forward.
Finally two came forward 61and declared, "This fellow said, 'I am able to
destroy the temple of God and rebuild it in
three days.' "
62Then the high priest stood up and said
to Jesus, "Are you not going to answer?
What is this testimony that these men are
bringing against you?" 63But Jesus
remained silent.
The high priest said to him, "I charge
you under oath by the living God: Tell us
if you are the Christ,[c] the Son of God."
64"Yes, it is as you say," Jesus replied.
"But I say to all of you: In the future you
will see the Son of Man sitting at the right
hand of the Mighty One and coming on the
clouds of heaven."
65Then the high priest tore his clothes
and said, "He has spoken blasphemy!
Why do we need any more witnesses?
Look, now you have heard the blasphemy.
66What do you think?"
"He is worthy of death," they answered.
67Then they spit in his face and struck
him with their fists. Others slapped him
68and said, "Prophesy to us, Christ. Who
hit you?"●

*Peter Disowns Jesus*

69Now Peter was sitting out in the courtyard, and a servant girl came to him. "You
also were with Jesus of Galilee," she said.
70But he denied it before them all. "I
don't know what you're talking about," he
said.
71Then he went out to the gateway,
where another girl saw him and said to the
people there, "This fellow was with Jesus
of Nazareth."
72He denied it again, with an oath: "I
don't know the man!"
73After a little while, those standing there
went up to Peter and said, "Surely you are
one of them, for your accent gives you
away."
74Then he began to call down curses on
himself and he swore to them, "I don't
know the man!"
Immediately a rooster crowed. 75Then
Peter remembered the word Jesus had
spoken: "Before the rooster crows, you
will disown me three times." And he went
outside and wept bitterly.●

[c]*63* Or *Messiah*; also in verse 68

KING JAMES

1. TRIAL BEFORE THE COUNCIL

PETER FOLLOWING

57 And they that had laid hold on Jesus
led *him* away to Cai'aphas the high priest,
where the scribes and the elders were assembled. 58 But Peter followed him afar
off unto the high priest's palace, and went
in, and sat with the servants, to see the
end. 59 Now the chief priests, and elders,
and all the council, sought false witness
against Jesus, to put him to death; 60 but
found none: yea, though many false witnesses came, *yet* found they none. At the
last came two false witnesses, 61 and said,
This *fellow* said, I am able to destroy the
temple of God, and to build it in three
days. 62 And the high priest arose, and
said unto him, Answerest thou nothing?
what *is it which* these witness against thee?
63 But Jesus held his peace. And the high
priest answered and said unto him, I adjure thee by the living God, that thou tell
us whether thou be the Christ, the Son of
God. 64 Jesus saith unto him, Thou hast
said: nevertheless I say unto you, Hereafter shall ye see the Son of man sitting on
the right hand of power, and coming in
the clouds of heaven. 65 Then the high
priest rent his clothes, saying, He hath
spoken blasphemy; what further need
have we of witnesses? behold, now ye
have heard his blasphemy. 66 What
think ye? They answered and said, He is
guilty of death. 67 Then did they spit in
his face, and buffeted him; and others
smote *him* with the palms of their hands,
68 saying, Prophesy unto us, thou Christ,
Who is he that smote thee?●

2. PETER'S DENIAL

69 Now Peter sat without in the palace:
and a damsel came unto him, saying,
Thou also wast with Jesus of Galilee.
70 But he denied before *them* all, saying,
I know not what thou sayest. 71 And
when he was gone out into the porch,
another *maid* saw him, and said unto them
that were there, This *fellow* was also with
Jesus of Nazareth. 72 And again he
denied with an oath, I do not know the
man. 73 And after a while came unto *him*
they that stood by, and said to Peter,
Surely thou also art *one* of them; for thy
speech betrayeth thee. 74 Then began
he to curse and to swear, *saying*, I know
not the man. And immediately the cock
crew. 75 And Peter remembered the
word of Jesus, which said unto him,
Before the cock crow, thou shalt deny me
thrice. And he went out, and wept bitterly.●

PETER WEEPING

*26:57-68* Who were Jesus' accusers?

What was Peter doing at this time?

Record the charges made against Jesus, and Jesus' answers.

*26:69-75* Record the progression of Peter's denials.

NEW INTERNATIONAL VERSION

This passage reveals different kinds of hearts of human beings. Record what you observe.

JEWISH RELIGIOUS LEADERS

JUDAS

PILATE

MULTITUDES

List applications of the passage which may be made.

*Judas Hangs Himself*

27 Early in the morning, all the chief
priests and the elders of the people
came to the decision to put Jesus to death.
2They bound him, led him away and handed him over to Pilate, the governor.●
3When Judas, who had betrayed him,
saw that Jesus was condemned, he was
seized with remorse and returned the thirty
silver coins to the chief priests and the elders. 4"I have sinned," he said, "for I
have betrayed innocent blood."
"What is that to us?" they replied.
"That's your responsibility."
5So Judas threw the money into the temple and left. Then he went away and
hanged himself.
6The chief priests picked up the coins
and said, "It is against the law to put this
into the treasury, since it is blood money."
7So they decided to use the money to buy
the potter's field as a burial place for foreigners. 8That is why it has been called the
Field of Blood to this day. 9Then what was
spoken by Jeremiah the prophet was fulfilled: "They took the thirty silver coins,
the price set on him by the people of Israel,
10and they used them to buy the potter's
field, as the Lord commanded me."[a]●

*Jesus Before Pilate*

11Meanwhile Jesus stood before the governor, and the governor asked him, "Are
you the king of the Jews?"
"Yes, it is as you say," Jesus replied.
12When he was accused by the chief
priests and the elders, he gave no answer.
13Then Pilate asked him, "Don't you hear
how many things they are accusing you
of?" 14But Jesus made no reply, not even
to a single charge—to the great amazement
of the governor.●

[a]*10* Zech. 11:12,13; Jer. 32:6-9

KING JAMES

—to Pilate

ENEMIES' COUNSEL

27 When the morning was come, all
the chief priests and elders of the
people took counsel against Jesus to put
him to death: 2 and when they had
bound him, they led *him* away, and delivered him to Pontius Pilate the governor. ●

1. DEATH OF JUDAS

3 Then Judas, which had betrayed him,
when he saw that he was condemned, repented himself, and brought again the
thirty pieces of silver to the chief priests
and elders, 4 saying, I have sinned in that
I have betrayed the innocent blood. And
they said, What *is that* to us? see thou *to
that*. 5 And he cast down the pieces of
silver in the temple, and departed, and
went and hanged himself. 6 And the chief
priests took the silver pieces, and said, It
is not lawful for to put them into the
treasury, because it is the price of blood.
7 And they took counsel, and bought with
them the potter's field, to bury strangers
in. 8 Wherefore that field was called, The
field of blood, unto this day. 9 Then
was fulfilled that which was spoken by
Jeremiah the prophet, saying,

Zech. 11:12-13

And they took the thirty pieces of
silver,
the price of him that was valued,
whom they of the children of Israel
did value;
10 and gave them for the potter's field,
as the Lord appointed me.●

2. PILATE QUESTIONS JESUS

11 And Jesus stood before the governor:
and the governor asked him, saying, Art
thou the King of the Jews? And Jesus
said unto him, Thou sayest. 12 And when
he was accused of the chief priests and
elders, he answered nothing. 13 Then said
Pilate unto him, Hearest thou not how
many things they witness against thee?
14 And he answered him to never a word;
insomuch that the governor marveled
greatly.●

JESUS' SILENCE

The story of this segment continues into the next one (27:15-26).

*27:1-2* Who instigated Jesus' death?

*27:3-10* What is revealed here about Judas?

*27:11-14* Account for Jesus' reactions.

NEW INTERNATIONAL VERSION

15Now it was the governor's custom at
the Feast to release a prisoner chosen by
the crowd. 16At that time they had a notori-
ous prisoner, called Barabbas. 17So when
the crowd had gathered, Pilate asked them,
"Which one do you want me to release to
you: Barabbas, or Jesus who is called
Christ?" 18For he knew it was out of envy
that they had handed Jesus over to him.
19While Pilate was sitting on the judge's
seat, his wife sent him this message:
"Don't have anything to do with that innocent man, for I have suffered a great deal
today in a dream because of him."
20But the chief priests and the elders persuaded the crowd to ask for Barabbas and
to have Jesus executed.
21"Which of the two do you want me to
release to you?" asked the governor.
"Barabbas," they answered.
22"What shall I do, then, with Jesus who
is called Christ?" Pilate asked.
They all answered, "Crucify him!"
23"Why? What crime has he committed?" asked Pilate.●
But they shouted all the louder, "Crucify him!"
24When Pilate saw that he was getting
nowhere, but that instead an uproar was
starting, he took water and washed his
hands in front of the crowd. "I am innocent
of this man's blood," he said. "It is your
responsibility!"
25All the people answered, "Let his
blood be on us and on our children!"
26Then he released Barabbas to them.
But he had Jesus flogged, and handed him
over to be crucified.●

Record spiritual lessons and applications of the passage. ______

KING JAMES

1.MULTITUDES REJECT JESUS

15 Now at *that* feast the governor was
wont to release unto the people a prisoner, whom they would. 16 And they had
then a notable prisoner, called Barab'bas.
17 Therefore when they were gathered together, Pilate said unto them, Whom will
ye that I release unto you? Barab'bas, or
Jesus which is called Christ? 18 For he
knew that for envy they had delivered him.
19 When he was set down on the judgment seat, his wife sent unto him, saying,
Have thou nothing to do with that just
man: for I have suffered many things this
day in a dream because of him. 20 But the
chief priests and elders persuaded the multitude that they should ask Barab'bas, and
destroy Jesus. 21 The governor answered
and said unto them, Whether of the twain
will ye that I release unto you? They said,
Barab'bas. 22 Pilate saith unto them,
What shall I do then with Jesus which is
called Christ? *They* all say unto him, Let
him be crucified. 23 And the governor
said, Why, what evil hath he done? But
they cried out the more, saying, Let him
be crucified.●

2.PILATE SENTENCES JESUS

24 When Pilate saw that he could prevail nothing, but *that* rather a tumult was
made, he took water, and washed *his*
hands before the multitude, saying, I am
innocent of the blood of this just person:
see ye *to it.* 25 Then answered all the
people, and said, His blood *be* on us, and
on our children. 26 Then released he
Barab'bas unto them: and when he had
scourged Jesus, he delivered *him* to be
crucified.●

GOVERNOR

CRIMINAL

This segment continues the story of the preceding segment.

Record observations in addition to those asked for below.

*27:15-23* What do you learn about the multitudes here?

What do you learn about Pilate?

*27:24-26* Note the contrasts of the paragraph.

Compare Pilate and the multitudes.

NEW INTERNATIONAL VERSION

Does Matthew record any reaction by Jesus to all the mockery?

What do you think was going through His mind and heart, based on earlier events of this Passion Week?

Christ died *in the place of* sinners, for their sins. This is the doctrine of substitutionary atonement. What would have happened to this doctrine if Christ had been delivered from this sacrificial death?

What are your impressions of this passage?

*The Soldiers Mock Jesus*

[27]Then the governor's soldiers took Jesus into the Praetorium and gathered the whole company of soldiers around him. [28]They stripped him and put a scarlet robe on him, [29]and then wove a crown of thorns and set it on his head. They put a staff in his right hand and knelt in front of him and mocked him. "Hail, King of the Jews!" they said. [30]They spit on him, and took the staff and struck him on the head again and again. [31]After they had mocked him, they took off the robe and put his own clothes on him. Then they led him away to crucify him.●

*The Crucifixion*

[32]As they were going out, they met a man from Cyrene, named Simon, and they forced him to carry the cross. [33]They came to a place called Golgotha (which means The Place of the Skull). [34]There they offered him wine to drink, mixed with gall; but after tasting it, he refused to drink it. [35]When they had crucified him, they divided up his clothes by casting lots.[a] [36]And sitting down, they kept watch over him there. [37]Above his head they placed the written charge against him: THIS IS JESUS, THE KING OF THE JEWS. [38]Two robbers were crucified with him, one on his right and one on his left. [39]Those who passed by hurled insults at him, shaking their heads [40]and saying, "You who are going to destroy the temple and build it in three days, save yourself! Come down from the cross, if you are the Son of God!"

[41]In the same way the chief priests, the teachers of the law and the elders mocked him. [42]"He saved others," they said, "but he can't save himself! He's the king of Israel! Let him come down now from the cross, and we will believe in him. [43]He trusts in God. Let God rescue him now if he wants him, for he said, 'I am the Son of God.' " [44]In the same way the robbers who were crucified with him also heaped insults on him.●

[a]35 A few late manuscripts *lots that the word spoken by the prophet might be fulfilled: "They divided my garments among themselves and cast lots for my clothing"* (Psalm 22:18)

KING JAMES

**1. SOLDIERS MOCK**

SOLDIERS

27 Then the soldiers of the governor
took Jesus into the common hall, and
gathered unto him the whole band *of*
*soldiers*. 28 And they stripped him, and
put on him a scarlet robe. 29 And when
they had platted a crown of thorns, they
put *it* upon his head, and a reed in his
right hand: and they bowed the knee before him, and mocked him, saying, Hail,
King of the Jews! 30 And they spit upon
him, and took the reed, and smote him on
the head. 31 And after that they had
mocked him, they took the robe off from
him, and put his own raiment on him, and
led him away to crucify *him*.●

**2. JESUS IS CRUCIFIED**

—Simon helps

32 And as they came out, they found a
man of Cyre'ne, Simon by name: him
they compelled to bear his cross. 33 And
when they were come unto a place called
Gol'gotha, that is to say, a place of a
skull, 34 they gave him vinegar to drink
mingled with gall: and when he had tasted
*thereof*, he would not drink. 35 And they
crucified him, and parted his garments,
casting lots: that it might be fulfilled
which was spoken by the prophet,

Ps. 22:18

They parted my garments among them,
and upon my vesture did they cast lots.

36 And sitting down they watched him
there; 37 and set up over his head his
accusation written, THIS IS JESUS THE
KING OF THE JEWS. 38 Then were there
two thieves crucified with him; one on
the right hand, and another on the left.●

**3. THE OTHERS MOCK**

39 And they that passed by reviled him,
wagging their heads, 40 and saying,
Thou that destroyest the temple, and
buildest *it* in three days, save thyself. If
thou be the Son of God, come down from
the cross. 41 Likewise also the chief priests
mocking *him*, with the scribes and elders,
said, 42 He saved others; himself he cannot save. If he be the King of Israel, let
him now come down from the cross, and
we will believe him. 43 He trusted in
God; let him deliver him now, if he will
have him: for he said, I am the Son of
God. 44 The thieves also, which were
crucified with him, cast the same in his
teeth.●

ROBBERS

*27:27-31* List all the things done in mockery.

*27:32-38* List the actions which Matthew chooses to include in the crucifixion story.

*27:39-44* What were the verbal insults cast at Jesus on the cross? Record your conclusions concerning each.

NEW INTERNATIONAL VERSION

What can be learned from the spoken words of these verses:

v.46 (JESUS)

v.49 (BYSTANDERS)

v.54 (SOLDIERS)

vv.63-64 (CHIEF PRIESTS AND PHARISEES)

Record other spiritual lessons taught here.

What impressions does the passage leave with you?

### *The Death of Jesus*

45From the sixth hour until the ninth
hour darkness came over all the land.
46About the ninth hour Jesus cried out in a
loud voice, *"Eloi, Eloi,*[b] *lama sabachthani?"*—which means, "My God, my
God, why have you forsaken me?"[c]
47When some of those standing there
heard this, they said, "He's calling Elijah."
48Immediately one of them ran and got a
sponge. He filled it with wine vinegar, put
it on a stick, and offered it to Jesus to
drink. 49But the rest said, "Leave him
alone. Let's see if Elijah comes to save
him."
50And when Jesus had cried out again in
a loud voice, he gave up his spirit.
51At that moment the curtain of the temple was torn in two from top to bottom.
The earth shook and the rocks split. 52The
tombs broke open and the bodies of many
holy people who had died were raised to
life. 53They came out of the tombs, and
after Jesus' resurrection they went into the
holy city and appeared to many people.●
54When the centurion and those with him
who were guarding Jesus saw the earthquake and all that had happened, they were
terrified, and exclaimed, "Surely he was
the Son[d] of God!"
55Many women were there, watching
from a distance. They had followed Jesus
from Galilee to care for his needs. 56Among
them were Mary Magdalene, Mary the
mother of James and Joseph, and the
mother of Zebedee's sons.●

### *The Burial of Jesus*

57As evening approached, there came a
rich man from Arimathea, named Joseph,
who had himself become a disciple of
Jesus. 58Going to Pilate, he asked for
Jesus' body, and Pilate ordered that it be
given to him. 59Joseph took the body,
wrapped it in a clean linen cloth, 60and
placed it in his own new tomb that he had
cut out of the rock. He rolled a big stone
in front of the entrance to the tomb and
went away. 61Mary Magdalene and the other Mary were sitting there across from the
tomb.●

### *The Guard at the Tomb*

62The next day, the one after Preparation
Day, the chief priests and the Pharisees
went to Pilate. 63"Sir," they said, "we
remember that while he was still alive that
deceiver said, 'After three days I will rise
again.' 64So give the order for the tomb to
be made secure until the third day. Otherwise, his disciples may come and steal the
body and tell the people that he has been
raised from the dead. This last deception
will be worse than the first."
65"Take a guard," Pilate answered.
"Go, make the tomb as secure as you
know how." 66So they went and made the
tomb secure by putting a seal on the stone
and posting the guard.●

[b]*46* Some manuscripts *Eli, Eli* [c]*46* Psalm 22:1
[d]*54* Or *a son*

KING JAMES

**1. DEATH**

**EARTH DARKNESS**

45 Now from the sixth hour there was darkness over all the land unto the ninth hour. 46 And about the ninth hour Jesus cried with a loud voice, saying, Eli, Eli, lama sabach′thani? that is to say, My God, my God, why hast thou forsaken me? 47 Some of them that stood there, when they heard *that*, said, This *man* calleth for Eli′jah. 48 And straightway one of them ran, and took a sponge, and filled *it* with vinegar, and put *it* on a reed, and gave him to drink. 49 The rest said, Let be, let us see whether Eli′jah will come to save him. 50 Jesus, when he had cried again with a loud voice, yielded up the ghost.

51 And, behold, the veil of the temple was rent in twain from the top to the bottom; and the earth did quake, and the rocks rent; 52 and the graves were opened; and many bodies of the saints which slept arose, 53 and came out of the graves after his resurrection, and went into the holy city, and appeared unto many.●

**2. REACTIONS**

54 Now when the centurion, and they that were with him, watching Jesus, saw the earthquake, and those things that were done, they feared greatly, saying, Truly this was the Son of God.

55 And many women were there beholding afar off, which followed Jesus from Galilee, ministering unto him: 56 among which was Mary Mag′dalene, and Mary the mother of James and Joses, and the mother of Zeb′edee's children.●

**3. BURIAL**

57 When the even was come, there came a rich man of Arimathe′a, named Joseph, who also himself was Jesus' disciple: 58 he went to Pilate, and begged the body of Jesus. Then Pilate commanded the body to be delivered. 59 And when Joseph had taken the body, he wrapped it in a clean linen cloth, 60 and laid it in his own new tomb, which he had hewn out in the rock: and he rolled a great stone to the door of the sepulchre, and departed. 61 And there was Mary Mag′dalene, and the other Mary, sitting over against the sepulchre.●

**4. TOMB GUARDED**

62 Now the next day, that followed the day of the preparation, the chief priests and Pharisees came together unto Pilate, 63 saying, Sir, we remember that that deceiver said, while he was yet alive, After three days I will rise again. 64 Command therefore that the sepulchre be made sure until the third day, lest his disciples come by night, and steal him away, and say unto the people, He is risen from the dead: so the last error shall be worse than the first. 65 Pilate said unto them, Ye have a watch: go your way, make *it* as sure as ye can. 66 So they went, and made the sepulchre sure, sealing the stone, and setting a watch.●

**GRAVE DARKNESS**

*27:45-53* Record the words spoken at this time.

What events attended Jesus' death?

*27:54-56* Account for the centurion's reaction.

Why did Matthew include verses 55-56?

*27:57-61* and *27:62-66* Compare the contents of these two paragraphs. For example, compare verse 61 and verse 66.

NEW INTERNATIONAL VERSION

What are your impressions about the spoken words of these:

ANGEL

JESUS TO THE WOMEN

COUNCIL

JESUS TO THE DISCIPLES

How are verses 18-20 a fitting conclusion to Matthew's gospel?

*The Resurrection*

28 After the Sabbath, at dawn on the first day of the week, Mary Magdalene and the other Mary went to look at the tomb.

2There was a violent earthquake, for an angel of the Lord came down from heaven and, going to the tomb, rolled back the stone and sat on it. 3His appearance was like lightning, and his clothes were white as snow. 4The guards were so afraid of him that they shook and became like dead men.

5The angel said to the women, "Do not be afraid, for I know that you are looking for Jesus, who was crucified. 6He is not here; he has risen, just as he said. Come and see the place where he lay. 7Then go quickly and tell his disciples: 'He has risen from the dead and is going ahead of you into Galilee. There you will see him.' Now I have told you."

8So the women hurried away from the tomb, afraid yet filled with joy, and ran to tell his disciples.● 9Suddenly Jesus met them. "Greetings," he said. They came to him, clasped his feet and worshiped him. 10Then Jesus said to them, "Do not be afraid. Go and tell my brothers to go to Galilee; there they will see me."●

*The Guards' Report*

11While the women were on their way, some of the guards went into the city and reported to the chief priests everything that had happened. 12When the chief priests had met with the elders and devised a plan, they gave the soldiers a large sum of money, 13telling them, "You are to say, 'His disciples came during the night and stole him away while we were asleep.' 14If this report gets to the governor, we will satisfy him and keep you out of trouble." 15So the soldiers took the money and did as they were instructed. And this story has been widely circulated among the Jews to this very day.●

*The Great Commission*

16Then the eleven disciples went to Galilee, to the mountain where Jesus had told them to go. 17When they saw him, they worshiped him; but some doubted. 18Then Jesus came to them and said, "All authority in heaven and on earth has been given to me. 19Therefore go and make disciples of all nations, baptizing them in[a] the name of the Father and of the Son and of the Holy Spirit, 20and teaching them to obey everything I have commanded you. And surely I will be with you always, to the very end of the age."●

[a] 19 Or *into;* see Acts 8:16; 19:5; Romans 6:3; 1 Corinthians 1:13; 10:2 and Galatians 3:27.

KING JAMES

1. RESURRECTION

TWO WOMEN

28 In the end of the sabbath, as it began to dawn toward the first *day* of
the week, came Mary Mag'dalene and the
other Mary to see the sepulchre. 2 And,
behold, there was a great earthquake: for
the angel of the Lord descended from
heaven, and came and rolled back the
stone from the door, and sat upon it.
3 His countenance was like lightning, and
his raiment white as snow: 4 and for fear
of him the keepers did shake, and became
as dead *men*. 5 And the angel answered
and said unto the women, Fear not ye:
for I know that ye seek Jesus, which was
crucified. 6 He is not here: for he is risen,
as he said. Come, see the place where the
Lord lay. 7 And go quickly, and tell his
disciples that he is risen from the dead;
and, behold, he goeth before you into
Galilee; there shall ye see him: lo, I have
told you. 8 And they departed quickly
from the sepulchre with fear and great
joy; and did run to bring his disciples
word.●

2. JESUS APPEARS TO THE WOMEN

9 And as they went to tell his disciples, behold, Jesus met them, saying, All
hail. And they came and held him by the
feet, and worshipped him. 10 Then said
Jesus unto them, Be not afraid: go tell my
brethren that they go into Galilee, and
there shall they see me.●

3. GUARDS' REPORT

11 Now when they were going, behold,
some of the watch came into the city, and
showed unto the chief priests all the things
that were done. 12 And when they were
assembled with the elders, and had taken
counsel, they gave large money unto the
soldiers, 13 saying, Say ye, His disciples
came by night, and stole him *away* while
we slept. 14 And if this come to the
governor's ears, we will persuade him,
and secure you. 15 So they took the
money, and did as they were taught: and
this saying is commonly reported among
the Jews until this day.●

4. JESUS APPEARS TO THE ELEVEN

16 Then the eleven disciples went away
into Galilee, into a mountain where
Jesus had appointed them. 17 And when
they saw him, they worshipped him: but
some doubted. 18 And Jesus came and
spake unto them, saying, All power is
given unto me in heaven and in earth.
19 Go ye therefore, and teach all nations,
baptizing them in the name of the Father,
and of the Son, and of the Holy Ghost:
20 teaching them to observe all things
whatsoever I have commanded you: and,
lo, I am with you alway, *even* unto the end
of the world. Amen.●

ALL THE NATIONS

*28:1-8* Is this paragraph more about the actual event of resurrection or sequels that followed?

Analyze the angel's word to the two women.

*28:9-10* Note the strength of each statement of the paragraph.

*28:11-15* One sin begets another. How is this truth illustrated here?

*28:16-20* Analyze the Great Commission (vv. 18-20) phrase by phrase.

# MARK

## AUTHORSHIP

The author is not identified by name in the gospel, but internal evidence from the text itself agrees with external witness of the early church Fathers that John Mark was the author. His mother Mary was a devout, wealthy woman (Acts 12:12), and he was the cousin of Barnabas (Col. 4:10). He was a close friend of the apostle Peter (1 Pet. 5:13).

## DATE

There are two main views as to the date of writing: early and late. The early date (in the 50's) shows Mark as the first of the four gospels to be written; the late date shows it to be the third gospel (e.g. A.D. 68, soon after Peter's death, and before the fall of Jerusalem A.D. 70).

## PURPOSE

Mark's gospel was especially directed to the Roman mind, which was impressed more by action and power than by discourse and dialogue. Mark's style stressed the actions, not so much the words, of Jesus.

## THEME

A key verse of Mark identifies very clearly the theme of Mark's gospel: "For even the Son of man did not come to be ministered unto, but to minister, and to give His life a ransom for many" (10:45).

## MARK: The Servant Jesus

| | |
|---|---|
| SERVICE OF JESUS | 1:1-9:1 |
| Presentation | 1:1-13 |
| Popularity and Opposition | 1:14-3:6 |
| Growing Ministry | 3:7-6:32 |
| Reaching a Peak | 6:33-8:26 |
| Turning Point | 8:27-9:1 |
| SACRIFICE OF JESUS | 9:2-15:47 |
| Jesus as Redeemer | 9:2-10:52 |
| Jesus as Lord | 11:1-13:37 |
| Jesus as Sacrifice | 14:1-15:47 |
| TRIUMPH OF JESUS | 16:1-20 |

# MARK

NEW INTERNATIONAL VERSION

These thirteen verses are how Mark begins the wonderful story of Jesus. Why do you think he chose to relate these:

*John's ministry* ______________________

______________________

______________________

______________________

______________________

*Jesus' baptism* ______________________

______________________

______________________

______________________

______________________

*Jesus' temptations* ______________________

______________________

______________________

______________________

______________________

Temptation to sin is not sin. Why do you think Jesus was subjected to Satan's temptations?

______________________

______________________

______________________

______________________

______________________

______________________

______________________

Record spiritual applications of the passage. ______________________

______________________

______________________

______________________

______________________

______________________

______________________

______________________

______________________

______________________

### *John the Baptist Prepares the Way*

1 The beginning of the gospel about Jesus Christ, the Son of God.[b] ●

2 It is written in Isaiah the prophet:

> "I will send my messenger ahead of you,
> who will prepare your way"[c]—
> 3 "a voice of one calling in the desert,
> 'Prepare the way for the Lord,
> make straight paths for him.' "[d]

4 And so John came, baptizing in the desert
region and preaching a baptism of repentance for the forgiveness of sins. 5 The
whole Judean countryside and all the
people of Jerusalem went out to him. Confessing their sins, they were baptized by
him in the Jordan River. 6 John wore clothing made of camel's hair, with a leather belt
around his waist, and he ate locusts and
wild honey. 7 And this was his message:
"After me will come one more powerful
than I, the thongs of whose sandals I am
not worthy to stoop down and untie. 8 I
baptize you with[e] water, but he will baptize you with the Holy Spirit." ●

### *The Baptism and Temptation of Jesus*

9 At that time Jesus came from Nazareth
in Galilee and was baptized by John in the
Jordan. 10 As Jesus was coming up out of
the water, he saw heaven being torn open
and the Spirit descending on him like a
dove. 11 And a voice came from heaven:
"You are my Son, whom I love; with you
I am well pleased." ●
12 At once the Spirit sent him out into the
desert, 13 and he was in the desert forty
days, being tempted by Satan. He was with
the wild animals, and angels attended him. ●

[b] 1 Some manuscripts do not have *the Son of God*.
[c] 2 Mal. 3:1 [d] 3 Isaiah 40:3 [e] 8 Or *in*

KING JAMES

# MARK

JESUS CAME:

1.ANNOUNCED BY JOHN

1 The beginning of the gospel of Jesus
Christ, the Son of God.●
2 As it is written in the prophets,
Behold, I send my messenger before
thy face,
which shall prepare thy way before
thee.
3 The voice of one crying in the wilderness,
Prepare ye the way of the Lord,
make his paths straight.
4 John did baptize in the wilderness, and
preach the baptism of repentance for the
remission of sins. 5 And there went out
unto him all the land of Judea, and they
of Jerusalem, and were all baptized of him
in the river of Jordan, confessing their
sins. 6 And John was clothed with camel's
hair, and with a girdle of a skin about his
loins; and he did eat locusts and wild
honey; 7 and preached, saying, There
cometh one mightier than I after me, the
latchet of whose shoes I am not worthy to
stoop down and unloose. 8 I indeed have
baptized you with water: but he shall baptize you with the Holy Ghost. ●

2.COMMENDED BY THE FATHER

9 And it came to pass in those days,
that Jesus came from Nazareth of Galilee,
and was baptized of John in Jordan.
10 And straightway coming up out of the
water, he saw the heavens opened, and the
Spirit like a dove descending upon him:
11 and there came a voice from heaven,
*saying*, Thou art my beloved Son, in
whom I am well pleased. ●

3.TEMPTED BY SATAN

12 And immediately the Spirit driveth
him into the wilderness. 13 And he was
there in the wilderness forty days tempted
of Satan; and was with the wild beasts;
and the angels ministered unto him. ●

SON OF GOD

Mal. 3:1

Isa. 40:3

SATAN

*1:1* Note how Mark begins his account. Think about each of these words:

gospel ______

Jesus ______

Christ ______

Son of God ______

*1:2-8* Who was the fulfillment of the prophecies of verses 2-3?

______

What did John emphasize in his preaching?

______

______

Whom did he magnify? ______

______

*1:9-11* Record Jesus' relation to:

man ______

______

______

Spirit ______

______

______

Father ______

______

______

*1:12-13* Record the various parts of this story (people, places, actions).

______

______

______

______

______

______

______

______

______

______

NEW INTERNATIONAL VERSION

Jesus was very active throughout His public ministry. Record what you learn about Him from this passage:

Record various spiritual lessons for everyday living which are taught here.

*The Calling of the First Disciples*

[14]After John was put in prison, Jesus
went into Galilee, proclaiming the good
news of God. [15]"The time has come," he
said. "The kingdom of God is near. Repent
and believe the good news!"●
[16]As Jesus walked beside the Sea of Galilee, he saw Simon and his brother Andrew
casting a net into the lake, for they were
fishermen. [17]"Come, follow me," Jesus
said, "and I will make you fishers of men."
[18]At once they left their nets and followed
him.
[19]When he had gone a little farther, he
saw James son of Zebedee and his brother
John in a boat, preparing their nets. [20]With-
out delay he called them, and they left their
father Zebedee in the boat with the hired
men and followed him.●

*Jesus Drives Out an Evil Spirit*

[21]They went to Capernaum, and when
the Sabbath came, Jesus went into the
synagogue and began to teach. [22]The
people were amazed at his teaching, because he taught them as one who had authority, not as the teachers of the law.
[23]Just then a man in their synagogue who
was possessed by an evil[a] spirit cried out,
[24]"What do you want with us, Jesus of
Nazareth? Have you come to destroy us?
I know who you are—the Holy One of
God!"
[25]"Be quiet!" said Jesus sternly. "Come
out of him!" [26]The evil spirit shook the
man violently and came out of him with a
shriek.
[27]The people were all so amazed that
they asked each other, "What is this? A
new teaching—and with authority! He
even gives orders to evil spirits and they
obey him." [28]News about him spread
quickly over the whole region of Galilee●

[a]23 Greek *unclean*; also in verses 26 and 27

KING JAMES

1.PREACHING

14 Now after that John was put in
prison, Jesus came into Galilee, preaching the gospel of the kingdom of God,
15 and saying, The time is fulfilled, and
the kingdom of God is at hand: repent
ye, and believe the gospel. ●

2.CALLING

16 Now as he walked by the sea of
Galilee, he saw Simon and Andrew his
brother casting a net into the sea: for they
were fishers. 17 And Jesus said unto
them, Come ye after me, and I will make
you to become fishers of men. 18 And
straightway they forsook their nets, and
followed him. 19 And when he had gone
a little further thence, he saw James the
*son* of Zeb'edee, and John his brother,
who also were in the ship mending their
nets. 20 And straightway he called them:
and they left their father Zeb'edee in the
ship with the hired servants, and went
after him. ●

3.DELIVERING

21 And they went into Caper'na-um;
and straightway on the sabbath day he
entered into the synagogue, and taught.
22 And they were astonished at his doctrine: for he taught them as one that had
authority, and not as the scribes. 23 And
there was in their synagogue a man
with an unclean spirit; and he cried out,
24 saying, Let *us* alone; what have we to
do with thee, thou Jesus of Nazareth? art
thou come to destroy us? I know thee
who thou art, the Holy One of God.
25 And Jesus rebuked him, saying, Hold
thy peace, and come out of him. 26 And
when the unclean spirit had torn him, and
cried with a loud voice, he came out of
him. 27 And they were all amazed, insomuch that they questioned among themselves, saying, What thing is this? what
new doctrine *is* this? for with authority
commandeth he even the unclean spirits,
and they do obey him. 28 And immediately his fame spread abroad throughout
all the region round about Galilee. ●

FIRST GOSPEL

*1:14-15* What was the subject of Jesus' preaching?

_______________

_______________

Record each of the phrases of His gospel message:

_______________

_______________

_______________

_______________

*1:16-20* What are the two key words of the call for disciples?

_______________

_______________

Who became disciples here? _______________

_______________

_______________

_______________

_______________

NEW TEACHING

*1:21-28* What does this paragraph teach about Jesus'

TEACHING MINISTRY _______________

_______________

_______________

_______________

_______________

_______________

_______________

_______________

AUTHORITY _______________

_______________

_______________

_______________

_______________

_______________

_______________

NEW INTERNATIONAL VERSION

Record what is taught here about:

FAITH

JESUS' COMPASSION

PRAYER

THE GOSPEL

OTHER

*Jesus Heals Many*

29 As soon as they left the synagogue,
they went with James and John to the home
of Simon and Andrew. 30 Simon's mother-
in-law was in bed with a fever, and they
told Jesus about her. 31 So he went to her,
took her hand and helped her up. The fever
left her and she began to wait on them.●
32 That evening after sunset the people
brought to Jesus all the sick and demon-
possessed. 33 The whole town gathered at
the door, 34 and Jesus healed many who had
various diseases. He also drove out many
demons, but he would not let the demons
speak because they knew who he was.●

*Jesus Prays in a Solitary Place*

35 Very early in the morning, while it was
still dark, Jesus got up, left the house and
went off to a solitary place, where he
prayed. 36 Simon and his companions went
to look for him, 37 and when they found
him, they exclaimed: "Everyone is looking
for you!"
38 Jesus replied, "Let us go somewhere
else—to the nearby villages—so I can
preach there also. That is why I have
come." 39 So he traveled throughout Galilee, preaching in their synagogues and
driving out demons.●

*A Man With Leprosy*

40 A man with leprosy[b] came to him and
begged him on his knees, "If you are willing, you can make me clean."
41 Filled with compassion, Jesus reached
out his hand and touched the man. "I am
willing," he said. "Be clean!" 42 Immediately the leprosy left him and he was cured.
43 Jesus sent him away at once with a
strong warning: 44 "See that you don't tell
this to anyone. But go, show yourself to
the priest and offer the sacrifices that
Moses commanded for your cleansing, as
a testimony to them." 45 Instead he went
out and began to talk freely, spreading the
news. As a result, Jesus could no longer
enter a town openly but stayed outside in
lonely places. Yet the people still came to
him from everywhere.●

[b] *40* The Greek word was used for various diseases affecting the skin—not necessarily leprosy.

## KING JAMES

1.HEALING ONE

29 And forthwith, when they were come
out of the synagogue, they entered into
the house of Simon and Andrew, with
James and John. 30 But Simon's wife's
mother lay sick of a fever; and anon they
tell him of her. 31 And he came and took
her by the hand, and lifted her up; and
immediately the fever left her, and she
ministered unto them. ●

HOUSE

2.HEALING MANY

32 And at even, when the sun did set,
they brought unto him all that were diseased, and them that were possessed with
devils. 33 And all the city was gathered together at the door. 34 And he healed many
that were sick of divers diseases, and cast
out many devils; and suffered not the
devils to speak, because they knew him. ●

3.PRAYING

35 And in the morning, rising up a
great while before day, he went out, and
departed into a solitary place, and there
prayed. 36 And Simon and they that were
with him followed after him. 37 And
when they had found him, they said unto
him, All *men* seek for thee. 38 And he
said unto them, Let us go into the next
towns, that I may preach there also: for
therefore came I forth. 39 And he
preached in their synagogues throughout
all Galilee, and cast out devils. ●

4.HEALING A LEPER

40 And there came a leper to him, beseeching him, and kneeling down to him,
and saying unto him, If thou wilt, thou
canst make me clean. 41 And Jesus,
moved with compassion, put forth *his*
hand, and touched him, and saith unto
him, I will; be thou clean. 42 And as soon
as he had spoken, immediately the leprosy
departed from him, and he was cleansed.
43 And he straitly charged him, and forthwith sent him away; 44 and saith unto
him, See thou say nothing to any man:
but go thy way, show thyself to the priest,
and offer for thy cleansing those things
which Moses commanded, for a testimony unto them. 45 But he went out, and
began to publish *it* much, and to blaze
abroad the matter, insomuch that Jesus
could no more openly enter into the city,
but was without in desert places: and they
came to him from every quarter. ●

UNPOPULATED AREAS

Three of the four paragraphs report healings by Jesus. Record different observations you make here about Jesus' healing ministry:

*1:29-31* ________________

*1:32-34* ________________

*1:40-45* ________________

*1:35-39* Record the different things revealed here about Jesus and His public ministry.

NEW INTERNATIONAL VERSION

What do you learn here about:

FAITH FOR HEALING ______

FORGIVENESS OF SINS ______

LOVING SINNERS ______

JESUS' AUTHORITY AND POWER ______

JESUS' OMNISCIENCE ______

OTHER ______

### *Jesus Heals a Paralytic*

2 A few days later, when Jesus again entered Capernaum, the people heard
that he had come home. 2So many gathered
that there was no room left, not even outside the door, and he preached the word to
them. 3Some men came, bringing to him a
paralytic, carried by four of them. 4Since
they could not get him to Jesus because of
the crowd, they made an opening in the
roof above Jesus and, after digging through
it, lowered the mat the paralyzed man was
lying on. 5When Jesus saw their faith, he
said to the paralytic, "Son, your sins are
forgiven."
6Now some teachers of the law were sitting there, thinking to themselves, 7"Why
does this fellow talk like that? He's blas-
pheming! Who can forgive sins but God
alone?" ●
8Immediately Jesus knew in his spirit
that this was what they were thinking in
their hearts, and he said to them, "Why are
you thinking these things? 9Which is easier:
to say to the paralytic, 'Your sins are forgiven,' or to say, 'Get up, take your mat
and walk'? 10But that you may know that
the Son of Man has authority on earth to
forgive sins . . . ." He said to the paralytic,
11"I tell you, get up, take your mat and go
home." 12He got up, took his mat and
walked out in full view of them all. This
amazed everyone and they praised God,
saying, "We have never seen anything like
this!" ●

### *The Calling of Levi*

13Once again Jesus went out beside the
lake. A large crowd came to him, and he
began to teach them. 14As he walked along,
he saw Levi son of Alphaeus sitting at the
tax collector's booth. "Follow me," Jesus
told him, and Levi got up and followed
him. ●
15While Jesus was having dinner at
Levi's house, many tax collectors and
"sinners" were eating with him and his
disciples, for there were many who followed him. 16When the teachers of the law
who were Pharisees saw him eating with
the "sinners" and tax collectors, they
asked his disciples: "Why does he eat with
tax collectors and 'sinners'?"
17On hearing this, Jesus said to them, "It
is not the healthy who need a doctor, but
the sick. I have not come to call the righteous, but sinners." ●

[a]11 Greek *unclean*; also in verse 30
[b]14 Some manuscripts do not have *designating them apostles.*

KING JAMES

**1. SINS FORGIVEN**

**TEACHING**

2 And again he entered into Caper′-
na-um after *some* days; and it was
noised that he was in the house. 2 And
straightway many were gathered together, insomuch that there was no room
to receive *them*, no, not so much as about
the door: and he preached the word unto
them. 3 And they come unto him, bringing one sick of the palsy, which was borne
of four. 4 And when they could not come
nigh unto him for the press, they uncovered the roof where he was: and when
they had broken *it* up, they let down the
bed wherein the sick of the palsy lay.
5 When Jesus saw their faith, he said unto
the sick of the palsy, Son, thy sins be forgiven thee. 6 But there were certain of the
scribes sitting there, and reasoning in their
hearts, 7 Why doth this *man* thus speak
blasphemies? who can forgive sins but

**2. BODY HEALED**

God only? ● 8 And immediately, when
Jesus perceived in his spirit that they so
reasoned within themselves, he said unto
them, Why reason ye these things in your
hearts? 9 whether is it easier to say to the
sick of the palsy, *Thy* sins be forgiven
thee; or to say, Arise, and take up thy
bed, and walk? 10 But that ye may know
that the Son of man hath power on earth
to forgive sins, (he saith to the sick of the
palsy,) 11 I say unto thee, Arise, and take
up thy bed, and go thy way into thine
house. 12 And immediately he arose,
took up the bed, and went forth before
them all; insomuch that they were all
amazed, and glorified God, saying, We
never saw it on this fashion. ●

**3. TAX GATHERER CALLED**

13 And he went forth again by the sea
side; and all the multitude resorted unto
him, and he taught them. 14 And as he
passed by, he saw Levi the *son* of Al′pheus
sitting at the receipt of custom, and said
unto him, Follow me. And he arose and
followed him. ●

**4. SINNERS BEFRIENDED**

15 And it came to pass, that, as Jesus
sat at meat in his house, many publicans
and sinners sat also together with Jesus
and his disciples; for there were many,
and they followed him. 16 And when the
scribes and Pharisees saw him eat with
publicans and sinners, they said unto his
disciples, How is it that he eateth and

**DINING**

drinketh with publicans and sinners?
17 When Jesus heard *it*, he saith unto
them, They that are whole have no need
of the physician, but they that are sick:
I came not to call the righteous, but sinners to repentance. ●

Early in Jesus' ministry He was challenged, privately or openly, by false teachers concerning His miracles and message. Record the two challenges of this passage, and Jesus' responses.

CHALLENGE *2:6-7* ________________

JESUS' RESPONSE *2:8-11* ________________

CHALLENGE *2:16* ________________

JESUS' RESPONSE *2:17* ________________

What does paragraph 2:13-14 contribute to this segment?

________________

NEW INTERNATIONAL VERSION

The false teachers challenged Jesus about violating Moses' legal code. Their interpretation was strictly legalistic. What do you learn from Jesus' replies as to the true and legitimate application of the laws to everyday living?

Record other practical lessons you have learned from this passage.

### *Jesus Questioned About Fasting*

18Now John's disciples and the Pharisees
were fasting. Some people came and asked
Jesus, "How is it that John's disciples and
the disciples of the Pharisees are fasting,
but yours are not?"
19Jesus answered, "How can the guests
of the bridegroom fast while he is with
them? They cannot, so long as they have
him with them. 20But the time will come
when the bridegroom will be taken from
them, and on that day they will fast.
21"No one sews a patch of unshrunk
cloth on an old garment. If he does, the
new piece will pull away from the old, making the tear worse. 22And no one pours new
wine into old wineskins. If he does, the
wine will burst the skins, and both the wine
and the wineskins will be ruined. No, he
pours new wine into new wineskins."●

### *Lord of the Sabbath*

23One Sabbath Jesus was going through
the grainfields, and as his disciples walked
along, they began to pick some heads of
grain. 24The Pharisees said to him, "Look,
why are they doing what is unlawful on the
Sabbath?"
25He answered, "Have you never read
what David did when he and his companions were hungry and in need? 26In the days
of Abiathar the high priest, he entered the
house of God and ate the consecrated
bread, which is lawful only for priests to
eat. And he also gave some to his companions."
27Then he said to them, "The Sabbath
was made for man, not man for the Sabbath. 28So the Son of Man is Lord even of
the Sabbath."●
3 Another time he went into the synagogue, and a man with a shriveled hand
was there. 2Some of them were looking for
a reason to accuse Jesus, so they watched
him closely to see if he would heal him on
the Sabbath. 3Jesus said to the man with
the shriveled hand, "Stand up in front of
everyone."
4Then Jesus asked them, "Which is lawful on the Sabbath: to do good or to do evil,
to save life or to kill?" But they remained
silent.
5He looked around at them in anger and,
deeply distressed at their stubborn hearts,
said to the man, "Stretch out your hand."
He stretched it out, and his hand was completely restored. 6Then the Pharisees went
out and began to plot with the Herodians
how they might kill Jesus.●

KING JAMES

NEEDS SATISFIED

1.JOY

18 And the disciples of John and of the
Pharisees used to fast: and they come and
say unto him, Why do the disciples of
John and of the Pharisees fast, but thy
disciples fast not? 19 And Jesus said unto them, Can the children of the bridechamber fast, while the bridegroom is
with them? as long as they have the bridegroom with them, they cannot fast.
20 But the days will come, when the bridegroom shall be taken away from them,
and then shall they fast in those days.
21 No man also seweth a piece of new
cloth on an old garment; else the new
piece that filled it up taketh away from the
old, and the rent is made worse. 22 And
no man putteth new wine into old bottles;
else the new wine doth burst the bottles,
and the wine is spilled, and the bottles will
be marred: but new wine must be put into
new bottles. ●

"WHY?"

2.FOOD

23 And it came to pass, that he went
through the corn fields on the sabbath
day; and his disciples began, as they
went, to pluck the ears of corn. 24 And
the Pharisees said unto him, Behold, why
do they on the sabbath day that which is
not lawful? 25 And he said unto them,
Have ye never read what David did, when
he had need, and was ahungered, he, and
they that were with him? 26 How he
went into the house of God in the days of
Abi'athar the high priest, and did eat the
showbread, which is not lawful to eat but
for the priests, and gave also to them
which were with him? 27 And he said
unto them, The sabbath was made for
man, and not man for the sabbath:
28 therefore the Son of man is Lord also
of the sabbath. ●

3.HEALING

3 And he entered again into the synagogue; and there was a man there
which had a withered hand. 2 And they
watched him, whether he would heal him
on the sabbath day; that they might accuse him. 3 And he saith unto the man
which had the withered hand, Stand forth.
4 And he saith unto them, Is it lawful to
do good on the sabbath days, or to do
evil? to save life, or to kill? But they held
their peace. 5 And when he had looked
round about on them with anger, being
grieved for the hardness of their hearts, he
saith unto the man, Stretch forth thine
hand. And he stretched *it* out: and his
hand was restored whole as the other.
6 And the Pharisees went forth, and
straightway took counsel with the Hero'-
di-ans against him, how they might
destroy him. ●

DESTROY!

Opposition against Jesus keeps building up to a climax of violence. Observe the progression of opposition in the segment. What is the last phrase of the segment?

Study the oppositions and Jesus' responses.

OPPOSITION *2:18*

JESUS' RESPONSE *2:19-22*

OPPOSITION *2:24*

JESUS' RESPONSE *2:25-28*

OPPOSITION *3:2,4b*

JESUS' RESPONSE *3:4-5*

COUNSEL TO DESTROY JESUS *3:6*

NEW INTERNATIONAL VERSION

What different kinds of opposition to Jesus appear in this account?

What does it mean to be Christ's disciple today?

List some practical lessons about discipleship taught here.

Record other practical truths.

*Crowds Follow Jesus*

[7]Jesus withdrew with his disciples to the lake, and a large crowd from Galilee followed. [8]When they heard all he was doing, many people came to him from Judea, Jerusalem, Idumea, and the regions across the Jordan and around Tyre and Sidon. [9]Because of the crowd he told his disciples to have a small boat ready for him, to keep the people from crowding him. [10]For he had healed many, so that those with diseases were pushing forward to touch him. [11]Whenever the evil[a] spirits saw him, they fell down before him and cried out, "You are the Son of God." [12]But he gave them strict orders not to tell who he was.

*The Appointing of the Twelve Apostles*

[13]Jesus went up into the hills and called to him those he wanted, and they came to him. [14]He appointed twelve—designating them apostles[b]—that they might be with him and that he might send them out to preach [15]and to have authority to drive out demons. [16]These are the twelve he appointed: Simon (to whom he gave the name Peter); [17]James son of Zebedee, and his brother John (to them he gave the name Boanerges, which means Sons of Thunder); [18]Andrew, Philip, Bartholomew, Matthew, Thomas, James son of Alphaeus, Thaddaeus, Simon the Zealot [19]and Judas Iscariot, who betrayed him.

*Jesus and Beelzebub*

[20]Then Jesus entered a house, and again a crowd gathered, so that he and his disciples were not even able to eat. [21]When his family heard about this, they went to take charge of him, for they said, "He is out of his mind."

[22]And the teachers of the law who came down from Jerusalem said, "He is possessed by Beelzebub[a]! By the prince of demons he is driving out demons."

[23]So Jesus called them and spoke to them in parables: "How can Satan drive out Satan? [24]If a kingdom is divided against itself, that kingdom cannot stand. [25]If a house is divided against itself, that house cannot stand. [26]And if Satan opposes himself and is divided, he cannot stand; his end has come. [27]In fact, no one can enter a strong man's house and carry off his possessions unless he first ties up the strong man. Then he can rob his house. [28]I tell you the truth, all the sins and blasphemies of men will be forgiven them. [29]But whoever blasphemes against the Holy Spirit will never be forgiven; he is guilty of an eternal sin."

[30]He said this because they were saying, "He has an evil spirit."

*Jesus' Mother and Brothers*

[31]Then Jesus' mother and brothers arrived. Standing outside, they sent someone in to call him. [32]A crowd was sitting around him, and they told him, "Your mother and brothers are outside looking for you."

[33]"Who are my mother and my brothers?" he asked.

[34]Then he looked at those seated in a circle around him and said, "Here are my mother and my brothers! [35]Whoever does God's will is my brother and sister and mother."

[a]22 Greek *Beezeboul* or *Beelzeboul*

KING JAMES

1. SCOPE OF THE MINISTRY

7 But Jesus withdrew himself with his
disciples to the sea: and a great multitude
from Galilee followed him, and from
Judea, 8 and from Jerusalem, and from
Idume'a, and *from* beyond Jordan; and
they about Tyre and Sidon, a great multitude, when they had heard what great
things he did, came unto him. 9 And he
spake to his disciples, that a small ship
should wait on him because of the multitude, lest they should throng him. 10 For
he had healed many; insomuch that they
pressed upon him for to touch him, as
many as had plagues. 11 And unclean
spirits, when they saw him, fell down before him, and cried, saying, Thou art the
Son of God. 12 And he straitly charged
them that they should not make him
known. ●

GREAT MULTITUDE

2. HELPERS IN THE MINISTRY

13 And he goeth up into a mountain,
and calleth *unto him* whom he would: and
they came unto him. 14 And he ordained
twelve, that they should be with him, and
that he might send them forth to preach,
15 and to have power to heal sicknesses,
and to cast out devils: 16 and Simon he
surnamed Peter; 17 and James the *son* of
Zeb'edee, and John the brother of James;
and he surnamed them Bo-aner'ges, which
is, The sons of thunder: 18 and Andrew,
and Philip, and Bartholomew, and Matthew, and Thomas, and James the *son* of
Al'pheus, and Thad'de-us, and Simon the
Canaanite, 19 and Judas Iscar'i-ot, which
also betrayed him.

3. HINDRANCES TO THE MINISTRY

And they went into a house.● 20 And the
multitude cometh together again, so that
they could not so much as eat bread.
21 And when his friends heard *of it*, they
went out to lay hold on him: for they said,
He is beside himself.● 22 And the scribes

4. OPPONENTS OF THE MINISTRY

which came down from Jerusalem said,
He hath Beel'zebub, and by the prince of
the devils casteth he out devils. 23 And
he called them *unto him*, and said unto
them in parables, How can Satan cast out
Satan? 24 And if a kingdom be divided
against itself, that kingdom cannot stand.
25 And if a house be divided against itself, that house cannot stand. 26 And if
Satan rise up against himself, and be
divided, he cannot stand, but hath an end.
27 No man can enter into a strong man's
house, and spoil his goods, except he will
first bind the strong man; and then he
will spoil his house.
28 Verily I say unto you, All sins shall
be forgiven unto the sons of men, and
blasphemies wherewith soever they shall
blaspheme: 29 but he that shall blaspheme against the Holy Ghost hath never
forgiveness, but is in danger of eternal
damnation: 30 because they said, He
hath an unclean spirit. ●
31 There came then his brethren and his
mother, and, standing without, sent unto
him, calling him. 32 And the multitude
sat about him, and they said unto him,
Behold, thy mother and thy brethren
without seek for thee. 33 And he answered them, saying, Who is my mother,
or my brethren? 34 And he looked round
about on them which sat about him, and
said, Behold my mother and my brethren!
35 For whosoever shall do the will of
God, the same is my brother, and my
sister, and mother. ●

MOTHER

At this point in his gospel Mark begins to record the growing ministry of Jesus despite the enemy's counsel to destroy Him (3:6). It is a CONFRONTATION of the servant Jesus and false religion.

*3:7-12* Record some of the things Mark writes which indicates how effective Jesus' ministry was:

______________________________

______________________________

______________________________

______________________________

______________________________

*3:13-19* What do the verses teach about the call to discipleship? (Note: At this point Jesus began to call the men also "apostles"—cf. Luke 6:13.)

______________________________

______________________________

______________________________

______________________________

______________________________

Record your main observations of the next three paragraphs.

*3:20-21* ______________________________

______________________________

______________________________

______________________________

______________________________

*3:22-30* ______________________________

______________________________

______________________________

______________________________

______________________________

*3:31-35* ______________________________

______________________________

______________________________

______________________________

______________________________

NEW INTERNATIONAL VERSION

Make a list of key words and phrases of this passage.

List various spiritual lessons taught by the second paragraph:

*The Parable of the Sower*

4 On another occasion Jesus began to
teach by the lake. The crowd that gathered around him was so large that he got
into a boat and sat in it out on the lake,
while all the people were along the shore at
the water's edge. 2He taught them many
things by parables, and in his teaching said:
3"Listen! A farmer went out to sow his
seed. 4As he was scattering the seed, some
fell along the path, and the birds came and
ate it up. 5Some fell on rocky places, where
it did not have much soil. It sprang up
quickly, because the soil was shallow. 6But
when the sun came up, the plants were
scorched, and they withered because they
had no root. 7Other seed fell among thorns,
which grew up and choked the plants, so
that they did not bear grain. 8Still other
seed fell on good soil. It came up, grew and
produced a crop, multiplying thirty, sixty,
or even a hundred times."
9Then Jesus said, "He who has ears to
hear, let him hear."●
10When he was alone, the Twelve and
the others around him asked him about the
parables. 11He told them, "The secret of
the kingdom of God has been given to you.
But to those on the outside everything is
said in parables 12so that,

" 'they may be ever seeing but
never perceiving,
and ever hearing but never
understanding;
otherwise they might turn and be
forgiven!'[b]"

13Then Jesus said to them, "Don't you
understand this parable? How then will
you understand any parable? 14The farmer
sows the word. 15Some people are like seed
along the path, where the word is sown. As
soon as they hear it, Satan comes and takes
away the word that was sown in them.
16Others, like seed sown on rocky places,
hear the word and at once receive it with
joy. 17But since they have no root, they last
only a short time. When trouble or persecution comes because of the word, they
quickly fall away. 18Still others, like seed
sown among thorns, hear the word; 19but
the worries of this life, the deceitfulness of
wealth and the desires for other things
come in and choke the word, making it
unfruitful. 20Others, like seed sown on
good soil, hear the word, accept it, and
produce a crop—thirty, sixty or even a
hundred times what was sown."●

*b12* Isaiah 6:9,10

KING JAMES

WITH THE MULTITUDES

4 And he began again to teach by the
sea side: and there was gathered unto
him a great multitude, so that he entered
into a ship, and sat in the sea; and the
whole multitude was by the sea on the

1. THE PARABLE

land. 2 And he taught them many things
by parables, and said unto them in his
doctrine, 3 Hearken; Behold, there went
out a sower to sow: 4 and it came to pass,
as he sowed, some fell by the wayside, and
the fowls of the air came and devoured it
up. 5 And some fell on stony ground,
where it had not much earth; and immediately it sprang up, because it had no
depth of earth: 6 but when the sun was
up, it was scorched; and because it had no
root, it withered away. 7 And some fell
among thorns, and the thorns grew up,
and choked it, and it yielded no fruit.
8 And other fell on good ground, and did
yield fruit that sprang up and increased,
and brought forth, some thirty, and some
sixty, and some a hundred. 9 And he said
unto them, He that hath ears to hear, let
him hear. ●

2. THE INTERPRETATION

WITH THE DISCIPLES

10 And when he was alone, they that
were about him with the twelve asked of
him the parable. 11 And he said unto
them, Unto you it is given to know the
mystery of the kingdom of God: but unto
them that are without, all *these* things are
done in parables:

Isa. 6:9

12 that seeing they may see, and not
perceive;
and hearing they may hear, and not
understand;
lest at any time they should be
converted,
and *their* sins should be forgiven
them.
13 And he said unto them, Know ye not
this parable? and how then will ye know
all parables? 14 The sower soweth the
word. 15 And these are they by the wayside, where the word is sown; but when
they have heard, Satan cometh immediately, and taketh away the word that was
sown in their hearts. 16 And these are
they likewise which are sown on stony
ground; who, when they have heard the
word, immediately receive it with gladness; 17 and have no root in themselves,
and so endure but for a time: afterward,
when affliction or persecution ariseth for
the word's sake, immediately they are
offended. 18 And these are they which
are sown among thorns; such as hear the
word, 19 and the cares of this world, and
the deceitfulness of riches, and the lusts of
other things entering in, choke the word,
and it becometh unfruitful. 20 And these
are they which are sown on good ground;
such as hear the word, and receive *it*, and
bring forth fruit, some thirtyfold, some
sixty, and some a hundred. ●

*4:1-9* Jesus liked to teach by parables because they made deep truths clear and simple. Record the different soils of this parable, and the outcomes of the plantings.

*4:10-20* Record the interpretations of the points of the parable of 4:1-9.

What does 4:21-25 reveal about the enlightening purposes of the parabolic method of teaching? In answering this, compare also the last phrase of verse 33.

Record what is taught in 4:26-32 about the kingdom of God.

What is taught by 4:21-25 about Christian stewardship and responsibility?

Record other applications of the passage.

## NEW INTERNATIONAL VERSION

*A Lamp on a Stand*

21He said to them, "Do you bring in a
lamp to put it under a bowl or a bed? Instead, don't you put it on its stand? 22For
whatever is hidden is meant to be disclosed, and whatever is concealed is meant
to be brought out into the open. 23If anyone
has ears to hear, let him hear."
24"Consider carefully what you hear,"
he continued. "With the measure you use,
it will be measured to you—and even
more. 25Whoever has will be given more;
whoever does not have, even what he has
will be taken from him."●

*The Parable of the Growing Seed*

26He also said, "This is what the kingdom of God is like. A man scatters seed on
the ground. 27Night and day, whether he
sleeps or gets up, the seed sprouts and
grows, though he does not know how. 28All
by itself the soil produces grain—first the
stalk, then the head, then the full kernel in
the head. 29As soon as the grain is ripe, he
puts the sickle to it, because the harvest
has come."●

*The Parable of the Mustard Seed*

30Again he said, "What shall we say the
kingdom of God is like, or what parable
shall we use to describe it? 31It is like a
mustard seed, which is the smallest seed
you plant in the ground. 32Yet when
planted, it grows and becomes the largest
of all garden plants, with such big branches
that the birds of the air can perch in its
shade."●
33With many similar parables Jesus
spoke the word to them, as much as they
could understand. 34He did not say anything to them without using a parable. But
when he was alone with his own disciples,
he explained everything.●

## KING JAMES

1. CANDLE AND BUSHEL

21 And he said unto them, Is a candle
brought to be put under a bushel, or under
a bed? and not to be set on a candlestick? 22 For there is nothing hid, which
shall not be manifested; neither was any
thing kept secret, but that it should come
abroad. 23 If any man have ears to hear,
let him hear. 24 And he said unto them,
Take heed what ye hear. With what
measure ye mete, it shall be measured to
you; and unto you that hear shall more
be given. 25 For he that hath, to him shall
be given; and he that hath not, from him
shall be taken even that which he
hath. ●

TO BE SEEN

2. SEED AND HARVEST

26 And he said, So is the kingdom of
God, as if a man should cast seed into the
ground; 27 and should sleep, and rise
night and day, and the seed should spring
and grow up, he knoweth not how. 28 For
the earth bringeth forth fruit of herself;
first the blade, then the ear, after that the
full corn in the ear. 29 But when the fruit
is brought forth, immediately he putteth in the sickle, because the harvest is
come. ●

3. MUSTARD SEED

30 And he said, Whereunto shall we
liken the kingdom of God? or with what
comparison shall we compare it? 31 *It is*
like a grain of mustard seed, which, when
it is sown in the earth, is less than all the
seeds that be in the earth: 32 but when it
is sown, it groweth up, and becometh
greater than all herbs, and shooteth out
great branches; so that the fowls of
the air may lodge under the shadow of
it. ●

TO BE-COME LARGE

—conclusion

33 And with many such parables spake
he the word unto them, as they were able
to hear *it*. 34 But without a parable spake
he not unto them: and when they were
alone, he expounded all things to his disciples. ●

This segment continues the teaching of Jesus reported in the preceding segment. Record the main point of each of the parables:

*4:21-25* ____________________

*4:26-29* ____________________

*4:30-32* ____________________

*4:33-34* What does this paragraph reveal about Jesus' method of teaching?

____________________

NEW INTERNATIONAL VERSION

List various spiritual applications taught by this passage.

What does the passage teach about Jesus?

### *Jesus Calms the Storm*

35 That day when evening came, he said
to his disciples, "Let us go over to the
other side." 36 Leaving the crowd behind,
they took him along, just as he was, in the
boat. There were also other boats with
him. 37 A furious squall came up, and the
waves broke over the boat, so that it was
nearly swamped. 38 Jesus was in the stern,
sleeping on a cushion. The disciples woke
him and said to him, "Teacher, don't you
care if we drown?"
39 He got up, rebuked the wind and said
to the waves, "Quiet! Be still!" Then the
wind died down and it was completely
calm.
40 He said to his disciples, "Why are you
so afraid? Do you still have no faith?"
41 They were terrified and asked each
other, "Who is this? Even the wind and the
waves obey him!"●

### *The Healing of a Demon-possessed Man*

5 They went across the lake to the region
of the Gerasenes.[a] 2 When Jesus got out
of the boat, a man with an evil[b] spirit came
from the tombs to meet him. 3 This man
lived in the tombs, and no one could bind
him any more, not even with a chain. 4 For
he had often been chained hand and foot,
but he tore the chains apart and broke the
irons on his feet. No one was strong
enough to subdue him. 5 Night and day
among the tombs and in the hills he would
cry out and cut himself with stones.
6 When he saw Jesus from a distance, he
ran and fell on his knees in front of him.
7 He shouted at the top of his voice, "What
do you want with me, Jesus, Son of the
Most High God? Swear to God that you
won't torture me!" 8 For Jesus was saying
to him, "Come out of this man, you evil
spirit!"
9 Then Jesus asked him, "What is your
name?"
"My name is Legion," he replied, "for
we are many." 10 And he begged Jesus
again and again not to send them out of the
area.
11 A large herd of pigs was feeding on the
nearby hillside. 12 The demons begged
Jesus, "Send us among the pigs; allow us
to go into them." 13 He gave them permission, and the evil spirits came out and went
into the pigs. The herd, about two thousand in number, rushed down the steep
bank into the lake and were drowned.●
14 Those tending the pigs ran off and reported this in the town and countryside,
and the people went out to see what had
happened. 15 When they came to Jesus,
they saw the man who had been possessed
by the legion of demons, sitting there,
dressed and in his right mind; and they
were afraid. 16 Those who had seen it told
the people what had happened to the demon-possessed man—and told about the
pigs as well. 17 Then the people began to
plead with Jesus to leave their region.●
18 As Jesus was getting into the boat, the
man who had been demon-possessed
begged to go with him. 19 Jesus did not let
him, but said, "Go home to your family
and tell them how much the Lord has done
for you, and how he has had mercy on
you." 20 So the man went away and began
to tell in the Decapolis[c] how much Jesus
had done for him. And all the people were
amazed.●

[a] *1* Some manuscripts *Gadarenes;* other manuscripts *Gergesenes*
[b] *2* Greek *unclean;* also in verses 8 and 13
[c] *20* That is, the Ten Cities

KING JAMES

1. POWER OVER NATURE

35 And the same day, when the even was come, he saith unto them, Let us pass over unto the other side. 36 And when they had sent away the multitude, they took him even as he was in the ship. And there were also with him other little ships. 37 And there arose a great storm of wind, and the waves beat into the ship, so that it was now full. 38 And he was in the hinder part of the ship, asleep on a pillow: and they awake him, and say unto him, Master, carest thou not that we perish? 39 And he arose, and rebuked the wind, and said unto the sea, Peace, be still. And the wind ceased, and there was a great calm. 40 And he said unto them, Why are ye so fearful? how is it that ye have no faith? 41 And they feared exceedingly, and said one to another, What manner of man is this, that even the wind and the sea obey him? ●

FEAR

2. POWER OVER DEMONS

5 And they came over unto the other side of the sea, into the country of the Gad'arenes. 2 And when he was come out of the ship, immediately there met him out of the tombs a man with an unclean spirit, 3 who had *his* dwelling among the tombs; and no man could bind him, no, not with chains: 4 because that he had been often bound with fetters and chains, and the chains had been plucked asunder by him, and the fetters broken in pieces: neither could any *man* tame him. 5 And always, night and day, he was in the mountains, and in the tombs, crying, and cutting himself with stones. 6 But when he saw Jesus afar off, he ran and worshipped him, 7 and cried with a loud voice, and said, What have I to do with thee, Jesus, *thou* Son of the most high God? I adjure thee by God, that thou torment me not. 8 For he said unto him, Come out of the man, *thou* unclean spirit. 9 And he asked him, What *is* thy name? And he answered, saying, My name *is* Legion: for we are many. 10 And he besought him much that he would not send them away out of the country. 11 Now there was there nigh unto the mountains a great herd of swine feeding. 12 And all the devils besought him, saying, Send us into the swine, that we may enter into them. 13 And forthwith Jesus gave them leave. And the unclean spirits went out, and entered into the swine; and the herd ran violently down a steep place into the sea, (they were about two thousand,) and were choked in the sea. ●

14 And they that fed the swine fled, and told *it* in the city, and in the country. And they went out to see what it was that was done. 15 And they come to Jesus, and see him that was possessed with the devil, and had the legion, sitting, and clothed, and in his right mind; and they were afraid. 16 And they that saw *it* told them how it befell to him that was possessed with the devil, and *also* concerning the swine. 17 And they began to pray him to depart out of their coasts. ● 18 And when he was come into the ship, he that had been possessed with the devil prayed him that he might be with him. 19 Howbeit Jesus suffered him not, but saith unto him, Go home to thy friends, and tell them how great things the Lord hath done for thee, and hath had compassion on thee. 20 And he departed, and began to publish in Decap'olis how great things Jesus had done for him: and all *men* did marvel. ●

DEMONS

*4:35-41* What do you learn about Jesus from His sleeping during the storm?

What do you learn about the disciples?

*5:1-17* Did Jesus perform this miracle in response to someone's faith?

What do you learn about demons here?

*5:18-20* Analyze Jesus' words of verse 19.

NEW INTERNATIONAL VERSION

Jesus performed the many miracles of these days and months of confrontation mainly to show people who He was. (Cf. 8:27-30.) What does this passage reveal as to His identity?

List various spiritual applications to be made from this segment, such as about faith.

*A Dead Girl and a Sick Woman*

21When Jesus had again crossed over by
boat to the other side of the lake, a large
crowd gathered around him. While he was
by the lake, 22one of the synagogue rulers,
named Jairus, came there. Seeing Jesus, he
fell at his feet 23and pleaded earnestly with
him, "My little daughter is dying. Please
come and put your hands on her so that she
will be healed and live." 24So Jesus went
with him.

A large crowd followed and pressed
around him. 25And a woman was there who
had been subject to bleeding for twelve
years. 26She had suffered a great deal under the care of many doctors and had spent
all she had, yet instead of getting better she
grew worse. 27When she heard about
Jesus, she came up behind him in the
crowd and touched his cloak, 28because
she thought, "If I just touch his clothes, I
will be healed." 29Immediately her bleeding stopped and she felt in her body that
she was freed from her suffering.

30At once Jesus realized that power had
gone out from him. He turned around in the
crowd and asked, "Who touched my
clothes?"

31"You see the people crowding against
you," his disciples answered, "and yet
you can ask, 'Who touched me?' "

32But Jesus kept looking around to see
who had done it. 33Then the woman, knowing what had happened to her, came and
fell at his feet and, trembling with fear, told
him the whole truth. 34He said to her,
"Daughter, your faith has healed you. Go
in peace and be freed from your suffering."

35While Jesus was still speaking, some
men came from the house of Jairus, the
synagogue ruler. "Your daughter is dead,"
they said. "Why bother the teacher any
more?"

36Ignoring what they said, Jesus told the
synagogue ruler, "Don't be afraid; just believe."

37He did not let anyone follow him except Peter, James and John the brother of
James. 38When they came to the home of
the synagogue ruler, Jesus saw a commotion, with people crying and wailing loudly. 39He went in and said to them, "Why all
this commotion and wailing? The child is
not dead but asleep." 40But they laughed at
him.

After he put them all out, he took the
child's father and mother and the disciples
who were with him, and went in where the
child was. 41He took her by the hand and
said to her, "*Talitha koum!*" (which
means, "Little girl, I say to you, get up!").
42Immediately the girl stood up and walked
around (she was twelve years old). At this
they were completely astonished. 43He
gave strict orders not to let anyone know
about this, and told them to give her something to eat.

KING JAMES

### 1. JAIRUS' FAITH

21 And when Jesus was passed over
again by ship unto the other side, much
people gathered unto him; and he was
nigh unto the sea. 22 And, behold, there
cometh one of the rulers of the synagogue, Jai'rus by name; and when he saw
him, he fell at his feet, 23 and besought
him greatly, saying, My little daughter
lieth at the point of death: *I pray thee*,
come and lay thy hands on her, that she
may be healed; and she shall live. 24 And
*Jesus* went with him.

PANIC

### 2. POWER OVER DISEASE

And much people followed him, and
thronged him.● 25 And a certain woman,
which had an issue of blood twelve years,
26 and had suffered many things of many
physicians, and had spent all that she had,
and was nothing bettered, but rather grew
worse, 27 when she had heard of Jesus,
came in the press behind, and touched his
garment. 28 For she said, If I may touch
but his clothes, I shall be whole. 29 And
straightway the fountain of her blood was
dried up; and she felt in *her* body that she
was healed of that plague. 30 And Jesus,
immediately knowing in himself that virtue had gone out of him, turned him about
in the press, and said, Who touched my
clothes? 31 And his disciples said unto
him, Thou seest the multitude thronging
thee, and sayest thou, Who touched me?
32 And he looked round about to see her
that had done this thing. 33 But the
woman fearing and trembling, knowing
what was done in her, came and fell down
before him, and told him all the truth.
34 And he said unto her, Daughter, thy
faith hath made thee whole; go in peace,
and be whole of thy plague. ●

### 3. POWER OVER DEATH

35 While he yet spake, there came from
the ruler of the synagogue's *house certain*
which said, Thy daughter is dead; why
troublest thou the Master any further?
36 As soon as Jesus heard the word that
was spoken, he saith unto the ruler of the
synagogue, Be not afraid, only believe.
37 And he suffered no man to follow him,
save Peter, and James, and John the
brother of James. 38 And he cometh to
the house of the ruler of the synagogue,
and seeth the tumult, and them that wept
and wailed greatly. 39 And when he was
come in, he saith unto them, Why make
ye this ado, and weep? the damsel is not
dead, but sleepeth. 40 And they laughed
him to scorn. But when he had put them
all out, he taketh the father and the
mother of the damsel, and them that were
with him, and entereth in where the damsel was lying. 41 And he took the damsel
by the hand, and said unto her, Tal'itha
cu'mi; which is, being interpreted, Damsel, (I say unto thee,) arise. 42 And
straightway the damsel arose, and walked;
for she was *of the age* of twelve years.
And they were astonished with a great
astonishment. 43 And he charged them
straitly that no man should know it; and
commanded that something should be
given her to eat. ●

ASTONISHMENT

*5:21-24* What kind of faith did Jairus have?

*5:25-34* What kind of a faith did the woman have?

*5:35-43* What is revealed here about Jesus?

NEW INTERNATIONAL VERSION

Record what you learn from this passage about the following:

HONOR

UNBELIEF

WITNESSING

What does the passage teach about human nature?

*A Prophet Without Honor*

6 Jesus left there and went to his home
town, accompanied by his disciples.
[2]When the Sabbath came, he began to
teach in the synagogue, and many who
heard him were amazed.
"Where did this man get these things?"
they asked. "What's this wisdom that has
been given him, that he even does miracles! [3]Isn't this the carpenter? Isn't this
Mary's son and the brother of James,
Joses, Judas and Simon? Aren't his sisters
here with us?" And they took offense at
him.
[4]Jesus said to them, "Only in his home
town, among his relatives and in his own
house is a prophet without honor." [5]He
could not do any miracles there, except lay
his hands on a few sick people and heal
them. [6]And he was amazed at their lack of
faith.●

*Jesus Sends Out the Twelve*

Then Jesus went around teaching from
village to village. [7]Calling the Twelve to
him, he sent them out two by two and gave
them authority over evil[a] spirits.
[8]These were his instructions: "Take
nothing for the journey except a staff—no
bread, no bag, no money in your belts.
[9]Wear sandals but not an extra tunic.
[10]Whenever you enter a house, stay there
until you leave that town. [11]And if any
place will not welcome you or listen to you,
shake the dust off your feet when you
leave, as a testimony against them."●
[12]They went out and preached that
people should repent. [13]They drove out
many demons and anointed many sick
people with oil and healed them.●

[a]7 Greek *unclean*

KING JAMES

1. HOME TOWN PROPHET

6 And he went out from thence, and
came into his own country; and his
disciples follow him. 2 And when the
sabbath day was come, he began to teach
in the synagogue: and many hearing *him*
were astonished, saying, From whence
hath this *man* these things? and what
wisdom *is* this which is given unto him,
that even such mighty works are wrought
by his hands? 3 Is not this the carpenter,
the son of Mary, the brother of James,
and Joses, and of Judas, and Simon? and
are not his sisters here with us? And they
were offended at him. 4 But Jesus said
unto them, A prophet is not without
honor, but in his own country, and
among his own kin, and in his own house.
5 And he could there do no mighty work,
save that he laid his hands upon a few
sick folk, and healed *them*. 6 And he
marveled because of their unbelief. ●

2. COMMISSIONED DISCIPLES

And he went round about the villages,
teaching.
7 And he called *unto him* the twelve,
and began to send them forth by two and
two; and gave them power over unclean
spirits; 8 and commanded them that they
should take nothing for *their* journey, save
a staff only; no scrip, no bread, no money
in *their* purse: 9 but *be* shod with sandals;
and not put on two coats. 10 And he said
unto them, In what place soever ye enter
into a house, there abide till ye depart
from that place. 11 And whosoever shall
not receive you, nor hear you, when ye
depart thence, shake off the dust under
your feet for a testimony against them.
Verily I say unto you, It shall be more
tolerable for Sodom and Gomor'rah in
the day of judgment, than for that city.●
12 And they went out, and preached that
men should repent. 13 And they cast out
many devils, and anointed with oil many
that were sick, and healed *them*. ●

DISCIPLES FOLLOWED HIM

DISCIPLES WENT OUT

Compare the disciples at the beginning of the segment with those of the ending.

_______________

*6:1-6a* What words or phrases describe the heart of the multitudes at this time?

v.2 _______________

v.3 _______________

v.6a _______________

*6:6b-11* Account for each of the instructions of verses 8-11.

_______________

*6:12-13* Why would Jesus give healing powers to His disciples?

_______________

NEW INTERNATIONAL VERSION

Most of this passage (vv.17-29) is a parenthesis in Mark's account. The main point is given in verses 14-16. What is it, in your own words?

Record what the passage teaches about:

WORLDLINESS

REVENGE

VIOLENCE

PERSECUTION

REST

Record other spiritual lessons.

### *John the Baptist Beheaded*

14King Herod heard about this, for Jesus'
name had become well known. Some were
saying,[b] "John the Baptist has been raised
from the dead, and that is why miraculous
powers are at work in him."
15Others said, "He is Elijah."
And still others claimed, "He is a
prophet, like one of the prophets of long
ago."
16But when Herod heard this, he said,
"John, the man I beheaded, has been
raised from the dead!"
17For Herod himself had given orders to
have John arrested, and he had him bound
and put in prison. He did this because of
Herodias, his brother Philip's wife, whom
he had married. 18For John had been saying to Herod, "It is not lawful for you to
have your brother's wife." 19So Herodias
nursed a grudge against John and wanted
to kill him. But she was not able to, 20be-
cause Herod feared John and protected
him, knowing him to be a righteous and
holy man. When Herod heard John, he was
greatly puzzled[a]; yet he liked to listen to
him.●
21Finally the opportune time came. On
his birthday Herod gave a banquet for his
high officials and military commanders and
the leading men of Galilee. 22When the
daughter of Herodias came in and danced,
she pleased Herod and his dinner guests.
The king said to the girl, "Ask me for
anything you want, and I'll give it to you."
23And he promised her with an oath,
"Whatever you ask I will give you, up to
half my kingdom."
24She went out and said to her mother,
"What shall I ask for?"
"The head of John the Baptist," she answered.
25At once the girl hurried in to the king
with the request: "I want you to give me
right now the head of John the Baptist on
a platter."
26The king was greatly distressed, but
because of his oaths and his dinner guests,
he did not want to refuse her. 27So he
immediately sent an executioner with orders to bring John's head. The man went,
beheaded John in the prison, 28and brought
back his head on a platter. He presented it
to the girl, and she gave it to her mother.
29On hearing of this, John's disciples came
and took his body and laid it in a tomb.●

### *Jesus Feeds the Five Thousand*

30The apostles gathered around Jesus
and reported to him all they had done and
taught. 31Then, because so many people
were coming and going that they did not
even have a chance to eat, he said to them,
"Come with me by yourselves to a quiet
place and get some rest."
32So they went away by themselves in a
boat to a solitary place.●

[b]14 Some early manuscripts *He was saying*
[a]20 Some early manuscripts *he did many things*

## KING JAMES

1.HEROD'S FEAR

WELL-KNOWN NAME

14 And king Herod heard *of him;* (for
his name was spread abroad;) and he said,
That John the Baptist was risen from the
dead, and therefore mighty works do
show forth themselves in him. 15 Others
said, That it is Eli'jah. And others said,
That it is a prophet, or as one of the
prophets. 16 But when Herod heard
*thereof,* he said, It is John, whom I beheaded: he is risen from the dead. 17 For
Herod himself had sent forth and laid hold
upon John, and bound him in prison for
Hero'di-as' sake, his brother Philip's
wife; for he had married her. 18 For
John had said unto Herod, It is not lawful for thee to have thy brother's wife.
19 Therefore Hero'di-as had a quarrel
against him, and would have killed him;
but she could not: 20 for Herod feared
John, knowing that he was a just man and
a holy, and observed him; and when he
heard him, he did many things, and heard
him gladly. ● 21 And when a convenient

2.HERODIAS' REVENGE

day was come, that Herod on his birthday
made a supper to his lords, high captains,
and chief *estates* of Galilee; 22 and when
the daughter of the said Hero'di-as came
in, and danced, and pleased Herod and
them that sat with him, the king said unto
the damsel, Ask of me whatsoever thou
wilt, and I will give *it* thee. 23 And he
sware unto her, Whatsoever thou shalt
ask of me, I will give *it* thee, unto the half
of my kingdom. 24 And she went forth,
and said unto her mother, What shall I
ask? And she said, The head of John the
Baptist. 25 And she came in straightway
with haste unto the king, and asked, saying, I will that thou give me by and by in
a charger the head of John the Baptist.
26 And the king was exceeding sorry; *yet*
for his oath's sake, and for their sakes
which sat with him, he would not reject
her. 27 And immediately the king sent an
executioner, and commanded his head to
be brought: and he went and beheaded
him in the prison, 28 and brought his
head in a charger, and gave it to the damsel; and the damsel gave it to her mother.
29 And when his disciples heard *of it,* they
came and took up his corpse, and laid it
in a tomb. ●

3.REST

30 And the apostles gathered themselves
together unto Jesus, and told him all
things, both what they had done, and
what they had taught. 31 And he said
unto them, Come ye yourselves apart into
a desert place, and rest a while: for there
were many coming and going, and they
had no leisure so much as to eat. 32 And
they departed into a desert place by ship
privately. ●

LONELY PLACE

*6:14-20* List the names of people of the paragraph, and what is said of each.

______________________________

*6:21-29* Record phrases of the paragraph which strike you.

______________________________

Compare verse 29 with verse 21. ______________________________

*6:30-32* What occupied the apostles' mind, as of verse 30?

______________________________

What was their need? ______________________________

NEW INTERNATIONAL VERSION

The tender heart of Jesus is clearly revealed here. Look for the different references to this tenderness, and record them:

What do you learn about:

POWER OF JESUS

COMPASSION OF JESUS

ORDERLINESS

FEAR

UNBELIEF

BELIEF

33But many who
saw them leaving recognized them and ran
on foot from all the towns and got there
ahead of them. 34When Jesus landed and
saw a large crowd, he had compassion on
them, because they were like sheep without a shepherd. So he began teaching them
many things.
35By this time it was late in the day, so
his disciples came to him. "This is a
remote place," they said, "and it's already
very late. 36Send the people away so they
can go to the surrounding countryside and
villages and buy themselves something to
eat."
37But he answered, "You give them
something to eat."
They said to him, "That would take eight
months of a man's wages[b]! Are we to go
and spend that much on bread and give it
to them to eat?"
38"How many loaves do you have?" he
asked. "Go and see."
When they found out, they said, "Five—
and two fish."
39Then Jesus directed them to have all
the people sit down in groups on the green
grass. 40So they sat down in groups of hundreds and fifties. 41Taking the five loaves
and the two fish and looking up to heaven,
he gave thanks and broke the loaves. Then
he gave them to his disciples to set before
the people. He also divided the two fish
among them all. 42They all ate and were
satisfied, 43and the disciples picked up
twelve basketfuls of broken pieces of
bread and fish. 44The number of the men
who had eaten was five thousand.●

*Jesus Walks on the Water*

45Immediately Jesus made his disciples
get into the boat and go on ahead of him to
Bethsaida, while he dismissed the crowd.
46After leaving them, he went into the hills
to pray.
47When evening came, the boat was in
the middle of the lake, and he was alone on
land. 48He saw the disciples straining at the
oars, because the wind was against them.
About the fourth watch of the night he
went out to them, walking on the lake. He
was about to pass by them, 49but when they
saw him walking on the lake, they thought
he was a ghost. They cried out, 50because
they all saw him and were terrified.
Immediately he spoke to them and said,
"Take courage! It is I. Don't be afraid."
51Then he climbed into the boat with them,
and the wind died down. They were completely amazed, 52for they had not understood about the loaves; their hearts were
hardened.●
53When they had crossed over, they
landed at Gennesaret and anchored there.
54As soon as they got out of the boat,
people recognized Jesus. 55They ran
throughout that whole region and carried
the sick on mats to wherever they heard he
was. 56And everywhere he went—into villages, towns or countryside—they placed
the sick in the marketplaces. They begged
him to let them touch even the edge of his
cloak, and all who touched him were
healed.●

[b]37 Greek *take two hundred denarii*

## KING JAMES

**1. NO FOOD**

—miracle of multiplication

33 And the people saw them
departing, and many knew him, and ran
afoot thither out of all cities, and outwent
them, and came together unto him.
34 And Jesus, when he came out, saw
much people, and was moved with compassion toward them, because they were
as sheep not having a shepherd: and he
began to teach them many things. 35 And
when the day was now far spent, his disciples came unto him, and said, This is a
desert place, and now the time *is* far
passed: 36 send them away, that they
may go into the country round about, and
into the villages, and buy themselves
bread: for they have nothing to eat.
37 He answered and said unto them, Give
ye them to eat. And they say unto him,
Shall we go and buy two hundred pennyworth of bread, and give them to eat?
38 He saith unto them, How many loaves
have ye? go and see. And when they
knew, they say, Five, and two fishes.
39 And he commanded them to make all
sit down by companies upon the green
grass. 40 And they sat down in ranks, by
hundreds, and by fifties. 41 And when he
had taken the five loaves and the two
fishes, he looked up to heaven, and
blessed, and brake the loaves, and gave
*them* to his disciples to set before them;
and the two fishes divided he among
them all. 42 And they did all eat, and
were filled. 43 And they took up twelve
baskets full of the fragments, and of the
fishes. 44 And they that did eat of
the loaves were about five thousand
men. ●

**2. STORM**

—miracle of subjugation

45 And straightway he constrained his
disciples to get into the ship, and to go to
the other side before unto Bethsai'da,
while he sent away the people. 46 And
when he had sent them away, he departed
into a mountain to pray. 47 And when
even was come, the ship was in the midst
of the sea, and he alone on the land.
48 And he saw them toiling in rowing;
for the wind was contrary unto them: and
about the fourth watch of the night he
cometh unto them, walking upon the sea,
and would have passed by them. 49 But
when they saw him walking upon the sea,
they supposed it had been a spirit, and
cried out: 50 for they all saw him, and
were troubled. And immediately he
talked with them, and saith unto them,
Be of good cheer: it is I; be not afraid.
51 And he went up unto them into the
ship; and the wind ceased: and they were
sore amazed in themselves beyond
measure, and wondered. 52 For they
considered not *the miracle* of the loaves;
for their heart was hardened. ●

**3. MIRACLE TOUCH**

—miracle of restoration

53 And when they had passed over,
they came into the land of Gennes'aret,
and drew to the shore. 54 And when they
were come out of the ship, straightway
they knew him, 55 and ran through that
whole region round about, and began to
carry about in beds those that were sick,
where they heard he was. 56 And whithersoever he entered, into villages, or cities,
or country, they laid the sick in the streets,
and besought him that they might touch
if it were but the border of his garment:
and as many as touched him were made
whole. ●

TEACHING MANY THINGS

HEALING MANY DISEASES

From this point on in Mark's gospel Jesus' ministry moves quickly to the peak and pivot point of 8:27-30.

Read this passage carefully and record what is taught about each of these subjects.

1) the disciples' needs ____________________

2) Jesus' training of the disciples ____________________

3) the multitude's needs ____________________

4) Jesus' ministry to the multitude ____________________

NEW INTERNATIONAL VERSION

What do you learn from this passage about:

WORSHIP

HEART

DEFILEMENT

HYPOCRISY

TRADITION OF MAN

WORD OF GOD

### *Clean and Unclean*

7 The Pharisees and some of the teachers
of the law who had come from Jerusalem gathered around Jesus and 2saw some
of his disciples eating food with "unclean"—that is, ceremonially unwashed—
hands. 3(The Pharisees and all the Jews do
not eat unless they give their hands a
ceremonial washing, holding to the tradition of the elders. 4When they come from
the marketplace they do not eat unless they
wash. And they observe many other traditions, such as the washing of cups, pitchers
and kettles.[a])
5So the Pharisees and teachers of the law
asked Jesus, "Why don't your disciples
live according to the tradition of the elders
instead of eating their food with 'unclean'
hands?"
6He replied, "Isaiah was right when he
prophesied about you hypocrites; as it is
written:

" 'These people honor me with their lips,
but their hearts are far from me.
7They worship me in vain;
their teachings are but rules taught by men.'[b]

8You have let go of the commands of God
and are holding on to the traditions of
men."
9And he said to them: "You have a fine
way of setting aside the commands of God
in order to observe[c] your own traditions!
10For Moses said, 'Honor your father and
mother,'[d] and, 'Anyone who curses his father or mother must be put to death.'[e]
11But you say that if a man says to his
father or mother: 'Whatever help you
might otherwise have received from me is
Corban' (that is, a gift devoted to God),
12then you no longer let him do anything for
his father or mother. 13Thus you nullify the
word of God by your tradition that you
have handed down. And you do many
things like that." ●
14Again Jesus called the crowd to him
and said, "Listen to me, everyone, and
understand this. 15Nothing outside a man
can make him 'unclean' by going into him.
Rather, it is what comes out of a man that
makes him 'unclean.'[f]"
17After he had left the crowd and entered
the house, his disciples asked him about
this parable. 18"Are you so dull?" he
asked. "Don't you see that nothing that
enters a man from the outside can make
him 'unclean'? 19For it doesn't go into his
heart but into his stomach, and then out of
his body." (In saying this, Jesus declared
all foods "clean.")
20He went on: "What comes out of a man
is what makes him 'unclean.' 21For from
within, out of men's hearts, come evil
thoughts, sexual immorality, theft, murder, adultery, 22greed, malice, deceit,
lewdness, envy, slander, arrogance and
folly. 23All these evils come from inside
and make a man 'unclean.' "

[a]4 Some early manuscripts *pitchers, kettles and dining couches*
[b]6,7 Isaiah 29:13
[c]9 Some manuscripts *set up*
[d]10 Exodus 20:12; Deut. 5:16
[e]10 Exodus 21:17; Lev. 20:9
[f]15 Some early manuscripts *'unclean.' 16If anyone has ears to hear, let him hear.*

KING JAMES

1. TRADITION

RELIGIOUS MEN

7 Then came together unto him the
Pharisees, and certain of the scribes,
which came from Jerusalem. 2 And when
they saw some of his disciples eat bread
with defiled, that is to say, with unwashen
hands, they found fault. 3 For the Pharisees,
and all the Jews, except they wash
*their* hands oft, eat not, holding the tradition
of the elders. 4 And *when they come*
from the market, except they wash, they
eat not. And many other things there be,
which they have received to hold, *as* the
washing of cups, and pots, brazen vessels,
and of tables. 5 Then the Pharisees and
scribes asked him, Why walk not thy disciples
according to the tradition of the
elders, but eat bread with unwashen
hands? 6 He answered and said unto
them, Well hath Isaiah prophesied of you
hypocrites, as it is written,

This people honoreth me with *their* lips,
but their heart is far from me. (Isa. 29:13)
7 Howbeit in vain do they worship me,
teaching *for* doctrines the commandments of men.

8 For laying aside the commandment of
God, ye hold the tradition of men, *as* the
washing of pots and cups: and many
other such like things ye do.
9 And he said unto them, Full well ye
reject the commandment of God, that ye
may keep your own tradition. 10 For
Moses said,

Honor thy father and thy mother; (Ex. 20:12)

and,

Whoso curseth father or mother,
let him die the death: (Ex. 21:17)

11 but ye say, If a man shall say to his
father or mother, *It is* Corban, that is to
say, a gift, by whatsoever thou mightest
be profited by me; *he shall be free.* 12 And
ye suffer him no more to do aught for his
father or his mother; 13 making the
word of God of none effect through your
tradition, which ye have delivered: and
many such like things do ye. ●

2. DEFILEMENT

14 And when he had called all the
people *unto him*, he said unto them,
Hearken unto me every one *of you*, and
understand: 15 there is nothing from
without a man, that entering into him can
defile him: but the things which come out
of him, those are they that defile the man.
16 If any man have ears to hear, let him
hear. 17 And when he was entered into
the house from the people, his disciples
asked him concerning the parable.
18 And he saith unto them, Are ye so
without understanding also? Do ye not
perceive, that whatsoever thing from
without entereth into the man, *it* cannot
defile him; 19 because it entereth not into
his heart, but into the belly, and goeth out
into the draught, purging all meats?
20 And he said, That which cometh out of
the man, that defileth the man. 21 For
from within, out of the heart of men, proceed
evil thoughts, adulteries, fornications,
murders, 22 thefts, covetousness, wickedness,
deceit, lasciviousness, an evil eye,
blasphemy, pride, foolishness: 23 all these
evil things come from within, and defile
the man. ●

A DEFILED MAN

Before analyzing this segment compare the two gatherings around Jesus described in 6:30 and 7:1:

*6:30* ______________________

*7:1* ______________________

In this discourse Jesus teaches much about the heart. Record your observations of this in the two paragraphs:

NEW INTERNATIONAL VERSION

What do you learn from this passage about purposes and procedures of Jesus' miracles?

Record things taught about Jesus' ministry.

What do you learn about FAITH in the passage?

Record other spiritual applications.

*The Faith of a Syrophoenician Woman*

24Jesus left that place and went to the
vicinity of Tyre.[g] He entered a house and
did not want anyone to know it; yet he
could not keep his presence secret. 25In
fact, as soon as she heard about him, a
woman whose little daughter was possessed by an evil[h] spirit came and fell at his
feet. 26The woman was a Greek, born in
Syrian Phoenicia. She begged Jesus to
drive the demon out of her daughter.
27"First let the children eat all they
want," he told her, "for it is not right to
take the children's bread and toss it to their
dogs."
28"Yes, Lord," she replied, "but even
the dogs under the table eat the children's
crumbs."
29Then he told her, "For such a reply,
you may go; the demon has left your
daughter."
30She went home and found her child
lying on the bed, and the demon gone.●

*The Healing of a Deaf and Dumb Man*

31Then Jesus left the vicinity of Tyre and
went through Sidon, down to the Sea of
Galilee and into the region of the Decapolis.[i] 32There some people brought a man to
him who was deaf and could hardly talk,
and they begged him to place his hand on
the man.
33After he took him aside, away from the
crowd, Jesus put his fingers into the man's
ears. Then he spit and touched the man's
tongue. 34He looked up to heaven and with
a deep sigh said to him, *"Ephphatha!"*
(which means, "Be opened!"). 35At this,
the man's ears were opened, his tongue
was loosened and he began to speak
plainly.
36Jesus commanded them not to tell anyone. But the more he did so, the more they
kept talking about it. 37People were overwhelmed with amazement. "He has done
everything well," they said. "He even
makes the deaf hear and the dumb speak."●

g24 Many early manuscripts *Tyre and Sidon*
h25 Greek *unclean* i31 That is, the Ten Cities

KING JAMES

1.A MOTHER INTERCEDES

DAUGHTER IN NEED

24 And from thence he arose, and went
into the borders of Tyre and Sidon, and
entered into a house, and would have no
man know *it*: but he could not be hid.
25 For a *certain* woman, whose young
daughter had an unclean spirit, heard of
him, and came and fell at his feet: 26 the
woman was a Greek, a Syrophoeni'cian
by nation; and she besought him that he
would cast forth the devil out of her
daughter. 27 But Jesus said unto her, Let
the children first be filled: for it is not
meet to take the children's bread, and to
cast *it* unto the dogs. 28 And she answered and said unto him, Yes, Lord: yet
the dogs under the table eat of the children's crumbs. 29 And he said unto her,
For this saying go thy way; the devil is
gone out of thy daughter. 30 And when
she was come to her house, she found the
devil gone out, and her daughter laid upon the bed. ●

2.FRIENDS INTERCEDE

MAN IN NEED

31 And again, departing from the
coasts of Tyre and Sidon, he came unto
the sea of Galilee, through the midst of
the coasts of Decap'olis. 32 And they
bring unto him one that was deaf, and
had an impediment in his speech; and
they beseech him to put his hand upon
him. 33 And he took him aside from the
multitude, and put his fingers into his
ears, and he spit, and touched his tongue;
34 and looking up to heaven, he sighed,
and saith unto him, Eph'phatha, that is,
Be opened. 35 And straightway his ears
were opened, and the string of his tongue
was loosed, and he spake plain. 36 And
he charged them that they should tell no
man: but the more he charged them, so
much the more a great deal they published *it*; 37 and were beyond measure
astonished, saying, He hath done all
things well: he maketh both the deaf to
hear, and the dumb to speak. ●

Observe the geography of both paragraphs.

What was significant about Jesus' ministering to Gentiles? (Cf. Matt. 15:21-24.)

*7:24-30* Why did Jesus heal the daughter?

*7:31-37* Decapolis was a region of Greek cities. Record the different steps of Jesus' healing.

What are your comments on verse 37?

NEW INTERNATIONAL VERSION

Record what you learn here about:

THE PURPOSE OF JESUS' MIRACLES

FAITH

THE MINISTRY OF JESUS

### *Jesus Feeds the Four Thousand*

8 During those days another large crowd
gathered. Since they had nothing to
eat, Jesus called his disciples to him and
said, 2"I have compassion for these
people; they have already been with me
three days and have nothing to eat. 3If I
send them home hungry, they will collapse
on the way, because some of them have
come a long distance."
4His disciples answered, "But where in
this remote place can anyone get enough
bread to feed them?"
5"How many loaves do you have?"
Jesus asked.
"Seven," they replied.
6He told the crowd to sit down on the
ground. When he had taken the seven
loaves and given thanks, he broke them
and gave them to his disciples to set before
the people, and they did so. 7They had a
few small fish as well; he gave thanks for
them also and told the disciples to distrib-
ute them. 8The people ate and were satisfied. Afterward the disciples picked up
seven basketfuls of broken pieces that
were left over. 9About four thousand men
were present. And having sent them away,
10he got into the boat with his disciples and
went to the region of Dalmanutha.●
11The Pharisees came and began to question Jesus. To test him, they asked him for
a sign from heaven. 12He sighed deeply and
said, "Why does this generation ask for a
miraculous sign? I tell you the truth, no
sign will be given to it." 13Then he left
them, got back into the boat and crossed to
the other side.●

### *The Yeast of the Pharisees and Herod*

14The disciples had forgotten to bring
bread, except for one loaf they had with
them in the boat. 15"Be careful," Jesus
warned them. "Watch out for the yeast of
the Pharisees and that of Herod."
16They discussed this with one another
and said, "It is because we have no
bread."
17Aware of their discussion, Jesus asked
them: "Why are you talking about having
no bread? Do you still not see or understand? Are your hearts hardened? 18Do you
have eyes but fail to see, and ears but fail
to hear? And don't you remember? 19When
I broke the five loaves for the five thousand, how many basketfuls of pieces did
you pick up?"
"Twelve," they replied.
20"And when I broke the seven loaves
for the four thousand, how many basketfuls of pieces did you pick up?"
They answered, "Seven."
21He said to them, "Do you still not understand?"●

### *The Healing of a Blind Man at Bethsaida*

22They came to Bethsaida, and some
people brought a blind man and begged
Jesus to touch him. 23He took the blind
man by the hand and led him outside the
village. When he had spit on the man's
eyes and put his hands on him, Jesus
asked, "Do you see anything?"
24He looked up and said, "I see people;
they look like trees walking around."
25Once more Jesus put his hands on the
man's eyes. Then his eyes were opened,
his sight was restored, and he saw everything clearly. 26Jesus sent him home, saying, "Don't go into the village.[a]"●

[a]26 Some manuscripts *Don't go and tell anyone in the village*

KING JAMES

1. MIRACLE OF FEEDING

GREAT MULTITUDE

8 In those days the multitude being very
great, and having nothing to eat,
Jesus called his disciples *unto him*, and
saith unto them, 2 I have compassion on
the multitude, because they have now been
with me three days, and have nothing to
eat: 3 and if I send them away fasting to
their own houses, they will faint by the
way: for divers of them came from far.
4 And his disciples answered him, From
whence can a man satisfy these *men* with
bread here in the wilderness? 5 And he
asked them, How many loaves have ye?
And they said, Seven. 6 And he commanded the people to sit down on the
ground: and he took the seven loaves, and
gave thanks, and brake, and gave to his
disciples to set before *them;* and they did
set *them* before the people. 7 And they
had a few small fishes: and he blessed, and
commanded to set them also before *them.*
8 So they did eat, and were filled: and
they took up of the broken *meat* that was
left seven baskets. 9 And they that had
eaten were about four thousand: and he
sent them away. 10 And straightway he
entered into a ship with his disciples,
and came into the parts of Dalmanu'-
tha. ●

—sign sought

—Pharisees

11 And the Pharisees came forth, and
began to question with him, seeking of
him a sign from heaven, tempting him.
12 And he sighed deeply in his spirit, and
saith, Why doth this generation seek after
a sign ? verily I say unto you, There shall
no sign be given unto this generation.
13 And he left them, and entering into
the ship again departed to the other
side. ●

—problem discussed

—disciples

14 Now *the disciples* had forgotten to
take bread, neither had they in the ship
with them more than one loaf. 15 And he
charged them, saying, Take heed, beware
of the leaven of the Pharisees, and *of* the
leaven of Herod. 16 And they reasoned
among themselves, saying, *It is* because
we have no bread. 17 And when Jesus
knew *it*, he saith unto them, Why reason
ye, because ye have no bread? perceive ye
not yet, neither understand? have ye your
heart yet hardened? 18 Having eyes, see
ye not? and having ears, hear ye not?
and do ye not remember? 19 When I
brake the five loaves among five thousand, how many baskets full of fragments
took ye up? They say unto him, Twelve.
20 And when the seven among four thousand, how many baskets full of fragments
took ye up? And they said, Seven.
21 And he said unto them, How is it that
ye do not understand? ●

2. MIRACLE OF HEALING

22 And he cometh to Bethsai'da; and
they bring a blind man unto him, and besought him to touch him. 23 And he took
the blind man by the hand, and led him
out of the town; and when he had spit on
his eyes, and put his hands upon him, he
asked him if he saw aught. 24 And he
looked up, and said, I see men as trees,
walking. 25 After that he put *his* hands
again upon his eyes, and made him look
up; and he was restored, and saw every
man clearly. 26 And he sent him away
to his house, saying, Neither go into
the town, nor tell *it* to any in the
town. ●

BLIND MAN

Observe the content of the two paragraphs located between those of the miracles. How does 8:11-13 relate to the first paragraph?

______________________________

______________________________

______________________________

______________________________

______________________________

______________________________

How does 8:14-21 relate to the first paragraph? The key verse for answering this is 8:21.

______________________________

______________________________

______________________________

______________________________

______________________________

*8:1-10* Record the various actions of Jesus.

______________________________

______________________________

______________________________

______________________________

______________________________

*8:11-13* The Pharisees sought "a sign from heaven." What do you think they had in mind?

______________________________

______________________________

______________________________

*8:14-21* Relate verse 15 to the other verses.

______________________________

______________________________

______________________________

______________________________

*8:22-26* What impresses you here? ______________________________

______________________________

______________________________

______________________________

______________________________

NEW INTERNATIONAL VERSION

There are many key spiritual truths taught in this passage.
Record what you see.

WHO JESUS IS

WHAT JESUS CAME TO DO

TRUE DISCIPLESHIP

What spiritual lessons does the passage teach?

### *Peter's Confession of Christ*

27 Jesus and his disciples went on to the
villages around Caesarea Philippi. On the
way he asked them, "Who do people say
I am?"
28 They replied, "Some say John the Baptist; others say Elijah; and still others, one
of the prophets."
29 "But what about you?" he asked.
"Who do you say I am?"
Peter answered, "You are the Christ.[b]"
30 Jesus warned them not to tell anyone
about him.●

### *Jesus Predicts His Death*

31 He then began to teach them that the
Son of Man must suffer many things and be
rejected by the elders, chief priests and
teachers of the law, and that he must be
killed and after three days rise again. 32 He
spoke plainly about this, and Peter took
him aside and began to rebuke him.
33 But when Jesus turned and looked at
his disciples, he rebuked Peter. "Out of my
sight, Satan!" he said. "You do not have
in mind the things of God, but the things of
men."●
34 Then he called the crowd to him along
with his disciples and said: "If anyone
would come after me, he must deny himself and take up his cross and follow me.
35 For whoever wants to save his life[a] will
lose it, but whoever loses his life for me
and for the gospel will save it. 36 What good
is it for a man to gain the whole world, yet
forfeit his soul? 37 Or what can a man give
in exchange for his soul? 38 If anyone is
ashamed of me and my words in this adulterous and sinful generation, the Son of
Man will be ashamed of him when he
comes in his Father's glory with the holy
angels."●
9 And he said to them, "I tell you the
truth, some who are standing here will
not taste death before they see the kingdom of God come with power."●

[b]29 Or *Messiah*. "The Christ" (Greek) and "the Messiah" (Hebrew) both mean "the Anointed One."
[a]35 The Greek word means either *life* or *soul*; also in verse 36.

KING JAMES

1.PERSON OF CHRIST

27 And Jesus went out, and his disciples, into the towns of Caesare'a Phil'-
ippi: and by the way he asked his disciples, saying unto them, Whom do men
say that I am? 28 And they answered,
John the Baptist: but some *say*, Eli'jah;
and others, One of the prophets. 29 And
he saith unto them, But whom say ye that
I am? And Peter answereth and saith unto him, Thou art the Christ. 30 And he
charged them that they should tell no
man of him. ●

THE CHRIST

2.WORK OF CHRIST

31 And he began to teach them, that the
Son of man must suffer many things, and
be rejected of the elders, and *of* the chief
priests, and scribes, and be killed, and
after three days rise again. 32 And he
spake that saying openly. And Peter took
him, and began to rebuke him. 33 But
when he had turned about and looked on
his disciples, he rebuked Peter, saying,
Get thee behind me, Satan: for thou
savorest not the things that be of God,
but the things that be of men. ●

3.FOLLOWERS OF CHRIST

34 And when he had called the people
*unto him* with his disciples also, he said
unto them, Whosoever will come after me,
let him deny himself, and take up his
cross, and follow me. 35 For whosoever
will save his life shall lose it; but whosoever shall lose his life for my sake and the
gospel's, the same shall save it. 36 For
what shall it profit a man, if he shall gain
the whole world, and lose his own soul?
37 Or what shall a man give in exchange
for his soul? 38 Whosoever therefore
shall be ashamed of me and of my words,
in this adulterous and sinful generation,
of him also shall the Son of man be
ashamed, when he cometh in the glory of
his Father with the holy angels. ●

4.KINGDOM OF GOD

9 1 And
he said unto them, Verily I say unto
you, That there be some of them that
stand here, which shall not taste of death,
till they have seen the kingdom of God
come with power. ●

THE KINGDOM

*8:27-30* This first paragraph is the pivotal point of Mark's gospel. Up to this point Jesus has been ministering in public to show the people WHO HE WAS. Now He asks the key question. What is it?

What was Peter's answer?

*8:31-33* Then Jesus began to reveal new things to His disciples. What was that?

Account for Peter's reaction.

*8:34-38* Relate this paragraph to the one preceding it.

*9:1* What do you think Jesus was referring to here?

NEW INTERNATIONAL VERSION

Record what the passage teaches about:

JESUS

PROPHETS

JOHN THE BAPTIST

RESURRECTION OF CHRIST

*The Transfiguration*

2After six days Jesus took Peter, James
and John with him and led them up a high
mountain, where they were all alone.
There he was transfigured before them.
3His clothes became dazzling white, whiter
than anyone in the world could bleach
them. 4And there appeared before them
Elijah and Moses, who were talking with
Jesus.
5Peter said to Jesus, "Rabbi, it is good
for us to be here. Let us put up three shelters—one for you, one for Moses and one
for Elijah." 6(He did not know what to say,
they were so frightened.)
7Then a cloud appeared and enveloped
them, and a voice came from the cloud:
"This is my Son, whom I love. Listen to
him!"
8Suddenly, when they looked around,
they no longer saw anyone with them except Jesus.●
9As they were coming down the mountain, Jesus gave them orders not to tell
anyone what they had seen until the Son of
Man had risen from the dead. 10They kept
the matter to themselves, discussing what
"rising from the dead" meant.
11And they asked him, "Why do the
teachers of the law say that Elijah must
come first?"
12Jesus replied, "To be sure, Elijah does
come first, and restores all things. Why
then is it written that the Son of Man must
suffer much and be rejected? 13But I tell
you, Elijah has come, and they have done
to him everything they wished, just as it is
written about him."●

## KING JAMES

**1. JESUS TRANSFIGURED**

2 And after six days Jesus taketh *with*
*him* Peter, and James, and John, and
leadeth them up into a high mountain
apart by themselves: and he was transfigured before them. 3 And his raiment
became shining, exceeding white as snow;
so as no fuller on earth can white them.
4 And there appeared unto them Eli'jah
with Moses: and they were talking with
Jesus. 5 And Peter answered and said to
Jesus, Master, it is good for us to be here:
and let us make three tabernacles; one for
thee, and one for Moses, and one for
Eli'jah. 6 For he wist not what to say;
for they were sore afraid. 7 And there
was a cloud that overshadowed them: and
a voice came out of the cloud, saying,
This is my beloved Son: hear him.
8 And suddenly, when they had looked
round about, they saw no man any more,
save Jesus only with themselves. ●

**2. ELIJAH HAD COME EARLIER**

9 And as they came down from the
mountain, he charged them that they
should tell no man what things they had
seen, till the Son of man were risen from
the dead. 10 And they kept that saying
with themselves, questioning one with
another what the rising from the dead
should mean. 11 And they asked him,
saying, Why say the scribes that Eli'jah
must first come? 12 And he answered
and told them, Eli'jah verily cometh first,
and restoreth all things; and how it is
written of the Son of man, that he must
suffer many things, and be set at nought.
13 But I say unto you, That Eli'jah is
indeed come, and they have done unto
him whatsoever they listed, as it is written
of him. ●

MOUNTAIN

VALLEY

Read 9:1 as the setting, six days earlier, of the story of this segment.

*9:2-8* Who were conversing with Jesus on the mountain?

____________________

____________________

____________________

Record the different things that happened then.

v.5 ____________________

v.6 ____________________

v.7 ____________________

v.8 ____________________

*9:9-13* What is the main point of verses 9-10?

____________________

What is the main point of verses 11-13?

____________________

How are the above two points related?

____________________

NEW INTERNATIONAL VERSION

Record what you learn here about:

DEMONISM

FAITH

PRAYER

DOUBT

List other spiritual applications which can be made from the passage:

### *The Healing of a Boy With an Evil Spirit*

14When they came to the other disciples,
they saw a large crowd around them and
the teachers of the law arguing with them.
15As soon as all the people saw Jesus, they
were overwhelmed with wonder and ran to
greet him.
16"What are you arguing with them
about?" he asked.
17A man in the crowd answered,
"Teacher, I brought you my son, who is
possessed by a spirit that has robbed him
of speech. 18Whenever it seizes him, it
throws him to the ground. He foams at the
mouth, gnashes his teeth and becomes rig-
id. I asked your disciples to drive out the
spirit, but they could not."
19"O unbelieving generation," Jesus replied, "how long shall I stay with you?
How long shall I put up with you? Bring the
boy to me."
20So they brought him. When the spirit
saw Jesus, it immediately threw the boy
into a convulsion. He fell to the ground and
rolled around, foaming at the mouth.
21Jesus asked the boy's father, "How
long has he been like this?"
"From childhood," he answered. 22"It
has often thrown him into fire or water to
kill him. But if you can do anything, take
pity on us and help us."
23" 'If you can'?" said Jesus. "Everything is possible for him who believes."
24Immediately the boy's father exclaimed, "I do believe; help me overcome
my unbelief!"●
25When Jesus saw that a crowd was running to the scene, he rebuked the evil[b]
spirit. "You deaf and dumb spirit," he
said, "I command you, come out of him
and never enter him again."
26The spirit shrieked, convulsed him violently and came out. The boy looked so
much like a corpse that many said, "He's
dead." 27But Jesus took him by the hand
and lifted him to his feet, and he stood up.●
28After Jesus had gone indoors, his disciples asked him privately, "Why couldn't
we drive it out?"
29He replied, "This kind can come out
only by prayer.[c]"●
30They left that place and passed through
Galilee. Jesus did not want anyone to know
where they were, 31because he was teaching his disciples. He said to them, "The
Son of Man is going to be betrayed into the
hands of men. They will kill him, and after
three days he will rise." 32But they did not
understand what he meant and were afraid
to ask him about it.●

[b]25 Greek *unclean*
[c]29 Some manuscripts *prayer and fasting*

KING JAMES

1. DEMON-POSSESSED BOY

14 And when he came to *his* disciples,
he saw a great multitude about them, and
the scribes questioning with them. 15 And
straightway all the people, when they beheld him, were greatly amazed, and running to *him* saluted him. 16 And he asked
the scribes, What question ye with them?
17 And one of the multitude answered
and said, Master, I have brought unto
thee my son, which hath a dumb spirit;
18 and wheresoever he taketh him, he
teareth him; and he foameth, and gnash-
eth with his teeth, and pineth away: and I
spake to thy disciples that they should cast
him out; and they could not. 19 He answereth him, and saith, O faithless generation, how long shall I be with you?
how long shall I suffer you? bring him
unto me. 20 And they brought him unto
him: and when he saw him, straightway
the spirit tare him; and he fell on the
ground, and wallowed foaming. 21 And
he asked his father, How long is it ago
since this came unto him? And he said,
Of a child. 22 And ofttimes it hath cast
him into the fire, and into the waters, to
destroy him: but if thou canst do any
thing, have compassion on us, and help us.
23 Jesus said unto him, If thou canst believe, all things *are* possible to him that
believeth. 24 And straightway the father
of the child cried out, and said with tears,
Lord, I believe; help thou mine unbelief. ●

2. DELIVERANCE

25 When Jesus saw that the people came
running together, he rebuked the foul
spirit, saying unto him, *Thou* dumb and
deaf spirit, I charge thee, come out of him,
and enter no more into him. 26 And *the*
*spirit* cried, and rent him sore, and came
out of him: and he was as one dead; insomuch that many said, He is dead. 27 But
Jesus took him by the hand, and lifted him
up; and he arose. ●

3. DISCIPLES' QUESTION

28 And when he was
come into the house, his disciples asked
him privately, Why could not we cast him
out? 29 And he said unto them, This kind
can come forth by nothing, but by prayer
and fasting. ●

4. JESUS PROPHESIES AGAIN

30 And they departed thence, and
passed through Galilee; and he would not
that any man should know *it*. 31 For he
taught his disciples, and said unto them,
The Son of man is delivered into the
hands of men, and they shall kill him; and
after that he is killed, he shall rise the
third day. 32 But they understood not
that saying, and were afraid to ask him. ●

POWER OF SATAN TO POSSESS

POWER OF GOD TO RESURRECT

These are the times in Jesus' public ministry when He was pressing the claim that He was truly the Messiah (cf. 8:29). After performing a miracle, He would often repeat the prophecy about His coming death and resurrection. See the last paragraph (9:30-32).

*9:14-24* What are the main parts of this story?

*9:25-27* What are your impressions?

*9:28-29* What is the implication of Jesus' answer?

*9:30-32* Your observations: ______

NEW INTERNATIONAL VERSION

What does this passage teach about:

TRUE GREATNESS

HUMILITY

CHILDREN

CHRISTIAN UNITY

HINDRANCES TO SPIRITUAL VITALITY

What are the spiritual lessons taught by "salt" in 9:49-50?

*Who Is the Greatest?*

[33]They came to Capernaum. When he
was in the house, he asked them, "What
were you arguing about on the road?"
[34]But they kept quiet because on the way
they had argued about who was the greatest.
[35]Sitting down, Jesus called the Twelve
and said, "If anyone wants to be first, he
must be the very last, and the servant of
all."
[36]He took a little child and had him stand
among them. Taking him in his arms, he
said to them, [37]"Whoever welcomes one of
these little children in my name welcomes
me; and whoever welcomes me does not
welcome me but the one who sent me."●

*Whoever Is Not Against Us Is for Us*

[38]"Teacher," said John, "we saw a man
driving out demons in your name and we
told him to stop, because he was not one of
us."
[39]"Do not stop him," Jesus said. "No
one who does a miracle in my name can in
the next moment say anything bad about
me, [40]for whoever is not against us is for
us. [41]I tell you the truth, anyone who gives
you a cup of water in my name because you
belong to Christ will certainly not lose his
reward.●

*Causing to Sin*

[42]"And if anyone causes one of these
little ones who believe in me to sin, it
would be better for him to be thrown into
the sea with a large millstone tied around
his neck. [43]If your hand causes you to sin,
cut it off. It is better for you to enter life
maimed than with two hands to go into
hell, where the fire never goes out.[a] [45]And
if your foot causes you to sin, cut it off. It
is better for you to enter life crippled than
to have two feet and be thrown into hell.[b]
[47]And if your eye causes you to sin, pluck
it out. It is better for you to enter the kingdom of God with one eye than to have two
eyes and be thrown into hell, [48]where

"'their worm does not die,
and the fire is not quenched.'[c]

[49]Everyone will be salted with fire.
[50]"Salt is good, but if it loses its saltiness, how can you make it salty again?
Have salt in yourselves, and be at peace
with each other."●

a43 Some manuscripts *out,* [44]*where / 'their worm does not die, / and the fire is not quenched'*
b45 Some manuscripts *hell,* [46]*where / 'their worm does not die, / and the fire is not quenched'*
c48 Isaiah 66:24

KING JAMES

1.GREAT-NESS

DISPUTE

33 And he came to Caper'na-um: and
being in the house he asked them, What
was it that ye disputed among yourselves
by the way? 34 But they held their peace:
for by the way they had disputed among
themselves, who *should be* the greatest.
35 And he sat down, and called the twelve,
and saith unto them, If any man desire to
be first, *the same* shall be last of all, and
servant of all. 36 And he took a child,
and set him in the midst of them: and
when he had taken him in his arms, he
said unto them, 37 Whosoever shall receive one of such children in my name,
receiveth me; and whosoever shall receive
me, receiveth not me, but him that sent
me. ●

2.UNITY

38 And John answered him, saying,
Master, we saw one casting out devils in
thy name, and he followeth not us; and
we forbade him, because he followeth not
us. 39 But Jesus said, Forbid him not: for
there is no man which shall do a miracle
in my name, that can lightly speak evil
of me. 40 For he that is not against us is
on our part. 41 For whosoever shall
give you a cup of water to drink in my
name, because ye belong to Christ, verily I
say unto you, he shall not lose his reward. ●

3.STUM-BLING BLOCKS

42 And whosoever shall offend one of
*these* little ones that believe in me, it is
better for him that a millstone were hanged
about his neck, and he were cast into the
sea. 43 And if thy hand offend thee, cut
it off: it is better for thee to enter into life
maimed, than having two hands to go into
hell, into the fire that never shall be
quenched: 44 where their worm dieth
not, and the fire is not quenched. 45 And
if thy foot offend thee, cut it off: it is
better for thee to enter halt into life, than
having two feet to be cast into hell, into
the fire that never shall be quenched:
46 where their worm dieth not, and the
fire is not quenched. 47 And if thine eye
offend thee, pluck it out: it is better for
thee to enter into the kingdom of God
with one eye, than having two eyes to be
cast into hell fire: 48 where their worm
dieth not, and the fire is not quenched.
49 For every one shall be salted with fire,
and every sacrifice shall be salted with
salt. 50 Salt *is* good: but if the salt have
lost his saltness, wherewith will ye season
it? Have salt in yourselves, and have
peace one with another. ●

PEACE

Jesus spent no little time training His disciples to be good followers of His, setting good examples for true righteousness. This segment reveals some of those things He was teaching.

*9:33-37* What recent event may have brought on the dispute reported here?

What was Jesus' method of correcting His disciples?

*9:38-41* Record important truths Jesus taught here.

*9:42-50* What are the key repeated words and phrases of the paragraph?

Compare "peace" of 9:50 with the dispute of 9:34.

NEW INTERNATIONAL VERSION

What does Jesus teach here about:

DIVORCE

ADULTERY

HUMILITY

CHILDREN

KINGDOM OF GOD

OTHER

*Divorce*

10 Jesus then left that place and went
into the region of Judea and across
the Jordan. Again crowds of people came
to him, and as was his custom, he taught
them.●
[2]Some Pharisees came and tested him by
asking, "Is it lawful for a man to divorce
his wife?"
[3]"What did Moses command you?" he
replied.
[4]They said, "Moses permitted a man to
write a certificate of divorce and send her
away."
[5]"It was because your hearts were hard
that Moses wrote you this law," Jesus replied. [6]"But at the beginning of creation
God 'made them male and female.'[d] [7]'For
this reason a man will leave his father and
mother and be united to his wife,[e] [8]and the
two will become one flesh.'[f] So they are no
longer two, but one. [9]Therefore what God
has joined together, let man not separate."●
[10]When they were in the house again, the
disciples asked Jesus about this. [11]He answered, "Anyone who divorces his wife
and marries another woman commits adultery against her. [12]And if she divorces her
husband and marries another man, she
commits adultery."●

*The Little Children and Jesus*

[13]People were bringing little children to
Jesus to have him touch them, but the disciples rebuked them. [14]When Jesus saw
this, he was indignant. He said to them,
"Let the little children come to me, and do
not hinder them, for the kingdom of God
belongs to such as these. [15]I tell you the
truth, anyone who will not receive the
kingdom of God like a little child will never
enter it." [16]And he took the children in his
arms, put his hands on them and blessed
them.●

*d6* Gen. 1:27
*e7* Some early manuscripts do not have *and be united to his wife.*
*f8* Gen. 2:24

## KING JAMES

ADULTS

**10** And he arose from thence, and cometh into the coasts of Judea by the
farther side of Jordan: and the people
resort unto him again; and, as he was
wont, he taught them again. ●

1. DIVORCE

2 And the Pharisees came to him, and
asked him, Is it lawful for a man to put
away *his* wife? tempting him. 3 And he
answered and said unto them, What did
Moses command you? 4 And they said,
Moses suffered to write a bill of divorcement, and to put *her* away. 5 And Jesus
answered and said unto them, For the
hardness of your heart he wrote you this
precept. 6 But from the beginning of the
creation God made them male and female. 7 For this cause shall a man leave
his father and mother, and cleave to his
wife; 8 and they twain shall be one flesh:
so then they are no more twain, but one
flesh. 9 What therefore God hath joined
together, let not man put asunder. ●

Deu. 24:1,3

2. THEN REMARRIAGE

10 And in the house his disciples asked
him again of the same *matter*. 11 And he
saith unto them, Whosoever shall put
away his wife, and marry another, committeth adultery against her. 12 And if a
woman shall put away her husband, and
be married to another, she committeth
adultery. ●

3. CHILDREN

13 And they brought young children to
him, that he should touch them; and *his*
disciples rebuked those that brought *them*.
14 But when Jesus saw *it*, he was much
displeased, and said unto them, Suffer the
little children to come unto me, and forbid
them not; for of such is the kingdom of
God. 15 Verily I say unto you, Whosoever shall not receive the kingdom of God
as a little child, he shall not enter therein.
16 And he took them up in his arms, put
*his* hands upon them, and blessed them. ●

CHILDREN

*10:1* How does verse 1 report Jesus' teaching ministry at this time?

Whom is Jesus teaching in each of the paragraphs?

*10:2-9* What was the Pharisees' question?

What was Jesus' answer?

*10:10-12* Why did the disciples still have a question in their mind?

*10:13-16* Account for the disciples' action of verse 13.

Compare Jesus and the disciples here.

NEW INTERNATIONAL VERSION

What does Jesus teach here about:

HOW TO BE SAVED

LAW OF GOD

WEALTH

KINGDOM OF GOD

POWER OF GOD

DISCIPLESHIP

REWARDS

*The Rich Young Man*

17 As Jesus started on his way, a man ran
up to him and fell on his knees before him.
"Good teacher," he asked, "what must I
do to inherit eternal life?"
18 "Why do you call me good?" Jesus
answered. "No one is good—except God
alone. 19 You know the commandments:
'Do not murder, do not commit adultery,
do not steal, do not give false testimony, do
not defraud, honor your father and
mother.'[g]"
20 "Teacher," he declared, "all these I
have kept since I was a boy."
21 Jesus looked at him and loved him.
"One thing you lack," he said. "Go, sell
everything you have and give to the poor,
and you will have treasure in heaven. Then
come, follow me."
22 At this the man's face fell. He went
away sad, because he had great wealth.
23 Jesus looked around and said to his
disciples, "How hard it is for the rich to
enter the kingdom of God!"
24 The disciples were amazed at his
words. But Jesus said again, "Children,
how hard it is[a] to enter the kingdom of
God! 25 It is easier for a camel to go through
the eye of a needle than for a rich man to
enter the kingdom of God."
26 The disciples were even more amazed,
and said to each other, "Who then can be
saved?"
27 Jesus looked at them and said, "With
man this is impossible, but not with God;
all things are possible with God."
28 Peter said to him, "We have left everything to follow you!"
29 "I tell you the truth," Jesus replied,
"no one who has left home or brothers or
sisters or mother or father or children or
fields for me and the gospel 30 will fail to
receive a hundred times as much in this
present age (homes, brothers, sisters,
mothers, children and fields—and with
them, persecutions) and in the age to
come, eternal life. 31 But many who are first
will be last, and the last first."

g 19 Exodus 20:12-16; Deut. 5:16-20

a 24 Some manuscripts *is for those who trust in riches*

KING JAMES

1. ETERNAL LIFE

17 And when he was gone forth into the
way, there came one running, and kneeled
to him, and asked him, Good Master,
what shall I do that I may inherit eternal
life? 18 And Jesus said unto him, Why
callest thou me good? *there is* none good
but one, *that is*, God. 19 Thou knowest
the commandments, Do not commit
adultery, Do not kill, Do not steal
Do not bear false witness, Defraud not,
Honor thy father and mother 20 And he
answered and said unto him, Master, all
these have I observed from my youth.
21 Then Jesus beholding him loved him,
and said unto him, One thing thou lackest:
go thy way, sell whatsoever thou hast, and
give to the poor, and thou shalt have
treasure in heaven: and come, take up the
cross, and follow me. 22 And he was sad
at that saying, and went away grieved: for
he had great possessions. ●

2. WEALTH

23 And Jesus looked round about, and
saith unto his disciples, How hardly shall
they that have riches enter into the kingdom of God! 24 And the disciples were
astonished at his words. But Jesus answereth again, and saith unto them,
Children, how hard is it for them that
trust in riches to enter into the kingdom
of God! 25 It is easier for a camel to go
through the eye of a needle, than for a
rich man to enter into the kingdom of
God. 26 And they were astonished out of
measure, saying among themselves, Who
then can be saved? 27 And Jesus looking
upon them saith, With men *it is* impossible, but not with God: for with God all
things are possible. ●

3. DISCIPLESHIP

28 Then Peter began
to say unto him, Lo, we have left all, and
have followed thee. 29 And Jesus answered and said, Verily I say unto you,
There is no man that hath left house, or
brethren, or sisters, or father, or mother,
or wife, or children, or lands, for my sake,
and the gospel's, 30 but he shall receive a
hundredfold now in this time, houses, and
brethren, and sisters, and mothers, and
children, and lands, with persecutions;
and in the world to come eternal life.
31 But many *that are* first shall be last;
and the last first. ●

ETERNITY

NOW

First observe Jesus' reference to the life hereafter, in each of the paragraphs. Note the repeated phrase "kingdom of God" in the second paragraph. What is the *time scope* of this kingdom?

For each of the paragraphs, record the questions (stated or implied) and Jesus' answers.

*10:17-22*

QUESTION

ANSWER

*10:23-27*

QUESTION

ANSWER

*10:28-31*

QUESTION

ANSWER

NEW INTERNATIONAL VERSION

Study the whole passage in light of the truths of verses 39b and 45. The believer is identified with Christ (39b), and Christ came to serve and to die (45). So what does this mean for the believer, in a practical way?

Record what the passage teaches about:

PRIDE

HONOR

*Jesus Again Predicts His Death*

32 They were on their way up to Jerusalem, with Jesus leading the way, and the
disciples were astonished, while those who
followed were afraid. Again he took the
Twelve aside and told them what was going
to happen to him. 33 "We are going up to
Jerusalem," he said, "and the Son of Man
will be betrayed to the chief priests and
teachers of the law. They will condemn
him to death and will hand him over to the
Gentiles, 34 who will mock him and spit on
him, flog him and kill him. Three days later
he will rise." ●

*The Request of James and John*

35 Then James and John, the sons of Zebedee, came to him. "Teacher," they said,
"we want you to do for us whatever we
ask."
36 "What do you want me to do for you?"
he asked.
37 They replied, "Let one of us sit at your
right and the other at your left in your
glory."
38 "You don't know what you are asking," Jesus said. "Can you drink the cup
I drink or be baptized with the baptism I
am baptized with?"
39 "We can," they answered.
Jesus said to them, "You will drink the
cup I drink and be baptized with the
baptism I am baptized with, 40 but to sit at
my right or left is not for me to grant. These
places belong to those for whom they have
been prepared." ●
41 When the ten heard about this, they
became indignant with James and John.
42 Jesus called them together and said,
"You know that those who are regarded as
rulers of the Gentiles lord it over them, and
their high officials exercise authority over
them. 43 Not so with you. Instead, whoever
wants to become great among you must be
your servant, 44 and whoever wants to be
first must be slave of all. 45 For even the
Son of Man did not come to be served, but
to serve, and to give his life as a ransom for
many." ●

*Blind Bartimaeus Receives His Sight*

46 Then they came to Jericho. As Jesus
and his disciples, together with a large
crowd, were leaving the city, a blind man,
Bartimaeus (that is, the Son of Timaeus),
was sitting by the roadside begging.
47 When he heard that it was Jesus of
Nazareth, he began to shout, "Jesus, Son
of David, have mercy on me!"
48 Many rebuked him and told him to be
quiet, but he shouted all the more, "Son of
David, have mercy on me!"
49 Jesus stopped and said, "Call him."
So they called to the blind man, "Cheer
up! On your feet! He's calling you."
50 Throwing his cloak aside, he jumped to
his feet and came to Jesus.
51 "What do you want me to do for you?"
Jesus asked him.
The blind man said, "Rabbi, I want to
see."
52 "Go," said Jesus, "your faith has
healed you." Immediately he received his
sight and followed Jesus along the road. ●

KING JAMES

1.DEATH PREDICTED

32 And they were in the way going up
to Jerusalem; and Jesus went before them:
and they were amazed; and as they followed, they were afraid. And he took
again the twelve, and began to tell them
what things should happen unto him,
33 *saying*, Behold, we go up to Jerusalem; and the Son of man shall be delivered unto the chief priests, and unto the
scribes; and they shall condemn him to
death, and shall deliver him to the Gentiles: 34 and they shall mock him, and
shall scourge him, and shall spit upon him,
and shall kill him; and the third day he
shall rise again. ●

2.LUST FOR HONOR

35 And James and John, the sons of
Zeb'edee, come unto him, saying, Master,
we would that thou shouldest do for us
whatsoever we shall desire. 36 And he
said unto them, What would ye that I
should do for you? 37 They said unto
him, Grant unto us that we may sit, one
on thy right hand, and the other on thy
left hand, in thy glory. 38 But Jesus said
unto them, Ye know not what ye ask: can
ye drink of the cup that I drink of? and be
baptized with the baptism that I am baptized with ? 39 And they said unto him,
We can. And Jesus said unto them, Ye
shall indeed drink of the cup that I drink
of; and with the baptism that I am baptized withal shall ye be baptized: 40 but
to sit on my right hand and on my left
hand is not mine to give; but *it shall be*
*given to them* for whom it is prepared.●

3.TRUE GREATNESS

41 And when the ten heard *it*, they began
to be much displeased with James and
John. 42 But Jesus called them *to him*,
and saith unto them, Ye know that they
which are accounted to rule over the
Gentiles exercise lordship over them; and
their great ones exercise authority upon
them. 43 But so shall it not be among
you: but whosoever will be great among
you, shall be your minister: 44 and whosoever of you will be the chiefest, shall be
servant of all. 45 For even the Son of
man came not to be ministered unto, but
to minister, and to give his life a ransom
for many. ●

4.SIGHT RESTORED

46 And they came to Jericho: and as he
went out of Jericho with his disciples and
a great number of people, blind Barti-
me'us, the son of Time'us, sat by the high-
way side begging. 47 And when he heard
that it was Jesus of Nazareth, he began to
cry out, and say, Jesus, *thou* Son of David,
have mercy on me. 48 And many charged
him that he should hold his peace: but he
cried the more a great deal, *Thou* Son of
David, have mercy on me. 49 And Jesus
stood still, and commanded him to be
called. And they call the blind man, saying unto him, Be of good comfort, rise;
he calleth thee. 50 And he, casting away
his garment, rose, and came to Jesus.
51 And Jesus answered and said unto him,
What wilt thou that I should do unto
thee? The blind man said unto him,
Lord, that I might receive my sight.
52 And Jesus said unto him, Go thy way;
thy faith hath made thee whole. And immediately he received his sight, and followed Jesus in the way.●

OMNISCIENCE

OMNIPOTENCE

A key verse for the gospel of Mark is 10:45. Study the verse especially in the context of the segment. Record the things of each paragraph related to the truths of the verse.

*10:32-34* ______

*10:35-40* ______

*10:41-45* ______

*10:46-52* ______

NEW INTERNATIONAL VERSION

Record things you learn here about:

THE PERSON OF JESUS

THE MINISTRY OF JESUS

THE AUTHORITY OF JESUS

PEOPLE'S HEARTS

(Note concerning the fig tree: The season was too early for fruit, but this tree showed evidence that it should have fruit on it, because it was in full leaf, which was the fruit indicator.)

*The Triumphal Entry*

11 As they approached Jerusalem and
came to Bethphage and Bethany at
the Mount of Olives, Jesus sent two of his
disciples, 2saying to them, "Go to the village ahead of you, and just as you enter it,
you will find a colt tied there, which no one
has ever ridden. Untie it and bring it here.
3If anyone asks you, 'Why are you doing
this?' tell him, 'The Lord needs it and will
send it back here shortly.' "
4They went and found a colt outside in
the street, tied at a doorway. As they untied it, 5some people standing there asked,
"What are you doing, untying that colt?"
6They answered as Jesus had told them to,
and the people let them go. 7When they
brought the colt to Jesus and threw their
cloaks over it, he sat on it. 8Many people
spread their cloaks on the road, while
others spread branches they had cut in the
fields. 9Those who went ahead and those
who followed shouted,

"Hosanna![a]"

"Blessed is he who comes in the
name of the Lord!"[b]

10"Blessed is the coming kingdom of
our father David!"

"Hosanna in the highest!"●

11Jesus entered Jerusalem and went to
the temple. He looked around at everything, but since it was already late, he went
out to Bethany with the Twelve.●

*Jesus Clears the Temple*

12The next day as they were leaving
Bethany, Jesus was hungry. 13Seeing in the
distance a fig tree in leaf, he went to find
out if it had any fruit. When he reached it,
he found nothing but leaves, because it was
not the season for figs. 14Then he said to
the tree, "May no one ever eat fruit from
you again." And his disciples heard him
say it.●

[a]9 A Hebrew expression meaning "Save!" which became an exclamation of praise; also in verse 10
[b]9 Psalm 118:25,26

KING JAMES

1.APPROACHING JERUSALEM

**11** And when they came nigh to Jerusalem, unto Bethphage and Bethany, at the mount of Olives, he sendeth
forth two of his disciples, 2 and saith unto them, Go your way into the village over
against you: and as soon as ye be entered
into it, ye shall find a colt tied, whereon
never man sat; loose him, and bring *him*. ANIMAL
3 And if any man say unto you, Why do
ye this? say ye that the Lord hath need of
him; and straightway he will send him
hither. 4 And they went their way, and
found the colt tied by the door without in
a place where two ways met; and they
loose him. 5 And certain of them that
stood there said unto them, What do ye,
loosing the colt? 6 And they said unto
them even as Jesus had commanded: and
they let them go. 7 And they brought the
colt to Jesus, and cast their garments on
him; and he sat upon him. 8 And many
spread their garments in the way; and
others cut down branches off the trees,
and strewed *them* in the way. 9 And they
that went before, and they that followed,
cried, saying,
Hosanna; Blessed *is* he that cometh Ps. 118:26
in the name of the Lord:
10 Blessed *be* the kingdom of our father
David,
that cometh in the name of the Lord:
Hosanna in the highest. ●

2.ENTERING THE TEMPLE

11 And Jesus entered into Jerusalem,
and into the temple: and when he had BUILDING
looked round about upon all things, and
now the eventide was come, he went out
unto Bethany with the twelve. ●

3.CURSING A TREE

12 And on the morrow, when they were
come from Bethany, he was hungry:
13 and seeing a fig tree afar off having TREE
leaves, he came, if haply he might find any
thing thereon: and when he came to it, he
found nothing but leaves; for the time of
figs was not *yet*. 14 And Jesus answered
and said unto it, No man eat fruit of thee
hereafter for ever. And his disciples
heard *it*. ●

This point in Mark's gospel begins Passion Week, the last week of Jesus' public ministry, climaxing in His death and resurrection. The week begins with people extolling Him (see verses 9-10), but before long He is mocked and rejected (e.g. 15:17).

*11:1-10* What prophecies did Jesus make, and when were they fulfilled?

What lesson was Jesus teaching His disciples through this?

Compare "Hosanna" (11:9) with "Crucify Him" (15:13).

*11:11* What do the different phrases suggest?

*11:12-14* What are your impressions?

NEW INTERNATIONAL VERSION

What does the passage teach about:

PLACE OF WORSHIP

PRAYER

FAITH

FORGIVENESS

AUTHORITY OF JESUS

15 On reaching Jerusalem, Jesus entered the temple area and began driving out those who were buying and selling there. He overturned the tables of the money changers and the benches of those selling doves, 16 and would not allow anyone to carry merchandise through the temple courts. 17 And as he taught them, he said, "Is it not written:

"'My house will be called
a house of prayer for all
nations'[c]?

But you have made it 'a den of robbers.'[d]"

18 The chief priests and the teachers of the law heard this and began looking for a way to kill him, for they feared him, because the whole crowd was amazed at his teaching.

19 When evening came, they[e] went out of the city.●

### *The Withered Fig Tree*

20 In the morning, as they went along, they saw the fig tree withered from the roots. 21 Peter remembered and said to Jesus, "Rabbi, look! The fig tree you cursed has withered!"

22 "Have[f] faith in God," Jesus answered. 23 "I tell you the truth, if anyone says to this mountain, 'Go, throw yourself into the sea,' and does not doubt in his heart but believes that what he says will happen, it will be done for him. 24 Therefore I tell you, whatever you ask for in prayer, believe that you have received it, and it will be yours. 25 And when you stand praying, if you hold anything against anyone, forgive him, so that your Father in heaven may forgive you your sins.[g]"●

### *The Authority of Jesus Questioned*

27 They arrived again in Jerusalem, and while Jesus was walking in the temple courts, the chief priests, the teachers of the law and the elders came to him. 28 "By what authority are you doing these things?" they asked. "And who gave you authority to do this?"

29 Jesus replied, "I will ask you one question. Answer me, and I will tell you by what authority I am doing these things. 30 John's baptism—was it from heaven, or from men? Tell me!"

31 They discussed it among themselves and said, "If we say, 'From heaven,' he will ask, 'Then why didn't you believe him?' 32 But if we say, 'From men'. . . ." (They feared the people, for everyone held that John really was a prophet.)

33 So they answered Jesus, "We don't know."

Jesus said, "Neither will I tell you by what authority I am doing these things."●

[c]17 Isaiah 56:7 [d]17 Jer. 7:11
[e]19 Some early manuscripts *he*
[f]22 Some early manuscripts *If you have*
[g]25 Some manuscripts *sins.* [26] *But if you do not forgive, neither will your Father who is in heaven forgive your sins.*

## KING JAMES

**1. CLEARING THE TEMPLE** — TEMPLE MERCHANTS

15 And they come to Jerusalem: and
Jesus went into the temple, and began to
cast out them that sold and bought in the
temple, and overthrew the tables of the
money changers, and the seats of them
that sold doves; 16 and would not suffer
that any man should carry *any* vessel
through the temple. 17 And he taught,
saying unto them, Is it not written, My
house shall be called of all nations the
house of prayer ? but ye have made it a
den of thieves. 18 And the scribes and
chief priests heard *it*, and sought how they
might destroy him: for they feared him,
because all the people was astonished at
his doctrine. 19 And when even was come,
he went out of the city. ●

Isa. 56:7

**2. TEACHING THE DISCIPLES** — DISCIPLES

20 And in the morning, as they passed
by, they saw the fig tree dried up from the
roots. 21 And Peter calling to remembrance saith unto him, Master, behold,
the fig tree which thou cursedst is withered
away. 22 And Jesus answering saith unto
them, Have faith in God. 23 For verily I
say unto you, That whosoever shall say
unto this mountain, Be thou removed,
and be thou cast into the sea; and shall
not doubt in his heart, but shall believe
that those things which he saith shall
come to pass; he shall have whatsoever
he saith. 24 Therefore I say unto you,
What things soever ye desire, when ye
pray, believe that ye receive *them*, and ye
shall have *them*. 25 And when ye stand
praying, forgive, if ye have aught against
any; that your Father also which is in
heaven may forgive you your trespasses.
26 But if ye do not forgive, neither will
your Father which is in heaven forgive
your trespasses. ●

**3. CHALLENGING THE OPPONENTS** — RELIGIOUS LEADERS

27 And they come again to Jerusalem:
and as he was walking in the temple, there
come to him the chief priests, and the
scribes, and the elders, 28 and say unto
him, By what authority doest thou these
things? and who gave thee this authority
to do these things? 29 And Jesus answered and said unto them, I will also ask
of you one question, and answer me, and
I will tell you by what authority I do these
things. 30 The baptism of John, was *it*
from heaven, or of men? answer me.
31 And they reasoned with themselves,
saying, If we shall say, From heaven; he
will say, Why then did ye not believe him?
32 But if we shall say, Of men; they feared
the people: for all *men* counted John, that
he was a prophet indeed. 33 And they answered and said unto Jesus, We cannot
tell. And Jesus answering saith unto
them, Neither do I tell you by what
authority I do these things. ●

---

Observe the variety of actions in this segment.
For each paragraph record
1) what leads into Jesus' speaking; and 2) what Jesus communicates.

*11:15-19* ____________________

*11:20-26* ____________________

*11:27-33* ____________________

NEW INTERNATIONAL VERSION

What is taught here about:

LOVE OF GOD

MINISTRY OF GOD'S SERVANTS

JESUS THE REJECTED SAVIOR

SACRIFICE OF JESUS

HEART OF UNBELIEF

JUDGMENT OF UNBELIEF

*The Parable of the Tenants*

12 He then began to speak to them in
parables: "A man planted a vine-
yard. He put a wall around it, dug a pit for
the winepress and built a watchtower.
Then he rented the vineyard to some farmers and went away on a journey. 2At harvest time he sent a servant to the tenants
to collect from them some of the fruit of the
vineyard. 3But they seized him, beat him
and sent him away empty-handed. 4Then
he sent another servant to them; they
struck this man on the head and treated
him shamefully. 5He sent still another, and
that one they killed. He sent many others;
some of them they beat, others they killed.
6"He had one left to send, a son, whom
he loved. He sent him last of all, saying,
'They will respect my son.'
7"But the tenants said to one another,
'This is the heir. Come, let's kill him, and
the inheritance will be ours.' 8So they took
him and killed him, and threw him out of
the vineyard.
9"What then will the owner of the vineyard do? He will come and kill those tenants and give the vineyard to others.
10Haven't you read this scripture:●

" 'The stone the builders rejected
has become the capstone[a];
11the Lord has done this,
and it is marvelous in our
eyes'[b]?"●

12Then they looked for a way to arrest
him because they knew he had spoken the
parable against them. But they were afraid
of the crowd; so they left him and went
away.●

[a]*10* Or *cornerstone* [b]*11* Psalm 118:22,23

KING JAMES

1.PARABLE

WORDS

12 And he began to speak unto them
by parables. A *certain* man planted
a vineyard, and set a hedge about *it*, and
digged *a place for* the winevat, and built a
tower, and let it out to husbandmen, and
went into a far country. 2 And at the
season he sent to the husbandmen a servant, that he might receive from the husbandmen of the fruit of the vineyard.
3 And they caught *him*, and beat him, and
sent *him* away empty. 4 And again he
sent unto them another servant; and at
him they cast stones, and wounded *him* in
the head, and sent *him* away shamefully
handled. 5 And again he sent another;
and him they killed, and many others;
beating some, and killing some. 6 Having
yet therefore one son, his well-beloved, he
sent him also last unto them, saying, They
will reverence my son. 7 But those husbandmen said among themselves, This is
the heir; come, let us kill him, and the inheritance shall be ours. 8 And they took
him, and killed *him*, and cast *him* out of
the vineyard. 9 What shall therefore the
lord of the vineyard do? he will come and
destroy the husbandmen, and will give the
vineyard unto others. ● 10 And have ye not
read this Scripture;

2.APPLICATION

Ps. 118:22

The stone which the builders rejected
is become the head of the corner:
11 this was the Lord's doing,
and it is marvelous in our eyes? ●

3.REACTION

CONVICTION

12 And they sought to lay hold on him,
but feared the people; for they knew
that he had spoken the parable against
them: and they left him, and went their
way. ●

Jesus taught much by parables. The subject of this parable is very vital because it involves man's rejection of God's love.

*12:1-9* Record the different parts of the parable:

*12:10-11* How does Jesus apply the parable to Himself, by these words?

*12:12* How is the people's reaction a fulfillment of the parable's story?

NEW INTERNATIONAL VERSION

What do you learn here about:

HYPOCRISY

CIVIL OBLIGATIONS OF CITIZENS

RESURRECTION BODY

MARRIAGE

HEAVEN

JESUS' WISDOM

GOD'S POWER

*Paying Taxes to Caesar*

13Later they sent some of the Pharisees
and Herodians to Jesus to catch him in his
words. 14They came to him and said,
"Teacher, we know you are a man of integrity. You aren't swayed by men, because
you pay no attention to who they are; but
you teach the way of God in accordance
with the truth. Is it right to pay taxes to
Caesar or not? 15Should we pay or
shouldn't we?"
But Jesus knew their hypocrisy. "Why
are you trying to trap me?" he asked.
"Bring me a denarius and let me look at
it." 16They brought the coin, and he asked
them, "Whose portrait is this? And whose
inscription?"
"Caesar's," they replied.
17Then Jesus said to them, "Give to Caesar what is Caesar's and to God what is
God's."
And they were amazed at him.●

*Marriage at the Resurrection*

18Then the Sadducees, who say there is
no resurrection, came to him with a question. 19"Teacher," they said, "Moses
wrote for us that if a man's brother dies and
leaves a wife but no children, the man must
marry the widow and have children for his
brother. 20Now there were seven brothers.
The first one married and died without
leaving any children. 21The second one
married the widow, but he also died, leaving no child. It was the same with the third.
22In fact, none of the seven left any children. Last of all, the woman died too. 23At
the resurrection[c] whose wife will she be,
since the seven were married to her?"
24Jesus replied, "Are you not in error
because you do not know the Scriptures or
the power of God? 25When the dead rise,
they will neither marry nor be given in marriage; they will be like the angels in heaven.
26Now about the dead rising—have you not
read in the book of Moses, in the account
of the bush, how God said to him, 'I am the
God of Abraham, the God of Isaac, and the
God of Jacob'[d]? 27He is not the God of the
dead, but of the living. You are badly mis-
taken!"●

c23 Some manuscripts *resurrection, when men rise from the dead,*
d26 Exodus 3:6

KING JAMES

1. PAYING TAXES

PHARISEES, HERODIANS

13 And they send unto him certain of
the Pharisees and of the Hero′dians, to
catch him in *his* words. 14 And when they
were come, they say unto him, Master,
we know that thou art true, and carest for
no man; for thou regardest not the person
of men, but teachest the way of God in
truth: Is it lawful to give tribute to
Caesar, or not? 15 Shall we give, or shall
we not give? But he, knowing their
hypocrisy, said unto them, Why tempt ye
me? bring me a penny, that I may see *it*.
16 And they brought *it*. And he saith unto them, Whose *is* this image and superscription? And they said unto him,
Caesar's. 17 And Jesus answering said
unto them, Render to Caesar the things
that are Caesar's, and to God the things
that are God's. And they marveled at
him. ●

2. RESURRECTION BODIES

SADDUCEES

18 Then come unto him the Sadducees,
which say there is no resurrection; and
they asked him, saying, 19 Master, Moses
wrote unto us, If a man's brother die, and
leave *his* wife *behind him*, and leave no
children, that his brother should take his
wife, and raise up seed unto his brother.
20 Now there were seven brethren: and
the first took a wife, and dying left no
seed. 21 And the second took her, and
died, neither left he any seed: and the
third likewise. 22 And the seven had her,
and left no seed: last of all the woman
died also. 23 In the resurrection therefore, when they shall rise, whose wife
shall she be of them? for the seven had
her to wife.
24 And Jesus answering said unto them,
Do ye not therefore err, because ye know
not the Scriptures, neither the power of
God? 25 For when they shall rise from
the dead, they neither marry, nor are
given in marriage; but are as the angels
which are in heaven. 26 And as touching
the dead, that they rise; have ye not read
in the book of Moses, how in the bush
God spake unto him, saying, I *am* the God
of Abraham, and the God of Isaac, and
the God of Jacob ? 27 He is not the God
of the dead, but the God of the living: ye
therefore do greatly err. ●

Deu. 25:5

Ex. 3:6

What religious groups tried to trap Jesus with questions reported in these two paragraphs? What is the atmosphere of this confrontation?

*12:13-17* Record:

THE QUESTION ____________________

JESUS' ANSWER ____________________

What does Jesus reveal about Himself by this reply?

*12:18-27*

THE QUESTION ____________________

JESUS' ANSWER ____________________

Why did Jesus speak the words of verses 26-27? (Cf. v.18a).

NEW INTERNATIONAL VERSION

Record what you learn here about:

THE COMMANDMENTS OF GOD

LOVE

WORKS

HYPOCRISY

GIVING

JESUS AS SON OF GOD

### *The Greatest Commandment*

28 One of the teachers of the law came
and heard them debating. Noticing that
Jesus had given them a good answer, he
asked him, "Of all the commandments,
which is the most important?"
29 "The most important one," answered
Jesus, "is this: 'Hear, O Israel, the Lord
our God, the Lord is one.[e] 30 Love the Lord
your God with all your heart and with all
your soul and with all your mind and with
all your strength.'[f] 31 The second is this:
'Love your neighbor as yourself.'[g] There is
no commandment greater than these."
32 "Well said, teacher," the man replied.
"You are right in saying that God is one
and there is no other but him. 33 To love him
with all your heart, with all your understanding and with all your strength, and to
love your neighbor as yourself is more important than all burnt offerings and sacrifices."
34 When Jesus saw that he had answered
wisely, he said to him, "You are not far
from the kingdom of God." And from then
on no one dared ask him any more questions.●

### *Whose Son Is the Christ?*

35 While Jesus was teaching in the temple
courts, he asked, "How is it that the
teachers of the law say that the Christ[h] is
the son of David? 36 David himself,
speaking by the Holy Spirit, declared:

> " 'The Lord said to my Lord:
> "Sit at my right hand
> until I put your enemies
> under your feet." '[i]

37 David himself calls him 'Lord.' How then
can he be his son?"
The large crowd listened to him with delight.●
38 As he taught, Jesus said, "Watch out
for the teachers of the law. They like to
walk around in flowing robes and be greeted in the marketplaces, 39 and have the
most important seats in the synagogues
and the places of honor at banquets.
40 They devour widows' houses and for a
show make lengthy prayers. Such men will
be punished most severely."●

### *The Widow's Offering*

41 Jesus sat down opposite the place
where the offerings were put and watched
the crowd putting their money into the
temple treasury. Many rich people threw
in large amounts. 42 But a poor widow came
and put in two very small copper coins,[a]
worth only a fraction of a penny.[b]
43 Calling his disciples to him, Jesus said,
"I tell you the truth, this poor widow has
put more into the treasury than all the
others. 44 They all gave out of their wealth;
but she, out of her poverty, put in everything—all she had to live on."●

[e]29 Or *the Lord our God is one Lord* [f]30 Deut. 6:4,5 [g]31 Lev. 19:18 [h]35 Or *Messiah* [i]36 Psalm 110:1 [a]42 Greek *two lepta* [b]42 Greek *kodrantes*

KING JAMES

1. JESUS ANSWERS A TRICK QUESTION

FOREMOST COMMANDMENT

28 And one of the scribes came, and
having heard them reasoning together,
and perceiving that he had answered them
well, asked him, Which is the first commandment of all? 29 And Jesus answered
him, The first of all the commandments *is*,
Hear, O Israel;
The Lord our God is one Lord:
30 and thou shalt love the Lord thy God
with all thy heart, and with all thy
soul,
and with all thy mind, and with all
thy strength:
this *is* the first commandment. 31 And
the second *is* like, *namely* this,
Thou shalt love thy neighbor as
thyself.
There is none other commandment greater than these. 32 And the scribe said unto
him, Well, Master, thou hast said the
truth: for there is one God; and there is
none other but he: 33 and to love him
with all the heart, and with all the understanding, and with all the soul, and with
all the strength, and to love *his* neighbor
as himself, is more than all whole burnt
offerings and sacrifices. 34 And when
Jesus saw that he answered discreetly, he
said unto him, Thou art not far from the
kingdom of God. And no man after that
durst ask him *any question*. ●

Deu. 6:4-5

Lev. 19:18

Deu. 4:35

Deu. 6:5

2. JESUS TEACHES

a.

35 And Jesus answered and said, while
he taught in the temple, How say the
scribes that Christ is the son of David?
36 For David himself said by the Holy
Ghost,
The LORD said to my Lord,
Sit thou on my right hand,
till I make thine enemies thy footstool.
37 David therefore himself calleth him
Lord; and whence is he *then* his son?
And the common people heard him
gladly. ●

Ps. 110:1

b.

38 And he said unto them in his doctrine, Beware of the scribes, which love to
go in long clothing, and *love* salutations
in the market places, 39 and the chief
seats in the synagogues, and the uppermost rooms at feasts: 40 which devour
widows' houses, and for a pretense make
long prayers: these shall receive greater
damnation. ●

c.

41 And Jesus sat over against the treasury, and beheld how the people cast
money into the treasury: and many that
were rich cast in much. 42 And there
came a certain poor widow, and she threw
in two mites, which make a farthing.
43 And he called *unto him* his disciples,
and saith unto them, Verily I say unto
you, That this poor widow hath cast more
in, than all they which have cast into the
treasury: 44 for all *they* did cast in of their
abundance; but she of her want did
cast in all that she had, *even* all her
living. ●

UTMOST GIVING

*12:28-34* What important teachings appear in this paragraph?

Explain Jesus' statement of verse 34.

*12:35-37* What is Jesus' main point?

Are the crowds still on His side?

*12:38-40* List the kinds of transgressions described here.

*12:41-44* Compare this account with the preceding paragraph. Whom is Jesus teaching here?

NEW INTERNATIONAL VERSION

Jesus did not prophesy the date of the end of the age. In this part of His prophetic discourse He prophesied events which would be indicators of the near impending calamity of the destruction of Jerusalem (v.2). One destruction of Jerusalem is now history—A.D. 70. The final destruction is yet to come—in end times.

In your own words, list the various signs of this passage: ______________

*Signs of the End of the Age*

13 As he was leaving the temple, one of
his disciples said to him, "Look,
Teacher! What massive stones! What mag-
nificent buildings!"
2"Do you see all these great buildings?"
replied Jesus. "Not one stone here will be
left on another; every one will be thrown
down."●
3As Jesus was sitting on the Mount of
Olives opposite the temple, Peter, James,
John and Andrew asked him privately,
4"Tell us, when will these things happen?
And what will be the sign that they are all
about to be fulfilled?"
5Jesus said to them: "Watch out that no
one deceives you. 6Many will come in my
name, claiming, 'I am he,' and will deceive
many. 7When you hear of wars and rumors
of wars, do not be alarmed. Such things
must happen, but the end is still to come.
8Nation will rise against nation, and kingdom against kingdom. There will be earthquakes in various places, and famines.
These are the beginning of birth pains.●
9"You must be on your guard. You will
be handed over to the local councils and
flogged in the synagogues. On account of
me you will stand before governors and
kings as witnesses to them. 10And the gospel must first be preached to all nations.
11Whenever you are arrested and brought
to trial, do not worry beforehand about
what to say. Just say whatever is given you
at the time, for it is not you speaking, but
the Holy Spirit.
12"Brother will betray brother to death,
and a father his child. Children will rebel
against their parents and have them put to
death. 13All men will hate you because of
me, but he who stands firm to the end will
be saved.●
14"When you see 'the abomination that
causes desolation'[c] standing where it[d] does
not belong—let the reader understand—
then let those who are in Judea flee to the
mountains. 15Let no one on the roof of his
house go down or enter the house to take
anything out. 16Let no one in the field go
back to get his cloak. 17How dreadful it will
be in those days for pregnant women and
nursing mothers! 18Pray that this will not
take place in winter, 19because those will
be days of distress unequaled from the beginning, when God created the world, until
now—and never to be equaled again. 20If
the Lord had not cut short those days, no
one would survive. But for the sake of the
elect, whom he has chosen, he has shortened them.● 21At that time if anyone says to
you, 'Look, here is the Christ[e]!' or, 'Look,
there he is!' do not believe it. 22For false
Christs and false prophets will appear and
perform signs and miracles to deceive the
elect—if that were possible. 23So be on
your guard; I have told you everything
ahead of time.●

[c]14 Daniel 9:27; 11:31; 12:11
[d]14 Or *he*; also in verse 29
[e]21 Or *Messiah*

KING JAMES

—setting

BEHOLD... STONES

**13** And as he went out of the temple,
one of his disciples saith unto him,
Master, see what manner of stones and
what buildings *are here!* 2 And Jesus answering said unto him, Seest thou these
great buildings? there shall not be left one
stone upon another, that shall not be
thrown down. ●

1.BEGINNING STAGE

3 And as he sat upon the mount of
Olives, over against the temple, Peter and
James and John and Andrew asked him
privately, 4 Tell us, when shall these
things be? and what *shall be* the sign when
all these things shall be fulfilled? 5 And
Jesus answering them began to say, Take
heed lest any *man* deceive you: 6 for
many shall come in my name, saying, I am
*Christ;* and shall deceive many. 7 And
when ye shall hear of wars and rumors of
wars, be ye not troubled: for *such things*
must needs be; but the end *shall* not *be*
yet. 8 For nation shall rise against nation,
and kingdom against kingdom: and there
shall be earthquakes in divers places,
and there shall be famines and troubles: these *are* the beginnings of sorrows. ●

2.TESTS OF ENDURANCE

9 But take heed to yourselves: for they
shall deliver you up to councils; and in the
synagogues ye shall be beaten: and ye
shall be brought before rulers and kings
for my sake, for a testimony against them.
10 And the gospel must first be published
among all nations. 11 But when they shall
lead *you,* and deliver you up, take no
thought beforehand what ye shall speak,
neither do ye premeditate: but whatsoever shall be given you in that hour, that
speak ye: for it is not ye that speak, but
the Holy Ghost. 12 Now the brother
shall betray the brother to death, and the
father the son; and children shall rise up
against *their* parents, and shall cause them
to be put to death. 13 And ye shall be
hated of all *men* for my name's sake: but
he that shall endure unto the end, the
same shall be saved. ●

3.WORST TRIBULATION

14 But when ye shall see the abomination of desolation, spoken of by Daniel
the prophet, standing where it ought not,
(let him that readeth understand,) then
let them that be in Judea flee to the mountains: 15 and let him that is on the housetop not go down into the house, neither
enter *therein,* to take any thing out of his
house: 16 and let him that is in the field
not turn back again for to take up his garment. 17 But woe to them that are with
child, and to them that give suck in those
days! 18 And pray ye that your flight be
not in the winter. 19 For *in* those days
shall be affliction, such as was not from
the beginning of the creation which God
created unto this time, neither shall be.
20 And except that the Lord had shortened those days, no flesh should be saved:
but for the elect's sake, whom he hath
chosen, he hath shortened the days. ●

4.FALSE CHRISTS

21 And then if any man shall say to you,
Lo, here *is* Christ; or, lo, *he is* there; believe *him* not: 22 for false Christs and
false prophets shall rise, and shall show
signs and wonders, to seduce, if *it were*
possible, even the elect. 23 But take ye
heed: behold, I have foretold you all
things. ●

BEHOLD... CHRIST

The preceding segment describes Jesus' last appearance in the temple before His death. Now, on leaving the temple (13:1), He gives a long discourse on prophecy (13:1-37).

Record:

a. the setting (vv.1,2) ____________________

____________________

____________________

b. the questions (v.4) ____________________

____________________

____________________

Now record the main points of the answer of Jesus:

*13:5-8* ____________________

____________________

____________________

____________________

*13:9-13* ____________________

____________________

____________________

____________________

____________________

*13:14-20* ____________________

____________________

____________________

____________________

____________________

____________________

____________________

(Read Luke 21:24 as happening between verses 20 and 21.)

*13:21-23* ____________________

____________________

____________________

____________________

____________________

____________________

NEW INTERNATIONAL VERSION

List all the truths (such as involving events and persons) which you observe in this passage.

Now record all the spiritual applications which you can make from the passage.

[24]"But in those days, following that distress,

" 'the sun will be darkened,
and the moon will not give its
light;
[25]the stars will fall from the sky,
and the heavenly bodies will be
shaken.'[f]

[26]"At that time men will see the Son of
Man coming in clouds with great power
and glory. [27]And he will send his angels and
gather his elect from the four winds, from
the ends of the earth to the ends of the
heavens.●
[28]"Now learn this lesson from the fig
tree: As soon as its twigs get tender and its
leaves come out, you know that summer is
near. [29]Even so, when you see these things
happening, you know that it is near, right
at the door. [30]I tell you the truth, this generation[g] will certainly not pass away until
all these things have happened. [31]Heaven
and earth will pass away, but my words
will never pass away.●

*The Day and Hour Unknown*

[32]"No one knows about that day or hour,
not even the angels in heaven, nor the Son,
but only the Father. [33]Be on guard! Be
alert[a]! You do not know when that time
will come. [34]It's like a man going away: He
leaves his house in charge of his servants,
each with his assigned task, and tells the
one at the door to keep watch.
[35]"Therefore keep watch because you
do not know when the owner of the house
will come back—whether in the evening,
or at midnight, or when the rooster crows,
or at dawn. [36]If he comes suddenly, do not
let him find you sleeping. [37]What I say to
you, I say to everyone: 'Watch!' "●

[f]25 Isaiah 13:10; 34:4 [g]30 Or *race*
[a]33 Some manuscripts *alert and pray*

KING JAMES

CHRIST'S COMING TO EARTH

1. THE EVENT

24 But in those days, after that tribulation, the sun shall be darkened, and the
moon shall not give her light, 25 and the
stars of heaven shall fall, and the powers
that are in heaven shall be shaken.
26 And then shall they see the Son of man
coming in the clouds with great power
and glory. 27 And then shall he send his
angels, and shall gather together his elect
from the four winds, from the uttermost
part of the earth to the uttermost part of
heaven. ●

2. THE WARNINGS

a. WHAT IS KNOWN

28 Now learn a parable of the fig tree:
When her branch is yet tender, and putteth
forth leaves, ye know that summer is
near: 29 so ye in like manner, when ye
shall see these things come to pass, know
that it is nigh, *even* at the doors. 30 Verily
I say unto you, that this generation shall
not pass, till all these things be done.
31 Heaven and earth shall pass away: but
my words shall not pass away. ●

b. WHAT IS NOT KNOWN

32 But of that day and *that* hour knoweth no man, no, not the angels which are
in heaven, neither the Son, but the Father.
33 Take ye heed, watch and pray: for ye
know not when the time is. 34 *For the
Son of man is* as a man taking a far journey, who left his house, and gave authority to his servants, and to every man his
work, and commanded the porter to
watch. 35 Watch ye therefore: for ye
know not when the master of the house
cometh, at even, or at midnight, or at the
cockcrowing, or in the morning: 36 lest
coming suddenly he find you sleeping.
37 And what I say unto you I say unto all,
Watch. ●

Read 13:19 first, noting the reference to "tribulation." Then read the opening verse (24) of this segment, and observe its reference to the tribulation.

*13:24-27* What is the great event prophesied here?

What signs of nature will attend Jesus' coming?

What will Jesus do at that time?

*13:28-31* What is the forewarning?

Consult commentaries for help in interpreting "this generation."

*13:32-37* What are the key words and phrases of this paragraph?

How is verse 37 an appropriate conclusion to Jesus' discourse?

NEW INTERNATIONAL VERSION

Record things taught about Jesus by this passage.

List important spiritual lessons taught:

*Jesus Anointed at Bethany*

14 Now the Passover and the Feast of
Unleavened Bread were only two
days away, and the chief priests and the
teachers of the law were looking for some
sly way to arrest Jesus and kill him. 2"But
not during the Feast," they said, "or the
people may riot."●
3While he was in Bethany, reclining at
the table in the home of a man known as
Simon the Leper, a woman came with an
alabaster jar of very expensive perfume,
made of pure nard. She broke the jar and
poured the perfume on his head.
4Some of those present were saying in-
dignantly to one another, "Why this waste
of perfume? 5It could have been sold for
more than a year's wages[b] and the money
given to the poor." And they rebuked her
harshly.
6"Leave her alone," said Jesus. "Why
are you bothering her? She has done a
beautiful thing to me. 7The poor you will
always have with you, and you can help
them any time you want. But you will not
always have me. 8She did what she could.
She poured perfume on my body beforehand to prepare for my burial. 9I tell you
the truth, wherever the gospel is preached
throughout the world, what she has done
will also be told, in memory of her."●
10Then Judas Iscariot, one of the
Twelve, went to the chief priests to betray
Jesus to them. 11They were delighted to
hear this and promised to give him money.
So he watched for an opportunity to hand
him over.●

[b]5 Greek *than three hundred denarii*

KING JAMES

1. RULERS' TREACHERY

BODY SOUGHT

14 After two days was *the feast of* the
passover, and of unleavened bread:
and the chief priests and the scribes
sought how they might take him by craft,
and put *him* to death. 2 But they said,
Not on the feast *day*, lest there be an uproar of the people. ●

2. WOMAN'S DEVOTION

3 And being in Bethany, in the house of
Simon the leper, as he sat at meat, there
came a woman having an alabaster box
of ointment of spikenard very precious;
and she brake the box, and poured *it* on
his head. 4 And there were some that
had indignation within themselves, and
said, Why was this waste of the ointment
made? 5 For it might have been sold for
more than three hundred pence, and have
been given to the poor. And they murmured against her. 6 And Jesus said, Let
her alone; why trouble ye her? she hath
wrought a good work on me. 7 For ye
have the poor with you always, and
whensoever ye will ye may do them good:
but me ye have not always. 8 She hath
done what she could: she is come afore-
hand to anoint my body to the burying.
9 Verily I say unto you, Wheresoever this
gospel shall be preached throughout the
whole world, *this* also that she hath done
shall be spoken of for a memorial of her. ●

BODY ANOINTED

3. JUDAS' OFFER

10 And Judas Iscar'i-ot, one of the
twelve, went unto the chief priests, to
betray him unto them. 11 And when they
heard *it*, they were glad, and promised to
give him money. And he sought how he
might conveniently betray him. ●

BODY BOUGHT

This segment is one of the moving dramas leading up to the arrest of Jesus in the Garden of Gethsemane. In your studies try to feel the pathos of it all.

*14:1-2* What holiday was only two days away?

Account for the preference indicated in verse 2:

*14:3-9*

ACTION

JESUS' WORDS

*14:10-11* Compare Judas with the woman of the previous paragraph.

NEW INTERNATIONAL VERSION

What does this passage teach about:

OLD TESTAMENT PROPHECY OF JESUS

OMNISCIENCE OF JESUS

SACRIFICIAL HEART OF JESUS

KINGDOM OF GOD

COMMUNION SERVICE

OTHER

*The Lord's Supper*

12 On the first day of the Feast of Unleavened Bread, when it was customary to sacrifice the Passover lamb, Jesus' disciples
asked him, "Where do you want us to go
and make preparations for you to eat the
Passover?"
13 So he sent two of his disciples, telling
them, "Go into the city, and a man carrying a jar of water will meet you. Follow
him. 14 Say to the owner of the house he
enters, 'The Teacher asks: Where is my
guest room, where I may eat the Passover
with my disciples?' 15 He will show you a
large upper room, furnished and ready.
Make preparations for us there."
16 The disciples left, went into the city
and found things just as Jesus had told
them. So they prepared the Passover.●
17 When evening came, Jesus arrived
with the Twelve. 18 While they were reclining at the table eating, he said, "I tell you
the truth, one of you will betray me—one
who is eating with me."
19 They were saddened, and one by one
they said to him, "Surely not I?"
20 "It is one of the Twelve," he replied,
"one who dips bread into the bowl with
me. 21 The Son of Man will go just as it is
written about him. But woe to that man
who betrays the Son of Man! It would be
better for him if he had not been born."●
22 While they were eating, Jesus took
bread, gave thanks and broke it, and gave
it to his disciples, saying, "Take it; this is
my body."
23 Then he took the cup, gave thanks and
offered it to them, and they all drank from
it.
24 "This is my blood of the[c] covenant,
which is poured out for many," he said to
them. 25 "I tell you the truth, I will not drink
again of the fruit of the vine until that day
when I drink it anew in the kingdom of
God."●

c24 Some manuscripts *the new*

KING JAMES

**1. PASSOVER PREPARED**

**BODY TO BE SACRIFICED**

12 And the first day of unleavened
bread, when they killed the passover, his
disciples said unto him, Where wilt thou
that we go and prepare that thou mayest
eat the passover? 13 And he sendeth
forth two of his disciples, and saith unto
them, Go ye into the city, and there shall
meet you a man bearing a pitcher of
water: follow him. 14 And wheresoever
he shall go in, say ye to the goodman of
the house, The Master saith, Where is the
guest chamber, where I shall eat the passover with my disciples? 15 And he will
show you a large upper room furnished
*and* prepared: there make ready for us.
16 And his disciples went forth, and came
into the city, and found as he had said
unto them: and they made ready the
passover. ●

**2. BETRAYER REVEALED**

17 And in the evening he cometh with
the twelve. 18 And as they sat and did eat,
Jesus said, Verily I say unto you, One of
you which eateth with me shall betray me.
19 And they began to be sorrowful, and
to say unto him one by one, *Is* it I? and
another *said*, *Is* it I? 20 And he answered
and said unto them, *It is* one of the twelve,
that dippeth with me in the dish. 21 The
Son of man indeed goeth, as it is written
of him:[c] but woe to that man by whom
the Son of man is betrayed! good were it
for that man if he had never been born. ●

**3. LAST SUPPER**

**BODY GLORIFIED**

22 And as they did eat, Jesus took
bread, and blessed, and brake *it*, and gave
to them, and said, Take, eat; this is my
body. 23 And he took the cup, and when
he had given thanks, he gave *it* to them:
and they all drank of it. 24 And he said
unto them, This is my blood of the new
testament, which is shed for many.
25 Verily I say unto you, I will drink no
more of the fruit of the vine, until that day
that I drink it new in the kingdom of God. ●

Review 14:1-11 before studying this segment. Compare 14:1 and 14:12.

Read the segment. Record the tone of each paragraph:

12-16 ______________________________

17-21 ______________________________

22-25 ______________________________

*14:12-16* Record the main parts of the paragraph.

*14:17-21* What is the main point here?

*14:22-25* Record the key words and phrases.

NEW INTERNATIONAL VERSION

Make lists of important truths taught in this passage about the following:

WEAKNESSES OF THE DISCIPLES

HEART OF JESUS

DIVINE SOVEREIGNTY

SCRIPTURES

Record some very practical lessons which can be learned from the passage:

26When they had sung a hymn, they went
out to the Mount of Olives.

*Jesus Predicts Peter's Denial*

27"You will all fall away," Jesus told
them, "for it is written:

> " 'I will strike the shepherd,
> and the sheep will be scattered.'[d]

28But after I have risen, I will go ahead of
you into Galilee."
29Peter declared, "Even if all fall away,
I will not."
30"I tell you the truth," Jesus answered,
"today—yes, tonight—before the rooster
crows twice[e] you yourself will disown me
three times."
31But Peter insisted emphatically,
"Even if I have to die with you, I will never
disown you." And all the others said the
same.

*Gethsemane*

32They went to a place called Gethsemane, and Jesus said to his disciples, "Sit
here while I pray." 33He took Peter, James
and John along with him, and he began to
be deeply distressed and troubled. 34"My
soul is overwhelmed with sorrow to the
point of death," he said to them. "Stay
here and keep watch."
35Going a little farther, he fell to the
ground and prayed that if possible the hour
might pass from him. 36 "*Abba*,[a] Father,"
he said, "everything is possible for you.
Take this cup from me. Yet not what I will,
but what you will."
37Then he returned to his disciples and
found them sleeping. "Simon," he said to
Peter, "are you asleep? Could you not
keep watch for one hour? 38Watch and pray
so that you will not fall into temptation.
The spirit is willing, but the body is weak."
39Once more he went away and prayed
the same thing. 40When he came back, he
again found them sleeping, because their
eyes were heavy. They did not know what
to say to him.
41Returning the third time, he said to
them, "Are you still sleeping and resting?
Enough! The hour has come. Look, the
Son of Man is betrayed into the hands of
sinners. 42Rise! Let us go! Here comes my
betrayer!"

*Jesus Arrested*

43Just as he was speaking, Judas, one of
the Twelve, appeared. With him was a
crowd armed with swords and clubs, sent
from the chief priests, the teachers of the
law, and the elders.
44Now the betrayer had arranged a signal
with them: "The one I kiss is the man;
arrest him and lead him away under
guard." 45Going at once to Jesus, Judas
said, "Rabbi!" and kissed him. 46The men
seized Jesus and arrested him. 47Then one
of those standing near drew his sword and
struck the servant of the high priest, cutting off his ear.
48"Am I leading a rebellion," said Jesus,
"that you have come out with swords and
clubs to capture me? 49Every day I was
with you, teaching in the temple courts,
and you did not arrest me. But the Scriptures must be fulfilled." 50Then everyone
deserted him and fled.
51A young man, wearing nothing but a
linen garment, was following Jesus. When
they seized him, 52he fled naked, leaving
his garment behind.

[d]27 Zech. 13:7
[e]30 Some early manuscripts do not have *twice*.
[a]36 Aramaic for *Father*

KING JAMES

**1. JESUS PREDICTS DESERTIONS**

26 And when they had sung a hymn,
they went out into the mount of Olives.
27 And Jesus saith unto them, All ye shall
be offended because of me this night: for
it is written,
I will smite the shepherd,
and the sheep shall be scattered.
28 But after that I am risen, I will go
before you into Galilee. 29 But Peter
said unto him, Although all shall be
offended, yet *will* not I. 30 And Jesus
saith unto him, Verily I say unto thee,
That this day, *even* in this night, before
the cock crow twice, thou shalt deny me
thrice. 31 But he spake the more vehemently, If I should die with thee, I will not
deny thee in any wise. Likewise also said
they all. ●

SHEEP SCATTERED

Zech. 13:7

**2. JESUS PRAYS**

32 And they came to a place which was
named Gethsem'ane: and he saith to his
disciples, Sit ye here, while I shall pray.
33 And he taketh with him Peter and
James and John, and began to be sore
amazed, and to be very heavy; 34 and
saith unto them, My soul is exceeding
sorrowful unto death: tarry ye here, and
watch. 35 And he went forward a little,
and fell on the ground, and prayed that,
if it were possible, the hour might pass
from him. 36 And he said, Abba, Father,
all things *are* possible unto thee; take
away this cup from me: nevertheless, not
what I will, but what thou wilt.●

**3. DISCIPLES SLEEP**

37 And
he cometh, and findeth them sleeping, and
saith unto Peter, Simon, sleepest thou?
couldest not thou watch one hour?
38 Watch ye and pray, lest ye enter into
temptation. The spirit truly *is* ready, but
the flesh *is* weak. 39 And again he went
away, and prayed, and spake the same
words. 40 And when he returned, he
found them asleep again, (for their eyes
were heavy,) neither wist they what to
answer him. 41 And he cometh the third
time, and saith unto them, Sleep on now,
and take *your* rest: it is enough, the hour
is come; behold, the Son of man is betrayed into the hands of sinners. 42 Rise
up, let us go; lo, he that betrayeth me is
at hand. ●

**4. JESUS ARRESTED**

43 And immediately, while he yet spake,
cometh Judas, one of the twelve, and with
him a great multitude with swords and
staves, from the chief priests and the
scribes and the elders. 44 And he that betrayed him had given them a token, saying, Whomsoever I shall kiss, that same
is he; take him, and lead *him* away safely.
45 And as soon as he was come, he goeth
straightway to him, and saith, Master,
Master; and kissed him. 46 And they
laid their hands on him, and took him.
47 And one of them that stood by drew a
sword, and smote a servant of the high
priest, and cut off his ear. 48 And Jesus
answered and said unto them, Are ye
come out, as against a thief, with swords
and *with* staves to take me? 49 I was
daily with you in the temple teaching, and
ye took me not: but the Scriptures must
be fulfilled.●

**5. DISCIPLES FLEE**

50 And they all forsook him,
and fled.
51 And there followed him a certain
young man, having a linen cloth cast
about *his* naked *body;* and the young
men laid hold on him: 52 and he left the
linen cloth, and fled from them naked.

DISCIPLES SCATTERED

There was no sleep for Jesus this Thursday night of Passion Week. The hours until midnight were spent in prayer (vv.32-42); and then came the arrest (vv.43-49).

Record your observations of key truths in each paragraph:

*14:26-31* ______________________

*14:32-36* ______________________

*14:37-42* ______________________

*14:43-49* ______________________

*14:50-52* ______________________

NEW INTERNATIONAL VERSION

Record your observations on these subjects:

FALSE WITNESSES ______

CLAIMS OF JESUS ______

PROPHECIES OF JESUS ______

DISLOYALTY ______

List spiritual applications taught in the passage. ______

*Before the Sanhedrin*

[53]They took Jesus to the high priest, and
all the chief priests, elders and teachers of
the law came together. [54]Peter followed
him at a distance, right into the courtyard
of the high priest. There he sat with the
guards and warmed himself at the fire.●
[55]The chief priests and the whole Sanhedrin were looking for evidence against
Jesus so that they could put him to death,
but they did not find any. [56]Many testified
falsely against him, but their statements
did not agree.
[57]Then some stood up and gave this false
testimony against him: [58]"We heard him
say, 'I will destroy this man-made temple
and in three days will build another, not
made by man.' " [59]Yet even then their testimony did not agree.
[60]Then the high priest stood up before
them and asked Jesus, "Are you not going
to answer? What is this testimony that
these men are bringing against you?" [61]But
Jesus remained silent and gave no answer.
Again the high priest asked him, "Are
you the Christ,[b] the Son of the Blessed
One?"
[62]"I am," said Jesus. "And you will see
the Son of Man sitting at the right hand of
the Mighty One and coming on the clouds
of heaven."
[63]The high priest tore his clothes. "Why
do we need any more witnesses?" he
asked. [64]"You have heard the blasphemy.
What do you think?"
They all condemned him as worthy of
death. [65]Then some began to spit at him;
they blindfolded him, struck him with their
fists, and said, "Prophesy!" And the
guards took him and beat him.●

*Peter Disowns Jesus*

[66]While Peter was below in the courtyard, one of the servant girls of the high
priest came by. [67]When she saw Peter
warming himself, she looked closely at
him.
"You also were with that Nazarene,
Jesus," she said.
[68]But he denied it. "I don't know or understand what you're talking about," he
said, and went out into the entryway.[c]
[69]When the servant girl saw him there,
she said again to those standing around,
"This fellow is one of them." [70]Again he
denied it.
After a little while, those standing near
said to Peter, "Surely you are one of them,
for you are a Galilean."
[71]He began to call down curses on himself, and he swore to them, "I don't know
this man you're talking about."
[72]Immediately the rooster crowed the
second time.[a] Then Peter remembered the
word Jesus had spoken to him: "Before the
rooster crows twice[b] you will disown me
three times." And he broke down and
wept.●

[b]61 Or *Messiah*
[c]68 Some early manuscripts *entryway and the rooster crowed*
[a]72 Some early manuscripts do not have *the second time.*
[b]72 Some early manuscripts do not have *twice.*

KING JAMES

1. PETER FOLLOWS AT A DISTANCE

53 And they led Jesus away to the high
priest: and with him were assembled all
the chief priests and the elders and the
scribes. 54 And Peter followed him afar
off, even into the palace of the high priest:
and he sat with the servants, and warmed
himself at the fire.●

2. JESUS BEFORE THE COUNCIL

55 And the chief priests
and all the council sought for witness
against Jesus to put him to death; and
found none. 56 For many bare false witness against him, but their witness agreed
not together. 57 And there arose certain,
and bare false witness against him, saying,
58 We heard him say, I will destroy this
temple that is made with hands, and within three days I will build another made
without hands. 59 But neither so did
their witness agree together. 60 And the
high priest stood up in the midst, and
asked Jesus, saying, Answerest thou
nothing? what *is it which* these witness
against thee? 61 But he held his peace,
and answered nothing. Again the high
priest asked him, and said unto him, Art
thou the Christ, the Son of the Blessed?
62 And Jesus said, I am: and ye shall see
the Son of man sitting on the right hand
of power, and coming in the clouds of
heaven. 63 Then the high priest rent his
clothes, and saith, What need we any
further witnesses? 64 Ye have heard the
blasphemy: what think ye? And they all
condemned him to be guilty of death.
65 And some began to spit on him, and to
cover his face, and to buffet him, and to say
unto him, Prophesy: and the servants did
strike him with the palms of their hands.●

COLDNESS

3. PETER DENIES JESUS

66 And as Peter was beneath in the
palace, there cometh one of the maids of
the high priest: 67 and when she saw
Peter warming himself, she looked upon
him, and said, And thou also wast with
Jesus of Nazareth. 68 But he denied,
saying, I know not, neither understand I
what thou sayest. And he went out into
the porch; and the cock crew. 69 And a
maid saw him again, and began to say to
them that stood by, This is *one* of them.
70 And he denied it again. And a little
after, they that stood by said again to
Peter, Surely thou art *one* of them: for
thou art a Galilean, and thy speech
agreeth *thereto*. 71 But he began to curse
and to swear, *saying*, I know not this man
of whom ye speak. 72 And the second
time the cock crew. And Peter called to
mind the word that Jesus said unto him,
Before the cock crow twice, thou shalt
deny me thrice. And when he thought
thereon, he wept.●

REMORSE

*14:53-54* What is suggested by the phrase "far off"?

*14:55-65* Why do you think Jesus refused to answer the false witnesses?

What question did He answer?

Relate this to 8:27-30.

What was the high priest's charge and the council's verdict?

*14:66-72* What key words and phrases stand out?

Compare the Peter of this paragraph and the accusers of the previous paragraph.

NEW INTERNATIONAL VERSION

Record all that the passage teaches about Jesus as King of the Jews:

What do you learn about Pilate here?

Record spiritual applications which can be made from this passage.

*Jesus Before Pilate*

15 Very early in the morning, the chief
priests, with the elders, the teachers
of the law and the whole Sanhedrin,
reached a decision. They bound Jesus, led
him away and handed him over to Pilate.
2"Are you the king of the Jews?" asked
Pilate.
"Yes, it is as you say," Jesus replied.
3The chief priests accused him of many
things. 4So again Pilate asked him, "Aren't
you going to answer? See how many things
they are accusing you of."
5But Jesus still made no reply, and Pilate
was amazed.●
6Now it was the custom at the Feast to
release a prisoner whom the people requested. 7A man called Barabbas was in
prison with the insurrectionists who had
committed murder in the uprising. 8The
crowd came up and asked Pilate to do for
them what he usually did.
9"Do you want me to release to you the
king of the Jews?" asked Pilate, 10knowing
it was out of envy that the chief priests had
handed Jesus over to him. 11But the chief
priests stirred up the crowd to have Pilate
release Barabbas instead.
12"What shall I do, then, with the one
you call the king of the Jews?" Pilate asked
them.
13"Crucify him!" they shouted.
14"Why? What crime has he committed?" asked Pilate.
But they shouted all the louder, "Crucify him!"
15Wanting to satisfy the crowd, Pilate
released Barabbas to them. He had Jesus
flogged, and handed him over to be crucified.●

*The Soldiers Mock Jesus*

16The soldiers led Jesus away into the
palace (that is, the Praetorium) and called
together the whole company of soldiers.
17They put a purple robe on him, then wove
a crown of thorns and set it on him. 18And
they began to call out to him, "Hail, King
of the Jews!" 19Again and again they
struck him on the head with a staff and spit
on him. Falling on their knees, they worshiped him.●

KING JAMES

1. ACCUSING JESUS

**15** And straightway in the morning the
chief priests held a consultation
with the elders and scribes and the whole
council, and bound Jesus, and carried *him*
away, and delivered *him* to Pilate. 2 And
Pilate asked him, Art thou the King of the
Jews? And he answering said unto him,
Thou sayest *it*. 3 And the chief priests
accused him of many things; but he answered nothing. 4 And Pilate asked him
again, saying, Answerest thou nothing?
behold how many things they witness
against thee. 5 But Jesus yet answered
nothing; so that Pilate marveled. ●

RELIGIOUS LEADERS

"Are you the King?"

2. REFUSING JESUS

6 Now at *that* feast he released unto
them one prisoner, whomsoever they
desired. 7 And there was *one* named Barab'bas, *which lay* bound with them that
had made insurrection with him, who had
committed murder in the insurrection.
8 And the multitude crying aloud began
to desire *him to do* as he had ever done
unto them. 9 But Pilate answered them,
saying, Will ye that I release unto you the
King of the Jews? 10 For he knew that
the chief priests had delivered him for
envy. 11 But the chief priests moved the
people, that he should rather release Barab'bas unto them. 12 And Pilate answered and said again unto them, What
will ye then that I shall do *unto him* whom
ye call the King of the Jews? 13 And they
cried out again, Crucify him. 14 Then
Pilate said unto them, Why, what evil
hath he done? And they cried out the
more exceedingly, Crucify him. 15 And
*so* Pilate, willing to content the people,
released Barab'bas unto them, and delivered Jesus, when he had scourged *him*,
to be crucified. ●

PEOPLE

3. MOCKING JESUS

16 And the soldiers led him away into
the hall, called Preto'ri-um; and they call
together the whole band. 17 And they
clothed him with purple, and platted a
crown of thorns, and put it about his
*head*, 18 and began to salute him, Hail,
King of the Jews! 19 And they smote him
on the head with a reed, and did spit upon
him, and bowing *their* knees worshipped
him. ●

SOLDIERS

"Hail, King!"

*15:1-5* Did Jesus answer Pilate's question about identity?

Did Jesus respond to the false accusations?

Compare the title of 15:2 with that of 14:61.

*15:6-15* As of this paragraph the multitudes have begun to turn against Jesus. Who stirred them up to do this?

Review earlier passages to see when they were last honoring and accepting Him.

*15:16-19* Record all the elements of mockery in verses 17-19.

NEW INTERNATIONAL VERSION

What do you learn here about: JESUS' ENEMIES

JESUS' FRIENDS

What do these verses teach you:

v.31

v.32

v.33

v.34

v.38

20And when they had mocked him, they took off the purple robe and put his own clothes on him. Then they led him out to crucify him.

*The Crucifixion*

21A certain man from Cyrene, Simon, the father of Alexander and Rufus, was passing by on his way in from the country, and they forced him to carry the cross. 22They brought Jesus to the place called Golgotha (which means The Place of the Skull). 23Then they offered him wine mixed with myrrh, but he did not take it. 24And they crucified him. Dividing up his clothes, they cast lots to see what each would get.

25It was the third hour when they crucified him. 26The written notice of the charge against him read: THE KING OF THE JEWS. 27They crucified two robbers with him, one on his right and one on his left.[c] 29Those who passed by hurled insults at him, shaking their heads and saying, "So! You who are going to destroy the temple and build it in three days, 30come down from the cross and save yourself!"

31In the same way the chief priests and the teachers of the law mocked him among themselves. "He saved others," they said, "but he can't save himself! 32Let this Christ,[d] this King of Israel, come down now from the cross, that we may see and believe." Those crucified with him also heaped insults on him.

*The Death of Jesus*

33At the sixth hour darkness came over the whole land until the ninth hour. 34And at the ninth hour Jesus cried out in a loud voice, *"Eloi, Eloi, lama sabachthani?"* —which means, "My God, my God, why have you forsaken me?"[e]

35When some of those standing near heard this, they said, "Listen, he's calling Elijah."

36One man ran, filled a sponge with wine vinegar, put it on a stick, and offered it to Jesus to drink. "Leave him alone now. Let's see if Elijah comes to take him down," he said.

37With a loud cry, Jesus breathed his last.

38The curtain of the temple was torn in two from top to bottom. 39And when the centurion, who stood there in front of Jesus, heard his cry and[a] saw how he died, he said, "Surely this man was the Son[b] of God!"

40Some women were watching from a distance. Among them were Mary Magdalene, Mary the mother of James the younger and of Joses, and Salome. 41In Galilee these women had followed him and cared for his needs. Many other women who had come up with him to Jerusalem were also there.

*The Burial of Jesus*

42It was Preparation Day (that is, the day before the Sabbath). So as evening approached, 43Joseph of Arimathea, a prominent member of the Council, who was himself waiting for the kingdom of God, went boldly to Pilate and asked for Jesus' body. 44Pilate was surprised to hear that he was already dead. Summoning the centurion, he asked him if Jesus had already died. 45When he learned from the centurion that it was so, he gave the body to Joseph. 46So Joseph bought some linen cloth, took down the body, wrapped it in the linen, and placed it in a tomb cut out of rock. Then he rolled a stone against the entrance of the tomb. 47Mary Magdalene and Mary the mother of Joses saw where he was laid.

c27 Some manuscripts *left* 28*and the scripture was fulfilled which says, "He was counted with the lawless ones"* (Isaiah 53:12)
d32 Or *Messiah* e34 Psalm 22:1
a39 Some manuscripts do not have *heard his cry and*. b39 Or *a son*

KING JAMES

1.TO CALVARY

LED TO THE CROSS

20 And when they had mocked him,
they took off the purple from him, and
put his own clothes on him, and led him
out to crucify him.
21 And they compel one Simon a Cyre'nian, who passed by, coming out of
the country, the father of Alexander and
Rufus, to bear his cross. 22 And they
bring him unto the place Gol'gotha,
which is, being interpreted, The place of
a skull.●

2.CRUCIFIXION

23 And they gave him to drink
wine mingled with myrrh: but he received
*it* not. 24 And when they had crucified
him, they parted his garments, casting lots
upon them, what every man should take.
25 And it was the third hour, and they
crucified him. 26 And the superscription
of his accusation was written over, THE
KING OF THE JEWS. 27 And with him they
crucify two thieves; the one on his right
hand, and the other on his left. 28 And
the Scripture was fulfilled, which saith,
And he was numbered with the transgressors. 29 And they that passed by
railed on him, wagging their heads, and
saying, Ah, thou that destroyest the
temple, and buildest *it* in three days,
30 save thyself, and come down from the
cross. 31 Likewise also the chief priests
mocking said among themselves with the
scribes, He saved others; himself he cannot save. 32 Let Christ the King of Israel
descend now from the cross, that we may
see and believe. And they that were crucified with him reviled him.●

Isa. 53:12

3.DEATH

33 And when the sixth hour was come,
there was darkness over the whole land
until the ninth hour. 34 And at the ninth
hour Jesus cried with a loud voice, saying,
E'lo-i, E'lo-i, lama sabach'thani? which is
being interpreted, My God, my God, why
hast thou forsaken me? 35 And some of
them that stood by, when they heard *it*,
said, Behold, he calleth Eli'jah. 36 And
one ran and filled a sponge full of vinegar,
and put *it* on a reed, and gave him to
drink, saying, Let alone; let us see
whether Eli'jah will come to take him
down. 37 And Jesus cried with a loud
voice, and gave up the ghost.●

4.MOURNING

38 And the
veil of the temple was rent in twain from
the top to the bottom. 39 And when the
centurion, which stood over against him,
saw that he so cried out, and gave up the
ghost, he said, Truly this man was the Son
of God.
40 There were also women looking on
afar off: among whom was Mary Mag'-
dalene, and Mary the mother of James the
less and of Joses, and Salo'me; 41 who
also, when he was in Galilee, followed
him, and ministered unto him; and many
other women which came up with him
unto Jerusalem.●

5.BURIAL

42 And now when the even was come,
because it was the preparation, that is, the
day before the sabbath, 43 Joseph of
Arimathe'a, an honorable counselor,
which also waited for the kingdom of
God, came, and went in boldly unto
Pilate, and craved the body of Jesus.
44 And Pilate marveled if he were already
dead: and calling *unto him* the centurion,
he asked him whether he had been any
while dead. 45 And when he knew *it* of
the centurion, he gave the body to Joseph.

BODY CARRIED AWAY

46 And he bought fine linen, and took
him down, and wrapped him in the linen,
and laid him in a sepulchre which was
hewn out of a rock, and rolled a stone
unto the door of the sepulchre. 47 And
Mary Mag'dalene and Mary *the mother*
of Joses beheld where he was laid.●

Here are some things to look for as you analyze the segment:

WORDS OF JESUS
WORDS OF OTHERS
REACTIONS
THINGS DONE TO JESUS

Record the main actions of each paragraph:

*15:20-22* ______

*15:23-32* ______

*15:33-37* ______

*15:38-41* ______

*15:42-47* ______

NEW INTERNATIONAL VERSION

What truths does the passage teach about:

RESURRECTION

UNBELIEF

BELIEF

OBEDIENCE

GOSPEL WITNESS

How is the last paragraph an appropriate conclusion to Mark's gospel?

*The Resurrection*

16 When the Sabbath was over, Mary
Magdalene, Mary the mother of
James, and Salome bought spices so that
they might go to anoint Jesus' body. 2Very
early on the first day of the week, just after
sunrise, they were on their way to the tomb
3and they asked each other, "Who will roll
the stone away from the entrance of the
tomb?"
4But when they looked up, they saw that
the stone, which was very large, had been
rolled away. 5As they entered the tomb,
they saw a young man dressed in a white
robe sitting on the right side, and they were
alarmed.
6"Don't be alarmed," he said. "You are
looking for Jesus the Nazarene, who was
crucified. He has risen! He is not here. See
the place where they laid him. 7But go, tell
his disciples and Peter, 'He is going ahead
of you into Galilee. There you will see him,
just as he told you.'"
8Trembling and bewildered, the women
went out and fled from the tomb. They said
nothing to anyone, because they were
afraid.●

[The two most reliable early manuscripts do not have Mark 16:9-20.]

9When Jesus rose early on the first day
of the week, he appeared first to Mary
Magdalene, out of whom he had driven
seven demons. 10She went and told those
who had been with him and who were
mourning and weeping. 11When they heard
that Jesus was alive and that she had seen
him, they did not believe it.●
12Afterward Jesus appeared in a different
form to two of them while they were walking in the country. 13These returned and
reported it to the rest; but they did not
believe them either.●
14Later Jesus appeared to the Eleven as
they were eating; he rebuked them for their
lack of faith and their stubborn refusal to
believe those who had seen him after he
had risen.
15He said to them, "Go into all the world
and preach the good news to all creation.
16Whoever believes and is baptized will be
saved, but whoever does not believe will
be condemned. 17And these signs will accompany those who believe: In my name
they will drive out demons; they will speak
in new tongues; 18they will pick up snakes
with their hands; and when they drink
deadly poison, it will not hurt them at all;
they will place their hands on sick people,
and they will get well."●
19After the Lord Jesus had spoken to
them, he was taken up into heaven and he
sat at the right hand of God. 20Then the
disciples went out and preached everywhere, and the Lord worked with them and
confirmed his word by the signs that accompanied it.●

KING JAMES

1. RESURRECTION

LEFT THE TOMB

16 And when the sabbath was past,
Mary Mag'dalene, and Mary the
*mother* of James, and Salo'me, had
bought sweet spices, that they might come
and anoint him. 2 And very early in the
morning, the first *day* of the week, they
came unto the sepulchre at the rising of
the sun. 3 And they said among themselves, Who shall roll us away the stone
from the door of the sepulchre? 4 And
when they looked, they saw that the stone
was rolled away: for it was very great.
5 And entering into the sepulchre, they
saw a young man sitting on the right side,
clothed in a long white garment; and they
were affrighted. 6 And he saith unto
them, Be not affrighted: ye seek Jesus of
Nazareth, which was crucified: he is risen;
he is not here: behold the place where they
laid him. 7 But go your way, tell his disciples and Peter that he goeth before you
into Galilee: there shall ye see him, as he
said unto you. 8 And they went out
quickly, and fled from the sepulchre; for
they trembled and were amazed: neither
said they any thing to any *man;* for they
were afraid.●

2. APPEARANCES

a.

9 Now when *Jesus* was risen early the
first *day* of the week, he appeared first to
Mary Mag'dalene, out of whom he had
cast seven devils. 10 *And* she went and
told them that had been with him, as they
mourned and wept. 11 And they, when
they had heard that he was alive, and had
been seen of her, believed not.●

b.

12 After that he appeared in another
form unto two of them, as they walked,
and went into the country. 13 And they
went and told *it* unto the residue: neither
believed they them.●

c.

14 Afterward he appeared unto the
eleven as they sat at meat, and upbraided
them with their unbelief and hardness of
heart, because they believed not them
which had seen him after he was risen.
15 And he said unto them, Go ye into all
the world, and preach the gospel to every
creature. 16 He that believeth and is
baptized shall be saved; but he that believeth not shall be damned. 17 And these
signs shall follow them that believe; In
my name shall they cast out devils; they
shall speak with new tongues; 18 they
shall take up serpents; and if they drink
any deadly thing, it shall not hurt them;
they shall lay hands on the sick, and they
shall recover.●

3. ASCENSION

RECEIVED UP INTO HEAVEN

19 So then, after the Lord had spoken
unto them, he was received up into
heaven, and sat on the right hand of
God. 20 And they went forth, and
preached every where, the Lord working
with *them*, and confirming the word with
signs following. Amen.●

*16:1-8* Why had the stone rolled away (v.4)?

Record:

FACTS (v.6) __________

INSTRUCTIONS (v.7) __________

REACTIONS (v.8) __________

*16:9-18* Record your observations on Jesus' appearances (9-14).

For what did Jesus reprove His disciples (v.14)?

What was the purpose of the signs (vv.17-18; cf. v.20)?

*16:19-20* Analyze carefully this last commission of Jesus.

# LUKE

## AUTHORSHIP

Luke the author was born of Greek parents, a heritage that made him probably the only Gentile writer of the New Testament. He was a physician (Col. 4:14), writer (he wrote Acts and this gospel) and evangelist. He may have been converted under the ministry of Paul. He was Paul's colaborer on the apostle's missionary journeys.

## DATE

Luke wrote this gospel around A.D. 60, not much earlier than writing Acts. Read Acts 1:1 for his reference to the gospel account as "the *former* treatise."

## PURPOSE AND THEME

Luke states his purpose in 1:1-4: to write an orderly account of the full truth of Jesus' ministry. The theme of Luke concerns "Jesus the Nazarene, which was a prophet mighty in deed and word before God and all the people" (24:19). He especially shows the humanity of Jesus—the Son of man among men (19:10), the perfect God-man (cf. 3:35). A key verse reflecting this is 19:10.

## LUKE: The Son of Man Among Men

| | |
|---|---|
| PREPARATION | 1:1-4:13 |
| Births of John and Jesus | 1:1-2:52 |
| Preaching of John, and Baptism and Temptations of Jesus | 3:1-4:13 |
| IDENTIFICATION | 4:14-9:50 |
| Jesus' Message Identified, Demonstrated and Opposed | 4:14-6:11 |
| Middle Galilean Ministry Begins | 6:12-7:50 |
| Last Months of Jesus' Galilean Ministry | 8:1-9:50 |
| INSTRUCTION | 9:51-19:27 |
| Ministries around Jerusalem | 9:51-11:54 |
| Teaching in Cities and Villages | 12:1-14:35 |
| Six Parables | 15:1-17:10 |
| Kingdom Teaching | 17:11-19:27 |
| SACRIFICE | 19:28-24:53 |
| Last Messages | 19:28-21:38 |
| The Great Sacrifice | 22:1-23:56 |
| The Grand Miracle | 24:1-53 |

# LUKE

NEW INTERNATIONAL VERSION

Record truths taught in this passage about:

RIGHTEOUS LIVING

SOVEREIGNTY AND POWER OF GOD

SERVING GOD

JOY

FAITH

DIVINE FAVOR

*Introduction*

1 Many have undertaken to draw up an
account of the things that have been
fulfilled[a] among us, 2just as they were
handed down to us by those who from the
first were eyewitnesses and servants of the
word. 3Therefore, since I myself have
carefully investigated everything from the
beginning, it seemed good also to me to
write an orderly account for you, most excellent Theophilus, 4so that you may know
the certainty of the things you have been
taught.●

*The Birth of John the Baptist Foretold*

5In the time of Herod king of Judea there
was a priest named Zechariah, who belonged to the priestly division of Abijah;
his wife Elizabeth was also a descendant of
Aaron. 6Both of them were upright in the
sight of God, observing all the Lord's commandments and regulations blamelessly.
7But they had no children, because Elizabeth was barren; and they were both well
along in years.●

8Once when Zechariah's division was on
duty and he was serving as priest before
God, 9he was chosen by lot, according to
the custom of the priesthood, to go into the
temple of the Lord and burn incense.
10And when the time for the burning of
incense came, all the assembled worshipers were praying outside.

11Then an angel of the Lord appeared to
him, standing at the right side of the altar
of incense. 12When Zechariah saw him, he
was startled and was gripped with fear.
13But the angel said to him: "Do not be
afraid, Zechariah; your prayer has been
heard. Your wife Elizabeth will bear you a
son, and you are to give him the name
John. 14He will be a joy and delight to you,
and many will rejoice because of his birth,
15for he will be great in the sight of the
Lord. He is never to take wine or other
fermented drink, and he will be filled with
the Holy Spirit even from birth.[b] 16Many of
the people of Israel will he bring back to
the Lord their God. 17And he will go on
before the Lord, in the spirit and power of
Elijah, to turn the hearts of the fathers to
their children and the disobedient to the
wisdom of the righteous—to make ready a
people prepared for the Lord."●

[a]1 Or *been surely believed*
[b]15 Or *from his mother's womb*

KING JAMES

# LUKE

—introduction

1 Forasmuch as many have taken in
hand to set forth in order a declaration of those things which are most surely
believed among us, 2 even as they delivered them unto us, which from the beginning were eyewitnesses, and ministers of
the word; 3 it seemed good to me also,
having had perfect understanding of all
things from the very first, to write unto
thee in order, most excellent The-oph'ilus,
4 that thou mightest know the certainty
of those things, wherein thou hast been
instructed.●

1.JOHN'S PARENTS

RIGHTEOUS BEFORE GOD

5 There was in the days of Herod, the
king of Judea, a certain priest named
Zechari'ah, of the course of Abi'jah: and
his wife *was* of the daughters of Aaron,
and her name *was* Elisabeth. 6 And they
were both righteous before God, walking
in all the commandments and ordinances
of the Lord blameless. 7 And they had
no child, because that Elisabeth was barren; and they both were *now* well stricken
in years.●

2.JOHN'S BIRTH FORETOLD

8 And it came to pass, that, while he
executed the priest's office before God in
the order of his course, 9 according to the
custom of the priest's office, his lot was to
burn incense when he went into the temple
of the Lord. 10 And the whole multitude
of the people were praying without at the
time of incense. 11 And there appeared
unto him an angel of the Lord standing on
the right side of the altar of incense.
12 And when Zechari'ah saw *him*, he was
troubled, and fear fell upon him. 13 But
the angel said unto him, Fear not, Zechari'ah: for thy prayer is heard; and thy wife
Elisabeth shall bear thee a son, and thou
shalt call his name John. 14 And thou
shalt have joy and gladness; and many
shall rejoice at his birth. 15 For he shall
be great in the sight of the Lord, and shall
drink neither wine nor strong drink; and
he shall be filled with the Holy Ghost,
even from his mother's womb. 16 And
many of the children of Israel shall he
turn to the Lord their God. 17 And he
shall go before him in the spirit and power
of Eli'jah, to turn the hearts of the fathers
to the children, and the disobedient to the
wisdom of the just; to make ready a people prepared for the Lord.●

MINISTRY OF THE UNRIGHTEOUS

Luke begins his account by alternating between the two persons: John the Baptist and Jesus. Here is the outline:

*Announcement of John's coming*
1:5-25
*Announcement of Jesus' coming*
1:26-56
*Birth of John*
1:57-58
*Birth of Jesus*
2:1-20

*1:1-4* What does Luke emphasize here?

______

______

______

______

*1:5-7* How does Luke describe Zacharias and Elizabeth?

______

______

______

______

______

*1:8-17*
ZACHARIAS' MINISTRY:

______

______

______

______

______

JOHN'S COMING MINISTRY: ______

______

______

______

______

______

______

______

______

NEW INTERNATIONAL VERSION

What does this passage teach about:

MIRACLE

FAITH

MINISTER OF GOD

GRACE OF GOD

FAVOR GIVEN TO WOMEN

18Zechariah asked the angel, "How can
I be sure of this? I am an old man and my
wife is well along in years."
19The angel answered, "I am Gabriel. I
stand in the presence of God, and I have
been sent to speak to you and to tell you
this good news. 20And now you will be
silent and not able to speak until the day
this happens, because you did not believe
my words, which will come true at their
proper time."●
21Meanwhile, the people were waiting
for Zechariah and wondering why he
stayed so long in the temple. 22When he
came out, he could not speak to them.
They realized he had seen a vision in the
temple, for he kept making signs to them
but remained unable to speak.
23When his time of service was completed, he returned home.● 24After this his
wife Elizabeth became pregnant and for
five months remained in seclusion. 25"The
Lord has done this for me," she said. "In
these days he has shown his favor and tak-
en away my disgrace among the people."●

KING JAMES

1.ZACHARIAS' UNBELIEF

18 And Zecha-
ri'ah said unto the angel, Whereby shall I
know this? for I am an old man, and my
wife well stricken in years. 19 And the
angel answering said unto him, I am
Gabriel, that stand in the presence of
God; and am sent to speak unto thee, and
to show thee these glad tidings. 20 And,
behold, thou shalt be dumb, and not able
to speak, until the day that these things
shall be performed, because thou believest
not my words, which shall be fulfilled in
their season.● 21 And the people waited
for Zechari'ah, and marveled that he tarried so long in the temple. 22 And when
he came out, he could not speak unto
them: and they perceived that he had
seen a vision in the temple; for he beckoned unto them, and remained speechless.
23 And it came to pass, that, as soon
as the days of his ministration were accomplished, he departed to his own
house.●

GOOD NEWS

2.ZACHARIAS MUTE

3.ELIZABETH CONCEIVES

24 And after those days his wife Elisabeth conceived, and hid herself five
months, saying, 25 Thus hath the Lord
dealt with me in the days wherein he
looked on *me*, to take away my reproach
among men.●

FAVOR

This segment should be studied with the preceding one, because the story is a continuous one. The angel Gabriel is prominent in the first segment; here Zacharias and Elizabeth are the main characters of the account.

*1:18-20* How does Gabriel identify his message (v.19)?

Account for the angel's words of verse 20. What verse reveals Zacharias' unbelief?

*1:21-23* What prophecy is fulfilled here?

What made the people realize Zacharias had seen a vision?

*1:24-25* Record observations of each phrase of Elizabeth's words (v.25).

NEW INTERNATIONAL VERSION

Record truths taught here about:

JESUS

FAITH

HUMILITY

DIVINE FAVOR

JOY

PRAISE

MERCY OF GOD

### *The Birth of Jesus Foretold*

26 In the sixth month, God sent the angel
Gabriel to Nazareth, a town in Galilee, 27 to
a virgin pledged to be married to a man
named Joseph, a descendant of David. The
virgin's name was Mary. 28 The angel went
to her and said, "Greetings, you who are
highly favored! The Lord is with you."
29 Mary was greatly troubled at his words
and wondered what kind of greeting this
might be. 30 But the angel said to her, "Do
not be afraid, Mary, you have found favor
with God. 31 You will be with child and give
birth to a son, and you are to give him the
name Jesus. 32 He will be great and will be
called the Son of the Most High. The Lord
God will give him the throne of his father
David, 33 and he will reign over the house of
Jacob forever; his kingdom will never
end."●
34 "How will this be," Mary asked the
angel, "since I am a virgin?"
35 The angel answered, "The Holy Spirit
will come upon you, and the power of the
Most High will overshadow you. So the
holy one to be born will be called[a] the Son
of God. 36 Even Elizabeth your relative is
going to have a child in her old age, and she
who was said to be barren is in her sixth
month. 37 For nothing is impossible with
God."
38 "I am the Lord's servant," Mary answered. "May it be to me as you have
said." Then the angel left her.●

[a]35 Or *So the child to be born will be called holy.*

KING JAMES

1.JESUS; BIRTH FORETOLD

26 And in the sixth month the angel
Gabriel was sent from God unto a city of
Galilee, named Nazareth, 27 to a virgin
espoused to a man whose name was
Joseph, of the house of David; and the
virgin's name *was* Mary. 28 And the
angel came in unto her, and said, Hail,
*thou that art* highly favored, the Lord *is*
with thee: blessed *art* thou among women.
29 And when she saw *him*, she was
troubled at his saying, and cast in her
mind what manner of salutation this
should be. 30 And the angel said unto
her, Fear not, Mary: for thou hast found
favor with God. 31 And, behold, thou
shalt conceive in thy womb, and bring
forth a son, and shalt call his name JESUS.
32 He shall be great, and shall be called
the Son of the Highest; and the Lord God
shall give unto him the throne of his father
David: 33 and he shall reign over the
house of Jacob for ever; and of his kingdom there shall be no end.●

MARY IS TROUBLED

2.MARY'S REACTIONS

34 Then said
Mary unto the angel, How shall this be,
seeing I know not a man? 35 And the
angel answered and said unto her, The
Holy Ghost shall come upon thee, and
the power of the Highest shall overshadow
thee: therefore also that holy thing which
shall be born of thee shall be called the
Son of God. 36 And, behold, thy cousin
Elisabeth, she hath also conceived a son
in her old age; and this is the sixth month
with her, who was called barren. 37 For
with God nothing shall be impossible.
38 And Mary said, Behold the handmaid
of the Lord; be it unto me according to
thy word. And the angel departed from
her.●

MARY SUBMITS

Who is the main earthly character of this passage? ______________________

Record all that is said about her,as you study the paragraphs.

*1:26-33*

What did Gabriel say about Jesus?

*1:34-38*

NEW INTERNATIONAL VERSION

Record what this passage teaches about:

JESUS

THE MOTHER OF JESUS

THE GOSPEL OF SALVATION

*Mary Visits Elizabeth*

39At that time Mary got ready and hurried to a town in the hill country of Judah,
40where she entered Zechariah's home and
greeted Elizabeth. 41When Elizabeth heard
Mary's greeting, the baby leaped in her
womb, and Elizabeth was filled with the
Holy Spirit. 42In a loud voice she exclaimed: "Blessed are you among women,
and blessed is the child you will bear! 43But
why am I so favored, that the mother of my
Lord should come to me? 44As soon as the
sound of your greeting reached my ears,
the baby in my womb leaped for joy.
45Blessed is she who has believed that what
the Lord has said to her will be accomplished!"●

*Mary's Song*

46And Mary said:

"My soul praises the Lord
47 and my spirit rejoices in God my Savior,
48for he has been mindful
of the humble state of his servant.
From now on all generations will call me blessed,
49 for the Mighty One has done great things for me—
holy is his name.
50His mercy extends to those who fear him,
from generation to generation.
51He has performed mighty deeds with his arm;
he has scattered those who are proud in their inmost thoughts.
52He has brought down rulers from their thrones
but has lifted up the humble.
53He has filled the hungry with good things
but has sent the rich away empty.
54He has helped his servant Israel,
remembering to be merciful
55to Abraham and his descendants forever,
even as he said to our fathers."●

56Mary stayed with Elizabeth for about
three months and then returned home.●

KING JAMES

1. MARY VISITS ELIZABETH

ELIZABETH'S HOME

39 And Mary arose in those days, and
went into the hill country with haste, into
a city of Judah; 40 and entered into the
house of Zechari'ah, and saluted Elisabeth. 41 And it came to pass, that, when
Elisabeth heard the salutation of Mary,
the babe leaped in her womb; and Elisabeth was filled with the Holy Ghost:
42 and she spake out with a loud voice,
and said, Blessed *art* thou among women,
and blessed *is* the fruit of thy womb.
43 And whence *is* this to me, that the
mother of my Lord should come to me?
44 For, lo, as soon as the voice of thy
salutation sounded in mine ears, the babe
leaped in my womb for joy. 45 And
blessed *is* she that believed: for there shall
be a performance of those things which
were told her from the Lord.● 46 And
Mary said,

2. MARY'S PRAISE

My soul doth magnify the Lord,
47 and my spirit hath rejoiced in God
my Saviour.
48 For he hath regarded the low estate
of his handmaiden:
for, behold, from henceforth all
generations shall call me blessed.
49 For he that is mighty hath done to
me great things;
and holy *is* his name.
50 And his mercy *is* on them that fear
him
from generation to generation.
51 He hath showed strength with his
arm;
he hath scattered the proud in the
imagination of their hearts.
52 He hath put down the mighty from
*their* seats,
and exalted them of low degree.
53 He hath filled the hungry with good
things;
and the rich he hath sent empty
away.
54 He hath holpen his servant Israel,
in remembrance of *his* mercy;
55 as he spake to our fathers,
to Abraham, and to his seed for
ever. ●

3. MARY RETURNS HOME

56 And Mary abode with her about three
months, and returned to her own house.●

MARY'S HOME

This segment reports the beautiful sequel to the announcement of the preceding segment. Review 1:26-38 before studying this passage.

*1:39-45* Record the different things Elizabeth said.

*1:46-55* Analyze these inspiring words of Mary. Record the main truths.

*1:56* What does this verse contribute to the story?

NEW INTERNATIONAL VERSION

Record the truths taught here about:

OBEDIENCE

FAITH

TESTIMONY TO OTHERS

PRAISE

GOD'S MERCY

JOHN'S MINISTRY

OTHER

*The Birth of John the Baptist*

57When it was time for Elizabeth to have
her baby, she gave birth to a son. 58Her
neighbors and relatives heard that the Lord
had shown her great mercy, and they
shared her joy.●
59On the eighth day they came to circumcise the child, and they were going to name
him after his father Zechariah, 60but his
mother spoke up and said, "No! He is to
be called John."
61They said to her, "There is no one
among your relatives who has that name."
62Then they made signs to his father, to
find out what he would like to name the
child. 63He asked for a writing tablet, and
to everyone's astonishment he wrote,
"His name is John." 64Immediately his
mouth was opened and his tongue was
loosed, and he began to speak, praising
God. 65The neighbors were all filled with
awe, and throughout the hill country of
Judea people were talking about all these
things. 66Everyone who heard this wondered about it, asking, "What then is this
child going to be?" For the Lord's hand
was with him.●

*Zechariah's Song*

67His father Zechariah was filled with the
Holy Spirit and prophesied:

68"Praise be to the Lord, the God of
Israel,
because he has come and has
redeemed his people.
69He has raised up a horn[b] of
salvation for us
in the house of his servant David
70(as he said through his holy
prophets of long ago),
71salvation from our enemies
and from the hand of all who
hate us—
72to show mercy to our fathers
and to remember his holy
covenant,
73 the oath he swore to our father
Abraham:
74to rescue us from the hand of our
enemies,
and to enable us to serve him
without fear
75 in holiness and righteousness
before him all our days.

76And you, my child, will be called a
prophet of the Most High;
for you will go on before the Lord
to prepare the way for him,
77to give his people the knowledge of
salvation
through the forgiveness of their
sins,
78because of the tender mercy of our
God,
by which the rising sun will come
to us from heaven
79to shine on those living in darkness
and in the shadow of death,
to guide our feet into the path of
peace."●

80And the child grew and became strong
in spirit; and he lived in the desert until he
appeared publicly to Israel.●

[b]69 *Horn* here symbolizes strength.

KING JAMES

1. JOHN'S BIRTH

57 Now Elisabeth's full time came that
she should be delivered; and she brought
forth a son. 58 And her neighbors and
her cousins heard how the Lord had
showed great mercy upon her; and they
rejoiced with her. ● 59 And it came to pass,

2. JOHN'S DEDICATION

that on the eighth day they came to circumcise the child;[f] and they called him
Zechari'ah, after the name of his father.
60 And his mother answered and said,
Not *so;* but he shall be called John.
61 And they said unto her, There is none
of thy kindred that is called by this name.
62 And they made signs to his father, how
he would have him called. 63 And he
asked for a writing table, and wrote, saying, His name is John. And they marveled
all. 64 And his mouth was opened immediately, and his tongue *loosed,* and he
spake, and praised God. 65 And fear
came on all that dwelt round about them:
and all these sayings were noised abroad
throughout all the hill country of Judea.
66 And all they that heard *them* laid *them*
up in their hearts, saying, What manner
of child shall this be? And the hand of the
Lord was with him. ●

NEW-BORN BABE AT HOME

3. ZACHARIAS' SONG

67 And his father Zechari'ah was filled
with the Holy Ghost, and prophesied,
saying,

68 Blessed *be* the Lord God of Israel;
for he hath visited and redeemed his people,
69 and hath raised up a horn of salvation for us
in the house of his servant David;
70 as he spake by the mouth of his holy prophets,
which have been since the world began:
71 that we should be saved from our enemies,
and from the hand of all that hate us;
72 to perform the mercy *promised* to our fathers,
and to remember his holy covenant;
73 the oath which he sware to our father Abraham,
74 that he would grant unto us, that we, being delivered out of the hand of our enemies,
might serve him without fear,
75 in holiness and righteousness before him, all the days of our life.
76 And thou, child, shalt be called the prophet of the Highest:
for thou shalt go before the face of the Lord to prepare his ways;[a]
77 to give knowledge of salvation unto his people
by the remission of their sins,
78 through the tender mercy of our God;
whereby the dayspring from on high hath visited us,
79 to give light to them that sit in darkness[b] and *in* the shadow of death,
to guide our feet into the way of peace. ●

4. JOHN'S MATURING YEARS

80 And the child grew, and waxed strong
in spirit, and was in the deserts till the day
of his showing unto Israel. ●

YOUTH LEAVES HOME

*1:59-66* What are the main parts of this paragraph? ______

Why did the parents name their son John? (1:13)

*1:67-79* Analyze Zacharias' praise and prophecy:

PRAISE (verses 67-75) ______

PROPHECY (verses 76-79) ______

*1:80* What is known about John from this verse?

NEW INTERNATIONAL VERSION

What does the passage teach about:

LORD'S GLORY

FEAR

WORSHIP

List spiritual applications which can be made from this passage.

*The Birth of Jesus*

2 In those days Caesar Augustus issued
a decree that a census should be taken
of the entire Roman world. [2](This was the
first census that took place while Quirinius
was governor of Syria.) [3]And everyone
went to his own town to register.
[4]So Joseph also went up from the town
of Nazareth in Galilee to Judea, to Bethlehem the town of David, because he belonged to the house and line of David. [5]He
went there to register with Mary, who was
pledged to be married to him and was expecting a child. [6]While they were there, the
time came for the baby to be born, [7]and she
gave birth to her firstborn, a son. She
wrapped him in cloths and placed him in a
manger, because there was no room for
them in the inn.●

*The Shepherds and the Angels*

[8]And there were shepherds living out in
the fields nearby, keeping watch over their
flocks at night. [9]An angel of the Lord appeared to them, and the glory of the Lord
shone around them, and they were terrified. [10]But the angel said to them, "Do not
be afraid. I bring you good news of great
joy that will be for all the people. [11]Today
in the town of David a Savior has been
born to you; he is Christ[a] the Lord. [12]This
will be a sign to you: You will find a baby
wrapped in cloths and lying in a manger."
[13]Suddenly a great company of the heavenly host appeared with the angel, praising
God and saying,

[14]"Glory to God in the highest,
and on earth peace to men on
whom his favor rests."●

[15]When the angels had left them and
gone into heaven, the shepherds said to
one another, "Let's go to Bethlehem and
see this thing that has happened, which the
Lord has told us about."
[16]So they hurried off and found Mary and
Joseph, and the baby, who was lying in the
manger. [17]When they had seen him, they
spread the word concerning what had been
told them about this child, [18]and all who
heard it were amazed at what the shepherds said to them. [19]But Mary treasured
up all these things and pondered them in
her heart. [20]The shepherds returned, glorifying and praising God for all the things
they had heard and seen, which were just
as they had been told.●

[a]11 Or *Messiah*. "The Christ" (Greek) and "the Messiah" (Hebrew) both mean "the Anointed One"; also in verse 26.

KING JAMES

1. JESUS BORN

COLD DECREE

2 And it came to pass in those days,
that there went out a decree from
Caesar Augustus, that all the world should
be taxed. 2 (*And* this taxing was first
made when Cy·re'ni-us was governor of
Syria.) 3 And all went to be taxed, every
one into his own city. 4 And Joseph also
went up from Galilee, out of the city of
Nazareth, into Judea, unto the city of
David, which is called Bethlehem, (because he was of the house and lineage of
David,) 5 to be taxed with Mary his
espoused wife, being great with child.
6 And so it was, that, while they were
there, the days were accomplished that
she should be delivered. 7 And she
brought forth her firstborn son, and
wrapped him in swaddling clothes, and
laid him in a manger; because there was
no room for them in the inn. ●

2. ANNOUNCEMENT TO SHEPHERDS

8 And there were in the same country
shepherds abiding in the field, keeping
watch over their flock by night. 9 And, lo,
the angel of the Lord came upon them,
and the glory of the Lord shone round
about them; and they were sore afraid.
10 And the angel said unto them, Fear
not: for, behold, I bring you good tidings
of great joy, which shall be to all people.
11 For unto you is born this day in the
city of David a Saviour, which is Christ
the Lord. 12 And this *shall be* a sign unto
you; Ye shall find the babe wrapped in
swaddling clothes, lying in a manger.
13 And suddenly there was with the angel
a multitude of the heavenly host praising
God, and saying,
14 Glory to God in the highest,
and on earth peace,
good will toward men. ●

3. SHEPHERDS VISIT BABY

15 And it came to pass, as the angels
were gone away from them into heaven,
the shepherds said one to another, Let us
now go even unto Bethlehem, and see this
thing which is come to pass, which the
Lord hath made known unto us. 16 And
they came with haste, and found Mary
and Joseph, and the babe lying in a
manger. 17 And when they had seen *it*,
they made known abroad the saying
which was told them concerning this
child. 18 And all they that heard *it* wondered at those things which were told
them by the shepherds. 19 But Mary
kept all these things, and pondered *them*
in her heart. 20 And the shepherds returned, glorifying and praising God for
all the things that they had heard and
seen, as it was told unto them. ●

WARM PRAISE

*2:1-7* What was the setting of Jesus' birth:

POLITICAL: ______________________

GEOGRAPHICAL: ______________________

ECONOMICAL: ______________________

*2:8-14* Record key words and phrases.

______________________

*2:15-20* What does the paragraph reveal about:

SHEPHERDS ______________________

MARY ______________________

PEOPLE ______________________

NEW INTERNATIONAL VERSION

Record what is taught here about:

SACRIFICE TO GOD

WORD OF GOD

VISION

FAITH

JESUS' MINISTRY

THANKSGIVING

OTHER

*Jesus Presented in the Temple*

21 On the eighth day, when it was time to circumcise him, he was named Jesus, the name the angel had given him before he had been conceived.●

22 When the time of their purification according to the Law of Moses had been completed, Joseph and Mary took him to Jerusalem to present him to the Lord 23 (as it is written in the Law of the Lord, "Every firstborn male is to be consecrated to the Lord"[b]), 24 and to offer a sacrifice in keeping with what is said in the Law of the Lord: "a pair of doves or two young pigeons."[c]●

25 Now there was a man in Jerusalem called Simeon, who was righteous and devout. He was waiting for the consolation of Israel, and the Holy Spirit was upon him. 26 It had been revealed to him by the Holy Spirit that he would not die before he had seen the Lord's Christ. 27 Moved by the Spirit, he went into the temple courts. When the parents brought in the child Jesus to do for him what the custom of the Law required, 28 Simeon took him in his arms and praised God, saying:

29 "Sovereign Lord, as you have promised,
you now dismiss[d] your servant in peace.
30 For my eyes have seen your salvation,
31 which you have prepared in the sight of all people,
32 a light for revelation to the Gentiles
and for glory to your people Israel."

33 The child's father and mother marveled at what was said about him. 34 Then Simeon blessed them and said to Mary, his mother: "This child is destined to cause the falling and rising of many in Israel, and to be a sign that will be spoken against, 35 so that the thoughts of many hearts will be revealed. And a sword will pierce your own soul too."●

36 There was also a prophetess, Anna, the daughter of Phanuel, of the tribe of Asher. She was very old; she had lived with her husband seven years after her marriage, 37 and then was a widow until she was eighty-four.[a] She never left the temple but worshiped night and day, fasting and praying. 38 Coming up to them at that very moment, she gave thanks to God and spoke about the child to all who were looking forward to the redemption of Jerusalem.●

39 When Joseph and Mary had done everything required by the Law of the Lord, they returned to Galilee to their own town of Nazareth.●

[b] 23 Exodus 13:2,12  [c] 24 Lev. 12:8
[d] 29 Or *promised, / now dismiss*
[a] 37 Or *widow for eighty-four years*

KING JAMES

**1. JESUS IS NAMED**

JESUS' NAME

21 And when eight days were accomplished for the circumcising of the child,
his name was called JESUS, which was so
named of the angel before he was conceived in the womb. ●

**2. JESUS IS DEDICATED**

22 And when the days of her purification according to the law of Moses were
accomplished, they brought him to Jerusalem, to present *him* to the Lord; 23 (as
it is written in the law of the Lord, Every
male that openeth the womb shall be
called holy to the Lord; ) 24 and to offer
a sacrifice according to that which is said
in the law of the Lord, A pair of turtle-
doves, or two young pigeons. ● 25 And,

Ex. 13:2

Lev. 5:11

**3. SIMEON'S PROPHECY**

behold, there was a man in Jerusalem,
whose name *was* Simeon; and the same
man *was* just and devout, waiting for the
consolation of Israel: and the Holy Ghost
was upon him. 26 And it was revealed
unto him by the Holy Ghost, that he
should not see death, before he had seen
the Lord's Christ. 27 And he came by the
Spirit into the temple: and when the
parents brought in the child Jesus, to do
for him after the custom of the law,
28 then took he him up in his arms, and
blessed God, and said,
29 Lord, now lettest thou thy servant
depart in peace,
according to thy word:
30 for mine eyes have seen thy salvation,
31 which thou hast prepared before the
face of all people;
32 a light to lighten the Gentiles,
and the glory of thy people Israel.
33 And Joseph and his mother marveled at those things which were spoken
of him. 34 And Simeon blessed them, and
said unto Mary his mother, Behold, this
*child* is set for the fall and rising again of
many in Israel; and for a sign which shall
be spoken against; 35 (yea, a sword shall
pierce through thy own soul also;) that
the thoughts of many hearts may be revealed. ●

**4. ANNA'S PRAISE**

36 And there was one Anna, a prophetess, the daughter of Phan'u-el, of the tribe
of Asher: she was of a great age, and had
lived with a husband seven years from her
virginity; 37 and she *was* a widow of
about fourscore and four years, which departed not from the temple, but served
*God* with fastings and prayers night and
day. 38 And she coming in that instant
gave thanks likewise unto the Lord, and
spake of him to all them that looked for
redemption in Jerusalem. ●

**5. FAMILY RETURNS HOME**

JESUS' HOME

39 And when they had performed all
things according to the law of the Lord,
they returned into Galilee, to their own
city Nazareth. ●

*2:21-24* Read Leviticus 12 for the Mosaic instructions followed in 2:21-24. Why did Jesus' parents fulfill the Mosaic Law?

______

*2:25-35* Record your observations about:

JESUS ______

SIMEON'S PRAISE (vv.29-43) ______

SIMEON'S PROPHECY (vv.34-35) ______

*2:36-38* Record what the paragraph reveals about Anna.

______

NEW INTERNATIONAL VERSION

How does verse 40 describe the healthy maturing of a well-rounded person?

What does Jesus' interest in the temple discussion reveal about Him?

What was Jesus' persuasion concerning His relation to the heavenly Father?

To what extent did Jesus submit to parental authority (v.51)?

What is suggested by the phrase "in favor with God and man" (v.52)?

Why do you think the Holy Spirit inspired Luke to include this story in his gospel?

40 And the child grew
and became strong; he was filled with wisdom, and the grace of God was upon him.●

*The Boy Jesus at the Temple*

41 Every year his parents went to Jerusalem for the Feast of the Passover. 42 When
he was twelve years old, they went up to
the Feast, according to the custom. 43 After
the Feast was over, while his parents were
returning home, the boy Jesus stayed behind in Jerusalem, but they were unaware
of it. 44 Thinking he was in their company,
they traveled on for a day. Then they began
looking for him among their relatives and
friends. 45 When they did not find him, they
went back to Jerusalem to look for him.
46 After three days they found him in the
temple courts, sitting among the teachers,
listening to them and asking them questions. 47 Everyone who heard him was
amazed at his understanding and his answers.● 48 When his parents saw him, they
were astonished. His mother said to him,
"Son, why have you treated us like this?
Your father and I have been anxiously
searching for you."
49 "Why were you searching for me?" he
asked. "Didn't you know I had to be in my
Father's house?" 50 But they did not understand what he was saying to them.
51 Then he went down to Nazareth with
them and was obedient to them. But his
mother treasured all these things in her
heart.● 52 And Jesus grew in wisdom and
stature, and in favor with God and men.●

## KING JAMES

1.CHILD JESUS GROWING

40 And the child grew,
and waxed strong in spirit, filled with wisdom; and the grace of God was upon him.●

GRACE OF GOD

2.FAMILY SEPARATION

41 Now his parents went to Jerusalem
every year at the feast of the passover.
42 And when he was twelve years old,
they went up to Jerusalem after the custom of the feast. 43 And when they had
fulfilled the days, as they returned, the
child Jesus tarried behind in Jerusalem;
and Joseph and his mother knew not *of it*.
44 But they, supposing him to have been
in the company, went a day's journey;
and they sought him among *their* kinsfolk
and acquaintance. 45 And when they
found him not, they turned back again to
Jerusalem, seeking him. 46 And it came
to pass, that after three days they found
him in the temple, sitting in the midst of
the doctors, both hearing them, and asking them questions. 47 And all that
heard him were astonished at his understanding and answers.● 48 And when they

3.JESUS' EXPLANATION

saw him, they were amazed: and his
mother said unto him, Son, why hast thou
thus dealt with us? behold, thy father and
I have sought thee sorrowing. 49 And he
said unto them, How is it that ye sought
me? wist ye not that I must be about my
Father's business? 50 And they understood not the saying which he spake unto
them. 51 And he went down with them,
and came to Nazareth, and was subject
unto them: but his mother kept all these
sayings in her heart. ●

4.YOUTH JESUS MATURING

52 And Jesus increased in wisdom and
stature, and in favor with God and man. ●

FAVOR WITH GOD

Only Luke records this experience of Jesus. Record your observations of the text, below.

2:40 ____________________

2:41-47 ____________________

2:48-51 ____________________

2:52 ____________________

NEW INTERNATIONAL VERSION

What was the message which John preached (vv.3-6,8,9)?

How was John's mission related to Christ (vv.4-5)?

What was the ultimate purpose of John's ministry (v.6)?

On what did John's hearers base their salvation (v.8)?

What did John say was the real test of salvation (vv.8,10-14)?

What is revealed about Christ in verses 15-17?

### *John the Baptist Prepares the Way*

3 In the fifteenth year of the reign of
Tiberius Caesar—when Pontius Pilate
was governor of Judea, Herod tetrarch of
Galilee, his brother Philip tetrarch of Itu-
rea and Traconitis, and Lysanias tetrarch
of Abilene— 2during the high priesthood of
Annas and Caiaphas, the word of God
came to John son of Zechariah in the
desert. 3He went into all the country
around the Jordan, preaching a baptism of
repentance for the forgiveness of sins. 4As
is written in the book of the words of Isaiah
the prophet:

"A voice of one calling in the
desert,
'Prepare the way for the Lord,
make straight paths for him.
5Every valley shall be filled in,
every mountain and hill made
low.
The crooked roads shall become
straight,
the rough ways smooth.
6And all mankind will see God's
salvation.' "[b] ●

7John said to the crowds coming out to
be baptized by him, "You brood of vipers!
Who warned you to flee from the coming
wrath? 8Produce fruit in keeping with repentance. And do not begin to say to yourselves, 'We have Abraham as our father.'
For I tell you that out of these stones God
can raise up children for Abraham. 9The ax
is already at the root of the trees, and every
tree that does not produce good fruit will
be cut down and thrown into the fire." ●
10"What should we do then?" the crowd
asked.
11John answered, "The man with two
tunics should share with him who has
none, and the one who has food should do
the same."
12Tax collectors also came to be baptized. "Teacher," they asked, "what
should we do?"
13"Don't collect any more than you are
required to," he told them.
14Then some soldiers asked him, "And
what should we do?" ●
He replied, "Don't extort money and
don't accuse people falsely—be content
with your pay."
15The people were waiting expectantly
and were all wondering in their hearts if
John might possibly be the Christ.[c] 16John
answered them all, "I baptize you with[a]
water. But one more powerful than I will
come, the thongs of whose sandals I am not
worthy to untie. He will baptize you with
the Holy Spirit and with fire. 17His win-
nowing fork is in his hand to clear his
threshing floor and to gather the wheat into
his barn, but he will burn up the chaff with
unquenchable fire." ● 18And with many other words John exhorted the people and
preached the good news to them.
19But when John rebuked Herod the tetrarch because of Herodias, his brother's
wife, and all the other evil things he had
done, 20Herod added this to them all: He
locked John up in prison. ●

[b]6 Isaiah 40:3-5 [c]15 Or *Messiah* [a]16 Or *in*

KING JAMES

1. JOHN CAME

JOHN IN THE WILDERNESS

**3** Now in the fifteenth year of the reign
of Tibe'ri-us Caesar, Pontius Pilate
being governor of Judea, and Herod being
tetrarch of Galilee, and his brother Philip
tetrarch of Iturae'a and of the region of
Trachoni'tis, and Lysa'ni-as the tetrarch
of Abile'ne, 2 Annas and Cai'aphas being
the high priests, the word of God came
unto John the son of Zechari'ah in the
wilderness. 3 And he came into all the
country about Jordan, preaching the baptism of repentance for the remission of
sins; 4 as it is written in the book of the
words of Isaiah the prophet, saying,

The voice of one crying in the wilderness,
Prepare ye the way of the Lord,
make his paths straight.
5 Every valley shall be filled,
and every mountain and hill shall be brought low;
and the crooked shall be made straight,
and the rough ways *shall be* made smooth;
6 and all flesh shall see the salvation of God. ●

Isa. 40:4-5

2. JOHN PREACHED

—bring forth fruits

7 Then said he to the multitude that
came forth to be baptized of him, O generation of vipers, who hath warned you
to flee from the wrath to come? 8 Bring
forth therefore fruits worthy of repentance, and begin not to say within yourselves, We have Abraham to *our* father:
for I say unto you, That God is able of
these stones to raise up children unto
Abraham. 9 And now also the axe is laid
unto the root of the trees: every tree therefore which bringeth not forth good fruit
is hewn down, and cast into the fire. ●

3. JOHN ANSWERED

examples

10 And the people asked him, saying,
What shall we do then? 11 He answereth
and saith unto them, He that hath two
coats, let him impart to him that hath
none; and he that hath meat, let him do
likewise. 12 Then came also publicans to
be baptized, and said unto him, Master,
what shall we do? 13 And he said unto
them, Exact no more than that which is
appointed you. 14 And the soldiers likewise demanded of him, saying, And what
shall we do? And he said unto them, Do
violence to no man, neither accuse *any*
falsely; and be content with your wages. ●

4. JOHN POINTED TO CHRIST

15 And as the people were in expectation, and all men mused in their hearts of
John, whether he were the Christ, or not;
16 John answered, saying unto *them* all, I
indeed baptize you with water; but one
mightier than I cometh, the latchet of
whose shoes I am not worthy to unloose:
he shall baptize you with the Holy Ghost
and with fire: 17 whose fan *is* in his hand,
and he will thoroughly purge his floor,
and will gather the wheat into his garner;
but the chaff he will burn with fire unquenchable. ●

5. JOHN IMPRISONED

JOHN IN PRISON

18 And many other things in his exhortation preached he unto the people.
19 But Herod the tetrarch, being reproved
by him for Hero'di-as his brother Philip's
wife, and for all the evils which Herod
had done, 20 added yet this above all,
that he shut up John in prison. ●

Scan the segment and observe who the main character is in each paragraph.

Record observations of key parts of each paragraph:

*3:1-6* ______________________

*3:7-9* ______________________

*3:10-14* ______________________

*3:15-17* ______________________

*3:18-20* ______________________

NEW INTERNATIONAL VERSION

What do you think Jesus was testifying about by His baptism?

Why was this an appropriate introduction to His public ministry?

Why were His Father's words also an appropriate introduction?

List spiritual truths taught directly or indirectly by the genealogy of 3:23-38.

*The Baptism and Genealogy of Jesus*

21When all the people were being baptized, Jesus was baptized too. And as he
was praying, heaven was opened 22and the
Holy Spirit descended on him in bodily
form like a dove. And a voice came from
heaven: "You are my Son, whom I love;
with you I am well pleased."●
23Now Jesus himself was about thirty
years old when he began his ministry. He
was the son, so it was thought, of Joseph,

the son of Heli, 24the son of
Matthat,
the son of Levi, the son of Melki,
the son of Jannai, the son of Joseph,
25the son of Mattathias, the son of
Amos,
the son of Nahum, the son of Esli,
the son of Naggai, 26the son of
Maath,
the son of Mattathias, the son of
Semein,
the son of Josech, the son of Joda,
27the son of Joanan, the son of Rhesa,
the son of Zerubbabel, the son of
Shealtiel,
the son of Neri, 28the son of Melki,
the son of Addi, the son of Cosam,
the son of Elmadam, the son of Er,
29the son of Joshua, the son of
Eliezer,
the son of Jorim, the son of Matthat,
the son of Levi, 30the son of
Simeon,
the son of Judah, the son of Joseph,
the son of Jonam, the son of
Eliakim,
31the son of Melea, the son of Menna,
the son of Mattatha, the son of
Nathan,
the son of David, 32the son of Jesse,
the son of Obed, the son of Boaz,
the son of Salmon,[b] the son of
Nahshon,
33the son of Amminadab, the son of
Ram,[c]
the son of Hezron, the son of Perez,
the son of Judah, 34the son of Jacob,
the son of Isaac, the son of
Abraham,
the son of Terah, the son of Nahor,
35the son of Serug, the son of Reu,
the son of Peleg, the son of Eber,
the son of Shelah, 36the son of
Cainan,
the son of Arphaxad, the son of
Shem,
the son of Noah, the son of
Lamech,
37the son of Methuselah, the son of
Enoch,
the son of Jared, the son of
Mahalaleel,
the son of Cainan, 38the son of
Enos,
the son of Seth, the son of Adam,
the son of God.●

c33 Some manuscripts *Amminadab, the son of Admin, the son of Arni;* other manuscripts vary widely.
b32 Some early manuscripts *Sala*

## KING JAMES

**1. JESUS' BAPTISM**

**JESUS THE SON OF GOD**

21 Now when all the people were baptized, it came to pass, that Jesus also being
baptized, and praying, the heaven was
opened, 22 and the Holy Ghost descended
in a bodily shape like a dove upon him,
and a voice came from heaven, which
said, Thou art my beloved Son; in thee
I am well pleased. ●

**2. JESUS' ANCESTORS**

23 And Jesus himself began to be about
thirty years of age, being (as was supposed) the son of Joseph, which was *the*
*son* of Heli, 24 which was *the son* of
Matthat, which was *the son* of Levi, which
was *the son* of Melchi, which was *the son*
of Janna, which was *the son* of Joseph,
25 which was *the son* of Mattathi'as,
which was *the son* of Amos, which was *the*
*son* of Nahum, which was *the son* of Esli,
which was *the son* of Nag'gai, 26 which
was *the son* of Ma'ath, which was *the son*
of Mattathi'as, which was *the son* of
Sem'e-i, which was *the son* of Joseph,
which was *the son* of Judah, 27 which was
*the son* of Joanna, which was *the son* of
Rhesa, which was *the son* of Zerub'babel,
which was *the son* of She-al'ti-el, which
was *the son* of Neri, 28 which was *the son*
of Melchi, which was *the son* of Addi,
which was *the son* of Cosam, which was
*the son* of Elmo'dam, which was *the son*
of Er, 29 which was *the son* of Jose,
which was *the son* of Eli-e'zer, which was
*the son* of Jorim, which was *the son* of
Matthat, which was *the son* of Levi,
30 which was *the son* of Simeon, which
was *the son* of Judah, which was *the son*
of Joseph, which was *the son* of Jonan,
which was *the son* of Eli'akim, 31 which
was *the son* of Me'le-a, which was *the son*
of Menan, which was *the son* of Mat'tatha,
which was *the son* of Nathan, which was
*the son* of David, 32 which was *the son*
of Jesse, which was *the son* of Obed,
which was *the son* of Boaz, which was
*the son* of Salmon, which was *the son* of
Nahshon, 33 which was *the son* of Ammin'adab, which was *the son* of Ram,
which was *the son* of Hezron, which was
*the son* of Pharez, which was *the son* of
Judah, 34 which was *the son* of Jacob,
which was *the son* of Isaac, which was *the*
*son* of Abraham, which was *the son* of
Terah, which was *the son* of Nahor,
35 which was *the son* of Serug, which was
*the son* of Re'u, which was *the son* of
Peleg, which was *the son* of Eber, which
was *the son* of Salah, 36 which was *the*
*son* of Ca-i'nan, which was *the son* of
Arphax'ad, which was *the son* of Shem,
which was *the son* of Noah, which was
*the son* of Lamech, 37 which was *the son*
of Methu'selah, which was *the son* of
Enoch, which was *the son* of Jared, which
was *the son* of Mahal'aleel, which was *the*
*son* of Ca-i'nan, 38 which was *the son* of
Enos, which was *the son* of Seth, which
was *the son* of Adam, which was *the son*
of God. ●

**ADAM, SON OF GOD**

These are the last things recorded by Luke before he begins to report Jesus' public ministry.

*3:21-22* What happened while Jesus was praying?

Record the words of the Father to the Son.

*3:23-38* Why does Luke record this paragraph?

Luke traces Jesus' line back to Adam (v.38). How does this emphasize the humanity of Christ?

How is Adam related to God (v.38)?

What is intended by the phrase "being (as was supposed) the son of Joseph" (v.23)?

NEW INTERNATIONAL VERSION

List spiritual applications of the text in these areas:

DEVIL'S TEMPTATIONS

VICTORY OVER TEMPTATION

SCRIPTURE

FOOD

WEALTH AND POWER

GOD'S PROTECTION

WORSHIP

*The Temptation of Jesus*

4 Jesus, full of the Holy Spirit, returned
from the Jordan and was led by the
Spirit in the desert, [2]where for forty days
he was tempted by the devil. He ate nothing during those days, and at the end of
them he was hungry.
[3]The devil said to him, "If you are the
Son of God, tell this stone to become
bread."
[4]Jesus answered, "It is written: 'Man
does not live on bread alone.'[d]" ●
[5]The devil led him up to a high place and
showed him in an instant all the kingdoms
of the world. [6]And he said to him, "I will
give you all their authority and splendor,
for it has been given to me, and I can give
it to anyone I want to. [7]So if you worship
me, it will all be yours."
[8]Jesus answered, "It is written: 'Worship the Lord your God and serve him
only.'[e]" ●
[9]The devil led him to Jerusalem and had
him stand on the highest point of the temple. "If you are the Son of God," he said,
"throw yourself down from here. [10]For it
is written:

" 'He will command his angels
concerning you
to guard you carefully;
[11]they will lift you up in their hands,
so that you will not strike your
foot against a stone.'[a]"

[12]Jesus answered, "It says: 'Do not put
the Lord your God to the test.'[b]" ●
[13]When the devil had finished all this
tempting, he left him until an opportune
time. ●

[d]4 Deut. 8:3 [e]8 Deut. 6:13
[a]11 Psalm 91:11,12 [b]12 Deut. 6:16

KING JAMES

1.BREAD

4 And Jesus being full of the Holy Ghost returned from Jordan, and was
led by the Spirit into the wilderness,
2 being forty days tempted of the devil.
And in those days he did eat nothing: and
when they were ended, he afterward
hungered. 3 And the devil said unto him,
If thou be the Son of God, command this
stone that it be made bread. 4 And Jesus
answered him, saying, It is written, That
man shall not live by bread alone, but
by every word of God. ● 5 And the devil,
taking him up into a high mountain,
showed unto him all the kingdoms of the
world in a moment of time. 6 And the
devil said unto him, All this power will I
give thee, and the glory of them: for that
is delivered unto me; and to whomsoever
I will, I give it. 7 If thou therefore wilt
worship me, all shall be thine. 8 And
Jesus answered and said unto him,
Get thee behind me, Satan: for it is
written,

Thou shalt worship the Lord thy God,
and him only shalt thou serve. ●

9 And he brought him to Jerusalem, and
set him on a pinnacle of the temple, and
said unto him, If thou be the Son of God,
cast thyself down from hence: 10 for it is
written,

He shall give his angels charge over thee, to keep thee:
11 and in *their* hands they shall bear thee up,
lest at any time thou dash thy foot against a stone.

12 And Jesus answering said unto him,
It is said, Thou shalt not tempt the Lord
thy God. ● 13 And when the devil had
ended all the temptation, he departed
from him for a season. ●

2.DOMAIN

3.PROTECTION

—conclusion

HOLY SPIRIT

Deu. 8:3

Deu. 6:13

Ps. 91:11,12

Deu. 6:16

DEVIL

*4:1-4* Record what is revealed in verses 1-3 about:

JESUS ______________________________

HOLY SPIRIT ______________________________

DEVIL ______________________________

What was the first temptation? ______________________________

How did Jesus respond? ______________________________

*4:5-8* Record:

TEMPTATION ______________________________

JESUS' ANSWER ______________________________

*4:9-12*

TEMPTATION ______________________________

JESUS' ANSWER ______________________________

*4:13*

What is taught here about Satan? ______________________________

NEW INTERNATIONAL VERSION

What does the passage teach about:

*JESUS'* ______

PERSON ______

WISDOM ______

POWER ______

MESSAGE ______

MINISTRY ______

PEOPLE'S HEARTS ______

SOVEREIGNTY OF GOD ______

*Jesus Rejected at Nazareth*

14 Jesus returned to Galilee in the power
of the Spirit, and news about him spread
through the whole countryside. 15 He
taught in their synagogues, and everyone
praised him.●
16 He went to Nazareth, where he had
been brought up, and on the Sabbath day
he went into the synagogue, as was his
custom. And he stood up to read. 17 The
scroll of the prophet Isaiah was handed to
him. Unrolling it, he found the place where
it is written:

18 "The Spirit of the Lord is on me,
because he has anointed me
to preach good news to the poor.
He has sent me to proclaim freedom
for the prisoners
and recovery of sight for the
blind,
to release the oppressed,
19 to proclaim the year of the Lord's
favor."[c]●

20 Then he rolled up the scroll, gave it
back to the attendant and sat down. The
eyes of everyone in the synagogue were
fastened on him, 21 and he began by saying
to them, "Today this scripture is fulfilled
in your hearing."
22 All spoke well of him and were amazed
at the gracious words that came from his
lips. "Isn't this Joseph's son?" they asked.
23 Jesus said to them, "Surely you will
quote this proverb to me: 'Physician, heal
yourself! Do here in your home town what
we have heard that you did in Capernaum.' "
24 "I tell you the truth," he continued,
"no prophet is accepted in his home town.
25 I assure you that there were many widows in Israel in Elijah's time, when the sky
was shut for three and a half years and
there was a severe famine throughout the
land. 26 Yet Elijah was not sent to any of
them, but to a widow in Zarephath in the
region of Sidon. 27 And there were many in
Israel with leprosy[d] in the time of Elisha
the prophet, yet not one of them was
cleansed—only Naaman the Syrian."●
28 All the people in the synagogue were
furious when they heard this. 29 They got
up, drove him out of the town, and took
him to the brow of the hill on which the
town was built, in order to throw him down
the cliff. 30 But he walked right through the
crowd and went on his way.●

[c] *19* Isaiah 61:1,2
[d] *27* The Greek word was used for various diseases affecting the skin—not necessarily leprosy.

KING JAMES

—to Galilee

PRAISE

14 And Jesus returned in the power of
the Spirit into Galilee: and there went out
a fame of him through all the region round
about. 15 And he taught in their synagogues, being glorified of all. ●

1.JESUS READS SCRIPTURE

16 And he came to Nazareth, where he
had been brought up: and, as his custom
was, he went into the synagogue on the
sabbath day, and stood up for to read.
17 And there was delivered unto him the
book of the prophet Isaiah. And when
he had opened the book, he found the
place where it was written,
18 The Spirit of the Lord *is* upon
me,
because he hath anointed me to
preach the gospel to the poor;
he hath sent me to heal the broken-
hearted,
to preach deliverance to the captives,
and recovering of sight to the
blind,
to set at liberty them that are bruised,
19 to preach the acceptable year of the
Lord. ●

Isa. 61:1-2

2.JESUS EX-PLAINS

20 And he closed the book, and he gave
*it* again to the minister, and sat down.
And the eyes of all them that were in the
synagogue were fastened on him. 21 And
he began to say unto them, This day is
this Scripture fulfilled in your ears.
22 And all bare him witness, and wondered at the gracious words which proceeded out of his mouth. And they said,
Is not this Joseph's son? 23 And he said
unto them, Ye will surely say unto me this
proverb, Physician, heal thyself: whatsoever we have heard done in Caper'na-um,
do also here in thy country. 24 And he
said, Verily I say unto you, No prophet is
accepted in his own country. 25 But I
tell you of a truth, many widows were in
Israel in the days of Eli'jah, when the
heaven was shut up three years and six
months, when great famine was throughout all the land; 26 but unto none of
them was Eli'jah sent, save unto Zar'e-
phath, *a city* of Sidon, unto a woman *that*
*was* a widow. 27 And many lepers were in
Israel in the time of Eli'sha the prophet;
and none of them was cleansed, saving
Na'aman the Syrian. ●28And all they in

3.JESUS CAST OUT OF CITY

the synagogue, when they heard these
things, were filled with wrath, 29 and
rose up, and thrust him out of the city,
and led him unto the brow of the hill
whereon their city was built, that they
might cast him down headlong. 30 But
he, passing through the midst of them,
went his way, ●

RAGE

This segment begins the Early Galilean ministry of Jesus. Luke skips over the events of Jesus' first-year Judean ministry. The section 4:14-9:50 is called IDENTIFICATION (see outline) because Jesus was trying to establish His true identity at the time.

*4:14-15* Underline key words in this introductory paragraph.

*4:16-19* Record what verses 18-19 say about Jesus.

*4:20-27* Observe the pairs of two illustrations: Israel, Sidon; and Israel, Syria. What is the main point of Jesus' words?

*4:28-30* Contrast verses 29 and 30: ______

What miracle is wrought in verse 30? ______

NEW INTERNATIONAL VERSION

Many important spiritual lessons can be learned from this passage. Record what you see.

The demons knew who Christ was (v.4). Why didn't Jesus want them to proclaim this?

Can you apply this to today, not involving demons?

*Jesus Drives Out an Evil Spirit*

[31]Then he went down to Capernaum, a
town in Galilee, and on the Sabbath began
to teach the people. [32]They were amazed at
his teaching, because his message had authority.●
[33]In the synagogue there was a man possessed by a demon, an evil[e] spirit. He cried
out at the top of his voice, [34]"Ha! What do
you want with us, Jesus of Nazareth? Have
you come to destroy us? I know who you
are—the Holy One of God!"
[35]"Be quiet!" Jesus said sternly. "Come
out of him!" Then the demon threw the
man down before them all and came out
without injuring him.
[36]All the people were amazed and said to
each other, "What is this teaching? With
authority and power he gives orders to evil
spirits and they come out!" [37]And the news
about him spread throughout the surrounding area.●

*Jesus Heals Many*

[38]Jesus left the synagogue and went to
the home of Simon. Now Simon's mother-
in-law was suffering from a high fever, and
they asked Jesus to help her. [39]So he bent
over her and rebuked the fever, and it left
her. She got up at once and began to wait
on them.
[40]When the sun was setting, the people
brought to Jesus all who had various kinds
of sickness, and laying his hands on each
one, he healed them. [41]Moreover, demons
came out of many people, shouting, "You
are the Son of God!" But he rebuked them
and would not allow them to speak, because they knew he was the Christ.[f]●
[42]At daybreak Jesus went out to a solitary place. The people were looking for
him and when they came to where he was,
they tried to keep him from leaving them.
[43]But he said, "I must preach the good
news of the kingdom of God to the other
towns also, because that is why I was
sent."● [44]And he kept on preaching in the
synagogues of Judea.[a]●

[e]33 Greek *unclean*; also in verse 36 [f]41 Or *Messiah*
[a]44 Or *the land of the Jews*; some manuscripts *Galilee*

## KING JAMES

31 and came down to Ca-
per'na-um, a city of Galilee, and taught
1.TEACHING them on the sabbath days. 32 And they AUTHOR-
were astonished at his doctrine: for his ITY
word was with power. ●
2.HEALING 33 And in the synagogue there was a
man, which had a spirit of an unclean
devil, and cried out with a loud voice,
a. 34 saying, Let *us* alone; what have we to
do with thee, *thou* Jesus of Nazareth? art
thou come to destroy us? I know thee
who thou art; the Holy One of God.
35 And Jesus rebuked him, saying, Hold
thy peace, and come out of him. And
when the devil had thrown him in the
midst, he came out of him, and hurt him
not. 36 And they were all amazed, and
spake among themselves, saying, What a
word *is* this! for with authority and power
he commandeth the unclean spirits, and
they come out. 37 And the fame of him
went out into every place of the country
round about. ●
b. 38 And he arose out of the synagogue,
and entered into Simon's house. And
Simon's wife's mother was taken with a
great fever; and they besought him for
her. 39 And he stood over her, and rebuked the fever; and it left her: and immediately she arose and ministered unto
them. ●
c. 40 Now when the sun was setting, all
they that had any sick with divers diseases
brought them unto him; and he laid his
hands on every one of them, and healed
them. 41 And devils also came out of
many, crying out, and saying, Thou art
Christ the Son of God. And he rebuking
*them* suffered them not to speak: for they
knew that he was Christ. ●
3.PREACH-ING 42 And when it was day, he departed
and went into a desert place: and the
people sought him, and came unto him,
and stayed him, that he should not depart
from them. 43 And he said unto them, I COMPUL-
must preach the kingdom of God to other SION
cities also: for therefore am I sent.● 44 And
he preached in the synagogues of Galilee.●

Record your main observations of each paragraph. Look especially for *identifications* of Jesus.

*4:31-37* ______________________

*4:38-39* ______________________

*4:40-41* ______________________

*4:42-43* ______________________

*4:44* ______________________

NEW INTERNATIONAL VERSION

What does this story teach about:

THE WORD OF GOD

FAITH

MIRACLES

SOUL WINNING

DISCIPLESHIP

OTHER

*The Calling of the First Disciples*

5 One day as Jesus was standing by the
Lake of Gennesaret,[b] with the people
crowding around him and listening to the
word of God, 2he saw at the water's edge
two boats, left there by the fishermen, who
were washing their nets. 3He got into one
of the boats, the one belonging to Simon,
and asked him to put out a little from shore.
Then he sat down and taught the people
from the boat.●
4When he had finished speaking, he said
to Simon, "Put out into deep water, and let
down[c] the nets for a catch."
5Simon answered, "Master, we've
worked hard all night and haven't caught
anything. But because you say so, I will let
down the nets."
6When they had done so, they caught
such a large number of fish that their nets
began to break. 7So they signaled their
partners in the other boat to come and help
them, and they came and filled both boats
so full that they began to sink.
8When Simon Peter saw this, he fell at
Jesus' knees and said, "Go away from me,
Lord; I am a sinful man!" 9For he and all
his companions were astonished at the
catch of fish they had taken, 10and so were
James and John, the sons of Zebedee, Simon's partners.
Then Jesus said to Simon, "Don't be
afraid; from now on you will catch men."●
11So they pulled their boats up on shore,
left everything and followed him.●

[b]*1* That is, Sea of Galilee
[c]*4* The Greek verb is plural.

## KING JAMES

1.INSTRUCTION

TEACHER

5 And it came to pass, that, as the people pressed upon him to hear the
word of God, he stood by the lake of
Gennes'aret, 2 and saw two ships standing by the lake: but the fishermen were
gone out of them, and were washing *their*
nets. 3 And he entered into one of the
ships, which was Simon's, and prayed him
that he would thrust out a little from the
land. And he sat down, and taught the
people out of the ship. ● 4 Now when he
had left speaking, he said unto Simon,

2.A MIRACLE

Launch out into the deep, and let down
your nets for a draught. 5 And Simon
answering said unto him, Master, we have
toiled all the night, and have taken nothing: nevertheless at thy word I will let
down the net. 6 And when they had this
done, they inclosed a great multitude of
fishes: and their net brake. 7 And they
beckoned unto *their* partners, which were
in the other ship, that they should come
and help them. And they came, and filled
both the ships, so that they began to sink.
8 When Simon Peter saw *it*, he fell down
at Jesus' knees, saying, Depart from me;
for I am a sinful man, O Lord. 9 For he
was astonished, and all that were with him,
at the draught of the fishes which they had
taken: 10 and so *was* also James, and
John, the sons of Zeb'edee, which were
partners with Simon. And Jesus said unto
Simon, Fear not; from henceforth thou
shalt catch men. ● 11 And when they had

3.A FOLLOWING

MASTER

brought their ships to land, they forsook
all, and followed him. ●

Observe how this segment begins with multitudes (v.1) and concludes with disciples (v.11). Jesus was ministering to both groups during His three years before death.

Record the main parts (words and actions) of each of the paragraphs:

*5:1-3* ____________________

*5:4-10* ____________________

*5:11* ____________________

NEW INTERNATIONAL VERSION

What do you learn from this passage about:

FAITH FOR HEALING ____________________

JESUS' DEITY ____________________

JESUS' POWER ____________________

FORGIVENESS OF SINS ____________________

OTHER ____________________

*The Man With Leprosy*

12While Jesus was in one of the towns, a man came along who was covered with leprosy.[d] When he saw Jesus, he fell with his face to the ground and begged him, "Lord, if you are willing, you can make me clean."

13Jesus reached out his hand and touched the man. "I am willing," he said. "Be clean!" And immediately the leprosy left him.

14Then Jesus ordered him, "Don't tell anyone, but go, show yourself to the priest and offer the sacrifices that Moses commanded for your cleansing, as a testimony to them."

15Yet the news about him spread all the more, so that crowds of people came to hear him and to be healed of their sicknesses. 16But Jesus often withdrew to lonely places and prayed.●

*Jesus Heals a Paralytic*

17One day as he was teaching, Pharisees and teachers of the law, who had come from every village of Galilee and from Judea and Jerusalem, were sitting there. And the power of the Lord was present for him to heal the sick. 18Some men came carrying a paralytic on a mat and tried to take him into the house to lay him before Jesus. 19When they could not find a way to do this because of the crowd, they went up on the roof and lowered him on his mat through the tiles into the middle of the crowd, right in front of Jesus.

20When Jesus saw their faith, he said, "Friend, your sins are forgiven."

21The Pharisees and the teachers of the law began thinking to themselves, "Who is this fellow who speaks blasphemy? Who can forgive sins but God alone?"

22Jesus knew what they were thinking and asked, "Why are you thinking these things in your hearts? 23Which is easier: to say, 'Your sins are forgiven,' or to say, 'Get up and walk'? 24But that you may know that the Son of Man has authority on earth to forgive sins. . . ." He said to the paralyzed man, "I tell you, get up, take your mat and go home." 25Immediately he stood up in front of them, took what he had been lying on and went home praising God.● 26Everyone was amazed and gave praise to God. They were filled with awe and said, "We have seen remarkable things today."●

*d12* The Greek word was used for various diseases affecting the skin—not necessarily leprosy.

## KING JAMES

**1. LEPER HEALED**

**BESEECHING JESUS**

12 And it came to pass, when he was in
a certain city, behold a man full of leprosy;
who seeing Jesus fell on *his* face, and besought him, saying, Lord, if thou wilt,
thou canst make me clean. 13 And he
put forth *his* hand, and touched him, saying, I will: be thou clean. And immediately the leprosy departed from him.
14 And he charged him to tell no man:
But go, and show thyself to the priest, and
offer for thy cleansing, according as Moses
commanded, for a testimony unto them.
15 But so much the more went there a
fame abroad of him: and great multitudes
came together to hear, and to be healed
by him of their infirmities. 16 And he
withdrew himself into the wilderness, and
prayed. ●

**2. PARALYTIC HEALED**

17 And it came to pass on a certain day,
as he was teaching, that there were Pharisees and doctors of the law sitting by,
which were come out of every town of
Galilee, and Judea, and Jerusalem: and
the power of the Lord was *present* to heal
them. 18 And, behold, men brought in a
bed a man which was taken with a palsy:
and they sought *means* to bring him in,
and to lay *him* before him. 19 And when
they could not find by what *way* they
might bring him in because of the multitude, they went upon the housetop, and
let him down through the tiling with *his*
couch into the midst before Jesus. 20 And
when he saw their faith, he said unto him,
Man, thy sins are forgiven thee. 21 And
the scribes and the Pharisees began to
reason, saying, Who is this which speaketh blasphemies? Who can forgive sins,
but God alone? 22 But when Jesus perceived their thoughts, he answering said
unto them, What reason ye in your hearts?
23 whether is easier, to say, Thy sins be
forgiven thee; or to say, Rise up and walk?
24 But that ye may know that the Son of
man hath power upon earth to forgive
sins, (he said unto the sick of the palsy,) I
say unto thee, Arise, and take up thy
couch, and go into thine house. 25 And
immediately he rose up before them, and
took up that whereon he lay, and departed to his own house, glorifying God.●
26 And they were all amazed, and they
glorified God, and were filled with fear,
saying, We have seen strange things today.●

**GLORIFYING GOD**

*5:12-16* Record the main words and actions of the healing situation:

What does Luke report in verses 15 and 16?

*5:17-25* What was the physical need here?

What was the spiritual need?

How did Jesus use this occasion to teach about the spiritual needs of man?

*5:26* Record the reactions:

NEW INTERNATIONAL VERSION

What are the dramatic moments and key utterances of this narrative? Write down at least five spiritual lessons you have learned here.

Record some ways you could share these lessons with others.

*The Calling of Levi*

27 After this, Jesus went out and saw a tax
collector by the name of Levi sitting at his
tax booth. "Follow me," Jesus said to
him, 28 and Levi got up, left everything and
followed him.●
29 Then Levi held a great banquet for
Jesus at his house, and a large crowd of tax
collectors and others were eating with
them. 30 But the Pharisees and the teachers
of the law who belonged to their sect complained to his disciples, "Why do you eat
and drink with tax collectors and 'sinners'?"
31 Jesus answered them, "It is not the
healthy who need a doctor, but the sick. 32 I
have not come to call the righteous, but
sinners to repentance."●

*Jesus Questioned About Fasting*

33 They said to him, "John's disciples
often fast and pray, and so do the disciples
of the Pharisees, but yours go on eating and
drinking."
34 Jesus answered, "Can you make the
guests of the bridegroom fast while he is
with them? 35 But the time will come when
the bridegroom will be taken from them; in
those days they will fast."
36 He told them this parable: "No one
tears a patch from a new garment and sews
it on an old one. If he does, he will have
torn the new garment, and the patch from
the new will not match the old. 37 And no
one pours new wine into old wineskins. If
he does, the new wine will burst the skins,
the wine will run out and the wineskins will
be ruined. 38 No, new wine must be poured
into new wineskins. 39 And no one after
drinking old wine wants the new, for he
says, 'The old is better.' "●

*Lord of the Sabbath*

6 One Sabbath Jesus was going through
the grainfields, and his disciples began
to pick some heads of grain, rub them in
their hands and eat the kernels. 2 Some of
the Pharisees asked, "Why are you doing
what is unlawful on the Sabbath?"
3 Jesus answered them, "Have you never
read what David did when he and his companions were hungry? 4 He entered the
house of God, and taking the consecrated
bread, he ate what is lawful only for priests
to eat. And he also gave some to his companions." 5 Then Jesus said to them, "The
Son of Man is Lord of the Sabbath."●
6 On another Sabbath he went into the
synagogue and was teaching, and a man
was there whose right hand was shriveled.
7 The Pharisees and the teachers of the law
were looking for a reason to accuse Jesus,
so they watched him closely to see if he
would heal on the Sabbath. 8 But Jesus
knew what they were thinking and said to
the man with the shriveled hand, "Get up
and stand in front of everyone." So he got
up and stood there.
9 Then Jesus said to them, "I ask you,
which is lawful on the Sabbath: to do good
or to do evil, to save life or to destroy it?"
10 He looked around at them all, and then
said to the man, "Stretch out your hand."
He did so, and his hand was completely
restored. 11 But they were furious and began to discuss with one another what they
might do to Jesus.●

KING JAMES

1. CALLING OF LEVI

FOLLOWING JESUS

**27 And after these things he went forth,
and saw a publican, named Levi, sitting
at the receipt of custom: and he said unto
him, Follow me. 28 And he left all, rose
up, and followed him.●**

2. OPPOSITION

a.

**29 And Levi made him a great feast in
his own house: and there was a great company of publicans and of others that sat
down with them. 30 But their scribes and
Pharisees murmured against his disciples,
saying, Why do ye eat and drink with publicans and sinners? 31 And Jesus answering said unto them, They that are whole
need not a physician; but they that are
sick. 32 I came not to call the righteous,
but sinners to repentance.●**

b.

**33 And they said unto him, Why do the
disciples of John fast often, and make
prayers, and likewise *the disciples* of the
Pharisees; but thine eat and drink?
34 And he said unto them, Can ye make
the children of the bridechamber fast,
while the bridegroom is with them?
35 But the days will come, when the bridegroom shall be taken away from them,
and then shall they fast in those days.
36 And he spake also a parable unto
them; No man putteth a piece of a new
garment upon an old; if otherwise, then
both the new maketh a rent, and the piece
that was *taken* out of the new agreeth not
with the old. 37 And no man putteth new
wine into old bottles; else the new wine
will burst the bottles, and be spilled, and
the bottles shall perish. 38 But new wine
must be put into new bottles; and both
are preserved. 39 No man also having
drunk old *wine* straightway desireth new;
for he saith, The old is better.●**

c.

**6 And it came to pass on the second
sabbath after the first, that he went
through the corn fields; and his disciples
plucked the ears of corn, and did eat,
rubbing *them* in *their* hands. 2 And certain of the Pharisees said unto them, Why
do ye that which is not lawful to do on the
sabbath days? 3 And Jesus answering
them said, Have ye not read so much as
this, what David did, when himself was
ahungered, and they which were with him;
4 how he went into the house of God, and
did take and eat the showbread, and gave
also to them that were with him; which
it is not lawful to eat but for the priests
alone? 5 And he said unto them, That
the Son of man is Lord also of the sabbath.●**

d.

**6 And it came to pass also on another
sabbath, that he entered into the synagogue and taught: and there was a man
whose right hand was withered. 7 And
the scribes and Pharisees watched him,
whether he would heal on the sabbath
day; that they might find an accusation
against him. 8 But he knew their thoughts,
and said to the man which had the withered hand, Rise up, and stand forth in the
midst. And he arose and stood forth.
9 Then said Jesus unto them, I will ask
you one thing; Is it lawful on the sabbath
days to do good, or to do evil? to save
life, or to destroy *it?* 10 And looking
round about upon them all, he said unto
the man, Stretch forth thy hand. And he
did so: and his hand was restored whole
as the other. 11 And they were filled**

PLOTTING AGAINST JESUS

**with madness; and communed one
with another what they might do to
Jesus.●**

Opposition to Jesus came quickly from the religious leaders. Compare the four cases of opposition cited here. For each case, observe the following:

a. who the objectors were

b. to whom they raised the objection

c. about whom the objection was

d. the objection itself

e. Jesus' answer

*5:30-32* ______

*5:33-39* ______

*6:1-5* ______

*6:6-11* ______

NEW INTERNATIONAL VERSION

Try answering these three questions:

1. Why would Jesus pray all night long? ______

2. Why did Jesus need a select, small group of apostles? ______

3. Why did Jesus choose Judas Iscariot, whom He knew would betray Him? ______

List important spiritual applications taught by this passage. ______

*The Twelve Apostles*

[12]One of those days Jesus went out into the hills to pray, and spent the night praying to God. [13]When morning came, he called his disciples to him and chose twelve of them, whom he also designated apostles: [14]Simon (whom he named Peter), his brother Andrew, James, John, Philip, Bartholomew, [15]Matthew, Thomas, James son of Alphaeus, Simon who was called the Zealot, [16]Judas son of James, and Judas Iscariot, who became a traitor.●

*Blessings and Woes*

[17]He went down with them and stood on a level place. A large crowd of his disciples was there and a great number of people from all over Judea, from Jerusalem, and from the seacoast of Tyre and Sidon, [18]who had come to hear him and to be healed of their diseases. Those troubled by evil[a] spirits were cured, [19]and the people all tried to touch him, because power was coming from him and healing them all.●

[20]Looking at his disciples, he said:

"Blessed are you who are poor,
for yours is the kingdom of God.
[21]Blessed are you who hunger now,
for you will be satisfied.
Blessed are you who weep now,
for you will laugh.
[22]Blessed are you when men hate you,
when they exclude you and insult you
and reject your name as evil,
because of the Son of Man.

[23]"Rejoice in that day and leap for joy, because great is your reward in heaven. For that is how their fathers treated the prophets.

[24]"But woe to you who are rich,
for you have already received your comfort.
[25]Woe to you who are well fed now,
for you will go hungry.
Woe to you who laugh now,
for you will mourn and weep.
[26]Woe to you when all men speak well of you,
for that is how their fathers
treated the false prophets.●

*Love for Enemies*

[27]"But I tell you who hear me: Love your enemies, do good to those who hate you, [28]bless those who curse you, pray for those who mistreat you. [29]If someone strikes you on one cheek, turn to him the other also. If someone takes your cloak, do not stop him from taking your tunic. [30]Give to everyone who asks you, and if anyone takes what belongs to you, do not demand it back. [31]Do to others as you would have them do to you.

[32]"If you love those who love you, what credit is that to you? Even 'sinners' love those who love them. [33]And if you do good to those who are good to you, what credit is that to you? Even 'sinners' do that. [34]And if you lend to those from whom you expect repayment, what credit is that to you? Even 'sinners' lend to 'sinners,' expecting to be repaid in full. [35]But love your enemies, do good to them, and lend to them without expecting to get anything back. Then your reward will be great, and you will be sons of the Most High, because he is kind to the ungrateful and wicked. [36]Be merciful, just as your Father is merciful.●

[a]18 Greek *unclean*

KING JAMES

1.12 DISCIPLES CALLED

PRAYER

12 And it came to pass in those days,
that he went out into a mountain to pray,
and continued all night in prayer to God.
13 And when it was day, he called *unto*
*him* his disciples: and of them he chose
twelve, whom also he named apostles;
14 Simon, (whom he also named Peter,)
and Andrew his brother, James and
John, Philip and Bartholomew, 15 Matthew and Thomas, James the *son* of
Al'pheus, and Simon called Zelo'tes,
16 and Judas *the brother* of James, and
Judas Iscar'i-ot, which also was the
traitor. ●

2.MULTITUDES HEALED

17 And he came down with them, and
stood in the plain, and the company of his
disciples, and a great multitude of people
out of all Judea and Jerusalem, and from
the seacoast of Tyre and Sidon, which
came to hear him, and to be healed of
their diseases; 18 and they that were
vexed with unclean spirits: and they were
healed. 19 And the whole multitude
sought to touch him: for there went
virtue out of him, and healed *them*
all. ●

3.BLESSINGS AND WOES

20 And he lifted up his eyes on his disciples, and said, Blessed *be ye* poor: for
yours is the kingdom of God.
21 Blessed *are ye* that hunger now: for
ye shall be filled. Blessed *are ye* that weep
now: for ye shall laugh.
22 Blessed are ye, when men shall hate
you, and when they shall separate you
*from their company*, and shall reproach
*you*, and cast out your name as evil, for
the Son of man's sake. 23 Rejoice ye in
that day, and leap for joy: for, behold,
your reward *is* great in heaven: for in the
like manner did their fathers unto the
prophets.
24 But woe unto you that are rich! for
ye have received your consolation.
25 Woe unto you that are full! for ye
shall hunger. Woe unto you that laugh
now! for ye shall mourn and weep.
26 Woe unto you, when all men shall
speak well of you! for so did their fathers
to the false prophets. ●

4.LOVING OUR ENEMIES

27 But I say unto you which hear, Love
your enemies, do good to them which
hate you, 28 bless them that curse you,
and pray for them which despitefully use
you. 29 And unto him that smiteth thee
on the *one* cheek offer also the other; and
him that taketh away thy cloak forbid not
*to take thy* coat also. 30 Give to every
man that asketh of thee; and of him that
taketh away thy goods ask *them* not
again. 31 And as ye would that men
should do to you, do ye also to them
likewise.
32 For if ye love them which love you,
what thank have ye? for sinners also love
those that love them. 33 And if ye do
good to them which do good to you, what
thank have ye? for sinners also do even
the same. 34 And if ye lend *to them* of
whom ye hope to receive, what thank
have ye? for sinners also lend to sinners,
to receive as much again. 35 But love ye
your enemies, and do good, and lend,
hoping for nothing again; and your reward shall be great, and ye shall be the
children of the Highest: for he is kind unto the unthankful and *to* the evil. 36 Be
ye therefore merciful, as your Father also
is merciful. ●

LOVE

*6:12-16* What are the prominent truths of this paragraph? ____________

*6:17-19* Observe the *context* of healing:
a. after prayer (v.12)
b. after calling the twelve (vv.13-16)
c. before the sermon (vv.20-26)
What are your impressions?

*6:20-26* Record observations of these words of Jesus. For example, who were the hearers?

*6:27-36* Record the main truths. ____________

NEW INTERNATIONAL VERSION

Does this sermon show unbelievers how to be saved, or instruct believers how to live the Christian life? Support your answer.

What is taught here about:

LOVE

WORKS

THE FUTURE

Record practical lessons from the promises and warnings of the sermon.

### *Judging Others*

37"Do not judge, and you will not be
judged. Do not condemn, and you will not
be condemned. Forgive, and you will be
forgiven. 38Give, and it will be given to
you. A good measure, pressed down, shak-
en together and running over, will be
poured into your lap. For with the measure
you use, it will be measured to you."
39He also told them this parable: "Can a
blind man lead a blind man? Will they not
both fall into a pit? 40A student is not above
his teacher, but everyone who is fully
trained will be like his teacher.
41"Why do you look at the speck of saw-
dust in your brother's eye and pay no attention to the plank in your own eye?
42How can you say to your brother, 'Brother, let me take the speck out of your eye,'
when you yourself fail to see the plank in
your own eye? You hypocrite, first take
the plank out of your eye, and then you will
see clearly to remove the speck from your
brother's eye.●

### *A Tree and Its Fruit*

43"No good tree bears bad fruit, nor does
a bad tree bear good fruit. 44Each tree is
recognized by its own fruit. People do not
pick figs from thornbushes, or grapes from
briers. 45The good man brings good things
out of the good stored up in his heart, and
the evil man brings evil things out of the
evil stored up in his heart. For out of the
overflow of his heart his mouth speaks.●

### *The Wise and Foolish Builders*

46"Why do you call me, 'Lord, Lord,'
and do not do what I say? 47I will show you
what he is like who comes to me and hears
my words and puts them into practice.
48He is like a man building a house, who
dug down deep and laid the foundation on
rock. When a flood came, the torrent
struck that house but could not shake it,
because it was well built. 49But the one
who hears my words and does not put them
into practice is like a man who built a house
on the ground without a foundation. The
moment the torrent struck that house, it
collapsed and its destruction was complete."●

## KING JAMES

### 1. JUDGING OTHERS

JUDGMENT

37 Judge not, and ye shall not be judged:
condemn not, and ye shall not be condemned: forgive, and ye shall be forgiven:
38 give, and it shall be given unto you;
good measure, pressed down, and shaken
together, and running over, shall men
give into your bosom. For with the same
measure that ye mete withal it shall be
measured to you again.
39 And he spake a parable unto them;
Can the blind lead the blind? shall they
not both fall into the ditch? 40 The disciple is not above his master: but every
one that is perfect shall be as his master.
41 And why beholdest thou the mote that
is in thy brother's eye, but perceivest not
the beam that is in thine own eye?
42 Either how canst thou say to thy
brother, Brother, let me pull out the mote
that is in thine eye, when thou thyself beholdest not the beam that is in thine own
eye? Thou hypocrite, cast out first the
beam out of thine own eye, and then shalt
thou see clearly to pull out the mote that
is in thy brother's eye. ●

### 2. A TREE AND ITS FRUIT

43 For a good tree bringeth not forth
corrupt fruit; neither doth a corrupt tree
bring forth good fruit. 44 For every tree
is known by his own fruit. For of thorns
men do not gather figs, nor of a bramble
bush gather they grapes. 45 A good man
out of the good treasure of his heart bringeth forth that which is good; and an evil
man out of the evil treasure of his heart
bringeth forth that which is evil: for of the
abundance of the heart his mouth
speaketh. ●

### 3. WISE AND FOOLISH BUILDERS

46 And why call ye me, Lord, Lord, and
do not the things which I say? 47 Whosoever cometh to me, and heareth my sayings, and doeth them, I will show you to
whom he is like: 48 he is like a man
which built a house, and digged deep, and
laid the foundation on a rock: and when
the flood arose, the stream beat vehemently upon that house, and could not
shake it; for it was founded upon a rock.
49 But he that heareth, and doeth not, is
like a man that without a foundation built
a house upon the earth; against which the
stream did beat vehemently, and immediately it fell; and the ruin of that house was
great. ●

COLLAPSE

This sermon began at 6:20 (cf. 6:17 and 7:1). Record your observations for each paragraph.

*6:37-42* __________

*6:43-45* __________

*6:46-49* __________

NEW INTERNATIONAL VERSION

What does the passage teach about:

MERCY

MERIT

FAITH

JESUS' COMPASSION

OTHER TRUTHS

*The Faith of the Centurion*

7 When Jesus had finished saying all this
in the hearing of the people, he entered
Capernaum. 2There a centurion's servant,
whom his master valued highly, was sick
and about to die. 3The centurion heard of
Jesus and sent some elders of the Jews to
him, asking him to come and heal his servant. 4When they came to Jesus, they
pleaded earnestly with him, "This man deserves to have you do this, 5because he
loves our nation and has built our synagogue." 6So Jesus went with them.
He was not far from the house when the
centurion sent friends to say to him:
"Lord, don't trouble yourself, for I do not
deserve to have you come under my roof.
7That is why I did not even consider myself
worthy to come to you. But say the word,
and my servant will be healed. 8For I myself am a man under authority, with soldiers under me. I tell this one, 'Go,' and he
goes; and that one, 'Come,' and he comes.
I say to my servant, 'Do this,' and he does
it."
9When Jesus heard this, he was amazed
at him, and turning to the crowd following
him, he said, "I tell you, I have not found
such great faith even in Israel." 10Then the
men who had been sent returned to the
house and found the servant well.

*Jesus Raises a Widow's Son*

11Soon afterward, Jesus went to a town
called Nain, and his disciples and a large
crowd went along with him. 12As he approached the town gate, a dead person was
being carried out—the only son of his
mother, and she was a widow. And a large
crowd from the town was with her. 13When
the Lord saw her, his heart went out to her
and he said, "Don't cry."
14Then he went up and touched the cof-
fin, and those carrying it stood still. He
said, "Young man, I say to you, get up!"
15The dead man sat up and began to talk,
and Jesus gave him back to his mother.
16They were all filled with awe and
praised God. "A great prophet has appeared among us," they said. "God has
come to help his people." 17This news
about Jesus spread throughout Judea[a] and
the surrounding country.

[a]17 Or *the land of the Jews*

## KING JAMES

—to Capernaum

1.HEALING

7 Now when he had ended all his sayings in the audience of the people, he
entered into Caper'na-um.● 2 And a certain centurion's servant, who was dear
unto him, was sick, and ready to die.
3 And when he heard of Jesus, he sent
unto him the elders of the Jews, beseeching him that he would come and heal his
servant. 4 And when they came to Jesus,
they besought him instantly, saying, That
he was worthy for whom he should do
this: 5 for he loveth our nation, and he
hath built us a synagogue. 6 Then Jesus
went with them. And when he was now
not far from the house, the centurion sent
friends to him, saying unto him, Lord,
trouble not thyself; for I am not worthy
that thou shouldest enter under my roof:
7 wherefore neither thought I myself
worthy to come unto thee: but say in a
word, and my servant shall be healed.
8 For I also am a man set under authority, having under me soldiers, and I say
unto one, Go, and he goeth; and to another, Come, and he cometh; and to my
servant, Do this, and he doeth *it*. 9 When
Jesus heard these things, he marveled at
him, and turned him about, and said unto
the people that followed him, I say unto
you, I have not found so great faith, no,
not in Israel. 10 And they that were sent,
returning to the house, found the servant
whole that had been sick. ●

ABOUT TO DIE

GOOD HEALTH

2.RAISING THE DEAD

11 And it came to pass the day after,
that he went into a city called Nain; and
many of his disciples went with him, and
much people. 12 Now when he came nigh
to the gate of the city, behold, there was
a dead man carried out, the only son of
his mother, and she was a widow: and
much people of the city was with her.
13 And when the Lord saw her, he had
compassion on her, and said unto her,
Weep not. 14 And he came and touched
the bier: and they that bare *him* stood still.
And he said, Young man, I say unto thee,
Arise. 15 And he that was dead sat up,
and began to speak. And he delivered
him to his mother. 16 And there came a
fear on all: and they glorified God, saying,
That a great prophet is risen up among
us; and, That God hath visited his people.
17 And this rumor of him went forth
throughout all Judea, and throughout all
the region round about. ●

DEAD

ALIVE

Compare these two instances of Jesus' miracle-working, as to the following:

a. the ones distressed, and extent of distress
b. the place of faith
c. Jesus' power
d. a recorded effect on the people

*7:2-10* __________

*7:11-17* __________

NEW INTERNATIONAL VERSION

Record what the passage teaches about:

A BELIEVER'S DOUBTS

JESUS' POWER

TRUE MESSENGERS OF GOD

TRUE GREATNESS

UNBELIEF

INCONSISTENCY

OTHER

*Jesus and John the Baptist*

[18]John's disciples told him about all
these things. Calling two of them, [19]he sent
them to the Lord to ask, "Are you the one
who was to come, or should we expect
someone else?"
[20]When the men came to Jesus, they
said, "John the Baptist sent us to you to
ask, 'Are you the one who was to come, or
should we expect someone else?' "
[21]At that very time Jesus cured many
who had diseases, sicknesses and evil
spirits, and gave sight to many who were
blind. [22]So he replied to the messengers,
"Go back and report to John what you
have seen and heard: The blind receive
sight, the lame walk, those who have leprosy[b] are cured, the deaf hear, the dead are
raised, and the good news is preached to
the poor. [23]Blessed is the man who does
not fall away on account of me."●
[24]After John's messengers left, Jesus began to speak to the crowd about John:
"What did you go out into the desert to
see? A reed swayed by the wind? [25]If not,
what did you go out to see? A man dressed
in fine clothes? No, those who wear expensive clothes and indulge in luxury are in
palaces. [26]But what did you go out to see?
A prophet? Yes, I tell you, and more than
a prophet. [27]This is the one about whom it
is written:

" 'I will send my messenger ahead
of you,
who will prepare your way before
you.'[c]

[28]I tell you, among those born of women
there is no one greater than John; yet the
one who is least in the kingdom of God is
greater than he."●
[29](All the people, even the tax collectors,
when they heard Jesus' words, acknowledged that God's way was right, because
they had been baptized by John. [30]But the
Pharisees and experts in the law rejected
God's purpose for themselves, because
they had not been baptized by John.)
[31]"To what, then, can I compare the
people of this generation? What are they
like? [32]They are like children sitting in the
marketplace and calling out to each other:

" 'We played the flute for you,
and you did not dance;
we sang a dirge,
and you did not cry.'

[33]For John the Baptist came neither eating
bread nor drinking wine, and you say, 'He
has a demon.' [34]The Son of Man came eating and drinking, and you say, 'Here is a
glutton and a drunkard, a friend of tax collectors and "sinners." ' [35]But wisdom is
proved right by all her children."●

[b]22 The Greek word was used for various diseases affecting the skin—not necessarily leprosy.
[c]27 Mal. 3:1

## KING JAMES

**1. JOHN'S QUESTION**

DOUBTS

18 And the disciples of John showed
him of all these things. 19 And John calling *unto him* two of his disciples sent *them*
to Jesus, saying, Art thou he that should
come? or look we for another? 20 When
the men were come unto him, they said,
John Baptist hath sent us unto thee, saying, Art thou he that should come? or
look we for another? 21 And in that
same hour he cured many of *their* infirmities and plagues, and of evil spirits; and
unto many *that were* blind he gave sight.
22 Then Jesus answering said unto them,
Go your way, and tell John what things
ye have seen and heard; how that the
blind see, the lame walk, the lepers are
cleansed, the deaf hear, the dead are
raised, to the poor the gospel is preached.
23 And blessed is *he*, whosoever shall not
be offended in me. ●

**2. JESUS' COMMENDATION**

24 And when the messengers of John
were departed, he began to speak unto the
people concerning John, What went ye
out into the wilderness for to see? A
reed shaken with the wind? 25 But what
went ye out for to see? A man clothed in
soft raiment? Behold, they which are
gorgeously appareled, and live delicately,
are in kings' courts. 26 But what went ye
out for to see? A prophet? Yea, I say
unto you, and much more than a prophet.
27 This is *he*, of whom it is written,

Mal. 3:1

> Behold, I send my messenger before
> thy face,
> which shall prepare thy way before
> thee.

28 For I say unto you, Among those that
are born of women there is not a greater
prophet than John the Baptist: but he
that is least in the kingdom of God is
greater than he.● 29 And all the people

**3. OPPONENTS' REJECTION**

that heard *him*, and the publicans, justified
God, being baptized with the baptism of
John. 30 But the Pharisees and lawyers
rejected the counsel of God against themselves, being not baptized of him.
31 And the Lord said, Whereunto then
shall I liken the men of this generation?
and to what are they like? 32 They are
like unto children sitting in the market
place, and calling one to another, and
saying,

> We have piped unto you, and ye have
> not danced;
> we have mourned to you, and ye have
> not wept.

33 For John the Baptist came neither
eating bread nor drinking wine; and ye
say, He hath a devil. 34 The Son of man
is come eating and drinking; and ye say,
Behold a gluttonous man, and a winebibber, a friend of publicans and sinners!
35 But wisdom is justified of all her
children. ●

ACCUSATION

---

Read 3:15-18,20, the last reference to John the Baptist. Try to account for the doubts that now are in John's heart.

*7:18-23* Analyze John's question and Jesus' answer.

*7:24-28* What was Jesus' estimate of John?

*7:29-35* What was Jesus' indictment against the unbelieving generation?

## NEW INTERNATIONAL VERSION

Record practical teachings here about:

GENUINE LOVE ____

GRATITUDE ____

DEVOTION ____

CONTRITION ____

FORGIVENESS ____

"Your faith has saved you" (7:50). What does it mean to be saved? ____

Who saves? ____

What did Jesus mean by the words, "Go in peace" (7:50)? ____

### *Jesus Anointed by a Sinful Woman*

[36]Now one of the Pharisees invited Jesus
to have dinner with him, so he went to the
Pharisee's house and reclined at the table.
[37]When a woman who had lived a sinful life
in that town learned that Jesus was eating
at the Pharisee's house, she brought an
alabaster jar of perfume, [38]and as she stood
behind him at his feet weeping, she began
to wet his feet with her tears. Then she
wiped them with her hair, kissed them and
poured perfume on them. ●
[39]When the Pharisee who had invited
him saw this, he said to himself, "If this
man were a prophet, he would know who
is touching him and what kind of woman
she is—that she is a sinner."
[40]Jesus answered him, "Simon, I have
something to tell you."
"Tell me, teacher," he said.
[41]"Two men owed money to a certain
moneylender. One owed him five hundred
denarii,[d] and the other fifty. [42]Neither of
them had the money to pay him back, so he
canceled the debts of both. Now which of
them will love him more?"
[43]Simon replied, "I suppose the one who
had the bigger debt canceled."●
"You have judged correctly," Jesus
said.
[44]Then he turned toward the woman and
said to Simon, "Do you see this woman? I
came into your house. You did not give me
any water for my feet, but she wet my feet
with her tears and wiped them with her
hair. [45]You did not give me a kiss, but this
woman, from the time I entered, has not
stopped kissing my feet. [46]You did not put
oil on my head, but she has poured perfume on my feet. [47]Therefore, I tell you,
her many sins have been forgiven—for she
loved much. But he who has been forgiven
little loves little."
[48]Then Jesus said to her, "Your sins are
forgiven."●
[49]The other guests began to say among
themselves, "Who is this who even for-
gives sins?"
[50]Jesus said to the woman, "Your faith
has saved you; go in peace."●

*d41* A denarius was a coin worth about a day's wages.

KING JAMES

1. LOVE FOR JESUS

36 And one of the Pharisees desired him
that he would eat with him. And he went
into the Pharisee's house, and sat down to
meat. 37 And, behold, a woman in the
city, which was a sinner, when she knew
that *Jesus* sat at meat in the Pharisee's
house, brought an alabaster box of ointment, 38 and stood at his feet behind *him*
weeping, and began to wash his feet with
tears, and did wipe *them* with the hairs of
her head, and kissed his feet, and anointed
*them* with the ointment. ●

2. LOVE COMMENDED

a.

39 Now when
the Pharisee which had bidden him saw *it*,
he spake within himself, saying, This man,
if he were a prophet, would have known
who and what manner of woman *this is*
that toucheth him; for she is a sinner.
40 And Jesus answering said unto him,
Simon, I have somewhat to say unto thee.
And he saith, Master, say on. 41 There
was a certain creditor which had two
debtors: the one owed five hundred pence,
and the other fifty. 42 And when they had
nothing to pay, he frankly forgave them
both. Tell me therefore, which of them
will love him most? 43 Simon answered
and said, I suppose that *he*, to whom he
forgave most. And he said unto him,
Thou hast rightly judged.●

b.

44 And he
turned to the woman, and said unto
Simon, Seest thou this woman? I entered into thine house, thou gavest me no
water for my feet: but she hath washed my
feet with tears, and wiped *them* with the
hairs of her head. 45 Thou gavest me no
kiss: but this woman, since the time I
came in, hath not ceased to kiss my feet.
46 My head with oil thou didst not anoint:
but this woman hath anointed my feet
with ointment. 47 Wherefore I say unto
thee, Her sins, which are many, are forgiven; for she loved much: but to whom
little is forgiven, *the same* loveth little.
48 And he said unto her, Thy sins are forgiven.●

3. GUEST'S REACTION

49 And they that sat at meat with
him began to say within themselves, Who
is this that forgiveth sins also? 50 And he
said to the woman, Thy faith hath saved
thee; go in peace.●

SEEKING SINNER

*7:36-38* Record things said here about the woman.

*7:39-43* What is revealed here about sinners?

How does Jesus relate love to forgiveness?

SAVED SINNER

*7:44-48* How does Jesus apply what He had said in verses 41-43?

*7:49-50* Explain verse 50.

NEW INTERNATIONAL VERSION

Can you think of situations today where the hearers of the gospel are like the three unfruitful places:

WAYSIDE

ROCK

THORNS

What kind of hearing is fruitful?

What are some important lessons on Christian witness to the lost which are taught by the parable of 8:5-15 and the illustration of 8:16-18?

Why did Jesus teach in parables? (8:10). Compare Matthew 13:10-17; 13:34-35.

*The Parable of the Sower*

8 After this, Jesus traveled about from
one town and village to another, proclaiming the good news of the kingdom of
God. The Twelve were with him, 2and also
some women who had been cured of evil
spirits and diseases: Mary (called Magdalene) from whom seven demons had come
out; 3Joanna the wife of Cuza, the manager
of Herod's household; Susanna; and many
others. These women were helping to support them out of their own means.●
4While a large crowd was gathering and
people were coming to Jesus from town
after town, he told this parable: 5"A farmer
went out to sow his seed. As he was scattering the seed, some fell along the path; it
was trampled on, and the birds of the air
ate it up. 6Some fell on rock, and when it
came up, the plants withered because they
had no moisture. 7Other seed fell among
thorns, which grew up with it and choked
the plants. 8Still other seed fell on good
soil. It came up and yielded a crop, a hundred times more than was sown."
When he said this, he called out, "He
who has ears to hear, let him hear."●
9His disciples asked him what this parable meant. 10He said, "The knowledge of
the secrets of the kingdom of God has been
given to you, but to others I speak in parables, so that,

"'though seeing, they may not see;
though hearing, they may not
understand.'[a]

11"This is the meaning of the parable:
The seed is the word of God. 12Those along
the path are the ones who hear, and then
the devil comes and takes away the word
from their hearts, so that they cannot believe and be saved. 13Those on the rock are
the ones who receive the word with joy
when they hear it, but they have no root.
They believe for a while, but in the time of
testing they fall away. 14The seed that fell
among thorns stands for those who hear,
but as they go on their way they are choked
by life's worries, riches and pleasures, and
they do not mature. 15But the seed on good
soil stands for those with a noble and good
heart, who hear the word, retain it, and by
persevering produce a crop.●

*A Lamp on a Stand*

16"No one lights a lamp and hides it in a
jar or puts it under a bed. Instead, he puts
it on a stand, so that those who come in can
see the light. 17For there is nothing hidden
that will not be disclosed, and nothing concealed that will not be known or brought
out into the open. 18Therefore consider
carefully how you listen. Whoever has will
be given more; whoever does not have,
even what he thinks he has will be taken
from him."●

*Jesus' Mother and Brothers*

19Now Jesus' mother and brothers came
to see him, but they were not able to get
near him because of the crowd. 20Someone
told him, "Your mother and brothers are
standing outside, wanting to see you."
21He replied, "My mother and brothers
are those who hear God's word and put it
into practice."●

[a]*10* Isaiah 6:9 [b]*26* Some manuscripts *Gadarenes;* other manuscripts *Gergesenes;* also in verse 37

KING JAMES

FINANCIAL SUPPORTERS

8 And it came to pass afterward, that
he went throughout every city and
village, preaching and showing the glad
tidings of the kingdom of God: and the
twelve *were* with him, 2 and certain
women, which had been healed of evil
spirits and infirmities, Mary called Mag'-
dalene, out of whom went seven devils,
3 and Joanna the wife of Chuza Herod's
steward, and Susanna, and many others,
which ministered unto him of their substance. ●

1. PARABLE

4 And when much people were gathered
together, and were come to him out of
every city, he spake by a parable: 5 A
sower went out to sow his seed: and as he
sowed, some fell by the wayside; and it
was trodden down, and the fowls of the
air devoured it. 6 And some fell upon a
rock; and as soon as it was sprung up, it
withered away, because it lacked moisture.
7 And some fell among thorns; and the
thorns sprang up with it, and choked it.
8 And other fell on good ground, and
sprang up, and bare fruit a hundredfold.
And when he had said these things, he
cried, He that hath ears to hear, let him
hear. ●

2. INTERPRETATION

9 And his disciples asked him, saying,
What might this parable be? 10 And he
said, Unto you it is given to know the
mysteries of the kingdom of God: but to
others in parables;
that seeing they might not see,
and hearing they might not understand.
11 Now the parable is this: The seed is the
word of God. 12 Those by the wayside
are they that hear; then cometh the devil,
and taketh away the word out of their
hearts, lest they should believe and be
saved. 13 They on the rock *are they*,
which, when they hear, receive the word
with joy; and these have no root, which
for a while believe, and in time of temptation fall away. 14 And that which fell
among thorns are they, which, when they
have heard, go forth, and are choked with
cares and riches and pleasures of *this* life,
and bring no fruit to perfection. 15 But
that on the good ground are they, which
in an honest and good heart, having heard
the word, keep *it*, and bring forth fruit
with patience. ●

3. ILLUSTRATION

16 No man, when he hath lighted a
candle, covereth it with a vessel, or putteth
*it* under a bed; but setteth *it* on a candlestick, that they which enter in may see the
light. 17 For nothing is secret, that shall
not be made manifest; neither *any thing*
hid, that shall not be known and come
abroad. 18 Take heed therefore how ye
hear: for whosoever hath, to him shall be
given; and whosoever hath not, from him
shall be taken even that which he seemeth
to have. ●

BLOOD RELATIVES

19 Then came to him *his* mother and
his brethren, and could not come at him
for the press. 20 And it was told him *by
certain* which said, Thy mother and thy
brethren stand without, desiring to see
thee. 21 And he answered and said unto
them, My mother and my brethren are
these which hear the word of God, and
do it. ●

This segment shows some of Jesus' effective teaching towards the end of the Galilean ministry.

*8:1-3* Record your observations:

______________________________

______________________________

______________________________

______________________________

______________________________

For the next two paragraphs record the main parts and the interpretations of each.

*8:4-8* ______________________________

______________________________

______________________________

______________________________

*8:9-15* ______________________________

______________________________

______________________________

______________________________

*8:16-18* ______________________________

ILLUSTRATION (v.16) ______________________________

______________________________

______________________________

______________________________

INTERPRETATION (v.17) ______________________________

______________________________

______________________________

______________________________

APPLICATION (v.18) ______________________________

______________________________

______________________________

______________________________

*8:19-21* Relate verse 21 ("hear") to the previous paragraph. ______________________________

______________________________

______________________________

______________________________

NEW INTERNATIONAL VERSION

Record what the text supplies for each of the two miracles.

| SUBJECT | STORM vv.22-25 | DEMONIAC vv.26-39 |
|---|---|---|
| Realm of miracle | | |
| Occasion | | |
| Persons involved | | |
| Appeal made | | |
| Faith demonstrated | | |
| Manner and extent of miracle | | |
| Effect | | |
| Main practical instruction of the miracle | | |

*Jesus Calms the Storm*

22 One day Jesus said to his disciples,
"Let's go over to the other side of the
lake." So they got into a boat and set out.
23 As they sailed, he fell asleep. A squall
came down on the lake, so that the boat
was being swamped, and they were in great
danger.

24 The disciples went and woke him, saying, "Master, Master, we're going to
drown!"

He got up and rebuked the wind and the
raging waters; the storm subsided, and all
was calm. 25 "Where is your faith?" he
asked his disciples.

In fear and amazement they asked one
another, "Who is this? He commands even
the winds and the water, and they obey
him." ●

*The Healing of a Demon-possessed Man*

26 They sailed to the region of the Gerasenes,[b] which is across the lake from Galilee. 27 When Jesus stepped ashore, he was
met by a demon-possessed man from the
town. For a long time this man had not
worn clothes or lived in a house, but had
lived in the tombs. 28 When he saw Jesus,
he cried out and fell at his feet, shouting at
the top of his voice, "What do you want
with me, Jesus, Son of the Most High God?
I beg you, don't torture me!" 29 For Jesus
had commanded the evil[a] spirit to come
out of the man. Many times it had seized
him, and though he was chained hand and
foot and kept under guard, he had broken
his chains and had been driven by the demon into solitary places.

30 Jesus asked him, "What is your
name?"

"Legion," he replied, because many demons had gone into him. 31 And they
begged him repeatedly not to order them to
go into the Abyss.

32 A large herd of pigs was feeding there
on the hillside. The demons begged Jesus
to let them go into them, and he gave them
permission. 33 When the demons came out
of the man, they went into the pigs, and the
herd rushed down the steep bank into the
lake and was drowned. ●

34 When those tending the pigs saw what
had happened, they ran off and reported
this in the town and countryside, 35 and the
people went out to see what had happened.
When they came to Jesus, they found the
man from whom the demons had gone out,
sitting at Jesus' feet, dressed and in his
right mind; and they were afraid. 36 Those
who had seen it told the people how the
demon-possessed man had been cured.
37 Then all the people of the region of the
Gerasenes asked Jesus to leave them, because they were overcome with fear. So he
got into the boat and left.

38 The man from whom the demons had
gone out begged to go with him, but Jesus
sent him away, saying, 39 "Return home
and tell how much God has done for you."
So the man went away and told all over
town how much Jesus had done for him. ●

[a] 29 Greek *unclean*

## KING JAMES

1. STORM

SLEEPING

22 Now it came to pass on a certain
day, that he went into a ship with his disciples: and he said unto them, Let us go
over unto the other side of the lake. And
they launched forth. 23 But as they
sailed, he fell asleep: and there came down
a storm of wind on the lake; and they were
filled *with water*, and were in jeopardy.
24 And they came to him, and awoke him,
saying, Master, Master, we perish. Then
he arose, and rebuked the wind and the
raging of the water: and they ceased, and
there was a calm. 25 And he said unto
them, Where is your faith? And they
being afraid wondered, saying one to another, What manner of man is this! for he
commandeth even the winds and water,
and they obey him. ●

—effect

2. DEMON POSSESSION

26 And they arrived at the country of
the Gad′arenes, which is over against
Galilee. 27 And when he went forth to
land, there met him out of the city a certain man, which had devils long time, and
ware no clothes, neither abode in *any*
house, but in the tombs. 28 When he saw
Jesus, he cried out, and fell down before
him, and with a loud voice said, What
have I to do with thee, Jesus, *thou* Son of
God most high? I beseech thee, torment
me not. 29 (For he had commanded the
unclean spirit to come out of the man.
For oftentimes it had caught him: and he
was kept bound with chains and in fetters;
and he brake the bands, and was driven of
the devil into the wilderness.) 30 And
Jesus asked him, saying, What is thy
name? And he said, Legion: because
many devils were entered into him.
31 And they besought him that he would
not command them to go out into the
deep. 32 And there was there a herd of
many swine feeding on the mountain: and
they besought him that he would suffer
them to enter into them. And he suffered
them. 33 Then went the devils out of the
man, and entered into the swine: and the
herd ran violently down a steep place into
the lake, and were choked. ●

—effect

34 When they that fed *them* saw what
was done, they fled, and went and told *it*
in the city and in the country. 35 Then
they went out to see what was done; and
came to Jesus, and found the man, out of
whom the devils were departed, sitting at
the feet of Jesus, clothed, and in his right
mind: and they were afraid. 36 They also
which saw *it* told them by what means he
that was possessed of the devils was
healed. 37 Then the whole multitude of
the country of the Gad′arenes round
about besought him to depart from them;
for they were taken with great fear: and
he went up into the ship, and returned
back again. 38 Now the man, out of
whom the devils were departed, besought
him that he might be with him: but Jesus
sent him away, saying, 39 Return to thine
own house, and show how great things
God hath done unto thee. And he went
his way, and published throughout the
whole city how great things Jesus had
done unto him. ●

DOING

Luke records four miracles in 8:22-56. Miracles abound in the IDENTIFICATION section of Luke.

*8:22-25* Record observations of:

MIRACLE ______

EFFECT ______

*8:26-39* Record observations of:

MIRACLE ______

EFFECT ______

Account for the great fear of verse 37.

Analyze carefully verse 39. ______

NEW INTERNATIONAL VERSION

what is recorded here about:

FAITH

HEALING POWER OF JESUS

COMPASSION OF JESUS

JESUS' UNDERSTANDING OF PEOPLE

Some practical lessons:

*A Dead Girl and a Sick Woman*

40Now when Jesus returned, a crowd
welcomed him, for they were all expecting
him. 41Just then a man named Jairus, a
ruler of the synagogue, came and fell at
Jesus' feet, pleading with him to come to
his house 42because his only daughter, a
girl of about twelve, was dying.
As Jesus was on his way, the crowds
almost crushed him. 43And a woman was
there who had been subject to bleeding for
twelve years,[b] but no one could heal her.
44She came up behind him and touched the
edge of his cloak, and immediately her
bleeding stopped.
45"Who touched me?" Jesus asked.
When they all denied it, Peter said,
"Master, the people are crowding and
pressing against you."
46But Jesus said, "Someone touched me;
I know that power has gone out from me."
47Then the woman, seeing that she could
not go unnoticed, came trembling and fell
at his feet. In the presence of all the people,
she told why she had touched him and how
she had been instantly healed. 48Then he
said to her, "Daughter, your faith has
healed you. Go in peace."
49While Jesus was still speaking, someone came from the house of Jairus, the
synagogue ruler. "Your daughter is dead,"
he said. "Don't bother the teacher any
more."
50Hearing this, Jesus said to Jairus,
"Don't be afraid; just believe, and she will
be healed."
51When he arrived at the house of Jairus,
he did not let anyone go in with him except
Peter, John and James, and the child's father and mother. 52Meanwhile, all the
people were wailing and mourning for her.
"Stop wailing," Jesus said. "She is not
dead but asleep."
53They laughed at him, knowing that she
was dead. 54But he took her by the hand
and said, "My child, get up!" 55Her spirit
returned, and at once she stood up. Then
Jesus told them to give her something to
eat. 56Her parents were astonished, but he
ordered them not to tell anyone what had
happened.

[b]43 Many manuscripts *years, and she had spent all she had on doctors*

KING JAMES

1. JAIRUS' APPEAL

BELIEF

40 And it came to pass, that, when
Jesus was returned, the people *gladly* received him: for they were all waiting for
him. 41 And, behold, there came a man
named Jai'rus, and he was a ruler of the
synagogue; and he fell down at Jesus'
feet, and besought him that he would
come into his house: 42 for he had one
only daughter, about twelve years of age,
and she lay a dying.
But as he went the people thronged him. ●

2. HEMORRHAGE

43 And a woman having an issue of blood
twelve years, which had spent all her living upon physicians, neither could be
healed of any, 44 came behind *him*, and
touched the border of his garment: and
immediately her issue of blood stanched.
45 And Jesus said, Who touched me?
When all denied, Peter and they that were
with him said, Master, the multitude
throng thee and press *thee*, and sayest
thou, Who touched me? 46 And Jesus
said, Somebody hath touched me: for I
perceive that virtue is gone out of me.
47 And when the woman saw that she was
not hid, she came trembling, and falling
down before him, she declared unto him
before all the people for what cause she
had touched him, and how she was healed
immediately. 48 And he said unto her,
Daughter, be of good comfort: thy faith
hath made thee whole; go in peace. ●

3. JAIRUS' DAUGHTER RAISED

49 While he yet spake, there cometh
one from the ruler of the synagogue's
*house*, saying to him, Thy daughter is
dead; trouble not the Master. 50 But
when Jesus heard *it*, he answered him,
saying, Fear not: believe only, and she
shall be made whole. 51 And when he
came into the house, he suffered no man
to go in, save Peter, and James, and John,
and the father and the mother of the
maiden. 52 And all wept, and bewailed
her: but he said, Weep not; she is not
dead, but sleepeth. 53 And they laughed
him to scorn, knowing that she was dead.
54 And he put them all out, and took her
by the hand, and called, saying, Maid,
arise. 55 And her spirit came again, and
she arose straightway: and he commanded
to give her meat. 56 And her parents were
astonished: but he charged them that they
should tell no man what was done. ●

AMAZEMENT

First review the two miracles of the preceding segment. Then study this narrative, observing similar *and* different patterns in Jesus' healing ministry. Record the main parts of each paragraph:

*8:40-42* ______________________

*8:43-48* ______________________

*8:49-56* ______________________

Compare Jairus' faith as of verse 41 with that of verse 56.

NEW INTERNATIONAL VERSION

Record what is taught here about:

WITNESSING FOR JESUS

THE CHRISTIAN WITNESS'S MESSAGE

OBEDIENCE TO CHRIST

THE SPIRITUAL HUNGER OF MAN

PRACTICAL CONCERNS OF JESUS

ORDERLINESS

OTHER

*Jesus Sends Out the Twelve*

9 When Jesus had called the Twelve together, he gave them power and authority to drive out all demons and to cure
diseases, 2and he sent them out to preach
the kingdom of God and to heal the sick.
3He told them: "Take nothing for the journey—no staff, no bag, no bread, no money,
no extra tunic. 4Whatever house you enter,
stay there until you leave that town. 5If
people do not welcome you, shake the dust
off your feet when you leave their town, as
a testimony against them." 6So they set out
and went from village to village, preaching
the gospel and healing people everywhere.●
7Now Herod the tetrarch heard about all
that was going on. And he was perplexed,
because some were saying that John had
been raised from the dead, 8others that Elijah had appeared, and still others that one
of the prophets of long ago had come back
to life. 9But Herod said, "I beheaded John.
Who, then, is this I hear such things
about?" And he tried to see him.●

*Jesus Feeds the Five Thousand*

10When the apostles returned, they reported to Jesus what they had done. Then
he took them with him and they withdrew
by themselves to a town called Bethsaida,
11but the crowds learned about it and followed him. He welcomed them and spoke
to them about the kingdom of God, and
healed those who needed healing.●
12Late in the afternoon the Twelve came
to him and said, "Send the crowd away so
they can go to the surrounding villages and
countryside and find food and lodging, because we are in a remote place here."
13He replied, "You give them something
to eat."
They answered, "We have only five
loaves of bread and two fish—unless we go
and buy food for all this crowd." 14(About
five thousand men were there.)
But he said to his disciples, "Have them
sit down in groups of about fifty each."
15The disciples did so, and everybody sat
down. 16Taking the five loaves and the two
fish and looking up to heaven, he gave
thanks and broke them. Then he gave them
to the disciples to set before the people.
17They all ate and were satisfied, and the
disciples picked up twelve basketfuls of
broken pieces that were left over.●

KING JAMES

1. THE TWELVE SENT OUT

9 Then he called his twelve disciples together, and gave them power and
authority over all devils, and to cure
diseases. 2 And he sent them to preach
the kingdom of God, and to heal the sick.
3 And he said unto them, Take nothing
for *your* journey, neither staves, nor scrip,
neither bread, neither money; neither
have two coats apiece. 4 And whatsoever
house ye enter into, there abide, and
thence depart. 5 And whosoever will not
receive you, when ye go out of that city,
shake off the very dust from your feet for
a testimony against them. 6 And they
departed, and went through the towns,
preaching the gospel, and healing every
where. ●
7 Now Herod the tetrarch heard of all
that was done by him: and he was perplexed, because that it was said of some,
that John was risen from the dead; 8 and
of some, that Eli'jah had appeared; and of
others, that one of the old prophets was
risen again. 9 And Herod said, John
have I beheaded; but who is this, of
whom I hear such things? And he desired to see him. ●
10 And the apostles, when they were
returned, told him all that they had done.
And he took them, and went aside privately into a desert place belonging to the
city called Bethsai'da. 11 And the people,
when they knew *it*, followed him: and he
received them, and spake unto them of the
kingdom of God, and healed them that
had need of healing.● 12 And when the day
began to wear away, then came the
twelve, and said unto him, Send the multitude away, that they may go into the
towns and country round about, and
lodge, and get victuals: for we are here in
a desert place. 13 But he said unto them,
Give ye them to eat. And they said, We
have no more but five loaves and two
fishes; except we should go and buy meat
for all this people. 14 For they were about
five thousand men. And he said to his disciples, Make them sit down by fifties in a
company. 15 And they did so, and made
them all sit down. 16 Then he took the
five loaves and the two fishes, and looking
up to heaven, he blessed them, and brake,
and gave to the disciples to set before the
multitude. 17 And they did eat, and were
all filled: and there was taken up of fragments that remained to them twelve
baskets. ●

2. MULTITUDES FED

12 APOSTLES

—a perplexed ruler

—a seeking multitude

12 BASKETS

Three main experiences of the apostles are described in 9:1-50: commission (9:1-6); testimony (9:18-20); and vision (9:28-36).

*9:1-6* What twofold ministry were the apostles to engage in?

How is the healing related to the preaching?

Account for the instructions of 9:3-5.

*9:7-9* Why did Luke include these verses in his story?

*9:10-11* What ministry of Jesus is recorded here?

*9:12-17* What things impress you about this paragraph?

NEW INTERNATIONAL VERSION

What does the passage teach about:

DISCIPLESHIP

VALUES

THE CRUCIFIED LIFE

PRAYER

FELLOWSHIP WITH JESUS

JESUS THE MESSIAH

JESUS THE SON OF GOD

OTHER

*Peter's Confession of Christ*

18Once when Jesus was praying in private and his disciples were with him, he
asked them, "Who do the crowds say I
am?"
19They replied, "Some say John the Baptist; others say Elijah; and still others, that
one of the prophets of long ago has come
back to life."
20"But what about you?" he asked.
"Who do you say I am?"
Peter answered, "The Christ[a] of God."
21Jesus strictly warned them not to tell
this to anyone. 22And he said, "The Son of
Man must suffer many things and be rejected by the elders, chief priests and
teachers of the law, and he must be killed
and on the third day be raised to life."●
23Then he said to them all: "If anyone
would come after me, he must deny himself and take up his cross daily and follow
me. 24For whoever wants to save his life
will lose it, but whoever loses his life for
me will save it. 25What good is it for a man
to gain the whole world, and yet lose or
forfeit his very self? 26If anyone is ashamed
of me and my words, the Son of Man will
be ashamed of him when he comes in his
glory and in the glory of the Father and of
the holy angels. 27I tell you the truth, some
who are standing here will not taste death
before they see the kingdom of God.●

*The Transfiguration*

28About eight days after Jesus said this,
he took Peter, John and James with him
and went up onto a mountain to pray. 29As
he was praying, the appearance of his face
changed, and his clothes became as bright
as a flash of lightning. 30Two men, Moses
and Elijah, 31appeared in glorious splendor, talking with Jesus. They spoke about
his departure, which he was about to bring
to fulfillment at Jerusalem. 32Peter and his
companions were very sleepy, but when
they became fully awake, they saw his glory and the two men standing with him. 33As
the men were leaving Jesus, Peter said to
him, "Master, it is good for us to be here.
Let us put up three shelters—one for you,
one for Moses and one for Elijah." (He did
not know what he was saying.)
34While he was speaking, a cloud appeared and enveloped them, and they were
afraid as they entered the cloud. 35A voice
came from the cloud, saying, "This is my
Son, whom I have chosen; listen to him."
36When the voice had spoken, they found
that Jesus was alone. The disciples kept
this to themselves, and told no one at that
time what they had seen.●

[a]20 Or *Messiah*

KING JAMES

1. WHAT MEN THINK OF CHRIST

18 And it came to pass, as he was alone
praying, his disciples were with him; and
he asked them, saying, Whom say the
people that I am? 19 They answering
said, John the Baptist; but some *say*, Eli'-
jah; and others *say*, that one of the old
prophets is risen again. 20 He said unto
them, But whom say ye that I am? Peter
answering said, The Christ of God.
21 And he straitly charged them, and
commanded *them* to tell no man that
thing; 22 saying, The Son of man must
suffer many things, and be rejected of the
elders and chief priests and scribes, and
be slain, and be raised the third day. ●

"THE CHRIST"

2. WHAT DISCIPLESHIP IS

23 And he said to *them* all, If any *man*
will come after me, let him deny himself,
and take up his cross daily, and follow me.
24 For whosoever will save his life shall
lose it: but whosoever will lose his life for
my sake, the same shall save it. 25 For
what is a man advantaged, if he gain the
whole world, and lose himself, or be cast
away? 26 For whosoever shall be ashamed
of me and of my words, of him shall the
Son of man be ashamed, when he shall
come in his own glory, and *in his* Father's,
and of the holy angels. 27 But I tell you
of a truth, there be some standing here,
which shall not taste of death, till they see
the kingdom of God. ●

3. WHAT GOD THINKS OF CHRIST

28 And it came to pass about an eight
days after these sayings, he took Peter and
John and James, and went up into a
mountain to pray. 29 And as he prayed,
the fashion of his countenance was al-
tered, and his raiment *was* white *and* glis-
tering. 30 And, behold, there talked with
him two men, which were Moses and
Eli'jah: 31 who appeared in glory, and
spake of his decease which he should accomplish at Jerusalem. 32 But Peter and
they that were with him were heavy with
sleep: and when they were awake, they
saw his glory, and the two men that stood
with him. 33 And it came to pass, as they
departed from him, Peter said unto Jesus,
Master, it is good for us to be here: and
let us make three tabernacles; one for
thee, and one for Moses, and one for Eli'-
jah: not knowing what he said. 34 While
he thus spake, there came a cloud, and
overshadowed them: and they feared as
they entered into the cloud. 35 And there
came a voice out of the cloud, saying,
This is my beloved Son: hear him.
36 And when the voice was past, Jesus
was found alone. And they kept *it* close,
and told no man in those days any of
those things which they had seen. ●

"MY SON"

The first paragraph of this segment ties in very closely with the name IDENTIFICATION of the section 4:14-9:50 of Luke's gospel. This was a turning point of Jesus' public ministry.

9:18-22 Analyze the paragraph carefully. What predictions did Jesus make in verse 22?

*9:23-27* Observe the emphasis on the voluntary (e.g. "if"), and on the "whosoever." What is the point?

9:28-36 What was Jesus engaged in when he experienced the transfiguration?

Who appeared with Him? ______

What was the topic of their conversation? ______

What was Peter's presumption, and how was he rebuked?

NEW INTERNATIONAL VERSION

Record spiritual lessons taught by the passage on these subjects:

CHRISTIAN SERVICE

HUMILITY

DEPENDENCE ON GOD

FAITH

UNBELIEF

TRUE GREATNESS

CHILDREN

BROTHERS IN CHRIST

### *The Healing of a Boy With an Evil Spirit*

37 The next day, when they came down
from the mountain, a large crowd met him.
38 A man in the crowd called out, "Teacher,
I beg you to look at my son, for he is my
only child. 39 A spirit seizes him and he
suddenly screams; it throws him into con-
vulsions so that he foams at the mouth. It
scarcely ever leaves him and is destroying
him. 40 I begged your disciples to drive it
out, but they could not."
41 "O unbelieving and perverse generation," Jesus replied, "how long shall I stay
with you and put up with you? Bring your
son here."
42 Even while the boy was coming, the
demon threw him to the ground in a convulsion. But Jesus rebuked the evil[b] spirit,
healed the boy and gave him back to his
father. 43 And they were all amazed at the
greatness of God.●
While everyone was marveling at all that
Jesus did, he said to his disciples, 44 "Listen carefully to what I am about to tell you:
The Son of Man is going to be betrayed into
the hands of men." 45 But they did not understand what this meant. It was hidden
from them, so that they did not grasp it,
and they were afraid to ask him about it.●

### *Who Will Be the Greatest?*

46 An argument started among the disciples as to which of them would be the
greatest. 47 Jesus, knowing their thoughts,
took a little child and had him stand beside
him. 48 Then he said to them, "Whoever
welcomes this little child in my name welcomes me; and whoever welcomes me welcomes the one who sent me. For he who is
least among you all—he is the greatest."
49 "Master," said John, "we saw a man
driving out demons in your name and we
tried to stop him, because he is not one of
us."
50 "Do not stop him," Jesus said, "for
whoever is not against you is for you."●

[b]42 Greek *unclean*

## KING JAMES

**LESSONS FOR THE DISCIPLES**

**1. SOURCE OF POWER**

**IMPOTENCE OF DISCIPLES**

37 And it came to pass, that on the
next day, when they were come down
from the hill, much people met him.
38 And, behold, a man of the company
cried out, saying, Master, I beseech thee,
look upon my son; for he is mine only
child. 39 And, lo, a spirit taketh him, and
he suddenly crieth out; and it teareth him
that he foameth again, and bruising him,
hardly departeth from him. 40 And I besought thy disciples to cast him out; and
they could not. 41 And Jesus answering
said, O faithless and perverse generation,
how long shall I be with you, and suffer
you? Bring thy son hither. 42 And as he
was yet a coming, the devil threw him
down, and tare *him*. And Jesus rebuked
the unclean spirit, and healed the child,
and delivered him again to his father.
43 And they were all amazed at the
mighty power of God. ●

**2. NEED FOR UNDERSTANDING**

But while they wondered every one at
all things which Jesus did, he said unto his
disciples, 44 Let these sayings sink down
into your ears: for the Son of man shall be
delivered into the hands of men. 45 But
they understood not this saying, and it was
hid from them, that they perceived it not:
and they feared to ask him of that saying. ●

**3. MEASURE OF GREATNESS**

46 Then there arose a reasoning among
them, which of them should be greatest.
47 And Jesus, perceiving the thought of
their heart, took a child, and set him by
him, 48 and said unto them, Whosoever
shall receive this child in my name receiveth
me; and whosoever shall receive me, receiveth him that sent me: for he that is least
among you all, the same shall be great.

**POWER OF A STRANGER**

49 And John answered and said,
Master, we saw one casting out devils in
thy name; and we forbade him, because
he followeth not with us. 50 And Jesus
said unto him, Forbid *him* not: for he that
is not against us is for us. ●

---

Verse 37 connects this paragraph with the preceding one about Jesus' transfiguration.

*9:37-43a* Compare verse 38 with 9:35.

Compare the apostles' impotency (v.40) with their power (9:1). How do you explain such a change?

Record your observations of this paragraph.

*9:43b-45* How is verse 44 related to verse 43b?

Explain verse 45.

*9:46-50* What may have brought on the argument of verse 46?

Relate verses 49-50 to verse 48.

NEW INTERNATIONAL VERSION

What does the passage teach about:

TAKING REVENGE

DISCIPLESHIP

PRIORITIES

Record other spiritual applications which can be made from the passage.

*Samaritan Opposition*

51As the time approached for him to be
taken up to heaven, Jesus resolutely set
out for Jerusalem, 52and he sent messengers on ahead. They went into a Samaritan
village to get things ready for him, 53but the
people there did not welcome him, because
he was heading for Jerusalem. 54When the
disciples James and John saw this, they
asked, "Lord, do you want us to call fire
down from heaven to destroy them[a]?"
55But Jesus turned and rebuked them,
56and[b] they went to another village.●

*The Cost of Following Jesus*

57As they were walking along the road, a
man said to him, "I will follow you
wherever you go."
58Jesus replied, "Foxes have holes and
birds of the air have nests, but the Son of
Man has no place to lay his head."
59He said to another man, "Follow me."
But the man replied, "Lord, first let me
go and bury my father."
60Jesus said to him, "Let the dead bury
their own dead, but you go and proclaim
the kingdom of God."
61Still another said, "I will follow you,
Lord; but first let me go back and say good-
by to my family."
62Jesus replied, "No one who puts his
hand to the plow and looks back is fit for
service in the kingdom of God."●

[a]54 Some manuscripts *them, even as Elijah did*
[b]55,56 Some manuscripts *them. And he said, "You do not know what kind of spirit you are of, for the Son of Man did not come to destroy men's lives, but to save them." 56And*

## KING JAMES

1.TO JERUSALEM

51 And it came to pass, when the time
was come that he should be received up,
he steadfastly set his face to go to Jerusalem, 52 and sent messengers before his
face: and they went, and entered into a
village of the Samaritans, to make ready
for him. 53 And they did not receive him,
because his face was as though he would
go to Jerusalem. 54 And when his disciples James and John saw *this*, they said,
Lord, wilt thou that we command fire to
come down from heaven, and consume
them, even as Eli'jah did ? 55 But he
turned, and rebuked them, and said, Ye
know not what manner of spirit ye are of.
56 For the Son of man is not come to
destroy men's lives, but to save *them*.
And they went to another village. ●

2.WOULD-BE FOLLOWERS

57 And it came to pass, that, as they
went in the way, a certain *man* said unto
him, Lord, I will follow thee whithersoever thou goest. 58 And Jesus said unto
him, Foxes have holes, and birds of the
air *have* nests; but the Son of man hath
not where to lay *his* head. 59 And he said
unto another, Follow me. But he said,
Lord, suffer me first to go and bury my
father. 60 Jesus said unto him, Let the
dead bury their dead: but go thou and
preach the kingdom of God. 61 And another also said, Lord, I will follow thee;
but let me first go bid them farewell,
which are at home at my house. 62 And
Jesus said unto him, No man, having put
his hand to the plow, and looking back,
is fit for the kingdom of God. ●

ASCENSION

KINGDOM

This segment begins the third main division (INSTRUCTION) of Luke's gospel. The *word* ministry (e.g. parables) of Jesus is prominent at this time. Jesus knew when it was time to move into the next and final phase of His ministry, culminating in His death, resurrection and ascension. Read 9:51.

*9:51-56* Why would not the Samaritans extend hospitality to Jesus on His journey?

What was Jesus' reaction toward such slight?

*9:57-62* What is a key word of the paragraph?

Analyze the responses of Jesus to the excuses made.

NEW INTERNATIONAL VERSION

What does the passage teach about:

HARVEST FIELD OF THE GOSPEL MINISTRY

LABORERS IN THE HARVEST

REJECTION OF THE GOSPEL

DISCIPLESHIP

AUTHORITY AND POWER IN WITNESSING

JOY

SPIRITUAL UNDERSTANDING

PERSON OF CHRIST

*Jesus Sends Out the Seventy-two*

10 After this the Lord appointed seventy-two[c] others and sent them two by
two ahead of him to every town and place
where he was about to go. 2He told them,
"The harvest is plentiful, but the workers
are few. Ask the Lord of the harvest, therefore, to send out workers into his harvest
field. 3Go! I am sending you out like lambs
among wolves. 4Do not take a purse or bag
or sandals; and do not greet anyone on the
road.
5"When you enter a house, first say,
'Peace to this house.' 6If a man of peace is
there, your peace will rest on him; if not,
it will return to you. 7Stay in that house,
eating and drinking whatever they give
you, for the worker deserves his wages. Do
not move around from house to house.
8"When you enter a town and are welcomed, eat what is set before you. 9Heal
the sick who are there and tell them, 'The
kingdom of God is near you.' 10But when
you enter a town and are not welcomed, go
into its streets and say, 11'Even the dust of
your town that sticks to our feet we wipe
off against you. Yet be sure of this: The
kingdom of God is near.' 12I tell you, it will
be more bearable on that day for Sodom
than for that town.●
13"Woe to you, Korazin! Woe to you,
Bethsaida! For if the miracles that were
performed in you had been performed in
Tyre and Sidon, they would have repented
long ago, sitting in sackcloth and ashes.
14But it will be more bearable for Tyre and
Sidon at the judgment than for you. 15And
you, Capernaum, will you be lifted up to
the skies? No, you will go down to the
depths.[d]
16"He who listens to you listens to me;
he who rejects you rejects me; but he who
rejects me rejects him who sent me."●
17The seventy-two returned with joy and
said, "Lord, even the demons submit to us
in your name."
18He replied, "I saw Satan fall like lightning from heaven. 19I have given you authority to trample on snakes and scorpions
and to overcome all the power of the enemy; nothing will harm you. 20However, do
not rejoice that the spirits submit to you,
but rejoice that your names are written in
heaven."●
21At that time Jesus, full of joy through
the Holy Spirit, said, "I praise you, Father, Lord of heaven and earth, because
you have hidden these things from the wise
and learned, and revealed them to little
children. Yes, Father, for this was your
good pleasure.
22"All things have been committed to me
by my Father. No one knows who the Son
is except the Father, and no one knows
who the Father is except the Son and those
to whom the Son chooses to reveal him."
23Then he turned to his disciples and said
privately, "Blessed are the eyes that see
what you see. 24For I tell you that many
prophets and kings wanted to see what you
see but did not see it, and to hear what you
hear but did not hear it."●

[c]1 Some manuscripts *seventy*; also in verse 17
[d]15 Greek *Hades*

KING JAMES

**1. MISSION OF THE SEVENTY**

**10** After these things the Lord appointed other seventy also, and sent
them two and two before his face into
every city and place, whither he himself
would come. 2 Therefore said he unto
them, The harvest truly *is* great, but the
laborers *are* few: pray ye therefore the
Lord of the harvest, that he would send
forth laborers into his harvest. 3 Go
your ways: behold, I send you forth as
lambs among wolves. 4 Carry neither
purse, nor scrip, nor shoes: and salute no
man by the way. 5 And into whatsoever
house ye enter, first say, Peace *be* to this
house. 6 And if the son of peace be there,
your peace shall rest upon it: if not, it
shall turn to you again. 7 And in the
same house remain, eating and drinking
such things as they give: for the laborer is
worthy of his hire. Go not from house
to house. 8 And into whatsoever city ye
enter, and they receive you, eat such things
as are set before you: 9 and heal the sick
that are therein, and say unto them, The
kingdom of God is come nigh unto you.
10 But into whatsoever city ye enter, and
they receive you not, go your ways out
into the streets of the same, and say,
11 Even the very dust of your city, which
cleaveth on us, we do wipe off against
you: notwithstanding, be ye sure of this,
that the kingdom of God is come nigh
unto you. 12 But I say unto you, that it
shall be more tolerable in that day for
Sodom, than for that city. ●

70 DISCIPLES

Much of the section 9:51-11:13 involves Jesus training His disciples to carry on the gospel ministry.

*10:1-12* Observe the context of the familiar verse 2.

Is an unresponding city (v.10) considered part of the great harvest (v.2)? If so, how?

**2. WOE TO REJECTORS**

13 Woe unto thee, Chora'zin! woe unto
thee, Bethsai'da! for if the mighty works
had been done in Tyre and Sidon, which
have been done in you, they had a great
while ago repented, sitting in sackcloth
and ashes. 14 But it shall be more tolerable for Tyre and Sidon at the judgment,
than for you. 15 And thou, Caper'na-um,
which art exalted to heaven, shalt be
thrust down to hell.
16 He that heareth you heareth me;
and he that despiseth you despiseth me;
and he that despiseth me despiseth him
that sent me. ●

WOE

*10:13-16* Record observations.

**3. JOY OF THE SEVENTY**

17 And the seventy returned again with
joy, saying, Lord, even the devils are subject unto us through thy name. 18 And he
said unto them, I beheld Satan as lightning fall from heaven. 19 Behold, I give
unto you power to tread on serpents and
scorpions, and over all the power of the
enemy; and nothing shall by any means
hurt you. 20 Notwithstanding, in this
rejoice not, that the spirits are subject unto you; but rather rejoice, because your
names are written in heaven. ●

JOY

*10:17-20* Record observations.

**4. JOY OF JESUS**

21 In that hour Jesus rejoiced in spirit,
and said, I thank thee, O Father, Lord of
heaven and earth, that thou hast hid these
things from the wise and prudent, and
hast revealed them unto babes: even so,
Father; for so it seemed good in thy sight.
22 All things are delivered to me of my
Father: and no man knoweth who the
Son is, but the Father; and who the
Father is, but the Son, and *he* to whom
the Son will reveal *him*.
23 And he turned him unto *his* disciples,
and said privately, Blessed *are* the eyes
which see the things that ye see:
24 for I
tell you, that many prophets and kings
have desired to see those things which ye
see, and have not seen *them;* and to hear
those things which ye hear, and have not
heard *them*. ●

JOY

MANY PROPHETS AND KINGS

*10:21-24* Analyze the various parts of this paragraph carefully.

NEW INTERNATIONAL VERSION

What does this passage teach about:

LOVE TO GOD

LOVE TO MAN

DEVOTION

CHRISTIAN SERVICE

What could the disciples have learned personally if they overheard Jesus' conversation with the lawyer?

*The Parable of the Good Samaritan*

25On one occasion an expert in the law
stood up to test Jesus. "Teacher," he
asked, "what must I do to inherit eternal
life?"
26"What is written in the Law?" he replied. "How do you read it?"
27He answered: " 'Love the Lord your
God with all your heart and with all your
soul and with all your strength and with all
your mind'[a]; and, 'Love your neighbor as
yourself.'[b]"
28"You have answered correctly," Jesus
replied. "Do this and you will live." ●
29But he wanted to justify himself, so he
asked Jesus, "And who is my neighbor?"
30In reply Jesus said: "A man was going
down from Jerusalem to Jericho, when he
fell into the hands of robbers. They
stripped him of his clothes, beat him and
went away, leaving him half dead. 31A
priest happened to be going down the same
road, and when he saw the man, he passed
by on the other side. 32So too, a Levite,
when he came to the place and saw him,
passed by on the other side. 33But a
Samaritan, as he traveled, came where the
man was; and when he saw him, he took
pity on him. 34He went to him and ban-
daged his wounds, pouring on oil and wine.
Then he put the man on his own donkey,
took him to an inn and took care of him.
35The next day he took out two silver
coins[c] and gave them to the innkeeper.
'Look after him,' he said, 'and when I return, I will reimburse you for any extra
expense you may have.'
36"Which of these three do you think
was a neighbor to the man who fell into the
hands of robbers?"
37The expert in the law replied, "The one
who had mercy on him."
Jesus told him, "Go and do likewise." ●

*At the Home of Martha and Mary*

38As Jesus and his disciples were on their
way, he came to a village where a woman
named Martha opened her home to him.
39She had a sister called Mary, who sat at
the Lord's feet listening to what he said.
40But Martha was distracted by all the
preparations that had to be made. She
came to him and asked, "Lord, don't you
care that my sister has left me to do the
work by myself? Tell her to help me!"
41"Martha, Martha," the Lord answered, "you are worried and upset about
many things, 42but only one thing is
needed.[d] Mary has chosen what is better,
and it will not be taken away from her." ●

[a]27 Deut. 6:5 [b]27 Lev. 19:18 [c]35 Greek *two denarii*
[d]42 Some manuscripts *but few things are needed—or only one*

KING JAMES

1. LAWYER

ETERNAL LIFE

—first question

**25 And, behold, a certain lawyer stood**
**up, and tempted him, saying, Master,**
**what shall I do to inherit eternal life?**
**26 He said unto him, What is written in**
**the law? how readest thou? 27 And he**
**answering said,**
**Thou shalt love the Lord thy God**
**with all thy heart, and with all thy soul,**
**and with all thy strength, and with all thy mind;**
**and thy neighbor as thyself.**
**28 And he said unto him, Thou hast**
**answered right: this do, and thou shalt**
**live.** ●

Deu. 6:5

Lev. 19:18

—second question

**29 But he, willing to justify himself,**
**said unto Jesus, And who is my neighbor?**
**30 And Jesus answering said, A certain**
***man* went down from Jerusalem to Jeri-**
**cho, and fell among thieves, which stripped**
**him of his raiment, and wounded *him*, and**
**departed, leaving *him* half dead. 31 And**
**by chance there came down a certain**
**priest that way; and when he saw him, he**
**passed by on the other side. 32 And like-**
**wise a Levite, when he was at the place,**
**came and looked *on him*, and passed by**
**on the other side. 33 But a certain Samar-**
**itan, as he journeyed, came where he was;**
**and when he saw him, he had compassion**
***on him*, 34 and went to *him*, and bound**
**up his wounds, pouring in oil and wine,**
**and set him on his own beast, and brought**
**him to an inn, and took care of him.**
**35 And on the morrow when he departed,**
**he took out two pence, and gave *them* to**
**the host, and said unto him, Take care of**
**him: and whatsoever thou spendest more,**
**when I come again, I will repay thee.**
**36 Which now of these three, thinkest**
**thou, was neighbor unto him that fell**
**among the thieves? 37 And he said, He**
**that showed mercy on him. Then said**
**Jesus unto him, Go, and do thou like-**
**wise.** ●

2. TWO SISTERS

**38 Now it came to pass, as they went,**
**that he entered into a certain village: and**
**a certain woman named Martha received**
**him into her house. 39 And she had a sis-**
**ter called Mary, which also sat at Jesus'**
**feet, and heard his word. 40 But Martha**
**was cumbered about much serving, and**
**came to him, and said, Lord, dost thou**
**not care that my sister hath left me to**
**serve alone? bid her therefore that she**
**help me. 41 And Jesus answered and said**
**unto her, Martha, Martha, thou art care-**
**ful and troubled about many things:**
**42 but one thing is needful; and Mary**
**hath chosen that good part, which shall**
**not be taken away from her.** ●

SERVING

*10:25-28* What was the lawyer's question? ________

How did Jesus answer it? ________

*10:29-37* Why did the lawyer ask the question of verse 29? ________

Analyze Jesus' answer. ________

What test question did Jesus give the lawyer? ________

Did the lawyer answer correctly? ________

*10:38-42* Compare the words "many" (v.41) and "one" (v.42). ________

Was Jesus rebuking Martha's labors, or her *overdoing* these things? ________

NEW INTERNATIONAL VERSION

Record what you learn from the model prayer:

THE ONE ADDRESSED ______

THE ORDER FOLLOWED ______

ATTITUDE ______

KINDS OF PETITIONS ______

Record other practical lessons taught by this passage. ______

*Jesus' Teaching on Prayer*

11 One day Jesus was praying in a certain place. When he finished, one of
his disciples said to him, "Lord, teach us
to pray, just as John taught his disciples."
2 He said to them, "When you pray, say:

" 'Father,[e]
hallowed be your name,
your kingdom come.[f]
3 Give us each day our daily bread.
4 Forgive us our sins,
for we also forgive everyone who
sins against us.[g]
And lead us not into temptation.[h]' "●

5 Then he said to them, "Suppose one of
you has a friend, and he goes to him at
midnight and says, 'Friend, lend me three
loaves of bread, 6 because a friend of mine
on a journey has come to me, and I have
nothing to set before him.'
7 "Then the one inside answers, 'Don't
bother me. The door is already locked, and
my children are with me in bed. I can't get
up and give you anything.' 8 I tell you,
though he will not get up and give him the
bread because he is his friend, yet because
of the man's persistence he will get up and
give him as much as he needs.●
9 "So I say to you: Ask and it will be
given to you; seek and you will find; knock
and the door will be opened to you. 10 For
everyone who asks receives; he who seeks
finds; and to him who knocks, the door will
be opened.
11 "Which of you fathers, if your son asks
for[i] a fish, will give him a snake instead?
12 Or if he asks for an egg, will give him a
scorpion? 13 If you then, though you are
evil, know how to give good gifts to your
children, how much more will your Father
in heaven give the Holy Spirit to those who
ask him!"●

[e]2 Some manuscripts *Our Father in heaven*
[f]2 Some manuscripts *come. May your will be done on earth as it is in heaven.*
[g]4 Greek *everyone who is indebted to us*
[h]4 Some manuscripts *temptation but deliver us from the evil one*
[i]11 Some manuscripts *for bread, will give him a stone; or if he asks for*

KING JAMES

1.PRAYER MODEL

11 And it came to pass, that, as he was
praying in a certain place, when he
ceased, one of his disciples said unto him,
Lord, teach us to pray, as John also
taught his disciples. 2 And he said unto
them, When ye pray, say,
Our Father which art in heaven,
Hallowed be thy name.
Thy kingdom come.
Thy will be done,
as in heaven, so in earth.
3 Give us day by day our daily bread.
4 And forgive us our sins;
for we also forgive every one that is
indebted to us.
And lead us not into temptation;
but deliver us from evil.

DISCIPLE PRAYS

2.PERSISTENCE IN PRAYER

5 And he said unto them, Which of you
shall have a friend, and shall go unto him
at midnight, and say unto him, Friend,
lend me three loaves; 6 for a friend of
mine in his journey is come to me, and I
have nothing to set before him? 7 And
he from within shall answer and say,
Trouble me not: the door is now shut, and
my children are with me in bed; I cannot
rise and give thee. 8 I say unto you,
Though he will not rise and give him, because he is his friend, yet because of his
importunity he will rise and give him as
many as he needeth. ● 9 And I say unto

3.ASKING AND RECEIVING

you, Ask, and it shall be given you; seek,
and ye shall find; knock, and it shall be
opened unto you. 10 For every one that
asketh receiveth; and he that seeketh findeth; and to him that knocketh it shall be
opened. 11 If a son shall ask bread of any
of you that is a father, will he give him a
stone? or if *he ask* a fish, will he for a fish
give him a serpent? 12 Or if he shall ask
an egg, will he offer him a scorpion? 13 If
ye then, being evil, know how to give good
gifts unto your children; how much more
shall *your* heavenly Father give the Holy
Spirit to them that ask him? ●

FATHER GIVES

*11:1-4* Analyze carefully the model prayer. For example, note the order of statements. Record your observations.

*11:5-8* What do these verses add to verses 1-4?

*11:9-13* What is taught here about:

THE ASKER

THE GIVER

NEW INTERNATIONAL VERSION

Record what this passage teaches about:

SATAN

UNBELIEF

FAITH

SIN

HAPPINESS

WORD OF GOD

JUDGMENT

CHRISTIAN WITNESS

PURITY

*Jesus and Beelzebub*

14Jesus was driving out a demon that was
mute. When the demon left, the man who
had been dumb spoke, and the crowd was
amazed. 15But some of them said, "By
Beelzebub,[a] the prince of demons, he is
driving out demons." 16Others tested him
by asking for a sign from heaven.
17Jesus knew their thoughts and said to
them: "Any kingdom divided against itself
will be ruined, and a house divided against
itself will fall. 18If Satan is divided against
himself, how can his kingdom stand? I say
this because you claim that I drive out demons by Beelzebub. 19Now if I drive out
demons by Beelzebub, by whom do your
followers drive them out? So then, they
will be your judges. 20But if I drive out
demons by the finger of God, then the kingdom of God has come to you.
21"When a strong man, fully armed,
guards his own house, his possessions are
safe. 22But when someone stronger attacks
and overpowers him, he takes away the
armor in which the man trusted and divides
up the spoils.
23"He who is not with me is against me,
and he who does not gather with me, scatters.●
24"When an evil[b] spirit comes out of a
man, it goes through arid places seeking
rest and does not find it. Then it says, 'I
will return to the house I left.' 25When it
arrives, it finds the house swept clean and
put in order. 26Then it goes and takes seven
other spirits more wicked than itself, and
they go in and live there. And the final
condition of that man is worse than the
first."●
27As Jesus was saying these things, a
woman in the crowd called out, "Blessed
is the mother who gave you birth and
nursed you."
28He replied, "Blessed rather are those
who hear the word of God and obey it."●

*The Sign of Jonah*

29As the crowds increased, Jesus said,
"This is a wicked generation. It asks for a
miraculous sign, but none will be given it
except the sign of Jonah. 30For as Jonah
was a sign to the Ninevites, so also will the
Son of Man be to this generation. 31The
Queen of the South will rise at the judgment with the men of this generation and
condemn them, for she came from the ends
of the earth to listen to Solomon's wisdom,
and now one[c] greater than Solomon is
here. 32The men of Nineveh will stand up
at the judgment with this generation and
condemn it, for they repented at the
preaching of Jonah, and now one greater
than Jonah is here.●

*The Lamp of the Body*

33"No one lights a lamp and puts it in a
place where it will be hidden, or under a
bowl. Instead he puts it on its stand, so that
those who come in may see the light.
34Your eye is the lamp of your body. When
your eyes are good, your whole body also
is full of light. But when they are bad, your
body also is full of darkness. 35See to it,
then, that the light within you is not darkness. 36Therefore, if your whole body is
full of light, and no part of it dark, it will be
completely lighted, as when the light of a
lamp shines on you."●

[a]*15* Greek *Beezeboul* or *Beelzeboul*; also in verses 18 and 19
[b]*24* Greek *unclean*
[c]*31* Or *something*; also in verse 32

KING JAMES

**1. JESUS AND BEELZEBUB**

POWER

14 And he was casting out a devil, and
it was dumb. And it came to pass, when
the devil was gone out, the dumb spake;
and the people wondered. 15 But some of
them said, He casteth out devils through
Beel'zebub the chief of the devils.
16 And others, tempting *him*, sought of
him a sign from heaven. 17 But he,
knowing their thoughts, said unto them,
Every kingdom divided against itself is
brought to desolation; and a house *divided*
against a house falleth. 18 If Satan also
be divided against himself, how shall his
kingdom stand? because ye say that I cast
out devils through Beel'zebub. 19 And if
I by Beel'zebub cast out devils, by whom
do your sons cast *them* out? therefore
shall they be your judges. 20 But if I with
the finger of God cast out devils, no doubt
the kingdom of God is come upon you.
21 When a strong man armed keepeth his
palace, his goods are in peace: 22 but
when a stronger than he shall come upon
him, and overcome him, he taketh
from him all his armor wherein he
trusted, and divideth his spoils. 23 He
that is not with me is against me;
and he that gathereth not with me scattereth. ●

**2. RETURN OF EVIL SPIRIT**

24 When the unclean spirit is gone out
of a man, he walketh through dry places,
seeking rest; and finding none, he saith, I
will return unto my house whence I came
out. 25 And when he cometh, he findeth
*it* swept and garnished. 26 Then goeth
he, and taketh *to him* seven other spirits
more wicked than himself; and they
enter in, and dwell there: and the last
*state* of that man is worse than the
first. ●

**3. TRUE HAPPINESS**

JOY

27 And it came to pass, as he spake
these things, a certain woman of the company lifted up her voice, and said unto
him, Blessed *is* the womb that bare thee,
and the paps which thou hast sucked.
28 But he said, Yea, rather, blessed *are*
they that hear the word of God, and keep
it. ●

**4. DEMAND FOR MIRACLE**

29 And when the people were gathered
thick together, he began to say, This is an
evil generation: they seek a sign; and
there shall no sign be given it, but the sign
of Jonah the prophet. 30 For as Jonah was
a sign unto the Nin'evites, so shall also
the Son of man be to this generation.
31 The queen of the south shall rise up in
the judgment with the men of this generation, and condemn them: for she came
from the utmost parts of the earth to hear
the wisdom of Solomon; and, behold, a
greater than Solomon *is* here. 32 The men
of Nin'eveh shall rise up in the judgment
with this generation, and shall condemn
it: for they repented at the preaching of
Jonah; and, behold, a greater than Jonah
*is* here. ●

**5. LIGHT OF THE BODY**

LIGHT

33 No man, when he hath lighted a
candle, putteth *it* in a secret place, neither
under a bushel, but on a candlestick,
that they which come in may see the light.
34 The light of the body is the eye: therefore when thine eye is single, thy whole
body also is full of light; but when *thine*
*eye* is evil, thy body also *is* full of darkness. 35 Take heed therefore, that the
light which is in thee be not darkness.
36 If thy whole body therefore *be* full of
light, having no part dark, the whole shall
be full of light, as when the bright shining
of a candle doth give thee light. ●

---

Scan the segment first, noting how the paragraphs alternate between evil things and good things.

*11:14-23* and *11:24-26* What is taught here about Satan and his domain?

______________________________

______________________________

______________________________

______________________________

______________________________

______________________________

*11:27-28* Compare this paragraph with the two paragraphs surrounding it.

______________________________

______________________________

______________________________

______________________________

______________________________

*11:29-32* What is Jesus' main point?

______________________________

______________________________

______________________________

______________________________

______________________________

______________________________

*11:33-36* Relate this paragraph to 11:29-32.

______________________________

______________________________

______________________________

______________________________

______________________________

______________________________

______________________________

______________________________

______________________________

NEW INTERNATIONAL VERSION

Record what the passage teaches about:

HYPOCRISY

TYRANNY

INJUSTICE

HATRED

JUDGMENT

OTHER

*Six Woes*

37When Jesus had finished speaking, a
Pharisee invited him to eat with him; so he
went in and reclined at the table. 38But the
Pharisee, noticing that Jesus did not first
wash before the meal, was surprised.
39Then the Lord said to him, "Now then,
you Pharisees clean the outside of the cup
and dish, but inside you are full of greed
and wickedness. 40You foolish people! Did
not the one who made the outside make the
inside also? 41But give what is inside ⌞the
dish⌟[d] to the poor, and everything will be
clean for you.●
42"Woe to you Pharisees, because you
give God a tenth of your mint, rue and all
other kinds of garden herbs, but you neglect justice and the love of God. You
should have practiced the latter without
leaving the former undone.
43"Woe to you Pharisees, because you
love the most important seats in the synagogues and greetings in the marketplaces.
44"Woe to you, because you are like unmarked graves, which men walk over without knowing it."●
45One of the experts in the law answered
him, "Teacher, when you say these things,
you insult us also."
46Jesus replied, "And you experts in the
law, woe to you, because you load people
down with burdens they can hardly carry,
and you yourselves will not lift one finger
to help them.
47"Woe to you, because you build tombs
for the prophets, and it was your forefathers who killed them. 48So you testify that
you approve of what your forefathers did;
they killed the prophets, and you build
their tombs. 49Because of this, God in his
wisdom said, 'I will send them prophets
and apostles, some of whom they will kill
and others they will persecute.' 50Therefore this generation will be held responsible for the blood of all the prophets that has
been shed since the beginning of the world,
51from the blood of Abel to the blood of
Zechariah, who was killed between the altar and the sanctuary. Yes, I tell you, this
generation will be held responsible for it
all.
52"Woe to you experts in the law, because you have taken away the key to
knowledge. You yourselves have not entered, and you have hindered those who
were entering."●
53When Jesus left there, the Pharisees
and the teachers of the law began to oppose
him fiercely and to besiege him with questions, 54waiting to catch him in something
he might say.●

[d]41 Or *what you have*

## KING JAMES

1. OCCASION

LUNCH WITH JESUS

37 And as he spake, a certain Pharisee
besought him to dine with him: and he
went in, and sat down to meat. 38 And
when the Pharisee saw *it*, he marveled that
he had not first washed before dinner.

2. ILLUSTRATION

39 And the Lord said unto him, Now do
ye Pharisees make clean the outside of the
cup and the platter; but your inward part
is full of ravening and wickedness. 40 *Ye*
fools, did not he, that made that which is
without, make that which is within also?
41 But rather give alms of such things as
ye have; and, behold, all things are clean
unto you. ●

3. APPLICATION

—Pharisees

42 But woe unto you, Pharisees! for ye
tithe mint and rue and all manner of
herbs, and pass over judgment and the
love of God: these ought ye to have done,
and not to leave the other undone. 43 Woe
unto you, Pharisees! for ye love the uppermost seats in the synagogues, and greetings in the markets. 44 Woe unto you,
scribes and Pharisees, hypocrites! for ye
are as graves which appear not, and the
men that walk over *them* are not aware
*of them*. ●

—Lawyers

45 Then answered one of the lawyers,
and said unto him, Master, thus saying
thou reproachest us also. 46 And he said,
Woe unto you also, *ye* lawyers! for ye
lade men with burdens grievous to be
borne, and ye yourselves touch not the
burdens with one of your fingers. 47 Woe
unto you! for ye build the sepulchres of
the prophets, and your fathers killed them.
48 Truly ye bear witness that ye allow the
deeds of your fathers: for they indeed
killed them, and ye build their sepulchres.
49 Therefore also said the wisdom of God,
I will send them prophets and apostles,
and *some* of them they shall slay and persecute: 50 that the blood of all the prophets, which was shed from the foundation
of the world, may be required of this
generation; 51 from the blood of Abel
unto the blood of Zechari'ah, which
perished between the altar and the temple:
verily I say unto you, It shall be required
of this generation. 52 Woe unto you, lawyers! for ye have taken away the key of
knowledge: ye entered not in yourselves,
and them that were entering in ye hindered. ●

4. OPPOSITION

PLOT AGAINST JESUS

53 And as he said these things unto
them, the scribes and the Pharisees began
to urge *him* vehemently, and to provoke
him to speak of many things: 54 laying
wait for him, and seeking to catch something out of his mouth, that they might
accuse him. ●

*11:37-41* What is Jesus' illustration, and how does He apply it, in general, to the Pharisees?

*11:42-44* What are the specific examples of hypocrisy here?

*11:45-52* Record all the indictments against the lawyers. Is hypocrisy involved in all?

*11:53-54* Record the verbs associated with "the Pharisees":

NEW INTERNATIONAL VERSION

Record what this passage teaches about:

HYPOCRISY

JUDGMENT

GODLY FEAR

PUBLIC TESTIMONY

PERSECUTION

HOLY SPIRIT

OTHER

*Warnings and Encouragements*

12 Meanwhile, when a crowd of many
thousands had gathered, so that
they were trampling on one another, Jesus
began to speak first to his disciples, saying:
"Be on your guard against the yeast of the
Pharisees, which is hypocrisy. 2There is
nothing concealed that will not be disclosed, or hidden that will not be made
known. 3What you have said in the dark
will be heard in the daylight, and what you
have whispered in the ear in the inner
rooms will be proclaimed from the
housetops.●
4"I tell you, my friends, do not be afraid
of those who kill the body and after that
can do no more. 5But I will show you
whom you should fear: Fear him who, after
the killing of the body, has power to throw
you into hell. Yes, I tell you, fear him. 6Are
not five sparrows sold for two pennies[a]?
Yet not one of them is forgotten by God.
7Indeed, the very hairs of your head are all
numbered. Don't be afraid; you are worth
more than many sparrows.●
8"I tell you, whoever acknowledges me
before men, the Son of Man will also acknowledge him before the angels of God.
9But he who disowns me before men will
be disowned before the angels of God.
10And everyone who speaks a word against
the Son of Man will be forgiven, but anyone who blasphemes against the Holy
Spirit will not be forgiven.
11"When you are brought before synagogues, rulers and authorities, do not worry about how you will defend yourselves or
what you will say, 12for the Holy Spirit will
teach you at that time what you should
say."●

[a]6 Greek *two assaria*

KING JAMES

1.HYPOCRISY

JESUS TEACHING

**12** In the mean time, when there were
gathered together an innumerable
multitude of people, insomuch that they
trode one upon another, he began to say
unto his disciples first of all, Beware ye of
the leaven of the Pharisees, which is
hypocrisy. 2 For there is nothing covered,
that shall not be revealed; neither hid,
that shall not be known. 3 Therefore,
whatsoever ye have spoken in darkness
shall be heard in the light; and that which
ye have spoken in the ear in closets shall
be proclaimed upon the housetops. ●

2.FEAR

fear

4 And I say unto you my friends, Be
not afraid of them that kill the body, and
after that have no more that they can do.
5 But I will forewarn you whom ye shall
fear: Fear him, which after he hath killed
hath power to cast into hell; yea, I say
unto you, Fear him. 6 Are not five sparrows sold for two farthings, and not one
of them is forgotten before God? 7 But
even the very hairs of your head are all
numbered. Fear not therefore: ye are of
more value than many sparrows. ●

do not fear

3.PUBLIC CONFESSION

8 Also I say unto you, Whosoever shall
confess me before men, him shall the Son
of man also confess before the angels of
God: 9 but he that denieth me before
men shall be denied before the angels of
God. 10 And whosoever shall speak a
word against the Son of man, it shall be
forgiven him: but unto him that blasphemeth against the Holy Ghost it shall not be
forgiven. 11 And when they bring you
unto the synagogues, and *unto* magistrates, and powers, take ye no thought
how or what thing ye shall answer, or
what ye shall say: 12 for the Holy Ghost
shall teach you in the same hour what ye
ought to say. ●

HOLY SPIRIT TEACHING

This segment continues the INSTRUCTION ministry of Jesus. From 12:1 to 13:21 the audience is mainly Jesus' followers, and the message is mainly about the walk of the believer. From 13:22 to 14:35 the audience is mainly Jesus' opposition, and the message is mainly about who will be saved.

Record observations of Jesus' teachings below.

*12:1-3* ____________________

*12:4-7* ____________________

*12:8-12* ____________________

NEW INTERNATIONAL VERSION

What is taught here about:

GREED ______

MATERIAL POSSESSIONS ______

REAL RICHES ______

ANXIETY ______

WORRY ______

GOD'S PROVIDENCE ______

OTHER ______

*The Parable of the Rich Fool*

[13]Someone in the crowd said to him, "Teacher, tell my brother to divide the inheritance with me."

[14]Jesus replied, "Man, who appointed me a judge or an arbiter between you?" [15]Then he said to them, "Watch out! Be on your guard against all kinds of greed; a man's life does not consist in the abundance of his possessions."

[16]And he told them this parable: "The ground of a certain rich man produced a good crop. [17]He thought to himself, 'What shall I do? I have no place to store my crops.'

[18]"Then he said, 'This is what I'll do. I will tear down my barns and build bigger ones, and there I will store all my grain and my goods. [19]And I'll say to myself, "You have plenty of good things laid up for many years. Take life easy; eat, drink and be merry." '

[20]"But God said to him, 'You fool! This very night your life will be demanded from you. Then who will get what you have prepared for yourself?'

[21]"This is how it will be with anyone who stores up things for himself but is not rich toward God."●

*Do Not Worry*

[22]Then Jesus said to his disciples: "Therefore I tell you, do not worry about your life, what you will eat; or about your body, what you will wear. [23]Life is more than food, and the body more than clothes. [24]Consider the ravens: They do not sow or reap, they have no storeroom or barn; yet God feeds them. And how much more valuable you are than birds! [25]Who of you by worrying can add a single hour to his life[b]? [26]Since you cannot do this very little thing, why do you worry about the rest?

[27]"Consider how the lilies grow. They do not labor or spin. Yet I tell you, not even Solomon in all his splendor was dressed like one of these. [28]If that is how God clothes the grass of the field, which is here today, and tomorrow is thrown into the fire, how much more will he clothe you, O you of little faith! [29]And do not set your heart on what you will eat or drink; do not worry about it. [30]For the pagan world runs after all such things, and your Father knows that you need them. [31]But seek his kingdom, and these things will be given to you as well.●

[32]"Do not be afraid, little flock, for your Father has been pleased to give you the kingdom. [33]Sell your possessions and give to the poor. Provide purses for yourselves that will not wear out, a treasure in heaven that will not be exhausted, where no thief comes near and no moth destroys. [34]For where your treasure is, there your heart will be also.●

[b]25 Or *single cubit to his height*

KING JAMES

1. RICHES

EARTHLY INHERITANCE

13 And one of the company said unto
him, Master, speak to my brother, that he
divide the inheritance with me. 14 And he
said unto him, Man, who made me a
judge or a divider over you? 15 And he
said unto them, Take heed, and beware
of covetousness: for a man's life consisteth
not in the abundance of the things which
he possesseth. 16 And he spake a parable
unto them, saying, The ground of a certain rich man brought forth plentifully:
17 and he thought within himself, saying,
What shall I do, because I have no room
where to bestow my fruits? 18 And he
said, This will I do: I will pull down my
barns, and build greater; and there will
I bestow all my fruits and my goods.
19 And I will say to my soul, Soul, thou
hast much goods laid up for many years;
take thine ease, eat, drink, *and* be merry.
20 But God said unto him, *Thou* fool, this
night thy soul shall be required of thee:
then whose shall those things be, which
thou hast provided? 21 So *is* he that
layeth up treasure for himself, and is not
rich toward God. ●

2. ANXIETY

22 And he said unto his disciples, Therefore I say unto you, Take no thought for
your life, what ye shall eat; neither for the
body, what ye shall put on. 23 The life is
more than meat, and the body *is more*
than raiment. 24 Consider the ravens: for
they neither sow nor reap; which neither
have storehouse nor barn; and God feedeth them: how much more are ye better
than the fowls? 25 And which of you with
taking thought can add to his stature one
cubit? 26 If ye then be not able to do that
thing which is least, why take ye thought
for the rest? 27 Consider the lilies how
they grow: they toil not, they spin not;
and yet I say unto you, that Solomon in
all his glory was not arrayed like one of
these. 28 If then God so clothe the grass,
which is today in the field, and tomorrow
is cast into the oven; how much more *will*
*he clothe* you, O ye of little faith? 29 And
seek not ye what ye shall eat, or what ye
shall drink, neither be ye of doubtful
mind. 30 For all these things do the nations of the world seek after: and your
Father knoweth that ye have need of these
things. 31 But rather seek ye the kingdom
of God; and all these things shall be added unto you. ●

3. TREASURE IN HEAVEN

32 Fear not, little flock; for it is your
Father's good pleasure to give you the
kingdom. 33 Sell that ye have, and give
alms; provide yourselves bags which wax
not old, a treasure in the heavens that faileth not, where no thief approacheth, neither moth corrupteth. 34 For where your
treasure is, there will your heart be also. ●

HEAVENLY TREASURE

Record the main parts of each of the three paragraphs.

*12:13-21* ______________________

*12:22-31* ______________________

*12:32-34* ______________________

NEW INTERNATIONAL VERSION

What does the passage teach about:

CHRIST'S SECOND COMING

READINESS OF THE BELIEVER

FAITHFULNESS

STEWARDSHIP

OTHER

*Watchfulness*

35 "Be dressed ready for service and keep
your lamps burning, 36 like men waiting for
their master to return from a wedding banquet, so that when he comes and knocks
they can immediately open the door for
him. 37 It will be good for those servants
whose master finds them watching when
he comes. I tell you the truth, he will dress
himself to serve, will have them recline at
the table and will come and wait on them.
38 It will be good for those servants whose
master finds them ready, even if he comes
in the second or third watch of the night.
39 But understand this: If the owner of the
house had known at what hour the thief
was coming, he would not have let his
house be broken into. 40 You also must be
ready, because the Son of Man will come
at an hour when you do not expect him."●
41 Peter asked, "Lord, are you telling this
parable to us, or to everyone?"
42 The Lord answered, "Who then is the
faithful and wise manager, whom the master puts in charge of his servants to give
them their food allowance at the proper
time? 43 It will be good for that servant
whom the master finds doing so when he
returns. 44 I tell you the truth, he will put
him in charge of all his possessions. 45 But
suppose the servant says to himself, 'My
master is taking a long time in coming,' and
he then begins to beat the menservants and
womenservants and to eat and drink and
get drunk. 46 The master of that servant will
come on a day when he does not expect
him and at an hour he is not aware of. He
will cut him to pieces and assign him a
place with the unbelievers.
47 "That servant who knows his master's
will and does not get ready or does not do
what his master wants will be beaten with
many blows. 48 But the one who does not
know and does things deserving punishment will be beaten with few blows. From
everyone who has been given much, much
will be demanded; and from the one who
has been entrusted with much, much more
will be asked.●

KING JAMES

1. READINESS

35 Let your loins be girded about, and
*your* lights burning; 36 and ye yourselves like unto men that wait for their
lord, when he will return from the wedding; that, when he cometh and knocketh,
they may open unto him immediately.
37 Blessed *are* those servants, whom the
lord when he cometh shall find watching:
verily I say unto you, that he shall gird
himself, and make them to sit down to
meat, and will come forth and serve them.
38 And if he shall come in the second
watch, or come in the third watch, and
find *them* so, blessed are those servants.
39 And this know, that if the goodman of
the house had known what hour the thief
would come, he would have watched, and
not have suffered his house to be broken
through. 40 Be ye therefore ready also:
for the Son of man cometh at an hour
when ye think not. ●

SERVANT

2. FAITHFULNESS

41 Then Peter said unto him, Lord,
speakest thou this parable unto us, or
even to all? 42 And the Lord said, Who
then is that faithful and wise steward,
whom *his* lord shall make ruler over his
household, to give *them their* portion of
meat in due season? 43 Blessed *is* that
servant, whom his lord when he cometh
shall find so doing. 44 Of a truth I say
unto you, that he will make him ruler over
all that he hath. 45 But and if that servant
say in his heart, My lord delayeth his coming; and shall begin to beat the menservants and maidens, and to eat and drink,
and to be drunken; 46 the lord of that
servant will come in a day when he looketh not for *him*, and at an hour when he is
not aware, and will cut him in sunder, and
will appoint him his portion with the unbelievers. 47 And that servant, which
knew his lord's will, and prepared not
*himself*, neither did according to his will,
shall be beaten with many *stripes*. 48 But
he that knew not, and did commit things
worthy of stripes, shall be beaten with few
*stripes*. For unto whomsoever much is
given, of him shall be much required; and
to whom men have committed much, of
him they will ask the more. ●

STEWARD

Study the segment in light of the second coming of Christ. Record observations. Look for repeated words.

*12:35-40* ____________________

*12:41-48* ____________________

NEW INTERNATIONAL VERSION

Record what is taught here about:

SUFFERINGS OF JESUS

CONFLICT IN THE WORLD

SIN

SIGNS OF END TIMES

JUSTICE

RIGHTEOUSNESS

*Not Peace but Division*

49"I have come to bring fire on the earth,
and how I wish it were already kindled!
50But I have a baptism to undergo, and how
distressed I am until it is completed! 51Do
you think I came to bring peace on earth?
No, I tell you, but division. 52From now on
there will be five in one family divided
against each other, three against two and
two against three. 53They will be divided,
father against son and son against father,
mother against daughter and daughter
against mother, mother-in-law against
daughter-in-law and daughter-in-law
against mother-in-law."●

*Interpreting the Times*

54He said to the crowd: "When you see
a cloud rising in the west, immediately you
say, 'It's going to rain,' and it does. 55And
when the south wind blows, you say, 'It's
going to be hot,' and it is. 56Hypocrites!
You know how to interpret the appearance
of the earth and the sky. How is it that you
don't know how to interpret this present
time?●

57"Why don't you judge for yourselves
what is right? 58As you are going with your
adversary to the magistrate, try hard to be
reconciled to him on the way, or he may
drag you off to the judge, and the judge
turn you over to the officer, and the officer
throw you into prison. 59I tell you, you will
not get out until you have paid the last
penny.[a]"●

[a]59 Greek *lepton*

KING JAMES

1. DIVISION

49 I am come to send fire on the earth;
and what will I, if it be already kindled?
50 But I have a baptism to be baptized
with; and how am I straitened till it be
accomplished! 51 Suppose ye that I am
come to give peace on earth? I tell you,
Nay; but rather division: 52 for from
henceforth there shall be five in one house
divided, three against two, and two
against three. 53 The father shall be divided against the son, and the son against
the father; the mother against the daughter, and the daughter against the mother;
the mother-in-law against her daughter-
in-law, and the daughter-in-law against
her mother-in-law. ●

FIRE

2. THE TIMES

54 And he said also to the people,
When ye see a cloud rise out of the west,
straightway ye say, There cometh a
shower; and so it is. 55 And when *ye see*
the south wind blow, ye say, There will be
heat; and it cometh to pass. 56 *Ye* hypocrites, ye can discern the face of the sky
and of the earth; but how is it that ye do
not discern this time? ●

3. THE RIGHT

57 Yea, and why even of yourselves
judge ye not what is right? 58 When thou
goest with thine adversary to the magistrate, *as thou art* in the way, give diligence
that thou mayest be delivered from him;
lest he hale thee to the judge, and the
judge deliver thee to the officer, and the
officer cast thee into prison. 59 I tell thee,
thou shalt not depart thence, till thou hast
paid the very last mite. ●

PRISON

This segment continues Jesus' teaching reported in the preceding segments.

*12:49-53* Is Jesus referring to His two comings here?

Record observations.

*12:54-56* Complete the wording of the key question: "Why do you not

?"

What does this mean?

*12:57-59* What is the main appeal of Jesus here?

NEW INTERNATIONAL VERSION

What does this passage teach about:

JUSTICE

JUDGMENT

REPENTANCE

GRACE

JESUS' POWER

KINGDOM OF GOD

OTHER

### *Repent or Perish*

13 Now there were some present at that time who told Jesus about the Galileans whose blood Pilate had mixed with their sacrifices. [2]Jesus answered, "Do you think that these Galileans were worse sinners than all the other Galileans because they suffered this way? [3]I tell you, no! But unless you repent, you too will all perish. [4]Or those eighteen who died when the tower in Siloam fell on them—do you think they were more guilty than all the others living in Jerusalem? [5]I tell you, no! But unless you repent, you too will all perish."●

[6]Then he told this parable: "A man had a fig tree, planted in his vineyard, and he went to look for fruit on it, but did not find any. [7]So he said to the man who took care of the vineyard, 'For three years now I've been coming to look for fruit on this fig tree and haven't found any. Cut it down! Why should it use up the soil?'

[8]" 'Sir,' the man replied, 'leave it alone for one more year, and I'll dig around it and fertilize it. [9]If it bears fruit next year, fine! If not, then cut it down.' "●

### *A Crippled Woman Healed on the Sabbath*

[10]On a Sabbath Jesus was teaching in one of the synagogues, [11]and a woman was there who had been crippled by a spirit for eighteen years. She was bent over and could not straighten up at all. [12]When Jesus saw her, he called her forward and said to her, "Woman, you are set free from your infirmity." [13]Then he put his hands on her, and immediately she straightened up and praised God.

[14]Indignant because Jesus had healed on the Sabbath, the synagogue ruler said to the people, "There are six days for work. So come and be healed on those days, not on the Sabbath."

[15]The Lord answered him, "You hypocrites! Doesn't each of you on the Sabbath untie his ox or donkey from the stall and lead it out to give it water? [16]Then should not this woman, a daughter of Abraham, whom Satan has kept bound for eighteen long years, be set free on the Sabbath day from what bound her?"

[17]When he said this, all his opponents were humiliated, but the people were delighted with all the wonderful things he was doing.●

### *The Parables of the Mustard Seed and the Yeast*

[18]Then Jesus asked, "What is the kingdom of God like? What shall I compare it to? [19]It is like a mustard seed, which a man took and planted in his garden. It grew, became a tree, and the birds of the air perched in its branches."

[20]Again he asked, "What shall I compare the kingdom of God to? [21]It is like yeast that a woman took and mixed into a large amount[a] of flour until it worked all through the dough."●

[a]21 Greek *three satas* (probably about 1/2 bushel or 22 liters)

KING JAMES

1.JUSTICE

HUMAN RULER

13 There were present at that season
some that told him of the Galileans,
whose blood Pilate had mingled with their
sacrifices. 2 And Jesus answering said unto them, Suppose ye that these Galileans
were sinners above all the Galileans, because they suffered such things? 3 I tell
you, Nay: but, except ye repent, ye shall
all likewise perish. 4 Or those eighteen,
upon whom the tower in Silo'am fell, and
slew them, think ye that they were sinners
above all men that dwelt in Jerusalem?
5 I tell you, Nay: but, except ye repent, ye
shall all likewise perish. ●

2.MERCY

6 He spake also this parable; A certain
*man* had a fig tree planted in his vineyard;
and he came and sought fruit thereon, and
found none. 7 Then said he unto the
dresser of his vineyard, Behold, these
three years I come seeking fruit on this fig
tree, and find none: cut it down; why
cumbereth it the ground? 8 And he answering said unto him, Lord, let it alone
this year also, till I shall dig about it, and
dung *it*: 9 and if it bear fruit, *well*: and if
not, *then* after that thou shalt cut it down.●

3.HEALING

10 And he was teaching in one of the
synagogues on the sabbath. 11 And, behold, there was a woman which had a
spirit of infirmity eighteen years, and was
bowed together, and could in no wise lift
up *herself*. 12 And when Jesus saw her,
he called *her to him*, and said unto her,
Woman, thou art loosed from thine infirmity. 13 And he laid *his* hands on her:
and immediately she was made straight,
and glorified God. 14 And the ruler of the
synagogue answered with indignation, because that Jesus had healed on the sabbath day, and said unto the people, There
are six days in which men ought to work:
in them therefore come and be healed, and
not on the sabbath day. 15 The Lord
then answered him, and said, *Thou* hypocrite, doth not each one of you on the
sabbath loose his ox or *his* ass from the
stall, and lead *him* away to watering?
16 And ought not this woman, being a
daughter of Abraham, whom Satan hath
bound, lo, these eighteen years, be loosed
from this bond on the sabbath day?
17 And when he had said these things, all
his adversaries were ashamed: and all the
people rejoiced for all the glorious things
that were done by him. ●

4.KINGDOM

18 Then said he, Unto what is the kingdom of God like? and whereunto shall I
resemble it? 19 It is like a grain of mustard seed, which a man took, and cast into
his garden; and it grew, and waxed a
great tree; and the fowls of the air lodged
in the branches of it.

GOD'S KINGDOM

20 And again he said, Whereunto shall
I liken the kingdom of God? 21 It is like
leaven, which a woman took and hid in
three measures of meal, till the whole was
leavened. ●

Record your observations of each paragraph below. Look especially for the main points.

*13:1-5* ______________________

*13:6-9* ______________________

*13:10-17* ______________________

*13:18-21* ______________________

NEW INTERNATIONAL VERSION

What is taught here about:

WHAT SALVATION IS

HOW TO BE SAVED

JUDGMENT OF LOST SOULS

JESUS' POWER

JESUS' COMPASSION

List important spiritual applications of the passage.

*The Narrow Door*

[22]Then Jesus went through the towns and
villages, teaching as he made his way to
Jerusalem. [23]Someone asked him, "Lord,
are only a few people going to be saved?"
He said to them, [24]"Make every effort to
enter through the narrow door, because
many, I tell you, will try to enter and will
not be able to. [25]Once the owner of the
house gets up and closes the door, you will
stand outside knocking and pleading, 'Sir,
open the door for us.'
"But he will answer, 'I don't know you
or where you come from.'
[26]"Then you will say, 'We ate and drank
with you, and you taught in our streets.'
[27]"But he will reply, 'I don't know you
or where you come from. Away from me,
all you evildoers!'
[28]"There will be weeping there, and
gnashing of teeth, when you see Abraham,
Isaac and Jacob and all the prophets in the
kingdom of God, but you yourselves
thrown out. [29]People will come from east
and west and north and south, and will take
their places at the feast in the kingdom of
God. [30]Indeed there are those who are last
who will be first, and first who will be
last."●

*Jesus' Sorrow for Jerusalem*

[31]At that time some Pharisees came to
Jesus and said to him, "Leave this place
and go somewhere else. Herod wants to
kill you."
[32]He replied, "Go tell that fox, 'I will
drive out demons and heal people today
and tomorrow, and on the third day I will
reach my goal.' [33]In any case, I must keep
going today and tomorrow and the next
day—for surely no prophet can die outside
Jerusalem!●
[34]"O Jerusalem, Jerusalem, you who kill
the prophets and stone those sent to you,
how often I have longed to gather your
children together, as a hen gathers her
chicks under her wings, but you were not
willing! [35]Look, your house is left to you
desolate. I tell you, you will not see me
again until you say, 'Blessed is he who
comes in the name of the Lord.'[b]"●

[b]35 Psalm 118:26

KING JAMES

1. SAVED SINNERS

ON HIS WAY TO JERUSALEM

22 And he went through the cities and
villages, teaching, and journeying toward
Jerusalem. 23 Then said one unto him,
Lord, are there few that be saved? And
he said unto them, 24 Strive to enter in at
the strait gate: for many, I say unto you,
will seek to enter in, and shall not be able.
25 When once the master of the house is
risen up, and hath shut to the door, and
ye begin to stand without, and to knock
at the door, saying, Lord, Lord, open unto us; and he shall answer and say unto
you, I know you not whence ye are:
26 then shall ye begin to say, We have
eaten and drunk in thy presence, and thou
hast taught in our streets. 27 But he shall
say, I tell you, I know you not whence ye
are; depart from me, all *ye* workers of
iniquity. 28 There shall be weeping and
gnashing of teeth, when ye shall see
Abraham, and Isaac, and Jacob, and all
the prophets, in the kingdom of God, and
you *yourselves* thrust out. 29 And they
shall come from the east, and *from* the
west, and from the north, and *from* the
south, and shall sit down in the kingdom
of God. 30 And, behold, there are last
which shall be first; and there are first
which shall be last. ●

2. INDESTRUCTIBLE SAVIOR

31 The same day there came certain of
the Pharisees, saying unto him, Get thee
out, and depart hence; for Herod will kill
thee. 32 And he said unto them, Go ye,
and tell that fox, Behold, I cast out devils,
and I do cures today and tomorrow, and
the third *day* I shall be perfected. 33 Nevertheless I must walk today, and tomorrow,
and the *day* following: for it cannot be
that a prophet perish out of Jerusalem.●

3. UNRESPONSIVE CITY

34 O Jerusalem, Jerusalem, which killest
the prophets, and stonest them that are
sent unto thee; how often would I have
gathered thy children together, as a hen
*doth gather* her brood under *her* wings,
and ye would not! 35 Behold, your house
is left unto you desolate: and verily I say
unto you, Ye shall not see me, until
*the time* come when ye shall say, Blessed
*is* he that cometh in the name of the
Lord. ●

"O JERUSALEM, JERUSALEM"

This is an interesting segment of three different but related paragraphs. Look especially for things common to all three paragraphs.

*13:22-30*

SAVED ______________________________

______________________________

______________________________

______________________________

UNSAVED ______________________________

______________________________

______________________________

______________________________

*13:31-33* Record truths about Jesus:

______________________________

______________________________

______________________________

______________________________

______________________________

______________________________

______________________________

*13:34-35* Record the main point of each verse:

v.34 ______________________________

______________________________

______________________________

______________________________

______________________________

______________________________

v.35 ______________________________

______________________________

______________________________

______________________________

______________________________

______________________________

______________________________

______________________________

______________________________

NEW INTERNATIONAL VERSION

Record truths taught here about:

CONDUCT ON THE LORD'S DAY

HONOR

HUMILITY

LOVE AND KINDNESS

EXCUSES

GOD'S GRACIOUS INVITATIONS

### *Jesus at a Pharisee's House*

14 One Sabbath, when Jesus went to
eat in the house of a prominent
Pharisee, he was being carefully watched.
2There in front of him was a man suffering
from dropsy. 3Jesus asked the Pharisees
and experts in the law, "Is it lawful to heal
on the Sabbath or not?" 4But they
remained silent. So taking hold of the man,
he healed him and sent him away.
5Then he asked them, "If one of you has
a son[c] or an ox that falls into a well on the
Sabbath day, will you not immediately pull
him out?" 6And they had nothing to say. ●
7When he noticed how the guests picked
the places of honor at the table, he told
them this parable: 8"When someone invites you to a wedding feast, do not take
the place of honor, for a person more dis-
tinguished than you may have been invited. 9If so, the host who invited both of
you will come and say to you, 'Give this
man your seat.' Then, humiliated, you will
have to take the least important place.
10But when you are invited, take the lowest
place, so that when your host comes, he
will say to you, 'Friend, move up to a better place.' Then you will be honored in the
presence of all your fellow guests. 11For
everyone who exalts himself will be humbled, and he who humbles himself will be
exalted."
12Then Jesus said to his host, "When
you give a luncheon or dinner, do not invite
your friends, your brothers or relatives, or
your rich neighbors; if you do, they may
invite you back and so you will be repaid.
13But when you give a banquet, invite the
poor, the crippled, the lame, the blind,
14and you will be blessed. Although they
cannot repay you, you will be repaid at the
resurrection of the righteous." ●

### *The Parable of the Great Banquet*

15When one of those at the table with him
heard this, he said to Jesus, "Blessed is the
man who will eat at the feast in the kingdom of God."
16Jesus replied: "A certain man was preparing a great banquet and invited many
guests. 17At the time of the banquet he sent
his servant to tell those who had been invited, 'Come, for everything is now
ready.'
18"But they all alike began to make excuses. The first said, 'I have just bought a
field, and I must go and see it. Please excuse me.'
19"Another said, 'I have just bought five
yoke of oxen, and I'm on my way to try
them out. Please excuse me.'
20"Still another said, 'I just got married,
so I can't come.'
21"The servant came back and reported
this to his master. Then the owner of the
house became angry and ordered his servant, 'Go out quickly into the streets and
alleys of the town and bring in the poor, the
crippled, the blind and the lame.'
22" 'Sir,' the servant said, 'what you ordered has been done, but there is still
room.'
23"Then the master told his servant, 'Go
out to the roads and country lanes and
make them come in, so that my house will
be full. 24I tell you, not one of those men
who were invited will get a taste of my
banquet.' " ●

c5 Some manuscripts *donkey*

KING JAMES

1. HEALING ON THE SABBATH

A PHARISEE'S LUNCH

14 And it came to pass, as he went into
the house of one of the chief Pharisees to eat bread on the sabbath day, that
they watched him. 2 And, behold, there
was a certain man before him which had
the dropsy. 3 And Jesus answering spake
unto the lawyers and Pharisees, saying, Is
it lawful to heal on the sabbath day?
4 And they held their peace. And he took
*him*, and healed him, and let him go;
5 and answered them, saying, Which of
you shall have an ass or an ox fallen into
a pit, and will not straightway pull him
out on the sabbath day? 6 And they
could not answer him again to these
things. ●

2. AMBITIOUS GUEST

7 And he put forth a parable to those
which were bidden, when he marked how
they chose out the chief rooms; saying
unto them, 8 When thou art bidden of
any *man* to a wedding, sit not down in the
highest room; lest a more honorable man
than thou be bidden of him; 9 and he
that bade thee and him come and say to
thee, Give this man place; and thou begin
with shame to take the lowest room.
10 But when thou art bidden, go and sit
down in the lowest room; that when he
that bade thee cometh, he may say unto
thee, Friend, go up higher: then shalt thou
have worship in the presence of them that
sit at meat with thee. 11 For whosoever
exalteth himself shall be abased; and he
that humbleth himself shall be exalted.
12 Then said he also to him that bade
him, When thou makest a dinner or a supper, call not thy friends, nor thy brethren,
neither thy kinsmen, nor *thy* rich neighbors; lest they also bid thee again, and a
recompense be made thee. 13 But when
thou makest a feast, call the poor, the
maimed, the lame, the blind: 14 and thou
shalt be blessed; for they cannot recompense thee: for thou shalt be recompensed
at the resurrection of the just. ●

3. GREAT BANQUET

15 And when one of them that sat at
meat with him heard these things, he said
unto him, Blessed *is* he that shall eat bread
in the kingdom of God. 16 Then said he
unto him, A certain man made a great
supper, and bade many: 17 and sent his
servant at supper time to say to them that
were bidden, Come; for all things are now
ready. 18 And they all with one *consent*
began to make excuse. The first said unto
him, I have bought a piece of ground, and
I must needs go and see it: I pray thee
have me excused. 19 And another said,
I have bought five yoke of oxen, and I go
to prove them: I pray thee have me excused. 20 And another said, I have
married a wife, and therefore I cannot
come. 21 So that servant came, and
showed his lord these things. Then the
master of the house being angry said to
his servant, Go out quickly into the streets
and lanes of the city, and bring in hither
the poor, and the maimed, and the halt,
and the blind. 22 And the servant said,
Lord, it is done as thou hast commanded,
and yet there is room. 23 And the lord
said unto the servant, Go out into the
highways and hedges, and compel *them*
to come in, that my house may be filled.
24 For I say unto you, That none of those
men which were bidden shall taste of my
supper. ●

JESUS' DINNER

*14:1-6* Account for the silence of the opponents at the two times (vv.4,6).

*14:7-14* A repeated key word of this and the next paragraphs is "bidden." Keep this in mind as you analyze each paragraph.

Record the main points of each paragraph.

*14:15-24*

NEW INTERNATIONAL VERSION

What does the passage teach about:

DISCIPLESHIP

LOYALTY TO CHRIST

COUNTING THE COST

CHRISTIAN INFLUENCE

LOVE OF CHRIST

COMPASSION FOR LOST SOULS

REPENTANCE

OTHER

### *The Cost of Being a Disciple*

25 Large crowds were traveling with
Jesus, and turning to them he said: 26 "If
anyone comes to me and does not hate his
father and mother, his wife and children,
his brothers and sisters—yes, even his own
life—he cannot be my disciple. 27 And anyone who does not carry his cross and follow me cannot be my disciple.
28 "Suppose one of you wants to build a
tower. Will he not first sit down and estimate the cost to see if he has enough
money to complete it? 29 For if he lays the
foundation and is not able to finish it,
everyone who sees it will ridicule him,
30 saying, 'This fellow began to build and
was not able to finish.'
31 "Or suppose a king is about to go to
war against another king. Will he not first
sit down and consider whether he is able
with ten thousand men to oppose the one
coming against him with twenty thousand?
32 If he is not able, he will send a delegation
while the other is still a long way off and
will ask for terms of peace. 33 In the same
way, any of you who does not give up
everything he has cannot be my disciple.
34 "Salt is good, but if it loses its saltiness, how can it be made salty again? 35 It
is fit neither for the soil nor for the manure
pile; it is thrown out.
"He who has ears to hear, let him hear." ●

### *The Parable of the Lost Sheep*

15 Now the tax collectors and "sinners" were all gathering around to
hear him. 2 But the Pharisees and the
teachers of the law muttered, "This man
welcomes sinners and eats with them."
3 Then Jesus told them this parable:
4 "Suppose one of you has a hundred sheep
and loses one of them. Does he not leave
the ninety-nine in the open country and go
after the lost sheep until he finds it? 5 And
when he finds it, he joyfully puts it on his
shoulders 6 and goes home. Then he calls
his friends and neighbors together and
says, 'Rejoice with me; I have found my
lost sheep.' 7 I tell you that in the same way
there is more rejoicing in heaven over one
sinner who repents than over ninety-nine
righteous persons who do not need to repent. ●

### *The Parable of the Lost Coin*

8 "Or suppose a woman has ten silver
coins[a] and loses one. Does she not light a
lamp, sweep the house and search carefully until she finds it? 9 And when she finds
it, she calls her friends and neighbors together and says, 'Rejoice with me; I have
found my lost coin.' 10 In the same way, I
tell you, there is rejoicing in the presence
of the angels of God over one sinner who
repents." ●

[a] 8 Greek *ten drachmas*, each worth about a day's wages

KING JAMES

1. DISCIPLESHIP COSTS

25 And there went great multitudes with
him: and he turned, and said unto them,
26 If any *man* come to me, and hate not
his father, and mother, and wife, and children, and brethren, and sisters, yea, and
his own life also, he cannot be my disciple. 27 And whosoever doth not bear
his cross, and come after me, cannot be
my disciple. 28 For which of you, intending to build a tower, sitteth not down
first, and counteth the cost, whether he
have *sufficient* to finish *it?* 29 Lest haply,
after he hath laid the foundation, and is
not able to finish *it*, all that behold *it*
begin to mock him, 30 saying, This man
began to build, and was not able to finish.
31 Or what king, going to make war
against another king, sitteth not down
first, and consulteth whether he be able
with ten thousand to meet him that cometh against him with twenty thousand?
32 Or else, while the other is yet a great
way off, he sendeth an ambassage, and
desireth conditions of peace. 33 So likewise, whosoever he be of you that for-
saketh not all that he hath, he cannot be
my disciple.
34 Salt *is* good: but if the salt have lost
his savor, wherewith shall it be seasoned?
35 It is neither fit for the land, nor yet for
the dunghill; *but* men cast it out. He that
hath ears to hear, let him hear. ●

SACRIFICIAL DISCIPLE

2. LOST SHEEP

15 Then drew near unto him all the
publicans and sinners for to hear
him. 2 And the Pharisees and scribes
murmured, saying, This man receiveth
sinners, and eateth with them.
3 And he spake this parable unto them,
saying, 4 What man of you, having a
hundred sheep, if he lose one of them,
doth not leave the ninety and nine in the
wilderness, and go after that which is lost,
until he find it? 5 And when he hath
found *it*, he layeth *it* on his shoulders,
rejoicing. 6 And when he cometh home,
he calleth together *his* friends and neighbors, saying unto them, Rejoice with me;
for I have found my sheep which was lost.
7 I say unto you, that likewise joy shall be
in heaven over one sinner that repenteth,
more than over ninety and nine just persons, which need no repentance. ●

3. LOST COIN

8 Either what woman having ten pieces
of silver, if she lose one piece, doth not
light a candle, and sweep the house, and
seek diligently till she find *it?* 9 And
when she hath found *it*, she calleth *her*
friends and *her* neighbors together, saying, Rejoice with me; for I have found the
piece which I had lost. 10 Likewise, I say
unto you, there is joy in the presence of
the angels of God over one sinner that
repenteth. ●

REPENTANT SINNER

Chapter 15 of Luke contains the three familiar parables of lost things: lost sheep, lost coin, and lost son. This segment includes the first two, which are introduced by important counsel about the cost of discipleship.

*14:25-35* Observe the different ways Jesus teaches about the cost of discipleship.

How are verses 34-35 related to the preceding verses?

*15:1-7* What brought on the parable? Record the main parts of the parable and the conclusion.

*15:8-10* Compare this parable with that of the lost sheep.

NEW INTERNATIONAL VERSION

Record practical applications which can be made from the experience of the two sons:

YOUNGER SON ______________________

OLDER SON ______________________

What was the father's answer to the older son's discontent? ______________________

Was this a fair arrangement? Support your answer. ______________________

List truths taught in the parable about the Heavenly Father. ______________________

*The Parable of the Lost Son*

11 Jesus continued: "There was a man
who had two sons. 12 The younger one said
to his father, 'Father, give me my share of
the estate.' So he divided his property between them.
13 "Not long after that, the younger son
got together all he had, set off for a distant
country and there squandered his wealth in
wild living. 14 After he had spent everything, there was a severe famine in that
whole country, and he began to be in need.
15 So he went and hired himself out to a
citizen of that country, who sent him to his
fields to feed pigs. 16 He longed to fill his
stomach with the pods that the pigs were
eating, but no one gave him anything.
17 "When he came to his senses, he said,
'How many of my father's hired men have
food to spare, and here I am starving to
death! 18 I will set out and go back to my
father and say to him: Father, I have sinned
against heaven and against you. 19 I am no
longer worthy to be called your son; make
me like one of your hired men.' 20 So he got
up and went to his father.●
"But while he was still a long way off,
his father saw him and was filled with compassion for him; he ran to his son, threw his
arms around him and kissed him.
21 "The son said to him, 'Father, I have
sinned against heaven and against you. I
am no longer worthy to be called your
son.[a]'
22 "But the father said to his servants,
'Quick! Bring the best robe and put it on
him. Put a ring on his finger and sandals on
his feet. 23 Bring the fattened calf and kill it.
Let's have a feast and celebrate. 24 For this
son of mine was dead and is alive again; he
was lost and is found.' So they began to
celebrate.●
25 "Meanwhile, the older son was in the
field. When he came near the house, he
heard music and dancing. 26 So he called
one of the servants and asked him what
was going on. 27 'Your brother has come,'
he replied, 'and your father has killed the
fattened calf because he has him back safe
and sound.'
28 "The older brother became angry and
refused to go in. So his father went out and
pleaded with him. 29 But he answered his
father, 'Look! All these years I've been
slaving for you and never disobeyed your
orders. Yet you never gave me even a
young goat so I could celebrate with my
friends. 30 But when this son of yours who
has squandered your property with prostitutes comes home, you kill the fattened
calf for him!'
31 " 'My son,' the father said, 'you are
always with me, and everything I have is
yours. 32 But we had to celebrate and be
glad, because this brother of yours was
dead and is alive again; he was lost and is
found.' "●

[a]21 Some early manuscripts *son. Make me like one of your hired men.*

KING JAMES

1.YOUNGER SON

"HE WAS DEAD"

11 And he said, A certain man had two
sons: 12 and the younger of them said to
*his* father, Father, give me the portion of
goods that falleth *to me*. And he divided
unto them *his* living. 13 And not many
days after the younger son gathered all together, and took his journey into a far
country, and there wasted his substance
with riotous living. 14 And when he had
spent all, there arose a mighty famine in
that land; and he began to be in want.
15 And he went and joined himself to a
citizen of that country; and he sent him
into his fields to feed swine. 16 And he
would fain have filled his belly with the
husks that the swine did eat: and no man
gave unto him. 17 And when he came to
himself, he said, How many hired servants of my father's have bread enough and
to spare, and I perish with hunger! 18 I
will arise and go to my father, and will
say unto him, Father, I have sinned
against heaven, and before thee, 19 and
am no more worthy to be called thy son:
make me as one of thy hired servants.
20 And he arose, and came to his father.●

2.FATHER

But when he was yet a great way off, his
father saw him, and had compassion, and
ran, and fell on his neck, and kissed him.
21 And the son said unto him, Father, I
have sinned against heaven, and in thy
sight, and am no more worthy to be called
thy son. 22 But the father said to his
servants, Bring forth the best robe, and
put *it* on him; and put a ring on his hand,
and shoes on *his* feet: 23 and bring hither
the fatted calf, and kill *it;* and let us eat,
and be merry: 24 for this my son was
dead, and is alive again; he was lost, and
is found. And they began to be merry.●

3.OLDER SON

25 Now his elder son was in the field:
and as he came and drew nigh to the
house, he heard music and dancing.
26 And he called one of the servants, and
asked what these things meant. 27 And
he said unto him, Thy brother is come;
and thy father hath killed the fatted calf,
because he hath received him safe and
sound. 28 And he was angry, and would
not go in: therefore came his father out,
and entreated him. 29 And he answering
said to *his* father, Lo, these many years
do I serve thee, neither transgressed I at
any time thy commandment; and yet
thou never gavest me a kid, that I might
make merry with my friends: 30 but as
soon as this thy son was come, which
hath devoured thy living with harlots,
thou hast killed for him the fatted calf.
31 And he said unto him, Son, thou art
ever with me, and all that I have is thine.
32 It was meet that we should make merry,
and be glad: for this thy brother was dead,
and is alive again; and was lost, and is
found.●

"HE HAS BEGUN TO LIVE"

Observe who the main subject is of each paragraph. Record your observations of the different parts of the paragraphs.

*15:11-20a* ______________________

*15:20b-24* ______________________

*15:25-32* ______________________

NEW INTERNATIONAL VERSION

What is taught here about:

STEWARDSHIP

FAITHFULNESS

HONESTY

SERVANT OF JESUS

RICHES

LAW

GOSPEL

HYPOCRISY

*The Parable of the Shrewd Manager*

16 Jesus told his disciples: "There was
a rich man whose manager was
accused of wasting his possessions. 2So he
called him in and asked him, 'What is this
I hear about you? Give an account of your
management, because you cannot be manager any longer.'
3"The manager said to himself, 'What
shall I do now? My master is taking away
my job. I'm not strong enough to dig, and
I'm ashamed to beg— 4I know what I'll do
so that, when I lose my job here, people
will welcome me into their houses.'
5"So he called in each one of his master's debtors. He asked the first, 'How
much do you owe my master?'
6" 'Eight hundred gallons[b] of olive oil,'
he replied.
"The manager told him, 'Take your bill,
sit down quickly, and make it four hundred.'
7"Then he asked the second, 'And how
much do you owe?'
" 'A thousand bushels[c] of wheat,' he replied.
"He told him, 'Take your bill and make
it eight hundred.'
8"The master commended the dishonest
manager because he had acted shrewdly.●
For the people of this world are more
shrewd in dealing with their own kind than
are the people of the light. 9I tell you, use
worldly wealth to gain friends for yourselves, so that when it is gone, you will be
welcomed into eternal dwellings.
10"Whoever can be trusted with very little can also be trusted with much, and whoever is dishonest with very little will also
be dishonest with much. 11So if you have
not been trustworthy in handling worldly
wealth, who will trust you with true riches?
12And if you have not been trustworthy
with someone else's property, who will
give you property of your own?
13"No servant can serve two masters.
Either he will hate the one and love the
other, or he will be devoted to the one and
despise the other. You cannot serve both
God and Money."●
14The Pharisees, who loved money,
heard all this and were sneering at Jesus.
15He said to them, "You are the ones who
justify yourselves in the eyes of men, but
God knows your hearts. What is highly
valued among men is detestable in God's
sight.
16"The Law and the Prophets were proclaimed until John. Since that time, the
good news of the kingdom of God is being
preached, and everyone is forcing his way
into it. 17It is easier for heaven and earth to
disappear than for the least stroke of a pen
to drop out of the Law.
18"Anyone who divorces his wife and
marries another woman commits adultery,
and the man who marries a divorced
woman commits adultery.●

[b]6 Greek *one hundred batous* (probably about 3 kiloliters)
[c]7 Greek *one hundred korous* (probably about 35 kiloliters)

KING JAMES

1.A SHREWD STEWARD

16 And he said also unto his disciples,
There was a certain rich man,
which had a steward; and the same was
accused unto him that he had wasted his
goods. 2 And he called him, and said unto him, How is it that I hear this of thee?
give an account of thy stewardship; for
thou mayest be no longer steward.
3 Then the steward said within himself,
What shall I do? for my lord taketh away
from me the stewardship: I cannot dig;
to beg I am ashamed. 4 I am resolved
what to do, that, when I am put out of the
stewardship, they may receive me into
their houses. 5 So he called every one of
his lord's debtors *unto him*, and said unto
the first, How much owest thou unto my
lord? 6 And he said, A hundred measures of oil. And he said unto him, Take
thy bill, and sit down quickly, and write
fifty. 7 Then said he to another, And how
much owest thou? And he said, A hundred measures of wheat. And he said unto him, Take thy bill, and write fourscore.
8 And the lord commended the unjust
steward, because he had done wisely ● for
the children of this world are in their generation wiser than the children of light.

2.A FAITHFUL STEWARD

9 And I say unto you, Make to yourselves
friends of the mammon of unrighteousness; that, when ye fail, they may receive
you into everlasting habitations.
10 He that is faithful in that which is
least is faithful also in much: and he that
is unjust in the least is unjust also in much.
11 If therefore ye have not been faithful in
the unrighteous mammon, who will commit to your trust the true *riches?* 12 And
if ye have not been faithful in that which
is another man's, who shall give you that
which is your own? 13 No servant can
serve two masters: for either he will hate
the one, and love the other; or else he will
hold to the one, and despise the other.
Ye cannot serve God and mammon. ●

3.THE UNFAILING LAW

14 And the Pharisees also, who were
covetous, heard all these things: and they
derided him. 15 And he said unto them,
Ye are they which justify yourselves before men; but God knoweth your hearts:
for that which is highly esteemed among
men is abomination in the sight of
God.
16 The law and the prophets *were* until
John: since that time the kingdom of God
is preached, and every man presseth into
it. 17 And it is easier for heaven and
earth to pass, than one tittle of the law to
fail.
18 Whosoever putteth away his wife,
and marrieth another, committeth adultery: and whosoever marrieth her that is
put away from *her* husband committeth
adultery. ●

EMPLOYEE IN TROUBLE

HUSBAND IN TROUBLE

Chapter 15 records three parables on RECOVERY, emphasizing God's Grace. The section 16:1-17:37 records three parables or illustrations on STEWARDSHIP, teaching man's responsibilities.

*16:1-8a* What does this parable teach? Interpret verse 8a in your answer.

*16:8b-13* How does Jesus apply the parable? (Compare the Living Bible text for an interpretation of this very difficult passage.) Note: Mammon means material riches.

*16:14-18* Note the repetition of the word "law." Record the main points of the paragraph:

NEW INTERNATIONAL VERSION

Record various spiritual lessons taught by this passage:

What are your reflections about these verses:

16:31

17:5

*The Rich Man and Lazarus*

19"There was a rich man who was
dressed in purple and fine linen and lived
in luxury every day. 20At his gate was laid
a beggar named Lazarus, covered with
sores 21and longing to eat what fell from the
rich man's table. Even the dogs came and
licked his sores.
22"The time came when the beggar died
and the angels carried him to Abraham's
side. The rich man also died and was buried. 23In hell,[a] where he was in torment, he
looked up and saw Abraham far away, with
Lazarus by his side. 24So he called to him,
'Father Abraham, have pity on me and
send Lazarus to dip the tip of his finger in
water and cool my tongue, because I am in
agony in this fire.'
25"But Abraham replied, 'Son, remember that in your lifetime you received your
good things, while Lazarus received bad
things, but now he is comforted here and
you are in agony. 26And besides all this,
between us and you a great chasm has been
fixed, so that those who want to go from
here to you cannot, nor can anyone cross
over from there to us.'
27"He answered, 'Then I beg you, father, send Lazarus to my father's house,
28for I have five brothers. Let him warn
them, so that they will not also come to this
place of torment.'
29"Abraham replied, 'They have Moses
and the Prophets; let them listen to them.'
30" 'No, father Abraham,' he said, 'but if
someone from the dead goes to them, they
will repent.'
31"He said to him, 'If they do not listen
to Moses and the Prophets, they will not be
convinced even if someone rises from the
dead.' "●

*Sin, Faith, Duty*

17 Jesus said to his disciples: "Things
that cause people to sin are bound to
come, but woe to that person through
whom they come. 2It would be better for
him to be thrown into the sea with a millstone tied around his neck than for him to
cause one of these little ones to sin. 3So
watch yourselves.
"If your brother sins, rebuke him, and if
he repents, forgive him. 4If he sins against
you seven times in a day, and seven times
comes back to you and says, 'I repent,'
forgive him."●
5The apostles said to the Lord, "Increase our faith!"
6He replied, "If you have faith as small
as a mustard seed, you can say to this mul-
berry tree, 'Be uprooted and planted in the
sea,' and it will obey you.●
7"Suppose one of you had a servant
plowing or looking after the sheep. Would
he say to the servant when he comes in
from the field, 'Come along now and sit
down to eat'? 8Would he not rather say,
'Prepare my supper, get yourself ready and
wait on me while I eat and drink; after that
you may eat and drink'? 9Would he thank
the servant because he did what he was
told to do? 10So you also, when you have
done everything you were told to do,
should say, 'We are unworthy servants; we
have only done our duty.' "●

[a]23 Greek *Hades*

KING JAMES

1. TRAGIC INADEQUACY OF RICHES

WASTED LIFE

19 There was a certain rich man, which
was clothed in purple and fine linen, and
fared sumptuously every day: 20 and
there was a certain beggar named Lazarus, which was laid at his gate, full of
sores, 21 and desiring to be fed with the
crumbs which fell from the rich man's
table: moreover the dogs came and licked
his sores. 22 And it came to pass, that the
beggar died, and was carried by the angels
into Abraham's bosom: the rich man also
died, and was buried; 23 and in hell he
lifted up his eyes, being in torments, and
seeth Abraham afar off, and Lazarus in
his bosom. 24 And he cried and said,
Father Abraham, have mercy on me, and
send Lazarus, that he may dip the tip of
his finger in water, and cool my tongue;
for I am tormented in this flame. 25 But
Abraham said, Son, remember that thou
in thy lifetime receivedst thy good things,
and likewise Lazarus evil things: but now
he is comforted, and thou art tormented.
26 And beside all this, between us and
you there is a great gulf fixed: so that they
which would pass from hence to you cannot; neither can they pass to us, that
*would come* from thence. 27 Then he said,
I pray thee therefore, father, that thou
wouldest send him to my father's house:
28 for I have five brethren; that he may
testify unto them, lest they also come into
this place of torment. 29 Abraham saith
unto him, They have Moses and the
prophets; let them hear them. 30 And he
said, Nay, father Abraham: but if one
went unto them from the dead, they will
repent. 31 And he said unto him, If they
hear not Moses and the prophets, neither
will they be persuaded, though one rose
from the dead.●

2. RIGHT ATTITUDES OF SERVICE

a.

17 Then said he unto the disciples, It
is impossible but that offenses will
come: but woe *unto him*, through whom
they come! 2 It were better for him that
a millstone were hanged about his neck,
and he cast into the sea, than that he
should offend one of these little ones.
3 Take heed to yourselves: If thy brother
trespass against thee, rebuke him; and
if he repent, forgive him. 4 And if he trespass against thee seven times in a day, and
seven times in a day turn again to thee,
saying, I repent; thou shalt forgive
him.●

b.

5 And the apostles said unto the Lord,
Increase our faith. 6 And the Lord said,
If ye had faith as a grain of mustard seed,
ye might say unto this sycamine tree, Be
thou plucked up by the root, and be thou
planted in the sea; and it should obey
you.●

c.

7 But which of you, having a servant
plowing or feeding cattle, will say unto
him by and by, when he is come from the
field, Go and sit down to meat? 8 and
will not rather say unto him, Make ready
wherewith I may sup, and gird thyself,
and serve me, till I have eaten and drunk-
en; and afterward thou shalt eat and
drink? 9 Doth he thank that servant because he did the things that were commanded him? I trow not. 10 So likewise
ye, when ye shall have done all those
things which are commanded you, say,
We are unprofitable servants: we have
done that which was our duty to do.●

DUTIFUL LABOR

*16:19-31* Is anything said here about the spiritual condition of the rich man and of the beggar?
From their two destinies after death, what may be concluded concerning this?

What is the main point of this story?

What additional truth is taught by verse 31?

*17:1-10* Record one right attitude of service taught by these verses:

1-2

3-4

5-6

7-10

NEW INTERNATIONAL VERSION

What is taught here about:

MERCY OF GOD ______

GRATITUDE ______

SIGNS OF CHRIST'S RETURN ______

SPIRITUAL APPLICATIONS ______

*Ten Healed of Leprosy*

11 Now on his way to Jerusalem, Jesus
traveled along the border between Samaria
and Galilee. 12 As he was going into a village, ten men who had leprosy[b] met him.
They stood at a distance 13 and called out in
a loud voice, "Jesus, Master, have pity on
us!"
14 When he saw them, he said, "Go,
show yourselves to the priests." And as
they went, they were cleansed.
15 One of them, when he saw he was
healed, came back, praising God in a loud
voice. 16 He threw himself at Jesus' feet and
thanked him—and he was a Samaritan.
17 Jesus asked, "Were not all ten
cleansed? Where are the other nine? 18 Was
no one found to return and give praise to
God except this foreigner?" 19 Then he said
to him, "Rise and go; your faith has made
you well."●

*The Coming of the Kingdom of God*

20 Once, having been asked by the Pharisees when the kingdom of God would
come, Jesus replied, "The kingdom of God
does not come visibly, 21 nor will people
say, 'Here it is,' or 'There it is,' because
the kingdom of God is within[a] you."●
22 Then he said to his disciples, "The
time is coming when you will long to see
one of the days of the Son of Man, but you
will not see it. 23 Men will tell you, 'There
he is!' or 'Here he is!' Do not go running
off after them. 24 For the Son of Man in his
day[b] will be like the lightning, which
flashes and lights up the sky from one end
to the other. 25 But first he must suffer
many things and be rejected by this generation.●
26 "Just as it was in the days of Noah, so
also will it be in the days of the Son of Man.
27 People were eating, drinking, marrying
and being given in marriage up to the day
Noah entered the ark. Then the flood came
and destroyed them all.
28 "It was the same in the days of Lot.
People were eating and drinking, buying
and selling, planting and building. 29 But the
day Lot left Sodom, fire and sulfur rained
down from heaven and destroyed them all.
30 "It will be just like this on the day the
Son of Man is revealed. 31 On that day no
one who is on the roof of his house, with
his goods inside, should go down to get
them. Likewise, no one in the field should
go back for anything. 32 Remember Lot's
wife! 33 Whoever tries to keep his life will
lose it, and whoever loses his life will preserve it. 34 I tell you, on that night two
people will be in one bed; one will be taken
and the other left. 35 Two women will be
grinding grain together; one will be taken
and the other left.[c]"
37 "Where, Lord?" they asked.
He replied, "Where there is a dead
body, there the vultures will gather."●

[b] *12* The Greek word was used for various diseases affecting the skin—not necessarily leprosy.
[a] *21* Or *among*
[b] *24* Some manuscripts do not have *in his day*.
[c] *35* Some manuscripts *left*. *36 Two men will be in the field; one will be taken and the other left.*

KING JAMES

PHYSICAL AND TEMPORAL REALM

1.OBJECTS OF JESUS' MERCY

11 And it came to pass, as he went to
Jerusalem, that he passed through the
midst of Samaria and Galilee. 12 And as
he entered into a certain village, there
met him ten men that were lepers, which
stood afar off: 13 and they lifted up *their*
voices, and said, Jesus, Master, have
mercy on us. 14 And when he saw *them*,
he said unto them, Go show yourselves
unto the priests. And it came to pass,
that, as they went, they were cleansed.
15 And one of them, when he saw that he
was healed, turned back, and with a loud
voice glorified God, 16 and fell down on
*his* face at his feet, giving him thanks: and
he was a Samaritan. 17 And Jesus answering said, Were there not ten cleansed?
but where *are* the nine? 18 There are not
found that returned to give glory to God,
save this stranger. 19 And he said unto
him, Arise, go thy way: thy faith hath
made thee whole. ●

2.TIME OF HIS RETURN

20 And when he was demanded of the
Pharisees, when the kingdom of God
should come, he answered them and said,
The kingdom of God cometh not with

a.

observation: 21 neither shall they say,
Lo here! or, lo there! for, behold, the
kingdom of God is within you.●

b.

22 And he said unto the disciples, The
days will come, when ye shall desire to see
one of the days of the Son of man, and ye
shall not see *it*. 23 And they shall say to
you, See here; or, see there: go not after
*them*, nor follow *them*. 24 For as the
lightning, that lighteneth out of the one
*part* under heaven, shineth unto the other
*part* under heaven; so shall also the Son
of man be in his day. 25 But first must he
suffer many things, and be rejected of this

c.

generation.● 26 And as it was in the days
of Noah, so shall it be also in the days of
the Son of man. 27 They did eat, they
drank, they married wives, they were
given in marriage, until the day that Noah
entered into the ark, and the flood came,
and destroyed them all. 28 Likewise also
as it was in the days of Lot; they did eat,
they drank, they bought, they sold, they
planted, they builded; 29 but the same
day that Lot went out of Sodom it rained
fire and brimstone from heaven, and destroyed *them* all. 30 Even thus shall it be
in the day when the Son of man is revealed. 31 In that day, he which shall be
upon the housetop, and his stuff in the
house, let him not come down to take it
away: and he that is in the field, let him
likewise not return back. 32 Remember
Lot's wife. 33 Whosoever shall seek to
save his life shall lose it; and whosoever
shall lose his life shall preserve it. 34 I
tell you, in that night there shall be two
*men* in one bed; the one shall be taken,
and the other shall be left. 35 Two *women*
shall be grinding together; the one shall
be taken, and the other left. 36 Two *men*
shall be in the field; the one shall be taken,
and the other left. 37 And they answered
and said unto him, Where, Lord? And
he said unto them, Wheresoever the
body *is*, thither will the eagles be gathered
together. ●

SPIRITUAL AND ETERNAL REALM

The section 17:11-19:27 covers Jesus' last words and works before He reached Jerusalem for the week of sacrifice and triumph. The main theme of His teaching was that of the Kingdom.

*17:11-19* Did all the lepers plead Jesus' mercy?

Who gave thanks? ____________________

*17:20-37* Record what the paragraphs teach about the time of Christ's return.

*17:20-21* ____________________

*17:22-25* ____________________

*17:26-37* ____________________

List various spiritual truths taught by the two parables. Most of these will be about prayer, but other subjects are also involved.

Try applying the above truths to everyday situations in your own life, and in the lives of others.

NEW INTERNATIONAL VERSION

*The Parable of the Persistent Widow*

18 Then Jesus told his disciples a parable to show them that they should
always pray and not give up. 2He said: "In
a certain town there was a judge who
neither feared God nor cared about men.
3And there was a widow in that town who
kept coming to him with the plea, 'Grant
me justice against my adversary.'
4"For some time he refused. But finally
he said to himself, 'Even though I don't
fear God or care about men, 5yet because
this widow keeps bothering me, I will see
that she gets justice, so that she won't
eventually wear me out with her coming!' "
6And the Lord said, "Listen to what the
unjust judge says. 7And will not God bring
about justice for his chosen ones, who cry
out to him day and night? Will he keep
putting them off? 8I tell you, he will see that
they get justice, and quickly. However,
when the Son of Man comes, will he find
faith on the earth?" ●

*The Parable of the Pharisee and the Tax Collector*

9To some who were confident of their
own righteousness and looked down on everybody else, Jesus told this parable:
10"Two men went up to the temple to pray,
one a Pharisee and the other a tax collector. 11The Pharisee stood up and prayed
about[d] himself: 'God, I thank you that I am
not like all other men—robbers, evildoers,
adulterers—or even like this tax collector.
12I fast twice a week and give a tenth of all
I get.'
13"But the tax collector stood at a distance. He would not even look up to
heaven, but beat his breast and said, 'God,
have mercy on me, a sinner.'
14"I tell you that this man, rather than
the other, went home justified before God.
For everyone who exalts himself will be
humbled, and he who humbles himself will
be exalted." ●

d11 Or *to*

KING JAMES

1.PERSIS-
TENCE

WIDOW

**18** And he spake a parable unto them
*to this end*, that men ought always
to pray, and not to faint; 2 saying, There
was in a city a judge, which feared not
God, neither regarded man: 3 and there
was a widow in that city; and she came
unto him, saying, Avenge me of mine adversary. 4 And he would not for a while:
but afterward he said within himself,
Though I fear not God, nor regard man;
5 yet because this widow troubleth me, I
will avenge her, lest by her continual coming she weary me. 6 And the Lord said,
Hear what the unjust judge saith. 7 And
shall not God avenge his own elect, which
cry day and night unto him, though he
bear long with them? 8 I tell you that he
will avenge them speedily. Nevertheless,
when the Son of man cometh, shall he
find faith on the earth?●

2.CONTRITE-
NESS

9 And he spake this parable unto certain which trusted in themselves that they
were righteous, and despised others:
10 Two men went up into the temple to
pray; the one a Pharisee, and the other a
publican. 11 The Pharisee stood and
prayed thus with himself, God, I thank
thee, that I am not as other men *are*, extortioners, unjust, adulterers, or even as
this publican. 12 I fast twice in the week,
I give tithes of all that I possess. 13 And
the publican, standing afar off, would not
lift up so much as *his* eyes unto heaven,
but smote upon his breast, saying, God be
merciful to me a sinner. 14 I tell you,
this man went down to his house justified
*rather* than the other: for every one
that exalteth himself shall be abased;
and he that humbleth himself shall be
exalted. ●

TAX-
GATHERER

These two parables teach important truths about prayer. Record your observations of the different parts of each parable and the main teaching:

*18:1-8* ______________________________

*18:9-14* ______________________________

NEW INTERNATIONAL VERSION

What does this passage teach about:

FAITH

LAW

TOTAL SURRENDER

HOW TO BE SAVED

ETERNAL LIFE

REWARDS

FULFILLED PROPHECY

GOD

*The Little Children and Jesus*

15People were also bringing babies to
Jesus to have him touch them. When the
disciples saw this, they rebuked them.
16But Jesus called the children to him and
said, "Let the little children come to me,
and do not hinder them, for the kingdom of
God belongs to such as these. 17I tell you
the truth, anyone who will not receive the
kingdom of God like a little child will never
enter it."●

*The Rich Ruler*

18A certain ruler asked him, "Good
teacher, what must I do to inherit eternal
life?"
19"Why do you call me good?" Jesus
answered. "No one is good—except God
alone. 20You know the commandments:
'Do not commit adultery, do not murder,
do not steal, do not give false testimony,
honor your father and mother.'[e]"
21"All these I have kept since I was a
boy," he said.
22When Jesus heard this, he said to him,
"You still lack one thing. Sell everything
you have and give to the poor, and you will
have treasure in heaven. Then come, follow me."
23When he heard this, he became very
sad, because he was a man of great wealth.
24Jesus looked at him and said, "How hard
it is for the rich to enter the kingdom of
God! 25Indeed, it is easier for a camel to go
through the eye of a needle than for a rich
man to enter the kingdom of God."
26Those who heard this asked, "Who
then can be saved?"
27Jesus replied, "What is impossible
with men is possible with God."●
28Peter said to him, "We have left all we
had to follow you!"
29"I tell you the truth," Jesus said to
them, "no one who has left home or wife
or brothers or parents or children for the
sake of the kingdom of God 30will fail to
receive many times as much in this age
and, in the age to come, eternal life."●

*Jesus Again Predicts His Death*

31Jesus took the Twelve aside and told
them, "We are going up to Jerusalem, and
everything that is written by the prophets
about the Son of Man will be fulfilled. 32He
will be handed over to the Gentiles. They
will mock him, insult him, spit on him, flog
him and kill him. 33On the third day he will
rise again."
34The disciples did not understand any of
this. Its meaning was hidden from them,
and they did not know what he was talking
about.●

[e]*20* Exodus 20:12-16; Deut. 5:16-20

## KING JAMES

**1. CHILD-LIKE ATTITUDE** — Disciples

15 And they brought unto him also infants, that he would touch them: but
when *his* disciples saw *it*, they rebuked
them. 16 But Jesus called them *unto him*,
and said, Suffer little children to come
unto me, and forbid them not: for of such
is the kingdom of God. 17 Verily I say
unto you, Whosoever shall not receive the
kingdom of God as a little child shall in
no wise enter therein. ●

**2. SACRIFICIAL ATTITUDE** — Rich ruler

18 And a certain ruler asked him, saying, Good Master, what shall I do to inherit eternal life? 19 And Jesus said unto
him, Why callest thou me good? none *is*
good, save one, *that is*, God. 20 Thou
knowest the commandments, Do not
commit adultery, Do not kill, Do not
steal, Do not bear false witness, Honor
thy father and thy mother. 21 And he
said, All these have I kept from my youth
up. 22 Now when Jesus heard these
things, he said unto him, Yet lackest thou
one thing: sell all that thou hast, and dis-
tribute unto the poor, and thou shalt have
treasure in heaven: and come, follow me.
23 And when he heard this, he was very
sorrowful: for he was very rich. 24 And
when Jesus saw that he was very sorrowful, he said, How hardly shall they that
have riches enter into the kingdom of
God! 25 For it is easier for a camel to go
through a needle's eye, than for a rich
man to enter into the kingdom of God.
26 And they that heard *it* said, Who then
can be saved? 27 And he said, The things
which are impossible with men are possible with God. ●

**3. REWARDS** — Peter

28 Then Peter said, Lo,
we have left all, and followed thee.
29 And he said unto them, Verily I say
unto you, There is no man that hath left
house, or parents, or brethren, or wife,
or children, for the kingdom of God's
sake, 30 who shall not receive manifold
more in this present time, and in the
world to come life everlasting. ●

**4. THE WAY OF JESUS** — The twelve

31 Then he took *unto him* the twelve,
and said unto them, Behold, we go up to
Jerusalem, and all things that are written
by the prophets concerning the Son of
man shall be accomplished. 32 For he
shall be delivered unto the Gentiles, and
shall be mocked, and spitefully entreated,
and spitted on: 33 and they shall scourge
*him*, and put him to death; and the third
day he shall rise again. 34 And they understood none of these things: and
this saying was hid from them, neither knew they the things which were
spoken. ●

---

Observe in the text where these words appear: kingdom, saved, eternal life, follow. Underline these and other key words in the text.

*18:15-17* What does Luke write about the kingdom of God?

*18:18-27* Analyze Jesus' answer to the ruler's question.

What do verses 24-27 add to Jesus' answer?

*18:28-30* What are the rewards?

*18:31-34* In the previous paragraphs Jesus was talking about following Him. How does this paragraph relate to that?

NEW INTERNATIONAL VERSION

What do you learn from this passage about:

FAITH

JESUS' MISSION

SALVATION

WORKS

ZEAL

OTHER

*A Blind Beggar Receives His Sight*

35As Jesus approached Jericho, a blind
man was sitting by the roadside begging.
36When he heard the crowd going by, he
asked what was happening. 37They told
him, "Jesus of Nazareth is passing by."
38He called out, "Jesus, Son of David,
have mercy on me!"
39Those who led the way rebuked him
and told him to be quiet, but he shouted all
the more, "Son of David, have mercy on
me!"
40Jesus stopped and ordered the man to
be brought to him. When he came near,
Jesus asked him, 41"What do you want me
to do for you?"
"Lord, I want to see," he replied.
42Jesus said to him, "Receive your sight;
your faith has healed you." 43Immediately
he received his sight and followed Jesus,
praising God. When all the people saw it,
they also praised God.●

*Zacchaeus the Tax Collector*

19 Jesus entered Jericho and was passing through. 2A man was there by
the name of Zacchaeus; he was a chief tax
collector and was wealthy. 3He wanted to
see who Jesus was, but being a short man
he could not, because of the crowd. 4So he
ran ahead and climbed a sycamore-fig tree
to see him, since Jesus was coming that
way.
5When Jesus reached the spot, he looked
up and said to him, "Zacchaeus, come
down immediately. I must stay at your
house today." 6So he came down at once
and welcomed him gladly.
7All the people saw this and began to
mutter, "He has gone to be the guest of a
'sinner.' "
8But Zacchaeus stood up and said to the
Lord, "Look, Lord! Here and now I give
half of my possessions to the poor, and if
I have cheated anybody out of anything, I
will pay back four times the amount."
9Jesus said to him, "Today salvation has
come to this house, because this man, too,
is a son of Abraham. 10For the Son of Man
came to seek and to save what was lost."●

## KING JAMES

### 1. FAITH FOR HEALING

BLIND MAN

35 And it came to pass, that as he was
come nigh unto Jericho, a certain blind
man sat by the wayside begging: 36 and
hearing the multitude pass by, he asked
what it meant. 37 And they told him,
that Jesus of Nazareth passeth by.
38 And he cried, saying, Jesus, *thou* Son
of David, have mercy on me. 39 And they
which went before rebuked him, that he
should hold his peace: but he cried so
much the more, *Thou* Son of David, have
mercy on me. 40 And Jesus stood, and
commanded him to be brought unto him:
and when he was come near, he asked him,
41 saying, What wilt thou that I shall do
unto thee? And he said, Lord, that I may
receive my sight. 42 And Jesus said unto
him, Receive thy sight: thy faith hath
saved thee. 43 And immediately he received his sight, and followed him, glorifying God: and all the people, when they
saw *it*, gave praise unto God. ●

### 2. FAITH FOR SALVATION

CHIEF TAX-GATHERER

19 And *Jesus* entered and passed
through Jericho. 2 And, behold,
*there was* a man named Zacche'us, which
was the chief among the publicans, and
he was rich. 3 And he sought to see Jesus
who he was; and could not for the press,
because he was little of stature. 4 And he
ran before, and climbed up into a syca-
more tree to see him; for he was to pass
that *way*. 5 And when Jesus came to the
place, he looked up, and saw him, and
said unto him, Zacche'us, make haste, and
come down; for today I must abide at thy
house. 6 And he made haste, and came
down, and received him joyfully. 7 And
when they saw *it*, they all murmured, saying, That he was gone to be guest with a
man that is a sinner. 8 And Zacche'us
stood, and said unto the Lord; Behold,
Lord, the half of my goods I give to the
poor; and if I have taken any thing from
any man by false accusation, I restore *him*
fourfold. 9 And Jesus said unto him,
This day is salvation come to this house,
forasmuch as he also is a son of Abraham.
10 For the Son of man is come to seek and
to save that which was lost. ●

Observe in these paragraphs what is revealed about the hearts of the persons. Also analyze carefully Jesus' words. Record your observations.

*18:35-43* ____________________

*19:1-10* ____________________

Compare verse 10 with verse 9.

NEW INTERNATIONAL VERSION

What is taught here about:

FAITHFULNESS

ACCOUNTABILITY

AUTHORITY

SUBJECTION

OBEDIENCE

REWARDS

JUSTICE

SECOND COMING OF CHRIST

*The Parable of the Ten Minas*

11While they were listening to this, he
went on to tell them a parable, because he
was near Jerusalem and the people thought
that the kingdom of God was going to appear at once. 12He said: "A man of noble
birth went to a distant country to have himself appointed king and then to return. 13So
he called ten of his servants and gave them
ten minas.[a] 'Put this money to work,' he
said, 'until I come back.'
14"But his subjects hated him and sent a
delegation after him to say, 'We don't want
this man to be our king.'●
15"He was made king, however, and returned home. Then he sent for the servants
to whom he had given the money, in order
to find out what they had gained with it.
16"The first one came and said, 'Sir,
your mina has earned ten more.'
17" 'Well done, my good servant!' his
master replied. 'Because you have been
trustworthy in a very small matter, take
charge of ten cities.'
18"The second came and said, 'Sir, your
mina has earned five more.'
19"His master answered, 'You take
charge of five cities.'●
20"Then another servant came and said,
'Sir, here is your mina; I have kept it laid
away in a piece of cloth. 21I was afraid of
you, because you are a hard man. You take
out what you did not put in and reap what
you did not sow.'
22"His master replied, 'I will judge you
by your own words, you wicked servant!
You knew, did you, that I am a hard man,
taking out what I did not put in, and reaping what I did not sow? 23Why then didn't
you put my money on deposit, so that
when I came back, I could have collected
it with interest?'
24"Then he said to those standing by,
'Take his mina away from him and give it
to the one who has ten minas.'
25" 'Sir,' they said, 'he already has ten!'●
26"He replied, 'I tell you that to everyone who has, more will be given, but as for
the one who has nothing, even what he has
will be taken away. 27But those enemies of
mine who did not want me to be king over
them—bring them here and kill them in
front of me.' "●

[a]*13* A mina was about three months' wages.

KING JAMES

1.EQUAL DISTRIBUTION

KING HIRES SUBJECTS

11 And as they heard these things, he
added and spake a parable, because he
was nigh to Jerusalem, and because they
thought that the kingdom of God should
immediately appear. 12 He said therefore, A certain nobleman went into a far
country to receive for himself a kingdom,
and to return. 13 And he called his ten
servants, and delivered them ten pounds,
and said unto them, Occupy till I come.
14 But his citizens hated him, and sent a
message after him, saying, We will not
have this *man* to reign over us.● 15And it

2.GOOD INVESTMENTS

came to pass, that when he was returned,
having received the kingdom, then he
commanded these servants to be called
unto him, to whom he had given the
money, that he might know how much
every man had gained by trading. 16 Then
came the first, saying, Lord, thy pound
hath gained ten pounds. 17 And he said
unto him, Well, thou good servant: because thou hast been faithful in a very
little, have thou authority over ten cities.
18 And the second came, saying, Lord,
thy pound hath gained five pounds.
19 And he said likewise to him, Be thou
also over five cities. ● 20 And another

3.EVIL HOARDING

came, saying, Lord, behold, *here is* thy
pound, which I have kept laid up in a
napkin: 21 for I feared thee, because thou
art an austere man: thou takest up that
thou layedst not down, and reapest that
thou didst not sow. 22 And he saith unto
him, Out of thine own mouth will I judge
thee, *thou* wicked servant. Thou knewest
that I was an austere man, taking up that
I laid not down, and reaping that I did
not sow: 23 wherefore then gavest not
thou my money into the bank, that at my
coming I might have required mine own
with usury? 24 And he said unto them
that stood by, Take from him the pound,
and give *it* to him that hath ten pounds.
25 (And they said unto him, Lord, he

4.DISPOSITION

hath ten pounds.)● 26For I say unto you,
That unto every one which hath shall be
given; and from him that hath not, even
that he hath shall be taken away from
him. 27 But those mine enemies, which
would not that I should reign over them,
bring hither, and slay *them* before me. ●

KING SLAYS ENEMIES

Record the main parts of each parable.

Observe that the parable invoves both slaves and citizens.

*19:11-14* ______

*19:15-19* ______

*19:20-25* ______

19*:26-27* ______

NEW INTERNATIONAL VERSION

What does this narrative teach about:

JESUS'

—DOMINION

—OMNISCIENCE

—COMPASSION

MIRACLES

PRAISE

WORSHIP

JUDGMENT

OTHER

### *The Triumphal Entry*

[28]After Jesus had said this, he went on
ahead, going up to Jerusalem. [29]As he approached Bethphage and Bethany at the
hill called the Mount of Olives, he sent two
of his disciples, saying to them, [30]"Go to
the village ahead of you, and as you enter
it, you will find a colt tied there, which no
one has ever ridden. Untie it and bring it
here. [31]If anyone asks you, 'Why are you
untying it?' tell him, 'The Lord needs it.' "
[32]Those who were sent ahead went and
found it just as he had told them. [33]As they
were untying the colt, its owners asked
them, "Why are you untying the colt?"
[34]They replied, "The Lord needs it."
[35]They brought it to Jesus, threw their
cloaks on the colt and put Jesus on it. ● [36]As
he went along, people spread their cloaks
on the road.
[37]When he came near the place where
the road goes down the Mount of Olives,
the whole crowd of disciples began joyfully
to praise God in loud voices for all the
miracles they had seen:

[38]"Blessed is the king who comes in
the name of the Lord!"[a]

"Peace in heaven and glory in the
highest!"

[39]Some of the Pharisees in the crowd
said to Jesus, "Teacher, rebuke your disciples!"
[40]"I tell you," he replied, "if they keep
quiet, the stones will cry out." ●
[41]As he approached Jerusalem and saw
the city, he wept over it [42]and said, "If you,
even you, had only known on this day what
would bring you peace—but now it is hidden from your eyes. [43]The days will come
upon you when your enemies will build an
embankment against you and encircle you
and hem you in on every side. [44]They will
dash you to the ground, you and the children within your walls. They will not leave
one stone on another, because you did not
recognize the time of God's coming to
you." ●

[a]38 Psalm 118:26 [b]46 Isaiah 56:7 [c]46 Jer. 7:11

KING JAMES

1. ENTRY INTO JERUSALEM

28 And when he had thus spoken, he
went before, ascending up to Jerusalem.
29 And it came to pass, when he was come
nigh to Bethphage and Bethany, at the
mount called *the mount* of Olives, he sent
two of his disciples, 30 saying, Go ye into
the village over against *you;* in the which
at your entering ye shall find a colt tied,
whereon yet never man sat: loose him,
and bring *him hither*. 31 And if any man
ask you, Why do ye loose *him?* thus shall
ye say unto him, Because the Lord hath
need of him. 32 And they that were sent
went their way, and found even as he had
said unto them. 33 And as they were
loosing the colt, the owners thereof said
unto them, Why loose ye the colt? 34 And
they said, The Lord hath need of him.
35 And they brought him to Jesus: and
they cast their garments upon the colt,
and they set Jesus thereon. ●

TO JERUSALEM FOR DEATH

2. PEOPLE PRAISE

36 And as he
went, they spread their clothes in the way.
37 And when he was come nigh, even now
at the descent of the mount of Olives, the
whole multitude of the disciples began to
rejoice and praise God with a loud voice
for all the mighty works that they had
seen; 38 saying,

Blessed *be* the King
that cometh in the name of the Lord:
peace in heaven,
and glory in the highest.

Ps. 118:26

39 And some of the Pharisees from among
the multitude said unto him, Master, rebuke thy disciples. 40 And he answered
and said unto them, I tell you that, if
these should hold their peace, the stones
would immediately cry out. ●

3. JESUS WEEPS

41 And when he was come near, he beheld the city, and wept over it, 42 saying,
If thou hadst known, even thou, at least
in this thy day, the things *which belong*
unto thy peace! but now they are hid
from thine eyes. 43 For the days shall
come upon thee, that thine enemies shall
cast a trench about thee, and compass thee
round, and keep thee in on every side,
44 and shall lay thee even with the ground,
and thy children within thee; and they
shall not leave in thee one stone upon
another; because thou knewest not the
time of thy visitation. ●

ABOUT JERUSALEM'S DESTRUCTION

This segment begins the fourth and last section of Luke (SACRIFICE). It is the story of Jesus' entry into Jerusalem. In six days He would be crucified.

*19:28-35* Study the paragraph around the repeated sentence, "The Lord hath need of him."

What miraculous elements appear in the paragraph?

*19:36-40* Analyze the words of the people, the Pharisees and Jesus.

*19:41-44* Why did Jesus weep over the city?

What did Jesus mean by the last phrase of verse 44?

NEW INTERNATIONAL VERSION

Record what is taught by the passage about:

PLACE OF WORSHIP

PRAYER

JESUS' AUTHORITY AND POWER

REJECTION OF JESUS

JUDGMENT

OTHER

*Jesus at the Temple*

45 Then he entered the temple area and
began driving out those who were selling.
46 "It is written," he said to them, " 'My
house will be a house of prayer'[b]; but you
have made it 'a den of robbers.'[c]"
47 Every day he was teaching at the temple. But the chief priests, the teachers of
the law and the leaders among the people
were trying to kill him. 48 Yet they could not
find any way to do it, because all the
people hung on his words.●

*The Authority of Jesus Questioned*

20 One day as he was teaching the
people in the temple courts and
preaching the gospel, the chief priests and
the teachers of the law, together with the
elders, came up to him. 2 "Tell us by what
authority you are doing these things," they
said. "Who gave you this authority?"
3 He replied, "I will also ask you a question. Tell me, 4 John's baptism—was it
from heaven, or from men?"
5 They discussed it among themselves
and said, "If we say, 'From heaven,' he
will ask, 'Why didn't you believe him?'
6 But if we say, 'From men,' all the people
will stone us, because they are persuaded
that John was a prophet."
7 So they answered, "We don't know
where it was from."
8 Jesus said, "Neither will I tell you by
what authority I am doing these things."●

*The Parable of the Tenants*

9 He went on to tell the people this parable: "A man planted a vineyard, rented it
to some farmers and went away for a long
time. 10 At harvest time he sent a servant to
the tenants so they would give him some of
the fruit of the vineyard. But the tenants
beat him and sent him away empty-handed. 11 He sent another servant, but that one
also they beat and treated shamefully and
sent away empty-handed. 12 He sent still a
third, and they wounded him and threw
him out.
13 "Then the owner of the vineyard said,
'What shall I do? I will send my son, whom
I love; perhaps they will respect him.'
14 "But when the tenants saw him, they
talked the matter over. 'This is the heir,'
they said. 'Let's kill him, and the inheritance will be ours.' 15 So they threw him out
of the vineyard and killed him.
"What then will the owner of the vineyard do to them? 16 He will come and kill
those tenants and give the vineyard to
others."
When the people heard this, they said,
"May this never be!"
17 Jesus looked directly at them and
asked, "Then what is the meaning of that
which is written:

" 'The stone the builders rejected
has become the capstone'[a][b]?

18 Everyone who falls on that stone will be
broken to pieces, but he on whom it falls
will be crushed."
19 The teachers of the law and the chief
priests looked for a way to arrest him
immediately, because they knew he had
spoken this parable against them. But they
were afraid of the people.●

[a] 17 Or *cornerstone* [b] 17 Psalm 118:22

KING JAMES

**1. CASTING OUT TRADERS**

**45 And he went into the temple, and be-
gan to cast out them that sold therein, and
them that bought; 46 saying unto them, It
is written, My house is the house of prayer; but ye have made it a den of thieves.**
47 And he taught daily in the temple.
But the chief priests and the scribes and
the chief of the people sought to destroy
him, 48 and could not find what they
might do: for all the people were very
attentive to hear him.●

Isa 56:7

TRYING TO DESTROY JESUS

**2. ANSWERING A QUESTION**

20 And it came to pass, *that* on one of
those days, as he taught the people
in the temple, and preached the gospel,
the chief priests and the scribes came upon
*him* with the elders, 2 and spake unto
him, saying, Tell us, by what authority
doest thou these things? or who is he that
gave thee this authority? 3 And he answered and said unto them, I will also ask
you one thing; and answer me: 4 The
baptism of John, was it from heaven, or
of men? 5 And they reasoned with themselves, saying, If we shall say, From
heaven; he will say, Why then believed ye
him not? 6 But and if we say, Of men;
all the people will stone us: for they be
persuaded that John was a prophet.
7 And they answered, that they could not
tell whence *it was*. 8 And Jesus said unto
them, Neither tell I you by what authority
I do these things.●

**3. TEACHING A PARABLE**

9 Then began he to speak to the people
this parable; A certain man planted a
vineyard, and let it forth to husbandmen,
and went into a far country for a long
time. 10 And at the season he sent a servant to the husbandmen, that they should
give him of the fruit of the vineyard: but
the husbandmen beat him, and sent *him*
away empty. 11 And again he sent another servant: and they beat him also, and
entreated *him* shamefully, and sent *him*
away empty. 12 And again he sent a
third: and they wounded him also, and
cast *him* out. 13 Then said the lord of the
vineyard, What shall I do? I will send my
beloved son: it may be they will reverence
*him* when they see him. 14 But when the
husbandmen saw him, they reasoned
among themselves, saying, This is the heir:
come, let us kill him, that the inheritance
may be ours. 15 So they cast him out of
the vineyard, and killed *him*. What therefore shall the lord of the vineyard do unto
them? 16 He shall come and destroy
these husbandmen, and shall give the vineyard to others. And when they heard *it*,
they said, God forbid. 17 And he beheld
them, and said, What is this then that is
written,

> The stone which the builders rejected,
> the same is become the head of the corner?

Ps. 118:22

18 Whosoever shall fall upon that stone
shall be broken; but on whomsoever it
shall fall, it will grind him to powder.
19 And the chief priests and the scribes
the same hour sought to lay hands on
him; and they feared the people: for they
perceived that he had spoken this parable
against them.●

TRYING TO LAY HANDS ON JESUS

The section 17:11-19:27 covers Jesus' last words and works before He reached Jerusalem for the week of sacrifice and triumph. The main theme of His teaching was that of the Kingdom.

*19:45-48* ______

*20:1-8* ______

*20:9-19* ______

Compare 20:19 with 19:47-48. ______

NEW INTERNATIONAL VERSION

What do you learn here about:

CITIZENSHIP ON EARTH

ALLEGIANCES

RESURRECTION FACT

RESURRECTION BODIES

GOD

JESUS

List five key spiritual applications.

*Paying Taxes to Caesar*

[20]Keeping a close watch on him, they
sent spies, who pretended to be honest.
They hoped to catch Jesus in something he
said so that they might hand him over to
the power and authority of the governor.
[21]So the spies questioned him: "Teacher,
we know that you speak and teach what is
right, and that you do not show partiality
but teach the way of God in accordance
with the truth. [22]Is it right for us to pay
taxes to Caesar or not?"
[23]He saw through their duplicity and said
to them, [24]"Show me a denarius. Whose
portrait and inscription are on it?"
[25]"Caesar's," they replied.
He said to them, "Then give to Caesar
what is Caesar's, and to God what is
God's."
[26]They were unable to trap him in what
he had said there in public. And astonished
by his answer, they became silent.●

*The Resurrection and Marriage*

[27]Some of the Sadducees, who say there
is no resurrection, came to Jesus with a
question. [28]"Teacher," they said, "Moses
wrote for us that if a man's brother dies and
leaves a wife but no children, the man must
marry the widow and have children for his
brother. [29]Now there were seven brothers.
The first one married a woman and died
childless. [30]The second [31]and then the third
married her, and in the same way the seven
died, leaving no children. [32]Finally, the
woman died too. [33]Now then, at the resurrection whose wife will she be, since the
seven were married to her?"●
[34]Jesus replied, "The people of this age
marry and are given in marriage. [35]But
those who are considered worthy of taking
part in that age and in the resurrection from
the dead will neither marry nor be given in
marriage, [36]and they can no longer die; for
they are like the angels. They are God's
children, since they are children of the
resurrection. [37]But in the account of the
bush, even Moses showed that the dead
rise, for he calls the Lord 'the God of Abraham, and the God of Isaac, and the God of
Jacob.'[c] [38]He is not the God of the dead,
but of the living, for to him all are alive."●
[39]Some of the teachers of the law re-
sponded, "Well said, teacher!" [40]And no
one dared to ask him any more questions.●

c37 Exodus 3:6

KING JAMES

1. PAYING TAXES

20 And they watched *him*,
and sent forth spies, which should feign
themselves just men, that they might take
hold of his words, that so they might deliver him unto the power and authority of
the governor. 21 And they asked him,
saying, Master, we know that thou sayest
and teachest rightly, neither acceptest
thou the person *of any*, but teachest the
way of God truly: 22 Is it lawful for us
to give tribute unto Caesar, or no? 23 But
he perceived their craftiness, and said unto them, Why tempt ye me? 24 Show me
a penny. Whose image and superscription
hath it? They answered and said, Caesar's.
25 And he said unto them, Render therefore unto Caesar the things which be
Caesar's, and unto God the things which
be God's. 26 And they could not take
hold of his words before the people: and
they marveled at his answer, and held
their peace. ●

DECEITFUL

2. RESURRECTION AND MARRIAGE

—question

27 Then came to *him* certain of the
Sadducees, which deny that there is any
resurrection; and they asked him, 28 saying, Master, Moses wrote unto us, If any
man's brother die, having a wife, and he
die without children, that his brother
should take his wife, and raise up seed
unto his brother. 29 There were therefore seven brethren: and the first took a
wife, and died without children. 30 And
the second took her to wife, and he died
childless. 31 And the third took her; and
in like manner the seven also: and they
left no children, and died. 32 Last of all
the woman died also. 33 Therefore in the
resurrection whose wife of them is she?
for seven had her to wife. ●

Deu. 25:5

—answer

34 And Jesus answering said unto them,
The children of this world marry, and are
given in marriage: 35 but they which shall
be accounted worthy to obtain that world,
and the resurrection from the dead, neither marry, nor are given in marriage:
36 neither can they die any more: for they
are equal unto the angels; and are the
children of God, being the children of the
resurrection. 37 Now that the dead are
raised, even Moses showed at the bush,
when he calleth the Lord the God of
Abraham, and the God of Isaac, and the
God of Jacob. 38 For he is not a God of
the dead, but of the living: for all live unto
him. ●

Ex. 3:6

3. REACTION

39 Then certain of the scribes answering said, Master, thou hast well said.
40 And after that they durst not ask him
any *question at all.* ●

COWARDLY

First read the opening verse (v.20) and concluding verses (vv.39-40). Study the remainder of the segment in light of this setting. Record your observations.

*20:20-26* ____________________

*20:27-33*

QUESTION ____________________

*20:34-38*

ANSWER ____________________

NEW INTERNATIONAL VERSION

Record truths taught here about:

JESUS

HYPOCRISY

DEVOTION

GIVING

OTHER

*Whose Son Is the Christ?*

41Then Jesus said to them, "How is it
that they say the Christ[d] is the Son of David? 42David himself declares in the Book
of Psalms:

" 'The Lord said to my Lord:
"Sit at my right hand
43until I make your enemies
a footstool for your feet." '[e]

44David calls him 'Lord.' How then can he
be his son?"●

45While all the people were listening,
Jesus said to his disciples, 46"Beware of
the teachers of the law. They like to walk
around in flowing robes and love to be
greeted in the marketplaces and have the
most important seats in the synagogues
and the places of honor at banquets.
47They devour widows' houses and for a
show make lengthy prayers. Such men will
be punished most severely."●

*The Widow's Offering*

21 As he looked up, Jesus saw the rich
putting their gifts into the temple
treasury. 2He also saw a poor widow put in
two very small copper coins.[f] 3"I tell you
the truth," he said, "this poor widow has
put in more than all the others. 4All these
people gave their gifts out of their wealth;
but she out of her poverty put in all she had
to live on."●

[d]*41* Or *Messiah* [e]*43* Psalm 110:1
[f]*2* Greek *two lepta*

KING JAMES

1. IDENTIFICATION

41 And he said unto them, How say
they that Christ is David's son? 42 And
David himself saith in the book of Psalms,
The LORD said unto my Lord,
Sit thou on my right hand,
43 till I make thine enemies thy footstool.
44 David therefore calleth him Lord, how
is he then his son? ●

HIGHEST POSITION

Ps. 110:1

2. CONDEMNATION

45 Then in the audience of all the people
he said unto his disciples, 46 Beware of
the scribes, which desire to walk in long robes, and love greetings in the markets, and the highest seats in the synagogues,
and the chief rooms at feasts; 47 which
devour widows' houses, and for a show make long prayers: the same shall receive greater damnation. ●

3. COMMENDATION

21 And he looked up, and saw the rich men casting their gifts into the treasury. 2 And he saw also a certain poor
widow casting in thither two mites.
3 And he said, Of a truth I say unto you, that this poor widow hath cast in more
than they all: 4 for all these have of their
abundance cast in unto the offerings of God: but she of her penury hath cast in all the living that she had. ●

UTMOST DEVOTION

The setting of this segment is still in the court of the Temple. The day is Tuesday of Passion Week. Luke records a few things spoken by Jesus at this time.

Analyze the short paragraphs carefully, and record your observations.

*20:41-44* ____________________

*20:45-47* ____________________

*21:1-4* ____________________

NEW INTERNATIONAL VERSION

Record what this prophetic discourse teaches about:

TRIBULATIONS

DELIVERANCES

EXHORTATIONS

*Signs of the End of the Age*
5Some of his disciples were remarking
about how the temple was adorned with
beautiful stones and with gifts dedicated to
God. But Jesus said, 6"As for what you see
here, the time will come when not one
stone will be left on another; every one of
them will be thrown down."
7"Teacher," they asked, "when will
these things happen? And what will be the
sign that they are about to take place?"●
8He replied: "Watch out that you are not
deceived. For many will come in my name,
claiming, 'I am he,' and, 'The time is near.'
Do not follow them. 9When you hear of
wars and revolutions, do not be frightened.
These things must happen first, but the end
will not come right away."●
10Then he said to them: "Nation will rise
against nation, and kingdom against kingdom. 11There will be great earthquakes,
famines and pestilences in various places,
and fearful events and great signs from
heaven.
12"But before all this, they will lay hands
on you and persecute you. They will deliver you to synagogues and prisons, and
you will be brought before kings and governors, and all on account of my name. 13This
will result in your being witnesses to them.
14But make up your mind not to worry
beforehand how you will defend yourselves. 15For I will give you words and
wisdom that none of your adversaries will
be able to resist or contradict. 16You will be
betrayed by parents, brothers, relatives
and friends, and they will put some of you
to death. 17All men will hate you because
of me. 18But not a hair of your head will
perish. 19By standing firm you will save
yourselves.●
20"When you see Jerusalem surrounded
by armies, you will know that its desolation is near. 21Then let those who are in
Judea flee to the mountains, let those in the
city get out, and let those in the country not
enter the city. 22For this is the time of punishment in fulfillment of all that has been
written. 23How dreadful it will be in those
days for pregnant women and nursing
mothers! There will be great distress in the
land and wrath against this people. 24They
will fall by the sword and will be taken as
prisoners to all the nations. Jerusalem will
be trampled on by the Gentiles until the
times of the Gentiles are fulfilled.●

KING JAMES

—setting

A BEAUTIFUL TEMPLE

**5 And as some spake of the temple, how**
**it was adorned with goodly stones and**
**gifts, he said, 6 *As for* these things which**
**ye behold, the days will come, in the**
**which there shall not be left one stone up-**
**on another, that shall not be thrown**
**down. 7 And they asked him, saying,**
**Master, but when shall these things be?**
**and what sign *will there be* when these**

1.FIRST SIGNS

**things shall come to pass? ● 8And he said,**
**Take heed that ye be not deceived: for**
**many shall come in my name, saying, I am**
***Christ;* and the time draweth near: go ye**
**not therefore after them. 9 But when ye**
**shall hear of wars and commotions, be not**
**terrified: for these things must first come**
**to pass; but the end *is* not by and by.●**

2.MORE SEVERE TIMES

**10 Then said he unto them, Nation**
**shall rise against nation, and kingdom**
**against kingdom: 11 and great earth-**
**quakes shall be in divers places, and**
**famines, and pestilences; and fearful**
**sights and great signs shall there be from**
**heaven. 12 But before all these, they shall**
**lay their hands on you, and persecute *you,***
**delivering *you* up to the synagogues, and**
**into prisons, being brought before kings**
**and rulers for my name's sake. 13 And it**
**shall turn to you for a testimony. 14 Settle**
***it* therefore in your hearts, not to medi-**
**tate before what ye shall answer: 15 for I**
**will give you a mouth and wisdom, which**
**all your adversaries shall not be able to**
**gainsay nor resist. 16 And ye shall be**
**betrayed both by parents, and brethren,**
**and kinsfolk, and friends; and *some* of**
**you shall they cause to be put to death.**
**17 And ye shall be hated of all *men* for my**
**name's sake. 18 But there shall not a hair**
**of your head perish. 19 In your patience**
**possess ye your souls.●**

3.FALL OF JERUSALEM

**20 And when ye shall see Jerusalem**
**compassed with armies, then know that**
**the desolation thereof is nigh. 21 Then let**
**them which are in Judea flee to the moun-**
**tains; and let them which are in the midst**
**of it depart out; and let not them that are**
**in the countries enter thereinto. 22 For**
**these be the days of vengeance, that all**
**things which are written may be fulfilled.**
**23 But woe unto them that are with child,**
**and to them that give suck, in those days!**
**for there shall be great distress in the land,**
**and wrath upon this people. 24 And they**
**shall fall by the edge of the sword, and**
**shall be led away captive into all nations:**
**and Jerusalem shall be trodden down of**
**the Gentiles, until the times of the Gen-**
**tiles be fulfilled.●**

A DESTROYED CITY

Luke 21 is Jesus' prophecy of end times, called the Olivet Discourse. (Cf. Matthew 24-25 and Mark 13.) There is a double perspective in the prophecy, involving the coming Fall of Jerusalem (A.D. 70) and the tribulation times before Christ's second coming.

*21:5-9* What brought on the discourse?

What do verses 8-9 prophesy?

*21:10-19* List the sequence of events.

*21:20-24* Interpret these prophecies especially as involving the fall of Jerusalem in A.D. 70. Then what does v.24b prophesy?

## NEW INTERNATIONAL VERSION

Record what this part of Jesus' discourse teaches about the signs of His coming in the end times.

List the different exhortations given in the passage.

25"There will be signs in the sun, moon
and stars. On the earth, nations will be in
anguish and perplexity at the roaring and
tossing of the sea. 26Men will faint from
terror, apprehensive of what is coming on
the world, for the heavenly bodies will be
shaken. 27At that time they will see the Son
of Man coming in a cloud with power and
great glory. 28When these things begin to
take place, stand up and lift up your heads,
because your redemption is drawing
near."●
29He told them this parable: "Look at the
fig tree and all the trees. 30When they
sprout leaves, you can see for yourselves
and know that summer is near. 31Even so,
when you see these things happening, you
know that the kingdom of God is near.
32"I tell you the truth, this generation[a]
will certainly not pass away until all these
things have happened. 33Heaven and earth
will pass away, but my words will never
pass away.●
34"Be careful, or your hearts will be
weighed down with dissipation, drunkenness and the anxieties of life, and that day
will close on you unexpectedly like a trap.
35For it will come upon all those who live
on the face of the whole earth. 36Be always
on the watch, and pray that you may be
able to escape all that is about to happen,
and that you may be able to stand before
the Son of Man."●
37Each day Jesus was teaching at the
temple, and each evening he went out to
spend the night on the hill called the Mount
of Olives, 38and all the people came early
in the morning to hear him at the temple.●

a32 Or *race*

KING JAMES

1. LAST SIGNS

KING

25 And there shall be signs in the sun,
and in the moon, and in the stars; and
upon the earth distress of nations, with
perplexity; the sea and the waves roaring;
26 men's hearts failing them for fear, and
for looking after those things which are
coming on the earth: for the powers of
heaven shall be shaken. 27 And then shall
they see the Son of man coming in a cloud
with power and great glory. 28 And when
these things begin to come to pass, then
look up, and lift up your heads; for your
redemption draweth nigh. ●

2. PARABLE

29 And he spake to them a parable;
Behold the fig tree, and all the trees;
30 when they now shoot forth, ye see and
know of your own selves that summer is
now nigh at hand. 31 So likewise ye,
when ye see these things come to pass,
know ye that the kingdom of God is nigh
at hand. 32 Verily I say unto you, This
generation shall not pass away, till all be
fulfilled. 33 Heaven and earth shall pass
away; but my words shall not pass away. ●

3. EXHORTATION

34 And take heed to yourselves, lest at
any time your hearts be overcharged with
surfeiting, and drunkenness, and cares of
this life, and *so* that day come upon you
unawares. 35 For as a snare shall it come
on all them that dwell on the face of the
whole earth. 36 Watch ye therefore, and
pray always, that ye may be accounted
worthy to escape all these things that shall
come to pass, and to stand before the
Son of man. ●

—Jesus' teaching ministry

TEACHER

37 And in the daytime he was teaching
in the temple; and at night he went out,
and abode in the mount that is called *the*
*mount* of Olives. 38 And all the people
came early in the morning to him in the
temple, for to hear him. ●

Since this segment is a continuation of the preceding one, review 21:5-24 before studying this.

*21:25-28*

LAST SIGNS (vv.25-26) __________

THE EVENT (v.27) __________

THE ADMONITION (v.28) __________

*21:29-33* Record your observations. __________

*21:34-36* Analyze the exhortations: __________

*21:37-38* How does this conclude the chapter? __________

NEW INTERNATIONAL VERSION

List all the things taught about each of the following:

JESUS

SATAN

JUDAS

PASSOVER

LORD'S TABLE

### *Judas Agrees to Betray Jesus*

22 Now the Feast of Unleavened
Bread, called the Passover, was approaching, 2and the chief priests and the
teachers of the law were looking for some
way to get rid of Jesus, for they were afraid
of the people. 3Then Satan entered Judas,
called Iscariot, one of the Twelve. 4And
Judas went to the chief priests and the officers of the temple guard and discussed
with them how he might betray Jesus.
5They were delighted and agreed to give
him money. 6He consented, and watched
for an opportunity to hand Jesus over to
them when no crowd was present.●

### *The Last Supper*

7Then came the day of Unleavened
Bread on which the Passover lamb had to
be sacrificed. 8Jesus sent Peter and John,
saying, "Go and make preparations for us
to eat the Passover."
9"Where do you want us to prepare for
it?" they asked.
10He replied, "As you enter the city, a
man carrying a jar of water will meet you.
Follow him to the house that he enters,
11and say to the owner of the house, 'The
Teacher asks: Where is the guest room,
where I may eat the Passover with my disciples?' 12He will show you a large upper
room, all furnished. Make preparations
there."
13They left and found things just as Jesus
had told them. So they prepared the Passover.●
14When the hour came, Jesus and his
apostles reclined at the table. 15And he said
to them, "I have eagerly desired to eat this
Passover with you before I suffer. 16For I
tell you, I will not eat it again until it finds
fulfillment in the kingdom of God."
17After taking the cup, he gave thanks
and said, "Take this and divide it among
you. 18For I tell you I will not drink again
of the fruit of the vine until the kingdom of
God comes."
19And he took bread, gave thanks and
broke it, and gave it to them, saying, "This
is my body given for you; do this in remembrance of me."
20In the same way, after the supper he
took the cup, saying, "This cup is the new
covenant in my blood, which is poured out
for you. 21But the hand of him who is going
to betray me is with mine on the table.
22The Son of Man will go as it has been
decreed, but woe to that man who betrays
him." 23They began to question among
themselves which of them it might be who
would do this.●

## KING JAMES

1. PLOT AGAINST JESUS

BETRAYER PLOTTING

22 Now the feast of unleavened bread
drew nigh, which is called the passover. 2 And the chief priests and scribes
sought how they might kill him; for they
feared the people.
3 Then entered Satan into Judas surnamed Iscar'i-ot, being of the number of
the twelve. 4 And he went his way, and
communed with the chief priests and captains, how he might betray him unto them.
5 And they were glad, and covenanted to
give him money. 6 And he promised, and
sought opportunity to betray him unto
them in the absence of the multitude.●

2. PASSOVER PREPARED

7 Then came the day of unleavened
bread, when the passover must be killed.
8 And he sent Peter and John, saying, Go
and prepare us the passover, that we may
eat. 9 And they said unto him, Where
wilt thou that we prepare? 10 And he
said unto them, Behold, when ye are
entered into the city, there shall a man
meet you, bearing a pitcher of water; follow him into the house where he entereth
in. 11 And ye shall say unto the goodman
of the house, The Master saith unto thee,
Where is the guest chamber, where I shall
eat the passover with my disciples?
12 And he shall show you a large upper
room furnished: there make ready.
13 And they went, and found as he had
said unto them: and they made ready the
passover.●

3. THE LAST SUPPER

14 And when the hour was come, he sat
down, and the twelve apostles with him.
15 And he said unto them, With desire I
have desired to eat this passover with you
before I suffer: 16 for I say unto you, I
will not any more eat thereof, until it be
fulfilled in the kingdom of God. 17 And
he took the cup, and gave thanks, and
said, Take this, and divide *it* among yourselves: 18 for I say unto you, I will not
drink of the fruit of the vine, until the
kingdom of God shall come. 19 And he
took bread, and gave thanks, and brake
*it*, and gave unto them, saying, This is my
body which is given for you: this do in
remembrance of me. 20 Likewise also the
cup after supper, saying, This cup *is* the
new testament in my blood, which is
shed for you. 21 But, behold, the hand of
him that betrayeth me *is* with me on the
table. 22 And truly the Son of man goeth,
as it was determined: but woe unto that
man by whom he is betrayed! 23 And
they began to inquire among themselves,
which of them it was that should do this
thing.●

BETRAYER EXPOSED

At 22:1 Luke begins recording the darkest experiences of Jesus' life, leading up to His death. Record the main parts of each paragraph.

*22:1-6* ______________________________

*22:7-13* What are your impressions? ______________

*22:14-23* Record observations of these three parts:

vv.14-16 ______________________________

vv.17-20 ______________________________

vv.21-23 ______________________________

NEW INTERNATIONAL VERSION

What does the passage teach about:

TRUE GREATNESS

BELIEVER'S FRAILTY

SATAN'S OPPOSITION

LORD'S HELP

JESUS' HUMANITY

PRAYER

24 Also a dispute arose among them as to
which of them was considered to be greatest. 25 Jesus said to them, "The kings of the
Gentiles lord it over them; and those who
exercise authority over them call themselves Benefactors. 26 But you are not to be
like that. Instead, the greatest among you
should be like the youngest, and the one
who rules like the one who serves. 27 For
who is greater, the one who is at the table
or the one who serves? Is it not the one
who is at the table? But I am among you as
one who serves. 28 You are those who have
stood by me in my trials. 29 And I confer on
you a kingdom, just as my Father conferred one on me, 30 so that you may eat and
drink at my table in my kingdom and sit on
thrones, judging the twelve tribes of Israel.●
31 "Simon, Simon, Satan has asked to sift
you[a] as wheat. 32 But I have prayed for you,
Simon, that your faith may not fail. And
when you have turned back, strengthen
your brothers."
33 But he replied, "Lord, I am ready to go
with you to prison and to death."
34 Jesus answered, "I tell you, Peter, before the rooster crows today, you will deny
three times that you know me."●
35 Then Jesus asked them, "When I sent
you without purse, bag or sandals, did you
lack anything?"
"Nothing," they answered.
36 He said to them, "But now if you have
a purse, take it, and also a bag; and if you
don't have a sword, sell your cloak and buy
one. 37 It is written: 'And he was numbered
with the transgressors'[b]; and I tell you that
this must be fulfilled in me. Yes, what is
written about me is reaching its fulfillment."
38 The disciples said, "See, Lord, here
are two swords."
"That is enough," he replied.●

*Jesus Prays on the Mount of Olives*

39 Jesus went out as usual to the Mount of
Olives, and his disciples followed him.
40 On reaching the place, he said to them,
"Pray that you will not fall into temptation." 41 He withdrew about a stone's
throw beyond them, knelt down and
prayed, 42 "Father, if you are willing, take
this cup from me; yet not my will, but
yours be done." 43 An angel from heaven
appeared to him and strengthened him.
44 And being in anguish, he prayed more
earnestly, and his sweat was like drops of
blood falling to the ground.[c]
45 When he rose from prayer and went
back to the disciples, he found them
asleep, exhausted from sorrow. 46 "Why
are you sleeping?" he asked them. "Get up
and pray so that you will not fall into temptation."●

[a] *31* The Greek is plural. [b] *37* Isaiah 53:12
[c] *44* Some early manuscripts do not have verses 43 and 44.

KING JAMES

1.TEACHING

DISCIPLES DISPUTING

24 And there was also a strife among
them, which of them should be accounted
the greatest. 25 And he said unto them,
The kings of the Gentiles exercise lordship over them; and they that exercise
authority upon them are called benefactors. 26 But ye *shall* not *be* so: but he that
is greatest among you, let him be as the
younger; and he that is chief, as he that
doth serve. 27 For whether *is* greater,
he that sitteth at meat, or he that serveth?
*is* not he that sitteth at meat? but I am
among you as he that serveth.

2.FORE-TELLING

a.

28 Ye are they which have continued
with me in my temptations. 29 And I appoint unto you a kingdom, as my Father
hath appointed unto me; 30 that ye may
eat and drink at my table in my kingdom,
and sit on thrones judging the twelve
tribes of Israel. ●

b.

31 And the Lord said, Simon, Simon,
behold, Satan hath desired *to have* you,
that he may sift *you* as wheat: 32 but I
have prayed for thee, that thy faith fail
not: and when thou art converted,
strengthen thy brethren. 33 And he said
unto him, Lord, I am ready to go with
thee, both into prison, and to death.
34 And he said, I tell thee, Peter, the cock
shall not crow this day, before that thou
shalt thrice deny that thou knowest me.●

c.

35 And he said unto them, When I sent
you without purse, and scrip, and shoes,
lacked ye any thing? And they said,
Nothing. 36 Then said he unto them, But
now, he that hath a purse, let him take *it*,
and likewise *his* scrip: and he that hath
no sword, let him sell his garment, and
buy one. 37 For I say unto you, that this
that is written must yet be accomplished
in me, And he was reckoned among the
transgressors: for the things concerning
me have an end. 38 And they said,
Lord, behold, here *are* two swords. And
he said unto them, It is enough.●

Isa. 53:12

3.PRAYING

39 And he came out, and went, as he
was wont, to the mount of Olives; and his
disciples also followed him. 40 And when
he was at the place, he said unto them,
Pray that ye enter not into temptation.
41 And he was withdrawn from them
about a stone's cast, and kneeled down,
and prayed, 42 saying, Father, if thou be
willing, remove this cup from me: nevertheless, not my will, but thine, be done.
43 And there appeared an angel unto him
from heaven, strengthening him. 44 And
being in an agony he prayed more
earnestly: and his sweat was as it were
great drops of blood falling down to the
ground. 45 And when he rose up from
prayer, and was come to his disciples, he
found them sleeping for sorrow, 46 and
said unto them, Why sleep ye? rise and
pray, lest ye enter into temptation.●

JESUS PRAYING

*22:24-30* Compare the strife of verse 24 with the discussion of 22:23.

What is the key word of verses 24-27?

What is the key word of verse 27? ______

Does Jesus' teaching on greatness resolve the disciples' question as to "which *one* of them" was the greatest?

*22:31-34* Compare the beginning of the paragraph with the ending.

*22:35-38* Observe the key phrase "But now" (v.36). How was this approaching hour different, both for Jesus and for His disciples, from the previous time?

*22:39-46* Record the different references to Jesus' human nature.

NEW INTERNATIONAL VERSION

What does the passage teach about:

JESUS' MINISTRY

JESUS' POWER

HUMAN FRAILTY

REMORSE

HATE

RELIGIOUS PREJUDICE

### *Jesus Arrested*

[47]While he was still speaking a crowd
came up, and the man who was called
Judas, one of the Twelve, was leading
them. He approached Jesus to kiss him,
[48]but Jesus asked him, "Judas, are you betraying the Son of Man with a kiss?"
[49]When Jesus' followers saw what was
going to happen, they said, "Lord, should
we strike with our swords?" [50]And one of
them struck the servant of the high priest,
cutting off his right ear.
[51]But Jesus answered, "No more of
this!" And he touched the man's ear and
healed him.
[52]Then Jesus said to the chief priests, the
officers of the temple guard, and the elders, who had come for him, "Am I leading
a rebellion, that you have come with
swords and clubs? [53]Every day I was with
you in the temple courts, and you did not
lay a hand on me. But this is your hour—
when darkness reigns."●

### *Peter Disowns Jesus*

[54]Then seizing him, they led him away
and took him into the house of the high
priest. Peter followed at a distance. [55]But
when they had kindled a fire in the middle
of the courtyard and had sat down together, Peter sat down with them. [56]A servant girl saw him seated there in the fire-
light. She looked closely at him and said,
"This man was with him."
[57]But he denied it. "Woman, I don't
know him," he said.
[58]A little later someone else saw him and
said, "You also are one of them."
"Man, I am not!" Peter replied.
[59]About an hour later another asserted,
"Certainly this fellow was with him, for he
is a Galilean."
[60]Peter replied, "Man, I don't know
what you're talking about!" Just as he was
speaking, the rooster crowed. [61]The Lord
turned and looked straight at Peter. Then
Peter remembered the word the Lord had
spoken to him: "Before the rooster crows
today, you will disown me three times."
[62]And he went outside and wept bitterly.●

### *The Soldiers Mock Jesus*

[63]The men who were guarding Jesus began mocking and beating him. [64]They
blindfolded him and demanded, "Prophesy! Who hit you?" [65]And they said many
other insulting things to him.●

### *Jesus Before Pilate and Herod*

[66]At daybreak the council of the elders of
the people, both the chief priests and
teachers of the law, met together, and
Jesus was led before them. [67]"If you are
the Christ,[a]" they said, "tell us."
Jesus answered, "If I tell you, you will
not believe me, [68]and if I asked you, you
would not answer. [69]But from now on, the
Son of Man will be seated at the right hand
of the mighty God."
[70]They all asked, "Are you then the Son
of God?"
He replied, "You are right in saying I
am."
[71]Then they said, "Why do we need any
more testimony? We have heard it from his
own lips."●

[a]67 Or *Messiah*

KING JAMES

1. JUDAS BETRAYS

BETRAYAL

47 And while he yet spake, behold a
multitude, and he that was called Judas,
one of the twelve, went before them, and
drew near unto Jesus to kiss him. 48 But
Jesus said unto him, Judas, betrayest thou
the Son of man with a kiss? 49 When
they which were about him saw what
would follow, they said unto him, Lord,
shall we smite with the sword? 50 And
one of them smote the servant of the high
priest, and cut off his right ear. 51 And
Jesus answered and said, Suffer ye thus
far. And he touched his ear, and healed
him. 52 Then Jesus said unto the chief
priests, and captains of the temple, and
the elders, which were come to him, Be
ye come out, as against a thief, with swords
and staves? 53 When I was daily with
you in the temple, ye stretched forth no
hands against me: but this is your hour,
and the power of darkness.●

2. PETER DENIES

54 Then took they him, and led *him*,
and brought him into the high priest's
house. And Peter followed afar off.
55 And when they had kindled a fire in the
midst of the hall, and were set down together, Peter sat down among them.
56 But a certain maid beheld him as he
sat by the fire, and earnestly looked upon
him, and said, This man was also with
him. 57 And he denied him, saying,
Woman, I know him not. 58 And after a
little while another saw him, and said,
Thou art also of them. And Peter said,
Man, I am not. 59 And about the space
of one hour after another confidently
affirmed, saying, Of a truth this *fellow* also
was with him; for he is a Galilean.
60 And Peter said, Man, I know not what
thou sayest. And immediately, while he
yet spake, the cock crew. 61 And the Lord
turned, and looked upon Peter. And
Peter remembered the word of the Lord,
how he had said unto him, Before the
cock crow, thou shalt deny me thrice.
62 And Peter went out, and wept bitterly.●

3. GUARDS BEAT JESUS

63 And the men that held Jesus mocked
him, and smote *him*. 64 And when they
had blindfolded him, they struck him on
the face, and asked him, saying, Prophesy,
who is it that smote thee? 65 And many
other things blasphemously spake they
against him.●

4. COUNCIL TRIES JESUS

66 And as soon as it was day, the elders
of the people and the chief priests and the
scribes came together, and led him into
their council, saying, 67 Art thou the
Christ? tell us. And he said unto them,
If I tell you, ye will not believe: 68 and if
I also ask *you*, ye will not answer me, nor
let *me* go. 69 Hereafter shall the Son of
man sit on the right hand of the power of
God. 70 Then said they all, Art thou
then the Son of God? And he said unto
them, Ye say that I am. 71 And they said,
What need we any further witness? for
we ourselves have heard of his own mouth.●

INDICTMENT

Jesus rose up from prayer (22:45) when He knew that the enemy's hour had arrived (22:53).

*22:47-53* Record:

CONTRASTS ______

______

______

______

______

MIRACLES ______

______

______

______

*22:54-62* Who is the main character? ______

______

Record the sequence, involving where Peter was, what he said, and what he did.

______

______

______

______

______

______

______

*22:63-65* What is the tone here? ______

______

*22:66-71* Record the names of Jesus. ______

______

______

______

Analyze Jesus' words. ______

______

______

______

______

______

______

NEW INTERNATIONAL VERSION

What do you learn from this passage about:

CHRIST

JUSTICE

POLITICS

HATE

FALSEHOOD

23 Then the whole assembly rose and
led him off to Pilate. 2And they began to accuse him, saying, "We have
found this man subverting our nation. He
opposes payment of taxes to Caesar and
claims to be Christ,[b] a king."
3So Pilate asked Jesus, "Are you the
king of the Jews?"
"Yes, it is as you say," Jesus replied.
4Then Pilate announced to the chief
priests and the crowd, "I find no basis for
a charge against this man."
5But they insisted, "He stirs up the
people all over Judea[c] by his teaching. He
started in Galilee and has come all the way
here."
6On hearing this, Pilate asked if the man
was a Galilean. 7When he learned that
Jesus was under Herod's jurisdiction, he
sent him to Herod, who was also in Jerusalem at that time. ●
8When Herod saw Jesus, he was greatly
pleased, because for a long time he had
been wanting to see him. From what he had
heard about him, he hoped to see him perform some miracle. 9He plied him with
many questions, but Jesus gave him no answer. 10The chief priests and the teachers
of the law were standing there, vehemently
accusing him. 11Then Herod and his soldiers ridiculed and mocked him. Dressing
him in an elegant robe, they sent him back
to Pilate. 12That day Herod and Pilate
became friends—before this they had been
enemies.●
13Pilate called together the chief priests,
the rulers and the people, 14and said to
them, "You brought me this man as one
who was inciting the people to rebellion. I
have examined him in your presence and
have found no basis for your charges
against him. 15Neither has Herod, for he
sent him back to us; as you can see, he has
done nothing to deserve death. 16There-
fore, I will punish him and then release
him.[d]"
18With one voice they cried out, "Away
with this man! Release Barabbas to us!"
19(Barabbas had been thrown into prison
for an insurrection in the city, and for murder.)
20Wanting to release Jesus, Pilate appealed to them again. 21But they kept
shouting, "Crucify him! Crucify him!"
22For the third time he spoke to them:
"Why? What crime has this man committed? I have found in him no grounds for the
death penalty. Therefore I will have him
punished and then release him."
23But with loud shouts they insistently
demanded that he be crucified, and their
shouts prevailed. 24So Pilate decided to
grant their demand. 25He released the man
who had been thrown into prison for insurrection and murder, the one they asked for,
and surrendered Jesus to their will.●

[b]2 Or *Messiah*; also in verses 35 and 39
[c]5 Or *over the land of the Jews*
[d]16 Some manuscripts *him.* 17*Now he was obliged to release one man to them at the Feast.*

KING JAMES

1. BEFORE PILATE

"NO GUILT"

**23** And the whole multitude of them
arose, and led him unto Pilate.
2 And they began to accuse him, saying,
We found this *fellow* perverting the nation,
and forbidding to give tribute to Caesar,
saying that he himself is Christ a king.
3 And Pilate asked him, saying, Art thou
the King of the Jews? And he answered
him and said, Thou sayest *it.* 4 Then said
Pilate to the chief priests and *to* the people,
I find no fault in this man. 5 And they
were the more fierce, saying, He stirreth
up the people, teaching throughout all
Jewry, beginning from Galilee to this
place.

6 When Pilate heard of Galilee, he
asked whether the man were a Galilean.
7 And as soon as he knew that he belonged unto Herod's jurisdiction, he sent
him to Herod, who himself also was at
Jerusalem at that time.●

2. BEFORE HEROD

8 And when
Herod saw Jesus, he was exceeding glad:
for he was desirous to see him of a long
*season*, because he had heard many things
of him; and he hoped to have seen some
miracle done by him. 9 Then he questioned with him in many words; but he
answered him nothing. 10 And the chief
priests and scribes stood and vehemently
accused him. 11 And Herod with his men
of war set him at nought, and mocked
*him*, and arrayed him in a gorgeous robe,
and sent him again to Pilate. 12 And the
same day Pilate and Herod were made
friends together; for before they were at
enmity between themselves.●

3. SENTENCED TO DEATH

13 And Pilate, when he had called together the chief priests and the rulers and
the people, 14 said unto them, Ye have
brought this man unto me, as one that
perverteth the people; and, behold, I,
having examined *him* before you, have
found no fault in this man touching those
things whereof ye accuse him: 15 no, nor
yet Herod: for I sent you to him; and, lo,
nothing worthy of death is done unto
him. 16 I will therefore chastise him, and
release *him.* 17 (For of necessity he must
release one unto them at the feast.)

18 And they cried out all at once, saying, Away with this *man*, and release unto
us Barab′bas: 19 (who for a certain sedition made in the city, and for murder, was
cast into prison.) 20 Pilate therefore, willing to release Jesus, spake again to them.
21 But they cried, saying, Crucify *him*,
crucify him. 22 And he said unto them
the third time, Why, what evil hath he
done? I have found no cause of death in
him: I will therefore chastise him, and let
*him* go. 23 And they were instant with
loud voices, requiring that he might be
crucified: and the voices of them and of
the chief priests prevailed. 24 And Pilate
gave sentence that it should be as they required. 25 And he released unto them
him that for sedition and murder was cast
into prison, whom they had desired; but
he delivered Jesus to their will.●

"CRUCIFY HIM!"

*23:1-7* Observe the charges against Jesus, and Pilate's thinking. Record.

______________________________

______________________________

______________________________

______________________________

*23:8-12* Account for the change in Herod's feelings about Jesus.

______________________________

______________________________

______________________________

*23:13-25* Record what the paragraph records about:

PEOPLE AND THE LEADERS ______________________________

______________________________

______________________________

______________________________

______________________________

PILATE ______________________________

______________________________

______________________________

______________________________

______________________________

Why did Pilate turn Jesus over to the will of the mobs? (v.25)

______________________________

______________________________

______________________________

______________________________

______________________________

______________________________

______________________________

______________________________

______________________________

______________________________

______________________________

NEW INTERNATIONAL VERSION

What do you learn here about:

GRIEF AND MOURNING

FORGIVENESS

SCOFFING

JUSTICE

MERCY

Record other spiritual lessons taught.

*The Crucifixion*

26 As they led him away, they seized Simon from Cyrene, who was on his way in
from the country, and put the cross on him
and made him carry it behind Jesus. 27 A
large number of people followed him, including women who mourned and wailed
for him. 28 Jesus turned and said to them,
"Daughters of Jerusalem, do not weep for
me; weep for yourselves and for your children. 29 For the time will come when you
will say, 'Blessed are the barren women,
the wombs that never bore and the breasts
that never nursed!' 30 Then

"'they will say to the mountains,
"Fall on us!"
and to the hills, "Cover us!"'[a]

31 For if men do these things when the tree
is green, what will happen when it is dry?"
32 Two other men, both criminals, were
also led out with him to be executed.
33 When they came to the place called The
Skull, there they crucified him, along with
the criminals—one on his right, the other
on his left. 34 Jesus said, "Father, forgive
them, for they do not know what they are
doing."[b] And they divided up his clothes
by casting lots.
35 The people stood watching, and the
rulers even sneered at him. They said, "He
saved others; let him save himself if he is
the Christ of God, the Chosen One."
36 The soldiers also came up and mocked
him. They offered him wine vinegar 37 and
said, "If you are the king of the Jews, save
yourself."
38 There was a written notice above him,
which read: THIS IS THE KING OF THE JEWS.
39 One of the criminals who hung there
hurled insults at him: "Aren't you the
Christ? Save yourself and us!"
40 But the other criminal rebuked him.
"Don't you fear God," he said, "since you
are under the same sentence? 41 We are
punished justly, for we are getting what our
deeds deserve. But this man has done
nothing wrong."
42 Then he said, "Jesus, remember me
when you come into your kingdom."
43 Jesus answered him, "I tell you the
truth, today you will be with me in paradise."

[a] *30* Hosea 10:8
[b] *34* Some early manuscripts do not have this sentence.

## KING JAMES

1. LAMEN- 26 And as they led him away, they laid CROSS
TATION hold upon one Simon, a Cyre'nian, coming out of the country, and on him they
laid the cross, that he might bear *it* after
Jesus. 27 And there followed him a great
company of people, and of women, which
also bewailed and lamented him. 28 But
Jesus turning unto them said, Daughters
of Jerusalem, weep not for me, but weep
for yourselves, and for your children.
29 For, behold, the days are coming, in
the which they shall say, Blessed *are* the
barren, and the wombs that never bare,
and the paps which never gave suck.
30 Then shall they begin to say to the
mountains, Fall on us; and to the hills,
Cover us. 31 For if they do these things
in a green tree, what shall be done in the
dry?
32 And there were also two others,
malefactors, led with him to be put to
2. MOCK- death.● 33 And when they were come to
ERY the place, which is called Calvary, there
they crucified him, and the malefactors,
one on the right hand, and the other on
the left. 34 Then said Jesus, Father, forgive them; for they know not what they
do. And they parted his raiment, and cast
lots. 35 And the people stood beholding.
And the rulers also with them derided
*him*, saying, He saved others; let him save
himself, if he be Christ, the chosen of God.
36 And the soldiers also mocked him,
coming to him, and offering him vinegar,
37 and saying, If thou be the King of the
Jews, save thyself. 38 And a superscription also was written over him in letters
of Greek, and Latin, and Hebrew, THIS
IS THE KING OF THE JEWS.●
3. REPEN- 39 And one of the malefactors which
TANCE were hanged railed on him, saying, If thou
be Christ, save thyself and us. 40 But the
other answering rebuked him, saying,
Dost not thou fear God, seeing thou art
in the same condemnation? 41 And we
indeed justly; for we receive the due reward of our deeds: but this man hath done
nothing amiss. 42 And he said unto
Jesus, Lord, remember me when thou
comest into thy kingdom. 43 And Jesus
said unto him, Verily I say unto thee, To- PARADISE
day shalt thou be with me in paradise.●

Study especially the words of Jesus, and the words of people. Record the highlights of each paragraph.

*23:26-32* To Calvary ______

*23:33-38* Crucifixion ______

*23:39-43* Two criminals ______

NEW INTERNATIONAL VERSION

Record truths and applications taught by this somber passage:

TRUTHS

APPLICATIONS

*Jesus' Death*

[44]It was now about the sixth hour, and
darkness came over the whole land until
the ninth hour, [45]for the sun stopped shining. And the curtain of the temple was torn
in two. [46]Jesus called out with a loud voice,
"Father, into your hands I commit my
spirit." When he had said this, he breathed
his last.
[47]The centurion, seeing what had happened, praised God and said, "Surely this
was a righteous man." [48]When all the
people who had gathered to witness this
sight saw what took place, they beat their
breasts and went away. [49]But all those who
knew him, including the women who had
followed him from Galilee, stood at a distance, watching these things.●

*Jesus' Burial*

[50]Now there was a man named Joseph, a
member of the Council, a good and upright
man, [51]who had not consented to their
decision and action. He came from the Judean town of Arimathea and he was waiting for the kingdom of God. [52]Going to
Pilate, he asked for Jesus' body. [53]Then he
took it down, wrapped it in linen cloth and
placed it in a tomb cut in the rock, one in
which no one had yet been laid. [54]It was
Preparation Day, and the Sabbath was
about to begin.
[55]The women who had come with Jesus
from Galilee followed Joseph and saw the
tomb and how his body was laid in it.
[56]Then they went home and prepared
spices and perfumes. But they rested on
the Sabbath in obedience to the commandment.●

KING JAMES

1. JESUS' COMMIT-TAL

44 And it was about the sixth hour, and
there was a darkness over all the earth
until the ninth hour. 45 And the sun was
darkened, and the veil of the temple was
rent in the midst. 46 And when Jesus had
cried with a loud voice, he said, Father,
into thy hands I commend my spirit: and
having said thus, he gave up the ghost.
47 Now when the centurion saw what was
done, he glorified God, saying, Certainly
this was a righteous man. 48 And all the
people that came together to that sight,
beholding the things which were done,
smote their breasts, and returned. 49 And
all his acquaintance, and the women that
followed him from Galilee, stood afar
off, beholding these things. ●

2. WOMAN'S DEVOTION

50 And, behold, *there was* a man named
Joseph, a counselor; *and he was* a good
man, and a just: 51 (the same had not
consented to the counsel and deed of
them:) *he was* of Arimathe'a, a city of the
Jews; who also himself waited for the
kingdom of God. 52 This *man* went unto
Pilate, and begged the body of Jesus.
53 And he took it down, and wrapped it
in linen, and laid it in a sepulchre that was
hewn in stone, wherein never man before
was laid. 54 And that day was the preparation, and the sabbath drew on. 55 And
the women also, which came with him
from Galilee, followed after, and beheld
the sepulchre, and how his body was laid.
56 And they returned, and prepared spices
and ointments; and rested the sabbath
day according to the commandment. ●

DARK WORLD

DARK TOMB

Review 23:26-43 before studying this passage. The two segments are one continuous account.

Record observations of all the main parts of each paragraph.

*23:44-49* What are Jesus' last words?

Compare these with the centurion's words.

*23:50-56* What is revealed here about:

JOSEPH

THE WOMEN

NEW INTERNATIONAL VERSION

What were the women's reactions after seeing the empty tomb?

What may have been going through their minds?

What do you learn from the words of the two men?

*question* (v.5)

*statement of fact* (v.6a)

*reminder of command* (v.6b)

Compare the reactions of the other disciples (v.ll) and Peter (v.l2) with the women's.

What are your strongest impressions of this passage?

*The Resurrection*

24 On the first day of the week, very
early in the morning, the women
took the spices they had prepared and went
to the tomb. 2They found the stone rolled
away from the tomb, 3but when they entered, they did not find the body of the
Lord Jesus.● 4While they were wondering
about this, suddenly two men in clothes
that gleamed like lightning stood beside
them. 5In their fright the women bowed
down with their faces to the ground, but
the men said to them, "Why do you look
for the living among the dead? 6He is not
here; he has risen! Remember how he told
you, while he was still with you in Galilee:
7'The Son of Man must be delivered into
the hands of sinful men, be crucified and on
the third day be raised again.' "● 8Then they
remembered his words.
9When they came back from the tomb,
they told all these things to the Eleven and
to all the others. 10It was Mary Magdalene,
Joanna, Mary the mother of James, and the
others with them who told this to the apostles. 11But they did not believe the women,
because their words seemed to them like
nonsense. 12Peter, however, got up and ran
to the tomb. Bending over, he saw the
strips of linen lying by themselves, and he
went away, wondering to himself what had
happened.●

KING JAMES

1. WITNESS

24 Now upon the first *day* of the week,
very early in the morning, they
came unto the sepulchre, bringing the
spices which they had prepared, and certain *others* with them. 2 And they found
the stone rolled away from the sepulchre.
3 And they entered in, and found not the
body of the Lord Jesus. ●

2. EXPLANATION

4 And it came to
pass, as they were much perplexed there-
about, behold, two men stood by them in
shining garments: 5 and as they were
afraid, and bowed down *their* faces to the
earth, they said unto them, Why seek ye
the living among the dead? 6 He is not
here, but is risen: remember how he spake
unto you when he was yet in Galilee,
7 saying, The Son of man must be delivered into the hands of sinful men, and
be crucified, and the third day rise again. ●

3. REPORT

8 And they remembered his words, 9 and
returned from the sepulchre, and told all
these things unto the eleven, and to all the
rest. 10 It was Mary Mag'dalene, and
Joanna, and Mary *the mother* of James,
and other *women that were* with them,
which told these things unto the apostles.
11 And their words seemed to them as
idle tales, and they believed them not.
12 Then arose Peter, and ran unto the
sepulchre; and stooping down, he beheld
the linen clothes laid by themselves, and
departed, wondering in himself at that
which was come to pass. ●

perplexed

terrified

marveling

Luke's account of the empty tomb is as bright as it is brief.

*24:1-3* Observe Luke's clear reporting of a first-hand witness. How many times does the word "they" appear?

*24:4-7* Analyze the words of the two men.

*24:8-12* Relate the three words "remembered," "returned," "told."

Compare the different reactions reported in verses 11 and 12.

NEW INTERNATIONAL VERSION

What do you learn from this passage about:

EYES DARKENED

SCRIPTURE

PROPHECY

JESUS THE MESSIAH

LORD'S TABLE

PRESENCE OF JESUS

UNBELIEF

REVELATION

*On the Road to Emmaus*

13Now that same day two of them were
going to a village called Emmaus, about
seven miles[a] from Jerusalem. 14They were
talking with each other about everything
that had happened. 15As they talked and
discussed these things with each other,
Jesus himself came up and walked along
with them; 16but they were kept from
recognizing him.
17He asked them, "What are you discussing together as you walk along?"
They stood still, their faces downcast.
18One of them, named Cleopas, asked him,
"Are you the only one living in Jerusalem
who doesn't know the things that have
happened there in these days?"
19"What things?" he asked.
"About Jesus of Nazareth," they replied. "He was a prophet, powerful in
word and deed before God and all the
people. 20The chief priests and our rulers
handed him over to be sentenced to death,
and they crucified him; 21but we had hoped
that he was the one who was going to redeem Israel. And what is more, it is the
third day since all this took place. 22In addition, some of our women amazed us. They
went to the tomb early this morning 23but
didn't find his body. They came and told us
that they had seen a vision of angels, who
said he was alive. 24Then some of our companions went to the tomb and found it just
as the women had said, but him they did
not see."●
25He said to them, "How foolish you
are, and how slow of heart to believe all
that the prophets have spoken! 26Did not
the Christ[b] have to suffer these things and
then enter his glory?" 27And beginning
with Moses and all the Prophets, he explained to them what was said in all the
Scriptures concerning himself.●
28As they approached the village to
which they were going, Jesus acted as if he
were going farther. 29But they urged him
strongly, "Stay with us, for it is nearly
evening; the day is almost over." So he
went in to stay with them.
30When he was at the table with them, he
took bread, gave thanks, broke it and began to give it to them. 31Then their eyes
were opened and they recognized him, and
he disappeared from their sight. 32They
asked each other, "Were not our hearts
burning within us while he talked with us
on the road and opened the Scriptures to
us?"●
33They got up and returned at once to
Jerusalem. There they found the Eleven
and those with them, assembled together
34and saying, "It is true! The Lord has ris-
en and has appeared to Simon." 35Then the
two told what had happened on the way,
and how Jesus was recognized by them
when he broke the bread.●

[a]13 Greek *sixty stadia* (about 11 kilometers)
[b]26 Or *Messiah*; also in verse 46

## KING JAMES

**1. BEWILDERMENT**

**NO RECOGNITION**

13 And, behold, two of them went that
same day to a village called Emma'us,
which was from Jerusalem *about* threescore furlongs. 14 And they talked together of all these things which had happened. 15 And it came to pass, that,
while they communed *together* and
reasoned, Jesus himself drew near, and
went with them. 16 But their eyes were
holden that they should not know him.
17 And he said unto them, What manner
of communications *are* these that ye have
one to another, as ye walk, and are sad?
18 And the one of them, whose name was
Cle'opas, answering said unto him, Art
thou only a stranger in Jerusalem, and
hast not known the things which are come
to pass there in these days? 19 And he
said unto them, What things? And they
said unto him, Concerning Jesus of Nazareth, which was a prophet mighty in
deed and word before God and all the
people: 20 and how the chief priests and
our rulers delivered him to be condemned
to death, and have crucified him. 21 But
we trusted that it had been he which
should have redeemed Israel: and beside
all this, today is the third day since these
things were done. 22 Yea, and certain
women also of our company made us
astonished, which were early at the sepulchre; 23 and when they found not his
body, they came, saying, that they had
also seen a vision of angels, which said
that he was alive. 24 And certain of them
which were with us went to the sepulchre,
and found *it* even so as the women had

**2. EXPLANATION**

said: but him they saw not. ● 25 Then he
said unto them, O fools, and slow of heart
to believe all that the prophets have
spoken: 26 ought not Christ to have
suffered these things, and to enter into his
glory? 27 And beginning at Moses and
all the prophets, he expounded unto them
in all the Scriptures the things concerning
himself. ●

**3. RECOGNITION**

28 And they drew nigh unto the village,
whither they went: and he made as
though he would have gone further.
29 But they constrained him, saying,
Abide with us; for it is toward evening,
and the day is far spent. And he went in
to tarry with them. 30 And it came to
pass, as he sat at meat with them, he took
bread, and blessed *it*, and brake, and
gave to them. 31 And their eyes were
opened, and they knew him; and he
vanished out of their sight. 32 And they
said one to another, Did not our heart
burn within us, while he talked with us
by the way, and while he opened to us the

**4. PROCLAMATION**

Scriptures? ● 33 And they rose up the
same hour, and returned to Jerusalem,
and found the eleven gathered together,
and them that were with them, 34 saying,
The Lord is risen indeed, and hath appeared to Simon. 35 And they told what
things *were done* in the way, and how he
was known of them in breaking of bread. ●

**RECOGNITION**

*24:13-24* Compare verses 16 and 31. Was there a divine purpose in keeping the disciples from recognizing Jesus at this time? If so, what may it have been?

What does verse 21a reveal about the disciples' concept of Messiahship?

*24:25-27* What was the basis for Jesus' rebuke?

What place did He give the Scriptures?

24:28-32 What is the significance of the action of verse 30 in view of the fact that Jesus was a Guest, not the Host?

Note the miracles of verse 31.

*24:33-35* What are your observations?

NEW INTERNATIONAL VERSION

Record truths and applications taught here about:

DOUBT

JESUS' PRESENCE

JOY

RESURRECTION BODY

SCRIPTURE

WITNESS

SPIRITUAL POWER

*Jesus Appears to the Disciples*

36While they were still talking about this,
Jesus himself stood among them and said
to them, "Peace be with you."
37They were startled and frightened,
thinking they saw a ghost. 38He said to
them, "Why are you troubled, and why do
doubts rise in your minds? 39Look at my
hands and my feet. It is I myself! Touch me
and see; a ghost does not have flesh and
bones, as you see I have."
40When he had said this, he showed them
his hands and feet. 41And while they still
did not believe it because of joy and amazement, he asked them, "Do you have anything here to eat?" 42They gave him a piece
of broiled fish, 43and he took it and ate it in
their presence.●
44He said to them, "This is what I told
you while I was still with you: Everything
must be fulfilled that is written about me in
the Law of Moses, the Prophets and the
Psalms."
45Then he opened their minds so they
could understand the Scriptures. 46He told
them, "This is what is written: The Christ
will suffer and rise from the dead on the
third day, 47and repentance and forgiveness of sins will be preached in his name to
all nations, beginning at Jerusalem. 48You
are witnesses of these things. 49I am going
to send you what my Father has promised;
but stay in the city until you have been
clothed with power from on high."●

*The Ascension*

50When he had led them out to the vicinity of Bethany, he lifted up his hands and
blessed them. 51While he was blessing
them, he left them and was taken up into
heaven. 52Then they worshiped him and
returned to Jerusalem with great joy. 53And
they stayed continually at the temple,
praising God.●

KING JAMES

1. PROOF

36 And as they thus spake, Jesus himself stood in the midst of them, and saith
unto them, Peace *be* unto you. 37 But
they were terrified and affrighted, and
supposed that they had seen a spirit.
38 And he said unto them, Why are ye
troubled? and why do thoughts arise in
your hearts? 39 Behold my hands and my
feet, that it is I myself: handle me, and
see; for a spirit hath not flesh and bones,
as ye see me have. 40 And when he had
thus spoken, he showed them *his* hands
and *his* feet. 41 And while they yet believed not for joy, and wondered, he said
unto them, Have ye here any meat?
42 And they gave him a piece of a broiled
fish, and of a honeycomb. 43 And he
took *it*, and did eat before them.●

2. INSTRUCTION

44 And he said unto them, These *are*
the words which I spake unto you, while I
was yet with you, that all things must be
fulfilled, which were written in the law of
Moses, and *in* the prophets, and *in* the
psalms, concerning me. 45 Then opened
he their understanding, that they might
understand the Scriptures, 46 and said
unto them, Thus it is written, and thus it
behooved Christ to suffer, and to rise
from the dead the third day: 47 and that
repentance and remission of sins should
be preached in his name among all nations, beginning at Jerusalem. 48 And ye
are witnesses of these things. 49 And, behold, I send the promise of my Father
upon you: but tarry ye in the city of
Jerusalem, until ye be endued with power
from on high.●

3. BLESSING

50 And he led them out as far as to
Bethany, and he lifted up his hands, and
blessed them. 51 And it came to pass,
while he blessed them, he was parted
from them, and carried up into heaven.
52 And they worshipped him, and returned to Jerusalem with great joy:
53 and were continually in the temple,
praising and blessing God. Amen.●

GREAT FEAR

GREAT JOY

This is the bright ending of Luke's gospel. Compare "in the midst of them" (v.36) with "parted from them" (v.51).

*24:36-43* What miracle brought on the reaction of verse 37?

What things did Jesus do to convince the disciples that what they were beholding was real?

*24:44-49* How did Jesus connect the accomplished facts (death and resurrection) with the unfinished task (witness)?

How did Jesus involve His disciples in verses 48-49?

*24-50-53* Record the bright references in each verse.

Account for the "great joy" of verse 52.

# JOHN

## AUTHORSHIP

The traditional view is that John the apostle is the author. In the book he is referred to only as "the disciple whom Jesus loved" (21:20,24).

The apostle John was a son of Zebedee (21:2) and Salome (cf. Matt. 27:56; Mark 15:40; and John 19:25). Since Salome was a sister of Jesus' mother Mary, Jesus and John were cousins. John was a brother of the apostle James.

John was a Palestinian Jew, a close companion of Peter, and a contemporary of the events of his gospel. He also wrote three epistles (1,2,3 John) and the book of Revelation.

## DATE

John wrote this Gospel around A.D. 85, while he was ministering at Ephesus.

## PURPOSE AND THEME

The advanced nature of this fourth Gospel, as compared with the other Gospels, points to the fact that the early church's need was for a restatement of the same story of Christ, but with more reflection and interpretation combined with the narrative. The evangelistic purpose, focusing on unsaved readers, is clearly stated in the account itself: "these [signs] are written, that ye might believe that Jesus is the Christ, the Son of God; and that believing ye might have life through His name" (20:31).

## JOHN: Life in Jesus, the Son of God

| | |
|---|---|
| ERA OF INCARNATION BEGINS | 1:1—4:54 |
| Prologue | 1:1-18 |
| Witnesses and Discoveries of Jesus | 1:19-51 |
| Miracle Worker and Voice of Authority | 2:1-25 |
| Teacher Come from God | 3:1-36 |
| "This Is Indeed the Christ" | 4:1-54 |
| YEARS OF CONFLICT | 5:1—12:36a |
| Persecution Against Jesus Begins | 5:1-47 |
| Bread of Life Refused | 6:1-71 |
| Attempts to Arrest Jesus | 7:1-53 |
| Light of the World Rejected | 8:1—9:41 |
| The Good Shepherd Spurned | 10:1-39 |
| The King of Israel Enters Jerusalem | 10:40—12:36a |
| DAY OF PREPARATION | 12:36b—17:26 |
| Events Attending the Last Supper | 12:36b—13:38 |
| Farewell Discourses | 14:1—16:33 |
| High Priestly Prayer | 17:1-26 |
| HOUR OF SACRIFICE | 18:1—19:42 |
| Arrested and Tried | 18:1—19:16a |
| Crucified and Buried | 19:16b-42 |
| DAWN OF VICTORY | 20:1—21:25 |
| Signs of the Resurrected Jesus | 20:1-31 |
| Postresurrection Appearances in Galilee | 21:1-25 |

# JOHN

NEW INTERNATIONAL VERSION

What does this prologue to John's Gospel teach about the following:

THE WORD

CREATION

HUMAN RACE

JESUS CHRIST

SALVATION

GRACE

LIFE

LIGHT

*The Word Became Flesh*

1 In the beginning was the Word, and the
Word was with God, and the Word was
God. 2He was with God in the beginning.
3Through him all things were made; without him nothing was made that has been
made. 4In him was life, and that life was the
light of men. 5The light shines in the darkness, but the darkness has not understood[a]
it.●
6There came a man who was sent from
God; his name was John. 7He came as a
witness to testify concerning that light, so
that through him all men might believe.
8He himself was not the light; he came only
as a witness to the light.● 9The true light that
gives light to every man was coming into
the world.[b]
10He was in the world, and though the
world was made through him, the world
did not recognize him. 11He came to that
which was his own, but his own did not
receive him. 12Yet to all who received him,
to those who believed in his name, he gave
the right to become children of God—
13children born not of natural descent,[c] nor
of human decision or a husband's will, but
born of God.●
14The Word became flesh and lived for a
while among us. We have seen his glory,
the glory of the one and only ⌊Son⌋,[d] who
came from the Father, full of grace and
truth.
15John testifies concerning him. He cries
out, saying, "This was he of whom I said,
'He who comes after me has surpassed me
because he was before me.' " 16From the
fullness of his grace we have all received
one blessing after another. 17For the law
was given through Moses; grace and truth
came through Jesus Christ. 18No one has
ever seen God, but God the only[e] ⌊Son⌋,[f]
who is at the Father's side, has made him
known.●

[a]5 Or *overcome* [b]9 Or *This was the true light that gives light to every man who comes into the world*
[c]13 Greek *of bloods* [d]14 Or *the Only Begotten*
[e]18 Or *but God the only begotten*
[f]18 Some manuscripts *but the only Son* (or *but the only begotten Son*)

KING JAMES

# JOHN

1. SOURCE OF LIGHT

JESUS IS GOD

**1** In the beginning was the Word, and
the Word was with God, and the
Word was God. 2 The same was in the
beginning with God. 3 All things were
made by him; and without him was not
any thing that was made. 4 In him
was life; and the life was the light of men.
5 And the light shineth in darkness; and
the darkness comprehended it not.●

2. WITNESS OF THE LIGHT

6 There was a man sent from God,
whose name *was* John. 7 The same
came for a witness, to bear witness of the
Light, that all *men* through him might
believe. 8 He was not that Light, but *was*
*sent* to bear witness of that Light.●

3. FOCUS OF THE LIGHT

9 *That* was the true Light, which light-
eth every man that cometh into the world.
10 He was in the world, and the world was
made by him, and the world knew him
not. 11 He came unto his own, and his
own received him not. 12 But as many as
received him, to them gave he power to
become the sons of God, *even* to them
that believe on his name: 13 which were
born, not of blood, nor of the will of the
flesh, nor of the will of man, but of God.●

4. GLORY OF THE LIGHT

14 And the Word was made flesh, and
dwelt among us, (and we beheld his glory,
the glory as of the only begotten of the
Father,) full of grace and truth. 15 John
bare witness of him, and cried, saying,
This was he of whom I spake, He that
cometh after me is preferred before me;
for he was before me. 16 And of his fulness have all we received, and grace for
grace. 17 For the law was given by
Moses, *but* grace and truth came by Jesus
Christ. 18 No man hath seen God at any
time; the only begotten Son, which is in
the bosom of the Father, he hath declared
*him*.●

JESUS REVEALS THE FATHER

John opens his gospel account by showing how the Creator Jesus was involved in His Father's plan of redemption for the fallen human race.

*1:1-5* Who is the "Word"? ______

What is said about Him here? ______

*1:6-8* Where in the segment does John reappear?

______

*1:9-13* Record what is said about Jesus here.

______

*1:14-18* Note the repeated word "grace." Record the main truths of the paragraph.

______

NEW INTERNATIONAL VERSION

What does this passage teach about:

WITNESSING ABOUT CHRIST

HUMILITY

LAMB OF GOD

SIN

BAPTISM

HUMANITY OF JESUS

DEITY OF JESUS

PRACTICAL LESSONS FROM JOHN'S MINISTRY

*John the Baptist Denies Being the Christ*

19 Now this was John's testimony when
the Jews of Jerusalem sent priests and Levites to ask him who he was. 20 He did not
fail to confess, but confessed freely, "I am
not the Christ.[g]"
21 They asked him, "Then who are you?
Are you Elijah?"
He said, "I am not."
"Are you the Prophet?"
He answered, "No."
22 Finally they said, "Who are you? Give
us an answer to take back to those who
sent us. What do you say about yourself?"
23 John replied in the words of Isaiah the
prophet, "I am the voice of one calling in
the desert, 'Make straight the way for the
Lord.' "[h] ●
24 Now some Pharisees who had been
sent 25 questioned him, "Why then do you
baptize if you are not the Christ, nor Elijah,
nor the Prophet?"
26 "I baptize with[i] water," John replied,
"but among you stands one you do not
know. 27 He is the one who comes after me,
the thongs of whose sandals I am not
worthy to untie."
28 This all happened at Bethany on the
other side of the Jordan, where John was
baptizing. ●

*Jesus the Lamb of God*

29 The next day John saw Jesus coming
toward him and said, "Look, the Lamb of
God, who takes away the sin of the world!
30 This is the one I meant when I said, 'A
man who comes after me has surpassed me
because he was before me.' 31 I myself did
not know him, but the reason I came baptizing with water was that he might be revealed to Israel."
32 Then John gave this testimony: "I saw
the Spirit come down from heaven as a
dove and remain on him. 33 I would not
have known him, except that the one who
sent me to baptize with water told me, 'The
man on whom you see the Spirit come
down and remain is he who will baptize
with the Holy Spirit.' 34 I have seen and I
testify that this is the Son of God." ●

[g] *20* Or *Messiah*. "The Christ" (Greek) and "the Messiah" (Hebrew) both mean "the Anointed One"; also in verse 25.
[h] *23* Isaiah 40:3
[i] *26* Or *in*; also in verses 31 and 33

KING JAMES

**1. WHO JOHN IS**

"WHO ART THOU?"

19 And this is the record of John, when
the Jews sent priests and Levites from
Jerusalem to ask him, Who art thou?
20 And he confessed, and denied not; but
confessed, I am not the Christ. 21 And
they asked him, What then? Art thou
Eli'jah ? And he saith, I am not. Art thou
that Prophet ? And he answered, No.
22 Then said they unto him, Who art
thou? that we may give an answer to them
that sent us. What sayest thou of thyself?
23 He said, I *am*
the voice of one crying in the wilderness,
Make straight the way of the Lord,
as said the prophet Isaiah. ●

Isa. 40:3

**2. JOHN AND JESUS COMPARED**

24 And they which were sent were of the
Pharisees. 25 And they asked him, and
said unto him, Why baptizest thou then,
if thou be not that Christ, nor Eli'jah,
neither that Prophet? 26 John answered
them, saying, I baptize with water: but
there standeth one among you, whom ye
know not; 27 he it is, who coming after
me is preferred before me, whose shoe-
latchet I am not worthy to unloose.
28 These things were done in Bethab'ara
beyond Jordan, where John was baptizing.●

**3. WHO JESUS IS**

29 The next day John seeth Jesus coming unto him, and saith, Behold the Lamb
of God, which taketh away the sin of the
world! 30 This is he of whom I said,
After me cometh a man which is preferred before me; for he was before me.
31 And I knew him not: but that he
should be made manifest to Israel, therefore am I come baptizing with water.
32 And John bare record, saying, I saw
the Spirit descending from heaven like a
dove, and it abode upon him. 33 And I
knew him not: but he that sent me to baptize with water, the same said unto me,
Upon whom thou shalt see the Spirit descending, and remaining on him, the
same is he which baptizeth with the Holy
Ghost. 34 And I saw, and bare record
that this is the Son of God.●

"THIS IS HE"

The writer John here reports more about John the Baptist's introduction of Jesus to His contemporaries.

Observe the main content of each of the three paragraphs. Where is the focus, in each case?

*1:19-23* Record what is said about John.

*1:24-28* How does John compare himself with Jesus?

*1:29-34* Record how John identifies Jesus.

NEW INTERNATIONAL VERSION

Record what the passage teaches about:

NAMES AND TITLES OF JESUS

ATTRIBUTES OF JESUS

PERSONAL EVANGELISM

DISCIPLESHIP

List practical lessons which you learn here.

### *Jesus' First Disciples*

[35]The next day John was there again with
two of his disciples. [36]When he saw Jesus
passing by, he said, "Look, the Lamb of
God!"
[37]When the two disciples heard him say
this, they followed Jesus. [38]Turning
around, Jesus saw them following and
asked, "What do you want?"
They said, "Rabbi" (which means
Teacher), "where are you staying?"
[39]"Come," he replied, "and you will
see."
So they went and saw where he was staying, and spent that day with him. It was
about the tenth hour.●
[40]Andrew, Simon Peter's brother, was
one of the two who heard what John had
said and who had followed Jesus. [41]The
first thing Andrew did was to find his
brother Simon and tell him, "We have
found the Messiah" (that is, the Christ).
[42]Then he brought Simon to Jesus, who
looked at him and said, "You are Simon
son of John. You will be called Cephas"
(which, when translated, is Peter[a]).●

### *Jesus Calls Philip and Nathanael*

[43]The next day Jesus decided to leave for
Galilee. Finding Philip, he said to him,
"Follow me."
[44]Philip, like Andrew and Peter, was
from the town of Bethsaida. [45]Philip found
Nathanael and told him, "We have found
the one Moses wrote about in the Law, and
about whom the prophets also wrote—
Jesus of Nazareth, the son of Joseph."
[46]"Nazareth! Can anything good come
from there?" Nathanael asked.
"Come and see," said Philip.●
[47]When Jesus saw Nathanael approaching, he said of him, "Here is a true Israelite, in whom there is nothing false."
[48]"How do you know me?" Nathanael
asked.
Jesus answered, "I saw you while you
were still under the fig tree before Philip
called you."
[49]Then Nathanael declared, "Rabbi, you
are the Son of God; you are the King of
Israel."
[50]Jesus said, "You believe[b] because I
told you I saw you under the fig tree. You
shall see greater things than that." [51]He
then added, "I tell you[c] the truth, you[c]
shall see heaven open, and the angels of
God ascending and descending on the Son
of Man."

[a]42 Both *Cephas* (Aramaic) and *Peter* (Greek) mean *rock*.
[b]50 Or *Do you believe . . . ?*
[c]51 The Greek is plural.

KING JAMES

GREAT DISCOVERIES

1. THROUGH SEEKING

2. THROUGH ABIDING

3. THROUGH FOLLOWING

4. THROUGH HONESTY

5. FROM HEAVEN

LAMB OF GOD

35 Again the next day after, John stood,
and two of his disciples; 36 and looking
upon Jesus as he walked, he saith, Behold
the Lamb of God! 37 And the two disciples heard him speak, and they followed
Jesus. 38 Then Jesus turned, and saw
them following, and saith unto them,
What seek ye? They said unto him,
Rabbi, (which is to say, being interpreted,
Master,) where dwellest thou? 39 He
saith unto them, Come and see. They
came and saw where he dwelt, and abode
with him that day: for it was about the
tenth hour. ● 40 One of the two which
heard John *speak*, and followed him, was
Andrew, Simon Peter's brother. 41 He
first findeth his own brother Simon,
and saith unto him, We have found
the Messiah, which is, being interpreted,
the Christ. 42 And he brought him
to Jesus. And when Jesus beheld
him, he said, Thou art Simon the
son of Jona: thou shalt be called Cephas, which is by interpretation, A
stone. ●
43 The day following Jesus would go
forth into Galilee, and findeth Philip,
and saith unto him, Follow me. 44 Now
Philip was of Bethsai'da, the city of
Andrew and Peter. 45 Philip findeth Nathan'a-el, and saith unto him, We have
found him, of whom Moses in the law,
and the prophets, did write, Jesus of
Nazareth, the son of Joseph. 46 And
Nathan'a-el said unto him, Can there any
good thing come out of Nazareth? Philip
saith unto him, Come and see. ● 47 Jesus
saw Nathan'a-el coming to him, and saith
of him, Behold an Israelite indeed, in
whom is no guile! 48 Nathan'a-el saith
unto him, Whence knowest thou me?
Jesus answered and said unto him, Before
that Philip called thee, when thou wast
under the fig tree, I saw thee. 49 Nathan'-
a-el answered and saith unto him, Rabbi,
thou art the Son of God; thou art the
King of Israel. 50 Jesus answered and
said unto him, Because I said unto thee, I
saw thee under the fig tree, believest thou?
thou shalt see greater things than these.
51 And he saith unto him, Verily, verily,
I say unto you, Hereafter ye shall see
heaven open, and the angels of God
ascending and descending upon the Son
of man. ●

SON OF MAN

Begin your study of the segment with the key statement, "We have found the Messiah" (v.41). Then follow the outline of GREAT DISCOVERIES and record observations for each paragraph.

*I:35-39* ______

*1:40-42* ______

*I:43-46* ______

*I:47-5I* ______

NEW INTERNATIONAL VERSION

Record what you learn about Jesus from this passage:

*JESUS'*
PRESENCE

PERFORMANCE

KNOWLEDGE

GLORY

ZEAL

AUTHORITY

DEATH

RESURRECTION

List five important applications of the passage.

### *Jesus Changes Water to Wine*

2 On the third day a wedding took place
at Cana in Galilee. Jesus' mother was
there, 2and Jesus and his disciples had also
been invited to the wedding. 3When the
wine was gone, Jesus' mother said to him,
"They have no more wine."
4"Dear woman, why do you involve
me?" Jesus replied, "My time has not yet
come."
5His mother said to the servants, "Do
whatever he tells you."
6Nearby stood six stone water jars, the
kind used by the Jews for ceremonial
washing, each holding from twenty to
thirty gallons.[d]
7Jesus said to the servants, "Fill the jars
with water"; so they filled them to the
brim.
8Then he told them, "Now draw some
out and take it to the master of the banquet."
They did so, 9and the master of the banquet tasted the water that had been turned
into wine. He did not realize where it had
come from, though the servants who had
drawn the water knew. Then he called the
bridegroom aside 10and said, "Everyone
brings out the choice wine first and then
the cheaper wine after the guests have had
too much to drink; but you have saved the
best till now."
11This, the first of his miraculous signs,
Jesus performed in Cana of Galilee. He
thus revealed his glory, and his disciples
put their faith in him.●

### *Jesus Clears the Temple*

12After this he went down to Capernaum
with his mother and brothers and his disciples. There they stayed for a few days.●
13When it was almost time for the Jewish
Passover, Jesus went up to Jerusalem. 14In
the temple courts he found men selling cattle, sheep and doves, and others sitting at
tables exchanging money. 15So he made a
whip out of cords, and drove all from the
temple area, both sheep and cattle; he scattered the coins of the money changers and
overturned their tables. 16To those who
sold doves he said, "Get these out of here!
How dare you turn my Father's house into
a market!"
17His disciples remembered that it is
written: "Zeal for your house will consume
me."[a]●
18Then the Jews demanded of him,
"What miraculous sign can you show us to
prove your authority to do all this?"
19Jesus answered them, "Destroy this
temple, and I will raise it again in three
days."
20The Jews replied, "It has taken forty-
six years to build this temple, and you are
going to raise it in three days?" 21But the
temple he had spoken of was his body.
22After he was raised from the dead, his
disciples recalled what he had said. Then
they believed the Scripture and the words
that Jesus had spoken.●
23Now while he was in Jerusalem at the
Passover Feast, many people saw the miraculous signs he was doing and believed in
his name.[b] 24But Jesus would not entrust
himself to them, for he knew all men. 25He
did not need man's testimony about man,
for he knew what was in a man.●

[d]6 Greek *two to three metretes* (probably about 75 to 115 liters)
[a]17 Psalm 69:9 [b]23 Or *and believed in him*

KING JAMES

1. MIRACLE

JESUS' POWER

2 And the third day there was a marriage in Cana of Galilee; and the
mother of Jesus was there: 2 and both
Jesus was called, and his disciples, to the
marriage. 3 And when they wanted wine,
the mother of Jesus saith unto him, They
have no wine. 4 Jesus saith unto her,
Woman, what have I to do with thee?
mine hour is not yet come. 5 His mother
saith unto the servants, Whatsoever he
saith unto you, do *it*. 6 And there were
set there six waterpots of stone, after the
manner of the purifying of the Jews, containing two or three firkins apiece.
7 Jesus saith unto them, Fill the waterpots
with water. And they filled them up to
the brim. 8 And he saith unto them,
Draw out now, and bear unto the governor of the feast. And they bare *it*.
9 When the ruler of the feast had tasted
the water that was made wine, and knew
not whence it was, (but the servants which
drew the water knew,) the governor of the
feast called the bridegroom, 10 and saith
unto him, Every man at the beginning
doth set forth good wine; and when men
have well drunk, then that which is worse:
*but* thou hast kept the good wine until
now. 11 This beginning of miracles did
Jesus in Cana of Galilee, and manifested
forth his glory; and his disciples believed
on him. ●

-transition-

12 After this he went down to Caper'-
na-um, he, and his mother, and his brethren, and his disciples; and they continued
there not many days. ●

2. SCOURGING

13 And the Jews' passover[c] was at hand,
and Jesus went up to Jerusalem, 14 and
found in the temple those that sold oxen
and sheep and doves, and the changers of
money sitting: 15 and when he had made
a scourge of small cords, he drove them
all out of the temple, and the sheep, and
the oxen; and poured out the changers'
money, and overthrew the tables; 16 and
said unto them that sold doves, Take
these things hence; make not my Father's
house a house of merchandise. 17 And
his disciples remembered that it was
written, The zeal of thine house hath

3. SIGN

eaten me up. ● 18 Then answered the Jews
and said unto him, What sign showest
thou unto us, seeing that thou doest these
things? 19 Jesus answered and said unto
them, Destroy this temple, and in three
days I will raise it up. 20 Then said the
Jews, Forty and six years was this temple
in building, and wilt thou rear it up in
three days? 21 But he spake of the temple
of his body. 22 When therefore he was
risen from the dead, his disciples remembered that he had said this unto them; and
they believed the Scripture, and the word
which Jesus had said. ●

23 Now when he was in Jerusalem at
the passover, in the feast *day*, many believed in his name, when they saw the
miracles which he did. 24 But Jesus did
not commit himself unto them, because
he knew all *men*, 25 and needed not that
any should testify of man; for he knew
what was in man. ●

JESUS' PERCEPTION

*2:1-11* Record observations, including:

JESUS' FEELINGS ____

ATTRIBUTES MANIFESTED ____

*2:13-17*
JESUS' FEELINGS ____

ATTRIBUTES MANIFESTED ____

*2:18-22* How is this paragraph related to the preceding one?

Record observations: ____

*2:23-25* Relate the word "man" to the first four words of chapter 3.

## NEW INTERNATIONAL VERSION

What is taught in this passage about:

REGENERATION

HOLY SPIRIT

SPIRITUAL UNDERSTANDING

FAITH

ETERNAL LIFE

EVIL

### *Jesus Teaches Nicodemus*

3 Now there was a man of the Pharisees
named Nicodemus, a member of the
Jewish ruling council. 2He came to Jesus at
night and said, "Rabbi, we know you are
a teacher who has come from God. For no
one could perform the miraculous signs
you are doing if God were not with him."
3In reply Jesus declared, "I tell you the
truth, unless a man is born again,[c] he cannot see the kingdom of God."
4"How can a man be born when he is
old?" Nicodemus asked. "Surely he cannot enter a second time into his mother's
womb to be born!"
5Jesus answered, "I tell you the truth,
unless a man is born of water and the
Spirit, he cannot enter the kingdom of
God. 6Flesh gives birth to flesh, but the
Spirit[d] gives birth to spirit. 7You should not
be surprised at my saying, 'You[e] must be
born again.' 8The wind blows wherever it
pleases. You hear its sound, but you cannot tell where it comes from or where it is
going. So it is with everyone born of the
Spirit."●
9"How can this be?" Nicodemus asked.
10"You are Israel's teacher," said Jesus,
"and do you not understand these things?
11I tell you the truth, we speak of what we
know, and we testify to what we have seen,
but still you people do not accept our testimony. 12I have spoken to you of earthly
things and you do not believe; how then
will you believe if I speak of heavenly
things? 13No one has ever gone into heaven
except the one who came from heaven—
the Son of Man.[f] 14Just as Moses lifted up
the snake in the desert, so the Son of Man
must be lifted up, 15that everyone who believes in him may have eternal life.[g]●
16"For God so loved the world that he
gave his one and only Son,[h] that whoever
believes in him shall not perish but have
eternal life. 17For God did not send his Son
into the world to condemn the world, but
to save the world through him. 18Whoever
believes in him is not condemned, but whoever does not believe stands condemned
already because he has not believed in the
name of God's one and only Son.[i] 19This is
the verdict: Light has come into the world,
but men loved darkness instead of light
because their deeds were evil. 20Everyone
who does evil hates the light, and will not
come into the light for fear that his deeds
will be exposed. 21But whoever lives by the
truth comes into the light, so that it may be
seen plainly that what he has done has been
done through God."[j]●

[c]*3* Or *born from above*; also in verse 7
[d]*6* Or *but spirit* [e]*7* The Greek is plural.
[f]*13* Some manuscripts *Man, who is in heaven*
[g]*15* Or *believes may have eternal life in him*
[h]*16* Or *his only begotten Son*
[i]*18* Or *God's only begotten Son*
[j]*21* Some interpreters end the quotation after verse 15.
[k]*28* Or *Messiah*

KING JAMES

1. NEW BIRTH

NEW BIRTH

3 There was a man of the Pharisees,
named Nicode'mus, a ruler of the
Jews: 2 the same came to Jesus by night,
and said unto him, Rabbi, we know that
thou art a teacher come from God: for no
man can do these miracles that thou doest,
except God be with him. 3 Jesus answered and said unto him, Verily, verily,
I say unto thee, Except a man be born
again, he cannot see the kingdom of God.
4 Nicode'mus saith unto him, How can a
man be born when he is old? can he enter
the second time into his mother's womb,
and be born? 5 Jesus answered, Verily,
verily, I say unto thee, Except a man be
born of water and *of* the Spirit, he cannot
enter into the kingdom of God. 6 That
which is born of the flesh is flesh; and
that which is born of the Spirit is spirit.
7 Marvel not that I said unto thee, Ye
must be born again. 8 The wind bloweth
where it listeth, and thou hearest the
sound thereof, but canst not tell whence
it cometh, and whither it goeth: so is every
one that is born of the Spirit.● 9 Nicode'-

2. KEY TO UNDER-STANDING

mus answered and said unto him, How
can these things be? 10 Jesus answered
and said unto him, Art thou a master of
Israel, and knowest not these things?
11 Verily, verily, I say unto thee, We
speak that we do know, and testify that
we have seen; and ye receive not our witness. 12 If I have told you earthly things,
and ye believe not, how shall ye believe,
if I tell you *of* heavenly things? 13 And
no man hath ascended up to heaven, but
he that came down from heaven, *even* the
Son of man which is in heaven. 14 And
as Moses lifted up the serpent in the wilderness, even so must the Son of man be
lifted up: 15 that whosoever believeth in
him should not perish, but have eternal
life.●

3. ETER-NAL LIFE

EVERLAST-ING LIFE

16 For God so loved the world, that he
gave his only begotten Son, that whosoever believeth in him should not perish,
but have everlasting life. 17 For God sent
not his Son into the world to condemn the
world; but that the world through him
might be saved. 18 He that believeth on
him is not condemned: but he that believeth not is condemned already, because
he hath not believed in the name of the
only begotten Son of God. 19 And this is
the condemnation, that light is come into
the world, and men loved darkness rather
than light, because their deeds were evil.
20 For every one that doeth evil hateth the
light, neither cometh to the light, lest his
deeds should be reproved. 21 But he that
doeth truth cometh to the light, that his
deeds may be made manifest, that they
are wrought in God.●

*3:1-8* Where does the subject of new birth begin in the paragraph?

____________________

What brought it on? ____________________

Record observations. ____________________

*3:9-15* What is Nicodemus' problem?

What is Jesus' answer? ____________________

How do verses 14-15 lead into the next paragraph?

*3:16-21* Record the various truths taught.

NEW INTERNATIONAL VERSION

What does this passage teach about:

WATER BAPTISM

CHRIST'S MINISTRY

CHRIST ABOVE ALL

THE GOSPEL

List spiritual applications.

*John the Baptist's Testimony*
*About Jesus*

22After this, Jesus and his disciples went
out into the Judean countryside, where he
spent some time with them, and baptized.
23Now John also was baptizing at Aenon
near Salim, because there was plenty of
water, and people were constantly coming
to be baptized. 24(This was before John
was put in prison.) 25An argument devel-
oped between some of John's disciples and
a certain Jew over the matter of ceremonial
washing. 26They came to John and said to
him, "Rabbi, that man who was with you
on the other side of the Jordan—the one
you testified about—well, he is baptizing,
and everyone is going to him."
27To this John replied, "A man can receive only what is given him from heaven.
28You yourselves can testify that I said, 'I
am not the Christ[k] but am sent ahead of
him.' 29The bride belongs to the bridegroom. The friend who attends the bridegroom waits and listens for him, and is full
of joy when he hears the bridegroom's
voice. That joy is mine, and it is now complete. 30He must become greater; I must
become less.
31"The one who comes from above is
above all; the one who is from the earth
belongs to the earth, and speaks as one
from the earth. The one who comes from
heaven is above all. 32He testifies to what
he has seen and heard, but no one accepts
his testimony. 33The man who has accepted it has certified that God is truthful.
34For the one whom God has sent speaks
the words of God; to him God gives the
Spirit without limit. 35The Father loves the
Son and has placed everything in his
hands. 36Whoever believes in the Son has
eternal life, but whoever rejects the Son
will not see life, for God's wrath remains
on him."[a]

[a]36 Some interpreters end the quotation after verse 30.

KING JAMES

-setting-

JESUS BAPTIZES

22 After these things came Jesus and
his disciples into the land of Judea; and
there he tarried with them, and baptized.
23 And John also was baptizing in Ae'non
near to Salim, because there was much
water there: and they came, and were
baptized. 24 For John was not yet cast
into prison. ●

I. JOHN EXALTS CHRIST

25 Then there arose a question between *some* of John's disciples and the
Jews about purifying. 26 And they came
unto John, and said unto him, Rabbi, he
that was with thee beyond Jordan, to
whom thou barest witness, behold, the
same baptizeth, and all *men* come to him.
27 John answered and said, A man can
receive nothing, except it be given him
from heaven. 28 Ye yourselves bear me
witness, that I said, I am not the Christ,
but that I am sent before him. 29 He that
hath the bride is the bridegroom: but the
friend of the bridegroom, which standeth
and heareth him, rejoiceth greatly because of the bridegroom's voice: this my
joy therefore is fulfilled. 30 He must increase, but I *must* decrease. ●

2. FATHER EXALTS HIS SON

31 He that cometh from above is above
all: he that is of the earth is earthly, and
speaketh of the earth: he that cometh
from heaven is above all. 32 And what
he hath seen and heard, that he testifieth;
and no man receiveth his testimony.
33 He that hath received his testimony
hath set to his seal that God is true.
34 For he whom God hath sent speaketh
the words of God: for God giveth not
the Spirit by measure *unto him*. 35 The
Father loveth the Son, and hath given all
things into his hand. 36 He that believeth on the Son hath everlasting life: and
he that believeth not the Son shall not see
life; but the wrath of God abideth on him. ●

JESUS GIVES ETERNAL LIFE

*3:22-24* What is the setting? ______

*3:25-30* How does John exalt Christ? ______

Explain verse 30. ______

*3:31-36* Compare the words "above all" (v.31) with verse 30.

How does this paragraph show a basis for such a testimony as that of verse 30?

How is verse 36 a summary for the entire chapter?

NEW INTERNATIONAL VERSION

What is said in this passage to support these statements:

For the castoff, there is contact.

For the unenlightened, there is teaching.

For the sinner, there is a way to God.

For the seeker, there is hope fulfilled.

Record what is taught here about:

JESUS AND SALVATION

TRUE WORSHIP

### *Jesus Talks With a Samaritan Woman*

4 The Pharisees heard that Jesus was
gaining and baptizing more disciples
than John, 2although in fact it was not
Jesus who baptized, but his disciples.
3When the Lord learned of this, he left
Judea and went back once more to Galilee.
4Now he had to go through Samaria. 5So
he came to a town in Samaria called
Sychar, near the plot of ground Jacob had
given to his son Joseph. 6Jacob's well was
there, and Jesus, tired as he was from the
journey, sat down by the well. It was about
the sixth hour.●
7When a Samaritan woman came to draw
water, Jesus said to her, "Will you give me
a drink?" 8(His disciples had gone into the
town to buy food.)
9The Samaritan woman said to him,
"You are a Jew and I am a Samaritan
woman. How can you ask me for a drink?"
(For Jews do not associate with Samaritans.[b])
10Jesus answered her, "If you knew the
gift of God and who it is that asks you for
a drink, you would have asked him and he
would have given you living water."
11"Sir," the woman said, "you have
nothing to draw with and the well is deep.
Where can you get this living water? 12Are
you greater than our father Jacob, who
gave us the well and drank from it himself,
as did also his sons and his flocks and
herds?"
13Jesus answered, "Everyone who
drinks this water will be thirsty again, 14but
whoever drinks the water I give him will
never thirst. Indeed, the water I give him
will become in him a spring of water well-
ing up to eternal life."
15The woman said to him, "Sir, give me
this water so that I won't get thirsty and
have to keep coming here to draw water."●
16He told her, "Go, call your husband
and come back."
17"I have no husband," she replied.
Jesus said to her, "You are right when
you say you have no husband. 18The fact
is, you have had five husbands, and the
man you now have is not your husband.
What you have just said is quite true."
19"Sir," the woman said, "I can see that
you are a prophet. 20Our fathers worshiped
on this mountain, but you Jews claim that
the place where we must worship is in
Jerusalem."
21Jesus declared, "Believe me, woman,
a time is coming when you will worship the
Father neither on this mountain nor in
Jerusalem. 22You Samaritans worship
what you do not know; we worship what
we do know, for salvation is from the Jews.
23Yet a time is coming and has now come
when the true worshipers will worship the
Father in spirit and truth, for they are the
kind of worshipers the Father seeks. 24God
is spirit, and his worshipers must worship
in spirit and in truth."
25The woman said, "I know that Messiah" (called Christ) "is coming. When he
comes, he will explain everything to us."
26Then Jesus declared, "I who speak to
you am he."●

[b]9 Or *do not use dishes Samaritans have used*

KING JAMES

-setting-

TRAVELER

4 When therefore the Lord knew how
the Pharisees had heard that Jesus
made and baptized more disciples than
John, 2 (though Jesus himself baptized
not, but his disciples,) 3 he left Judea, and
departed again into Galilee. 4 And he
must needs go through Samaria. 5 Then
cometh he to a city of Samaria, which is
called Sychar, near to the parcel of ground
that Jacob gave to his son Joseph.
6 Now Jacob's well was there. Jesus
therefore, being wearied with *his* journey,
sat thus on the well: *and* it was about the
sixth hour.●

I. LIVING WATER

7 There cometh a woman of Samaria
to draw water: Jesus saith unto her, Give
me to drink. 8 (For his disciples were
gone away unto the city to buy meat.)
9 Then saith the woman of Samaria unto
him, How is it that thou, being a Jew,
askest drink of me, which am a woman of
Samaria? for the Jews have no dealings
with the Samaritans. 10 Jesus answered
and said unto her, If thou knewest the gift
of God, and who it is that saith to thee,
Give me to drink; thou wouldest have
asked of him, and he would have given
thee living water. 11 The woman saith
unto him, Sir, thou hast nothing to draw
with, and the well is deep: from whence
then hast thou that living water? 12 Art
thou greater than our father Jacob, which
gave us the well, and drank thereof himself, and his children, and his cattle?
13 Jesus answered and said unto her,
Whosoever drinketh of this water shall
thirst again: 14 but whosoever drinketh
of the water that I shall give him shall
never thirst; but the water that I shall give
him shall be in him a well of water springing up into everlasting life. 15 The woman
saith unto him, Sir, give me this water,
that I thirst not, neither come hither to
draw.●

2.TRUE WORSHIP

16 Jesus saith unto her, Go, call thy
husband, and come hither. 17 The
woman answered and said, I have no husband. Jesus said unto her, Thou hast well
said, I have no husband: 18 for thou hast
had five husbands; and he whom thou
now hast is not thy husband: in that saidst
thou truly. 19 The woman saith unto him,
Sir, I perceive that thou art a prophet.
20 Our fathers worshipped in this mountain; and ye say, that in Jerusalem is the
place where men ought to worship.
21 Jesus saith unto her, Woman, believe
me, the hour cometh, when ye shall neither in this mountain, nor yet at Jerusalem, worship the Father. 22 Ye worship ye know not what: we know what we
worship; for salvation is of the Jews.
23 But the hour cometh, and now is,
when the true worshippers shall worship
the Father in spirit and in truth: for the
Father seeketh such to worship him.
24 God *is* a Spirit: and they that worship
him must worship *him* in spirit and in
truth. 25 The woman saith unto him, I
know that Messiah cometh, which is
called Christ: when he is come, he will
tell us all things. 26 Jesus saith unto her,
I that speak unto thee am *he*.●

MESSIAH

*4:1-6* The setting is that of a Jew (Jesus) in contact with a Samaritan (the woman). Associate these three verses: verses 4, 9 and 20.

______________________________

______________________________

______________________________

In the next two paragraphs record what is revealed about Jesus and the woman.

*4:7-15*

THE WOMAN ______________________________

______________________________

______________________________

______________________________

______________________________

______________________________

JESUS ______________________________

______________________________

______________________________

______________________________

______________________________

______________________________

*4:16-26*

THE WOMAN ______________________________

______________________________

______________________________

______________________________

______________________________

______________________________

JESUS ______________________________

______________________________

______________________________

______________________________

______________________________

______________________________

______________________________

______________________________

______________________________

______________________________

NEW INTERNATIONAL VERSION

Record what this passage teaches about:

BEARING WITNESS

CHRISTIAN SERVICE

THE WORD

FAITH

ASSURANCE

OTHER

*The Disciples Rejoin Jesus*

27 Just then his disciples returned and
were surprised to find him talking with a
woman. But no one asked, "What do you
want?" or "Why are you talking with
her?"
28 Then, leaving her water jar, the woman
went back to the town and said to the
people, 29 "Come, see a man who told me
everything I ever did. Could this be the
Christ[c]?" 30 They came out of the town and
made their way toward him.●
31 Meanwhile his disciples urged him,
"Rabbi, eat something."
32 But he said to them, "I have food to eat
that you know nothing about."
33 Then his disciples said to each other,
"Could someone have brought him food?"
34 "My food," said Jesus, "is to do the
will of him who sent me and to finish his
work. 35 Do you not say, 'Four months
more and then the harvest'? I tell you, open
your eyes and look at the fields! They are
ripe for harvest. 36 Even now the reaper
draws his wages, even now he harvests the
crop for eternal life, so that the sower and
the reaper may be glad together. 37 Thus the
saying 'One sows and another reaps' is
true. 38 I sent you to reap what you have not
worked for. Others have done the hard
work, and you have reaped the benefits of
their labor."●

*Many Samaritans Believe*

39 Many of the Samaritans from that town
believed in him because of the woman's
testimony, "He told me everything I ever
did." 40 So when the Samaritans came to
him, they urged him to stay with them, and
he stayed two days. 41 And because of his
words many more became believers.
42 They said to the woman, "We no longer believe just because of what you said;
now we have heard for ourselves, and we
know that this man really is the Savior of
the world."●

c29 Or *Messiah*

KING JAMES

1. WOMAN'S TESTIMONY

27 And upon this came his disciples,
and marveled that he talked with the
woman: yet no man said, What seekest
thou? or, Why talkest thou with her?
28 The woman then left her waterpot, and
went her way into the city, and saith to the
men, 29 Come, see a man, which told me
all things that ever I did: is not this the
Christ? 30 Then they went out of the city,
and came unto him.●

"Is not this the Christ?"

2. JESUS' TEACHING

31 In the mean while his disciples
prayed him, saying, Master, eat. 32 But
he said unto them, I have meat to eat that
ye know not of. 33 Therefore said the
disciples one to another, Hath any man
brought him *aught* to eat? 34 Jesus saith
unto them, My meat is to do the will of
him that sent me, and to finish his work.
35 Say not ye, There are yet four months,
and *then* cometh harvest? behold, I say
unto you, Lift up your eyes, and look on
the fields; for they are white already to
harvest. 36 And he that reapeth receiveth
wages, and gathereth fruit unto life eternal: that both he that soweth and he that
reapeth may rejoice together. 37 And
herein is that saying true, One soweth, and
another reapeth. 38 I sent you to reap
that whereupon ye bestowed no labor:
other men labored, and ye are entered
into their labors.●

3. SAMARITAN'S CONVERSION

39 And many of the Samaritans of that
city believed on him for the saying of the
woman, which testified, He told me all
that ever I did. 40 So when the Samaritans were come unto him, they besought
him that he would tarry with them: and
he abode there two days. 41 And many
more believed because of his own word;
42 and said unto the woman, Now we
believe, not because of thy saying: for we
have heard *him* ourselves, and know that
this is indeed the Christ, the Saviour of
the world.●

"This is indeed the Christ"

Good results came of Jesus' encounter with the Samaritan woman. List these, paragraph by paragraph:

*4:27-30* Concerning the woman: ____________

*4:31-38* Concerning the disciples: ____________

*4:39-42* Concerning the Samaritans: ____________

NEW INTERNATIONAL VERSION

Record what this passage teaches about Jesus and about faith:

JESUS

FAITH

List some spiritual applications which can be made from this account.

*Jesus Heals the Official's Son*

43 After the two days he left for Galilee.
44 (Now Jesus himself had pointed out that
a prophet has no honor in his own country.) 45 When he arrived in Galilee, the Galileans welcomed him. They had seen all
that he had done in Jerusalem at the Passover Feast, for they also had been there.●
46 Once more he visited Cana in Galilee,
where he had turned the water into wine.
And there was a certain royal official
whose son lay sick at Capernaum. 47 When
this man heard that Jesus had arrived in
Galilee from Judea, he went to him and
begged him to come and heal his son, who
was close to death.
48 "Unless you people see miraculous
signs and wonders," Jesus told him, "you
will never believe."
49 The royal official said, "Sir, come
down before my child dies."
50 Jesus replied, "You may go. Your son
will live."
The man took Jesus at his word and departed.● 51 While he was still on the way, his
servants met him with the news that his
boy was living. 52 When he inquired as to
the time when his son got better, they said
to him, "The fever left him yesterday at the
seventh hour."
53 Then the father realized that this was
the exact time at which Jesus had said to
him, "Your son will live." So he and all his
household believed.
54 This was the second miraculous sign
that Jesus performed, having come from
Judea to Galilee.●

KING JAMES

-setting-

NO HONOR

43 Now after two days he departed
thence, and went into Galilee. 44 For
Jesus himself testified, that a prophet hath
no honor in his own country. 45 Then
when he was come into Galilee, the Galileans received him, having seen all the
things that he did at Jerusalem at the
feast: for they also went unto the feast.●

1. FAITH EXER-CISED

46 So Jesus came again into Cana of
Galilee, where he made the water wine.
And there was a certain nobleman, whose
son was sick at Caper'na-um. 47 When
he heard that Jesus was come out of Judea
into Galilee, he went unto him, and besought him that he would come down,
and heal his son: for he was at the point
of death. 48 Then said Jesus unto him,
Except ye see signs and wonders, ye will
not believe. 49 The nobleman saith unto
him, Sir, come down ere my child die.
50 Jesus saith unto him, Go thy way; thy
son liveth. And the man believed the
word that Jesus had spoken unto him, and
he went his way.●

2. FAITH RE-WARDED

51 And as he was now
going down, his servants met him, and
told *him*, saying, Thy son liveth. 52 Then
inquired he of them the hour when he
began to amend. And they said unto him,
Yesterday at the seventh hour the fever
left him. 53 So the father knew that *it*
*was* at the same hour, in the which Jesus
said unto him, Thy son liveth: and himself believed, and his whole house.
54 This *is* again the second miracle *that*
Jesus did, when he was come out of Judea
into Galilee.●

GREAT POWER

*4:43-45* Try to explain verse 45a, in light of verse 44.

*4:46-50* Relate verse 48 to the key verse of John, 20:3l.

Compare the man's "Come" (v.49) and Jesus' "Go" (v.50).

Observe how verse 50 records a *believing without seeing.* How is this a test of genuine faith?

*4:51-54* Observe the influence of the nobleman upon his whole house (v.53). Record.

NEW INTERNATIONAL VERSION

What do you learn here about:

LEGALISM

MIRACLE

FAITH

FORGIVENESS

JESUS

Record some spiritual applications:

*The Healing at the Pool*

5 Some time later, Jesus went up to Jerusalem for a feast of the Jews. 2Now there is in Jerusalem near the Sheep Gate a pool, which in Aramaic is called Bethesda[a] and which is surrounded by five covered colonnades. 3Here a great number of disabled people used to lie—the blind, the lame, the paralyzed.[b] 5One who was there had been an invalid for thirty-eight years. 6When Jesus saw him lying there and learned that he had been in this condition for a long time, he asked him, "Do you want to get well?"

7"Sir," the invalid replied, "I have no one to help me into the pool when the water is stirred. While I am trying to get in, someone else goes down ahead of me."

8Then Jesus said to him, "Get up! Pick up your mat and walk." 9At once the man was cured; he picked up his mat and walked.

The day on which this took place was a Sabbath,● 10and so the Jews said to the man who had been healed, "It is the Sabbath; the law forbids you to carry your mat."

11But he replied, "The man who made me well said to me, 'Pick up your mat and walk.'"

12So they asked him, "Who is this fellow who told you to pick it up and walk?"

13The man who was healed had no idea who it was, for Jesus had slipped away into the crowd that was there.●

14Later Jesus found him at the temple and said to him, "See, you are well again. Stop sinning or something worse may happen to you." 15The man went away and told the Jews that it was Jesus who had made him well.●

*Life Through the Son*

16So, because Jesus was doing these things on the Sabbath, the Jews persecuted him. 17Jesus said to them, "My Father is always at his work to this very day, and I, too, am working." 18For this reason the Jews tried all the harder to kill him; not only was he breaking the Sabbath, but he was even calling God his own Father, making himself equal with God.●

[a]2 Some manuscripts *Bethzatha;* other manuscripts *Bethsaida*

[b]3 Some manuscripts *paralyzed—and they waited for the moving of the waters;* some less important manuscripts continue *4From time to time an angel of the Lord would come down and stir up the waters. The first one into the pool after each such disturbance would be cured of whatever disease he had.*

KING JAMES

1. PHYSICAL HEALING

FEAST TO WORSHIP GOD

5 After this there was a feast of the
Jews; and Jesus went up to Jerusalem.
2 Now there is at Jerusalem by the
sheep *market* a pool, which is called in
the Hebrew tongue Bethes'da, having five
porches. 3 In these lay a great multitude
of impotent folk, of blind, halt, withered,
waiting for the moving of the water.
4 For an angel went down at a certain
season into the pool, and troubled the
water: whosoever then first after the
troubling of the water stepped in was
made whole of whatsoever disease he
had. 5 And a certain man was there,
which had an infirmity thirty and eight
years. 6 When Jesus saw him lie, and knew
that he had been now a long time *in that*
*case*, he saith unto him, Wilt thou be made
whole? 7 The impotent man answered
him, Sir, I have no man, when the water
is troubled, to put me into the pool: but
while I am coming, another steppeth
down before me. 8 Jesus saith unto him,
Rise, take up thy bed, and walk. 9 And
immediately the man was made whole,
and took up his bed, and walked: and on
the same day was the sabbath.●

2. INQUIRY

10 The Jews therefore said unto him
that was cured, It is the sabbath day: it is
not lawful for thee to carry *thy* bed.
11 He answered them, He that made me
whole, the same said unto me, Take up
thy bed, and walk. 12 Then asked they
him, What man is that which said unto
thee, Take up thy bed, and walk? 13 And
he that was healed wist not who it was:
for Jesus had conveyed himself away, a
multitude being in *that* place.●

3. SPIRITUAL HEALING

14 After-
ward Jesus findeth him in the temple, and
said unto him, Behold, thou art made
whole: sin no more, lest a worse thing
come unto thee. 15 The man departed,
and told the Jews that it was Jesus, which
had made him whole.●

4. PERSECUTION

16 And therefore
did the Jews persecute Jesus, and sought
to slay him, because he had done these
things on the sabbath day. 17 But Jesus
answered them, My Father worketh
hitherto, and I work. 18 Therefore the
Jews sought the more to kill him, because
he not only had broken the sabbath, but
said also that God was his Father, making
himself equal with God.●

PLOT TO KILL GOD

Chapter 5 begins a new section in John: YEARS OF CONFLICT. (See outline.) Here the author begins to record instances of open opposition to Jesus by the Jewish rulers. (See 5:16.)

*5:1-9* Compare the two methods of healing.

*5:10-13* Compare the Jews' objection of verse 10 with that of verse 16.

*5:14-15* Compare the phrases "thou art made whole" and "sin no more" (v.14).

*5:16-18* Analyze especially verses 17-18.

NEW INTERNATIONAL VERSION

What is taught here about:

JESUS' AUTHORITY AND POWER

RESURRECTION

JUDGMENT

INVITATION TO SALVATION

PROPHECY

OTHER

19 Jesus gave them this answer: "I tell
you the truth, the Son can do nothing by
himself; he can do only what he sees his
Father doing, because whatever the Father
does the Son also does. 20 For the Father
loves the Son and shows him all he does.
Yes, to your amazement he will show him
even greater things than these. 21 For just as
the Father raises the dead and gives them
life, even so the Son gives life to whom he
is pleased to give it. 22 Moreover, the Father judges no one, but has entrusted all
judgment to the Son, 23 that all may honor
the Son just as they honor the Father. He
who does not honor the Son does not honor
the Father, who sent him. ●
24 "I tell you the truth, whoever hears my
word and believes him who sent me has
eternal life and will not be condemned; he
has crossed over from death to life. ● 25 I tell
you the truth, a time is coming and has now
come when the dead will hear the voice of
the Son of God and those who hear will
live. 26 For as the Father has life in himself,
so he has granted the Son to have life in
himself. 27 And he has given him authority
to judge because he is the Son of Man. ●
28 "Do not be amazed at this, for a time
is coming when all who are in their graves
will hear his voice 29 and come out—those
who have done good will rise to live, and
those who have done evil will rise to be
condemned. ●

KING JAMES

I. DOCTRINE

VERILY, VERILY

19 Then answered Jesus and said unto
them, Verily, verily, I say unto you, The
Son can do nothing of himself, but what
he seeth the Father do: for what things
soever he doeth, these also doeth the Son
likewise. 20 For the Father loveth the
Son, and showeth him all things that himself doeth: and he will show him greater
works than these, that ye may marvel.
21 For as the Father raiseth up the dead,
and quickeneth *them;* even so the Son
quickeneth whom he will. 22 For the
Father judgeth no man, but hath committed all judgment unto the Son: 23 that
all *men* should honor the Son, even as they
honor the Father. He that honoreth not
the Son honoreth not the Father which

2. INVITATION

hath sent him.● 24 Verily, verily, I say unto
you, He that heareth my word, and believeth on him that sent me, hath everlasting
life, and shall not come into condemnation; but is passed from death unto life.●

3. PROPHECY

25 Verily, verily, I say unto you, The
hour is coming, and now is, when the dead
shall hear the voice of the Son of God:
and they that hear shall live. 26 For as the
Father hath life in himself; so hath he
given to the Son to have life in himself;
27 and hath given him authority to execute judgment also, because he is the Son

4. APPEAL

of man.● 28 Marvel not at this: for the
hour is coming, in the which all that are
in the graves shall hear his voice, 29 and
shall come forth; they that have done
good, unto the resurrection of life; and
they that have done evil, unto the resurrection of damnation. ●

MARVEL NOT

Read the passage to answer these questions: What two things has the Father given the Son authority to do?

1. __________

2. __________

What verses are in the first person ("I")--not including the phrase "I say unto you"?

*5:19-23* List the doctrines taught:

*5:24* Relate this verse to the preceding paragraph.

*5:25-27* What does Jesus prophesy?

*5:28-29* Account for the words "Marvel not." Compare the last phrase of verse 20.

NEW INTERNATIONAL VERSION

Record what this passage teaches about:

TRUTH

WITNESSES TO JESUS

JESUS' FATHER

SCRIPTURES

HUMAN HEART

List some spiritual applications:

[30]By myself I can do nothing;
I judge only as I hear, and my judgment is
just, for I seek not to please myself but him
who sent me.

*Testimonies About Jesus*

[31]"If I testify about myself, my testimony is not valid. [32]There is another who
testifies in my favor, and I know that his
testimony about me is valid.
[33]"You have sent to John and he has
testified to the truth. [34]Not that I accept
human testimony; but I mention it that you
may be saved. [35]John was a lamp that
burned and gave light, and you chose for a
time to enjoy his light.
[36]"I have testimony weightier than that
of John. For the very work that the Father
has given me to finish, and which I am
doing, testifies that the Father has sent me.
[37]And the Father who sent me has himself
testified concerning me. You have never
heard his voice nor seen his form, [38]nor
does his word dwell in you, for you do not
believe the one he sent. ● [39]You diligently
study[a] the Scriptures because you think
that by them you possess eternal life.
These are the Scriptures that testify about
me, [40]yet you refuse to come to me to have
life.
[41]"I do not accept praise from men, [42]but
I know you. I know that you do not have
the love of God in your hearts. [43]I have
come in my Father's name, and you do not
accept me; but if someone else comes in his
own name, you will accept him. [44]How can
you believe if you accept praise from one
another, yet make no effort to obtain the
praise that comes from the only God[b]? ●
[45]"But do not think I will accuse you
before the Father. Your accuser is Moses,
on whom your hopes are set. [46]If you believed Moses, you would believe me, for
he wrote about me. [47]But since you do not
believe what he wrote, how are you going
to believe what I say?" ●

[a]39 Or *Study diligently* (the imperative)
[b]44 Some early manuscripts *the Only One*

KING JAMES

1. WITNESSES OF JESUS

FATHER'S WILL

30 I can of mine own self do nothing:
as I hear, I judge: and my judgment is
just; because I seek not mine own will, but
the will of the Father which hath sent me.
31 If I bear witness of myself, my witness
is not true. 32 There is another that beareth witness of me; and I know that the
witness which he witnesseth of me is true.
33 Ye sent unto John, and he bare witness
unto the truth. 34 But I receive not testimony from man: but these things I say,
that ye might be saved. 35 He was a burning and a shining light: and ye were willing for a season to rejoice in his light.
36 But I have greater witness than *that* of
John: for the works which the Father hath
given me to finish, the same works that I
do, bear witness of me, that the Father
hath sent me. 37 And the Father himself,
which hath sent me, hath borne witness of
me. Ye have neither heard his voice at
any time, nor seen his shape. 38 And ye
have not his word abiding in you: for
whom he hath sent, him ye believe not.●

2. REJECTORS OF JESUS

39 Search the Scriptures; for in them ye
think ye have eternal life: and they are
they which testify of me. 40 And ye will
not come to me, that ye might have life.
41 I receive not honor from men. 42 But
I know you, that ye have not the love of
God in you. 43 I am come in my Father's
name, and ye receive me not: if another
shall come in his own name, him ye will
receive. 44 How can ye believe, which
receive honor one of another, and seek
not the honor that *cometh* from God only?●

3. THE LAW CONDEMNS

MOSES' WRITINGS

45 Do not think that I will accuse you to
the Father: there is *one* that accuseth you,
*even* Moses, in whom ye trust. 46 For had
ye believed Moses, ye would have believed me: for he wrote of me. 47 But if
ye believe not his writings, how shall ye
believe my words?●

*5:30-38* What is a key repeated word of the paragraph?

____________________

List the various witnesses which Jesus cites as proof that He was doing the work of God.

____________________

*5:39-44* What is a key repeated word of this paragraph?

____________________

Why do the people reject Jesus? __________

*5:45-47* Analyze Jesus' logical approach here..

____________________

NEW INTERNATIONAL VERSION

Record things taught here about:

SOLITUDE

PRAYER

*JESUS'* COMPASSION

POWER

PRESENCE

KINGSHIP

TROUBLE

Record practical lessons which can be learned:

*Jesus Feeds the Five Thousand*

6 Some time after this, Jesus crossed to
the far shore of the Sea of Galilee (that
is, the Sea of Tiberias), 2and a great crowd
of people followed him because they saw
the miraculous signs he had performed on
the sick. 3Then Jesus went up on the hillside and sat down with his disciples. 4The
Jewish Passover Feast was near.
5When Jesus looked up and saw a great
crowd coming toward him, he said to
Philip, "Where shall we buy bread for
these people to eat?" 6He asked this only
to test him, for he already had in mind what
he was going to do.
7Philip answered him, "Eight months'
wages[c] would not buy enough bread for
each one to have a bite!"
8Another of his disciples, Andrew, Simon Peter's brother, spoke up, 9"Here is
a boy with five small barley loaves and two
small fish, but how far will they go among
so many?"
10Jesus said, "Have the people sit
down." There was plenty of grass in that
place, and the men sat down, about five
thousand of them. 11Jesus then took the
loaves, gave thanks, and distributed to
those who were seated as much as they
wanted. He did the same with the fish.
12When they had all had enough to eat,
he said to his disciples, "Gather the pieces
that are left over. Let nothing be wasted."
13So they gathered them and filled twelve
baskets with the pieces of the five barley
loaves left over by those who had eaten.
14After the people saw the miraculous
sign that Jesus did, they began to say,
"Surely this is the Prophet who is to come
into the world." 15Jesus, knowing that they
intended to come and make him king by
force, withdrew again into the hills by himself.

*Jesus Walks on the Water*

16When evening came, his disciples went
down to the lake, 17where they got into a
boat and set off across the lake for Capernaum. By now it was dark, and Jesus had
not yet joined them. 18A strong wind was
blowing and the waters grew rough.
19When they had rowed three or three and
a half miles,[a] they saw Jesus approaching
the boat, walking on the water; and they
were terrified. 20But he said to them, "It is
I; don't be afraid." 21Then they were willing to take him into the boat, and immediately the boat reached the shore where
they were heading.

[c]7 Greek *two hundred denarii*

[a]19 Greek *rowed twenty-five or thirty stadia* (about 5 or 6 kilometers)

KING JAMES

-setting-

DISCIPLES IN FELLOWSHIP WITH JESUS

6 After these things Jesus went over the
sea of Galilee, which is *the sea* of Tibe'ri-as. 2 And a great multitude followed him, because they saw his miracles
which he did on them that were diseased.
3 And Jesus went up into a mountain, and
there he sat with his disciples. 4 And the
passover, a feast of the Jews, was nigh. ●

I. MIRACLE

5 When Jesus then lifted up *his* eyes, and
saw a great company come unto him, he
saith unto Philip, Whence shall we buy
bread, that these may eat? 6 And this he
said to prove him: for he himself knew
what he would do. 7 Philip answered him,
Two hundred pennyworth of bread is not
sufficient for them, that every one of them
may take a little. 8 One of his disciples,
Andrew, Simon Peter's brother, saith unto him, 9 There is a lad here, which hath
five barley loaves, and two small fishes:
but what are they among so many?
10 And Jesus said, Make the men sit
down. Now there was much grass in the
place. So the men sat down, in number
about five thousand. 11 And Jesus took
the loaves; and when he had given thanks,
he distributed to the disciples, and the
disciples to them that were set down; and
likewise of the fishes as much as they
would. 12 When they were filled, he said
unto his disciples, Gather up the fragments that remain, that nothing be lost.
13 Therefore they gathered *them* together,
and filled twelve baskets with the fragments of the five barley loaves, which remained over and above unto them that
had eaten.●

DISCIPLES IN SERVICE

2. REACTION

14 Then those men, when they
had seen the miracle that Jesus did, said,
This is of a truth that Prophet that should
come into the world.
15 When Jesus therefore perceived that
they would come and take him by force,
to make him a king, he departed again
into a mountain himself alone.●

DISCIPLES PARTED FROM JESUS

3. MIRACLE

16 And when even was *now* come, his
disciples went down unto the sea, 17 and
entered into a ship, and went over the sea
toward Caper'na-um. And it was now
dark, and Jesus was not come to them.
18 And the sea arose by reason of a great
wind that blew. 19 So when they had
rowed about five and twenty or thirty
furlongs, they see Jesus walking on the
sea, and drawing nigh unto the ship: and
they were afraid. 20 But he saith unto
them, It is I; be not afraid. 21 Then they
willingly received him into the ship: and
immediately the ship was at the land
whither they went.●

DISCIPLES IN TROUBLE

There is a one-year interlude between chapters 5 and 6. (Compare 5:1 and 6:4). Record observations for each paragraph

*6:1-4* ____________________

*6:5-13* ____________________

*6:14-15* What kind of king did the people want to make Jesus?

____________________

*6:16-21* ____________________

NEW INTERNATIONAL VERSION

Record all the things taught in this passage about JESUS AS THE BREAD.

List spiritual applications to be made from this passage.

[22]The next day the crowd that had stayed
on the opposite shore of the lake realized
that only one boat had been there, and that
Jesus had not entered it with his disciples,
but that they had gone away alone. [23]Then
some boats from Tiberias landed near the
place where the people had eaten the bread
after the Lord had given thanks. [24]Once the
crowd realized that neither Jesus nor his
disciples were there, they got into the
boats and went to Capernaum in search of
Jesus.●

*Jesus the Bread of Life*

[25]When they found him on the other side
of the lake, they asked him, "Rabbi, when
did you get here?"
[26]Jesus answered, "I tell you the truth,
you are looking for me, not because you
saw miraculous signs but because you ate
the loaves and had your fill. [27]Do not work
for food that spoils, but for food that en-
dures to eternal life, which the Son of Man
will give you. On him God the Father has
placed his seal of approval."
[28]Then they asked him, "What must we
do to do the works God requires?"
[29]Jesus answered, "The work of God is
this: to believe in the one he has sent."
[30]So they asked him, "What miraculous
sign then will you give that we may see it
and believe you? What will you do? [31]Our
forefathers ate the manna in the desert; as
it is written: 'He gave them bread from
heaven to eat.'[b]"
[32]Jesus said to them, "I tell you the
truth, it is not Moses who has given you the
bread from heaven, but it is my Father who
gives you the true bread from heaven.
[33]For the bread of God is he who comes
down from heaven and gives life to the
world."
[34]"Sir," they said, "from now on give us
this bread."●
[35]Then Jesus declared, "I am the bread
of life. He who comes to me will never go
hungry, and he who believes in me will
never be thirsty. [36]But as I told you, you
have seen me and still you do not believe.
[37]All that the Father gives me will come to
me, and whoever comes to me I will never
drive away. [38]For I have come down from
heaven not to do my will but to do the will
of him who sent me. [39]And this is the will
of him who sent me, that I shall lose none
of all that he has given me, but raise them
up at the last day. [40]For my Father's will is
that everyone who looks to the Son and
believes in him shall have eternal life, and
I will raise him up at the last day."●

[b]31 Exodus 16:4; Psalm 78:24

KING JAMES

-setting-

SEEKING JESUS

22 The day following, when the people,
which stood on the other side of the sea,
saw that there was none other boat there,
save that one whereinto his disciples were
entered, and that Jesus went not with his
disciples into the boat, but *that* his disciples were gone away alone; 23 (howbeit
there came other boats from Tibe'ri-as
nigh unto the place where they did eat
bread, after that the Lord had given
thanks:) 24 when the people therefore
saw that Jesus was not there, neither his
disciples, they also took shipping, and
came to Caper'na-um, seeking for Jesus.●

I. BREAD FROM HEAVEN

25 And when they had found him on
the other side of the sea, they said unto
him, Rabbi, when camest thou hither?
26 Jesus answered them and said, Verily,
verily, I say unto you, Ye seek me, not because ye saw the miracles, but because ye
did eat of the loaves, and were filled.
27 Labor not for the meat which perisheth, but for that meat which endureth unto everlasting life, which the Son of man
shall give unto you: for him hath God the
Father sealed. 28 Then said they unto
him, What shall we do, that we might
work the works of God? 29 Jesus answered and said unto them, This is the
work of God, that ye believe on him
whom he hath sent. 30 They said therefore unto him, What sign showest thou
then, that we may see, and believe thee?
what dost thou work? 31 Our fathers did
eat manna in the desert; as it is written,
He gave them bread from heaven to eat.
32 Then Jesus said unto them, Verily,
verily, I say unto you, Moses gave you
not that bread from heaven; but my
Father giveth you the true bread from
heaven. 33 For the bread of God is he
which cometh down from heaven, and
giveth life unto the world. 34 Then said
they unto him, Lord, evermore give us
this bread.●

"GIVE US THIS BREAD"

2. JESUS IS THE BREAD

35 And Jesus said unto them, I am the
bread of life: he that cometh to me shall
never hunger; and he that believeth on me
shall never thirst. 36 But I said unto you,
That ye also have seen me, and believe
not. 37 All that the Father giveth me
shall come to me; and him that cometh
to me I will in no wise cast out. 38 For I
came down from heaven, not to do mine
own will, but the will of him that sent me.
39 And this is the Father's will which hath
sent me, that of all which he hath given
me I should lose nothing, but should raise
it up again at the last day. 40 And this is
the will of him that sent me, that every
one which seeth the Son, and believeth
on him, may have everlasting life: and I
will raise him up at the last day.●

Center your study about Jesus' key testimony: "I am the bread of life" (v.35).

*6:22-24* What is the main point of this setting?

*6:25-34* Why were the people hunting for Jesus? (v.26)

What is the basic difference between seeing a miracle and eating miraculous bread (v.26)?

*6:35-40* Jesus clearly identifies who the bread of life is, in verse 35. Had He done this in the preceding paragraph?

What does Jesus say of His heavenly Father?

NEW INTERNATIONAL VERSION

Record what this passage teaches about:

THE SOVEREIGN FATHER

SALVATION

LIFE AND ETERNAL LIFE

PARTAKING OF JESUS' FLESH AND BLOOD

List practical lessons:

41At this the Jews began to grumble
about him because he said, "I am the bread
that came down from heaven." 42They
said, "Is this not Jesus, the son of Joseph,
whose father and mother we know? How
can he now say, 'I came down from
heaven'?"
43"Stop grumbling among yourselves,"
Jesus answered. 44"No one can come to
me unless the Father who sent me draws
him, and I will raise him up at the last day.
45It is written in the Prophets: 'They will all
be taught by God.'[c] Everyone who listens
to the Father and learns from him comes to
me. 46No one has seen the Father except
the one who is from God; only he has seen
the Father. 47I tell you the truth, he who
believes has everlasting life. 48I am the
bread of life. 49Your forefathers ate the
manna in the desert, yet they died. 50But
here is the bread that comes down from
heaven, which a man may eat and not die.
51I am the living bread that came down
from heaven. If a man eats of this bread, he
will live forever. This bread is my flesh,
which I will give for the life of the world."
52Then the Jews began to argue sharply
among themselves, "How can this man
give us his flesh to eat?"
53Jesus said to them, "I tell you the
truth, unless you eat the flesh of the Son of
Man and drink his blood, you have no life
in you. 54Whoever eats my flesh and drinks
my blood has eternal life, and I will raise
him up at the last day. 55For my flesh is real
food and my blood is real drink. 56Whoever
eats my flesh and drinks my blood remains
in me, and I in him. 57Just as the living
Father sent me and I live because of the
Father, so the one who feeds on me will
live because of me. 58This is the bread that
came down from heaven. Our forefathers
ate manna and died, but he who feeds on
this bread will live forever." 59He said this
while teaching in the synagogue in Capernaum.

[c]45 Isaiah 54:13

KING JAMES

**I. SOVEREIGN FATHER**

41 The Jews then murmured at him, because he said, I am the bread which came
down from heaven. 42 And they said, Is
not this Jesus, the son of Joseph, whose
father and mother we know? how is it
then that he saith, I came down from
heaven? 43 Jesus therefore answered and
said unto them, Murmur not among yourselves. 44 No man can come to me, except
the Father which hath sent me draw him:
and I will raise him up at the last day.
45 It is written in the prophets, And they
shall be all taught of God. Every man
therefore that hath heard, and hath
learned of the Father, cometh unto me.
46 Not that any man hath seen the
Father, save he which is of God, he hath
seen the Father.●

**2. EVERLASTING LIFE**

47 Verily, verily, I say
unto you, He that believeth on me hath
everlasting life. 48 I am that bread of life.
49 Your fathers did eat manna in the
wilderness, and are dead. 50 This is the
bread which cometh down from heaven,
that a man may eat thereof, and not die.
51 I am the living bread which came
down from heaven: if any man eat of
this bread, he shall live for ever: and
the bread that I will give is my flesh,
which I will give for the life of the
world.●

**3. FLESH AND BLOOD OF JESUS**

52 The Jews therefore strove among
themselves, saying, How can this man
give us *his* flesh to eat? 53 Then Jesus
said unto them, Verily, verily, I say unto
you, Except ye eat the flesh of the Son of
man, and drink his blood, ye have no life
in you. 54 Whoso eateth my flesh, and
drinketh my blood, hath eternal life; and
I will raise him up at the last day. 55 For
my flesh is meat indeed, and my blood is
drink indeed. 56 He that eateth my flesh,
and drinketh my blood, dwelleth in me,
and I in him. 57 As the living Father hath
sent me, and I live by the Father; so he
that eateth me, even he shall live by me.
58 This is that bread which came down
from heaven: not as your fathers did eat
manna, and are dead: he that eateth of
this bread shall live for ever. 59 These
things said he in the synagogue, as he
taught in Caper'na-um.●

"I am the bread"

"Eat this bread"

*6:41-46* Note the different references to Jesus' Father. What is taught here about this relationship?

______

*6:47-51* What is a key repeated truth of this paragraph?

______

*6:52-59* What is the key repeated word of this paragraph?

______

Record the various key truths. ______

NEW INTERNATIONAL VERSION

This is a short passage, but it contains many important truths, and vital spiritual applications can be made from the text. Record these.

MAIN TRUTHS

SPIRITUAL APPLICATIONS

*Many Disciples Desert Jesus*

60On hearing it, many of his disciples
said, "This is a hard teaching. Who can
accept it?"
61Aware that his disciples were grumbling about this, Jesus said to them, "Does
this offend you? 62What if you see the Son
of Man ascend to where he was before!
63The Spirit gives life; the flesh counts for
nothing. The words I have spoken to you
are spirit[a] and they are life. 64Yet there are
some of you who do not believe." For
Jesus had known from the beginning which
of them did not believe and who would
betray him. 65He went on to say, "This is
why I told you that no one can come to me
unless the Father has enabled him."
66From this time many of his disciples
turned back and no longer followed him.●
67"You do not want to leave too, do
you?" Jesus asked the Twelve.
68Simon Peter answered him, "Lord, to
whom shall we go? You have the words of
eternal life. 69We believe and know that
you are the Holy One of God."●
70Then Jesus replied, "Have I not chosen you, the Twelve? Yet one of you is a
devil!" 71(He meant Judas, the son of Simon Iscariot, who, though one of the
Twelve, was later to betray him.)●

[a]63 Or *Spirit*

KING JAMES

I. UNBELIEF — MANY

60 Many therefore of his disciples,
when they had heard *this*, said, This is a
hard saying; who can hear it? 61 When
Jesus knew in himself that his disciples
murmured at it, he said unto them, Doth
this offend you? 62 *What* and if ye shall
see the Son of man ascend up where he
was before? 63 It is the Spirit that quickeneth; the flesh profiteth nothing: the
words that I speak unto you, *they* are
spirit, and *they* are life. 64 But there are
some of you that believe not. For Jesus
knew from the beginning who they were
that believed not, and who should betray
him. 65 And he said, Therefore said I
unto you, that no man can come unto
me, except it were given unto him of my
Father.
66 From that *time* many of his disciples
went back, and walked no more with him. ●

2. BELIEF — TWELVE

67 Then said Jesus unto the twelve, Will
ye also go away? 68 Then Simon Peter
answered him, Lord, to whom shall we
go? thou hast the words of eternal life.
69 And we believe and are sure that thou
art that Christ, the Son of the living
God. ●

3. BETRAYAL — ONE

70 Jesus answered them, Have not
I chosen you twelve, and one of you is a
devil? 71 He spake of Judas Iscar'i-ot *the
son* of Simon: for he it was that should
betray him, being one of the twelve. ●

*6:60-66* What was the stumbling block for many of Jesus' followers at this time?

*6:67-69* Compare the testimony of Peter, in verse 69, with the key verse 20:31.

*6:70-71* How do you reconcile the two main parts of verse 70?

NEW INTERNATIONAL VERSION

What do you learn here about:

JESUS' HOUR OF SACRIFICE

PERSECUTION

REPUTATION

JESUS THE TEACHER

TRUE DOCTRINE

LAW OF MOSES

OTHER

### *Jesus Goes to the Feast of Tabernacles*

7 After this, Jesus went around in Galilee, purposely staying away from Judea because the Jews there were waiting to take his life. [2]But when the Jewish Feast of Tabernacles was near, [3]Jesus' brothers said to him, "You ought to leave here and go to Judea, so that your disciples may see the miracles you do. [4]No one who wants to become a public figure acts in secret. Since you are doing these things, show yourself to the world." [5]For even his own brothers did not believe in him.

[6]Therefore Jesus told them, "The right time for me has not yet come; for you any time is right. [7]The world cannot hate you, but it hates me because I testify that what it does is evil. [8]You go to the Feast. I am not yet[b] going up to this Feast, because for me the right time has not yet come." [9]Having said this, he stayed in Galilee.●

[10]However, after his brothers had left for the Feast, he went also, not publicly, but in secret. [11]Now at the Feast the Jews were watching for him and asking, "Where is that man?"

[12]Among the crowds there was widespread whispering about him. Some said, "He is a good man."

Others replied, "No, he deceives the people." [13]But no one would say anything publicly about him for fear of the Jews.●

### *Jesus Teaches at the Feast*

[14]Not until halfway through the Feast did Jesus go up to the temple courts and begin to teach. [15]The Jews were amazed and asked, "How did this man get such learning without having studied?"

[16]Jesus answered, "My teaching is not my own. It comes from him who sent me. [17]If any one chooses to do God's will, he will find out whether my teaching comes from God or whether I speak on my own. [18]He who speaks on his own does so to gain honor for himself, but he who works for the honor of the one who sent him is a man of truth; there is nothing false about him. [19]Has not Moses given you the law? Yet not one of you keeps the law. Why are you trying to kill me?"

[20]"You are demon-possessed," the crowd answered. "Who is trying to kill you?"

[21]Jesus said to them, "I did one miracle, and you are all astonished. [22]Yet, because Moses gave you circumcision (though actually it did not come from Moses, but from the patriarchs), you circumcise a child on the Sabbath. [23]Now if a child can be circumcised on the Sabbath so that the law of Moses may not be broken, why are you angry with me for healing the whole man on the Sabbath? [24]Stop judging by mere appearances, and make a right judgment."●

[b]8 Some early manuscripts do not have *yet*.

KING JAMES

### I. JESUS' BROTHERS ADVISE HIM

*Jesus and Jerusalem: absence*

**7** After these things Jesus walked in Galilee: for he would not walk in Jewry, because the Jews sought to kill him. 2 Now the Jews' feast of tabernacles was at hand. 3 His brethren therefore said unto him, Depart hence, and go into Judea, that thy disciples also may see the works that thou doest. 4 For *there is* no man *that* doeth any thing in secret, and he himself seeketh to be known openly. If thou do these things, show thyself to the world. 5 For neither did his brethren believe in him. 6 Then Jesus said unto them, My time is not yet come: but your time is always ready. 7 The world cannot hate you; but me it hateth, because I testify of it, that the works thereof are evil. 8 Go ye up unto this feast: I go not up yet unto this feast; for my time is not yet full come. 9 When he had said these words unto them, he abode *still* in Galilee.●

### 2. JEWS SEEK JESUS

*secret presence*

10 But when his brethren were gone up, then went he also up unto the feast, not openly, but as it were in secret. 11 Then the Jews sought him at the feast, and said, Where is he? 12 And there was much murmuring among the people concerning him: for some said, He is a good man: others said, Nay; but he deceiveth the people. 13 Howbeit no man spake openly of him for fear of the Jews.●

### 3. JESUS TEACHES

*public appearance*

14 Now about the midst of the feast Jesus went up into the temple, and taught. 15 And the Jews marveled, saying, How knoweth this man letters, having never learned? 16 Jesus answered them, and said, My doctrine is not mine, but his that sent me. 17 If any man will do his will, he shall know of the doctrine, whether it be of God, or *whether* I speak of myself. 18 He that speaketh of himself seeketh his own glory: but he that seeketh his glory that sent him, the same is true, and no unrighteousness is in him. 19 Did not Moses give you the law, and *yet* none of you keepeth the law? Why go ye about to kill me? 20 The people answered and said, Thou hast a devil: who goeth about to kill thee? 21 Jesus answered and said unto them, I have done one work, and ye all marvel. 22 Moses therefore gave unto you circumcision; (not because it is of Moses, but of the fathers; ) and ye on the sabbath day circumcise a man. 23 If a man on the sabbath day receive circumcision, that the law of Moses should not be broken; are ye angry at me, because I have made a man every whit whole on the sabbath day? 24 Judge not according to the appearance, but judge righteous judgment.●

---

The two most prominent truths of chapter 7 are (1) Jesus' clear consciousness of His mission (7:8,29); and (2) the enemies' failure to seize Him (7:30).

*7:1-9* Account for the advice of Jesus' brothers and Jesus' response.

*7:10-13* Account for the two different reputations of Jesus.

*7:14-24* Analyze Jesus' teaching. What is the main point of verses 19-24?

NEW INTERNATIONAL VERSION

What does this passage teach about the Jews' expectation of the Messiah?

What does the passage teach about Christ?

List applications which may be made of the passage:

*Is Jesus the Christ?*

25At that point some of the people of
Jerusalem began to ask, "Isn't this the man
they are trying to kill? 26Here he is,
speaking publicly, and they are not saying
a word to him. Have the authorities really
concluded that he is the Christ[c]? 27But we
know where this man is from; when the
Christ comes, no one will know where he
is from."

28Then Jesus, still teaching in the temple
courts, cried out, "Yes, you know me, and
you know where I am from. I am not here
on my own, but he who sent me is true.
You do not know him, 29but I know him
because I am from him and he sent me."●

30At this they tried to seize him, but no
one laid a hand on him, because his time
had not yet come. 31Still, many in the
crowd put their faith in him. They said,
"When the Christ comes, will he do more
miraculous signs than this man?"●

32The Pharisees heard the crowd whispering such things about him. Then the
chief priests and the Pharisees sent temple
guards to arrest him.

33Jesus said, "I am with you for only a
short time, and then I go to the one who
sent me. 34You will look for me, but you
will not find me; and where I am, you cannot come."

35The Jews said to one another, "Where
does this man intend to go that we cannot
find him? Will he go where our people live
scattered among the Greeks, and teach the
Greeks? 36What did he mean when he said,
'You will look for me, but you will not find
me,' and 'Where I am, you cannot
come'?"●

[c]26 Or *Messiah*; also in verses 27, 31, 41 and 42

KING JAMES

I. SOME QUESTION JESUS

25 Then said some of them of Jerusalem, Is not this he, whom they seek to kill?
26 But, lo, he speaketh boldly, and they
say nothing unto him. Do the rulers
know indeed that this is the very Christ?
27 Howbeit we know this man whence he
is: but when Christ cometh, no man knoweth whence he is. 28 Then cried Jesus in
the temple as he taught, saying, Ye both
know me, and ye know whence I am: and
I am not come of myself, but he that sent
me is true, whom ye know not. 29 But I
know him; for I am from him, and he
hath sent me.● 30 Then they sought to
take him: but no man laid hands on him,
because his hour was not yet come.
31 And many of the people believed on
him, and said, When Christ cometh, will
he do more miracles than these which this
*man* hath done?●

2. MANY BELIEVE JESUS

3. RELIGIOUS RULERS MOVE AGAINST HIM

32 The Pharisees heard that the people
murmured such things concerning him;
and the Pharisees and the chief priests
sent officers to take him. 33 Then said
Jesus unto them, Yet a little while am I
with you, and *then* I go unto him that sent
me. 34 Ye shall seek me, and shall not
find *me:* and where I am, *thither* ye cannot come. 35 Then said the Jews among
themselves, Whither will he go, that we
shall not find him? will he go unto the
dispersed among the Gentiles, and teach
the Gentiles? 36 What *manner of* saying
is this that he said, Ye shall seek me, and
shall not find *me:* and where I am, *thither*
ye cannot come?●

WHO?

WHERE?

The opposition against Jesus begins to intensify at this time. As you study the passage, observe
1) the opposition: words and deeds
2) Jesus' words
3) believers or neutral observers

Record these things in the spaces below.

*7:25-29* ______

*7:30-31* ______

*7:32-36* ______

NEW INTERNATIONAL VERSION

What do you learn here about:

LIFE

HOLY SPIRIT

IDENTITY OF JESUS

JUSTICE

PROPHECY

OTHER

[37]On the last and greatest day of the
Feast, Jesus stood and said in a loud voice,
"If a man is thirsty, let him come to me and
drink. [38]Whoever believes in me,[a] as the
Scripture has said, streams of living water
will flow from within him." [39]By this he
meant the Spirit, whom those who believed in him were later to receive. Up to
that time the Spirit had not been given,
since Jesus had not yet been glorified.●
[40]On hearing his words, some of the
people said, "Surely this man is the
Prophet."
[41]Others said, "He is the Christ."
Still others asked, "How can the Christ
come from Galilee? [42]Does not the Scripture say that the Christ will come from
David's family[b] and from Bethlehem, the
town where David lived?" [43]Thus the
people were divided because of Jesus.
[44]Some wanted to seize him, but no one
laid a hand on him.●

*Unbelief of the Jewish Leaders*

[45]Finally the temple guards went back to
the chief priests and Pharisees, who asked
them, "Why didn't you bring him in?"
[46]"No one ever spoke the way this man
does," the guards declared.
[47]"You mean he has deceived you
also?" the Pharisees retorted. [48]"Has any
of the rulers or of the Pharisees believed in
him? [49]No! But this mob that knows nothing of the law—there is a curse on them."
[50]Nicodemus, who had gone to Jesus
earlier and who was one of their own number, asked, [51]"Does our law condemn a
man without first hearing him to find out
what he is doing?"
[52]They replied, "Are you from Galilee,
too? Look into it, and you will find that a
prophet[c] does not come out of Galilee."●

---

[The earliest and most reliable manuscripts do not have John 7:53-8:11.]

[a]38 Or *If a man is thirsty, / let him come to me. / And let him drink, / who believes in me*
[b]42 Greek *seed*
[c]52 Two early manuscripts *the Prophet*

KING JAMES

I. JESUS SPEAKS

37 In the last day, that great *day* of the
feast, Jesus stood and cried, saying, If
any man thirst, let him come unto me, and
drink. 38 He that believeth on me, as the
Scripture hath said, out of his belly shall
flow rivers of living water. 39 (But this
spake he of the Spirit, which they that
believe on him should receive: for the
Holy Ghost was not yet *given;* because
that Jesus was not yet glorified.) ●

INVITATION

2. PEOPLE ARE DIVIDED

40 Many of the people therefore, when
they heard this saying, said, Of a truth
this is the Prophet. 41 Others said, This
is the Christ. But some said, Shall Christ
come out of Galilee? 42 Hath not the
Scripture said, That Christ cometh of the
seed of David, and out of the town of
Bethlehem, where David was? 43 So
there was a division among the people
because of him. 44 And some of them
would have taken him; but no man laid
hands on him.●

3. PHARISEES MOCK

45 Then came the officers to the chief
priests and Pharisees; and they said unto
them, Why have ye not brought him?
46 The officers answered, Never man
spake like this man. 47 Then answered
them the Pharisees, Are ye also deceived?
48 Have any of the rulers or of the Pharisees believed on him? 49 But this people
who knoweth not the law are cursed.
50 Nicode'mus saith unto them, (he that
came to Jesus by night, being one of
them,) 51 Doth our law judge *any* man,
before it hear him, and know what he
doeth? 52 They answered and said unto
him, Art thou also of Galilee? Search,
and look: for out of Galilee ariseth no
prophet.●

REJECTION

*7:37-39* Analyze carefully Jesus' words.

INVITATION ______

PROMISE ______

*7:40-44* Record the reactions: ______

Account for verse 44. ______

*7:45-52* Compare the officers, the Pharisees, and Nicodemus.

NEW INTERNATIONAL VERSION

What does this passage teach about:

JESUS' TEACHING MINISTRY

LAW

SIN

MERCY AND GRACE

CONDEMNATION

FORGIVENESS

53 Then each went to his own home.
8 But Jesus went to the Mount of Olives.
2 At dawn he appeared again in the temple courts, where all the people gathered around him, and he sat down to teach
them. 3 The teachers of the law and the Pharisees brought in a woman caught in adultery. They made her stand before the
group 4 and said to Jesus, "Teacher, this woman was caught in the act of adultery.
5 In the Law Moses commanded us to stone such women. Now what do you say?"
6 They were using this question as a trap, in order to have a basis for accusing him. ●
But Jesus bent down and started to write on the ground with his finger. 7 When they
kept on questioning him, he straightened up and said to them, "If any one of you is without sin, let him be the first to throw a
stone at her." 8 Again he stooped down and wrote on the ground.
9 At this, those who heard began to go away one at a time, the older ones first, until only Jesus was left, with the woman
still standing there. ● 10 Jesus straightened up and asked her, "Woman, where are they? Has no one condemned you?"
11 "No one, sir," she said.
"Then neither do I condemn you," Jesus declared. "Go now and leave your life of sin." ●

KING JAMES

1. THE CHARGE

ADULTERY

53 And every man went unto his own
8 house. 1 Jesus went unto the mount
of Olives. 2 And early in the morning
he came again into the temple, and all the
people came unto him; and he sat down,
and taught them. 3 And the scribes and
Pharisees brought unto him a woman
taken in adultery; and when they had set
her in the midst, 4 they say unto him,
Master, this woman was taken in adultery,
in the very act. 5 Now Moses in the law
commanded us, that such should be
stoned: but what sayest thou? 6 This
they said, tempting him, that they might
have to accuse him.●

2. JESUS CONFRONTS THE ACCUSERS

But Jesus stooped
down, and with *his* finger wrote on the
ground, *as though he heard them not.* 7 So
when they continued asking him, he lifted
up himself, and said unto them, He that is
without sin among you, let him first cast
a stone at her. 8 And again he stooped
down, and wrote on the ground. 9 And
they which heard *it*, being convicted by
*their own* conscience, went out one by one,
beginning at the eldest, *even* unto the last:
and Jesus was left alone, and the woman
standing in the midst.●

3. JESUS ABSOLVES THE WOMAN

"SIN NO MORE"

10 When Jesus had
lifted up himself, and saw none but the
woman, he said unto her, Woman, where
are those thine accusers? hath no man
condemned thee? 11 She said, No man,
Lord. And Jesus said unto her, Neither
do I condemn thee: go, and sin no
more. ●

Compare the three paragraphs as to the persons and groups involved.

*7:53—8:6a* Compare verses 2 and 3.

What may the accusers have had in mind in verse 6a?

*8:6b-9* Speculate as to what Jesus wrote on the ground (vv.6b,8).

*8:10-11* Explain Jesus' words of verse 11.

NEW INTERNATIONAL VERSION

What would you know about Jesus if this was the only Scripture revealing Him? It may surprise you how much is revealed in this passage.

*The Validity of Jesus' Testimony*

12When Jesus spoke again to the people,
he said, "I am the light of the world. Whoever follows me will never walk in darkness, but will have the light of life."
13The Pharisees challenged him, "Here
you are, appearing as your own witness;
your testimony is not valid."
14Jesus answered, "Even if I testify on
my own behalf, my testimony is valid, for
I know where I came from and where I am
going. But you have no idea where I come
from or where I am going. 15You judge by
human standards; I pass judgment on no
one. 16But if I do judge, my decisions are
right, because I am not alone. I stand with
the Father who sent me.● 17In your own
Law it is written that the testimony of two
men is valid. 18I am one who testifies for
myself; my other witness is the one who
sent me—the Father."
19Then they asked him, "Where is your
father?"
"You do not know me or my Father,"
Jesus replied. "If you knew me, you would
know my Father also." 20He spoke these
words while teaching in the temple area
near the place where the offerings were
put. Yet no one seized him, because his
time had not yet come.●
21Once more Jesus said to them, "I am
going away, and you will look for me, and
you will die in your sin. Where I go, you
cannot come."
22This made the Jews ask, "Will he kill
himself? Is that why he says, 'Where I go,
you cannot come'?"
23But he continued, "You are from
below; I am from above. You are of this
world; I am not of this world. 24I told you
that you would die in your sins; if you do
not believe that I am ⌊the one I claim to be⌋,[a]
you will indeed die in your sins."●
25"Who are you?" they asked.
"Just what I have been claiming all
along," Jesus replied. 26"I have much to
say in judgment of you. But he who sent
me is reliable, and what I have heard from
him I tell the world."
27They did not understand that he was
telling them about his Father. 28So Jesus
said, "When you have lifted up the Son of
Man, then you will know who I am[b] and
that I do nothing on my own but speak just
what the Father has taught me. 29The one
who sent me is with me; he has not left me
alone, for I always do what pleases him."
30Even as he spoke, many put their faith in
him.●

[a]24 Or *I am he* [b]28 Or *know that I am he*

KING JAMES

1. JESUS' WITNESS OF HIMSELF

PHARISEES REJECT JESUS

12 Then spake Jesus again unto them,
saying, I am the light of the world: he
that followeth me shall not walk in darkness, but shall have the light of life.
13 The Pharisees therefore said unto him,
Thou bearest record of thyself; thy record
is not true. 14 Jesus answered and said
unto them, Though I bear record of myself, *yet* my record is true: for I know
whence I came, and whither I go; but ye
cannot tell whence I come, and whither I
go. 15 Ye judge after the flesh; I judge
no man. 16 And yet if I judge, my judgment is true: for I am not alone, but I and
the Father that sent me. ● 17 It is also

2. FATHER'S WITNESS OF JESUS

written in your law, that the testimony of
two men is true. 18 I am one that bear
witness of myself, and the Father that sent
me beareth witness of me. 19 Then said
they unto him, Where is thy Father?
Jesus answered, Ye neither know me, nor
my Father: if ye had known me, ye should
have known my Father also. 20 These
words spake Jesus in the treasury, as he
taught in the temple: and no man laid
hands on him; for his hour was not yet
come. ●

3. JESUS' HEAVENLY HOME

21 Then said Jesus again unto them, I
go my way, and ye shall seek me, and shall
die in your sins: whither I go, ye cannot
come. 22 Then said the Jews, Will he kill
himself? because he saith, Whither I go,
ye cannot come. 23 And he said unto
them, Ye are from beneath; I am from
above: ye are of this world; I am not of
this world. 24 I said therefore unto you,
that ye shall die in your sins: for if ye believe not that I am *he*, ye shall die in your
sins. ● 25 Then said they unto him, Who art

4. JESUS' EARTHLY MINISTRY

thou? And Jesus saith unto them, Even
*the same* that I said unto you from the
beginning. 26 I have many things to say
and to judge of you: but he that sent me
is true; and I speak to the world those
things which I have heard of him. 27 They
understood not that he spake to them of
the Father. 28 Then said Jesus unto them,
When ye have lifted up the Son of man,
then shall ye know that I am *he*, and *that*
I do nothing of myself; but as my Father
hath taught me, I speak these things.
29 And he that sent me is with me: the
Father hath not left me alone; for I do
always those things that please him.
30 As he spake these words, many believed on him. ●

MANY BELIEVE ON JESUS

Observe the key question of verse 25. Study the segment with this in view. Underline every appearance of the identifying words "I am."
Record in the right-hand margin all the identifications of Jesus (e.g. LIGHT).
Record the main claims made by Jesus in each paragraph.

*8:12-16* ______

8:17-20 ______

*8:21-24* ______

*8:25-30* ______

NEW INTERNATIONAL VERSION

What is taught here about:

TRUTH

FREEDOM

DISCIPLESHIP

TRADITION

THE DEVIL

JESUS

*The Children of Abraham*

[31]To the Jews who had believed him, Jesus said, "If you hold to my teaching, you are really my disciples. [32]Then you will know the truth, and the truth will set you free."

[33]They answered him, "We are Abraham's descendants[c] and have never been slaves of anyone. How can you say that we shall be set free?"●

[34]Jesus replied, "I tell you the truth, everyone who sins is a slave to sin. [35]Now a slave has no permanent place in the family, but a son belongs to it forever. [36]So if the Son sets you free, you will be free indeed. [37]I know you are Abraham's descendants. Yet you are ready to kill me, because you have no room for my word. [38]I am telling you what I have seen in the Father's presence, and you do what you have heard from your father.[d]"●

[39]"Abraham is our father," they answered.

"If you were Abraham's children," said Jesus, "then you would[e] do the things Abraham did. [40]As it is, you are determined to kill me, a man who has told you the truth that I heard from God. Abraham did not do such things. [41]You are doing the things your own father does."

"We are not illegitimate children," they protested. "The only Father we have is God himself."

*The Children of the Devil*

[42]Jesus said to them, "If God were your Father, you would love me, for I came from God and now am here. I have not come on my own; but he sent me. [43]Why is my language not clear to you? Because you are unable to hear what I say. [44]You belong to your father, the devil, and you want to carry out your father's desire. He was a murderer from the beginning, not holding to the truth, for there is no truth in him. When he lies, he speaks his native language, for he is a liar and the father of lies. [45]Yet because I tell the truth, you do not believe me! [46]Can any of you prove me guilty of sin? If I am telling the truth, why don't you believe me? [47]He who belongs to God hears what God says. The reason you do not hear is that you do not belong to God."●

[c]33 Greek *seed;* also in verse 37
[d]38 Or *presence. Therefore do what you have heard from the Father.*
[e]39 Some early manuscripts *"If you are Abraham's children," said Jesus, "then*

KING JAMES

1. CHILDREN OF ABRAHAM

a.
31 Then said Jesus to those Jews which
believed on him, If ye continue in my
word, *then* are ye my disciples indeed;
32 and ye shall know the truth, and the
truth shall make you free. 33 They answered him, We be Abraham's seed, and
were never in bondage to any man:
how sayest thou, Ye shall be made
free? ●

b.
34 Jesus answered them, Verily, verily,
I say unto you, Whosoever committeth
sin is the servant of sin. 35 And the servant abideth not in the house for ever: *but*
the Son abideth ever. 36 If the Son therefore shall make you free, ye shall be free
indeed. 37 I know that ye are Abraham's
seed; but ye seek to kill me, because my
word hath no place in you. 38 I speak
that which I have seen with my Father:
and ye do that which ye have seen with
your father. ●

c.
39 They answered and said unto him,
Abraham is our father. Jesus saith unto
them, If ye were Abraham's children, ye
would do the works of Abraham. 40 But
now ye seek to kill me, a man that hath
told you the truth, which I have heard of
God: this did not Abraham. 41 Ye do the
deeds of your father. Then said they to
him, We be not born of fornication; we
have one Father, *even* God. ●

2. CHILDREN OF THE DEVIL

42 Jesus said
unto them, If God were your Father, ye
would love me: for I proceeded forth and
came from God; neither came I of myself, but he sent me. 43 Why do ye not
understand my speech? *even* because ye
cannot hear my word. 44 Ye are of *your*
father the devil, and the lusts of your
father ye will do: he was a murderer from
the beginning, and abode not in the truth,
because there is no truth in him. When he
speaketh a lie, he speaketh of his own: for
he is a liar, and the father of it. 45 And
because I tell *you* the truth, ye believe me
not. 46 Which of you convinceth me of
sin? And if I say the truth, why do ye not
believe me? 47 He that is of God heareth
God's words: ye therefore hear *them* not,
because ye are not of God. ●

TRUTH AND JESUS' WORD

TRUTH AND GOD'S WORDS

Read the segment. Is Jesus speaking to the same group in all the paragraphs? If not, identify.

______

______

Are the believers of verse 31 *true* disciples?

______

CHILDREN OF ABRAHAM

Record what Jesus teaches about this relationship in the three paragraphs:

*8:31-33* ______

*8:34-38* ______

*8:39-41* ______

CHILDREN OF THE DEVIL
*8:42-47* Record your observations.

______

NEW INTERNATIONAL VERSION

What do you learn here about:

JESUS

LIFE

RESURRECTION

TRADITION

RELIGION

MIRACLE

Record some practical applications.

*The Claims of Jesus About Himself*

48The Jews answered him, "Aren't we
right in saying that you are a Samaritan and
demon-possessed?"
49"I am not possessed by a demon," said
Jesus, "but I honor my Father and you
dishonor me. 50I am not seeking glory for
myself; but there is one who seeks it, and
he is the judge. 51I tell you the truth, if a
man keeps my word, he will never see
death."●
52At this the Jews exclaimed, "Now we
know that you are demon-possessed!
Abraham died and so did the prophets, yet
you say that if a man keeps your word, he
will never taste death. 53Are you greater
than our father Abraham? He died, and so
did the prophets. Who do you think you
are?"
54Jesus replied, "If I glorify myself, my
glory means nothing. My Father, whom
you claim as your God, is the one who
glorifies me. 55Though you do not know
him, I know him. If I said I did not, I would
be a liar like you, but I do know him and
keep his word. 56Your father Abraham rejoiced at the thought of seeing my day; he
saw it and was glad."
57"You are not yet fifty years old," the
Jews said to him, "and you have seen
Abraham!"
58"I tell you the truth," Jesus answered,
"before Abraham was born, I am!"● 59At
this, they picked up stones to stone him,
but Jesus hid himself, slipping away from
the temple grounds.●

KING JAMES

**1. FIRST ACCUSATION AND REPLY**

**ACCUSING WORDS**

48 Then answered the Jews, and said
unto him, Say we not well that thou art a
Samaritan, and hast a devil? 49 Jesus
answered, I have not a devil; but I honor
my Father, and ye do dishonor me.
50 And I seek not mine own glory: there
is one that seeketh and judgeth. 51 Verily,
verily, I say unto you, If a man keep my
saying, he shall never see death.●

**2. SECOND ACCUSATION AND REPLY**

52 Then
said the Jews unto him, Now we know
that thou hast a devil. Abraham is dead,
and the prophets; and thou sayest, If a
man keep my saying, he shall never taste
of death. 53 Art thou greater than our
father Abraham, which is dead? and the
prophets are dead: whom makest thou
thyself? 54 Jesus answered, If I honor
myself, my honor is nothing: it is my
Father that honoreth me; of whom ye say,
that he is your God: 55 yet ye have not
known him; but I know him: and if I
should say, I know him not, I shall be a
liar like unto you: but I know him, and
keep his saying. 56 Your father Abraham
rejoiced to see my day: and he saw *it*, and
was glad. 57 Then said the Jews unto him,
Thou art not yet fifty years old, and hast
thou seen Abraham? 58 Jesus said unto
them, Verily, verily, I say unto you,
Before Abraham was, I am.●

**3. ESCAPE**

**MURDEROUS STONES**

59 Then
took they up stones to cast at him: but
Jesus hid himself, and went out of the
temple, going through the midst of them,
and so passed by.●

Compare the first two paragraphs, noting the sequence of accusation followed by reply.
Record your observations of these parts of the paragraphs.

*8:48-51*

JEWS' ACCUSATION ____________________

JESUS' REPLY ____________________

*8:52-58*

JEWS' ACCUSATIONS ____________________

JESUS' REPLY ____________________

Compare verse 58 with verse 51. ____________________

*8:59* What miracle is reported here? ____________________

NEW INTERNATIONAL VERSION

Record what this passage teaches about the following:

JESUS

SOVEREIGNTY OF GOD

SPIRITUAL BLINDNESS

UNBELIEF

Record spiritual applications which can be made from the passage.

### *Jesus Heals a Man Born Blind*

9 As he went along, he saw a man blind
from birth. [2]His disciples asked him,
"Rabbi, who sinned, this man or his parents, that he was born blind?"
[3]"Neither this man nor his parents
sinned," said Jesus, "but this happened so
that the work of God might be displayed in
his life. [4]As long as it is day, we must do
the work of him who sent me. Night is
coming, when no one can work. [5]While I
am in the world, I am the light of the
world."
[6]Having said this, he spit on the ground,
made some mud with the saliva, and put it
on the man's eyes. [7]"Go," he told him,
"wash in the pool of Siloam" (this word
means Sent). So the man went and washed,
and came home seeing.
[8]His neighbors and those who had formerly seen him begging asked, "Isn't this
the same man who used to sit and beg?"
[9]Some claimed that he was.
Others said, "No, he only looks like
him."
But he himself insisted, "I am the man."
[10]"How then were your eyes opened?"
they demanded.
[11]He replied, "The man they call Jesus
made some mud and put it on my eyes. He
told me to go to Siloam and wash. So I
went and washed, and then I could see."
[12]"Where is this man?" they asked him.
"I don't know," he said.●

### *The Pharisees Investigate the Healing*

[13]They brought to the Pharisees the man
who had been blind. [14]Now the day on
which Jesus had made the mud and opened
the man's eyes was a Sabbath. [15]Therefore
the Pharisees also asked him how he had
received his sight. "He put mud on my
eyes," the man replied, "and I washed,
and now I see."
[16]Some of the Pharisees said, "This man
is not from God, for he does not keep the
Sabbath."
But others asked, "How can a sinner do
such miraculous signs?" So they were divided.
[17]Finally they turned again to the blind
man, "What have you to say about him? It
was your eyes he opened."●
The man replied, "He is a prophet."
[18]The Jews still did not believe that he
had been blind and had received his sight
until they sent for the man's parents. [19]"Is
this your son?" they asked. "Is this the
one you say was born blind? How is it that
now he can see?"
[20]"We know he is our son," the parents
answered, "and we know he was born
blind. [21]But how he can see now, or who
opened his eyes, we don't know. Ask him.
He is of age; he will speak for himself."
[22]His parents said this because they were
afraid of the Jews, for already the Jews had
decided that anyone who acknowledged
that Jesus was the Christ[a] would be put out
of the synagogue. [23]That was why his parents said, "He is of age; ask him."●

[a]22 Or *Messiah*

KING JAMES

1. MIRACLE

9 And as *Jesus* passed by, he saw a man
which was blind from *his* birth.
2 And his disciples asked him, saying,
Master, who did sin, this man, or his
parents, that he was born blind? 3 Jesus
answered, Neither hath this man sinned,
nor his parents: but that the works of God
should be made manifest in him. 4 I must
work the works of him that sent me, while
it is day: the night cometh, when no man
can work. 5 As long as I am in the world,
I am the light of the world. 6 When he
had thus spoken, he spat on the ground,
and made clay of the spittle, and he
anointed the eyes of the blind man with
the clay, 7 and said unto him, Go, wash
in the pool of Silo'am, (which is by interpretation,
Sent.) He went his way therefore,
and washed, and came seeing. 8 The
neighbors therefore, and they which before
had seen him that he was blind, said,
Is not this he that sat and begged?
9 Some said, This is he: others *said*, He is
like him: *but* he said, I am *he*. 10 Therefore
said they unto him, How were thine
eyes opened? 11 He answered and said,
A man that is called Jesus made clay, and
anointed mine eyes, and said unto me, Go
to the pool of Silo'am, and wash: and I
went and washed, and I received sight.
12 Then said they unto him, Where is he?
He said, I know not.●

2. DIVISION

13 They brought to the Pharisees him
that aforetime was blind. 14 And it was
the sabbath day when Jesus made the clay,
and opened his eyes. 15 Then again the
Pharisees also asked him how he had received
his sight. He said unto them, He
put clay upon mine eyes, and I washed,
and do see. 16 Therefore said some of the
Pharisees, This man is not of God, because
he keepeth not the sabbath day.
Others said, How can a man that is a sinner
do such miracles? And there was a
division among them. 17 They say unto
the blind man again, What sayest thou of
him, that he hath opened thine eyes? He
said, He is a prophet.●

3. SKEPTICISM

18 But the Jews did not believe concerning
him, that he had been blind, and
received his sight, until they called the
parents of him that had received his sight.
19 And they asked them, saying, Is this
your son, who ye say was born blind?
how then doth he now see? 20 His parents
answered them and said, We know that
this is our son, and that he was born
blind: 21 but by what means he now
seeth, we know not; or who hath opened
his eyes, we know not: he is of age; ask
him: he shall speak for himself. 22 These
*words* spake his parents, because they
feared the Jews: for the Jews had agreed
already, that if any man did confess that
he was Christ, he should be put out of the
synagogue. 23 Therefore said his parents,
He is of age; ask him.●

BLIND MAN

INTIMIDATED PARENTS

Chapter 8 showed Jesus with power to forgive sins. Chapter 9 shows Him demonstrating His power over nature. The latter accredits the authority of the former.
When you study these paragraphs, look for references to Jesus:
who He was, and what He came to do.

*9:1-12* Why was the man born blind? ____________________

*9:13-17* ____________________

*9:18-23* ____________________

NEW INTERNATIONAL VERSION

What is taught here about:

SPIRITUAL BLINDNESS

SAVING FAITH

LIGHT OF THE WORLD

SIN

Record spiritual applications:

24 A second time they summoned the man
who had been blind. "Give glory to
God,[b]" they said. "We know this man is a
sinner."
25 He replied, "Whether he is a sinner or
not, I don't know. One thing I do know. I
was blind but now I see!"
26 Then they asked him, "What did he do
to you? How did he open your eyes?"
27 He answered, "I have told you already
and you did not listen. Why do you want to
hear it again? Do you want to become his
disciples, too?"
28 Then they hurled insults at him and
said, "You are this fellow's disciple! We
are disciples of Moses! 29 We know that
God spoke to Moses, but as for this fellow,
we don't even know where he comes
from."
30 The man answered, "Now that is
remarkable! You don't know where he
comes from, yet he opened my eyes. 31 We
know that God does not listen to sinners.
He listens to the godly man who does his
will. 32 Nobody has ever heard of opening
the eyes of a man born blind. 33 If this man
were not from God, he could do nothing."
34 To this they replied, "You were
steeped in sin at birth; how dare you lecture us!" And they threw him out.●

*Spiritual Blindness*

35 Jesus heard that they had thrown him
out, and when he found him, he said, "Do
you believe in the Son of Man?"
36 "Who is he, sir?" the man asked. "Tell
me so that I may believe in him."
37 Jesus said, "You have now seen him;
in fact, he is the one speaking with you."
38 Then the man said, "Lord, I believe,"
and he worshiped him.●
39 Jesus said, "For judgment I have come
into this world, so that the blind will see
and those who see will become blind."
40 Some Pharisees who were with him
heard him say this and asked, "What? Are
we blind too?"
41 Jesus said, "If you were blind, you
would not be guilty of sin; but now that you
claim you can see, your guilt remains.●

[b]24 A solemn charge to tell the truth (see Joshua 7:19)

KING JAMES

**1. HEALED MAN DEFENDS JESUS**

**JESUS A SINNER?**

24 Then again called they the man that
was blind, and said unto him, Give God
the praise: we know that this man is a
sinner. 25 He answered and said, Whether
he be a sinner *or no*, I know not: one thing
I know, that, whereas I was blind, now
I see. 26 Then said they to him again,
What did he to thee? how opened he
thine eyes? 27 He answered them, I have
told you already, and ye did not hear:
wherefore would ye hear *it* again? will ye
also be his disciples? 28 Then they reviled him, and said, Thou art his disciple;
but we are Moses' disciples. 29 We know
that God spake unto Moses: *as for* this
*fellow*, we know not from whence he is.
30 The man answered and said unto them,
Why herein is a marvelous thing, that ye
know not from whence he is, and *yet* he
hath opened mine eyes. 31 Now we know
that God heareth not sinners: but if any
man be a worshipper of God, and doeth
his will, him he heareth. 32 Since the
world began was it not heard that any
man opened the eyes of one that was born
blind. 33 If this man were not of God, he
could do nothing. 34 They answered and
said unto him, Thou wast altogether born
in sins, and dost thou teach us? And they
cast him out.●

**2. HEALED MAN BELIEVES**

35 Jesus heard that they had cast him
out; and when he had found him, he said
unto him, Dost thou believe on the Son
of God? 36 He answered and said, Who
is he, Lord, that I might believe on him?
37 And Jesus said unto him, Thou hast
both seen him, and it is he that talketh
with thee. 38 And he said, Lord, I believe. And he worshipped him.●

**3. SPIRITUAL BLINDNESS**

**"YOUR SIN REMAINETH"**

39 And
Jesus said, For judgment I am come into
this world, that they which see not might
see; and that they which see might be
made blind. 40 And *some* of the Pharisees which were with him heard these
words, and said unto him, Are we blind
also? 41 Jesus said unto them, If ye were
blind, ye should have no sin: but now ye
say, We see; therefore your sin remaineth.●

This segment reports the sequel to the previous segment.

*9:24-34* Analyze the argument between the healed man and his opponents. Record the main parts.

*9:35-38* What are the key statements of the paragraph?

*9:39-41* What does Jesus mean by verse 39?

What does He mean by verse 41?

NEW INTERNATIONAL VERSION

Record as many practical truths as you can see in this passage about Jesus as Shepherd and about His sheep.

*The Shepherd and His Flock*

10 "I tell you the truth, the man who
does not enter the sheep pen by the
gate, but climbs in by some other way, is
a thief and a robber. 2The man who enters
by the gate is the shepherd of his sheep.
3The watchman opens the gate for him, and
the sheep listen to his voice. He calls his
own sheep by name and leads them out.
4When he has brought out all his own, he
goes on ahead of them, and his sheep follow him because they know his voice. 5But
they will never follow a stranger; in fact,
they will run away from him because they
do not recognize a stranger's voice."
6Jesus used this figure of speech, but they
did not understand what he was telling
them. ●

7Therefore Jesus said again, "I tell you
the truth, I am the gate for the sheep. 8All
who ever came before me were thieves and
robbers, but the sheep did not listen to
them. 9I am the gate; whoever enters
through me will be saved.[a] He will come in
and go out, and find pasture. 10The thief
comes only to steal and kill and destroy; I
have come that they may have life, and
have it to the full.

11"I am the good shepherd. The good
shepherd lays down his life for the sheep.
12The hired hand is not the shepherd who
owns the sheep. So when he sees the wolf
coming, he abandons the sheep and runs
away. Then the wolf attacks the flock and
scatters it. 13The man runs away because
he is a hired hand and cares nothing for the
sheep.

14"I am the good shepherd; I know my
sheep and my sheep know me— 15just as
the Father knows me and I know the Father—and I lay down my life for the sheep.
16I have other sheep that are not of this
sheep pen. I must bring them also. They
too will listen to my voice, and there shall
be one flock and one shepherd. 17The reason my Father loves me is that I lay down
my life—only to take it up again. 18No one
takes it from me, but I lay it down of my
own accord. I have authority to lay it down
and authority to take it up again. This command I received from my Father." ●

19At these words the Jews were again
divided. 20Many of them said, "He is demon-possessed and raving mad. Why listen to him?"

21But others said, "These are not the
sayings of a man possessed by a demon.
Can a demon open the eyes of the blind?" ●

[a]9 Or *kept safe*

KING JAMES

1. PARABLE

**10** Verily, verily, I say unto you, He
that entereth not by the door into
the sheepfold, but climbeth up some other
way, the same is a thief and a robber.
2 But he that entereth in by the door is the
shepherd of the sheep. 3 To him the porter openeth; and the sheep hear his voice:
and he calleth his own sheep by name, and
leadeth them out. 4 And when he putteth
forth his own sheep, he goeth before them,
and the sheep follow him: for they know
his voice. 5 And a stranger will they not
follow, but will flee from him; for they
know not the voice of strangers. 6 This
parable spake Jesus unto them; but they
understood not what things they were
which he spake unto them.●

2. INTERPRETATION

7 Then said Jesus unto them again,
Verily, verily, I say unto you, I am the
door of the sheep. 8 All that ever came
before me are thieves and robbers: but the
sheep did not hear them. 9 I am the door:
by me if any man enter in, he shall be
saved, and shall go in and out, and find
pasture. 10 The thief cometh not, but for
to steal, and to kill, and to destroy: I am
come that they might have life, and that
they might have *it* more abundantly. 11 I
am the good shepherd: the good shepherd
giveth his life for the sheep. 12 But he
that is a hireling, and not the shepherd,
whose own the sheep are not, seeth the
wolf coming, and leaveth the sheep, and
fleeth; and the wolf catcheth them, and
scattereth the sheep. 13 The hireling
fleeth, because he is a hireling, and careth
not for the sheep. 14 I am the good shepherd, and know my *sheep*, and am known
of mine. 15 As the Father knoweth me,
even so know I the Father: and I lay
down my life for the sheep. 16 And other
sheep I have, which are not of this fold:
them also I must bring, and they shall
hear my voice; and there shall be one
fold, *and* one shepherd. 17 Therefore
doth my Father love me, because I lay
down my life, that I might take it again.
18 No man taketh it from me, but I lay it
down of myself. I have power to lay it
down, and I have power to take it again.
This commandment have I received of my
Father.●

3. REACTIONS

19 There was a division therefore again
among the Jews for these sayings. 20 And
many of them said, He hath a devil, and
is mad; why hear ye him? 21 Others said,
These are not the words of him that hath
a devil. Can a devil open the eyes of the
blind?●

SHEPHERD

DEVIL

First read 9:34-38. Jesus brought the man into fellowship with Himself. Relate this setting to this segment about the good shepherd

*10:1-6* Record the main parts of the parable.

*10:7-18* Record the teachings of Jesus about the shepherd and the sheep.

SHEPHERD ____________

SHEEP ____________

*10:19-21* What are your observations here?

NEW INTERNATIONAL VERSION

What does this passage teach about:

MIRACLES AS SIGNS

CREDENTIALS OF JESUS' DEITY

THE FATHER

Record spiritual applications to be made from this passage.

*The Unbelief of the Jews*

22Then came the Feast of Dedication[b] at
Jerusalem. It was winter, 23and Jesus was
in the temple area walking in Solomon's
Colonnade. 24The Jews gathered around
him, saying, "How long will you keep us
in suspense? If you are the Christ,[c] tell us
plainly."

25Jesus answered, "I did tell you, but
you do not believe. The miracles I do in my
Father's name speak for me, 26but you do
not believe because you are not my sheep.
27My sheep listen to my voice; I know
them, and they follow me. 28I give them
eternal life, and they shall never perish; no
one can snatch them out of my hand. 29My
Father, who has given them to me, is
greater than all[d]; no one can snatch them
out of my Father's hand. 30I and the Father
are one."●

31Again the Jews picked up stones to
stone him, 32but Jesus said to them, "I
have shown you many great miracles from
the Father. For which of these do you
stone me?"

33"We are not stoning you for any of
these," replied the Jews, "but for blasphemy, because you, a mere man, claim to be
God."

34Jesus answered them, "Is it not written
in your Law, 'I have said you are gods'[e]?
35If he called them 'gods,' to whom the
word of God came—and the Scripture cannot be broken— 36what about the one
whom the Father set apart as his very own
and sent into the world? Why then do you
accuse me of blasphemy because I said, 'I
am God's Son'? 37Do not believe me unless
I do what my Father does. 38But if I do it,
even though you do not believe me, believe
the miracles, that you may learn and understand that the Father is in me, and I in
the Father." 39Again they tried to seize
him, but he escaped their grasp.●

40Then Jesus went back across the Jordan to the place where John had been baptizing in the early days. Here he stayed
41and many people came to him. They said,
"Though John never performed a miraculous sign, all that John said about this man
was true." 42And in that place many believed in Jesus.●

[b]22 That is, Hanukkah
[c]24 Or *Messiah*
[d]29 Many early manuscripts *What my Father has given me is greater than all*
[e]34 Psalm 82:6

KING JAMES

1. JEWS QUESTION JESUS

IN THE TEMPLE: MIRACLES DENIED

22 And it was at Jerusalem the feast of
the dedication, and it was winter. 23 And
Jesus walked in the temple in Solomon's
porch. 24 Then came the Jews round
about him, and said unto him, How long
dost thou make us to doubt? If thou be
the Christ, tell us plainly. 25 Jesus answered them, I told you, and ye believed
not: the works that I do in my Father's
name, they bear witness of me. 26 But ye
believe not, because ye are not of my
sheep, as I said unto you. 27 My sheep
hear my voice, and I know them, and they
follow me: 28 and I give unto them eternal life; and they shall never perish, neither shall any *man* pluck them out of my
hand. 29 My Father, which gave *them* me,
is greater than all; and no *man* is able to
pluck *them* out of my Father's hand.
30 I and *my* Father are one.●

2. JEWS CHARGE JESUS

31 Then the Jews took up stones again
to stone him. 32 Jesus answered them,
Many good works have I showed you from
my Father; for which of those works do
ye stone me? 33 The Jews answered him,
saying, For a good work we stone thee
not; but for blasphemy; and because that
thou, being a man, makest thyself God.
34 Jesus answered them, Is it not written
in your law, I said, Ye are gods ? 35 If he
called them gods, unto whom the word of
God came, and the Scripture cannot be
broken; 36 say ye of him, whom the
Father hath sanctified, and sent into the
world, Thou blasphemest; because I said,
I am the Son of God? 37 If I do not the
works of my Father, believe me not.
38 But if I do, though ye believe not me,
believe the works; that ye may know,
and believe, that the Father *is* in me, and
I in him.

Ps. 82:6

39 Therefore they sought again to take
him; but he escaped out of their hand,●

3. SOME PEOPLE BELIEVE

BEYOND THE JORDAN: MIRACLES BELIEVED

40 and went away again beyond Jordan
into the place where John at first baptized; and there he abode. 41 And many
resorted unto him and said, John did no
miracle: but all things that John spake of
this man were true. 42 And many believed on him there.●

There is an interval of about 2 months between the preceding segment and this one. Luke 10-13 records events of this interval.

For a connection in John's reporting, compare 10:3 and 10:27.

*10:22-30* What did the Jews want to know?

What was Jesus' answer?

Analyze verses 27-30 carefully.

*10:31-39* What did the Jews charge Jesus with?

Analyze Jesus' reply.

*10:40-42* Record your observations.

NEW INTERNATIONAL VERSION

Record what this passage teaches about:

GLORY OF GOD

FAITH

DEATH

LIFE

List some practical lessons taught here.

*The Death of Lazarus*

11 Now a man named Lazarus was
sick. He was from Bethany, the village of Mary and her sister Martha. 2This
Mary, whose brother Lazarus now lay
sick, was the same one who poured perfume on the Lord and wiped his feet with
her hair. 3So the sisters sent word to Jesus,
"Lord, the one you love is sick."
4When he heard this, Jesus said, "This
sickness will not end in death. No, it is for
God's glory so that God's Son may be
glorified through it." ● 5Jesus loved Martha
and her sister and Lazarus. 6Yet when he
heard that Lazarus was sick, he stayed
where he was two more days.
7Then he said to his disciples, "Let us go
back to Judea."
8"But Rabbi," they said, "a short while
ago the Jews tried to stone you, and yet
you are going back there?"
9Jesus answered, "Are there not twelve
hours of daylight? A man who walks by day
will not stumble, for he sees by this world's
light. 10It is when he walks by night that he
stumbles, for he has no light." ●
11After he had said this, he went on to tell
them, "Our friend Lazarus has fallen
asleep; but I am going there to wake him
up."
12His disciples replied, "Lord, if he
sleeps, he will get better." 13Jesus had
been speaking of his death, but his disciples thought he meant natural sleep.
14So then he told them plainly, "Lazarus
is dead, 15and for your sake I am glad I was
not there, so that you may believe. But let
us go to him."
16Then Thomas (called Didymus) said to
the rest of the disciples, "Let us also go,
that we may die with him." ●

KING JAMES

1. LAZARUS IS SICK

11 Now a certain *man* was sick, *named*
Lazarus, of Bethany, the town of
Mary and her sister Martha. 2 (It was
*that* Mary which anointed the Lord with
ointment, and wiped his feet with her
hair, whose brother Lazarus was sick.)
3 Therefore his sisters sent unto him,
saying, Lord, behold, he whom thou
lovest is sick. 4 When Jesus heard
*that*, he said, This sickness is not unto
death, but for the glory of God, that
the Son of God might be glorified
thereby. ●

GLORY OF GOD

2. JESUS TARRIES

5 Now Jesus loved Martha, and her
sister, and Lazarus. 6 When he had heard
therefore that he was sick, he abode two
days still in the same place where he was.
7 Then after that saith he to *his* disciples,
Let us go into Judea again. 8 *His* disciples say unto him, Master, the Jews of
late sought to stone thee; and goest thou
thither again? 9 Jesus answered, Are
there not twelve hours in the day? If any
man walk in the day, he stumbleth not,
because he seeth the light of this world.
10 But if a man walk in the night, he
stumbleth, because there is no light in
him. ●

3. LAZARUS IS DEAD

11 These things said he: and after
that he saith unto them, Our friend Lazarus sleepeth; but I go, that I may awake
him out of sleep. 12 Then said his disciples, Lord, if he sleep, he shall do well.
13 Howbeit Jesus spake of his death: but
they thought that he had spoken of taking
of rest in sleep. 14 Then said Jesus unto
them plainly, Lazarus is dead. 15 And I
am glad for your sakes that I was not
there, to the intent ye may believe; nevertheless let us go unto him. 16 Then said
Thomas, which is called Did'ymus, unto
his fellow disciples, Let us also go, that
we may die with him. ●

BELIEF OF DISCIPLES

Jesus was in Perea when the report of Lazarus' sickness came to Him. What was Lazarus' home town?
Fit the geography of verse 7 into this picture.

Record observations for each paragraph:

*11:1-4*

EVENTS (1-3)

JESUS' TEACHING (4)

*11:5-10*

EVENTS (5-8)

JESUS' TEACHING (9-10)

*11:11-16* Explain these two verses:

*verse 15*

*verse 16*

NEW INTERNATIONAL VERSION

What do you learn here about:

RESURRECTION OF THE BODY

ETERNAL LIFE

FAITH

DEATH

GRIEF

LOVE OF JESUS

OTHER

*Jesus Comforts the Sisters*

17On his arrival, Jesus found that Lazarus had already been in the tomb for four
days. 18Bethany was less than two miles[a]
from Jerusalem, 19and many Jews had
come to Martha and Mary to comfort them
in the loss of their brother. 20When Martha
heard that Jesus was coming, she went out
to meet him, but Mary stayed at home.
21"Lord," Martha said to Jesus, "if you
had been here, my brother would not have
died. 22But I know that even now God will
give you whatever you ask."
23Jesus said to her, "Your brother will
rise again."
24Martha answered, "I know he will rise
again in the resurrection at the last day."
25Jesus said to her, "I am the resurrection and the life. He who believes in me
will live, even though he dies; 26and whoever lives and believes in me will never die.
Do you believe this?"
27"Yes, Lord," she told him, "I believe
that you are the Christ,[b] the Son of God,
who was to come into the world."●
28And after she had said this, she went
back and called her sister Mary aside.
"The Teacher is here," she said, "and is
asking for you." 29When Mary heard this,
she got up quickly and went to him. 30Now
Jesus had not yet entered the village, but
was still at the place where Martha had met
him. 31When the Jews who had been with
Mary in the house, comforting her, noticed
how quickly she got up and went out, they
followed her, supposing she was going to
the tomb to mourn there.●
32When Mary reached the place where
Jesus was and saw him, she fell at his feet
and said, "Lord, if you had been here, my
brother would not have died."
33When Jesus saw her weeping, and the
Jews who had come along with her also
weeping, he was deeply moved in spirit
and troubled. 34"Where have you laid
him?" he asked.
"Come and see, Lord," they replied.
35Jesus wept.
36Then the Jews said, "See how he loved
him!"
37But some of them said, "Could not he
who opened the eyes of the blind man have
kept this man from dying?"●

[a] *18* Greek *fifteen stadia* (about 3 kilometers)
[b] *27* Or *Messiah*

KING JAMES

**1. MARTHA'S FAITH**

17 Then when Jesus came, he found
that he had *lain* in the grave four days
already. 18 Now Bethany was nigh unto
Jerusalem, about fifteen furlongs off:
19 and many of the Jews came to Martha
and Mary, to comfort them concerning
their brother. 20 Then Martha, as soon
as she heard that Jesus was coming, went
and met him: but Mary sat *still* in the
house. 21 Then said Martha unto Jesus,
Lord, if thou hadst been here, my brother
had not died. 22 But I know, that even
now, whatsoever thou wilt ask of God,
God will give *it* thee. 23 Jesus saith unto
her, Thy brother shall rise again.
24 Martha saith unto him, I know that
he shall rise again in the resurrection at
the last day. 25 Jesus said unto her, I am
the resurrection, and the life: he that believeth in me, though he were dead,
yet shall he live: 26 and whosoever
liveth and believeth in me shall never
die. Believest thou this? 27 She
saith unto him, Yea, Lord: I believe
that thou art the Christ, the Son of
God, which should come into the
world.●

**JESUS GIVES LIFE**

**2. MARY GOES TO JESUS**

28 And when she had so said, she went
her way, and called Mary her sister secretly, saying, The Master is come, and
calleth for thee. 29 As soon as she heard
*that*, she arose quickly, and came unto
him. 30 Now Jesus was not yet come into
the town, but was in that place where
Martha met him. 31 The Jews then which
were with her in the house, and comforted
her, when they saw Mary, that she rose up
hastily and went out, followed her, saying,
She goeth unto the grave to weep there.●

**3. MARY'S GRIEF**

32 Then when Mary was come where
Jesus was, and saw him, she fell down at
his feet, saying unto him, Lord, if thou
hadst been here, my brother had not died.
33 When Jesus therefore saw her weeping,
and the Jews also weeping which came
with her, he groaned in the spirit, and was
troubled, 34 and said, Where have ye
laid him? They say unto him, Lord, come
and see. 35 Jesus wept. 36 Then said the
Jews, Behold how he loved him! 37 And
some of them said, Could not this man,
which opened the eyes of the blind, have
caused that even this man should not have
died?●

**JESUS SHARES LOVE**

Man's worst predicament is that he wants to live but he must die. Study this passage with this in mind.

*11:17-27* Record the teachings of verses 22-27:

MARTHA ______________________________

JESUS ______________________________

*11:28-31* Compare verses 29 and 21.

*11:32-37* Compare verse 32 with verse 21.

Then compare verses 33ff. with verses 22ff.

NEW INTERNATIONAL VERSION

Record everything you see taught by this passage, whether directly or indirectly, about MIRACLES.

List various spiritual applications which can be made from the story of Lazarus (11:1-46).

### *Jesus Raises Lazarus From the Dead*

38 Jesus, once more deeply moved, came
to the tomb. It was a cave with a stone laid
across the entrance. 39 "Take away the
stone," he said.
"But, Lord," said Martha, the sister of
the dead man, "by this time there is a bad
odor, for he has been there four days."
40 Then Jesus said, "Did I not tell you
that if you believed, you would see the
glory of God?"
41 So they took away the stone. Then
Jesus looked up and said, "Father, I thank
you that you have heard me. 42 I knew that
you always hear me, but I said this for the
benefit of the people standing here, that
they may believe that you sent me."●
43 When he had said this, Jesus called in
a loud voice, "Lazarus, come out!" 44 The
dead man came out, his hands and feet
wrapped with strips of linen, and a cloth
around his face.
Jesus said to them, "Take off the grave
clothes and let him go."●

### *The Plot to Kill Jesus*

45 Therefore many of the Jews who had
come to visit Mary, and had seen what
Jesus did, put their faith in him. 46 But some
of them went to the Pharisees and told
them what Jesus had done●

KING JAMES

**1. JESUS PRAYS**

BELIEVING TO SEE

38 Jesus therefore again groaning in
himself cometh to the grave. It was a
cave, and a stone lay upon it. 39 Jesus
said, Take ye away the stone. Martha, the
sister of him that was dead, saith unto
him, Lord, by this time he stinketh: for he
hath been *dead* four days. 40 Jesus saith
unto her, Said I not unto thee, that, if
thou wouldest believe, thou shouldest see
the glory of God? 41 Then they took
away the stone *from the place* where the
dead was laid. And Jesus lifted up *his*
eyes, and said, Father, I thank thee that
thou hast heard me. 42 And I knew that
thou hearest me always: but because of
the people which stand by I said *it*, that
they may believe that thou hast sent me.●

**2. LAZARUS COMES FORTH**

43 And when he thus had spoken, he
cried with a loud voice, Lazarus, come
forth. 44 And he that was dead came
forth, bound hand and foot with grave-
clothes; and his face was bound about
with a napkin. Jesus saith unto them,
Loose him, and let him go.●

**3. REACTIONS OF THE JEWS**

BELIEVING FOR SEEING

45 Then many of the Jews which came
to Mary, and had seen the things which
Jesus did, believed on him. 46 But some
of them went their ways to the Pharisees,
and told them what things Jesus had done.●

*11:38-42* Record what is taught by these verses:

*verse 40* __________

*verses 41-42* __________

*11:43-44* What are your impressions? __________

*11:45-46* Compare verses 45 and 46. __________

NEW INTERNATIONAL VERSION

List every reference to opposition to Jesus in this passage.

What do you learn about Jesus here?

[47]Then the
chief priests and the Pharisees called a
meeting of the Sanhedrin.
"What are we accomplishing?" they
asked. "Here is this man performing many
miraculous signs. [48]If we let him go on like
this, everyone will believe in him, and then
the Romans will come and take away both
our place[a] and our nation."
[49]Then one of them, named Caiaphas,
who was high priest that year, spoke up,
"You know nothing at all! [50]You do not
realize that it is better for you that one man
die for the people than that the whole nation perish."
[51]He did not say this on his own, but as
high priest that year he prophesied that
Jesus would die for the Jewish nation,
[52]and not only for that nation but also for
the scattered children of God, to bring
them together and make them one.● [53]So
from that day on they plotted to take his
life.
[54]Therefore Jesus no longer moved
about publicly among the Jews. Instead he
withdrew to a region near the desert, to a
village called Ephraim, where he stayed
with his disciples.●
[55]When it was almost time for the Jewish
Passover, many went up from the country
to Jerusalem for their ceremonial cleansing
before the Passover. [56]They kept looking
for Jesus, and as they stood in the temple
area they asked one another, "What do
you think? Isn't he coming to the Feast at
all?" [57]But the chief priests and Pharisees
had given orders that if anyone found out
where Jesus was, he should report it so that
they might arrest him.●

[a]48 Or *temple*

KING JAMES

1. HIGH PRIEST'S PROPHECY

47 Then gathered the chief priests and the
Pharisees a council, and said, What do
we? for this man doeth many miracles.
48 If we let him thus alone, all *men* will
believe on him; and the Romans shall
come and take away both our place and
nation. 49 And one of them, *named*
Cai'aphas, being the high priest that same
year, said unto them, Ye know nothing
at all, 50 nor consider that it is expedient
for us, that one man should die for the
people, and that the whole nation perish
not. 51 And this spake he not of himself:
but being high priest that year, he prophesied that Jesus should die for that nation;
52 and not for that nation only, but that
also he should gather together in one the
children of God that were scattered
abroad. ●

TAKE US AWAY

2. JESUS HIDES

53 Then from that day forth they
took counsel together for to put him to
death.
54 Jesus therefore walked no more
openly among the Jews; but went thence
unto a country near to the wilderness, into
a city called E'phra-im, and there continued with his disciples. ●

3. PEOPLE SEEK JESUS

55 And the Jews' passover was nigh at
hand: and many went out of the country
up to Jerusalem before the passover, to
purify themselves. 56 Then sought they
for Jesus, and spake among themselves,
as they stood in the temple, What think
ye, that he will not come to the feast?
57 Now both the chief priests and the
Pharisees had given a commandment,
that, if any man knew where he were, he
should show *it*, that they might take
him. ●

TAKE HIM

This is the first of two sequels to the raising of Lazarus.

*11:47-52* What was the religious leaders' predicament?

Compare Caiaphas' prophecy (v.50) and John's commentary on it (vv.51-52).

*11:53-54* Record your observations and impressions.

*11:55-57* Record observations and impressions.

NEW INTERNATIONAL VERSION

Record what the passage teaches about:

HUMILITY

DEVOTION

PROPHECY

WORSHIP

Record spiritual applications below:

*Jesus Anointed at Bethany*

12 Six days before the Passover, Jesus
arrived at Bethany, where Lazarus
lived, whom Jesus had raised from the
dead. 2Here a dinner was given in Jesus'
honor. Martha served, while Lazarus was
among those reclining at the table with
him. 3Then Mary took about a pint[b] of pure
nard, an expensive perfume; she poured it
on Jesus' feet and wiped his feet with her
hair. And the house was filled with the
fragrance of the perfume.
4But one of his disciples, Judas Iscariot,
who was later to betray him, objected,
5"Why wasn't this perfume sold and the
money given to the poor? It was worth a
year's wages.[c]" 6He did not say this because he cared about the poor but because
he was a thief; as keeper of the money bag,
he used to help himself to what was put
into it.
7"Leave her alone," Jesus replied. "It
was meant that she should save this perfume for the day of my burial. 8You will
always have the poor among you, but you
will not always have me."●
9Meanwhile a large crowd of Jews found
out that Jesus was there and came, not only
because of him but also to see Lazarus,
whom he had raised from the dead. 10So
the chief priests made plans to kill Lazarus
as well, 11for on account of him many of the
Jews were going over to Jesus and putting
their faith in him.●

*The Triumphal Entry*

12The next day the great crowd that had
come for the Feast heard that Jesus was on
his way to Jerusalem. 13They took palm
branches and went out to meet him, shouting,

"Hosanna![d]"

"Blessed is he who comes in the
name of the Lord!"[e]

"Blessed is the King of Israel!"

14Jesus found a young donkey and sat upon
it, as it is written,

15"Do not be afraid, O Daughter of
Zion;
see, your king is coming,
seated on a donkey's colt."[f]●

16At first his disciples did not understand
all this. Only after Jesus was glorified did
they realize that these things had been
written about him and that they had done
these things to him.
17Now the crowd that was with him had
continued to spread the word that he had
called Lazarus from the tomb, raising him
from the dead.[a] 18Many people, because
they had heard that he had given this miraculous sign, went out to meet him. 19So
the Pharisees said to one another, "See,
this is getting us nowhere. Look how the
whole world has gone after him!"●

[b]3 Greek *a litra* (probably about 0.5 liter)
[c]5 Greek *three hundred denarii*
[d]13 A Hebrew expression meaning "Save!" which became an exclamation of praise
[e]13 Psalm 118:25, 26 [f]15 Zech. 9:9
[a]17 Or *Now the crowd that had been with him when he called Lazarus from the tomb and raised him from the dead were telling everyone*

KING JAMES

1. SUPPER IN BETHANY

INNER CIRCLE

12 Then Jesus six days before the passover came to Bethany, where Lazarus was which had been dead, whom he
raised from the dead. 2 There they made
him a supper; and Martha served: but
Lazarus was one of them that sat at the
table with him. 3 Then took Mary a
pound of ointment of spikenard, very
costly, and anointed the feet of Jesus, and
wiped his feet with her hair: and the
house was filled with the odor of the ointment. 4 Then saith one of his disciples,
Judas Iscar'i-ot, Simon's *son*, which
should betray him, 5 Why was not this
ointment sold for three hundred pence,
and given to the poor? 6 This he said, not
that he cared for the poor; but because he
was a thief, and had the bag, and bare*
what was put therein. 7 Then said Jesus,
Let her alone: against the day of my burying hath she kept this. 8 For the poor
always ye have with you; but me ye have
not always.●

2. PLOT AGAINST LAZARUS

9 Much people of the Jews therefore
knew that he was there: and they came
not for Jesus' sake only, but that they
might see Lazarus also, whom he had
raised from the dead. 10 But the chief
priests consulted that they might put
Lazarus also to death; 11 because that
by reason of him many of the Jews went
away, and believed on Jesus.●

3. ENTRY INTO JERUSALEM

12 On the next day much people that
were come to the feast, when they heard
that Jesus was coming to Jerusalem,
13 took branches of palm trees, and went
forth to meet him, and cried,

Hosanna:
Blessed *is* the King of Israel
that cometh in the name of the Lord. Ps. 118:25f.

14 And Jesus, when he had found a young
ass, sat thereon; as it is written, Zech. 9:9

15 Fear not, daughter of Zion:
behold, thy King cometh,
sitting on an ass's colt. ●

4. DIFFERENT REACTIONS

16 These things understood not his disciples at the first: but when Jesus was
glorified, then remembered they that these
things were written of him, and *that* they
had done these things unto him. 17 The
people therefore that was with him when
he called Lazarus out of his grave, and
raised him from the dead, bare record.
18 For this cause the people also met him,
for that they heard that he had done this
miracle. 19 The Pharisees therefore said
among themselves, Perceive ye how ye
prevail nothing? behold, the world is
gone after him.●

WHOLE WORLD

Jesus' march into Jerusalem (vv.12ff.) took place on Sunday, the first of the six days of Passion Week. On Friday Jesus would be hanging on the cross.

*12:1-8* What did the ointment symbolize (v.7)?

*12:9-11* What does this paragraph reveal about the Lazarus miracle? (Cf. vv.17-18)

*12:12-15* Do you see any contrasts in the two Old Testament quotations?

*12:16-19* Record the different reactions.

NEW INTERNATIONAL VERSION

What is taught here about:

SON OF MAN

CRUCIFIXION OF JESUS

DISCIPLESHIP

GLORIFICATION OF FATHER

SPIRITUAL DARKNESS

OTHER

*Jesus Predicts His Death*

20Now there were some Greeks among
those who went up to worship at the Feast.
21They came to Philip, who was from Bethsaida in Galilee, with a request. "Sir,"
they said, "we would like to see Jesus."
22Philip went to tell Andrew; Andrew and
Philip in turn told Jesus.
23Jesus replied, "The hour has come for
the Son of Man to be glorified. 24I tell you
the truth, unless a kernel of wheat falls to
the ground and dies, it remains only a single seed. But if it dies, it produces many
seeds. 25The man who loves his life will
lose it, while the man who hates his life in
this world will keep it for eternal life.
26Whoever serves me must follow me; and
where I am, my servant also will be. My
Father will honor the one who serves me.●
27"Now my heart is troubled, and what
shall I say? 'Father, save me from this
hour'? No, it was for this very reason I
came to this hour. 28Father, glorify your
name!"

Then a voice came from heaven, "I have
glorified it, and will glorify it again." 29The
crowd that was there and heard it said it
had thundered; others said an angel had
spoken to him.
30Jesus said, "This voice was for your
benefit, not mine. 31Now is the time for
judgment on this world; now the prince of
this world will be driven out. 32But I, when
I am lifted up from the earth, will draw all
men to myself." 33He said this to show the
kind of death he was going to die.
34The crowd spoke up, "We have heard
from the Law that the Christ[b] will remain
forever, so how can you say, 'The Son of
Man must be lifted up'? Who is this 'Son of
Man'?"●
35Then Jesus told them, "You are going
to have the light just a little while longer.
Walk while you have the light, before darkness overtakes you. The man who walks in
the dark does not know where he is going.
36Put your trust in the light while you have
it, so that you may become sons of light."●

[b]34 Or *Messiah*

## KING JAMES

**1. GREEKS SEEK JESUS**

20 And there were certain Greeks
among them that came up to worship at
the feast: 21 the same came therefore to
Philip, which was of Bethsai′da of Galilee, and desired him, saying, Sir, we
would see Jesus. 22 Philip cometh and
telleth Andrew: and again Andrew and
Philip tell Jesus. 23 And Jesus answered
them, saying, The hour is come, that the
Son of man should be glorified. 24 Verily,
verily, I say unto you, Except a corn of
wheat fall into the ground and die, it
abideth alone: but if it die, it bringeth
forth much fruit. 25 He that loveth his
life shall lose it; and he that hateth his life
in this world shall keep it unto life eternal.
26 If any man serve me, let him follow
me; and where I am, there shall also my
servant be: if any man serve me, him will
*my* Father honor.●

**2. JESUS FORETELLS HIS DEATH**

27 Now is my soul troubled; and what
shall I say? Father, save me from this
hour: but for this cause came I unto this
hour. 28 Father, glorify thy name. Then
came there a voice from heaven, *saying*, I
have both glorified *it*, and will glorify *it*
again. 29 The people therefore that stood
by, and heard *it*, said that it thundered:
others said, An angel spake to him.
30 Jesus answered and said, This voice
came not because of me, but for your
sakes. 31 Now is the judgment of this
world: now shall the prince of this world
be cast out. 32 And I, if I be lifted up
from the earth, will draw all *men* unto me.
33 This he said, signifying what death he
should die. 34 The people answered him,
We have heard out of the law that Christ
abideth for ever: and how sayest thou,
The Son of man must be lifted up? who is
this Son of man?●

**3. JESUS AS THE LIGHT**

35 Then Jesus said unto
them, Yet a little while is the light with
you. Walk while ye have the light, lest
darkness come upon you: for he that
walketh in darkness knoweth not whither
he goeth. 36 While ye have light, believe
in the light, that ye may be the children
of light.●

HOUR OF CHRIST'S GLORIFICATION

REDEMPTION

REVELATION

This is the concluding passage of the section of John's gospel called YEARS OF CONFLICT. What makes verse 21 significant, in view of the increasing opposition against Jesus at this time?

*12:20-26* What was Jesus' response to the Greeks' quest?

*12:27-34* Record observations.

*12:35-36a* Compare the two command words, "Walk" and "Believe."

NEW INTERNATIONAL VERSION

What do you learn here about:

THE PURPOSE OF MIRACLES

BELIEF

UNBELIEF

HARDNESS OF HEART

JUDGMENT

FATHER-SON RELATIONSHIP

OTHER

When he had finished speaking, Jesus left
and hid himself from them.

*The Jews Continue in Their Unbelief*

37Even after Jesus had done all these miraculous signs in their presence, they still
would not believe in him. 38This was to
fulfill the word of Isaiah the prophet:

"Lord, who has believed our
message
and to whom has the arm of the
Lord been revealed?"[c]

39For this reason they could not believe,
because, as Isaiah says elsewhere:

40"He has blinded their eyes
and deadened their hearts,
so they can neither see with their
eyes,
nor understand with their hearts,
nor turn—and I would heal
them."[d]

41Isaiah said this because he saw Jesus'
glory and spoke about him.
42Yet at the same time many even among
the leaders believed in him. But because of
the Pharisees they would not confess their
faith for fear they would be put out of the
synagogue; 43for they loved praise from
men more than praise from God.●
44Then Jesus cried out, "When a man
believes in me, he does not believe in me
only, but in the one who sent me. 45When
he looks at me, he sees the one who sent
me. 46I have come into the world as a light,
so that no one who believes in me should
stay in darkness.
47"As for the person who hears my
words but does not keep them, I do not
judge him. For I did not come to judge the
world, but to save it. 48There is a judge for
the one who rejects me and does not accept
my words; that very word which I spoke
will condemn him at the last day. 49For I
did not speak of my own accord, but the
Father who sent me commanded me what
to say and how to say it. 50I know that his
command leads to eternal life. So whatever
I say is just what the Father has told me to
say."●

c38 Isaiah 53:1 d40 Isaiah 6:10

## KING JAMES

### 1. PEOPLE'S UNBELIEF

JESUS REJECTED BY PEOPLE

These things spake Jesus, and departed,
and did hide himself from them. 37 But
though he had done so many miracles
before them, yet they believed not on him:
38 that the saying of Isaiah the prophet
might be fulfilled, which he spake,
Lord, who hath believed our report?
and to whom hath the arm of the
Lord been revealed?
39 Therefore they could not believe, because that Isaiah said again,
40 He hath blinded their eyes, and
hardened their heart;
that they should not see with *their*
eyes,
nor understand with *their* heart,
and be converted, and I should heal
them.
41 These things said Isaiah, when he saw
his glory, and spake of him. 42 Nevertheless among the chief rulers also many
believed on him; but because of the Pharisees they did not confess *him*, lest they
should be put out of the synagogue:
43 for they loved the praise of men more
than the praise of God.●

Isa. 53:1

Isa. 6:10

### 2. JUDGMENT BY THE WORLD

44 Jesus cried and said, He that believeth on me, believeth not on me, but on
him that sent me. 45 And he that seeth
me seeth him that sent me. 46 I am come
a light into the world, that whosoever believeth on me should not abide in darkness. 47 And if any man hear my words,
and believe not, I judge him not: for I
came not to judge the world, but to save
the world. 48 He that rejecteth me, and
receiveth not my words, hath one that
judgeth him: the word that I have spoken,
the same shall judge him in the last day.
49 For I have not spoken of myself; but
the Father which sent me, he gave me a
commandment, what I should say, and
what I should speak. 50 And I know that
his commandment is life everlasting:
whatsoever I speak therefore, even as the
Father said unto me, so I speak.●

JESUS SENT BY THE FATHER

At this point in his gospel John begins to concentrate on Jesus' private ministry to His disciples. This segment is a transition from the public ministry recorded in the earlier section to the private ministry that follows (cf.13:1ff).

*12:36b-43* Observe John's three comments on the people's unbelief:
-not logical (12:37)
-foretold (12:38)
-from hardness of heart (12:39-40)

Record the statements that follow these words (vv.42-43):

nevertheless ______________________

______________________

______________________

______________________

but ______________________

______________________

______________________

______________________

lest ______________________

______________________

______________________

______________________

for ______________________

______________________

______________________

______________________

*12:44-50* Record observations

______________________

______________________

______________________

______________________

______________________

______________________

______________________

______________________

______________________

______________________

NEW INTERNATIONAL VERSION

What do you learn here about:

LOVE

CLEAN HEART

HUMILITY

SERVICE

FELLOWSHIP

OBEDIENCE

OTHER

*Jesus Washes His Disciples' Feet*

13 It was just before the Passover
Feast. Jesus knew that the time had
come for him to leave this world and go to
the Father. Having loved his own who
were in the world, he now showed them the
full extent of his love.[e]
2 The evening meal was being served, and
the devil had already prompted Judas Iscariot, son of Simon, to betray Jesus.
3 Jesus knew that the Father had put all
things under his power, and that he had
come from God and was returning to God;
4 so he got up from the meal, took off his
outer clothing, and wrapped a towel
around his waist. 5 After that, he poured
water into a basin and began to wash his
disciples' feet, drying them with the towel
that was wrapped around him.●
6 He came to Simon Peter, who said to
him, "Lord, are you going to wash my
feet?"
7 Jesus replied, "You do not realize now
what I am doing, but later you will understand."
8 "No," said Peter, "you shall never
wash my feet."
Jesus answered, "Unless I wash you,
you have no part with me."
9 "Then, Lord," Simon Peter replied,
"not just my feet but my hands and my
head as well!"
10 Jesus answered, "A person who has
had a bath needs only to wash his feet; his
whole body is clean. And you are clean,
though not every one of you." 11 For he
knew who was going to betray him, and
that was why he said not every one was
clean.●
12 When he had finished washing their
feet, he put on his clothes and returned to
his place. "Do you understand what I have
done for you?" he asked them. 13 "You call
me 'Teacher' and 'Lord,' and rightly so,
for that is what I am. 14 Now that I, your
Lord and Teacher, have washed your feet,
you also should wash one another's feet.
15 I have set you an example that you
should do as I have done for you. 16 I tell
you the truth, no servant is greater than his
master, nor is a messenger greater than the
one who sent him. 17 Now that you know
these things, you will be blessed if you do
them.●

*Jesus Predicts His Betrayal*

18 "I am not referring to all of you; I know
those I have chosen. But this is to fulfill the
scripture: 'He who shares my bread has
lifted up his heel against me.'[a]
19 "I am telling you now before it happens, so that when it does happen you will
believe that I am He. 20 I tell you the truth,
whoever accepts anyone I send accepts
me; and whoever accepts me accepts the
one who sent me."●

[e] *1* Or *he loved them to the last*
[a] *18* Psalm 41:9

KING JAMES

**1. JESUS WASHES DISCIPLES' FEET**

LOVE

13 Now before the feast of the passover, when Jesus knew that his hour
was come that he should depart out of
this world unto the Father, having loved
his own which were in the world, he loved
them unto the end. 2 And supper being
ended, the devil having now put into the
heart of Judas Iscar'i-ot, Simon's *son*, to
betray him; 3 Jesus knowing that the
Father had given all things into his hands,
and that he was come from God, and
went to God; 4 he riseth from supper,
and laid aside his garments; and took a
towel, and girded himself. 5 After that he
poureth water into a basin, and began to
wash the disciples' feet, and to wipe *them*
with the towel wherewith he was girded.●

**2. PETER OBJECTS**

6 Then cometh he to Simon Peter: and
Peter saith unto him, Lord, dost thou
wash my feet? 7 Jesus answered and said
unto him, What I do thou knowest not
now; but thou shalt know hereafter.
8 Peter saith unto him, Thou shalt never
wash my feet. Jesus answered him, If I
wash thee not, thou hast no part with me.
9 Simon Peter saith unto him, Lord, not
my feet only, but also *my* hands and *my*
head. 10 Jesus saith to him, He that is
washed needeth not save to wash *his* feet,
but is clean every whit: and ye are clean,
but not all. 11 For he knew who should
betray him; therefore said he, Ye are not
all clean.●

**3. JESUS EXPLAINS**

12 So after he had washed their feet,
and had taken his garments, and was set
down again, he said unto them, Know ye
what I have done to you? 13 Ye call me
Master and Lord: and ye say well; for *so*
I am. 14 If I then, *your* Lord and Master,
have washed your feet; ye also ought to
wash one another's feet. 15 For I have
given you an example, that ye should do
as I have done to you. 16 Verily, verily,
I say unto you, The servant is not greater
than his lord; neither he that is sent
greater than he that sent him. 17 If ye
know these things, happy are ye if ye do
them.●

**4. BETRAYAL PREDICTED**

18 I speak not of you all: I know
whom I have chosen: but that the Scripture may be fulfilled,

> He that eateth bread with me
> hath lifted up his heel against me.

19 Now I tell you before it come, that, — Ps. 41:9
when it is come to pass, ye may believe
that I am *he*. 20 Verily, verily, I say unto
you, He that receiveth whomsoever I send
receiveth me; and he that receiveth me
receiveth him that sent me. ●

ACCEPTANCE

---

Read the four paragraphs and note the different references to Judas Iscariot.

*13:1-5* Record your observations of these two parts:

*verses 1-3* ______

*verses 4-5* ______

*13:6-11* What prominent truth is Jesus teaching here?

______

*13:12-17* What prominent truth is Jesus teaching here?

______

*13:18-20* What is the point of verses 18-19?

______

How is verse 20 related to that point? ______

NEW INTERNATIONAL VERSION

Record what this passage teaches about:

UNBELIEF

SATAN

GLORY OF GOD

CHRISTIAN LOVE

VOWS

OTHER

[21]After he had said this, Jesus was troubled in spirit and testified, "I tell you the
truth, one of you is going to betray me."
[22]His disciples stared at one another, at
a loss to know which of them he meant.
[23]One of them, the disciple whom Jesus
loved, was reclining next to him. [24]Simon
Peter motioned to this disciple and said,
"Ask him which one he means."
[25]Leaning back against Jesus, he asked
him, "Lord, who is it?"
[26]Jesus answered, "It is the one to whom
I will give this piece of bread when I have
dipped it in the dish." Then, dipping the
piece of bread, he gave it to Judas Iscariot,
son of Simon. [27]As soon as Judas took the
bread, Satan entered into him.
"What you are about to do, do quickly,"
Jesus told him, [28]but no one at the meal
understood why Jesus said this to him.
[29]Since Judas had charge of the money,
some thought Jesus was telling him to buy
what was needed for the Feast, or to give
something to the poor. [30]As soon as Judas
had taken the bread, he went out. And it
was night.●

*Jesus Predicts Peter's Denial*

[31]When he was gone, Jesus said, "Now
is the Son of Man glorified and God is glorified in him. [32]If God is glorified in him,[b]
God will glorify the Son in himself, and will
glorify him at once.
[33]"My children, I will be with you only
a little longer. You will look for me, and
just as I told the Jews, so I tell you now:
Where I am going, you cannot come.
[34]"A new command I give you: Love one
another. As I have loved you, so you must
love one another. [35]All men will know that
you are my disciples if you love one another."●
[36]Simon Peter asked him, "Lord, where
are you going?"
Jesus replied, "Where I am going, you
cannot follow now, but you will follow
later."
[37]Peter asked, "Lord, why can't I follow
you now? I will lay down my life for you."
[38]Then Jesus answered, "Will you really
lay down your life for me? I tell you the
truth, before the rooster crows, you will
disown me three times!●

[b]32 Many early manuscripts do not have *If God is glorified in him.*

KING JAMES

**1. BETRAYAL FORETOLD**

**JESUS AND THE TWELVE**

21 When Jesus had thus said, he was
troubled in spirit, and testified, and said,
Verily, verily, I say unto you, that one of
you shall betray me. 22 Then the disciples
looked one on another, doubting of whom
he spake. 23 Now there was leaning on
Jesus' bosom one of his disciples, whom
Jesus loved. 24 Simon Peter therefore
beckoned to him, that he should ask who
it should be of whom he spake. 25 He
then lying on Jesus' breast saith unto him,
Lord, who is it? 26 Jesus answered, He it
is, to whom I shall give a sop, when I have
dipped *it*. And when he had dipped the
sop, he gave *it* to Judas Iscar'i-ot, *the son*
of Simon. 27 And after the sop Satan
entered into him. Then said Jesus unto
him, That thou doest, do quickly. 28 Now
no man at the table knew for what intent
he spake this unto him. 29 For some *of*
*them* thought, because Judas had the bag,
that Jesus had said unto him, Buy *those*
*things* that we have need of against the
feast; or, that he should give something
to the poor. 30 He then, having received
the sop, went immediately out; and it
was night.●

**2. DEPARTURE FORETOLD**

31 Therefore, when he was gone out,
Jesus said, Now is the Son of man glorified, and God is glorified in him. 32 If
God be glorified in him, God shall also
glorify him in himself, and shall straightway glorify him. 33 Little children, yet
a little while I am with you. Ye shall seek
me; and as I said unto the Jews, Whither
I go, ye cannot come; so now I say to you.
34 A new commandment I give unto you,
That ye love one another; as I have
loved you, that ye also love one another.
35 By this shall all *men* know that ye are
my disciples, if ye have love one to
another.●

**3. DENIAL FORETOLD**

36 Simon Peter said unto him, Lord,
whither goest thou? Jesus answered him,
Whither I go, thou canst not follow me
now; but thou shalt follow me afterward.
37 Peter said unto him, Lord, why cannot
I follow thee now? I will lay down my
life for thy sake. 38 Jesus answered him,
Wilt thou lay down thy life for my sake?
Verily, verily, I say unto thee, The cock
shall not crow, till thou hast denied me
thrice.●

**JESUS AND PETER**

Observe that this segment begins with Jesus' foretelling *betrayal*, and ends with His foretelling *denial*. Still, He can talk about GLORY and LOVE (middle paragraph).

*13:21-30* What does the paragraph teach about:

JESUS ______________________

SATAN ______________________

THE DISCIPLES ______________________

*13:31-35* Record your observations. ______________________

*13:36-38* Compare Peter's vow with his concern in verse 24.

NEW INTERNATIONAL VERSION

What do you learn from this passage about:

HEAVEN

THE FATHER

FAITH

MIRACLES

PRAYER

*Jesus Comforts His Disciples*

14 "Do not let your hearts be troubled.
Trust in God[c]; trust also in me. 2In
my Father's house are many rooms; if it
were not so, I would have told you. I am
going there to prepare a place for you.
3And if I go and prepare a place for you, I
will come back and take you to be with me
that you also may be where I am. 4You
know the way to the place where I am
going."

*Jesus the Way to the Father*

5Thomas said to him, "Lord, we don't
know where you are going, so how can we
know the way?"
6Jesus answered, "I am the way and the
truth and the life. No one comes to the
Father except through me. 7If you really
knew me, you would know[a] my Father as
well. From now on, you do know him and
have seen him."●
8Philip said, "Lord, show us the Father
and that will be enough for us."
9Jesus answered: "Don't you know me,
Philip, even after I have been among you
such a long time? Anyone who has seen me
has seen the Father. How can you say,
'Show us the Father'? 10Don't you believe
that I am in the Father, and that the Father
is in me? The words I say to you are not just
my own. Rather, it is the Father, living in
me, who is doing his work. 11Believe me
when I say that I am in the Father and the
Father is in me; or at least believe on the
evidence of the miracles themselves.● 12I
tell you the truth, anyone who has faith in
me will do what I have been doing. He will
do even greater things than these, because
I am going to the Father. 13And I will do
whatever you ask in my name, so that the
Son may bring glory to the Father. 14You
may ask me for anything in my name, and
I will do it.●

c1 Or *You trust in God*
a7 Some early manuscripts *If you really have known me, you will know*

KING JAMES

1. HEAVEN

**14** Let not your heart be troubled: ye — BELIEVE
believe in God, believe also in me.
2 In my Father's house are many man-
sions: if *it were* not *so*, I would have told
you. I go to prepare a place for you.
3 And if I go and prepare a place for you,
I will come again, and receive you unto
myself; that where I am, *there* ye may be
also. 4 And whither I go ye know, and the
way ye know. 5 Thomas saith unto him,
Lord, we know not whither thou goest;
and how can we know the way? 6 Jesus
saith unto him, I am the way, the truth,
and the life: no man cometh unto the
Father, but by me. 7 If ye had known
me, ye should have known my Father
also: and from henceforth ye know him,
and have seen him.●

2. THE FATHER

8 Philip saith unto him, Lord, show us
the Father, and it sufficeth us. 9 Jesus
saith unto him, Have I been so long time
with you, and yet hast thou not known
me, Philip? he that hath seen me hath
seen the Father; and how sayest thou
*then*, Show us the Father? 10 Believest
thou not that I am in the Father, and the
Father in me? the words that I speak unto
you I speak not of myself: but the Father
that dwelleth in me, he doeth the works.
11 Believe me that I *am* in the Father, and
the Father in me: or else believe me for the
very works' sake.●

3. WORKS

12 Verily, verily, I say unto you, He
that believeth on me, the works that I do
shall he do also; and greater *works* than
these shall he do; because I go unto my
Father. 13 And whatsoever ye shall ask
in my name, that will I do, that the Father
may be glorified in the Son. 14 If ye shall — ASK
ask any thing in my name, I will do *it*.●

This segment begins a series of farewell discourses by Jesus, which may be identified this way:

*The Father's House* 14:1-31

*Vine and the Branches* 15:1—16:4a

*Promises of Jesus* 16:4b-33

*14:1-7* What are the two main subjects of the paragraph?

*14:8-11* What is the key repeated word of the paragraph?

What is the main point of Jesus' words?

*14:12-14* What two similar words are the key words of the paragraph?

NEW INTERNATIONAL VERSION

Record what this passage teaches about:

THE PERSON OF THE HOLY SPIRIT

THE MINISTRIES OF THE HOLY SPIRIT

JESUS AND HIS FATHER

LOVE

PEACE OF HEART

PROPHECY

### *Jesus Promises the Holy Spirit*

15"If you love me, you will obey what I
command. 16And I will ask the Father, and
he will give you another Counselor to be
with you forever— 17the Spirit of truth.
The world cannot accept him, because it
neither sees him nor knows him. But you
know him, for he lives with you and will
be[b] in you.● 18I will not leave you as orphans; I will come to you. 19Before long,
the world will not see me anymore, but you
will see me. Because I live, you also will
live. 20On that day you will realize that I am
in my Father, and you are in me, and I am
in you. 21Whoever has my commands and
obeys them, he is the one who loves me.
He who loves me will be loved by my Father, and I too will love him and show myself to him."
22Then Judas (not Judas Iscariot) said,
"But, Lord, why do you intend to show
yourself to us and not to the world?"
23Jesus replied, "If anyone loves me, he
will obey my teaching. My Father will love
him, and we will come to him and make our
home with him. 24He who does not love me
will not obey my teaching. These words
you hear are not my own; they belong to
the Father who sent me.●
25"All this I have spoken while still with
you. 26But the Counselor, the Holy Spirit,
whom the Father will send in my name,
will teach you all things and will remind
you of everything I have said to you.●
27Peace I leave with you; my peace I give
you. I do not give to you as the world gives.
Do not let your hearts be troubled and do
not be afraid.
28"You heard me say, 'I am going away
and I am coming back to you.' If you loved
me, you would be glad that I am going to
the Father, for the Father is greater than I.
29I have told you now before it happens, so
that when it does happen you will believe.
30I will not speak with you much longer, for
the prince of this world is coming. He has
no hold on me, 31but the world must learn
that I love the Father and that I do exactly
what my Father has commanded me.
"Come now; let us leave.●

[b]17 Some early manuscripts *and is*

KING JAMES

1. HOLY SPIRIT PROMISED

LOVE ME

15 If ye love me, keep my commandments. 16 And I will pray the Father, and
he shall give you another Comforter, that
he may abide with you for ever; 17 *even*
the Spirit of truth; whom the world cannot receive, because it seeth him not, neither knoweth him: but ye know him; for
he dwelleth with you, and shall be in you.●

2. JESUS' PRESENCE PROMISED

18 I will not leave you comfortless: I
will come to you. 19 Yet a little while,
and the world seeth me no more; but ye
see me: because I live, ye shall live also.
20 At that day ye shall know that I *am* in
my Father, and ye in me, and I in you.
21 He that hath my commandments, and
keepeth them, he it is that loveth me: and
he that loveth me shall be loved of my
Father, and I will love him, and will manifest myself to him. 22 Judas saith unto
him, not Iscar'i-ot, Lord, how is it that
thou wilt manifest thyself unto us, and
not unto the world? 23 Jesus answered
and said unto him, If a man love me, he
will keep my words: and my Father will
love him, and we will come unto him, and
make our abode with him. 24 He that
loveth me not keepeth not my sayings:
and the word which ye hear is not mine,
but the Father's which sent me.●

3. HOLY SPIRIT PROMISED

25 These things have I spoken unto
you, being *yet* present with you. 26 But
the Comforter, *which is* the Holy Ghost,
whom the Father will send in my name,
he shall teach you all things, and bring all
things to your remembrance, whatsoever
I have said unto you.●

4. PEACE PROMISED

27 Peace I leave
with you, my peace I give unto you: not
as the world giveth, give I unto you. Let
not your heart be troubled, neither let it
be afraid. 28 Ye have heard how I said
unto you, I go away, and come *again* unto
you. If ye loved me, ye would rejoice,
because I said, I go unto the Father: for my
Father is greater than I. 29 And now I
have told you before it come to pass, that,
when it is come to pass, ye might believe.
30 Hereafter I will not talk much with
you: for the prince of this world cometh,
and hath nothing in me. 31 But that the
world may know that I love the Father;
and as the Father gave me commandment, even so I do. Arise, let us go
hence.●

I LOVE THE FATHER

This segment concludes Jesus' first farewell discourse. (Read the last sentence.)

*14:15-17* What is said here about the Holy Spirit?

*14:18-24* Record your observations.

*14:25-26* Compare this paragraph with the first paragraph.

*14:27-31* Record your observations.

NEW INTERNATIONAL VERSION

List as many spiritual applications which can be made of these subjects:

ABIDING IN CHRIST ______________________

SPIRITUAL FRUIT ______________________

LOVING CHRIST ______________________

LOVING ONE ANOTHER ______________________

SOVEREIGN LORD ______________________

OTHER ______________________

*The Vine and the Branches*

15 "I am the true vine and my Father is the gardener. 2He cuts off every branch in me that bears no fruit, while every branch that does bear fruit he trims clean so that it will be even more fruitful. 3You are already clean because of the word I have spoken to you. 4Remain in me, and I will remain in you. No branch can bear fruit by itself; it must remain in the vine. Neither can you bear fruit unless you remain in me.●

5"I am the vine; you are the branches. If a man remains in me and I in him, he will bear much fruit; apart from me you can do nothing. 6If anyone does not remain in me, he is like a branch that is thrown away and withers; such branches are picked up, thrown into the fire and burned. 7If you remain in me and my words remain in you, ask whatever you wish, and it will be given you. 8This is to my Father's glory, that you bear much fruit, showing yourselves to be my disciples.●

9"As the Father has loved me, so have I loved you. Now remain in my love. 10If you obey my commands, you will remain in my love, just as I have obeyed my Father's commands and remain in his love. 11I have told you this so that my joy may be in you and that your joy may be complete. 12My command is this: Love each other as I have loved you. 13Greater love has no one than this, that one lay down his life for his friends. 14You are my friends if you do what I command. 15I no longer call you servants, because a servant does not know his master's business. Instead, I have called you friends, for everything that I learned from my Father I have made known to you. 16You did not choose me, but I chose you to go and bear fruit—fruit that will last. Then the Father will give you whatever you ask in my name. 17This is my command: Love each other.●

KING JAMES

1. BEAR FRUIT **15** I am the true vine, and my Father MORE
is the husbandman. 2 Every branch FRUIT
in me that beareth not fruit he taketh
away: and every *branch* that beareth fruit,
he purgeth it, that it may bring forth more
fruit. 3 Now ye are clean through the
word which I have spoken unto you.
4 Abide in me, and I in you. As the
branch cannot bear fruit of itself, except
it abide in the vine; no more can ye, ex-
2. ABIDE cept ye abide in me. ● 5 I am the vine, ye
*are* the branches. He that abideth in me,
and I in him, the same bringeth forth
much fruit; for without me ye can do
nothing. 6 If a man abide not in me, he
is cast forth as a branch, and is withered;
and men gather them, and cast *them* into
the fire, and they are burned. 7 If ye
abide in me, and my words abide in you,
ye shall ask what ye will, and it shall be
done unto you. 8 Herein is my Father
glorified, that ye bear much fruit; so shall
3. LOVE ye be my disciples. ● 9 As the Father hath
loved me, so have I loved you: continue
ye in my love. 10 If ye keep my commandments, ye shall abide in my love;
even as I have kept my Father's commandments, and abide in his love.
11 These things have I spoken unto you,
that my joy might remain in you, and *that*
your joy might be full.
12 This is my commandment, That ye
love one another, as I have loved you.
13 Greater love hath no man than this,
that a man lay down his life for his
friends. 14 Ye are my friends, if ye do
whatsoever I command you. 15 Henceforth I call you not servants; for the servant knoweth not what his lord doeth: but
I have called you friends; for all things
that I have heard of my Father I have
made known unto you. 16 Ye have not
chosen me, but I have chosen you, and
ordained you, that ye should go and
bring forth fruit, and *that* your fruit
should remain; that whatsoever ye shall
ask of the Father in my name, he may FRUIT
give it you. 17 These things I command ALWAYS
you, that ye love one another. ●

Analyze each paragraph carefully, recording your observations. Note especially key repeated words.

*15:1-4* Compare the first sentence with that of verse 5

*15:5-8*

*15:9-17* Underline the repeated word "love". Record the main statements of Jesus:

NEW INTERNATIONAL VERSION

Record what this passage teaches about:

PERSECUTION OF CHRISTIANS

HOLY SPIRIT

JESUS

FATHER

List some important spiritual applications.

*The World Hates the Disciples*

[18]"If the world hates you, keep in mind
that it hated me first. [19]If you belonged to
the world, it would love you as its own. As
it is, you do not belong to the world, but I
have chosen you out of the world. That is
why the world hates you. [20]Remember the
words I spoke to you: 'No servant is
greater than his master.'[a] If they persecuted me, they will persecute you also. If they
obeyed my teaching, they will obey yours
also. [21]They will treat you this way because of my name, for they do not know
the One who sent me. [22]If I had not come
and spoken to them, they would not be
guilty of sin. Now, however, they have no
excuse for their sin. [23]He who hates me
hates my Father as well. [24]If I had not done
among them what no one else did, they
would not be guilty of sin. But now they
have seen these miracles, and yet they
have hated both me and my Father. [25]But
this is to fulfill what is written in their Law:
'They hated me without reason.'[b]●
[26]"When the Counselor comes, whom I
will send to you from the Father, the Spirit
of truth who goes out from the Father, he
will testify about me; [27]but you also must
testify, for you have been with me from the
beginning.●

16 "All this I have told you so that you
will not go astray. [2]They will put
you out of the synagogue; in fact, a time is
coming when anyone who kills you will
think he is offering a service to God. [3]They
will do such things because they have not
known the Father or me. [4]I have told you
this, so that when the time comes you will
remember that I warned you.●

[a]*20* John 13:16 [b]*25* Psalms 35:19; 69:4

## KING JAMES

**1. THE WORLD'S HATE**

18 If the world hate you, ye know that
it hated me before *it hated* you. 19 If ye
were of the world, the world would love
his own; but because ye are not of the
world, but I have chosen you out of the
world, therefore the world hateth you.
20 Remember the word that I said unto
you, The servant is not greater than his
lord. If they have persecuted me, they
will also persecute you; if they have kept
my saying, they will keep yours also.
21 But all these things will they do unto
you for my name's sake, because they
know not him that sent me. 22 If I had
not come and spoken unto them, they had
not had sin; but now they have no cloak
for their sin. 23 He that hateth me hateth
my Father also. 24 If I had not done
among them the works which none other
man did, they had not had sin: but now
have they both seen and hated both me
and my Father. 25 But *this cometh to
pass*, that the word might be fulfilled that
is written in their law, They hated me
without a cause. ●

HATE

Ps. 35:19

**2. THE SPIRIT'S HELP**

26 But when the Com-
forter is come, whom I will send unto you
from the Father, *even* the Spirit of truth,
which proceedeth from the Father, he
shall testify of me: 27 and ye also shall
bear witness, because ye have been with
me from the beginning.●

**3. JESUS' FORE-WARNING**

16 These things have I spoken unto
you, that ye should not be offended.
2 They shall put you out of the synagogues: yea, the time cometh, that whosoever killeth you will think that he doeth
God service. 3 And these things will they
do unto you, because they have not known
the Father, nor me. 4 But these things
have I told you, that when the time shall
come, ye may remember that I told you
of them.●

HELP

Review the preceding segment (15:1-17) to see how this segment is related to it.
Record the main truths of each paragraph.

*15:18-25* ____________________

*15:26-27* ____________________

*16:1-4a* ____________________

NEW INTERNATIONAL VERSION

Record truths taught here about:

SECOND COMING OF JESUS

HOLY SPIRIT'S MINISTRY

TRUTH

RELATION OF HOLY SPIRIT TO CHRIST

SORROW

JOY

PRAYER

I did not tell
you this at first because I was with you.

*The Work of the Holy Spirit*

5"Now I am going to him who sent me,
yet none of you asks me, 'Where are you
going?' 6Because I have said these things,
you are filled with grief. 7But I tell you the
truth: It is for your good that I am going
away. Unless I go away, the Counselor will
not come to you; but if I go, I will send him
to you. 8When he comes, he will convict
the world of guilt in regard to sin and righteousness and judgment: 9in regard to sin,
because men do not believe in me; 10in regard to righteousness, because I am going
to the Father, where you can see me no
longer; 11and in regard to judgment, because the prince of this world now stands
condemned.●
12"I have much more to say to you, more
than you can now bear. 13But when he, the
Spirit of truth, comes, he will guide you
into all truth. He will not speak on his own;
he will speak only what he hears, and he
will tell you what is yet to come. 14He will
bring glory to me by taking from what is
mine and making it known to you. 15All
that belongs to the Father is mine. That is
why I said the Spirit will take from what is
mine and make it known to you.●
16"In a little while you will see me no
more, and then after a little while you will
see me."

*The Disciples' Grief Will Turn to Joy*

17Some of his disciples said to one another, "What does he mean by saying, 'In
a little while you will see me no more, and
then after a little while you will see me,'
and 'Because I am going to the Father'?"
18They kept asking, "What does he mean
by 'a little while'? We don't understand
what he is saying."
19Jesus saw that they wanted to ask him
about this, so he said to them, "Are you
asking one another what I meant when I
said, 'In a little while you will see me no
more, and then after a little while you will
see me'? 20I tell you the truth, you will
weep and mourn while the world rejoices.
You will grieve, but your grief will turn to
joy. 21A woman giving birth to a child has
pain because her time has come; but when
her baby is born she forgets the anguish
because of her joy that a child is born into
the world. 22So with you: Now is your time
of grief, but I will see you again and you
will rejoice, and no one will take away your
joy. 23In that day you will no longer ask me
anything. I tell you the truth, my Father
will give you whatever you ask in my
name. 24Until now you have not asked for
anything in my name. Ask and you will
receive, and your joy will be complete.●

KING JAMES

1. HOLY SPIRIT AS CONVICTER

SORROW

And these things I said not unto you at
the beginning, because I was with you.
5 But now I go my way to him that sent
me; and none of you asketh me, Whither
goest thou? 6 But because I have said
these things unto you, sorrow hath filled
your heart. 7 Nevertheless I tell you the
truth; It is expedient for you that I go
away: for if I go not away, the Comforter will not come unto you; but if I
depart, I will send him unto you. 8 And
when he is come, he will reprove the
world of sin, and of righteousness, and
of judgment: 9 of sin, because they believe not on me; 10 of righteousness,
because I go to my Father, and ye see me
no more; 11 of judgment, because the
prince of this world is judged.●

2. HOLY SPIRIT AS GUIDE

12 I have yet many things to say unto
you, but ye cannot bear them now.
13 Howbeit when he, the Spirit of truth,
is come, he will guide you into all truth:
for he shall not speak of himself; but
whatsoever he shall hear, *that* shall he
speak: and he will show you things to
come. 14 He shall glorify me: for he shall
receive of mine, and shall show *it* unto
you. 15 All things that the Father hath
are mine: therefore said I, that he shall
take of mine, and shall show *it* unto you.●

3. SORROW INTO JOY

16 A little while, and ye shall not see
me: and again, a little while, and ye shall
see me, because I go to the Father.
17 Then said *some* of his disciples among
themselves, What is this that he saith unto
us, A little while, and ye shall not see me:
and again, a little while, and ye shall see
me: and, Because I go to the Father?
18 They said therefore, What is this that
he saith, A little while? we cannot tell
what he saith. 19 Now Jesus knew that
they were desirous to ask him, and said
unto them, Do ye inquire among yourselves of that I said, A little while, and ye
shall not see me: and again, a little while,
and ye shall see me? 20 Verily, verily, I
say unto you, That ye shall weep and
lament, but the world shall rejoice; and
ye shall be sorrowful, but your sorrow
shall be turned into joy. 21 A woman
when she is in travail hath sorrow, because her hour is come: but as soon as she
is delivered of the child, she remembereth
no more the anguish, for joy that a man
is born into the world. 22 And ye now
therefore have sorrow: but I will see you
again, and your heart shall rejoice, and
your joy no man taketh from you. 23 And
in that day ye shall ask me nothing.
Verily, verily, I say unto you, Whatsoever
ye shall ask the Father in my name, he
will give *it* you. 24 Hitherto have ye
asked nothing in my name: ask, and ye
shall receive, that your joy may be full.●

JOY

The third farewell discourse of Jesus (16:4b-33) contains many promises to Jesus' disciples. Be alert to these as you study the text.

*16:4b-11* What is the main point of these two parts of the paragraph:

*verses 4b-7a* ______

*verses 7b-11* ______

*16:12-15* Analyze carefully. Record your observations.

*16:16-24* What is the main point of these two parts of the paragraph:

*verses 16-19* ______

*verses 20-24* ______

NEW INTERNATIONAL VERSION

Record what this passage teaches about:

REVELATION

LOVE

MINISTRIES OF JESUS

FAITH

PERSECUTION

PEACE

OTHER

25 "Though I have been speaking figuratively, a time is coming when I will no
longer use this kind of language but will tell
you plainly about my Father. 26 In that day
you will ask in my name. I am not saying
that I will ask the Father on your behalf.
27 No, the Father himself loves you because
you have loved me and have believed that
I came from God. 28 I came from the Father
and entered the world; now I am leaving
the world and going back to the Father." ●
29 Then Jesus' disciples said, "Now you
are speaking clearly and without figures of
speech. 30 Now we can see that you know
all things and that you do not even need to
have anyone ask you questions. This
makes us believe that you came from
God."
31 "You believe at last!"[a] Jesus answered. 32 "But a time is coming, and has
come, when you will be scattered, each to
his own home. You will leave me all alone.
Yet I am not alone, for my Father is with
me. ●
33 "I have told you these things, so that
in me you may have peace. In this world
you will have trouble. But take heart! I
have overcome the world." ●

[a]31 Or *"Do you now believe?"*

KING JAMES

1. MANNER OF CHRIST'S SPEAKING

LOVE

25 These things have I spoken unto
you in proverbs: but the time cometh,
when I shall no more speak unto you in
proverbs, but I shall show you plainly of
the Father. 26 At that day ye shall ask in
my name: and I say not unto you, that I
will pray the Father for you: 27 for the
Father himself loveth you, because ye
have loved me, and have believed that I
came out from God. 28 I came forth
from the Father, and am come into the
world: again, I leave the world, and go to
the Father.●

2. EFFECTIVENESS OF CHRIST'S SPEAKING

29 His disciples said unto him, Lo, now
speakest thou plainly, and speakest no
proverb. 30 Now are we sure that thou
knowest all things, and needest not that
any man should ask thee: by this we believe
that thou camest forth from God.
31 Jesus answered them, Do ye now believe?
32 Behold, the hour cometh, yea,
is now come, that ye shall be scattered,
every man to his own, and shall leave me
alone: and yet I am not alone, because the

3. PURPOSE OF CHRIST'S SPEAKING

Father is with me.● 33 These things I have
spoken unto you, that in me ye might
have peace. In the world ye shall have
tribulation: but be of good cheer; I have
overcome the world.●

PEACE

This segment is the conclusion of Jesus' third farewell discourse (16:4b-33). Review the preceding segment to see how it leads to this passage.

*16:25-28* What ministries of Jesus appear here?

*16:29-32* The word "now" appears in every verse. Record what is said in each case.

*16:33* What are the key words of this concluding verse?

NEW INTERNATIONAL VERSION

What does this passage teach about:

CHRIST'S GLORY

ETERNAL LIFE

RELATION OF CHRIST TO THE FATHER

INTERCESSION OF CHRIST

JOY

SANCTIFICATION

What are your impressions of this part of Christ's prayer?

*Jesus Prays for Himself*

17 After Jesus said this, he looked
toward heaven and prayed:
"Father, the time has come. Glorify
your Son, that your Son may glorify
you. 2For you granted him authority
over all people that he might give eternal life to all those you have given him.
3Now this is eternal life: that they may
know you, the only true God, and
Jesus Christ, whom you have sent. 4I
have brought you glory on earth by
completing the work you gave me to
do. 5And now, Father, glorify me in
your presence with the glory I had
with you before the world began.●

*Jesus Prays for His Disciples*

6"I have revealed you[b] to those
whom you gave me out of the world.
They were yours; you gave them to me
and they have obeyed your word.
7Now they know that everything you
have given me comes from you. 8For
I gave them the words you gave me
and they accepted them. They knew
with certainty that I came from you,
and they believed that you sent me. 9I
pray for them. I am not praying for the
world, but for those you have given
me, for they are yours. 10All I have is
yours, and all you have is mine. And
glory has come to me through them. 11I
will remain in the world no longer, but
they are still in the world, and I am
coming to you. Holy Father, protect
them by the power of your name—the
name you gave me—so that they may
be one as we are one. 12While I was
with them, I protected them and kept
them safe by that name you gave me.
None has been lost except the one
doomed to destruction so that Scripture would be fulfilled.●
13"I am coming to you now, but I
say these things while I am still in the
world, so that they may have the full
measure of my joy within them. 14I
have given them your word and the
world has hated them, for they are not
of the world any more than I am of the
world. 15My prayer is not that you take
them out of the world but that you
protect them from the evil one. 16They
are not of the world, even as I am not
of it. 17Sanctify[c] them by the truth;
your word is truth. 18As you sent me
into the world, I have sent them into
the world. 19For them I sanctify myself, that they too may be truly sanctified.●

[b]6 Greek *your name;* also in verse 26
[c]17 Greek *hagiazo (set apart for sacred use* or *make holy);* also in verse 19

## KING JAMES

### 1. JESUS PRAYS FOR HIMSELF

GLORY OF THE SON

17 These words spake Jesus, and lifted
up his eyes to heaven, and said,
Father, the hour is come; glorify thy Son,
that thy Son also may glorify thee: 2 as
thou hast given him power over all flesh,
that he should give eternal life to as many
as thou hast given him. 3 And this is life
eternal, that they might know thee the
only true God, and Jesus Christ, whom
thou hast sent. 4 I have glorified thee on
the earth: I have finished the work which
thou gavest me to do. 5 And now, O
Father, glorify thou me with thine own
self with the glory which I had with thee
before the world was.●

### 2. JESUS PRAYS FOR HIS DISCIPLES' PROTECTION

6 I have manifested thy name unto the
men which thou gavest me out of the
world: thine they were, and thou gavest
them me; and they have kept thy word.
7 Now they have known that all things
whatsoever thou hast given me are of
thee. 8 For I have given unto them the
words which thou gavest me; and they
have received *them*, and have known
surely that I came out from thee, and they
have believed that thou didst send me.
9 I pray for them: I pray not for the
world, but for them which thou hast given
me; for they are thine. 10 And all mine
are thine, and thine are mine; and I am
glorified in them. 11 And now I am no
more in the world, but these are in the
world, and I come to thee. Holy Father,
keep through thine own name those whom
thou hast given me, that they may be one,
as we *are*. 12 While I was with them in the
world, I kept them in thy name: those that
thou gavest me I have kept, and none of
them is lost, but the son of perdition; that
the Scripture might be fulfilled. ●

### 3. JESUS PRAYS FOR HIS DISCIPLES' SANCTIFICATION

13 And
now come I to thee; and these things I
speak in the world, that they might have
my joy fulfilled in themselves. 14 I have
given them thy word; and the world hath
hated them, because they are not of the
world, even as I am not of the world.
15 I pray not that thou shouldest take
them out of the world, but that thou
shouldest keep them from the evil.
16 They are not of the world, even as I
am not of the world. 17 Sanctify them
through thy truth: thy word is truth.
18 As thou hast sent me into the world,
even so have I also sent them into the
world. 19 And for their sakes I sanctify
myself, that they also might be sanctified
through the truth.●

HOLINESS OF THE SON

Chapter 17 is Jesus' high-priestly prayer, because in most of it He is interceding for others.

*17:1-5* What is the basic petition of verse 1?

What is the key repeated word of the paragraph?

*17:6-12* Who are "the men which thou gavest me"?

What is the one petition of the paragraph?

*17:13-19* What are the petitions of this paragraph?

NEW INTERNATIONAL VERSION

What do you learn from this part of Jesus' prayer about these subjects:

FELLOWSHIP ______

GLORY ______

PERFECTION ______

LOVE ______

If you are a believer, show how this prayer relates to you. ______

*Jesus Prays for All Believers*

20 "My prayer is not for them alone.
I pray also for those who will believe
in me through their message, 21 that all
of them may be one, Father, just as
you are in me and I am in you. May
they also be in us so that the world
may believe that you have sent me. 22 I
have given them the glory that you
gave me, that they may be one as we
are one: 23 I in them and you in me.
May they be brought to complete unity
to let the world know that you sent me
and have loved them even as you have
loved me.●
24 "Father, I want those you have
given me to be with me where I am,
and to see my glory, the glory you
have given me because you loved me
before the creation of the world.
25 "Righteous Father, though the
world does not know you, I know you,
and they know that you have sent me.
26 I have made you known to them, and
will continue to make you known in
order that the love you have for me
may be in them and that I myself may
be in them."●

KING JAMES

Jesus prays for all believers:

1. UNITY

2. GLORY

20 Neither pray I for these alone, but
for them also which shall believe on me
through their word; 21 that they all may
be one; as thou, Father, *art* in me, and I
in thee, that they also may be one in us:
that the world may believe that thou hast
sent me. 22 And the glory which thou
gavest me I have given them; that they
may be one, even as we are one: 23 I in
them, and thou in me, that they may be
made perfect in one; and that the world
may know that thou hast sent me, and
hast loved them, as thou hast loved me.●
24 Father, I will that they also, whom
thou hast given me, be with me where I
am; that they may behold my glory,
which thou hast given me: for thou lovedst
me before the foundation of the world.
25 O righteous Father, the world hath not
known thee: but I have known thee, and
these have known that thou hast sent me.
26 And I have declared unto them thy
name, and will declare *it;* that the love
wherewith thou hast loved me may be in
them, and I in them.●

MAY BE ONE

MAY BEHOLD GLORY

This segment continues Jesus' prayer, which is of three parts:

JESUS PRAYS FOR HIMSELF 1-5

JESUS PRAYS FOR HIS DISCIPLES 6-19

JESUS PRAYS FOR THE CHURCH 20-26

Analyze each paragraph carefully, recording your observations.

*17:20-23*

PETITION: ____________________

*17:24-26*

PETITION ____________________

NEW INTERNATIONAL VERSION

Record what is taught by this passage about:

SOVEREIGN WILL OF THE FATHER

JESUS' COMPASSION

JESUS' POWER

JESUS' OBEDIENCE TO HIS FATHER

Write some spiritual applications which may be made from the passage.

*Jesus Arrested*

18 When he had finished praying, Jesus
left with his disciples and crossed
the Kidron Valley. On the other side there
was an olive grove, and he and his disciples
went into it.
2Now Judas, who betrayed him, knew
the place, because Jesus had often met
there with his disciples. 3So Judas came to
the grove, guiding a detachment of soldiers
and some officials from the chief priests
and Pharisees. They were carrying
torches, lanterns and weapons. ●
4Jesus, knowing all that was going to
happen to him, went out and asked them,
"Who is it you want?"
5"Jesus of Nazareth," they replied.
"I am he," Jesus said. (And Judas the
traitor was standing there with them.)
6When Jesus said, "I am he," they drew
back and fell to the ground.
7Again he asked them, "Who is it you
want?"
And they said, "Jesus of Nazareth."
8"I told you that I am he," Jesus answered. "If you are looking for me, then let
these men go." 9This happened so that the
words he had spoken would be fulfilled: "I
have not lost one of those you gave me."[a] ●
10Then Simon Peter, who had a sword,
drew it and struck the high priest's servant,
cutting off his right ear. (The servant's
name was Malchus.)
11Jesus commanded Peter, "Put your
sword away! Shall I not drink the cup the
Father has given me?" ●

[a]9 John 6:39

KING JAMES

1. SETTING

**18** When Jesus had spoken these
words, he went forth with his disciples over the brook Cedron, where was
a garden, into the which he entered, and
his disciples. 2 And Judas also, which
betrayed him, knew the place: for Jesus
ofttimes resorted thither with his disciples.
3 Judas then, having received a band *of*
*men* and officers from the chief priests and
Pharisees, cometh thither with lanterns

2.MEETING

and torches and weapons. ● 4 Jesus therefore, knowing all things that should come
upon him, went forth, and said unto them,
Whom seek ye? 5 They answered him,
Jesus of Nazareth. Jesus saith unto them,
I am *he*. And Judas also, which betrayed
him, stood with them. 6 As soon then as
he had said unto them, I am *he*, they went
backward, and fell to the ground. 7 Then
asked he them again, Whom seek ye?
And they said, Jesus of Nazareth. 8 Jesus
answered, I have told you that I am *he*:
if therefore ye seek me, let these go their
way: 9 that the saying might be fulfilled,
which he spake, Of them which thou

3. REACTION

gavest me have I lost none. ● 10 Then
Simon Peter having a sword drew it, and
smote the high priest's servant, and cut
off his right ear. The servant's name was
Malchus. 11 Then said Jesus unto Peter,
Put up thy sword into the sheath: the
cup which my Father hath given me,
shall I not drink it? ●

GARDEN

CUP

As you study this segment try to visualize all the action and also the thoughts of the people involved. Record as many observations as you can.

*18:1-3* Record the different parts of the setting.

*18:4-9* Who takes the initiative here?

Account for verse 6.

Who are the "these" of verse 8?

*18:10-11* Compare Peter's action and Jesus' words.

NEW INTERNATIONAL VERSION

What is taught here about:

UNFAITHFULNESS

TRUTH

FALSEHOOD

List some spiritual applications which may be made from this account.

### *Jesus Taken to Annas*

12Then the detachment of soldiers with
its commander and the Jewish officials arrested Jesus. They bound him 13and
brought him first to Annas, who was the
father-in-law of Caiaphas, the high priest
that year. 14Caiaphas was the one who had
advised the Jews that it would be good if
one man died for the people.●

### *Peter's First Denial*

15Simon Peter and another disciple were
following Jesus. Because this disciple was
known to the high priest, he went with
Jesus into the high priest's courtyard, 16but
Peter had to wait outside at the door. The
other disciple, who was known to the high
priest, came back, spoke to the girl on duty
there and brought Peter in.
17"Surely you are not another of this
man's disciples?" the girl at the door asked
Peter.
He replied, "I am not."
18It was cold, and the servants and officials stood around a fire they had made to
keep warm. Peter also was standing with
them, warming himself.●

### *The High Priest Questions Jesus*

19Meanwhile, the high priest questioned
Jesus about his disciples and his teaching.
20"I have spoken openly to the world,"
Jesus replied. "I always taught in synagogues or at the temple, where all the Jews
come together. I said nothing in secret.
21Why question me? Ask those who heard
me. Surely they know what I said."
22When Jesus said this, one of the officials nearby struck him in the face. "Is that
any way to answer the high priest?" he
demanded.
23"If I said something wrong," Jesus replied, "testify as to what is wrong. But if
I spoke the truth, why did you strike me?"
24Then Annas sent him, still bound, to
Caiaphas the high priest.[b]●

### *Peter's Second and Third Denials*

25As Simon Peter stood warming himself, he was asked, "Surely you are not
another of his disciples?"
He denied it, saying, "I am not."
26One of the high priest's servants, a
relative of the man whose ear Peter had cut
off, challenged him, "Didn't I see you with
him in the olive grove?" 27Again Peter denied it, and at that moment a rooster began
to crow.●

[b]24 Or *(Now Annas had sent him, still bound, to Caiaphas the high priest.)*

KING JAMES

1. JESUS IS ARRESTED

12 Then the band and the captain and
officers of the Jews took Jesus, and bound
him, 13 and led him away to Annas first;
for he was father-in-law to Cai'aphas,
which was the high priest that same year.
14 Now Cai'aphas was he, which gave
counsel to the Jews, that it was expedient that one man should die for the
people. ●

2. PETER DENIES JESUS

15 And Simon Peter followed Jesus,
and *so did* another disciple: that disciple
was known unto the high priest, and
went in with Jesus into the palace of the
high priest. 16 But Peter stood at the
door without. Then went out that other
disciple, which was known unto the high
priest, and spake unto her that kept the
door, and brought in Peter. 17 Then saith
the damsel that kept the door unto Peter,
Art not thou also *one* of this man's disciples? He saith, I am not. 18 And the
servants and officers stood there, who had
made a fire of coals, for it was cold; and
they warmed themselves: and Peter stood
with them, and warmed himself.●

3. ANNAS QUESTIONS JESUS

19 The high priest then asked Jesus of
his disciples, and of his doctrine. 20 Jesus
answered him, I spake openly to the
world; I ever taught in the synagogue, and
in the temple, whither the Jews always
resort; and in secret have I said nothing.
21 Why askest thou me? ask them which
heard me, what I have said unto them:
behold, they know what I said. 22 And
when he had thus spoken, one of the
officers which stood by struck Jesus with
the palm of his hand, saying, Answerest
thou the high priest so? 23 Jesus answered him, If I have spoken evil, bear
witness of the evil: but if well, why smitest
thou me? 24 Now Annas had sent him
bound unto Cai'aphas the high priest.●

4. TWO MORE DENIALS BY PETER

25 And Simon Peter stood and warmed
himself. They said therefore unto him,
Art not thou also *one* of his disciples?
He denied *it*, and said, I am not. 26 One
of the servants of the high priest, being
*his* kinsman whose ear Peter cut off, saith,
Did not I see thee in the garden with him?
27 Peter then denied again; and immediately the cock crew.●

JESUS BOUND BY HIS ENEMIES

JESUS DENIED BY HIS DISCIPLE

After His arrest Jesus was tried by both Jewish religious authorities and Roman political rulers. This segment is the first of His Jewish trials.

*18:12-14* Who are the people of this paragraph?

Read John 11:50 for the earlier advice of Caiaphas.

*18:15-18* What is written here about Peter?

*18:19-24* Note: the high priest of verse 19 is Annas—he served in that capacity because he was ex-high priest. Also, follow the Living Bible translation of verse 24.

*18:25-27* Record the two questions.

NEW INTERNATIONAL VERSION

What does this passage teach about:

JESUS' KINGDOM

JESUS' MINISTRY

TRUTH

Record spiritual applications of the passage:

*Jesus Before Pilate*

28Then the Jews led Jesus from Caiaphas
to the palace of the Roman governor. By
now it was early morning, and to avoid
ceremonial uncleanness the Jews did not
enter the palace; they wanted to be able to
eat the Passover. 29So Pilate came out to
them and asked, "What charges are you
bringing against this man?"
30"If he were not a criminal," they replied, "we would not have handed him
over to you."
31Pilate said, "Take him yourselves and
judge him by your own law."
"But we have no right to execute anyone," the Jews objected. 32This happened
so that the words Jesus had spoken indicating the kind of death he was going to die
would be fulfilled.●
33Pilate then went back inside the palace,
summoned Jesus and asked him, "Are you
the king of the Jews?"
34"Is that your own idea," Jesus asked,
"or did others talk to you about me?"
35"Do you think I am a Jew?" Pilate replied. "It was your people and your chief
priests who handed you over to me. What
is it you have done?"
36Jesus said, "My kingdom is not of this
world. If it were, my servants would fight
to prevent my arrest by the Jews. But now
my kingdom is from another place."
37"You are a king, then!" said Pilate.
Jesus answered, "You are right in saying
I am a king. In fact, for this reason I was
born, and for this I came into the world, to
testify to the truth. Everyone on the side of
truth listens to me."
38"What is truth?" Pilate asked.●

## KING JAMES

### 1. PILATE AND THE JEWISH ACCUSERS

28 Then led they Jesus from Cai'aphas
unto the hall of judgment: and it was
early; and they themselves went not into
the judgment hall, lest they should be defiled; but that they might eat the passover.
29 Pilate then went out unto them, and
said, What accusation bring ye against
this man? 30 They answered and said
unto him, If he were not a malefactor, we
would not have delivered him up unto
thee. 31 Then said Pilate unto them,
Take ye him, and judge him according to
your law. The Jews therefore said unto
him, It is not lawful for us to put any man
to death: 32 that the saying of Jesus
might be fulfilled, which he spake, signifying what death he should die. ●

"What is your charge?"

### 2. PILATE AND JESUS

33 Then Pilate entered into the judgment hall again, and called Jesus, and said
unto him, Art thou the King of the Jews?
34 Jesus answered him, Sayest thou this
thing of thyself, or did others tell it thee
of me? 35 Pilate answered, Am I a Jew?
Thine own nation and the chief priests
have delivered thee unto me: what hast
thou done? 36 Jesus answered, My kingdom is not of this world: if my kingdom
were of this world, then would my servants fight, that I should not be delivered
to the Jews: but now is my kingdom not
from hence. 37 Pilate therefore said unto
him, Art thou a king then? Jesus answered, Thou sayest that I am a king. To
this end was I born, and for this cause
came I into the world, that I should bear
witness unto the truth. Every one that is
of the truth heareth my voice. 38 Pilate
saith unto him, What is truth?●

"What is truth?"

This segment records Jesus' first appearance before Pilate, a Roman governor of Palestine. It is early morning, on Friday.

18:28-32 (Note on v.32: Jesus predicted He would be crucified, which was a Roman method of punishment; the Jews used stoning.)

*18:33-38a* Examine Pilate's questions and Jesus' answers.

NEW INTERNATIONAL VERSION

What does this passage teach about:

JUSTICE

RIGHTEOUSNESS

JESUS' POWER

JESUS' MINISTRY

OTHER

With
this he went out again to the Jews and said,
"I find no basis for a charge against him.
39But it is your custom for me to release to
you one prisoner at the time of the Passover. Do you want me to release 'the king
of the Jews'?"
40They shouted back, "No, not him!
Give us Barabbas!" Now Barabbas had
taken part in a rebellion.●

*Jesus Sentenced to be Crucified*

19 Then Pilate took Jesus and had him
flogged. 2The soldiers twisted together a crown of thorns and put it on his
head. They clothed him in a purple robe
3and went up to him again and again, saying, "Hail, O king of the Jews!" And they
struck him in the face.
4Once more Pilate came out and said to
the Jews, "Look, I am bringing him out to
you to let you know that I find no basis for
a charge against him." 5When Jesus came
out wearing the crown of thorns and the
purple robe, Pilate said to them, "Here is
the man!"
6As soon as the chief priests and their
officials saw him, they shouted, "Crucify!
Crucify!"
But Pilate answered, "You take him and
crucify him. As for me, I find no basis for
a charge against him."
7The Jews insisted, "We have a law, and
according to that law he must die, because
he claimed to be the Son of God."●
8When Pilate heard this, he was even
more afraid, 9and he went back inside the
palace. "Where do you come from?" he
asked Jesus, but Jesus gave him no answer. 10"Do you refuse to speak to me?"
Pilate said. "Don't you realize I have
power either to free you or to crucify
you?"
11Jesus answered, "You would have no
power over me if it were not given to you
from above. Therefore the one who handed me over to you is guilty of a greater
sin."●
12From then on, Pilate tried to set Jesus
free, but the Jews kept shouting, "If you
let this man go, you are no friend of Caesar. Anyone who claims to be a king opposes Caesar."
13When Pilate heard this, he brought
Jesus out and sat down on the judge's seat
at a place known as The Stone Pavement
(which in Aramaic is Gabbatha). 14It was
the day of Preparation of Passover Week,
about the sixth hour.
"Here is your king," Pilate said to the
Jews.
15But they shouted, "Take him away!
Take him away! Crucify him!"
"Shall I crucify your king?" Pilate
asked.
"We have no king but Caesar," the chief
priests answered.
16Finally Pilate handed him over to them
to be crucified.●

## KING JAMES

JESUS:

1. SPURNED

BARABBAS, NOT JESUS

And when he had said this, he went out
again unto the Jews, and saith unto them,
I find in him no fault *at all.* 39 But ye
have a custom, that I should release unto
you one at the passover: will ye therefore
that I release unto you the King of the
Jews? 40 Then cried they all again, saying, Not this man, but Barab'bas. Now
Barab'bas was a robber.●

2. SCOURGED

**19** Then Pilate therefore took Jesus,
and scourged *him.* 2 And the soldiers platted a crown of thorns, and put
*it* on his head, and they put on him a
purple robe, 3 and said, Hail, King of the
Jews! and they smote him with their
hands. 4 Pilate therefore went forth
again, and saith unto them, Behold, I
bring him forth to you, that ye may know
that I find no fault in him. 5 Then came
Jesus forth, wearing the crown of thorns,
and the purple robe. And *Pilate* saith unto them, Behold the man! 6 When the
chief priests therefore and officers saw
him, they cried out, saying, Crucify *him,*
crucify *him.* Pilate saith unto them, Take
ye him, and crucify *him:* for I find no
fault in him. 7 The Jews answered him,
We have a law, and by our law he ought
to die, because he made himself the Son

3. INTIMIDATED

of God.● 8When Pilate therefore heard
that saying, he was the more afraid;
9 and went again into the judgment hall,
and saith unto Jesus, Whence art thou?
But Jesus gave him no answer. 10 Then
saith Pilate unto him, Speakest thou not
unto me? knowest thou not that I have
power to crucify thee, and have power to
release thee? 11 Jesus answered, Thou
couldest have no power *at all* against me,
except it were given thee from above:
therefore he that delivered me unto thee
hath the greater sin.●

4. DELIVERED TO BE CRUCIFIED

12 And from thenceforth Pilate sought
to release him: but the Jews cried out,
saying, If thou let this man go, thou art
not Caesar's friend: whosoever maketh
himself a king speaketh against Caesar.
13 When Pilate therefore heard that saying, he brought Jesus forth, and sat down
in the judgment seat in a place that is
called the Pavement, but in the Hebrew,
Gab'batha. 14 And it was the preparation of the passover, and about the sixth
hour: and he saith unto the Jews, Behold
your King! 15 But they cried out, Away
with *him,* away with *him,* crucify him.
Pilate saith unto them, Shall I crucify
your King? The chief priests answered,
We have no king but Caesar. 16 Then
delivered he him therefore unto them to
be crucified.●

CAESAR, NOT JESUS

This segment records Jesus' final appearance before Pilate. As you analyze each paragraph, record observations on Pilate, Jesus, and the accusers.

*18:38b-40*

PILATE ______________________________

JESUS ______________________________

ACCUSERS ______________________________

*19:1-7*

PILATE ______________________________

JESUS ______________________________

ACCUSERS ______________________________

*19:8-11*

PILATE ______________________________

JESUS ______________________________

ACCUSERS ______________________________

*19:12-16a*

PILATE ______________________________

JESUS ______________________________

ACCUSERS ______________________________

NEW INTERNATIONAL VERSION

What does this account teach about:

JESUS ______________________________

SCRIPTURE ______________________________

UNBELIEVING HEART ______________________________

OTHER ______________________________

*The Crucifixion*

So the soldiers took charge of Jesus.
[17]Carrying his own cross, he went out to
The Place of the Skull (which in Aramaic
is called Golgotha). [18]Here they crucified
him, and with him two others—one on
each side and Jesus in the middle.
[19]Pilate had a notice prepared and fastened to the cross. It read: JESUS OF
NAZARETH, THE KING OF THE JEWS. [20]Many
of the Jews read this sign, for the place
where Jesus was crucified was near the
city, and the sign was written in Aramaic,
Latin and Greek. [21]The chief priests of the
Jews protested to Pilate, "Do not write
'The King of the Jews,' but that this man
claimed to be king of the Jews."
[22]Pilate answered, "What I have written,
I have written."●
[23]When the soldiers crucified Jesus, they
took his clothes, dividing them into four
shares, one for each of them, with the un-
dergarment remaining. This garment was
seamless, woven in one piece from top to
bottom.
[24]"Let's not tear it," they said to one
another. "Let's decide by lot who will
get it."
This happened that the scripture might
be fulfilled which said,

> "They divided my garments among
> them
> and cast lots for my clothing."[a]●

So this is what the soldiers did.
[25]Near the cross of Jesus stood his
mother, his mother's sister, Mary the wife
of Clopas, and Mary of Magdala. [26]When
Jesus saw his mother there, and the disciple whom he loved standing nearby, he
said to his mother, "Dear woman, here is
your son," [27]and to the disciple, "Here is
your mother." From that time on, this disciple took her into his home.

*The Death of Jesus*

[28]Later, knowing that all was now completed, and so that the Scripture would be
fulfilled, Jesus said, "I am thirsty." [29]A jar
of wine vinegar was there, so they soaked
a sponge in it, put the sponge on a stalk of
the hyssop plant, and lifted it to Jesus' lips.
[30]When he had received the drink, Jesus
said, "It is finished." With that, he bowed
his head and gave up his spirit.●
[31]Now it was the day of Preparation, and
the next day was to be a special Sabbath.
Because the Jews did not want the bodies
left on the crosses during the Sabbath, they
asked Pilate to have the legs broken and
the bodies taken down. [32]The soldiers
therefore came and broke the legs of the
first man who had been crucified with
Jesus, and then those of the other. [33]But
when they came to Jesus and found that he
was already dead, they did not break his
legs. [34]Instead, one of the soldiers pierced
Jesus' side with a spear, bringing a sudden
flow of blood and water. [35]The man who
saw it has given testimony, and his testimony is true. He knows that he tells the
truth, and he testifies so that you also may
believe. [36]These things happened so that
the scripture would be fulfilled: "Not one
of his bones will be broken,"[a] [37]and, as
another scripture says, "They will look on
the one they have pierced."[b]●

[a]24 Psalm 22:18
[a]36 Exodus 12:46; Num. 9:12; Psalm 34:20
[b]37 Zech. 12:10
[c]39 Greek *a hundred litrai* (about 34 kilograms)

KING JAMES

*JESUS'* CRUCIFIED

1. IDENTITY RECOGNIZED

And they took Jesus, and
led *him* away.
17 And he bearing his cross went forth
into a place called *the place* of a skull,
which is called in the Hebrew Gol'gotha:
18 where they crucified him, and two
others with him, on either side one, and
Jesus in the midst. 19 And Pilate wrote a
title, and put *it* on the cross. And the
writing was, JESUS OF NAZARETH THE KING
OF THE JEWS. 20 This title then read
many of the Jews; for the place where
Jesus was crucified was nigh to the city:
and it was written in Hebrew, *and* Greek,
*and* Latin. 21 Then said the chief priests
of the Jews to Pilate, Write not, The King
of the Jews; but that he said, I am King
of the Jews. 22 Pilate answered, What I
have written I have written.●

2. GOODS CONFISCATED

23 Then the soldiers, when they had
crucified Jesus, took his garments, and
made four parts, to every soldier a part;
and also *his* coat: now the coat was without
seam, woven from the top throughout.
24 They said therefore among themselves,
Let us not rend it, but cast lots for
it, whose it shall be: that the Scripture
might be fulfilled, which saith,

*Ps. 22:18*

> They parted my raiment among them,
> and for my vesture they did cast lots.

These things therefore the soldiers did.●

3. MOTHER CARED FOR

25 Now there stood by the cross of
Jesus his mother, and his mother's sister,
Mary the *wife* of Cle'ophas, and Mary
Mag'dalene. 26 When Jesus therefore
saw his mother, and the disciple standing
by, whom he loved, he saith unto his
mother, Woman, behold thy son! 27 Then
saith he to the disciple, Behold thy mother!
And from that hour that disciple took her
unto his own *home*.●

4. LIFE GIVEN

28 After this, Jesus knowing that all
things were now accomplished, that the
Scripture might be fulfilled, saith, I thirst.
29 Now there was set a vessel full of vinegar:
and they filled a sponge with vinegar,
and put *it* upon hyssop, and put *it* to his
mouth. 30 When Jesus therefore had
received the vinegar, he said, It is finished:
and he bowed his head, and gave up the
ghost.●

5. DEATH VERIFIED

31 The Jews therefore, because it was
the preparation, that the bodies should
not remain upon the cross on the sabbath
day, (for that sabbath day was a high
day,) besought Pilate that their legs might
be broken, and *that* they might be taken
away. 32 Then came the soldiers, and
brake the legs of the first, and of the other
which was crucified with him. 33 But
when they came to Jesus, and saw that he
was dead already, they brake not his legs:
34 but one of the soldiers with a spear
pierced his side, and forthwith came there
out blood and water. 35 And he that
saw *it* bare record, and his record is true;
and he knoweth that he saith true, that ye
might believe. 36 For these things were
done, that the Scripture should be fulfilled,
A bone of him shall not be broken.
37 And again another Scripture saith,
They shall look on him whom they
pierced. ●

*Ex. 12:46*

*Zech. 12:10* PIERCED

What paragraphs of the segment record Jesus' words?

Why are the second and third paragraphs included in the story of Jesus' crucifixion?

Record the main parts of each paragraph:

*19:16b-22*

*19:23-24*

*19:25-27*

*19:28-30*

*19:31-37*

NEW INTERNATIONAL VERSION

List different impressions and reactions which this account leaves you with.

Why is it important that the Bible records the real death, burial and resurrection of Jesus?

*The Burial of Jesus*

38Later, Joseph of Arimathea asked Pilate for the body of Jesus. Now Joseph was
a disciple of Jesus, but secretly because he
feared the Jews. With Pilate's permission,
he came and took the body. 39He was accompanied by Nicodemus, the man who
earlier had visited Jesus at night. Nicodemus brought a mixture of myrrh and aloes,
about seventy-five pounds.[c] 40Taking
Jesus' body, the two of them wrapped it,
with the spices, in strips of linen. This was
in accordance with Jewish burial customs.
41At the place where Jesus was crucified,
there was a garden, and in the garden a new
tomb, in which no one had ever been laid.
42Because it was the Jewish day of Preparation and since the tomb was nearby, they
laid Jesus there.●

*The Empty Tomb*

20 Early on the first day of the week,
while it was still dark, Mary of Magdala went to the tomb and saw that the
stone had been removed from the entrance. 2So she came running to Simon Peter and the other disciple, the one Jesus
loved, and said, "They have taken the
Lord out of the tomb, and we don't know
where they have put him!"
3So Peter and the other disciple started
for the tomb. 4Both were running, but the
other disciple outran Peter and reached the
tomb first. 5He bent over and looked in at
the strips of linen lying there but did not go
in. 6Then Simon Peter, who was behind
him, arrived and went into the tomb. He
saw the strips of linen lying there, 7as well
as the burial cloth that had been around
Jesus' head. The cloth was folded up by
itself, separate from the linen. 8Finally the
other disciple, who had reached the tomb
first, also went inside. He saw and believed. 9(They still did not understand from
Scripture that Jesus had to rise from the
dead.)

*Jesus Appears to Mary of Magdala*

10Then the disciples went back to their
homes, ●

KING JAMES

1. BURIAL

BODY FOR THE TOMB

38 And after this Joseph of Arimathe'a,
being a disciple of Jesus, but secretly for
fear of the Jews, besought Pilate that he
might take away the body of Jesus: and
Pilate gave *him* leave. He came therefore,
and took the body of Jesus. 39 And there
came also Nicode'mus, which at the first
came to Jesus by night, and brought a
mixture of myrrh and aloes, about a
hundred pound *weight*. 40 Then took
they the body of Jesus, and wound it in
linen clothes with the spices, as the manner of the Jews is to bury. 41 Now in the
place where he was crucified there was a
garden; and in the garden a new sepulchre, wherein was never man yet laid.
42 There laid they Jesus therefore because
of the Jews' preparation *day;* for the
sepulchre was nigh at hand.●

*19:38-42* Record your observations.

2. RESURRECTION

TOMB WITHOUT THE BODY

20 The first *day* of the week cometh
Mary Mag'dalene early, when it
was yet dark, unto the sepulchre, and
seeth the stone taken away from the
sepulchre. 2 Then she runneth, and
cometh to Simon Peter, and to the other
disciple, whom Jesus loved, and saith unto
them, They have taken away the Lord out
of the sepulchre, and we know not where
they have laid him. 3 Peter therefore
went forth, and that other disciple, and
came to the sepulchre. 4 So they ran
both together: and the other disciple did
outrun Peter, and came first to the sepulchre. 5 And he stooping down, *and looking in*, saw the linen clothes lying; yet
went he not in. 6 Then cometh Simon
Peter following him, and went into the
sepulchre, and seeth the linen clothes lie,
7 and the napkin, that was about his head,
not lying with the linen clothes, but
wrapped together in a place by itself.
8 Then went in also that other disciple,
which came first to the sepulchre, and he
saw, and believed. 9 For as yet they knew
not the Scripture, that he must rise again
from the dead. 10 Then the disciples
went away again unto their own home.●

*20:1-10* Analyze this paragraph carefully. The three words "saw" (v.5), "seeth" (v.6) and "saw" (v.8) translate three different Greek words. The last word has the strength of *perception*. How would you account for this (as over against mere observing)?

NEW INTERNATIONAL VERSION

Record what you learn from this passage about:

GRIEF

THE RESURRECTED CHRIST

MIRACLE

PEACE AND GLADNESS

COMMISSION

HOLY SPIRIT

FORGIVENESS OF SINS

[11]but Mary stood outside the tomb
crying. As she wept, she bent over to look
into the tomb [12]and saw two angels in
white, seated where Jesus' body had been,
one at the head and the other at the foot.
[13]They asked her, "Woman, why are
you crying?"
"They have taken my Lord away," she
said, "and I don't know where they have
put him." [14]At this, she turned around and
saw Jesus standing there, but she did not
realize that it was Jesus.
[15]"Woman," he said, "why are you crying? Who is it you are looking for?"
Thinking he was the gardener, she said,
"Sir, if you have carried him away, tell me
where you have put him, and I will get
him."
[16]Jesus said to her, "Mary."
She turned toward him and cried out in
Aramaic, "Rabboni!" (which means
Teacher).
[17]Jesus said, "Do not hold on to me, for
I have not yet returned to the Father. Go
instead to my brothers and tell them, 'I am
returning to my Father and your Father, to
my God and your God.' "
[18]Mary of Magdala went to the disciples
with the news: "I have seen the Lord!"
And she told them that he had said these
things to her.●

*Jesus Appears to His Disciples*

[19]On the evening of that first day of the
week, when the disciples were together,
with the doors locked for fear of the Jews,
Jesus came and stood among them and
said, "Peace be with you!" [20]After he said
this, he showed them his hands and side.
The disciples were overjoyed when they
saw the Lord.●
[21]Again Jesus said, "Peace be with you!
As the Father has sent me, I am sending
you." [22]And with that he breathed on them
and said, "Receive the Holy Spirit. [23]If
you forgive anyone his sins, they are forgiven; if you do not forgive them, they are
not forgiven."●

KING JAMES

## 1. JESUS APPEARS TO MARY

WEEPING HEART

11 But Mary stood without at the
sepulchre weeping: and as she wept, she
stooped down, *and looked* into the sepulchre, 12 and seeth two angels in white
sitting, the one at the head, and the other
at the feet, where the body of Jesus had
lain. 13 And they say unto her, Woman,
why weepest thou? She saith unto them,
Because they have taken away my Lord,
and I know not where they have laid him.
14 And when she had thus said, she
turned herself back, and saw Jesus standing, and knew not that it was Jesus.
15 Jesus saith unto her, Woman, why
weepest thou? whom seekest thou? She,
supposing him to be the gardener, saith
unto him, Sir, if thou have borne him
hence, tell me where thou hast laid him,
and I will take him away. 16 Jesus saith
unto her, Mary. She turned herself, and
saith unto him, Rabbo'ni; which is to say,
Master. 17 Jesus saith unto her, Touch
me not; for I am not yet ascended to my
Father: but go to my brethren, and say
unto them, I ascend unto my Father, and
your Father; and *to* my God, and your
God. 18 Mary Mag'dalene came and told
the disciples that she had seen the Lord,
and *that* he had spoken these things unto
her.●

## 2. JESUS APPEARS TO THE DISCIPLES

19 Then the same day at evening, being
the first *day* of the week, when the doors
were shut where the disciples were assembled for fear of the Jews, came Jesus
and stood in the midst, and saith unto
them, Peace *be* unto you. 20 And when
he had so said, he showed unto them *his*
hands and his side. Then were the disciples glad, when they saw the Lord.●

## 3. COMMISSION TO THE DISCIPLES

21 Then said Jesus to them again, Peace
*be* unto you: as *my* Father hath sent me,
even so send I you. 22 And when he had
said this, he breathed on *them*, and saith
unto them, Receive ye the Holy Ghost:
23 whosesoever sins ye remit, they are
remitted unto them; *and* whosesoever
*sins* ye retain, they are retained. ●

FORGIVEN HEARTS

*20:11-18* Why do you think Mary recognized Jesus as of verse 16 but not as of verse 15?

______

______

______

______

______

______

What doctrines did Jesus teach Mary? ______

______

______

______

______

______

______

______

*20:19-20* Record the main parts of this paragraph.

______

______

______

______

______

______

*20:21-23* Analyze Jesus' different messages to the disciples.

______

______

______

______

______

______

______

______

______

NEW INTERNATIONAL VERSION

Record all that is taught by this passage about:

SKEPTICISM

FAITH FOR SEEING

FAITH FOR NOT SEEING

MIRACLES

JESUS AS THE SON OF GOD

OTHER

*Jesus Appears to Thomas*

24Now Thomas (called Didymus), one of
the Twelve, was not with the disciples
when Jesus came. 25When the other disciples told him that they had seen the Lord,
he declared, "Unless I see the nail marks
in his hands and put my finger where the
nails were, and put my hand into his side,
I will not believe it."●
26A week later his disciples were in the
house again, and Thomas was with them.
Though the doors were locked, Jesus came
and stood among them and said, "Peace be
with you!" 27Then he said to Thomas, "Put
your finger here; see my hands. Reach out
your hand and put it into my side. Stop
doubting and believe."
28Thomas said to him, "My Lord and my
God!"
29Then Jesus told him, "Because you
have seen me, you have believed; blessed
are those who have not seen and yet have
believed."●
30Jesus did many other miraculous signs
in the presence of his disciples, which are
not recorded in this book. 31But these are
written that you may[a] believe that Jesus is
the Christ, the Son of God, and that by
believing you may have life in his name.●

[a]31 Some manuscripts *may continue to*

KING JAMES

1. SKEPTIC THOMAS

24 But Thomas, one of the twelve,
called Did'ymus, was not with them when
Jesus came. 25 The other disciples therefore said unto him, We have seen the
Lord. But he said unto them, Except I
shall see in his hands the print of the nails,
and put my finger into the print of the
nails, and thrust my hand into his side, I
will not believe.●

SKEPTICISM

2. BELIEVING THOMAS

26 And after eight days again his disciples were within, and Thomas with
them: *then* came Jesus, the doors being
shut, and stood in the midst, and said,
Peace *be* unto you. 27 Then saith he to
Thomas, Reach hither thy finger, and behold my hands; and reach hither thy
hand, and thrust *it* into my side; and be
not faithless, but believing. 28 And
Thomas answered and said unto him,
My Lord and my God. 29 Jesus saith unto him, Thomas, because thou hast seen
me, thou hast believed: blessed *are*
they that have not seen, and *yet* have
believed.●

-purpose of the book

30 And many other signs truly did Jesus
in the presence of his disciples, which are
not written in this book: 31 but these are
written, that ye might believe that Jesus
is the Christ, the Son of God; and that
believing ye might have life through his
name.●

BELIEF

*20:24-25* What word was unconvincing to Thomas?

______________________________

*20:26-29* Compare the three things Jesus said to Thomas:

v.26 ______________________________

______________________________

v.27 ______________________________

______________________________

v.29 ______________________________

______________________________

What is significant about each part of Thomas' affirmation, "My Lord and my God"?

______________________________

______________________________

______________________________

______________________________

______________________________

______________________________

*20:30-31* Record the different truths taught by these verses.

______________________________

______________________________

______________________________

______________________________

______________________________

______________________________

______________________________

______________________________

______________________________

______________________________

______________________________

______________________________

______________________________

______________________________

______________________________

NEW INTERNATIONAL VERSION

Record what this passage teaches about:

MIRACLES

FAITH

RESURRECTED CHRIST

OTHER

### *Jesus and the Miraculous Catch of Fish*

**21** Afterward Jesus appeared again to his disciples by the Sea of Tiberias.[b] It happened this way: 2Simon Peter, Thomas (called Didymus), Nathanael from Cana in Galilee, the sons of Zebedee, and two other disciples were together. 3"I'm going out to fish," Simon Peter told them, and they said, "We'll go with you." So they went out and got into the boat, but that night they caught nothing.●

4Early in the morning, Jesus stood on the shore, but the disciples did not realize that it was Jesus.

5He called out to them, "Friends, haven't you any fish?"

"No," they answered.

6He said, "Throw your net on the right side of the boat and you will find some." When they did, they were unable to haul the net in because of the large number of fish.

7Then the disciple whom Jesus loved said to Peter, "It is the Lord!" As soon as Simon Peter heard him say, "It is the Lord," he wrapped his outer garment around him (for he had taken it off) and jumped into the water. 8The other disciples followed in the boat, towing the net full of fish, for they were not far from shore, about a hundred yards.[c]● 9When they landed, they saw a fire of burning coals there with fish on it, and some bread.

10Jesus said to them, "Bring some of the fish you have just caught."

11Simon Peter climbed aboard and dragged the net ashore. It was full of large fish, 153, but even with so many the net was not torn. 12Jesus said to them, "Come and have breakfast." None of the disciples dared ask him, "Who are you?" They knew it was the Lord. 13Jesus came, took the bread and gave it to them, and did the same with the fish. 14This was now the third time Jesus appeared to his disciples after he was raised from the dead.●

[b]*1* That is, Sea of Galilee
[c]*8* Greek *about two hundred cubits* (about 90 meters)

KING JAMES

1. SETTING

NO FISH

**21** After these things Jesus showed
himself again to the disciples at the
sea of Tibe'ri-as; and on this wise showed
he *himself*. 2 There were together Simon
Peter, and Thomas called Did'ymus, and
Nathan'a-el of Cana in Galilee, and the
*sons* of Zeb'edee, and two other of his
disciples. 3 Simon Peter saith unto them,
I go a fishing. They say unto him, We also
go with thee. They went forth, and entered
into a ship immediately; and that night
they caught nothing. ●

2. MIRACLE

4 But when the morning was now come,
Jesus stood on the shore; but the disciples
knew not that it was Jesus. 5 Then Jesus
saith unto them, Children, have ye any
meat? They answered him, No. 6 And
he said unto them, Cast the net on the
right side of the ship, and ye shall find.
They cast therefore, and now they were
not able to draw it for the multitude of
fishes. 7 Therefore that disciple whom
Jesus loved saith unto Peter, It is the Lord.
Now when Simon Peter heard that it was
the Lord, he girt *his* fisher's coat *unto him*,
(for he was naked,) and did cast himself
into the sea. 8 And the other disciples
came in a little ship, (for they were not
far from land, but as it were two hundred
cubits,) dragging the net with fishes.●

3. RECOGNITION

9 As soon then as they were come to
land, they saw a fire of coals there, and
fish laid thereon, and bread. 10 Jesus
saith unto them, Bring of the fish which
ye have now caught. 11 Simon Peter went
up, and drew the net to land full of great
fishes, a hundred and fifty and three: and
for all there were so many, yet was not the
net broken. 12 Jesus saith unto them,
Come *and* dine. And none of the disciples
durst ask him, Who art thou? knowing
that it was the Lord. 13 Jesus then
cometh, and taketh bread, and giveth
them, and fish likewise. 14 This is now
the third time that Jesus showed himself
to his disciples, after that he was risen
from the dead.●

FISH DINNER

*21:1-3* What are the main parts of the setting?

*21:4-8* Why do you think only one disciple (John) recognized Jesus (v.7)?

*21:9-14* Record your observations

NEW INTERNATIONAL VERSION

What do you learn here about:

LOVE FOR JESUS

DISCIPLESHIP

WILL OF CHRIST

OTHER

*Jesus Reinstates Peter*

15When they had finished eating, Jesus
said to Simon Peter, "Simon son of John,
do you truly love me more than these?"
"Yes, Lord," he said, "you know that I
love you."
Jesus said, "Feed my lambs."
16Again Jesus said, "Simon son of John,
do you truly love me?"
He answered, "Yes, Lord, you know
that I love you."
Jesus said, "Take care of my sheep."
17The third time he said to him, "Simon
son of John, do you love me?"
Peter was hurt because Jesus asked him
the third time, "Do you love me?" He said,
"Lord, you know all things; you know that
I love you."
Jesus said, "Feed my sheep. 18I tell you
the truth, when you were younger you
dressed yourself and went where you
wanted; but when you are old you will
stretch out your hands, and someone else
will dress you and lead you where you do
not want to go." 19Jesus said this to indicate the kind of death by which Peter
would glorify God. Then he said to him,
"Follow me!"●
20Peter turned and saw that the disciple
whom Jesus loved was following them.
(This was the one who had leaned back
against Jesus at the supper and had said,
"Lord, who is going to betray you?")
21When Peter saw him, he asked, "Lord,
what about him?"
22Jesus answered, "If I want him to
remain alive until I return, what is that to
you? You must follow me." 23Because of
this, the rumor spread among the brothers
that this disciple would not die. But Jesus
did not say that he would not die; he only
said, "If I want him to remain alive until I
return, what is that to you?"●
24This is the disciple who testifies to
these things and who wrote them down.
We know that his testimony is true.
25Jesus did many other things as well. If
every one of them were written down, I
suppose that even the whole world would
not have room for the books that would be
written.●

## KING JAMES

1. CHALLENGE

LOVE ME

15 So when they had dined, Jesus saith
to Simon Peter, Simon, *son* of Jona,
lovest thou me more than these? He
saith unto him, Yea, Lord; thou knowest
that I love thee. He saith unto him, Feed
my lambs. 16 He saith to him again the
second time, Simon, *son* of Jona, lovest
thou me? He saith unto him, Yea, Lord;
thou knowest that I love thee. He saith
unto him, Feed my sheep. 17 He saith
unto him the third time, Simon, *son* of
Jona, lovest thou me? Peter was grieved
because he said unto him the third time,
Lovest thou me? And he said unto him,
Lord, thou knowest all things; thou
knowest that I love thee. Jesus saith unto
him, Feed my sheep. 18 Verily, verily, I
say unto thee, When thou wast young,
thou girdedst thyself, and walkedst
whither thou wouldest: but when thou
shalt be old, thou shalt stretch forth thy
hands, and another shall gird thee, and
carry *thee* whither thou wouldest not.
19 This spake he, signifying by what death
he should glorify God. And when he had
spoken this, he saith unto him, Follow me.●

2. CORRECTION

FOLLOW ME

20 Then Peter, turning about, seeth the
disciple whom Jesus loved following;
which also leaned on his breast at supper,
and said, Lord, which is he that betrayeth
thee? 21 Peter seeing him saith to Jesus,
Lord, and what *shall* this man *do?*
22 Jesus saith unto him, If I will that he
tarry till I come, what *is that* to thee?
follow thou me. 23 Then went this saying
abroad among the brethren, that that
disciple should not die: yet Jesus said not
unto him, He shall not die; but, If I will
that he tarry till I come, what *is that* to
thee?●

-conclusion

24 This is the disciple which testifieth
of these things, and wrote these things:
and we know that his testimony is true.
25 And there are also many other things
which Jesus did, the which, if they should
be written every one, I suppose that even
the world itself could not contain the
books that should be written. Amen.●

Recall Peter's triple denial of Christ, as background for this segment.

*21:15-19* Analyze Jesus' questions, Peter's answers, and Jesus' responses.

*21:20-23* Who is the one being corrected here?

*21:24-25* Compare verse 25 with 20:30-31

# ACTS

## AUTHORSHIP

Luke is the author (cf. Acts 1:1 with Luke 1:1-4). He was a Gentile, and about the same age as Paul. He and Paul were constant companions and co-workers for about the last twenty years of Paul's life. Luke was a gifted scholar and physician, and was probably converted under Paul's ministry.

## DATE

Luke apparently finished writing Acts around A.D. 61 while Paul was still imprisoned in Rome (Acts 28). The Holy Spirit's design was not to include any more of Paul's life nor of the church's experience in this book, and so He inspired Luke to write at this time.

## PURPOSE AND THEME

Acts is a connecting link: the sequel to the Gospels that precede it, and the background to the Epistles that follow it. It is the historical record that attests the success of Jesus' earthly ministry by showing how the risen Lord works in the present age in the hearts of men. The explanations and interpretations of the tremendous events of Acts are given in the Epistles.

The verse most frequently recognized as the key verse of Acts is 1:8: "But ye shall receive power, after that the Holy Ghost is come upon you: and ye shall be witnesses unto me both in Jerusalem, and in all Judea, and in Samaria, and unto the uttermost part of the earth."

## ACTS: Birth, Growth and Mission of the First Church

| | |
|---|---|
| THE CHURCH IS BORN | 1:1-2:47 |
| The Church's Work | 1:1-14 |
| The Church's Workers | 1:15-26 |
| The Church's Spirit Baptism | 2:1-21 |
| The Church's Gospel | 2:22-47 |
| THE CHURCH GROWS THROUGH TESTING | 3:1-8:1a |
| The Test of Popularity | 3:1-26 |
| The Test of Loyalty | 4:1-22 |
| The Test of Things | 4:23-5:11 |
| The Test of Fortitude | 5:12-42 |
| The Test of Responsibility | 6:1-15 |
| The Test of Grace | 7:1-8:1a |
| THE CHURCH IS SCATTERED | 8:1b-9:31 |
| Samaritans Saved | 8:1b-25 |
| An Ethiopian Saved | 8:26-40 |
| Saul Saved | 9:1-19a |
| Saul's First Ministries | 9:19b-31 |
| THE CHURCH EMBRACES GENTILES | 9:32-12:25 |
| Peter's Outlook Changes Through a Vision | 9:32-11:18 |
| Mission-Minded Church at Antioch | 11:19-30 |
| God's Deliverance of Peter from Prison | 12:1-25 |
| THE CHURCH EXTENDS OVERSEAS | 13:1-21:17 |
| First Missionary Journey | 13:1-14:28 |
| Jerusalem Council | 15:1-35 |
| Second Missionary Journey | 15:36-18:22 |
| Third Missionary Journey | 18:23-21:17 |
| THE CHURCH'S LEADER ON TRIAL | 21:18-28:31 |
| Paul Before the Mob and Council | 21:18-23:30 |
| Paul Before the Governors | 23:31-25:12 |
| Paul Before a King | 25:13-26:32 |
| Paul Reaches Rome | 27:1-28:31 |

# ACTS

NEW INTERNATIONAL VERSION

The things Jesus talked about after His resurrection and before His ascension were very important. According to verses 3-8, what were those important subjects?

How does the commission of verse 8 apply to the church today, geographically?

List practical lessons taught by this passage:

### *Jesus Taken Up Into Heaven*

1 In my former book, Theophilus, I
wrote about all that Jesus began to do
and to teach 2until the day he was taken up
to heaven, after giving instructions through
the Holy Spirit to the apostles he had chosen. 3After his suffering, he showed himself to these men and gave many convinc-
ing proofs that he was alive. He appeared
to them over a period of forty days and
spoke about the kingdom of God. 4On one
occasion, while he was eating with them,
he gave them this command: "Do not leave
Jerusalem, but wait for the gift my Father
promised, which you have heard me speak
about. 5For John baptized with[a] water, but
in a few days you will be baptized with the
Holy Spirit."●
6So when they met together, they asked
him, "Lord, are you at this time going to
restore the kingdom to Israel?"
7He said to them: "It is not for you to
know the times or dates the Father has set
by his own authority. 8But you will receive
power when the Holy Spirit comes on you;
and you will be my witnesses in Jerusalem,
and in all Judea and Samaria, and to the
ends of the earth."
9After he said this, he was taken up before their very eyes, and a cloud hid him
from their sight.
10They were looking intently up into the
sky as he was going, when suddenly two
men dressed in white stood beside them.
11"Men of Galilee," they said, "why do
you stand here looking into the sky? This
same Jesus, who has been taken from you
into heaven, will come back in the same
way you have seen him go into heaven."●

### *Matthias Chosen to Replace Judas*

12Then they returned to Jerusalem from
the hill called the Mount of Olives, a Sabbath day's walk[b] from the city. 13When
they arrived, they went upstairs to the
room where they were staying. Those
present were Peter, John, James and Andrew; Philip and Thomas, Bartholomew
and Matthew; James son of Alphaeus and
Simon the Zealot, and Judas son of James.
14They all joined together constantly in
prayer, along with the women and Mary
the mother of Jesus, and his brothers.●

[a]5 Or *in*

[b]12 That is, about 3/4 mile (about 1,100 meters)

KING JAMES

# ACTS

1\. INSTRUCTED WITNESSES

VISIBLE CONTACT WITH JESUS

1 The former treatise have I made, O
The-oph'ilus, of all that Jesus began
both to do and teach, 2 until the day in
which he was taken up, after that he
through the Holy Ghost had given commandments unto the apostles whom he
had chosen: 3 to whom also he showed
himself alive after his passion by many
infallible proofs, being seen of them forty
days, and speaking of the things pertaining to the kingdom of God: 4 and, being
assembled together with *them*, commanded them that they should not depart
from Jerusalem, but wait for the promise
of the Father, which, *saith he*, ye have
heard of me. 5 For John truly baptized
with water; but ye shall be baptized with
the Holy Ghost not many days hence.●

2\. EMPOWERED WITNESSES

6 When they therefore were come together, they asked of him, saying, Lord,
wilt thou at this time restore again the
kingdom to Israel? 7 And he said unto
them, It is not for you to know the times
or the seasons, which the Father hath put
in his own power. 8 But ye shall receive
power, after that the Holy Ghost is come
upon you: and ye shall be witnesses unto
me both in Jerusalem, and in all Judea,
and in Samaria, and unto the uttermost
part of the earth. 9 And when he had
spoken these things, while they beheld, he
was taken up; and a cloud received him
out of their sight. 10 And while they
looked steadfastly toward heaven as he
went up, behold, two men stood by them
in white apparel; 11 which also said, Ye
men of Galilee, why stand ye gazing up
into heaven? this same Jesus, which is
taken up from you into heaven, shall so
come in like manner as ye have seen him
go into heaven.●

3\. PRAYING WITNESSES

12 Then returned they unto Jerusalem
from the mount called Ol'ivet, which is
from Jerusalem a sabbath day's journey.
13 And when they were come in, they
went up into an upper room, where abode
both Peter, and James, and John, and
Andrew, Philip, and Thomas, Bartholomew, and Matthew, James *the son* of
Al'pheus, and Simon Zelo'tes, and Judas
*the brother* of James. 14 These all continued with one accord in prayer and supplication, with the women, and Mary the
mother of Jesus, and with his brethren.●

INVISIBLE CONTACT WITH JESUS

*1:1-5* What were the two activities of Jesus' public ministry (v.1)?

For how long was Jesus on earth after His resurrection (v.3)?

What person of the trinity continued Jesus' work on earth (v.5)?

*1:6-11* The important thing for the disciples was not to know

but to receive Where would this come from?

The disciples were to be witnesses in

a.

b.

c.

*1:12-14* Relate verse 12 to verse 4. What different things does verse 14 teach about the upper room prayer times?

NEW INTERNATIONAL VERSION

What is there about the Bible that makes it *necessary* for its prophecies to be fulfilled?

How did God punish Judas' betrayal of Jesus?

What practical lessons do you learn from these statements:

"You know every heart"(v.25)

"Show us which...you have chosen"(v.25)

What is the prominent warning taught by this passage?

Record other practical truths taught by the passage.

15In those days Peter stood up among the
believers[c] (a group numbering about a hundred and twenty) 16and said, "Brothers,
the Scripture had to be fulfilled which the
Holy Spirit spoke long ago through the
mouth of David concerning Judas, who
served as guide for those who arrested
Jesus— 17he was one of our number and
shared in this ministry."
18(With the reward he got for his wickedness, Judas bought a field; there he fell
headlong, his body burst open and all his
intestines spilled out. 19Everyone in
Jerusalem heard about this, so they called
that field in their language Akeldama, that
is, Field of Blood.)
20"For," said Peter, "it is written in the
book of Psalms,

" 'May his place be deserted;
let there be no one to dwell in
it,'[a]

and,

" 'May another take his place of
leadership.'[b]

21Therefore it is necessary to choose one of
the men who have been with us the whole
time the Lord Jesus went in and out among
us, 22beginning from John's baptism to the
time when Jesus was taken up from us. For
one of these must become a witness with us
of his resurrection."●
23So they proposed two men: Joseph
called Barsabbas (also known as Justus)
and Matthias. 24Then they prayed, "Lord,
you know everyone's heart. Show us
which of these two you have chosen 25to
take over this apostolic ministry, which
Judas left to go where he belongs." 26Then
they drew lots, and the lot fell to Matthias;
so he was added to the eleven apostles.●

[c]*15* Greek *brothers*
[a]*20* Psalm 69:25 [b]*20* Psalm 109:8

KING JAMES

1. TRAITOR

**15** And in those days Peter stood up in
the midst of the disciples, and said, (the
number of names together were about a
hundred and twenty,) **16** Men *and* brethren, this Scripture must needs have been
fulfilled, which the Holy Ghost by the
mouth of David spake before concerning
Judas, which was guide to them that took
Jesus. **17** For he was numbered with us,
and had obtained part of this ministry.
**18** Now this man purchased a field with
the reward of iniquity; and falling headlong, he burst asunder in the midst, and
all his bowels gushed out. **19** And it was
known unto all the dwellers at Jerusalem;
insomuch as that field is called, in their
proper tongue, Acel'dama, that is to say,
The field of blood. **20** For it is written
in the book of Psalms,
Let his habitation be desolate,
and let no man dwell therein:
and,
His bishopric let another take.
**21** Wherefore of these men which have
companied with us all the time that the
Lord Jesus went in and out among us,
**22** beginning from the baptism of John,
unto that same day that he was taken up
from us, must one be ordained to be a
witness with us of his resurrection.●

2. RE-PLACE-MENT CHOSEN

**23** And they appointed two, Joseph called
Barsabas, who was surnamed Justus, and
Matthi'as. **24** And they prayed, and said,
Thou, Lord, which knowest the hearts of
all *men*, show whether of these two thou
hast chosen, **25** that he may take part of
this ministry and apostleship, from which
Judas by transgression fell, that he might
go to his own place. **26** And they gave
forth their lots; and the lot fell upon
Matthi'as; and he was numbered with the
eleven apostles.●

120 brethren

Ps. 69:25

Ps. 109:8

11 apostles plus one

List the ministries or experiences of Jesus as they appear in the passage. Record these also in the right-hand margin, with single words.

a. ____

b. ____

c. ____

d. ____

e. ____

What would you know about these four men, if this was the only passage referring to them:

Peter ____

Judas ____

Joseph ____

Matthias ____

What was the ministry of the following in the choice of Matthias?

Scripture (vv.16-18) ____

Lord (vv.24-25) ____

lots (v.26) ____

NEW INTERNATIONAL VERSION

The day of Pentecost was a holy day (holiday), fifty days after the Passover ceremonies, when Christ was crucified. (See Lev. 23:16)
What things happened on this day? (vv.2-4)

What person of the trinity was prominent?

Who were personally involved (v.1)?

What were the reactions of the multitudes? (vv.5-13)

Peter quoted the prophecy of Joel 2:28-32 to the people (vv.17-21). By inspiration of the Holy Spirit he adds the words "In the last days." What part of the prophecy were the multitudes seeing fulfilled?

In end times, before the day of the Lord arrives, what sign would be given?

Why is verse 21 such an important verse in the Bible?

### *The Holy Spirit Comes at Pentecost*

2 When the day of Pentecost came, they
were all together in one place. 2 Suddenly a sound like the blowing of a violent
wind came from heaven and filled the
whole house where they were sitting.
3 They saw what seemed to be tongues of
fire that separated and came to rest on each
of them. 4 All of them were filled with the
Holy Spirit and began to speak in other
tongues[c] as the Spirit enabled them. ●
5 Now there were staying in Jerusalem
God-fearing Jews from every nation under
heaven. 6 When they heard this sound, a
crowd came together in bewilderment, because each one heard them speaking in his
own language. 7 Utterly amazed, they
asked: "Are not all these men who are
speaking Galileans? 8 Then how is it that
each of us hears them in his own native
language? 9 Parthians, Medes and Elamites;
residents of Mesopotamia, Judea and Cap-
padocia, Pontus and Asia, 10 Phrygia and
Pamphylia, Egypt and the parts of Libya
near Cyrene; visitors from Rome 11 (both
Jews and converts to Judaism); Cretans
and Arabs—we hear them declaring the
wonders of God in our own tongues!"
12 Amazed and perplexed, they asked one
another, "What does this mean?"
13 Some, however, made fun of them and
said, "They have had too much wine.[d]" ●

### *Peter Addresses the Crowd*

14 Then Peter stood up with the Eleven,
raised his voice and addressed the crowd:
"Fellow Jews and all of you who are in
Jerusalem, let me explain this to you; listen
carefully to what I say. 15 These men are
not drunk, as you suppose. It's only nine
in the morning! 16 No, this is what was
spoken by the prophet Joel:

17 " 'In the last days, God says,
I will pour out my Spirit on all
people.
Your sons and daughters will
prophesy,
your young men will see visions,
your old men will dream dreams.
18 Even on my servants, both men and
women,
I will pour out my Spirit in those
days,
and they will prophesy.
19 I will show wonders in the heaven
above
and signs on the earth below,
blood and fire and billows of
smoke.
20 The sun will be turned to darkness
and the moon to blood
before the coming of the great
and glorious day of the Lord.
21 And everyone who calls
on the name of the Lord will be
saved.'[e] ●

[c] 4 Or *languages*; also in verse 11
[d] 13 Or *sweet wine*
[e] 21 Joel 2:28-32

KING JAMES

1. EVENT

**2** And when the day of Pentecost was
fully come, they were all with one
accord in one place. 2 And suddenly
there came a sound from heaven as of a
rushing mighty wind, and it filled all the
house where they were sitting. 3 And
there appeared unto them cloven tongues
like as of fire, and it sat upon each of them.
4 And they were all filled with the Holy
Ghost, and began to speak with other
tongues, as the Spirit gave them utterance.●

DAY OF PENTECOST HAD COME

2. REACTION

5 And there were dwelling at Jerusalem
Jews, devout men, out of every nation
under heaven. 6 Now when this was
noised abroad, the multitude came together, and were confounded, because
that every man heard them speak in his
own language. 7 And they were all
amazed and marveled, saying one to another, Behold, are not all these which
speak Galileans? 8 And how hear we
every man in our own tongue, wherein we
were born? 9 Par'thi-ans, and Medes,
and E'lamites, and the dwellers in Meso-
pota'mi-a, and in Judea, and Cappa-
do'cia, in Pontus, and Asia, 10 Phryg'i-a,
and Pamphyl'i-a, in Egypt, and in the
parts of Libya about Cyre'ne, and
strangers of Rome, Jews and proselytes,
11 Cretes and Arabians, we do hear them
speak in our tongues the wonderful works
of God. 12 And they were all amazed,
and were in doubt, saying one to another,
What meaneth this? 13 Others mocking said, These men are full of new
wine.●

3. EXPLANATION

14 But Peter, standing up with the
eleven, lifted up his voice, and said unto
them, Ye men of Judea, and all *ye* that
dwell at Jerusalem, be this known unto
you, and hearken to my words: 15 for
these are not drunken, as ye suppose,
seeing it is *but* the third hour of the day.
16 But this is that which was spoken by
the prophet Joel;

17 And it shall come to pass in the last days, saith God,
I will pour out of my Spirit upon all flesh:
and your sons and your daughters shall prophesy,
and your young men shall see visions,
and your old men shall dream dreams:
18 and on my servants and on my handmaidens
I will pour out in those days of my Spirit;
and they shall prophesy:
19 and I will show wonders in heaven above,
and signs in the earth beneath;
blood, and fire, and vapor of smoke:
20 the sun shall be turned into darkness,
and the moon into blood,
before that great and notable day of the Lord come:
21 and it shall come to pass, *that* whosoever shall call on the name of the Lord shall be saved. ●

Joel 2:28-32

DAY OF THE LORD SHALL COME

*2:1-4* Jesus' promise concerning the soon coming of the Holy Spirit (1:5) was fulfilled on this day of Pentecost. Was the large group of believers in a meeting at the time?

______

What happened? ______

______

______

______

What was the source of the tongues speaking (v.4)?

______

______

______

*2:5-13* What does this paragraph tell about the multitudes?

______

______

______

______

What was the subject of the tongues speaking (v.11)?

______

______

______

*2:14-21* What does this paragraph teach about God?

______

______

______

______

What was the object or purpose of the tongues speaking (v.21)?

______

______

______

______

NEW INTERNATIONAL VERSION

Record all that you see taught in this passage about:

JESUS

SCRIPTURE

ISRAEL

List some spiritual applications:

[22]"Men of Israel, listen to this: Jesus of
Nazareth was a man accredited by God to
you by miracles, wonders and signs, which
God did among you through him, as you
yourselves know. [23]This man was handed
over to you by God's set purpose and foreknowledge; and you, with the help of
wicked men, put him to death by nailing
him to the cross. [24]But God raised him
from the dead, freeing him from the agony
of death, because it was impossible for
death to keep its hold on him. [25]David said
about him:

" 'I saw the Lord always before
me.
Because he is at my right hand,
I will not be shaken.
[26]Therefore my heart is glad and my
tongue rejoices;
my body also will live in hope,
[27]because you will not abandon me to
the grave,
nor will you let your Holy One
see decay.
[28]You have made known to me the
paths of life;
you will fill me with joy in your
presence.'[f] ●

[29]"Brothers, I can tell you confidently
that the patriarch David died and was buried, and his tomb is here to this day. [30]But
he was a prophet and knew that God had
promised him on oath that he would place
one of his descendants on his throne.
[31]Seeing what was ahead, he spoke of the
resurrection of the Christ,[a] that he was not
abandoned to the grave, nor did his body
see decay. [32]God has raised this Jesus to
life, and we are all witnesses of the fact.
[33]Exalted to the right hand of God, he has
received from the Father the promised
Holy Spirit and has poured out what you
now see and hear. [34]For David did not ascend to heaven, and yet he said,

"The Lord said to my Lord:
"Sit at my right hand
[35]until I make your enemies
a footstool for your feet." '[b]

[36]"Therefore let all Israel be assured of
this: God has made this Jesus, whom you
crucified, both Lord and Christ."●

[f]28 Psalm 16:8-11
[a]31 Or *Messiah*. "The Christ" (Greek) and "the Messiah" (Hebrew) both mean "the Anointed One"; also in verse 36.
[b]35 Psalm 110:1

KING JAMES

1. JESUS IS ALIVE

JESUS OF NAZARETH

22 Ye men of Israel, hear these words;
Jesus of Nazareth, a man approved of
God among you by miracles and wonders
and signs, which God did by him in the
midst of you, as ye yourselves also know:
23 him, being delivered by the deter-
minate counsel and foreknowledge of
God, ye have taken, and by wicked hands
have crucified and slain: 24 whom God
hath raised up, having loosed the pains
of death: because it was not possible that
he should be holden of it. 25 For David
speaketh concerning him,

Ps. 16:8-11

I foresaw the Lord always before my
face;
for he is on my right hand, that I
should not be moved:
26 therefore did my heart rejoice, and
my tongue was glad;
moreover also my flesh shall rest in
hope:
27 because thou wilt not leave my soul
in hell,
neither wilt thou suffer thine Holy
One to see corruption.
28 Thou hast made known to me the
ways of life;
thou shalt make me full of joy with
thy countenance. ●

2. DAVID IS DEAD

29 Men *and* brethren, let me freely
speak unto you of the patriarch David,
that he is both dead and buried, and his
sepulchre is with us unto this day.
30 Therefore being a prophet, and knowing that God had sworn with an oath to
him, that of the fruit of his loins, according to the flesh, he would raise up Christ
to sit on his throne; 31 he, seeing this
before, spake of the resurrection of Christ,
that his soul was not left in hell, neither
his flesh did see corruption. 32 This Jesus
hath God raised up, whereof we all are
witnesses. 33 Therefore being by the
right hand of God exalted, and having
received of the Father the promise of the
Holy Ghost, he hath shed forth this,
which ye now see and hear. 34 For David
is not ascended into the heavens: but he
saith himself,

The LORD said unto my Lord,
Sit thou on my right hand,
35 until I make thy foes thy footstool.

Ps. 110:1

36 Therefore let all the house of Israel
know assuredly, that God hath made that
same Jesus, whom ye have crucified, both
Lord and Christ. ●

LORD AND CHRIST

This segment continues Peter's sermon begun at 2:14. It is his arraignment of those who rejected Jesus.

*2:22-28* Complete this charge: "Jesus of Nazareth ... ye have ________ "(vv.22,23).

What is Peter's next triumphant statement? "God hath ________ "(v.24).

*2:29-36* Record what is written here about David:

______________________________

______________________________

______________________________

______________________________

______________________________

______________________________

______________________________

______________________________

______________________________

______________________________

______________________________

______________________________

______________________________

______________________________

______________________________

Analyze verse 36 carefully, as the conclusion of Peter's sermon.

______________________________

______________________________

______________________________

______________________________

______________________________

______________________________

______________________________

______________________________

______________________________

______________________________

______________________________

______________________________

NEW INTERNATIONAL VERSION

What does this passage teach about:

GUILT

REPENTANCE

REMISSION OF SINS

GRACE OF GOD

GROWING AS YOUNG CHRISTIAN CONVERTS

JOY IN CHRIST

List other spiritual applications:

[37]When the people heard this, they were
cut to the heart and said to Peter and the
other apostles, "Brothers, what shall we
do?"
[38]Peter replied, "Repent and be baptized, every one of you, in the name of
Jesus Christ so that your sins may be forgiven. And you will receive the gift of the
Holy Spirit. [39]The promise is for you and
your children and for all who are far off—
for all whom the Lord our God will call."
[40]With many other words he warned
them; and he pleaded with them, "Save
yourselves from this corrupt generation."
[41]Those who accepted his message were
baptized, and about three thousand were
added to their number that day.

*The Fellowship of the Believers*

[42]They devoted themselves to the apostles' teaching and to the fellowship, to the
breaking of bread and to prayer. [43]Every-
one was filled with awe, and many wonders and miraculous signs were done by
the apostles. [44]All the believers were together and had everything in common.
[45]Selling their possessions and goods, they
gave to anyone as he had need. [46]Every
day they continued to meet together in the
temple courts. They broke bread in their
homes and ate together with glad and sincere hearts, [47]praising God and enjoying
the favor of all the people. And the Lord
added to their number daily those who
were being saved.

c18 Or *Messiah*; also in verse 20

KING JAMES

1. CONVICTION OF SIN

37 Now when they heard *this*, they were
pricked in their heart, and said unto Peter
and to the rest of the apostles, Men *and*
brethren, what shall we do? 38 Then
Peter said unto them, Repent, and be baptized every one of you in the name of
Jesus Christ for the remission of sins, and
ye shall receive the gift of the Holy Ghost.
39 For the promise is unto you, and to
your children, and to all that are afar off,
*even* as many as the Lord our God shall
call. 40 And with many other words did
he testify and exhort, saying, Save yourselves from this untoward generation.●

2. REGENERATION

41 Then they that gladly received his
word were baptized: and the same day
there were added *unto them* about three
thousand souls. 42 And they continued
steadfastly in the apostles' doctrine and
fellowship, and in breaking of bread, and
in prayers.●

3. DAILY VICTORY

43 And fear came upon every soul: and
many wonders and signs were done by the
apostles. 44 And all that believed were
together, and had all things common;
45 and sold their possessions and goods,
and parted them to all *men*, as every man
had need. 46 And they, continuing daily
with one accord in the temple, and breaking bread from house to house, did eat
their meat with gladness and singleness
of heart, 47 praising God, and having
favor with all the people. And the Lord
added to the church daily such as should
be saved. ●

GUILT

PRAISE

This segment records the response of the people to Peter's sermon.

*2:37-40* Compare the people's reactions and Peter's answer.

*2:41-42* What are the main items of this paragraph?

*2:43-47* Record the different things that transpired at this time.

NEW INTERNATIONAL VERSION

Where were Peter and John going when this event happened?

What do you think impelled Peter to say what he said?

What do you learn from the man's praising God?

What does this passage teach about:

CHRISTIAN SERVICE

COMPASSION

PRIORITIES

OTHER

*Peter Heals the Crippled Beggar*

3 One day Peter and John were going up
to the temple at the time of prayer—at
three in the afternoon. 2Now a man crippled from birth was being carried to the
temple gate called Beautiful, where he was
put every day to beg from those going into
the temple courts. 3When he saw Peter and
John about to enter, he asked them for
money. 4Peter looked straight at him, as
did John. Then Peter said, "Look at us!"
5So the man gave them his attention, expecting to get something from them.●
6Then Peter said, "Silver or gold I do not
have, but what I have I give you. In the
name of Jesus Christ of Nazareth, walk."
7Taking him by the right hand, he helped
him up, and instantly the man's feet and
ankles became strong. 8He jumped to his
feet and began to walk. Then he went with
them into the temple courts, walking and
jumping, and praising God.● 9When all the
people saw him walking and praising God,
10they recognized him as the same man
who used to sit begging at the temple gate
called Beautiful, and they were filled with
wonder and amazement at what had happened to him.●

KING JAMES

1. LAME MAN

NEED

3 Now Peter and John went up together into the temple at the hour of
prayer, *being* the ninth *hour*. 2 And a
certain man lame from his mother's
womb was carried, whom they laid daily
at the gate of the temple which is called
Beautiful, to ask alms of them that entered
into the temple; 3 who, seeing Peter and
John about to go into the temple, asked
an alms. 4 And Peter, fastening his eyes
upon him with John, said, Look on us.
5 And he gave heed unto them, expecting
to receive something of them. ●

2. HEALED MAN

HEALING

6 Then
Peter said, Silver and gold have I none;
but such as I have give I thee: In the name
of Jesus Christ of Nazareth rise up and
walk. 7 And he took him by the right
hand, and lifted *him* up: and immediately
his feet and ankle bones received strength.
8 And he leaping up stood, and walked,
and entered with them into the temple,
walking, and leaping, and praising God.●

3. AMAZED PEOPLE

REACTION

9 And all the people saw him walking and
praising God: 10 and they knew that it
was he which sat for alms at the Beautiful
gate of the temple: and they were filled
with wonder and amazement at that
which had happened unto him.●

This story repeats a common pattern of Jesus' ministry: NEED, HEALING, REACTION. Why would this give credentials for the apostles' ministry?

____________________

____________________

____________________

____________________

Record your observations of the main parts of each paragraph.

*3:1-5* ____________________

*3:6-8* ____________________

*3:9-10* ____________________

NEW INTERNATIONAL VERSION

List all the facts of the gospel message which Peter cited in this sermon:

What does the passage teach about:

REPENTANCE

GRACE OF GOD

SCRIPTURE

JUDGMENT

FAITH

OTHER

*Peter Speaks to the Onlookers*

11 While the beggar held on to Peter and
John, all the people were astonished and
came running to them in the place called
Solomon's Colonnade. 12 When Peter saw
this, he said to them: "Men of Israel, why
does this surprise you? Why do you stare
at us as if by our own power or godliness
we had made this man walk? 13 The God of
Abraham, Isaac and Jacob, the God of our
fathers, has glorified his servant Jesus.
You handed him over to be killed, and you
disowned him before Pilate, though he had
decided to let him go. 14 You disowned the
Holy and Righteous One and asked that a
murderer be released to you. 15 You killed
the author of life, but God raised him from
the dead. We are witnesses of this. 16 By
faith in the name of Jesus, this man whom
you see and know was made strong. It is
Jesus' name and the faith that comes
through him that has given this complete
healing to him, as you can all see.●

17 "Now, brothers, I know that you acted
in ignorance, as did your leaders. 18 But this
is how God fulfilled what he had foretold
through all the prophets, saying that his
Christ[c] would suffer.● 19 Repent, then, and
turn to God, so that your sins may be
wiped out, that times of refreshing may
come from the Lord, 20 and that he may
send the Christ, who has been appointed
for you—even Jesus. 21 He must remain in
heaven until the time comes for God to
restore everything, as he promised long
ago through his holy prophets. 22 For
Moses said, 'The Lord your God will raise
up for you a prophet like me from among
your own people; you must listen to everything he tells you. 23 Anyone who does not
listen to him will be completely cut off from
among his people.'[a]

24 "Indeed, all the prophets from Samuel
on, as many as have spoken, have foretold
these days. 25 And you are heirs of the
prophets and of the covenant God made
with your fathers. He said to Abraham,
'Through your offspring all peoples on
earth will be blessed.'[b] 26 When God raised
up his servant, he sent him first to you to
bless you by turning each of you from your
wicked ways."●

[a] *23* Deut. 18:15,18,19
[b] *25* Gen. 22:18; 26:4

KING JAMES

**1. EXPLANATION**

JESUS THE OBJECT OF ISRAEL'S HATE

**11** And as the lame man which was healed held Peter and John, all the people ran together unto them in the porch that is called Solomon's, greatly wondering. **12** And when Peter saw *it*, he answered unto the people, Ye men of Israel, why marvel ye at this? or why look ye so earnestly on us, as though by our own power or holiness we had made this man to walk? **13** The God of Abraham, and of Isaac, and of Jacob, the God of our fathers, hath glorified his Son Jesus; whom ye delivered up, and denied him in the presence of Pilate, when he was determined to let *him* go. **14** But ye denied the Holy One and the Just, and desired a murderer to be granted unto you; **15** and killed the Prince of life, whom God hath raised from the dead; whereof we are witnesses. **16** And his name. through faith in his name, hath made this man strong, whom ye see and know: yea, the faith which is by him hath given him this perfect soundness in the presence of you all.●

**17** And now, brethren, I wot that through ignorance ye did *it*, as *did* also your rulers. **18** But those things, which God before had showed by the mouth of all his prophets, that Christ should suffer, he hath so fulfilled.●

**2. APPEAL**

ISRAEL THE OBJECT OF GOD'S LOVE

**19** Repent ye therefore, and be converted, that your sins may be blotted out, when the times of refreshing shall come from the presence of the Lord; **20** and he shall send Jesus Christ, which before was preached unto you: **21** whom the heaven must receive until the times of restitution of all things, which God hath spoken by the mouth of all his holy prophets since the world began. **22** For Moses truly said unto the fathers,

Deu. 15:18-19

> A Prophet shall the Lord your God
> raise up unto you of your brethren,
> like unto me;
> him shall ye hear in all things whatsoever he shall say unto you.
> **23** And it shall come to pass, *that* every soul, which will not hear that Prophet,
> shall be destroyed from among the people.

**24** Yea, and all the prophets from Samuel and those that follow after, as many as have spoken, have likewise foretold of these days. **25** Ye are the children of the prophets, and of the covenant which God made with our fathers, saying unto Abraham, And in thy seed shall all the kindreds of the earth be blessed. **26** Unto you first God, having raised up his Son Jesus, sent him to bless you, in turning away every one of you from his iniquities.●

Gen. 22:18

This segment reports the sequel to the lame man's healing (preceding segment). Peter first explains everything, then he gives a spiritual appeal.

"God...hath his Son Jesus" (v.13) "Ye the Holy One" (v.14)

*3:17-18* Compare the brethren and God.

*3:19-26* What is Peter's command?

What is promised for obeying the command? (vv.20-21)

What do verses 22-26 teach?

NEW INTERNATIONAL VERSION

What does this passage teach about:

PERSECUTION

POWER OF GOD

SALVATION

BOLDNESS IN WITNESSING

OBEDIENCE TO GOD

IMPOTENCE OF MAN

OTHER

*Peter and John Before the Sanhedrin*

4 The priests and the captain of the temple guard and the Sadducees came up
to Peter and John while they were speaking
to the people. 2They were greatly disturbed
because the apostles were teaching the
people and proclaiming in Jesus the resurrection of the dead. 3They seized Peter and
John, and because it was evening, they put
them in jail until the next day. 4But many
who heard the message believed, and the
number of men grew to about five thousand.●
5The next day the rulers, elders and
teachers of the law met in Jerusalem. 6An-
nas the high priest was there, and so were
Caiaphas, John, Alexander and the other
men of the high priest's family. 7They had
Peter and John brought before them and
began to question them: "By what power
or what name did you do this?"
8Then Peter, filled with the Holy Spirit,
said to them: "Rulers and elders of the
people! 9If we are being called to account
today for an act of kindness shown to a
cripple and are asked how he was healed,
10then know this, you and everyone else in
Israel: It is by the name of Jesus Christ of
Nazareth, whom you crucified but whom
God raised from the dead, that this man
stands before you completely healed. 11He
is

"'the stone you builders rejected,
which has become the
capstone.'[c,d]

12Salvation is found in no one else, for
there is no other name under heaven given
to men by which we must be saved."●
13When they saw the courage of Peter
and John and realized that they were un-
schooled, ordinary men, they were astonished and they took note that these men
had been with Jesus. 14But since they could
see the man who had been healed standing
there with them, there was nothing they
could say. 15So they ordered them to withdraw from the Sanhedrin and then conferred together. 16"What are we going to
do with these men?" they asked. "Everybody living in Jerusalem knows they have
done an outstanding miracle, and we cannot deny it. 17But to stop this thing from
spreading any further among the people,
we must warn these men to speak no longer
to anyone in this name."
18Then they called them in again and
commanded them not to speak or teach at
all in the name of Jesus. 19But Peter and
John replied, "Judge for yourselves
whether it is right in God's sight to obey
you rather than God. 20For we cannot help
speaking about what we have seen and
heard."
21After further threats they let them go.
They could not decide how to punish them,
because all the people were praising God
for what had happened. 22For the man who
was miraculously healed was over forty
years old.●

[c]11 Or *cornerstone* [d]11 Psalm 118:22

## KING JAMES

1. RESULTS

SOULS SAVED

4 And as they spake unto the people,
the priests, and the captain of the
temple, and the Sadducees, came upon
them, 2 being grieved that they taught the
people, and preached through Jesus the
resurrection from the dead. 3 And they
laid hands on them, and put *them* in hold
unto the next day: for it was now eventide. 4 Howbeit many of them which
heard the word believed; and the number
of the men was about five thousand.●

2. EXAMINATION

5 And it came to pass on the morrow,
that their rulers, and elders, and scribes,
6 and Annas the high priest, and Cai'a-
phas, and John, and Alexander, and as
many as were of the kindred of the high
priest, were gathered together at Jerusalem. 7 And when they had set them in
the midst, they asked, By what power, or
by what name, have ye done this? 8 Then
Peter, filled with the Holy Ghost, said
unto them, Ye rulers of the people, and
elders of Israel, 9 if we this day be examined of the good deed done to the impotent man, by what means he is made
whole; 10 be it known unto you all, and
to all the people of Israel, that by the
name of Jesus Christ of Nazareth, whom
ye crucified, whom God raised from the
dead, *even* by him doth this man stand
here before you whole. 11 This is the
stone which was set at nought of you
builders, which is become the head of the
corner. 12 Neither is there salvation in
any other: for there is none other name
under heaven given among men, whereby
we must be saved.●

Ps. 118:22

3. DISPOSITION

13 Now when they saw the boldness of
Peter and John, and perceived that they
were unlearned and ignorant men, they
marveled; and they took knowledge of
them, that they had been with Jesus.
14 And beholding the man which was
healed standing with them, they could say
nothing against it. 15 But when they had
commanded them to go aside out of the
council, they conferred among themselves, 16 saying, What shall we do to
these men? for that indeed a notable
miracle hath been done by them *is* manifest to all them that dwell in Jerusalem;
and we cannot deny *it*. 17 But that it
spread no further among the people, let
us straitly threaten them, that they speak
henceforth to no man in this name.
18 And they called them, and commanded
them not to speak at all nor teach in the
name of Jesus. 19 But Peter and John
answered and said unto them, Whether it
be right in the sight of God to hearken
unto you more than unto God, judge ye.
20 For we cannot but speak the things
which we have seen and heard. 21 So
when they had further threatened them,
they let them go, finding nothing how they
might punish them, because of the people:
for all *men* glorified God for that which
was done. 22 For the man was above
forty years old, on whom this miracle of
healing was showed.●

GOD GLORIFIED

*4:1-4* What doctrine about Jesus was being proclaimed?

How many people were saved at this time?

*4:5-12* What explanation did Peter give for the miracle?

What did he teach about the way of salvation?

*4:13-22* Compare the people and the two apostles:

PEOPLE: ______

PETER and JOHN: ______

What does verse 21 add to this story?

NEW INTERNATIONAL VERSION

What do you learn here about:

PRAYER

LAW OF REAPING

SOVEREIGN GOD

FAITH

GRACE

FEAR

CHRISTIAN FELLOWSHIP

*The Believers' Prayer*

23On their release, Peter and John went
back to their own people and reported all
that the chief priests and elders had said to
them. 24When they heard this, they raised
their voices together in prayer to God.
"Sovereign Lord," they said, "you made
the heaven and the earth and the sea, and
everything in them. 25You spoke by the
Holy Spirit through the mouth of your servant, our father David:

"'Why do the nations rage
and the peoples plot in vain?
26The kings of the earth take their
stand
and the rulers gather together
against the Lord
and against his Anointed One.'[e][f]

27Indeed Herod and Pontius Pilate met together with the Gentiles and the people of
Israel in this city to conspire against your
holy servant Jesus, whom you anointed.
28They did what your power and will had
decided beforehand should happen.
29Now, Lord, consider their threats and
enable your servants to speak your word
with great boldness. 30Stretch out your
hand to heal and perform miraculous signs
and wonders through the name of your
holy servant Jesus."
31After they prayed, the place where
they were meeting was shaken. And they
were all filled with the Holy Spirit and
spoke the word of God boldly.●

*The Believers Share Their Possessions*

32All the believers were one in heart and
mind. No one claimed that any of his
possessions was his own, but they shared
everything they had. 33With great power
the apostles continued to testify to the
resurrection of the Lord Jesus, and much
grace was upon them all. 34There were no
needy persons among them. For from time
to time those who owned lands or houses
sold them, brought the money from the
sales 35and put it at the apostles' feet, and
it was distributed to anyone as he had
need.
36Joseph, a Levite from Cyprus, whom
the apostles called Barnabas (which means
Son of Encouragement), 37sold a field he
owned and brought the money and put it at
the apostles' feet.●

[e]26 That is, Christ or Messiah [f]26 Psalm 2:1,2

KING JAMES

1. PRAYER

REPORT SHARED

**23 And being let go, they went to their
own company, and reported all that the
chief priests and elders had said unto
them. 24 And when they heard that, they
lifted up their voice to God with one
accord, and said, Lord, thou *art* God,
which hast made heaven, and earth, and
the sea, and all that in them is; 25 who
by the mouth of thy servant David hast
said,**

**Why did the heathen rage,
and the people imagine vain things?**
**26 The kings of the earth stood up,
and the rulers were gathered together
against the Lord, and against his
Christ.**

Ps. 2:1,2

**27 For of a truth against thy holy child
Jesus, whom thou hast anointed, both
Herod, and Pontius Pilate, with the
Gentiles, and the people of Israel, were
gathered together, 28 for to do whatsoever thy hand and thy counsel determined
before to be done. 29 And now, Lord,
behold their threatenings: and grant unto
thy servants, that with all boldness they
may speak thy word, 30 by stretching
forth thine hand to heal; and that signs
and wonders may be done by the name of
thy holy child Jesus. 31 And when they
had prayed, the place was shaken where
they were assembled together; and they
were all filled with the Holy Ghost, and
they spake the word of God with boldness.●**

2. FELLOWSHIP

**32 And the multitude of them that be-
lieved were of one heart and of one soul:
neither said any *of them* that aught of the
things which he possessed was his own;
but they had all things common. 33 And
with great power gave the apostles witness
of the resurrection of the Lord Jesus: and
great grace was upon them all. 34 Neither
was there any among them that lacked:
for as many as were possessors of lands or
houses sold them, and brought the prices
of the things that were sold, 35 and laid
*them* down at the apostles' feet: and distribution was made unto every man according as he had need. 36 And Joses,
who by the apostles was surnamed Barnabas, (which is, being interpreted, The
son of consolation,) a Levite, *and* of the
country of Cyprus, 37 having land, sold
*it*, and brought the money, and laid *it* at
the apostles' feet.●**

MONEY SHARED

This segment reports what happened after Peter and John were released by the Council (4:21).

*4:23-31* Who prays the prayer of verses 24-30?

Where does the first specific petition appear?

What is it?

What is the subject of verses 24-28?

*4:32-37* Record all the notes of common-ness in this paragraph.

NEW INTERNATIONAL VERSION

*Ananias and Sapphira*

5 Now a man named Ananias, together
with his wife Sapphira, also sold a
piece of property. 2With his wife's full
knowledge he kept back part of the money
for himself, but brought the rest and put it
at the apostles' feet.
3Then Peter said, "Ananias, how is it
that Satan has so filled your heart that you
have lied to the Holy Spirit and have kept
for yourself some of the money you received for the land? 4Didn't it belong to you
before it was sold? And after it was sold,
wasn't the money at your disposal? What
made you think of doing such a thing? You
have not lied to men but to God."
5When Ananias heard this, he fell down
and died. And great fear seized all who
heard what had happened. 6Then the
young men came forward, wrapped up his
body, and carried him out and buried him.●
7About three hours later his wife came
in, not knowing what had happened. 8Peter
asked her, "Tell me, is this the price you
and Ananias got for the land?"
"Yes," she said, "that is the price."
9Peter said to her, "How could you agree
to test the Spirit of the Lord? Look! The
feet of the men who buried your husband
are at the door, and they will carry you out
also."
10At that moment she fell down at his feet
and died. Then the young men came in and,
finding her dead, carried her out and buried
her beside her husband. 11Great fear seized
the whole church and all who heard about
these events.●

What are your impressions of this account? ______

What do you learn here about:

HONESTY ______

DECEPTION ______

GOD AS JUDGE ______

In your own words, what timeless, universal truth does this story teach, which applies to today?

KING JAMES

1. ANANIAS DROPS DEAD

**5** But a certain man named Anani'as,
with Sapphi'ra his wife, sold a possession, 2 and kept back *part* of the price,
his wife also being privy *to it*, and brought
a certain part, and laid *it* at the apostles'
feet. 3 But Peter said, Anani'as, why hath
Satan filled thine heart to lie to the Holy
Ghost, and to keep back *part* of the price
of the land? 4 While it remained, was it
not thine own? and after it was sold, was
it not in thine own power? why hast thou
conceived this thing in thine heart? thou
hast not lied unto men, but unto God.
5 And Anani'as hearing these words fell
down, and gave up the ghost: and great
fear came on all them that heard these
things. 6 And the young men arose,
wound him up, and carried *him* out, and
buried *him*.●

2. SAPPHIRA ALSO DIES

7 And it was about the space of three
hours after, when his wife, not knowing
what was done, came in. 8 And Peter answered unto her, Tell me whether ye sold
the land for so much? And she said, Yea,
for so much. 9 Then Peter said unto her,
How is it that ye have agreed together to
tempt the Spirit of the Lord? behold, the
feet of them which have buried thy husband *are* at the door, and shall carry thee
out. 10 Then fell she down straightway
at his feet, and yielded up the ghost: and
the young men came in, and found her
dead, and, carrying *her* forth, buried *her*
by her husband. 11 And great fear came
upon all the church, and upon as many as
heard these things.●

DECEPTION

FEAR

Review 4:32-37 as background for this segment.

*5:1-6* How do you think Peter learned of Ananias' deception?

Did Peter pronounce any judgment on Ananias?

*5:7-11* Compare this paragraph with the first one.

NEW INTERNATIONAL VERSION

Record the different things of this account which helped to establish the Church in its life and testimony.

What does the passage teach about:

DIVINE POWER

PERSECUTION

Record spiritual applications:

*The Apostles Heal Many*

[12]The apostles performed many miraculous signs and wonders among the people. And all the believers used to meet together in Solomon's Colonnade. [13]No one else dared join them, even though they were highly regarded by the people. [14]Nevertheless, more and more men and women believed in the Lord and were added to their number. [15]As a result, people brought the sick into the streets and laid them on beds and mats so that at least Peter's shadow might fall on some of them as he passed by. [16]Crowds gathered also from the towns around Jerusalem, bringing their sick and those tormented by evil[a] spirits, and all of them were healed.●

*The Apostles Persecuted*

[17]Then the high priest and all his associates, who were members of the party of the Sadducees, were filled with jealousy. [18]They arrested the apostles and put them in the public jail. [19]But during the night an angel of the Lord opened the doors of the jail and brought them out. [20]"Go, stand in the temple courts," he said, "and tell the people the full message of this new life."

[21]At daybreak they entered the temple courts, as they had been told, and began to teach the people.●

When the high priest and his associates arrived, they called together the Sanhedrin—the full assembly of the elders of Israel—and sent to the jail for the apostles. [22]But on arriving at the jail, the officers did not find them there. So they went back and reported, [23]"We found the jail securely locked, with the guards standing at the doors; but when we opened them, we found no one inside." [24]On hearing this report, the captain of the temple guard and the chief priests were puzzled, wondering what would come of this.

[25]Then someone came and said, "Look! The men you put in jail are standing in the temple courts teaching the people." [26]At that, the captain went with his officers and brought the apostles. They did not use force, because they feared that the people would stone them.●

[a]16 Greek *unclean*

## KING JAMES

**1. SIGNS AND WONDERS**

**APOSTLES MAGNIFIED BY PEOPLE**

12 And by the hands of the apostles
were many signs and wonders wrought
among the people; (and they were all with
one accord in Solomon's porch. 13 And
of the rest durst no man join himself to
them: but the people magnified them.
14 And believers were the more added to
the Lord, multitudes both of men and
women;) 15 insomuch that they brought
forth the sick into the streets, and laid
*them* on beds and couches, that at the
least the shadow of Peter passing by
might overshadow some of them. 16 There
came also a multitude *out* of the cities
round about unto Jerusalem, bringing
sick folks, and them which were vexed
with unclean spirits: and they were healed
every one.●

**2. IN AND OUT OF JAIL**

17 Then the high priest rose up, and all
they that were with him, (which is the sect
of the Sadducees,) and were filled with indignation, 18 and laid their hands on the
apostles, and put them in the common
prison. 19 But the angel of the Lord by
night opened the prison doors, and
brought them forth, and said, 20 Go,
stand and speak in the temple to the people all the words of this life. 21 And when
they heard *that*, they entered into the
temple early in the morning, and taught.●

**3. ESCAPE REPORTED**

But the high priest came, and they that
were with him, and called the council together, and all the senate of the children
of Israel, and sent to the prison to have
them brought. 22 But when the officers
came, and found them not in the prison,
they returned, and told, 23 saying, The
prison truly found we shut with all safety,
and the keepers standing without before
the doors: but when we had opened, we
found no man within. 24 Now when the
high priest and the captain of the temple
and the chief priests heard these things,
they doubted of them whereunto this
would grow. 25 Then came one and told
them, saying, Behold, the men whom ye
put in prison are standing in the temple,
and teaching the people. 26 Then went
the captain with the officers, and brought
them without violence: for they feared
the people, lest they should have been
stoned.●

**APOSTLES ARRESTED BY POLICE**

This is another experience of the apostles in the section of Acts called CHURCH ESTABLISHED (see outline). As you study the chapters in this section, observe the experiences of the Church which God brought to establish that community of believers.

*5:12-16* Try reading verses 12-15 without the parenthesis. What does the parenthesis add to the main point of the verses?

*5:17-21a* Record key words of this paragraph.

*5:21b-26* Record observations.

NEW INTERNATIONAL VERSION

What do you learn here about:

BOLDNESS IN CHRISTIAN SERVICE

OBEDIENCE TO GOD

OPPOSITION TO GOD

POWER OF GOD

FAITHFULNESS IN WITNESSING

OTHER

27 Having brought the apostles, they
made them appear before the Sanhedrin to
be questioned by the high priest. 28 "We
gave you strict orders not to teach in this
name," he said. "Yet you have filled
Jerusalem with your teaching and are determined to make us guilty of this man's
blood."
29 Peter and the other apostles replied:
"We must obey God rather than men!
30 The God of our fathers raised Jesus from
the dead—whom you had killed by hanging
him on a tree. 31 God exalted him to his own
right hand as Prince and Savior that he
might give repentance and forgiveness of
sins to Israel. 32 We are witnesses of these
things, and so is the Holy Spirit, whom
God has given to those who obey him."●
33 When they heard this, they were furious and wanted to put them to death. 34 But
a Pharisee named Gamaliel, a teacher of
the law, who was honored by all the
people, stood up in the Sanhedrin and ordered that the men be put outside for a little
while. 35 Then he addressed them: "Men of
Israel, consider carefully what you intend
to do to these men. 36 Some time ago Theu-
das appeared, claiming to be somebody,
and about four hundred men rallied to him.
He was killed, all his followers were dispersed, and it all came to nothing. 37 After
him, Judas the Galilean appeared in the
days of the census and led a band of people
in revolt. He too was killed, and all his
followers were scattered. 38 Therefore, in
the present case I advise you: Leave these
men alone! Let them go! For if their purpose or activity is of human origin, it will
fail. 39 But if it is from God, you will not be
able to stop these men; you will only find
yourselves fighting against God."●
40 His speech persuaded them. They
called the apostles in and had them
flogged. Then they ordered them not to
speak in the name of Jesus, and let them
go.
41 The apostles left the Sanhedrin, rejoicing because they had been counted worthy
of suffering disgrace for the Name. 42 Day
after day, in the temple courts and from
house to house, they never stopped teaching and proclaiming the good news that
Jesus is the Christ.[a]●

[a]42 Or *Messiah*

KING JAMES

1. EN-
COUNTER

OBEYING
GOD

27 And when they had brought them,
they set *them* before the council: and the
high priest asked them, 28 saying, Did
not we straitly command you that ye
should not teach in this name? and, behold, ye have filled Jerusalem with your
doctrine, and intend to bring this man's
blood upon us. 29 Then Peter and the
*other* apostles answered and said, We
ought to obey God rather than men.
30 The God of our fathers raised up Jesus,
whom ye slew and hanged on a tree.
31 Him hath God exalted with his right
hand *to be* a Prince and a Saviour, for to
give repentance to Israel, and forgiveness
of sins. 32 And we are his witnesses of
these things; and *so is* also the Holy
Ghost, whom God hath given to them
that obey him.●

2. ADVICE

33 When they heard *that*, they were cut
*to the heart*, and took counsel to slay them.
34 Then stood there up one in the council,
a Pharisee, named Gama'li-el, a doctor of
the law, had in reputation among all the
people, and commanded to put the
apostles forth a little space; 35 and said
unto them, Ye men of Israel, take heed to
yourselves what ye intend to do as touching these men. 36 For before these days
rose up Theu'das, boasting himself to be
somebody; to whom a number of men,
about four hundred, joined themselves:
who was slain; and all, as many as obeyed
him, were scattered, and brought to
nought. 37 After this man rose up Judas
of Galilee in the days of the taxing, and
drew away much people after him: he also
perished; and all, *even* as many as obeyed
him, were dispersed. 38 And now I say
unto you, Refrain from these men, and
let them alone: for if this counsel or this
work be of men, it will come to nought:
39 but if it be of God, ye cannot overthrow it; lest haply ye be found even to
fight against God.●

3. OUT-
COME

PREACH-
ING JESUS

40 And to him they agreed: and when
they had called the apostles, and beaten
*them*, they commanded that they should
not speak in the name of Jesus, and let
them go. 41 And they departed from the
presence of the council, rejoicing that they
were counted worthy to suffer shame for
his name. 42 And daily in the temple, and
in every house, they ceased not to teach
and preach Jesus Christ.●

*5:27-32* Analyze the reply of the apostles carefully. What did they say about the persons of the Trinity:

FATHER ("God") ______________________

______________________

______________________

______________________

______________________

______________________

JESUS ______________________

______________________

______________________

______________________

______________________

______________________

HOLY SPIRIT ______________________

______________________

______________________

______________________

______________________

______________________

*5:33-39* What are your impressions of Gamaliel and his advice?

______________________

______________________

______________________

______________________

______________________

______________________

*5:40-42* What does this paragraph reveal about the apostles?

______________________

______________________

______________________

______________________

______________________

______________________

NEW INTERNATIONAL VERSION

What are the different references to the word of God in this passage?

What does the passage teach about:

PRAYER

TOTAL MINISTRY OF THE CHURCH

FAITH

CHRISTIAN SERVICE

PERSECUTION

FALSE ACCUSATION

OTHER

### *The Choosing of the Seven*

6 In those days when the number of disciples was increasing, the Grecian
Jews among them complained against
those of the Aramaic-speaking[b] community because their widows were being
overlooked in the daily distribution of
food. 2So the Twelve gathered all the disciples together and said, "It would not be
right for us to neglect the ministry of the
word of God in order to wait on tables.
3Brothers, choose seven men from among
you who are known to be full of the Spirit
and wisdom. We will turn this responsibility over to them 4and will give our attention
to prayer and the ministry of the word."
5This proposal pleased the whole group.
They chose Stephen, a man full of faith and
of the Holy Spirit; also Philip, Procorus,
Nicanor, Timon, Parmenas, and Nicolas
from Antioch, a convert to Judaism. 6They
presented these men to the apostles, who
prayed and laid their hands on them.
7So the word of God spread. The number
of disciples in Jerusalem increased rapidly,
and a large number of priests became
obedient to the faith.●

### *Stephen Seized*

8Now Stephen, a man full of God's grace
and power, did great wonders and miraculous signs among the people. 9Opposition
arose, however, from members of the
Synagogue of the Freedmen (as it was
called)—Jews of Cyrene and Alexandria as
well as the provinces of Cilicia and Asia.
These men began to argue with Stephen,
10but they could not stand up against his
wisdom or the Spirit by which he spoke.
11Then they secretly persuaded some
men to say, "We have heard Stephen
speak words of blasphemy against Moses
and against God."
12So they stirred up the people and the
elders and the teachers of the law. They
seized Stephen and brought him before the
Sanhedrin. 13They produced false witnesses, who testified, "This fellow never
stops speaking against the holy place and
against the law. 14For we have heard him
say that this Jesus of Nazareth will destroy
this place and change the customs Moses
handed down to us."
15All who were sitting in the Sanhedrin
looked intently at Stephen, and they saw
that his face was like the face of an angel.●

b1 Or possibly *Hebrew-speaking*

KING JAMES

1. SEVEN DEACONS CHOSEN

6 And in those days, when the number
of the disciples was multiplied, there
arose a murmuring of the Gre'cians
against the Hebrews, because their widows
were neglected in the daily ministration.
2 Then the twelve called the multitude of
the disciples *unto them*, and said, It is not
reason that we should leave the word of
God, and serve tables. 3 Wherefore,
brethren, look ye out among you seven
men of honest report, full of the Holy
Ghost and wisdom, whom we may appoint over this business. 4 But we will
give ourselves continually to prayer, and
to the ministry of the word. 5 And the
saying pleased the whole multitude: and
they chose Stephen, a man full of faith
and of the Holy Ghost, and Philip, and
Proch'orus, and Nica'nor, and Timon,
and Par'menas, and Nicolas a proselyte
of An'ti-och; 6 whom they set before the
apostles: and when they had prayed, they
laid *their* hands on them.
7 And the word of God increased; and
the number of the disciples multiplied in
Jerusalem greatly; and a great company
of the priests were obedient to the faith.●

2. STEPHEN ARRESTED

8 And Stephen, full of faith and power,
did great wonders and miracles among the
people. 9 Then there arose certain of the
synagogue, which is called *the synagogue*
of the Libertines, and Cyre'nians, and
Alexandrians, and of them of Cili'cia and
of Asia, disputing with Stephen. 10 And
they were not able to resist the wisdom
and the spirit by which he spake. 11 Then
they suborned men, which said, We have
heard him speak blasphemous words
against Moses, and *against* God. 12 And
they stirred up the people, and the elders,
and the scribes, and came upon *him*, and
caught him, and brought *him* to the
council, 13 and set up false witnesses,
which said, This man ceaseth not to speak
blasphemous words against this holy
place, and the law: 14 for we have heard
him say, that this Jesus of Nazareth shall
destroy this place, and shall change the
customs which Moses delivered us.
15 And all that sat in the council, looking
steadfastly on him, saw his face as it had
been the face of an angel.●

BELIEVERS MURMURING

UNBELIEVERS LYING

This is the place in Acts for Luke to introduce Stephen, who becomes the focal point of intense persecution yet to come (cf.8:1b).

*6:1-7* Record:

COMPLAINT: __________

SOLUTION: __________

APPROVAL. __________

BLESSING: __________

*6:8-15* Compare:

FAIR ARGUMENT (vv.8-10) __________

FALSE ACCUSATION (vv.11-14) __________

NEW INTERNATIONAL VERSION

See how many practical lessons you can learn from this passage, and record them here:

*Stephen's Speech to the Sanhedrin*

7 Then the high priest asked him, "Are
these charges true?"
[2]To this he replied: "Brothers and fathers, listen to me! The God of glory appeared to our father Abraham while he was
still in Mesopotamia, before he lived in
Haran. [3]'Leave your country and your
people,' God said, 'and go to the land I will
show you.'[c]
[4]"So he left the land of the Chaldeans
and settled in Haran. After the death of his
father, God sent him to this land where you
are now living. [5]He gave him no inheritance here, not even a foot of ground. But
God promised him that he and his descendants after him would possess the land, even
though at that time Abraham had no child.
[6]God spoke to him in this way: 'Your descendants will be strangers in a country not
their own, and they will be enslaved and
mistreated four hundred years. [7]But I will
punish the nation they serve as slaves,'
God said, 'and afterward they will come
out of that country and worship me in this
place.'[a] [8]Then he gave Abraham the covenant of circumcision. And Abraham
became the father of Isaac and circumcised
him eight days after his birth. Later Isaac
became the father of Jacob, and Jacob
became the father of the twelve patriarchs.
[9]"Because the patriarchs were jealous of
Joseph, they sold him as a slave into
Egypt. But God was with him [10]and rescued him from all his troubles. He gave
Joseph wisdom and enabled him to gain the
goodwill of Pharaoh king of Egypt; so he
made him ruler over Egypt and all his palace.
[11]"Then a famine struck all Egypt and
Canaan, bringing great suffering, and our
fathers could not find food. [12]When Jacob
heard that there was grain in Egypt, he sent
our fathers on their first visit. [13]On their
second visit, Joseph told his brothers who
he was, and Pharaoh learned about Joseph's family. [14]After this, Joseph sent for
his father Jacob and his whole family, seventy-five in all. [15]Then Jacob went down to
Egypt, where he and our fathers died.
[16]Their bodies were brought back to Shechem and placed in the tomb that Abraham
had bought from the sons of Hamor at Shechem for a certain sum of money.●
[17]"As the time drew near for God to fulfill his promise to Abraham, the number of
our people in Egypt greatly increased.
[18]Then another king, who knew nothing
about Joseph, became ruler of Egypt. [19]He
dealt treacherously with our people and
oppressed our forefathers by forcing them
to throw out their newborn babies so that
they would die.●

*c3* Gen. 12:1 *a7* Gen. 15:13,14

KING JAMES

1. ABRAHAM

ONE MAN

7 Then said the high priest, Are these
things so? 2 And he said,
Men, brethren, and fathers, hearken;
The God of glory appeared unto our
father Abraham, when he was in Meso-
pota'mi-a, before he dwelt in Haran,
3 and said unto him, Get thee out of thy
country, and from thy kindred, and come
into the land which I shall show thee.
4 Then came he out of the land of the
Chalde'ans, and dwelt in Haran: and
from thence, when his father was dead,
he removed him into this land, wherein ye
now dwell. 5 And he gave him none inheritance in it, no, not *so much as* to set
his foot on: yet he promised that he
would give it to him for a possession, and
to his seed after him, when *as yet* he had
no child. 6 And God spake on this wise,
That his seed should sojourn in a strange
land; and that they should bring them
into bondage, and entreat *them* evil four
hundred years. 7 And the nation to
whom they shall be in bondage will I
judge, said God: and after that shall they
come forth, and serve me in this place.
8 And he gave him the covenant of circumcision: and so *Abraham* begat Isaac,
and circumcised him the eighth day; and
Isaac *begat* Jacob; and Jacob *begat* the
twelve patriarchs. ●

2. JOSEPH

9 And the patriarchs, moved with envy,
sold Joseph into Egypt: but God was
with him, 10 and delivered him out of all
his afflictions, and gave him favor and
wisdom in the sight of Pharaoh king of
Egypt; and he made him governor over
Egypt and all his house. 11 Now there
came a dearth over all the land of Egypt
and Canaan, and great affliction: and
our fathers found no sustenance. 12 But
when Jacob heard that there was corn in
Egypt, he sent out our fathers first.
13 And at the second *time* Joseph was
made known to his brethren; and
Joseph's kindred was made known unto
Pharaoh. 14 Then sent Joseph, and
called his father Jacob to *him*, and all his
kindred, threescore and fifteen souls.
15 So Jacob went down into Egypt, and
died, he, and our fathers, 16 and were
carried over into Shechem, and laid in
the sepulchre that Abraham bought for a
sum of money of the sons of Hamor, *the
father* of Shechem. ●

3. JEWS MULTIPLY

17 But when the time of the promise
drew nigh, which God had sworn to
Abraham, the people grew and multiplied
in Egypt, 18 till another king arose,
which knew not Joseph. 19 The same
dealt subtilely with our kindred, and evil
entreated our fathers, so that they cast
out their young children, to the end they
might not live. ●

LARGE NATION

This segment is the first part of Stephen's speech, which concludes at 7:53. The entire speech is a summary of the highlights of Israel's history. Record for each paragraph those highlights.

*7:1-8* ________________

*7:9-16* ________________

*7:17-19* ________________

NEW INTERNATIONAL VERSION

What do you learn from this passage about:

THE HEART OF MAN

SOVEREIGNTY OF GOD

VISION OF THE LORD

CALL TO THE LORD'S SERVICE

Record some practical lessons learned:

[20]"At that time Moses was born, and he
was no ordinary child.[b] For three months
he was cared for in his father's house.
[21]When he was placed outside, Pharaoh's
daughter took him and brought him up as
her own son. [22]Moses was educated in all
the wisdom of the Egyptians and was powerful in speech and action.●
[23]"When Moses was forty years old, he
decided to visit his fellow Israelites. [24]He
saw one of them being mistreated by an
Egyptian, so he went to his defense and
avenged him by killing the Egyptian.
[25]Moses thought that his own people would
realize that God was using him to rescue
them, but they did not. [26]The next day
Moses came upon two Israelites who were
fighting. He tried to reconcile them by saying, 'Men, you are brothers; why do you
want to hurt each other?'
[27]"But the man who was mistreating the
other pushed Moses aside and said, 'Who
made you ruler and judge over us? [28]Do
you want to kill me as you killed the Egyptian yesterday?'[c] [29]When Moses heard
this, he fled to Midian, where he settled as
a foreigner and had two sons.●
[30]"After forty years had passed, an angel
appeared to Moses in the flames of a burning bush in the desert near Mount Sinai.
[31]When he saw this, he was amazed at the
sight. As he went over to look more closely, he heard the Lord's voice: [32]'I am the
God of your fathers, the God of Abraham,
Isaac and Jacob.'[d] Moses trembled with
fear and did not dare to look.
[33]"Then the Lord said to him, 'Take off
your sandals; the place where you are
standing is holy ground. [34]I have indeed
seen the oppression of my people in Egypt.
I have heard their groaning and have come
down to set them free. Now come, I will
send you back to Egypt.'[e]●

[b]20 Or *was fair in the sight of God* [c]28 Exodus 2:14
[d]32 Exodus 3:6 [e]34 Exodus 3:5,7,8,10

## KING JAMES

**1. BIRTH OF MOSES**

**MOSES AND PHARAOH'S DAUGHTER**

20 In which time Moses
was born, and was exceeding fair, and
nourished up in his father's house three
months: 21 and when he was cast out,
Pharaoh's daughter took him up, and
nourished him for her own son. 22 And
Moses was learned in all the wisdom of
the Egyptians, and was mighty in words
and in deeds. ●

**2. FLIGHT TO MIDIAN**

23 And when he was full forty years old,
it came into his heart to visit his brethren
the children of Israel. 24 And seeing one
*of them* suffer wrong, he defended *him*,
and avenged him that was oppressed, and
smote the Egyptian: 25 for he supposed
his brethren would have understood how
that God by his hand would deliver them;
but they understood not. 26 And the
next day he showed himself unto them as
they strove, and would have set them at
one again, saying, Sirs, ye are brethren;
why do ye wrong one to another? 27 But
he that did his neighbor wrong thrust him
away, saying, Who made thee a ruler and
a judge over us? 28 Wilt thou kill me, as
thou didst the Egyptian yesterday?
29 Then fled Moses at this saying, and was
a stranger in the land of Mid'i-an, where
he begat two sons. ●

**3. VISION AND CALL**

30 And when forty years were expired,
there appeared to him in the wilderness of
mount Si'nai an angel of the Lord in a
flame of fire in a bush. 31 When Moses
saw *it*, he wondered at the sight: and as he
drew near to behold *it*, the voice of the
Lord came unto him, 32 *saying*, I *am* the
God of thy fathers, the God of Abraham
and the God of Isaac, and the God of
Jacob. Then Moses trembled, and durst
not behold. 33 Then said the Lord to him,
Put off thy shoes from thy feet: for the
place where thou standest is holy ground.
34 I have seen, I have seen the affliction
of my people which is in Egypt, and I
have heard their groaning, and am come
down to deliver them. And now come, I
will send thee into Egypt. ●

**MOSES AND GOD**

The preceding segment was about Abraham, Isaac, Jacob and Joseph. Now Stephen speaks about another key man in Israel's past, Moses.

*7:20-22* What do these verses teach about Moses?

*7:23-29* What do these verses teach about Moses?

*7:30-34* This is a classic passage in the Bible. Record your observations of Moses' vision and and call.

NEW INTERNATIONAL VERSION

What do you learn from this passage about:

SERVANT OF GOD

SINFUL HEART

IDOLATRY

JUDGMENT

DIVINE DELIVERANCE

WORSHIP

GOD'S CREATION

OTHER

35"This is the same Moses whom they
had rejected with the words, 'Who made
you ruler and judge?' He was sent to be
their ruler and deliverer by God himself,
through the angel who appeared to him in
the bush. 36He led them out of Egypt and
did wonders and miraculous signs in
Egypt, at the Red Sea[f] and for forty years
in the desert. 37This is that Moses who told
the Israelites, 'God will send you a prophet
like me from your own people.'[g] 38He was
in the assembly in the desert, with our fathers and with the angel who spoke to him
on Mount Sinai; and he received living
words to pass on to us.
39"But our fathers refused to obey him.
Instead, they rejected him and in their
hearts turned back to Egypt. 40They told
Aaron, 'Make us gods who will go before
us. As for this fellow Moses who led us out
of Egypt—we don't know what has happened to him!'[h] ● 41That was the time they
made an idol in the form of a calf. They
brought sacrifices to it and held a celebration in honor of what their hands had made.
42But God turned away and gave them over
to the worship of the heavenly bodies. This
agrees with what is written in the book of
the prophets:

" 'Did you bring me sacrifices and
offerings
forty years in the desert, O house
of Israel?
43You have lifted up the shrine of
Moloch
and the star of your god Rephan,
the idols you made to worship.
Therefore I will send you into
exile'[a] beyond Babylon. ●

44"Our forefathers had the tabernacle of
Testimony with them in the desert. It had
been made as God directed Moses, according to the pattern he had seen. 45Having
received the tabernacle, our fathers under
Joshua brought it with them when they
took the land from the nations God drove
out before them. It remained in the land
until the time of David, 46who enjoyed
God's favor and asked that he might provide a dwelling place for the God of Jacob.[b]
47But it was Solomon who built the house
for him.
48"However, the Most High does not
live in houses made by men. As the
prophet says:

49" 'Heaven is my throne,
and the earth is my footstool.
What kind of house will you build
for me?
says the Lord.
Or where will my resting place
be?
50Has not my hand made all these
things?'[c] ●

*f36* That is, Sea of Reeds *g37* Deut. 18:15
*h40* Exodus 32:1 *a43* Amos 5:25-27
*b46* Some early manuscripts *the house of Jacob*
*c50* Isaiah 66:1,2

KING JAMES

1. MOSES AS LEADER

LEADER MOSES

35 This Moses whom they refused,
saying, Who made thee a ruler and a
judge? the same did God send *to be* a
ruler and a deliverer by the hand of the
angel which appeared to him in the bush.
36 He brought them out, after that he had
showed wonders and signs in the land of
Egypt, and in the Red sea, and in the
wilderness forty years. 37 This is that
Moses, which said unto the children of
Israel, A Prophet shall the Lord your God
raise up unto you of your brethren, like
unto me; him shall ye hear. 38 This is
he, that was in the church in the wilderness with the angel which spake to him in
the mount Si'nai, and *with* our fathers:
who received the lively oracles to give unto us: 39 to whom our fathers would not
obey, but thrust *him* from them, and in
their hearts turned back again into
Egypt, 40 saying unto Aaron, Make us
gods to go before us: for *as for* this Moses,
which brought us out of the land of
Egypt, we wot not what is become of him. ●

2. ISRAEL'S IDOLATRY

41 And they made a calf in those days,
and offered sacrifice unto the idol, and rejoiced in the works of their own hands.
42 Then God turned, and gave them up to
worship the host of heaven; as it is written
in the book of the prophets,

Amos 5:25-27

O ye house of Israel,
have ye offered to me slain beasts and
sacrifices
*by the space of* forty years in the
wilderness?
43 Yea, ye took up the tabernacle of
Moloch,
and the star of your god Rem-
phan,
figures which ye made to worship
them:
and I will carry you away beyond
Babylon. ●

3. LEADERS IN CANAAN

44 Our fathers had the tabernacle of
witness in the wilderness, as he had appointed, speaking unto Moses, that he
should make it according to the fashion
that he had seen. 45 Which also our
fathers that came after brought in with
Joshua into the possession of the Gentiles, whom God drave out before the face
of our fathers, unto the days of David;
46 who found favor before God, and
desired to find a tabernacle for the God of
Jacob. 47 But Solomon built him a
house. 48 Howbeit the Most High dwelleth not in temples made with hands; as
saith the prophet,

KING SOLOMON

49 Heaven *is* my throne,
and earth *is* my footstool:
what house will ye build me? saith
the Lord:
or what *is* the place of my rest?
50 Hath not my hand made all these
things? ●

Isa. 66:1-2

*7:35-40* Record what Stephen said about:

MOSES ______________________________

GOD ______________________________

ISRAELITES ______________________________

*7:41-43* Compare:

THE PEOPLE ______________________________

GOD ______________________________

*7:44-50* Record the ministry of each:

MOSES ______________________________

JOSHUA ______________________________

DAVID ______________________________

SOLOMON ______________________________

NEW INTERNATIONAL VERSION

Record what the passage teaches about:

STUBBORN UNBELIEF

HOLY SPIRIT

GLORY OF GOD

JESUS

FORGIVENESS

OTHER

51"You stiff-necked people, with uncircumcised hearts and ears! You are just like
your fathers: You always resist the Holy
Spirit! 52Was there ever a prophet your fathers did not persecute? They even killed
those who predicted the coming of the
Righteous One. And now you have betrayed and murdered him— 53you who
have received the law that was put into
effect through angels but have not obeyed
it."●

*The Stoning of Stephen*

54When they heard this, they were furious and gnashed their teeth at him. 55But
Stephen, full of the Holy Spirit, looked up
to heaven and saw the glory of God, and
Jesus standing at the right hand of God.
56"Look," he said, "I see heaven open and
the Son of Man standing at the right hand
of God."●
57At this they covered their ears and,
yelling at the top of their voices, they all
rushed at him, 58dragged him out of the city
and began to stone him. Meanwhile, the
witnesses laid their clothes at the feet of a
young man named Saul.
59While they were stoning him, Stephen
prayed, "Lord Jesus, receive my spirit."
60Then he fell on his knees and cried out,
"Lord, do not hold this sin against them."
When he had said this, he fell asleep.
8 And Saul was there, giving approval to
his death.●

KING JAMES

1. CHARGE

51 Ye stiffnecked and uncircumcised in
heart and ears, ye do always resist the
Holy Ghost: as your fathers *did*, so *do* ye.
52 Which of the prophets have not your
fathers persecuted? and they have slain
them which showed before of the coming
of the Just One; of whom ye have
been now the betrayers and murderers:
53 who have received the law by the disposition of angels, and have not kept
*it*.●

PROPHETS SLAIN

2. VISION

54 When they heard these things, they
were cut to the heart, and they gnashed
on him with *their* teeth. 55 But he, being
full of the Holy Ghost, looked up steadfastly into heaven, and saw the glory of
God, and Jesus standing on the right hand
of God, 56 and said, Behold, I see the
heavens opened, and the Son of man
standing on the right hand of God.●

3. DEATH

57 Then they cried out with a loud voice,
and stopped their ears, and ran upon him
with one accord, 58 and cast *him* out of
the city, and stoned *him*: and the witnesses laid down their clothes at a young
man's feet, whose name was Saul. 59 And
they stoned Stephen, calling upon *God*,
and saying, Lord Jesus, receive my spirit.
60 And he kneeled down, and cried with
a loud voice, Lord, lay not this sin to their
charge. And when he had said this, he
8 fell asleep. 1 And Saul was consenting unto his death.●

STEPHEN STONED

This is a short segment, but it has many solid truths. Study it carefully.

*7:51-53* Compare this paragraph with the last one.

*7:54-56* Record each significant phrase relating to Stephen's experience.

*7:57—8:1a* Compare:

THE MOBS

STEPHEN

Note Saul's introduction to the story of Acts.

NEW INTERNATIONAL VERSION

What does this passage teach about:

PERSECUTION

SATAN

SIGNS AND WONDERS

POWER OF GOD

CONVERSION

Record spiritual applications:

*The Church Persecuted and Scattered*

On that day a great persecution broke
out against the church at Jerusalem, and all
except the apostles were scattered
throughout Judea and Samaria. 2Godly
men buried Stephen and mourned deeply
for him. 3But Saul began to destroy the
church. Going from house to house, he
dragged off men and women and put them
in prison.●

*Philip in Samaria*

4Those who had been scattered preached
the word wherever they went. 5Philip went
down to a city in Samaria and proclaimed
the Christ[d] there. 6When the crowds heard
Philip and saw the miraculous signs he did,
they all paid close attention to what he
said. 7With shrieks, evil[e] spirits came out
of many, and many paralytics and cripples
were healed. 8So there was great joy in that
city.●

*Simon the Sorcerer*

9Now for some time a man named Simon
had practiced sorcery in the city and
amazed all the people of Samaria. He
boasted that he was someone great, 10and
all the people, both high and low, gave him
their attention and exclaimed, "This man
is the divine power known as the Great
Power." 11They followed him because he
had amazed them for a long time with his
magic. 12But when they believed Philip as
he preached the good news of the kingdom
of God and the name of Jesus Christ, they
were baptized, both men and women. 13Si-
mon himself believed and was baptized.
And he followed Philip everywhere, astonished by the great signs and miracles he
saw.●

[d]5 Or *Messiah* [e]7 Greek *unclean*

KING JAMES

1. PERSECUTION IN JERUSALEM

BELIEVERS SCATTERED

And at that time there was a great persecution against the church which was at
Jerusalem; and they were all scattered
abroad throughout the regions of Judea
and Samaria, except the apostles. 2 And
devout men carried Stephen *to his burial*,
and made great lamentation over him.
3 As for Saul, he made havoc of the
church, entering into every house, and
haling men and women committed *them*
to prison. ●

2. JOY IN SAMARIA

4 Therefore they that were scattered
abroad went every where preaching the
word. 5 Then Philip went down to the
city of Samaria, and preached Christ unto
them. 6 And the people with one accord
gave heed unto those things which Philip
spake, hearing and seeing the miracles
which he did. 7 For unclean spirits, crying with loud voice, came out of many
that were possessed *with them*: and many
taken with palsies, and that were lame,
were healed. 8 And there was great joy
in that city. ●

3. SORCERER SAVED

9 But there was a certain man, called
Simon, which beforetime in the same city
used sorcery, and bewitched the people
of Samaria, giving out that himself was
some great one: 10 to whom they all gave
heed, from the least to the greatest, saying, This man is the great power of God.
11 And to him they had regard, because
that of long time he had bewitched them
with sorceries. 12 But when they believed
Philip preaching the things concerning the
kingdom of God, and the name of Jesus
Christ, they were baptized, both men and
women. 13 Then Simon himself believed
also: and when he was baptized, he continued with Philip, and wondered, beholding
the miracles and signs which were done. ●

SORCERER CONVERTED

This segment begins a new section in Acts called CHURCH SCATTERED. (See Outline.) Persecution of believers always brings forth good fruit. How is this illustrated in this passage? (Cf. verses 1,13)

*8:1b-3* Who are the characters of this paragraph?

Why do you think the apostles didn't leave Jerusalem (v.1)?

*8:4-8* Record the fruits of the scattering:

*8:9-13* Record the different stages of Simon's experience.

NEW INTERNATIONAL VERSION

What is taught here about:

PREACHING

GOSPEL

HOLY SPIRIT

BAPTISM

COVETOUSNESS

OTHER

14When the apostles in Jerusalem heard
that Samaria had accepted the word of
God, they sent Peter and John to them.
15When they arrived, they prayed for them
that they might receive the Holy Spirit,
16because the Holy Spirit had not yet come
upon any of them; they had simply been
baptized into[a] the name of the Lord Jesus.
17Then Peter and John placed their hands
on them, and they received the Holy Spirit.●
18When Simon saw that the Spirit was
given at the laying on of the apostles'
hands, he offered them money and said,
19"Give me also this ability so that everyone on whom I lay my hands may receive
the Holy Spirit."
20Peter answered: "May your money
perish with you, because you thought you
could buy the gift of God with money!
21You have no part or share in this ministry, because your heart is not right before
God. 22Repent of this wickedness and pray
to the Lord. Perhaps he will forgive you for
having such a thought in your heart. 23For
I see that you are full of bitterness and
captive to sin."
24Then Simon answered, "Pray to the
Lord for me so that nothing you have said
may happen to me."●
25When they had testified and proclaimed the word of the Lord, Peter and
John returned to Jerusalem, preaching the
gospel in many Samaritan villages.●

[a]16 Or *in*

## KING JAMES

**1. SAMARITANS RECEIVE THE HOLY SPIRIT**

GIFT OF THE SPIRIT

14 Now when the apostles which were
at Jerusalem heard that Samaria had received the word of God, they sent unto
them Peter and John: 15 who, when they
were come down, prayed for them, that
they might receive the Holy Ghost:
16 (for as yet he was fallen upon none of
them: only they were baptized in the
name of the Lord Jesus.) 17 Then laid
they *their* hands on them, and they received the Holy Ghost.●

**2. SIMON'S COVETOUSNESS**

18 And when
Simon saw that through laying on of the
apostles' hands the Holy Ghost was given,
he offered them money, 19 saying, Give
me also this power, that on whomsoever
I lay hands, he may receive the Holy
Ghost. 20 But Peter said unto him, Thy
money perish with thee, because thou
hast thought that the gift of God may be
purchased with money. 21 Thou hast
neither part nor lot in this matter: for thy
heart is not right in the sight of God.
22 Repent therefore of this thy wickedness, and pray God, if perhaps the
thought of thine heart may be forgiven
thee. 23 For I perceive that thou art in
the gall of bitterness, and *in* the bond of
iniquity. 24 Then answered Simon, and
said, Pray ye to the Lord for me, that
none of these things which ye have spoken
come upon me.●

**3. APOSTLES RETURN**

25 And they, when they had testified
and preached the word of the Lord, returned to Jerusalem, and preached the
gospel in many villages of the Samaritans.●

WORD OF THE LORD

*8:14-17* Who were the apostles sent to Samaria?

What was their mission?

Would this ministry by leaders of the Jerusalem church help to identify the Samaritan believers with the Jerusalem believers? If so, how?

*8:18-24* What is revealed here about Simon?

Compare the above with 8:9-13

*8:25* What are the strong words and phrases of this verse?

NEW INTERNATIONAL VERSION

This is a classic passage on personal evangelism. List what you learn about this ministry from the passage.

Record what is also taught here about:

CHRIST'S DEATH

FULFILLED PROPHECY

FAITH FOR SALVATION

WATER BAPTISM

OTHER

*Philip and the Ethiopian*

[26]Now an angel of the Lord said to
Philip, "Go south to the road—the desert
road—that goes down from Jerusalem to
Gaza." [27]So he started out, and on his way
he met an Ethiopian[b] eunuch, an important
official in charge of all the treasury of Candace, queen of the Ethiopians. This man
had gone to Jerusalem to worship, [28]and on
his way home was sitting in his chariot
reading the book of Isaiah the prophet.
[29]The Spirit told Philip, "Go to that chariot
and stay near it."●
[30]Then Philip ran up to the chariot and
heard the man reading Isaiah the prophet.
"Do you understand what you are reading?" Philip asked.
[31]"How can I," he said, "unless someone explains it to me?" So he invited Philip
to come up and sit with him.
[32]The eunuch was reading this passage of
Scripture:

"He was led like a sheep to the
slaughter,
and as a lamb before the shearer
is silent,
so he did not open his mouth.
[33]In his humiliation he was deprived
of justice.
Who can speak of his
descendants?
For his life was taken from the
earth."[c]

[34]The eunuch asked Philip, "Tell me,
please, who is the prophet talking about,
himself or someone else?" [35]Then Philip
began with that very passage of Scripture
and told him the good news about Jesus.●
[36]As they traveled along the road, they
came to some water and the eunuch said,
"Look, here is water. Why shouldn't I be
baptized?"[d] [38]And he ordered the chariot
to stop. Then both Philip and the eunuch
went down into the water and Philip baptized him. [39]When they came up out of the
water, the Spirit of the Lord suddenly took
Philip away, and the eunuch did not see
him again, but went on his way rejoicing.
[40]Philip, however, appeared at Azotus and
traveled about, preaching the gospel in all
the towns until he reached Caesarea.●

[b]*27* That is, from the upper Nile region
[c]*33* Isaiah 53:7,8
[d]*36* Some late manuscripts *baptized?" [37]Philip said, "If you believe with all your heart, you may." The official answered, "I believe that Jesus Christ is the Son of God."*

KING JAMES

1. MEETING

A SEEKING GENTILE

26 And the angel of the Lord spake unto Philip, saying, Arise, and go toward the
south, unto the way that goeth down from
Jerusalem unto Gaza, which is desert.
27 And he arose and went: and, behold,
a man of Ethiopia, a eunuch of great
authority under Candace queen of the
Ethiopians, who had the charge of all her
treasure, and had come to Jerusalem for
to worship, 28 was returning, and sitting
in his chariot read Isaiah the prophet.
29 Then the Spirit said unto Philip, Go
near, and join thyself to this chariot.●

2. CONVERSATION

30 And Philip ran thither to *him*, and
heard him read the prophet Isaiah, and
said, Understandest thou what thou
readest? 31 And he said, How can I, except some man should guide me? And he
desired Philip that he would come up and
sit with him. 32 The place of the Scripture which he read was this,

Isa. 53:7-8

He was led as a sheep to the slaughter;
and like a lamb dumb before his shearer,
so opened he not his mouth:
33 in his humiliation his judgment was taken away:
and who shall declare his generation?
for his life is taken from the earth.

34 And the eunuch answered Philip, and
said, I pray thee, of whom speaketh the
prophet this? of himself, or of some other
man? 35 Then Philip opened his mouth,
and began at the same Scripture, and
preached unto him Jesus.●

3. CONVERSION

36 And as they
went on *their* way, they came unto a certain water: and the eunuch said, See, *here*
*is* water; what doth hinder me to be baptized? 37 And Philip said, If thou believest with all thine heart, thou mayest.
And he answered and said, I believe that
Jesus Christ is the Son of God. 38 And
he commanded the chariot to stand still:
and they went down both into the water,
both Philip and the eunuch; and he baptized him. 39 And when they were come
up out of the water, the Spirit of the Lord
caught away Philip, that the eunuch saw
him no more: and he went on his way rejoicing. 40 But Philip was found at
Azo'tus: and passing through he preached
in all the cities, till he came to Caesare'a.●

A REJOICING CHRISTIAN

This segment shows an early extension of the church's witness into the south.

*8:26-29* What are the main parts of the setting?

*8:30-35* Study the questions and answers of this conversation. Record them:

*8:36-40* What do you think is the key statement of the paragraph?

Account for the miracle of verse 39.

NEW INTERNATIONAL VERSION

What do you learn here about:

REVELATION FROM GOD

POWER OF GOD

CONVERSION

MIRACLE

VISIONS

SOVEREIGN WILL OF GOD

OTHER

*Saul's Conversion*

9 Meanwhile, Saul was still breathing
out murderous threats against the
Lord's disciples. He went to the high priest
2and asked him for letters to the synagogues in Damascus, so that if he found
any there who belonged to the Way,
whether men or women, he might take
them as prisoners to Jerusalem. 3As he
neared Damascus on his journey, suddenly
a light from heaven flashed around him.
4He fell to the ground and heard a voice say
to him, "Saul, Saul, why do you persecute
me?"
5"Who are you, Lord?" Saul asked.
"I am Jesus, whom you are persecuting," he replied. 6"Now get up and go into
the city, and you will be told what you
must do."
7The men traveling with Saul stood there
speechless; they heard the sound but did
not see anyone. 8Saul got up from the
ground, but when he opened his eyes he
could see nothing. So they led him by the
hand into Damascus. 9For three days he
was blind, and did not eat or drink anything.●
10In Damascus there was a disciple
named Ananias. The Lord called to him in
a vision, "Ananias!"
"Yes, Lord," he answered.
11The Lord told him, "Go to the house of
Judas on Straight Street and ask for a man
from Tarsus named Saul, for he is praying.
12In a vision he has seen a man named
Ananias come and place his hands on him
to restore his sight."
13"Lord," Ananias answered, "I have
heard many reports about this man and all
the harm he has done to your saints in
Jerusalem. 14And he has come here with
authority from the chief priests to arrest all
who call on your name."
15But the Lord said to Ananias, "Go!
This man is my chosen instrument to carry
my name before the Gentiles and their
kings and before the people of Israel. 16I
will show him how much he must suffer for
my name."●
17Then Ananias went to the house and
entered it. Placing his hands on Saul, he
said, "Brother Saul, the Lord—Jesus, who
appeared to you on the road as you were
coming here—has sent me so that you may
see again and be filled with the Holy
Spirit." 18Immediately, something like
scales fell from Saul's eyes, and he could
see again. He got up and was baptized,
19and after taking some food, he regained
his strength.●

KING JAMES

1. SAUL'S CONVERSION

9 And Saul, yet breathing out threatenings and slaughter against the disciples of the Lord, went unto the high
priest, 2 and desired of him letters to
Damascus to the synagogues, that if he
found any of this way, whether they were
men or women, he might bring them
bound unto Jerusalem. 3 And as he journeyed, he came near Damascus: and suddenly there shined round about him a
light from heaven: 4 and he fell to the
earth, and heard a voice saying unto him,
Saul, Saul, why persecutest thou me?
5 And he said, Who art thou, Lord? And
the Lord said, I am Jesus whom thou persecutest: *it is* hard for thee to kick against
the pricks. 6 And he trembling and astonished said, Lord, what wilt thou have
me to do? And the Lord *said* unto him,
Arise, and go into the city, and it shall be
told thee what thou must do. 7 And the
men which journeyed with him stood
speechless, hearing a voice, but seeing no
man. 8 And Saul arose from the earth;
and when his eyes were opened, he saw no
man: but they led him by the hand, and
brought *him* into Damascus. 9 And he
was three days without sight, and neither
did eat nor drink.●

BREATHING MURDER

2. ANANIAS' VISION

10 And there was a certain disciple at
Damascus, named Anani'as; and to him
said the Lord in a vision, Anani'as. And
he said, Behold, I *am here*, Lord. 11 And
the Lord *said* unto him, Arise, and go into
the street which is called Straight, and
inquire in the house of Judas for *one*
called Saul, of Tarsus: for, behold, he
prayeth, 12 and hath seen in a vision a
man named Anani'as coming in, and
putting *his* hand on him, that he might
receive his sight. 13 Then Anani'as answered, Lord, I have heard by many of
this man, how much evil he hath done to
thy saints at Jerusalem: 14 and here he
hath authority from the chief priests to
bind all that call on thy name. 15 But the
Lord said unto him, Go thy way: for he
is a chosen vessel unto me, to bear my
name before the Gentiles, and kings, and
the children of Israel: 16 for I will show
him how great things he must suffer for
my name's sake.●

3. SAUL'S BAPTISM

17 And Anani'as went
his way, and entered into the house; and
putting his hands on him said, Brother
Saul, the Lord, *even* Jesus, that appeared
unto thee in the way as thou camest, hath
sent me, that thou mightest receive thy
sight, and be filled with the Holy Ghost.
18 And immediately there fell from his
eyes as it had been scales: and he received
sight forthwith, and arose, and was baptized. 19 And when he had received meat,
he was strengthened.●

FILLED WITH HOLY SPIRIT

*9:1-9* Compare the Saul of verse 1 with Saul of verses 8-9.

What are the main parts of Saul's experience of this paragraph?

*9:10-16* Compare Ananias' balking (vv.13-14) with Saul's submission (vv.6-9).

What do verses 15-16 reveal about Saul's coming ministry?

*9:17-19a* What happened to Saul?

What were the purposes of these experiences?

NEW INTERNATIONAL VERSION

What is taught in this passage about:

CHRISTIAN FELLOWSHIP

CHRISTIAN GROWTH

CARE OF NEW CONVERTS

THE GOSPEL MESSAGE

HUMILIATION

CHRISTIAN WITNESS

List spiritual applications which may be made of verse 31.

*Saul in Damascus and Jerusalem*

Saul spent several days with the disciples in Damascus. 20At once he began to
preach in the synagogues that Jesus is the
Son of God. 21All those who heard him
were astonished and asked, "Isn't he the
man who raised havoc in Jerusalem among
those who call on this name? And hasn't he
come here to take them as prisoners to the
chief priests?" 22Yet Saul grew more and
more powerful and baffled the Jews living
in Damascus by proving that Jesus is the
Christ.[a]
23After many days had gone by, the Jews
conspired to kill him, 24but Saul learned of
their plan. Day and night they kept close
watch on the city gates in order to kill him.
25But his followers took him by night and
lowered him in a basket through an opening in the wall.●
26When he came to Jerusalem, he tried to
join the disciples, but they were all afraid
of him, not believing that he really was a
disciple. 27But Barnabas took him and
brought him to the apostles. He told them
how Saul on his journey had seen the Lord
and that the Lord had spoken to him, and
how in Damascus he had preached fearlessly in the name of Jesus. 28So Saul
stayed with them and moved about freely
in Jerusalem, speaking boldly in the name
of the Lord. 29He talked and debated with
the Grecian Jews, but they tried to kill him.
30When the brothers learned of this, they
took him down to Caesarea and sent him
off to Tarsus.●
31Then the church throughout Judea,
Galilee and Samaria enjoyed a time of
peace. It was strengthened; and encouraged by the Holy Spirit, it grew in
numbers, living in the fear of the Lord.●

[a]22 Or *Messiah*

KING JAMES

**1. PAUL MINISTERS IN DAMASCUS**

**PERSECUTION**

Then was Saul certain days with the
disciples which were at Damascus. 20 And
straightway he preached Christ in the
synagogues, that he is the Son of God.
21 But all that heard *him* were amazed,
and said; Is not this he that destroyed
them which called on this name in Jerusalem, and came hither for that intent,
that he might bring them bound unto the
chief priests? 22 But Saul increased the
more in strength, and confounded the
Jews which dwelt at Damascus, proving
that this is very Christ.
23 And after that many days were fulfilled, the Jews took counsel to kill him:
24 but their laying wait was known of
Saul. And they watched the gates day and
night to kill him. 25 Then the disciples
took him by night, and let *him* down by
the wall in a basket. ●

**2. PAUL MINISTERS IN JERUSALEM**

26 And when Saul was come to Jerusalem, he assayed to join himself to the
disciples: but they were all afraid of him,
and believed not that he was a disciple.
27 But Barnabas took him, and brought
*him* to the apostles, and declared unto
them how he had seen the Lord in the
way, and that he had spoken to him, and
how he had preached boldly at Damascus
in the name of Jesus. 28 And he was with
them coming in and going out at Jerusalem. 29 And he spake boldly in the
name of the Lord Jesus, and disputed
against the Gre'cians: but they went
about to slay him. 30 *Which* when the
brethren knew, they brought him down
to Caesare'a, and sent him forth to
Tarsus. ●

**3. CHURCHES ARE EDIFIED**

31 Then had the churches rest throughout all Judea and Galilee and Samaria,
and were edified; and walking in the fear
of the Lord, and in the comfort of the
Holy Ghost, were multiplied. ●

**REST**

*9:19b-25* Record what is written here about:

SAUL: ______________________

______________________

______________________

THE PEOPLE: ______________________

______________________

______________________

THE JEWS: ______________________

______________________

______________________

DISCIPLES: ______________________

______________________

______________________

*9:26-30* Record what is written about:

SAUL: ______________________

______________________

______________________

BARNABAS: ______________________

______________________

______________________

APOSTLES: ______________________

______________________

______________________

*9:31* How is this verse a conclusion to the story of Saul's conversion?

______________________

______________________

______________________

______________________

______________________

______________________

______________________

______________________

______________________

______________________

______________________

NEW INTERNATIONAL VERSION

What does this passage teach about:

MIRACLES AS SIGNS

GOOD WORKS

DEATH AND LIFE

DIVINE POWER

List some spiritual applications which may be made of this passage.

The gospel was for Gentiles as well as Jews. Apply this truth to today.

*Aeneas and Dorcas*

32As Peter traveled about the country, he
went to visit the saints in Lydda. 33There
he found a man named Aeneas, a paralytic
who had been bedridden for eight years.
34"Aeneas," Peter said to him, "Jesus
Christ heals you. Get up and take care of
your mat." Immediately Aeneas got up.
35All those who lived in Lydda and Sharon
saw him and turned to the Lord.●
36In Joppa there was a disciple named
Tabitha (which, when translated, is Dorcas[b]), who was always doing good and
helping the poor. 37About that time she
became sick and died, and her body was
washed and placed in an upstairs room.
38Lydda was near Joppa; so when the disciples heard that Peter was in Lydda, they
sent two men to him and urged him,
"Please come at once!"
39Peter went with them, and when he
arrived he was taken upstairs to the room.
All the widows stood around him, crying
and showing him the robes and other clothing that Dorcas had made while she was
still with them.●
40Peter sent them all out of the room;
then he got down on his knees and prayed.
Turning toward the dead woman, he said,
"Tabitha, get up." She opened her eyes,
and seeing Peter she sat up. 41He took her
by the hand and helped her to her feet.
Then he called the believers and the widows and presented her to them alive. 42This
became known all over Joppa, and many
people believed in the Lord. 43Peter stayed
in Joppa for some time with a tanner named
Simon.●

[b]36 Both *Tabitha* (Aramaic) and *Dorcas* (Greek) mean *gazelle*.

KING JAMES

1. AENEAS HEALED

32 And it came to pass, as Peter passed
throughout all *quarters*, he came down
also to the saints which dwelt at Lydda.
33 And there he found a certain man
named Aene'as, which had kept his bed
eight years, and was sick of the palsy.
34 And Peter said unto him, Aene'as,
Jesus Christ maketh thee whole: arise,
and make thy bed. And he arose immediately. 35 And all that dwelt at Lydda
and Sharon saw him, and turned to the
Lord.●

RISEN FROM SICK BED

2. DORCAS DIES

36 Now there was at Joppa a certain
disciple named Tab'itha, which by interpretation is called Dorcas: this woman
was full of good works and almsdeeds
which she did. 37 And it came to pass in
those days, that she was sick, and died:
whom when they had washed, they laid
*her* in an upper chamber. 38 And forasmuch as Lydda was nigh to Joppa, and
the disciples had heard that Peter was
there, they sent unto him two men, desiring *him* that he would not delay to come
to them. 39 Then Peter arose and went
with them. When he was come, they
brought him into the upper chamber: and
all the widows stood by him weeping, and
showing the coats and garments which
Dorcas made, while she was with them.●

3. DORCAS RESTORED TO LIFE

40 But Peter put them all forth, and
kneeled down, and prayed; and turning
*him* to the body said, Tab'itha, arise. And
she opened her eyes: and when she saw
Peter, she sat up. 41 And he gave her *his*
hand, and lifted her up; and when he had
called the saints and widows, he presented
her alive. 42 And it was known throughout all Joppa; and many believed in the
Lord. 43 And it came to pass, that he
tarried many days in Joppa with one
Simon a tanner.●

RISEN FROM THE DEAD

Beginning at this point in Acts God shows the apostles and other believers that the gospel was for Gentiles as well as Jews. This new period of His working is covered by the section 9:32-12:25. In this segment God uses the sign of MIRACLES to accredit the ministry to Gentiles.

*9:32-35* Record:

*PETER'S WORDS* __________

*PEOPLE'S REACTION* __________

*9:36-39* Record what is known about Dorcas here:

*9:40-43* Record your observations:

THE MIRACLE: __________

THE EFFECT: __________

NEW INTERNATIONAL VERSION

What is taught here about:

DEVOUT LIVING

PRAYER

VISIONS

OBEDIENCE

LEGALISM

Apply verse 15b to today, in different kinds of situations.

*Cornelius Calls for Peter*

10 At Caesarea there was a man named
Cornelius, a centurion in what was
known as the Italian Regiment. 2He and all
his family were devout and God-fearing; he
gave generously to those in need and
prayed to God regularly. 3One day at about
three in the afternoon he had a vision. He
distinctly saw an angel of God, who came
to him and said, "Cornelius!"
4Cornelius stared at him in fear. "What
is it, Lord?" he asked.
The angel answered, "Your prayers and
gifts to the poor have come up as a remembrance before God. 5Now send men to Joppa to bring back a man named Simon who
is called Peter. 6He is staying with Simon
the tanner, whose house is by the sea."
7When the angel who spoke to him had
gone, Cornelius called two of his servants
and one of his soldiers who was a devout
man. 8He told them everything that had
happened and sent them to Joppa.●

*Peter's Vision*

9About noon the following day as they
were approaching the city, Peter went up
on the roof to pray. 10He became hungry
and wanted something to eat, and while the
meal was being prepared, he fell into a
trance. 11He saw heaven opened and something like a large sheet being let down to
earth by its four corners. 12It contained all
kinds of four-footed animals, as well as
reptiles of the earth and birds of the air.
13Then a voice told him, "Get up, Peter.
Kill and eat."
14"Surely not, Lord!" Peter replied. "I
have never eaten anything impure or unclean."
15The voice spoke to him a second time,
"Do not call anything impure that God has
made clean."
16This happened three times, and
immediately the sheet was taken back to
heaven.●

## KING JAMES

**1. CORNELIUS' VISION**

**A PRAYING CENTURION**

10 There was a certain man in Caesare'a called Cornelius, a centurion of
the band called the Italian *band*, 2 *a*
devout *man*, and one that feared God with
all his house, which gave much alms to the
people, and prayed to God always.
3 He saw in a vision evidently, about the
ninth hour of the day, an angel of God
coming in to him, and saying unto him,
Cornelius. 4 And when he looked on him,
he was afraid, and said, What is it, Lord?
And he said unto him, Thy prayers and
thine alms are come up for a memorial
before God. 5 And now send men to
Joppa, and call for *one* Simon, whose surname is Peter: 6 he lodgeth with one
Simon a tanner, whose house is by the
sea side: he shall tell thee what thou
oughtest to do. 7 And when the angel
which spake unto Cornelius was departed,
he called two of his household servants,
and a devout soldier of them that waited
on him continually; 8 and when he had
declared all *these* things unto them, he
sent them to Joppa.●

**2. PETER'S VISION**

**A PRAYING APOSTLE**

9 On the morrow, as they went on their
journey, and drew nigh unto the city,
Peter went up upon the housetop to pray
about the sixth hour: 10 and he became
very hungry, and would have eaten: but
while they made ready, he fell into a
trance, 11 and saw heaven opened, and
a certain vessel descending unto him, as
it had been a great sheet knit at the four
corners, and let down to the earth:
12 wherein were all manner of fourfooted
beasts of the earth, and wild beasts, and
creeping things, and fowls of the air.
13 And there came a voice to him, Rise,
Peter; kill, and eat. 14 But Peter said,
Not so, Lord; for I have never eaten any
thing that is common or unclean. 15 And
the voice *spake* unto him again the second
time, What God hath cleansed, *that* call
not thou common. 16 This was done
thrice: and the vessel was received up
again into heaven.●

This segment records the visions of a centurion and an apostle. The connection between the two will be seen in the succeeding segments. It involves the credentials supplied by the sign of visions.

*10:1-8* CORNELIUS: ______

THE VISION: ______

*10:9-16*

SETTING (vv.9-10) ______

VISION (vv.11-12) ______

CONVERSATION (vv.13-16) ______

NEW INTERNATIONAL VERSION

What do you learn here about:

SPIRITUAL UNDERSTANDING

OBEDIENCE

RESPECT

PREJUDICE

PRAYER

SEEKING GOD

DIVINE COMMUNICATION

17While Peter was wondering about the
meaning of the vision, the men sent by
Cornelius found out where Simon's house
was and stopped at the gate. 18They called
out, asking if Simon who was known as
Peter was staying there.
19While Peter was still thinking about the
vision, the Spirit said to him, "Simon,
three[a] men are looking for you. 20So get up
and go downstairs. Do not hesitate to go
with them, for I have sent them."
21Peter went down and said to the men,
"I'm the one you're looking for. Why have
you come?"
22The men replied, "We have come from
Cornelius the centurion. He is a righteous
and God-fearing man, who is respected by
all the Jewish people. A holy angel told him
to have you come to his house so that he
could hear what you have to say." 23Then
Peter invited the men into the house to be
his guests.●

*Peter at Cornelius' House*

The next day Peter started out with
them, and some of the brothers from Joppa
went along. 24The following day he arrived
in Caesarea. Cornelius was expecting them
and had called together his relatives and
close friends. 25As Peter entered the house,
Cornelius met him and fell at his feet in
reverence. 26But Peter made him get up.
"Stand up," he said, "I am only a man
myself."
27Talking with him, Peter went inside
and found a large gathering of people. 28He
said to them: "You are well aware that it
is against our law for a Jew to associate
with a Gentile or visit him. But God has
shown me that I should not call any man
impure or unclean. 29So when I was sent
for, I came without raising any objection.
May I ask why you sent for me?"●
30Cornelius answered: "Four days ago I
was in my house praying at this hour, at
three in the afternoon. Suddenly a man in
shining clothes stood before me 31and said,
'Cornelius, God has heard your prayer and
remembered your gifts to the poor. 32Send
to Joppa for Simon who is called Peter. He
is a guest in the home of Simon the tanner,
who lives by the sea.' 33So I sent for you
immediately, and it was good of you to
come. Now we are all here in the presence
of God to listen to everything the Lord has
commanded you to tell us."●

[a]19 One early manuscript *two*; other manuscripts do not have the number.

KING JAMES

**1. INVITATION**

**VISION'S MEANING**

17 Now while Peter doubted in himself
what this vision which he had seen should
mean, behold, the men which were sent
from Cornelius had made inquiry for
Simon's house, and stood before the gate,
18 and called, and asked whether Simon,
which was surnamed Peter, were lodged
there. 19 While Peter thought on the
vision, the Spirit said unto him, Behold,
three men seek thee. 20 Arise therefore,
and get thee down, and go with them,
doubting nothing: for I have sent them.
21 Then Peter went down to the men
which were sent unto him from Cornelius; and said, Behold, I am he whom
ye seek: what *is* the cause wherefore ye are
come? 22 And they said, Cornelius the
centurion, a just man, and one that feareth God, and of good report among all
the nation of the Jews, was warned from
God by a holy angel to send for thee into
his house, and to hear words of thee.
23 Then called he them in, and lodged
*them*. ●

**2. MEETING**

And on the morrow Peter went away
with them, and certain brethren from
Joppa accompanied him. 24 And the
morrow after they entered into Caesare'a.
And Cornelius waited for them, and had
called together his kinsmen and near
friends. 25 And as Peter was coming in,
Cornelius met him, and fell down at his
feet, and worshipped *him*. 26 But Peter
took him up, saying, Stand up; I myself
also am a man. 27 And as he talked with
him, he went in, and found many that
were come together. 28 And he said unto
them, Ye know how that it is an unlawful
thing for a man that is a Jew to keep company, or come unto one of another nation;
but God hath showed me that I should
not call any man common or unclean.
29 Therefore came I *unto you* without
gainsaying, as soon as I was sent for: I
ask therefore for what intent ye have sent
for me? ●

**3. OPPORTUNITY**

30 And Cornelius said, Four days ago
I was fasting until this hour; and at the
ninth hour I prayed in my house, and,
behold, a man stood before me in bright
clothing, 31 and said, Cornelius, thy
prayer is heard, and thine alms are had
in remembrance in the sight of God.
32 Send therefore to Joppa, and call
hither Simon, whose surname is Peter; he
is lodged in the house of *one* Simon a tanner by the sea side: who, when he cometh,
shall speak unto thee. 33 Immediately
therefore I sent to thee; and thou hast
well done that thou art come. Now therefore are we all here present before God, to
hear all things that are commanded thee
of God. ●

**VISION'S PURPOSE**

The credentials of the ministry to Gentiles are also supported by the sign of conversion. These are recorded in the section 10:17—11:30.

*10:17-23a* What was Peter's curiosity (v.17)?

What does verse 21 reveal about Peter?

Why did Cornelius want to meet Peter (v.22)?

*10:23b-29* How does Peter here apply the spiritual teaching of the vision he had seen earlier?

*10:30-33* Compare verses 33 and 22.

NEW INTERNATIONAL VERSION

What is taught here about:

GOD NO RESPECTOR OF PERSONS

GOSPEL MESSAGE

JESUS' MINISTRY

SALVATION INVITATION

GIFT OF THE HOLY SPIRIT

WATER BAPTISM

OTHER

34Then Peter began to speak: "I now
realize how true it is that God does not
show favoritism 35but accepts men from
every nation who fear him and do what is
right. 36This is the message God sent to the
people of Israel, telling the good news of
peace through Jesus Christ, who is Lord of
all. 37You know what has happened
throughout Judea, beginning in Galilee after the baptism that John preached— 38how
God anointed Jesus of Nazareth with the
Holy Spirit and power, and how he went
around doing good and healing all who
were under the power of the devil, because
God was with him.

39"We are witnesses of everything he did
in the country of the Jews and in Jerusalem. They killed him by hanging him on a
tree, 40but God raised him from the dead on
the third day and caused him to be seen.
41He was not seen by all the people, but by
witnesses whom God had already chos-
en—by us who ate and drank with him after
he rose from the dead. 42He commanded us
to preach to the people and to testify that
he is the one whom God appointed as judge
of the living and the dead. 43All the prophets testify about him that everyone who
believes in him receives forgiveness of sins
through his name."●

44While Peter was still speaking these
words, the Holy Spirit came on all who
heard the message. 45The circumcised believers who had come with Peter were astonished that the gift of the Holy Spirit had
been poured out even on the Gentiles.
46For they heard them speaking in tongues[a]
and praising God.

Then Peter said, 47"Can anyone keep
these people from being baptized with
water? They have received the Holy Spirit
just as we have." 48So he ordered that they
be baptized in the name of Jesus Christ.
Then they asked Peter to stay with them
for a few days.●

[a]46 Or *other languages*

KING JAMES

## 1. PETER'S SPEECH

EVERY NATION

34 Then Peter opened *his* mouth, and
said, Of a truth I perceive that God is no
respecter of persons: 35 but in every
nation he that feareth him, and worketh
righteousness, is accepted with him.
36 The word which *God* sent unto the
children of Israel, preaching peace by
Jesus Christ: (he is Lord of all:) 37 that
word, *I say*, ye know, which was published throughout all Judea, and began
from Galilee, after the baptism which
John preached; 38 how God anointed
Jesus of Nazareth with the Holy Ghost
and with power: who went about doing
good, and healing all that were oppressed
of the devil; for God was with him.
39 And we are witnesses of all things
which he did both in the land of the Jews,
and in Jerusalem; whom they slew and
hanged on a tree: 40 him God raised up
the third day, and showed him openly;
41 not to all the people, but unto witnesses chosen before of God, *even* to us,
who did eat and drink with him after he
rose from the dead. 42 And he commanded us to preach unto the people, and
to testify that it is he which was ordained
of God *to be* the Judge of quick and dead.
43 To him give all the prophets witness,
that through his name whosoever believeth in him shall receive remission of sins.●

## 2. THE GENTILES RECEIVE THE HOLY SPIRIT

GENTILES ALSO

44 While Peter yet spake these words,
the Holy Ghost fell on all them which
heard the word. 45 And they of the circumcision which believed were astonished,
as many as came with Peter, because that
on the Gentiles also was poured out the
gift of the Holy Ghost. 46 For they heard
them speak with tongues, and magnify
God. Then answered Peter, 47 Can any
man forbid water, that these should not
be baptized, which have received the Holy
Ghost as well as we? 48 And he commanded them to be baptized in the name
of the Lord. Then prayed they him to
tarry certain days.●

*10:34-43* How does Peter apply his vision, in verses 34-35?

Compare "the word...unto the children of Israel" (v.36) with "that word...ye know"(v.37).

Record the main truths of the gospel message (vv.38-43):

How does the word "whosoever"(v.43) relate to Peter's vision?

*10:44-48* Record the effects of Peter's speaking:

NEW INTERNATIONAL VERSION

What does this passage teach about:

DISSENSION

GOSPEL FOR GENTILES

SPIRIT BAPTISM

WATER BAPTISM

LOVE

OTHER

*Peter Explains His Actions*

11 The apostles and the brothers
throughout Judea heard that the
Gentiles also had received the word of
God. 2So when Peter went up to Jerusalem,
the circumcised believers criticized him
3and said, "You went into the house of
uncircumcised men and ate with them."
4Peter began and explained everything to
them precisely as it had happened● 5"I was
in the city of Joppa praying, and in a trance
I saw a vision. I saw something like a large
sheet being let down from heaven by its
four corners, and it came down to where I
was. 6I looked into it and saw four-footed
animals of the earth, wild beasts, reptiles,
and birds of the air. 7Then I heard a voice
telling me, 'Get up, Peter. Kill and eat.'
8"I replied, 'Surely not, Lord! Nothing
impure or unclean has ever entered my
mouth.'
9"The voice spoke from heaven a second
time, 'Do not call anything impure that
God has made clean.' 10This happened
three times, and then it was all pulled up to
heaven again.
11"Right then three men who had been
sent to me from Caesarea stopped at the
house where I was staying. 12The Spirit
told me to have no hesitation about going
with them. These six brothers also went
with me, and we entered the man's house.
13He told us how he had seen an angel
appear in his house and say, 'Send to Joppa
for Simon who is called Peter. 14He will
bring you a message through which you
and all your household will be saved.'
15"As I began to speak, the Holy Spirit
came on them as he had come on us at the
beginning. 16Then I remembered what the
Lord had said, 'John baptized with[b] water,
but you will be baptized with the Holy
Spirit.' 17So if God gave them the same gift
as he gave us, who believed in the Lord
Jesus Christ, who was I to think that I
could oppose God!"●
18When they heard this, they had no further objections and praised God, saying,
"So then, God has even granted the Gentiles repentance unto life."

[b]16 Or *in*

## KING JAMES

1. OBJECTION

CONTENTION

**11** And the apostles and brethren that
were in Judea heard that the Gentiles had also received the word of God.
2 And when Peter was come up to Jerusalem, they that were of the circumcision
contended with him, 3 saying, Thou
wentest in to men uncircumcised, and
didst eat with them. 4 But Peter rehearsed *the matter* from the beginning,
and expounded *it* by order unto them,
saying,● 5 I was in the city of Joppa praying: and in a trance I saw a vision, a certain vessel descend, as it had been a great
sheet, let down from heaven by four corners; and it came even to me: 6 upon the
which when I had fastened mine eyes, I
considered, and saw fourfooted beasts of
the earth, and wild beasts, and creeping
things, and fowls of the air. 7 And I
heard a voice saying unto me, Arise,
Peter; slay and eat. 8 But I said, Not so,
Lord: for nothing common or unclean
hath at any time entered into my mouth.
9 But the voice answered me again from
heaven, What God hath cleansed, *that*
call not thou common. 10 And this was
done three times: and all were drawn up
again into heaven. 11 And, behold, immediately there were three men already
come unto the house where I was, sent
from Caesare'a unto me. 12 And the
Spirit bade me go with them, nothing
doubting. Moreover these six brethren
accompanied me, and we entered into the
man's house: 13 and he showed us how
he had seen an angel in his house, which
stood and said unto him, Send men to
Joppa, and call for Simon, whose surname is Peter; 14 who shall tell thee
words, whereby thou and all thy house
shall be saved. 15 And as I began to
speak, the Holy Ghost fell on them, as on
us at the beginning. 16 Then remembered
I the word of the Lord, how that he said,
John indeed baptized with water; but ye
shall be baptized with the Holy Ghost.
17 Forasmuch then as God gave them the
like gift as *he did* unto us, who believed on
the Lord Jesus Christ, what was I, that I
could withstand God?● 18 When they
heard these things, they held their peace,
and glorified God, saying, Then hath God
also to the Gentiles granted repentance
unto life.●

2. EXPLANATION

3. SATISFACTION

PEACE

*11:1-4* Compare the report (v.1) with the accusation (v.3).

*11:5-17* According to verse 14 was Cornelius a Christian before meeting Peter?

Note the references to persons of the trinity in the paragraph. What is written about each?

What convinced Peter that the gospel was for Gentiles as well as for Jews (vv.15-17)?

*11:18* What three notes of *acceptance* do you see here?

NEW INTERNATIONAL VERSION

Record what you have learned from this passage about:

SPIRITUAL GROWTH

MINISTRY OF THE WORD

CHRISTIANS

HAND OF THE LORD

GRACE OF GOD

MINISTRY OF TEACHING

GOOD WORKS

OTHER

*The Church in Antioch*

19Now those who had been scattered by
the persecution in connection with Stephen traveled as far as Phoenicia, Cyprus
and Antioch, telling the message only to
Jews. 20Some of them, however, men from
Cyprus and Cyrene, went to Antioch and
began to speak to Greeks also, telling them
the good news about the Lord Jesus. 21The
Lord's hand was with them, and a great
number of people believed and turned to
the Lord.●

22News of this reached the ears of the
church at Jerusalem, and they sent Barnabas to Antioch. 23When he arrived and
saw the evidence of the grace of God, he
was glad and encouraged them all to
remain true to the Lord with all their
hearts. 24He was a good man, full of the
Holy Spirit and faith, and a great number
of people were brought to the Lord.●

25Then Barnabas went to Tarsus to look
for Saul, 26and when he found him, he
brought him to Antioch. So for a whole
year Barnabas and Saul met with the
church and taught great numbers of
people. The disciples were first called
Christians at Antioch.●

27During this time some prophets came
down from Jerusalem to Antioch. 28One of
them, named Agabus, stood up and
through the Spirit predicted that a severe
famine would spread over the entire Roman world. (This happened during the
reign of Claudius.) 29The disciples, each
according to his ability, decided to provide
help for the brothers living in Judea. 30This
they did, sending their gift to the elders by
Barnabas and Saul.●

## KING JAMES

**1. CON-VERSIONS**

**GOSPEL FROM JERUSALEM**

19 Now they which were scattered
abroad upon the persecution that arose
about Stephen traveled as far as Phoeni'cia, and Cyprus, and An'ti-och, preaching the word to none but unto the Jews
only. 20 And some of them were men of
Cyprus and Cyre'ne, which, when they
were come to An'ti-och, spake unto the
Gre'cians, preaching the Lord Jesus.
21 And the hand of the Lord was with
them: and a great number believed, and

**2. EXHOR-TATIONS**

turned unto the Lord.● 22 Then tidings of
these things came unto the ears of the
church which was in Jerusalem: and they
sent forth Barnabas, that he should go as
far as An'ti-och. 23 Who, when he came,
and had seen the grace of God, was glad,
and exhorted them all, that with purpose
of heart they would cleave unto the Lord.
24 For he was a good man, and full of the
Holy Ghost and of faith: and much peo-

**3. TEACH-ING**

ple was added unto the Lord. ● 25 Then
departed Barnabas to Tarsus, for to seek
Saul: 26 and when he had found him, he
brought him unto An'ti-och. And it came
to pass, that a whole year they assembled
themselves with the church, and taught
much people. And the disciples were
called Christians first in An'ti-och.●

**4. APPLICA-TION**

27 And in these days came prophets
from Jerusalem unto An'ti-och. 28 And
there stood up one of them named Ag'a-
bus, and signified by the Spirit that there
should be great dearth throughout all the
world: which came to pass in the days of
Claudius Caesar. 29 Then the disciples,
every man according to his ability, determined to send relief unto the brethren

**GIFTS TO JERUSALEM**

which dwelt in Judea: 30 which also they
did, and sent it to the elders by the hands
of Barnabas and Saul.●

Before studying this segment review 8:1,4. Also compare 11:18 and 11:20.

*11:19-21* Compare the audiences of this gospel preaching of verses 19 and 20.

______________________

______________________

______________________

______________________

What was the fruit of the ministry in Antioch?

______________________

______________________

*11:22-24*

CHURCH'S CONCERN: ______________________

______________________

______________________

THE MAN BARNABAS: ______________________

______________________

______________________

BARNABAS' MINISTRY: ______________________

______________________

______________________

*11:25-26* What was the main ministry at this time?

______________________

______________________

______________________

______________________

*11:27-30* What are your impressions of this paragraph?

______________________

______________________

______________________

______________________

______________________

______________________

______________________

______________________

NEW INTERNATIONAL VERSION

Record what this passage teaches about:

PERSECUTION

VISIONS

OBEDIENCE

DELIVERANCE

PRAYER

DOUBT

OTHER

### *Peter's Miraculous Escape From Prison*

12 It was about this time that King Herod arrested some who belonged to
the church, intending to persecute them.
2He had James, the brother of John, put to
death with the sword. 3When he saw that
this pleased the Jews, he proceeded to
seize Peter also. This happened during the
Feast of Unleavened Bread. 4After arresting him, he put him in prison, handing him
over to be guarded by four squads of four
soldiers each. Herod intended to bring him
out for public trial after the Passover.
5So Peter was kept in prison, but the
church was earnestly praying to God for
him.●
6The night before Herod was to bring
him to trial, Peter was sleeping between
two soldiers, bound with two chains, and
sentries stood guard at the entrance. 7Sud-
denly an angel of the Lord appeared and a
light shone in the cell. He struck Peter on
the side and woke him up. "Quick, get
up!" he said, and the chains fell off Peter's
wrists.
8Then the angel said to him, "Put on
your clothes and sandals." And Peter did
so. "Wrap your cloak around you and follow me," the angel told him. 9Peter followed him out of the prison, but he had no
idea that what the angel was doing was
really happening; he thought he was seeing
a vision. 10They passed the first and second
guards and came to the iron gate leading to
the city. It opened for them by itself, and
they went through it. When they had
walked the length of one street, suddenly
the angel left him.
11Then Peter came to himself and said,
"Now I know without a doubt that the
Lord sent his angel and rescued me from
Herod's clutches and from everything the
Jewish people were anticipating."●
12When this had dawned on him, he went
to the house of Mary the mother of John,
also called Mark, where many people had
gathered and were praying. 13Peter
knocked at the outer entrance, and a servant girl named Rhoda came to answer the
door. 14When she recognized Peter's
voice, she was so overjoyed she ran back
without opening it and exclaimed, "Peter
is at the door!"
15"You're out of your mind," they told
her. When she kept insisting that it was so,
they said, "It must be his angel."
16But Peter kept on knocking, and when
they opened the door and saw him, they
were astonished. 17Peter motioned with his
hand for them to be quiet and described
how the Lord had brought him out of prison. "Tell James and the brothers about
this," he said, and then he left for another
place.●

KING JAMES

1. ARREST

PETER IN PRISON

12 Now about that time Herod the
king stretched forth *his* hands to
vex certain of the church. 2 And he killed
James the brother of John with the sword.
3 And because he saw it pleased the Jews,
he proceeded further to take Peter also.
(Then were the days of unleavened bread.)
4 And when he had apprehended him, he
put *him* in prison, and delivered *him* to
four quaternions of soldiers to keep him;
intending after Easter to bring him forth
to the people. 5 Peter therefore was kept
in prison: but prayer was made without
ceasing of the church unto God for him.●

2. DELIVERANCE

6 And when Herod would have brought
him forth, the same night Peter was sleeping between two soldiers, bound with two
chains: and the keepers before the door
kept the prison. 7 And, behold, the angel
of the Lord came upon *him*, and a light
shined in the prison: and he smote Peter
on the side, and raised him up, saying,
Arise up quickly. And his chains fell off
from *his* hands. 8 And the angel said unto him, Gird thyself, and bind on thy sandals. And so he did. And he saith unto
him, Cast thy garment about thee, and
follow me. 9 And he went out, and followed him; and wist not that it was true
which was done by the angel; but thought
he saw a vision. 10 When they were past
the first and the second ward, they came
unto the iron gate that leadeth unto the
city; which opened to them of his own
accord: and they went out, and passed on
through one street; and forthwith the
angel departed from him. 11 And when
Peter was come to himself, he said, Now
I know of a surety, that the Lord hath
sent his angel, and hath delivered me out
of the hand of Herod, and *from* all the
expectation of the people of the Jews.●

3. VISITATION

12 And when he had considered *the*
*thing*, he came to the house of Mary the
mother of John, whose surname was
Mark; where many were gathered together praying. 13 And as Peter knocked
at the door of the gate, a damsel came to
hearken, named Rhoda. 14 And when
she knew Peter's voice, she opened not the
gate for gladness, but ran in, and told how
Peter stood before the gate. 15 And they
said unto her, Thou art mad. But she
constantly affirmed that it was even so.
Then said they, It is his angel. 16 But
Peter continued knocking: and when they
had opened *the door*, and saw him, they
were astonished. 17 But he, beckoning
unto them with the hand to hold their
peace, declared unto them how the Lord
had brought him out of the prison. And
he said, Go show these things unto James,
and to the brethren. And he departed,
and went into another place.●

PETER FREE

Record items for each paragraph as shown:

*12:1-5*

THE PERSECUTIONS __________

PRAYER __________

*12:6-11*

PETER'S EXPERIENCES (vv.7-10) __________

PETER'S INTERPRETATION (v.11) __________

*12:12-17*

ACTIONS AND ACTIVITIES __________

REACTIONS __________

NEW INTERNATIONAL VERSION

What does this passage teach about:

RIGHTEOUSNESS

IDOLATRY

JUDGMENT

GLORY OF GOD

WORD OF GOD

List some spiritual applications of the passage:

18 In the morning, there was a great commotion among the soldiers. "What could
have happened to Peter?" they asked.
19 After Herod had a thorough search made
for him and did not find him, he cross-
examined the guards and ordered that they
be executed.●

*Herod's Death*

Then Herod went from Judea to Caesarea and stayed there a while. 20 He had
been quarreling with the people of Tyre
and Sidon; they now joined together and
sought an audience with him. Having
secured the support of Blastus, a trusted
personal servant of the king, they asked for
peace, because they depended on the
king's country for their food supply.
21 On the appointed day Herod, wearing
his royal robes, sat on his throne and delivered a public address to the people.
22 They shouted, "This is the voice of a
god, not of a man." 23 Immediately, because Herod did not give praise to God, an
angel of the Lord struck him down, and he
was eaten by worms and died.●
24 But the word of God continued to increase and spread.
25 When Barnabas and Saul had finished
their mission, they returned from[a] Jerusalem, taking with them John, also called
Mark.●

[a]25 Some manuscripts *to*

KING JAMES

1. JAIL-KEEPERS SEN—TENCED TO DEATH

18 Now as soon as it was day, there was
no small stir among the soldiers, what was
become of Peter. 19 And when Herod
had sought for him, and found him not,
he examined the keepers, and commanded
that *they* should be put to death. And he
went down from Judea to Caesare'a, and
*there* abode. ●

2. HEROD SMITTEN BY GOD

20 And Herod was highly displeased
with them of Tyre and Sidon: but they
came with one accord to him, and, having
made Blastus the king's chamberlain their
friend, desired peace; because their country was nourished by the king's *country*.
21 And upon a set day Herod, arrayed in
royal apparel, sat upon his throne, and
made an oration unto them. 22 And the
people gave a shout, *saying*, *It is* the voice
of a god, and not of a man. 23 And immediately the angel of the Lord smote
him, because he gave not God the glory:
and he was eaten of worms, and gave up
the ghost. ●

3. THE WORD MULTI-PLIES

24 But the word of God grew and
multiplied.
25 And Barnabas and Saul returned
from Jerusalem, when they had fulfilled
*their* ministry, and took with them John,
whose surname was Mark. ●

AN APOSTLE NOT BOUND

WORD OF GOD NOT BOUND

This is the last segment of the section of Acts called CHURCH SCATTERED. The missionary journeys to "the uttermost parts" (1:8) begin in the next segment.

*12:18-19* Compare the three situations:

SOLDIERS ______________________________

______________________________

______________________________

PETER ______________________________

______________________________

______________________________

HEROD ______________________________

______________________________

______________________________

*12:20-23* Does the text give a reason for Herod's displeasure of verse 20?

______________________________

Compare the Herod of verse 20 with the Herod of verse 21.

______________________________

______________________________

______________________________

Identify *sin* and *judgment* of verses 21-23:

PEOPLE: ______________________________

______________________________

______________________________

HEROD: ______________________________

______________________________

______________________________

*12:24-25* What are your reflections of verse 24?

______________________________

______________________________

______________________________

______________________________

______________________________

______________________________

______________________________

NEW INTERNATIONAL VERSION

What does the passage teach about:

MISSIONARY VISION ______________________________

HOLY SPIRIT ______________________________

PRAYER ______________________________

MISSIONARY WORK ______________________________

OPPOSITION TO GOD ______________________________

FAITH ______________________________

JUDGMENT ______________________________

OTHER ______________________________

*Barnabas and Saul Sent Off*

13 In the church at Antioch there were
prophets and teachers: Barnabas,
Simeon called Niger, Lucius of Cyrene,
Manaen (who had been brought up with
Herod the tetrarch) and Saul. 2While they
were worshiping the Lord and fasting, the
Holy Spirit said, "Set apart for me Barnabas and Saul for the work to which I
have called them." 3So after they had fasted and prayed, they placed their hands on
them and sent them off.●

*On Cyprus*

4The two of them, sent on their way by
the Holy Spirit, went down to Seleucia and
sailed from there to Cyprus. 5When they
arrived at Salamis, they proclaimed the
word of God in the Jewish synagogues.
John was with them as their helper.
6They traveled through the whole island
until they came to Paphos. There they met
a Jewish sorcerer and false prophet named
Bar-Jesus, 7who was an attendant of the
proconsul, Sergius Paulus. The proconsul,
an intelligent man, sent for Barnabas and
Saul because he wanted to hear the word
of God. 8But Elymas the sorcerer (for that
is what his name means) opposed them and
tried to turn the proconsul from the faith.●
9Then Saul, who was also called Paul, filled
with the Holy Spirit, looked straight at
Elymas and said, 10"You are a child of the
devil and an enemy of everything that is
right! You are full of all kinds of deceit and
trickery. Will you never stop perverting
the right ways of the Lord? 11Now the hand
of the Lord is against you. You are going
to be blind, and for a time you will be unable to see the light of the sun."
Immediately mist and darkness came
over him, and he groped about, seeking
someone to lead him by the hand. 12When
the proconsul saw what had happened, he
believed, for he was amazed at the teaching about the Lord.●

KING JAMES

1. COMMISSIONING

**13** Now there were in the church that
was at An'ti-och certain prophets
and teachers; as Barnabas, and Simeon
that was called Niger, and Lucius of Cyre'ne, and Man'a-en, which had been
brought up with Herod the tetrarch, and
Saul. 2 As they ministered to the Lord,
and fasted, the Holy Ghost said, Separate
me Barnabas and Saul for the work whereunto I have called them. 3 And when they
had fasted and prayed, and laid *their*
hands on them, they sent *them* away.●

2. FIRST MINISTRY

4 So they, being sent forth by the Holy
Ghost, departed unto Seleu'cia; and from
thence they sailed to Cyprus. 5 And
when they were at Sal'amis, they preached
the word of God in the synagogues of the
Jews: and they had also John to *their*
minister. 6 And when they had gone
through the isle unto Paphos, they found
a certain sorcerer, a false prophet, a Jew,
whose name *was* Bar-jesus: 7 which was
with the deputy of the country, Sergius
Paulus, a prudent man; who called for
Barnabas and Saul, and desired to hear
the word of God. 8 But El'ymas the sorcerer (for so is his name by interpretation)
withstood them, seeking to turn away the
deputy from the faith.●

3. TWO RESULTS

9 Then Saul, (who
also *is called* Paul,) filled with the Holy
Ghost, set his eyes on him, 10 and said,
O full of all subtilty and all mischief, *thou*
child of the devil, *thou* enemy of all righteousness, wilt thou not cease to pervert
the right ways of the Lord? 11 And now,
behold, the hand of the Lord *is* upon thee,
and thou shalt be blind, not seeing the sun
for a season. And immediately there fell
on him a mist and a darkness; and he
went about seeking some to lead him by
the hand. 12 Then the deputy, when he
saw what was done, believed, being astonished at the doctrine of the Lord.●

FIRST COMMISSIONING

FIRST JOURNEY

FIRST CONVERT

Chapter 13 begins an entirely new section in Acts. Here are recorded the first extensions of the gospel ministry to the ends of the world.

*13:1-3* Record these:

PLACE: ______________________

TITLES: ______________________

NAMES: ______________________

COMMISSIONER: ______________________

*13:4-8* Who had joined Barnabas and Saul?

______________________

What was their ministry? (v.5) ______________________

Compare these two:

BAR-JESUS: ______________________

SERGIUS PAULUS: ______________________

*13:9-12* What happened to each:

BAR-JESUS: ______________________

SERGIUS PAULUS: ______________________

NEW INTERNATIONAL VERSION

There are many suggestions of spiritual applications which may be made of this passage. See how many you can find, and record these.

*In Pisidian Antioch*

13From Paphos, Paul and his companions sailed to Perga in Pamphylia, where
John left them to return to Jerusalem.
14From Perga they went on to Pisidian Antioch. On the Sabbath they entered the
synagogue and sat down. 15After the reading from the Law and the Prophets, the
synagogue rulers sent word to them, saying, "Brothers, if you have a message of
encouragement for the people, please
speak."●

16Standing up, Paul motioned with his
hand and said: "Men of Israel and you
Gentiles who worship God, listen to me!
17The God of the people of Israel chose our
fathers and made the people prosper during their stay in Egypt. With mighty power
he led them out of that country 18and endured their conduct[a] forty years in the
desert. 19He overthrew seven nations in
Canaan and gave their land to his people as
their inheritance. 20All this took about 450
years.

"After this, God gave them judges until
the time of Samuel the prophet. 21Then the
people asked for a king, and he gave them
Saul son of Kish, of the tribe of Benjamin,
who ruled forty years. 22After removing
Saul, he made David their king. He testified concerning him: 'I have found David
son of Jesse a man after my own heart; he
will do everything I want him to do.'

23"From this man's descendants God
has brought to Israel the Savior Jesus, as
he promised. 24Before the coming of Jesus,
John preached repentance and baptism to
all the people of Israel. 25As John was completing his work, he said: 'Who do you
think I am? I am not that one. No, but he
is coming after me, whose sandals I am not
worthy to untie.'●

[a]18 Some manuscripts *and cared for them*

## KING JAMES

1. AT ANTIOCH

PAUL

13 Now when Paul and his company
loosed from Paphos, they came to Perga
in Pamphyl'i-a: and John departing from
them returned to Jerusalem. 14 But when
they departed from Perga, they came to
An'ti-och in Pisid'i-a, and went into the
synagogue on the sabbath day, and sat
down. 15 And after the reading of the
law and the prophets, the rulers of the
synagogue sent unto them, saying, *Ye*
men *and* brethren, if ye have any word of
exhortation for the people, say on.●

2. SERMON

16 Then Paul stood up, and beckoning
with *his* hand said,
Men of Israel, and ye that fear God,
give audience. 17 The God of this people
of Israel chose our fathers, and exalted the
people when they dwelt as strangers in
the land of Egypt, and with a high arm
brought he them out of it. 18 And about
the time of forty years suffered he their
manners in the wilderness. 19 And when
he had destroyed seven nations in the
land of Canaan, he divided their land
to them by lot. 20 And after that he gave
*unto them* judges about the space of four
hundred and fifty years, until Samuel the
prophet. 21 And afterward they desired
a king: and God gave unto them Saul the
son of Kish, a man of the tribe of Benjamin, by the space of forty years. 22 And
when he had removed him, he raised up
unto them David to be their king; to
whom also he gave testimony, and said, I
have found David the *son* of Jesse, a man
after mine own heart, which shall fulfil all
my will. 23 Of this man's seed hath God,
according to *his* promise, raised unto
Israel a Saviour, Jesus: 24 when John
had first preached before his coming the
baptism of repentance to all the people
of Israel. 25 And as John fulfilled his
course, he said, Whom think ye that I
am? I am not *he*. But, behold, there
cometh one after me, whose shoes of *his*
feet I am not worthy to loose. ●

JOHN THE BAPTIST

The sermon of this segment concludes with the next segment.

*13:13-15* What was the setting which opened the door for Paul to speak?

Who separated from Paul and Barnabas at this time?

*13:16-25* Paul here rehearses the past history of the Jewish nation. The reason for his doing this will be seen in the next segment.
Record the highlights of Paul's summary:

NEW INTERNATIONAL VERSION

What do you learn from this passage about:

SALVATION

GRACE OF GOD

RESURRECTION OF CHRIST

FORGIVENESS OF SINS

LAW OF MOSES

DAY OF INVITATION

EARTHLY LIFE OF CHRIST

26 "Brothers, children of Abraham, and
you God-fearing Gentiles, it is to us that
this message of salvation has been sent.
27 The people of Jerusalem and their rulers
did not recognize Jesus, yet in condemning
him they fulfilled the words of the prophets
that are read every Sabbath. 28 Though they
found no proper ground for a death sentence, they asked Pilate to have him executed. 29 When they had carried out all
that was written about him, they took him
down from the tree and laid him in a tomb.
30 But God raised him from the dead, 31 and
for many days he was seen by those who
had traveled with him from Galilee to
Jerusalem. They are now his witnesses to
our people.●
32 "We tell you the good news: What God
promised our fathers 33 he has fulfilled for
us, their children, by raising up Jesus. As
it is written in the second Psalm:

" 'You are my Son;
today I have become your
Father.'[b,c]

34 The fact that God raised him from the
dead, never to decay, is stated in these
words:

" 'I will give you the holy and sure
blessings promised to
David.'[d]

35 So it is stated elsewhere:

" 'You will not let your Holy One
see decay.'[e]

36 "For when David had served God's
purpose in his own generation, he fell
asleep; he was buried with his fathers and
his body decayed. 37 But the one whom
God raised from the dead did not see
decay.●
38 "Therefore, my brothers, I want you to
know that through Jesus the forgiveness of
sins is proclaimed to you. 39 Through him
everyone who believes is justified from
everything you could not be justified from
by the law of Moses. 40 Take care that what
the prophets have said does not happen to
you:

41 " 'Look, you scoffers,
wonder and perish,
for I am going to do something in
your days
that you would never believe,
even if someone told you.'[f]"●

[b]33 Or *have begotten you* [c]33 Psalm 2:7
[d]34 Isaiah 55:3 [e]35 Psalm 16:10 [f]41 Hab. 1:5

KING JAMES

1. JEWS CRUCIFIED JESUS

TO YOU THE WORD IS SENT

26 Men *and* brethren, children of the
stock of Abraham, and whosoever among
you feareth God, to you is the word of
this salvation sent. 27 For they that dwell
at Jerusalem, and their rulers, because
they knew him not, nor yet the voices of
the prophets which are read every sabbath day, they have fulfilled *them* in condemning *him*. 28 And though they found
no cause of death *in him*, yet desired they
Pilate that he should be slain. 29 And
when they had fulfilled all that was written of him, they took *him* down from the
tree, and laid *him* in a sepulchre. 30 But
God raised him from the dead: 31 and he
was seen many days of them which came
up with him from Galilee to Jerusalem,
who are his witnesses unto the people.●

2. JESUS WAS RESURRECTED

32 And we declare unto you glad tidings,
how that the promise which was made unto the fathers, 33 God hath fulfilled the
same unto us their children, in that he
hath raised up Jesus again; as it is also
written in the second psalm,

Thou art my Son,
this day have I begotten thee. — Ps. 2:7

34 And as concerning that he raised him
up from the dead, *now* no more to return
to corruption, he said on this wise, — Is. 55:3

I will give you the sure mercies of
David.

35 Wherefore he saith also in another
*psalm*,

Thou shalt not suffer thine Holy One
to see corruption. — Ps. 16:10

36 For David, after he had served his own
generation by the will of God, fell on
sleep, and was laid unto his fathers, and
saw corruption: 37 but he, whom God
raised again, saw no corruption.●

3. SALVATION IS BY JESUS

38 Be it
known unto you therefore, men *and* brethren, that through this man is preached
unto you the forgiveness of sins: 39 and
by him all that believe are justified from
all things, from which ye could not be
justified by the law of Moses. 40 Beware
therefore, lest that come upon you, which
is spoken of in the prophets;

41 Behold, ye despisers, and wonder,
and perish:
for I work a work in your days,
a work which ye shall in no wise
believe,
though a man declare it unto you. ● — Hab. 1:5

BELIEVE IT!

---

This segment shows how Paul related the Jews' history to his hearers, and appealed to them to accept Jesus as their Messiah.

Before analyzing each paragraph, compare the opening verse of each. How does Paul involve his hearers?

v.26

v.32

v.38

*13:26-31* What is the main point of the paragraph?

*13:32-37* What is the main point here?

*13:38-41* Record the truths:

vv.38-39:

vv.40-41:

NEW INTERNATIONAL VERSION

Record what the passage teaches about:

ENVY

BOLDNESS TO WITNESS

UNIVERSAL GOSPEL

ETERNAL LIFE

FAITH

OPPOSITION TO GOD

OTHER

42As Paul and Barnabas were leaving the
synagogue, the people invited them to
speak further about these things on the
next Sabbath. 43When the congregation
was dismissed, many of the Jews and devout converts to Judaism followed Paul
and Barnabas, who talked with them and
urged them to continue in the grace of God.●

44On the next Sabbath almost the whole
city gathered to hear the word of the Lord.
45When the Jews saw the crowds, they
were filled with jealousy and talked abusively against what Paul was saying.
46Then Paul and Barnabas answered
them boldly: "We had to speak the word of
God to you first. Since you reject it and do
not consider yourselves worthy of eternal
life, we now turn to the Gentiles. 47For this
is what the Lord has commanded us:

"'I have made you[a] a light for the
Gentiles,
that you[a] may bring salvation to
the ends of the earth.'[b]"●

48When the Gentiles heard this, they
were glad and honored the word of the
Lord; and all who were appointed for eternal life believed.
49The word of the Lord spread through
the whole region. 50But the Jews incited
the God-fearing women of high standing
and the leading men of the city. They
stirred up persecution against Paul and
Barnabas, and expelled them from their
region. 51So they shook the dust from their
feet in protest against them and went to
Iconium. 52And the disciples were filled
with joy and with the Holy Spirit.●

[a]47 The Greek is singular. [b]47 Isaiah 49:6

## KING JAMES

**1. MIXED REACTIONS**

42 And when the Jews were gone out of
the synagogue, the Gentiles besought that
these words might be preached to them
the next sabbath. 43 Now when the congregation was broken up, many of the
Jews and religious proselytes followed
Paul and Barnabas; who, speaking to
them, persuaded them to continue in the
grace of God.●

APOSTLES ARE FOLLOWED

**2. JEWISH LEADERS OPPOSE**

44 And the next sabbath day came almost the whole city together to hear the
word of God. 45 But when the Jews saw
the multitudes, they were filled with envy,
and spake against those things which were
spoken by Paul, contradicting and blas-
pheming. 46 Then Paul and Barnabas
waxed bold, and said, It was necessary
that the word of God should first have
been spoken to you: but seeing ye put it
from you, and judge yourselves unworthy
of everlasting life, lo, we turn to the
Gentiles. 47 For so hath the Lord commanded us, *saying*,

> I have set thee to be a light of the Gentiles, (Is. 49:6)
> that thou shouldest be for salvation unto the ends of the earth. ●

**3. GENTILES BELIEVE**

48 And when the Gentiles heard this,
they were glad, and glorified the word of
the Lord: and as many as were ordained
to eternal life believed. 49 And the word
of the Lord was published throughout all
the region. 50 But the Jews stirred up the
devout and honorable women, and the
chief men of the city, and raised persecution against Paul and Barnabas, and expelled them out of their coasts. 51 But
they shook off the dust of their feet
against them, and came unto Ico'ni-um.
52 And the disciples were filled with joy,
and with the Holy Ghost.●

APOSTLES ARE EXPELLED

The effects of Paul's preaching at Antioch are described here.

*13:42-43* Record the mixed reactions:

______________________________

______________________________

______________________________

______________________________

*13:44-47* What principles are taught in verses 46-47?

______________________________

______________________________

______________________________

______________________________

______________________________

______________________________

______________________________

______________________________

______________________________

______________________________

*13:48-52* Record what each verse adds to the story:

48 ______________________________

______________________________

______________________________

49 ______________________________

______________________________

______________________________

50 ______________________________

______________________________

______________________________

51 ______________________________

______________________________

______________________________

52 ______________________________

______________________________

______________________________

NEW INTERNATIONAL VERSION

What may be learned here about:

BELIEF

UNBELIEF

MIRACLES

PERSECUTION

IDOLATRY

HUMAN NATURE

GOD

OTHER

*In Iconium*

14 At Iconium Paul and Barnabas went
as usual into the Jewish synagogue.
There they spoke so effectively that a great
number of Jews and Gentiles believed.
2But the Jews who refused to believe
stirred up the Gentiles and poisoned their
minds against the brothers. 3So Paul and
Barnabas spent considerable time there,
speaking boldly for the Lord, who confirmed the message of his grace by enabling
them to do miraculous signs and wonders.
4The people of the city were divided; some
sided with the Jews, others with the apostles. 5There was a plot afoot among the
Gentiles and Jews, together with their
leaders, to mistreat them and stone them.
6But they found out about it and fled to the
Lycaonian cities of Lystra and Derbe and
to the surrounding country, 7where they
continued to preach the good news.●

*In Lystra and Derbe*

8In Lystra there sat a man crippled in his
feet, who was lame from birth and had never walked. 9He listened to Paul as he was
speaking. Paul looked directly at him, saw
that he had faith to be healed 10and called
out, "Stand up on your feet!" At that, the
man jumped up and began to walk.
11When the crowd saw what Paul had
done, they shouted in the Lycaonian language, "The gods have come down to us in
human form!" 12Barnabas they called
Zeus, and Paul they called Hermes because he was the chief speaker. 13The
priest of Zeus, whose temple was just outside the city, brought bulls and wreaths to
the city gates because he and the crowd
wanted to offer sacrifices to them.●
14But when the apostles Barnabas and
Paul heard of this, they tore their clothes
and rushed out into the crowd, shouting:
15"Men, why are you doing this? We too
are only men, human like you. We are
bringing you good news, telling you to turn
from these worthless things to the living
God, who made heaven and earth and sea
and everything in them. 16In the past, he let
all nations go their own way. 17Yet he has
not left himself without testimony: He has
shown kindness by giving you rain from
heaven and crops in their seasons; he provides you with plenty of food and fills your
hearts with joy." 18Even with these words,
they had difficulty keeping the crowd from
sacrificing to them.●

KING JAMES

**1. AT ICONIUM**

**THE MESSAGE BELIEVED**

14 And it came to pass in Ico′ni-um,
that they went both together into
the synagogue of the Jews, and so spake,
that a great multitude both of the Jews
and also of the Greeks believed. 2 But the
unbelieving Jews stirred up the Gentiles,
and made their minds evil affected against
the brethren. 3 Long time therefore abode
they speaking boldly in the Lord, which
gave testimony unto the word of his grace,
and granted signs and wonders to be done
by their hands. 4 But the multitude of the
city was divided: and part held with the
Jews, and part with the apostles. 5 And
when there was an assault made both of
the Gentiles, and also of the Jews with
their rulers, to use *them* despitefully, and
to stone them, 6 they were ware of *it*, and
fled unto Lystra and Derbe, cities of Lyca-
o′nia, and unto the region that lieth
round about: 7 and there they preached
the gospel.●

**2. AT LYSTRA**

8 And there sat a certain man at Lystra,
impotent in his feet, being a cripple from
his mother's womb, who never had
walked: 9 the same heard Paul speak:
who steadfastly beholding him, and perceiving that he had faith to be healed,
10 said with a loud voice, Stand upright
on thy feet. And he leaped and walked.
11 And when the people saw what Paul
had done, they lifted up their voices, saying in the speech of Lyca-o′nia, The gods
are come down to us in the likeness of
men. 12 And they called Barnabas, Jupiter; and Paul, Mercu′ri-us, because he
was the chief speaker. 13 Then the priest
of Jupiter, which was before their city,
brought oxen and garlands unto the gates,
and would have done sacrifice with the
people.● 14 *Which* when the apostles,
Barnabas and Paul, heard *of*, they rent
their clothes, and ran in among the people, crying out, 15 and saying, Sirs, why
do ye these things? We also are men of
like passions with you, and preach unto
you that ye should turn from these vani-
ties unto the living God, which made
heaven, and earth, and the sea, and all
things that are therein: 16 who in times
past suffered all nations to walk in their
own ways. 17 Nevertheless he left not
himself without witness, in that he did
good, and gave us rain from heaven, and
fruitful seasons, filling our hearts with
food and gladness. 18 And with these
sayings scarce restrained they the people,
that they had not done sacrifice unto
them.●

**THE MEN IDOLIZED**

*14:1-7* Record:

APOSTLES' MINISTRIES: __________

REACTIONS: __________

*14:8-13*

APOSTLES' MINISTRIES: __________

REACTIONS: __________

*14:14-18* Analyze the apostles' objections (vv.14-17):

NEW INTERNATIONAL VERSION

Record what you learn here about:

PERSEVERANCE

TRIBULATION

FORGIVING SPIRIT

COMPASSION

CHRISTIAN FELLOWSHIP

List some spiritual applicatons.

19Then some Jews came from Antioch
and Iconium and won the crowd over.
They stoned Paul and dragged him outside
the city, thinking he was dead. 20But after
the disciples had gathered around him, he
got up and went back into the city. The
next day he and Barnabas left for Derbe.●

*The Return to Antioch in Syria*

21They preached the good news in that
city and won a large number of disciples.
Then they returned to Lystra, Iconium and
Antioch, 22strengthening the disciples and
encouraging them to remain true to the
faith. "We must go through many hardships to enter the kingdom of God," they
said. 23Paul and Barnabas appointed elders[c] for them in each church and, with
prayer and fasting, committed them to the
Lord in whom they had put their trust.●
24After going through Pisidia, they came
into Pamphylia, 25and when they had
preached the word in Perga, they went
down to Attalia.
26From Attalia they sailed back to Antioch, where they had been committed to the
grace of God for the work they had now
completed. 27On arriving there, they gathered the church together and reported all
that God had done through them and how
he had opened the door of faith to the Gentiles. 28And they stayed there a long time
with the disciples.●

[c]23 Or *Barnabas ordained elders*; or *Barnabas had elders elected*

KING JAMES

1. PAUL STONED

AMONG ENEMIES

19 And there came thither *certain* Jews
from An'ti-och and Ico'ni-um, who persuaded the people, and, having stoned
Paul, drew *him* out of the city, supposing
he had been dead. 20 Howbeit, as the
disciples stood round about him, he rose
up, and came into the city: and the next
day he departed with Barnabas to Derbe.●

2. FOLLOW-UP WORK

21 And when they had preached the gospel to that city, and had taught many, they
returned again to Lystra, and *to* Ico'ni-
um, and An'ti-och, 22 confirming the
souls of the disciples, *and* exhorting them
to continue in the faith, and that we must
through much tribulation enter into the
kingdom of God. 23 And when they had
ordained them elders in every church, and
had prayed with fasting, they commended
them to the Lord, on whom they believed.●

3. RETURN HOME

WITH FRIENDS

24 And after they had passed throughout Pisid'i-a, they came to Pamphyl'i-a.
25 And when they had preached the word
in Perga, they went down into Attali'a:
26 and thence sailed to An'ti-och, from
whence they had been recommended to
the grace of God for the work which they
fulfilled. 27 And when they were come,
and had gathered the church together,
they rehearsed all that God had done with
them, and how he had opened the door of
faith unto the Gentiles. 28 And there they
abode long time with the disciples.●

*14:19-20* Do you see miracles here? If so, where:

*14:21-23* What was significant about the apostles returning to the cities of Lystra, Iconium and Antioch?

What was their ministry in this return stage?

*14:24-28* Record what you learn from verses 26-28:

NEW INTERNATIONAL VERSION

What does this passage teach about:

WAY OF SALVATION ______

LAW OF MOSES ______

LEGALISM ______

FAITH AND GRACE ______

GOSPEL TO NON-JEWS ______

### *The Council at Jerusalem*

15 Some men came down from Judea
to Antioch and were teaching the
brothers: "Unless you are circumcised, according to the custom taught by Moses,
you cannot be saved." 2This brought Paul
and Barnabas into sharp dispute and debate with them. So Paul and Barnabas
were appointed, along with some other believers, to go up to Jerusalem to see the
apostles and elders about this question.
3The church sent them on their way, and as
they traveled through Phoenicia and Samaria, they told how the Gentiles had been
converted. This news made all the brothers
very glad. 4When they came to Jerusalem,
they were welcomed by the church and the
apostles and elders, to whom they reported
everything God had done through them.
5Then some of the believers who belonged to the party of the Pharisees stood
up and said, "The Gentiles must be circumcised and required to obey the law of
Moses."●
6The apostles and elders met to consider
this question. 7After much discussion, Peter got up and addressed them: "Brothers,
you know that some time ago God made a
choice among you that the Gentiles might
hear from my lips the message of the gospel
and believe. 8God, who knows the heart,
showed that he accepted them by giving
the Holy Spirit to them, just as he did to us.
9He made no distinction between us and
them, for he purified their hearts by faith.
10Now then, why do you try to test God by
putting on the necks of the disciples a yoke
that neither we nor our fathers have been
able to bear? 11No! We believe it is through
the grace of our Lord Jesus that we are
saved, just as they are."●
12The whole assembly became silent as
they listened to Barnabas and Paul telling
about the miraculous signs and wonders
God had done among the Gentiles through
them. 13When they finished, James spoke
up: "Brothers, listen to me. 14Simon[a] has
described to us how God at first showed his
concern by taking from the Gentiles a
people for himself. 15The words of the
prophets are in agreement with this, as it is
written:

16" 'After this I will return
and rebuild David's fallen tent.
Its ruins I will rebuild,
and I will restore it,
17that the remnant of men may seek
the Lord,
and all the Gentiles who bear my
name,
says the Lord, who does these
things'[b]
18 that have been known for ages.[c]

19"It is my judgment, therefore, that we
should not make it difficult for the Gentiles
who are turning to God. 20Instead we
should write to them, telling them to abstain from food polluted by idols, from sexual immorality, from the meat of strangled
animals and from blood. 21For Moses has
been preached in every city from the earliest times and is read in the synagogues on
every Sabbath."●

[a]*14* Greek *Simeon*, a variant of *Simon;* that is, Peter
[b]*17* Amos 9:11,12
[c]*17,18* Some manuscripts *things'— / 18known to the Lord for ages is his work*

KING JAMES

1. A PROBLEM ARISES

15 And certain men which came down
from Judea taught the brethren,
*and said*, Except ye be circumcised after
the manner of Moses, ye cannot be
saved. 2 When therefore Paul and Barnabas had no small dissension and dis-
putation with them, they determined that
Paul and Barnabas, and certain other of
them, should go up to Jerusalem unto the
apostles and elders about this question.
3 And being brought on their way by the
church, they passed through Phoeni'cia
and Samaria, declaring the conversion of
the Gentiles: and they caused great joy
unto all the brethren. 4 And when they
were come to Jerusalem, they were received of the church, and *of* the apostles
and elders, and they declared all things
that God had done with them. 5 But
there rose up certain of the sect of the
Pharisees which believed, saying, That it
was needful to circumcise them, and to
command *them* to keep the law of Moses.●

EXCLUSIVE VIEW

2. PETER'S VIEW

6 And the apostles and elders came together for to consider of this matter.
7 And when there had been much disputing, Peter rose up, and said unto them,
Men *and* brethren, ye know how that a
good while ago God made choice among
us, that the Gentiles by my mouth should
hear the word of the gospel, and believe.
8 And God, which knoweth the hearts,
bare them witness, giving them the Holy
Ghost, even as *he did* unto us; 9 and
put no difference between us and them,
purifying their hearts by faith. 10 Now
therefore why tempt ye God, to put a yoke
upon the neck of the disciples, which neither our fathers nor we were able to bear?
11 But we believe that through the grace
of the Lord Jesus Christ we shall be saved,
even as they. ●

3. OTHER VIEWS

12 Then all the multitude kept silence,
and gave audience to Barnabas and Paul,
declaring what miracles and wonders God
had wrought among the Gentiles by them.
13 And after they had held their peace,
James answered, saying, Men *and* brethren, hearken unto me: 14 Simeon hath
declared how God at the first did visit the
Gentiles, to take out of them a people for
his name. 15 And to this agree the words
of the prophets; as it is written,

Amos 9:11-12

16 After this I will return,
and will build again the tabernacle of
David, which is fallen down;
and I will build again the ruins
thereof,
and I will set it up:
17 that the residue of men might seek
after the Lord,
and all the Gentiles, upon whom my
name is called, saith the Lord,
who doeth all these things.
18 Known unto God are all his works
from the beginning of the world.
19 Wherefore my sentence is, that we
trouble not them, which from among the
Gentiles are turned to God: 20 but that
we write unto them, that they abstain
from pollutions of idols, and *from* fornication, and *from* things strangled, and
*from* blood. 21 For Moses of old time
hath in every city them that preach him,
being read in the synagogues every sabbath day. ●

INCLUSIVE VIEW

*15:1-5* Identify the problem which arose.

How was the problem disposed of by the Antioch church?

*15:6-11* Record the different points of Peter's argument:

*15:12-21* Record the arguments of these:

BARNABAS AND PAUL:

JAMES:

NEW INTERNATIONAL VERSION

What does this passage teach about:

HOLY SPIRIT

UNITY OF BELIEVERS

EDIFICATION OF SAINTS

MODERATION

CLEANLINESS

LAW OF MOSES

Apply chapter 15 in different ways regarding these subjects:

CHRISTIAN LIVING

HOW TO DEAL WITH DIVISIONS IN THE CHURCH

### *The Council's Letter to Gentile Believers*

22Then the apostles and elders, with the
whole church, decided to choose some of
their own men and send them to Antioch
with Paul and Barnabas. They chose Judas
(called Barsabbas) and Silas, two men who
were leaders among the brothers. 23With
them they sent the following letter:

The apostles and elders, your brothers,

To the Gentile believers in Antioch, Syria and Cilicia:

Greetings.

24We have heard that some went out
from us without our authorization and
disturbed you, troubling your minds
by what they said. 25So we all agreed
to choose some men and send them to
you with our dear friends Barnabas
and Paul— 26men who have risked
their lives for the name of our Lord
Jesus Christ. 27Therefore we are sending
Judas and Silas to confirm by word
of mouth what we are writing. 28It
seemed good to the Holy Spirit and to
us not to burden you with anything
beyond the following requirements:
29You are to abstain from food sacrificed
to idols, from blood, from the
meat of strangled animals and from
sexual immorality. You will do well to
avoid these things.

Farewell. ●

30The men were sent off and went down
to Antioch, where they gathered the
church together and delivered the letter.
31The people read it and were glad for its
encouraging message. 32Judas and Silas,
who themselves were prophets, said much
to encourage and strengthen the brothers.
33After spending some time there, they
were sent off by the brothers with the
blessing of peace to return to those who
had sent them.[a] 35But Paul and Barnabas
remained in Antioch, where they and many
others taught and preached the word of the
Lord. ●

[a]33 Some manuscripts *them, 34but Silas decided to remain there*

KING JAMES

1. LETTER TO ANTIOCH

UNITY IN CHURCH AT JERUSALEM

22 Then pleased it the apostles and
elders, with the whole church, to send
chosen men of their own company to An′-
ti-och with Paul and Barnabas; *namely*,
Judas surnamed Barsabas, and Silas,
chief men among the brethren: 23 and
they wrote *letters* by them after this manner; The apostles and elders and brethren
*send* greeting unto the brethren which are
of the Gentiles in An′ti-och and Syria and
Cili′cia: 24 Forasmuch as we have heard,
that certain which went out from us have
troubled you with words, subverting your
souls, saying, *Ye must* be circumcised, and
keep the law; to whom we gave no *such*
commandment: 25 it seemed good unto
us, being assembled with one accord, to
send chosen men unto you with our beloved Barnabas and Paul, 26 men that
have hazarded their lives for the name of
our Lord Jesus Christ. 27 We have sent
therefore Judas and Silas, who shall also
tell *you* the same things by mouth. 28 For
it seemed good to the Holy Ghost, and to
us, to lay upon you no greater burden
than these necessary things; 29 that ye
abstain from meats offered to idols, and
from blood, and from things strangled,
and from fornication: from which if ye
keep yourselves, ye shall do well. Fare
ye well. ●

2. PROBLEM RESOLVED

30 So when they were dismissed, they
came to An′ti-och: and when they had
gathered the multitude together, they delivered the epistle: 31 *which* when they
had read, they rejoiced for the consolation.
32 And Judas and Silas, being prophets
also themselves, exhorted the brethren
with many words, and confirmed *them*.
33 And after they had tarried *there* a
space, they were let go in peace from the
brethren unto the apostles. 34 Notwithstanding it pleased Silas to abide there
still. 35 Paul also and Barnabas continued in An′ti-och, teaching and preaching the word of the Lord, with many
others also. ●

UNITY IN CHURCH AT ANTIOCH

*15:22-29* Record the parts of the letter:

THE PROBLEM (v.24) ____________________

EMISSARIES (vv.25-27) ____________________

RECOMMENDATION (vv.28-29) ____________________

*15:30-35*

MINISTRIES: ____________________

SENTIMENTS: ____________________

NEW INTERNATIONAL VERSION

What do you learn from this passage about:

SETTLING DIFFERENCES OF OPINION

NURTURING OF NEW CONVERTS

THE WORK OF GOD

List some practical lessons taught by the passage.

### *Disagreement Between Paul and Barnabas*

36Some time later Paul said to Barnabas,
"Let us go back and visit the brothers in all
the towns where we preached the word of
the Lord and see how they are doing."
37Barnabas wanted to take John, also
called Mark, with them, 38but Paul did not
think it wise to take him, because he had
deserted them in Pamphylia and had not
continued with them in the work. 39They
had such a sharp disagreement that they
parted company. Barnabas took Mark and
sailed for Cyprus, 40but Paul chose Silas
and left, commended by the brothers to the
grace of the Lord. 41He went through Syria
and Cilicia, strengthening the churches.●

### *Timothy Joins Paul and Silas*

16 He came to Derbe and then to Lystra, where a disciple named Timothy lived, whose mother was a Jewess and
a believer, but whose father was a Greek.
2The brothers at Lystra and Iconium spoke
well of him. 3Paul wanted to take him along
on the journey, so he circumcised him because of the Jews who lived in that area,
for they all knew that his father was a
Greek. 4As they traveled from town to
town, they delivered the decisions reached
by the apostles and elders in Jerusalem for
the people to obey. 5So the churches were
strengthened in the faith and grew daily in
numbers.●

KING JAMES

1. BARNABAS AND PAUL PART

36 And some days after, Paul said unto
Barnabas, Let us go again and visit our
brethren in every city where we have
preached the word of the Lord, *and see*
how they do. 37 And Barnabas determined to take with them John, whose
surname was Mark. 38 But Paul thought
not good to take him with them, who departed from them from Pamphyl'i-a, and
went not with them to the work. 39 And
the contention was so sharp between
them, that they departed asunder one
from the other: and so Barnabas took
Mark, and sailed unto Cyprus; 40 and
Paul chose Silas, and departed, being recommended by the brethren unto the grace
of God. 41 And he went through Syria
and Cili'cia, confirming the churches.●

PLAN TO VISIT

2. TIMOTHY JOINS PAUL

16 Then came he to Derbe and Lystra:
and, behold, a certain disciple was
there, named Timothy, the son of a
certain woman, which was a Jewess, and
believed; but his father *was* a Greek:
2 which was well reported of by the brethren that were at Lystra and Ico'ni-um.
3 Him would Paul have to go forth with
him; and took and circumcised him because of the Jews which were in those
quarters: for they knew all that his father
was a Greek. 4 And as they went through
the cities, they delivered them the decrees
for to keep, that were ordained of the
apostles and elders which were at Jerusalem. 5 And so were the churches established in the faith, and increased in number daily.●

VISIT FRUITFUL

*15:36-41*

PLAN ______

DISAGREEMENT ______

OUTCOME ______

*16:1-5* What is written here about Timothy?

Why did Paul circumcise Timothy? ______

Why the action of verse 4? ______

What does verse 5 reveal? ______

NEW INTERNATIONAL VERSION

What does the passage teach about:

PREACHING

SPIRIT'S DIRECTION

LORD'S CALLING

VISION

FAITHFULNESS

ASSURANCE

FAITH

*Paul's Vision of the Man of Macedonia*

6 Paul and his companions traveled
throughout the region of Phrygia and
Galatia, having been kept by the Holy
Spirit from preaching the word in the province of Asia. 7 When they came to the border of Mysia, they tried to enter Bithynia,
but the Spirit of Jesus would not allow
them to. 8 So they passed by Mysia and
went down to Troas. 9 During the night Paul
had a vision of a man of Macedonia standing and begging him, "Come over to Macedonia and help us." 10 After Paul had seen
the vision, we got ready at once to leave for
Macedonia, concluding that God had
called us to preach the gospel to them.●

*Lydia's Conversion in Philippi*

11 From Troas we put out to sea and
sailed straight for Samothrace, and the
next day on to Neapolis. 12 From there we
traveled to Philippi, a Roman colony and
the leading city of that district of Macedonia. And we stayed there several days.
13 On the Sabbath we went outside the
city gate to the river, where we expected to
find a place of prayer. We sat down and
began to speak to the women who had
gathered there. 14 One of those listening
was a woman named Lydia, a dealer in
purple cloth from the city of Thyatira, who
was a worshiper of God. The Lord opened
her heart to respond to Paul's message.
15 When she and the members of her
household were baptized, she invited us to
her home. "If you consider me a believer
in the Lord," she said, "come and stay at
my house." And she persuaded us.●

KING JAMES

**1. VISION AT TROAS**

6 Now when they had gone throughout
Phryg'i-a and the region of Galatia, and
were forbidden of the Holy Ghost to
preach the word in Asia, 7 after they were
come to My'si-a, they assayed to go into
Bithyn'i-a: but the Spirit suffered them
not. 8 And they passing by My'si-a came
down to Tro'as. 9 And a vision appeared
to Paul in the night; There stood a man of
Macedonia, and prayed him, saying,
Come over into Macedonia, and help us.
10 And after he had seen the vision, immediately we endeavored to go into
Macedonia, assuredly gathering that the
Lord had called us for to preach the gospel unto them.●

"Don't go there"

**2. CONVERSION OF LYDIA**

11 Therefore loosing from Tro'as, we
came with a straight course to Samo-
thracia, and the next *day* to Ne-ap'olis;
12 and from thence to Phil'ippi, which is
the chief city of that part of Macedonia,
*and* a colony: and we were in that city
abiding certain days. 13 And on the sabbath we went out of the city by a river
side, where prayer was wont to be made;
and we sat down, and spake unto the
women which resorted *thither*. 14 And a
certain woman named Lydia, a seller of
purple, of the city of Thy-ati'ra, which
worshipped God, heard *us*: whose heart
the Lord opened, that she attended unto
the things which were spoken of Paul.
15 And when she was baptized, and her
household, she besought *us*, saying, If ye
have judged me to be faithful to the Lord,
come into my house, and abide *there*.
And she constrained us.●

"Abide here"

*16:6-10* Note the change of pronoun from "they" (v.6) to "we" (v.10). What does this indicate? (Recall that Luke is writing.)

Record the vision that came to Paul.

Compare the forbidding of verses 6 and 7 with the go-ahead of verse 9.

*16:11-15* Record Paul's activities:

What does the paragraph reveal about Lydia?

NEW INTERNATIONAL VERSION

What do you learn here about:

SATAN

POWER OVER DEMONS

PERSECUTION

PRAYER

PRAISE

OMNIPOTENCE OF GOD

PEACE OF HEART

OTHER

*Paul and Silas in Prison*

16 Once when we were going to the place
of prayer, we were met by a slave girl who
had a spirit by which she predicted the
future. She earned a great deal of money
for her owners by fortune-telling. 17 This
girl followed Paul and the rest of us, shouting, "These men are servants of the Most
High God, who are telling you the way to
be saved." 18 She kept this up for many
days. Finally Paul became so troubled that
he turned around and said to the spirit, "In
the name of Jesus Christ I command you to
come out of her!" At that moment the
spirit left her.●
19 When the owners of the slave girl realized that their hope of making money was
gone, they seized Paul and Silas and
dragged them into the marketplace to face
the authorities. 20 They brought them before the magistrates and said, "These men
are Jews, and are throwing our city into an
uproar 21 by advocating customs unlawful
for us Romans to accept or practice."
22 The crowd joined in the attack against
Paul and Silas, and the magistrates ordered
them to be stripped and beaten. 23 After
they had been severely flogged, they were
thrown into prison, and the jailer was commanded to guard them carefully. 24 Upon
receiving such orders, he put them in the
inner cell and fastened their feet in the
stocks.●
25 About midnight Paul and Silas were
praying and singing hymns to God, and the
other prisoners were listening to them.
26 Suddenly there was such a violent earthquake that the foundations of the prison
were shaken. At once all the prison doors
flew open, and everybody's chains came
loose. 27 The jailer woke up, and when he
saw the prison doors open, he drew his
sword and was about to kill himself because he thought the prisoners had escaped. 28 But Paul shouted, "Don't harm
yourself! We are all here!"●

KING JAMES

**1. EVIL SPIRIT CAST OUT** — SATAN

16 And it came to pass, as we went to
prayer, a certain damsel possessed with a
spirit of divination met us, which brought
her masters much gain by soothsaying:
17 the same followed Paul and us, and
cried, saying, These men are the servants
of the most high God, which show unto
us the way of salvation. 18 And this did
she many days. But Paul, being grieved,
turned and said to the spirit, I command
thee in the name of Jesus Christ to come
out of her. And he came out the same
hour.●

**2. APOSTLES IMPRISONED** — MAN

19 And when her masters saw that the
hope of their gains was gone, they caught
Paul and Silas, and drew *them* into the
market place unto the rulers, 20 and
brought them to the magistrates, saying,
These men, being Jews, do exceedingly
trouble our city, 21 and teach customs,
which are not lawful for us to receive,
neither to observe, being Romans. 22 And
the multitude rose up together against
them; and the magistrates rent off their
clothes, and commanded to beat *them*.
23 And when they had laid many stripes
upon them, they cast *them* into prison,
charging the jailer to keep them safely: 24 who, having received such a
charge, thrust them into the inner prison, and made their feet fast in the
stocks.●

**3. EARTHQUAKE** — GOD

25 And at midnight Paul and Silas
prayed, and sang praises unto God: and
the prisoners heard them. 26 And suddenly there was a great earthquake, so
that the foundations of the prison were
shaken: and immediately all the doors
were opened, and every one's bands were
loosed. 27 And the keeper of the prison
awaking out of his sleep, and seeing the
prison doors open, he drew out his sword,
and would have killed himself, supposing
that the prisoners had been fled. 28 But
Paul cried with a loud voice, saying, Do
thyself no harm: for we are all here.●

The story of this segment continues into the next segment.

*16:16-18* What was the setting (v.16)?

________________________________________

________________________________________

________________________________________

________________________________________

What did the demon-possessed woman say about the apostles?

________________________________________

________________________________________

________________________________________

What was Paul's response? ________________

________________________________________

________________________________________

________________________________________

*16:19-24* Record what is written here about:

GIRL'S MASTERS: ________________________

________________________________________

MULTITUDES: ____________________________

________________________________________

MAGISTRATES: __________________________

________________________________________

________________________________________

*16:25-28*

SETTING: ______________________________

________________________________________

________________________________________

________________________________________

________________________________________

ACTIONS: ______________________________

________________________________________

________________________________________

________________________________________

________________________________________

________________________________________

NEW INTERNATIONAL VERSION

What does the passage teach about:

FEAR OF GOD

SAVING FAITH

JOY

CHRISTIAN TESTIMONY

COURAGE

PRUDENCE

CHRISTIAN FELLOWSHIP

List some spiritual applications which may be made.

29The jailer called for lights, rushed in
and fell trembling before Paul and Silas.
30He then brought them out and asked,
"Sirs, what must I do to be saved?"
31They replied, "Believe in the Lord
Jesus, and you will be saved—you and
your household." 32Then they spoke the
word of the Lord to him and to all the
others in his house. 33At that hour of the
night the jailer took them and washed their
wounds; then immediately he and all his
family were baptized. 34The jailer brought
them into his house and set a meal before
them, and the whole family was filled with
joy, because they had come to believe in
God.●
35When it was daylight, the magistrates
sent their officers to the jailer with the order: "Release those men." 36The jailer told
Paul, "The magistrates have ordered that
you and Silas be released. Now you can
leave. Go in peace."
37But Paul said to the officers: "They
beat us publicly without a trial, even
though we are Roman citizens, and threw
us into prison. And now do they want to
get rid of us quietly? No! Let them come
themselves and escort us out."
38The officers reported this to the magistrates, and when they heard that Paul and
Silas were Roman citizens, they were
alarmed. 39They came to appease them and
escorted them from the prison, requesting
them to leave the city. 40After Paul and
Silas came out of the prison, they went to
Lydia's house, where they met with the
brothers and encouraged them. Then they
left.●

## KING JAMES

**1. JAILOR SAVED**

**FEAR OF AN UNBELIEVER**

29 Then he called for a light, and sprang
in, and came trembling, and fell down
before Paul and Silas, 30 and brought
them out, and said, Sirs, what must I do
to be saved? 31 And they said, Believe on
the Lord Jesus Christ, and thou shalt be
saved, and thy house. 32 And they spake
unto him the word of the Lord, and to all
that were in his house. 33 And he took
them the same hour of the night, and
washed *their* stripes; and was baptized,
he and all his, straightway. 34 And when
he had brought them into his house,
he set meat before them, and rejoiced, believing in God with all his
house.●

**2. APOSTLES RELEASED**

35 And when it was day, the magistrates sent the sergeants, saying, Let those
men go. 36 And the keeper of the prison
told this saying to Paul, The magistrates
have sent to let you go: now therefore
depart, and go in peace. 37 But Paul said
unto them, They have beaten us openly
uncondemned, being Romans, and have
cast *us* into prison; and now do they
thrust us out privily? nay verily; but let
them come themselves and fetch us out.
38 And the sergeants told these words
unto the magistrates: and they feared,
when they heard that they were Romans.
39 And they came and besought them,
and brought *them* out, and desired *them*
to depart out of the city. 40 And they
went out of the prison, and entered into
*the house of* Lydia: and when they had
seen the brethren, they comforted them,
and departed.●

**COMFORT OF BELIEVERS**

Review the preceding segment before studying this one.

*16:29-34* Record:

JAILER'S HEART: ____________________

QUESTION: ____________________

ANSWER: ____________________

INSTRUCTION: ____________________

TESTIMONY: ____________________

FELLOWSHIP: ____________________

*16:35-40* Account for Paul's action of verse 37.

____________________

How does the story end (v.40)? ____________________

NEW INTERNATIONAL VERSION

What do you learn from this passage about:

SCRIPTURE

GOSPEL MESSAGE

JESUS AS MESSIAH AND KING

CONVERSION

PERSECUTION

BIBLE STUDY

List some spiritual applications.

*In Thessalonica*

17 When they had passed through Amphipolis and Apollonia, they came to Thessalonica, where there was a Jewish synagogue. [2]As his custom was, Paul went into the synagogue, and on three Sabbath days he reasoned with them from the Scriptures, [3]explaining and proving that the Christ[a] had to suffer and rise from the dead. "This Jesus I am proclaiming to you is the Christ,[a]" he said. [4]Some of the Jews were persuaded and joined Paul and Silas, as did a large number of God-fearing Greeks and not a few prominent women.●

[5]But the Jews were jealous; so they rounded up some bad characters from the marketplace, formed a mob and started a riot in the city. They rushed to Jason's house in search of Paul and Silas in order to bring them out to the crowd.[b] [6]But when they did not find them, they dragged Jason and some other brothers before the city officials, shouting: "These men who have caused trouble all over the world have now come here, [7]and Jason has welcomed them into his house. They are all defying Caesar's decrees, saying that there is another king, one called Jesus." [8]When they heard this, the crowd and the city officials were thrown into turmoil. [9]Then they made Jason and the others post bond and let them go.●

*In Berea*

[10]As soon as it was night, the brothers sent Paul and Silas away to Berea. On arriving there, they went to the Jewish synagogue. [11]Now the Bereans were of more noble character than the Thessalonians, for they received the message with great eagerness and examined the Scriptures every day to see if what Paul said was true. [12]Many of the Jews believed, as did also a number of prominent Greek women and many Greek men.

[13]When the Jews in Thessalonica learned that Paul was preaching the word of God at Berea, they went there too, agitating the crowds and stirring them up. [14]The brothers immediately sent Paul to the coast, but Silas and Timothy stayed at Berea. [15]The men who accompanied Paul brought him to Athens and then left with instructions for Silas and Timothy to join him as soon as possible.●

[a]3 Or *Messiah* [b]5 Or *the assembly of the people*

KING JAMES

1. MISSION AT THESSALONICA

PEACE

**17** Now when they had passed through
Amphip'olis and Apollo'ni-a, they
came to Thessaloni'ca, where was a synagogue of the Jews: 2 and Paul, as his
manner was, went in unto them, and three
sabbath days reasoned with them out of
the Scriptures, 3 opening and alleging,
that Christ must needs have suffered, and
risen again from the dead; and that this
Jesus, whom I preach unto you, is Christ.
4 And some of them believed, and con-
sorted with Paul and Silas; and of the
devout Greeks a great multitude, and of
the chief women not a few.●

2. TROUBLE

5 But the Jews
which believed not, moved with envy,
took unto them certain lewd fellows of the
baser sort, and gathered a company, and
set all the city on an uproar, and assaulted
the house of Jason, and sought to bring
them out to the people. 6 And when they
found them not, they drew Jason and certain brethren unto the rulers of the city,
crying, These that have turned the world
upside down are come hither also;
7 whom Jason hath received: and these all
do contrary to the decrees of Caesar, saying that there is another king, *one* Jesus.
8 And they troubled the people and the
rulers of the city, when they heard these
things. 9 And when they had taken security of Jason, and of the others, they
let them go.●

3. MISSION AT BEREA

10 And the brethren immediately sent
away Paul and Silas by night unto Beroe'a:
who coming *thither* went into the synagogue of the Jews. 11 These were more
noble than those in Thessaloni'ca, in that
they received the word with all readiness
of mind, and searched the Scriptures
daily, whether those things were so.
12 Therefore many of them believed; also
of honorable women which were Greeks,
and of men, not a few. 13 But when the
Jews of Thessaloni'ca had knowledge that
the word of God was preached of Paul at
Beroe'a, they came thither also, and stirred
up the people. 14 And then immediately
the brethren sent away Paul to go as it
were to the sea: but Silas and Timothy
abode there still. 15 And they that conducted Paul brought him unto Athens:
and receiving a commandment unto Silas
and Timothy for to come to him with
all speed, they departed.●

PERSECUTION

*17:1-4*

PAUL'S MESSAGE (vv.2-3) ______

RESULTS (v.4) ______

*17:5-9* What were the accusations against the missionaries?

______

*17:10-15* Compare the Thessalonian and Berean Christians.

______

What was Paul's message at Berea? ______

What were the results of his ministry? ______

NEW INTERNATIONAL VERSION

Record what this passage teaches about:

MAN ______

RESURRECTION OF JESUS ______

IDOLATRY ______

GOD ______

TRUE WORSHIP ______

FUTURE JUDGMENT ______

*In Athens*
16While Paul was waiting for them in
Athens, he was greatly distressed to see
that the city was full of idols. 17So he reasoned in the synagogue with the Jews and
the God-fearing Greeks, as well as in the
marketplace day by day with those who
happened to be there. 18A group of Epicu-
rean and Stoic philosophers began to dispute with him. Some of them asked,
"What is this babbler trying to say?"
Others remarked, "He seems to be advocating foreign gods." They said this because Paul was preaching the good news
about Jesus and the resurrection. 19Then
they took him and brought him to a meeting
of the Areopagus, where they said to him,
"May we know what this new teaching is
that you are presenting? 20You are bringing
some strange ideas to our ears, and we
want to know what they mean." 21(All the
Athenians and the foreigners who lived
there spent their time doing nothing but
talking about and listening to the latest
ideas.)●

22Paul then stood up in the meeting of the
Areopagus and said: "Men of Athens! I see
that in every way you are very religious.
23For as I walked around and observed
your objects of worship, I even found an
altar with this inscription: TO AN UNKNOWN
GOD. Now what you worship as something
unknown I am going to proclaim to you.
24"The God who made the world and
everything in it is the Lord of heaven and
earth and does not live in temples built by
hands. 25And he is not served by human
hands, as if he needed anything, because
he himself gives all men life and breath and
everything else. 26From one man he made
every nation of men, that they should inhabit the whole earth; and he determined
the times set for them and the exact places
where they should live. 27God did this so
that men would seek him and perhaps
reach out for him and find him, though he
is not far from each one of us. 28'For in him
we live and move and have our being.' As
some of your own poets have said, 'We are
his offspring.'

29"Therefore since we are God's offspring, we should not think that the divine
being is like gold or silver or stone—an
image made by man's design and skill. 30In
the past God overlooked such ignorance,
but now he commands all people everywhere to repent. 31For he has set a day
when he will judge the world with justice
by the man he has appointed. He has given
proof of this to all men by raising him from
the dead."●

32When they heard about the resurrection of the dead, some of them sneered, but
others said, "We want to hear you again on
this subject." 33At that, Paul left the Council. 34A few men became followers of Paul
and believed. Among them was Dionysius,
a member of the Areopagus, also a woman
named Damaris, and a number of others.●

KING JAMES

1. INVITATION

IDOLATRY EVERYWHERE

16 Now while Paul waited for them at
Athens, his spirit was stirred in him, when
he saw the city wholly given to idolatry.
17 Therefore disputed he in the synagogue with the Jews, and with the devout
persons, and in the market daily with
them that met with him. 18 Then certain
philosophers of the Epicure'ans, and of
the Sto'ics, encountered him. And some
said, What will this babbler say? other
some, He seemeth to be a setter forth of
strange gods: because he preached unto
them Jesus, and the resurrection. 19 And
they took him, and brought him unto
Areop'agus, saying, May we know what
this new doctrine, whereof thou speakest,
*is?* 20 For thou bringest certain strange
things to our ears: we would know therefore what these things mean. 21 (For all
the Athenians, and strangers which were
there, spent their time in nothing else, but
either to tell or to hear some new thing.)●

2. SERMON

22 Then Paul stood in the midst of
Mars' hill, and said, *Ye* men of Athens,
I perceive that in all things ye are too
superstitious. 23 For as I passed by, and
beheld your devotions, I found an altar
with this inscription, TO THE UNKNOWN
GOD. Whom therefore ye ignorantly worship, him declare I unto you. 24 God that
made the world and all things therein,
seeing that he is Lord of heaven and earth,
dwelleth not in temples made with hands;
25 neither is worshipped with men's
hands, as though he needed any thing,
seeing he giveth to all life, and breath, and
all things; 26 and hath made of one
blood all nations of men for to dwell on
all the face of the earth, and hath determined the times before appointed, and the
bounds of their habitation; 27 that they
should seek the Lord, if haply they might
feel after him, and find him, though he be
not far from every one of us: 28 for in him
we live, and move, and have our being; as
certain also of your own poets have said,
For we are also his offspring.
29 Forasmuch then as we are the offspring of God, we ought not to think that
the Godhead is like unto gold, or silver,
or stone, graven by art and man's device.
30 And the times of this ignorance God
winked at; but now commandeth all men
every where to repent: 31 because he hath
appointed a day, in the which he will
judge the world in righteousness by *that*
man whom he hath ordained; *whereof* he
hath given assurance unto all *men*, in that
he hath raised him from the dead.●

3. REACTIONS

32 And when they heard of the resurrection of the dead, some mocked: and
others said, We will hear thee again of
this *matter*. 33 So Paul departed from
among them. 34 Howbeit certain men
clave unto him, and believed: among the
which *was* Di-onys'ius the Areop'agite,
and a woman named Dam'aris, and others
with them.●

SOME BELIEVERS

*17:16-21* What kind of thinkers encountered Paul (v.18)?

What did Paul preach which stirred up these Athenians?

*17:22-31* Record the highlights of Paul's sermon.

*17:32-34* REACTIONS:

NEW INTERNATIONAL VERSION

What do you learn here about:

UNIVERSAL GOSPEL

PERSECUTION

FAITH

SALVATION

VISION

PROVIDENCE OF GOD

TEACHING MINISTRY

*In Corinth*

18 After this, Paul left Athens and went
to Corinth. [2]There he met a Jew
named Aquila, a native of Pontus, who had
recently come from Italy with his wife Priscilla, because Claudius had ordered all the
Jews to leave Rome. Paul went to see
them, [3]and because he was a tentmaker as
they were, he stayed and worked with
them. [4]Every Sabbath he reasoned in the
synagogue, trying to persuade Jews and
Greeks.●

[5]When Silas and Timothy came from
Macedonia, Paul devoted himself exclusively to preaching, testifying to the Jews
that Jesus was the Christ.[a] [6]But when the
Jews opposed Paul and became abusive,
he shook out his clothes in protest and said
to them, "Your blood be on your own
heads! I am clear of my responsibility.
From now on I will go to the Gentiles."

[7]Then Paul left the synagogue and went
next door to the house of Titius Justus, a
worshiper of God. [8]Crispus, the synagogue
ruler, and his entire household believed in
the Lord; and many of the Corinthians who
heard him believed and were baptized.

[9]One night the Lord spoke to Paul in a
vision: "Do not be afraid; keep on
speaking, do not be silent. [10]For I am with
you, and no one is going to attack and harm
you, because I have many people in this
city." [11]So Paul stayed for a year and a
half, teaching them the word of God.●

[a]5 Or *Messiah*; also in verse 28

KING JAMES

1. PAUL SPEAKS TO JEWS AND GENTILES

**18** After these things Paul departed
from Athens, and came to Corinth;
2 and found a certain Jew named Aquila,
born in Pontus, lately come from Italy,
with his wife Priscilla, (because that
Claudius had commanded all Jews to depart from Rome,) and came unto them.
3 And because he was of the same craft,
he abode with them, and wrought: (for
by their occupation they were tentmakers.)
4 And he reasoned in the synagogue every
sabbath, and persuaded the Jews and the
Greeks.●

FELLOWSHIP WITH JEWS

2. JEWS OPPOSE THE GOSPEL

5 And when Silas and Timothy were
come from Macedonia, Paul was pressed
in the spirit, and testified to the Jews *that*
Jesus *was* Christ. 6 And when they opposed themselves, and blasphemed, he
shook *his* raiment, and said unto them,
Your blood *be* upon your own heads; I
*am* clean: from henceforth I will go unto
the Gentiles. 7 And he departed thence,
and entered into a certain *man's* house,
named Justus, *one* that worshipped God,
whose house joined hard to the synagogue. 8 And Crispus, the chief ruler of
the synagogue, believed on the Lord with
all his house; and many of the Corinthians hearing believed, and were baptized. 9 Then spake the Lord to Paul in
the night by a vision, Be not afraid, but
speak, and hold not thy peace: 10 for I
am with thee, and no man shall set on thee
to hurt thee: for I have much people in
this city. 11 And he continued *there* a
year and six months, teaching the word
of God among them.●

MINISTRY TO GENTILES

*18:1-4* Record what is written here about:

JEWS ____________________

____________________

____________________

____________________

PAUL ____________________

____________________

____________________

____________________

*18:5-11* What change of Paul's ministry is reported here?

____________________

____________________

____________________

____________________

____________________

____________________

Record observations on:

PAUL ____________________

____________________

____________________

____________________

____________________

____________________

____________________

____________________

GENTILES ____________________

____________________

____________________

____________________

____________________

____________________

____________________

____________________

____________________

NEW INTERNATIONAL VERSION

[12]While Gallio was proconsul of Achaia,
the Jews made a united attack on Paul and
brought him into court. [13]"This man,"
they charged, "is persuading the people to
worship God in ways contrary to the law."
[14]Just as Paul was about to speak, Gallio
said to the Jews, "If you Jews were making
a complaint about some misdemeanor or
serious crime, it would be reasonable for
me to listen to you. [15]But since it involves
questions about words and names and your
own law—settle the matter yourselves. I
will not be a judge of such things." [16]So he
had them ejected from the court. [17]Then
they all turned on Sosthenes the synagogue
ruler and beat him in front of the court. But
Gallio showed no concern whatever. ●

*Priscilla, Aquila and Apollos*

[18]Paul stayed on in Corinth for some
time. Then he left the brothers and sailed
for Syria, accompanied by Priscilla and
Aquila. Before he sailed, he had his hair
cut off at Cenchrea because of a vow he
had taken. [19]They arrived at Ephesus,
where Paul left Priscilla and Aquila. He
himself went into the synagogue and reasoned with the Jews. [20]When they asked
him to spend more time with them, he de-
clined. [21]But as he left, he promised, "I
will come back if it is God's will." Then he
set sail from Ephesus. [22]When he landed at
Caesarea, he went up and greeted the
church and then went down to Antioch. ●

What does this passage teach about:

THE HUMAN HEART

OPPOSITION TO THE GOSPEL

VOWS

WILL OF GOD

List some spiritual lessons taught by this passage:

KING JAMES

**1. GALLIO PROTECTS PAUL**

PERSECUTION

12 And when Gal'li-o was the deputy
of Achai'a, the Jews made insurrection
with one accord against Paul, and brought
him to the judgment seat, 13 saying, This
*fellow* persuadeth men to worship God
contrary to the law. 14 And when Paul
was now about to open *his* mouth, Gal'-
li-o said unto the Jews, If it were a matter
of wrong or wicked lewdness, O *ye* Jews,
reason would that I should bear with you:
15 but if it be a question of words and
names, and *of* your law, look ye *to it;* for
I will be no judge of such *matters.* 16 And
he drave them from the judgment seat.
17 Then all the Greeks took Sos'thenes,
the chief ruler of the synagogue, and beat
*him* before the judgment seat. And Gal'-
li-o cared for none of those things.●

**2. FAREWELL AT EPHESUS**

18 And Paul *after this* tarried *there* yet
a good while, and then took his leave of
the brethren, and sailed thence into Syria,
and with him Priscilla and Aquila; having
shorn *his* head in Cen'chre-ae: for he had
a vow. 19 And he came to Ephesus, and
left them there: but he himself entered into the synagogue, and reasoned with the
Jews. 20 When they desired *him* to tarry
longer time with them, he consented not;
21 but bade them farewell, saying, I must
by all means keep this feast that cometh
in Jerusalem: but I will return again unto
you, if God will. And he sailed from
Ephesus.

SALUTATION

22 And when he had landed at Caesare'a, and gone up, and saluted the church,
he went down to An'ti-och.●

This passage describes the last phases of Paul's second missionary journey.

*18:12-17* Record what is written about:

JEWS

GENTILES

GALLIO

*18:18-22* Record what happened at Ephesus.

Where was the church of verse 22 located?

The Antioch of verse 22 was where the missionary journey started. See 15:35-36.

NEW INTERNATIONAL VERSION

What do you learn here about:

FOLLOW-UP MINISTRY TO YOUNG CONVERTS

FERVENT CHRISTIAN SPIRIT

NEED FOR BIBLE INSTRUCTION

BAPTISM OF HOLY SPIRIT

UNBELIEF

OTHER

23 After spending some time in Antioch,
Paul set out from there and traveled from
place to place throughout the region of
Galatia and Phrygia, strengthening all the
disciples.●
24 Meanwhile a Jew named Apollos, a native of Alexandria, came to Ephesus. He
was a learned man, with a thorough knowledge of the Scriptures. 25 He had been instructed in the way of the Lord, and he
spoke with great fervor and taught about
Jesus accurately, though he knew only the
baptism of John. 26 He began to speak boldly in the synagogue. When Priscilla and
Aquila heard him, they invited him to their
home and explained to him the way of God
more adequately.
27 When Apollos wanted to go to Achaia,
the brothers encouraged him and wrote to
the disciples there to welcome him. On arriving, he was a great help to those who by
grace had believed. 28 For he vigorously
refuted the Jews in public debate, proving
from the Scriptures that Jesus was the
Christ.

*Paul in Ephesus*

19 While Apollos was at Corinth, Paul
took the road through the interior
and arrived at Ephesus. There he found
some disciples 2 and asked them, "Did you
receive the Holy Spirit when[a] you believed?"
They answered, "No, we have not even
heard that there is a Holy Spirit."
3 So Paul asked, "Then what baptism did
you receive?"
"John's baptism," they replied.
4 Paul said, "John's baptism was a
baptism of repentance. He told the people
to believe in the one coming after him, that
is, in Jesus." 5 On hearing this, they were
baptized into[b] the name of the Lord Jesus.
6 When Paul placed his hands on them, the
Holy Spirit came on them, and they spoke
in tongues[c] and prophesied. 7 There were
about twelve men in all.●
8 Paul entered the synagogue and spoke
boldly there for three months, arguing per-
suasively about the kingdom of God. 9 But
some of them became obstinate; they
refused to believe and publicly maligned
the Way. So Paul left them. He took the
disciples with him and had discussions
daily in the lecture hall of Tyrannus. 10 This
went on for two years, so that all the Jews
and Greeks who lived in the province of
Asia heard the word of the Lord.●

[a]2 Or *after* [b]5 Or *in* [c]6 Or *other languages*

KING JAMES

**1. JOURNEY BEGINS**

23 And after
he had spent some time *there*, he departed,
and went over *all* the country of Galatia
and Phryg'i-a in order, strengthening all
the disciples.●

**2. APOLLOS AT EPHESUS**

24 And a certain Jew named Apol'los,
born at Alexandria, an eloquent man, *and*
mighty in the Scriptures, came to Ephesus. 25 This man was instructed in the
way of the Lord; and being fervent in the
spirit, he spake and taught diligently
the things of the Lord, knowing only the
baptism of John. 26 And he began to
speak boldly in the synagogue: whom
when Aquila and Priscilla had heard, they
took him unto *them*, and expounded unto
him the way of God more perfectly.
27 And when he was disposed to pass into
Achai'a, the brethren wrote, exhorting the
disciples to receive him: who, when he
was come, helped them much which had
believed through grace: 28 for he mightily convinced the Jews, *and that* publicly,
showing by the Scriptures that Jesus was
Christ.●

**3. PAUL AT EPHESUS**

19 And it came to pass, that, while
Apol'los was at Cŏrinth, Paul having passed through the upper coasts came
to Ephesus; and finding certain disciples,
2 he said unto them, Have ye received the
Holy Ghost since ye believed? And they
said unto him, We have not so much as
heard whether there be any Holy Ghost.
3 And he said unto them, Unto what then
were ye baptized? And they said, Unto
John's baptism. 4 Then said Paul, John
verily baptized with the baptism of repentance, saying unto the people, that
they should believe on him which should
come after him, that is, on Christ Jesus.
5 When they heard *this*, they were baptized in the name of the Lord Jesus.
6 And when Paul had laid *his* hands upon
them, the Holy Ghost came on them; and
they spake with tongues, and prophesied.
7 And all the men were about twelve.●

**4. TEACHING MINISTRY**

8 And he went into the synagogue, and
spake boldly for the space of three
months, disputing and persuading the
things concerning the kingdom of God.
9 But when divers were hardened, and believed not, but spake evil of that way
before the multitude, he departed from
them, and separated the disciples, disputing daily in the school of one Tyran'nus.
10 And this continued by the space of two
years; so that all they which dwelt in Asia
heard the word of the Lord Jesus, both
Jews and Greeks.●

BELIEVERS ARE STRENGTHENED

BELIEVERS ARE INSTRUCTED

This segment reports the beginnings of Paul's third missionary journey. The entire passage is 18:23—21:17.

*18:23* Where did Paul spend "some time"?

What was involved in the "strengthening" ministry?

*18:24-28* Record what is reported here about:

THE MAN APOLLOS

HIS DOCTRINE

HIS REVISED DOCTRINE

*19:1-7* What particular ministry did Paul have at this time?

*19:8-10* Compare verses 8 and 10. Account for the difference.

NEW INTERNATIONAL VERSION

What does this passage teach about:

GENUINE POWER

EXORCISM

JESUS MAGNIFIED

BLACK MAGIC

WORD OF GOD

MAKING PLANS

OTHER

11God did extraordinary miracles
through Paul. 12Handkerchiefs and aprons
that had touched him were taken to the
sick, and their illnesses were cured and the
evil spirits left them.
13Some Jews who went around driving
out evil spirits tried to invoke the name of
the Lord Jesus over those who were demon-possessed. They would say, "In the
name of Jesus, whom Paul preaches, I
command you to come out." 14Seven sons
of Sceva, a Jewish chief priest, were doing
this. 15The evil spirit answered them,
"Jesus I know and Paul I know about, but
who are you?" 16Then the man who had the
evil spirit jumped on them and overpow-
ered them all. He gave them such a beating
that they ran out of the house naked and
bleeding.●
17When this became known to the Jews
and Greeks living in Ephesus, they were all
seized with fear, and the name of the Lord
Jesus was held in high honor. 18Many of
those who believed now came and openly
confessed their evil deeds. 19A number
who had practiced sorcery brought their
scrolls together and burned them publicly.
When they calculated the value of the
scrolls, the total came to fifty thousand
drachmas.[d] 20In this way the word of the
Lord spread widely and grew in power.●
21After all this had happened, Paul decided to go to Jerusalem, passing through
Macedonia and Achaia. "After I have been
there," he said, "I must visit Rome also."
22He sent two of his helpers, Timothy and
Erastus, to Macedonia, while he stayed in
the province of Asia a little longer.●

*d19* A drachma was a silver coin worth about a day's wages.

## KING JAMES

**1. MIRACLES BY PAUL** — POWER DEMONSTRATED

11 And God wrought special miracles
by the hands of Paul: 12 so that from his
body were brought unto the sick hand-
kerchiefs or aprons, and the diseases departed from them, and the evil spirits
went out of them. 13 Then certain of the
vagabond Jews, exorcists, took upon
them to call over them which had evil
spirits the name of the Lord Jesus, saying,
We adjure you by Jesus whom Paul
preacheth. 14 And there were seven sons
of *one* Sceva, a Jew, *and* chief of the
priests, which did so. 15 And the evil
spirit answered and said, Jesus I know,
and Paul I know; but who are ye? 16 And
the man in whom the evil spirit was
leaped on them, and overcame them, and
prevailed against them, so that they fled
out of that house naked and wounded.●

**2. EFFECTS**

17 And this was known to all the Jews and
Greeks also dwelling at Ephesus; and
fear fell on them all, and the name of the
Lord Jesus was magnified. 18 And many
that believed came, and confessed, and
showed their deeds. 19 Many of them
also which used curious arts brought their
books together, and burned them before
all *men:* and they counted the price of
them, and found *it* fifty thousand *pieces*
of silver. 20 So mightily grew the word
of God and prevailed.●

**3. TARRYING AT EPHESUS** — PLANS MADE

21 After these things were ended, Paul
purposed in the spirit, when he had passed
through Macedonia and Achai'a, to go to
Jerusalem, saying, After I have been
there, I must also see Rome. 22 So he
sent into Macedonia two of them that
ministered unto him, Timothy and
Eras'tus; but he himself stayed in Asia
for a season.●

---

*19:11-16* Compare the ministry of Paul with that of the itinerant exorcists:

PAUL: ____________________

EXORCISTS: ____________________

*19:17-20* Record the different effects of what had happened up until now.

*19:21-22* What were Paul's plans? ____________________

NEW INTERNATIONAL VERSION

What do you learn here about:

IDOLATRY

GREED

MOB HYSTERIA

JUSTICE

OTHER

*The Riot in Ephesus*

23 About that time there arose a great disturbance about the Way. 24 A silversmith
named Demetrius, who made silver shrines
of Artemis, brought in no little business for
the craftsmen. 25 He called them together,
along with the workmen in related trades,
and said: "Men, you know we receive a
good income from this business. 26 And you
see and hear how this fellow Paul has convinced and led astray large numbers of
people here in Ephesus and in practically
the whole province of Asia. He says that
man-made gods are no gods at all. 27 There
is danger not only that our trade will lose
its good name, but also that the temple of
the great goddess Artemis will be discredit-
ed, and the goddess herself, who is worshiped throughout the province of Asia and
the world, will be robbed of her divine
majesty." ●
28 When they heard this, they were furious and began shouting: "Great is Artemis
of the Ephesians!" 29 Soon the whole city
was in an uproar. The people seized Gaius
and Aristarchus, Paul's traveling companions from Macedonia, and rushed as one
man into the theater. 30 Paul wanted to appear before the crowd, but the disciples
would not let him. 31 Even some of the officials of the province, friends of Paul, sent
him a message begging him not to venture
into the theater.
32 The assembly was in confusion: Some
were shouting one thing, some another.
Most of the people did not even know why
they were there. 33 The Jews pushed Alexander to the front, and some of the crowd
shouted instructions to him. He motioned
for silence in order to make a defense before the people. 34 But when they realized
he was a Jew, they all shouted in unison for
about two hours: "Great is Artemis of the
Ephesians!" ●
35 The city clerk quieted the crowd and
said: "Men of Ephesus, doesn't all the
world know that the city of Ephesus is the
guardian of the temple of the great Artemis
and of her image, which fell from heaven?
36 Therefore, since these facts are undeni-
able, you ought to be quiet and not do anything rash. 37 You have brought these men
here, though they have neither robbed
temples nor blasphemed our goddess. 38 If,
then, Demetrius and his fellow craftsmen
have a grievance against anybody, the
courts are open and there are proconsuls.
They can press charges. 39 If there is anything further you want to bring up, it must
be settled in a legal assembly. 40 As it is, we
are in danger of being charged with rioting
because of today's events. In that case we
would not be able to account for this commotion, since there is no reason for it."
41 After he had said this, he dismissed the
assembly. ●

KING JAMES

1. SILVERSMITHS STIRRED UP

23 And the same time there arose no
small stir about that way. 24 For a certain *man* named Deme'tri-us, a silversmith, which made silver shrines for
Diana, brought no small gain unto the
craftsmen; 25 whom he called together
with the workmen of like occupation, and
said, Sirs, ye know that by this craft we
have our wealth. 26 Moreover ye see and
hear, that not alone at Ephesus, but almost throughout all Asia, this Paul hath
persuaded and turned away much people,
saying that they be no gods, which are
made with hands: 27 so that not only
this our craft is in danger to be set at
nought; but also that the temple of the
great goddess Diana should be despised,
and her magnificence should be destroyed,
whom all Asia and the world worshippeth.●

2. CITY RIOTS

28 And when they heard *these sayings*,
they were full of wrath, and cried out,
saying, Great *is* Diana of the Ephesians.
29 And the whole city was filled with confusion: and having caught Gai'us and
Aristar'chus, men of Macedonia, Paul's
companions in travel, they rushed with
one accord into the theater. 30 And when
Paul would have entered in unto the
people, the disciples suffered him not.
31 And certain of the chief of Asia, which
were his friends, sent unto him, desiring
*him* that he would not adventure himself
into the theater. 32 Some therefore cried
one thing, and some another: for the assembly was confused; and the more part
knew not wherefore they were come together. 33 And they drew Alexander out
of the multitude, the Jews putting him forward. And Alexander beckoned with the
hand, and would have made his defense
unto the people. 34 But when they knew
that he was a Jew, all with one voice about
the space of two hours cried out, Great *is*
Diana of the Ephesians.●

3. MAYOR CALMS THE MOB

35 And when the
townclerk had appeased the people, he
said, *Ye* men of Ephesus, what man is
there that knoweth not how that the city
of the Ephesians is a worshipper of the
great goddess Diana, and of the *image*
which fell down from Jupiter? 36 Seeing
then that these things cannot be spoken
against, ye ought to be quiet, and to do
nothing rashly. 37 For ye have brought
hither these men, which are neither robbers of churches, nor yet blasphemers of
your goddess. 38 Wherefore if Deme'-
tri-us, and the craftsmen which are with
him, have a matter against any man, the
law is open, and there are deputies: let
them implead one another. 39 But if ye
inquire any thing concerning other matters, it shall be determined in a lawful
assembly. 40 For we are in danger to be
called in question for this day's uproar,
there being no cause whereby we may
give an account of this concourse. 41 And
when he had thus spoken, he dismissed
the assembly.●

BUSINESSMAN

RULER

*19:23-27* What were the points of Demetrius' argument?

*19:28-34* Compare the beginning and end of the paragraph.

What happens in between?

*19:35-41* Record the different points of the townclerk's argument:

NEW INTERNATIONAL VERSION

What does this passage teach about:

CHRISTIAN LOVE

CHRISTIAN FELLOWSHIP

MISSIONARY WORK

PREACHING

MIRACLE

PLANNING

List some spiritual applications.

*Through Macedonia and Greece*

20 When the uproar had ended, Paul
sent for the disciples and, after encouraging them, said good-by and set out
for Macedonia. [2]He traveled through that
area, speaking many words of encouragement to the people, and finally arrived in
Greece, [3]where he stayed three months.
Because the Jews made a plot against him
just as he was about to sail for Syria, he
decided to go back through Macedonia.
[4]He was accompanied by Sopater son of
Pyrrhus from Berea, Aristarchus and
Secundus from Thessalonica, Gaius from
Derbe, Timothy also, and from the province of Asia Tychicus and Trophimus.
[5]These men went on ahead and waited for
us at Troas. [6]But we sailed from Philippi
after the Feast of Unleavened Bread, and
five days later joined the others at Troas,
where we stayed seven days.●

*Eutychus Raised From the Dead at Troas*

[7]On the first day of the week we came
together to break bread. Paul spoke to the
people and, because he intended to leave
the next day, kept on talking until midnight. [8]There were many lamps in the upstairs room where we were meeting. [9]Seat-
ed in a window was a young man named
Eutychus, who was sinking into a deep
sleep as Paul talked on and on. When he
was sound asleep, he fell to the ground
from the third story and was picked up
dead. [10]Paul went down, threw himself on
the young man and put his arms around
him. "Don't be alarmed," he said. "He's
alive!" [11]Then he went upstairs again and
broke bread and ate. After talking until
daylight, he left. [12]The people took the
young man home alive and were greatly
comforted.●

*Paul's Farewell to the Ephesian Elders*

[13]We went on ahead to the ship and
sailed for Assos, where we were going to
take Paul aboard. He had made this arrangement because he was going there on
foot. [14]When he met us at Assos, we took
him aboard and went on to Mitylene. [15]The
next day we set sail from there and arrived
off Kios. The day after that we crossed
over to Samos, and on the following day
arrived at Miletus. [16]Paul had decided to
sail past Ephesus to avoid spending time in
the province of Asia, for he was in a hurry
to reach Jerusalem, if possible, by the day
of Pentecost.●

KING JAMES

**1. MACEDONIA AND GREECE**

**PAUL LEAVES EPHESUS**

**20** And after the uproar was ceased,
Paul called unto *him* the disciples,
and embraced *them*, and departed for to
go into Macedonia. 2 And when he had
gone over those parts, and had given them
much exhortation, he came into Greece,
3 and *there* abode three months. And
when the Jews laid wait for him, as he was
about to sail into Syria, he purposed to
return through Macedonia. 4 And there
accompanied him into Asia So'pater of
Beroe'a; and of the Thessalo'ni-ans, Aristar'chus and Secun'dus; and Gai'us of
Derbe, and Timothy; and of Asia, Tych'-
icus and Troph'imus. 5 These going
before tarried for us at Tro'as. 6 And we
sailed away from Phil'ippi after the days
of unleavened bread, and came unto them
to Tro'as in five days; where we abode
seven days.●

**2. TROAS**

7 And upon the first *day* of the week,
when the disciples came together to break
bread, Paul preached unto them, ready
to depart on the morrow; and continued
his speech until midnight. 8 And there
were many lights in the upper chamber,
where they were gathered together. 9 And
there sat in a window a certain young man
named Eu'tychus, being fallen into a deep
sleep: and as Paul was long preaching, he
sunk down with sleep, and fell down from
the third loft, and was taken up dead.
10 And Paul went down, and fell on him,
and embracing *him* said, Trouble not
yourselves; for his life is in him. 11 When
he therefore was come up again, and had
broken bread, and eaten, and talked a
long while, even till break of day, so he
departed. 12 And they brought the young
man alive, and were not a little comforted.●

**3. TO MILETUS**

13 And we went before to ship, and
sailed unto Assos, there intending to take
in Paul: for so had he appointed, minding
himself to go afoot. 14 And when he met
with us at Assos, we took him in, and
came to Mityle'ne. 15 And we sailed
thence, and came the next *day* over against
Chi'os; and the next *day* we arrived at
Samos, and tarried at Trogyl'li-um; and
the next *day* we came to Mile'tus. 16 For
Paul had determined to sail by Ephesus,
because he would not spend the time in
Asia: for he hasted, if it were possible for
him, to be at Jerusalem the day of Pentecost.●

**PAUL PASSES BY EPHESUS**

*20:1-6* What references are here about Paul's ministry?

______________________________

______________________________

______________________________

______________________________

______________________________

Where did Luke join Paul? (Note the first appearance of the word "us".)

______________________________

______________________________

______________________________

*20:7-12* List the main parts of this story. ______

______________________________

______________________________

______________________________

______________________________

______________________________

Why do you think this story was included in the Acts account?

______________________________

______________________________

______________________________

______________________________

______________________________

*20:13-16* List the main parts of this itinerary.

______________________________

______________________________

______________________________

______________________________

______________________________

______________________________

______________________________

______________________________

______________________________

______________________________

## NEW INTERNATIONAL VERSION

Record different examples for Christian living which you observe from Paul's testimony.

17 From Miletus, Paul sent to Ephesus for the elders of the church. 18 When they arrived, he said to them: "You know how I lived the whole time I was with you, from the first day I came into the province of Asia. 19 I served the Lord with great humility and with tears, although I was severely tested by the plots of the Jews. 20 You know that I have not hesitated to preach anything that would be helpful to you but have taught you publicly and from house to house. 21 I have declared to both Jews and Greeks that they must turn to God in repentance and have faith in our Lord Jesus.

22 "And now, compelled by the Spirit, I am going to Jerusalem, not knowing what will happen to me there. 23 I only know that in every city the Holy Spirit warns me that prison and hardships are facing me. 24 However, I consider my life worth nothing to me, if only I may finish the race and complete the task the Lord Jesus has given me—the task of testifying to the gospel of God's grace.

25 "Now I know that none of you among whom I have gone about preaching the kingdom will ever see me again. 26 Therefore, I declare to you today that I am innocent of the blood of all men. 27 For I have not hesitated to proclaim to you the whole will of God. 28 Keep watch over yourselves and all the flock of which the Holy Spirit has made you overseers.[a] Be shepherds of the church of God,[b] which he bought with his own blood. 29 I know that after I leave, savage wolves will come in among you and will not spare the flock. 30 Even from your own number men will arise and distort the truth in order to draw away disciples after them. 31 So be on your guard! Remember that for three years I never stopped warning each of you night and day with tears.

32 "Now I commit you to God and to the word of his grace, which can build you up and give you an inheritance among all those who are sanctified. 33 I have not coveted anyone's silver or gold or clothing. 34 You yourselves know that these hands of mine have supplied my own needs and the needs of my companions. 35 In everything I did, I showed you that by this kind of hard work we must help the weak, remembering the words the Lord Jesus himself said: 'It is more blessed to give than to receive.' "

36 When he had said this, he knelt down with all of them and prayed. 37 They all wept as they embraced him and kissed him. 38 What grieved them most was his statement that they would never see his face again. Then they accompanied him to the ship.

[a] 28 Traditionally *bishops*
[b] 28 Many manuscripts *of the Lord*

KING JAMES

PAUL'S EXAMPLE:

1. COMMITTED TO A TASK

TEARS IN TRIALS

17 And from Mile'tus he sent to Ephesus, and called the elders of the church.
18 And when they were come to him, he
said unto them,
Ye know, from the first day that I came
into Asia, after what manner I have been
with you at all seasons, 19 serving the
Lord with all humility of mind, and with
many tears, and temptations, which befell
me by the lying in wait of the Jews:
20 *and* how I kept back nothing that was
profitable *unto you*, but have showed you,
and have taught you publicly, and from
house to house, 21 testifying both to the
Jews, and also to the Greeks, repentance
toward God, and faith toward our Lord
Jesus Christ.● 22And now, behold, I go
bound in the spirit unto Jerusalem, not
knowing the things that shall befall me
there: 23 save that the Holy Ghost witnesseth in every city, saying that bonds
and afflictions abide me. 24 But none of
these things move me, neither count I my
life dear unto myself, so that I might
finish my course with joy, and the ministry, which I have received of the Lord
Jesus, to testify the gospel of the grace of
God. ● 25And now, behold, I know that
ye all, among whom I have gone preaching the kingdom of God, shall see my
face no more. 26 Wherefore I take you to
record this day, that I *am* pure from the
blood of all *men*. 27 For I have not
shunned to declare unto you all the
counsel of God. 28 Take heed therefore
unto yourselves, and to all the flock, over
the which the Holy Ghost hath made you
overseers, to feed the church of God,
which he hath purchased with his own
blood. 29 For I know this, that after my
departing shall grievous wolves enter in
among you, not sparing the flock. 30 Also
of your own selves shall men arise, speaking perverse things, to draw away disciples after them. 31 Therefore watch,
and remember, that by the space of three
years I ceased not to warn every one night
and day with tears. 32 And now, brethren, I commend you to God, and to the
word of his grace, which is able to build
you up, and to give you an inheritance
among all them which are sanctified.● 33 I
have coveted no man's silver, or gold, or
apparel. 34 Yea, ye yourselves know,
that these hands have ministered unto my
necessities, and to them that were with
me. 35 I have showed you all things, how
that so laboring ye ought to support the
weak, and to remember the words of the
Lord Jesus, how he said, It is more blessed
to give than to receive.●
36 And when he had thus spoken, he
kneeled down, and prayed with them all.
37 And they all wept sore, and fell on
Paul's neck, and kissed him, 38 sorrowing most of all for the words which he
spake, that they should see his face no
more. And they accompanied him unto
the ship.●

2. CRUCIFIED TO SELF

3. CON—CERN FOR THE FLOCK

4. COVETING NOTHING

5. COMPASSION FOR BRETHREN

TEARS IN SEPARATION

Paul's testimony gives many good examples to follow. Some of these appear in the segment outline.
Record the different experiences of Paul cited in each paragraph:

*20:17-21* ______________________________

*20:22-24* ______________________________

*20:25-32* ______________________________

*20:33-35* ______________________________

*20:36-38* ______________________________

NEW INTERNATIONAL VERSION

What does this passage teach about:

HOLY SPIRIT

PRAYER

GIFT OF PROPHECY

PERSECUTION

LORD'S WILL

CHRISTIAN FELLOWSHIP

OTHER

### *On to Jerusalem*

**21** After we had torn ourselves away
from them, we put out to sea and
sailed straight to Cos. The next day we
went to Rhodes and from there to Patara.
[2]We found a ship crossing over to Phoenicia, went on board and set sail. [3]After
sighting Cyprus and passing to the south of
it, we sailed on to Syria. We landed at
Tyre, where our ship was to unload its cargo. [4]Finding the disciples there, we stayed
with them seven days. Through the Spirit
they urged Paul not to go on to Jerusalem.
[5]But when our time was up, we left and
continued on our way. All the disciples and
their wives and children accompanied us
out of the city, and there on the beach we
knelt to pray. [6]After saying good-by to
each other, we went aboard the ship, and
they returned home.●

[7]We continued our voyage from Tyre
and landed at Ptolemais, where we greeted
the brothers and stayed with them for a
day. [8]Leaving the next day, we reached
Caesarea and stayed at the house of Philip
the evangelist, one of the Seven. [9]He had
four unmarried daughters who prophesied.

[10]After we had been there a number of
days, a prophet named Agabus came down
from Judea. [11]Coming over to us, he took
Paul's belt, tied his own hands and feet
with it and said, "The Holy Spirit says, 'In
this way the Jews of Jerusalem will bind
the owner of this belt and will hand him
over to the Gentiles.'"

[12]When we heard this, we and the people
there pleaded with Paul not to go up to
Jerusalem. [13]Then Paul answered, "Why
are you weeping and breaking my heart? I
am ready not only to be bound, but also to
die in Jerusalem for the name of the Lord
Jesus." [14]When he would not be dissuad-
ed, we gave up and said, "The Lord's will
be done."●

[15]After this, we got ready and went up to
Jerusalem. [16]Some of the disciples from
Caesarea accompanied us and brought us
to the home of Mnason, where we were to
stay. He was a man from Cyprus and one
of the early disciples.

### *Paul's Arrival at Jerusalem*

[17]When we arrived at Jerusalem, the
brothers received us warmly.●

KING JAMES

1. AT TYRE

WARNING NOT TO GO

21 And it came to pass, that after we
were gotten from them, and had
launched, we came with a straight course
unto Co'os, and the *day* following unto
Rhodes, and from thence unto Pat'ara:
2 and finding a ship sailing over unto
Phoeni'cia, we went aboard, and set forth.
3 Now when we had discovered Cyprus,
we left it on the left hand, and sailed into
Syria, and landed at Tyre: for there the
ship was to unlade her burden. 4 And
finding disciples, we tarried there seven
days: who said to Paul through the Spirit,
that he should not go up to Jerusalem.
5 And when we had accomplished those
days, we departed and went our way; and
they all brought us on our way, with
wives and children, till *we were* out of the
city: and we kneeled down on the shore,
and prayed. 6 And when we had taken
our leave one of another, we took ship;
and they returned home again.●

2. AT CAESAREA

7 And when we had finished *our* course
from Tyre, we came to Ptolema'is, and
saluted the brethren, and abode with
them one day. 8 And the next *day* we that
were of Paul's company departed, and
came unto Caesare'a; and we entered into
the house of Philip the evangelist, which
was *one* of the seven; and abode with him.
9 And the same man had four daughters,
virgins, which did prophesy. 10 And as
we tarried *there* many days, there came
down from Judea a certain prophet,
named Ag'abus. 11 And when he was
come unto us, he took Paul's girdle, and
bound his own hands and feet, and said,
Thus saith the Holy Ghost, So shall the
Jews at Jerusalem bind the man that own-
eth this girdle, and shall deliver *him* into
the hands of the Gentiles. 12 And when
we heard these things, both we, and they
of that place, besought him not to go up
to Jerusalem. 13 Then Paul answered,
What mean ye to weep and to break mine
heart? for I am ready not to be bound
only, but also to die at Jerusalem for the
name of the Lord Jesus. 14 And when he
would not be persuaded, we ceased, saying, The will of the Lord be done.●

3. ARRIVAL AT JERUSALEM

JOY OVER COMING

15 And after those days we took up our
carriages, and went up to Jerusalem.
16 There went with us also *certain* of the
disciples of Caesare'a, and brought with
them one Mnason of Cyprus, an old disciple, with whom we should lodge.
17 And when we were come to Jerusalem, the brethren received us gladly.●

*21:1-6* Why do you think Luke records the details of the itinerary of verses 1-3?

What different things impress you in verses 4-5?

*21:7-14* What was Paul urged to do?

Compare this with verse 4.

What was Paul's reply?

*21:15-17* What is the bright note of this paragraph?

NEW INTERNATIONAL VERSION

What does this passage teach about:

GOSPEL TO NON-JEWS

HEBREW CHRISTIANS

LEGALISM

LAW OF GOD

PERSECUTION

FALSE ACCUSATION

CIVIL RULERS

18The next
day Paul and the rest of us went to see
James, and all the elders were present.
19Paul greeted them and reported in detail
what God had done among the Gentiles
through his ministry.
20When they heard this, they praised
God. Then they said to Paul: "You see,
brother, how many thousands of Jews
have believed, and all of them are zealous
for the law. 21They have been informed
that you teach all the Jews who live among
the Gentiles to turn away from Moses, telling them not to circumcise their children or
live according to our customs. 22What shall
we do? They will certainly hear that you
have come, 23so do what we tell you. There
are four men with us who have made a
vow. 24Take these men, join in their purification rites and pay their expenses, so that
they can have their heads shaved. Then
everybody will know there is no truth in
these reports about you, but that you yourself are living in obedience to the law. 25As
for the Gentile believers, we have written
to them our decision that they should abstain from food sacrificed to idols, from
blood, from the meat of strangled animals
and from sexual immorality."
26The next day Paul took the men and
purified himself along with them. Then he
went to the temple to give notice of the
date when the days of purification would
end and the offering would be made for
each of them.●

*Paul Arrested*

27When the seven days were nearly over,
some Jews from the province of Asia saw
Paul at the temple. They stirred up the
whole crowd and seized him, 28shouting,
"Men of Israel, help us! This is the man
who teaches all men everywhere against
our people and our law and this place. And
besides, he has brought Greeks into the
temple area and defiled this holy place."
29(They had previously seen Trophimus
the Ephesian in the city with Paul and as-
sumed that Paul had brought him into the
temple area.)●
30The whole city was aroused, and the
people came running from all directions.
Seizing Paul, they dragged him from the
temple, and immediately the gates were
shut. 31While they were trying to kill him,
news reached the commander of the Roman troops that the whole city of Jerusalem was in an uproar. 32He at once took
some officers and soldiers and ran down to
the crowd. When the rioters saw the commander and his soldiers, they stopped
beating Paul.
33The commander came up and arrested
him and ordered him to be bound with two
chains. Then he asked who he was and
what he had done. 34Some in the crowd
shouted one thing and some another, and
since the commander could not get at the
truth because of the uproar, he ordered
that Paul be taken into the barracks.
35When Paul reached the steps, the violence of the mob was so great he had to be
carried by the soldiers. 36The crowd that
followed kept shouting, "Away with him!"●

KING JAMES

1. PAUL TAKES A VOW

AMONG FRIENDS

18 And the *day* following Paul went in
with us unto James; and all the elders
were present. 19 And when he had
saluted them, he declared particularly
what things God had wrought among the
Gentiles by his ministry. 20 And when
they heard *it*, they glorified the Lord, and
said unto him, Thou seest, brother, how
many thousands of Jews there are which
believe; and they are all zealous of the
law: 21 and they are informed of thee,
that thou teachest all the Jews which are
among the Gentiles to forsake Moses,
saying that they ought not to circumcise
*their* children, neither to walk after the
customs. 22 What is it therefore? the
multitude must needs come together: for
they will hear that thou art come. 23 Do
therefore this that we say to thee: We
have four men which have a vow on them;
24 them take, and purify thyself with them,
and be at charges with them, that they
may shave *their* heads: and all may know
that those things, whereof they were informed concerning thee, are nothing; but
*that* thou thyself also walkest orderly,
and keepest the law. 25 As touching the
Gentiles which believe, we have written
*and* concluded that they observe no such
thing, save only that they keep themselves from *things* offered to idols, and
from blood, and from strangled, and from
fornication. 26 Then Paul took the men,
and the next day purifying himself with
them entered into the temple, to signify
the accomplishment of the days of purification, until that an offering should be
offered for every one of them. ●

2. PAUL IS FALSELY ACCUSED

27 And when the seven days were almost ended, the Jews which were of Asia,
when they saw him in the temple, stirred
up all the people, and laid hands on him,
28 crying out, Men of Israel, help: This is
the man, that teacheth all *men* every
where against the people, and the law, and
this place: and further brought Greeks
also into the temple, and hath polluted
this holy place. 29 (For they had seen
before with him in the city Troph'imus
an Ephesian, whom they supposed that
Paul had brought into the temple.) ●

3. PAUL IS ARRESTED

30 And all the city was moved, and the
people ran together: and they took Paul,
and drew him out of the temple: and
forthwith the doors were shut. 31 And as
they went about to kill him, tidings came
unto the chief captain of the band, that all
Jerusalem was in an uproar: 32 who immediately took soldiers and centurions,
and ran down unto them: and when they
saw the chief captain and the soldiers,
they left beating of Paul. 33 Then the
chief captain came near, and took him,
and commanded *him* to be bound with
two chains; and demanded who he was,
and what he had done. 34 And some
cried one thing, some another, among the
multitude: and when he could not know
the certainty for the tumult, he commanded him to be carried into the castle.
35 And when he came upon the stairs, so
it was, that he was borne of the soldiers
for the violence of the people. 36 For the
multitude of the people followed after,
crying, Away with him. ●

AMONG ENEMIES

The tone of the book of Acts changes radically at this point—to one of intensity and violence. From this point on in Acts Paul is no longer missionary, rather PRISONER.

*21:18-26* What report of his third journey did Paul give (v.19)?

______

______

______

What was the elders' response and recommendation (vv.20-24)?

______

______

______

______

______

What does verse 26 reveal about Paul? ______

______

______

______

______

______

*21:27-29* What were the charges against Paul?

______

______

______

______

______

______

*21:30-36* Record the events: ______

______

______

______

______

______

______

______

NEW INTERNATIONAL VERSION

What do you learn here about:

EDUCATION

ZEAL

FALSE RIGHTEOUSNESS

CONVERSION EXPERIENCE

GLORY OF GOD

COMMISSION TO SERVE THE LORD

*Paul Speaks to the Crowd*

37 As the soldiers were about to take Paul
into the barracks, he asked the commander, "May I say something to you?"
"Do you speak Greek?" he replied.
38 "Aren't you the Egyptian who started a
revolt and led four thousand terrorists out
into the desert some time ago?"
39 Paul answered, "I am a Jew, from Tarsus in Cilicia, a citizen of no ordinary city.
Please let me speak to the people."●
40 Having received the commander's permission, Paul stood on the steps and motioned to the crowd. When they were
all silent, he said to them in Aramaic[a]:
22 1 "Brothers and fathers, listen now
to my defense."
2 When they heard him speak to them in
Aramaic, they became very quiet.
Then Paul said: 3 "I am a Jew, born in
Tarsus of Cilicia, but brought up in this
city. Under Gamaliel I was thoroughly
trained in the law of our fathers and was
just as zealous for God as any of you are
today. 4 I persecuted the followers of this
Way to their death, arresting both men and
women and throwing them into prison, 5 as
also the high priest and all the council can
testify. I even obtained letters from them
to their brothers in Damascus, and went
there to bring these people as prisoners to
Jerusalem to be punished.●
6 "About noon as I came near Damascus,
suddenly a bright light from heaven flashed
around me. 7 I fell to the ground and heard
a voice say to me, 'Saul! Saul! Why do you
persecute me?'
8 " 'Who are you, Lord?' I asked.
" 'I am Jesus of Nazareth, whom you are
persecuting,' he replied. 9 My companions
saw the light, but they did not understand
the voice of him who was speaking to me.
10 " 'What shall I do, Lord?' I asked.
" 'Get up,' the Lord said, 'and go into
Damascus. There you will be told all that
you have been assigned to do.' 11 My companions led me by the hand into Damascus,
because the brilliance of the light had
blinded me.●
12 "A man named Ananias came to see
me. He was a devout observer of the law
and highly respected by all the Jews living
there. 13 He stood beside me and said,
'Brother Saul, receive your sight!' And at
that very moment I was able to see him.
14 "Then he said: 'The God of our fathers
has chosen you to know his will and to see
the Righteous One and to hear words from
his mouth. 15 You will be his witness to all
men of what you have seen and heard.
16 And now what are you waiting for? Get
up, be baptized and wash your sins away,
calling on his name.'●

[a]40 Or possibly *Hebrew;* also in verse 2

KING JAMES

**SPEAKING TO THE CROWD**

1. PAUL ASKS TO SPEAK

37 And as Paul was to be led into the
castle, he said unto the chief captain, May
I speak unto thee? Who said, Canst thou
speak Greek? 38 Art not thou that
Egyptian, which before these days madest
an uproar, and leddest out into the wilderness four thousand men that were murderers? 39 But Paul said, I am a man
*which am* a Jew of Tarsus, *a city* in Cili′-
cia, a citizen of no mean city: and, I beseech thee, suffer me to speak unto the
people.● 40 And when he had given him
license, Paul stood on the stairs, and
beckoned with the hand unto the people.
And when there was made a great silence,
he spake unto *them* in the Hebrew tongue,
saying,

2. PRE-CONVERSION YEARS

22 Men, brethren, and fathers, hear ye
my defense *which I make* now unto
you.
2 (And when they heard that he spake
in the Hebrew tongue to them, they kept
the more silence: and he saith,)
3 I am verily a man *which am* a Jew,
born in Tarsus, *a city* in Cili′cia, yet
brought up in this city at the feet of Ga-
ma′li-el, *and* taught according to the perfect manner of the law of the fathers, and
was zealous toward God, as ye all are this
day. 4 And I persecuted this way unto the
death, binding and delivering into prisons
both men and women. 5 As also the high
priest doth bear me witness, and all the
estate of the elders: from whom also I
received letters unto the brethren, and
went to Damascus, to bring them which
were there bound unto Jerusalem, for to
be punished. ●

3. CONVERSION DAY

6 And it came to pass, that, as I made
my journey, and was come nigh unto
Damascus about noon, suddenly there
shone from heaven a great light round
about me. 7 And I fell unto the ground,
and heard a voice saying unto me, Saul,
Saul, why persecutest thou me? 8 And I
answered, Who art thou, Lord? And he
said unto me, I am Jesus of Nazareth,
whom thou persecutest. 9 And they that
were with me saw indeed the light, and
were afraid; but they heard not the voice
of him that spake to me. 10 And I said,
What shall I do, Lord? And the Lord
said unto me, Arise, and go into Damascus; and there it shall be told thee of all
things which are appointed for thee to do.
11 And when I could not see for the glory
of that light, being led by the hand of
them that were with me, I came into
Damascus.●

4. COMMISSION FROM GOD

12 And one Anani′as, a devout man
according to the law, having a good report of all the Jews which dwelt *there*,
13 came unto me, and stood, and said
unto me, Brother Saul, receive thy sight.
And the same hour I looked up upon him.
14 And he said, The God of our fathers
hath chosen thee, that thou shouldest
know his will, and see that Just One, and
shouldest hear the voice of his mouth.
15 For thou shalt be his witness unto
all men of what thou hast seen and
heard. 16 And now why tarriest thou?
arise, and be baptized, and wash away
thy sins, calling on the name of the
Lord.●

**WITNESS UNTO ALL MEN**

Paul's speech reported in this segment continues into the next one, concluding at 22:21.

*21:37-39* Compare the tone of the chief captain's words with that of Paul's.

*21:40—22:5* Record the main parts of Paul's testimony of the preconversion years.

*22:6-11* Record Paul's two questions and the Lord's answer to each.

*22:12-16* What were Paul's main experiences at this time?

NEW INTERNATIONAL VERSION

What does this passage teach about:

LORD'S WILL AND DIRECTION

OBEDIENCE

PERSECUTION

CHRISTIAN GRACE

PERSEVERANCE

SPIRITUAL STRENGTH

List other important lessons:

17"When I returned to Jerusalem and
was praying at the temple, I fell into a
trance 18and saw the Lord speaking.
'Quick!' he said to me. 'Leave Jerusalem
immediately, because they will not accept
your testimony about me.'
19" 'Lord,' I replied, 'these men know
that I went from one synagogue to another
to imprison and beat those who believe in
you. 20And when the blood of your martyr[a]
Stephen was shed, I stood there giving my
approval and guarding the clothes of those
who were killing him.'
21"Then the Lord said to me, 'Go; I will
send you far away to the Gentiles.' "●

*Paul the Roman Citizen*

22The crowd listened to Paul until he said
this. Then they raised their voices and
shouted, "Rid the earth of him! He's not fit
to live!"
23As they were shouting and throwing off
their cloaks and flinging dust into the air,
24the commander ordered Paul to be taken
into the barracks. He directed that he be
flogged and questioned in order to find out
why the people were shouting at him like
this.● 25As they stretched him out to flog
him, Paul said to the centurion standing
there, "Is it legal for you to flog a Roman
citizen who hasn't even been found
guilty?"
26When the centurion heard this, he went
to the commander and reported it. "What
are you going to do?" he asked. "This man
is a Roman citizen."
27The commander went to Paul and
asked, "Tell me, are you a Roman citizen?"
"Yes, I am," he answered.
28Then the commander said, "I had to
pay a big price for my citizenship."
"But I was born a citizen," Paul replied.
29Those who were about to question him
withdrew immediately. The commander
himself was alarmed when he realized that
he had put Paul, a Roman citizen, in
chains.●

[a]20 Or *witness*

KING JAMES

1. PAUL AT JERU-SALEM

17 And it came to pass, that, when I
was come again to Jerusalem, even while
I prayed in the temple, I was in a trance;
18 and saw him saying unto me, Make
haste, and get thee quickly out of Jerusalem: for they will not receive thy testimony concerning me. 19 And I said,
Lord, they know that I imprisoned and
beat in every synagogue them that believed on thee: 20 and when the blood
of thy martyr Stephen was shed, I also
was standing by, and consenting unto his
death, and kept the raiment of them that
slew him. 21 And he said unto me,
Depart: for I will send thee far hence unto
the Gentiles.●

PAUL THE CHRISTIAN

2. ANGER OF THE CROWD

22 And they gave him audience unto
this word, and *then* lifted up their voices,
and said, Away with such a *fellow* from
the earth: for it is not fit that he should
live. 23 And as they cried out, and cast
off *their* clothes, and threw dust into the
air, 24 the chief captain commanded him
to be brought into the castle, and bade
that he should be examined by scourging;
that he might know wherefore they cried
so against him.● 25 And as they bound him

3. FEAR OF THE CHIEF CAPTAIN

with thongs, Paul said unto the centurion
that stood by, Is it lawful for you to
scourge a man that is a Roman, and uncondemned? 26 When the centurion
heard *that*, he went and told the chief captain, saying, Take heed what thou doest;
for this man is a Roman. 27 Then the
chief captain came, and said unto him,
Tell me, art thou a Roman? He said, Yea.
28 And the chief captain answered, With
a great sum obtained I this freedom. And
Paul said, But I was *free*-born. 29 Then
straightway they departed from him
which should have examined him: and the
chief captain also was afraid, after he
knew that he was a Roman, and because
he had bound him.●

PAUL A ROMAN

The first paragraph of this segment concludes Paul's speech to the crowd.

*22:17-21* What was the Lord's command to Paul, via the vision (v.18)?

How did Paul justify staying in Jerusalem?

What is the key word of verse 21? (see verse 22.)

*22:22-24* Account for the anger of the crowd.

*22:25-29* What is the key repeated word of the paragraph?

How did Paul's citizenship help him at this time?

NEW INTERNATIONAL VERSION

What do you learn from this passage about:

GOOD CONSCIENCE

COURAGE

HONESTY

RESURRECTION

PROVIDENCE OF GOD

COMMISSION TO SERVE

CHEER OF THE LORD

OTHER

*Before the Sanhedrin*

30The next day, since the commander
wanted to find out exactly why Paul was
being accused by the Jews, he released him
and ordered the chief priests and all the
Sanhedrin to assemble. Then he brought
Paul and had him stand before them.
23 Paul looked straight at the Sanhedrin and said, "My brothers, I have
fulfilled my duty to God in all good conscience to this day." 2At this the high
priest Ananias ordered those standing near
Paul to strike him on the mouth. 3Then
Paul said to him, "God will strike you, you
whitewashed wall! You sit there to judge
me according to the law, yet you yourself
violate the law by commanding that I be
struck!"
4Those who were standing near Paul
said, "You dare to insult God's high
priest?"
5Paul replied, "Brothers, I did not realize that he was the high priest; for it is
written: 'Do not speak evil about the ruler
of your people.'[b]"●
6Then Paul, knowing that some of them
were Sadducees and the others Pharisees,
called out in the Sanhedrin, "My brothers,
I am a Pharisee, the son of a Pharisee. I
stand on trial because of my hope in the
resurrection of the dead." 7When he said
this, a dispute broke out between the
Pharisees and the Sadducees, and the assembly was divided. 8(The Sadducees say
that there is no resurrection, and that there
are neither angels nor spirits, but the Pharisees acknowledge them all.)
9There was a great uproar, and some of
the teachers of the law who were Pharisees
stood up and argued vigorously. "We find
nothing wrong with this man," they said.
"What if a spirit or an angel has spoken to
him?"● 10The dispute became so violent that
the commander was afraid Paul would be
torn to pieces by them. He ordered the
troops to go down and take him away from
them by force and bring him into the barracks.●
11The following night the Lord stood
near Paul and said, "Take courage! As you
have testified about me in Jerusalem, so
you must also testify in Rome."●

[b]5 Exodus 22:28

KING JAMES

1. DEFENSE

30 On the morrow, because he would
have known the certainty wherefore he
was accused of the Jews, he loosed him
from *his* bands, and commanded the chief
priests and all their council to appear, and
brought Paul down, and set him before
them.
23 And Paul, earnestly beholding the
council, said, Men *and* brethren, I
have lived in all good conscience before
God until this day. 2 And the high priest
Anani'as commanded them that stood by
him to smite him on the mouth. 3 Then
said Paul unto him, God shall smite thee,
*thou* whited wall: for sittest thou to judge
me after the law, and commandest me to
be smitten contrary to the law? 4 And
they that stood by said, Revilest thou
God's high priest? 5 Then said Paul,
I wist not, brethren, that he was the
high priest: for it is written, Thou
shalt not speak evil of the ruler of thy
people. ●

2. DISSENSION

6 But when Paul perceived that the one
part were Sadducees, and the other Pharisees, he cried out in the council, Men *and*
brethren, I am a Pharisee, the son of a
Pharisee: of the hope and resurrection of
the dead I am called in question. 7 And
when he had so said, there arose a dissension between the Pharisees and the
Sadducees: and the multitude was divided. 8 For the Sadducees say that there
is no resurrection, neither angel, nor
spirit: but the Pharisees confess both.
9 And there arose a great cry: and the
scribes *that were* of the Pharisees' part
arose, and strove, saying, We find no evil
in this man: but if a spirit or an angel hath
spoken to him, let us not fight against
God. ●

3. TRANSFER

10 And when there arose a great
dissension, the chief captain, fearing lest
Paul should have been pulled in pieces of
them, commanded the soldiers to go
down, and to take him by force from
among them, and to bring *him* into the
castle. ●

4. ENCOURAGEMENT

11 And the night following the Lord
stood by him, and said, Be of good cheer,
Paul: for as thou hast testified of me in
Jerusalem, so must thou bear witness also
at Rome. ●

WITNESSING AT JERUSALEM

WITNESSING AT ROME

This segment begins with the chief captain delivering Paul to the Council to be examined. First read the whole segment. Are any charges made against Paul for his missionary activities?

*22:30—23:5* Account for Ananias' action of verse 2.

Compare the two references to law in verse 3.

*23:6-9* What was Paul's strategy here?

Was Paul successful?

*23:10* What are your observations?

*23:11* How would the Lord's words assure Paul concerning any persecution to come?

NEW INTERNATIONAL VERSION

What does this passage teach about:

DECEPTION

CONSPIRACY

DIVINE PROVIDENCE

CIVIL RULERS

Record spiritual applications to be made of the passage.

### *The Plot to Kill Paul*

12The next morning the Jews formed a
conspiracy and bound themselves with an
oath not to eat or drink until they had killed
Paul. 13More than forty men were involved
in this plot. 14They went to the chief priests
and elders and said, "We have taken a
solemn oath not to eat anything until we
have killed Paul. 15Now then, you and the
Sanhedrin petition the commander to bring
him before you on the pretext of wanting
more accurate information about his case.
We are ready to kill him before he gets
here."●

16But when the son of Paul's sister heard
of this plot, he went into the barracks and
told Paul.
17Then Paul called one of the centurions
and said, "Take this young man to the
commander; he has something to tell him."
18So he took him to the commander.

The centurion said, "Paul, the prisoner,
sent for me and asked me to bring this
young man to you because he has something to tell you."

19The commander took the young man
by the hand, drew him aside and asked,
"What is it you want to tell me?"
20He said: "The Jews have agreed to ask
you to bring Paul before the Sanhedrin tomorrow on the pretext of wanting more
accurate information about him. 21Don't
give in to them, because more than forty of
them are waiting in ambush for him. They
have taken an oath not to eat or drink until
they have killed him. They are ready now,
waiting for your consent to their request."
22The commander dismissed the young
man and cautioned him, "Don't tell anyone that you have reported this to me."●

### *Paul Transferred to Caesarea*

23Then he called two of his centurions
and ordered them, "Get ready a detachment of two hundred soldiers, seventy
horsemen and two hundred spearmen to go
to Caesarea at nine tonight. 24Provide
mounts for Paul so that he may be taken
safely to Governor Felix."
25He wrote a letter as follows:●

KING JAMES

**1. PLOT TO KILL PAUL**

12 And when it was day, certain of the
Jews banded together, and bound themselves under a curse, saying that they
would neither eat nor drink till they had
killed Paul. 13 And they were more than
forty which had made this conspiracy.
14 And they came to the chief priests and
elders, and said, We have bound ourselves under a great curse, that we will eat
nothing until we have slain Paul. 15 Now
therefore ye with the council signify to the
chief captain that he bring him down unto
you tomorrow, as though ye would inquire something more perfectly concerning him: and we, or ever he come near,
are ready to kill him. ●

FORTY CONSPIRATORS

**2. PLOT REVEALED**

16 And when Paul's sister's son heard
of their lying in wait, he went and entered
into the castle, and told Paul. 17 Then
Paul called one of the centurions unto
*him*, and said, Bring this young man unto
the chief captain: for he hath a certain
thing to tell him. 18 So he took him, and
brought *him* to the chief captain, and said,
Paul the prisoner called me unto *him*, and
prayed me to bring this young man unto
thee, who hath something to say unto thee.
19 Then the chief captain took him by the
hand, and went *with him* aside privately,
and asked *him*, What is that thou hast to
tell me? 20 And he said, The Jews have
agreed to desire thee that thou wouldest
bring down Paul tomorrow into the
council, as though they would inquire
somewhat of him more perfectly. 21 But
do not thou yield unto them: for there lie
in wait for him of them more than forty
men, which have bound themselves with
an oath, that they will neither eat nor
drink till they have killed him: and now
are they ready, looking for a promise
from thee. 22 So the chief captain *then*
let the young man depart, and charged
*him*, *See thou* tell no man that thou hast
showed these things to me. ●

**3. CAPTAIN'S HELP**

23 And he called unto *him* two centurions, saying, Make ready two hundred
soldiers to go to Caesare'a, and horsemen
threescore and ten, and spearmen two
hundred, at the third hour of the night;
24 and provide *them* beasts, that they may
set Paul on, and bring *him* safe unto Felix
the governor. 25 And he wrote a letter
after this manner: ●

ONE PROTECTOR

---

*23:12-15* What three different groups or persons are involved in this reporting of the plot?

Compare each of the above, as to what you think was going through their minds at this time.

*23:16-22* What does the paragraph reveal about:

PAUL'S NEPHEW

CHIEF CAPTAIN

What are your reflections on the phrase "looking for a promise from thee"?

*23:23-25* Record the different verbs of the paragraph. What are your impressions?

NEW INTERNATIONAL VERSION

What do you learn here about:

JUSTICE

INJUSTICE

FLATTERY

FALSEHOOD

List spiritual applications:

26Claudius Lysias,
To His Excellency, Governor Felix:
Greetings.

27This man was seized by the Jews
and they were about to kill him, but I
came with my troops and rescued him,
for I had learned that he is a Roman
citizen. 28I wanted to know why they
were accusing him, so I brought him to
their Sanhedrin. 29I found that the accusation had to do with questions
about their law, but there was no
charge against him that deserved death
or imprisonment. 30When I was informed of a plot to be carried out
against the man, I sent him to you at
once. I also ordered his accusers to
present to you their case against him.●

31So the soldiers, carrying out their orders, took Paul with them during the night
and brought him as far as Antipatris. 32The
next day they let the cavalry go on with
him, while they returned to the barracks.
33When the cavalry arrived in Caesarea,
they delivered the letter to the governor
and handed Paul over to him. 34The governor read the letter and asked what province
he was from. Learning that he was from
Cilicia, 35he said, "I will hear your case
when your accusers get here." Then he
ordered that Paul be kept under guard in
Herod's palace.●

*The Trial Before Felix*

24 Five days later the high priest
Ananias went down to Caesarea
with some of the elders and a lawyer
named Tertullus, and they brought their
charges against Paul before the governor.
2When Paul was called in, Tertullus
presented his case before Felix: "We have
enjoyed a long period of peace under you,
and your foresight has brought about re-
forms in this nation. 3Everywhere and in
every way, most excellent Felix, we acknowledge this with profound gratitude.
4But in order not to weary you further, I
would request that you be kind enough to
hear us briefly.
5"We have found this man to be a trou-
blemaker, stirring up riots among the Jews
all over the world. He is a ringleader of the
Nazarene sect 6and even tried to desecrate
the temple; so we seized him. 8By[a] examining him yourself you will be able to learn
the truth about all these charges we are
bringing against him."
9The Jews joined in the accusation, as-
serting that these things were true.●

[a]6-8 Some manuscripts *him and wanted to judge him according to our law. 7But the commander, Lysias, came and with the use of much force snatched him from our hands 8and ordered his accusers to come before you. By*

KING JAMES

1. LETTER

INTERCESSION

26 Claudius Lys'i-as unto the most excellent governor Felix *sendeth* greeting.
27 This man was taken of the Jews, and
should have been killed of them: then
came I with an army, and rescued him,
having understood that he was a Roman.
28 And when I would have known the
cause wherefore they accused him, I
brought him forth into their council:
29 whom I perceived to be accused of
questions of their law, but to have nothing
laid to his charge worthy of death or of
bonds. 30 And when it was told me how
that the Jews laid wait for the man, I sent
straightway to thee, and gave commandment to his accusers also to say before
thee what *they had* against him. Farewell. ●

2. ARRIVAL

31 Then the soldiers, as it was commanded them, took Paul, and brought
*him* by night to Antip'atris. 32 On the
morrow they left the horsemen to go with
him, and returned to the castle: 33 who,
when they came to Caesare'a, and delivered the epistle to the governor, presented Paul also before him. 34 And
when the governor had read *the letter*, he
asked of what province he was. And
when he understood that *he was* of Cili'-
cia; 35 I will hear thee, said he, when
thine accusers are also come. And he
commanded him to be kept in Herod's
judgment hall. ●

3. ACCUSATIONS

24 And after five days Anani'as the
high priest descended with the
elders, and *with* a certain orator *named*
Tertul'lus, who informed the governor
against Paul. 2 And when he was called
forth, Tertul'lus began to accuse *him*,
saying,
Seeing that by thee we enjoy great
quietness, and that very worthy deeds are
done unto this nation by thy providence,
3 we accept *it* always, and in all places,
most noble Felix, with all thankfulness.
4 Notwithstanding, that I be not further
tedious unto thee, I pray thee that thou
wouldest hear us of thy clemency a few
words. 5 For we have found this man *a*
pestilent *fellow*, and a mover of sedition
among all the Jews throughout the world,
and a ringleader of the sect of the Naz-
arenes: 6 who also hath gone about to
profane the temple: whom we took, and
would have judged according to our law.
7 But the chief captain Lys'i-as came
*upon us*, and with great violence took *him*
away out of our hands, 8 commanding
his accusers to come unto thee: by examining of whom thyself mayest take
knowledge of all these things, whereof we
accuse him.
9 And the Jews also assented, saying
that these things were so. ●

ACCUSATION

*23:26-30* Record the main points of Claudius' letter:

______

______

______

______

______

*23:31-35* List the events reported here.

______

______

______

______

______

______

______

*24:1-9* What is Tertullus trying to do in verses 2-4?

______

______

______

What are the accusations against Paul? (vv.5-6)

______

______

______

What is Tertullus trying to accomplish by the words of verses 7-8?

______

______

______

______

______

______

NEW INTERNATIONAL VERSION

What does this passage teach about:

JUSTICE

TRUTH

FALSEHOOD

CONSCIENCE

WAY OF SALVATION

RESURRECTION

[10]When the governor motioned for him
to speak, Paul replied: "I know that for a
number of years you have been a judge
over this nation; so I gladly make my defense. [11]You can easily verify that no more
than twelve days ago I went up to Jerusalem to worship. [12]My accusers did not find
me arguing with anyone at the temple, or
stirring up a crowd in the synagogues or
anywhere else in the city. [13]And they cannot prove to you the charges they are now
making against me.● [14]However, I admit
that I worship the God of our fathers, as a
follower of the Way, which they call a sect.
I believe everything that agrees with the
Law and that is written in the Prophets,
[15]and I have the same hope in God as these
men, that there will be a resurrection of
both the righteous and the wicked. [16]So I
strive always to keep my conscience clear
before God and man.●

[17]"After an absence of several years, I
came to Jerusalem to bring my people gifts
for the poor and to present offerings. [18]I
was ceremonially clean when they found
me in the temple courts doing this. There
was no crowd with me, nor was I involved
in any disturbance. [19]But there are some
Jews from the province of Asia, who ought
to be here before you and bring charges if
they have anything against me. [20]Or these
who are here should state what crime they
found in me when I stood before the Sanhedrin— [21]unless it was this one thing I shouted as I stood in their presence: 'It is concerning the resurrection of the dead that I
am on trial before you today.' "●

[22]Then Felix, who was well acquainted
with the Way, adjourned the proceedings.
"When Lysias the commander comes," he
said, "I will decide your case." [23]He ordered the centurion to keep Paul under
guard but to give him some freedom and
permit his friends to take care of his needs.●

[24]Several days later Felix came with his
wife Drusilla, who was a Jewess. He sent
for Paul and listened to him as he spoke
about faith in Christ Jesus. [25]As Paul dis-
coursed on righteousness, self-control and
the judgment to come, Felix was afraid and
said, "That's enough for now! You may
leave. When I find it convenient, I will
send for you." [26]At the same time he was
hoping that Paul would offer him a bribe,
so he sent for him frequently and talked
with him.

[27]When two years had passed, Felix was
succeeded by Porcius Festus, but because
Felix wanted to grant a favor to the Jews,
he left Paul in prison.●

KING JAMES

**1. PAUL'S DEFENSE**

**PAUL HONORS FELIX**

10 Then Paul, after that the governor
had beckoned unto him to speak, answered,
Forasmuch as I know that thou hast
been of many years a judge unto this
nation, I do the more cheerfully answer
for myself: 11 because that thou mayest
understand, that there are yet but twelve
days since I went up to Jerusalem for to
worship. 12 And they neither found me
in the temple disputing with any man,
neither raising up the people, neither in
the synagogues, nor in the city: 13 neither
can they prove the things whereof they
now accuse me.● 14But this I confess unto
thee, that after the way which they call
heresy, so worship I the God of my
fathers, believing all things which are
written in the law and in the prophets:
15 and have hope toward God, which
they themselves also allow, that there shall
be a resurrection of the dead, both of the
just and unjust. 16 And herein do I exercise myself, to have always a conscience
void of offense toward God, and *toward*
men.● 17Now after many years I came to
bring alms to my nation, and offerings.
18 Whereupon certain Jews from Asia
found me purified in the temple, neither
with multitude, nor with tumult. 19 Who
ought to have been here before thee, and
object, if they had aught against me.
20 Or else let these same *here* say, if they
have found any evildoing in me, while I
stood before the council, 21 except it be
for this one voice, that I cried standing
among them, Touching the resurrection
of the dead I am called in question by
you this day. ●

**2. CASE ADJOURNED**

22 And when Felix heard these things,
having more perfect knowledge of *that*
way, he deferred them, and said, When
Lys'i-as the chief captain shall come
down, I will know the uttermost of your
matter. 23 And he commanded a centurion to keep Paul, and to let *him* have
liberty, and that he should forbid none of
his acquaintance to minister or come unto
him.●

**3. FELIX CONFERS OFTEN**

24 And after certain days, when Felix
came with his wife Drusil'la, which was a
Jewess, he sent for Paul, and heard him
concerning the faith in Christ. 25 And as
he reasoned of righteousness, temperance,
and judgment to come, Felix trembled,
and answered, Go thy way for this time;
when I have a convenient season, I will
call for thee. 26 He hoped also that
money should have been given him of
Paul, that he might loose him: wherefore
he sent for him the oftener, and communed with him. 27 But after two years
Por'ci-us Festus came into Felix' room:
and Felix, willing to show the Jews a
pleasure, left Paul bound.●

**FELIX FAVORS THE JEWS**

Paul's defense before Felix was powerful. Study each of the three parts, and summarize the things Paul said.

*24:10-13* ______________________

*24:14-16* ______________________

*24:17-21* ______________________

What is the last point made by Paul? ______________________

*24:22-23* Account for Felix's kind treatment of Paul.

______________________

*24:24-27* What are the things which Paul and Felix discussed?

______________________

What does this paragraph reveal about Felix?

______________________

NEW INTERNATIONAL VERSION

What do you learn here about:

DEECEIT

JUSTICE

FALSEHOOD

POLITICS

CIVIL LAW

LAW OF GOD

OTHER

*The Trial Before Festus*

25 Three days after arriving in the
province, Festus went up from Caesarea to Jerusalem, 2where the chief priests
and Jewish leaders appeared before him
and presented the charges against Paul.
3They urgently requested Festus, as a favor to them, to have Paul transferred to
Jerusalem, for they were preparing an ambush to kill him along the way. 4Festus
answered, "Paul is being held at Caesarea,
and I myself am going there soon. 5Let
some of your leaders come with me and
press charges against the man there, if he
has done anything wrong."●
6After spending eight or ten days with
them, he went down to Caesarea, and the
next day he convened the court and ordered that Paul be brought before him.
7When Paul appeared, the Jews who had
come down from Jerusalem stood around
him, bringing many serious charges against
him, which they could not prove.
8Then Paul made his defense: "I have
done nothing wrong against the law of the
Jews or against the temple or against Caesar."●
9Festus, wishing to do the Jews a favor,
said to Paul, "Are you willing to go up to
Jerusalem and stand trial before me there
on these charges?"
10Paul answered: "I am now standing before Caesar's court, where I ought to be
tried. I have not done any wrong to the
Jews, as you yourself know very well. 11If,
however, I am guilty of doing anything deserving death, I do not refuse to die. But if
the charges brought against me by these
Jews are not true, no one has the right to
hand me over to them. I appeal to Caesar!"●
12After Festus had conferred with his
council, he declared: "You have appealed
to Caesar. To Caesar you will go!"●

## KING JAMES

**1. FESTUS IN CHARGE**

**25** Now when Festus was come into
the province, after three days he ascended from Caesare'a to Jerusalem.
2 Then the high priest and the chief of the
Jews informed him against Paul, and besought him, 3 and desired favor against
him, that he would send for him to Jerusalem, laying wait in the way to kill him.
4 But Festus answered, that Paul should
be kept at Caesare'a, and that he himself
would depart shortly *thither*. 5 Let them
therefore, said he, which among you are
able, go down with *me*, and accuse this
man, if there be any wickedness in him.●

**2. JEWS ACCUSE IN VAIN**

6 And when he had tarried among them
more than ten days, he went down unto
Caesare'a; and the next day sitting on the
judgment seat commanded Paul to be
brought. 7 And when he was come, the
Jews which came down from Jerusalem
stood round about, and laid many and
grievous complaints against Paul, which
they could not prove. 8 While he answered for himself, Neither against the
law of the Jews, neither against the
temple, nor yet against Caesar, have I
offended any thing at all.●

**3. PAUL APPEALS TO CAESAR**

9 But Festus,
willing to do the Jews a pleasure, answered Paul, and said, Wilt thou go up to
Jerusalem, and there be judged of these
things before me? 10 Then said Paul, I
stand at Caesar's judgment seat, where
I ought to be judged: to the Jews have I
done no wrong, as thou very well knowest. 11 For if I be an offender, or have
committed any thing worthy of death, I
refuse not to die: but if there be none of
these things whereof these accuse me, no
man may deliver me unto them. I appeal
unto Caesar.● 12 Then Festus, when he
had conferred with the council, answered,
Hast thou appealed unto Caesar? unto
Caesar shalt thou go.●

GOVERNOR

EMPEROR

This segment is a study of political maneuvering, where Paul is the object of all the action. Study the segment, and record who makes these statements involving *place:*

Bring Paul to Jerusalem. ____________________

Come to Caesarea. ____________________

Will you go up to Jerusalem? ____________________

*25:1-5* Compare Festus with the enemies of Paul:

FESTUS ____________________

ENEMIES ____________________

*25:6-8* Compare Paul with his enemies:

PAUL ____________________

ENEMIES ____________________

*25:9-11* What is Paul's appeal? ____________________

*25:12* What was Festus' response to Paul?

____________________

NEW INTERNATIONAL VERSION

Think about Festus' reference to "someone called Jesus who died, but Paul insists is alive!"(v.19). In the account of Acts thus far has Luke reported the Jews as talking about this? Also, has Paul said much about *resurrection* in referring to the charges against him?

What does this passage teach about:

JUSTICE

INJUSTICE

OTHER

*Festus Consults King Agrippa*

13 A few days later King Agrippa and Bernice arrived at Caesarea to pay their re-
spects to Festus. 14 Since they were spending many days there, Festus discussed
Paul's case with the king. He said: "There
is a man here whom Felix left as a prisoner.
15 When I went to Jerusalem, the chief
priests and elders of the Jews brought
charges against him and asked that he be
condemned.
16 "I told them that it is not the Roman
custom to hand over any man before he has
faced his accusers and has had an opportunity to defend himself against their
charges. 17 When they came here with me,
I did not delay the case, but convened the
court the next day and ordered the man to
be brought in. 18 When his accusers got up
to speak, they did not charge him with any
of the crimes I had expected. 19 Instead,
they had some points of dispute with him
about their own religion and about a dead
man named Jesus who Paul claimed was
alive. 20 I was at a loss how to investigate
such matters; so I asked if he would be
willing to go to Jerusalem and stand trial
there on these charges. 21 When Paul made
his appeal to be held over for the Emper-
or's decision, I ordered him held until I
could send him to Caesar."
22 Then Agrippa said to Festus, "I would
like to hear this man myself."
He replied, "Tomorrow you will hear
him."●

*Paul Before Agrippa*

23 The next day Agrippa and Bernice
came with great pomp and entered the
audience room with the high ranking officers and the leading men of the city. At the
command of Festus, Paul was brought in.
24 Festus said: "King Agrippa, and all who
are present with us, you see this man! The
whole Jewish community has petitioned
me about him in Jerusalem and here in Caesarea, shouting that he ought not to live
any longer. 25 I found he had done nothing
deserving of death, but because he made
his appeal to the Emperor I decided to send
him to Rome. 26 But I have nothing definite
to write to His Majesty about him. Therefore I have brought him before all of you,
and especially before you, King Agrippa,
so that as a result of this investigation I
may have something to write. 27 For I think
it is unreasonable to send on a prisoner
without specifying the charges against
him."●

KING JAMES

1. INFORMAL CONFERENCE

SEEKING JUDGMENT

13 And after certain days king Agrip'-
pa and Bernice came unto Caesare'a to
salute Festus. 14 And when they had
been there many days, Festus declared
Paul's cause unto the king, saying, There
is a certain man left in bonds by Felix:
15 about whom, when I was at Jerusalem,
the chief priests and the elders of the Jews
informed *me*, desiring *to have* judgment
against him. 16 To whom I answered,
It is not the manner of the Romans to
deliver any man to die, before that he
which is accused have the accusers face to
face, and have license to answer for himself concerning the crime laid against him.
17 Therefore, when they were come
hither, without any delay on the morrow
I sat on the judgment seat, and commanded the man to be brought forth.
18 Against whom when the accusers
stood up, they brought none accusation
of such things as I supposed: 19 but had
certain questions against him of their own
superstition, and of one Jesus, which was
dead, whom Paul affirmed to be alive.
20 And because I doubted of such manner
of questions, I asked *him* whether he
would go to Jerusalem, and there be
judged of these matters. 21 But when
Paul had appealed to be reserved unto the
hearing of Augustus, I commanded him
to be kept till I might send him to Caesar.
22 Then Agrip'pa said unto Festus, I
would also hear the man myself. Tomorrow, said he, thou shalt hear him.●

2. FORMAL PRESENTATION

23 And on the morrow, when Agrip'pa
was come, and Bernice, with great pomp,
and was entered into the place of hearing,
with the chief captains, and principal men
of the city, at Festus' commandment Paul
was brought forth. 24 And Festus said,
King Agrip'pa, and all men which are
here present with us, ye see this man,
about whom all the multitude of the Jews
have dealt with me, both at Jerusalem,
and *also* here, crying that he ought not to
live any longer. 25 But when I found that
he had committed nothing worthy of
death, and that he himself hath appealed
to Augustus, I have determined to send
him. 26 Of whom I have no certain thing
to write unto my lord. Wherefore I have
brought him forth before you, and specially before thee, O king Agrip'pa, that,
after examination had, I might have somewhat to write. 27 For it seemeth to me
unreasonable to send a prisoner, and not
withal to signify the crimes *laid* against
him.●

SEEKING JUSTICE

King Agrippa, a ruler of regions in North Palestine, was visiting Festus at this time. Festus hoped Agrippa would help him compose a letter to Caesar, referring Paul for trial. Festus' problem had been that he was not convinced of any guilt by Paul.

*25:13-22* What one reference to Jesus does Festus make?

______________________________

______________________________

From the way Festus spoke of this, what do you think were his own beliefs?

______________________________

______________________________

______________________________

______________________________

What was Agrippa's reaction to Festus' summary of the case?

______________________________

______________________________

______________________________

*25:23-27* List the ones who were present at this occasion.

______________________________

______________________________

______________________________

______________________________

______________________________

______________________________

What is your impression of the occasion?

______________________________

______________________________

______________________________

______________________________

______________________________

______________________________

______________________________

______________________________

NEW INTERNATIONAL VERSION

What does this passage teach about:

RELIGION

SELF-RIGHTEOUSNESS

ZEAL

RESURRECTION HOPE

CONVERSION

MINISTRY OF THE GOSPEL

FORGIVENESS OF SINS

OTHER

26 Then Agrippa said to Paul, "You
have permission to speak for yourself."
So Paul motioned with his hand and began his defense: 2"King Agrippa, I consider myself fortunate to stand before you
today as I make my defense against all the
accusations of the Jews, 3and especially so
because you are well acquainted with all
the Jewish customs and controversies.
Therefore, I beg you to listen to me patiently.●
4"The Jews all know the way I have
lived ever since I was a child, from the
beginning of my life in my own country,
and also in Jerusalem. 5They have known
me for a long time and can testify, if they
are willing, that according to the strictest
sect of our religion, I lived as a Pharisee.
6And now it is because of my hope in what
God has promised our fathers that I am on
trial today. 7This is the promise our twelve
tribes are hoping to see fulfilled as they
earnestly serve God day and night. O king,
it is because of this hope that the Jews are
accusing me. 8Why should any of you consider it incredible that God raises the dead?●
9"I too was convinced that I ought to do
all that was possible to oppose the name of
Jesus of Nazareth. 10And that is just what
I did in Jerusalem. On the authority of the
chief priests I put many of the saints in
prison, and when they were put to death,
I cast my vote against them. 11Many a time
I went from one synagogue to another to
have them punished, and I tried to force
them to blaspheme. In my obsession
against them, I even went to foreign cities
to persecute them.●
12"On one of these journeys I was going
to Damascus with the authority and commission of the chief priests. 13About noon,
O king, as I was on the road, I saw a light
from heaven, brighter than the sun, blazing
around me and my companions. 14We all
fell to the ground, and I heard a voice saying to me in Aramaic,[a] 'Saul, Saul, why do
you persecute me? It is hard for you to kick
against the goads.'
15"Then I asked, 'Who are you, Lord?'
"'I am Jesus, whom you are persecuting,' the Lord replied. 16'Now get up and
stand on your feet. I have appeared to you
to appoint you as a servant and as a witness
of what you have seen of me and what I will
show you. 17I will rescue you from your
own people and from the Gentiles. I am
sending you 18to open their eyes and turn
them from darkness to light, and from the
power of Satan to God, so that they may
receive forgiveness of sins and a place
among those who are sanctified by faith in
me.'●

[a]14 Or *Hebrew*

KING JAMES

-salutation-

**26** Then Agrip'pa said unto Paul, Thou
art permitted to speak for thyself.
Then Paul stretched forth the hand, and
answered for himself:
2 I think myself happy, king Agrip'pa,
because I shall answer for myself this day
before thee touching all the things whereof I am accused of the Jews: 3 especially
*because I know* thee to be expert in all customs and questions which are among the
Jews: wherefore I beseech thee to hear me
patiently.●

1. PAUL THE PHARISEE

RELIGIOUS

4 My manner of life from my youth,
which was at the first among mine own
nation at Jerusalem, know all the Jews;
5 which knew me from the beginning, if
they would testify, that after the most
straitest sect of our religion I lived a Pharisee. 6 And now I stand and am judged
for the hope of the promise made of God
unto our fathers: 7 unto which *promise*
our twelve tribes, instantly serving *God*
day and night, hope to come. For which
hope's sake, king Agrip'pa, I am accused
of the Jews. 8 Why should it be thought
a thing incredible with you, that God
should raise the dead?●

2. PAUL THE PERSECUTOR

9 I verily thought with myself, that I
ought to do many things contrary to the
name of Jesus of Nazareth. 10 Which
thing I also did in Jerusalem: and many
of the saints did I shut up in prison, having received authority from the chief
priests; and when they were put to death,
I gave my voice against *them.* 11 And I
punished them oft in every synagogue,
and compelled *them* to blaspheme; and
being exceedingly mad against them,
I persecuted *them* even unto strange
cities. ●

3. THE NEW PAUL

12 Whereupon as I went to Damascus
with authority and commission from the
chief priests, 13 at midday, O king, I saw
in the way a light from heaven, above the
brightness of the sun, shining round about
me and them which journeyed with me.
14 And when we were all fallen to the
earth, I heard a voice speaking unto me,
and saying in the Hebrew tongue, Saul,
Saul, why persecutest thou me? *it is* hard
for thee to kick against the pricks. 15 And
I said, Who art thou, Lord? And he said,
I am Jesus whom thou persecutest.
16 But rise, and stand upon thy feet: for I
have appeared unto thee for this purpose,
to make thee a minister and a witness
both of these things which thou hast seen,
and of those things in the which I will
appear unto thee; 17 delivering thee from
the people, and *from* the Gentiles, unto
whom now I send thee, 18 to open their
eyes, *and* to turn *them* from darkness to
light, and *from* the power of Satan unto
God, that they may receive forgiveness
of sins, and inheritance among them
which are sanctified by faith that is in
me.●

FORGIVEN

*26:1-3* Why does Paul say these things at this time?

*26:4-8* What does Paul say of himself in verse 5?

*26:9-11* What verbs did Paul use to describe this part of his life?

*26:12-18* Record your observations of these two parts:

VISION (vv.12-15)

COMMISSION (vv.16-18)

NEW INTERNATIONAL VERSION

What do you learn here about:

OBEDIENCE

REPENTANCE

GOD'S HELP

CHRISTIAN WITNESS

CHRIST'S MISSION

GOSPEL TO GENTILES

SAVING FAITH

OTHER

19"So then, King Agrippa, I was not
disobedient to the vision from heaven.
20First to those in Damascus, then to those
in Jerusalem and in all Judea, and to the
Gentiles also, I preached that they should
repent and turn to God and prove their
repentance by their deeds. 21That is why
the Jews seized me in the temple courts
and tried to kill me. 22But I have had God's
help to this very day, and so I stand here
and testify to small and great alike. I am
saying nothing beyond what the prophets
and Moses said would happen— 23that the
Christ[b] would suffer and, as the first to rise
from the dead, would proclaim light to his
own people and to the Gentiles."●

24At this point Festus interrupted Paul's
defense. "You are out of your mind,
Paul!" he shouted. "Your great learning is
driving you insane."

25"I am not insane, most excellent Festus," Paul replied. "What I am saying is
true and reasonable. 26The king is familiar
with these things, and I can speak freely to
him. I am convinced that none of this has
escaped his notice, because it was not done
in a corner.● 27King Agrippa, do you believe
the prophets? I know you do."

28Then Agrippa said to Paul, "Do you
think that in such a short time you can
persuade me to be a Christian?"

29Paul replied, "Short time or long—I
pray God that not only you but all who are
listening to me today may become what I
am, except for these chains."●

30The king rose, and with him the governor and Bernice and those sitting with
them. 31They left the room, and while talking with one another, they said, "This man
is not doing anything that deserves death
or imprisonment."

32Agrippa said to Festus, "This man
could have been set free, if he had not
appealed to Caesar."●

[b]23 Or *Messiah*

KING JAMES

**1. PAUL'S OBEDIENCE TO THE VISION**

OBEDIENT

19 Whereupon, O king Agrip'pa, I was
not disobedient unto the heavenly vision:
20 but showed first unto them of Damascus, and at Jerusalem, and throughout
all the coasts of Judea, and *then* to the
Gentiles, that they should repent and turn
to God, and do works meet for repentance. 21 For these causes the Jews
caught me in the temple, and went about
to kill *me*. 22 Having therefore obtained
help of God, I continue unto this day,
witnessing both to small and great, saying
none other things than those which the
prophets and Moses did say should come:
23 that Christ should suffer, *and* that
he should be the first that should
rise from the dead, and should show
light unto the people, and to the Gentiles. ●

**2. FESTUS REACTS**

24 And as he thus spake for himself,
Festus said with a loud voice, Paul, thou
art beside thyself; much learning doth
make thee mad. 25 But he said, I am not
mad, most noble Festus; but speak forth
the words of truth and soberness. 26 For
the king knoweth of these things, before
whom also I speak freely: for I am persuaded that none of these things are hidden from him; for this thing was not done
in a corner. ●

**3. AGRIPPA REACTS**

27 King Agrip'pa, believest
thou the prophets? I know that thou believest. 28 Then Agrip'pa said unto Paul,
Almost thou persuadest me to be a
Christian. 29 And Paul said, I would to
God, that not only thou, but also all that
hear me this day, were both almost, and
altogether such as I am, except these
bonds. ●

**4. DECISION**

30 And when he had thus spoken, the
king rose up, and the governor, and
Bernice, and they that sat with them:
31 and when they were gone aside, they
talked between themselves, saying, This
man doeth nothing worthy of death or of
bonds. 32 Then said Agrip'pa unto
Festus, This man might have been set at
liberty, if he had not appealed unto
Caesar. ●

NOT GUILTY

The first paragraph of this segment concludes Paul's defense. The next paragraphs show the reactions of the rulers.

*26:19-23* Paul was obedient to the Lord's commission to witness to the world. What was his message:

v.20 ______

v.23 ______

*26:24-26*

FESTUS: ______

PAUL: ______

*26:27-29*

AGRIPPA: ______

PAUL: ______

*26:30-32* What did the rulers conclude?

______

NEW INTERNATIONAL VERSION

What do you learn from this passage about:

FRIENDS

THE MAN PAUL

FULFILLED PROPHECY

NATURAL ELEMENTS

List some spiritual lessons of the passage:

*Paul Sails for Rome*

27 When it was decided that we would
sail for Italy, Paul and some other
prisoners were handed over to a centurion
named Julius, who belonged to the Imperi-
al Regiment. 2We boarded a ship from
Adramyttium about to sail for ports along
the coast of the province of Asia, and we
put out to sea. Aristarchus, a Macedonian
from Thessalonica, was with us.
3The next day we landed at Sidon; and
Julius, in kindness to Paul, allowed him to
go to his friends so they might provide for
his needs. 4From there we put out to sea
again and passed to the lee of Cyprus because the winds were against us. 5When we
had sailed across the open sea off the coast
of Cilicia and Pamphylia, we landed at
Myra in Lycia. 6There the centurion found
an Alexandrian ship sailing for Italy and
put us on board. 7We made slow headway
for many days and had difficulty arriving
off Cnidus. When the wind did not allow us
to hold our course, we sailed to the lee of
Crete, opposite Salmone. 8We moved
along the coast with difficulty and came to
a place called Fair Havens, near the town
of Lasea.●
9Much time had been lost, and sailing
had already become dangerous because by
now it was after the Fast.[a] So Paul warned
them, 10"Men, I can see that our voyage is
going to be disastrous and bring great loss
to ship and cargo, and to our own lives
also." 11But the centurion, instead of listening to what Paul said, followed the advice of the pilot and of the owner of the
ship. 12Since the harbor was unsuitable to
winter in, the majority decided that we
should sail on, hoping to reach Phoenix
and winter there. This was a harbor in
Crete, facing both southwest and northwest.●

*The Storm*

13When a gentle south wind began to
blow, they thought they had obtained what
they wanted; so they weighed anchor and
sailed along the shore of Crete. 14Before
very long, a wind of hurricane force, called
the "Northeaster," swept down from the
island. 15The ship was caught by the storm
and could not head into the wind; so we
gave way to it and were driven along. 16As
we passed to the lee of a small island called
Cauda, we were hardly able to make the
lifeboat secure. 17When the men had hoisted it aboard, they passed ropes under the
ship itself to hold it together. Fearing that
they would run aground on the sandbars of
Syrtis, they lowered the sea anchor and let
the ship be driven along. 18We took such a
violent battering from the storm that the
next day they began to throw the cargo
overboard. 19On the third day, they threw
the ship's tackle overboard with their own
hands. 20When neither sun nor stars appeared for many days and the storm continued raging, we finally gave up all hope
of being saved.●

[a]9 That is, the Day of Atonement (Yom Kippur)

KING JAMES

1. CAESAREA TO FAIR HAVENS

**27** And when it was determined that we should sail into Italy, they delivered Paul and certain other prisoners unto *one* named Julius, a centurion of Augustus' band. 2 And entering into a ship of Adramyt'ti-um, we launched, meaning to sail by the coasts of Asia; *one* Aristar'chus, a Macedo'nian of Thessaloni'ca, being with us. 3 And the next *day* we touched at Sidon. And Julius courteously entreated Paul, and gave *him* liberty to go unto his friends to refresh himself. 4 And when we had launched from thence, we sailed under Cyprus, because the winds were contrary. 5 And when we had sailed over the sea of Cili'cia and Pamphyl'i-a, we came to Myra, *a city* of Ly'ci-a. 6 And there the centurion found a ship of Alexandria sailing into Italy; and he put us therein. 7 And when we had sailed slowly many days, and scarce were come over against Cnidus, the wind not suffering us, we sailed under Crete, over against Salmo'ne; 8 and, hardly passing it, came unto a place which is called the Fair Havens; nigh whereunto was the city *of* Lase'a.●

2. PAUL'S ADVICE

9 Now when much time was spent, and when sailing was now dangerous, because the fast was now already past, Paul admonished *them*, 10 and said unto them, Sirs, I perceive that this voyage will be with hurt and much damage, not only of the lading and ship, but also of our lives. 11 Nevertheless the centurion believed the master and the owner of the ship, more than those things which were spoken by Paul. 12 And because the haven was not commodious to winter in, the more part advised to depart thence also, if by any means they might attain to Phoenix, *and there* to winter; *which is* a haven of Crete, and lieth toward the southwest and northwest.●

3. STORM

13 And when the south wind blew softly, supposing that they had obtained *their* purpose, loosing *thence*, they sailed close by Crete. 14 But not long after there arose against it a tempestuous wind, called Euroc'lydon. 15 And when the ship was caught, and could not bear up into the wind, we let *her* drive. 16 And running under a certain island which is called Clauda, we had much work to come by the boat: 17 which when they had taken up, they used helps, undergirding the ship; and, fearing lest they should fall into the quicksands, struck sail, and so were driven. 18 And we being exceedingly tossed with a tempest, the next *day* they lightened the ship; 19 and the third *day* we cast out with our own hands the tackling of the ship. 20 And when neither sun nor stars in many days appeared, and no small tempest lay on *us*, all hope that we should be saved was then taken away.●

PEACEFUL BEGINNING

STORM

This segment begins the story of Paul's voyage to Rome. Read the following references in Acts to the apostle's going to Rome. Record the words and who speaks the words:

19:21 ______

23:11 ______

25:12 ______

27:24 ______

28:14 ______

Record the main parts of the voyage in each of the paragraphs.

*27:1-8* ______

*27:9-12* ______

*27:13-20* ______

NEW INTERNATIONAL VERSION

What do you learn from this passage about:

ANGELS

GOD'S PROTECTION

FAITH

THANKSGIVING

PROPHECY

OTHER

21 After the men had gone a long time
without food, Paul stood up before them
and said: "Men, you should have taken my
advice not to sail from Crete; then you
would have spared yourselves this damage
and loss. 22 But now I urge you to keep up
your courage, because not one of you will
be lost; only the ship will be destroyed.
23 Last night an angel of the God whose I am
and whom I serve stood beside me 24 and
said, 'Do not be afraid, Paul. You must
stand trial before Caesar; and God has graciously given you the lives of all who sail
with you.' 25 So keep up your courage,
men, for I have faith in God that it will
happen just as he told me. 26 Nevertheless,
we must run aground on some island." ●

*The Shipwreck*

27 On the fourteenth night we were still
being driven across the Adriatic[b] Sea,
when about midnight the sailors sensed
they were approaching land. 28 They took
soundings and found that the water was a
hundred and twenty feet[c] deep. A short
time later they took soundings again and
found it was ninety feet[d] deep. 29 Fearing
that we would be dashed against the rocks,
they dropped four anchors from the stern
and prayed for daylight. 30 In an attempt to
escape from the ship, the sailors let the
lifeboat down into the sea, pretending they
were going to lower some anchors from the
bow. 31 Then Paul said to the centurion and
the soldiers, "Unless these men stay with
the ship, you cannot be saved." 32 So the
soldiers cut the ropes that held the lifeboat
and let it fall away. ●

33 Just before dawn Paul urged them all to
eat. "For the last fourteen days," he said,
"you have been in constant suspense and
have gone without food—you haven't eat-
en anything. 34 Now I urge you to take some
food. You need it to survive. Not one of
you will lose a single hair from his head."
35 After he said this, he took some bread
and gave thanks to God in front of them all.
Then he broke it and began to eat. 36 They
were all encouraged and ate some food
themselves. 37 Altogether there were 276 of
us on board. 38 When they had eaten as
much as they wanted, they lightened the
ship by throwing the grain into the sea. ●

39 When daylight came, they did not
recognize the land, but they saw a bay with
a sandy beach, where they decided to run
the ship aground if they could. 40 Cutting
loose the anchors, they left them in the sea
and at the same time untied the ropes that
held the rudders. Then they hoisted the
foresail to the wind and made for the
beach. 41 But the ship struck a sandbar and
ran aground. The bow stuck fast and would
not move, and the stern was broken to
pieces by the pounding of the surf.

42 The soldiers planned to kill the prisoners to prevent any of them from swimming
away and escaping. 43 But the centurion
wanted to spare Paul's life and kept them
from carrying out their plan. He ordered
those who could swim to jump overboard
first and get to land. 44 The rest were to get
there on planks or on pieces of the ship. In
this way everyone reached land in safety. ●

[b]*27* In ancient times the name referred to an area extending well south of Italy.
[c]*28* Greek *twenty orguias* (about 37 meters)
[d]*28* Greek *fifteen orguias* (about 27 meters)

KING JAMES

1. PAUL'S PROPHECIES

ALL WILL SURVIVE

21 But after long abstinence, Paul stood
forth in the midst of them, and said, Sirs,
ye should have hearkened unto me, and
not have loosed from Crete, and to have
gained this harm and loss. 22 And now I
exhort you to be of good cheer: for there
shall be no loss of *any man's* life among
you, but of the ship. 23 For there stood
by me this night the angel of God, whose
I am, and whom I serve, 24 saying, Fear
not, Paul; thou must be brought before
Caesar: and, lo, God hath given thee all
them that sail with thee. 25 Wherefore,
sirs, be of good cheer: for I believe God,
that it shall be even as it was told me.
26 Howbeit we must be cast upon a certain island.●

2. APPROACHING LAND

27 But when the fourteenth night was
come, as we were driven up and down in
A'dria, about midnight the shipmen
deemed that they drew near to some
country; 28 and sounded, and found *it*
twenty fathoms: and when they had gone
a little further, they sounded again, and
found *it* fifteen fathoms. 29 Then fearing
lest we should have fallen upon rocks,
they cast four anchors out of the stern,
and wished for the day. 30 And as the
shipmen were about to flee out of the ship,
when they had let down the boat into the
sea, under color as though they would
have cast anchors out of the foreship,
31 Paul said to the centurion and to the
soldiers, Except these abide in the ship, ye
cannot be saved. 32 Then the soldiers cut
off the ropes of the boat, and let her fall
off.●

3. FOOD FOR ALL

33 And while the day was coming on,
Paul besought *them* all to take meat, saying, This day is the fourteenth day that ye
have tarried and continued fasting, having
taken nothing. 34 Wherefore I pray you
to take *some* meat; for this is for your
health: for there shall not a hair fall from
the head of any of you. 35 And when he
had thus spoken, he took bread, and gave
thanks to God in presence of them all;
and when he had broken *it*, he began to
eat. 36 Then were they all of good cheer,
and they also took *some* meat. 37 And
we were in all in the ship two hundred
threescore and sixteen souls. 38 And
when they had eaten enough, they lightened the ship, and cast out the wheat into
the sea.●

4. ARRIVAL AT LAND

39 And when it was day, they knew not
the land: but they discovered a certain
creek with a shore, into the which they
were minded, if it were possible, to thrust
in the ship. 40 And when they had taken
up the anchors, they committed *themselves* unto the sea, and loosed the rudder
bands, and hoisted up the mainsail to the
wind, and made toward shore. 41 And
falling into a place where two seas met,
they ran the ship aground; and the forepart stuck fast, and remained unmovable,
but the hinder part was broken with the
violence of the waves. 42 And the soldiers' counsel was to kill the prisoners,
lest any of them should swim out, and
escape. 43 But the centurion, willing to
save Paul, kept them from *their* purpose;
and commanded that they which could
swim should cast *themselves* first *into the sea*, and get to land:
44 and the rest,
some on boards, and some on *broken pieces* of the ship. And so it came
to pass, that they escaped all safe to
land.●

ALL DO SURVIVE

Most of this passage records details of Paul's voyvoyage from Clauda to Melita. In which paragraphs are words of Paul reported?

___

___

For each paragraph record your observations of the main items, especially the words of Paul.

*27:21-26* ___

*27:27-32* ___

*27:33-38* ___

*27:39-44* What phrases in verses 43 and 44 are key phrases of the story?

v.43 ___

v.44 ___

NEW INTERNATIONAL VERSION

What do you learn here about:

KINDNESS

MIRACLES

IDOLATRY

CHRISTIAN FELLOWSHIP

List some spiritual applications of the passage.

*Ashore on Malta*

28 Once safely on shore, we found out
that the island was called Malta.
2The islanders showed us unusual kindness. They built a fire and welcomed us all
because it was raining and cold. 3Paul gathered a pile of brushwood and, as he put it
on the fire, a viper, driven out by the heat,
fastened itself on his hand. 4When the islanders saw the snake hanging from his
hand, they said to each other, "This man
must be a murderer; for though he escaped
from the sea, Justice has not allowed him
to live." 5But Paul shook the snake off into
the fire and suffered no ill effects. 6The
people expected him to swell up or suddenly fall over dead, but after waiting a long
time and seeing nothing unusual happen to
him, they changed their minds and said he
was a god.●
7There was an estate nearby that belonged to Publius, the chief official of the
island. He welcomed us to his home and
for three days entertained us hospitably.
8His father was sick in bed, suffering from
fever and dysentery. Paul went in to see
him and, after prayer, placed his hands on
him and healed him. 9When this had happened, the rest of the sick on the island
came and were cured. 10They honored us
in many ways and when we were ready to
sail, they furnished us with the supplies we
needed.●

*Arrival at Rome*

11After three months we put out to sea in
a ship that had wintered in the island. It
was an Alexandrian ship with the figure-
head of the twin gods Castor and Pollux.
12We put in at Syracuse and stayed there
three days. 13From there we set sail and
arrived at Rhegium. The next day the south
wind came up, and on the following day we
reached Puteoli. 14There we found some
brothers who invited us to spend a week
with them. ●

## KING JAMES

**1. PAUL SURVIVES SNAKE BITE**

**FRIENDLY BARBARIANS**

28 And when they were escaped, then
they knew that the island was called
Meli'ta. 2 And the barbarous people
showed us no little kindness: for they
kindled a fire, and received us every one,
because of the present rain, and because
of the cold. 3 And when Paul had gathered
a bundle of sticks, and laid *them* on the
fire, there came a viper out of the heat,
and fastened on his hand. 4 And when
the barbarians saw the *venomous* beast
hang on his hand, they said among themselves, No doubt this man is a murderer,
whom, though he hath escaped the sea,
yet vengeance suffereth not to live. 5 And
he shook off the beast into the fire, and
felt no harm. 6 Howbeit they looked
when he should have swollen, or fallen
down dead suddenly: but after they had
looked a great while, and saw no harm
come to him, they changed their minds,
and said that he was a god.●

**2. PAUL HEALS A MAN**

7 In the same quarters were possessions
of the chief man of the island, whose
name was Pub'li-us; who received us, and
lodged us three days courteously. 8 And
it came to pass, that the father of Pub'li-us
lay sick of a fever and of a bloody flux:
to whom Paul entered in, and prayed, and
laid his hands on him, and healed him.
9 So when this was done, others also,
which had diseases in the island, came,
and were healed: 10 who also honored us
with many honors; and when we departed,
they laded *us* with such things as were
necessary.●

**3. SAILING ON TO ROME**

11 And after three months we departed
in a ship of Alexandria, which had wintered in the isle, whose sign was Castor
and Pollux. 12 And landing at Syracuse,
we tarried *there* three days. 13 And from
thence we fetched a compass, and came
to Rhe'gi-um: and after one day the south
wind blew, and we came the next day to
Pute'oli: 14 where we found brethren,
and were desired to tarry with them seven
days:●

**FRIENDLY BRETHREN**

*28:1-6* Record these three different views and attitudes of natives in the course of this paragraph:

v.2 ______________________________

______________________________

______________________________

v.4 ______________________________

______________________________

______________________________

v.6 ______________________________

______________________________

______________________________

*28:7-10* Why do you think God brought about this miracle (and the one of the previous paragraph) at this time?

______________________________

______________________________

______________________________

What is the parallel paraphrase of the word "possessions"(v.7)?

______________________________

*28:11-14a* What is the warm and bright verse of this paragraph?

______________________________

What is the parallel paraphrase of the phrase "we fetched a compass"(v.13)?

______________________________

______________________________

______________________________

______________________________

______________________________

______________________________

______________________________

______________________________

______________________________

______________________________

______________________________

______________________________

NEW INTERNATIONAL VERSION

What does this concluding passage teach about:

PAUL

KINGDOM OF GOD

TEACHING THE WORD

GOSPEL TO NON-JEWS

BOLDNESS IN WITNESS

OTHER

And so we went to Rome. 15The
brothers there had heard that we were
coming, and they traveled as far as the
Forum of Appius and the Three Taverns to
meet us. At the sight of these men Paul
thanked God and was encouraged. 16When
we got to Rome, Paul was allowed to live
by himself, with a soldier to guard him. ●

*Paul Preaches at Rome Under Guard*

17Three days later he called together the
leaders of the Jews. When they had assembled, Paul said to them: "My brothers, although I have done nothing against our
people or against the customs of our ancestors, I was arrested in Jerusalem and handed over to the Romans. 18They examined
me and wanted to release me, because I
was not guilty of any crime deserving
death. 19But when the Jews objected, I was
compelled to appeal to Caesar—not that I
had any charge to bring against my own
people. 20For this reason I have asked to
see you and talk with you. It is because of
the hope of Israel that I am bound with this
chain."

21They replied, "We have not received
any letters from Judea concerning you, and
none of the brothers who has come from
there has reported or said anything bad
about you. 22But we want to hear what
your views are, for we know that people
everywhere are talking against this sect." ●

23They arranged to meet Paul on a certain day, and came in even larger numbers
to the place where he was staying. From
morning till evening he explained and declared to them the kingdom of God and
tried to convince them about Jesus from
the Law of Moses and from the Prophets.
24Some were convinced by what he said,
but others would not believe. ● 25They dis-
agreed among themselves and began to
leave after Paul had made this final
statement: "The Holy Spirit spoke the
truth to your forefathers when he said
through Isaiah the prophet:

26" 'Go to this people and say,
"You will be ever hearing but never
understanding;
you will be ever seeing but never
perceiving."
27For this people's heart has become
calloused;
they hardly hear with their ears,
and they have closed their eyes.
Otherwise they might see with their
eyes,
hear with their ears,
understand with their hearts
and turn and I would heal them.'[a]

28"Therefore I want you to know that
God's salvation has been sent to the Gentiles, and they will listen!"[b] ●

30For two whole years Paul stayed there
in his own rented house and welcomed all
who came to see him. 31Boldly and without
hindrance he preached the kingdom of God
and taught about the Lord Jesus Christ. ●

[a]27 Isaiah 6:9,10
[b]28 Some manuscripts *listen!"* 29*After he said this, the Jews left, arguing vigorously among themselves.*

KING JAMES

### 1. ARRIVAL AT ROME

ENCOURAGEMENT OF FELLOWSHIP

and so we went toward Rome.
15 And from thence, when the brethren
heard of us, they came to meet us as far
as Ap′pi-i Forum, and the Three Taverns;
whom when Paul saw, he thanked God,
and took courage. 16 And when we came
to Rome, the centurion delivered the
prisoners to the captain of the guard: but
Paul was suffered to dwell by himself with
a soldier that kept him.●

### 2. PAUL DEFENDS HIMSELF

17 And it came to pass, that after three
days Paul called the chief of the Jews together: and when they were come together, he said unto them, Men *and*
brethren, though I have committed nothing against the people, or customs of our
fathers, yet was I delivered prisoner from
Jerusalem into the hands of the Romans:
18 who, when they had examined me,
would have let *me* go, because there was
no cause of death in me. 19 But when the
Jews spake against *it*, I was constrained to
appeal unto Caesar; not that I had aught
to accuse my nation of. 20 For this cause
therefore have I called for you, to see *you*,
and to speak with *you*: because that for
the hope of Israel I am bound with this
chain. 21 And they said unto him, We
neither received letters out of Judea concerning thee, neither any of the brethren
that came showed or spake any harm of
thee. 22 But we desire to hear of thee
what thou thinkest: for as concerning this
sect, we know that every where it is spoken
against.●

### 3. PAUL PREACHES THE GOSPEL

23 And when they had appointed him a
day, there came many to him into *his*
lodging; to whom he expounded and testified the kingdom of God, persuading
them concerning Jesus, both out of the
law of Moses, and *out of* the prophets,
from morning till evening. 24 And some
believed the things which were spoken,
and some believed not.●

### 4. THE JEWS LEAVE

25And when they
agreed not among themselves, they departed, after that Paul had spoken one
word, Well spake the Holy Ghost by
Isaiah the prophet unto our fathers,
26 saying,

Isa. 6:9-10

Go unto this people, and say,
Hearing ye shall hear, and shall not
understand;
and seeing ye shall see, and not
perceive:
27 for the heart of this people is waxed
gross,
and their ears are dull of hearing,
and their eyes have they closed;
lest they should see with *their* eyes,
and hear with *their* ears,
and understand with *their* heart,
and should be converted, and I
should heal them.
28 Be it known therefore unto you, that
the salvation of God is sent unto the
Gentiles, and *that* they will hear it.
29 And when he had said these words, the
Jews departed, and had great reasoning
among themselves. ●

### 5. CONCLUSION

LIBERTY OF WITNESS

30 And Paul dwelt two whole years in
his own hired house, and received all that
came in unto him, 31 preaching the kingdom of God, and teaching those things
which concern the Lord Jesus Christ, with
all confidence, no man forbidding him.●

---

The book of Acts concludes with this passage. Read the whole segment with this in mind.

*28:14-16* Compare the first and last paragraphs as to Paul's situation:

*28:17-22* What is Paul saying here?

How does Paul use the phrase "the hope of Israel"?

*28:23-34* Note the reference to "kingdom of God.' How does the remainder of verse 23 expand on this subject?

*28:25-29* What was the one word (v.25)?

What does the Old Testament quotation teach?

*28:30-31* What words expand on the phrase, "kingdom of God"?

How appropriate is the last phrase, as a conclusion for Acts?

# ROMANS

## AUTHORSHIP

The apostle Paul was the author. Read 1:1. He sent this letter "to all that be in Rome, beloved of God, called to be saints" (1:7).

## DATE

Paul wrote Romans from Corinth toward the end of his third missionary journey, around A.D. 56.

## PURPOSE

The underlying purpose of the Epistle was to give instruction to the Christians at Rome regarding the basic truths of salvation and Christian living. This doctrinal and practical purpose has been fulfilled for readers ever since the letter was first penned.

## THEME

The central theme of Romans is the imparting of God's righteousness to the sinner who believes on the Lord Jesus Christ. Woven into this theme are such truths as: all people are sinners; sin brings eternal death; there is only one way of salvation; God is no respecter of persons; salvation is a gift of God; and the power of God is the source of all Christian living.

## ROMANS: God's Salvation for Sinners

| | |
|---|---|
| PROLOGUE | 1:1-17 |
| DOCTRINE | 1:18-11:36 |
| God's Holiness in Condemning Sin | 1:18-3:20 |
| God's Grace in Justifying Sinners | 3:21-5:21 |
| God's Power in Sanctifying Believers | 6:1-8:39 |
| God's Sovereignty in Saving Jew and Gentile | 9:1-11:36 |
| PRACTICE | 12:1-15:13 |
| The Christian Servant | 12:1-21 |
| The Christian Citizen | 13:1-14 |
| The Christian Brother | 14:1-15:13 |
| EPILOGUE | 15:14-16:27 |

# ROMANS

NEW INTERNATIONAL VERSION

Record what this passage teaches about:

A SERVANT OF JESUS

JESUS CHRIST

GRACE AND FAITH

PRAYER

LOVE

RIGHTEOUSNESS

List spiritual applications of the passage.

**1** Paul, a servant of Christ Jesus, called to be an apostle and set apart for the gospel of God— [2]the gospel he promised beforehand through his prophets in the Holy Scriptures [3]regarding his Son, who as to his human nature was a descendant of David, [4]and who through the Spirit[c] of holiness was declared with power to be the Son of God[d] by his resurrection from the dead: Jesus Christ our Lord. [5]Through him and for his name's sake, we received grace and apostleship to call people from among all the Gentiles to the obedience that comes from faith. [6]And you also are among those who are called to belong to Jesus Christ.

[7]To all in Rome who are loved by God and called to be saints:

Grace and peace to you from God our Father and from the Lord Jesus Christ.●

*Paul's Longing to Visit Rome*

[8]First, I thank my God through Jesus Christ for all of you, because your faith is being reported all over the world. [9]God, whom I serve with my whole heart in preaching the gospel of his Son, is my witness how constantly I remember you [10]in my prayers at all times; and I pray that now at last by God's will the way may be opened for me to come to you.

[11]I long to see you so that I may impart to you some spiritual gift to make you strong— [12]that is, that you and I may be mutually encouraged by each other's faith. [13]I do not want you to be unaware, brothers, that I planned many times to come to you (but have been prevented from doing so until now) in order that I might have a harvest among you, just as I have had among the other Gentiles.

[14]I am obligated both to Greeks and non-Greeks, both to the wise and the foolish. [15]That is why I am so eager to preach the gospel also to you who are at Rome.●

[16]I am not ashamed of the gospel, because it is the power of God for the salvation of everyone who believes: first for the Jew, then for the Gentile. [17]For in the gospel a righteousness from God is revealed, a righteousness that is by faith from first to last,[e] just as it is written: "The righteous will live by faith."[f]●

c4 Or *who as to his spirit*
d4 Or *was appointed to be the Son of God with power*
e17 Or *is from faith to faith*
f17 Hab. 2:4

KING JAMES

# ROMANS

1. PAUL THE SERVANT

GOSPEL OF GOD

1 Paul, a servant of Jesus Christ, called
*to be* an apostle, separated unto the
gospel of God, 2 (which he had promised
afore by his prophets in the holy Scriptures,) 3 concerning his Son Jesus Christ
our Lord, which was made of the seed of
David according to the flesh; 4 and declared *to be* the Son of God with power,
according to the Spirit of holiness, by the
resurrection from the dead: 5 by whom
we have received grace and apostleship, for obedience to the faith among
all nations, for his name: 6 among
whom are ye also the called of Jesus
Christ:
7 To all that be in Rome, beloved of
God, called *to be* saints:
Grace to you, and peace, from God our
Father and the Lord Jesus Christ.●

2. PAUL THE DEBTOR

GOSPEL OF HIS SON

8 First, I thank my God through Jesus
Christ for you all, that your faith is spoken
of throughout the whole world. 9 For
God is my witness, whom I serve with my
spirit in the gospel of his Son, that without ceasing I make mention of you always
in my prayers; 10 making request, if by
any means now at length I might have a
prosperous journey by the will of God to
come unto you. 11 For I long to see you,
that I may impart unto you some spiritual
gift, to the end ye may be established;
12 that is, that I may be comforted together with you by the mutual faith both
of you and me. 13 Now I would not have
you ignorant, brethren, that oftentimes I
purposed to come unto you, (but was
let hitherto,) that I might have some fruit
among you also, even as among other
Gentiles. 14 I am debtor both to the
Greeks, and to the Barbarians; both to
the wise, and to the unwise. 15 So, as
much as in me is, I am ready to preach
the gospel to you that are at Rome
also.●

3. PAUL UNASHAMED

GOSPEL OF CHRIST

16 For I am not ashamed of the gospel
of Christ: for it is the power of God unto
salvation to every one that believeth; to
the Jew first, and also to the Greek. 17 For
therein is the righteousness of God revealed from faith to faith: as it is written,
The just shall live by faith.●

Hab. 2:4

The epistle to the Romans teaches the ABC's of the gospel. A suggested title for the book is GOD'S SALVATION FOR SINNERS. Key verses of the book appear in this opening salutation: verses 16-17.

*1:1-7* Record what is revealed in this salutation about:

PAUL: ______

______

______

GOSPEL: ______

______

______

JESUS: ______

______

______

*1:8-15* Record Paul's many statements beginning with "I".

______

______

______

______

______

______

______

______

______

*1:16-17* What are the many truths of these key verses?

______

______

______

______

______

______

______

______

______

NEW INTERNATIONAL VERSION

What do you learn here about:

UNRIGHTEOUSNESS

DIVINE LIGHT FOR THE SOUL

MERCY OF GOD

FREE WILL OF MAN

WRATH AND JUDGMENT OF GOD

*God's Wrath Against Mankind*

18The wrath of God is being revealed
from heaven against all the godlessness
and wickedness of men who suppress the
truth by their wickedness, 19since what
may be known about God is plain to them,
because God has made it plain to them.
20For since the creation of the world God's
invisible qualities—his eternal power and
divine nature—have been clearly seen, being understood from what has been made,
so that men are without excuse.
21For although they knew God, they
neither glorified him as God nor gave
thanks to him, but their thinking became
futile and their foolish hearts were darkened. 22Although they claimed to be wise,
they became fools 23and exchanged the glory of the immortal God for images made to
look like mortal man and birds and animals
and reptiles.●
24Therefore God gave them over in the
sinful desires of their hearts to sexual impurity for the degrading of their bodies
with one another. 25They exchanged the
truth of God for a lie, and worshiped and
served created things rather than the Creator—who is forever praised. Amen.●
26Because of this, God gave them over to
shameful lusts. Even their women exchanged natural relations for unnatural
ones. 27In the same way the men also abandoned natural relations with women and
were inflamed with lust for one another.
Men committed indecent acts with other
men, and received in themselves the due
penalty for their perversion.●
28Furthermore, since they did not think
it worthwhile to retain the knowledge of
God, he gave them over to a depraved
mind, to do what ought not to be done.
29They have become filled with every kind
of wickedness, evil, greed and depravity.
They are full of envy, murder, strife, deceit
and malice. They are gossips, 30slanderers,
God-haters, insolent, arrogant and boastful; they invent ways of doing evil; they
disobey their parents; 31they are senseless,
faithless, heartless, ruthless. 32Although
they know God's righteous decree that
those who do such things deserve death,
they not only continue to do these very
things but also approve of those who practice them.●

KING JAMES

1. GOD HATH REVEALED

WRATH OF GOD

18 For the wrath of God is revealed
from heaven against all ungodliness and
unrighteousness of men, who hold the
truth in unrighteousness; 19 because that
which may be known of God is manifest
in them; for God hath showed *it* unto
them. 20 For the invisible things of him
from the creation of the world are clearly
seen, being understood by the things that
are made, *even* his eternal power and Godhead; so that they are without excuse:
21 because that, when they knew God,
they glorified *him* not as God, neither
were thankful; but became vain in their
imaginations, and their foolish heart was
darkened. 22 Professing themselves to be
wise, they became fools, 23 and changed
the glory of the uncorruptible God into an
image made like to corruptible man, and
to birds, and four-footed beasts, and
creeping things.●

2. GOD GAVE THEM OVER

a.

24 Wherefore God also gave them up to
uncleanness, through the lusts of their
own hearts, to dishonor their own bodies
between themselves: 25 who changed the
truth of God into a lie, and worshipped
and served the creature more than
the Creator, who is blessed for ever.
Amen.●

b.

26 For this cause God gave them up
unto vile affections: for even their women
did change the natural use into that which
is against nature: 27 and likewise also the
men, leaving the natural use of the woman, burned in their lust one toward another; men with men working that which
is unseemly, and receiving in themselves
that recompense of their error which was
meet.●

c.

28 And even as they did not like to retain God in *their* knowledge, God gave
them over to a reprobate mind, to do those
things which are not convenient; 29 being
filled with all unrighteousness, fornication, wickedness, covetousness, maliciousness; full of envy, murder, debate, deceit,
malignity; whisperers, 30 backbiters,
haters of God, despiteful, proud, boasters,
inventors of evil things, disobedient to
parents, 31 without understanding, cov-
enant-breakers, without natural affection,
implacable, unmerciful: 32 who, knowing
the judgment of God, that they which
commit such things are worthy of death,
not only do the same, but have pleasure in
them that do them.●

JUDGMENT OF GOD

The first section (1:18—3:20) of this epistle of Salvation is about SIN because that brings on man's *need* for salvation.

________________

*1:18-23* Record what you observe: ________

LIGHT FROM GOD: ________

________________

________________

________________

________________

REJECTION OF THAT LIGHT: ________

________________

________________

________________

CONDEMNATION (v.18): ________

________________

________________

________________

In 1:24-32 Paul shows the recompense for the sinner's rejection of God's light. Complete the statements of each of the three paragraphs, and list the sins reproved.

*1:24-25* "God gave them up to" ________

________________

________________

________________

________________

*1:26-27* "God gave them up unto" ________

________________

________________

________________

*1:28-32* "God gave them over to" ________

________________

________________

________________

________________

________________

________________

NEW INTERNATIONAL VERSION

What does this passage teach about:

SELF-RIGHTEOUS MORALIST ______

JUDGMENT OF GOD ______

JUSTICE ______

GRACE OF GOD ______

REPENTANCE ______

SIN ______

LAW ______

OTHER ______

### *God's Righteous Judgment*

2 You, therefore, have no excuse, you
who pass judgment on someone else,
for at whatever point you judge the other,
you are condemning yourself, because you
who pass judgment do the same things.
2Now we know that God's judgment
against those who do such things is based
on truth. 3So when you, a mere man, pass
judgment on them and yet do the same
things, do you think you will escape God's
judgment? 4Or do you show contempt for
the riches of his kindness, tolerance and
patience, not realizing that God's kindness
leads you toward repentance?●
5But because of your stubbornness and
your unrepentant heart, you are storing up
wrath against yourself for the day of God's
wrath, when his righteous judgment will be
revealed. 6God "will give to each person
according to what he has done."[a] 7To
those who by persistence in doing good
seek glory, honor and immortality, he will
give eternal life. 8But for those who are
self-seeking and who reject the truth and
follow evil, there will be wrath and anger.
9There will be trouble and distress for
every human being who does evil: first for
the Jew, then for the Gentile; 10but glory,
honor and peace for everyone who does
good: first for the Jew, then for the Gentile.
11For God does not show favoritism.●
12All who sin apart from the law will also
perish apart from the law, and all who sin
under the law will be judged by the law.
13For it is not those who hear the law who
are righteous in God's sight, but it is those
who obey the law who will be declared
righteous. 14(Indeed, when Gentiles, who
do not have the law, do by nature things
required by the law, they are a law for
themselves, even though they do not have
the law, 15since they show that the requirements of the law are written on their
hearts, their consciences also bearing witness, and their thoughts now accusing,
now even defending them.) 16This will take
place on the day when God will judge
men's secrets through Jesus Christ, as my
gospel declares.●

[a]6 Psalm 62:12; Prov. 24:12

KING JAMES

1. JUDGMENT BY GOD

2. JUDGMENT ACCORDING TO DEEDS

3. JUDGMENT BY GOSPEL

**2** Therefore thou art inexcusable, O
man, whosoever thou art that judgest: for wherein thou judgest another,
thou condemnest thyself; for thou that
judgest doest the same things. 2 But we
are sure that the judgment of God is according to truth against them which commit such things. 3 And thinkest thou
this, O man, that judgest them which do
such things, and doest the same, that thou
shalt escape the judgment of God? 4 Or
despisest thou the riches of his goodness
and forbearance and long-suffering; not
knowing that the goodness of God leadeth thee to repentance?● 5 but, after thy
hardness and impenitent heart, treasurest
up unto thyself wrath against the day of
wrath and revelation of the righteous
judgment of God; 6 who will render to
every man according to his deeds: 7 to
them who by patient continuance in well
doing seek for glory and honor and immortality, eternal life: 8 but unto them
that are contentious, and do not obey the
truth, but obey unrighteousness, indignation and wrath, 9 tribulation and
anguish, upon every soul of man that
doeth evil; of the Jew first, and also of the
Gentile; 10 but glory, honor, and peace,
to every man that worketh good; to the
Jew first, and also to the Gentile: 11 for
there is no respect of persons with God.●
12 For as many as have sinned without
law shall also perish without law; and as
many as have sinned in the law shall be
judged by the law; 13 (for not the hearers of the law *are* just before God, but the
doers of the law shall be justified. 14 For
when the Gentiles, which have not the
law, do by nature the things contained in
the law, these, having not the law, are a
law unto themselves: 15 which show the
work of the law written in their hearts,
their conscience also bearing witness, and
*their* thoughts the mean while accusing or
else excusing one another;) 16 in the day
when God shall judge the secrets of men
by Jesus Christ according to my gospel.●

MAN JUDGING

GOD JUDGING

*2:1-4* Judgments by what two persons are compared here?

God's judgment is according to what?

What does verse 4 contribute to this paragraph?

*2:5-11* Verse 6 is a key to this paragraph. What does it teach?

Compare this with verse 11.

How does the paragraph illustrate the principle of verse 6?

*2:12-16* What is a key repeated word of the paragraph?

How are the written law and law of the heart compared?

According to verse 16 judgment is by what?

NEW INTERNATIONAL VERSION

What does this passage teach about:

THE JEWS AS A FAVORED PEOPLE ____________________

SIN ____________________

LAW OF GOD ____________________

DISOBEDIENCE ____________________

HYPOCRISY ____________________

RESPONSIBILITY ____________________

*The Jews and the Law*

17Now you, if you call yourself a Jew; if
you rely on the law and brag about your
relationship to God; 18if you know his will
and approve of what is superior because
you are instructed by the law; 19if you are
convinced that you are a guide for the
blind, a light for those who are in the dark,
20an instructor of the foolish, a teacher of
infants, because you have in the law the
embodiment of knowledge and truth—
21you, then, who teach others, do you not
teach yourself? You who preach against
stealing, do you steal? 22You who say that
people should not commit adultery, do you
commit adultery? You who abhor idols, do
you rob temples? 23You who brag about the
law, do you dishonor God by breaking the
law? 24As it is written: "God's name is
blasphemed among the Gentiles because of
you."[b] ●

25Circumcision has value if you observe
the law, but if you break the law, you have
become as though you had not been circumcised. 26If those who are not circumcised keep the law's requirements, will
they not be regarded as though they were
circumcised? 27The one who is not circumcised physically and yet obeys the law will
condemn you who, even though you have
the[c] written code and circumcision, are a
lawbreaker.

28A man is not a Jew if he is only one
outwardly, nor is circumcision merely outward and physical. 29No, a man is a Jew if
he is one inwardly; and circumcision is circumcision of the heart, by the Spirit, not by
the written code. Such a man's praise is not
from men, but from God. ●

*God's Faithfulness*

3 What advantage, then, is there in being
a Jew, or what value is there in circumcision? 2Much in every way! First of all,
they have been entrusted with the very
words of God.

3What if some did not have faith? Will
their lack of faith nullify God's faithfulness? 4Not at all! Let God be true, and
every man a liar. As it is written:

> "So that you may be proved right
> in your words
> and prevail in your judging."[a]

5But if our unrighteousness brings out
God's righteousness more clearly, what
shall we say? That God is unjust in bringing
his wrath on us? (I am using a human argument.) 6Certainly not! If that were so, how
could God judge the world? 7Someone
might argue, "If my falsehood enhances
God's truthfulness and so increases his
glory, why am I still condemned as a sinner?" 8Why not say—as we are being slanderously reported as saying and as some
claim that we say—"Let us do evil that
good may result"? Their condemnation is
deserved. ●

[b]24 Isaiah 52:5; Ezek. 36:22
[c]27 Or *who, by means of a*
[a]4 Psalm 51:4

KING JAMES

1. CONDEMNED FOR DISOBEDIENCE

JEWS FAVORED

17 Behold, thou art called a Jew, and
restest in the law, and makest thy boast of
God, 18 and knowest *his* will, and ap-
provest the things that are more excellent,
being instructed out of the law; 19 and
art confident that thou thyself art a guide
of the blind, a light of them which are in
darkness, 20 an instructor of the foolish,
a teacher of babes, which hast the form of
knowledge and of the truth in the law.
21 Thou therefore which teachest another,
teachest thou not thyself? thou that
preachest a man should not steal, dost
thou steal? 22 thou that sayest a man
should not commit adultery, dost thou
commit adultery? thou that abhorrest
idols, dost thou commit sacrilege?
23 thou that makest thy boast of the law,
through breaking the law dishonorest
thou God? 24 For the name of God is
blasphemed among the Gentiles through
you, as it is written.●

2. CONDEMNED FOR HYPOCRISY

25 For circumcision verily profiteth, if
thou keep the law: but if thou be a breaker
of the law, thy circumcision is made uncircumcision. 26 Therefore, if the uncircumcision keep the righteousness of the
law, shall not his uncircumcision be
counted for circumcision? 27 And shall
not uncircumcision which is by nature, if
it fulfil the law, judge thee, who by the
letter and circumcision dost transgress the
law? 28 For he is not a Jew, which is one
outwardly; neither *is that* circumcision,
which is outward in the flesh: 29 but he
*is* a Jew, which is one inwardly; and circumcision *is that* of the heart, in the spirit,
*and* not in the letter; whose praise *is* not
of men, but of God.●

3. CONDEMNED ABSOLUTELY

3 What advantage then hath the Jew?
or what profit *is there* of circumcision? 2 Much every way: chiefly, because that unto them were committed the
oracles of God. 3 For what if some did
not believe? shall their unbelief make the
faith of God without effect? 4 God forbid: yea, let God be true, but every man a
liar; as it is written,

> That thou mightest be justified in thy
> sayings,
> and mightest overcome when thou
> art judged.

Ps. 51:4

5 But if our unrighteousness commend the
righteousness of God, what shall we say?
*Is* God unrighteous who taketh vengeance? (I speak as a man) 6 God forbid:
for then how shall God judge the world?
7 For if the truth of God hath more
abounded through my lie unto his glory;
why yet am I also judged as a sinner?
8 and not *rather*, (as we be slanderously
reported, and as some affirm that we say,)
Let us do evil, that good may come?
whose damnation is just.●

BUT STILL SINFUL

*2:17-24* List the boasts and privileges of the Jews (vv.17-20):

_______________

What basic sin are such Jews guilty of (vv.21-23)?

_______________

*2:25-29* What is the repeated word of the paragraph?

_______________

What was the rite of circumcision? (v.28,LB) _______________

What is the Jews' sin of verses 28-29? _______________

*3:1-8* All Jews are judged by God according to His absolute principles of justice. How is this taught by the paragraph?

_______________

NEW INTERNATIONAL VERSION

What do you learn here about:

UNIVERSALITY OF SIN

RIGHTEOUSNESS

UNRIGHTEOUSNESS

LAW OF GOD

JUSTIFICATION

OTHER

*No One Is Righteous*

9What shall we conclude then? Are we
any better[b]? Not at all! We have already
made the charge that Jews and Gentiles
alike are all under sin. 10As it is written:

"There is no one righteous, not
even one;
11 there is no one who understands,
no one who seeks God.
12All have turned away,
they have together become
worthless;
there is no one who does good,
not even one."[c] ●
13"Their throats are open graves;
their tongues practice deceit."[d]
"The poison of vipers is on their
lips."[e]
14 "Their mouths are full of cursing
and bitterness."[f]
15"Their feet are swift to shed blood;●
16 ruin and misery mark their ways,
17and the way of peace they do not
know."[g]
18 "There is no fear of God before
their eyes."[h]

19Now we know that whatever the law
says, it says to those who are under the
law, so that every mouth may be silenced
and the whole world held accountable to
God. 20Therefore no one will be declared
righteous in his sight by observing the law;
rather, through the law we become conscious of sin.●

[b]9 Or *worse*
[c]12 Psalms 14:1-3; 53:1-3; Eccles. 7:20
[d]13 Psalm 5:9
[e]13 Psalm 140:3
[f]14 Psalm 10:7
[g]17 Isaiah 59:7,8
[h]18 Psalm 36:1

KING JAMES

1. UNIVERSALITY OF SIN

9 What then? are we better *than they?*
No, in no wise: for we have before proved
both Jews and Gentiles, that they are all
under sin; 10 as it is written,
There is none righteous, no, not
one:
11 there is none that understandeth,
there is none that seeketh after God.
12 They are all gone out of the way,
they are together become unprofitable;
there is none that doeth good, no, not
one.●

SIN

Ps. 14:1-3

2. DESCRIPTION OF SINNER

13 Their throat *is* an open sepulchre;
with their tongues they have used
deceit;
the poison of asps *is* under their
lips:
14 whose mouth *is* full of cursing and
bitterness:
15 their feet *are* swift to shed blood:
16 destruction and misery *are* in their
ways:
17 and the way of peace have they not
known:[f]
18 there is no fear of God before their
eyes.●

Ps. 5:9

Ps. 10:7
Isa. 59:7f.

Ps. 36:1

3. REVEALER OF SIN

19 Now we know that what things soever the law saith, it saith to them who are
under the law: that every mouth may be
stopped, and all the world may become
guilty before God. 20 Therefore by the
deeds of the law there shall no flesh be justified in his sight: for by the law *is* the
knowledge of sin.●

LAW

This segment is the summation of the case which Paul began describing at 1:18. Who are condemned in the text of these segments:

1:18-32 ______

2:1-16 ______

2:17—3:8 ______

Now how does Paul identify the ones under condemnation? (v.9)

*3:9-12* In what different ways does Paul teach that *all* are sinners?

*3:13-18* How are sinners described here?

*3:19-20* How does Paul here relate law and sin?

NEW INTERNATIONAL VERSION

Record definitions of each of these doctrinal words. (See the Living Bible paraphrases.)

JUSTIFICATION

REMISSION

REDEMPTION

PROPITIATION

What does this passage teach about:

RIGHTEOUSNESS OF GOD

SAVING FAITH

Record other teachings of the passage:

### *Righteousness Through Faith*

[21]But now a righteousness from God,
apart from law, has been made known, to
which the Law and the Prophets testify.
[22]This righteousness from God comes
through faith in Jesus Christ to all who
believe. There is no difference, [23]for all
have sinned and fall short of the glory of
God, [24]and are justified freely by his grace
through the redemption that came by
Christ Jesus. [25]God presented him as a sacrifice of atonement,[i] through faith in his
blood. He did this to demonstrate his
justice, because in his forbearance he had
left the sins committed beforehand unpun-
ished— [26]he did it to demonstrate his
justice at the present time, so as to be just
and the one who justifies the man who has
faith in Jesus.
[27]Where, then, is boasting? It is excluded. On what principle? On that of observing the law? No, but on that of faith.
[28]For we maintain that a man is justified by
faith apart from observing the law. [29]Is
God the God of Jews only? Is he not the
God of Gentiles too? Yes, of Gentiles too,
[30]since there is only one God, who will
justify the circumcised by faith and the uncircumcised through that same faith. [31]Do
we, then, nullify the law by this faith? Not
at all! Rather, we uphold the law.

[i]25 Or *as the one who would turn aside his wrath, taking away sin*

KING JAMES

1. RIGHTEOUSNESS BY FAITH

LAW APPLIED

21 But now the righteousness of God
without the law is manifested, being witnessed by the law and the prophets;
22 even the righteousness of God *which is*
by faith of Jesus Christ unto all and upon
all them that believe; for there is no difference: 23 for all have sinned, and come
short of the glory of God; 24 being justified freely by his grace through the redemption that is in Christ Jesus: ● 25 whom

2. PROPITIATION THROUGH FAITH

God hath set forth *to be* a propitiation
through faith in his blood, to declare his
righteousness for the remission of sins
that are past, through the forbearance of
God; 26 to declare, *I say*, at this time his
righteousness: that he might be just, and
the justifier of him which believeth in
Jesus. ●

3. JUSTIFIED BY FAITH

27 Where *is* boasting then? It is excluded. By what law? of works? Nay;
but by the law of faith. 28 Therefore we
conclude that a man is justified by faith
without the deeds of the law. 29 *Is he* the
God of the Jews only? *is he* not also of
the Gentiles? Yes, of the Gentiles also:
30 seeing *it is* one God, which shall justify the circumcision by faith, and uncircumcision through faith. 31 Do we
then make void the law through faith?
God forbid: yea, we establish the
law. ●

LAW ESTABLISHED

Paul now begins to write about the way to heaven—a way to get right with God—which God has revealed through His Son. The subject of the second section of Romans (3:21—5:21) is GOD'S GRACE IN JUSTIFYING SINNERS

*3:21-24* Record the strong doctrinal words of this paragraph:

How are those words related to each other in the paragraph?

*3:25-26* Record the strong doctrinal words of this paragraph:

What does the paragraph teach about:

GOD:

JESUS:

*3:27-31* What is the key repeated word of the paragraph?

What does Paul conclude from what he has written thus far (v.28)?

NEW INTERNATIONAL VERSION

What do you learn here about:

WORKS ____________________

SAVING FAITH ____________________

RELIGION ____________________

LAW ____________________

PROMISE OF GOD ____________________

OTHER ____________________

*Abraham Justified by Faith*

4 What then shall we say that Abraham,
our forefather, discovered in this matter? [2]If, in fact, Abraham was justified by
works, he had something to boast about—
but not before God. [3]What does the Scripture say? "Abraham believed God, and it
was credited to him as righteousness."[j]
[4]Now when a man works, his wages are
not credited to him as a gift, but as an
obligation. [5]However, to the man who
does not work but trusts God who justifies
the wicked, his faith is credited as righteousness. [6]David says the same thing when
he speaks of the blessedness of the man to
whom God credits righteousness apart
from works:

[7]"Blessed are they
whose transgressions are forgiven,
whose sins are covered.
[8]Blessed is the man
whose sin the Lord will never
count against him."[a] ●

[9]Is this blessedness only for the circumcised, or also for the uncircumcised? We
have been saying that Abraham's faith was
credited to him as righteousness. [10]Under
what circumstances was it credited? Was it
after he was circumcised, or before? It was
not after, but before! [11]And he received the
sign of circumcision, a seal of the righteousness that he had by faith while he was
still uncircumcised. So then, he is the father of all who believe but have not been
circumcised, in order that righteousness
might be credited to them. [12]And he is also
the father of the circumcised who not only
are circumcised but who also walk in the
footsteps of the faith that our father Abraham had before he was circumcised. ●
[13]It was not through law that Abraham
and his offspring received the promise that
he would be heir of the world, but through
the righteousness that comes by faith.
[14]For if those who live by law are heirs,
faith has no value and the promise is worthless, [15]because law brings wrath. And
where there is no law there is no transgression. ●

[j]3 Gen. 15:6; also in verse 22
[a]8 Psalm 32:1,2

KING JAMES

1. APART FROM WORKS

FATHER OF ISRAEL

4 What shall we say then that Abraham
our father, as pertaining to the flesh,
hath found? 2 For if Abraham were justified by works, he hath *whereof* to glory;
but not before God. 3 For what saith the
Scripture? Abraham believed God, and
it was counted unto him for righteousness. 4 Now to him that worketh is the
reward not reckoned of grace, but of debt.
5 But to him that worketh not, but believeth on him that justifieth the ungodly,
his faith is counted for righteousness.
6 Even as David also describeth the
blessedness of the man, unto whom God
imputeth righteousness without works,
7 *saying*,

Ps. 32:1-2

Blessed *are* they whose iniquities are
forgiven, and whose sins are
covered.
8 Blessed *is* the man to whom the Lord
will not impute sin.●

2. APART FROM RELIGION

9 *Cometh* this blessedness then upon the
circumcision *only*, or upon the uncircumcision also? for we say that faith was
reckoned to Abraham for righteousness.
10 How was it then reckoned? when he
was in circumcision, or in uncircumcision?
Not in circumcision, but in uncircumcision. 11 And he received the sign of circumcision, a seal of the righteousness of
the faith which *he had yet* being uncircumcised: that he might be the father of
all them that believe, though they be not
circumcised; that righteousness might be
imputed unto them also: 12 and the
father of circumcision to them who are
not of the circumcision only, but who also
walk in the steps of that faith of our father
Abraham, which *he had* being *yet* uncircumcised.●

3. APART FROM THE LAW

13 For the promise, that he should be
the heir of the world, *was* not to Abraham, or to his seed, through the law, but
through the righteousness of faith. 14 For
if they which are of the law *be* heirs, faith
is made void, and the promise made of
none effect: 15 because the law worketh
wrath: for where no law is, *there is* no
transgression.●

HEIR OF THE WORLD

In this segment Paul uses Abraham as an illustration of the doctrine of justification. Underline all the appearances of the name Abraham in the text.

*4:1-8* Record the different ways WORKS and FAITH are compared.

What does the word "impute" mean (v.8)? (See Living Bible)

*4:9-12* Circumcision was a religious rite of the nation of Israel. Uncircumcision identifies non-Jews. How does the paragraph illustrate that *religion* does not justify a sinner?

*4:13-15* Observe the repeated word "law." What does this paragraph teach from the life of Abraham?

NEW INTERNATIONAL VERSION

What does this passage teach about:

SAVING FAITH

GRACE

HOPE

UNIVERSAL GOSPEL

IMPUTATION

JUSTIFICATION

OTHER

[16]Therefore, the promise comes by faith,
so that it may be by grace and may be
guaranteed to all Abraham's offspring—
not only to those who are of the law but
also to those who are of the faith of Abraham. He is the father of us all. [17]As it is
written: "I have made you a father of many
nations."[b] He is our father in the sight of
God, in whom he believed—the God who
gives life to the dead and calls things that
are not as though they were.●
[18]Against all hope, Abraham in hope believed and so became the father of many
nations, just as it had been said to him, "So
shall your offspring be."[c] [19]Without weak-
ening in his faith, he faced the fact that his
body was as good as dead—since he was
about a hundred years old—and that Sarah's womb was also dead. [20]Yet he did not
waver through unbelief regarding the
promise of God, but was strengthened in
his faith and gave glory to God, [21]being
fully persuaded that God had power to do
what he had promised. [22]This is why "it
was credited to him as righteousness."●
[23]The words "it was credited to him" were
written not for him alone, [24]but also for us,
to whom God will credit righteousness—
for us who believe in him who raised Jesus
our Lord from the dead. [25]He was delivered over to death for our sins and was
raised to life for our justification.●

[b]17 Gen. 17:5 [c]18 Gen. 15:5

## KING JAMES

1. SALVATION IS OFFERED TO ALL

16 Therefore *it is* of faith, that *it might*
*be* by grace; to the end the promise might
be sure to all the seed; not to that only
which is of the law, but to that also which
is of the faith of Abraham; who is the
father of us all, 17 (as it is written, I
have made thee a father of many nations, )
before him whom he believed, *even* God,
who quickeneth the dead, and calleth
those things which be not as though they
were:●18 who against hope believed in
hope, that he might become the father of
many nations, according to that which
was spoken, So shall thy seed be. 19 And
being not weak in faith, he considered not
his own body now dead, when he was
about a hundred years old, neither yet the
deadness of Sarah's womb: 20 he stag-
gered not at the promise of God through
unbelief; but was strong in faith, giving
glory to God; 21 and being fully persuaded, that what he had promised, he
was able also to perform. 22 And therefore it was imputed to him for righteousness.●23 Now it was not written for his
sake alone, that it was imputed to him;
24 but for us also, to whom it shall be
imputed, if we believe on him that raised
up Jesus our Lord from the dead; 25 who
was delivered for our offenses, and was
raised again for our justification.●

2. ABRAHAM RECEIVED IT

3. SO MAY WE

PROMISE TO ALL

INCLUDING US

This segment continues the illustration of Abraham's experience of saving faith. The emphasized truth here is that the gift of salvation is offered to *everyone*, not only to Jews. Read the passage and choose a key verse which represents this.

______________________________

*4:16-17* The key word here is "all". Note where it appears. What does the paragraph teach?

______________________________

______________________________

______________________________

______________________________

______________________________

______________________________

______________________________

*4:18-22* What is emphasized in this paragraph?

______________________________

______________________________

______________________________

______________________________

List all the references to Abraham's faith: ______

______________________________

______________________________

______________________________

______________________________

______________________________

*4:23-25* What is the main point here? ______

______________________________

______________________________

______________________________

______________________________

______________________________

What is taught about Jesus? ______

______________________________

______________________________

______________________________

______________________________

NEW INTERNATIONAL VERSION

What do you learn here about:

PEACE WITH GOD

RIGHTEOUSNESS

CHRIST'S DEATH

ATONEMENT

ADAM

GRACE

SIN

*Peace and Joy*

5 Therefore, since we have been justified
through faith, we[d] have peace with
God through our Lord Jesus Christ,
2through whom we have gained access by
faith into this grace in which we now stand.
And we[d] rejoice in the hope of the glory of
God. 3Not only so, but we[d] also rejoice in
our sufferings, because we know that suffering produces perseverance; 4persever-
ance, character; and character, hope. 5And
hope does not disappoint us, because God
has poured out his love into our hearts by
the Holy Spirit, whom he has given us.●
6You see, at just the right time, when we
were still powerless, Christ died for the
ungodly. 7Very rarely will anyone die for a
righteous man, though for a good man
someone might possibly dare to die. 8But
God demonstrates his own love for us in
this: While we were still sinners, Christ
died for us.
9Since we have now been justified by his
blood, how much more shall we be saved
from God's wrath through him! 10For if,
when we were God's enemies, we were
reconciled to him through the death of his
Son, how much more, having been reconciled, shall we be saved through his life!
11Not only is this so, but we also rejoice in
God through our Lord Jesus Christ,
through whom we have now received
reconciliation.●

*Death Through Adam, Life Through Christ*

12Therefore, just as sin entered the world
through one man, and death through sin,
and in this way death came to all men,
because all sinned— 13for before the law
was given, sin was in the world. But sin is
not taken into account when there is no
law. 14Nevertheless, death reigned from
the time of Adam to the time of Moses,
even over those who did not sin by breaking a command, as did Adam, who was a
pattern of the one to come.
15But the gift is not like the trespass. For
if the many died by the trespass of the one
man, how much more did God's grace and
the gift that came by the grace of the one
man, Jesus Christ, overflow to the many!
16Again, the gift of God is not like the result
of the one man's sin: The judgment followed one sin and brought condemnation,
but the gift followed many trespasses and
brought justification. 17For if, by the trespass of the one man, death reigned through
that one man, how much more will those
who receive God's abundant provision of
grace and of the gift of righteousness reign
in life through the one man, Jesus Christ.●
18Consequently, just as the result of one
trespass was condemnation for all men, so
also the result of one act of righteousness
was justification that brings life for all men.
19For just as through the disobedience of
the one man the many were made sinners,
so also through the obedience of the one
man the many will be made righteous.
20The law was added so that the trespass
might increase. But where sin increased,
grace increased all the more, 21so that, just
as sin reigned in death, so also grace might
reign through righteousness to bring eternal life through Jesus Christ our Lord.●

d1,2,3 Or *let us*

KING JAMES

1. PEACE

5 Therefore being justified by faith, we
have peace with God through our
Lord Jesus Christ: 2 by whom also we
have access by faith into this grace wherein we stand, and rejoice in hope of the
glory of God. 3 And not only *so*, but we
glory in tribulations also; knowing that
tribulation worketh patience; 4 and patience, experience; and experience, hope:
5 and hope maketh not ashamed; because
the love of God is shed abroad in our
hearts by the Holy Ghost which is given
unto us. ●

-therefore

2. ASSUR-ANCE

6 For when we were yet without
strength, in due time Christ died for the
ungodly. 7 For scarcely for a righteous
man will one die: yet peradventure for a
good man some would even dare to die.
8 But God commendeth his love toward
us, in that, while we were yet sinners,
Christ died for us. 9 Much more then,
being now justified by his blood, we shall
be saved from wrath through him. 10 For
if, when we were enemies, we were reconciled to God by the death of his Son; much
more, being reconciled, we shall be saved
by his life. 11 And not only *so*, but we
also joy in God through our Lord Jesus
Christ, by whom we have now received
the atonement. ●

-for

3. GRACE

12 Wherefore, as by one man sin entered into the world, and death by sin;
and so death passed upon all men, for
that all have sinned: 13 (for until the law
sin was in the world: but sin is not imputed when there is no law. 14 Nevertheless death reigned from Adam to Moses,
even over them that had not sinned after
the similitude of Adam's transgression,
who is the figure of him that was to come.
15 But not as the offense, so also *is* the
free gift: for if through the offense of one
many be dead, much more the grace of
God, and the gift by grace, *which is* by one
man, Jesus Christ, hath abounded unto
many. 16 And not as *it was* by one that
sinned, *so is* the gift: for the judgment *was*
by one to condemnation, but the free gift
*is* of many offenses unto justification.
17 For if by one man's offense death
reigned by one; much more they which
receive abundance of grace and of the gift
of righteousness shall reign in life by one,
Jesus Christ.) ●

-wherefore

4. ETERNAL LIFE

18 Therefore, as by the offense of one
*judgment came* upon all men to condemnation; even so by the righteousness of
one *the free gift came* upon all men unto
justification of life. 19 For as by one
man's disobedience many were made sinners, so by the obedience of one shall
many be made righteous. 20 Moreover
the law entered, that the offense might
abound. But where sin abounded, grace
did much more abound: 21 that as sin
hath reigned unto death, even so might
grace reign through righteousness unto
eternal life by Jesus Christ our Lord. ●

-therefore

This segment describes the fruits, or blessings, which come to those who are justified by faith.

*5:1-5* Note the repeated pronoun "we." List the fruits of justification:

*5:6-11* What experience of Jesus' ministry is repeated in these verses?

List blessings:

*5:12-17* For clarity, omit the word "as" in verse 12 and the parenthetical brackets enclosing verses 13-17.

What two facts are compared in the paragraph?

*5:18-21* Observe the repeated word "righteous." How is righteousness a fruit of justification?

NEW INTERNATIONAL VERSION

What does this passage teach about:

DEATH OF CHRIST

DEATH PRINCIPLE IN CHRISTIAN LIVING

RESURRECTION OF CHRIST

LIFE PRINCIPLE IN CHRISTIAN LIVING

SIN

SERVANT OF GOD

List some practical applications:

*Dead to Sin, Alive in Christ*

6 What shall we say, then? Shall we go
on sinning so that grace may increase?
2By no means! We died to sin; how can we
live in it any longer? 3Or don't you know
that all of us who were baptized into Christ
Jesus were baptized into his death? 4We
were therefore buried with him through
baptism into death in order that, just as
Christ was raised from the dead through
the glory of the Father, we too may live a
new life.●
5If we have been united with him in his
death, we will certainly also be united with
him in his resurrection. 6For we know that
our old self was crucified with him so that
the body of sin might be rendered powerless, that we should no longer be slaves to
sin— 7because anyone who has died has
been freed from sin.
8Now if we died with Christ, we believe
that we will also live with him. 9For we
know that since Christ was raised from the
dead, he cannot die again; death no longer
has mastery over him. 10The death he died,
he died to sin once for all; but the life he
lives, he lives to God.
11In the same way, count yourselves
dead to sin but alive to God in Christ Jesus.●
12Therefore do not let sin reign in your
mortal body so that you obey its evil desires. 13Do not offer the parts of your body
to sin, as instruments of wickedness, but
rather offer yourselves to God, as those
who have been brought from death to life;
and offer the parts of your body to him as
instruments of righteousness. 14For sin
shall not be your master, because you are
not under law, but under grace.●

## KING JAMES

**1. WALKING IN NEWNESS OF LIFE**

6 What shall we say then? Shall we
continue in sin, that grace may
abound? 2 God forbid. How shall we,
that are dead to sin, live any longer therein? 3 Know ye not, that so many of us as
were baptized into Jesus Christ were baptized into his death? 4 Therefore we are
buried with him by baptism into death:
that like as Christ was raised up from the
dead by the glory of the Father, even
so we also should walk in newness of
life.●

**2. LIVING WITH CHRIST**

5 For if we have been planted together
in the likeness of his death, we shall be
also *in the likeness* of *his* resurrection:
6 knowing this, that our old man is crucified with *him*, that the body of sin might
be destroyed, that henceforth we should
not serve sin. 7 For he that is dead is
freed from sin. 8 Now if we be dead with
Christ, we believe that we shall also live
with him: 9 knowing that Christ being
raised from the dead dieth no more;
death hath no more dominion over him.
10 For in that he died, he died unto sin
once: but in that he liveth, he liveth unto
God. 11 Likewise reckon ye also yourselves to be dead indeed unto sin, but
alive unto God through Jesus Christ our
Lord.●

**3. YIELDING TO GOD**

12 Let not sin therefore reign in your
mortal body, that ye should obey it in the
lusts thereof. 13 Neither yield ye your
members *as* instruments of unrighteousness unto sin: but yield yourselves unto
God, as those that are alive from the dead,
and your members *as* instruments of righteousness unto God. 14 For sin shall not
have dominion over you: for ye are not
under the law, but under grace.●

PRACTICE OF SIN

DOMINION OF SIN

This passage begins the third section of Romans, 6:1—8:39 (see outline), where Paul writes about how to live the Christian life. This is the present experiential aspect of salvation.

The believer has a double identification: dead and alive. Record what is said about each, in the first two paragraphs:

*6:1-4* __________

DEAD __________

ALIVE __________

What exhortation does the paragraph conclude with?

*6:5-11* __________

DEAD __________

ALIVE __________

What command does the paragraph conclude with?

*6:12-14* Record the commands: __________

How does the paragraph conclude? __________

NEW INTERNATIONAL VERSION

What do you learn here about:

OBEDIENCE TO GOD

FREEDOM FROM SIN

SERVANTS OF RIGHTEOUSNESS

GIFT OF GOD

LAW'S DOMINION

List spiritual applications:

*Slaves to Righteousness*

[15]What then? Shall we sin because we are not under law but under grace? By no means! [16]Don't you know that when you offer yourselves to someone to obey him as slaves, you are slaves to the one whom you obey—whether you are slaves to sin, which leads to death, or to obedience, which leads to righteousness? [17]But thanks be to God that, though you used to be slaves to sin, you wholeheartedly obeyed the form of teaching to which you were entrusted. [18]You have been set free from sin and have become slaves to righteousness.

[19]I put this in human terms because you are weak in your natural selves. Just as you used to offer the parts of your body in slavery to impurity and to ever-increasing wickedness, so now offer them in slavery to righteousness leading to holiness.● [20]When you were slaves to sin, you were free from the control of righteousness. [21]What benefit did you reap at that time from the things you are now ashamed of? Those things result in death! [22]But now that you have been set free from sin and have become slaves to God, the benefit you reap leads to holiness, and the result is eternal life. [23]For the wages of sin is death, but the gift of God is eternal life in[a] Christ Jesus our Lord.●

*An Illustration From Marriage*

7 Do you not know, brothers—for I am speaking to men who know the law—that the law has authority over a man only as long as he lives? [2]For example, by law a married woman is bound to her husband as long as he is alive, but if her husband dies, she is released from the law of marriage. [3]So then, if she marries another man while her husband is still alive, she is called an adulteress. But if her husband dies, she is released from that law and is not an adulteress, even though she marries another man.●

[4]So, my brothers, you also died to the law through the body of Christ, that you might belong to another, to him who was raised from the dead, in order that we might bear fruit to God. [5]For when we were controlled by the sinful nature,[b] the sinful passions aroused by the law were at work in our bodies, so that we bore fruit for death. [6]But now, by dying to what once bound us, we have been released from the law so that we serve in the new way of the Spirit, and not in the old way of the written code.●

[a]23 Or *through* [b]5 Or *the flesh;* also in verse 25

KING JAMES

1. NEW BONDAGE
-before and now

GRACE

15 What then? shall we sin, because we
are not under the law, but under grace?
God forbid. 16 Know ye not, that to
whom ye yield yourselves servants to
obey, his servants ye are to whom ye obey;
whether of sin unto death, or of obedience
unto righteousness? 17 But God be
thanked, that ye were the servants of sin,
but ye have obeyed from the heart that
form of doctrine which was delivered you.
18 Being then made free from sin, ye became the servants of righteousness. 19 I
speak after the manner of men because of
the infirmity of your flesh: for as ye have
yielded your members servants to uncleanness and to iniquity unto iniquity;
even so now yield your members servants
to righteousness unto holiness.●
20 For when ye were the servants of sin,
ye were free from righteousness. 21 What
fruit had ye then in those things whereof
ye are now ashamed? for the end of those
things *is* death. 22 But now being made
free from sin, and become servants to
God, ye have your fruit unto holiness, and
the end everlasting life. 23 For the wages
of sin *is* death; but the gift of God *is*
eternal life through Jesus Christ our
Lord.●

2. TOTAL LIBERATION
-old and new

7 Know ye not, brethren, (for I speak
to them that know the law,) how that
the law hath dominion over a man as long
as he liveth? 2 For the woman which
hath a husband is bound by the law to
*her* husband so long as he liveth; but if the
husband be dead, she is loosed from the
law of *her* husband. 3 So then if, while
*her* husband liveth, she be married to
another man, she shall be called an adulteress: but if her husband be dead, she is
free from that law; so that she is no adulteress, though she be married to another
man.●
4 Wherefore, my brethren, ye also are
become dead to the law by the body of
Christ; that ye should be married to another, *even* to him who is raised from the
dead, that we should bring forth fruit unto
God. 5 For when we were in the flesh, the
motions of sins, which were by the law,
did work in our members to bring forth
fruit unto death. 6 But now we are delivered from the law, that being dead
wherein we were held; that we should
serve in newness of spirit, and not *in* the
oldness of the letter.●

NEWNESS OF SPIRIT

Paul continues the theme of principles of Christian living begun in the preceding segment.

*6:15-23* Paul compares the *before* and *now* of the believer as to his servitude. Record the comparisons:

*BEFORE* ______

*NOW* ______

How does verse 23 relate to the above? ______

*7:1-6* What truth do verses 2-3 illustrate? ______

How is this truth applied in verses 4-6? ______

What does it mean to "serve in newness of spirit" (v.6)?

______

NEW INTERNATIONAL VERSION

What does this passage teach about:

LAW OF GOD

LAW OF SIN

TWO NATURES OF THE BELIEVER

SPIRITUAL CONFLICT OF THE HEART

HOW TO DO WHAT IS RIGHT

OTHER

*Struggling With Sin*

7What shall we say, then? Is the law sin?
Certainly not! Indeed I would not have
known what sin was except through the
law. For I would not have known what it
was to covet if the law had not said, "Do
not covet."[a] 8But sin, seizing the opportunity afforded by the commandment, produced in me every kind of covetous desire.
For apart from law, sin is dead. 9Once I
was alive apart from law; but when the
commandment came, sin sprang to life and
I died. 10I found that the very commandment that was intended to bring life actually brought death. 11For sin, seizing the opportunity afforded by the commandment,
deceived me, and through the commandment put me to death. 12So then, the law is
holy, and the commandment is holy, righteous and good.

13Did that which is good, then, become
death to me? By no means! But in order
that sin might be recognized as sin, it produced death in me through what was good,
so that through the commandment sin
might become utterly sinful.●

14We know that the law is spiritual; but
I am unspiritual, sold as a slave to sin. 15I
do not understand what I do. For what I
want to do I do not do, but what I hate I do.
16And if I do what I do not want to do, I
agree that the law is good. 17As it is, it is
no longer I myself who do it, but it is sin
living in me. 18I know that nothing good
lives in me, that is, in my sinful nature.[b]
For I have the desire to do what is good,
but I cannot carry it out. 19For what I do is
not the good I want to do; no, the evil I do
not want to do—this I keep on doing.
20Now if I do what I do not want to do, it
is no longer I who do it, but it is sin living
in me that does it.●

21So I find this law at work: When I want
to do good, evil is right there with me.
22For in my inner being I delight in God's
law; 23but I see another law at work in the
members of my body, waging war against
the law of my mind and making me a prisoner of the law of sin at work within my
members. 24What a wretched man I am!
Who will rescue me from this body of
death? 25Thanks be to God—through Jesus
Christ our Lord!

So then, I myself in my mind am a slave
to God's law, but in the sinful nature a
slave to the law of sin.●

[a]7 Exodus 20:17; Deut. 5:21 [b]18 Or *my flesh*

## KING JAMES

### 1. GOD'S LAW

LAW OF GOD

7 What shall we say then? *Is* the law
sin? God forbid. Nay, I had not known
sin, but by the law: for I had not known
lust, except the law had said, Thou shalt
not covet. 8 But sin, taking occasion by
the commandment, wrought in me all
manner of concupiscence. For without
the law sin *was* dead. 9 For I was alive
without the law once: but when the commandment came, sin revived, and I died.
10 And the commandment, which *was or-*
*dained* to life, I found *to be* unto death.
11 For sin, taking occasion by the commandment, deceived me, and by it slew
*me.* 12 Wherefore the law *is* holy, and
the commandment holy, and just, and
good.
13 Was then that which is good made
death unto me? God forbid. But sin, that
it might appear sin, working death in me
by that which is good; that sin by the
commandment might become exceeding
sinful.● 14 For we know that the law is
spiritual: but I am carnal, sold under sin.
15 For that which I do, I allow not: for
what I would, that do I not; but what I
hate, that do I. 16 If then I do that which
I would not, I consent unto the law that
*it is* good. 17 Now then it is no more I
that do it, but sin that dwelleth in me.
18 For I know that in me (that is, in my
flesh,) dwelleth no good thing: for to will
is present with me; but *how* to perform
that which is good I find not. 19 For the
good that I would, I do not: but the evil
which I would not, that I do. 20 Now if I
do that I would not, it is no more I that
do it, but sin that dwelleth in me.●
21 I find then a law, that, when I would
do good, evil is present with me. 22 For I
delight in the law of God after the inward
man: 23 but I see another law in my members, warring against the law of my mind,
and bringing me into captivity to the law
of sin which is in my members. 24 O
wretched man that I am! who shall deliver
me from the body of this death? 25 I
thank God through Jesus Christ our
Lord. So then with the mind I myself
serve the law of God; but with the flesh
the law of sin.●

### 2. CHRISTIAN'S CONFLICT

### 3. CHRIST THE ANSWER

LAW OF SIN

Paul says the practical problem of Christians is "how to perform that which is good"(v.18). Study this segment with this in mind.

*7:7-13* How does this paragraph show that the law of God is good?

*7:14-20* What is the conflict in the Christian's heart?

*7:21-25* How are these compared:

LAW OF GOD

LAW OF SIN

What is the answer to the conflict mentioned above?

NEW INTERNATIONAL VERSION

Record what the passage teaches about:

THE CARNAL CHRISTIAN

THE CRUCIFIED LIFE

THE BELIEVER'S RELATION TO GOD

Make a list of practical applications of the passage to everyday living.

In your own words, what is the source of power for living the Christian life?

*Life Through the Spirit*

8 Therefore, there is now no condemnation for those who are in Christ Jesus,[c]
2because through Christ Jesus the law of
the Spirit of life set me free from the law of
sin and death. 3For what the law was powerless to do in that it was weakened by the
sinful nature,[d] God did by sending his own
Son in the likeness of sinful man to be a sin
offering.[e] And so he condemned sin in sinful man, 4in order that the righteous requirements of the law might be fully met in
us, who do not live according to the sinful
nature but according to the Spirit.
5Those who live according to the sinful
nature have their minds set on what that
nature desires; but those who live in accordance with the Spirit have their minds set
on what the Spirit desires. 6The mind of
sinful man is death, but the mind controlled
by the Spirit is life and peace; 7the sinful
mind is hostile to God. It does not submit
to God's law, nor can it do so. 8Those controlled by the sinful nature cannot please
God.●
9You, however, are controlled not by the
sinful nature but by the Spirit, if the Spirit
of God lives in you. And if anyone does not
have the Spirit of Christ, he does not belong to Christ. 10But if Christ is in you,
your body is dead because of sin, yet your
spirit is alive because of righteousness.
11And if the Spirit of him who raised Jesus
from the dead is living in you, he who
raised Christ from the dead will also give
life to your mortal bodies through his
Spirit, who lives in you.●
12Therefore, brothers, we have an obligation—but it is not to the sinful nature, to
live according to it. 13For if you live according to the sinful nature, you will die;
but if by the Spirit you put to death the
misdeeds of the body, you will live, 14be-
cause those who are led by the Spirit of
God are sons of God. 15For you did not
receive a spirit that makes you a slave
again to fear, but you received the Spirit of
sonship.[f] And by him we cry, "*Abba*,[g] Father." 16The Spirit himself testifies with
our spirit that we are God's children.
17Now if we are children, then we are
heirs—heirs of God and co-heirs with
Christ, if indeed we share in his sufferings
in order that we may also share in his glory.●

c1 Some later manuscripts *Jesus, who do not live according to the sinful nature but according to the Spirit,*
d3 Or *the flesh;* also in verses 4, 5, 8, 9, 12 and 13
e3 Or *man, for sin*  f15 Or *adoption*
g15 Aramaic for *Father*

KING JAMES

1. WALKING BY THE SPIRIT

NO CONDEMNATION

8 *There is* therefore now no condemnation to them which are in Christ Jesus,
who walk not after the flesh, but after the
Spirit. 2 For the law of the Spirit of life
in Christ Jesus hath made me free from
the law of sin and death. 3 For what the
law could not do, in that it was weak
through the flesh, God sending his own
Son in the likeness of sinful flesh, and for
sin, condemned sin in the flesh: 4 that the
righteousness of the law might be fulfilled
in us, who walk not after the flesh, but
after the Spirit. 5 For they that are after
the flesh do mind the things of the flesh;
but they that are after the Spirit, the things
of the Spirit. 6 For to be carnally minded
*is* death; but to be spiritually minded *is*
life and peace. 7 Because the carnal mind
*is* enmity against God: for it is not subject
to the law of God, neither indeed can be.
8 So then they that are in the flesh cannot
please God. ●

2. LIFE BY THE SPIRIT

9 But ye are not in the flesh, but in the
Spirit, if so be that the Spirit of God dwell
in you. Now if any man have not the
Spirit of Christ, he is none of his. 10 And
if Christ *be* in you, the body *is* dead because of sin; but the Spirit *is* life because
of righteousness. 11 But if the Spirit of
him that raised up Jesus from the dead
dwell in you, he that raised up Christ from
the dead shall also quicken your mortal
bodies by his Spirit that dwelleth in you. ●

3. ASSURANCE BY THE SPIRIT

12 Therefore, brethren, we are debtors,
not to the flesh, to live after the flesh.
13 For if ye live after the flesh, ye shall die:
but if ye through the Spirit do mortify the
deeds of the body, ye shall live. 14 For as
many as are led by the Spirit of God, they
are the sons of God. 15 For ye have not
received the spirit of bondage again to
fear; but ye have received the Spirit of
adoption, whereby we cry, Abba, Father.
16 The Spirit itself beareth witness with
our spirit, that we are the children of God:
17 and if children, then heirs; heirs of
God, and joint-heirs with Christ, if so be
that we suffer with *him*, that we may be
also glorified together. ●

HEIRS

The apostle writes about the *power* of Christian living in this and the following segment. Underline the name Spirit throughout the whole segment.

*8:1-8* What contrast is made in verse 1? ______

______

______

______

______

Record what is taught here about: ______

SPIRIT ______

______

______

______

______

CHRIST ______

______

______

*8:9-11* Record what is taught about: ______

FATHER ______

______

______

______

SON ______

______

______

______

SPIRIT ______

______

______

______

*8:12-17* What does this paragraph teach about the believer?

______

______

______

______

______

NEW INTERNATIONAL VERSION

What do you learn here about:

SUFFERING

FUTURE GLORY

HOPE

PHYSICAL BODY

PRAYER

HOLY SPIRIT

List some practical applications:

*Future Glory*

18I consider that our present sufferings
are not worth comparing with the glory
that will be revealed in us. 19The creation
waits in eager expectation for the sons of
God to be revealed. 20For the creation was
subjected to frustration, not by its own
choice, but by the will of the one who subjected it, in hope 21that the creation itself
will be liberated from its bondage to decay
and brought into the glorious freedom of
the children of God.●
22We know that the whole creation has
been groaning as in the pains of childbirth
right up to the present time. 23Not only so,
but we ourselves, who have the firstfruits
of the Spirit, groan inwardly as we wait
eagerly for our adoption as sons, the redemption of our bodies. 24For in this hope
we were saved. But hope that is seen is no
hope at all. Who hopes for what he already
has? 25But if we hope for what we do not
yet have, we wait for it patiently.●
26In the same way, the Spirit helps us in
our weakness. We do not know what[a] we
ought to pray, but the Spirit himself intercedes for us with groans that words cannot
express. 27And he who searches our hearts
knows the mind of the Spirit, because the
Spirit intercedes for the saints in accordance with God's will.●

[a]26 Or *how*

## KING JAMES

1. GLORY

18 For I reckon that the sufferings of
this present time *are* not worthy *to be compared*
*pared* with the glory which shall be revealed in us. 19 For the earnest expectation of the creature waiteth for the
manifestation of the sons of God. 20 For
the creature was made subject to vanity,
not willingly, but by reason of him who
hath subjected *the same* in hope; 21 because the creature itself also shall be
delivered from the bondage of corruption
into the glorious liberty of the children of
God.● 22 For we know that the whole
creation groaneth and travaileth in pain
together until now. 23 And not only *they*,
but ourselves also, which have the firstfruits of the Spirit, even we ourselves
groan within ourselves, waiting for the
adoption, *to wit*, the redemption of our
body. 24 For we are saved by hope: but
hope that is seen is not hope: for what a
man seeth, why doth he yet hope for?
25 But if we hope for that we see not, *then*
do we with patience wait for *it*.●
26 Likewise the Spirit also helpeth our
infirmities: for we know not what we
should pray for as we ought: but the Spirit
itself maketh intercession for us with
groanings which cannot be uttered.
27 And he that searcheth the hearts
knoweth what *is* the mind of the Spirit,
because he maketh intercession for the
saints according to *the will of* God.●

2. HOPE

3. INTERCESSION

SUFFERINGS

INFIRMITIES

*8:18-21* What is the key word of verse 18? ____

How is this contrasted with present sufferings? ____

What is meant by "the manifestation of the sons of God"(v.19)?

*8:22-25* Are verses 22-23 about the physical body?

What is meant by "the redemption of our body" (v.23)?

How are verses 24-25 related to verses 22-23?

*8:26-27* How is this paragraph related to the two preceding ones?

Who of the Trinity helps the Christian in his prayer life?

NEW INTERNATIONAL VERSION

What does this passage teach about:

PREDESTINATION

DIVINE CALLING

JUSTIFICATION

GLORIFICATION

MINISTRIES OF CHRIST

LOVE OF GOD

PERSECUTION AND TRIAL

PERSEVERANCE OF THE SAINTS

OTHER

*More Than Conquerors*

28 And we know that in all things God
works for the good of those who love him,[b]
who have been called according to his purpose. 29 For those God foreknew he also
predestined to be conformed to the likeness of his Son, that he might be the firstborn among many brothers. 30 And those he
predestined, he also called; those he
called, he also justified; those he justified,
he also glorified.●

31 What, then, shall we say in response to
this? If God is for us, who can be against
us? 32 He who did not spare his own Son,
but gave him up for us all—how will he not
also, along with him, graciously give us all
things? 33 Who will bring any charge against
those whom God has chosen? It is God
who justifies. 34 Who is he that condemns?
Christ Jesus, who died—more than that,
who was raised to life—is at the right hand
of God and is also interceding for us.●
35 Who shall separate us from the love of
Christ? Shall trouble or hardship or persecution or famine or nakedness or danger or
sword? 36 As it is written:

> "For your sake we face death all
> day long;
> we are considered as sheep to be
> slaughtered."[c]

37 No, in all these things we are more than
conquerors through him who loved us.
38 For I am convinced that neither death nor
life, neither angels nor demons,[d] neither
the present nor the future, nor any powers,
39 neither height nor depth, nor anything
else in all creation, will be able to separate
us from the love of God that is in Christ
Jesus our Lord.●

[b] 28 Some manuscripts *And we know that all things work together for good to those who love God*
[c] 36 Psalm 44:22 [d] 38 Or *nor heavenly rulers*

KING JAMES

**1. THE CONQUERORS**

WE LOVE GOD

28 And we know that all things work
together for good to them that love God,
to them who are the called according to
*his* purpose. 29 For whom he did fore-
know, he also did predestinate *to be* conformed to the image of his Son, that he
might be the firstborn among many brethren. 30 Moreover, whom he did predestinate, them he also called: and whom he
called, them he also justified: and whom
he justified, them he also glorified.●

**2. THE HELP OF GOD**

31 What shall we then say to these
things? If God *be* for us, who *can be*
against us? 32 He that spared not his own
Son, but delivered him up for us all, how
shall he not with him also freely give us all
things? 33 Who shall lay any thing to the
charge of God's elect? *It is* God that justifieth. 34 Who *is* he that condemneth?
*It is* Christ that died, yea rather, that is
risen again, who is even at the right hand
of God, who also maketh intercession for
us.●

**3. NO SEPARATION**

35 Who shall separate us from the
love of Christ? *shall* tribulation, or distress, or persecution, or famine, or nakedness, or peril, or sword? 36 As it is
written,

> For thy sake we are killed all the day long;
> we are accounted as sheep for the slaughter.

Ps.44:22

37 Nay, in all these things we are more
than conquerors through him that loved
us. 38 For I am persuaded, that neither
death, nor life, nor angels, nor principalities, nor powers, nor things present, nor
things to come, 39 nor height, nor depth,
nor any other creature, shall be able to
separate us from the love of God, which
is in Christ Jesus our Lord.●

GOD LOVES US

This is the last segment of the section about the believer's sanctification (6:1—8:39). Choose a key verse reflecting the title, "More than Conquerors."

*8:28-30* How does Paul describe the conquering life in verse 28?

List the works of God in the life of the believer:

*8:31-34* Record the questions and answers.

*8:35-39* What key word is common to verses 35 and 39?

Compare the lists of verses 35 and 38-39.

NEW INTERNATIONAL VERSION

What do you learn here about:

PAUL

TRUE ISRAEL

MERCY OF GOD

SOVEREIGNTY OF GOD

Record spiritual lessons taught by this passage, which can be applied to your everyday living.

*God's Sovereign Choice*

9 I speak the truth in Christ—I am not lying, my conscience confirms it in the Holy Spirit— 2 I have great sorrow and unceasing anguish in my heart. 3 For I could wish that I myself were cursed and cut off from Christ for the sake of my brothers, those of my own race, 4 the people of Israel. Theirs is the adoption as sons; theirs the divine glory, the covenants, the receiving of the law, the temple worship and the promises. 5 Theirs are the patriarchs, and from them is traced the human ancestry of Christ, who is God over all, forever praised![e] Amen.●

6 It is not as though God's word had failed. For not all who are descended from Israel are Israel. 7 Nor because they are his descendants are they all Abraham's children. On the contrary, "It is through Isaac that your offspring will be reckoned."[f] 8 In other words, it is not the natural children who are God's children, but it is the children of the promise who are regarded as Abraham's offspring. 9 For this was how the promise was stated: "At the appointed time I will return, and Sarah will have a son."[g]

10 Not only that, but Rebecca's children had one and the same father, our father Isaac. 11 Yet, before the twins were born or had done anything good or bad—in order that God's purpose in election might stand: 12 not by works but by him who calls—she was told, "The older will serve the younger."[h] 13 Just as it is written: "Jacob I loved, but Esau I hated."[i]●

14 What then shall we say? Is God unjust? Not at all! 15 For he says to Moses,

> "I will have mercy on whom I have mercy,
> and I will have compassion on whom I have compassion."[a]

16 It does not, therefore, depend on man's desire or effort, but on God's mercy. 17 For the Scripture says to Pharaoh: "I raised you up for this very purpose, that I might display my power in you and that my name might be proclaimed in all the earth."[b] 18 Therefore God has mercy on whom he wants to have mercy, and he hardens whom he wants to harden.●

[e] 5 Or *Christ, who is over all. God be forever praised!* Or *Christ. God who is over all be forever praised!*
[f] 7 Gen. 21:12 [g] 9 Gen. 18:10,14 [h] 12 Gen. 25:23
[i] 13 Mal. 1:2,3 [a] 15 Exodus 33:19 [b] 17 Exodus 9:16

KING JAMES

1. PAUL'S COMPASSION FOR ISRAEL

PAUL'S COMPASSION

9 I say the truth in Christ, I lie not, my
conscience also bearing me witness in
the Holy Ghost, 2 that I have great heaviness and continual sorrow in my heart.
3 For I could wish that myself were accursed from Christ for my brethren, my
kinsmen according to the flesh: 4 who
are Israelites; to whom *pertaineth* the
adoption, and the glory, and the covenants, and the giving of the law, and the
service *of God*, and the promises; 5 whose
*are* the fathers, and of whom as concerning the flesh Christ *came*, who is over all,
God blessed for ever. Amen.●

2. TRUE ISRAEL

6 Not as though the word of God hath
taken none effect. For they *are* not all
Israel, which are of Israel: 7 neither, because they are the seed of Abraham, *are
they* all children: but, In Isaac shall thy
seed be called. 8 That is, They which are
the children of the flesh, these *are* not the
children of God: but the children of the
promise are counted for the seed. 9 For
this *is* the word of promise, At this time
will I come, and Sarah shall have a son.
10 And not only *this;* but when Rebecca
also had conceived by one, *even* by our
father Isaac, 11 (for *the children* being
not yet born, neither having done any
good or evil, that the purpose of God according to election might stand, not of
works, but of him that calleth;) 12 it was
said unto her, The elder shall serve the
younger. 13 As it is written, Jacob have
I loved, but Esau have I hated.●

3. GOD'S RIGHTEOUS SOVEREIGNTY

14 What shall we say then? *Is there* unrighteousness with God? God forbid.
15 For he saith to Moses,

I will have mercy on whom I will have mercy,
and I will have compassion on whom I will have compassion. (Ex. 33:19)

16 So then *it is* not of him that willeth, nor
of him that runneth, but of God that
showeth mercy. 17 For the Scripture
saith unto Pharaoh, (Ex. 9:16)

Even for this same purpose have I raised thee up,
that I might show my power in thee,
and that my name might be declared throughout all the earth.

18 Therefore hath he mercy on whom he
will *have mercy*, and whom he will he
hardeneth.●

GOD'S SOVEREIGNTY

---

This segment begins the fourth section of Romans, 9:1—11:36, GOD'S SOVEREIGNTY IN SAVING JEW AND GENTILE. (See outline.)

*9:1-5* List the favors bestowed on Israel: ______

*9:6-13* What is the main point of this paragraph? ______

How does verse 6a introduce this? ______

*9:14-18* Compare the illustrations:

MOSES ______

PHARAOH ______

What is the main point of the paragraph? ______

NEW INTERNATIONAL VERSION

What does this passage teach about:

SOVEREIGN CREATOR

SOVEREIGN SAVIOR

SOVEREIGN JUDGE

MERCY OF GOD

OTHER

19One of you will say to me: "Then why
does God still blame us? For who resists
his will?" 20But who are you, O man, to
talk back to God? "Shall what is formed
say to him who formed it, 'Why did you
make me like this?' "[c] 21Does not the potter have the right to make out of the same
lump of clay some pottery for noble purposes and some for common use?
22What if God, choosing to show his
wrath and make his power known, bore
with great patience the objects of his
wrath—prepared for destruction? 23What if
he did this to make the riches of his glory
known to the objects of his mercy, whom
he prepared in advance for glory— 24even
us, whom he also called, not only from the
Jews but also from the Gentiles? 25As he
says in Hosea:

"I will call them 'my people' who
are not my people;
and I will call her 'my loved one'
who is not my loved one,"[d]

26and,

"It will happen that in the very
place where it was said
to them,
'You are not my people,'
they will be called 'sons of the
living God.' "[e] ●

27Isaiah cries out concerning Israel:

"Though the number of the
Israelites be like the
sand by the sea,
only the remnant will be saved.
28For the Lord will carry out
his sentence on earth with speed
and finality."[f]

29It is just as Isaiah said previously:

"Unless the Lord Almighty
had left us descendants,
we would have become like Sodom,
and we would have been like
Gomorrah."[g] ●

[c] *20* Isaiah 29:16; 45:9 [d] *25* Hosea 2:23 [e] *26* Hosea 1:10
[f] *28* Isaiah 10:22,23 [g] *29* Isaiah 1:9

KING JAMES

1. SOVEREIGNTY OF THE POTTER

19 Thou wilt say then unto me, Why doth he yet find fault? For who hath resisted his will? 20 Nay but, O man, who art thou that repliest against God? Shall the thing formed say to him that formed *it*, Why hast thou made me thus?
21 Hath not the potter power over the clay, of the same lump to make one vessel unto honor, and another unto dishonor?
22 *What* if God, willing to show *his* wrath, and to make his power known, endured with much long-suffering the vessels of wrath fitted to destruction: 23 and that he might make known the riches of his glory on the vessels of mercy, which he had afore prepared unto glory, 24 even us, whom he hath called, not of the Jews only, but also of the Gentiles? 25 As he saith also in Hose'a,

I will call them my people,
which were not my people;
and her beloved,
which was not beloved.
26 And it shall come to pass,
*that* in the place where it was said unto them, Ye *are* not my people;
there shall they be called the children of the living God.●

POTTER

Hos. 2:23

Hos. 1:10

2. REMNANT OF ISRAEL SAVED

27 Isaiah also crieth concerning Israel,
Though the number of the children of Israel be as the sand of the sea,
a remnant shall be saved:
28 for he will finish the work, and cut *it* short in righteousness:
because a short work will the Lord make upon the earth.
29 And as Isaiah said before,
Except the Lord of Sab'a-oth had left us a seed,
we had been as Sodom,
and been made like unto Gomor'rah.●

Isa. 10:22-23

Isa. 1:9

LORD

First read 9:18 for its connection with 9:19.

*9:19-26* Record what the passage says about:

POTTER ______

CLAY ______

VESSELS OF WRATH ______

VESSELS OF MERCY ______

JEW ______

GENTILE ______

*9:27-29* What attribute of God is prominent here?

______

What is the bright phrase of the paragraph?

______

Compare verse 27 with verses 28-29. ______

NEW INTERNATIONAL VERSION

What do you learn from this passage about:

TRUE RIGHTEOUSNESS

LAW OF GOD

CHRIST

HOW TO BE SAVED

OTHER

*Israel's Unbelief*

30What then shall we say? That the Gentiles, who did not pursue righteousness,
have obtained it, a righteousness that is by
faith; 31but Israel, who pursued a law of
righteousness, has not attained it. 32Why
not? Because they pursued it not by faith
but as if it were by works. They stumbled
over the "stumbling stone." 33As it is written:

"See, I lay in Zion a stone that
causes men to stumble
and a rock that makes them fall,
and the one who trusts in him will
never be put to shame."[h] ●

10 Brothers, my heart's desire and
prayer to God for the Israelites is
that they may be saved. 2For I can testify
about them that they are zealous for God,
but their zeal is not based on knowledge.
3Since they did not know the righteousness
that comes from God and sought to establish their own, they did not submit to God's
righteousness. 4Christ is the end of the law
so that there may be righteousness for
everyone who believes.●
5Moses describes in this way the righteousness that is by the law: "The man who
does these things will live by them."[i] 6But
the righteousness that is by faith says: "Do
not say in your heart, 'Who will ascend
into heaven?'[j]" (that is, to bring Christ
down) 7"or 'Who will descend into the
deep?'[k]" (that is, to bring Christ up from
the dead). 8But what does it say? "The
word is near you; it is in your mouth and
in your heart,"[l] that is, the word of faith
we are proclaiming: 9That if you confess
with your mouth, "Jesus is Lord," and
believe in your heart that God raised him
from the dead, you will be saved. 10For it
is with your heart that you believe and are
justified, and it is with your mouth that you
confess and are saved. 11As the Scripture
says, "Everyone who trusts in him will
never be put to shame."[m] 12For there is no
difference between Jew and Gentile—the
same Lord is Lord of all and richly blesses
all who call on him, 13for, "Everyone who
calls on the name of the Lord will be
saved."[n]●

h33 Isaiah 8:14; 28:16 i5 Lev. 18:5 j6 Deut. 30:12 k7 Deut. 30:13 l8 Deut. 30:14 m11 Isaiah 28:16 n13 Joel 2:32

KING JAMES

1. SAVED AND UNSAVED

GENTILES AND ISRAEL

**30 What shall we say then? That the
Gentiles, which followed not after righteousness, have attained to righteousness,
even the righteousness which is of faith.
31 But Israel, which followed after the
law of righteousness, hath not attained to
the law of righteousness. 32 Wherefore?
Because *they sought it* not by faith, but as
it were by the works of the law. For they
stumbled at that stumblingstone; 33 as it
is written,**

**Behold, I lay in Zion a stumbling-
stone
and rock of offense:
and whosoever believeth on him shall
not be ashamed.●**

Isa. 28:16

2. PRAYER FOR ISRAEL

**10 Brethren, my heart's desire and
prayer to God for Israel is, that
they might be saved. 2 For I bear them
record that they have a zeal of God, but
not according to knowledge. 3 For they,
being ignorant of God's righteousness,
and going about to establish their own
righteousness, have not submitted themselves unto the righteousness of God.●**

3. WAY OF SALVATION

**4 For Christ *is* the end of the law for
righteousness to every one that believeth.
5 For Moses describeth the righteousness which is of the law, That the man
which doeth those things shall live by
them. 6 But the righteousness which is
of faith speaketh on this wise, Say not in
thine heart, Who shall ascend into heaven?
(that is, to bring Christ down *from above*:)
7 or, Who shall descend into the deep?
(that is, to bring up Christ again from the
dead.) 8 But what saith it? The word is
nigh thee, *even* in thy mouth, and in thy
heart: that is, the word of faith, which
we preach; 9 that if thou shalt confess
with thy mouth the Lord Jesus, and shalt
believe in thine heart that God hath raised
him from the dead, thou shalt be saved.
10 For with the heart man believeth unto
righteousness; and with the mouth confession is made unto salvation. 11 For the
Scripture saith, Whosoever believeth on
him shall not be ashamed. 12 For there
is no difference between the Jew and the
Greek: for the same Lord over all is rich
unto all that call upon him. 13 For whosoever shall call upon the name of the
Lord shall be saved.●**

WHOSOEVER

*9:30-33* What is written here about:

GENTILES ______

JEWS ______

CHRIST ______

*10:1-3*

PAUL'S PRAYER ______

JEWS ______

*10:4-13*

CHRIST ______

WAY OF SALVATION ______

NEW INTERNATIONAL VERSION

What does this passage teach about:

PREACHING

CALL TO WITNESSING

HEARING AND BELIEVING

GENTILES

JEWS

List spiritual applications of the passage.

14 How, then, can they call on the one
they have not believed in? And how can
they believe in the one of whom they have
not heard? And how can they hear without
someone preaching to them? 15 And how
can they preach unless they are sent? As it
is written, "How beautiful are the feet of
those who bring good news!"[a] ●
16 But not all the Israelites accepted the
good news. For Isaiah says, "Lord, who
has believed our message?"[b] 17 Conse-
quently, faith comes from hearing the message, and the message is heard through the
word of Christ. ● 18 But I ask, Did they not
hear? Of course they did:

> "Their voice has gone out into all
> the earth,
> their words to the ends of the
> world."[c]

19 Again I ask, did Israel not understand?
First, Moses says,

> "I will make you envious by those
> who are not a nation;
> I will make you angry by a nation
> that has no understanding."[d]

20 And Isaiah boldly says,

> "I was found by those who did not
> seek me;
> I revealed myself to those who
> did not ask for me."[e]

21 But concerning Israel he says,

> "All day long I have held out my
> hands
> to a disobedient and obstinate
> people."[f] ●

[a] *15* Isaiah 52:7 [b] *16* Isaiah 53:1 [c] *18* Psalm 19:4
[d] *19* Deut. 32:21 [e] *20* Isaiah 65:1 [f] *21* Isaiah 65:2

## KING JAMES

**1. GOSPEL IS PREACHED**

14 How then shall they call on him in
whom they have not believed? and how
shall they believe in him of whom they
have not heard? and how shall they hear
without a preacher? 15 and how shall
they preach, except they be sent? as it is
written, FEET
How beautiful are the feet of them
that preach the gospel of peace, Isa. 52:7
and bring glad tidings of good
things! ●

**2. NOT ALL BELIEVE**

16 But they have not all obeyed the gospel. For Isaiah saith, Lord, who hath
believed our report? 17 So then faith Isa. 53:1
*cometh* by hearing, and hearing by the
word of God. ●

**3. JEWS KEEP ON REJECTING**

18 But I say, Have they not heard?
Yes verily,
Their sound went into all the earth,
and their words unto the ends of the Ps. 19:4
world.
19 But I say, Did not Israel know? First
Moses saith,
I will provoke you to jealousy by Deu. 32:21
*them that are* no people,
*and* by a foolish nation I will anger
you.
20 But Isaiah is very bold, and saith,
I was found of them that sought me Isa. 65:1
not;
I was made manifest unto them that
asked not after me.
21 But to Israel he saith, Isa. 65:2
All day long I have stretched forth
my hands
unto a disobedient and gainsaying HANDS
people. ●

*10:14-15* List the order of activity and experience in the communication of the gospel to souls of men:

How is this paragraph related to 10:13?

*10:16-17* Record the strong words of the paragraph:

*10:18-21* Who are the "they" of verse 18?

What does "their" (v.18) refer to?

What is the question of verse 19?

How is it answered in the verses:

v.19

v.20

v.21

NEW INTERNATIONAL VERSION

What do you learn here about:

REMNANT OF BELIEVING JEWS

GRACE OF GOD

WORKS AND SALVATION

PREDESTINATION

OTHER

*The Remnant of Israel*

11 I ask then, Did God reject his
people? By no means! I am an Israelite myself, a descendant of Abraham,
from the tribe of Benjamin. 2God did not
reject his people, whom he foreknew.
Don't you know what the Scripture says in
the passage about Elijah—how he appealed to God against Israel: 3"Lord, they
have killed your prophets and torn down
your altars; I am the only one left, and they
are trying to kill me"[g]? 4And what was
God's answer to him? "I have reserved for
myself seven thousand who have not
bowed the knee to Baal."[h] 5So too, at the
present time there is a remnant chosen by
grace. 6And if by grace, then it is no longer
by works; if it were, grace would no longer
be grace.[i] ●
7What then? What Israel sought so earnestly it did not obtain, but the elect did.
The others were hardened, 8as it is written:

"God gave them a spirit of stupor,
eyes so that they could not see
and ears so that they could not
hear,
to this very day."[j]

9And David says:

"May their table become a snare
and a trap,
a stumbling block and a
retribution for them.
10May their eyes be darkened so they
cannot see,
and their backs be bent forever."[k] ●

[g]*3* 1 Kings 19:10,14 [h]*4* 1 Kings 19:18
[i]*6* Some manuscripts *by grace. But if by works, then it is no longer grace; if it were, work would no longer be work.*
[j]*8* Deut. 29:4; Isaiah 29:10 [k]*10* Psalm 69:22,23

KING JAMES

**1. REMNANT AND GRACE**

PAUL A JEWISH BELIEVER

11 I say then, Hath God cast away his
people? God forbid. For I also am
an Israelite, of the seed of Abraham, *of*
the tribe of Benjamin. 2 God hath not
cast away his people which he foreknew.
Wot ye not what the Scripture saith of
Eli'jah? how he maketh intercession to I Ki. 19:10
God against Israel, saying,
3 Lord, they have killed thy prophets,
and digged down thine altars;
and I am left alone,
and they seek my life.
4 But what saith the answer of God unto
him? I Ki. 19:18
I have reserved to myself seven thousand men,
who have not bowed the knee to *the image of* Ba'al.
5 Even so then at this present time also
there is a remnant according to the election of grace. 6 And if by grace, then *is it*
no more of works: otherwise grace is no
more grace. But if *it be* of works, then is
it no more grace: otherwise work is no
more work.●

**2. NON-REMNANT AND DARKNESS**

7 What then? Israel hath not obtained
that which he seeketh for; but the election
hath obtained it, and the rest were blinded
8 (according as it is written,
God hath given them the spirit of slumber, Deu. 29:4
eyes that they should not see,
and ears that they should not hear;)
unto this day.
9 And David saith,
Let their table be made a snare, and a trap, Ps. 69:22f.
and a stumblingblock, and a recompense unto them:
10 let their eyes be darkened, that they may not see,
and bow down their back alway.●

JEWISH NON-BELIEVERS

*11:1-6* What different things are written here about the Jewish remnant?

Was Paul of the Jewish remnant?

Was there a remnant in Paul's time?

Why does Paul write here about grace? (vv.5-6)

*11:7-10* What does Paul write about the non-remnant?

NEW INTERNATIONAL VERSION

What is taught here about:

UNBELIEVING JEWS

GOSPEL TO THE GENTILES

A SECOND CHANCE

FRUITS OF JUDGMENT

BOASTING

FAITH

GRACE OF GOD

*Ingrafted Branches*

11Again I ask, Did they stumble so as to
fall beyond recovery? Not at all! Rather,
because of their transgression, salvation
has come to the Gentiles to make Israel
envious. 12But if their transgression means
riches for the world, and their loss means
riches for the Gentiles, how much greater
riches will their fullness bring!
13I am talking to you Gentiles. Inasmuch
as I am the apostle to the Gentiles, I make
much of my ministry 14in the hope that I
may somehow arouse my own people to
envy and save some of them. 15For if their
rejection is the reconciliation of the world,
what will their acceptance be but life from
the dead? 16If the part of the dough offered
as firstfruits is holy, then the whole batch
is holy; if the root is holy, so are the
branches.●
17If some of the branches have been broken off, and you, though a wild olive shoot,
have been grafted in among the others and
now share in the nourishing sap from the
olive root, 18do not boast over those
branches. If you do, consider this: You do
not support the root, but the root supports
you. 19You will say then, "Branches were
broken off so that I could be grafted in."
20Granted. But they were broken off because of unbelief, and you stand by faith.
Do not be arrogant, but be afraid. 21For if
God did not spare the natural branches, he
will not spare you either.●
22Consider therefore the kindness and
sternness of God: sternness to those who
fell, but kindness to you, provided that you
continue in his kindness. Otherwise, you
also will be cut off. 23And if they do not
persist in unbelief, they will be grafted in,
for God is able to graft them in again. 24Af-
ter all, if you were cut out of an olive tree
that is wild by nature, and contrary to nature were grafted into a cultivated olive
tree, how much more readily will these, the
natural branches, be grafted into their own
olive tree!●

KING JAMES

1. ISRAEL'S FALL—GENTILES' SALVATION

SALVATION TO GENTILES

11 I say then, Have they stumbled that
they should fall? God forbid: but *rather*
through their fall salvation *is come* unto
the Gentiles, for to provoke them to
jealousy. 12 Now if the fall of them *be* the
riches of the world, and the diminishing of
them the riches of the Gentiles; how much
more their fulness?
13 For I speak to you Gentiles, inasmuch as I am the apostle of the Gentiles,
I magnify mine office: 14 if by any means
I may provoke to emulation *them which
are* my flesh, and might save some of them.
15 For if the casting away of them *be* the
reconciling of the world, what *shall* the receiving *of them be*, but life from the dead?
16 For if the firstfruit *be* holy, the lump *is*
also *holy*: and if the root *be* holy, so *are*
the branches.●

2. WARNING TO GENTILES

17 And if some of the branches be
broken off, and thou, being a wild olive
tree, wert graffed in among them, and with
them partakest of the root and fatness of
the olive tree; 18 boast not against the
branches. But if thou boast, thou bearest
not the root, but the root thee. 19 Thou
wilt say then, The branches were broken
off, that I might be graffed in. 20 Well;
because of unbelief they were broken off,
and thou standest by faith. Be not high-
minded, but fear: 21 for if God spared
not the natural branches, *take heed* lest he
also spare not thee.●

3. GOD'S SAVING WORK

22 Behold therefore
the goodness and severity of God: on
them which fell, severity; but toward thee,
goodness, if thou continue in *his* goodness: otherwise thou also shalt be cut off.
23 And they also, if they abide not still in
unbelief, shall be graffed in: for God is
able to graff them in again. 24 For if thou
wert cut out of the olive tree which is wild
by nature, and wert graffed contrary to
nature into a good olive tree; how much
more shall these, which be the natural
*branches*, be graffed into their own olive
tree?●

HOPE YET FOR JEWS

This segment shows how the gospel reached the Gentiles via the Jews. How are the Gentiles referred to in each paragraph?

To whom is Paul speaking in each paragraph?

*11:11-16* Compare what is written about:

GENTILES

JEWS

*11:17-21* List the warnings and commands to the Gentiles.

*11:22-24* What is written about:

GENTILES

JEWS

NEW INTERNATIONAL VERSION

What does this passage teach about:

ISRAELITES

GENTILES

END TIMES

MERCY OF GOD

ATTRIBUTES OF GOD

MIND OF GOD

OTHER

### *All Israel Will Be Saved*

25I do not want you to be ignorant of this
mystery, brothers, so that you may not be
conceited: Israel has experienced a hardening in part until the full number of the
Gentiles has come in. 26And so all Israel
will be saved, as it is written:

"The deliverer will come from Zion;
he will turn godlessness away
from Jacob.●
27And this is[a] my covenant with them
when I take away their sins."[b]

28As far as the gospel is concerned, they
are enemies on your account; but as far as
election is concerned, they are loved on
account of the patriarchs, 29for God's gifts
and his call are irrevocable. 30Just as you
who were at one time disobedient to God
have now received mercy as a result of
their disobedience, 31so they too have now
become disobedient in order that they too
may now[c] receive mercy as a result of
God's mercy to you. 32For God has bound
all men over to disobedience so that he
may have mercy on them all.●

### *Doxology*

33Oh, the depth of the riches of the
wisdom and[d] knowledge of
God!
How unsearchable his judgments,
and his paths beyond tracing out!
34"Who has known the mind of the
Lord?
Or who has been his counselor?"[e]
35"Who has ever given to God,
that God should repay him?"[f]
36For from him and through him and
to him are all things.
To him be the glory forever!
Amen.●

[a]27 Or *will be* [b]27 Isaiah 59:20,21; 27:9
[c]31 Some manuscripts do not have *now*.
[d]33 Or *riches and the wisdom and the*
[e]34 Isaiah 40:13 [f]35 Job 41:11

KING JAMES

1. ALL ISRAEL TO BE SAVED

MYSTERY

25 For I would not, brethren, that ye
should be ignorant of this mystery, lest ye
should be wise in your own conceits, that
blindness in part is happened to Israel,
until the fulness of the Gentiles be come
in. 26 And so all Israel shall be saved:
as it is written,
There shall come out of Zion the
Deliverer,
and shall turn away ungodliness from
Jacob:
27 for this *is* my covenant unto them,
when I shall take away their sins.●

Isa. 59:20,21

Isa. 27:9

2. MERCY

28 As concerning the gospel, *they are*
enemies for your sakes: but as touching
the election, *they are* beloved for the
fathers' sakes. 29 For the gifts and calling
of God *are* without repentance. 30 For as
ye in times past have not believed God,
yet have now obtained mercy through
their unbelief: 31 even so have these also
now not believed, that through your mercy
they also may obtain mercy. 32 For God
hath concluded them all in unbelief, that
he might have mercy upon all.●

DOXOLOGY

33 O the depth of the riches both of the
wisdom and knowledge of God! how unsearchable *are* his judgments, and his ways
past finding out! 34 For who hath known
the mind of the Lord? or who hath been
his counselor? 35 or who hath first given
to him, and it shall be recompensed unto
him again? 36 For of him, and through
him, and to him, *are* all things: to whom
*be* glory for ever. Amen.●

PAST FINDING OUT

This segment concludes the section of Romans, GOD'S SOVEREIGNTY IN SAVING JEW AND GENTILE (9:1—11:36).

*11:25-27* List the sequence of spiritual states mentioned here:

What is meant by the phrase, "until the fulness of the Gentiles be come in" (v.25)? (See Living Bible.)

*11:28-32* What is meant by these verses:

v.28

v.29

Relate verse 31 to verse 26:

*11:33-36* List the parts of this doxology:

NEW INTERNATIONAL VERSION

What does this passage teach about:

THE TRANSFORMED LIFE

HUMILITY

THE CHURCH

SPIRITUAL GIFTS

CHRISTIAN LOVE

CHRISTIAN SERVICE

List your favorite commands or exhortations of this passage:

*Living Sacrifices*

12 Therefore, I urge you, brothers, in
view of God's mercy, to offer your
bodies as living sacrifices, holy and pleasing to God—which is your spiritual worship. 2 Do not conform any longer to the
pattern of this world, but be transformed
by the renewing of your mind. Then you
will be able to test and approve what God's
will is—his good, pleasing and perfect will.
3 For by the grace given me I say to every
one of you: Do not think of yourself more
highly than you ought, but rather think of
yourself with sober judgment, in accordance with the measure of faith God has
given you. 4 Just as each of us has one body
with many members, and these members
do not all have the same function, 5 so in
Christ we who are many form one body,
and each member belongs to all the others.
6 We have different gifts, according to the
grace given us. If a man's gift is prophesying, let him use it in proportion to his faith.
7 If it is serving, let him serve; if it is teaching, let him teach; 8 if it is encouraging, let
him encourage; if it is contributing to the
needs of others, let him give generously; if
it is leadership, let him govern diligently; if
it is showing mercy, let him do it cheerfully.●

*Love*

9 Love must be sincere. Hate what is evil;
cling to what is good. 10 Be devoted to one
another in brotherly love. Honor one another above yourselves. 11 Never be lacking in zeal, but keep your spiritual fervor,
serving the Lord. 12 Be joyful in hope, patient in affliction, faithful in prayer. 13 Share
with God's people who are in need. Practice hospitality.●
14 Bless those who persecute you; bless
and do not curse. 15 Rejoice with those who
rejoice; mourn with those who mourn.
16 Live in harmony with one another. Do
not be proud, but be willing to associate
with people of low position.[g] Do not be
conceited.
17 Do not repay anyone evil for evil. Be
careful to do what is right in the eyes of
everybody. 18 If it is possible, as far as it
depends on you, live at peace with everyone. 19 Do not take revenge, my friends, but
leave room for God's wrath, for it is written: "It is mine to avenge; I will repay,"[h]
says the Lord. 20 On the contrary:

> "If your enemy is hungry, feed him;
> if he is thirsty, give him
> something to drink.
> In doing this, you will heap burning
> coals on his head."[i]

21 Do not be overcome by evil, but overcome evil with good.●

[g] *16* Or *willing to do menial work* [h] *19* Deut. 32:35 [i] *20* Prov. 25:21,22

KING JAMES

1. CONSECRATION

HOLY

12 I beseech you therefore, brethren,
by the mercies of God, that ye present your bodies a living sacrifice, holy,
acceptable unto God, *which is* your reasonable service. 2 And be not conformed to
this world: but be ye transformed by the
renewing of your mind, that ye may prove
what *is* that good, and acceptable, and
perfect will of God.●

2. GIFTS FOR SERVICE

3 For I say, through the grace given
unto me, to every man that is among you,
not to think *of himself* more highly than
he ought to think; but to think soberly,
according as God hath dealt to every man
the measure of faith. 4 For as we have
many members in one body, and all members have not the same office: 5 so we,
*being* many, are one body in Christ, and
every one members one of another.
6 Having then gifts differing according to
the grace that is given to us, whether
prophecy, *let us prophesy* according to the
proportion of faith; 7 or ministry, *let us
wait* on *our* ministering; or he that teacheth, on teaching; 8 or he that exhorteth,
on exhortation: he that giveth, *let him do
it* with simplicity; he that ruleth, with
diligence; he that showeth mercy, with
cheerfulness.●

3. OBLIGATIONS TO OTHERS

—saints

9 *Let* love be without dissimulation.
Abhor that which is evil; cleave to that
which is good. 10 *Be* kindly affectioned
one to another with brotherly love; in
honor preferring one another; 11 not
slothful in business; fervent in spirit;
serving the Lord; 12 rejoicing in hope;
patient in tribulation; continuing instant
in prayer; 13 distributing to the necessity
of saints; given to hospitality.●

—world

14 Bless them which persecute you:
bless, and curse not. 15 Rejoice with them
that do rejoice, and weep with them that
weep. 16 *Be* of the same mind one toward
another. Mind not high things, but con-
descend to men of low estate. Be not wise
in your own conceits. 17 Recompense to
no man evil for evil. Provide things honest
in the sight of all men. 18 If it be possible,
as much as lieth in you, live peaceably
with all men. 19 Dearly beloved, avenge
not yourselves, but *rather* give place unto
wrath: for it is written, Vengeance *is*
mine; I will repay, saith the Lord.
20 Therefore if thine enemy hunger, feed
him; if he thirst, give him drink: for in so
doing thou shalt heap coals of fire on his
head. 21 Be not overcome of evil, but
overcome evil with good.●

GOOD

This segment begins the *practical* section of Romans. Recall this outline of the book:

DOCTRINE 1:18—11:36
PRACTICE 12:1—15:13

*12:1-2* What is written about:

GOD ____________________

COMMANDS ____________________

*12:3-8* What is the theme of verses 3-5? ____________________

List the gifts (vv.6-8): ____________________

*12:9-21* List the commands. Look for any groupings according to common areas.

____________________

NEW INTERNATIONAL VERSION

What do you learn here about:

CHRISTIAN CITIZEN

CIVIL AUTHORITY

TAXES

LOVE

TEN COMMANDMENTS

HONESTY

OTHER

*Submission to the Authorities*

13 Everyone must submit himself to the governing authorities, for there is no authority except that which God has established. The authorities that exist have been established by God. 2Consequently, he who rebels against the authority is rebelling against what God has instituted, and those who do so will bring judgment on themselves. 3For rulers hold no terror for those who do right, but for those who do wrong. Do you want to be free from fear of the one in authority? Then do what is right and he will commend you. 4For he is God's servant to do you good. But if you do wrong, be afraid, for he does not bear the sword for nothing. He is God's servant, an agent of wrath to bring punishment on the wrongdoer. 5Therefore, it is necessary to submit to the authorities, not only because of possible punishment but also because of conscience.

6This is also why you pay taxes, for the authorities are God's servants, who give their full time to governing. 7Give everyone what you owe him: If you owe taxes, pay taxes; if revenue, then revenue; if respect, then respect; if honor, then honor.●

*Love, for the Day Is Near*

8Let no debt remain outstanding, except the continuing debt to love one another, for he who loves his fellow man has fulfilled the law. 9The commandments, "Do not commit adultery," "Do not murder," "Do not steal," "Do not covet,"[a] and whatever other commandment there may be, are summed up in this one rule: "Love your neighbor as yourself."[b] 10Love does no harm to its neighbor. Therefore love is the fulfillment of the law.●

11And do this, understanding the present time. The hour has come for you to wake up from your slumber, because our salvation is nearer now than when we first believed. 12The night is nearly over; the day is almost here. So let us put aside the deeds of darkness and put on the armor of light. 13Let us behave decently, as in the daytime, not in orgies and drunkenness, not in sexual immorality and debauchery, not in dissension and jealousy. 14Rather, clothe yourselves with the Lord Jesus Christ, and do not think about how to gratify the desires of the sinful nature.[c] ●

a9 Exodus 20:13-15,17; Deut. 5:17-19,21
b9 Lev. 19:18 c14 Or *the flesh*

KING JAMES

### 1. SUBJECTION TO AUTHORITIES

POWER

13 Let every soul be subject unto the
higher powers. For there is no
power but of God: the powers that be are
ordained of God. 2 Whosoever therefore
resisteth the power, resisteth the ordinance
of God: and they that resist shall receive
to themselves damnation. 3 For rulers
are not a terror to good works, but to the
evil. Wilt thou then not be afraid of the
power? do that which is good, and thou
shalt have praise of the same: 4 for he is
the minister of God to thee for good. But
if thou do that which is evil, be afraid; for
he beareth not the sword in vain: for he is
the minister of God, a revenger to *execute*
wrath upon him that doeth evil. 5 Wherefore *ye* must needs be subject, not only for
wrath, but also for conscience' sake.
6 For, for this cause pay ye tribute also:
for they are God's ministers, attending
continually upon this very thing. 7 Render therefore to all their dues: tribute to
whom tribute *is due;* custom to whom
custom; fear to whom fear; honor to
whom honor.●

### 2. ATTITUDE OF LOVE

8 Owe no man any thing, but to love
one another: for he that loveth another
hath fulfilled the law. 9 For this, Thou
shalt not commit adultery, Thou shalt
not kill, Thou shalt not steal, Thou shalt
not bear false witness, Thou shalt not
covet; and if *there be* any other commandment, it is briefly comprehended in
this saying, namely, Thou shalt love thy
neighbor as thyself. 10 Love worketh no
ill to his neighbor: therefore love *is* the
fulfilling of the law.●

Ex. 20:13ff.

### 3. ARMOR OF LIGHT

11 And that, knowing the time, that
now *it is* high time to awake out of sleep:
for now *is* our salvation nearer than when
we believed. 12 The night is far spent, the
day is at hand: let us therefore cast off
the works of darkness, and let us put on
the armor of light. 13 Let us walk honestly, as in the day; not in rioting and
drunkenness, not in chambering and wantonness, not in strife and envying: 14 but
put ye on the Lord Jesus Christ, and make
not provision for the flesh, to *fulfil* the
lusts *thereof.*●

ARMOR

*13:1-7* Observe the different references to *subjection*. The paragraph is made up of commands and statements of fact. Record these.

COMMANDS

FACTS

*13:8-10* Record the references to love:

*13:11-14* Record at least five strong phrases of this paragraph.

NEW INTERNATIONAL VERSION

What does this passage teach about:

WEAK CHRISTIAN BROTHERS

STUMBLING BLOCKS

LORDSHIP OF CHRIST

WORKS

JUDGING OTHERS

KINGDOM OF GOD

FAITH

*The Weak and the Strong*

**14** Accept him whose faith is weak, without passing judgment on disputable matters. 2One man's faith allows him to eat everything, but another man, whose faith is weak, eats only vegetables. 3The man who eats everything must not look down on him who does not, and the man who does not eat everything must not condemn the man who does, for God has accepted him. 4Who are you to judge someone else's servant? To his own master he stands or falls. And he will stand, for the Lord is able to make him stand.●

5One man considers one day more sacred than another; another man considers every day alike. Each one should be fully convinced in his own mind. 6He who regards one day as special, does so to the Lord. He who eats meat, eats to the Lord, for he gives thanks to God; and he who abstains, does so to the Lord and gives thanks to God. 7For none of us lives to himself alone and none of us dies to himself alone. 8If we live, we live to the Lord; and if we die, we die to the Lord. So, whether we live or die, we belong to the Lord.

9For this very reason, Christ died and returned to life so that he might be the Lord of both the dead and the living.● 10You, then, why do you judge your brother? Or why do you look down on your brother? For we will all stand before God's judgment seat. 11It is written:

> " 'As surely as I live,' says the Lord,
> 'Every knee will bow before me;
> every tongue will confess to God.' "[d]

12So then, each of us will give an account of himself to God.

13Therefore let us stop passing judgment on one another. Instead, make up your mind not to put any stumbling block or obstacle in your brother's way. 14As one who is in the Lord Jesus, I am fully convinced that no food is unclean in itself. But if anyone regards something as unclean, then for him it is unclean. 15If your brother is distressed because of what you eat, you are no longer acting in love. Do not by your eating destroy your brother for whom Christ died. 16Do not allow what you consider good to be spoken of as evil. 17For the kingdom of God is not a matter of eating and drinking, but of righteousness, peace and joy in the Holy Spirit, 18because anyone who serves Christ in this way is pleasing to God and approved by men.

19Let us therefore make every effort to do what leads to peace and to mutual edification.● 20Do not destroy the work of God for the sake of food. All food is clean, but it is wrong for a man to eat anything that causes someone else to stumble. 21It is better not to eat meat or drink wine or to do anything else that will cause your brother to fall.

22So whatever you believe about these things keep between yourself and God. Blessed is the man who does not condemn himself by what he approves. 23But the man who has doubts is condemned if he eats, because his eating is not from faith; and everything that does not come from faith is sin.●

*d11* Isaiah 49:18; 45:23

KING JAMES

1.FELLOWSHIP

WEAK IN THE FAITH

14 Him that is weak in the faith receive
ye, *but* not to doubtful disputations.
2 For one believeth that he may eat all
things: another, who is weak, eateth herbs.
3 Let not him that eateth despise him that
eateth not; and let not him which eateth
not judge him that eateth: for God hath
received him. 4 Who art thou that judgest
another man's servant? to his own master
he standeth or falleth. Yea, he shall be
holden up: for God is able to make him
stand. ●

2.DEVOTION

5 One man esteemeth one day above
another: another esteemeth every day
*alike*. Let every man be fully persuaded
in his own mind. 6 He that regardeth the
day, regardeth *it* unto the Lord; and he
that regardeth not the day, to the Lord he
doth not regard *it*. He that eateth, eateth
to the Lord, for he giveth God thanks;
and he that eateth not, to the Lord he eateth not, and giveth God thanks. 7 For
none of us liveth to himself, and no man
dieth to himself. 8 For whether we live,
we live unto the Lord; and whether we
die, we die unto the Lord: whether we live
therefore, or die, we are the Lord's. 9 For
to this end Christ both died, and rose,
and revived, that he might be Lord both
of the dead and living. ●

3.NO JUDGING

10 But why dost thou judge thy brother?
or why dost thou set at nought thy
brother? for we shall all stand before the
judgment seat of Christ. 11 For it is
written,

Isa. 45:23

*As* I live, saith the Lord,
every knee shall bow to me,
and every tongue shall confess to
God.

12 So then every one of us shall give account of himself to God.
13 Let us not therefore judge one another any more: but judge this rather, that
no man put a stumblingblock or an occasion to fall in *his* brother's way. 14 I
know, and am persuaded by the Lord
Jesus, that *there is* nothing unclean of itself: but to him that esteemeth any thing
to be unclean, to him *it is* unclean. 15 But
if thy brother be grieved with *thy* meat,
now walkest thou not charitably. Destroy
not him with thy meat, for whom Christ
died. 16 Let not then your good be evil
spoken of: 17 for the kingdom of God is
not meat and drink; but righteousness,
and peace, and joy in the Holy Ghost.
18 For he that in these things serveth
Christ *is* acceptable to God, and approved
of men. 19 Let us therefore follow after
the things which make for peace, and
things wherewith one may edify another. ●

4.FAITH

20 For meat destroy not the work of God.
All things indeed *are* pure; but *it is* evil
for that man who eateth with offense.
21 *It is* good neither to eat flesh, nor to
drink wine, nor *any thing* whereby thy
brother stumbleth, or is offended, or is
made weak. 22 Hast thou faith? have *it*
to thyself before God. Happy *is* he that
condemneth not himself in that thing
which he alloweth. 23 And he that doubt-
eth is damned if he eat, because *he eateth*
not of faith: for whatsoever *is* not of faith
is sin. ●

NOT OF FAITH

First read the entire segment to see the many references to a Christian's relation to other believers.

*14:1-4* A key word is "receive." What is written here about this?

________________

*14:5-9* Note the repeated phrase "unto the Lord," and similar references. Record key truths here.

________________

*14:10-19* What is the main point? ________________

Record the different exhortations introduced by "Let us."

________________

*14:20-23* What is the point of this paragraph?

________________

NEW INTERNATIONAL VERSION

What do you learn here about:

HELPING OTHER CHRISTIANS

CHRIST

HOPE

GLORY OF GOD

JEW

GENTILE

OTHER

15 We who are strong ought to bear
with the failings of the weak and not
to please ourselves. [2]Each of us should
please his neighbor for his good, to build
him up. [3]For even Christ did not please
himself but, as it is written: "The insults of
those who insult you have fallen on me."[a]
[4]For everything that was written in the past
was written to teach us, so that through
endurance and the encouragement of the
Scriptures we might have hope.●
[5]May the God who gives endurance and
encouragement give you a spirit of unity
among yourselves as you follow Christ
Jesus, [6]so that with one heart and mouth
you may glorify the God and Father of our
Lord Jesus Christ.●
[7]Accept one another, then, just as Christ
accepted you, in order to bring praise to
God. [8]For I tell you that Christ has become
a servant of the Jews[b] on behalf of God's
truth, to confirm the promises made to the
patriarchs [9]so that the Gentiles may glorify
God for his mercy, as it is written:

> "Therefore I will praise you among
> the Gentiles;
> I will sing hymns to your name."[c]

[10]Again, it says,

> "Rejoice, O Gentiles, with his
> people."[d]

[11]And again,

> "Praise the Lord, all you Gentiles,
> and sing praises to him, all you
> peoples."[e]

[12]And again, Isaiah says,

> "The root of Jesse will spring up,
> one who will arise to rule over
> the nations;
> the Gentiles will hope in him."[f]●

[13]May the God of hope fill you with all
joy and peace as you trust in him, so that
you may overflow with hope by the power
of the Holy Spirit.●

*a3* Psalm 69:9 *b8* Greek *circumcision*
*c9* 2 Samuel 22:50; Psalm 18:49 *d10* Deut. 32:43
*e11* Psalm 117:1 *f12* Isaiah 11:10

## KING JAMES

1.PLEASE OTHERS

**15** We then that are strong ought to
bear the infirmities of the weak, and
not to please ourselves. 2 Let every one
of us please *his* neighbor for *his* good to
edification. 3 For even Christ pleased not
himself; but, as it is written, The reproaches of them that reproached thee
fell on me. 4 For whatsoever things were
written aforetime were written for our
learning, that we through patience and
comfort of the Scriptures might have hope.●

—BENEDICTION

5 Now the God of patience and consolation grant you to be likeminded one toward another according to Christ Jesus:
6 that ye may with one mind *and* one
mouth glorify God, even the Father of our
Lord Jesus Christ.●

2.RECEIVE OTHERS

7 Wherefore receive ye one another, as
Christ also received us, to the glory of
God. 8 Now I say that Jesus Christ was a
minister of the circumcision for the truth
of God, to confirm the promises *made* unto the fathers: 9 and that the Gentiles
might glorify God for *his* mercy; as it is
written,

For this cause I will confess to thee
among the Gentiles,
and sing unto thy name.

10 And again he saith,

Rejoice, ye Gentiles, with his people.

11 And again,

Praise the Lord, all ye Gentiles;
and laud him, all ye people.

12 And again, Isaiah saith,

There shall be a root of Jesse,
and he that shall rise to reign over the
Gentiles;
in him shall the Gentiles trust.●

—BENEDICTION

13 Now the God of hope fill you with all
joy and peace in believing, that ye may
abound in hope, through the power of the
Holy Ghost.●

STRONG CHRISTIANS

Ps. 69:9

2 Sam. 22:50

Deu. 32:43

Ps. 117:1

Isa. 11:10

POWER OF THE SPIRIT

Observe the two places where a benediction appears.

*15:1-4* What is the main point of the paragraph? ______

What is Christ's example? ______

How does verse 4 relate to the preceding verses?

*15:5-6* Record the main parts of the benediction:

*15:7-12* What is the main point of verse 7?

According to this paragraph, how was Christ's ministry directed to both Jew and Gentile?

*15:13* Record the main parts of this benediction:

NEW INTERNATIONAL VERSION

What does this passage teach about:

MINISTRY OF THE GOSPEL

HOLY SPIRIT

WILL OF GOD

GIFTS TO THE POOR

INTERCESSORY PRAYER

JOY

OTHER

### *Paul the Minister to the Gentiles*

[14]I myself am convinced, my brothers, that you yourselves are full of goodness, complete in knowledge and competent to instruct one another. [15]I have written you quite boldly on some points, as if to remind you of them again, because of the grace God gave me [16]to be a minister of Christ Jesus to the Gentiles with the priestly duty of proclaiming the gospel of God, so that the Gentiles might become an offering acceptable to God, sanctified by the Holy Spirit.

[17]Therefore I glory in Christ Jesus in my service to God. [18]I will not venture to speak of anything except what Christ has accomplished through me in leading the Gentiles to obey God by what I have said and done— [19]by the power of signs and miracles, through the power of the Spirit. So from Jerusalem all the way around to Illyricum, I have fully proclaimed the gospel of Christ. [20]It has always been my ambition to preach the gospel where Christ was not known, so that I would not be building on someone else's foundation. [21]Rather, as it is written:

> "Those who were not told about
> him will see,
> and those who have not heard
> will understand."[g]

[22]This is why I have often been hindered from coming to you.●

### *Paul's Plan to Visit Rome*

[23]But now that there is no more place for me to work in these regions, and since I have been longing for many years to see you, [24]I plan to do so when I go to Spain. I hope to visit you while passing through and to have you assist me on my journey there, after I have enjoyed your company for a while. [25]Now, however, I am on my way to Jerusalem in the service of the saints there. [26]For Macedonia and Achaia were pleased to make a contribution for the poor among the saints in Jerusalem. [27]They were pleased to do it, and indeed they owe it to them. For if the Gentiles have shared in the Jews' spiritual blessings, they owe it to the Jews to share with them their material blessings. [28]So after I have completed this task and have made sure that they have received this fruit, I will go to Spain and visit you on the way. [29]I know that when I come to you, I will come in the full measure of the blessing of Christ.●

[30]I urge you, brothers, by our Lord Jesus Christ and by the love of the Spirit, to join me in my struggle by praying to God for me. [31]Pray that I may be rescued from the unbelievers in Judea and that my service in Jerusalem may be acceptable to the saints there, [32]so that by God's will I may come to you with joy and together with you be refreshed. [33]The God of peace be with you all. Amen.●

[g]*21* Isaiah 52:15

KING JAMES

1. PAST: PREACHING EVERYWHERE

14 And I myself also am persuaded of
you, my brethren, that ye also are full of
goodness, filled with all knowledge, able
also to admonish one another. 15 Nevertheless, brethren, I have written the more
boldly unto you in some sort, as putting
you in mind, because of the grace that is
given to me of God, 16 that I should be
the minister of Jesus Christ to the Gentiles, ministering the gospel of God, that
the offering up of the Gentiles might be
acceptable, being sanctified by the Holy
Ghost. 17 I have therefore whereof I may
glory through Jesus Christ in those things
which pertain to God. 18 For I will not
dare to speak of any of those things which
Christ hath not wrought by me, to make
the Gentiles obedient, by word and deed,
19 through mighty signs and wonders, by
the power of the Spirit of God; so that
from Jerusalem, and round about unto
Illyr'icum, I have fully preached the gospel of Christ. 20 Yea, so have I strived to
preach the gospel, not where Christ was
named, lest I should build upon another
man's foundation: 21 but as it is written,

> To whom he was not spoken of, they
> shall see:
> and they that have not heard shall
> understand.

22 For which cause also I have been
much hindered from coming to you.●

2. FUTURE: MINISTRY AT ROME

23 But now having no more place in these
parts, and having a great desire these
many years to come unto you; 24 whensoever I take my journey into Spain, I will
come to you: for I trust to see you in my
journey, and to be brought on my way
thitherward by you, if first I be somewhat
filled with your *company*. 25 But now I
go unto Jerusalem to minister unto the
saints. 26 For it hath pleased them of
Macedonia and Achai'a to make a certain
contribution for the poor saints which are
at Jerusalem. 27 It hath pleased them
verily; and their debtors they are. For if
the Gentiles have been made partakers of
their spiritual things, their duty is also to
minister unto them in carnal things.
28 When therefore I have performed this,
and have sealed to them this fruit, I will
come by you into Spain. 29 And I am
sure that, when I come unto you, I shall
come in the fulness of the blessing of the
gospel of Christ.●

3. PRESENT: MINISTRY AT JERUSALEM

30 Now I beseech you, brethren, for the
Lord Jesus Christ's sake, and for the love
of the Spirit, that ye strive together with
me in *your* prayers to God for me;
31 that I may be delivered from them that
do not believe in Judea; and that my
service which *I have* for Jerusalem may be
accepted of the saints; 32 that I may
come unto you with joy by the will of
God, and may with you be refreshed.
33 Now the God of peace *be* with you all.
Amen.●

GOODNESS AND KNOWLEDGE

Isa. 52:15

JOY AND PEACE

At this point Paul begins the last part of his letter, the epilogue, which contains various personal notes, such as testimony and greeting.

*15:14-22* Relate verse 14 to 15:13. ________

Why did Paul write this letter, according to verses 15-16?

What is Paul's testimony, in verses 17-21?

How does his testimony lead into verse 22?

*15:23-29* What is the parenthesis of verses 25-27 about?

What were Paul's future plans? ________

*15:30-33* List all the bright words and phrases of the paragraph.

NEW INTERNATIONAL VERSION

It may surprise you how many spiritual lessons are taught by this passage. Record as many as you can:

*Personal Greetings*

16 I commend to you our sister
Phoebe, a servant[a] of the church in
Cenchrea. 2I ask you to receive her in the
Lord in a way worthy of the saints and to
give her any help she may need from you,
for she has been a great help to many
people, including me.●

3Greet Priscilla[b] and Aquila, my fellow workers in Christ Jesus. 4They
risked their lives for me. Not only I but all the churches of the Gentiles are grateful to them.
5Greet also the church that meets at their house.
Greet my dear friend Epenetus, who was the first convert to Christ in the province of Asia.
6Greet Mary, who worked very hard for you.
7Greet Andronicus and Junias, my relatives who have been in prison with me. They are outstanding among the apostles, and they were in Christ before I was.
8Greet Ampliatus, whom I love in the Lord.
9Greet Urbanus, our fellow worker in Christ, and my dear friend Stachys.
10Greet Apelles, tested and approved in Christ.
Greet those who belong to the household of Aristobulus.
11Greet Herodion, my relative.
Greet those in the household of Narcissus who are in the Lord.
12Greet Tryphena and Tryphosa, those women who work hard in the Lord.
Greet my dear friend Persis, another woman who has worked very hard in the Lord.
13Greet Rufus, chosen in the Lord, and his mother, who has been a mother to me, too.
14Greet Asyncritus, Phlegon, Hermes, Patrobas, Hermas and the brothers with them.
15Greet Philologus, Julia, Nereus and his sister, and Olympas and all the saints with them.
16Greet one another with a holy kiss.
All the churches of Christ send greetings.●

[a]1 Or *deaconess*
[b]3 Greek *Prisca*, a variant of *Priscilla*

KING JAMES

1.COMMENDATION

SISTER IN CHRIST

**16** I commend unto you Phoebe our
sister, which is a servant of the
church which is at Cen'chre-ae: 2 that ye
receive her in the Lord, as becometh
saints, and that ye assist her in whatsoever business she hath need of you: for
she hath been a succorer of many, and of
myself also.●

2.GREETINGS

3 Greet Priscilla and Aquila, my
helpers in Christ Jesus: 4 who have for
my life laid down their own necks: unto
whom not only I give thanks, but also all
the churches of the Gentiles. 5 Likewise
*greet* the church that is in their house.
Salute my well-beloved Epe'netus, who is
the firstfruits of Achai'a unto Christ.
6 Greet Mary, who bestowed much labor
on us. 7 Salute Andron'icus and Ju'ni-a,
my kinsmen, and my fellow prisoners,
who are of note among the apostles, who
also were in Christ before me. 8 Greet
Am'pli-as, my beloved in the Lord.
9 Salute Ur'bane, our helper in Christ,
and Stachys my beloved. 10 Salute Apel'-
les approved in Christ. Salute them which
are of Aristob'ulus' *household*. 11 Salute
Hero'di-on my kinsman. Greet them that
be of the *household* of Narcissus, which
are in the Lord. 12 Salute Tryphae'na and
Trypho'sa, who labor in the Lord. Salute
the beloved Persis, which labored much
in the Lord. 13 Salute Rufus chosen in
the Lord, and his mother and mine.
14 Salute Asyn'critus, Phlegon, Hermas,
Pat'robas, Hermes, and the brethren
which are with them. 15 Salute Philol'o-
gus, and Julia, Ne'reus, and his sister, and
Olym'pas, and all the saints which are
with them. 16 Salute one another with a
holy kiss. The churches of Christ salute
you.●

CHURCHES OF CHRIST

*16:1-2* What is revealed here about Phoebe?

*16:3-16* What *different kinds* of people are mentioned in this long list (e.g., men, women)?

Make a list of the names and how the people are identified.

NEW INTERNATIONAL VERSION

17 I urge you, brothers, to watch out for
those who cause divisions and put obsta-
cles in your way that are contrary to the
teaching you have learned. Keep away
from them. 18 For such people are not serving our Lord Christ, but their own appe-
tites. By smooth talk and flattery they deceive the minds of naive people. 19 Everyone has heard about your obedience, so I
am full of joy over you; but I want you to
be wise about what is good, and innocent
about what is evil.
20 The God of peace will soon crush Satan
under your feet.
The grace of our Lord Jesus be with
you.●
21 Timothy, my fellow worker, sends his
greetings to you, as do Lucius, Jason and
Sosipater, my relatives.
22 I, Tertius, who wrote down this letter,
greet you in the Lord.
23 Gaius, whose hospitality I and the
whole church here enjoy, sends you his
greetings.
Erastus, who is the city's director of
public works, and our brother Quartus
send you their greetings.[c]●
25 Now to him who is able to establish
you by my gospel and the proclamation of
Jesus Christ, according to the revelation of
the mystery hidden for long ages past,
26 but now revealed and made known
through the prophetic writings by the command of the eternal God, so that all nations
might believe and obey him— 27 to the only
wise God be glory forever through Jesus
Christ! Amen.●

c23 Some manuscripts *their greetings. 24 May the grace of our Lord Jesus Christ be with all of you. Amen.*

What does this concluding passage teach about:

ENEMIES OF THE GOSPEL

DECEIT

FAITHFUL WITNESSES

SATAN

FELLOW WORKERS

GOD

JESUS CHRIST

List spiritual applications of the passage.

KING JAMES

1.WARNING

TROUBLE

17 Now I beseech you, brethren, mark
them which cause divisions and offenses
contrary to the doctrine which ye have
learned; and avoid them. **18** For they
that are such serve not our Lord Jesus
Christ, but their own belly; and by good
words and fair speeches deceive the hearts
of the simple. **19** For your obedience is
come abroad unto all *men*. I am glad
therefore on your behalf: but yet I would
have you wise unto that which is good,
and simple concerning evil. **20** And the
God of peace shall bruise Satan under
your feet shortly. The grace of our Lord
Jesus Christ *be* with you. Amen.●

2.GREETING

21 Timothy my workfellow, and
Lucius, and Jason, and Sosip'ater, my
kinsmen, salute you.
22 I Tertius, who wrote *this* epistle,
salute you in the Lord.
23 Gai'us mine host, and of the whole
church, saluteth you. Eras'tus the chamberlain of the city saluteth you, and
Quartus a brother. **24** The grace of our
Lord Jesus Christ *be* with you all. Amen.●

3.DOXOL-
OGY

25 Now to him that is of power to
stablish you according to my gospel, and
the preaching of Jesus Christ, according
to the revelation of the mystery, which
was kept secret since the world began,
**26** but now is made manifest, and by the
Scriptures of the prophets, according to
the commandment of the everlasting God,
made known to all nations for the obedience of faith: **27** to God only wise, *be*
glory through Jesus Christ for ever.
Amen.●

GLORY

*16:17-20* What is written here about:

TROUBLE MAKERS ____________________

CHRISTIANS AT HOME ____________________

GOD ____________________

JESUS CHRIST ____________________

*16:21-24* Record your observations. ____________________

*16:25-27* Record the parts of the doxology:

TO: ____________________

BE: ____________________

# 1 CORINTHIANS

## AUTHORSHIP

Paul wrote this letter to the church at Corinth. The apostle wrote the letter on his third missionary journey, toward the end of a three-year ministry in the city of Ephesus (16:8).

## DATE

A.D. 55-56.

## OCCASION

The gospel was first preached in Corinth by Paul, on his second missionary journey, A.D. 50. Paul carried the burden of the spiritual care of this church from the very day it was founded with a small nucleus of new converts (2 Cor. 11:28). The apostle learned about spiritual problems in the church through reports (see 1:11 and 5:1) and inquiries (e.g. 7:1,25) originating with members and leaders of the church.

## PURPOSES

Among Paul's purposes in writing were these: (1) to identify the problems underlying the reports and inquiries; (2) to offer solutions by way of doctrine and example; (3) to give extended teaching on related doctrines; (4) to give a defense of his apostleship; (5) to exhort the believers in the ways of a full, mature, Christian life.

## THEME

First Corinthians is about spiritual problems of a local church, and their solutions.

## 1 CORINTHIANS: Problems of A Local Church

| | |
|---|---|
| Introduction | 1:1-9 |
| DIVISIONS | 1:10-4:21 |
| Party Strife | 1:10-31 |
| The Mysteries of God Revealed | 2:1-16 |
| The Unity of God's Servants | 3:1-23 |
| Paul's Defense of His Ministry | 4:1-21 |
| DEPRAVITIES | 5:1-6:20 |
| Licentiousness | 5:1-13 |
| Lawsuits | 6:1-11 |
| Libertinism | 6:12-20 |
| PERSONAL PROBLEMS | 7:1-11:1 |
| To Marry or Not to Marry | 7:1-40 |
| Boundaries of Christian Liberty | 8:1-11:1 |
| WORSHIP SERVICE PROBLEMS | 11:2-15:58 |
| Place of Women and Men | 11:2-16 |
| Observing the Lord's Supper | 11:17-34 |
| Spiritual Gifts | 12:1-14:40 |
| Doctrinal Questions: the Resurrection | 15:1-58 |
| Conclusion | 16:1-24 |

# 1 CORINTHIANS

NEW INTERNATIONAL VERSION

What does this passage teach about:

SERVANT OF JESUS

LOCAL CHURCH

SAINTS

JESUS

GRACE OF GOD

SECOND COMING OF CHRIST

OTHER

1 Paul, called to be an apostle of Christ
Jesus by the will of God, and our brother Sosthenes,

2To the church of God in Corinth, to
those sanctified in Christ Jesus and called
to be holy, together with all those everywhere who call on the name of our Lord
Jesus Christ—their Lord and ours:

3Grace and peace to you from God our
Father and the Lord Jesus Christ. ●

*Thanksgiving*

4I always thank God for you because of
his grace given you in Christ Jesus. 5For in
him you have been enriched in every
way—in all your speaking and in all your
knowledge— 6because our testimony
about Christ was confirmed in you. 7There-
fore you do not lack any spiritual gift as
you eagerly wait for our Lord Jesus Christ
to be revealed. 8He will keep you strong to
the end, so that you will be blameless on
the day of our Lord Jesus Christ. ● 9God,
who has called you into fellowship with his
Son Jesus Christ our Lord, is faithful. ●

KING JAMES

# 1 CORINTHIANS

1.SALUTATION

1 Paul, called *to be* an apostle of Jesus
Christ through the will of God, and
Sos'thenes *our* brother,
2 Unto the church of God which is at
Corinth, to them that are sanctified in
Christ Jesus, called *to be* saints, with all
that in every place call upon the name of
Jesus Christ our Lord, both theirs and
ours:
3 Grace *be* unto you, and peace, from
God our Father, and *from* the Lord Jesus
Christ. ●

2.GRATITUDE

4 I thank my God always on your behalf, for the grace of God which is given
you by Jesus Christ; 5 that in every thing
ye are enriched by him, in all utterance,
and *in* all knowledge; 6 even as the testimony of Christ was confirmed in you:
7 so that ye come behind in no gift; waiting for the coming of our Lord Jesus
Christ: 8 who shall also confirm you unto
the end, *that ye may be* blameless in the
day of our Lord Jesus Christ.●

3.GOD AND HIS SON

9 God *is*
faithful, by whom ye were called unto the
fellowship of his Son Jesus Christ our
Lord.●

AN APOSTLE AND JESUS

THE CHURCH AND JESUS

1 Corinthians is about problems of a local church, but the opening verses give no clue to this. Account for Paul's bright and positive introduction.

*1:1-3* Record what is written about:

PAUL

CHURCH AT CORINTH

*1:4-8* Record what is further revealed about the church at Corinth:

*1:9* What are the strong words and phrases of the text?

NEW INTERNATIONAL VERSION

What do you learn here about:

CHRISTIAN LOVE

UNITY OF BELIEVERS

WATER BAPTISM

CROSS OF CHRIST

TRUE WISDOM

VAIN GLORY

### *Divisions in the Church*

[10]I appeal to you, brothers, in the name
of our Lord Jesus Christ, that all of you
agree with one another so that there may
be no divisions among you and that you
may be perfectly united in mind and
thought. [11]My brothers, some from
Chloe's household have informed me that
there are quarrels among you. [12]What I
mean is this: One of you says, "I follow
Paul"; another, "I follow Apollos"; another, "I follow Cephas[a]"; still another, "I
follow Christ."
[13]Is Christ divided? Was Paul crucified
for you? Were you baptized into[b] the name
of Paul? [14]I am thankful that I did not baptize any of you except Crispus and Gaius,
[15]so no one can say that you were baptized
into my name. [16](Yes, I also baptized the
household of Stephanas; beyond that, I
don't remember if I baptized anyone else.)
[17]For Christ did not send me to baptize, but
to preach the gospel—not with words of
human wisdom, lest the cross of Christ be
emptied of its power.●

### *Christ the Wisdom and Power of God*

[18]For the message of the cross is foolishness to those who are perishing, but to us
who are being saved it is the power of God.
[19]For it is written:

> "I will destroy the wisdom of the
> wise;
> the intelligence of the intelligent I
> will frustrate."[c]

[20]Where is the wise man? Where is the
scholar? Where is the philosopher of this
age? Has not God made foolish the wisdom
of the world? [21]For since in the wisdom of
God the world through its wisdom did not
know him, God was pleased through the
foolishness of what was preached to save
those who believe. [22]Jews demand miraculous signs and Greeks look for wisdom,
[23]but we preach Christ crucified: a stumbling block to Jews and foolishness to Gentiles, [24]but to those whom God has called,
both Jews and Greeks, Christ the power of
God and the wisdom of God. [25]For the foolishness of God is wiser than man's wisdom, and the weakness of God is stronger
than man's strength.●
[26]Brothers, think of what you were when
you were called. Not many of you were
wise by human standards; not many were
influential; not many were of noble birth.
[27]But God chose the foolish things of the
world to shame the wise; God chose the
weak things of the world to shame the
strong. [28]He chose the lowly things of this
world and the despised things—and the
things that are not—to nullify the things
that are, [29]so that no one may boast before
him. [30]It is because of him that you are in
Christ Jesus, who has become for us wisdom from God—that is, our righteousness,
holiness and redemption. [31]Therefore, as it
is written: "Let him who boasts boast in
the Lord."[d]●

[a] *12* That is, Peter
[b] *13* Or *in*; also in verse 15
[c] *19* Isaiah 29:14
[d] *31* Jer. 9:24

## KING JAMES

**1. CHURCH UNITY**

LOVE

10 Now I beseech you, brethren, by the
name of our Lord Jesus Christ, that ye all
speak the same thing, and *that* there be
no divisions among you; but *that* ye be
perfectly joined together in the same mind
and in the same judgment. 11 For it hath
been declared unto me of you, my brethren, by them *which are of the house* of
Chlo'e, that there are contentions among
you. 12 Now this I say, that every one of
you saith, I am of Paul; and I of Apol'-
los; and I of Cephas; and I of Christ.
13 Is Christ divided? was Paul crucified
for you? or were ye baptized in the name
of Paul? 14 I thank God that I baptized
none of you, but Crispus and Gai'us;
15 lest any should say that I had baptized
in mine own name. 16 And I baptized
also the household of Steph'anas: besides, I know not whether I baptized any
other. 17 For Christ sent me not to baptize, but to preach the gospel: not with
wisdom of words, lest the cross of Christ
should be made of none effect.●

**2. TRUE WISDOM**

18 For the preaching of the cross is to
them that perish, foolishness; but unto
us which are saved, it is the power of God.
19 For it is written,
I will destroy the wisdom of the wise, (Isa. 29:14)
and will bring to nothing the understanding of the prudent.
20 Where *is* the wise? where *is* the scribe?
where *is* the disputer of this world? hath
not God made foolish the wisdom of this
world? 21 For after that in the wisdom
of God the world by wisdom knew not
God, it pleased God by the foolishness of
preaching to save them that believe.
22 For the Jews require a sign, and the
Greeks seek after wisdom: 23 but we
preach Christ crucified, unto the Jews a
stumblingblock, and unto the Greeks
foolishness; 24 but unto them which are
called, both Jews and Greeks, Christ the
power of God, and the wisdom of God.
25 Because the foolishness of God is wiser
than men; and the weakness of God is
stronger than men.●

**3. GOD'S GLORY**

26 For ye see your calling, brethren,
how that not many wise men after the
flesh, not many mighty, not many noble,
*are called:* 27 but God hath chosen the
foolish things of the world to confound
the wise; and God hath chosen the weak
things of the world to confound the things
which are mighty; 28 and base things of
the world, and things which are despised,
hath God chosen, *yea*, and things which
are not, to bring to nought things that are:
29 that no flesh should glory in his
presence. 30 But of him are ye in Christ
Jesus, who of God is made unto us wisdom, and righteousness, and sanctifica-
tion, and redemption: 31 that, according (Jer. 9:23f)
as it is written, He that glorieth, let him
glory in the Lord.●

HUMILITY

---

This segment begins the section DIVISIONS (1:10—4:21).

*1:10-17* What words of verses 10 and 11 identify the problem?

Record the different cliques:

What is a key repeated word of verses 13-17?

*1:18-25* What two words are contrasted throughout?

Record the different references to the cross.

*1:26-31* What key word is a key to the main emphasis of the paragraph?

What are the strong words of verse 30?

NEW INTERNATIONAL VERSION

What does this passage teach about:

THE CRUCIFIED LIFE ____________________

HUMILITY ____________________

WISDOM OF THE WORLD ____________________

REVELATION FROM GOD ____________________

SPIRITUAL UNDERSTANDING ____________________

NATURAL MAN ____________________

OTHER ____________________

2 When I came to you, brothers, I did not
come with eloquence or superior wisdom as I proclaimed to you the testimony
about God.[a] 2For I resolved to know nothing while I was with you except Jesus
Christ and him crucified. 3I came to you in
weakness and fear, and with much trembling. 4My message and my preaching were
not with wise and persuasive words, but
with a demonstration of the Spirit's power,
5so that your faith might not rest on men's
wisdom, but on God's power.●

*Wisdom From the Spirit*

6We do, however, speak a message of
wisdom among the mature, but not the wisdom of this age or of the rulers of this age,
who are coming to nothing. 7No, we speak
of God's secret wisdom, a wisdom that has
been hidden and that God destined for our
glory before time began. 8None of the rulers of this age understood it, for if they
had, they would not have crucified the
Lord of glory. 9However, as it is written:

"No eye has seen,
no ear has heard,
no mind has conceived
what God has prepared for those
who love him"[b]— ●

10but God has revealed it to us by his Spirit.
The Spirit searches all things, even the
deep things of God. 11For who among men
knows the thoughts of a man except the
man's spirit within him? In the same way
no one knows the thoughts of God except
the Spirit of God. 12We have not received
the spirit of the world but the Spirit who is
from God, that we may understand what
God has freely given us. 13This is what we
speak, not in words taught us by human
wisdom but in words taught by the Spirit,
expressing spiritual truths in spiritual
words.[c] 14The man without the Spirit does
not accept the things that come from the
Spirit of God, for they are foolishness to
him, and he cannot understand them, because they are spiritually discerned. 15The
spiritual man makes judgments about all
things, but he himself is not subject to any
man's judgment:

16"For who has known the mind of
the Lord
that he may instruct him?"[d]

But we have the mind of Christ.●

[a] *1* Some manuscripts *as I proclaimed to you God's mystery*
[b] *9* Isaiah 64:4
[c] *13* Or *Spirit, interpreting spiritual truths to spiritual men*
[d] *16* Isaiah 40:13

KING JAMES

1.METHOD OF PAUL'S PREACHING

TESTIMONY OF GOD

**2** And I, brethren, when I came to you,
came not with excellency of speech or
of wisdom, declaring unto you the testimony of God. 2 For I determined not to
know any thing among you, save Jesus
Christ, and him crucified. 3 And I was
with you in weakness, and in fear, and in
much trembling. 4 And my speech and
my preaching *was* not with enticing words
of man's wisdom, but in demonstration of
the Spirit and of power: 5 that your faith
should not stand in the wisdom of men,
but in the power of God.●

2.MESSAGE OF PAUL'S PREACHING

6 Howbeit we speak wisdom among
them that are perfect: yet not the wisdom
of this world, nor of the princes of this
world, that come to nought: 7 but we
speak the wisdom of God in a mystery,
*even* the hidden *wisdom*, which God ordained before the world unto our glory;
8 which none of the princes of this world
knew: for had they known *it*, they would
not have crucified the Lord of glory.
9 But as it is written,

Isa. 64:4

Eye hath not seen, nor ear heard,
neither have entered into the heart
of man,
the things which God hath prepared
for them that love him.●

3.SOURCE OF PAUL'S MESSAGE

10 But God hath revealed *them* unto us by
his Spirit: for the Spirit searcheth all
things, yea, the deep things of God.
11 For what man knoweth the things of a
man, save the spirit of man which is in
him? even so the things of God knoweth
no man, but the Spirit of God. 12 Now
we have received, not the spirit of the
world, but the Spirit which is of God;
that we might know the things that are
freely given to us of God. 13 Which
things also we speak, not in the words
which man's wisdom teacheth, but which
the Holy Ghost teacheth; comparing
spiritual things with spiritual.
14 But the natural man receiveth not
the things of the Spirit of God: for they
are foolishness unto him: neither can he
know *them*, because they are spiritually
discerned. 15 But he that is spiritual
judgeth all things, yet he himself is judged
of no man. 16 For who hath known the
mind of the Lord, that he may instruct
him? But we have the mind of Christ.●

MIND OF CHRIST

*2:1-5* Record how Paul preached:

v.1 ________

v.3 ________

v.4 ________

What were Paul's purposes?

v.2 ________

v.5 ________

*2:6-9* What was Paul's message? ________

*2:10-16* Observe the references to the three persons of the Trinity.
How does a Christian understand spiritual truth?

Compare verses 10 and 16, observing the ministries of Father, Son and Holy Spirit.

NEW INTERNATIONAL VERSION

What is taught here about:

CARNAL CHRISTIANS

CHRISTIAN UNITY

WORKS

TEMPLE OF GOD

TRUE WISDOM

FUTURE JUDGMENT

*On Divisions in the Church*

3 Brothers, I could not address you as
spiritual but as worldly—mere infants
in Christ. [2]I gave you milk, not solid food,
for you were not yet ready for it. Indeed,
you are still not ready. [3]You are still worldly. For since there is jealousy and quarreling among you, are you not worldly? Are
you not acting like mere men? [4]For when
one says, "I follow Paul," and another, "I
follow Apollos," are you not mere men?
[5]What, after all, is Apollos? And what is
Paul? Only servants, through whom you
came to believe—as the Lord has assigned
to each his task. [6]I planted the seed, Apollos watered it, but God made it grow. [7]So
neither he who plants nor he who waters is
anything, but only God, who makes things
grow. [8]The man who plants and the man
who waters have one purpose, and each
will be rewarded according to his own labor. [9]For we are God's fellow workers; you
are God's field, God's building.●
[10]By the grace God has given me, I laid
a foundation as an expert builder, and
someone else is building on it. But each
one should be careful how he builds. [11]For
no one can lay any foundation other than
the one already laid, which is Jesus Christ.
[12]If any man builds on this foundation using gold, silver, costly stones, wood, hay
or straw, [13]his work will be shown for what
it is, because the Day will bring it to light.
It will be revealed with fire, and the fire
will test the quality of each man's work.
[14]If what he has built survives, he will receive his reward. [15]If it is burned up, he will
suffer loss; he himself will be saved, but
only as one escaping through the flames.●
[16]Don't you know that you yourselves
are God's temple and that God's Spirit
lives in you? [17]If anyone destroys God's
temple, God will destroy him; for God's
temple is sacred, and you are that temple.●
[18]Do not deceive yourselves. If any one
of you thinks he is wise by the standards of
this age, he should become a "fool" so that
he may become wise. [19]For the wisdom of
this world is foolishness in God's sight. As
it is written: "He catches the wise in their
craftiness"[e]; [20]and again, "The Lord
knows that the thoughts of the wise are
futile."[f] [21]So then, no more boasting about
men! All things are yours, [22]whether Paul
or Apollos or Cephas[g] or the world or life
or death or the present or the future—all
are yours, [23]and you are of Christ, and
Christ is of God.●

[e]*19* Job 5:13 [f]*20* Psalm 94:11 [g]*22* That is, Peter

## KING JAMES

**1. ONE FIELD**

**BABES IN CHRIST**

3 And I, brethren, could not speak unto
you as unto spiritual, but as unto carnal, *even* as unto babes in Christ. 2 I have
fed you with milk, and not with meat:
for hitherto ye were not able *to bear it*,
neither yet now are ye able. 3 For ye are
yet carnal: for whereas *there is* among you
envying, and strife, and divisions, are
ye not carnal, and walk as men? 4 For
while one saith, I am of Paul; and another, I *am* of Apol'los; are ye not carnal?
5 Who then is Paul, and who *is* Apol'-
los, but ministers by whom ye believed,
even as the Lord gave to every man? 6 I
have planted, Apol'los watered; but
God gave the increase. 7 So then neither
is he that planteth any thing, neither he
that watereth; but God that giveth the
increase. 8 Now he that planteth and he
that watereth are one: and every man
shall receive his own reward according to
his own labor. 9 For we are laborers together with God: ye are God's husbandry,
*ye are* God's building.●

**2. ONE BUILDING**

10 According to the grace of God which
is given unto me, as a wise masterbuilder,
I have laid the foundation, and another
buildeth thereon. But let every man take
heed how he buildeth thereupon. 11 For
other foundation can no man lay than
that is laid, which is Jesus Christ. 12 Now
if any man build upon this foundation
gold, silver, precious stones, wood, hay,
stubble; 13 every man's work shall be
made manifest: for the day shall declare it,
because it shall be revealed by fire; and the
fire shall try every man's work of what
sort it is. 14 If any man's work abide
which he hath built thereupon, he shall
receive a reward. 15 If any man's work
shall be burned, he shall suffer loss: but
he himself shall be saved; yet so as by fire.●

**3. ONE TEMPLE**

16 Know ye not that ye are the temple
of God, and *that* the Spirit of God dwelleth in you? 17 If any man defile the
temple of God, him shall God destroy;
for the temple of God is holy, which
*temple* ye are.●

**4. ONE CHRIST**

18 Let no man deceive himself. If any
man among you seemeth to be wise in this
world, let him become a fool, that he may
be wise. 19 For the wisdom of this world
is foolishness with God: for it is written,

> He taketh the wise in their own craft-
> iness. (Job 5:13)

20 And again,

> The Lord knoweth the thoughts of
> the wise,
> that they are vain. (Ps. 94:11)

21 Therefore let no man glory in men: for
all things are yours; 22 whether Paul, or
Apol'los, or Cephas, or the world, or life,
or death, or things present, or things to
come; all are yours; 23 and ye are
Christ's; and Christ *is* God's.●

**YE ARE CHRIST'S**

---

*3:1-9* How does verse 3 identify the problem?

______________________________

______________________________

What one word of verses 3-4 describes the Corinthians' spiritual condition?

______________________________

______________________________

Record different references to unity in verses 5-9.

______________________________

______________________________

*3:10-15* The last phrase of verse 9 introduces this paragraph.
Identify each of the following:

THE BUILDING ______________________________

______________________________

______________________________

OWNER OF THE BUILDING ______________________________

______________________________

______________________________

BUILDER OF STRUCTURE ______________________________

______________________________

______________________________

BUILDING MATERIALS ______________________________

______________________________

______________________________

TEST OF BUILDING ______________________________

______________________________

______________________________

*13:16-17* What is the key word? ______________________________

______________________________

*13:18-23* Complete the phrase,
"ye are ______________________________."

Relate this to the other parts of the paragraph.

______________________________

______________________________

______________________________

NEW INTERNATIONAL VERSION

What do you learn from this passage about:

WHAT IS REQUIRED IN CHRISTIAN SERVICE

THE JUDGE OF THE BELIEVER'S SERVICE

TRUE HUMILITY

*Apostles of Christ*

4 So then, men ought to regard us as servants of Christ and as those entrusted with the secret things of God. [2]Now it is required that those who have been given a trust must prove faithful. [3]I care very little if I am judged by you or by any human court; indeed, I do not even judge myself. [4]My conscience is clear, but that does not make me innocent. It is the Lord who judges me. [5]Therefore judge nothing before the appointed time; wait till the Lord comes. He will bring to light what is hidden in darkness and will expose the motives of men's hearts. At that time each will receive his praise from God.●

[6]Now, brothers, I have applied these things to myself and Apollos for your benefit, so that you may learn from us the meaning of the saying, "Do not go beyond what is written." Then you will not take pride in one man over against another. [7]For who makes you different from anyone else? What do you have that you did not receive? And if you did receive it, why do you boast as though you did not?

[8]Already you have all you want! Already you have become rich! You have become kings—and that without us! How I wish that you really had become kings so that we might be kings with you! [9]For it seems to me that God has put us apostles on display at the end of the procession, like men condemned to die in the arena. We have been made a spectacle to the whole universe, to angels as well as to men. [10]We are fools for Christ, but you are so wise in Christ! We are weak, but you are strong! You are honored, we are dishonored! [11]To this very hour we go hungry and thirsty, we are in rags, we are brutally treated, we are homeless. [12]We work hard with our own hands. When we are cursed, we bless; when we are persecuted, we endure it; [13]when we are slandered, we answer kindly. Up to this moment we have become the scum of the earth, the refuse of the world.●

[14]I am not writing this to shame you, but to warn you, as my dear children. [15]Even though you have ten thousand guardians in Christ, you do not have many fathers, for in Christ Jesus I became your father through the gospel. [16]Therefore I urge you to imitate me. [17]For this reason I am sending to you Timothy, my son whom I love, who is faithful in the Lord. He will remind you of my way of life in Christ Jesus, which agrees with what I teach everywhere in every church.●

[18]Some of you have become arrogant, as if I were not coming to you. [19]But I will come to you very soon, if the Lord is willing, and then I will find out not only how these arrogant people are talking, but what power they have. [20]For the kingdom of God is not a matter of talk but of power. [21]What do you prefer? Shall I come to you with a whip, or in love and with a gentle spirit?●

KING JAMES

1.CHRIST: JUDGE AND REWARDER

FAITHFUL SERVICE

4 Let a man so account of us, as of the
ministers of Christ, and stewards of
the mysteries of God. 2 Moreover it is
required in stewards, that a man be found
faithful. 3 But with me it is a very small
thing that I should be judged of you, or
of man's judgment: yea, I judge not mine
own self. 4 For I know nothing by myself; yet am I not hereby justified: but he
that judgeth me is the Lord. 5 Therefore
judge nothing before the time, until the
Lord come, who both will bring to light
the hidden things of darkness, and will
make manifest the counsels of the hearts:
and then shall every man have praise of
God. ●

2.TRUE HUMILITY

6 And these things, brethren, I have in
a figure transferred to myself and *to*
A·pol'los for your sakes; that ye might
learn in us not to think *of men* above that
which is written, that no one of you be
puffed up for one against another. 7 For
who maketh thee to differ *from another?*
and what hast thou that thou didst not
receive? now if thou didst receive *it*, why
dost thou glory, as if thou hadst not received *it?*
8 Now ye are full, now ye are rich, ye
have reigned as kings without us: and I
would to God ye did reign, that we also
might reign with you. 9 For I think that
God hath set forth us the apostles last, as
it were appointed to death: for we are
made a spectacle unto the world, and to
angels, and to men. 10 We *are* fools for
Christ's sake, but ye *are* wise in Christ;
we *are* weak, but ye *are* strong; ye *are*
honorable, but we *are* despised. 11 Even
unto this present hour we both hunger,
and thirst, and are naked, and are buffeted, and have no certain dwelling place;
12 and labor, working with our own
hands: being reviled, we bless; being persecuted, we suffer it: 13 being defamed,
we entreat: we are made as the filth of the
world, *and are* the offscouring of all things
unto this day. ●

3.PAUL: FATHER AND EX-AMPLE

14 I write not these things to shame
you, but as my beloved sons I warn *you.*
15 For though ye have ten thousand in-
structors in Christ, yet *have ye* not many
fathers: for in Christ Jesus I have begotten
you through the gospel. 16 Wherefore I
beseech you, be ye followers of me.
17 For this cause have I sent unto you
Timothy, who is my beloved son, and
faithful in the Lord, who shall bring you
into remembrance of my ways which be
in Christ, as I teach every where in every

—conclusion

church. ● 18 Now some are puffed up, as
though I would not come to you. 19 But
I will come to you shortly, if the Lord will,
and will know, not the speech of them
which are puffed up, but the power.
20 For the kingdom of God *is* not in
word, but in power. 21 What will ye?
shall I come unto you with a rod, or in
love, and *in* the spirit of meekness? ●

OBEDIENT SERVICE

*4:1-5* What two words does Paul use in verse 1 to identify his work?

Record the different references to *judge* and *judgment.*

*4:6-13* Read verse 8 as irony (see Living Bible text). How do verses 6-7 lead up to this?

What is Paul saying in verses 9-13?

*4:14-17* In what ways does Paul describe his ministry here?

*4:18-21* This paragraph concludes the section of the epistle about DIVISIONS (1:10—4:21). In what ways does it conclude?

NEW INTERNATIONAL VERSION

What does this passage teach about:

IMMORALITY

CHURCH DISCIPLINE

SATAN

DAY OF THE LORD

SANCTIFICATION

FELLOWSHIP

List spiritual applications of the passage.

*Expel the Immoral Brother!*

5 It is actually reported that there is sexual immorality among you, and of a
kind that does not occur even among pagans: A man has his father's wife. [2]And
you are proud! Shouldn't you rather have
been filled with grief and have put out of
your fellowship the man who did this?
[3]Even though I am not physically present,
I am with you in spirit. And I have already
passed judgment on the one who did this,
just as if I were present. [4]When you are
assembled in the name of our Lord Jesus
and I am with you in spirit, and the power
of our Lord Jesus is present, [5]hand this
man over to Satan, so that the sinful nature[a] may be destroyed and his spirit saved
on the day of the Lord.●
[6]Your boasting is not good. Don't you
know that a little yeast works through the
whole batch of dough? [7]Get rid of the old
yeast that you may be a new batch without
yeast—as you really are. For Christ, our
Passover lamb, has been sacrificed.
[8]Therefore let us keep the Festival, not
with the old yeast, the yeast of malice and
wickedness, but with bread without yeast,
the bread of sincerity and truth.●
[9]I have written you in my letter not to
associate with sexually immoral people—
[10]not at all meaning the people of this world
who are immoral, or the greedy and swindlers, or idolaters. In that case you would
have to leave this world. [11]But now I am
writing you that you must not associate
with anyone who calls himself a brother
but is sexually immoral or greedy, an idolater or a slanderer, a drunkard or a swindler.
With such a man do not even eat.
[12]What business is it of mine to judge
those outside the church? Are you not to
judge those inside? [13]God will judge those
outside. "Expel the wicked man from
among you."[b]●

[a]5 Or *that his body*; or *that the flesh*
[b]13 Deut. 17:7; 19:19; 22:21,24; 24:7

KING JAMES

1. JUDGING THE SIN

5 It is reported commonly *that there is*
fornication among you, and such fornication as is not so much as named
among the Gentiles, that one should
have his father's wife. 2 And ye are
puffed up, and have not rather mourned,
that he that hath done this deed might be
taken away from among you.
3 For I verily, as absent in body, but
present in spirit, have judged already, as
though I were present, *concerning* him
that hath so done this deed, 4 in the name
of our Lord Jesus Christ, when ye are
gathered together, and my spirit, with the
power of our Lord Jesus Christ, 5 to deliver such a one unto Satan for the destruction of the flesh, that the spirit may be
saved in the day of the Lord Jesus.●

2. PURGING THE CHURCH

6 Your glorying *is* not good. Know ye
not that a little leaven leaveneth the whole
lump? 7 Purge out therefore the old
leaven, that ye may be a new lump, as ye
are unleavened. For even Christ our passover is sacrificed for us: 8 therefore let us
keep the feast, not with old leaven, neither
with the leaven of malice and wickedness;
but with the unleavened *bread* of sincerity and truth.●

3. GUARDING THE CIRCLE

9 I wrote unto you in an epistle not to
company with fornicators: 10 yet not altogether with the fornicators of this world,
or with the covetous, or extortioners, or
with idolaters; for then must ye needs go
out of the world. 11 But now I have written unto you not to keep company, if any
man that is called a brother be a fornica-
tor, or covetous, or an idolater, or a railer,
or a drunkard, or an extortioner; with
such a one, no, not to eat. 12 For what
have I to do to judge them also that are
without? do not ye judge them that are
within? 13 But them that are without God judgeth. Therefore put away
from among yourselves that wicked
person.●

FORNICATION

EXPULSION

*5:1-5* What two sins are mentioned in verses 1-2?

Record the different parts of Paul's recommendation of verses 4-5:

*5:6-8* What is the repeated word of the paragraph?

What are contrasted here?

How does the paragraph relate to the problem of the first paragraph?

*5:9-13* Note the references to immoral believers and immoral professing believers. What is Paul's command (v.11)?

What is the last command of the segment?

NEW INTERNATIONAL VERSION

What do you learn here about:

SETTLING STRIFE AMONG CHRISTIANS

PLACE OF CIVIL COURTS

BELIEVER'S POSITION IN CHRIST

KINGDOM OF GOD

PHYSICAL BODY

FORNICATION

### *Lawsuits Among Believers*

6 If any of you has a dispute with another, dare he take it before the ungodly for judgment instead of before the saints? [2]Do you not know that the saints will judge the world? And if you are to judge the world, are you not competent to judge trivial cases? [3]Do you not know that we will judge angels? How much more the things of this life! [4]Therefore, if you have disputes about such matters, appoint as judges even men of little account in the church![a] [5]I say this to shame you. Is it possible that there is nobody among you wise enough to judge a dispute between believers? [6]But instead, one brother goes to law against another—and this in front of unbelievers!

[7]The very fact that you have lawsuits among you means you have been completely defeated already. Why not rather be wronged? Why not rather be cheated? [8]Instead, you yourselves cheat and do wrong, and you do this to your brothers.●

[9]Do you not know that the wicked will not inherit the kingdom of God? Do not be deceived: Neither the sexually immoral nor idolaters nor adulterers nor male prostitutes nor homosexual offenders [10]nor thieves nor the greedy nor drunkards nor slanderers nor swindlers will inherit the kingdom of God. [11]And that is what some of you were. But you were washed, you were sanctified, you were justified in the name of the Lord Jesus Christ and by the Spirit of our God.●

### *Sexual Immorality*

[12]"Everything is permissible for me"—but not everything is beneficial. "Everything is permissible for me"—but I will not be mastered by anything. [13]"Food for the stomach and the stomach for food"—but God will destroy them both. The body is not meant for sexual immorality, but for the Lord, and the Lord for the body. [14]By his power God raised the Lord from the dead, and he will raise us also. [15]Do you not know that your bodies are members of Christ himself? Shall I then take the members of Christ and unite them with a prostitute? Never! [16]Do you not know that he who unites himself with a prostitute is one with her in body? For it is said, "The two will become one flesh."[b] [17]But he who unites himself with the Lord is one with him in spirit.

[18]Flee from sexual immorality. All other sins a man commits are outside his body, but he who sins sexually sins against his own body. [19]Do you not know that your body is a temple of the Holy Spirit, who is in you, whom you have received from God? You are not your own; [20]you were bought at a price. Therefore honor God with your body.●

*a4* Or *matters, do you appoint as judges men of little account in the church?*
*b16* Gen. 2:24

KING JAMES

1.PROBLEM: LAWSUITS

SUING BROTHERS

6 Dare any of you, having a matter
against another, go to law before the
unjust, and not before the saints? 2 Do
ye not know that the saints shall judge the
world? and if the world shall be judged by
you, are ye unworthy to judge the smallest
matters? 3 Know ye not that we shall
judge angels? how much more things that
pertain to this life? 4 If then ye have
judgments of things pertaining to this life,
set them to judge who are least esteemed
in the church. 5 I speak to your shame.
Is it so, that there is not a wise man among
you? no, not one that shall be able to
judge between his brethren? 6 but brother
goeth to law with brother, and that before
the unbelievers.
7 Now therefore there is utterly a fault
among you, because ye go to law one with
another. Why do ye not rather take
wrong? Why do ye not rather *suffer yourselves to* be defrauded? 8 Nay, ye do
wrong, and defraud, and that *your*
brethren. ●

2.DOCTRINE

9 Know ye not that the unrighteous
shall not inherit the kingdom of God?
Be not deceived: neither fornicators, nor
idolaters, nor adulterers, nor effeminate,
nor abusers of themselves with mankind,
10 nor thieves, nor covetous, nor drunkards, nor revilers, nor extortioners, shall
inherit the kingdom of God. 11 And such
were some of you: but ye are washed, but
ye are sanctified, but ye are justified in the
name of the Lord Jesus, and by the Spirit
of our God. ●

3.PROBLEM: IMMORALITY

12 All things are lawful unto me, but all
things are not expedient: all things are
lawful for me, but I will not be brought
under the power of any. 13 Meats for the
belly, and the belly for meats: but God
shall destroy both it and them. Now the
body *is* not for fornication, but for the
Lord; and the Lord for the body. 14 And
God hath both raised up the Lord, and
will also raise up us by his own power.
15 Know ye not that your bodies are the
members of Christ? shall I then take the
members of Christ, and make *them*
the members of a harlot? God forbid.
16 What! know ye not that he which is
joined to a harlot is one body? for two,
saith he, shall be one flesh. 17 But he
that is joined unto the Lord is one spirit.
18 Flee fornication. Every sin that a man
doeth is without the body; but he that
committeth fornication sinneth against his
own body. 19 What! know ye not that
your body is the temple of the Holy Ghost
*which is* in you, which ye have of God,
and ye are not your own? 20 For ye are
bought with a price: therefore glorify God
in your body, and in your spirit, which
are God's. ●

GLORIFYING GOD

*6:1-8* Record two key repeated words of the paragraph:

______________________

What is the problem? ______________________

______________________

______________________

______________________

What does Paul recommend? ______________________

______________________

______________________

______________________

______________________

*6:9-11* What is the Christian's *position,* according to verse 11?

______________________

______________________

______________________

______________________

How are verses 9-10 related to verse 11? ____

______________________

______________________

______________________

*6:12-20* This paragraph is about the Christian and his body. Record:

DOCTRINES ______________________

______________________

______________________

______________________

______________________

______________________

COMMANDS ______________________

______________________

______________________

______________________

______________________

______________________

NEW INTERNATIONAL VERSION

What is taught here about:

CELIBACY

MARRIAGE

UNEQUAL YOKE

CALLING OF GOD

*Marriage*

7 Now for the matters you wrote about: It is good for a man not to marry. [2]But since there is so much immorality, each man should have his own wife, and each woman her own husband. [3]The husband should fulfill his marital duty to his wife, and likewise the wife to her husband. [4]The wife's body does not belong to her alone but also to her husband. In the same way, the husband's body does not belong to him alone but also to his wife. [5]Do not deprive each other except by mutual consent and for a time, so that you may devote yourselves to prayer. Then come together again so that Satan will not tempt you because of your lack of self-control. [6]I say this as a concession, not as a command. [7]I wish that all men were as I am. But each man has his own gift from God; one has this gift, another has that.

[8]Now to the unmarried and the widows I say: It is good for them to stay unmarried, as I am. [9]But if they cannot control themselves, they should marry, for it is better to marry than to burn with passion.●

[10]To the married I give this command (not I, but the Lord): A wife must not separate from her husband. [11]But if she does, she must remain unmarried or else be reconciled to her husband. And a husband must not divorce his wife.●

[12]To the rest I say this (I, not the Lord): If any brother has a wife who is not a believer and she is willing to live with him, he must not divorce her. [13]And if a woman has a husband who is not a believer and he is willing to live with her, she must not divorce him. [14]For the unbelieving husband has been sanctified through his wife, and the unbelieving wife has been sanctified through her believing husband. Otherwise your children would be unclean, but as it is, they are holy.

[15]But if the unbeliever leaves, let him do so. A believing man or woman is not bound in such circumstances; God has called us to live in peace. [16]How do you know, wife, whether you will save your husband? Or, how do you know, husband, whether you will save your wife?●

[17]Nevertheless, each one should retain the place in life that the Lord assigned to him and to which God has called him. This is the rule I lay down in all the churches. [18]Was a man already circumcised when he was called? He should not become uncircumcised. Was a man uncircumcised when he was called? He should not be circumcised. [19]Circumcision is nothing and uncircumcision is nothing. Keeping God's commands is what counts. [20]Each one should remain in the situation which he was in when God called him. [21]Were you a slave when you were called? Don't let it trouble you—although if you can gain your freedom, do so. [22]For he who was a slave when he was called by the Lord is the Lord's freedman; similarly, he who was a free man when he was called is Christ's slave. [23]You were bought at a price; do not become slaves of men. [24]Brothers, each man, as responsible to God, should remain in the situation God called him to.●

KING JAMES

1.CELIBACY AND MARRIAGE ARE GOOD

HUSBAND AND WIFE

7 Now concerning the things whereof
ye wrote unto me: *It is* good for a man
not to touch a woman. 2 Nevertheless, *to*
*avoid* fornication, let every man have his
own wife, and let every woman have her
own husband. 3 Let the husband render
unto the wife due benevolence: and
likewise also the wife unto the husband.
4 The wife hath not power of her own
body, but the husband: and likewise also
the husband hath not power of his own
body, but the wife. 5 Defraud ye not one
the other, except *it be* with consent for a
time, that ye may give yourselves to fasting and prayer; and come together
again, that Satan tempt you not for your
incontinency. 6 But I speak this by permission, *and* not of commandment. 7 For
I would that all men were even as I myself.
But every man hath his proper gift of
God, one after this manner, and another
after that.
8 I say therefore to the unmarried and
widows, It is good for them if they abide
even as I. 9 But if they cannot contain,
let them marry: for it is better to marry
than to burn.●

2.MARRIAGE IS INDISSOLUBLE

10 And unto the married I command,
*yet* not I, but the Lord, Let not the wife
depart from *her* husband: 11 but and if
she depart, let her remain unmarried, or
be reconciled to *her* husband: and let not
the husband put away *his* wife.●

3.UNEQUAL YOKE

12 But to the rest speak I, not the Lord:
If any brother hath a wife that believeth
not, and she be pleased to dwell with him,
let him not put her away. 13 And the
woman which hath a husband that believeth not, and if he be pleased to dwell
with her, let her not leave him. 14 For the
unbelieving husband is sanctified by the
wife, and the unbelieving wife is sanctified
by the husband: else were your children
unclean; but now are they holy. 15 But if
the unbelieving depart, let him depart. A
brother or a sister is not under bondage in
such *cases:* but God hath called us to
peace. 16 For what knowest thou, O wife,
whether thou shalt save *thy* husband? or
how knowest thou, O man, whether thou
shalt save *thy* wife?●

4.OBEDIENCE TO LORD'S CALLING

17 But as God hath distributed to every
man, as the Lord hath called every one,
so let him walk. And so ordain I in all
churches. 18 Is any man called being circumcised? let him not become uncircumcised. Is any called in uncircumcision?
let him not be circumcised. 19 Circumcision is nothing, and uncircumcision is
nothing, but the keeping of the commandments of God. 20 Let every man abide in
the same calling wherein he was called.
21 Art thou called *being* a servant? care
not for it: but if thou mayest be made free,
use *it* rather. 22 For he that is called in
the Lord, *being* a servant, is the Lord's
freeman: likewise also he that is called,
*being* free, is Christ's servant. 23 Ye are
bought with a price; be not ye the servants
of men. 24 Brethren, let every man,
wherein he is called, therein abide with
God.●

LORD AND SERVANT

*7:1-9* How does Paul value celibacy? ______

How does he value marriage? ______

Read verse 7b. How is this truth the key to answering the question to marry or not marry?

______

*7:10-11* What is commanded here? ______

*7:12-16* This is a paragraph about married couples where one mate is an unbeliever. What is Paul's counsel?

______

*7:17-24* What is the key repeated word? ______

What does the paragraph teach? ______

How does this answer the original question of the segment?

______

NEW INTERNATIONAL VERSION

Go through this passage again and list the things Paul writes about marrying and not marrying:

MARRYING

NOT MARRYING

25 Now about virgins: I have no command
from the Lord, but I give a judgment as one
who by the Lord's mercy is trustworthy.
26 Because of the present crisis, I think that
it is good for you to remain as you are.
27 Are you married? Do not seek a divorce.
Are you unmarried? Do not look for a wife.
28 But if you do marry, you have not sinned;
and if a virgin marries, she has not sinned.
But those who marry will face many troubles in this life, and I want to spare you
this.
29 What I mean, brothers, is that the time
is short. From now on those who have
wives should live as if they had none;
30 those who mourn, as if they did not; those
who are happy, as if they were not; those
who buy something, as if it were not theirs
to keep; 31 those who use the things of the
world, as if not engrossed in them. For this
world in its present form is passing away.●
32 I would like you to be free from concern. An unmarried man is concerned
about the Lord's affairs—how he can
please the Lord. 33 But a married man is
concerned about the affairs of this world—
how he can please his wife— 34 and his interests are divided. An unmarried woman
or virgin is concerned about the Lord's
affairs: Her aim is to be devoted to the
Lord in both body and spirit. But a married
woman is concerned about the affairs of
this world—how she can please her husband. 35 I am saying this for your own good,
not to restrict you, but that you may live in
a right way in undivided devotion to the
Lord.●
36 If anyone thinks he is acting improper-
ly toward the virgin he is engaged to, and
if she is getting along in years and he feels
he ought to marry, he should do as he
wants. He is not sinning. They should get
married. 37 But the man who has settled the
matter in his own mind, who is under no
compulsion but has control over his own
will, and who has made up his mind not to
marry the virgin—this man also does the
right thing. 38 So then, he who marries the
virgin does right, but he who does not
marry her does even better.[a]
39 A woman is bound to her husband as
long as he lives. But if her husband dies,
she is free to marry anyone she wishes, but
he must belong to the Lord. 40 In my judgment, she is happier if she stays as she
is—and I think that I too have the Spirit of
God.●

[a] 36-38 Or *36 If anyone thinks he is not treating his daughter properly, and if she is getting along in years, and he feels she ought to marry, he should do as he wants. He is not sinning. They should get married. 37 But the man who has settled the matter in his own mind, who is under no compulsion but has control over his own will, and who has made up his mind to keep the virgin unmarried—this man also does the right thing. 38 So then, he who gives his virgin in marriage does right, but he who does not give her in marriage does even better.*

KING JAMES

1.SITUATION

MERCY GIVEN TO ME

25 Now concerning virgins I have no
commandment of the Lord: yet I give my
judgment, as one that hath obtained
mercy of the Lord to be faithful. 26 I
suppose therefore that this is good for the
present distress, *I say*, that *it is* good for a
man so to be. 27 Art thou bound unto a
wife? seek not to be loosed. Art thou
loosed from a wife? seek not a wife.
28 But and if thou marry, thou hast not
sinned; and if a virgin marry, she hath
not sinned. Nevertheless such shall have
trouble in the flesh: but I spare you.
29 But this I say, brethren, the time *is*
short: it remaineth, that both they that
have wives be as though they had none;
30 and they that weep, as though they
wept not; and they that rejoice, as though
they rejoiced not; and they that buy, as
though they possessed not; 31 and they
that use this world, as not abusing *it*: for
the fashion of this world passeth away.●

2.MOTIVATION

32 But I would have you without carefulness. He that is unmarried careth for
the things that belong to the Lord, how
he may please the Lord: 33 but he that is
married careth for the things that are of
the world, how he may please *his* wife.
34 There is difference *also* between a wife
and a virgin. The unmarried woman
careth for the things of the Lord, that she
may be holy both in body and in spirit:
but she that is married careth for the
things of the world, how she may please
*her* husband. 35 And this I speak for
your own profit; not that I may cast a
snare upon you, but for that which is
comely, and that ye may attend upon the
Lord without distraction.●

3.COMPARISON

36 But if any man think that he be-
haveth himself uncomely toward his virgin, if she pass the flower of *her* age, and
need so require, let him do what he will,
he sinneth not: let them marry. 37 Nevertheless he that standeth steadfast in his
heart, having no necessity, but hath power
over his own will, and hath so decreed in
his heart that he will keep his virgin, doeth
well. 38 So then he that giveth *her* in
marriage doeth well; but he that giveth
*her* not in marriage doeth better.
39 The wife is bound by the law as long
as her husband liveth; but if her husband
be dead, she is at liberty to be married to
whom she will; only in the Lord. 40 But
she is happier if she so abide, after my
judgment: and I think also that I have the
Spirit of God.●

SPIRIT GIVEN TO ME

*7:25-31* In this paragraph Paul refers to the hard times which beset the Corinthians when he was writing. What words or phrases suggest this?

How would such a situation affect one's decision as to whether to marry, at that time?

*7:32-35* What motivations does Paul write about here?

How are these related to the question to marry or not marry?

*7:36-40* Compare this paragraph with 7:1-11.

What two persons are mentioned in verse 38? Are these the persons of verses 36 and 37?

NEW INTERNATIONAL VERSION

What do you learn from this passage about:

THE LIBERTY WHICH A CHRISTIAN HAS ______

HOW A WEAK CHRISTIAN CAN BE WOUNDED BY A STRONGER CHRISTIAN ______

WHEN THE STRONGER CHRISTIAN MUST FOREGO HIS LIBERTY

HOW CHRIST IS PART OF THIS PICTURE ______

List some situations of the present day which involve the same spiritual principles of this "meat" problem.

*Food Sacrificed to Idols*

8 Now about food sacrificed to idols: We
know that we all possess knowledge.[b]
Knowledge puffs up, but love builds up.
2The man who thinks he knows something
does not yet know as he ought to know.
3But the man who loves God is known by
God.
4So then, about eating food sacrificed to
idols: We know that an idol is nothing at all
in the world and that there is no God but
one. 5For even if there are so-called gods,
whether in heaven or on earth (as indeed
there are many "gods" and many
"lords"), 6yet for us there is but one God,
the Father, from whom all things came and
for whom we live; and there is but one
Lord, Jesus Christ, through whom all
things came and through whom we live.●
7But not everyone knows this. Some
people are still so accustomed to idols that
when they eat such food they think of it as
having been sacrificed to an idol, and since
their conscience is weak, it is defiled. 8But
food does not bring us near to God; we are
no worse if we do not eat, and no better if
we do.●
9Be careful, however, that the exercise
of your freedom does not become a stumbling block to the weak. 10For if anyone
with a weak conscience sees you who have
this knowledge eating in an idol's temple,
won't he be emboldened to eat what has
been sacrificed to idols? 11So this weak
brother, for whom Christ died, is destroyed by your knowledge. 12When you
sin against your brothers in this way and
wound their weak conscience, you sin
against Christ. 13Therefore, if what I eat
causes my brother to fall into sin, I will
never eat meat again, so that I will not
cause him to fall.●

b1 Or *"We all possess knowledge," as you say*

KING JAMES

1.QUESTION AND SITUATION

EDIFY

8 Now as touching things offered unto
idols, we know that we all have
knowledge. Knowledge puffeth up, but
charity edifieth. 2 And if any man think
that he knoweth any thing, he knoweth
nothing yet as he ought to know. 3 But if
any man love God, the same is known of
him.
4 As concerning therefore the eating of
those things that are offered in sacrifice
unto idols, we know that an idol *is* nothing in the world, and that *there is* none
other God but one. 5 For though there
be that are called gods, whether in heaven
or in earth, (as there be gods many, and
lords many,) 6 but to us *there is but* one
God, the Father, of whom *are* all things,
and we in him; and one Lord Jesus Christ,
by whom *are* all things, and we by
him. ●

2.FIRST PROBLEM

7 Howbeit *there is* not in every man that
knowledge: for some with conscience of
the idol unto this hour eat *it* as a thing
offered unto an idol; and their conscience
being weak is defiled. 8 But meat commendeth us not to God: for neither, if we
eat, are we the better; neither, if we eat
not, are we the worse. ●

3.SECOND PROBLEM

9 But take heed
lest by any means this liberty of yours become a stumblingblock to them that are
weak. 10 For if any man see thee which
hast knowledge sit at meat in the idol's
temple, shall not the conscience of him
which is weak be emboldened to eat those
things which are offered to idols; 11 and
through thy knowledge shall the weak
brother perish, for whom Christ died?
12 But when ye sin so against the brethren, and wound their weak conscience, ye
sin against Christ. 13 Wherefore, if meat
make my brother to offend, I will eat no
flesh while the world standeth, lest I make
my brother to offend. ●

DON'T OFFEND

This segment identifies another question the Corinthians asked Paul. __________

*8:1-6* What was the Corinthians' question, according to verse 4? __________

What facts does Paul cite to describe the situation which brought on the question? __________

*8:7-8* What problem is recognized here? __________

What is the answer? __________

*8:9-13* What is the problem here? __________

What is the answer? __________

NEW INTERNATIONAL VERSION

What do you learn here about:

CHRISTIAN LIBERTY

RIGHTS OF A CHRISTIAN SERVANT

CHURCH'S FINANCIAL OBLIGATION TO CHRISTIAN WORKERS

AVOIDING OFFENSE

GOSPEL OF CHRIST

SELFLESSNESS

*The Rights of an Apostle*

9 Am I not free? Am I not an apostle?
Have I not seen Jesus our Lord? Are
you not the result of my work in the Lord?
[2]Even though I may not be an apostle to
others, surely I am to you! For you are the
seal of my apostleship in the Lord.●
[3]This is my defense to those who sit in
judgment on me. [4]Don't we have the right
to food and drink? [5]Don't we have the right
to take a believing wife along with us, as do
the other apostles and the Lord's brothers
and Cephas[a]? [6]Or is it only I and Barnabas
who must work for a living?
[7]Who serves as a soldier at his own expense? Who plants a vineyard and does not
eat of its grapes? Who tends a flock and
does not drink of the milk? [8]Do I say this
merely from a human point of view?
Doesn't the Law say the same thing? [9]For
it is written in the Law of Moses: "Do not
muzzle an ox while it is treading out the
grain."[b] Is it about oxen that God is concerned? [10]Surely he says this for us,
doesn't he? Yes, this was written for us,
because when the plowman plows and the
thresher threshes, they ought to do so in
the hope of sharing in the harvest. [11]If we
have sown spiritual seed among you, is it
too much if we reap a material harvest from
you? [12]If others have this right of support
from you, shouldn't we have it all the
more?
But we did not use this right. On the
contrary, we put up with anything rather
than hinder the gospel of Christ. [13]Don't
you know that those who work in the temple get their food from the temple, and
those who serve at the altar share in what
is offered on the altar? [14]In the same way,
the Lord has commanded that those who
preach the gospel should receive their living from the gospel.●
[15]But I have not used any of these rights.
And I am not writing this in the hope that
you will do such things for me. I would
rather die than have anyone deprive me of
this boast. [16]Yet when I preach the gospel,
I cannot boast, for I am compelled to
preach. Woe to me if I do not preach the
gospel! [17]If I preach voluntarily, I have a
reward; if not voluntarily, I am simply dis-
charging the trust committed to me. [18]What
then is my reward? Just this: that in preaching the gospel I may offer it free of charge,
and so not make use of my rights in preaching it.●

[a]5 That is, Peter   [b]9 Deut. 25:4

KING JAMES

1.OFFICE

THE MESSENGER

9 Am I not an apostle? am I not free?
have I not seen Jesus Christ our Lord?
are not ye my work in the Lord? 2 If I be
not an apostle unto others, yet doubtless
I am to you: for the seal of mine apostleship are ye in the Lord.●

2.RIGHTS

3 Mine answer to them that do examine
me is this: 4 Have we not power to eat
and to drink? 5 Have we not power to
lead about a sister, a wife, as well as other
apostles, and *as* the brethren of the Lord,
and Cephas? 6 Or I only and Barnabas,
have not we power to forbear working?
7 Who goeth a warfare any time at his
own charges? who planteth a vineyard,
and eateth not of the fruit thereof? or who
feedeth a flock, and eateth not of the milk
of the flock?
8 Say I these things as a man? or saith
not the law the same also? 9 For it is
written in the law of Moses, (Deu. 25:4)

Thou shalt not muzzle the mouth of
the ox
that treadeth out the corn.

Doth God take care for oxen? 10 or saith
he *it* altogether for our sakes? For our
sakes, no doubt, *this* is written: that he
that ploweth should plow in hope; and
that he that thresheth in hope should be
partaker of his hope. 11 If we have sown
unto you spiritual things, *is it* a great
thing if we shall reap your carnal things?
12 If others be partakers of *this* power
over you, *are* not we rather?
Nevertheless we have not used this
power; but suffer all things, lest we should
hinder the gospel of Christ. 13 Do ye not
know that they which minister about holy
things live *of the things* of the temple? and
they which wait at the altar are partakers
with the altar? 14 Even so hath the Lord
ordained that they which preach the gospel should live of the gospel.●

3.SURRENDER

15 But I have used none of these things:
neither have I written these things, that it
should be so done unto me: for *it were*
better for me to die, than that any man
should make my glorying void. 16 For
though I preach the gospel, I have nothing
to glory of: for necessity is laid upon me;
yea, woe is unto me, if I preach not the
gospel! 17 For if I do this thing willingly,
I have a reward: but if against my will, a
dispensation *of the gospel* is committed
unto me. 18 What is my reward then?
*Verily* that, when I preach the gospel, I
may make the gospel of Christ without
charge, that I abuse not my power in the
gospel.●

THE MESSAGE

*9:1-2* What is the key repeated word? ________

What does Paul write here about apostleship?

*9:3-14* What problem does Paul raise here?

What are the apostle's rights? ________

Why didn't Paul use those rights? ________

*9:15-18* What does Paul further say about using those rights?

NEW INTERNATIONAL VERSION

What does this passage teach about:

ATTITUDE OF SERVING OTHERS

DISCIPLINE OF THE BODY

List different ways this passage can be applied to situations involving Christians today.

[19]Though I am free and belong to no
man, I make myself a slave to everyone, to
win as many as possible. [20]To the Jews I
became like a Jew, to win the Jews. To
those under the law I became like one under the law (though I myself am not under
the law), so as to win those under the law.
[21]To those not having the law I became like
one not having the law (though I am not
free from God's law but am under Christ's
law), so as to win those not having the law.
[22]To the weak I became weak, to win the
weak. I have become all things to all men
so that by all possible means I might save
some. [23]I do all this for the sake of the
gospel, that I may share in its blessings.●
[24]Do you not know that in a race all the
runners run, but only one gets the prize?
Run in such a way as to get the prize.
[25]Everyone who competes in the games
goes into strict training. They do it to get
a crown that will not last; but we do it to
get a crown that will last forever. [26]There-
fore I do not run like a man running aim-
lessly; I do not fight like a man beating the
air. [27]No, I beat my body and make it my
slave so that after I have preached to
others, I myself will not be disqualified for
the prize.●

KING JAMES

1.SUBSERVIENCE

19 For though I be free from all *men*,
yet have I made myself servant unto all,
that I might gain the more. 20 And unto
the Jews I became as a Jew, that I might
gain the Jews; to them that are under the
law, as under the law, that I might gain
them that are under the law; 21 to them
that are without law, as without law,
(being not without law to God, but under
the law to Christ,) that I might gain them
that are without law. 22 To the weak became I as weak, that I might gain the
weak: I am made all things to all *men*,
that I might by all means save some.
23 And this I do for the gospel's sake, that
I might be partaker thereof with *you*.●

2.DISCIPLINE

24 Know ye not that they which run in
a race run all, but one receiveth the prize?
So run, that ye may obtain. 25 And every
man that striveth for the mastery is temperate in all things. Now they *do it* to
obtain a corruptible crown; but we an
incorruptible. 26 I therefore so run, not
as uncertainly; so fight I, not as one that
beateth the air: 27 but I keep under my
body, and bring *it* into subjection: lest
that by any means, when I have preached
to others, I myself should be a cast-
away.●

SERVANT

CAST-AWAY

*9:19-23* Compare:

"servant unto" (v.19) ______

"partaker with" (v.23) ______

What does this paragraph emphasize? ______

How is subservience a solution to the problem of chapter 8?

______

*9:24-27* Record what Paul writes here about:

DISCIPLINE ______

MOTIVATIONS ______

NEW INTERNATIONAL VERSION

What may be learned here about:

DISOBEDIENCE

IDOLATRY

FAIR WARNING FROM GOD

TEMPTATION

DIVINE JUDGMENT

OTHER

*Warnings From Israel's History*

10 For I do not want you to be ignorant
of the fact, brothers, that our forefathers were all under the cloud and that they
all passed through the sea. 2They were all
baptized into Moses in the cloud and in the
sea. 3They all ate the same spiritual food
4and drank the same spiritual drink; for
they drank from the spiritual rock that accompanied them, and that rock was Christ.
5Nevertheless, God was not pleased with
most of them; their bodies were scattered
over the desert.●
6Now these things occurred as examples,[c] to keep us from setting our hearts on
evil things as they did. 7Do not be idolaters, as some of them were; as it is written:
"The people sat down to eat and drink and
got up to indulge in pagan revelry."[d] 8We
should not commit sexual immorality, as
some of them did—and in one day twenty-
three thousand of them died. 9We should
not test the Lord, as some of them did—
and were killed by snakes. 10And do not
grumble, as some of them did—and were
killed by the destroying angel.●
11These things happened to them as examples and were written down as warnings
for us, on whom the fulfillment of the ages
has come. 12So, if you think you are standing firm, be careful that you don't fall! 13No
temptation has seized you except what is
common to man. And God is faithful; he
will not let you be tempted beyond what
you can bear. But when you are tempted,
he will also provide a way out so that you
can stand up under it.●

[c]6 Or *types*; also in verse 11 [d]7 Exodus 32:6

KING JAMES

1. ISRAEL'S EXPERIENCE

PASSED THROUGH

**10** Moreover, brethren, I would not
that ye should be ignorant, how
that all our fathers were under the cloud,
and all passed through the sea; 2 and
were all baptized unto Moses in the cloud
and in the sea; 3 and did all eat the same
spiritual meat; 4 and did all drink the
same spiritual drink; for they drank of
that spiritual Rock that followed them:
and that Rock was Christ. 5 But with
many of them God was not well pleased:
for they were overthrown in the wilderness.●

2. SPECIFIC LESSONS

6 Now these things were our examples,
to the intent we should not lust after evil
things, as they also lusted. 7 Neither be
ye idolaters, as *were* some of them; as it is
written, The people sat down to eat and
drink, and rose up to play. 8 Neither let
us commit fornication, as some of them
committed, and fell in one day three and
twenty thousand. 9 Neither let us tempt
Christ, as some of them also tempted,
and were destroyed of serpents. 10 Neither murmur ye, as some of them also
murmured, and were destroyed of the destroyer.●

3. GENERAL WARNING

11 Now all these things happened unto them for ensamples: and they
are written for our admonition, upon
whom the ends of the world are come.
12 Wherefore let him that thinketh he
standeth take heed lest he fall. 13 There
hath no temptation taken you but such as
is common to man: but God *is* faithful,
who will not suffer you to be tempted
above that ye are able; but will with the
temptation also make a way to escape,
that ye may be able to bear *it*.●

A WAY TO ESCAPE

*10:1-5* What kinds of experiences are cited here?

How many Israelites were involved? (Note the repeated word.)

What are the main parts of verse 5?

How does verse 5 relate to verses 1-4?

*10:6-10* Record the experiences and the lessons.

*10:11-13* What is the key repeated word of this paragraph?

What is the teaching of the paragraph?

NEW INTERNATIONAL VERSION

Record what you learn here about:

THE RIGHTS WHICH A CHRISTIAN HAS

THE CHRISTIAN'S ATTITUDE IN EVERYTHING HE DOES

SELFLESS LIVING FOR OTHERS

Apply the motivations of 10:23—11:1 to present-day situations.

*Idol Feasts and the Lord's Supper*

14Therefore, my dear friends, flee from
idolatry. 15I speak to sensible people; judge
for yourselves what I say. 16Is not the cup
of thanksgiving for which we give thanks a
participation in the blood of Christ? And is
not the bread that we break a participation
in the body of Christ? 17Because there is
one loaf, we, who are many, are one body,
for we all partake of the one loaf.

18Consider the people of Israel: Do not
those who eat the sacrifices participate in
the altar? 19Do I mean then that a sacrifice
offered to an idol is anything, or that an
idol is anything? 20No, but the sacrifices of
pagans are offered to demons, not to God,
and I do not want you to be participants
with demons. 21You cannot drink the cup
of the Lord and the cup of demons too; you
cannot have a part in both the Lord's table
and the table of demons. 22Are we trying to
arouse the Lord's jealousy? Are we stronger than he?●

*The Believer's Freedom*

23"Everything is permissible"—but not
everything is beneficial. "Everything is
permissible"—but not everything is con-
structive. 24Nobody should seek his own
good, but the good of others.

25Eat anything sold in the meat market
without raising questions of conscience,
26for, "The earth is the Lord's, and everything in it."[a]

27If some unbeliever invites you to a
meal and you want to go, eat whatever is
put before you without raising questions of
conscience. 28But if anyone says to you,
"This has been offered in sacrifice," then
do not eat it, both for the sake of the man
who told you and for conscience' sake[b]—
29the other man's conscience, I mean, not
yours. For why should my freedom be
judged by another's conscience? 30If I take
part in the meal with thankfulness, why am
I denounced because of something I thank
God for?

31So whether you eat or drink or whatever you do, do it all for the glory of God.
32Do not cause anyone to stumble, whether
Jews, Greeks or the church of God—
33even as I try to please everybody in every
way. For I am not seeking my own good
but the good of many, so that they may be
11 saved. 1Follow my example, as I follow the example of Christ.●

[b]28 Some manuscripts *conscience' sake, for "the earth is the Lord's and everything in it"*
[a]26 Psalm 24:1

KING JAMES

1.FLEE FROM IDOLATRY

14 Wherefore, my dearly beloved, flee
from idolatry. 15 I speak as to wise men;
judge ye what I say. 16 The cup of blessing which we bless, is it not the communion of the blood of Christ? The
bread which we break, is it not the communion of the body of Christ? 17 For
we *being* many are one bread, *and* one
body: for we are all partakers of that one
bread. 18 Behold Israel after the flesh:
are not they which eat of the sacrifices partakers of the altar? 19 What say I then?
that the idol is any thing, or that which is
offered in sacrifice to idols is any thing?
20 But *I say*, that the things which the
Gentiles sacrifice, they sacrifice to devils,
and not to God: and I would not that ye
should have fellowship with devils. 21 Ye
cannot drink the cup of the Lord, and the
cup of devils: ye cannot be partakers of
the Lord's table, and of the table of devils.
22 Do we provoke the Lord to jealousy?
are we stronger than he?●

2.FOREGO YOUR LIBERTY

23 All things are lawful for me, but all
things are not expedient: all things are
lawful for me, but all things edify not.
24 Let no man seek his own, but every
man another's *wealth*. 25 Whatsoever is
sold in the shambles, *that* eat, asking no
question for conscience' sake: 26 for the
earth *is* the Lord's, and the fulness thereof. 27 If any of them that believe not bid
you *to a feast*, and ye be disposed to go;
whatsoever is set before you, eat, asking
no question for conscience' sake. 28 But
if any man say unto you, This is offered in
sacrifice unto idols, eat not for his sake
that showed it, and for conscience' sake:
for the earth *is* the Lord's, and the fulness
thereof: 29 conscience, I say, not thine
own, but of the other: for why is my
liberty judged of another *man's* conscience? 30 For if I by grace be a partaker, why am I evil spoken of for that for
which I give thanks?
31 Whether therefore ye eat, or drink,
or whatsoever ye do, do all to the glory of
God. 32 Give none offense, neither to the
Jews, nor to the Gentiles, nor to the
church of God: 33 even as I please all
*men* in all *things*, not seeking mine own
profit, but the *profit* of many, that they
may be saved.
11 1 Be ye followers of
me, even as I also *am* of Christ.●

BLOOD OF CHRIST

FOLLOWER OF CHRIST

First read 11:1. Study the whole segment in light of this key verse.

*10:14-22* Paul writes here about three different altars. Identify each altar, and the spiritual truth he is teaching:

vv.16-17

v.18

vv.19-21

*10:23—11:1* This is the final paragraph referring to the original problem of eating meat. List the different motivations for Christian action cited here.

NEW INTERNATIONAL VERSION

What does this passage teach about:

RELATION OF MAN AND WOMAN ____________________

ACTIVITIES AND DRESS OF MEN IN WORSHIP SERVICE ____________________

ACTIVITIES AND DRESS OF WOMEN IN WORSHIP SERVICE ____________________

CHRIST ____________________

List spiritual applications of the passage. ____________________

*Propriety in Worship*

2 I praise you for remembering me in
everything and for holding to the teachings,[c] just as I passed them on to you.
3 Now I want you to realize that the head
of every man is Christ, and the head of the
woman is man, and the head of Christ is
God. 4 Every man who prays or prophesies
with his head covered dishonors his head.
5 And every woman who prays or prophesies with her head uncovered dishonors
her head—it is just as though her head were
shaved. 6 If a woman does not cover her
head, she should have her hair cut off; and
if it is a disgrace for a woman to have her
hair cut or shaved off, she should cover her
head. 7 A man ought not to cover his head,[d]
since he is the image and glory of God; but
the woman is the glory of man. 8 For man
did not come from woman, but woman
from man; 9 neither was man created for
woman, but woman for man. 10 For this reason, and because of the angels, the woman
ought to have a sign of authority on her
head.●
11 In the Lord, however, woman is not
independent of man, nor is man independent of woman. 12 For as woman came from
man, so also man is born of woman. But
everything comes from God.● 13 Judge for
yourselves: Is it proper for a woman to
pray to God with her head uncovered?
14 Does not the very nature of things teach
you that if a man has long hair, it is a disgrace to him, 15 but that if a woman has long
hair, it is her glory? For long hair is given
to her as a covering. 16 If anyone wants to
be contentious about this, we have no other practice—nor do the churches of God.●

c2 Or *traditions*

d4-7 Or *4Every man who prays or prophesies with long hair dishonors his head. 5And every woman who prays or prophesies with no covering* ⌊*of hair*⌋ *on her head dishonors her head—she is just like one of the "shorn women." 6If a woman has no covering, let her be for now with short hair, but since it is a disgrace for a woman to have her hair shorn or shaved, she should grow it again. 7A man ought not to have long hair*

KING JAMES

1. PRINCIPLE OF DIFFERENCES

FOLLOWING THE RULES

2 Now I praise you, brethren, that ye
remember me in all things, and keep the
ordinances, as I delivered *them* to you.
3 But I would have you know, that the
head of every man is Christ; and the head
of the woman *is* the man; and the head of
Christ *is* God. 4 Every man praying or
prophesying, having *his* head covered, dishonoreth his head. 5 But every woman
that prayeth or prophesieth with *her* head
uncovered dishonoreth her head: for that
is even all one as if she were shaven. 6 For
if the woman be not covered, let her also
be shorn: but if it be a shame for a woman
to be shorn or shaven, let her be covered.
7 For a man indeed ought not to cover *his*
head, forasmuch as he is the image and
glory of God: but the woman is the glory
of the man. 8 For the man is not of the
woman; but the woman of the man.
9 Neither was the man created for the
woman; but the woman for the man.
10 For this cause ought the woman to
have power on *her* head because of the
angels.●

2. PRINCIPLE OF DEPENDENCIES

11 Nevertheless neither is the man
without the woman, neither the woman
without the man, in the Lord. 12 For as
the woman *is* of the man, even so *is* the
man also by the woman; but all things of
God.●

—conclusion

CHALLENGING THE RULES

13 Judge in yourselves: is it comely
that a woman pray unto God uncovered?
14 Doth not even nature itself teach you,
that, if a man have long hair, it is a shame
unto him? 15 But if a woman have long
hair, it is a glory to her: for *her* hair is
given her for a covering. 16 But if any
man seem to be contentious, we have no
such custom, neither the churches of
God.●

At this point Paul begins to write about problems of the worship service (11:2—14:40).

*11:2-10* What are the three different levels cited in verse 3?

What public function do verses 4-10 refer to?

How should the position of men and women be reflected in their public appearance at the worship service, according to verses 4-7?

*11:11-12* What is the main point?

Compare this with the first paragraph.

*11:13-16* What different things does Paul teach here?

NEW INTERNATIONAL VERSION

Record what this passage teaches about the communion service (Lord's Table):

ATMOSPHERE AND SETTING

SYMBOLIC MEANING OF THE BROKEN BREAD

SYMBOLIC MEANING OF THE CUP

FREQUENCY OF OBSERVING

PURPOSES OF OBSERVING

ABUSES OF PARTICIPATING

*The Lord's Supper*

17In the following directives I have no
praise for you, for your meetings do more
harm than good. 18In the first place, I hear
that when you come together as a church,
there are divisions among you, and to some
extent I believe it. 19No doubt there have
to be differences among you to show which
of you have God's approval. 20When you
come together, it is not the Lord's Supper
you eat, 21for as you eat, each of you goes
ahead without waiting for anybody else.
One remains hungry, another gets drunk.
22Don't you have homes to eat and drink
in? Or do you despise the church of God
and humiliate those who have nothing?
What shall I say to you? Shall I praise you
for this? Certainly not! ●

23For I received from the Lord what I
also passed on to you: The Lord Jesus, on
the night he was betrayed, took bread,
24and when he had given thanks, he broke
it and said, "This is my body, which is for
you; do this in remembrance of me." 25In
the same way, after supper he took the
cup, saying, "This cup is the new covenant
in my blood; do this, whenever you drink
it, in remembrance of me." 26For whenever you eat this bread and drink this cup,
you proclaim the Lord's death until he
comes.●

27Therefore, whoever eats the bread or
drinks the cup of the Lord in an unworthy
manner will be guilty of sinning against the
body and blood of the Lord. 28A man ought
to examine himself before he eats of the
bread and drinks of the cup. 29For anyone
who eats and drinks without recognizing
the body of the Lord eats and drinks judgment on himself. 30That is why many
among you are weak and sick, and a number of you have fallen asleep. 31But if we
judged ourselves, we would not come under judgment. 32When we are judged by the
Lord, we are being disciplined so that we
will not be condemned with the world.

33So then, my brothers, when you come
together to eat, wait for each other. 34If
anyone is hungry, he should eat at home,
so that when you meet together it may not
result in judgment.

And when I come I will give further directions.●

## KING JAMES

1.ABUSE

DIVISIONS

17 Now in this that I declare *unto you* I
praise *you* not, that ye come together not
for the better, but for the worse. 18 For
first of all, when ye come together in the
church, I hear that there be divisions
among you; and I partly believe it. 19 For
there must be also heresies among you,
that they which are approved may be
made manifest among you. 20 When ye
come together therefore into one place,
*this* is not to eat the Lord's supper. 21 For
in eating every one taketh before *other* his
own supper: and one is hungry, and another is drunken. 22 What! have ye not
houses to eat and to drink in? or despise
ye the church of God, and shame them
that have not? What shall I say to you?
shall I praise you in this? I praise *you*
not.●

2.THE ORDINANCE

23 For I have received of the Lord that
which also I delivered unto you, That the
Lord Jesus, the *same* night in which he
was betrayed, took bread: 24 and when
he had given thanks, he brake *it*, and said,
Take, eat; this is my body, which is
broken for you: this do in remembrance
of me. 25 After the same manner also *he*
*took* the cup, when he had supped, saying,
This cup is the new testament in my
blood: this do ye, as oft as ye drink *it*, in
remembrance of me. 26 For as often as
ye eat this bread, and drink this cup, ye
do show the Lord's death till he come.●

3.PARTICI-PATING UN-WORTHILY

27 Wherefore whosoever shall eat this
bread, and drink *this* cup of the Lord, un-
worthily, shall be guilty of the body and
blood of the Lord. 28 But let a man examine himself, and so let him eat of *that*
bread, and drink of *that* cup. 29 For he
that eateth and drinketh unworthily, eateth and drinketh damnation to himself,
not discerning the Lord's body. 30 For
this cause many *are* weak and sickly
among you, and many sleep. 31 For if we
would judge ourselves, we should not be
judged. 32 But when we are judged, we
are chastened of the Lord, that we should
not be condemned with the world.
33 Wherefore, my brethren, when ye
come together to eat, tarry one for another. 34 And if any man hunger, let him
eat at home; that ye come not together
unto condemnation. And the rest will I
set in order when I come.●

NO PREFERENCE

*11:17-22* What is the problem here? ______

How does Paul deal with the problem? ______

*11:23-26* This paragraph describes the parts of the communion service. Record these.

*11:27-34* What does it mean to partake unworthily of the elements?

What is the judgment for this sin? ______

How can this be averted? ______

NEW INTERNATIONAL VERSION

What does this passage teach about:

THE TRINITY

ONE BODY OF BELIEVERS

PURPOSE OF SPIRITUAL GIFTS

KINDS OF SPIRITUAL GIFTS

Record spiritual applications of the passage.

*Spiritual Gifts*

12 Now about spiritual gifts, brothers,
I do not want you to be ignorant.
2You know that when you were pagans,
somehow or other you were influenced and
led astray to dumb idols. 3Therefore I tell
you that no one who is speaking by the
Spirit of God says, "Jesus be cursed," and
no one can say, "Jesus is Lord," except by
the Holy Spirit.●
4There are different kinds of gifts, but the
same Spirit. 5There are different kinds of
service, but the same Lord. 6There are different kinds of working, but the same God
works all of them in all men.
7Now to each one the manifestation of
the Spirit is given for the common good.
8To one there is given through the Spirit
the message of wisdom, to another the
message of knowledge by means of the
same Spirit, 9to another faith by the same
Spirit, to another gifts of healing by that
one Spirit, 10to another miraculous powers, to another prophecy, to another the
ability to distinguish between spirits, to another the ability to speak in different kinds
of tongues,[a] and to still another the interpretation of tongues.[a] 11All these are the
work of one and the same Spirit, and he
gives them to each one, just as he determines.●

*One Body, Many Parts*

12The body is a unit, though it is made up
of many parts; and though all its parts are
many, they form one body. So it is with
Christ. 13For we were all baptized by[b] one
Spirit into one body—whether Jews or
Greeks, slave or free—and we were all giv-
en the one Spirit to drink.●

[a]10 Or *languages*; also in verse 28
[b]13 Or *with*; or *in*

KING JAMES

—introduction

12 Now concerning spiritual *gifts*,
brethren, I would not have you ignorant. 2 Ye know that ye were Gentiles,
carried away unto these dumb idols, even
as ye were led. 3 Wherefore I give you to
understand, that no man speaking by the
Spirit of God calleth Jesus accursed: and
*that* no man can say that Jesus is the Lord,
but by the Holy Ghost.●

MANY GIFTS

1. ONE SOURCE

4 Now there are diversities of gifts, but
the same Spirit. 5 And there are differences of administrations, but the same
Lord. 6 And there are diversities of
operations, but it is the same God which
worketh all in all. 7 But the manifestation
of the Spirit is given to every man to
profit withal. 8 For to one is given by the
Spirit the word of wisdom; to another the
word of knowledge by the same Spirit;
9 to another faith by the same Spirit; to
another the gifts of healing by the same
Spirit; 10 to another the working of
miracles; to another prophecy; to another discerning of spirits; to another
*divers* kinds of tongues; to another the
interpretation of tongues: 11 but all these
worketh that one and the selfsame Spirit,
dividing to every man severally as he will.●

2. ONE BODY

12 For as the body is one, and hath
many members and all the members of
that one body, being many, are one body:
so also *is* Christ. 13 For by one Spirit
are we all baptized into one body, whether
*we be* Jews or Gentiles, whether *we be*
bond or free; and have been all made to
drink into one Spirit.●

ONE SPIRIT

*12:1-3* Is it implied in verse 3 that the speakers are using spiritual gifts?
If so, what is a purpose of spiritual gifts?

*12:4-11* Note the references to the Trinity in verses 4-6. Note the repetition of "same Spirit" in verses 7-11. What is this contrasted with?

What is the point?

*12:12-13* How many times does the word "one" appear?

What is the point of this emphasis?

What group is meant by "one body"?

NEW INTERNATIONAL VERSION

What do you learn here about:

HOW CHRISTIANS ARE RELATED TO EACH OTHER

CHRIST AND HIS BODY

SPIRITUAL GIFTS

OTHER

14 Now the body is not made up of one
part but of many. 15 If the foot should say,
"Because I am not a hand, I do not belong
to the body," it would not for that reason
cease to be part of the body. 16 And if the
ear should say, "Because I am not an eye,
I do not belong to the body," it would not
for that reason cease to be part of the body.
17 If the whole body were an eye, where
would the sense of hearing be? If the whole
body were an ear, where would the sense
of smell be? 18 But in fact God has arranged
the parts in the body, every one of them,
just as he wanted them to be. 19 If they were
all one part, where would the body be?
20 As it is, there are many parts, but one
body.

21 The eye cannot say to the hand, "I
don't need you!" And the head cannot say
to the feet, "I don't need you!" 22 On the
contrary, those parts of the body that seem
to be weaker are indispensable, 23 and the
parts that we think are less honorable we
treat with special honor. And the parts that
are unpresentable are treated with special
modesty, 24 while our presentable parts
need no special treatment. But God has
combined the members of the body and has
given greater honor to the parts that lacked
it, 25 so that there should be no division in
the body, but that its parts should have
equal concern for each other. 26 If one part
suffers, every part suffers with it; if one
part is honored, every part rejoices with it.●

27 Now you are the body of Christ, and
each one of you is a part of it. 28 And in the
church God has appointed first of all apostles, second prophets, third teachers, then
workers of miracles, also those having gifts
of healing, those able to help others, those
with gifts of administration, and those
speaking in different kinds of tongues.
29 Are all apostles? Are all prophets? Are all
teachers? Do all work miracles? 30 Do all
have gifts of healing? Do all speak in
tongues[a]? Do all interpret? 31 But eagerly
desire[b] the greater gifts.●

[a]30 Or *other languages*
[b]31 Or *But you are eagerly desiring*

KING JAMES

1.DIF-
FERENT
MEMBERS

MANY
MEMBERS

14 For the body is not one member, but
many. 15 If the foot shall say, Because I
am not the hand, I am not of the body; is
it therefore not of the body? 16 And if the
ear shall say, Because I am not the eye, I
am not of the body; is it therefore not of
the body? 17 If the whole body *were* an
eye, where *were* the hearing? If the whole
*were* hearing, where *were* the smelling?
18 But now hath God set the members
every one of them in the body, as it hath
pleased him. 19 And if they were all one
member, where *were* the body? 20 But
now *are they* many members, yet but one
body. 21 And the eye cannot say unto the
hand, I have no need of thee: nor again
the head to the feet, I have no need of you.
22 Nay, much more those members of the
body, which seem to be more feeble, are
necessary: 23 and those *members* of the
body, which we think to be less honorable, upon these we bestow more abundant honor; and our uncomely *parts* have
more abundant comeliness. 24 For our
comely *parts* have no need: but God hath
tempered the body together, having given
more abundant honor to that *part* which
lacked: 25 that there should be no schism
in the body; but *that* the members should
have the same care one for another.
26 And whether one member suffer, all
the members suffer with it; or one member be honored, all the members rejoice
with it.●

2.DIF-
FERENT
GIFTS

27 Now ye are the body of Christ, and
members in particular. 28 And God hath
set some in the church, first apostles,
secondarily prophets, thirdly teachers,[c]
after that miracles, then gifts of healings,
helps, governments, diversities of tongues.
29 *Are* all apostles? *are* all prophets? *are*
all teachers? *are* all workers of miracles?
30 have all the gifts of healing? do all
speak with tongues? do all interpret?
31 But covet earnestly the best gifts.

BEST
GIFTS

And yet show I unto you a more excellent way.●

*12:14-26* Record the truths taught by these verses:

15-16 ______________________________

______________________________

______________________________

17,19 ______________________________

______________________________

______________________________

18 ______________________________

______________________________

______________________________

21 ______________________________

______________________________

______________________________

22,23 ______________________________

______________________________

______________________________

24,25 ______________________________

______________________________

______________________________

26 ______________________________

______________________________

______________________________

*12:27-31* How does this paragraph relate to the first paragraph?

______________________________

______________________________

______________________________

List the various spiritual gifts. ______________________________

______________________________

______________________________

______________________________

What does the last sentence point to?

______________________________

______________________________

______________________________

NEW INTERNATIONAL VERSION

Go through the verses one by one and apply the verse, whenever possible, to a present-day situation in your own experience:

*Love*

And now I will show you the most excellent way.

13 If I speak in the tongues[c] of men and
of angels, but have not love, I am
only a resounding gong or a clanging cymbal. [2]If I have the gift of prophecy and can
fathom all mysteries and all knowledge,
and if I have a faith that can move mountains, but have not love, I am nothing. [3]If
I give all I possess to the poor and surrender my body to the flames,[d] but have not
love, I gain nothing.●

[4]Love is patient, love is kind. It does not
envy, it does not boast, it is not proud. [5]It
is not rude, it is not self-seeking, it is not
easily angered, it keeps no record of
wrongs. [6]Love does not delight in evil but
rejoices with the truth. [7]It always protects,
always trusts, always hopes, always perseveres.●

[8]Love never fails. But where there are
prophecies, they will cease; where there
are tongues, they will be stilled; where
there is knowledge, it will pass away. [9]For
we know in part and we prophesy in part,
[10]but when perfection comes, the imper-
fect disappears. [11]When I was a child, I
talked like a child, I thought like a child, I
reasoned like a child. When I became a
man, I put childish ways behind me. [12]Now
we see but a poor reflection; then we shall
see face to face. Now I know in part; then
I shall know fully, even as I am fully
known.

[13]And now these three remain: faith,
hope and love. But the greatest of these is
love.●

c1 Or *languages*
d3 Some early manuscripts *body that I may boast*

KING JAMES

1.VALUES OF LOVE

**13** Though I speak with the tongues of
men and of angels, and have not
charity, I am become *as* sounding brass,
or a tinkling cymbal. 2 And though I
have *the gift of* prophecy, and understand
all mysteries, and all knowledge; and
though I have all faith, so that I could
remove mountains, and have not charity,
I am nothing. 3 And though I bestow all
my goods to feed *the poor*, and though I
give my body to be burned, and have not
charity, it profiteth me nothing.●

2.CHARACTERISTICS OF LOVE

4 Charity suffereth long, *and* is kind;
charity envieth not; charity vaunteth not
itself, is not puffed up, 5 doth not behave
itself unseemly, seeketh not her own, is
not easily provoked, thinketh no evil;
6 rejoiceth not in iniquity, but rejoiceth
in the truth; 7 beareth all things, believeth all things, hopeth all things, endureth all things.●

3.ABIDING NATURE OF LOVE

8 Charity never faileth: but whether
*there be* prophecies, they shall fail;
whether *there be* tongues, they shall cease;
whether *there be* knowledge, it shall vanish
away. 9 For we know in part, and we
prophesy in part. 10 But when that which
is perfect is come, then that which is in
part shall be done away. 11 When I was
a child, I spake as a child, I understood
as a child, I thought as a child: but when
I became a man, I put away childish
things. 12 For now we see through a
glass, darkly, but then face to face: now I
know in part; but then shall I know even
as also I am known. 13 And now abideth
faith, hope, charity, these three; but the
greatest of these *is* charity.●

SPEAKING

*13:1-3* Love is evaluated here by grading a Christian who lacks love. What gifts and virtues are cited:

v.1 ______________________________

______________________________

v.2 ______________________________

______________________________

v.3 ______________________________

______________________________

What is the grade, in each case:

v.1 ______________________________

______________________________

v.2 ______________________________

______________________________

v.3 ______________________________

______________________________

*13:4-7* List the different qualities of this Christ-like love:

______________________________

______________________________

______________________________

______________________________

______________________________

KNOWING

*13:8-13* What non-enduring gifts does Paul cite?

______________________________

______________________________

______________________________

______________________________

______________________________

What future event do you think is meant by verse 10?

______________________________

______________________________

______________________________

______________________________

______________________________

NEW INTERNATIONAL VERSION

What kinds of ministries are involved in the gift of prophecy? (e.g. vv.3-4)

Why is clarity an important test of speaking in tongues?

Record different ways the Christian can edify the church through special abilities given by the Holy Spirit.

### *Gifts of Prophecy and Tongues*

14 Follow the way of love and eagerly
desire spiritual gifts, especially the
gift of prophecy. 2For anyone who speaks
in a tongue[e] does not speak to men but to
God. Indeed, no one understands him; he
utters mysteries with his spirit.[f] 3But
everyone who prophesies speaks to men
for their strengthening, encouragement
and comfort. 4He who speaks in a tongue
edifies himself, but he who prophesies edifies the church. 5I would like every one of
you to speak in tongues,[g] but I would
rather have you prophesy. He who prophesies is greater than one who speaks in
tongues,[g] unless he interprets, so that the
church may be edified.●
6Now, brothers, if I come to you and
speak in tongues, what good will I be to
you, unless I bring you some revelation or
knowledge or prophecy or word of instruction? 7Even in the case of lifeless things
that make sounds, such as the flute or harp,
how will anyone know what tune is being
played unless there is a distinction in the
notes? 8Again, if the trumpet does not
sound a clear call, who will get ready for
battle? 9So it is with you. Unless you speak
intelligible words with your tongue, how
will anyone know what you are saying?
You will just be speaking into the air.
10Undoubtedly there are all sorts of languages in the world, yet none of them is
without meaning. 11If then I do not grasp
the meaning of what someone is saying, I
am a foreigner to the speaker, and he is a
foreigner to me. 12So it is with you. Since
you are eager to have spiritual gifts, try to
excel in gifts that build up the church.●

[e]2 Or *another language;* also in verses 4, 13, 14, 19, 26 and 27
[f]2 Or *by the Spirit*
[g]5 Or *other languages;* also in verses 6, 18, 22, 23 and 39
[h]16 Or *among the inquirers*

KING JAMES

1.TEST OF EDIFICATION

DESIRE

**14** Follow after charity, and desire
spiritual *gifts*, but rather that ye
may prophesy. 2 For he that speaketh in
an *unknown* tongue speaketh not unto
men, but unto God: for no man understandeth *him;* howbeit in the spirit he
speaketh mysteries. 3 But he that prophesieth speaketh unto men *to* edification,
and exhortation, and comfort. 4 He that
speaketh in an *unknown* tongue edifieth
himself; but he that prophesieth edifieth
the church. 5 I would that ye all spake
with tongues, but rather that ye prophesied: for greater *is* he that prophesieth
than he that speaketh with tongues, except he interpret, that the church may
receive edifying. ●

2.TEST OF CLARITY

6 Now, brethren, if I come unto you
speaking with tongues, what shall I profit
you, except I shall speak to you either by
revelation, or by knowledge, or by prophesying, or by doctrine? 7 And even things
without life giving sound, whether pipe or
harp, except they give a distinction in the
sounds, how shall it be known what is
piped or harped? 8 For if the trumpet
give an uncertain sound, who shall prepare himself to the battle? 9 So likewise
ye, except ye utter by the tongue words
easy to be understood, how shall it be
known what is spoken? for ye shall speak
into the air. 10 There are, it may be, so
many kinds of voices in the world, and
none of them *is* without signification.
11 Therefore if I know not the meaning of
the voice, I shall be unto him that speaketh a barbarian, and he that speaketh *shall*
*be* a barbarian unto me. 12 Even so ye,
forasmuch as ye are zealous of spiritual
*gifts*, seek that ye may excel to the edifying
of the church. ●

ZEAL

Read the segment. What two gifts are compared?

*14:1-5* What are the three parts of verse 1?

What is taught here about edification?

*14:6-12* What four things are not communicated via tongues (v.6)?

What is taught here about the test of charity?

NEW INTERNATIONAL VERSION

What does this passage teach about:

SPEAKING IN TONGUES

PROPHESYING (See The Living Bible, verse 22, for an identification of this.)

PRAYER

SIGNS

WITNESS TO UNBELIEVERS

OTHER

13For this reason the man who speaks in
a tongue should pray that he may interpret
what he says. 14For if I pray in a tongue,
my spirit prays, but my mind is unfruitful.
15So what shall I do? I will pray with my
spirit, but I will also pray with my mind; I
will sing with my spirit, but I will also sing
with my mind. 16If you are praising God
with your spirit, how can one who finds
himself among those who do not understand[h] say "Amen" to your thanksgiving,
since he does not know what you are saying? 17You may be giving thanks well
enough, but the other man is not edified.
18I thank God that I speak in tongues
more than all of you. 19But in the church I
would rather speak five intelligible words
to instruct others than ten thousand words
in a tongue.●
20Brothers, stop thinking like children.
In regard to evil be infants, but in
your thinking be adults. 21In the Law it is
written:

"Through men of strange tongues
and through the lips of foreigners
I will speak to this people,
but even then they will not listen
to me,"[a]
says the Lord.

22Tongues, then, are a sign, not for believers but for unbelievers; prophecy, however, is for believers, not for unbelievers.
23So if the whole church comes together
and everyone speaks in tongues, and some
who do not understand[b] or some unbelievers come in, will they not say that you are
out of your mind? 24But if an unbeliever or
someone who does not understand[c] comes
in while everybody is prophesying, he will
be convinced by all that he is a sinner and
will be judged by all, 25and the secrets of
his heart will be laid bare. So he will fall
down and worship God, exclaiming, "God
is really among you!"●

[a]*21* Isaiah 28:11,12; Deut. 28:49
[b]*23* Or *some inquirers*
[c]*24* Or *or some inquirer*

KING JAMES

1. MINISTRY TO BELIEVERS

TONGUE SPEAKING

13 Wherefore let him that speaketh in
an *unknown* tongue pray that he may interpret. 14 For if I pray in an *unknown*
tongue, my spirit prayeth, but my understanding is unfruitful. 15 What is it then?
I will pray with the spirit, and I will pray
with the understanding also: I will sing
with the spirit, and I will sing with the
understanding also. 16 Else, when thou
shalt bless with the spirit, how shall he
that occupieth the room of the unlearned
say Amen at thy giving of thanks, seeing
he understandeth not what thou sayest?
17 For thou verily givest thanks well, but
the other is not edified. 18 I thank my
God, I speak with tongues more than ye
all: 19 yet in the church I had rather
speak five words with my understanding,
that *by my voice* I might teach others also,
than ten thousand words in an *unknown*
tongue.●

2. MINISTRY TO UNBELIEVERS

PROPHESYING

20 Brethren, be not children in understanding: howbeit in malice be ye children, but in understanding be men. 21 In
the law it is written,

> With *men of* other tongues and other lips
> will I speak unto this people;
> and yet for all that will they not hear me, saith the Lord.

Isa. 28:11f.

22 Wherefore tongues are for a sign, not
to them that believe, but to them that believe not: but prophesying *serveth* not for
them that believe not, but for them which
believe. 23 If therefore the whole church
be come together into one place, and all
speak with tongues, and there come in
*those that are* unlearned, or unbelievers,
will they not say that ye are mad? 24 But
if all prophesy, and there come in one
that believeth not, or *one* unlearned, he is
convinced of all, he is judged of all:
25 and thus are the secrets of his heart
made manifest; and so falling down on
*his* face he will worship God, and report
that God is in you of a truth.●

*14:13-19* The setting is a worship service of Paul's day, where believers were gathered. What were some of the spoken activities of the service?

How could speaking in tongues be of help to those attending the service?

*14:20-25* Paul writes that genuine tongues were miraculous signs to whom (v.2a)?

How did prophesying minister to unbelievers attending the worship service?

NEW INTERNATIONAL VERSION

After you have observed the many parts of this passage, record the different things taught about the worship service. Apply the passage to the present-day church.

*Orderly Worship*

[26]What then shall we say, brothers?
When you come together, everyone has a
hymn, or a word of instruction, a revelation, a tongue or an interpretation. All of
these must be done for the strengthening of
the church. [27]If anyone speaks in a tongue,
two—or at the most three—should speak,
one at a time, and someone must interpret.
[28]If there is no interpreter, the speaker
should keep quiet in the church and speak
to himself and God.
[29]Two or three prophets should speak,
and the others should weigh carefully what
is said. [30]And if a revelation comes to
someone who is sitting down, the first
speaker should stop. [31]For you can all
prophesy in turn so that everyone may be
instructed and encouraged. [32]The spirits of
prophets are subject to the control of
prophets. [33]For God is not a God of disorder but of peace.
As in all the congregations of the saints,
[34]women should remain silent in the
churches. They are not allowed to speak,
but must be in submission, as the Law
says. [35]If they want to inquire about something, they should ask their own husbands
at home; for it is disgraceful for a woman
to speak in the church. [36]Did the word of
God originate with you? Or are you the
only people it has reached?
[37]If anybody thinks he is a prophet or
spiritually gifted, let him acknowledge that
what I am writing to you is the Lord's command. [38]If he ignores this, he himself will
be ignored.[d]
[39]Therefore, my brothers, be eager to
prophesy, and do not forbid speaking in
tongues. [40]But everything should be done
in a fitting and orderly way.

[d]38 Some manuscripts *this, let him ignore this*

KING JAMES

1.ORDER

EDIFICATION

26 How is it then, brethren? when ye
come together, every one of you hath a
psalm, hath a doctrine, hath a tongue,
hath a revelation, hath an interpretation.
Let all things be done unto edifying. 27 If
any man speak in an *unknown* tongue, *let*
*it be* by two, or at the most *by* three, and
*that* by course; and let one interpret.
28 But if there be no interpreter, let him
keep silence in the church; and let him
speak to himself, and to God. 29 Let the
prophets speak two or three, and let the
other judge. 30 If *any thing* be revealed to
another that sitteth by, let the first hold
his peace. 31 For ye may all prophesy one
by one, that all may learn, and all may be
comforted. 32 And the spirits of the
prophets are subject to the prophets.
33 For God is not *the author* of confusion,
but of peace, ● as in all churches of the
saints.

2.THE WOMEN

34 Let your women keep silence in the
churches: for it is not permitted unto
them to speak; but *they are commanded*
to be under obedience, as also saith the
law. 35 And if they will learn any thing,
let them ask their husbands at home: for
it is a shame for women to speak in the
church. ●

—summary

36 What! came the word of God
out from you? or came it unto you only?
37 If any man think himself to be a
prophet, or spiritual, let him acknowledge
that the things that I write unto you are
the commandments of the Lord. 38 But
if any man be ignorant, let him be ignorant. 39 Wherefore, brethren, covet to
prophesy, and forbid not to speak with
tongues. 40 Let all things be done decently and in order. ●

ORDER

*14:26-33a* Record the following, about the early church's worship service:

PARTICIPATORS (vv.27,29-32) ______

ACTIVITIES (v.26) ______

PURPOSES (vv.26,31) ______

ATMOSPHERE (v.33) ______

*14:33b-35* This paragraph suggests a situation of confusion in the worship service. What was that?

______

*14:36-40* What is Paul saying in verses 36-38?

______

What are the commands of verses 39-40?

______

How do these summarize chapter 14?

______

NEW INTERNATIONAL VERSION

What does this passage teach about:

THE GOSPEL

FOUNDATIONAL FACTS OF CHRIST'S MINISTRY

RESURRECTION OF CHRIST

PAUL

GRACE OF GOD

OTHER

*The Resurrection of Christ*

15 Now, brothers, I want to remind
you of the gospel I preached to you,
which you received and on which you have
taken your stand. [2]By this gospel you are
saved, if you hold firmly to the word I
preached to you. Otherwise, you have believed in vain.●
[3]For what I received I passed on to you
as of first importance[e]: that Christ died for
our sins according to the Scriptures, [4]that
he was buried, that he was raised on the
third day according to the Scriptures, [5]and
that he appeared to Peter,[f] and then to the
Twelve. [6]After that, he appeared to more
than five hundred of the brothers at the
same time, most of whom are still living,
though some have fallen asleep. [7]Then he
appeared to James, then to all the apostles,●
[8]and last of all he appeared to me also, as
to one abnormally born.
[9]For I am the least of the apostles and do
not even deserve to be called an apostle,
because I persecuted the church of God.
[10]But by the grace of God I am what I am,
and his grace to me was not without effect.
No, I worked harder than all of them—yet
not I, but the grace of God that was with
me. [11]Whether, then, it was I or they, this
is what we preach, and this is what you
believed.●

[e]3 Or *you at the first* [f]5 Greek *Cephas*

## KING JAMES

1. THE PREACHED GOSPEL

GOSPEL IS RECEIVED

15 Moreover, brethren, I declare unto
you the gospel which I preached
unto you, which also ye have received,
and wherein ye stand; 2 by which also ye
are saved, if ye keep in memory what I
preached unto you, unless ye have believed in vain. ●

2. HISTORICAL FACTS

3 For I delivered unto you first of all
that which I also received, how that Christ
died for our sins according to the Scriptures; 4 and that he was buried, and
that he rose again the third day according
to the Scriptures: 5 and that he was seen
of Cephas, then of the twelve: 6 after
that, he was seen of above five hundred
brethren at once; of whom the greater
part remain unto this present, but some
are fallen asleep. 7 After that, he was seen
of James; then of all the apostles. ● 8 And

3. WITNESS OF PAUL

last of all he was seen of me also, as of
one born out of due time. 9 For I am the
least of the apostles, that am not meet to
be called an apostle, because I persecuted
the church of God. 10 But by the grace
of God I am what I am: and his grace
which *was bestowed* upon me was not in
vain; but I labored more abundantly than
they all: yet not I, but the grace of God
which was with me. 11 Therefore whether
*it were* I or they, so we preach, and so ye
believed. ●

GOSPEL IS BELIEVED

Chapter 15 is the New Testament's classic chapter on the resurrection body. The *FACT* of the bodily resurrection is the theme of 15:1-34.
First read the segment. How does it introduce the subject of resurrection?

*15:1-2* Record what is said here about:

PAUL

CORINTHIANS

GOSPEL

*15:3-7* List the historical facts:

*15:8-11* What are Paul's credentials as a witness?

Compare verse 11 with verse 1.

NEW INTERNATIONAL VERSION

What do you learn here about:

HOPE OF RESURRECTION

FUTURE REIGN OF CHRIST

FUTURE JUDGMENT

DEATH

CRUCIFIED LIFE OF THE BELIEVER

OTHER

*The Resurrection of the Dead*

[12]But if it is preached that Christ has
been raised from the dead, how can some
of you say that there is no resurrection of
the dead? [13]If there is no resurrection of the
dead, then not even Christ has been raised.
[14]And if Christ has not been raised, our
preaching is useless and so is your faith.
[15]More than that, we are then found to be
false witnesses about God, for we have
testified about God that he raised Christ
from the dead. But he did not raise him if
in fact the dead are not raised. [16]For if the
dead are not raised, then Christ has not
been raised either. [17]And if Christ has not
been raised, your faith is futile; you are still
in your sins. [18]Then those also who have
fallen asleep in Christ are lost. [19]If only for
this life we have hope in Christ, we are to
be pitied more than all men.●

[20]But Christ has indeed been raised from
the dead, the firstfruits of those who have
fallen asleep. [21]For since death came
through a man, the resurrection of the dead
comes also through a man. [22]For as in
Adam all die, so in Christ all will be made
alive. [23]But each in his own turn: Christ,
the firstfruits; then, when he comes, those
who belong to him. [24]Then the end will
come, when he hands over the kingdom to
God the Father after he has destroyed all
dominion, authority and power. [25]For he
must reign until he has put all his enemies
under his feet. [26]The last enemy to be destroyed is death. [27]For he "has put everything under his feet."[a] Now when it says
that "everything" has been put under him,
it is clear that this does not include God
himself, who put everything under Christ.
[28]When he has done this, then the Son himself will be made subject to him who put
everything under him, so that God may be
all in all.●

[29]Now if there is no resurrection, what
will those do who are baptized for the
dead? If the dead are not raised at all, why
are people baptized for them? [30]And as for
us, why do we endanger ourselves every
hour? [31]I die every day—I mean that,
brothers—just as surely as I glory over you
in Christ Jesus our Lord. [32]If I fought wild
beasts in Ephesus for merely human reasons, what have I gained? If the dead are
not raised,

> "Let us eat and drink,
> for tomorrow we die."[b]

[33]Do not be misled: "Bad company corrupts good character." [34]Come back to
your senses as you ought, and stop sinning;
for there are some who are ignorant of
God—I say this to your shame.●

[a]27 Psalm 8:6 [b]32 Isaiah 22:13

KING JAMES

1. BELIEVER'S RESURRECTION

NO RESURRECTION?

12 Now if Christ be preached that he
rose from the dead, how say some among
you that there is no resurrection of the
dead? 13 But if there be no resurrection
of the dead, then is Christ not risen:
14 and if Christ be not risen, then *is* our
preaching vain, and your faith *is* also vain.
15 Yea, and we are found false witnesses
of God; because we have testified of God
that he raised up Christ: whom he raised
not up, if so be that the dead rise not.
16 For if the dead rise not, then is not
Christ raised: 17 and if Christ be not
raised, your faith *is* vain; ye are yet in
your sins. 18 Then they also which are
fallen asleep in Christ are perished. 19 If
in this life only we have hope in Christ, we
are of all men most miserable.●

2. BELIEVER'S FUTURE

20 But now is Christ risen from the
dead, *and* become the firstfruits of them
that slept. 21 For since by man *came*
death, by man *came* also the resurrection
of the dead. 22 For as in Adam all die,
even so in Christ shall all be made alive.
23 But every man in his own order: Christ
the firstfruits; afterward they that are
Christ's at his coming. 24 Then *cometh*
the end, when he shall have delivered up
the kingdom to God, even the Father;
when he shall have put down all rule, and
all authority and power. 25 For he must
reign, till he hath put all enemies under
his feet. 26 The last enemy *that* shall be
destroyed *is* death. 27 For he hath put all
things under his feet. But when he saith,
All things are put under *him*, *it is* manifest that he is excepted, which did put all
things under him. 28 And when all
things shall be subdued unto him, then
shall the Son also himself be subject unto
him that put all things under him, that
God may be all in all.●

3. BELIEVER'S PRESENT

29 Else what shall they do which are
baptized for the dead, if the dead rise not
at all? why are they then baptized for the
dead? 30 and why stand we in jeopardy
every hour? 31 I protest by your rejoicing which I have in Christ Jesus our Lord,
I die daily. 32 If after the manner of men
I have fought with beasts at Ephesus,
what advantageth it me, if the dead rise
not? let us eat and drink; for tomorrow
we die. 33 Be not deceived: evil communications corrupt good manners.
34 Awake to righteousness, and sin not;
for some have not the knowledge of God:
I speak *this* to your shame.●

NO KNOWLEDGE!

*15:12-19* Record what Paul establishes here:

IF CHRIST IS NOT RISEN: __________

IF CHRIST IS RISEN: __________

*15:20-28* What is the tone of the opening statement?

What does Paul write about the future, in verses 23-28?

*15:29-34* What is the believer's present state, *if* Christ is not risen?

NEW INTERNATIONAL VERSION

What does this passage teach about:

SPIRITUAL BODIES IN HEAVEN

INCORRUPTION

DEATH

HOPE

CHRISTIAN SERVICE

*The Resurrection Body*

35 But someone may ask, "How are the
dead raised? With what kind of body will
they come?" 36 How foolish! What you sow
does not come to life unless it dies. 37 When
you sow, you do not plant the body that
will be, but just a seed, perhaps of wheat
or of something else. 38 But God gives it a
body as he has determined, and to each
kind of seed he gives its own body. 39 All
flesh is not the same: Men have one kind of
flesh, animals have another, birds another
and fish another. 40 There are also heavenly
bodies and there are earthly bodies; but the
splendor of the heavenly bodies is one
kind, and the splendor of the earthly bodies
is another. 41 The sun has one kind of splendor, the moon another and the stars another; and star differs from star in splendor.

42 So will it be with the resurrection of the
dead. The body that is sown is perishable,
it is raised imperishable; 43 it is sown in dishonor, it is raised in glory; it is sown in
weakness, it is raised in power; 44 it is sown
a natural body, it is raised a spiritual body.

If there is a natural body, there is also a
spiritual body. 45 So it is written: "The first
man Adam became a living being"[c]; the
last Adam, a life-giving spirit. 46 The spiritual did not come first, but the natural, and
after that the spiritual. 47 The first man was
of the dust of the earth, the second man
from heaven. 48 As was the earthly man, so
are those who are of the earth; and as is the
man from heaven, so also are those who
are of heaven. 49 And just as we have borne
the likeness of the earthly man, so shall
we[d] bear the likeness of the man from
heaven.

50 I declare to you, brothers, that flesh
and blood cannot inherit the kingdom of
God, nor does the perishable inherit the
imperishable. 51 Listen, I tell you a mystery: We will not all sleep, but we will all
be changed— 52 in a flash, in the twinkling
of an eye, at the last trumpet. For the trumpet will sound, the dead will be raised imperishable, and we will be changed. 53 For
the perishable must clothe itself with the
imperishable, and the mortal with immortality. 54 When the perishable has been
clothed with the imperishable, and the
mortal with immortality, then the saying
that is written will come true: "Death has
been swallowed up in victory."[e]

> 55 "Where, O death, is your victory?
> Where, O death, is your sting?"[f]

56 The sting of death is sin, and the power
of sin is the law. 57 But thanks be to God!
He gives us the victory through our Lord
Jesus Christ.

58 Therefore, my dear brothers, stand
firm. Let nothing move you. Always give
yourselves fully to the work of the Lord,
because you know that your labor in the
Lord is not in vain.

c45 Gen. 2:7 d49 Some early manuscripts *so let us*
e54 Isaiah 25:8 f55 Hosea 13:14

KING JAMES

PHYSICAL WORK OF GOD

1. SUPERNATURAL BODY

35 But some *man* will say, How are the
dead raised up? and with what body do
they come? 36 *Thou* fool, that which
thou sowest is not quickened, except it
die: 37 and that which thou sowest, thou
sowest not that body that shall be, but
bare grain, it may chance of wheat, or of
some other *grain:* 38 but God giveth it a
body as it hath pleased him, and to every
seed his own body. ●

2. HEAVENLY IMAGE

39 All flesh *is* not the
same flesh: but *there is* one *kind of* flesh of
men, another flesh of beasts, another of
fishes, *and* another of birds. 40 *There are*
also celestial bodies, and bodies terrestrial: but the glory of the celestial *is* one,
and the *glory* of the terrestrial *is* another.
41 *There is* one glory of the sun, and another glory of the moon, and another
glory of the stars; for *one* star differeth
from *another* star in glory.
42 So also *is* the resurrection of the
dead. It is sown in corruption, it is raised
in incorruption: 43 it is sown in dishonor,
it is raised in glory: it is sown in weakness, it is raised in power: 44 it is sown a
natural body, it is raised a spiritual body.
There is a natural body, and there is a
spiritual body. 45 And so it is written,
The first man Adam was made a living
soul; the last Adam *was made* a quicken-
ing spirit. 46 Howbeit that *was* not first
which is spiritual, but that which is natural; and afterward that which is spiritual. 47 The first man *is* of the earth,
earthy: the second man *is* the Lord from
heaven. 48 As *is* the earthy, such *are* they
also that are earthy: and as *is* the heavenly,
such *are* they also that are heavenly.
49 And as we have borne the image of the
earthy, we shall also bear the image of the
heavenly. ●

3. INCORRUPTIBLE CHARACTER

50 Now this I say, brethren,
that flesh and blood cannot inherit the
kingdom of God; neither doth corruption inherit incorruption.
51 Behold, I show you a mystery; We
shall not all sleep, but we shall all be
changed, 52 in a moment, in the twinkling of an eye, at the last trump: for the
trumpet shall sound, and the dead shall be
raised incorruptible, and we shall be
changed. 53 For this corruptible must
put on incorruption, and this mortal *must*
put on immortality. 54 So when this corruptible shall have put on incorruption,
and this mortal shall have put on immortality, then shall be brought to pass
the saying that is written, Death is
swallowed up in victory. 55 O death,
where *is* thy sting? O grave, where *is*
thy victory? 56 The sting of death *is*
sin; and the strength of sin *is* the law.
57 But thanks *be* to God, which giveth
us the victory through our Lord Jesus
Christ.

SPIRITUAL WORK OF THE LORD

58 Therefore, my beloved brethren, be
ye steadfast, unmovable, always abounding in the work of the Lord, forasmuch as
ye know that your labor is not in vain in
the Lord. ●

*15:35-38* What picture does Paul use to describe what the resurrection body will be like?

_______________

*15:39-49* Read verse 49 first. This is a summary of the paragraph.

List the contrasts: _______________

*15:50-58* What event mocks the transformation of corruptible bodies to incorruptible bodies?

_______________

What do verses 55-57 teach? _______________

How is verse 58 an appropriate appeal for the resurrection theme?

_______________

NEW INTERNATIONAL VERSION

What is taught here about:

CHRISTIAN LOVE

COMPASSION

THE WILL OF GOD

COURAGE

List some practical applications of the passage.

*The Collection for God's People*

16 Now about the collection for God's
people: Do what I told the Galatian
churches to do. [2]On the first day of every
week, each one of you should set aside a
sum of money in keeping with his income,
saving it up, so that when I come no collec-
tions will have to be made. [3]Then, when I
arrive, I will give letters of introduction to
the men you approve and send them with
your gift to Jerusalem. [4]If it seems advis-
able for me to go also, they will accompany
me.●

*Personal Requests*

[5]After I go through Macedonia, I will
come to you—for I will be going through
Macedonia. [6]Perhaps I will stay with you
awhile, or even spend the winter, so that
you can help me on my journey, wherever
I go. [7]I do not want to see you now and
make only a passing visit; I hope to spend
some time with you, if the Lord permits.
[8]But I will stay on at Ephesus until Pentecost, [9]because a great door for effective
work has opened to me, and there are
many who oppose me.●
[10]If Timothy comes, see to it that he has
nothing to fear while he is with you, for he
is carrying on the work of the Lord, just as
I am. [11]No one, then, should refuse to accept him. Send him on his way in peace so
that he may return to me. I am expecting
him along with the brothers.●
[12]Now about our brother Apollos: I
strongly urged him to go to you with the
brothers. He was quite unwilling to go
now, but he will go when he has the opportunity.●
[13]Be on your guard; stand firm in the
faith; be men of courage; be strong. [14]Do
everything in love.
[15]You know that the household of Stephanas were the first converts in Achaia, and
they have devoted themselves to the service of the saints. I urge you, brothers, [16]to
submit to such as these and to everyone
who joins in the work, and labors at it. [17]I
was glad when Stephanas, Fortunatus and
Achaicus arrived, because they have supplied what was lacking from you. [18]For
they refreshed my spirit and yours also.
Such men deserve recognition.●

*Final Greetings*

[19]The churches in the province of Asia
send you greetings. Aquila and Priscilla[a]
greet you warmly in the Lord, and so does
the church that meets at their house. [20]All
the brothers here send you greetings.
Greet one another with a holy kiss.●
[21]I, Paul, write this greeting in my own
hand.
[22]If anyone does not love the Lord—a
curse be on him. Come, O Lord[b]!
[23]The grace of the Lord Jesus be with
you.
[24]My love to all of you in Christ Jesus.
Amen.[c]●

[a]19 Greek *Prisca*, a variant of *Priscilla*
[b]22 In Aramaic the expression *Come, O Lord* is *Marana tha*
[c]24 Some manuscripts do not have *Amen*.

KING JAMES

1.THE COL-
LECTION

GIFTS

**16** Now concerning the collection for
the saints, as I have given order to
the churches of Galatia, even so do ye.
2 Upon the first *day* of the week let every
one of you lay by him in store, as *God*
hath prospered him, that there be no
gatherings when I come. 3 And when I
come, whomsoever ye shall approve by
*your* letters, them will I send to bring
your liberality unto Jerusalem. 4 And if
it be meet that I go also, they shall go
with me.●

2.VISITS
—Paul

5 Now I will come unto you, when I
shall pass through Macedonia: for I do
pass through Macedonia. 6 And it may
be that I will abide, yea, and winter with
you, that ye may bring me on my journey
whithersoever I go. 7 For I will not see
you now by the way; but I trust to tarry
a while with you, if the Lord permit.
8 But I will tarry at Ephesus until Pentecost. 9 For a great door and effectual
is opened unto me, and *there are* many
adversaries.●

—Timothy

10 Now if Timothy come, see that
he may be with you without fear: for he
worketh the work of the Lord, as I also
*do*. 11 Let no man therefore despise him:
but conduct him forth in peace, that he
may come unto me: for I look for him
with the brethren.●

—Apollos

12 As touching *our* brother Apol'los,
I greatly desired him to come unto you
with the brethren: but his will was not
at all to come at this time; but he will
come when he shall have convenient
time.●

3.EXHORTA-
TIONS

13 Watch ye, stand fast in the faith,
quit you like men, be strong. 14 Let all
your things be done with charity.●
15 I beseech you, brethren, (ye know
the house of Steph'anas, that it is the
firstfruits of Achai'a, and *that* they have
addicted themselves to the ministry of the
saints,) 16 that ye submit yourselves unto
such, and to every one that helpeth with
*us*, and laboreth. 17 I am glad of the
coming of Steph'anas and Fortuna'tus
and Acha'icus: for that which was lacking
on your part they have supplied. 18 For
they have refreshed my spirit and yours:
therefore acknowledge ye them that are
such.●

4.GREET-
INGS

19 The churches of Asia salute you.
Aquila and Priscilla salute you much
in the Lord, with the church that is in
their house. 20 All the brethren greet
you. Greet ye one another with a holy
kiss.●

5.BENEDIC-
TION

21 The salutation of *me* Paul with mine
own hand. 22 If any man love not the
Lord Jesus Christ, let him be Anath'ema,
Maranath'a. 23 The grace of our Lord
Jesus Christ *be* with you. 24 My love *be*
with you all in Christ Jesus. Amen.●

LOVE

This is Paul's conclusion to the epistle. It is a practical demonstration of Christianity in everyday life.

*16:1-4* Record key phrases: ____________

____________

____________

____________

____________

*16:5-12* Record important truths in connection with each man's visit:

PAUL ____________

____________

____________

____________

____________

TIMOTHY ____________

____________

____________

____________

____________

APOLLOS ____________

____________

____________

____________

____________

*16:13-18* Record the exhortations. ____________

____________

____________

____________

____________

*16:19-24* Record the highlights. ____________

____________

____________

____________

____________

____________

____________

# 2 CORINTHIANS

## AUTHORSHIP

Paul the apostle was the author of this Epistle (1:1). He wrote it to the church at Corinth about a year after he wrote 1 Corinthians.

## DATE

Around A.D. 56-57.

## PURPOSE AND THEME

At least three main purposes can be seen in the Epistle: a) to give instruction in doctrine and practical exhortation; b) to give further instructions for the offering being gathered for the poor saints in Jerusalem; c) to make an extended defense of Paul's apostleship in view of false accusations by some in the Corinthian church. A suggested theme is: Paul's ministry in the light of the indescribable gift of God's Son.

## 2 CORINTHIANS: Paul's Apostolic Ministry

| | |
|---|---|
| SKETCH OF PAUL'S MINISTRY | 1:1-7:16 |
| Comfort in Tribulation | 1:1-11 |
| Maintaining Good Relations with Fellow Christians | 1:12-2:13 |
| Ministry of Proclaiming Christ | 2:14-4:6 |
| God's Treasure in Common Clay Vessels | 4:7-5:10 |
| An Ambassador for Christ | 5:11-7:3 |
| Joy in Tribulation | 7:4-16 |
| APPEAL ABOUT GIVING | 8:1-9:15 |
| Macedonians' Gift | 8:1-9 |
| Corinthians' Gift | 8:10-9:15 |
| VINDICATION OF PAUL'S MINISTRY | 10:1-13:14 |
| Authority and Approval of a True Ministry | 10:1-18 |
| True and False Apostles | 11:1-15 |
| Credentials of a True Ministry | 11:16-12:13 |
| "Prepare for My Visit" | 12:14-13:14 |

# 2 CORINTHIANS

NEW INTERNATIONAL VERSION

What does this passage teach about:

TRIBULATION

COMFORT

SUFFERING OF CHRIST

CHRISTIAN FELLOWSHIP

TRUST

PRAYER

List practical applications of the passage.

1 Paul, an apostle of Christ Jesus by the will of God, and Timothy our brother,

To the church of God in Corinth, together with all the saints throughout Achaia:

2Grace and peace to you from God our Father and the Lord Jesus Christ.●

*The God of All Comfort*

3Praise be to the God and Father of our
Lord Jesus Christ, the Father of compassion and the God of all comfort, 4who comforts us in all our troubles, so that we can
comfort those in any trouble with the comfort we ourselves have received from God.
5For just as the sufferings of Christ flow
over into our lives, so also through Christ
our comfort overflows. 6If we are distressed, it is for your comfort and salvation; if we are comforted, it is for your
comfort, which produces in you patient endurance of the same sufferings we suffer.
7And our hope for you is firm, because we
know that just as you share in our sufferings, so also you share in our comfort.●
8We do not want you to be uninformed,
brothers, about the hardships we suffered
in the province of Asia. We were under
great pressure, far beyond our ability to
endure, so that we despaired even of life.
9Indeed, in our hearts we felt the sentence
of death. But this happened that we might
not rely on ourselves but on God, who
raises the dead. 10He has delivered us from
such a deadly peril, and he will deliver us.
On him we have set our hope that he will
continue to deliver us, 11as you help us by
your prayers. Then many will give thanks
on our[d] behalf for the gracious favor
granted us in answer to the prayers of
many.●

[d]11 Many manuscripts *your*

KING JAMES

# 2 CORINTHIANS

—salutation

1 Paul, an apostle of Jesus Christ by the will of God, and Timothy *our* brother, unto the church of God which is at Corinth, with all the saints which are in all Achai'a:
2 Grace *be* to you, and peace, from God our Father, and *from* the Lord Jesus Christ.●

LETTER TO THE CHURCH

1.COMFORT IN TRIBULATION

3 Blessed *be* God, even the Father of our Lord Jesus Christ, the Father of mercies, and the God of all comfort; 4 who
comforteth us in all our tribulation, that we may be able to comfort them which are in any trouble, by the comfort wherewith we ourselves are comforted of God.
5 For as the sufferings of Christ abound in us, so our consolation also aboundeth
by Christ. 6 And whether we be afflicted,
*it is* for your consolation and salvation, which is effectual in the enduring of the same sufferings which we also suffer: or whether we be comforted, *it is* for your
consolation and salvation. 7 And our
hope of you *is* steadfast, knowing, that as ye are partakers of the sufferings, so *shall ye be* also of the consolation.●

2.PAUL'S EXPERIENCE

8 For we would not, brethren, have you ignorant of our trouble which came to us in Asia, that we were pressed out of measure, above strength, insomuch that
we despaired even of life: 9 but we had
the sentence of death in ourselves, that we should not trust in ourselves, but in God
which raiseth the dead: 10 who delivered
us from so great a death, and doth deliver: in whom we trust that he will yet deliver *us*;
11 ye also helping together by prayer for us, that for the gift *bestowed* upon us by the means of many persons thanks may be given by many on our behalf.●

PRAYER BY THE CHURCH

After the salutation of 1:1-2, Paul begins to write a sketch of his ministry. This testimony is the section 1:3—7:16.

*1:1-2* What are the parts of the salutation?

*1:3-7* Underline the word "tribulation" and all other similar terms. Do this for the word "comfort" and similar terms. What is the theme of the paragraph?

*1:8-11* What was Paul's experience?

What did Paul learn from the experience?

NEW INTERNATIONAL VERSION

What do you learn here about:

SINCERITY AND HONESTY

JOY

FICKLENESS

PLANS AND THE WILL OF GOD

TRINITY

LOVE

OTHER

*Paul's Change of Plans*

12Now this is our boast: Our conscience
testifies that we have conducted ourselves
in the world, and especially in our relations
with you, in the holiness and sincerity that
are from God. We have done so not according to worldly wisdom but according
to God's grace. 13For we do not write you
anything you cannot read or understand.
And I hope that, 14as you have understood
us in part, you will come to understand
fully that you can boast of us just as we will
boast of you in the day of the Lord Jesus.●

15Because I was confident of this, I
planned to visit you first so that you might
benefit twice. 16I planned to visit you on
my way to Macedonia and to come back to
you from Macedonia, and then to have you
send me on my way to Judea. 17When I
planned this, did I do it lightly? Or do I
make my plans in a worldly manner so that
in the same breath I say, "Yes, yes" and
"No, no"?

18But as surely as God is faithful, our
message to you is not "Yes" and "No."
19For the Son of God, Jesus Christ, who
was preached among you by me and Silas[a]
and Timothy, was not "Yes" and "No,"
but in him it has always been "Yes." 20For
no matter how many promises God has
made, they are "Yes" in Christ. And so
through him the "Amen" is spoken by us
to the glory of God. 21Now it is God who
makes both us and you stand firm in Christ.
He anointed us, 22set his seal of ownership
on us, and put his Spirit in our hearts as a
deposit, guaranteeing what is to come.●

23I call God as my witness that it was in
order to spare you that I did not return to
Corinth. 24Not that we lord it over your
faith, but we work with you for your joy,
because it is by faith you stand firm.

2 1So I made up my mind that I would not
make another painful visit to you. 2For if I
grieve you, who is left to make me glad but
you whom I have grieved? 3I wrote as I did
so that when I came I should not be distressed by those who ought to make me
rejoice. I had confidence in all of you, that
you would all share my joy. 4For I wrote
you out of great distress and anguish of
heart and with many tears, not to grieve
you but to let you know the depth of my
love for you.●

[a]*19* Greek *Silvanus*, a variant of *Silas*

KING JAMES

1. PAUL AND THE CORINTHIANS

12 For our rejoicing is this, the testimony of our conscience, that in simplicity
and godly sincerity, not with fleshly wisdom, but by the grace of God, we have
had our conversation in the world, and
more abundantly to you-ward. 13 For we
write none other things unto you, than
what ye read or acknowledge; and I trust
ye shall acknowledge even to the end;
14 as also ye have acknowledged us in
part, that we are your rejoicing, even as
ye also *are* ours in the day of the Lord
Jesus.●

JOY

2. CHANGED PLAN

15 And in this confidence I was minded
to come unto you before, that ye might
have a second benefit; 16 and to pass by
you into Macedonia, and to come again
out of Macedonia unto you, and of you
to be brought on my way toward Judea.
17 When I therefore was thus minded, did
I use lightness? or the things that I purpose, do I purpose according to the flesh,
that with me there should be yea, yea, and
nay, nay? 18 But *as* God *is* true, our
word toward you was not yea and nay.
19 For the Son of God, Jesus Christ, who
was preached among you by us, *even* by
me and Silva'nus and Timothy, was
not yea and nay, but in him was yea.
20 For all the promises of God in him *are*
yea, and in him Amen, unto the glory of
God by us. 21 Now he which stablisheth
us with you in Christ, and hath anointed
us, *is* God; 22 who hath also sealed us,
and given the earnest of the Spirit in our
hearts.●

3. REASONS FOR CHANGE

23 Moreover I call God for a record
upon my soul, that to spare you I came
not as yet unto Corinth. 24 Not for that
we have dominion over your faith, but
are helpers of your joy: for by faith ye
2 stand. 1 But I determined this with
myself, that I would not come again
to you in heaviness. 2 For if I make you
sorry, who is he then that maketh me
glad, but the same which is made sorry by
me? 3 And I wrote this same unto you,
lest, when I came, I should have sorrow
from them of whom I ought to rejoice;
having confidence in you all, that my joy
is *the joy* of you all. 4 For out of much
affliction and anguish of heart I wrote unto you with many tears; not that ye
should be grieved, but that ye might
know the love which I have more abundantly unto you.●

TEARS

*1:12-14* Paul writes about his relations with the Corinthians. Record these:

PAST ______________________________

PRESENT ______________________________

FUTURE ______________________________

*1:15-22* What was Paul's original travel plan (vv.15,16)?

______________________________

Verses 17 and 23 refer to a change of plan. How does Paul defend change? (vv.18-22)

______________________________

What else does he say in this paragraph?

______________________________

*1:23—2:4* According to this paragraph why did Paul delay his visit to Corinth?

______________________________

NEW INTERNATIONAL VERSION

What does the passage teach about these aspects of forgiveness:

WHAT OFFENDED ONES OWE THE OFFENDER

INDIVIDUAL AND GROUP FORGIVENESS

BASIS OF FORGIVENESS

CONSEQUENCES OF A NON-FORGIVING SPIRIT

List other practical applications of the passage.

*Forgiveness for the Sinner*

5If anyone has caused grief, he has not so
much grieved me as he has grieved all of
you, to some extent—not to put it too
severely. 6The punishment inflicted on him
by the majority is sufficient for him. 7Now
instead, you ought to forgive and comfort
him, so that he will not be overwhelmed by
excessive sorrow. 8I urge you, therefore,
to reaffirm your love for him. 9The reason
I wrote you was to see if you would stand
the test and be obedient in everything. 10If
you forgive anyone, I also forgive him.
And what I have forgiven—if there was
anything to forgive—I have forgiven in the
sight of Christ for your sake, 11in order that
Satan might not outwit us. For we are not
unaware of his schemes.●

*Ministers of the New Covenant*

12Now when I went to Troas to preach
the gospel of Christ and found that the
Lord had opened a door for me, 13I still had
no peace of mind, because I did not find my
brother Titus there. So I said good-by to
them and went on to Macedonia.●

KING JAMES

1. FORGIVENESS

5 But if any have caused grief, he hath
not grieved me, but in part: that I may
not overcharge you all. 6 Sufficient to
such a man *is* this punishment, which *was*
*inflicted* of many. 7 So that contrariwise
ye *ought* rather to forgive *him*, and comfort *him*, lest perhaps such a one should
be swallowed up with overmuch sorrow.
8 Wherefore I beseech you that ye would
confirm *your* love toward him. 9 For to
this end also did I write, that I might
know the proof of you, whether ye be
obedient in all things. 10 To whom ye
forgive any thing, I *forgive* also: for if I
forgave any thing, to whom I forgave *it*,
for your sakes *forgave I it* in the person of
Christ; 11 lest Satan should get an advantage of us: for we are not ignorant of
his devices.●

GRIEF

2. WITNESS

12 Furthermore, when I came to Tro'as
to *preach* Christ's gospel, and a door was
opened unto me of the Lord, 13 I had no
rest in my spirit, because I found not
Titus my brother; but taking my leave of
them, I went from thence into Macedonia.●

NO REST

It is not known who the offender of 2:5 was, or what was his offense against Paul.

*2:5-11* What is a key repeated word? ________

List the persons or groups referred to in the paragraph:

What godly traits are associated here with forgiveness?

*2:12-13* Note the two geographical names. It was Paul's going to Macedonia first, rather than to Corinth first, that offended the Corinthians.

What are the key phrases of the paragraph?

NEW INTERNATIONAL VERSION

What do you learn here about:

VICTORY THROUGH CHRIST

PREACHERS OF THE GOSPEL

THE HOLY SPIRIT

GOD'S HELP FOR HIS WORKERS

GLORY

OTHER

[14]But thanks be to God, who always
leads us in triumphal procession in Christ
and through us spreads everywhere the
fragrance of the knowledge of him. [15]For
we are to God the aroma of Christ among
those who are being saved and those who
are perishing. [16]To the one we are the smell
of death; to the other, the fragrance of life.●
And who is equal to such a task? [17]Unlike
so many, we do not peddle the word of God
for profit. On the contrary, in Christ we
speak before God with sincerity, like men
sent from God.

3 Are we beginning to commend ourselves again? Or do we need, like some
people, letters of recommendation to you
or from you? [2]You yourselves are our letter, written on our hearts, known and read
by everybody. [3]You show that you are a
letter from Christ, the result of our ministry, written not with ink but with the Spirit
of the living God, not on tablets of stone
but on tablets of human hearts.
[4]Such confidence as this is ours through
Christ before God. [5]Not that we are
competent to claim anything for ourselves,
but our competence comes from God. [6]He
has made us competent as ministers of a
new covenant—not of the letter but of the
Spirit; for the letter kills, but the Spirit
gives life.●

*The Glory of the New Covenant*

[7]Now if the ministry that brought death,
which was engraved in letters on stone,
came with glory, so that the Israelites
could not look steadily at the face of Moses
because of its glory, fading though it was,
[8]will not the ministry of the Spirit be even
more glorious? [9]If the ministry that condemns men is glorious, how much more
glorious is the ministry that brings righteousness! [10]For what was glorious has no
glory now in comparison with the surpassing glory. [11]And if what was fading away
came with glory, how much greater is the
glory of that which lasts!●

KING JAMES

1. SWEET FRAGRANCE OF CHRIST

14 Now thanks *be* unto God, which
always causeth us to triumph in Christ,
and maketh manifest the savor of his
knowledge by us in every place. 15 For
we are unto God a sweet savor of Christ,
in them that are saved, and in them that
perish: 16 to the one *we are* the savor of
death unto death; and to the other the
savor of life unto life.● And who *is* suffi-

2. SUFFICIENCY OF GOD

cient for these things? 17 For we are not
as many, which corrupt the word of God:
but as of sincerity, but as of God, in the
sight of God speak we in Christ.
3 Do we begin again to commend ourselves? or need we, as some *others*,
epistles of commendation to you, or
*letters* of commendation from you? 2 Ye
are our epistle written in our hearts,
known and read of all men: 3 *forasmuch
as ye are* manifestly declared to be the
epistle of Christ ministered by us, written
not with ink, but with the Spirit of the
living God; not in tables of stone, but in
fleshly tables of the heart.
4 And such trust have we through
Christ to God-ward: 5 not that we are
sufficient of ourselves to think any thing
as of ourselves; but our sufficiency *is* of
God; 6 who also hath made us able
ministers of the new testament; not of
the letter, but of the spirit: for the letter
killeth, but the spirit giveth life.●

3. UNEXCELLED GLORY

7 But if the ministration of death,
written *and* engraven in stones, was glorious, so that the children of Israel could
not steadfastly behold the face of Moses
for the glory of his countenance; which
*glory* was to be done away; 8 how shall
not the ministration of the spirit be rather
glorious? 9 For if the ministration of
condemnation *be* glory, much more doth
the ministration of righteousness exceed
in glory. 10 For even that which was
made glorious had no glory in this respect,
by reason of the glory that excelleth.
11 For if that which is done away *was*
glorious, much more that which remaineth *is* glorious.●

TRIUMPH

GLORY

In the section 2:14—4:6 Paul writes about his ministry as preacher of the gospel. This segment is the first half of that testimony.

*2:14-16a* Observe the repeated phrase, "unto God." What is rendered unto God in each case?

______

______

______

______

______

______

What is the key repeated word of the paragraph?

______

What does this mean? ______

______

______

*2:16b—3:6* What is the opening question of the paragraph?

______

______

______

______

How is it answered in the paragraph? ______

______

______

______

______

*3:7-11* What are the key repeated words of the paragraph?

______

______

______

What is the theme of the paragraph? ______

______

______

______

NEW INTERNATIONAL VERSION

What does this passage teach about:

HOPE

BOLDNESS

STRENGTH

WITNESSES OF THE GOSPEL

PREACHING CHRIST JESUS AS LORD

ENLIGHTENED HEARTS

GLORY OF THE LORD

12Therefore, since we have such a hope,
we are very bold. 13We are not like Moses,
who would put a veil over his face to keep
the Israelites from gazing at it while the
radiance was fading away. 14But their
minds were made dull, for to this day the
same veil remains when the old covenant
is read. It has not been removed, because
only in Christ is it taken away. 15Even to
this day when Moses is read, a veil covers
their hearts. 16But whenever anyone turns
to the Lord, the veil is taken away. 17Now
the Lord is the Spirit, and where the Spirit
of the Lord is, there is freedom. 18And we,
who with unveiled faces all reflect[a] the
Lord's glory, are being transformed into
his likeness with ever-increasing glory,
which comes from the Lord, who is the
Spirit.●

*Treasures in Jars of Clay*

4 Therefore, since through God's mercy
we have this ministry, we do not lose
heart. 2Rather, we have renounced secret
and shameful ways; we do not use deception, nor do we distort the word of God. On
the contrary, by setting forth the truth
plainly we commend ourselves to every
man's conscience in the sight of God. 3And
even if our gospel is veiled, it is veiled to
those who are perishing. 4The god of this
age has blinded the minds of unbelievers,
so that they cannot see the light of the
gospel of the glory of Christ, who is the
image of God. 5For we do not preach ourselves, but Jesus Christ as Lord, and ourselves as your servants for Jesus' sake.
6For God, who said, "Let light shine out of
darkness,"[b] made his light shine in our
hearts to give us the light of the knowledge
of the glory of God in the face of Christ.●

[a]18 Or *contemplate* [b]6 Gen. 1:3

KING JAMES

1. PREACHING BOLDLY

12 Seeing then that we have such hope,
we use great plainness of speech: 13 and
not as Moses, *which* put a veil over his
face, that the children of Israel could not
steadfastly look to the end of that which
is abolished: 14 but their minds were
blinded: for until this day remaineth the
same veil untaken away in the reading of
the old testament; which *veil* is done
away in Christ. 15 But even unto this
day, when Moses is read, the veil is upon
their heart. 16 Nevertheless, when it shall
turn to the Lord, the veil shall be taken
away. 17 Now the Lord is that Spirit: and
where the Spirit of the Lord *is*, there *is*
liberty. 18 But we all, with open face beholding as in a glass the glory of the Lord,
are changed into the same image from
glory to glory, *even* as by the Spirit of the
Lord.●

HOPE

2. PREACHING CHRIST JESUS

4 Therefore, seeing we have this ministry, as we have received mercy, we
faint not; 2 but have renounced the hidden things of dishonesty, not walking in
craftiness, nor handling the word of God
deceitfully; but, by manifestation of the
truth, commending ourselves to every
man's conscience in the sight of God.
3 But if our gospel be hid, it is hid to them
that are lost: 4 in whom the god of this
world hath blinded the minds of them
which believe not, lest the light of the
glorious gospel of Christ, who is the
image of God, should shine unto them.
5 For we preach not ourselves, but Christ
Jesus the Lord; and ourselves your servants for Jesus' sake. 6 For God, who
commanded the light to shine out of darkness, hath shined in our hearts, to *give*
the light of the knowledge of the glory of
God in the face of Jesus Christ.●

LIGHT

This segment continues the theme begun at 2:14.

*3:12-18* What is the key repeated word of the paragraph?

______________________________

What does a veil symbolize, spiritually? ______________________________

______________________________

______________________________

______________________________

______________________________

What can take away the veil? ______________________________

______________________________

______________________________

______________________________

______________________________

______________________________

*4:1-6* According to verse 5, what was the object and subject of Paul's preaching?

______________________________

______________________________

______________________________

What were Paul's methods (v.2)? ______________________________

______________________________

______________________________

______________________________

______________________________

Who is the enemy of verse 4? ______________________________

______________________________

______________________________

Compare that enemy with the God of verse 6.

______________________________

______________________________

______________________________

______________________________

______________________________

______________________________

______________________________

NEW INTERNATIONAL VERSION

What do you learn here about:

PHYSICAL BODY

TRIALS

FAITH

ENDURANCE

HEAVEN

RESURRECTION

JUDGMENT SEAT OF CHRIST

7But we have this treasure in jars of clay
to show that this all-surpassing power is
from God and not from us. 8We are hard
pressed on every side, but not crushed;
perplexed, but not in despair; 9persecuted,
but not abandoned; struck down, but not
destroyed. 10We always carry around in
our body the death of Jesus, so that the life
of Jesus may also be revealed in our body.
11For we who are alive are always being
given over to death for Jesus' sake, so that
his life may be revealed in our mortal body.
12So then, death is at work in us, but life is
at work in you.●
13It is written: "I believed; therefore I
have spoken."[c] With that same spirit of
faith we also believe and therefore speak,
14because we know that the one who raised
the Lord Jesus from the dead will also raise
us with Jesus and present us with you in his
presence. 15All this is for your benefit, so
that the grace that is reaching more and
more people may cause thanksgiving to
overflow to the glory of God.●
16Therefore we do not lose heart.
Though outwardly we are wasting away,
yet inwardly we are being renewed day by
day. 17For our light and momentary troubles are achieving for us an eternal glory
that far outweighs them all. 18So we fix our
eyes not on what is seen, but on what is
unseen. For what is seen is temporary, but
what is unseen is eternal.●

### *Our Heavenly Dwelling*

5 Now we know that if the earthly tent
we live in is destroyed, we have a
building from God, an eternal house in
heaven, not built by human hands. 2Mean-
while we groan, longing to be clothed with
our heavenly dwelling, 3because when we
are clothed, we will not be found naked.
4For while we are in this tent, we groan and
are burdened, because we do not wish to
be unclothed but to be clothed with our
heavenly dwelling, so that what is mortal
may be swallowed up by life. 5Now it is
God who has made us for this very purpose
and has given us the Spirit as a deposit,
guaranteeing what is to come.●
6Therefore we are always confident and
know that as long as we are at home in the
body we are away from the Lord. 7We live
by faith, not by sight. 8We are confident, I
say, and would prefer to be away from the
body and at home with the Lord. 9So we
make it our goal to please him, whether we
are at home in the body or away from it.
10For we must all appear before the judgment seat of Christ, that each one may
receive what is due him for the things done
while in the body, whether good or bad.●

*c13* Psalm 116:10

KING JAMES

1. PRESERVED IN TRIAL

7 But we have this treasure in earthen
vessels, that the excellency of the power
may be of God, and not of us. 8 *We are*
troubled on every side, yet not distressed;
*we are* perplexed, but not in despair;
9 persecuted, but not forsaken; cast down,
but not destroyed; 10 always bearing
about in the body the dying of the Lord
Jesus, that the life also of Jesus might be
made manifest in our body. 11 For we
which live are alway delivered unto death
for Jesus' sake, that the life also of Jesus
might be made manifest in our mortal
flesh. 12 So then death worketh in us, but
life in you.●

TREASURE

2. INSPIRED BY HOPE OF RESURRECTION

13 We having the same spirit of faith,
according as it is written, I believed, and
therefore have I spoken; we also believe,
and therefore speak; 14 knowing that he
which raised up the Lord Jesus shall raise
up us also by Jesus, and shall present *us*
with you. 15 For all things *are* for your
sakes, that the abundant grace might
through the thanksgiving of many re-
dound to the glory of God.●

Ps. 16:10

3. RENEWED DAILY

16 For which cause we faint not; but
though our outward man perish, yet the
inward *man* is renewed day by day. 17 For
our light affliction, which is but for a
moment, worketh for us a far more exceeding *and* eternal weight of glory;
18 while we look not at the things which
are seen, but at the things which are not
seen: for the things which are seen *are*
temporal; but the things which are not
seen *are* eternal.●

4. DESTINED FOR HEAVEN

5 For we know that, if our earthly house
of *this* tabernacle were dissolved, we
have a building of God, a house not made
with hands, eternal in the heavens. 2 For
in this we groan, earnestly desiring to be
clothed upon with our house which is
from heaven: 3 if so be that being clothed
we shall not be found naked. 4 For we
that are in *this* tabernacle do groan, being
burdened: not for that we would be unclothed, but clothed upon, that mortality
might be swallowed up of life. 5 Now he
that hath wrought us for the selfsame
thing *is* God, who also hath given unto us
the earnest of the Spirit.●

5. APPROVED IN FUTURE JUDGMENT

6 Therefore *we are* always confident,
knowing that, whilst we are at home in
the body, we are absent from the Lord:
7 (for we walk by faith, not by sight:)
8 we are confident, *I say*, and willing
rather to be absent from the body, and to
be present with the Lord. 9 Wherefore
we labor, that, whether present or absent,
we may be accepted of him. 10 For we
must all appear before the judgment seat
of Christ; that every one may receive the
things *done* in *his* body, according to that
he hath done, whether *it be* good or bad.●

JUDGMENT SEAT

*4:7-12* What does "earthen vessels" refer to? ______

______

Record:

TRIALS: ______

______

______

______

PRESERVED: ______

______

______

______

*4:13-15* What is the key doctrine here? ______

______

______

What are the key words of the paragraph?

______

______

______

*4:16-18* List the contrasts: ______

______

______

______

______

*5:1-5* What is the main point of the paragraph?

______

______

______

*5:6-10* Record every verb whose subject is "we."

______

______

______

______

Who are the "we" of verse 10? ______

______

NEW INTERNATIONAL VERSION

Make a list of spiritual lessons taught by this passage. ______

### *The Ministry of Reconciliation*

11 Since, then, we know what it is to fear
the Lord, we try to persuade men. What
we are is plain to God, and I hope it is also
plain to your conscience. 12 We are not trying to commend ourselves to you again,
but are giving you an opportunity to take
pride in us, so that you can answer those
who take pride in what is seen rather than
in what is in the heart. 13 If we are out of our
mind, it is for the sake of God; if we are in
our right mind, it is for you. 14 For Christ's
love compels us, because we are convinced that one died for all, and therefore
all died. 15 And he died for all, that those
who live should no longer live for themselves but for him who died for them and
was raised again.●

16 So from now on we regard no one from
a worldly point of view. Though we once
regarded Christ in this way, we do so no
longer. 17 Therefore, if anyone is in Christ,
he is a new creation; the old has gone, the
new has come! 18 All this is from God, who
reconciled us to himself through Christ and
gave us the ministry of reconciliation:
19 that God was reconciling the world to
himself in Christ, not counting men's sins
against them. And he has committed to us
the message of reconciliation. 20 We are
therefore Christ's ambassadors, as though
God were making his appeal through us.
We implore you on Christ's behalf: Be reconciled to God. 21 God made him who had
no sin to be sin[a] for us, so that in him we
might become the righteousness of God.●

6 As God's fellow workers we urge you
not to receive God's grace in vain. 2 For
he says,

> "In the time of my favor I heard
> you,
> and in the day of salvation I
> helped you."[b]

I tell you, now is the time of God's favor,
now is the day of salvation.

### *Paul's Hardships*

3 We put no stumbling block in anyone's
path, so that our ministry will not be dis-
credited. 4 Rather, as servants of God we
commend ourselves in every way: in great
endurance; in troubles, hardships and distresses; 5 in beatings, imprisonments and riots; in hard work, sleepless nights and hunger; 6 in purity, understanding, patience
and kindness; in the Holy Spirit and in sincere love; 7 in truthful speech and in the
power of God; with weapons of righteousness in the right hand and in the left;
8 through glory and dishonor, bad report
and good report; genuine, yet regarded as
impostors; 9 known, yet regarded as unknown; dying, and yet we live on; beaten,
and yet not killed; 10 sorrowful, yet always
rejoicing; poor, yet making many rich; having nothing, and yet possessing everything.●

[a] 21 Or *be a sin offering* [b] 2 Isaiah 49:8

KING JAMES

1. MOTIVATIONS

PERSUADING MEN

11 Knowing therefore the terror of the
Lord, we persuade men; but we are made
manifest unto God; and I trust also are
made manifest in your consciences.
12 For we commend not ourselves again
unto you, but give you occasion to glory
on our behalf, that ye may have somewhat to *answer* them which glory in appearance, and not in heart. 13 For
whether we be beside ourselves, *it is* to
God: or whether we be sober, *it is* for
your cause. 14 For the love of Christ con-
straineth us; because we thus judge, that
if one died for all, then were all dead:
15 and *that* he died for all, that they which
live should not henceforth live unto themselves, but unto him which died for them,
and rose again.●

2. MESSAGE

16 Wherefore henceforth know we no
man after the flesh: yea, though we have
known Christ after the flesh, yet now
henceforth know we *him* no more.
17 Therefore if any man *be* in Christ, *he is*
a new creature: old things are passed
away; behold, all things are become new.
18 And all things *are* of God, who hath
reconciled us to himself by Jesus Christ,
and hath given to us the ministry of reconciliation;
19 to wit, that God was in
Christ, reconciling the world unto himself, not imputing their trespasses unto
them; and hath committed unto us the
word of reconciliation. 20 Now then we
are ambassadors for Christ, as though
God did beseech *you* by us: we pray *you*
in Christ's stead, be ye reconciled to God.
21 For he hath made him *to be* sin for us,
who knew no sin; that we might be made
the righteousness of God in him.●

3. MARKS

6 We then, *as* workers together *with*
*him*, beseech *you* also that ye receive
not the grace of God in vain. 2 (For he
saith,

Isa. 49:8

> I have heard thee in a time accepted,
> and in the day of salvation have I
> succored thee:

Behold, now *is* the accepted time; behold,
now *is* the day of salvation.) 3 Giving no
offense in any thing, that the ministry be
not blamed: 4 but in all *things* approving
ourselves as the ministers of God, in much
patience, in afflictions, in necessities, in
distresses, 5 in stripes, in imprisonments,
in tumults, in labors, in watchings, in
fastings; 6 by pureness, by knowledge,
by longsuffering, by kindness, by the Holy
Ghost, by love unfeigned, 7 by the word
of truth, by the power of God, by the
armor of righteousness on the right hand
and on the left, 8 by honor and dishonor,
by evil report and good report: as deceivers, and *yet* true;
9 as unknown, and
*yet* well known; as dying, and, behold,
we live; as chastened, and not killed;
10 as sorrowful, yet alway rejoicing; as
poor, yet making many rich; as having
nothing, and *yet* possessing all things.●

MAKING MANY RICH

First read 5:20. What are the duties of an ambassador?

*5:11-15* Record the different motivations:

*5:16-21* What is the repeated strong word of verse 20?

How else is the ambassador's message identified in the paragraph?

*6:1-10* What marks of an ambassador for Christ do you see here?

NEW INTERNATIONAL VERSION

What is taught by this passage about:

CHRISTIAN FELLOWSHIP

LOVE

LOYALTY

PURITY

SEPARATION FROM THE WORLD

OTHER

11 We have spoken freely to you, Corinthians, and opened wide our hearts to you.
12 We are not withholding our affection
from you, but you are withholding yours
from us. 13 As a fair exchange—I speak as
to my children—open wide your hearts
also.●

*Do Not Be Yoked With Unbelievers*

14 Do not be yoked together with unbelievers. For what do righteousness and
wickedness have in common? Or what fellowship can light have with darkness?
15 What harmony is there between Christ
and Belial[c]? What does a believer have in
common with an unbeliever? 16 What agreement is there between the temple of God
and idols? For we are the temple of the
living God. As God has said: "I will live
with them and walk among them, and I will
be their God, and they will be my
people."[d]

17 "Therefore come out from them
and be separate,
says the Lord.
Touch no unclean thing,
and I will receive you."[e]
18 "I will be a Father to you,
and you will be my sons and
daughters,
says the Lord Almighty."[f]

7 Since we have these promises, dear
friends, let us purify ourselves from
everything that contaminates body and
spirit, perfecting holiness out of reverence
for God.●

*Paul's Joy*

2 Make room for us in your hearts. We
have wronged no one, we have corrupted
no one, we have exploited no one. 3 I do not
say this to condemn you; I have said before
that you have such a place in our hearts
that we would live or die with you.●

*c15* Greek *Beliar*, a variant of *Belial*
*d16* Lev. 26:12; Jer. 32:38; Ezek. 37:27
*e17* Isaiah 52:11; Ezek. 20:34,41
*f18* 2 Samuel 7:14; 7:8

KING JAMES

1.MUTUALLY DEVOTED

11 O *ye* Corinthians, our mouth is open
unto you, our heart is enlarged. 12 Ye are
not straitened in us, but ye are straitened
in your own bowels. 13 Now for a recompense in the same, (I speak as unto
*my* children,) be ye also enlarged. ●

ALL MY HEART

2.OF LIKE MIND

14 Be ye not unequally yoked together
with unbelievers: for what fellowship hath
righteousness with unrighteousness? and
what communion hath light with darkness? 15 And what concord hath Christ
with Be'li-al? or what part hath he that
believeth with an infidel? 16 And what
agreement hath the temple of God with
idols? for ye are the temple of the living
God; as God hath said,

I will dwell in them, and walk in *them;* (Ex. 29:45)
and I will be their God,
and they shall be my people.

17 Wherefore come out from among them, (Isa. 52:11)
and be ye separate,
saith the Lord,
and touch not the unclean *thing;*
and I will receive you,
18 and will be a Father unto you,
and ye shall be my sons and daughters, (Isa. 43:6)
saith the Lord Almighty.

7 Having therefore these promises,
dearly beloved, let us cleanse ourselves from all filthiness of the flesh and
spirit, perfecting holiness in the fear of
God. ●

3.LOYAL UNTO DEATH

2 Receive us; we have wronged no man,
we have corrupted no man, we have defrauded no man. 3 I speak not *this* to
condemn *you:* for I have said before,
that ye are in our hearts to die and live
with *you.* ●

IN MY HEART

*6:11-13* What does verse 12 mean? ____________

How does verse 13 answer to verse 11? ____________

*6:14—7:1* Record:

CONTRASTS ____________

RELATIONSHIP TO GOD ____________

SEPARATION ____________

*7:2-3* What are the strong phrases of this paragraph?

NEW INTERNATIONAL VERSION

What do you learn here about:

TRIBULATION

JOY

SORROW

COMFORT

CHRISTIAN WORKERS

CHRISTIAN FELLOWSHIP

REPENTANCE

[4]I have
great confidence in you; I take great pride
in you. I am greatly encouraged; in all our
troubles my joy knows no bounds.
[5]For when we came into Macedonia, this
body of ours had no rest, but we were
harassed at every turn—conflicts on the
outside, fears within. [6]But God, who comforts the downcast, comforted us by the
coming of Titus, [7]and not only by his coming but also by the comfort you had given
him. He told us about your longing for me,
your deep sorrow, your ardent concern for
me, so that my joy was greater than ever.●
[8]Even if I caused you sorrow by my letter, I do not regret it. Though I did regret
it—I see that my letter hurt you, but only
for a little while— [9]yet now I am happy, not
because you were made sorry, but because
your sorrow led you to repentance. For
you became sorrowful as God intended
and so were not harmed in any way by us.
[10]Godly sorrow brings repentance that
leads to salvation and leaves no regret, but
worldly sorrow brings death. [11]See what
this godly sorrow has produced in you:
what earnestness, what eagerness to clear
yourselves, what indignation, what alarm,
what longing, what concern, what readiness to see justice done. At every point you
have proved yourselves to be innocent in
this matter. [12]So even though I wrote to
you, it was not on account of the one who
did the wrong or of the injured party, but
rather that before God you could see for
yourselves how devoted to us you are.
[13]By all this we are encouraged.
In addition to our own encouragement,●
we were especially delighted to see how
happy Titus was, because his spirit has
been refreshed by all of you. [14]I had boasted to him about you, and you have not
embarrassed me. But just as everything we
said to you was true, so our boasting about
you to Titus has proved to be true as well.
[15]And his affection for you is all the greater
when he remembers that you were all
obedient, receiving him with fear and trembling. [16]I am glad I can have complete confidence in you.●

## KING JAMES

1.COMFORT

4 Great *is* my boldness of
speech toward you, great *is* my glorying
of you: I am filled with comfort, I am exceeding joyful in all our tribulation.
5 For, when we were come into Macedonia, our flesh had no rest, but we were
troubled on every side; without *were*
fightings, within *were* fears. 6 Nevertheless God, that comforteth those that are
cast down, comforted us by the coming
of Titus; 7 and not by his coming only,
but by the consolation wherewith he was
comforted in you, when he told us your
earnest desire, your mourning, your fervent mind toward me; so that I rejoiced
the more.● 8 For though I made you sorry
with a letter, I do not repent, though I did
repent: for I perceive that the same epistle
hath made you sorry, though *it were* but
for a season. 9 Now I rejoice, not that ye
were made sorry, but that ye sorrowed to
repentance: for ye were made sorry after
a godly manner, that ye might receive
damage by us in nothing. 10 For godly
sorrow worketh repentance to salvation
not to be repented of: but the sorrow of
the world worketh death. 11 For behold
this selfsame thing, that ye sorrowed after
a godly sort, what carefulness it wrought
in you, yea, *what* clearing of yourselves,
yea, *what* indignation, yea, *what* fear, yea,
*what* vehement desire, yea, *what* zeal, yea,
*what* revenge! In all *things* ye have approved yourselves to be clear in this
matter. 12 Wherefore, though I wrote
unto you, *I did it* not for his cause that
had done the wrong, nor for his cause that
suffered wrong, but that our care for you
in the sight of God might appear unto you.
13 Therefore we were comforted in your
comfort: ●yea, and exceedingly the more
joyed we for the joy of Titus, because his
spirit was refreshed by you all. 14 For if
I have boasted any thing to him of you, I
am not ashamed; but as we spake all
things to you in truth, even so our boasting, which *I made* before Titus, is found a
truth. 15 And his inward affection is more
abundant toward you, whilst he remembereth the obedience of you all, how with
fear and trembling ye received him. 16 I
rejoice therefore that I have confidence in
you in all *things*.●

GLORYING OF YOU

2.SPIRITUAL FRUIT

3.WARM RECEPTION

CONFIDENCE IN YOU

This is the last segment in the testimonial section of Paul's letter (1:3—7:16).

*7:4-7* What is Paul's testimony of verse 4?

How does he support this testimony with personal experiences (vv.5-7)?

*7:8-13a* Note the repetition of the word "sorry" (and related terms).
What spiritual fruit came of Paul's dealings with the Corinthians?

*7:13b-16* Who is the main person of the paragraph?

What is said about him?

How did this involve Paul?

NEW INTERNATIONAL VERSION

What does this passage teach about:

GENEROSITY

THANKSGIVING

GIVING

LOVE

CHRIST

OTHER

*Generosity Encouraged*

8 And now, brothers, we want you to
know about the grace that God has giv-
en the Macedonian churches. [2]Out of the
most severe trial, their overflowing joy and
their extreme poverty welled up in rich
generosity. [3]For I testify that they gave as
much as they were able, and even beyond
their ability. Entirely on their own, [4]they
urgently pleaded with us for the privilege
of sharing in this service to the saints. [5]And
they did not do as we expected, but they
gave themselves first to the Lord and then
to us in keeping with God's will. ● [6]So we
urged Titus, since he had earlier made a
beginning, to bring also to completion this
act of grace on your part. [7]But just as you
excel in everything—in faith, in speech, in
knowledge, in complete earnestness and in
your love for us[a]—see that you also excel
in this grace of giving.
[8]I am not commanding you, but I want to
test the sincerity of your love by comparing it with the earnestness of others. [9]For
you know the grace of our Lord Jesus
Christ, that though he was rich, yet for
your sakes he became poor, so that you
through his poverty might become rich. ●

[a]7 Some manuscripts *in our love for you*

KING JAMES

1. EXAMPLE

GRACE OF GOD

Macedonians' grace

8 Moreover, brethren, we do you to
wit of the grace of God bestowed on
the churches of Macedonia; 2 how that
in a great trial of affliction, the abundance
of their joy and their deep poverty
abounded unto the riches of their liberality. 3 For to *their* power, I bear record,
yea, and beyond *their* power *they were*
willing of themselves; 4 praying us with
much entreaty that we would receive the
gift, and *take upon us* the fellowship of the
ministering to the saints. 5 And *this they*
*did*, not as we hoped, but first gave their
own selves to the Lord, and unto us by the
will of God.● 6 Insomuch that we desired

2. INCENTIVE

Corinthians' grace

GRACE OF JESUS

Titus, that as he had begun, so he would
also finish in you the same grace also.
7 Therefore, as ye abound in every *thing*,
*in* faith, and utterance, and knowledge,
and *in* all diligence, and *in* your love to us,
*see* that ye abound in this grace also.
8 I speak not by commandment, but by
occasion of the forwardness of others, and
to prove the sincerity of your love. 9 For
ye know the grace of our Lord Jesus
Christ, that, though he was rich, yet for
your sakes he became poor, that ye
through his poverty might be rich. ●

This segment begins the second main section of the epistle. The subject is that of GIVING. Involved was a fund-raising project which the Corinthians had begun a year earlier. (Cf. 1 Cor. 16:1.)

*8:1-5* What is revealed about the churches of Macedonia?

What does Paul write about their giving?

*8:6-9* What spiritual qualities of the Corinthians does Paul recognize in verses 7-8?

How does Paul use this as an incentive for the Corinthians' giving?

NEW INTERNATIONAL VERSION

What is taught here about:

ENTHUSIASM

KEEPING PLEDGES

SHARING

HONESTY

LOVE

OTHER

[10]And here is my advice about what is
best for you in this matter: Last year you
were the first not only to give but also to
have the desire to do so. [11]Now finish the
work, so that your eager willingness to do
it may be matched by your completion of
it, according to your means. [12]For if the
willingness is there, the gift is acceptable
according to what one has, not according
to what he does not have.
[13]Our desire is not that others might be
relieved while you are hard pressed, but
that there might be equality. [14]At the
present time your plenty will supply what
they need, so that in turn their plenty will
supply what you need. Then there will be
equality, [15]as it is written: "He that gathered much did not have too much, and he
that gathered little did not have too little."[b] ●

*Titus Sent to Corinth*

[16]I thank God, who put into the heart of
Titus the same concern I have for you.
[17]For Titus not only welcomed our appeal,
but he is coming to you with much enthusiasm and on his own initiative. [18]And
we are sending along with him the brother
who is praised by all the churches for his
service to the gospel. [19]What is more, he
was chosen by the churches to accompany
us as we carry the offering, which we administer in order to honor the Lord himself
and to show our eagerness to help. [20]We
want to avoid any criticism of the way we
administer this liberal gift. [21]For we are
taking pains to do what is right, not only in
the eyes of the Lord but also in the eyes of
men.
[22]In addition, we are sending with them
our brother who has often proved to us in
many ways that he is zealous, and now
even more so because of his great confidence in you. [23]As for Titus, he is my partner and fellow worker among you; as for
our brothers, they are representatives of
the churches and an honor to Christ.
[24]Therefore show these men the proof of
your love and the reason for our pride in
you, so that the churches can see it. ●

[b]*15* Exodus 16:18

## KING JAMES

**1. THE DONORS**

ENTHUSIASM

10 And
herein I give *my* advice: for this is expedient for you, who have begun before,
not only to do, but also to be forward a
year ago. 11 Now therefore perform the
doing *of it;* that as *there was* a readiness
to will, so *there may be* a performance
also out of that which ye have. 12 For if
there be first a willing mind, *it is* accepted
according to that a man hath, *and* not according to that he hath not. 13 For *I*
*mean* not that other men be eased, and ye
burdened: 14 but by an equality, *that*
now at this time your abundance *may be*
*a supply* for their want, that their abundance also may be *a supply* for your want;
that there may be equality: 15 as it is
written,

> He that *had gathered* much had nothing over;
> and he that *had gathered* little had no lack.●

Ex. 16:18

**2. THE COLLECTORS**

16 But thanks *be* to God, which put the
same earnest care into the heart of Titus
for you. 17 For indeed he accepted the
exhortation; but being more forward, of
his own accord he went unto you. 18 And
we have sent with him the brother, whose
praise *is* in the gospel throughout all the
churches; 19 and not *that* only, but who
was also chosen of the churches to travel
with us with this grace, which is administered by us to the glory of the same Lord,
and *declaration of* your ready mind:
20 avoiding this, that no man should
blame us in this abundance which is administered by us: 21 providing for honest
things, not only in the sight of the Lord,
but also in the sight of men. 22 And we
have sent with them our brother, whom
we have oftentimes proved diligent in
many things, but now much more diligent,
upon the great confidence which *I have* in
you. 23 Whether *any do inquire* of Titus,
*he is* my partner and fellow helper concerning you: or our brethren *be inquired*
*of, they are* the messengers of the churches,
*and* the glory of Christ. 24 Wherefore
show ye to them, and before the churches,
the proof of your love, and of our boasting on your behalf.●

LOVE

*8:10-15* Record what is said here about the donors (Corinthians) and recipients (Jerusalem saints).

DONORS ______________________________

______________________________

______________________________

______________________________

______________________________

______________________________

______________________________

RECIPIENTS ______________________________

______________________________

______________________________

______________________________

______________________________

______________________________

______________________________

*8:16-24* What different persons are involved in the projects of collecting and delivering?

______________________________

______________________________

______________________________

______________________________

______________________________

______________________________

What spiritual principles does Paul cite here?

______________________________

______________________________

______________________________

______________________________

______________________________

______________________________

______________________________

______________________________

______________________________

NEW INTERNATIONAL VERSION

What do you learn here about:

CHRISTIAN GIVING

HEART

CHEERFUL GIVING

FRUITS OF RIGHTEOUSNESS

THANKSGIVING

GOD

9 There is no need for me to write to you
about this service to the saints. [2]For I
know your eagerness to help, and I have
been boasting about it to the Macedonians,
telling them that since last year you in
Achaia were ready to give; and your enthusiasm has stirred most of them to action. [3]But I am sending the brothers in order that our boasting about you in this matter should not prove hollow, but that you
may be ready, as I said you would be. [4]For
if any Macedonians come with me and find
you unprepared, we—not to say anything
about you—would be ashamed of having
been so confident. [5]So I thought it necessary to urge the brothers to visit you in
advance and finish the arrangements for
the generous gift you had promised. Then
it will be ready as a generous gift, not as
one grudgingly given.●

*Sowing Generously*

[6]Remember this: Whoever sows sparingly will also reap sparingly, and whoever
sows generously will also reap generously.
[7]Each man should give what he has decided in his heart to give, not reluctantly or
under compulsion, for God loves a cheerful giver. [8]And God is able to make all
grace abound to you, so that in all things at
all times, having all that you need, you will
abound in every good work. [9]As it is written:

> "He has scattered abroad his gifts
> to the poor;
> his righteousness endures
> forever."[a]

[10]Now he who supplies seed to the sower
and bread for food will also supply and
increase your store of seed and will enlarge
the harvest of your righteousness. [11]You
will be made rich in every way so that you
can be generous on every occasion, and
through us your generosity will result in
thanksgiving to God.●

[12]This service that you perform is not
only supplying the needs of God's people
but is also overflowing in many expres-
sions of thanks to God. [13]Because of the
service by which you have proved yourselves, men will praise God for the obedience that accompanies your confession of
the gospel of Christ, and for your generosity in sharing with them and with everyone
else. [14]And in their prayers for you their
hearts will go out to you, because of the
surpassing grace God has given you.
[15]Thanks be to God for his indescribable
gift!●

[a]9 Psalm 112:9

KING JAMES

1. WITH ZEAL

MONEY GIFT

9 For as touching the ministering to the
saints, it is superfluous for me to
write to you: 2 for I know the forwardness of your mind, for which I boast of
you to them of Macedonia, that Achai'a
was ready a year ago; and your zeal hath
provoked very many. 3 Yet have I sent
the brethren, lest our boasting of you
should be in vain in this behalf; that, as I
said, ye may be ready: 4 lest haply if they
of Macedonia come with me, and find
you unprepared, we (that we say not, ye)
should be ashamed in this same confident
boasting. 5 Therefore I thought it necessary to exhort the brethren, that they
would go before unto you, and make up
beforehand your bounty, whereof ye had
notice before, that the same might be
ready, as *a matter of* bounty, and not as
*of* covetousness.●

2. WITH CHEER

6 But this *I say*, He which soweth
sparingly shall reap also sparingly; and he
which soweth bountifully shall reap also
bountifully. 7 Every man according as he
purposeth in his heart, *so let him give;*
not grudgingly, or of necessity: for God
loveth a cheerful giver. 8 And God *is*
able to make all grace abound toward
you; that ye, always having all sufficiency
in all *things*, may abound to every good
work: 9 (as it is written,

He hath dispersed abroad;
he hath given to the poor:
his righteousness remaineth for ever.

Ps. 112:9

10 Now he that ministereth seed to the
sower both minister bread for *your* food,
and multiply your seed sown, and increase
the fruits of your righteousness:) 11 being
enriched in every thing to all bountiful-
ness, which causeth through us thanksgiving to God.● 12 For the administration

3. TO GOD'S GLORY

of this service not only supplieth the want
of the saints, but is abundant also by
many thanksgivings unto God; 13 while
by the experiment of this ministration
they glorify God for your professed subjection unto the gospel of Christ, and for
*your* liberal distribution unto them, and
unto all *men;* 14 and by their prayer
for you, which long after you for the
exceeding grace of God in you.
15 Thanks *be* unto God for his unspeakable gift.●

UNSPEAKABLE GIFT

*9:1-5* What was Paul's concern?

How does he commend the Corinthians?

*9:6-11* What does Paul write here about heart gifts?

*9:12-15* What spiritual fruits would the Corinthians' gift bring forth in the lives of the Jerusalem saints?

How is verse 15 a climax to chapter 8-9?

NEW INTERNATIONAL VERSION

What does this passage teach about:

APOSTLESHIP

DIVINE AUTHORITY

OUTWARD APPEARANCES

BOASTING

MEASURING CHRISTIAN SERVICE

THE LORD

*Paul's Defense of His Ministry*

10 By the meekness and gentleness of
Christ, I appeal to you—I, Paul,
who am "timid" when face to face with
you, but "bold" when away! 2I beg you
that when I come I may not have to be as
bold as I expect to be toward some people
who think that we live by the standards of
this world. 3For though we live in the
world, we do not wage war as the world
does. 4The weapons we fight with are not
the weapons of the world. On the contrary,
they have divine power to demolish strongholds. 5We demolish arguments and every
pretension that sets itself up against the
knowledge of God, and we take captive
every thought to make it obedient to
Christ. 6And we will be ready to punish
every act of disobedience, once your
obedience is complete.●

7You are looking only on the surface of
things.[b] If anyone is confident that he belongs to Christ, he should consider again
that we belong to Christ just as much as he.
8For even if I boast somewhat freely about
the authority the Lord gave us for building
you up rather than pulling you down, I will
not be ashamed of it. 9I do not want to seem
to be trying to frighten you with my letters.
10For some say, "His letters are weighty
and forceful, but in person he is unimpres-
sive and his speaking amounts to nothing."
11Such people should realize that what we
are in our letters when we are absent, we
will be in our actions when we are present.●

12We do not dare to classify or compare
ourselves with some who commend themselves. When they measure themselves by
themselves and compare themselves with
themselves, they are not wise. 13We, however, will not boast beyond proper limits,
but will confine our boasting to the field
God has assigned to us, a field that reaches
even to you. 14We are not going too far in
our boasting, as would be the case if we
had not come to you, for we did get as far
as you with the gospel of Christ. 15Neither
do we go beyond our limits by boasting of
work done by others.[c] Our hope is that, as
your faith continues to grow, our area of
activity among you will greatly expand,
16so that we can preach the gospel in the
regions beyond you. For we do not want to
boast about work already done in another
man's territory. 17But, "Let him who
boasts boast in the Lord."[d] 18For it is not
the one who commends himself who is approved, but the one whom the Lord commends.●

[b]7 Or *Look at the obvious facts*
[c]13-15 Or *13We, however, will not boast about things that cannot be measured, but we will boast according to the standard of measurement that the God of measure has assigned us—a measurement that relates even to you. 14 . . . . 15Neither do we boast about things that cannot be measured in regard to the work done by others.*
[d]17 Jer. 9:24

KING JAMES

1.WEAPONS

MEEKNESS OF CHRIST

10 Now I Paul myself beseech you by
the meekness and gentleness of
Christ, who in presence *am* base among
you, but being absent am bold toward
you: 2 but I beseech *you*, that I may not
be bold when I am present with that confidence, wherewith I think to be bold
against some, which think of us as if we
walked according to the flesh. 3 For
though we walk in the flesh, we do not
war after the flesh: 4 (for the weapons of
our warfare *are* not carnal, but mighty
through God to the pulling down of
strongholds;) 5 casting down imaginations, and every high thing that exalteth
itself against the knowledge of God, and
bringing into captivity every thought to
the obedience of Christ; 6 and having in
a readiness to revenge all disobedience,
when your obedience is fulfilled.●

2.AUTHORITY

7 Do ye look on things after the outward appearance? If any man trust to
himself that he is Christ's, let him of himself think this again, that, as he *is* Christ's,
even so *are* we Christ's. 8 For though I
should boast somewhat more of our
authority, which the Lord hath given us
for edification, and not for your destruction, I should not be ashamed: 9 that I
may not seem as if I would terrify you by
letters. 10 For *his* letters, say they, *are*
weighty and powerful; but *his* bodily
presence *is* weak, and *his* speech con-
temptible. 11 Let such a one think this,
that, such as we are in word by letters
when we are absent, such *will we be* also
in deed when we are present.●12 For we

3.EXTENT

dare not make ourselves of the number,
or compare ourselves with some that
commend themselves: but they, measuring themselves by themselves, and comparing themselves among themselves, are
not wise.
13 But we will not boast of things without *our* measure, but according to the
measure of the rule which God hath distributed to us, a measure to reach even
unto you. 14 For we stretch not ourselves beyond *our measure*, as though we
reached not unto you; for we are come as
far as to you also in *preaching* the gospel
of Christ: 15 not boasting of things without *our* measure, *that is*, of other men's
labors; but having hope, when your faith
is increased, that we shall be enlarged by
you according to our rule abundantly,
16 to preach the gospel in the *regions* beyond you, *and* not to boast in another
man's line of things made ready to our
hand. 17 But he that glorieth, let him
glory in the Lord. 18 For not he that
commendeth himself is approved, but
whom the Lord commendeth.●

Jer. 9:24

GLORY OF THE LORD

This segment begins the third and final section of 2 Corinthians. Paul's purpose is to vindicate his apostolic ministry, since his authority was being challenged by some (Cf. 13:3).

*10:1-6* What does Paul write about:

HIS WALK ____________________

HIS WEAPONS ____________________

*10:7-11* What charges were made against Paul?

What does the apostle write about his authority?

*10:12-18* Note the repetitions of "measure" and similar terms. How did false apostles measure things (v.12)?

How did Paul measure his ministry (v.13)?

NEW INTERNATIONAL VERSION

What do you learn here about:

FALSE MESSENGERS OF THE GOSPEL

A CHRISTIAN'S NEED FOR DISCERNMENT

HOW TO DEAL WITH FALSE TEACHERS

SATAN

CHRIST

FINANCES IN CHRISTIAN WORK

OTHER

*Paul and the False Apostles*

11 I hope you will put up with a little of
my foolishness; but you are already
doing that. 2I am jealous for you with a
godly jealousy. I promised you to one husband, to Christ, so that I might present you
as a pure virgin to him. 3But I am afraid that
just as Eve was deceived by the serpent's
cunning, your minds may somehow be led
astray from your sincere and pure devotion
to Christ. 4For if someone comes to you
and preaches a Jesus other than the Jesus
we preached, or if you receive a different
spirit from the one you received, or a different gospel from the one you accepted,
you put up with it easily enough. 5But I do
not think I am in the least inferior to those
"super-apostles." 6I may not be a trained
speaker, but I do have knowledge. We
have made this perfectly clear to you in
every way.●
7Was it a sin for me to lower myself in
order to elevate you by preaching the gospel of God to you free of charge? 8I robbed
other churches by receiving support from
them so as to serve you. 9And when I was
with you and needed something, I was not
a burden to anyone, for the brothers who
came from Macedonia supplied what I
needed. I have kept myself from being a
burden to you in any way, and will continue to do so. 10As surely as the truth of
Christ is in me, nobody in the regions of
Achaia will stop this boasting of mine.
11Why? Because I do not love you? God
knows I do! 12And I will keep on doing
what I am doing in order to cut the ground
from under those who want an opportunity
to be considered equal with us in the things
they boast about.●
13For such men are false apostles, deceitful workmen, masquerading as apostles of
Christ. 14And no wonder, for Satan himself
masquerades as an angel of light. 15It is not
surprising, then, if his servants mas-
querade as servants of righteousness.
Their end will be what their actions deserve.●

KING JAMES

1.PREACHING

TRUE APOSTLE

**11** Would to God ye could bear with
me a little in *my* folly: and indeed
bear with me. 2 For I am jealous over
you with godly jealousy: for I have espoused you to one husband, that I may
present *you as* a chaste virgin to Christ.
3 But I fear, lest by any means, as the serpent beguiled Eve through his subtilty,
so your minds should be corrupted from
the simplicity that is in Christ. 4 For if
he that cometh preacheth another Jesus,
whom we have not preached, or *if* ye receive another spirit, which ye have not
received, or another gospel, which ye have
not accepted, ye might well bear with *him*.
5 For I suppose I was not a whit behind
the very chiefest apostles. 6 But though
*I be* rude in speech, yet not in knowledge;
but we have been thoroughly made manifest among you in all things.●

2.FINANCIAL SUPPORT

7 Have I committed an offense in abas-
ing myself that ye might be exalted, because I have preached to you the gospel
of God freely? 8 I robbed other churches,
taking wages *of them*, to do you service.
9 And when I was present with you, and
wanted, I was chargeable to no man: for
that which was lacking to me the brethren which came from Macedonia supplied: and in all *things* I have kept myself
from being burdensome unto you, and *so*
will I keep *myself*. 10 As the truth of
Christ is in me, no man shall stop me of
this boasting in the regions of Achai'a.
11 Wherefore? because I love you not?
God knoweth.
12 But what I do, that I will do, that I
may cut off occasion from them which
desire occasion; that wherein they glory,
they may be found even as we.●13 For

3.MINISTRY

such *are* false apostles, deceitful workers,
transforming themselves into the apostles
of Christ. 14 And no marvel; for Satan
himself is transformed into an angel of
light. 15 Therefore *it is* no great thing if
his ministers also be transformed as the
ministers of righteousness; whose end
shall be according to their works.●

FALSE APOSTLE

*11:1-6* Record what is written here about:

PAUL ______________________

FALSE APOSTLES ______________________

*11:7-12* How was Paul supported financially?

Why did he choose that arrangement? ______

*11:13-15* Record the things written here about false apostles.

NEW INTERNATIONAL VERSION

Record what this passage teaches about:

RIGHTEOUS BOASTING

VAIN BOASTING

TRIBULATION IN CHRISTIAN SERVICE

HUMILIATION

Record spiritual applications of the passage.

*Paul Boasts About His Sufferings*

16I repeat: Let no one take me for a fool.
But if you do, then receive me just as you
would a fool, so that I may do a little boasting. 17In this self-confident boasting I am
not talking as the Lord would, but as a fool.
18Since many are boasting in the way the
world does, I too will boast. 19You gladly
put up with fools since you are so wise! 20In
fact, you even put up with anyone who
enslaves you or exploits you or takes advantage of you or pushes himself forward
or slaps you in the face. 21To my shame I
admit that we were too weak for that!●

What anyone else dares to boast about—
I am speaking as a fool—I also dare to
boast about. 22Are they Hebrews? So am I.
Are they Israelites? So am I. Are they
Abraham's descendants? So am I. 23Are
they servants of Christ? (I am out of my
mind to talk like this.) I am more. I have
worked much harder, been in prison more
frequently, been flogged more severely,
and been exposed to death again and again.
24Five times I received from the Jews the
forty lashes minus one. 25Three times I was
beaten with rods, once I was stoned, three
times I was shipwrecked, I spent a night
and a day in the open sea, 26I have been
constantly on the move. I have been in
danger from rivers, in danger from bandits,
in danger from my own countrymen, in
danger from Gentiles; in danger in the city,
in danger in the country, in danger at sea;
and in danger from false brothers. 27I have
labored and toiled and have often gone
without sleep; I have known hunger and
thirst and have often gone without food; I
have been cold and naked. 28Besides
everything else, I face daily the pressure of
my concern for all the churches. 29Who is
weak, and I do not feel weak? Who is led
into sin, and I do not inwardly burn?●

30If I must boast, I will boast of the things
that show my weakness. 31The God and
Father of the Lord Jesus, who is to be
praised forever, knows that I am not lying.
32In Damascus the governor under King
Aretas had the city of the Damascenes
guarded in order to arrest me. 33But I was
lowered in a basket from a window in the
wall and slipped through his hands.●

KING JAMES

—introduction

PAUL DEFENDING

16 I say again, Let no man think me a
fool; if otherwise, yet as a fool receive me,
that I may boast myself a little. 17 That
which I speak, I speak *it* not after the
Lord, but as it were foolishly, in this confidence of boasting. 18 Seeing that many
glory after the flesh, I will glory also.
19 For ye suffer fools gladly, seeing ye
*yourselves* are wise. 20 For ye suffer, if
a man bring you into bondage, if a man
devour *you*, if a man take *of you*, if a man
exalt himself, if a man smite you on the
face. 21 I speak as concerning reproach,
as though we had been weak.●

1.TRIBULATION

Howbeit, whereinsoever any is bold, (I
speak foolishly,) I am bold also. 22 Are
they Hebrews? so *am* I. Are they Israelites? so *am* I. Are they the seed of Abraham? so *am* I. 23 Are they ministers of
Christ? (I speak as a fool,) I *am* more;
in labors more abundant, in stripes above
measure, in prisons more frequent, in
deaths oft. 24 Of the Jews five times received I forty *stripes* save one. 25 Thrice
was I beaten with rods, once was I
stoned, thrice I suffered shipwreck, a
night and a day I have been in the deep;
26 *in* journeyings often, *in* perils of waters,
*in* perils of robbers, *in* perils by *mine own*
countrymen, *in* perils by the heathen,
*in* perils in the city, *in* perils in the wilderness, *in* perils in the sea, *in* perils among
false brethren; 27 in weariness and pain-
fulness, in watchings often, in hunger and
thirst, in fastings often, in cold and nakedness. 28 Beside those things that are without, that which cometh upon me daily, the
care of all the churches. 29 Who is weak,
and I am not weak? who is offended, and
I burn not?●

2.HUMILIATION

30 If I must needs glory, I will glory of
the things which concern mine infirmities.
31 The God and Father of our Lord Jesus
Christ, which is blessed for evermore,
knoweth that I lie not. 32 In Damascus
the governor under Ar′etas the king kept
the city of the Dam′ascenes with a gar-
rison, desirous to apprehend me: 33 and
through a window in a basket was I let
down by the wall, and escaped his hands.●

PAUL ESCAPING

In 11:16—12:13 Paul writes about the credentials of a true ministry. This segment begins that section.

*11:16-21a* What is Paul trying to establish in these introductory sentences?

*11:21b-29* Summarize the credentials of these groups:

v.22

vv.23-27

vv.28-29

*11:30-33* What is the main point of each verse:

v.30

v.31

v.32

v.33

NEW INTERNATIONAL VERSION

What do you learn here about:

VISIONS FROM HEAVEN

SPIRITUAL EXPERIENCES

AFFLICTION

GRACE OF THE LORD

CHRISTIAN STRENGTH

POWER OF CHRISTIAN WITNESSES

OTHER

### *Paul's Vision and His Thorn*

12 I must go on boasting. Although
there is nothing to be gained, I will
go on to visions and revelations from the
Lord. 2I know a man in Christ who fourteen years ago was caught up to the third
heaven. Whether it was in the body or out
of the body I do not know—God knows.
3And I know that this man—whether in the
body or apart from the body I do not know,
but God knows— 4was caught up to Paradise. He heard inexpressible things, things
that man is not permitted to tell. 5I will
boast about a man like that, but I will not
boast about myself, except about my
weaknesses. 6Even if I should choose to
boast, I would not be a fool, because I
would be speaking the truth. But I refrain,
so no one will think more of me than is
warranted by what I do or say.●

7To keep me from becoming conceited
because of these surpassingly great revelations, there was given me a thorn in my
flesh, a messenger of Satan, to torment me.
8Three times I pleaded with the Lord to
take it away from me. 9But he said to me,
"My grace is sufficient for you, for my
power is made perfect in weakness."
Therefore I will boast all the more gladly
about my weaknesses, so that Christ's
power may rest on me. 10That is why, for
Christ's sake, I delight in weaknesses, in
insults, in hardships, in persecutions, in
difficulties. For when I am weak, then I am
strong.●

### *Paul's Concern for the Corinthians*

11I have made a fool of myself, but you
drove me to it. I ought to have been commended by you, for I am not in the least
inferior to the "super-apostles," even
though I am nothing. 12The things that
mark an apostle—signs, wonders and miracles—were done among you with great
perseverance. 13How were you inferior to
the other churches, except that I was never
a burden to you? Forgive me this wrong!●

## KING JAMES

1.VISION

VISIONS SEEN

**12** It is not expedient for me doubtless
to glory. I will come to visions and
revelations of the Lord. 2 I knew a man
in Christ above fourteen years ago,
(whether in the body, I cannot tell; or
whether out of the body, I cannot tell: God
knoweth;) such a one caught up to the
third heaven. 3 And I knew such a man,
(whether in the body, or out of the body,
I cannot tell: God knoweth;) 4 how that
he was caught up into paradise, and heard
unspeakable words, which it is not lawful
for a man to utter. 5 Of such a one will I
glory: yet of myself I will not glory, but in
mine infirmities. 6 For though I would
desire to glory, I shall not be a fool; for I
will say the truth: but *now* I forbear, lest
any man should think of me above that
which he seeth me *to be*, or *that* he heareth
of me.●

2.AF-FLICTION

7 And lest I should be exalted
above measure through the abundance of
the revelations, there was given to me a
thorn in the flesh, the messenger of Satan
to buffet me, lest I should be exalted above
measure. 8 For this thing I besought the
Lord thrice, that it might depart from me.
9 And he said unto me, My grace is sufficient for thee: for my strength is made
perfect in weakness. Most gladly therefore will I rather glory in my infirmities,
that the power of Christ may rest upon
me. 10 Therefore I take pleasure in infirmities, in reproaches, in necessities, in
persecutions, in distresses for Christ's
sake: for when I am weak, then am I
strong.●

3.COMPE-TITION

11 I am become a fool in glorying; ye
have compelled me: for I ought to have
been commended of you: for in nothing
am I behind the very chiefest apostles,
though I be nothing. 12 Truly the signs
of an apostle were wrought among you
in all patience, in signs, and wonders, and
mighty deeds. 13 For what is it wherein
ye were inferior to other churches, except
*it be* that I myself was not burdensome to
you? forgive me this wrong.●

SIGNS WROUGHT

*12:1-6* How does verse 5 support the view that the man of verse 2 was Paul?

What was the vision about? ______

Why doesn't Paul share details of the vision?

Why does he write about this? ______

*12:7-10* Record:

THE AFFLICTION ______

LORD'S WORD ______

EFFECT ON PAUL ______

Why does Paul write about affliction here?

*12:11-13* Record:

PAUL'S TESTIMONY (v.11) ______

PAUL'S WORKS (v.12) ______

NEW INTERNATIONAL VERSION

What does this passage teach about:

LOVE FOR THE BRETHREN ______

EDIFYING OTHER CHRISTIANS ______

SINS OF CHRISTIANS ______

THE CRUCIFIED LIFE ______

EMPOWERED CHRISTIANS ______

OTHER ______

14 Now I am ready to visit you for the
third time, and I will not be a burden to
you, because what I want is not your
possessions but you. After all, children
should not have to save up for their parents, but parents for their children. 15 So I
will very gladly spend for you everything I
have and expend myself as well. If I love
you more, will you love me less? 16 Be that
as it may, I have not been a burden to you.
Yet, crafty fellow that I am, I caught you
by trickery! 17 Did I exploit you through
any of the men I sent you? 18 I urged Titus
to go to you and I sent our brother with
him. Titus did not exploit you, did he? Did
we not act in the same spirit and follow the
same course?●
19 Have you been thinking all along that
we have been defending ourselves to you?
We have been speaking in the sight of God
as those in Christ; and everything we do,
dear friends, is for your strengthening.
20 For I am afraid that when I come I may
not find you as I want you to be, and you
may not find me as you want me to be. I
fear that there may be quarreling, jealousy,
outbursts of anger, factions, slander, gos-
sip, arrogance and disorder. 21 I am afraid
that when I come again my God will humble me before you, and I will be grieved
over many who have sinned earlier and
have not repented of the impurity, sexual
sin and debauchery in which they have in-
dulged.●

*Final Warnings*

13 This will be my third visit to you.
"Every matter must be established
by the testimony of two or three witnesses."[a] 2 I already gave you a warning
when I was with you the second time. I
now repeat it while absent: On my return
I will not spare those who sinned earlier or
any of the others, 3 since you are demanding proof that Christ is speaking through
me. He is not weak in dealing with you, but
is powerful among you. 4 For to be sure, he
was crucified in weakness, yet he lives by
God's power. Likewise, we are weak in
him, yet by God's power we will live with
him to serve you.●

[a] 1 Deut. 19:15

KING JAMES

1. LOVE

NO BURDEN

14 Behold, the third time I am ready to
come to you; and I will not be burdensome to you: for I seek not yours, but you:
for the children ought not to lay up for the
parents, but the parents for the children.
15 And I will very gladly spend and be
spent for you; though the more abundantly I love you, the less I be loved.
16 But be it so, I did not burden you:
nevertheless, being crafty, I caught you
with guile. 17 Did I make a gain of you
by any of them whom I sent unto you?
18 I desired Titus, and with *him* I sent a
brother. Did Titus make a gain of you?
walked we not in the same spirit? *walked*
*we* not in the same steps?●

2. EDIFICATION

19 Again, think ye that we excuse ourselves unto you? we speak before God in
Christ: but *we do* all things, dearly beloved, for your edifying. 20 For I fear,
lest, when I come, I shall not find you
such as I would, and *that* I shall be found
unto you such as ye would not: lest *there*
*be* debates, envyings, wraths, strifes, back-
bitings, whisperings, swellings, tumults:
21 *and* lest, when I come again, my God
will humble me among you, and *that* I
shall bewail many which have sinned already, and have not repented of the uncleanness and fornication and lasciviousness which they have committed.●

3. PROOF

13 This *is* the third *time* I am coming
to you. In the mouth of two or
three witnesses shall every word be established. 2 I told you before, and foretell you, as if I were present, the second
time; and being absent now I write to
them which heretofore have sinned, and
to all other, that, if I come again, I will
not spare: 3 since ye seek a proof of
Christ speaking in me, which to you-ward
is not weak, but is mighty in you. 4 For
though he was crucified through weakness, yet he liveth by the power of God.
For we also are weak in him, but we shall
live with him by the power of God toward
you.●

POWER

This and the following segment (13:5-14) conclude Paul's letter to the Corinthians. Paul is saying, in effect, "Prepare for my visit to you." (Read 12:14 and 13:1.)

*12:14-18* Record things Paul wrote showing his motive of love.

*12:19-21* Record motives of edification.

What was Paul's fear?

*13:1-4* What did the Corinthians want proof of?

What did this make Paul do?

NEW INTERNATIONAL VERSION

What do you learn from these final words of the letter about:

PROFESSION OF FAITH

APPROVAL IN THE TEST OF FAITH

HONESTY AND TRUTH

EDIFICATION

LOVE

TRINITY

OTHER

[5]Examine yourselves to see whether you
are in the faith; test yourselves. Do you not
realize that Christ Jesus is in you—unless,
of course, you fail the test? [6]And I trust
that you will discover that we have not
failed the test. [7]Now we pray to God that
you will not do anything wrong. Not that
people will see that we have stood the test
but that you will do what is right even
though we may seem to have failed. [8]For
we cannot do anything against the truth,
but only for the truth. [9]We are glad whenever we are weak but you are strong; and
our prayer is for your perfection. [10]This is
why I write these things when I am absent,
that when I come I may not have to be
harsh in my use of authority—the authority
the Lord gave me for building you up, not
for tearing you down.●

*Final Greetings*

[11]Finally, brothers, good-by. Aim for
perfection, listen to my appeal, be of one
mind, live in peace. And the God of love
and peace will be with you.
[12]Greet one another with a holy kiss.
[13]All the saints send their greetings.●
[14]May the grace of the Lord Jesus Christ,
and the love of God, and the fellowship of
the Holy Spirit be with you all.●

KING JAMES

1. EXHORTATION

CHRIST IN YOU?

5 Examine yourselves, whether ye be in
the faith; prove your own selves. Know
ye not your own selves, how that Jesus
Christ is in you, except ye be reprobates?
6 But I trust that ye shall know that we
are not reprobates. 7 Now I pray to God
that ye do no evil; not that we should
appear approved, but that ye should do
that which is honest, though we be as
reprobates. 8 For we can do nothing
against the truth, but for the truth. 9 For
we are glad, when we are weak, and ye
are strong: and this also we wish, *even*
your perfection. 10 Therefore I write
these things being absent, lest being
present I should use sharpness, according to the power which the Lord hath
given me to edification, and not to
destruction.●

2. FAREWELL

11 Finally, brethren, farewell. Be perfect, be of good comfort, be of one mind,
live in peace; and the God of love and
peace shall be with you. 12 Greet one
another with a holy kiss. 13 All the saints
salute you.●

3. BENEDICTION

GRACE BE WITH YOU

14 The grace of the Lord Jesus Christ,
and the love of God, and the communion
of the Holy Ghost, *be* with you all. Amen.●

*13:5-10* Record:

COMMANDS ____________________

QUESTION ____________________

PRAYER OF PAUL ____________________

PURPOSE OF WRITING ____________________

*13:11-13* Record:

COMMANDS ____________________

PROMISE ____________________

SALUTATION ____________________

*13:14* Record the three parts of the benediction.

# GALATIANS

## AUTHORSHIP

The text identifies the writer as "Paul, an apostle" (1:1, cf. 6:11).

## DATE

Assigning a date to the writing depends on the identification of the name "Galatia" in 1:2. The "North Galatian View" interprets this as *geographical* Galatia which included the area of north central Asia Minor, not reached by Paul on his first missionary journey. The "South Galatian View" interprets the term as *political* Galatia, the Roman province in the south including Lystra, Derbe and other cities which Paul visited on his first journey.

If the South Galatian view is correct, Paul wrote this Epistle around A.D. 48, after the first missionary journey (Acts 13-14) and before the Jerusalem Council (Acts 15). If the North Galatian view is correct, Paul wrote the letter A.D. 53-55, after the Jerusalem Council and second missionary journey. The South Galatian view is held by most students.

## PURPOSE AND THEME

Some of the main purposes of Paul in writing this Epistle were a) to expose the false teachings of the Judaizers who were undermining the faith of the new converts; b) to defend Paul's apostleship which was being challenged by these Judaizers; c) to emphasize that salvation is through faith alone, not faith plus law; d) to exhort the Galatian Christians to live in the liberty bought by Christ (5:1), bringing forth fruit of the Spirit (5:22-23). A key verse is 5:1, which represents the letter's theme: "Stand fast therefore in the liberty wherewith Christ hath made us free, and be not entangled again with the yoke of bondage."

## GALATIANS: Set Free from Bondage

| | |
|---|---|
| SOURCE OF THE GOSPEL | 1:1-2:21 |
| Introduction | 1:1-10 |
| Paul's Message from God | 1:11-24 |
| Confirmation by Jerusalem Leaders | 2:1-10 |
| Confrontation with Peter | 2:11-21 |
| DEFENSE OF THE GOSPEL | 3:1-5:1 |
| Faith and Law Compared | 3:1-24 |
| Freedom in Christ | 3:25-5:1 |
| APPLICATION OF THE GOSPEL | 5:2-6:18 |
| New Walk of Christians | 5:2-26 |
| Obligations Attending Christian Liberty | 6:1-18 |

# GALATIANS

NEW INTERNATIONAL VERSION

What does this passage teach about:

THE TRINITY

THE TRUE GOSPEL

CHRISTIAN SERVICE

List some spiritual applications of the passage.

1 Paul, an apostle—sent not from men
nor by man, but by Jesus Christ and
God the Father, who raised him from the
dead— 2and all the brothers with me,

To the churches in Galatia:

3Grace and peace to you from God our
Father and the Lord Jesus Christ, 4who
gave himself for our sins to rescue us from
the present evil age, according to the will
of our God and Father, 5to whom be glory
for ever and ever. Amen.●

*No Other Gospel*

6I am astonished that you are so quickly
deserting the one who called you by the
grace of Christ and are turning to a different gospel— 7which is really no gospel at
all. Evidently some people are throwing
you into confusion and are trying to pervert the gospel of Christ. 8But even if we
or an angel from heaven should preach a
gospel other than the one we preached to
you, let him be eternally condemned! 9As
we have already said, so now I say again:
If anybody is preaching to you a gospel
other than what you accepted, let him be
eternally condemned!●

10Am I now trying to win the approval of
men, or of God? Or am I trying to please
men? If I were still trying to please men, I
would not be a servant of Christ.●

KING JAMES

# GALATIANS

—salutation and benediction

1 Paul, an apostle, (not of men, neither
by man, but by Jesus Christ, and
God the Father, who raised him from the
dead;) 2 and all the brethren which are
with me,
Unto the churches of Galatia:
3 Grace *be* to you, and peace, from God
the Father, and *from* our Lord Jesus
Christ, 4 who gave himself for our sins,
that he might deliver us from this present
evil world, according to the will of God
and our Father: 5 to whom *be* glory for
ever and ever. Amen.●

NOT OF MEN

1. THE PROBLEM

6 I marvel that ye are so soon removed
from him that called you into the grace of
Christ unto another gospel: 7 which is
not another; but there be some that
trouble you, and would pervert the gospel
of Christ. 8 But though we, or an angel
from heaven, preach any other gospel unto you than that which we have preached
unto you, let him be accursed. 9 As we
said before, so say I now again, If any
*man* preach any other gospel unto you
than that ye have received, let him be
accursed.●

2. PAUL'S MOTIVES

10 For do I now persuade men, or God?
or do I seek to please men? for if I yet
pleased men, I should not be the servant
of Christ.●

NOT PLEASING MEN

These opening words of Paul reveal in a general way the reason for his writing.

*1:1-5* Note the reference to "men" in verse 1. Compare this with the references in verse 10. Does this suggest a problem in the Galatian church's view about Paul?

Record the parts of the benediction:

*1:6-9* What are the key repeated words of the paragraph?

What is suggested by the phrase "another gospel"?

*1:10* Compare the reference to God and to Christ.

NEW INTERNATIONAL VERSION

What does this passage teach about:

SOURCE OF THE GOSPEL

REVELATION

CONVERSION

PREACHING

List spiritual applications of the passage.

*Paul Called by God*

[11]I want you to know, brothers, that the
gospel I preached is not something that
man made up. [12]I did not receive it from
any man, nor was I taught it; rather, I received it by revelation from Jesus Christ.
[13]For you have heard of my previous
way of life in Judaism, how intensely I persecuted the church of God and tried to destroy it. [14]I was advancing in Judaism
beyond many Jews of my own age and was
extremely zealous for the traditions of my
fathers. [15]But when God, who set me apart
from birth[a] and called me by his grace, was
pleased [16]to reveal his Son in me so that I
might preach him among the Gentiles, I did
not consult any man, [17]nor did I go up to
Jerusalem to see those who were apostles
before I was, but I went immediately into
Arabia and later returned to Damascus.
[18]Then after three years, I went up to
Jerusalem to get acquainted with Peter[b]
and stayed with him fifteen days. [19]I saw
none of the other apostles—only James,
the Lord's brother. [20]I assure you before
God that what I am writing you is no lie.
[21]Later I went to Syria and Cilicia. [22]I was
personally unknown to the churches of
Judea that are in Christ. [23]They only heard
the report: "The man who formerly persecuted us is now preaching the faith he
once tried to destroy." [24]And they praised
God because of me.

[a]15 Or *from my mother's womb*
[b]18 Greek *Cephas*

KING JAMES

—theme introduced

11 But I certify you, brethren, that the
gospel which was preached of me is not
after man. 12 For I neither received it of
man, neither was I taught *it*, but by the
revelation of Jesus Christ. ● 13 For ye have
heard of my conversation in time past in
the Jews' religion, how that beyond
measure I persecuted the church of God,
and wasted it: 14 and profited in the
Jews' religion above many my equals in
mine own nation, being more exceedingly
zealous of the traditions of my fathers.
15 But when it pleased God, who separated me from my mother's womb, and
called *me* by his grace, 16 to reveal his
Son in me, that I might preach him
among the heathen; immediately I conferred not with flesh and blood: 17 neither went I up to Jerusalem to them which
were apostles before me; but I went into
Arabia, and returned again unto Damascus. ●

REVELATION OF JESUS

1. BEFORE AND AFTER CONVERSION

2. LIMITED CONTACTS

18 Then after three years I went up to
Jerusalem to see Peter, and abode with
him fifteen days. 19 But other of the
apostles saw I none, save James the
Lord's brother. 20 Now the things which
I write unto you, behold, before God, I
lie not. 21 Afterward I came into the
regions of Syria and Cili'cia; 22 and was
unknown by face unto the churches of
Judea which were in Christ: 23 but they
had heard only, That he which persecuted
us in times past now preacheth the faith
which once he destroyed. 24 And they
glorified God in me. ●

GLORY OF GOD

In the first section (1:11—2:21) of the epistle Paul identifies the *source* of the gospel he preached.

*1:11-12* What is Paul claiming here?

What is meant by "revelation of Jesus Christ"?

*1:13-17* Compare Paul before and after his conversion.

What words describe his conversion?

What is significant about the words "I conferred not with flesh and blood" (v.16)?

*1:18-24* Do these verses support the theme that Paul's gospel came from God, not from men? If so, how?

NEW INTERNATIONAL VERSION

What do you learn here about:

GOSPEL FOR JEWS

GOSPEL FOR NON-JEWS

LEGALISM

CHRISTIAN LEADERS

CHRISTIAN FELLOWSHIP

List spiritual applications of the passage.

*Paul Accepted by the Apostles*

2 Fourteen years later I went up again to
Jerusalem, this time with Barnabas. I
took Titus along also. 2I went in response
to a revelation and set before them the gospel that I preach among the Gentiles. But
I did this privately to those who seemed to
be leaders, for fear that I was running or
had run my race in vain. 3Yet not even
Titus, who was with me, was compelled to
be circumcised, even though he was a
Greek. 4⌊This matter arose⌋ because some
false brothers had infiltrated our ranks to
spy on the freedom we have in Christ Jesus
and to make us slaves. 5We did not give in
to them for a moment, so that the truth of
the gospel might remain with you.●
6As for those who seemed to be important—whatever they were makes no difference to me; God does not judge by external
appearance—those men added nothing to
my message. 7On the contrary, they saw
that I had been given the task of preaching
the gospel to the Gentiles,[c] just as Peter
had been given the task of preaching the
gospel to the Jews.[d] 8For God, who was at
work in the ministry of Peter as an apostle
to the Jews, was also at work in my ministry as an apostle to the Gentiles. 9James,
Peter[e] and John, those reputed to be pillars, gave me and Barnabas the right hand
of fellowship when they recognized the
grace given to me. They agreed that we
should go to the Gentiles, and they to the
Jews. 10All they asked was that we should
continue to remember the poor, the very
thing I was eager to do.●

[c]7 Greek *uncircumcised*
[d]7 Greek *circumcised*; also in verses 8 and 9
[e]9 Greek *Cephas*; also in verses 11 and 14

## KING JAMES

**1. PAUL STATES HIS CASE**

**COMMUNICATION**

**2** Then fourteen years after I went up
again to Jerusalem with Barnabas,
and took Titus with *me* also. 2 And I
went up by revelation, and communicated
unto them that gospel which I preach
among the Gentiles, but privately to them
which were of reputation, lest by any
means I should run, or had run, in vain.
3 But neither Titus, who was with me,
being a Greek, was compelled to be circumcised: 4 and that because of false
brethren unawares brought in, who came
in privily to spy out our liberty which we
have in Christ Jesus, that they might bring
us into bondage: 5 to whom we gave
place by subjection, no, not for an hour;
that the truth of the gospel might continue with you. ●

**2. PAUL GETS SUPPORT**

6 But of those who seemed
to be somewhat, (whatsoever they were,
it maketh no matter to me: God accepteth
no man's person: ) for they who seemed *to
be somewhat* in conference added nothing to me: 7 but contrariwise, when they
saw that the gospel of the uncircumcision
was committed unto me, as *the gospel* of
the circumcision *was* unto Peter; 8 (for
he that wrought effectually in Peter to the
apostleship of the circumcision, the same
was mighty in me toward the Gentiles;)
9 and when James, Cephas, and John,
who seemed to be pillars, perceived
the grace that was given unto me, they
gave to me and Barnabas the right
hands of fellowship; that we *should
go* unto the heathen, and they unto
the circumcision. 10 Only *they would*
that we should remember the poor;
the same which I also was forward to
do. ●

**FELLOWSHIP**

*2:1-5* To whom did Paul talk, privately (v.2)? ______

What was the conference about? ______

Was Paul's message and ministry supported? ______

What opposition did Paul have in this meeting? ______

*2:6-10* What is the key repeated pronoun of the paragraph? ______

What two things did the leaders recognize had been given to Paul (vv.7,9)? ______

Compare the missions of Paul and Peter. ______

NEW INTERNATIONAL VERSION

What does this passage teach about:

JUSTIFICATION BY FAITH

MINISTRY OF GOD'S LAW

HYPOCRISY

THE CRUCIFIED LIFE

LIFE IN CHRIST

OTHER

*Paul Opposes Peter*

[11]When Peter came to Antioch, I opposed him to his face, because he was in
the wrong. [12]Before certain men came from
James, he used to eat with the Gentiles.
But when they arrived, he began to draw
back and separate himself from the Gentiles because he was afraid of those who
belonged to the circumcision group. [13]The
other Jews joined him in his hypocrisy, so
that by their hypocrisy even Barnabas was
led astray.●
[14]When I saw that they were not acting
in line with the truth of the gospel, I said
to Peter in front of them all, "You are a
Jew, yet you live like a Gentile and not like
a Jew. How is it, then, that you force Gentiles to follow Jewish customs?
[15]"We who are Jews by birth and not
'Gentile sinners' [16]know that a man is not
justified by observing the law, but by faith
in Jesus Christ. So we, too, have put our
faith in Christ Jesus that we may be justified by faith in Christ and not by observing
the law, because by observing the law no
one will be justified.●
[17]"If, while we seek to be justified in
Christ, it becomes evident that we ourselves are sinners, does that mean that
Christ promotes sin? Absolutely not! [18]If I
rebuild what I destroyed, I prove that I am
a lawbreaker. [19]For through the law I died
to the law so that I might live for God. [20]I
have been crucified with Christ and I no
longer live, but Christ lives in me. The life
I live in the body, I live by faith in the Son
of God, who loved me and gave himself for
me. [21]I do not set aside the grace of God,
for if righteousness could be gained
through the law, Christ died for nothing!"[a]●

[a]21 Some interpreters end the quotation after verse 14.

KING JAMES

1. PROBLEM SITUATION

11 But when Peter was come to An'ti-
och, I withstood him to the face, because
he was to be blamed. 12 For before that
certain came from James, he did eat with
the Gentiles: but when they were come,
he withdrew and separated himself, fearing them which were of the circumcision.
13 And the other Jews dissembled likewise with him; insomuch that Barnabas
also was carried away with their dissimulation. ●

2. PETER REBUKED

14 But when I saw that they
walked not uprightly according to the
truth of the gospel, I said unto Peter before *them* all, If thou, being a Jew, livest
after the manner of Gentiles, and not as
do the Jews, why compellest thou the
Gentiles to live as do the Jews? 15 We
*who are* Jews by nature, and not sinners
of the Gentiles, 16 knowing that a man
is not justified by the works of the law,
but by the faith of Jesus Christ, even we
have believed in Jesus Christ, that we
might be justified by the faith of Christ,
and not by the works of the law: for by the
works of the law shall no flesh be justified.●

3. THE TRUE DOCTRINE

17 But if, while we seek to be justified by
Christ, we ourselves also are found sinners, *is* therefore Christ the minister of
sin? God forbid. 18 For if I build again
the things which I destroyed, I make myself a transgressor. 19 For I through the
law am dead to the law, that I might live
unto God. 20 I am crucified with Christ:
nevertheless I live; yet not I, but Christ
liveth in me: and the life which I now live
in the flesh I live by the faith of the Son of
God, who loved me, and gave himself for
me. 21 I do not frustrate the grace of
God: for if righteousness *come* by the
law, then Christ is dead in vain.●

LAW

GRACE

*2:11-13* What group is "of the circumcision"? (See The Living Bible.)

______________________________

What wrong had Peter done? ______________________________

______________________________

How would Peter's action confuse the Gentiles with whom he had been eating?

______________________________

______________________________

______________________________

*2:14-16* Where do Paul's words to Peter begin?

______________________________

______________________________

Where do they end, according to The Living Bible punctuation?

______________________________

______________________________

What was Paul's rebuke of Peter? ______________________________

______________________________

______________________________

In what sense had Peter compelled the Jews "to live as do the Jews"?

______________________________

______________________________

______________________________

*2:17-21* What different doctrinal *salvation* words appear here?

______________________________

______________________________

______________________________

______________________________

What is the main contrast of the paragraph?

______________________________

______________________________

______________________________

NEW INTERNATIONAL VERSION

What is taught here about:

THE HOLY SPIRIT

CHRISTIAN GROWTH

SAVING FAITH

JUSTIFICATION

CURSE OF THE LAW

DEATH OF CHRIST

OTHER

*Faith or Observance of the Law*

3 You foolish Galatians! Who has bewitched you? Before your very eyes
Jesus Christ was clearly portrayed as
crucified. [2]I would like to learn just one
thing from you: Did you receive the Spirit
by observing the law, or by believing what
you heard? [3]Are you so foolish? After beginning with the Spirit, are you now trying
to attain your goal by human effort? [4]Have
you suffered so much for nothing—if it
really was for nothing? [5]Does God give you
his Spirit and work miracles among you
because you observe the law, or because
you believe what you heard?●

[6]Consider Abraham: "He believed God,
and it was credited to him as righteousness."[b] [7]Understand, then, that those who
believe are children of Abraham. [8]The
Scripture foresaw that God would justify
the Gentiles by faith, and announced the
gospel in advance to Abraham: "All nations will be blessed through you."[c] [9]So
those who have faith are blessed along with
Abraham, the man of faith.●

[10]All who rely on observing the law are
under a curse, for it is written: "Cursed is
everyone who does not continue to do
everything written in the Book of the
Law."[d] [11]Clearly no one is justified before
God by the law, because, "The righteous
will live by faith."[e] [12]The law is not based
on faith; on the contrary, "The man who
does these things will live by them."[f]
[13]Christ redeemed us from the curse of the
law by becoming a curse for us, for it is
written: "Cursed is everyone who is hung
on a tree."[g] [14]He redeemed us in order that
the blessing given to Abraham might come
to the Gentiles through Christ Jesus, so
that by faith we might receive the promise
of the Spirit.●

*b6* Gen. 15:6 *c8* Gen. 12:3; 18:18; 22:18
*d10* Deut. 27:26 *e11* Hab. 2:4
*f12* Lev. 18:5 *g13* Deut. 21:23

KING JAMES

1. GALATIANS' EXPERIENCE

3 O foolish Galatians, who hath bewitched you, that ye should not obey
the truth, before whose eyes Jesus Christ
hath been evidently set forth, crucified
among you? 2 This only would I learn
of you, Received ye the Spirit by the
works of the law, or by the hearing of
faith? 3 Are ye so foolish? having begun
in the Spirit, are ye now made perfect by
the flesh? 4 Have ye suffered so many
things in vain? if *it be* yet in vain. 5 He
therefore that ministereth to you the
Spirit, and worketh miracles among you,
*doeth he it* by the works of the law, or by
the hearing of faith? ●

OBEY THE TRUTH

2. ABRAHAM'S EXPERIENCE

6 Even as Abraham believed God, and
it was accounted to him for righteousness. 7 Know ye therefore that they
which are of faith, the same are the children of Abraham. 8 And the Scripture,
foreseeing that God would justify the
heathen through faith, preached before
the gospel unto Abraham, *saying*, In thee
shall all nations be blessed. 9 So then
they which be of faith are blessed with
faithful Abraham. ●

3. REDEEMED FROM THE CURSE

10 For as many as are of the works of
the law are under the curse: for it is
written,

Cursed *is* every one that continueth
not in all things
which are written in the book of the
law to do them. Deu. 27:26

11 But that no man is justified by the law
in the sight of God, *it is* evident: for, The
just shall live by faith. 12 And the law is
not of faith: but, The man that doeth
them shall live in them. 13 Christ hath
redeemed us from the curse of the law,
being made a curse for us: for it is written,
Cursed *is* every one that hangeth on a
tree: 14 that the blessing of Abraham
might come on the Gentiles through Jesus
Christ; that we might receive the promise
of the Spirit through faith. ●

Deu. 21:23

BELIEVE THE TRUTH

This segment begins the second of the three major sections of the letter: DEFENSE OF THE GOSPEL, 3:1—5:1.

*3:1-5* How many questions appear here?

What answer does Paul expect in each case?

What references are made to the Spirit?

What is the main point of the paragraph?

*3:6-9* What brought salvation to Abraham?

What blessings came of that salvation?

*3:10-14* Underline the repeated word "curse."
How is this curse related to God's law?

How is the sinner redeemed from the curse of the law?

NEW INTERNATIONAL VERSION

What does this passage teach about:

GOD'S PROMISE OF SALVATION FOR MAN

THE MINISTRIES OF CHRIST

MINISTRIES OF GOD'S LAW

SAVING FAITH

OTHER

*The Law and the Promise*

[15]Brothers, let me take an example from
everyday life. Just as no one can set aside
or add to a human covenant that has been
duly established, so it is in this case. [16]The
promises were spoken to Abraham and to
his seed. The Scripture does not say "and
to seeds," meaning many people, but "and
to your seed,"[h] meaning one person, who
is Christ. [17]What I mean is this: The law,
introduced 430 years later, does not set
aside the covenant previously established
by God and thus do away with the promise.
[18]For if the inheritance depends on the law,
then it no longer depends on a promise; but
God in his grace gave it to Abraham
through a promise.●

[19]What, then, was the purpose of the
law? It was added because of transgressions until the Seed to whom the promise
referred had come. The law was put into
effect through angels by a mediator. [20]A
mediator, however, does not represent just
one party; but God is one.

[21]Is the law, therefore, opposed to the
promises of God? Absolutely not! For if a
law had been given that could impart life,
then righteousness would certainly have
come by the law. [22]But the Scripture declares that the whole world is a prisoner of
sin, so that what was promised, being giv-
en through faith in Jesus Christ, might be
given to those who believe.●

[23]Before this faith came, we were held
prisoners by the law, locked up until faith
should be revealed. [24]So the law was put in
charge to lead us to Christ[a] that we might
be justified by faith.●

[h]*16* Gen. 12:7; 13:15; 24:7
[a]*24* Or *charge until Christ came*

KING JAMES

1. UNBREAKABLE PROMISE

15 Brethren, I speak after the manner of
men; Though *it be* but a man's covenant,
yet *if it be* confirmed, no man disannul-
leth, or addeth thereto. 16 Now to Abraham and his seed were the promises made.
He saith not, And to seeds, as of many;
but as of one, And to thy seed, which is
Christ. 17 And this I say, *that* the covenant, that was confirmed before of God in
Christ, the law, which was four hundred
and thirty years after, cannot disannul,
that it should make the promise of none
effect. 18 For if the inheritance *be* of the
law, *it is* no more of promise: but God
gave *it* to Abraham by promise.●

2. FUNCTIONAL LAW

19 Wherefore then *serveth* the law? It
was added because of transgressions, till
the seed should come to whom the promise was made; *and it was* ordained by
angels in the hand of a mediator. 20 Now
a mediator is not *a mediator* of one, but
God is one.
21 *Is* the law then against the promises
of God? God forbid: for if there had
been a law given which could have given
life, verily righteousness should have been
by the law. 22 But the Scripture hath
concluded all under sin, that the promise
by faith of Jesus Christ might be given to
them that believe.●
23 But before faith came, we were kept
under the law, shut up unto the faith
which should afterward be revealed.
24 Wherefore the law was our schoolmaster *to bring us* unto Christ, that we
might be justified by faith.●

PROMISE

LAW

*3:15-18* Which came first, law or promise?

_______________

Did the law annul the promise? _______________

What was the original promise made to Abraham and his seed?

_______________

_______________

_______________

Who is Abraham's seed? _______________

_______________

What is the main point of this paragraph?

_______________

_______________

*3:19-24* What is the opening question?

_______________

_______________

List the various references to the law of God:

_______________

_______________

_______________

_______________

_______________

_______________

_______________

_______________

_______________

_______________

_______________

_______________

_______________

_______________

_______________

_______________

_______________

_______________

_______________

NEW INTERNATIONAL VERSION

What do you learn here about:

CHILDREN OF GOD

SONS OF GOD

HEIRS OF GOD

BEING KNOWN OF GOD

BONDAGE OF THE LAW

NEW STANDING IN CHRIST

OTHER

25Now that faith has
come, we are no longer under the super-
vision of the law.

*Sons of God*

26You are all sons of God through faith in
Christ Jesus, 27for all of you who were baptized into Christ have clothed yourselves
with Christ. 28There is neither Jew nor
Greek, slave nor free, male nor female, for
you are all one in Christ Jesus. 29If you
belong to Christ, then you are Abraham's
seed, and heirs according to the promise. ●
4 What I am saying is that as long as the
heir is a child, he is no different from
a slave, although he owns the whole estate.
2He is subject to guardians and trustees
until the time set by his father. 3So also,
when we were children, we were in slavery
under the basic principles of the world.
4But when the time had fully come, God
sent his Son, born of a woman, born under
law, 5to redeem those under law, that we
might receive the full rights of sons. 6Be-
cause you are sons, God sent the Spirit of
his Son into our hearts, the Spirit who calls
out, "*Abba*,[b] Father." 7So you are no
longer a slave, but a son; and since you are
a son, God has made you also an heir. ●

*Paul's Concern for the Galatians*

8Formerly, when you did not know God,
you were slaves to those who by nature are
not gods. 9But now that you know God—or
rather are known by God—how is it that
you are turning back to those weak and
miserable principles? Do you wish to be
enslaved by them all over again? 10You are
observing special days and months and
seasons and years! 11I fear for you, that
somehow I have wasted my efforts on you. ●

[b]6 Aramaic for *Father*

KING JAMES

1. CHILDREN OF GOD

25 But after FAITH
that faith is come, we are no longer under
a schoolmaster. 26 For ye are all the
children of God by faith in Christ Jesus.
27 For as many of you as have been baptized into Christ have put on Christ.
28 There is neither Jew nor Greek, there
is neither bond nor free, there is neither
male nor female: for ye are all one in
Christ Jesus. 29 And if ye *be* Christ's,
then are ye Abraham's seed, and heirs
according to the promise. ●

2. HEIR OF GOD

4 Now I say, *That* the heir, as long as
he is a child, differeth nothing from a
servant, though he be lord of all; 2 but is
under tutors and governors until the time
appointed of the father. 3 Even so we,
when we were children, were in bondage
under the elements of the world: 4 but
when the fulness of the time was come,
God sent forth his Son, made of a woman,
made under the law, 5 to redeem them
that were under the law, that we might
receive the adoption of sons. 6 And because ye are sons, God hath sent forth the
Spirit of his Son into your hearts, crying,
Abba, Father. 7 Wherefore thou art no
more a servant, but a son; and if a son,
then an heir of God through Christ. ●

3. KNOWN OF GOD

8 Howbeit then, when ye knew not God,
ye did service unto them which by nature
are no gods. 9 But now, after that ye have
known God, or rather are known of God,
how turn ye again to the weak and beggarly elements, whereunto ye desire again
to be in bondage? 10 Ye observe days,
and months, and times, and years. 11 I
am afraid of you, lest I have bestowed WORKS
upon you labor in vain. ●

*3:25-29* What is the "schoolmaster" of verse 25?

Record the different references to Christ:

*4:1-7* What is meant by each of these:

CHILD

SON

HEIR

What is the main point of the paragraph?

*4:8-11* What is meant by "the weak and beggarly elements"?

What is the point of this paragraph?

NEW INTERNATIONAL VERSION

What do you learn here about:

COMPASSION FOR OTHER CHRISTIANS

LIBERTY THROUGH CHRIST

BONDAGE OF THE LAW

OTHER

[12]I plead with you, brothers, become like
me, for I became like you. You have done
me no wrong. [13]As you know, it was because of an illness that I first preached the
gospel to you. [14]Even though my illness
was a trial to you, you did not treat me with
contempt or scorn. Instead, you welcomed
me as if I were an angel of God, as if I were
Christ Jesus himself. [15]What has happened
to all your joy? I can testify that, if you
could have done so, you would have torn
out your eyes and given them to me.
[16]Have I now become your enemy by telling you the truth?

[17]Those people are zealous to win you
over, but for no good. What they want is to
alienate you ⌊from us⌋, so that you may be
zealous for them. [18]It is fine to be zealous,
provided the purpose is good, and to be so
always and not just when I am with you.
[19]My dear children, for whom I am again in
the pains of childbirth until Christ is
formed in you, [20]how I wish I could be with
you now and change my tone, because I am
perplexed about you!●

*Hagar and Sarah*

[21]Tell me, you who want to be under the
law, are you not aware of what the law
says? [22]For it is written that Abraham had
two sons, one by the slave woman and the
other by the free woman. [23]His son by the
slave woman was born in the ordinary way;
but his son by the free woman was born as
the result of a promise.

[24]These things may be taken figuratively,
for the women represent two covenants.
One covenant is from Mount Sinai and
bears children who are to be slaves: This is
Hagar. [25]Now Hagar stands for Mount
Sinai in Arabia and corresponds to the
present city of Jerusalem, because she is in
slavery with her children. [26]But the Jerusalem that is above is free, and she is our
mother. [27]For it is written:

"Be glad, O barren woman,
who bears no children;
break forth and cry aloud,
you who have no labor pains;
because more are the children of
the desolate woman
than of her who has a husband."[c]

[28]Now you, brothers, like Isaac, are children of promise. [29]At that time the son
born in the ordinary way persecuted the
son born by the power of the Spirit. It is the
same now. [30]But what does the Scripture
say? "Get rid of the slave woman and her
son, for the slave woman's son will never
share in the inheritance with the free
woman's son."[d] [31]Therefore, brothers, we
are not children of the slave woman, but of
the free woman.

*Freedom in Christ*

5 It is for freedom that Christ has set us
free. Stand firm, then, and do not let
yourselves be burdened again by a yoke of
slavery.●

[c]27 Isaiah 54:1 [d]30 Gen. 21:10

KING JAMES

—parenthesis

12 Brethren, I beseech you, be as I *am;*
for I *am* as ye *are:* ye have not injured me
at all. 13 Ye know how through infirmity
of the flesh I preached the gospel unto you
at the first. 14 And my temptation which
was in my flesh ye despised not, nor rejected; but received me as an angel of
God, *even* as Christ Jesus. 15 Where is
then the blessedness ye spake of? for I
bear you record, that, if *it had been* possible, ye would have plucked out your
own eyes, and have given them to me.
16 Am I therefore become your enemy,
because I tell you the truth? 17 They
zealously affect you, *but* not well; yea,
they would exclude you, that ye might
affect them. 18 But *it is* good to be zealously affected always in *a* good *thing,* and
not only when I am present with you.
19 My little children, of whom I travail in
birth again until Christ be formed in you,
20 I desire to be present with you now,
and to change my voice; for I stand in
doubt of you.●

BONDAGE OR FREEDOM

DESIRE BONDAGE?

21 Tell me, ye that desire to be under
the law, do ye not hear the law? 22 For
it is written, that Abraham had two sons,
the one by a bondmaid, the other by a
free woman. 23 But he *who was* of the
bondwoman was born after the flesh; but
he of the free woman *was* by promise.
24 Which things are an allegory: for these
are the two covenants; the one from the
mount Si'nai, which gendereth to bondage, which is Hagar. 25 For this Hagar is
mount Si'nai in Arabia, and answereth to
Jerusalem which now is, and is in bondage
with her children. 26 But Jerusalem
which is above is free, which is the mother
of us all. 27 For it is written, Isa. 54:1

Rejoice, thou barren that bearest
not;
break forth and cry, thou that trav-
ailest not:
for the desolate hath many more
children
than she which hath a husband.

28 Now we, brethren, as Isaac was, are
the children of promise. 29 But as then
he that was born after the flesh persecuted
him *that was born* after the Spirit, even
so *it is* now. 30 Nevertheless what saith Gen. 21:10, 12
the Scripture?

Cast out the bondwoman and her
son:
for the son of the bondwoman shall
not be heir
with the son of the free woman.

31 So then, brethren, we are not children
of the bondwoman, but of the free.

STAY FREE!

5 Stand fast therefore in the liberty
wherewith Christ hath made us free,
and be not entangled again with the yoke
of bondage.●

*4:12-20* This is a parenthesis in the letter, before Paul writes about the believer's freedom through Christ. Compare these two parts of Paul's testimony:

vv.12-15 ______

vv.16-20 ______

*4:21—5:1* What is the concluding verse? Study the paragraph in light of this. Record what Paul writes about these:

BONDAGE ______

FREEDOM ______

NEW INTERNATIONAL VERSION

List truths taught here about:

THE HOLY SPIRIT

JESUS CHRIST

WALK OF THE CHRISTIAN

FRUIT OF THE SPIRIT

WORKS OF THE FLESH

[2]Mark my words! I, Paul, tell you that if
you let yourselves be circumcised, Christ
will be of no value to you at all. [3]Again I
declare to every man who lets himself be
circumcised that he is obligated to obey the
whole law. [4]You who are trying to be justified by law have been alienated from
Christ; you have fallen away from grace.
[5]But by faith we eagerly await through the
Spirit the righteousness for which we
hope. [6]For in Christ Jesus neither circumcision nor uncircumcision has any value.
The only thing that counts is faith expressing itself through love.●
[7]You were running a good race. Who cut
in on you and kept you from obeying the
truth? [8]That kind of persuasion does not
come from the one who calls you. [9]"A little
yeast works through the whole batch of
dough." [10]I am confident in the Lord that
you will take no other view. The one who
is throwing you into confusion will pay the
penalty, whoever he may be. [11]Brothers, if
I am still preaching circumcision, why am
I still being persecuted? In that case the
offense of the cross has been abolished.
[12]As for those agitators, I wish they would
go the whole way and emasculate themselves!●

*Life by the Spirit*

[13]You, my brothers, were called to be
free. But do not use your freedom to indulge the sinful nature[a]; rather, serve one
another in love. [14]The entire law is
summed up in a single command: "Love
your neighbor as yourself."[b] [15]If you keep
on biting and devouring each other, watch
out or you will be destroyed by each other.●
[16]So I say, live by the Spirit, and you will
not gratify the desires of the sinful nature.
[17]For the sinful nature desires what is contrary to the Spirit, and the Spirit what is
contrary to the sinful nature. They are in
conflict with each other, so that you do not
do what you want. [18]But if you are led by
the Spirit, you are not under law.
[19]The acts of the sinful nature are obvious: sexual immorality, impurity and debauchery; [20]idolatry and witchcraft; hatred, discord, jealousy, fits of rage, selfish
ambition, dissensions, factions [21]and envy;
drunkenness, orgies, and the like. I warn
you, as I did before, that those who live
like this will not inherit the kingdom of
God.
[22]But the fruit of the Spirit is love, joy,
peace, patience, kindness, goodness, faithfulness, [23]gentleness and self-control.
Against such things there is no law.
[24]Those who belong to Christ Jesus have
crucified the sinful nature with its passions
and desires. [25]Since we live by the Spirit,
let us keep in step with the Spirit. [26]Let us
not become conceited, provoking and envying each other.●

[a]13 Or *the flesh;* also in verses 16, 17, 19 and 24
[b]14 Lev. 19:18

KING JAMES

1.WALK IN LIBERTY

EFFICACY BY CHRIST

2 Behold, I Paul say unto you, that if ye
be circumcised, Christ shall profit you
nothing. 3 For I testify again to every
man that is circumcised, that he is a debtor
to do the whole law. 4 Christ is become
of no effect unto you, whosoever of you
are justified by the law; ye are fallen from
grace. 5 For we through the Spirit wait
for the hope of righteousness by faith.
6 For in Jesus Christ neither circumcision
availeth any thing, nor uncircumcision;
but faith which worketh by love.● 7 Ye did
run well; who did hinder you that ye
should not obey the truth? 8 This persuasion *cometh* not of him that calleth
you. 9 A little leaven leaveneth the whole
lump. 10 I have confidence in you
through the Lord, that ye will be none
otherwise minded: but he that troubleth
you shall bear his judgment, whosoever
he be. 11 And I, brethren, if I yet preach
circumcision, why do I yet suffer persecution? then is the offense of the cross
ceased. 12 I would they were even cut off
which trouble you.●

—parenthesis

2.WALK IN LOVE

13 For, brethren, ye have been called
unto liberty; only *use* not liberty for an
occasion to the flesh, but by love serve one
another. 14 For all the law is fulfilled in
one word, *even* in this; Thou shalt love
thy neighbor as thyself. 15 But if ye
bite and devour one another, take
heed that ye be not consumed one of
another.●

3.WALK IN THE SPIRIT

16 *This* I say then, Walk in the Spirit,
and ye shall not fulfil the lust of the flesh.
17 For the flesh lusteth against the Spirit,
and the Spirit against the flesh: and these
are contrary the one to the other; so that
ye cannot do the things that ye would.
18 But if ye be led of the Spirit, ye are not
under the law. 19 Now the works of
the flesh are manifest, which are *these*,
adultery, fornication, uncleanness, lasciviousness, 20 idolatry, witchcraft, hatred,
variance, emulations, wrath, strife, sedi-
tions, heresies, 21 envyings, murders,
drunkenness, revelings, and such like:
of the which I tell you before, as I have
also told *you* in time past, that they
which do such things shall not inherit the
kingdom of God. 22 But the fruit of the
Spirit is love, joy, peace, long-suffering,
gentleness, goodness, faith, 23 meekness,
temperance: against such there is no law.
24 And they that are Christ's have crucified the flesh with the affections and
lusts.

LEADING BY THE SPIRIT

25 If we live in the Spirit, let us also
walk in the Spirit. 26 Let us not be desirous of vainglory, provoking one another, envying one another.●

Paul now begins the third and final section (5:2—6:18) of his letter. It emphasizes the practical APPLICATION OF THE GOSPEL.

*5:2-6* What word of verse 3 suggests the opposite of liberty?

______

What is Paul's point here? ______

______

______

______

*5:7-12* What are the references to troublemakers who were teaching false doctrines in the churches?

______

______

______

______

______

*5:13-15* Record the references to love:

______

______

______

*5:16-26* Underline every reference to Spirit. What is the practical exhortation of verse 25? List these:

WORKS OF THE FLESH ______

______

______

______

______

______

______

FRUIT OF THE SPIRIT ______

______

______

______

______

______

______

NEW INTERNATIONAL VERSION

List spiritual applications of this passage, in the following areas:

HELPING OTHER CHRISTIANS

JUST RECOMPENSE

THE CRUCIFIED LIFE

FALSE BOASTING

OTHER

### *Doing Good to All*

6 Brothers, if someone is caught in a sin,
you who are spiritual should restore
him gently. But watch yourself, or you also
may be tempted. [2]Carry each other's burdens, and in this way you will fulfill the law
of Christ. [3]If anyone thinks he is something
when he is nothing, he deceives himself.
[4]Each one should test his own actions.
Then he can take pride in himself, without
comparing himself to somebody else, [5]for
each one should carry his own load.●
[6]Anyone who receives instruction in the
word must share all good things with his
instructor.
[7]Do not be deceived: God cannot be
mocked. A man reaps what he sows. [8]The
one who sows to please his sinful nature,
from that nature[c] will reap destruction; the
one who sows to please the Spirit, from the
Spirit will reap eternal life. [9]Let us not
become weary in doing good, for at the
proper time we will reap a harvest if we do
not give up. [10]Therefore, as we have opportunity, let us do good to all people,
especially to those who belong to the
family of believers.●

### *Not Circumcision but a New Creation*

[11]See what large letters I use as I write to
you with my own hand!●
[12]Those who want to make a good impression outwardly are trying to compel
you to be circumcised. The only reason
they do this is to avoid being persecuted for
the cross of Christ. [13]Not even those who
are circumcised obey the law, yet they
want you to be circumcised that they may
boast about your flesh. [14]May I never boast
except in the cross of our Lord Jesus
Christ, through which the world has been
crucified to me, and I to the world.
[15]Neither circumcision nor uncircumcision
means anything; what counts is a new creation. [16]Peace and mercy to all who follow
this rule, even to the Israel of God.●
[17]Finally, let no one cause me trouble,
for I bear on my body the marks of Jesus.●
[18]The grace of our Lord Jesus Christ be
with your spirit, brothers. Amen.●

c8 Or *his flesh, from the flesh*

KING JAMES

1.LAW OF CHRIST

MEEKNESS

**6** Brethren, if a man be overtaken in a
fault, ye which are spiritual, restore
such a one in the spirit of meekness; con-
sidering thyself, lest thou also be tempted.
2 Bear ye one another's burdens, and so
fulfil the law of Christ. 3 For if a man
think himself to be something, when he is
nothing, he deceiveth himself. 4 But let
every man prove his own work, and then
shall he have rejoicing in himself alone,
and not in another. 5 For every man
shall bear his own burden.●

2.LAW OF REAPING

6 Let him that is taught in the word
communicate unto him that teacheth in
all good things.
7 Be not deceived; God is not mocked:
for whatsoever a man soweth, that shall
he also reap. 8 For he that soweth to his
flesh shall of the flesh reap corruption;
but he that soweth to the Spirit shall of
the Spirit reap life everlasting. 9 And let
us not be weary in well doing: for in due
season we shall reap, if we faint not.
10 As we have therefore opportunity, let
us do good unto all *men*, especially unto
them who are of the household of faith.●

—personal note

11 Ye see how large a letter I have
written unto you with mine own hand.●

3.TRUE AND FALSE VALUES

12 As many as desire to make a fair show
in the flesh, they constrain you to be circumcised; only lest they should suffer persecution for the cross of Christ. 13 For
neither they themselves who are circumcised keep the law; but desire to have you
circumcised, that they may glory in your
flesh. 14 But God forbid that I should
glory, save in the cross of our Lord Jesus
Christ, by whom the world is crucified
unto me, and I unto the world. 15 For in
Christ Jesus neither circumcision availeth
any thing, nor uncircumcision, but a new
creature. 16 And as many as walk according to this rule, peace *be* on them, and
mercy, and upon the Israel of God.●

—personal note

17 From henceforth let no man trouble
me: for I bear in my body the marks of the
Lord Jesus.●

BENEDICTION

GRACE

18 Brethren, the grace of our Lord
Jesus Christ *be* with your spirit. Amen.●

*6:1-5* What is the "law of Christ" (v.2)?

Compare verse 5 with verse 2.

*6:6-10* What is the law of reaping?

*6:12-16* Observe the references to the cross or crucifixion.
Record the different things written about this.

What is "this rule" of verse 16?

*6:17* Why does Paul write this?

*6:18* Relate this verse to the theme of Galatians.

# EPHESIANS

## AUTHORSHIP

Paul is identified as author twice in the text (1:1;3:1). Paul was around sixty-five years of age when he wrote this letter.

## DATE

The letter was written in A.D. 61, during Paul's first imprisonment in Rome. Ephesians, Philippians, Colossians and Philemon are sometimes referred to as the Prison Epistles, since they were all written during Paul's first imprisonment.

## OCCASION AND PURPOSE

The young Christians of the church at Ephesus had spiritual problems similar to those of other churches (e.g. at Colosse). But Paul does not cite specific problems in the letter. The basic need of the Christians was to grow spiritually in the Lord, by (1) an increasing awareness of their relationship to Him and His ministry to them through the Spirit, and (2) the day-to-day experience of walking in that light. The apostle was inspired to address the epistle to that need. The theme is the believer's heritage and life in Christ.

## EPHESIANS: Christ and the Church

| | |
|---|---|
| OUR HERITAGE IN CHRIST | 1:1-3:21 |
| Spiritual Blessings in Christ | 1:1-14 |
| Prayer for Spiritual Wisdom | 1:15-23 |
| Once Dead, Now Alive | 2:1-22 |
| Paul's Testimony and Prayer | 3:1-21 |
| OUR LIFE IN CHRIST | 4:1-6:24 |
| Preserving Church Unity | 4:1-16 |
| Daily Walk of Christians | 4:17-5:20 |
| Conduct in the Christian Home | 5:21-6:9 |
| The Christian's Armor | 6:10-24 |

# EPHESIANS

NEW INTERNATIONAL VERSION

Record truths or practical applications of the following verses:

1:4—chosen in Christ

1:5-6a—predestined by Jesus Christ

1:6b—favored in the Beloved

1:7-8—redeemed in Christ

1:9-10—all things gathered together in Christ

1:11-13a—given an inheritance in Christ

1:13b-14—sealed with the Holy Spirit

1 Paul, an apostle of Christ Jesus by the
will of God,
To the saints in Ephesus,[a] the faithful[b] in
Christ Jesus:
2 Grace and peace to you from God our
Father and the Lord Jesus Christ.●

*Spiritual Blessings in Christ*

3 Praise be to the God and Father of our
Lord Jesus Christ, who has blessed us in
the heavenly realms with every spiritual
blessing in Christ. 4 For he chose us in him
before the creation of the world to be holy
and blameless in his sight. In love 5 he[c]
predestined us to be adopted as his sons
through Jesus Christ, in accordance with
his pleasure and will— 6 to the praise of his
glorious grace, which he has freely given
us in the One he loves. 7 In him we have
redemption through his blood, the forgiveness of sins, in accordance with the riches
of God's grace 8 that he lavished on us with
all wisdom and understanding. 9 And he[d]
made known to us the mystery of his will
according to his good pleasure, which he
purposed in Christ, 10 to be put into effect
when the times will have reached their fulfillment—to bring all things in heaven and
on earth together under one head, even
Christ.●
11 In him we were also chosen,[e] having
been predestined according to the plan of
him who works out everything in conform-
ity with the purpose of his will, 12 in order
that we, who were the first to hope in
Christ, might be for the praise of his glory.
13 And you also were included in Christ
when you heard the word of truth, the gospel of your salvation. Having believed, you
were marked in him with a seal, the promised Holy Spirit, 14 who is a deposit guaranteeing our inheritance until the redemption
of those who are God's possession—to the
praise of his glory.●

a1 Some early manuscripts do not have *in Ephesus.*
b1 Or *believers who are*
c4,5 Or *sight in love. 5He*
d8,9 Or *us. With all wisdom and understanding, 9he*
e11 Or *were made heirs*

KING JAMES

# EPHESIANS

—salutation

**1** Paul, an apostle of Jesus Christ by the
will of God,
To the saints which are at Ephesus,
and to the faithful in Christ Jesus:
2 Grace *be* to you, and peace, from God
our Father, and *from* the Lord Jesus
Christ.●

1. ADOPTION

3 Blessed *be* the God and Father of our
Lord Jesus Christ, who hath blessed us
with all spiritual blessings in heavenly
*places* in Christ: 4 according as he hath
chosen us in him before the foundation of
the world, that we should be holy and
without blame before him in love: 5 having predestinated us unto the adoption of
children by Jesus Christ to himself, according to the good pleasure of his will,
6 to the praise of the glory of his grace,
wherein he hath made us accepted in the
beloved: 7 in whom we have redemption
through his blood, the forgiveness of sins,
according to the riches of his grace;
8 wherein he hath abounded toward us in
all wisdom and prudence; 9 having made
known unto us the mystery of his will, according to his good pleasure which he
hath purposed in himself: 10 that in the
dispensation of the fulness of times he
might gather together in one all things in
Christ, both which are in heaven, and
which are on earth; *even* in him.●

2. INHERITANCE

11 In whom also we have obtained an
inheritance, being predestinated according
to the purpose of him who worketh all
things after the counsel of his own will:
12 that we should be to the praise of his
glory, who first trusted in Christ. 13 In
whom ye also *trusted*, after that ye heard
the word of truth, the gospel of your salvation: in whom also, after that ye believed, ye were sealed with that Holy
Spirit of promise, 14 which is the earnest
of our inheritance until the redemption of
the purchased possession, unto the praise
of his glory.●

PAST AND PRESENT

The first half of this epistle is about the believer's HERITAGE IN CHRIST (chapters 1-3). This first segment reveals much about this.

*1:1-2* Observe the three different references to Jesus in this salutation.

*1:3-10* Underline the repeated key phrase "in Christ" (and similar phrases, such as "in him"). Then list the various blessings which the believer has in Christ:

FUTURE

*1:11-14* Repeat the procedure suggested above.

NEW INTERNATIONAL VERSION

What does this passage teach about:

THE EPHESIAN CHRISTIANS

PRAYER

SPIRITUAL KNOWLEDGE

POWER OF GOD

THE CHURCH

CHRIST

List spiritual applications of the passage.

*Thanksgiving and Prayer*

[15]For this reason, ever since I heard
about your faith in the Lord Jesus and your
love for all the saints, [16]I have not stopped
giving thanks for you, remembering you in
my prayers. [17]I keep asking that the God of
our Lord Jesus Christ, the glorious Father,
may give you the Spirit[f] of wisdom and
revelation, so that you may know him better. [18]I pray also that the eyes of your heart
may be enlightened in order that you may
know the hope to which he has called you,
the riches of his glorious inheritance in the
saints, [19]and his incomparably great power
for us who believe. That power is like the
working of his mighty strength, [20]which he
exerted in Christ when he raised him from
the dead and seated him at his right hand
in the heavenly realms, [21]far above all rule
and authority, power and dominion, and
every title that can be given, not only in the
present age but also in the one to come.
[22]And God placed all things under his feet
and appointed him to be head over everything for the church, [23]which is his body,
the fullness of him who fills everything in
every way.●

f17 *Or a spirit*

## KING JAMES

1.PRAYER

JESUS THE LORD

15 Wherefore I also, after I heard of
your faith in the Lord Jesus, and love unto all the saints, 16 cease not to give
thanks for you, making mention of you
in my prayers; 17 that the God of our
Lord Jesus Christ, the Father of glory,
may give unto you the spirit of wisdom
and revelation in the knowledge of him:
18 the eyes of your understanding being

2.KNOWL-EDGE

enlightened; that ye may know what is the
hope of his calling, and what the riches of
the glory of his inheritance in the saints,
19 and what *is* the exceeding greatness of

3.POWER

his power to us-ward who believe, according to the working of his mighty power,
20 which he wrought in Christ, when he
raised him from the dead, and set *him* at
his own right hand in the heavenly *places*,
21 far above all principality, and power,
and might, and dominion, and every
name that is named, not only in this
world, but also in that which is to come:
22 and hath put all *things* under his feet,
and gave him *to be* the head over all
*things* to the church, 23 which is his
body, the fulness of him that filleth all
in all.●

JESUS THE HEAD

This segment is one long sentence, and so is kept as one paragraph.
What two spiritual activities does Paul mention in verse 16?

______________________________

______________________________

What does Paul pray that God would give the saints at Ephesus (vv.17,18a)?

______________________________

______________________________

What are the three things Paul prays the saints would know (vv.18b,19)?

______________________________

______________________________

______________________________

List the different ways God's power is described (vv.19-22).

______________________________

NEW INTERNATIONAL VERSION

What do you learn here about:

SIN

SEPARATION FROM GOD

GOD'S MERCY

SALVATION

WAY OF SALVATION

WALK OF THE CHRISTIAN

OTHER

*Made Alive in Christ*

2 As for you, you were dead in your
transgressions and sins, 2in which you
used to live when you followed the ways of
this world and of the ruler of the kingdom
of the air, the spirit who is now at work in
those who are disobedient. 3All of us also
lived among them at one time, gratifying
the cravings of our sinful nature[g] and following its desires and thoughts. Like the
rest, we were by nature objects of wrath.●
4But because of his great love for us, God,
who is rich in mercy, 5made us alive with
Christ even when we were dead in transgressions—it is by grace you have been
saved. 6And God raised us up with Christ
and seated us with him in the heavenly
realms in Christ Jesus, 7in order that in the
coming ages he might show the incompara-
ble riches of his grace, expressed in his
kindness to us in Christ Jesus. 8For it is by
grace you have been saved, through
faith—and this not from yourselves, it is
the gift of God— 9not by works, so that no
one can boast. 10For we are God's workmanship, created in Christ Jesus to do
good works, which God prepared in advance for us to do.●

g3 Or *our flesh*

KING JAMES

1.PAST

2 And you *hath he quickened*, who were DEAD
dead in trespasses and sins; 2 wherein
in time past ye walked according to the
course of this world, according to the
prince of the power of the air, the spirit
that now worketh in the children of disobedience: 3 among whom also we all
had our conversation in times past in the
lusts of our flesh, fulfilling the desires of
the flesh and of the mind; and were by
nature the children of wrath, even as

2.PRESENT

others. ● 4 But God, who is rich in mercy,
for his great love wherewith he loved us,
5 even when we were dead in sins, hath
quickened us together with Christ, (by
grace ye are saved;) 6 and hath raised *us*
up together, and made *us* sit together in
heavenly *places* in Christ Jesus: 7 that in
the ages to come he might show the exceeding riches of his grace, in *his* kindness
toward us, through Christ Jesus. 8 For by
grace are ye saved through faith; and that
not of yourselves: *it is* the gift of God:
9 not of works, lest any man should boast.
10 For we are his workmanship, created
in Christ Jesus unto good works, which WALK-
God hath before ordained that we should ING
walk in them. ●

Paul's appeal in chapter 2 is that the saints would *remember* their state before conversion.

*2:1-3* Record the different phrases describing the saints' *past*.

*2:4-10* What are the first two words of the paragraph?

What do they suggest?

Record the different phrases describing the saints' *present* and *future*.

NEW INTERNATIONAL VERSION

What does this passage teach about:

GOSPEL FOR JEW AND GENTILE

RECONCILIATION

THE TRANSFORMED LIFE

THE BODY OF CHRIST

JESUS CHRIST

THE HOLY SPIRIT

OTHER

*One in Christ*

[11]Therefore, remember that formerly
you who are Gentiles by birth and called
"uncircumcised" by those who call themselves "the circumcision" (that done in the
body by the hands of men)— [12]remember
that at that time you were separate from
Christ, excluded from citizenship in Israel
and foreigners to the covenants of the
promise, without hope and without God in
the world.● [13]But now in Christ Jesus you
who once were far away have been brought
near through the blood of Christ.

[14]For he himself is our peace, who has
made the two one and has destroyed the
barrier, the dividing wall of hostility, [15]by
abolishing in his flesh the law with its commandments and regulations. His purpose
was to create in himself one new man out
of the two, thus making peace, [16]and in this
one body to reconcile both of them to God
through the cross, by which he put to death
their hostility. [17]He came and preached
peace to you who were far away and peace
to those who were near. [18]For through him
we both have access to the Father by one
Spirit.●

[19]Consequently, you are no longer foreigners and aliens, but fellow citizens with
God's people and members of God's
household, [20]built on the foundation of the
apostles and prophets, with Christ Jesus
himself as the chief cornerstone. [21]In him
the whole building is joined together and
rises to become a holy temple in the Lord.
[22]And in him you too are being built together to become a dwelling in which God
lives by his Spirit.●

KING JAMES

1. SEPARATED

11 Wherefore remember, that ye *being*
in time past Gentiles in the flesh, who are
called Uncircumcision by that which is
called the Circumcision in the flesh made
by hands; 12 that at that time ye were
without Christ, being aliens from the com-
monwealth of Israel, and strangers from
the covenants of promise, having no hope,
and without God in the world: ● 13 but
now, in Christ Jesus, ye who sometime
were far off are made nigh by the blood of
Christ. 14 For he is our peace, who hath
made both one, and hath broken down
the middle wall of partition *between us;*
15 having abolished in his flesh the enmity, *even* the law of commandments *contained* in ordinances; for to make in himself of twain one new man, *so* making
peace; 16 and that he might reconcile
both unto God in one body by the cross,
having slain the enmity thereby: 17 and
came and preached peace to you which
were afar off, and to them that were nigh.
18 For through him we both have access
by one Spirit unto the Father. ● 19 Now
therefore ye are no more strangers and
foreigners, but fellow citizens with the
saints, and of the household of God;
20 and are built upon the foundation of
the apostles and prophets, Jesus Christ
himself being the chief corner *stone;* 21 in
whom all the building fitly framed together groweth unto a holy temple in the
Lord: 22 in whom ye also are builded together for a habitation of God through
the Spirit. ●

2. RECONCILED

3. HABITATION OF GOD

WITHOUT CHRIST

IN CHRIST

*2:11-12* Note the references to Gentiles and Jews. What were the Ephesian Christians?

______________________________

How had they been alienated from:

CHRIST ______________________________

______________________________

______________________________

ISRAEL ______________________________

______________________________

______________________________

*2:13-18* What are the first two words of the paragraph?

______________________________

What does Paul write about these two reconciliations?

Ephesian Gentiles and Israel ______________________________

______________________________

______________________________

Sinners and Christ ______________________________

______________________________

______________________________

*2:19-22* What is written here about:

HOUSEHOLD ______________________________

______________________________

FOUNDATION ______________________________

______________________________

CORNER STONE ______________________________

______________________________

BUILDING ______________________________

______________________________

TEMPLE ______________________________

______________________________

______________________________

HABITATION ______________________________

______________________________

______________________________

NEW INTERNATIONAL VERSION

What do you learn here about:

MINISTER OF THE GOSPEL

RICHES OF CHRIST

GOD'S:

ETERNAL PURPOSE

SOVEREIGN WILL

GRACE

POWER

WISDOM

LOVE

*Paul the Preacher to the Gentiles*

3 For this reason I, Paul, the prisoner of
Christ Jesus for the sake of you Gentiles—
[2]Surely you have heard about the administration of God's grace that was given
to me for you, [3]that is, the mystery made
known to me by revelation, as I have already written briefly. [4]In reading this,
then, you will be able to understand my
insight into the mystery of Christ, [5]which
was not made known to men in other generations as it has now been revealed by the
Spirit to God's holy apostles and prophets.
[6]This mystery is that through the gospel the
Gentiles are heirs together with Israel,
members together of one body, and shar-
ers together in the promise in Christ Jesus.●
[7]I became a servant of this gospel by the
gift of God's grace given me through the
working of his power. [8]Although I am less
than the least of all God's people, this
grace was given me: to preach to the Gentiles the unsearchable riches of Christ,
[9]and to make plain to everyone the administration of this mystery, which for
ages past was kept hidden in God, who
created all things. [10]His intent was that
now, through the church, the manifold wisdom of God should be made known to the
rulers and authorities in the heavenly
realms, [11]according to his eternal purpose
which he accomplished in Christ Jesus our
Lord. [12]In him and through faith in him we
may approach God with freedom and confidence. [13]I ask you, therefore, not to be
discouraged because of my sufferings for
you, which are your glory.●

*A Prayer for the Ephesians*

[14]For this reason I kneel before the Father, [15]from whom his whole family[a] in
heaven and on earth derives its name. [16]I
pray that out of his glorious riches he may
strengthen you with power through his
Spirit in your inner being, [17]so that Christ
may dwell in your hearts through faith.
And I pray that you, being rooted and
established in love, [18]may have power, together with all the saints, to grasp how
wide and long and high and deep is the love
of Christ, [19]and to know this love that surpasses knowledge—that you may be filled
to the measure of all the fullness of God.●
[20]Now to him who is able to do im-
measurably more than all we ask or imagine, according to his power that is at work
within us, [21]to him be glory in the church
and in Christ Jesus throughout all generations, for ever and ever! Amen.●

[a]15 Or *whom all fatherhood*

KING JAMES

1.TESTI-
MONY

GRACE
OF GOD

3 For this cause I Paul, the prisoner of
Jesus Christ for you Gentiles, 2 if ye
have heard of the dispensation of the
grace of God which is given me to you-
ward: 3 how that by revelation he made
known unto me the mystery; (as I wrote
afore in few words; 4 whereby, when ye
read, ye may understand my knowledge
in the mystery of Christ,) 5 which in
other ages was not made known unto the
sons of men, as it is now revealed unto his
holy apostles and prophets by the Spirit;
6 that the Gentiles should be fellow
heirs, and of the same body, and partakers of his promise in Christ by the
gospel. ●
7 Whereof I was made a minister, according to the gift of the grace of God
given unto me by the effectual working of
his power. 8 Unto me, who am less than
the least of all saints, is this grace given,
that I should preach among the Gentiles
the unsearchable riches of Christ; 9 and to
make all *men* see what *is* the fellowship
of the mystery, which from the beginning
of the world hath been hid in God, who
created all things by Jesus Christ: 10 to
the intent that now unto the principalities
and powers in heavenly *places* might be
known by the church the manifold wisdom of God, 11 according to the eternal
purpose which he purposed in Christ
Jesus our Lord: 12 in whom we have
boldness and access with confidence by
the faith of him. 13 Wherefore I desire
that ye faint not at my tribulations for
you, which is your glory.●

2.PRAYER

14 For this cause I bow my knees unto
the Father of our Lord Jesus Christ, 15 of
whom the whole family in heaven and
earth is named, 16 that he would grant
you, according to the riches of his glory,
to be strengthened with might by his
Spirit in the inner man; 17 that Christ
may dwell in your hearts by faith; that ye,
being rooted and grounded in love,
18 may be able to comprehend with all
saints what *is* the breadth, and length, and
depth, and height; 19 and to know the
love of Christ, which passeth knowledge,
that ye might be filled with all the fulness
of God.●

3.DOX-
OLOGY

FULL-
NESS OF
GOD

20 Now unto him that is able to do exceeding abundantly above all that we ask
or think, according to the power that
worketh in us, 21 unto him *be* glory in the
church by Christ Jesus throughout all
ages, world without end. Amen.●

*3:1-13* Record everything Paul writes about his ministry:

*3:14-19* Record the different prayer requests of Paul:

*3:20-21* Record the strong phrases:

NEW INTERNATIONAL VERSION

What does this passage teach about:

UNITY OF BELIEVERS

TRINITY

SPIRITUAL GIFTS FOR SERVICE

BODY OF CHRIST

FALSE TEACHING

TRUTH

LOVE

*Unity in the Body of Christ*

4 As a prisoner for the Lord, then, I urge
you to live a life worthy of the calling
you have received. [2]Be completely humble
and gentle; be patient, bearing with one
another in love. [3]Make every effort to keep
the unity of the Spirit through the bond of
peace. [4]There is one body and one Spirit—
just as you were called to one hope when
you were called— [5]one Lord, one faith,
one baptism; [6]one God and Father of all,
who is over all and through all and in all.●
[7]But to each one of us grace has been
given as Christ apportioned it. [8]This is why
it[b] says:

"When he ascended on high,
he led captives in his train
and gave gifts to men."[a]

[9](What does "he ascended" mean except
that he also descended to the lower, earthly regions? [10]He who descended is the very
one who ascended higher than all the heavens, in order to fill the whole universe.) [11]It
was he who gave some to be apostles,
some to be prophets, some to be evange-
lists, and some to be pastors and teachers,
[12]to prepare God's people for works of service, so that the body of Christ may be
built up [13]until we all reach unity in the
faith and in the knowledge of the Son of
God and become mature, attaining to the
whole measure of the fullness of Christ.●
[14]Then we will no longer be infants,
tossed back and forth by the waves, and
blown here and there by every wind of
teaching and by the cunning and craftiness
of men in their deceitful scheming. [15]In-
stead, speaking the truth in love, we will in
all things grow up into him who is the
Head, that is, Christ. [16]From him the
whole body, joined and held together by
every supporting ligament, grows and
builds itself up in love, as each part does its
work.●

[b]8 Or *God*
[a]8 Psalm 68:18

KING JAMES

1. RIGHT ATTITUDES

WALK

**4** I therefore, the prisoner of the Lord,
beseech you that ye walk worthy of
the vocation wherewith ye are called,
2 with all lowliness and meekness, with
long-suffering, forbearing one another in
love; 3 endeavoring to keep the unity of
the Spirit in the bond of peace. 4 *There is*
one body, and one Spirit, even as ye are
called in one hope of your calling; 5 one
Lord, one faith, one baptism, 6 one God
and Father of all, who *is* above all, and
through all, and in you all. ● 7 But unto

2. EXERCISE OF GIFTS

every one of us is given grace according
to the measure of the gift of Christ.
8 Wherefore he saith,

> When he ascended up on high, he led
> captivity captive,
> and gave gifts unto men.

Ps. 68:18

9 (Now that he ascended, what is it but
that he also descended first into the lower
parts of the earth? 10 He that descended
is the same also that ascended up far
above all heavens, that he might fill all
things.) 11 And he gave some, apostles;
and some, prophets; and some, evange-
lists; and some, pastors and teachers;
12 for the perfecting of the saints, for the
work of the ministry, for the edifying of
the body of Christ: 13 till we all come in
the unity of the faith, and of the knowledge of the Son of God, unto a perfect
man, unto the measure of the stature of
the fulness of Christ: ● 14 that we *hence-*

3. SPEAKING TRUTH IN LOVE

*forth* be no more children, tossed to and
fro, and carried about with every wind of
doctrine, by the sleight of men, *and* cunning craftiness, whereby they lie in wait to
deceive; 15 but speaking the truth in
love, may grow up into him in all things,
which is the head, *even* Christ: 16 from
whom the whole body fitly joined together and compacted by that which every
joint supplieth, according to the effectual
working in the measure of every part,
maketh increase of the body unto the
edifying of itself in love. ●

GROW UP

At this point in his letter Paul begins to write about the Christian's *walk*. Read 4:1 to see how he introduces this practical subject.

*4:1-6* Record your observations:

ATTITUDES ____________________

CHURCH UNITY ____________________

*4:7-13* Record:

GIFTS ____________________

THEIR PURPOSES ____________________

*4:14-16* Compare verse 14 with verse 15.

____________________

What do verses 15 and 16 say about the unity of believers?

____________________

NEW INTERNATIONAL VERSION

Write a list of spiritual applications of this very practical message. Include in your list both positive and negative applications (e.g., "I should" and "I should not").

*Living as Children of Light*

17So I tell you this, and insist on it in the
Lord, that you must no longer live as the
Gentiles do, in the futility of their thinking.
18They are darkened in their understanding
and separated from the life of God because
of the ignorance that is in them due to the
hardening of their hearts. 19Having lost all
sensitivity, they have given themselves
over to sensuality so as to indulge in every
kind of impurity, with a continual lust for
more.
20You, however, did not come to know
Christ that way. 21Surely you heard of him
and were taught in him in accordance with
the truth that is in Jesus. 22You were
taught, with regard to your former way of
life, to put off your old self, which is being
corrupted by its deceitful desires; 23to be
made new in the attitude of your minds;
24and to put on the new self, created to be
like God in true righteousness and holiness.●
25Therefore each of you must put off
falsehood and speak truthfully to his neighbor, for we are all members of one body.
26"In your anger do not sin"[b]: Do not let
the sun go down while you are still angry,
27and do not give the devil a foothold. 28He
who has been stealing must steal no longer,
but must work, doing something useful
with his own hands, that he may have
something to share with those in need.
29Do not let any unwholesome talk come
out of your mouths, but only what is helpful for building others up according to their
needs, that it may benefit those who listen.
30And do not grieve the Holy Spirit of God,
with whom you were sealed for the day of
redemption. 31Get rid of all bitterness, rage
and anger, brawling and slander, along
with every form of malice. 32Be kind and
compassionate to one another, forgiving
each other, just as in Christ God forgave
you.●

5 Be imitators of God, therefore, as dearly loved children 2and live a life of love,
just as Christ loved us and gave himself up
for us as a fragrant offering and sacrifice to
God.●

[b]26 Psalm 4:4

## KING JAMES

**1. NEW MAN**

VANITY

17 This I say therefore, and testify in the
Lord, that ye henceforth walk not as other
Gentiles walk, in the vanity of their mind,
18 having the understanding darkened,
being alienated from the life of God
through the ignorance that is in them, because of the blindness of their heart:
19 who being past feeling have given
themselves over unto lasciviousness, to
work all uncleanness with greediness.
20 But ye have not so learned Christ;
21 if so be that ye have heard him, and
have been taught by him, as the truth is in
Jesus: 22 that ye put off concerning the
former conversation the old man, which
is corrupt according to the deceitful lusts;
23 and be renewed in the spirit of your
mind; 24 and that ye put on the new
man, which after God is created in righteousness and true holiness. ●

**2. NEW WALK**

25 Wherefore putting away lying, speak
every man truth with his neighbor: for we
are members one of another. 26 Be ye
angry, and sin not: let not the sun go
down upon your wrath: 27 neither give
place to the devil. 28 Let him that stole
steal no more: but rather let him labor,
working with *his* hands the thing which is
good, that he may have to give to him
that needeth. 29 Let no corrupt communication proceed out of your mouth,
but that which is good to the use of edifying, that it may minister grace unto the
hearers. 30 And grieve not the Holy
Spirit of God, whereby ye are sealed unto
the day of redemption. 31 Let all bitterness, and wrath, and anger, and clamor,
and evil speaking, be put away from you,
with all malice: 32 and be ye kind one to
another, tender-hearted, forgiving one
another, even as God for Christ's sake
hath forgiven you. ●

**3. FOLLOWERS OF GOD**

5 Be ye therefore followers of God, as
dear children; 2 and walk in love, as
Christ also hath loved us, and hath given
himself for us an offering and a sacrifice
to God for a sweetsmelling savor. ●

LOVE

*4:17-24* What is contrasted in the paragraph?

Record the descriptions:

OLD MAN

NEW MAN

*4:25-32* Record the different commands of Christian living:

*5:1-2* Record your observations:

NEW INTERNATIONAL VERSION

Record what is taught here about:

IMPURITY

KINGDOM OF CHRIST

FRUIT OF THE SPIRIT

WORKS OF DARKNESS

WILL OF GOD

FULLNESS OF THE SPIRIT

SONG

THANKSGIVING

[3]But among you there must not be even
a hint of sexual immorality, or of any kind
of impurity, or of greed, because these are
improper for God's holy people. [4]Nor
should there be obscenity, foolish talk or
coarse joking, which are out of place, but
rather thanksgiving. [5]For of this you can be
sure: No immoral, impure or greedy person—such a man is an idolater—has any
inheritance in the kingdom of Christ and of
God.[c] [6]Let no one deceive you with empty
words, for because of such things God's
wrath comes on those who are disobedient. [7]Therefore do not be partners with
them.

[8]For you were once darkness, but now
you are light in the Lord. Live as children
of light [9](for the fruit of the light consists in
all goodness, righteousness and truth)
[10]and find out what pleases the Lord.
[11]Have nothing to do with the fruitless
deeds of darkness, but rather expose them.
[12]For it is shameful even to mention what
the disobedient do in secret. [13]But everything exposed by the light becomes visible,
[14]for it is light that makes everything visible. This is why it is said:

"Wake up, O sleeper,
rise from the dead,
and Christ will shine on you."

[15]Be very careful, then, how you live—
not as unwise but as wise, [16]making the
most of every opportunity, because the
days are evil. [17]Therefore do not be foolish, but understand what the Lord's will is.
[18]Do not get drunk on wine, which leads to
debauchery. Instead, be filled with the
Spirit. [19]Speak to one another with psalms,
hymns and spiritual songs. Sing and make
music in your heart to the Lord, [20]always
giving thanks to God the Father for everything, in the name of our Lord Jesus Christ.

[c]5 Or *kingdom of the Christ and God*

## KING JAMES

1. IN PURITY

3 But fornication, and all uncleanness,
or covetousness, let it not be once named
among you, as becometh saints; 4 neither
filthiness, nor foolish talking, nor jesting,
which are not convenient: but rather giving of thanks. 5 For this ye know, that no
whoremonger, nor unclean person, nor
covetous man, who is an idolater, hath
any inheritance in the kingdom of Christ
and of God.● 6 Let no man deceive you

2. IN LIGHT

with vain words: for because of these
things cometh the wrath of God upon the
children of disobedience. 7 Be not ye
therefore partakers with them. 8 For ye
were sometime darkness, but now *are*
*ye* light in the Lord: walk as children of
light; 9 (for the fruit of the Spirit *is* in all
goodness and righteousness and truth;)
10 proving what is acceptable unto the
Lord. 11 And have no fellowship with the
unfruitful works of darkness, but rather
reprove *them.* 12 For it is a shame even
to speak of those things which are done of
them in secret. 13 But all things that are
reproved are made manifest by the light:
for whatsoever doth make manifest is
light. 14 Wherefore he saith,

Awake thou that sleepest,
and arise from the dead,
and Christ shall give thee light.●

3. IN WISDOM

15 See then that ye walk circumspectly,
not as fools, but as wise, 16 redeeming
the time, because the days are evil.
17 Wherefore be ye not unwise, but understanding what the will of the Lord *is.*
18 And be not drunk with wine, wherein
is excess; but be filled with the Spirit;
19 speaking to yourselves in psalms and
hymns and spiritual songs, singing and
making melody in your heart to the Lord;
20 giving thanks always for all things unto
God and the Father in the name of our
Lord Jesus Christ; ●

ABSTINENCE ALWAYS

Isa. 26:19

THANKS ALWAYS

*5:3-5* Record the three lists of sins.

What is written at the end of each list?

*5:6-14* Underline the repeated contrasting words "light" and "darkness."
Record the commands of the paragraph.

*5:15-20* Note the references to the three persons of the Trinity.
Record the commands.

NEW INTERNATIONAL VERSION

Make a list of practical applications of this passage to the home of today.

Make a list of all the things taught about Christ.

21Submit to one another out of reverence
for Christ.

*Wives and Husbands*

22Wives, submit to your husbands as to
the Lord. 23For the husband is the head of
the wife as Christ is the head of the church,
his body, of which he is the Savior. 24Now
as the church submits to Christ, so also
wives should submit to their husbands in
everything.●

25Husbands, love your wives, just as
Christ loved the church and gave himself
up for her 26to make her holy, cleansing[a]
her by the washing with water through the
word, 27and to present her to himself as a
radiant church, without stain or wrinkle or
any other blemish, but holy and blameless.
28In this same way, husbands ought to love
their wives as their own bodies. He who
loves his wife loves himself. 29After all, no
one ever hated his own body, but he feeds
and cares for it, just as Christ does the
church— 30for we are members of his
body. 31"For this reason a man will leave
his father and mother and be united to his
wife, and the two will become one flesh."[b]
32This is a profound mystery—but I am
talking about Christ and the church.
33However, each one of you also must love
his wife as he loves himself, and the wife
must respect her husband.●

*Children and Parents*

6 Children, obey your parents in the
Lord, for this is right. 2"Honor your
father and mother"—which is the first
commandment with a promise— 3"that it
may go well with you and that you may
enjoy long life on the earth."[c]●

4Fathers, do not exasperate your children; instead, bring them up in the training
and instruction of the Lord.●

*Slaves and Masters*

5Slaves, obey your earthly masters with
respect and fear, and with sincerity of
heart, just as you would obey Christ.
6Obey them not only to win their favor
when their eye is on you, but like slaves of
Christ, doing the will of God from your
heart. 7Serve wholeheartedly, as if you
were serving the Lord, not men, 8because
you know that the Lord will reward everyone for whatever good he does, whether he
is slave or free.●

9And masters, treat your slaves in the
same way. Do not threaten them, since you
know that he who is both their Master and
yours is in heaven, and there is no favoritism with him.●

[a]26 Or *having cleansed* [b]31 Gen. 2:24 [c]3 Deut. 5:16

KING JAMES

1.WIVES

FEAR OF GOD

21 submitting your-
selves one to another in the fear of God.
22 Wives, submit yourselves unto your
own husbands, as unto the Lord. 23 For
the husband is the head of the wife, even
as Christ is the head of the church: and he
is the saviour of the body. 24 Therefore
as the church is subject unto Christ, so *let*
the wives *be* to their own husbands in
every thing. ●

2.HUS-BANDS

25 Husbands, love your
wives, even as Christ also loved the
church, and gave himself for it; 26 that
he might sanctify and cleanse it with the
washing of water by the word, 27 that he
might present it to himself a glorious
church, not having spot, or wrinkle, or
any such thing; but that it should be holy
and without blemish. 28 So ought men to
love their wives as their own bodies. He
that loveth his wife loveth himself.
29 For no man ever yet hated his own
flesh; but nourisheth and cherisheth it,
even as the Lord the church: 30 for we
are members of his body, of his flesh, and
of his bones. 31 For this cause shall a
man leave his father and mother, and
shall be joined unto his wife, and they two
shall be one flesh. 32 This is a great
mystery: but I speak concerning Christ
and the church. 33 Nevertheless, let every
one of you in particular so love his wife
even as himself; and the wife *see* that she
reverence *her* husband. ●

3.CHIL-DREN

6 Children, obey your parents in the
Lord: for this is right. 2 Honor thy
father and mother; which is the first commandment with promise; 3 that it may
be well with thee, and thou mayest live
long on the earth. ●

4.FATHERS

4 And, ye fathers,
provoke not your children to wrath: but
bring them up in the nurture and admonition of the Lord. ●

5.SERVANTS

5 Servants, be obedient to them that are
*your* masters according to the flesh, with
fear and trembling, in singleness of your
heart, as unto Christ; 6 not with eyeservice, as menpleasers; but as the servants of Christ, doing the will of God from
the heart; 7 with good will doing service,
as to the Lord, and not to men: 8 knowing that whatsoever good thing any man
doeth, the same shall he receive of the
Lord, whether *he be* bond or free. ●

6.MASTERS

9 And, ye masters, do the same things unto them, forbearing threatening: knowing
that your Master also is in heaven; neither is there respect of persons with him. ●

MASTER IN HEAVEN

What does verse 21 teach? ______

Keep this in mind as you study the entire segment.
Record commands, reasons for keeping the commands, references to Christ, and rewards for each of the paragraphs:

*5:21-24* ______

*5:25-33* ______

*6:1-3* ______

*6:4* ______

*6:5-8* ______

*6:9* ______

NEW INTERNATIONAL VERSION

What do you learn here about:

SPIRITUAL WARFARE

ARMOR AND STRENGTH OF THE CHRISTIAN

PRAYER

INTERCESSION

LOVE FOR THE BRETHREN

*The Armor of God*

[10]Finally, be strong in the Lord and in his mighty power. [11]Put on the full armor of God so that you can take your stand against the devil's schemes. [12]For our struggle is not against flesh and blood, but against the rulers, against the authorities, against the powers of this dark world and against the spiritual forces of evil in the heavenly realms. [13]Therefore put on the full armor of God, so that when the day of evil comes, you may be able to stand your ground, and after you have done everything, to stand.● [14]Stand firm then, with the belt of truth buckled around your waist, with the breastplate of righteousness in place, [15]and with your feet fitted with the readiness that comes from the gospel of peace. [16]In addition to all this, take up the shield of faith, with which you can extinguish all the flaming arrows of the evil one. [17]Take the helmet of salvation and the sword of the Spirit, which is the word of God.● [18]And pray in the Spirit on all occasions with all kinds of prayers and requests. With this in mind, be alert and always keep on praying for all the saints.

[19]Pray also for me, that whenever I open my mouth, words may be given me so that I will fearlessly make known the mystery of the gospel, [20]for which I am an ambassador in chains. Pray that I may declare it fearlessly, as I should.●

*Final Greetings*

[21]Tychicus, the dear brother and faithful servant in the Lord, will tell you everything, so that you also may know how I am and what I am doing. [22]I am sending him to you for this very purpose, that you may know how we are, and that he may encourage you.●

[23]Peace to the brothers, and love with faith from God the Father and the Lord Jesus Christ. [24]Grace to all who love our Lord Jesus Christ with an undying love.●

KING JAMES

1. ENEMY

STRENGTH

10 Finally, my brethren, be strong in
the Lord, and in the power of his might.
11 Put on the whole armor of God, that
ye may be able to stand against the wiles
of the devil. 12 For we wrestle not against
flesh and blood, but against principalities,
against powers, against the rulers of the
darkness of this world, against spiritual
wickedness in high *places*. 13 Wherefore
take unto you the whole armor of God,
that ye may be able to withstand in the
evil day, and having done all, to stand. ●

2. ARMOR

14 Stand therefore, having your loins girt
about with truth, and having on the
breastplate of righteousness; 15 and
your feet shod with the preparation of the
gospel of peace; 16 above all, taking the
shield of faith, wherewith ye shall be able
to quench all the fiery darts of the wicked.
17 And take the helmet of salvation, and
the sword of the Spirit, which is the word
of God: ●

3. PRAYER

18 praying always with all prayer
and supplication in the Spirit, and watching
thereunto with all perseverance and
supplication for all saints; 19 and for me,
that utterance may be given unto me, that
I may open my mouth boldly, to make
known the mystery of the gospel, 20 for
which I am an ambassador in bonds; that
therein I may speak boldly, as I ought to
speak. ●

BOLDNESS

—personal note

21 But that ye also may know my affairs,
*and* how I do, Tych'icus, a beloved
brother and faithful minister in the Lord,
shall make known to you all things:
22 whom I have sent unto you for the
same purpose, that ye might know our
affairs, and *that* he might comfort your
hearts. ●

BENEDICTION

23 Peace *be* to the brethren, and love
with faith, from God the Father and the
Lord Jesus Christ. 24 Grace *be* with all
them that love our Lord Jesus Christ in
sincerity. Amen. ●

*6:10-13* Record the comments.

Record the enemies cited in verse 12.

*6:14-17* Record each piece of armor and what it symbolizes:

*6:18-20* Record the different references to prayer.

*6:21-22* Compare the two purposes given in verse 22.

*6:23-24* List five Christian attributes cited here.

# PHILIPPIANS

## AUTHORSHIP

Paul was the author of this Epistle. He names his colaborer Timothy in the salutation of 1:1 because Timothy was with him when he wrote the letter, joining in the sentiments expressed.

## DATE

Paul wrote this letter around A.D. 61-62 from his prison quarters at Rome.

## PURPOSE AND THEME

Three of Paul's purposes in writing were: 1) to encourage the saints to put Christ first in everyday living; 2) to urge them to correct spiritual problems; 3) to instruct in Christian doctrines. One of the main subjects of the letter is the abiding joy of living in Christ.

## PHILIPPIANS: Life in Christ

| | |
|---|---|
| Salutation | 1:1-2 |
| CHRIST OUR LIFE | 1:3-26 |
| CHRIST OUR PATTERN | 1:27-2:30 |
| CHRIST OUR GOAL | 3:1-4:1 |
| CHRIST OUR SUFFICIENCY | 4:2-20 |
| Greetings and Benediction | 4:21-23 |

# PHILIPPIANS

NEW INTERNATIONAL VERSION

What does this passage teach about:

SERVANTS OF CHRIST

THANKSGIVING

INTERCESSION FOR OTHER CHRISTIANS

PRAYER

DAY OF JESUS CHRIST

LOVE FOR THE BRETHREN

CHRISTIAN LIVING

OTHER

1 Paul and Timothy, servants of Christ
Jesus,
To all the saints in Christ Jesus at
Philippi, together with the overseers[a] and
deacons:
2Grace and peace to you from God our
Father and the Lord Jesus Christ.●

*Thanksgiving and Prayer*

3I thank my God every time I remember
you. 4In all my prayers for all of you, I
always pray with joy 5because of your part-
nership in the gospel from the first day until
now, 6being confident of this, that he who
began a good work in you will carry it on
to completion until the day of Christ Jesus.
7It is right for me to feel this way about
all of you, since I have you in my heart; for
whether I am in chains or defending and
confirming the gospel, all of you share in
God's grace with me. 8God can testify how
I long for all of you with the affection of
Christ Jesus.●
9And this is my prayer: that your love
may abound more and more in knowledge
and depth of insight, 10so that you may be
able to discern what is best and may be
pure and blameless until the day of Christ,
11filled with the fruit of righteousness that
comes through Jesus Christ—to the glory
and praise of God.●

[a]1 Traditionally *bishops*

KING JAMES

# PHILIPPIANS

—salutation

1 Paul and Timothy, the servants of
Jesus Christ,
To all the saints in Christ Jesus which
are at Phil'ippi, with the bishops and
deacons:
2 Grace *be* unto you, and peace, from
God our Father and *from* the Lord Jesus
Christ.●

1. THANKSGIVING

3 I thank my God upon every remembrance of you, 4 always in every prayer
of mine for you all making request with
joy, 5 for your fellowship in the gospel
from the first day until now; 6 being confident of this very thing, that he which
hath begun a good work in you will perform *it* until the day of Jesus Christ:
7 even as it is meet for me to think this of
you all, because I have you in my heart;
inasmuch as both in my bonds, and in the
defense and confirmation of the gospel, ye
all are partakers of my grace. 8 For God
is my record, how greatly I long after you
all in the bowels of Jesus Christ.●

2. PRAYER

9 And
this I pray, that your love may abound yet
more and more in knowledge and *in* all
judgment; 10 that ye may approve things
that are excellent; that ye may be sincere
and without offense till the day of Christ;
11 being filled with the fruits of righteousness, which are by Jesus Christ, unto the
glory and praise of God.●

PEACE FROM GOD

PRAISE OF GOD

Philippians is an epistle of joy. Observe the bright note of this opening segment.

*1:1-2* Compare "servants of Jesus Christ" and "saints in Christ Jesus."

______

How does Paul identify himself with Timothy?

______

*1:3-8* What are the main points of the paragraph?

______

*1:9-11* What are the four things which Paul prayed for?

v.9 ______

v.10a ______

v.10b ______

v.11 ______

NEW INTERNATIONAL VERSION

What do you learn here about:

PERSECUTION

GOSPEL

MOTIVES IN CHRISTIAN SERVICE

CHRIST MAGNIFIED

PRAYER

DEATH FOR THE CHRISTIAN

List practical applications of the passage.

*Paul's Chains Advance the Gospel*

12Now I want you to know, brothers,
that what has happened to me has really
served to advance the gospel. 13As a result,
it has become clear throughout the whole
palace guard[b] and to everyone else that I
am in chains for Christ. 14Because of my
chains, most of the brothers in the Lord
have been encouraged to speak the word of
God more courageously and fearlessly.●
15It is true that some preach Christ out of
envy and rivalry, but others out of good
will. 16The latter do so in love, knowing
that I am put here for the defense of the
gospel. 17The former preach Christ out of
selfish ambition, not sincerely, supposing
that they can stir up trouble for me while
I am in chains. 18But what does it matter?
The important thing is that in every way,
whether from false motives or true, Christ
is preached. And because of this I rejoice.
Yes, and I will continue to rejoice,● 19for
I know that through your prayers and the
help given by the Spirit of Jesus Christ,
what has happened to me will turn out for
my deliverance.[c] 20I eagerly expect and
hope that I will in no way be ashamed, but
will have sufficient courage so that now as
always Christ will be exalted in my body,
whether by life or by death.● 21For to me, to
live is Christ and to die is gain. 22If I am to
go on living in the body, this will mean
fruitful labor for me. Yet what shall I
choose? I do not know! 23I am torn between the two: I desire to depart and be
with Christ, which is better by far; 24but it
is more necessary for you that I remain in
the body. 25Convinced of this, I know that
I will remain, and I will continue with all of
you for your progress and joy in the faith,
26so that through my being with you again
your joy in Christ Jesus will overflow on
account of me.●

[b]13 Or *whole palace* [c]19 Or *salvation*

## KING JAMES

1.BONDS

BOUND

12 But I would ye should understand,
brethren, that the things *which happened*
unto me have fallen out rather unto the
furtherance of the gospel; 13 so that my
bonds in Christ are manifest in all the
palace, and in all other *places;* 14 and
many of the brethren in the Lord, wax-
ing confident by my bonds, are much
more bold to speak the word without
fear.●

2.PREACH-
ING

15 Some indeed preach Christ even of
envy and strife; and some also of good
will: 16 the one preach Christ of contention, not sincerely, supposing to add
affliction to my bonds: 17 but the other of
love, knowing that I am set for the defense
of the gospel. 18 What then? notwithstanding, every way, whether in pretense,

3.PRAYER

or in truth, Christ is preached;● and
I therein do rejoice, yea, and will rejoice.
19 For I know that this shall turn to my
salvation through your prayer, and the
supply of the Spirit of Jesus Christ,
20 according to my earnest expectation
and *my* hope, that in nothing I shall be
ashamed, but *that* with all boldness, as
always, *so* now also Christ shall be magnified in my body, whether *it be* by life, or

4.LABOR

by death.● 21 For to me to live *is* Christ,
and to die *is* gain. 22 But if I live in the
flesh, this *is* the fruit of my labor: yet
what I shall choose I wot not. 23 For I
am in a strait betwixt two, having a desire
to depart, and to be with Christ; which is
far better: 24 nevertheless to abide in the
flesh *is* more needful for you. 25 And
having this confidence, I know that I shall
abide and continue with you all for your
furtherance and joy of faith; 26 that your
rejoicing may be more abundant in Jesus
Christ for me by my coming to you
again.●

FREE
AGAIN

*1:12-14* What does Paul write about bonds?

What does Paul write about Christ?

*1:15-18a* Record what is written about preaching in each verse:

v.15

v.16

v.17

v.18a

*1:18b-20* What does Paul write here about Christ?

*1:21-26* Compare the phrases "far better" and "more needful." Who is the beneficiary in each case?

What is written in this paragraph about Christ?

NEW INTERNATIONAL VERSION

What does this passage teach about:

PERSECUTION

JOY

LOVE

SERVING OTHERS

HUMILIATION

EXALTATION OF CHRIST

WORK AND WORKS

BLAMELESS CHRISTIAN LIVING

27 Whatever happens, conduct yourselves in a manner worthy of the gospel of
Christ. Then, whether I come and see you
or only hear about you in my absence, I
will know that you stand firm in one spirit,
contending as one man for the faith of the
gospel 28 without being frightened in any
way by those who oppose you. This is a
sign to them that they will be destroyed,
but that you will be saved—and that by
God. 29 For it has been granted to you on
behalf of Christ not only to believe on him,
but also to suffer for him, 30 since you are
going through the same struggle you saw I
had, and now hear that I still have.●

*Imitating Christ's Humility*

2 If you have any encouragement from
being united with Christ, if any comfort
from his love, if any fellowship with the
Spirit, if any tenderness and compassion,
2 then make my joy complete by being likeminded, having the same love, being one in
spirit and purpose. 3 Do nothing out of selfish ambition or vain conceit, but in humility consider others better than yourselves.
4 Each of you should look not only to your
own interests, but also to the interests of
others.●
5 Your attitude should be the same as that
of Christ Jesus:

6 Who, being in very nature[a] God,
did not consider equality with
God something to be grasped,
7 but made himself nothing,
taking the very nature[b] of a
servant,
being made in human likeness.
8 And being found in appearance as a
man,
he humbled himself
and became obedient to death—
even death on a cross!
9 Therefore God exalted him to the
highest place
and gave him the name that is
above every name,
10 that at the name of Jesus every
knee should bow,
in heaven and on earth and under
the earth,
11 and every tongue confess that Jesus
Christ is Lord,
to the glory of God the Father.●

*Shining as Stars*

12 Therefore, my dear friends, as you
have always obeyed—not only in my presence, but now much more in my absence—
continue to work out your salvation with
fear and trembling, 13 for it is God who
works in you to will and to act according to
his good purpose.●
14 Do everything without complaining or
arguing, 15 so that you may become blameless and pure, children of God without fault
in a crooked and depraved generation, in
which you shine like stars in the universe
16 as you hold out[c] the word of life—in order that I may boast on the day of Christ
that I did not run or labor for nothing. 17 But
even if I am being poured out like a drink
offering on the sacrifice and service coming from your faith, I am glad and rejoice
with all of you. 18 So you too should be glad
and rejoice with me.●

[a] 6 Or *in the form of* [b] 7 Or *the form* [c] 16 Or *hold on to*

## KING JAMES

1.SAME CONFLICT

27 Only let your conversation be as
it becometh the gospel of Christ: that
whether I come and see you, or else be
absent, I may hear of your affairs, that ye
stand fast in one spirit, with one mind
striving together for the faith of the gospel; 28 and in nothing terrified by your
adversaries: which is to them an evident
token of perdition, but to you of salvation,
and that of God. 29 For unto you it is
given in the behalf of Christ, not only to
believe on him, but also to suffer for his
sake; 30 having the same conflict which
ye saw in me, and now hear *to be* in
me.●

GLAD TIDINGS

2.SAME LOVE

2 If *there be* therefore any consolation
in Christ, if any comfort of love, if any
fellowship of the Spirit, if any bowels and
mercies, 2 fulfil ye my joy, that ye be likeminded, having the same love, *being* of
one accord, of one mind. 3 *Let* nothing
*be done* through strife or vainglory; but in
lowliness of mind let each esteem other
better than themselves. 4 Look not every
man on his own things, but every man also
on the things of others. ●

3.SAME MIND

5 Let this mind
be in you, which was also in Christ Jesus:
6 who, being in the form of God, thought
it not robbery to be equal with God:
7 but made himself of no reputation, and
took upon him the form of a servant, and
was made in the likeness of men: 8 and being found in fashion as a man, he humbled himself, and became obedient unto
death, even the death of the cross.
9 Wherefore God also hath highly exalted
him, and given him a name which is above
every name: 10 that at the name of Jesus
every knee should bow, of *things* in
heaven, and *things* in earth, and *things*
under the earth; 11 and *that* every tongue
should confess that Jesus Christ *is* Lord,
to the glory of God the Father.●

4.SAME GOD

12 Wherefore, my beloved, as ye have
always obeyed, not as in my presence only,
but now much more in my absence, work
out your own salvation with fear and
trembling: 13 for it is God which worketh
in you both to will and to do of *his* good
pleasure.●

5.SAME JOY

14 Do all things without murmurings
and disputings: 15 that ye may be blameless and harmless, the sons of God, without rebuke, in the midst of a crooked and
perverse nation, among whom ye shine
as lights in the world; 16 holding forth
the word of life; that I may rejoice in the
day of Christ, that I have not run in vain,
neither labored in vain. 17 Yea, and if I
be offered upon the sacrifice and service
of your faith, I joy, and rejoice with you
all. 18 For the same cause also do ye joy,
and rejoice with me.●

JOY

First read 2:5, which suggests the title "Christ Our Pattern."

*1:27-30* What is written here about the Philippian saints?

*2:1-4* Record the commands:

*2:5-11* What is written about:

CHRIST

THE FATHER

ALL CREATURES

*2:12-13* Compare the two references to "work."

*2:14-18* Record:

REFERENCES TO JOY

CAUSES OF REJOICING

NEW INTERNATIONAL VERSION

Record what you learn here about:

CHRIST-CENTERED LIVES

COMPASSION FOR OTHERS

CHRISTIAN SERVICE

CHRISTIAN JOY

List other spiritual applications:

*Timothy and Epaphroditus*

19I hope in the Lord Jesus to send Timothy to you soon, that I also may be cheered
when I receive news about you. 20I have no
one else like him, who takes a genuine interest in your welfare. 21For everyone
looks out for his own interests, not those of
Jesus Christ. 22But you know that Timothy
has proved himself, because as a son with
his father he has served with me in the
work of the gospel. 23I hope, therefore, to
send him as soon as I see how things go
with me. 24And I am confident in the Lord
that I myself will come soon.●
25But I think it is necessary to send back
to you Epaphroditus, my brother, fellow
worker and fellow soldier, who is also your
messenger, whom you sent to take care of
my needs. 26For he longs for all of you and
is distressed because you heard he was ill.
27Indeed he was ill, and almost died. But
God had mercy on him, and not on him
only but also on me, to spare me sorrow
upon sorrow. 28Therefore I am all the more
eager to send him, so that when you see
him again you may be glad and I may have
less anxiety. 29Welcome him in the Lord
with great joy, and honor men like him,
30because he almost died for the work of
Christ, risking his life to make up for the
help you could not give me.●

KING JAMES

1.TIMOTHY

19 But I trust in the Lord Jesus to send
Timothy shortly unto you, that I also
may be of good comfort, when I know
your state. 20 For I have no man likeminded, who will naturally care for your
state. 21 For all seek their own, not the
things which are Jesus Christ's. 22 But
ye know the proof of him, that, as a son
with the father, he hath served with me in
the gospel. 23 Him therefore I hope to
send presently, so soon as I shall see how
it will go with me. 24 But I trust in the
Lord that I also myself shall come shortly.●

COM-FORT

2.EPAPHRODITUS

25 Yet I supposed it necessary to send
to you Epaphrodi'tus, my brother, and
companion in labor, and fellow soldier,
but your messenger, and he that ministered to my wants. 26 For he longed after
you all, and was full of heaviness, because
that ye had heard that he had been sick.
27 For indeed he was sick nigh unto
death: but God had mercy on him; and
not on him only, but on me also, lest I
should have sorrow upon sorrow. 28 I
sent him therefore the more carefully,
that, when ye see him again, ye may rejoice, and that I may be the less sorrowful. 29 Receive him therefore in the Lord
with all gladness; and hold such in reputation: 30 because for the work of Christ
he was nigh unto death, not regarding his
life, to supply your lack of service toward
me.●

SERVICE

Read the two paragraphs. What is common to both? ______

What is different? ______

Note that this segment concludes the section 1:27—2:30.

*2:19-24* Record what is known about each of the following from this paragraph that follows:

TIMOTHY ______

PAUL ______

PHILIPPIAN SAINTS ______

*2:25-30* EPAPHRODITUS ______

What are Paul's requests to the Philippians? ______

NEW INTERNATIONAL VERSION

What does this passage teach about:

FALSE RIGHTEOUSNESS

MOTIVES AND GOALS

FELLOWSHIP WITH CHRIST

RETURN OF CHRIST

RESURRECTION BODY OF THE SAINTS

*No Confidence in the Flesh*

3 Finally, my brothers, rejoice in the
Lord! It is no trouble for me to write
the same things to you again, and it is a
safeguard for you.
[2]Watch out for those dogs, those men
who do evil, those mutilators of the flesh.
[3]For it is we who are the circumcision, we
who worship by the Spirit of God, who
glory in Christ Jesus, and who put no confidence in the flesh● [4]though I myself have
reasons for such confidence.
If anyone else thinks he has reasons to
put confidence in the flesh, I have more:
[5]circumcised on the eighth day, of the
people of Israel, of the tribe of Benjamin,
a Hebrew of Hebrews; in regard to the law,
a Pharisee; [6]as for zeal, persecuting the
church; as for legalistic righteousness,
faultless.●
[7]But whatever was to my profit I now
consider loss for the sake of Christ. [8]What
is more, I consider everything a loss compared to the surpassing greatness of knowing Christ Jesus my Lord, for whose sake
I have lost all things. I consider them rub-
bish, that I may gain Christ [9]and be found
in him, not having a righteousness of my
own that comes from the law, but that
which is through faith in Christ—the righteousness that comes from God and is by
faith. [10]I want to know Christ and the
power of his resurrection and the fellowship of sharing in his sufferings, becoming
like him in his death, [11]and so, somehow,
to attain to the resurrection from the dead.

*Pressing on Toward the Goal*

[12]Not that I have already obtained all
this, or have already been made perfect,
but I press on to take hold of that for which
Christ Jesus took hold of me. [13]Brothers, I
do not consider myself yet to have taken
hold of it. But one thing I do: Forgetting
what is behind and straining toward what
is ahead, [14]I press on toward the goal to win
the prize for which God has called me
heavenward in Christ Jesus.●
[15]All of us who are mature should take
such a view of things. And if on some point
you think differently, that too God will
make clear to you. [16]Only let us live up to
what we have already attained.
[17]Join with others in following my example, brothers, and take note of those who
live according to the pattern we gave you.
[18]For, as I have often told you before and
now say again even with tears, many live
as enemies of the cross of Christ. [19]Their
destiny is destruction, their god is their
stomach, and their glory is in their shame.
Their mind is on earthly things.● [20]But our
citizenship is in heaven. And we eagerly
await a Savior from there, the Lord Jesus
Christ, [21]who, by the power that enables
him to bring everything under his control,
will transform our lowly bodies so that
they will be like his glorious body.
4 Therefore, my brothers, you whom I
love and long for, my joy and crown,
that is how you should stand firm in the
Lord, dear friends!●

## KING JAMES

1.COMMANDS

REJOICE

**3** Finally, my brethren, rejoice in the
Lord. To write the same things to
you, to me indeed *is* not grievous, but for
you *it is* safe.
2 Beware of dogs, beware of evil workers, beware of the concision. 3 For we are
the circumcision, which worship God in
the spirit, and rejoice in Christ Jesus, and
have no confidence in the flesh.● 4 Though

2.TESTIMONIES

I might also have confidence in the flesh.
If any other man thinketh that he hath
whereof he might trust in the flesh, I more:
5 circumcised the eighth day, of the stock
of Israel, *of* the tribe of Benjamin, a
Hebrew of the Hebrews; as touching the
law, a Pharisee; 6 concerning zeal, persecuting the church; touching the righteousness which is in the law, blameless.●
7 But what things were gain to me, those
I counted loss for Christ. 8 Yea doubtless, and I count all things *but* loss for the
excellency of the knowledge of Christ
Jesus my Lord: for whom I have suffered
the loss of all things, and do count them
*but* dung, that I may win Christ, 9 and be
found in him, not having mine own righteousness, which is of the law, but that
which is through the faith of Christ, the
righteousness which is of God by faith:
10 that I may know him, and the power
of his resurrection, and the fellowship of
his sufferings, being made conformable
unto his death; 11 if by any means I
might attain unto the resurrection of the
dead.
12 Not as though I had already attained, either were already perfect: but I
follow after, if that I may apprehend that
for which also I am apprehended of Christ
Jesus. 13 Brethren, I count not myself to
have apprehended: but *this* one thing *I do*,
forgetting those things which are behind,
and reaching forth unto those things
which are before, 14 I press toward the
mark for the prize of the high calling of

3.APPEALS

God in Christ Jesus. ● 15 Let us therefore,
as many as be perfect, be thus minded:
and if in any thing ye be otherwise minded,
God shall reveal even this unto you.
16 Nevertheless, whereto we have already
attained, let us walk by the same rule, let
us mind the same thing.
17 Brethren, be followers together of
me, and mark them which walk so as ye
have us for an ensample. 18 (For many
walk, of whom I have told you often, and
now tell you even weeping, *that they are*
the enemies of the cross of Christ:
19 whose end *is* destruction, whose God
*is their* belly, and *whose* glory *is* in their
shame, who mind earthly things.) ● 20 For
our conversation is in heaven; from
whence also we look for the Saviour, the
Lord Jesus Christ: 21 who shall change
our vile body, that it may be fashioned
like unto his glorious body, according to
the working whereby he is able even to
subdue all things unto himself.

STAND FAST

**4** Therefore, my brethren dearly beloved and longed for, my joy and
crown, so stand fast in the Lord, *my*
dearly beloved.●

*3:1-3* Compare the command of verse 1 with that of verse 2.

*3:4-6* What is the point of the paragraph?

Compare this with the last phrase of verse 3 and the first of verse 7.

*3:7-14* Record the different phrases introduced by "that I may."

Record the different references to Christ.

*3:15-19* Record the commands and exhortations.

*3:20—4:1* Relate 4:1 to 3:20-21.

NEW INTERNATIONAL VERSION

What do you learn here about:

CHRISTIAN UNITY

CHRISTIAN JOY

PRAYER

THE CHRISTIAN'S THOUGHT LIFE

SUFFICIENCY OF CHRIST

MEMBERS OF CHRIST'S BODY

*Exhortations*

2 I plead with Euodia and I plead with
Syntyche to agree with each other in the
Lord. 3 Yes, and I ask you, loyal yokefellow,[a] help these women who have contended at my side in the cause of the gospel, along with Clement and the rest of my
fellow workers, whose names are in the
book of life.●
4 Rejoice in the Lord always. I will say it
again: Rejoice! 5 Let your gentleness be evident to all. The Lord is near. 6 Do not be
anxious about anything, but in everything,
by prayer and petition, with thanksgiving,
present your requests to God. 7 And the
peace of God, which transcends all understanding, will guard your hearts and your
minds in Christ Jesus.●
8 Finally, brothers, whatever is true,
whatever is noble, whatever is right, whatever is pure, whatever is lovely, whatever
is admirable—if anything is excellent or
praiseworthy—think about such things.
9 Whatever you have learned or received or
heard from me, or seen in me—put it into
practice. And the God of peace will be with
you.●

*Thanks for Their Gifts*

10 I rejoice greatly in the Lord that at last
you have renewed your concern for me.
Indeed, you have been concerned, but you
had no opportunity to show it. 11 I am not
saying this because I am in need, for I have
learned to be content whatever the circumstances. 12 I know what it is to be in need,
and I know what it is to have plenty. I have
learned the secret of being content in any
and every situation, whether well fed or
hungry, whether living in plenty or in want.
13 I can do everything through him who
gives me strength.
14 Yet it was good of you to share in my
troubles. 15 Moreover, as you Philippians
know, in the early days of your acquaintance with the gospel, when I set out from
Macedonia, not one church shared with me
in the matter of giving and receiving, except you only; 16 for even when I was in
Thessalonica, you sent me aid again and
again when I was in need. 17 Not that I am
looking for a gift, but I am looking for what
may be credited to your account. 18 I have
received full payment and even more; I am
amply supplied, now that I have received
from Epaphroditus the gifts you sent. They
are a fragrant offering, an acceptable sacrifice, pleasing to God. 19 And my God will
meet all your needs according to his glorious riches in Christ Jesus.
20 To our God and Father be glory for
ever and ever. Amen.●

*Final Greetings*

21 Greet all the saints in Christ Jesus. The
brothers who are with me send greetings.
22 All the saints send you greetings, especially those who belong to Caesar's
household.
23 The grace of the Lord Jesus Christ be
with your spirit. Amen.[b]●

[a]3 Or *loyal Syzygus*

[b]23 Some manuscripts do not have *Amen*.

KING JAMES

1. I BESEECH

TWO SAINTS

2 I beseech Eu-o'di-as, and beseech
Syn'tyche, that they be of the same mind
in the Lord. 3 And I entreat thee also,
true yokefellow, help those women which
labored with me in the gospel, with
Clement also, and *with* other my fellow
laborers, whose names *are* in the book of
life.●
4 Rejoice in the Lord always: *and* again
I say, Rejoice. 5 Let your moderation be
known unto all men. The Lord *is* at hand.
6 Be careful for nothing; but in every
thing by prayer and supplication with
thanksgiving let your requests be made
known unto God. 7 And the peace of
God, which passeth all understanding,
shall keep your hearts and minds through
Christ Jesus.●
8 Finally, brethren, whatsoever things
are true, whatsoever things *are* honest,
whatsoever things *are* just, whatsoever
things *are* pure, whatsoever things *are*
lovely, whatsoever things *are* of good
report; if *there be* any virtue, and if *there*
*be* any praise, think on these things.
9 Those things, which ye have both
learned, and received, and heard, and seen
in me, do: and the God of peace shall be
with you.●

2. THANK YOU

10 But I rejoiced in the Lord greatly,
that now at the last your care of me hath
flourished again; wherein ye were also
careful, but ye lacked opportunity. 11 Not
that I speak in respect of want: for I have
learned, in whatsoever state I am, *there-*
*with* to be content. 12 I know both how
to be abased, and I know how to abound:
every where and in all things I am instructed both to be full and to be hungry,
both to abound and to suffer need. 13 I
can do all things through Christ which
strengtheneth me.
14 Notwithstanding, ye have well done,
that ye did communicate with my affliction. 15 Now ye Philippians know also,
that in the beginning of the gospel, when
I departed from Macedonia, no church
communicated with me as concerning
giving and receiving, but ye only. 16 For
even in Thessaloni'ca ye sent once and
again unto my necessity. 17 Not because I desire a gift: but I desire fruit that
may abound to your account. 18 But I
have all, and abound: I am full, having
received of Epaphrodi'tus the things *which*
*were sent* from you, an odor of a sweet
smell, a sacrifice acceptable, well-pleasing
to God. 19 But my God shall supply all
your need according to his riches in glory
by Christ Jesus. 20 Now unto God and
our Father *be* glory for ever and ever.
Amen.●

3. FAREWELL

21 Salute every saint in Christ Jesus.
The brethren which are with me greet you.
22 All the saints salute you, chiefly they
that are of Caesar's household.
23 The grace of our Lord Jesus Christ
*be* with you all. Amen.●

EVERY SAINT

*4:2-3* Record key phrases of the paragraph:

*4:4-7* List the commands and exhortations:

*4:8-9* What are the two *command* words?

*4:10-20* Record what is revealed here about:

PAUL

THE PHILIPPIANS

*4:21-23* What are your observations?

# COLOSSIANS

## AUTHORSHIP

Colossians 1:1 identifies the author as "Paul, an apostle of Jesus Christ by the will of God."

## DATE

Paul wrote the Epistle around A.D. 61 from prison at Rome.

## OCCASION AND PURPOSE

The immediate occasion for writing this letter was heresies in the church. Among these were 1) a Judaistic legalism; 2) a severe asceticism; 3) worship of angels; and 4) a glorification and worship of human knowledge. Paul challenges and explodes these heresies on a positive note, by a pure presentation of counter-truths about the person and work of Jesus Christ. This magnification of Christ is stated in a key verse: "Christ is all, and in all" (3:11).

## COLOSSIANS: Christ is All and In All

| | |
|---|---|
| Opening Benediction | 1:1-2 |
| TRUE DOCTRINE | 1:3-2:3 |
| Thanksgiving and Intercession | 1:3-12 |
| Person and Work of Christ | 1:13-2:3 |
| FALSE DOCTRINE | 2:4-3:4 |
| Heresies Exposed | 2:4-3:4 |
| CHRISTIAN LIVING | 3:5-4:18 |
| Christianity in Action | 3:5-4:6 |
| Personal Greetings | 4:7-18a |
| Closing Benediction | 4:18b |

# COLOSSIANS

NEW INTERNATIONAL VERSION

Record what this passage teaches about:

INTERCESSORY PRAYER

CHRISTIAN GRATITUDE

HEAVEN

GOSPEL

GRACE OF GOD

Apply the passage to everyday Christian living.

1 Paul, an apostle of Christ Jesus by the
will of God, and Timothy our brother,
2To the holy and faithful[a] brothers in
Christ at Colosse:
Grace and peace to you from God our
Father.[b] ●

*Thanksgiving and Prayer*

3We always thank God, the Father of our
Lord Jesus Christ, when we pray for you,
4because we have heard of your faith in
Christ Jesus and of the love you have for
all the saints— 5the faith and love that
spring from the hope that is stored up for
you in heaven and that you have already
heard about in the word of truth, the gospel
6that has come to you. All over the world
this gospel is producing fruit and growing,
just as it has been doing among you since
the day you heard it and understood God's
grace in all its truth. 7You learned it from
Epaphras, our dear fellow servant, who is
a faithful minister of Christ on our[c] behalf,
8and who also told us of your love in the
Spirit. ●
9For this reason, since the day we heard
about you, we have not stopped praying
for you and asking God to fill you with the
knowledge of his will through all spiritual
wisdom and understanding. 10And we pray
this in order that you may live a life worthy
of the Lord and may please him in every
way: bearing fruit in every good work,
growing in the knowledge of God, 11being
strengthened with all power according to
his glorious might so that you may have
great endurance and patience, and joyfully
12giving thanks to the Father, who has
qualified you[d] to share in the inheritance of
the saints in the kingdom of light. ●

a2 Or *believing*
b2 Some manuscripts *Father and the Lord Jesus Christ*
c7 Some manuscripts *your*
d12 Some manuscripts *us*

KING JAMES

# COLOSSIANS

—salutation

1 Paul, an apostle of Jesus Christ by
the will of God, and Timothy *our*
brother,
2 To the saints and faithful brethren in
Christ which are at Colos'sae:
Grace *be* unto you, and peace, from
God our Father and the Lord Jesus Christ.●

APOSTLE

1. THANKSGIVING

3 We give thanks to God and the Father
of our Lord Jesus Christ, praying always
for you, 4 since we heard of your faith in
Christ Jesus, and of the love *which ye have*
to all the saints, 5 for the hope which is
laid up for you in heaven, whereof ye
heard before in the word of the truth of
the gospel; 6 which is come unto you, as
*it is* in all the world; and bringeth forth
fruit, as *it doth* also in you, since the day
ye heard *of it*, and knew the grace of God
in truth: 7 as ye also learned of Ep'a-
phras our dear fellow servant, who is for
you a faithful minister of Christ; 8 who
also declared unto us your love in the
Spirit.●

2. INTERCESSION

9 For this cause we also, since the day
we heard *it*, do not cease to pray for you,
and to desire that ye might be filled with
the knowledge of his will in all wisdom and
spiritual understanding; 10 that ye might
walk worthy of the Lord unto all pleasing, being fruitful in every good work,
and increasing in the knowledge of God;
11 strengthened with all might, according
to his glorious power, unto all patience
and long-suffering with joyfulness; 12 giving thanks unto the Father, which hath
made us meet to be partakers of the inheritance of the saints in light: ●

SAINTS

*1:1-2* Record the different designations of persons or groups (e.g. "apostle").

______________________________

______________________________

______________________________

______________________________

______________________________

______________________________

*1:3-8* What are the opening three words?

______________________________

______________________________

Would you say that the things Paul writes about in verses 4-8 are things for which he was thankful? If so, list these:

______________________________

______________________________

______________________________

______________________________

______________________________

______________________________

______________________________

______________________________

______________________________

______________________________

______________________________

______________________________

*1:9-12* List the objects of Paul's intercessory prayers:

______________________________

______________________________

______________________________

______________________________

______________________________

______________________________

______________________________

______________________________

NEW INTERNATIONAL VERSION

Put yourself in the heart of this passage, and record 2 lists:

WHAT CHRIST DOES FOR YOU

WHAT YOU CAN DO FOR CHRIST

[13]For he has rescued us from the dominion of darkness and brought us into the kingdom of the Son he loves, [14]in whom we have redemption,[e] the forgiveness of sins.

*The Supremacy of Christ*

[15]He is the image of the invisible God, the firstborn over all creation. [16]For by him all things were created: things in heaven and on earth, visible and invisible, whether thrones or powers or rulers or authorities; all things were created by him and for him. [17]He is before all things, and in him all things hold together. [18]And he is the head of the body, the church; he is the beginning and the firstborn from among the dead, so that in everything he might have the supremacy. [19]For God was pleased to have all his fullness dwell in him, [20]and through him to reconcile to himself all things, whether things on earth or things in heaven, by making peace through his blood, shed on the cross.●

[21]Once you were alienated from God and were enemies in your minds because of your evil behavior. [22]But now he has reconciled you by Christ's physical body through death to present you holy in his sight, without blemish and free from accusation— [23]if you continue in your faith, established and firm, not moved from the hope held out in the gospel. This is the gospel that you heard and that has been proclaimed to every creature under heaven, and of which I, Paul, have become a servant.●

*Paul's Labor for the Church*

[24]Now I rejoice in what was suffered for you, and I fill up in my flesh what is still lacking in regard to Christ's afflictions, for the sake of his body, which is the church. [25]I have become its servant by the commission God gave me to present to you the word of God in its fullness— [26]the mystery that has been kept hidden for ages and generations, but is now disclosed to the saints. [27]To them God has chosen to make known among the Gentiles the glorious riches of this mystery, which is Christ in you, the hope of glory.

[28]We proclaim him, admonishing and teaching everyone with all wisdom, so that we may present everyone perfect in Christ. [29]To this end I labor, struggling with all his energy, which so powerfully works in me.●

2 I want you to know how much I am struggling for you and for those at Laodicea, and for all who have not met me personally. [2]My purpose is that they may be encouraged in heart and united in love, so that they may have the full riches of complete understanding, in order that they may know the mystery of God, namely, Christ,[a] [3]in whom are hidden all the treasures of wisdom and knowledge.●

[e]14 A few late manuscripts *redemption through his blood*
[a]2 Some manuscripts *God, even the Father, and of Christ*

KING JAMES

1.CHRIST'S MINISTRY TO THE WORLD

POWER OF DARKNESS

13 who
hath delivered us from the power of darkness, and hath translated *us* into the kingdom of his dear Son.
14 In whom we have redemption
through his blood, *even* the forgiveness of
sins: 15 who is the image of the invisible
God, the firstborn of every creature:
16 for by him were all things created, that
are in heaven, and that are in earth, visible
and invisible, whether *they be* thrones, or
dominions, or principalities, or powers:
all things were created by him, and for
him: 17 and he is before all things, and by
him all things consist: 18 and he is the
head of the body, the church: who is the
beginning, the firstborn from the dead;
that in all things he might have the preeminence. 19 For it pleased *the Father*
that in him should all fulness dwell;
20 and, having made peace through the
blood of his cross, by him to reconcile all
things unto himself; by him, *I say*, whether
*they be* things in earth, or things in
heaven. ●
21 And you, that were sometime alienated and enemies in *your* mind by wicked
works, yet now hath he reconciled 22 in
the body of his flesh through death, to
present you holy and unblamable and un-
reprovable in his sight: 23 if ye continue
in the faith grounded and settled, and *be*
not moved away from the hope of the
gospel, which ye have heard, *and* which
was preached to every creature which is
under heaven; whereof I Paul am made a
minister; ● 24 who now rejoice in my sufferings for you, and fill up that which is behind of the afflictions of Christ in my flesh
for his body's sake, which is the church:
25 whereof I am made a minister, according to the dispensation of God which is
given to me for you, to fulfil the word of
God; 26 *even* the mystery which hath been
hid from ages and from generations, but
now is made manifest to his saints: 27 to
whom God would make known what *is* the
riches of the glory of this mystery among
the Gentiles; which is Christ in you, the
hope of glory: 28 whom we preach, warning every man, and teaching every man in
all wisdom; that we may present every
man perfect in Christ Jesus: 29 whereunto I also labor, striving according
to his working, which worketh in me
mightily.●

2.PAUL's MINISTRY FOR CHRIST

2 For I would that ye knew what great
conflict I have for you, and *for* them
at La-odice'a, and *for* as many as have
not seen my face in the flesh; 2 that their
hearts might be comforted, being knit together in love, and unto all riches of the
full assurance of understanding, to the
acknowledgment of the mystery of God,
and of the Father, and of Christ; 3 in
whom are hid all the treasures of wisdom
and knowledge.●

WISDOM AND KNOWLEDGE

Record your observations of the person and work of Christ in the first two paragraphs:

*1:13-23*

PERSON OF CHRIST ______

WORK OF CHRIST ______

*1:24-29* Record:

PAUL'S MINISTRY ______

PAUL'S MESSAGE ______

*2:1-3* List Paul's different burdens: ______

NEW INTERNATIONAL VERSION

What do you learn here about:

JOY

STEADFAST FAITH

VAIN PHILOSOPHY

THE BELIEVER'S POSITION IN CHRIST

WORK OF CHRIST

List practical applications of the passage.

4 I tell you
this so that no one may deceive you by
fine-sounding arguments. 5 For though I am
absent from you in body, I am present with
you in spirit and delight to see how orderly
you are and how firm your faith in Christ
is.

*Freedom From Human Regulations*
*Through Life With Christ*

6 So then, just as you received Christ
Jesus as Lord, continue to live in him,
7 rooted and built up in him, strengthened in
the faith as you were taught, and overflowing with thankfulness.●
8 See to it that no one takes you captive
through hollow and deceptive philosophy,
which depends on human tradition and the
basic principles of this world rather than on
Christ.
9 For in Christ all the fullness of the Deity
lives in bodily form, 10 and you have been
given fullness in Christ, who is the head
over every power and authority. 11 In him
you were also circumcised, in the putting
off of the sinful nature,[b] not with a circumcision done by the hands of men but with
the circumcision done by Christ, 12 having
been buried with him in baptism and raised
with him through your faith in the power of
God, who raised him from the dead.●
13 When you were dead in your sins and
in the uncircumcision of your sinful nature,[c] God made you[d] alive with Christ. He
forgave us all our sins, 14 having canceled
the written code, with its regulations, that
was against us and that stood opposed to
us; he took it away, nailing it to the cross.
15 And having disarmed the powers and authorities, he made a public spectacle of
them, triumphing over them by the cross.[e]●

[b]11 Or *the flesh* [c]13 Or *your flesh*
[d]13 Some manuscripts *us* [e]15 Or *them in him*
[f]4 Some manuscripts *our*

KING JAMES

1.APPEAL

4 And this I say, lest any
man should beguile you with enticing
words. 5 For though I be absent in the
flesh, yet am I with you in the spirit, joying
and beholding your order, and the stead-
fastness of your faith in Christ.
6 As ye have therefore received Christ
Jesus the Lord, *so* walk ye in him:
7 rooted and built up in him, and stab-
lished in the faith, as ye have been taught,
abounding therein with thanksgiving.●

BEGUILING

2.POSITION

8 Beware lest any man spoil you
through philosophy and vain deceit, after
the tradition of men, after the rudiments
of the world, and not after Christ. 9 For
in him dwelleth all the fulness of the Godhead bodily. 10 And ye are complete in
him, which is the head of all principality
and power: 11 in whom also ye are circumcised with the circumcision made
without hands, in putting off the body of
the sins of the flesh by the circumcision of
Christ: 12 buried with him in baptism,
wherein also ye are risen with *him* through
the faith of the operation of God, who
hath raised him from the dead. ● 13And
you, being dead in your sins and the uncircumcision of your flesh, hath he quickened together with him, having forgiven
you all trespasses; 14 blotting out the
handwriting of ordinances that was
against us, which was contrary to us, and
took it out of the way, nailing it to his
cross; 15 *and* having spoiled principalities and powers, he made a show of
them openly, triumphing over them in
it.●

TRIUMPHING

This segment continues into the segment that follows. The entire passage (2:4—3:4) is about heresies in the church at Colosse, which Paul attempts to expose.

*2:4-7* What is the cause of Paul's joy?

What is his appeal?

*2:8-15* What is the warning of verse 8?

What is the subject of the remaining verses (9-15)?

Record what is written about:

CHRIST

THE BELIEVER

NEW INTERNATIONAL VERSION

What does this passage teach about:

LEGALISM

ASCETICISM

PLEASING CHRIST

NEW LIFE IN CHRIST

SECOND COMING OF CHRIST

Apply this passage to everyday living today:

16Therefore do not let anyone judge you
by what you eat or drink, or with regard to
a religious festival, a New Moon celebration or a Sabbath day. 17These are a shadow of the things that were to come; the
reality, however, is found in Christ. 18Do
not let anyone who delights in false humility and the worship of angels disqualify you
for the prize. Such a person goes into great
detail about what he has seen, and his unspiritual mind puffs him up with idle no-
tions. 19He has lost connection with the
Head, from whom the whole body, supported and held together by its ligaments
and sinews, grows as God causes it to
grow.●
20Since you died with Christ to the basic
principles of this world, why, as though
you still belonged to it, do you submit to its
rules: 21"Do not handle! Do not taste! Do
not touch!"? 22These are all destined to
perish with use, because they are based on
human commands and teachings. 23Such
regulations indeed have an appearance of
wisdom, with their self-imposed worship,
their false humility and their harsh treatment of the body, but they lack any value
in restraining sensual indulgence.●

*Rules for Holy Living*

3 Since, then, you have been raised with
Christ, set your hearts on things above,
where Christ is seated at the right hand of
God. 2Set your minds on things above, not
on earthly things. 3For you died, and your
life is now hidden with Christ in God.
4When Christ, who is your[f] life, appears,
then you also will appear with him in glory.●

KING JAMES

1. HERESIES

JUDGED BY MAN

16 Let no man therefore judge you in
meat, or in drink, or in respect of a holy-
day, or of the new moon, or of the sabbath *days:* 17 which are a shadow of
things to come; but the body *is* of Christ.
18 Let no man beguile you of your reward
in a voluntary humility and worshipping
of angels, intruding into those things
which he hath not seen, vainly puffed up
by his fleshly mind, 19 and not holding
the Head, from which all the body by
joints and bands having nourishment
ministered, and knit together, increaseth
with the increase of God. ●
20 Wherefore if ye be dead with Christ
from the rudiments of the world, why, as
though living in the world, are ye subject
to ordinances, 21 (touch not; taste not;
handle not; 22 which all are to perish
with the using;) after the commandments
and doctrines of men? 23 which things
have indeed a show of wisdom in will-
worship, and humility, and neglecting of
the body; not in any honor to the satisfy-
ing of the flesh. ●

2. APPEALS

3 If ye then be risen with Christ, seek
those things which are above, where
Christ sitteth on the right hand of God.
2 Set your affection on things above, not
on things on the earth. 3 For ye are dead,
and your life is hid with Christ in God.
4 When Christ, *who is* our life, shall appear, then shall ye also appear with him
in glory. ●

REIGNING WITH CHRIST

*2:16-19* What false teachings does Paul refer to here?

How does he expose each?

*2:20-23* Record Paul's criticisms of:

LEGALISM

ASCETICISM

*3:1-4* Record:

CHRISTIAN'S POSITION AND HOPE

COMMANDS

NEW INTERNATIONAL VERSION

Record the different motives for Christian living taught by this passage.

Make a list of practical applications of the passage.

[5]Put to death, therefore, whatever belongs to your earthly nature: sexual immorality, impurity, lust, evil desires and
greed, which is idolatry. [6]Because of these,
the wrath of God is coming.[g] [7]You used to
walk in these ways, in the life you once
lived. [8]But now you must rid yourselves of
all such things as these: anger, rage, malice, slander, and filthy language from your
lips. [9]Do not lie to each other, since you
have taken off your old self with its practices [10]and have put on the new self, which
is being renewed in knowledge in the image
of its Creator. [11]Here there is no Greek or
Jew, circumcised or uncircumcised, barbarian, Scythian, slave or free, but Christ
is all, and is in all.●
[12]Therefore, as God's chosen people,
holy and dearly loved, clothe yourselves
with compassion, kindness, humility, gentleness and patience. [13]Bear with each other and forgive whatever grievances you
may have against one another. Forgive as
the Lord forgave you. [14]And over all these
virtues put on love, which binds them all
together in perfect unity.
[15]Let the peace of Christ rule in your
hearts, since as members of one body you
were called to peace. And be thankful.
[16]Let the word of Christ dwell in you richly
as you teach and admonish one another
with all wisdom, and as you sing psalms,
hymns and spiritual songs with gratitude in
your hearts to God. [17]And whatever you
do, whether in word or deed, do it all in the
name of the Lord Jesus, giving thanks to
God the Father through him.●

[g]6 Some early manuscripts *coming on those who are disobedient*

## KING JAMES

1.PUT OFF

IDOLATRY

5 Mortify therefore your members
which are upon the earth; fornication,
uncleanness, inordinate affection, evil
concupiscence, and covetousness, which
is idolatry: 6 for which things' sake the
wrath of God cometh on the children of
disobedience: 7 in the which ye also
walked sometime, when ye lived in them.
8 But now ye also put off all these; anger,
wrath, malice, blasphemy, filthy communication out of your mouth. 9 Lie not
one to another, seeing that ye have put off
the old man with his deeds; 10 and have
put on the new *man*, which is renewed in
knowledge after the image of him that
created him: 11 where there is neither
Greek nor Jew, circumcision nor uncircumcision, Barbarian, Scyth'i-an, bond
*nor* free: but Christ *is* all, and in all.●

2.PUT ON

12 Put on therefore, as the elect of God,
holy and beloved, bowels of mercies,
kindness, humbleness of mind, meekness,
long-suffering; 13 forbearing one another, and forgiving one another, if any
man have a quarrel against any: even as
Christ forgave you, so also *do* ye. 14 And
above all these things *put on* charity,
which is the bond of perfectness. 15 And
let the peace of God rule in your hearts,
to the which also ye are called in one
body; and be ye thankful. 16 Let the
word of Christ dwell in you richly in all
wisdom; teaching and admonishing one
another in psalms and hymns and spiritual songs, singing with grace in your
hearts to the Lord. 17 And whatsoever
ye do in word or deed, *do* all in the name
of the Lord Jesus, giving thanks to God
and the Father by him. ●

RIGHTEOUS LIFE

*3:5-11* Are all the commands of this paragraph negative or positive? List them:

Compare v.9b with v.10a.

Record the doctrinal statements of the paragraph:

*3:12-17* Is this paragraph mainly negative or positive? (Note the first two words.) Record the different teachings about Christ.

NEW INTERNATIONAL VERSION

Make a list of practical applications of this passage to the Christian home today.

How can the verses about servants and masters (3:22—4:1) be applied to today, in view of the fact that most homes do not have servants?

*Rules for Christian Households*

[18]Wives, submit to your husbands, as is
fitting in the Lord.
[19]Husbands, love your wives and do not
be harsh with them.●
[20]Children, obey your parents in everything, for this pleases the Lord.
[21]Fathers, do not embitter your children,
or they will become discouraged.●
[22]Slaves, obey your earthly masters in
everything; and do it, not only when their
eye is on you and to win their favor, but
with sincerity of heart and reverence for
the Lord. [23]Whatever you do, work at it
with all your heart, as working for the
Lord, not for men, [24]since you know that
you will receive an inheritance from the
Lord as a reward. It is the Lord Christ you
are serving. [25]Anyone who does wrong will
be repaid for his wrong, and there is no
favoritism.●
4 Masters, provide your slaves with
what is right and fair, because you
know that you also have a Master in
heaven.●

*Further Instructions*

[2]Devote yourselves to prayer, being
watchful and thankful. [3]And pray for us,
too, that God may open a door for our
message, so that we may proclaim the mystery of Christ, for which I am in chains.
[4]Pray that I may proclaim it clearly, as I
should. [5]Be wise in the way you act toward
outsiders; make the most of every opportunity. [6]Let your conversation be always full
of grace, seasoned with salt, so that you
may know how to answer everyone.●

KING JAMES

1.SPECIFIC COMMANDS

SUBMISSION

18 Wives, submit yourselves unto your
own husbands, as it is fit in the Lord.
19 Husbands, love *your* wives, and be not
bitter against them. ● 20 Children, obey
*your* parents in all things: for this is well-
pleasing unto the Lord. 21 Fathers, provoke not your children *to anger*, lest they
be discouraged. ● 22 Servants, obey in all
things *your* masters according to the
flesh; not with eyeservice, as menpleasers;
but in singleness of heart, fearing God:
23 and whatsoever ye do, do *it* heartily, as
to the Lord, and not unto men; 24 knowing that of the Lord ye shall receive the
reward of the inheritance: for ye serve
the Lord Christ. 25 But he that doeth
wrong shall receive for the wrong which
he hath done: and there is no respect of
persons. ●
4 Masters, give unto *your* servants that
which is just and equal; knowing that
ye also have a Master in heaven. ●

2.FINAL EXHORTATIONS

2 Continue in prayer, and watch in the
same with thanksgiving; 3 withal praying
also for us, that God would open unto us
a door of utterance, to speak the mystery
of Christ, for which I am also in bonds:
4 that I may make it manifest, as I ought
to speak.
5 Walk in wisdom toward them that are
without, redeeming the time. 6 Let your
speech *be* always with grace, seasoned
with salt, that ye may know how ye ought
to answer every man.●

GRACE

*3:18—4:1* Record the six members (or groups) of a Christian household in Paul's day, and the commands given to each.

*4:2-6* What are the commands of this paragraph?

How appropriate are they as concluding commands of the main section of the epistle?

NEW INTERNATIONAL VERSION

Go through this passage again and make a list of practical applications to everyday Christian living today.

*Final Greetings*

7 Tychicus will tell you all the news about
me. He is a dear brother, a faithful minister
and fellow servant in the Lord. 8 I am sending him to you for the express purpose that
you may know about our[a] circumstances
and that he may encourage your hearts.
9 He is coming with Onesimus, our faithful
and dear brother, who is one of you. They
will tell you everything that is happening
here.
10 My fellow prisoner Aristarchus sends
you his greetings, as does Mark, the cousin
of Barnabas. (You have received instructions about him; if he comes to you, welcome him.) 11 Jesus, who is called Justus,
also sends greetings. These are the only
Jews among my fellow workers for the
kingdom of God, and they have proved a
comfort to me. 12 Epaphras, who is one of
you and a servant of Christ Jesus, sends
greetings. He is always wrestling in prayer
for you, that you may stand firm in all the
will of God, mature and fully assured. 13 I
vouch for him that he is working hard for
you and for those at Laodicea and
Hierapolis. 14 Our dear friend Luke, the
doctor, and Demas send greetings. 15 Give
my greetings to the brothers at Laodicea,
and to Nympha and the church in her
house.
16 After this letter has been read to you,
see that it is also read in the church of the
Laodiceans and that you in turn read the
letter from Laodicea.
17 Tell Archippus: "See to it that you
complete the work you have received in
the Lord."
18 I, Paul, write this greeting in my own
hand. Remember my chains. Grace be with
you.

[a]8 Some manuscripts *that he may know about your*

KING JAMES

1.TYCHICUS AND ONESIMUS

7 All my state shall Tych'icus declare
unto you, *who is* a beloved brother, and a
faithful minister and fellow servant in the
Lord: 8 whom I have sent unto you for
the same purpose, that he might know
your estate, and comfort your hearts;
9 with Ones'imus, a faithful and beloved
brother, who is *one* of you. They shall
make known unto you all things which
*are done* here. ●

BOND SERVANT

2.OTHER CO-LABORERS

10 Aristar'chus my fellow prisoner saluteth you, and Mark, sister's son to
Barnabas, (touching whom ye received
commandments: if he come unto you, receive him;) 11 and Jesus, which is called
Justus, who are of the circumcision.
These only *are my* fellow workers unto
the kingdom of God, which have been a
comfort unto me. 12 Ep'aphras, who is
*one* of you, a servant of Christ, saluteth
you, always laboring fervently for you in
prayers, that ye may stand perfect and
complete in all the will of God. 13 For I
bear him record, that he hath a great zeal
for you, and them *that are* in La-odice'a,
and them in Hi-erap'olis. 14 Luke, the
beloved physician, and Demas, greet
you. ●

3.COLOSSIAN CHURCH

15 Salute the brethren which are in
La-odice'a, and Nymphas, and the church
which is in his house. 16 And when this
epistle is read among you, cause that it be
read also in the church of the La-odice'ans; and that ye likewise read the
*epistle* from La-odice'a. 17 And say to
Archip'pus, Take heed to the ministry
which thou hast received in the Lord, that
thou fulfil it. ●

4.PAUL

18 The salutation by the hand of me
Paul. Remember my bonds. Grace *be*
with you. Amen. ●

PRISON BONDS

Each paragraph of this final personal section is about personalities close to Paul and his work. For each paragraph record the names, and what is written about each.

*4:7-9* ______

*4:10-14* ______

*4:15-17* ______

*4:18* ______

# 1 THESSALONIANS

## AUTHORSHIP

The author was Paul, identified by name twice in the text: 1:1; 2:18.

## DATE

The letter was written around A.D. 52. Paul was at Corinth at the time, where he was ministering for about eighteen months.

## PURPOSES

The church at Thessalonica was one of those founded by Paul on his second missionary journey. The apostle kept in constant touch with the young converts in these local fellowships, and he often wrote to help them in their daily walk.

Some of the purposes Paul had in mind when he wrote 1 Thessalonians were:

1) to commend the Christians for their faith (3:6)
2) to expose sins (e.g. fornication, 4:3, and idleness, 4:11)
3) to correct misapprehensions of doctrine (e.g., about the second coming of Christ, 4:13-17)
4) to exhort the young converts in their new spiritual experience (e.g., 4:1-12)
5) to answer false charges against his ministry

A key doctrine taught in the Epistle is the second coming of Christ. Each chapter ends with a reference to this.

1 THESSALONIANS:
The Lord Jesus Is Coming Again

| | |
|---|---|
| LOOKING BACK | 1:1-3:13 |
| A Dynamic Local Church | 1:1-10 |
| A Successful Christian Worker | 2:1-16 |
| Ministering to Christians at a Distance | 2:17-3:13 |
| LOOKING FORWARD | 4:1-5:28 |
| The Life That Pleases God | 4:1-12 |
| The Lord's Return | 4:13-5:11 |
| The Believer's Walk | 5:12-28 |

# 1 THESSALONIANS

NEW INTERNATIONAL VERSION

What does this opening passage teach about:

THE BELIEVER'S POSITION IN CHRIST

THE GOSPEL

HOLY SPIRIT

THE CHRISTIAN'S TESTIMONY

CHRISTIAN SERVICE

SECOND COMING OF CHRIST

OTHER

1 Paul, Silas[b] and Timothy,
To the church of the Thessalonians in
God the Father and the Lord Jesus Christ:
Grace and peace to you.[c] ●

*Thanksgiving for the Thessalonians' Faith*

2We always thank God for all of you,
mentioning you in our prayers. 3We continually remember before our God and Father your work produced by faith, your
labor prompted by love, and your endurance inspired by hope in our Lord Jesus
Christ.
4Brothers loved by God, we know that
he has chosen you, 5because our gospel
came to you not simply with words, but
also with power, with the Holy Spirit and
with deep conviction. You know how we
lived among you for your sake.● 6You
became imitators of us and of the Lord; in
spite of severe suffering, you welcomed
the message with the joy given by the Holy
Spirit. 7And so you became a model to all
the believers in Macedonia and Achaia.
8The Lord's message rang out from you not
only in Macedonia and Achaia—your faith
in God has become known everywhere.
Therefore we do not need to say anything
about it, 9for they themselves report what
kind of reception you gave us. They tell
how you turned to God from idols to serve
the living and true God, 10and to wait for
his Son from heaven, whom he raised from
the dead—Jesus, who rescues us from the
coming wrath.●

[b]*1* Greek *Silvanus,* a variant of *Silas*
[c]*1* Some early manuscripts *you from God our Father and the Lord Jesus Christ*

KING JAMES

# 1 THESSALONIANS

—salutation

1 Paul, and Silva'nus, and Timothy,
Unto the church of the Thessa-
lo'ni-ans *which is* in God the Father, and
*in* the Lord Jesus Christ:
Grace *be* unto you, and peace, from
God our Father, and the Lord Jesus
Christ. ●

1.THANKSGIVING — WORKING

2 We give thanks to God always for
you all, making mention of you in our
prayers; 3 remembering without ceasing
your work of faith, and labor of love, and
patience of hope in our Lord Jesus Christ,
in the sight of God and our Father;
4 knowing, brethren beloved, your election of God. 5 For our gospel came not
unto you in word only, but also in power,
and in the Holy Ghost, and in much assurance; as ye know what manner of men
we were among you for your sake. ●

2.EXAMPLES

6 And
ye became followers of us, and of the
Lord, having received the word in much
affliction, with joy of the Holy Ghost:
7 so that ye were ensamples to all that believe in Macedonia and Achai'a. 8 For
from you sounded out the word of the
Lord not only in Macedonia and Achai'a,
but also in every place your faith to God-
ward is spread abroad; so that we need
not to speak any thing. 9 For they themselves show of us what manner of entering
in we had unto you, and how ye turned to
God from idols to serve the living and

WAITING

true God; 10 and to wait for his Son
from heaven, whom he raised from the
dead, *even* Jesus, which delivered us from
the wrath to come. ●

*1:1* What does the word "in" suggest?

____________________

____________________

Record each name of the Godhead. What does each name suggest to you?

____________________

____________________

____________________

____________________

____________________

____________________

*1:2-5* Record what is written about:

THE THESSALONIANS ____________________

____________________

____________________

____________________

PAUL ____________________

____________________

____________________

____________________

*1:6-10* Who is the example of verse 6?

____________________

of verse 7? ____________________

What is the last reference to Christ in the segment?

____________________

____________________

____________________

____________________

____________________

____________________

____________________

____________________

____________________

____________________

____________________

NEW INTERNATIONAL VERSION

What do you learn here about:

CHRISTIAN LIVING

WITNESSING FOR CHRIST

LOVE OF THE BRETHREN

WORD OF GOD

PERSECUTION OF BELIEVERS

OTHER

*Paul's Ministry in Thessalonica*

2 You know, brothers, that our visit to
you was not a failure. 2We had previously suffered and been insulted in
Philippi, as you know, but with the help of
our God we dared to tell you his gospel in
spite of strong opposition. 3For the appeal
we make does not spring from error or impure motives, nor are we trying to trick
you. 4On the contrary, we speak as men
approved by God to be entrusted with the
gospel. We are not trying to please men but
God, who tests our hearts. 5You know we
never used flattery, nor did we put on a
mask to cover up greed—God is our witness. 6We were not looking for praise from
men, not from you or anyone else.●
7As apostles of Christ we could have
been a burden to you, but we were gentle
among you, like a mother caring for her
little children. 8We loved you so much that
we were delighted to share with you not
only the gospel of God but our lives as
well, because you had become so dear to
us. 9Surely you remember, brothers, our
toil and hardship; we worked night and day
in order not to be a burden to anyone while
we preached the gospel of God to you.
10You are witnesses, and so is God, of
how holy, righteous and blameless we
were among you who believed. 11For you
know that we dealt with each of you as a
father deals with his own children, 12en-
couraging, comforting and urging you to
live lives worthy of God, who calls you into
his kingdom and glory.●
13And we also thank God continually because, when you received the word of
God, which you heard from us, you accepted it not as the word of men, but as it
actually is, the word of God, which is at
work in you who believe. 14For you, brothers, became imitators of God's churches in
Judea, which are in Christ Jesus: You suffered from your own countrymen the same
things those churches suffered from the
Jews, 15who killed the Lord Jesus and the
prophets and also drove us out. They dis-
please God and are hostile to all men 16in
their effort to keep us from speaking to the
Gentiles so that they may be saved. In this
way they always heap up their sins to the
limit. The wrath of God has come upon
them at last.[a]●

[a]16 Or *them fully*

KING JAMES

1. SPEAKING THE GOSPEL

BOLD TO SPEAK

2 For yourselves, brethren, know our
entrance in unto you, that it was not
in vain: 2 but even after that we had
suffered before, and were shamefully entreated, as ye know, at Phil'ippi, we were
bold in our God to speak unto you the
gospel of God with much contention.
3 For our exhortation *was* not of deceit,
nor of uncleanness, nor in guile: 4 but as
we were allowed of God to be put in trust
with the gospel, even so we speak; not as
pleasing men, but God, which trieth our
hearts. 5 For neither at any time used we
flattering words, as ye know, nor a cloak
of covetousness; God *is* witness: 6 nor of
men sought we glory, neither of you, nor
*yet* of others, when we might have been
burdensome, as the apostles of Christ. ●

2. LIVING THE GOSPEL

7 But we were gentle among you, even as
a nurse cherisheth her children: 8 so being
affectionately desirous of you, we were
willing to have imparted unto you, not
the gospel of God only, but also our
own souls, because ye were dear unto
us.
9 For ye remember, brethren, our labor
and travail: for laboring night and day,
because we would not be chargeable unto
any of you, we preached unto you the
gospel of God. 10 Ye *are* witnesses, and
God *also*, how holily and justly and un-
blamably we behaved ourselves among
you that believe: 11 as ye know how we
exhorted and comforted and charged
every one of you, as a father *doth* his children, 12 that ye would walk worthy of
God, who hath called you unto his kingdom and glory. ●

3. SEEING THE GOSPEL RECEIVED

13 For this cause also thank we God
without ceasing, because, when ye received the word of God which ye heard of
us, ye received *it* not *as* the word of men,
but, as it is in truth, the word of God,
which effectually worketh also in you that
believe. 14 For ye, brethren, became followers of the churches of God which in
Judea are in Christ Jesus: for ye also have
suffered like things of your own countrymen, even as they *have* of the Jews:
15 who both killed the Lord Jesus, and
their own prophets, and have persecuted
us; and they please not God, and are
contrary to all men: 16 forbidding us to
speak to the Gentiles that they might be
saved, to fill up their sins always: for the
wrath is come upon them to the uttermost. ●

FORBIDDEN TO SPEAK

Chapter 1 was mainly about the Thessalonian believers. Read this segment. Whom is it mainly about?

______

*2:1-6* Record the references to God.

______

______

______

______

______

______

List the things Paul did *not* do, in sharing the gospel.

______

______

______

______

______

______

*2:7-12* Record things written about *how* Paul lived as a Christian.

______

______

______

______

______

*2:13-16* What is the commendation of verse 13?

______

______

What is written in verses 14-16 about the fellowship of suffering for the gospel?

______

______

______

______

______

NEW INTERNATIONAL VERSION

What does this passage teach about:

SATAN

REWARDS FOR CHRISTIAN SERVICE

STRENGTHENING OTHER CHRISTIANS

FAITH

JOY

LOVE

CHRISTIAN GROWTH

OTHER

### *Paul's Longing to See the Thessalonians*

17 But, brothers, when we were torn
away from you for a short time (in person,
not in thought), out of our intense longing
we made every effort to see you. 18 For we
wanted to come to you—certainly I, Paul,
did, again and again—but Satan stopped
us. 19 For what is our hope, our joy, or the
crown in which we will glory in the presence of our Lord Jesus when he comes? Is
it not you? 20 Indeed, you are our glory and
joy.●

3 So when we could stand it no longer,
we thought it best to be left by ourselves in Athens. 2 We sent Timothy, who
is our brother and God's fellow worker[b] in
spreading the gospel of Christ, to strength-
en and encourage you in your faith, 3 so that
no one would be unsettled by these trials.
You know quite well that we were destined
for them. 4 In fact, when we were with you,
we kept telling you that we would be persecuted. And it turned out that way, as you
well know. 5 For this reason, when I could
stand it no longer, I sent to find out about
your faith. I was afraid that in some way
the tempter might have tempted you and
our efforts might have been useless.●

### *Timothy's Encouraging Report*

6 But Timothy has just now come to us
from you and has brought good news about
your faith and love. He has told us that you
always have pleasant memories of us and
that you long to see us, just as we also long
to see you. 7 Therefore, brothers, in all our
distress and persecution we were encouraged about you because of your faith.
8 For now we really live, since you are
standing firm in the Lord. 9 How can we
thank God enough for you in return for all
the joy we have in the presence of our God
because of you? 10 Night and day we pray
most earnestly that we may see you again
and supply what is lacking in your faith.●
11 Now may our God and Father himself
and our Lord Jesus clear the way for us to
come to you. 12 May the Lord make your
love increase and overflow for each other
and for everyone else, just as ours does for
you. 13 May he strengthen your hearts so
that you will be blameless and holy in the
presence of our God and Father when our
Lord Jesus comes with all his holy ones.●

[b]2 Some manuscripts *brother and fellow worker;* other manuscripts *brother and God's servant*

KING JAMES

1. SATAN'S HINDRANCE

SEPARATION FROM THE BRETHREN

17 But we, brethren, being taken from
you for a short time in presence, not in
heart, endeavored the more abundantly to
see your face with great desire. 18 Wherefore we would have come unto you, even
I Paul, once and again; but Satan hindered us. 19 For what *is* our hope, or joy,
or crown of rejoicing? *Are* not even ye in
the presence of our Lord Jesus Christ at
his coming? 20 For ye are our glory and
joy. ●

2. TIMOTHY'S MINISTRY

3 Wherefore when we could no longer
forbear, we thought it good to be left
at Athens alone; 2 and sent Timothy,
our brother, and minister of God, and our
fellow laborer in the gospel of Christ, to
establish you, and to comfort you concerning your faith: 3 that no man should
be moved by these afflictions: for yourselves know that we are appointed thereunto. 4 For verily, when we were with
you, we told you before that we should
suffer tribulation; even as it came to pass,
and ye know. 5 For this cause, when I
could no longer forbear, I sent to know
your faith, lest by some means the tempter
have tempted you, and our labor be in
vain. ●

3. TIMOTHY'S REPORT

6 But now when Timothy came from
you unto us, and brought us good tidings of your faith and charity, and that
ye have good remembrance of us always,
desiring greatly to see us, as we also *to see*
you: 7 therefore, brethren, we were comforted over you in all our affliction and
distress by your faith: 8 for now we live,
if ye stand fast in the Lord. 9 For what
thanks can we render to God again for
you, for all the joy wherewith we joy for
your sakes before our God; 10 night and
day praying exceedingly that we might see
your face, and might perfect that which is
lacking in your faith? ●

4. GOD'S DIRECTION

11 Now God himself and our Father,
and our Lord Jesus Christ, direct our way
unto you. 12 And the Lord make you to
increase and abound in love one toward
another, and toward all *men*, even as we
*do* toward you: 13 to the end he may
stablish your hearts unblamable in holiness before God, even our Father, at the
coming of our Lord Jesus Christ with all
his saints. ●

PRESENCE WITH CHRIST

---

How does verse 17 introduce Paul's ministry *in absentia*?

*2:17-20* Record the two contrasting kinds of things written:

DARK

BRIGHT

*3:1-5* Record what you learn here about:

PAUL

TIMOTHY

*3:6-10* Record:

TIMOTHY'S REPORT

REPORT'S EFFECT ON PAUL

*3:11-13* What different things did Paul desire for the Thessalonians?

NEW INTERNATIONAL VERSION

What do you learn here about:

WILL OF GOD

SANCTIFICATION

PURITY OF THOUGHT AND DEED

LOVE OF THE BRETHREN

WORK

HONESTY

List other practical applications of the passage.

*Living to Please God*

4 Finally, brothers, we instructed you
how to live in order to please God, as
in fact you are living. Now we ask you and
urge you in the Lord Jesus to do this more
and more. 2You know what instructions we
gave you by the authority of the Lord
Jesus.
3It is God's will that you should be holy;
that you should avoid sexual immorality;
4that each of you should learn to control his
own body[a] in a way that is holy and honorable, 5not in passionate lust like the heathen, who do not know God; 6and that in
this matter no one should wrong his brother or take advantage of him. The Lord will
punish men for all such sins, as we have
already told you and warned you. 7For God
did not call us to be impure, but to live a
holy life. 8Therefore, he who rejects this
instruction does not reject man but God,
who gives you his Holy Spirit.●
9Now about brotherly love we do not
need to write to you, for you yourselves
have been taught by God to love each other. 10And in fact, you do love all the brothers throughout Macedonia. Yet we urge
you, brothers, to do so more and more.
11Make it your ambition to lead a quiet
life, to mind your own business and to
work with your hands, just as we told you,
12so that your daily life may win the respect
of outsiders and so that you will not be
dependent on anybody.●

[a]4 Or *learn to live with his own wife;* or *learn to acquire a wife*

KING JAMES

1. PURITY

4 Furthermore then we beseech you,
brethren, and exhort *you* by the Lord
Jesus, that as ye have received of us how
ye ought to walk and to please God, *so* ye
would abound more and more. 2 For ye
know what commandments we gave you
by the Lord Jesus. 3 For this is the will of
God, *even* your sanctification, that ye
should abstain from fornication: 4 that
every one of you should know how to
possess his vessel in sanctification and
honor; 5 not in the lust of concupiscence,
even as the Gentiles which know not God:
6 that no *man* go beyond and defraud his
brother in *any* matter: because that the
Lord *is* the avenger of all such, as we also
have forewarned you and testified. 7 For
God hath not called us unto uncleanness,
but unto holiness. 8 He therefore that
despiseth, despiseth not man, but God,
who hath also given unto us his Holy
Spirit.●

2. BROTHERLY LOVE

9 But as touching brotherly love ye need
not that I write unto you: for ye yourselves are taught of God to love one another. 10 And indeed ye do it toward all
the brethren which are in all Macedonia:
but we beseech you, brethren, that ye increase more and more; 11 and that ye
study to be quiet, and to do your own
business, and to work with your own
hands, as we commanded you; 12 that ye
may walk honestly toward them that are
without, and *that* ye may have lack of
nothing.●

ABOUND

LACK NOTHING

The first three chapters of 1 Thessalonians are mainly personal and historical in content. At 4:1 Paul begins to concentrate more on teaching and exhortations.

*4:1-8* Record what is written about:

GOD ______

NEGATIVE APPEALS ______

POSITIVE APPEALS ______

*4:9-12* Record the different appeals of this paragraph:

NEW INTERNATIONAL VERSION

What does this passage teach about:

THE RAPTURE OF THE SAINTS WHO ARE ALIVE

THE RESURRECTION OF THE DECEASED SAINTS

DAY OF THE LORD

JUDGMENT

THE CHRISTIAN LIFE

OTHER

*The Coming of the Lord*

13 Brothers, we do not want you to be ignorant about those who fall asleep, or to grieve like the rest of men, who have no hope. 14 We believe that Jesus died and rose again and so we believe that God will bring with Jesus those who have fallen asleep in him. 15 According to the Lord's own word, we tell you that we who are still alive, who are left till the coming of the Lord, will certainly not precede those who have fallen asleep. 16 For the Lord himself will come down from heaven, with a loud command, with the voice of the archangel and with the trumpet call of God, and the dead in Christ will rise first. 17 After that, we who are still alive and are left will be caught up with them in the clouds to meet the Lord in the air. And so we will be with the Lord forever. 18 Therefore encourage each other with these words.●

5 Now, brothers, about times and dates we do not need to write to you, 2 for you know very well that the day of the Lord will come like a thief in the night. 3 While people are saying, "Peace and safety," destruction will come on them suddenly, as labor pains on a pregnant woman, and they will not escape.

4 But you, brothers, are not in darkness so that this day should surprise you like a thief. 5 You are all sons of the light and sons of the day. We do not belong to the night or to the darkness.● 6 So then, let us not be like others, who are asleep, but let us be alert and self-controlled. 7 For those who sleep, sleep at night, and those who get drunk, get drunk at night. 8 But since we belong to the day, let us be self-controlled, putting on faith and love as a breastplate, and the hope of salvation as a helmet. 9 For God did not appoint us to suffer wrath but to receive salvation through our Lord Jesus Christ. 10 He died for us so that, whether we are awake or asleep, we may live together with him. 11 Therefore encourage one another and build each other up, just as in fact you are doing.●

KING JAMES

1.BLESSED RESURRECTION

**13 But I would not have you to be ig-
norant, brethren, concerning them which
are asleep, that ye sorrow not, even as
others which have no hope. 14 For if we
believe that Jesus died and rose again,
even so them also which sleep in Jesus
will God bring with him. 15 For this we
say unto you by the word of the Lord, that
we which are alive *and* remain unto the
coming of the Lord shall not prevent
them which are asleep. 16 For the Lord
himself shall descend from heaven with a
shout, with the voice of the archangel, and
with the trump of God: and the dead in
Christ shall rise first: 17 then we which
are alive *and* remain shall be caught up
together with them in the clouds, to meet
the Lord in the air: and so shall we ever
be with the Lord. 18 Wherefore comfort one another with these words.●**

SORROW

2.SUDDEN DESTRUCTION

**5 But of the times and the seasons,
brethren, ye have no need that I write
unto you. 2 For yourselves know perfectly that the day of the Lord so cometh
as a thief in the night. 3 For when they
shall say, Peace and safety; then sudden
destruction cometh upon them, as travail
upon a woman with child; and they shall
not escape. 4 But ye, brethren, are not in
darkness, that that day should overtake
you as a thief. 5 Ye are all the children of
light, and the children of the day: we are
not of the night, nor of darkness.●**

3.SOBER CHALLENGE

**6 There-
fore let us not sleep, as *do* others; but let
us watch and be sober. 7 For they that
sleep sleep in the night; and they that be
drunken are drunken in the night. 8 But
let us, who are of the day, be sober, putting
on the breastplate of faith and love; and
for a helmet, the hope of salvation.
9 For God hath not appointed us to
wrath, but to obtain salvation by our Lord
Jesus Christ, 10 who died for us, that,
whether we wake or sleep, we should live
together with him. 11 Wherefore comfort yourselves together, and edify one
another, even as also ye do.●**

COMFORT

*4:13-18* Record the events attending Christ's rapture of the church:

What truth is the rapture founded upon (v.14)?

*5:1-5* How will the "day of the Lord" come (v.2)?

What is associated with this "day" (v.3)?

Who will be affected (v.3)?

*5:6-11* What is the appeal to believers?

What do these verses contribute:

vv.9-10

v.11

NEW INTERNATIONAL VERSION

What do you learn here about:

CHURCH OFFICERS

CHURCH UNITY

SANCTIFICATION

Make a list of spiritual guidelines for living today, based on this passage.

*Final Instructions*

12Now we ask you, brothers, to respect
those who work hard among you, who are
over you in the Lord and who admonish
you. 13Hold them in the highest regard in
love because of their work. Live in peace
with each other. 14And we urge you, brothers, warn those who are idle, encourage
the timid, help the weak, be patient with
everyone. 15Make sure that nobody pays
back wrong for wrong, but always try
to be kind to each other and to everyone
else.
16Be joyful always; 17pray continually;
18give thanks in all circumstances, for this
is God's will for you in Christ Jesus.
19Do not put out the Spirit's fire; 20do not
treat prophecies with contempt. 21Test
everything. Hold on to the good. 22Avoid
every kind of evil.●
23May God himself, the God of peace,
sanctify you through and through. May
your whole spirit, soul and body be kept
blameless at the coming of our Lord Jesus
Christ. 24The one who calls you is faithful
and he will do it.●

25Brothers, pray for us. 26Greet all the
brothers with a holy kiss. 27I charge you
before the Lord to have this letter read to
all the brothers.
28The grace of our Lord Jesus Christ be
with you.●

KING JAMES

1. WALK OF THE BELIEVER

A FEW LEADERS

12 And we beseech you, brethren, to
know them which labor among you, and
are over you in the Lord, and admonish
you; 13 and to esteem them very highly
in love for their work's sake. *And* be at
peace among yourselves. 14 Now we exhort you, brethren, warn them that are
unruly, comfort the feeble-minded, support the weak, be patient toward all *men.*
15 See that none render evil for evil unto
any *man;* but ever follow that which is
good, both among yourselves, and to all
*men.* 16 Rejoice evermore. 17 Pray without ceasing. 18 In every thing give thanks:
for this is the will of God in Christ
Jesus concerning you. 19 Quench not the
Spirit. 20 Despise not prophesyings.
21 Prove all things; hold fast that which
is good. 22 Abstain from all appearance*
of evil.●

2. WORK OF GOD

23 And the very God of peace sanctify you wholly; and *I pray God* your
whole spirit and soul and body be
preserved blameless unto the coming
of our Lord Jesus Christ. 24 Faithful
*is* he that calleth you, who also will do
*it.*●

3. FELLOWSHIP OF THE BELIEVERS

ALL THE MEMBERS

25 Brethren, pray for us.
26 Greet all the brethren with a holy
kiss.
27 I charge you by the Lord, that this
epistle be read unto all the holy brethren.●

—benediction

28 The grace of our Lord Jesus Christ
*be* with you. Amen.●

*5:12-22* List the commands and exhortations of this compact paragraph. Look for any groupings in the list, according to area of life.

*5:23-24* What ministries of God and Christ are mentioned here?

*5:25-27* What word is repeated in each verse?

*5:28* What does grace mean?

# 2 THESSALONIANS

## AUTHORSHIP

Paul is identified by name at 1:1 and 3:17.

## DATE

Around A.D. 52. This letter followed the first by no more than a few months. Paul was still ministering at Corinth, on his second missionary journey, when he wrote the letter.

## OCCASION AND PURPOSES

After Paul's first letter to the Thessalonians had been delivered, report came back to Paul concerning the present state of the church. The good parts of the report are the subjects of Paul's commendations for the saints. A negative report was that Paul's teaching about the Lord's coming had been misrepresented—some false teachers were saying the Lord had already come. Paul is quick to correct the error and rebuke those involved. So the purposes of the letter were (a) commendation and (b) doctrinal and practical correction.

## 2 THESSALONIANS: Waiting for The Lord's Return

| | |
|---|---|
| Salutation | 1:1-2 |
| BEFORE THE RAPTURE: PERSECUTION | 1:3-12 |
| BEFORE THE REVELATION: ANTICHRIST | 2:1-17 |
| HOW CHRISTIANS SHOULD LIVE NOW | 3:1-15 |
| Benediction | 3:16-18 |

# 2 THESSALONIANS

NEW INTERNATIONAL VERSION

What does this passage teach about:

THANKSGIVING

PRAYER

SUFFERING OF THE SAINTS

JUDGMENT OF UNBELIEVERS

NAME OF CHRIST

OTHER

1 Paul, Silas[a] and Timothy,
To the church of the Thessalonians in
God our Father and the Lord Jesus Christ:
2Grace and peace to you from God the
Father and the Lord Jesus Christ.●

*Thanksgiving and Prayer*

3We ought always to thank God for you,
brothers, and rightly so, because your faith
is growing more and more, and the love
every one of you has for each other is increasing. 4Therefore, among God's
churches we boast about your perseverance and faith in all the persecutions and
trials you are enduring.●
5All this is evidence that God's judgment
is right, and as a result you will be counted
worthy of the kingdom of God, for which
you are suffering. 6God is just: He will pay
back trouble to those who trouble you 7and
give relief to you who are troubled, and to
us as well. This will happen when the Lord
Jesus is revealed from heaven in blazing
fire with his powerful angels. 8He will punish those who do not know God and do not
obey the gospel of our Lord Jesus. 9They
will be punished with everlasting destruction and shut out from the presence of the
Lord and from the majesty of his power
10on the day he comes to be glorified in his
holy people and to be marveled at among
all those who have believed. This includes
you, because you believed our testimony
to you.●
11With this in mind, we constantly pray
for you, that our God may count you
worthy of his calling, and that by his power
he may fulfill every good purpose of yours
and every act prompted by your faith.
12We pray this so that the name of our Lord
Jesus may be glorified in you, and you in
him, according to the grace of our God and
the Lord Jesus Christ.[b]●

[a] 1 Greek *Silvanus*, a variant of *Silas*
[b] 12 Or *God and Lord, Jesus Christ*

KING JAMES

# 2 THESSALONIANS

—salutation

THANKSGIVING

1 Paul, and Silva'nus, and Timothy,
Unto the church of the Thessa-
lo'ni-ans in God our Father and the
Lord Jesus Christ:
2 Grace unto you, and peace, from
God our Father and the Lord Jesus
Christ.●

1.COMMENDATION

3 We are bound to thank God always
for you, brethren, as it is meet, because
that your faith groweth exceedingly, and
the charity of every one of you all toward
each other aboundeth; 4 so that we ourselves glory in you in the churches of God,
for your patience and faith in all your persecutions and tribulations that ye endure:●

2.EXPLANATION

5 *which is* a manifest token of the righteous judgment of God, that ye may be
counted worthy of the kingdom of God,
for which ye also suffer: 6 seeing *it is* a
righteous thing with God to recompense
tribulation to them that trouble you;
7 and to you who are troubled rest with
us, when the Lord Jesus shall be revealed
from heaven with his mighty angels, 8 in
flaming fire taking vengeance on them
that know not God, and that obey not the
gospel of our Lord Jesus Christ: 9 who
shall be punished with everlasting destruction from the presence of the Lord,
and from the glory of his power; 10 when
he shall come to be glorified in his saints,
and to be admired in all them that believe
(because our testimony among you was
believed) in that day.●

3.INSPIRATION

11 Wherefore also we pray always for
you, that our God would count you
worthy of *this* calling, and fulfil all the
good pleasure of *his* goodness, and the
work of faith with power: 12 that the
name of our Lord Jesus Christ may be
glorified in you, and ye in him, according
to the grace of our God and the Lord
Jesus Christ.●

PRAYER

*1:1-2* What is suggested by the combination "grace...and peace"?

*1:3-4* For what things are the Thessalonian saints commended?

*1:5-10* What does Paul write about:

SUFFERING BY THE THESSALONIANS

JUDGMENT OF UNBELIEVERS

*1:11-12* Record the things prayed for:

NEW INTERNATIONAL VERSION

What do you learn here about:

ANTICHRIST

SECOND COMING OF CHRIST

SATAN

SOVEREIGNTY OF GOD

PERSEVERANCE OF THE SAINTS

DIVINE HELP FOR THE BELIEVER

### *The Man of Lawlessness*

2 Concerning the coming of our Lord
Jesus Christ and our being gathered to
him, we ask you, brothers, 2not to become
easily unsettled or alarmed by some prophecy, report or letter supposed to have
come from us, saying that the day of the
Lord has already come. 3Don't let anyone
deceive you in any way, for ⌊that day will
not come⌋ until the rebellion occurs and the
man of lawlessness[c] is revealed, the man
doomed to destruction. 4He opposes and
exalts himself over everything that is
called God or is worshiped, and even sets
himself up in God's temple, proclaiming
himself to be God.●
5Don't you remember that when I was
with you I used to tell you these things?
6And now you know what is holding him
back, so that he may be revealed at the
proper time. 7For the secret power of lawlessness is already at work; but the one
who now holds it back will continue to do
so till he is taken out of the way. 8And then
the lawless one will be revealed, whom the
Lord Jesus will overthrow with the breath
of his mouth and destroy by the splendor
of his coming. 9The coming of the lawless
one will be in accordance with the work of
Satan displayed in all kinds of counterfeit
miracles, signs and wonders, 10and in
every sort of evil that deceives those who
are perishing. They perish because they
refused to love the truth and so be saved.
11For this reason God sends them a powerful delusion so that they will believe the lie
12and so that all will be condemned who
have not believed the truth but have delighted in wickedness.●

### *Stand Firm*

13But we ought always to thank God for
you, brothers loved by the Lord, because
from the beginning God chose you[a] to be
saved through the sanctifying work of the
Spirit and through belief in the truth. 14He
called you to this through our gospel, that
you might share in the glory of our Lord
Jesus Christ. 15So then, brothers, stand
firm and hold to the teachings[b] we passed
on to you, whether by word of mouth or by
letter.●
16May our Lord Jesus Christ himself and
God our Father, who loved us and by his
grace gave us eternal encouragement and
good hope, 17encourage your hearts and
strengthen you in every good deed and
word.●

[c]3 Some manuscripts *sin*

[a]13 Some manuscripts *because God chose you as his firstfruits* [b]15 Or *traditions*

KING JAMES

1. ANTI-CHRIST'S APPEAR-ANCE

SHAKEN

2 Now we beseech you, brethren, by the
coming of our Lord Jesus Christ, and
*by* our gathering together unto him,
2 that ye be not soon shaken in mind, or
be troubled, neither by spirit, nor by word,
nor by letter as from us, as that the day of
Christ is at hand. 3 Let no man deceive
you by any means: for *that day shall not*
*come*, except there come a falling away
first, and that man of sin be revealed, the
son of perdition; 4 who opposeth and
exalteth himself above all that is called
God, or that is worshipped; so that he as
God sitteth in the temple of God, showing himself that he is God.●

2. ANTI-CHRIST'S OVER-THROW

5 Remember ye
not, that, when I was yet with you, I told
you these things? 6 And now ye know
what withholdeth that he might be revealed in his time. 7 For the mystery of
iniquity doth already work: only he who
now letteth *will let*, until he be taken out
of the way. 8 And then shall that Wicked
be revealed, whom the Lord shall consume with the spirit of his mouth, and
shall destroy with the brightness of his
coming: 9 *even him*, whose coming is
after the working of Satan with all power
and signs and lying wonders, 10 and
with all deceivableness of unrighteousness in them that perish; because they received not the love of the truth, that they
might be saved. 11 And for this cause
God shall send them strong delusion, that
they should believe a lie: 12 that they all
might be damned who believed not the
truth, but had pleasure in unrighteousness.●

3. ENCOUR-AGEMENT

13 But we are bound to give thanks always to God for you, brethren beloved of
the Lord, because God hath from the beginning chosen you to salvation through
sanctification of the Spirit and belief of
the truth: 14 whereunto he called you by
our gospel, to the obtaining of the glory
of our Lord Jesus Christ. 15 Therefore,
brethren, stand fast, and hold the traditions which ye have been taught, whether
by word, or our epistle.●

—benedic-tion

16 Now our Lord Jesus Christ himself,
and God, even our Father, which hath
loved us, and hath given *us* everlasting
consolation and good hope through
grace, 17 comfort your hearts, and stablish you in every good word and work.●

ESTAB-LISHED

The Wicked One of verse 8 is usually referred to as Antichrist.

*2:1-4* How else is Antichrist identified in this paragraph?

Read "is at hand" (v.2) as "has already begun" (Living Bible text). Why would the rumor of verse 2 disturb the Thessalonians?

*2:5-12* Record the sequence of events to take place.

*2:13-15* Record:

ASSURANCES

EXHORTATIONS

*2:16-17* What are the parts of this benediction?

NEW INTERNATIONAL VERSION

What does this concluding passage teach about:

THE LOCAL CHURCH FELLOWSHIP ______________________

IDLENESS ______________________

WORKS ______________________

### *Request for Prayer*

3 Finally, brothers, pray for us that the
message of the Lord may spread rapidly and be honored, just as it was with you.
[2]And pray that we may be delivered from
wicked and evil men, for not everyone has
faith. [3]But the Lord is faithful, and he will
strengthen and protect you from the evil
one. [4]We have confidence in the Lord that
you are doing and will continue to do the
things we command. [5]May the Lord direct
your hearts into God's love and Christ's
perseverance.●

### *Warning Against Idleness*

[6]In the name of the Lord Jesus Christ,
we command you, brothers, to keep away
from every brother who is idle and does not
live according to the teaching[c] you received from us. [7]For you yourselves know
how you ought to follow our example. We
were not idle when we were with you, [8]nor
did we eat anyone's food without paying
for it. On the contrary, we worked night
and day, laboring and toiling so that we
would not be a burden to any of you. [9]We
did this, not because we do not have the
right to such help, but in order to make
ourselves a model for you to follow. [10]For
even when we were with you, we gave you
this rule: "If a man will not work, he shall
not eat."

[11]We hear that some among you are idle.
They are not busy; they are busybodies.
[12]Such people we command and urge in the
Lord Jesus Christ to settle down and earn
the bread they eat. [13]And as for you, brothers, never tire of doing what is right.

[14]If anyone does not obey our instruction
in this letter, take special note of him. Do
not associate with him, in order that he
may feel ashamed. [15]Yet do not regard him
as an enemy, but warn him as a brother.●

### *Final Greetings*

[16]Now may the Lord of peace himself
give you peace at all times and in every
way. The Lord be with all of you.

[17]I, Paul, write this greeting in my own
hand, which is the distinguishing mark in
all my letters. This is how I write.

[18]The grace of our Lord Jesus Christ be
with you all.●

[c]6 Or *tradition*

KING JAMES

1. HELP OF THE LORD

WICKED MEN

3 Finally, brethren, pray for us, that the
word of the Lord may have *free*
course, and be glorified, even as *it is* with
you: 2 and that we may be delivered from
unreasonable and wicked men: for all *men*
have not faith. 3 But the Lord is faithful,
who shall stablish you, and keep *you* from
evil. 4 And we have confidence in the
Lord touching you, that ye both do and
will do the things which we command
you. 5 And the Lord direct your hearts
into the love of God, and into the patient
waiting for Christ.●

2. SIN OF IDLENESS

6 Now we command you, brethren, in
the name of our Lord Jesus Christ, that ye
withdraw yourselves from every brother
that walketh disorderly, and not after the
tradition which he received of us. 7 For
yourselves know how ye ought to follow
us: for we behaved not ourselves disorderly among you; 8 neither did we eat
any man's bread for nought; but wrought
with labor and travail night and day, that
we might not be chargeable to any of you:
9 not because we have not power, but to
make ourselves an ensample unto you to
follow us. 10 For even when we were with
you, this we commanded you, that if any
would not work, neither should he eat.
11 For we hear that there are some which
walk among you disorderly, working not
at all, but are busybodies. 12 Now them
that are such we command and exhort by
our Lord Jesus Christ, that with quietness
they work, and eat their own bread.
13 But ye, brethren, be not weary in well
doing.
14 And if any man obey not our word
by this epistle, note that man, and have no
company with him, that he may be
ashamed. 15 Yet count *him* not as an
enemy, but admonish *him* as a brother.● BROTHER

—benedictions

16 Now the Lord of peace himself give
you peace always by all means. The Lord
*be* with you all.
17 The salutation of Paul with mine
own hand, which is the token in every
epistle: so I write. 18 The grace of our
Lord Jesus Christ *be* with you all. Amen.●

*3:1-5* Record Paul's prayer requests:

What help of the Lord is recognized here?

*3:6-15* What is the paragraph mainly about:

Why is the sin of idleness so disruptive of the Christian fellowship?

Record the commands of the paragraph.

*3:16-18* Compare the two benedictions.

# 1 TIMOTHY

## AUTHORSHIP

Paul wrote this letter to his friend and co-laborer Timothy, who was ministering as an interim pastor in the church at Ephesus. Paul was probably in Macedonia at the time.

## DATE

Around A.D. 62.

## OCCASION AND PURPOSE

The situation at the church of Ephesus was the reason for Paul's writing to Timothy. There are direct or indirect references to various problems or needs, such as: spread of false doctrine, spiritual coldness, personnel problems, problems of the worship service and church offices, and the care of widows. And Paul's immediate purpose in writing was to urge Timothy to remain at Ephesus, ministering to help solve and correct the existing problems and evils. A theme of the letter is godliness and pastoral care.

## 1 TIMOTHY: Godliness and Pastoral Care

| | |
|---|---|
| CHARGE TO TIMOTHY | 1:1-20 |
| Sound Doctrine | 1:1-11 |
| Grace and Warfare | 1:12-20 |
| INSTRUCTIONS TO TIMOTHY | 2:1-6:21 |
| Public Worship in the Church | 2:1-15 |
| Church Officers | 3:1-16 |
| Antidote for False Teaching | 4:1-16 |
| Widows, Elders and Slaves | 5:1-6:2a |
| Final Instructions and Exhortations | 6:2b-21 |

# 1 TIMOTHY

NEW INTERNATIONAL VERSION

What do you learn here about:

FALSE DOCTRINE ____________________

LAW ____________________

GOSPEL ____________________

CHRISTIAN MINISTRY ____________________

GRACE ____________________

SPIRITUAL WARFARE ____________________

1 Paul, an apostle of Christ Jesus by the
command of God our Savior and of
Christ Jesus our hope,

2 To Timothy my true son in the faith:

Grace, mercy and peace from God the
Father and Christ Jesus our Lord.●

*Warning Against False Teachers of the Law*

3 As I urged you when I went into Macedonia, stay there in Ephesus so that you
may command certain men not to teach
false doctrines any longer 4 nor to devote
themselves to myths and endless genealogies. These promote controversies rather
than God's work—which is by faith. 5 The
goal of this command is love, which comes
from a pure heart and a good conscience
and a sincere faith. 6 Some have wandered
away from these and turned to meaningless
talk. 7 They want to be teachers of the law,
but they do not know what they are talking
about or what they so confidently affirm.
8 We know that the law is good if a man
uses it properly. 9 We also know that law is
made not for good men but for lawbreakers
and rebels, the ungodly and sinful, the unholy and irreligious; for those who kill their
fathers or mothers, for murderers, 10 for
adulterers and perverts, for slave traders
and liars and perjurers—and for whatever
else is contrary to the sound doctrine 11 that
conforms to the glorious gospel of the
blessed God, which he entrusted to me.●

*The Lord's Grace to Paul*

12 I thank Christ Jesus our Lord, who has
given me strength, that he considered me
faithful, appointing me to his service.
13 Even though I was once a blasphemer
and a persecutor and a violent man, I was
shown mercy because I acted in ignorance
and unbelief. 14 The grace of our Lord was
poured out on me abundantly, along with
the faith and love that are in Christ Jesus.
15 Here is a trustworthy saying that deserves full acceptance: Christ Jesus came
into the world to save sinners—of whom I
am the worst. 16 But for that very reason I
was shown mercy so that in me, the worst
of sinners, Christ Jesus might display his
unlimited patience as an example for those
who would believe on him and receive
eternal life. 17 Now to the King eternal, immortal, invisible, the only God, be honor
and glory for ever and ever. Amen.●
18 Timothy, my son, I give you this instruction in keeping with the prophecies
once made about you, so that by following
them you may fight the good fight, 19 holding on to faith and a good conscience.
Some have rejected these and so have shipwrecked their faith. 20 Among them are Hymenaeus and Alexander, whom I have
handed over to Satan to be taught not to
blaspheme.●

KING JAMES

# 1 TIMOTHY

—salutation

1 Paul, an apostle of Jesus Christ by the
commandment of God our Saviour,
and Lord Jesus Christ, *which is* our hope;
2 Unto Timothy, *my* own son in the
faith:
Grace, mercy, *and* peace, from God our
Father, and Jesus Christ our Lord.●

1.SOUND DOCTRINE

3 As I besought thee to abide still at
Ephesus, when I went into Macedonia,
that thou mightest charge some that they
teach no other doctrine, 4 neither give
heed to fables and endless genealogies,
which minister questions, rather than
godly edifying which is in faith: *so do.*
5 Now the end of the commandment is
charity out of a pure heart, and *of* a good
conscience, and *of* faith unfeigned: 6 from
which some having swerved have turned
aside unto vain jangling; 7 desiring to be
teachers of the law; understanding neither what they say, nor whereof they
affirm.
8 But we know that the law *is* good, if a
man use it lawfully; 9 knowing this, that
the law is not made for a righteous man,
but for the lawless and disobedient, for
the ungodly and for sinners, for unholy
and profane, for murderers of fathers and
murderers of mothers, for manslayers,
10 for whoremongers, for them that defile
themselves with mankind, for menstealers,
for liars, for perjured persons, and if there
be any other thing that is contrary to
sound doctrine; 11 according to the
glorious gospel of the blessed God, which
was committed to my trust.●

FALSE DOCTRINE

2.ABUNDANT GRACE

12 And I thank Christ Jesus our Lord,
who hath enabled me, for that he counted
me faithful, putting me into the ministry;
13 who was before a blasphemer, and a
persecutor, and injurious: but I obtained
mercy, because I did *it* ignorantly in unbelief. 14 And the grace of our Lord was
exceeding abundant with faith and love
which is in Christ Jesus. 15 This *is* a
faithful saying, and worthy of all acceptation, that Christ Jesus came into the
world to save sinners; of whom I am
chief. 16 Howbeit for this cause I obtained mercy, that in me first Jesus Christ
might show forth all long-suffering, for a
pattern to them which should hereafter
believe on him to life everlasting. 17 Now
unto the King eternal, immortal, invisible,
the only wise God, *be* honor and glory for
ever and ever. Amen.●

3.GOOD WARFARE

18 This charge I commit unto thee, son
Timothy, according to the prophecies
which went before on thee, that thou by
them mightest war a good warfare;
19 holding faith, and a good conscience;
which some having put away, concerning
faith have made shipwreck: 20 of whom
is Hymene'us and Alexander; whom I
have delivered unto Satan, that they may
learn not to blaspheme.●

BLASPHEMY

*1:1-2* Record the *doctrinal* words of the salutation, not including names;

______

______

______

______

______

*1:3-11* Where does the word "doctrine" appear in the paragraph?

______

______

What false doctrines does Paul mention?

______

______

______

What are the different references to the law?

______

______

______

______

______

______

*1:12-17* What are the different references to mercy and grace?

______

______

______

How does Paul relate grace to his ministry?

______

______

______

*1:18-20* What is a "good warfare"? ______

______

______

______

______

NEW INTERNATIONAL VERSION

What does this passage teach about:

INTERCESSORY PRAYER

SALVATION

WORK OF CHRIST

CHRISTIAN MINISTRY

PLACE OF WOMEN IN THE CHURCH

MOTHERS

OTHER

*Instructions on Worship*

2 I urge, then, first of all, that requests,
prayers, intercession and thanksgiving
be made for everyone— 2for kings and all
those in authority, that we may live peaceful and quiet lives in all godliness and holiness. 3This is good, and pleases God our
Savior, 4who wants all men to be saved and
to come to a knowledge of the truth. 5For
there is one God and one mediator between
God and men, the man Christ Jesus, 6who
gave himself as a ransom for all men—the
testimony given in its proper time. 7And for
this purpose I was appointed a herald and
an apostle—I am telling the truth, I am not
lying—and a teacher of the true faith to the
Gentiles.
8I want men everywhere to lift up holy
hands in prayer, without anger or disputing.●
9I also want women to dress modestly,
with decency and propriety, not with
braided hair or gold or pearls or expensive
clothes, 10but with good deeds, appropriate
for women who profess to worship God.
11A woman should learn in quietness and
full submission. 12I do not permit a woman
to teach or to have authority over a man;
she must be silent. 13For Adam was formed
first, then Eve. 14And Adam was not the
one deceived; it was the woman who was
deceived and became a sinner. 15But
women will be kept safe[a] through childbirth, if they continue in faith, love and
holiness with propriety.●

[a]15 Or *be saved*

KING JAMES

1.PRAYER

2 I exhort therefore, that, first of all,
supplications, prayers, intercessions,
*and* giving of thanks, be made for all men;
2 for kings, and *for* all that are in authority; that we may lead a quiet and peaceable life in all godliness and honesty.
3 For this *is* good and acceptable in the
sight of God our Saviour; 4 who will
have all men to be saved, and to come unto the knowledge of the truth. 5 For
*there is* one God, and one mediator between God and men, the man Christ
Jesus; 6 who gave himself a ransom for
all, to be testified in due time. 7 Whereunto I am ordained a preacher, and an
apostle, (I speak the truth in Christ, *and*
lie not,) a teacher of the Gentiles in faith
and verity.
8 I will therefore that men pray every
where, lifting up holy hands, without
wrath and doubting.● 9 In like manner
also, that women adorn themselves in
modest apparel, with shamefacedness and
sobriety; not with braided hair, or gold,
or pearls, or costly array; 10 but (which
becometh women professing godliness)
with good works. 11 Let the woman
learn in silence with all subjection. 12 But
I suffer not a woman to teach, nor to
usurp authority over the man, but to be
in silence. 13 For Adam was first formed,
then Eve. 14 And Adam was not deceived, but the woman being deceived was
in the transgression. 15 Notwithstanding
she shall be saved in childbearing, if they
continue in faith and charity and holiness
with sobriety.●

2.WOMEN

RULERS

MOTHERS

In this segment Paul begins to write about subjects particularly involving the church services.

*2:1-8* Record what is written about:

PRAYER ____________________

CHRIST ____________________

PAUL'S MISSION ____________________

*2:9-15* What is written in each of these parts:

vv.9-10 ____________________

vv.11-12 ____________________

vv.13-15 ____________________

NEW INTERNATIONAL VERSION

In your own words list the qualifications of a pastor. Apply these to the local church situation today.

Do the same for deacons:

Record what 3:14-16 teaches about:

HOUSE OF GOD

LIFE OF CHRIST

*Overseers and Deacons*

3 Here is a trustworthy saying: If anyone
sets his heart on being an overseer,[b] he
desires a noble task. 2Now the overseer
must be above reproach, the husband of
but one wife, temperate, self-controlled,
respectable, hospitable, able to teach, 3not
given to much wine, not violent but gentle,
not quarrelsome, not a lover of money. 4He
must manage his own family well and see
that his children obey him with proper respect. 5(If anyone does not know how to
manage his own family, how can he take
care of God's church?) 6He must not be a
recent convert, or he may become conceited and fall under the same judgment as the
devil. 7He must also have a good reputation with outsiders, so that he will not fall
into disgrace and into the devil's trap.●
8Deacons, likewise, are to be men
worthy of respect, sincere, not indulging in
much wine, and not pursuing dishonest
gain. 9They must keep hold of the deep
truths of the faith with a clear conscience.
10They must first be tested; and then if
there is nothing against them, let them
serve as deacons.
11In the same way, their wives[c] are to be
women worthy of respect, not malicious
talkers but temperate and trustworthy in
everything.
12A deacon must be the husband of but
one wife and must manage his children and
his household well. 13Those who have
served well gain an excellent standing and
great assurance in their faith in Christ
Jesus.●
14Although I hope to come to you soon,
I am writing you these instructions so that,
15if I am delayed, you will know how
people ought to conduct themselves in
God's household, which is the church of
the living God, the pillar and foundation of
the truth. 16Beyond all question, the mystery of godliness is great:

He[d] appeared in a body,
was vindicated by the Spirit,
was seen by angels,
was preached among the nations,
was believed on in the world,
was taken up in glory.●

[b]*1* Traditionally *bishop*; also in verse 2
[c]*11* Or *way, deaconesses*
[d]*16* Some manuscripts *God*

KING JAMES

1. PASTOR

GOOD WORK

**3** This *is* a true saying, If a man desire
the office of a bishop, he desireth a
good work. 2 A bishop then must be
blameless, the husband of one wife, vigilant, sober, of good behavior, given to
hospitality, apt to teach; 3 not given to
wine, no striker, not greedy of filthy lucre;
but patient, not a brawler, not covetous;
4 one that ruleth well his own house, having his children in subjection with all
gravity; 5 (for if a man know not how to
rule his own house, how shall he take care
of the church of God?) 6 not a novice,
lest being lifted up with pride he fall into
the condemnation of the devil. 7 Moreover he must have a good report of them
which are without; lest he fall into reproach and the snare of the devil.●

2. DEACON

8 Likewise *must* the deacons *be* grave,
not double-tongued, not given to much
wine, not greedy of filthy lucre; 9 holding
the mystery of the faith in a pure conscience. 10 And let these also first be
proved; then let them use the office of a
deacon, being *found* blameless. 11 Even
so *must their* wives *be* grave, not slanderers, sober, faithful in all things. 12 Let
the deacons be the husbands of one wife,
ruling their children and their own houses
well. 13 For they that have used the office
of a deacon well purchase to themselves a
good degree, and great boldness in the
faith which is in Christ Jesus.●

3. HOUSE OF GOD

14 These things write I unto thee, hoping to come unto thee shortly: 15 but if I
tarry long, that thou mayest know how
thou oughtest to behave thyself in the
house of God, which is the church of the
living God, the pillar and ground of
the truth. 16 And without controversy
great is the mystery of godliness:

GREAT MYSTERY

God was manifest in the flesh,
justified in the Spirit,
seen of angels,
preached unto the Gentiles,
believed on in the world,
received up into glory.●

*3:1-7* List the qualifications of a bishop (lit. "overseer"). Look for any groupings of the qualifications, and mark these on the list.

*3:8-13* List the qualifications of the deacon.

*3:14-16* This paragraph is the climax of the first half of the epistle.
What are the subjects of the paragraph?

NEW INTERNATIONAL VERSION

What do you learn here about:

FALSE TEACHING

MINISTER OF JESUS CHRIST

MINISTRIES OF A PASTOR

Apply this passage to all Christians living and serving Christ today. Make a list of these applications.

*Instructions to Timothy*

4 The Spirit clearly says that in later
times some will abandon the faith and
follow deceiving spirits and things taught
by demons. 2Such teachings come through
hypocritical liars, whose consciences have
been seared as with a hot iron. 3They forbid people to marry and order them to abstain from certain foods, which God
created to be received with thanksgiving
by those who believe and who know the
truth. 4For everything God created is good,
and nothing is to be rejected if it is received
with thanksgiving, 5because it is consecrated by the word of God and prayer.●
6If you point these things out to the
brothers, you will be a good minister of
Christ Jesus, brought up in the truths of the
faith and of the good teaching that you
have followed. 7Have nothing to do with
godless myths and old wives' tales; rather,
train yourself to be godly. 8For physical
training is of some value, but godliness has
value for all things, holding promise for
both the present life and the life to come.
9This is a trustworthy saying that deserves full acceptance 10(and for this we
labor and strive), that we have put our
hope in the living God, who is the Savior
of all men, and especially of those who
believe.●
11Command and teach these things.
12Don't let anyone look down on you because you are young, but set an example
for the believers in speech, in life, in love,
in faith and in purity. 13Until I come,
devote yourself to the public reading of
Scripture, to preaching and to teaching.
14Do not neglect your gift, which was given
you through a prophetic message when the
body of elders laid their hands on you.
15Be diligent in these matters; give yourself wholly to them, so that everyone may
see your progress. 16Watch your life and
doctrine closely. Persevere in them, because if you do, you will save both yourself
and your hearers.●

KING JAMES

1.FALSE TEACHING

BACK-SLIDING

4 Now the Spirit speaketh expressly,
that in the latter times some shall
depart from the faith, giving heed to se-
ducing spirits, and doctrines of devils;
2 speaking lies in hypocrisy; having their
conscience seared with a hot iron; 3 forbidding to marry, *and commanding* to abstain from meats, which God hath created
to be received with thanksgiving of them
which believe and know the truth. 4 For
every creature of God *is* good, and nothing to be refused, if it be received with
thanksgiving: 5 for it is sanctified by the
word of God and prayer.●

2.MINISTER OF CHRIST

6 If thou put the brethren in remembrance of these things, thou shalt be a
good minister of Jesus Christ, nourished
up in the words of faith and of good doctrine, whereunto thou hast attained.
7 But refuse profane and old wives' fables,
and exercise thyself *rather* unto godliness.
8 For bodily exercise profiteth little: but
godliness is profitable unto all things,
having promise of the life that now is, and
of that which is to come. 9 This *is* a faithful saying, and worthy of all acceptation.
10 For therefore we both labor and suffer
reproach, because we trust in the living
God, who is the Saviour of all men,
specially of those that believe.●

3.THE MINISTRY

11 These things command and teach.
12 Let no man despise thy youth; but be
thou an example of the believers, in word,
in conversation, in charity, in spirit, in
faith, in purity. 13 Till I come, give
attendance to reading, to exhortation, to
doctrine. 14 Neglect not the gift that is in
thee, which was given thee by prophecy,
with the laying on of the hands of the
presbytery. 15 Meditate upon these
things; give thyself wholly to them; that
thy profiting may appear to all. 16 Take
heed unto thyself, and unto the doctrine;
continue in them: for in doing this thou
shalt both save thyself, and them that
hear thee.●

BEING CAREFUL

*4:1-5* What is the main point of each part:

vv.1-2 ______________________________

v.3 ______________________________

vv.4-5 ______________________________

*4:6-10* Record the qualities of a good minister:

______________________________

*4:11-16* Record what is written about the ministry itself.

______________________________

NEW INTERNATIONAL VERSION

Organize your own list, based on this passage, of the church's obligations to widows.

Make another list of practical applications of the passage to the everyday life of the believer.

*Advice About Widows, Elders and Slaves*

5 Do not rebuke an older man harshly,
but exhort him as if he were your father. Treat younger men as brothers, [2]old-
er women as mothers, and younger women
as sisters, with absolute purity.●
[3]Give proper recognition to those widows who are really in need. [4]But if a widow
has children or grandchildren, these should
learn first of all to put their religion into
practice by caring for their own family and
so repaying their parents and grandpar-
ents, for this is pleasing to God. [5]The
widow who is really in need and left all
alone puts her hope in God and continues
night and day to pray and to ask God for
help. [6]But the widow who lives for pleasure is dead even while she lives. [7]Give the
people these instructions, too, so that no
one may be open to blame. [8]If anyone does
not provide for his relatives, and especially
for his immediate family, he has denied the
faith and is worse than an unbeliever.
[9]No widow may be put on the list of
widows unless she is over sixty, has been
faithful to her husband,[a] [10]and is well
known for her good deeds, such as bringing
up children, showing hospitality, washing
the feet of the saints, helping those in trouble and devoting herself to all kinds of good
deeds.●
[11]As for younger widows, do not put
them on such a list. For when their sensual
desires overcome their dedication to
Christ, they want to marry. [12]Thus they
bring judgment on themselves, because
they have broken their first pledge. [13]Be-
sides, they get into the habit of being idle
and going about from house to house. And
not only do they become idlers, but also
gossips and busybodies, saying things they
ought not to. [14]So I counsel younger widows to marry, to have children, to manage
their homes and to give the enemy no opportunity for slander. [15]Some have in fact
already turned away to follow Satan.●
[16]If any woman who is a believer has
widows in her family, she should help them
and not let the church be burdened with
them, so that the church can help those
widows who are really in need.●

[a]9 Or *has had but one husband*

KING JAMES

—the congregation

ELDERS

5 Rebuke not an elder, but entreat
*him* as a father; *and* the younger men
as brethren; 2 the elder women as mothers; the younger as sisters, with all purity.●

1. OLDER WIDOWS

3 Honor widows that are widows indeed. 4 But if any widow have children
or nephews, let them learn first to show
piety at home, and to requite their parents: for that is good and acceptable before God. 5 Now she that is a widow
indeed, and desolate, trusteth in God, and
continueth in supplications and prayers
night and day. 6 But she that liveth in
pleasure is dead while she liveth. 7 And
these things give in charge, that they may
be blameless. 8 But if any provide not for
his own, and specially for those of his
own house, he hath denied the faith, and
is worse than an infidel.
9 Let not a widow be taken into the
number under threescore years old, having been the wife of one man, 10 well reported of for good works; if she have
brought up children, if she have lodged
strangers, if she have washed the saints'
feet, if she have relieved the afflicted, if
she have diligently followed every good
work.●

2. YOUNGER WIDOWS

11 But the younger widows refuse:
for when they have begun to wax wanton
against Christ, they will marry; 12 having
damnation, because they have cast off
their first faith. 13 And withal they learn
*to be* idle, wandering about from house to
house; and not only idle, but tattlers also
and busybodies, speaking things which
they ought not. 14 I will therefore that
the younger women marry, bear children,
guide the house, give none occasion to the
adversary to speak reproachfully. 15 For
some are already turned aside after Satan.●

WIDOWS

16 If any man or woman that believeth
have widows, let them relieve them, and
let not the church be charged; that it may
relieve them that are widows indeed.●

*5:1-2* What are the two age groups mentioned?

What is Paul's counsel to Timothy regarding these relationships?

*5:3-10* Two groups of widows are discussed here: those for whose care the church is responsible (*real* widows), and those not an obligation to the church. Read what Paul writes about each group:

(1) Real widows— verses 3,5,9-10

(2) Widows who are not the church's obligation—verses 4,6-8,16. Note the word "but" at verses 4,6,8.

*5:11-15* What is Paul's counsel concerning younger widows?

*5:16* What does this verse add to what Paul has already written?

NEW INTERNATIONAL VERSION

Make a list of practical truths about elders (or pastors) and their work, based on this passage.

In what different ways can the paragraph 6:1-2a be applied to today?

17The elders who direct the affairs of the
church well are worthy of double honor,
especially those whose work is preaching
and teaching. 18For the Scripture says,
"Do not muzzle the ox while it is treading
out the grain,"[b] and "The worker deserves
his wages."[c] 19Do not entertain an accusation against an elder unless it is brought by
two or three witnesses. 20Those who sin
are to be rebuked publicly, so that the
others may take warning.●
21I charge you, in the sight of God and
Christ Jesus and the elect angels, to keep
these instructions without partiality, and to
do nothing out of favoritism.
22Do not be hasty in the laying on of
hands, and do not share in the sins of
others. Keep yourself pure.
23Stop drinking only water, and use a
little wine because of your stomach and
your frequent illnesses.●
24The sins of some men are obvious,
reaching the place of judgment ahead of
them; the sins of others trail behind them.
25In the same way, good deeds are obvious, and even those that are not cannot be
hidden.●
6 All who are under the yoke of slavery
should consider their masters worthy
of full respect, so that God's name and our
teaching may not be slandered. 2Those
who have believing masters are not to
show less respect for them because they
are brothers. Instead, they are to serve
them even better, because those who benefit from their service are believers, and
dear to them.●

[b]18 Deut. 25:4 [c]18 Luke 10:7

## KING JAMES

1.ELDERS

GOOD ELDERS

17 Let the elders that rule well be
counted worthy of double honor, especially they who labor in the word and
doctrine. 18 For the Scripture saith,
Thou shalt not muzzle the ox
that treadeth out the corn.
And,
The laborer *is* worthy of his reward.
19 Against an elder receive not an accusation, but before two or three witnesses.
20 Them that sin rebuke before all, that
others also may fear.● 21 I charge *thee*
before God, and the Lord Jesus Christ,
and the elect angels, that thou observe
these things without preferring one before
another, doing nothing by partiality.
22 Lay hands suddenly on no man, neither be partaker of other men's sins: keep
thyself pure.
23 Drink no longer water, but use a
little wine for thy stomach's sake and
thine often infirmities.●
24 Some men's sins are open beforehand, going before to judgment; and
some *men* they follow after. 25 Likewise
also the good works *of some* are manifest
beforehand; and they that are otherwise
cannot be hid.●

Deu. 25:4

Lk. 10:7

2.SERVANTS

GOOD MASTERS

6 Let as many servants as are under the
yoke count their own masters worthy
of all honor, that the name of God and
*his* doctrine be not blasphemed. 2 And
they that have believing masters, let them
not despise *them*, because they are brethren; but rather do *them* service, because
they are faithful and beloved, partakers
of the benefit.●

In what verses does the word "elder(s)" appear? ______

The context seems to indicate that verses 17-25 are about the office of the elder. Record what each paragraph says about elders:

*5:17-20* ______

*5:21-23* ______

*5:24-25* ______

*6:1-2a* This paragraph is about whom? ______

Record the different things written: ______

NEW INTERNATIONAL VERSION

Record what this passage teaches about:

RICHES ______

LIFE ______

THE FUTURE ______

PERSON AND WORK OF CHRIST (e.g. verses 15-16) ______

COUNSEL TO A YOUNG PASTOR ______

These are the things you are
to teach and urge on them.

*Love of Money*

[3]If anyone teaches false doctrines and
does not agree to the sound instruction of
our Lord Jesus Christ and to godly teaching, [4]he is conceited and understands nothing. He has an unhealthy interest in controversies and arguments that result in envy,
quarreling, malicious talk, evil suspicions
[5]and constant friction between men of corrupt mind, who have been robbed of the
truth and who think that godliness is a
means to financial gain.●
[6]But godliness with contentment is great
gain. [7]For we brought nothing into the
world, and we can take nothing out of it.
[8]But if we have food and clothing, we will
be content with that. [9]People who want to
get rich fall into temptation and a trap and
into many foolish and harmful desires that
plunge men into ruin and destruction. [10]For
the love of money is a root of all kinds of
evil. Some people, eager for money, have
wandered from the faith and pierced themselves with many griefs.●

*Paul's Charge to Timothy*

[11]But you, man of God, flee from all this,
and pursue righteousness, godliness, faith,
love, endurance and gentleness. [12]Fight
the good fight of the faith. Take hold of the
eternal life to which you were called when
you made your good confession in the
presence of many witnesses. [13]In the sight
of God, who gives life to everything, and of
Christ Jesus, who while testifying before
Pontius Pilate made the good confession, I
charge you [14]to keep this commandment
without spot or blame until the appearing
of our Lord Jesus Christ, [15]which God will
bring about in his own time—God, the
blessed and only Ruler, the King of kings
and Lord of lords, [16]who alone is immortal
and who lives in unapproachable light,
whom no one has seen or can see. To him
be honor and might forever. Amen.●

[17]Command those who are rich in this
present world not to be arrogant nor to put
their hope in wealth, which is so uncertain,
but to put their hope in God, who richly
provides us with everything for our enjoy-
ment. [18]Command them to do good, to be
rich in good deeds, and to be generous and
willing to share. [19]In this way they will lay
up treasure for themselves as a firm foundation for the coming age, so that they may
take hold of the life that is truly life.●
[20]Timothy, guard what has been entrusted to your care. Turn away from godless chatter and the opposing ideas of what
is falsely called knowledge, [21]which some
have professed and in so doing have wandered from the faith.
Grace be with you.●

KING JAMES

1.DOCTRINE

FALSE TEACHING

These things teach and exhort. 3 If any
man teach otherwise, and consent not to
wholesome words, *even* the words of our
Lord Jesus Christ, and to the doctrine
which is according to godliness; 4 he is
proud, knowing nothing, but doting about
questions and strifes of words, whereof
cometh envy, strife, railings, evil surmis-
ings, 5 perverse disputings of men of corrupt minds, and destitute of the truth,
supposing that gain is godliness: from

2.THINGS

such withdraw thyself.● 6 But godliness
with contentment is great gain. 7 For we
brought nothing into *this* world, *and it is*
certain we can carry nothing out. 8 And
having food and raiment, let us be therewith content. 9 But they that will be rich
fall into temptation and a snare, and *into*
many foolish and hurtful lusts, which
drown men in destruction and perdition.
10 For the love of money is the root of all
evil: which while some coveted after, they
have erred from the faith, and pierced
themselves through with many sorrows.●

3.PRACTICE

11 But thou, O man of God, flee these
things; and follow after righteousness,
godliness, faith, love, patience, meekness.
12 Fight the good fight of faith, lay hold
on eternal life, whereunto thou art also
called, and hast professed a good profession before many witnesses. 13 I give
thee charge in the sight of God, who
quickeneth all things, and *before* Christ
Jesus, who before Pontius Pilate witnessed a good confession; 14 that thou
keep *this* commandment without spot,
unrebukable, until the appearing of our
Lord Jesus Christ: 15 which in his times
he shall show, *who is* the blessed and only
Potentate, the King of kings, and Lord of
lords; 16 who only hath immortality,
dwelling in the light which no man can
approach unto; whom no man hath seen,
nor can see: to whom *be* honor and power
everlasting. Amen.●

4.TRUE RICHES

17 Charge them that are rich in this
world, that they be not high-minded, nor
trust in uncertain riches, but in the living
God, who giveth us richly all things to
enjoy; 18 that they do good, that they be
rich in good works, ready to distrib-
ute, willing to communicate; 19 laying
up in store for themselves a good
foundation against the time to come,
that they may lay hold on eternal
life.●

—final words

20 O Timothy, keep that which is committed to thy trust, avoiding profane *and*
vain babblings, and oppositions of sci-

FALSE KNOWLEDGE

ence falsely so called: 21 which some
professing have erred concerning the
faith.
Grace *be* with thee. Amen.●

*6:2b-5* What does Paul write about

TRUE DOCTRINE

FALSE DOCTRINE

*6:6-10* What is the appeal here?

*6:11-16* Record the commands to Timothy:

*6:17-19* What is the repeated key word? What is the main point of the paragraph?

*6:20-21* What is Paul's command to Timothy?

# 2 TIMOTHY

## AUTHORSHIP

Paul wrote this letter from prison at Rome—his second imprisonment there.

## DATE

A.D. 67. About five years intervened between the writing of 1 and 2 Timothy.

## OCCASION AND PURPOSE

The immediate occasion of the letter was Paul's desire to see his friends Timothy and Mark again (4:9,11,12), and to have Timothy bring Paul's cloak, books and parchments which the apostle had left at Troas (4:13).

Paul's main purpose in writing was to inspire and challenge Timothy to take up the torch of the gospel ministry which the apostle was handing over due to his imminent death. Paul knew that he would soon be executed for his faith and ministry (4:6). A theme of the letter is endurance and separation in the gospel ministry.

## 2 TIMOTHY: Endurance and Separation in the Ministry

| | |
|---|---|
| Salutation | 1:1-2 |
| FOUNDATIONS OF CHRISTIAN SERVICE | 1:1-18 |
| A GOOD SOLDIER OF JESUS CHRIST | 2:1-26 |
| PERILOUS TIMES AND THE CHRISTIAN SERVANT | 3:1-17 |
| PAUL'S FAREWELL | 4:1-18 |
| Greetings and Benediction | 4:19-22 |

# 2 TIMOTHY

NEW INTERNATIONAL VERSION

What does this passage teach about:

CHRISTIAN SERVICE

THE HOME

SALVATION

THE CHRISTIAN'S ASSURANCE AND POWER

PERSECUTION

CHRISTIAN FELLOWSHIP

1 Paul, an apostle of Christ Jesus by the
will of God, according to the promise
of life that is in Christ Jesus,

2 To Timothy, my dear son:

Grace, mercy and peace from God the
Father and Christ Jesus our Lord.

*Encouragement to Be Faithful*

3 I thank God, whom I serve, as my
forefathers did, with a clear conscience, as
night and day I constantly remember you
in my prayers. 4 Recalling your tears, I long
to see you, so that I may be filled with joy.
5 I have been reminded of your sincere
faith, which first lived in your grandmother
Lois and in your mother Eunice and, I am
persuaded, now lives in you also. 6 For this
reason I remind you to fan into flame the
gift of God, which is in you through the
laying on of my hands. 7 For God did not
give us a spirit of timidity, but a spirit of
power, of love and of self-discipline.
8 So do not be ashamed to testify about
our Lord, or ashamed of me his prisoner.
But join with me in suffering for the gospel,
by the power of God, 9 who has saved us
and called us to a holy life—not because of
anything we have done but because of his
own purpose and grace. This grace was
given us in Christ Jesus before the beginning of time, 10 but it has now been revealed
through the appearing of our Savior, Christ
Jesus, who has destroyed death and has
brought life and immortality to light
through the gospel. 11 And of this gospel I
was appointed a herald and an apostle and
a teacher. 12 That is why I am suffering as
I am. Yet I am not ashamed, because I
know whom I have believed, and am convinced that he is able to guard what I have
entrusted to him for that day.
13 What you heard from me, keep as the
pattern of sound teaching, with faith and
love in Christ Jesus. 14 Guard the good deposit that was entrusted to you—guard it
with the help of the Holy Spirit who lives
in us.
15 You know that everyone in the province of Asia has deserted me, including
Phygelus and Hermogenes.
16 May the Lord show mercy to the
household of Onesiphorus, because he
often refreshed me and was not ashamed of
my chains. 17 On the contrary, when he was
in Rome, he searched hard for me until he
found me. 18 May the Lord grant that he will
find mercy from the Lord on that day! You
know very well in how many ways he
helped me in Ephesus.

KING JAMES

# 2 TIMOTHY

—salutation

1 Paul, an apostle of Jesus Christ by the
will of God, according to the promise
of life which is in Christ Jesus,
2 To Timothy, *my* dearly beloved son:
Grace, mercy, *and* peace, from God the
Father and Christ Jesus our Lord.●

1. HOME TRAINING

3 I thank God, whom I serve from *my*
forefathers with pure conscience, that
without ceasing I have remembrance of
thee in my prayers night and day;
4 greatly desiring to see thee, being mindful of thy tears, that I may be filled with
joy; 5 when I call to remembrance the
unfeigned faith that is in thee, which
dwelt first in thy grandmother Lois, and
thy mother Eunice; and I am persuaded
that in thee also.●

RELATIVES

2. GOD'S WORK

6 Wherefore I put thee
in remembrance, that thou stir up the gift
of God, which is in thee by the putting on
of my hands. 7 For God hath not given
us the spirit of fear; but of power, and of
love, and of a sound mind.
8 Be not thou therefore ashamed of the
testimony of our Lord, nor of me his
prisoner: but be thou partaker of the
afflictions of the gospel according to the
power of God; 9 who hath saved us, and
called *us* with a holy calling, not according
to our works, but according to his own
purpose and grace, which was given us in
Christ Jesus before the world began;
10 but is now made manifest by the appearing of our Saviour Jesus Christ, who
hath abolished death, and hath brought
life and immortality to light through the
gospel:●

3. DIVINE CALL TO SERVE

11 whereunto I am appointed a
preacher, and an apostle, and a teacher of
the Gentiles. 12 For the which cause I
also suffer these things: nevertheless I am
not ashamed; for I know whom I have
believed, and am persuaded that he is able
to keep that which I have committed unto
him against that day. 13 Hold fast the
form of sound words, which thou hast
heard of me, in faith and love which is in
Christ Jesus. 14 That good thing which
was committed unto thee keep by the
Holy Ghost which dwelleth in us.●

4. FELLOW LABORERS

15 This thou knowest, that all they
which are in Asia be turned away from
me; of whom are Phygel'lus and Her-
mog'enes. 16 The Lord give mercy unto
the house of Onesiph'orus; for he oft refreshed me, and was not ashamed of my
chain: 17 but, when he was in Rome, he
sought me out very diligently, and found
*me*. 18 The Lord grant unto him that he
may find mercy of the Lord in that day:
and in how many things he ministered unto me at Ephesus, thou knowest very well.●

FRIEND

*1:1-2* Record the main phrases of the salutation:

______________________________

______________________________

______________________________

______________________________

*1:3-5* What is written about:

PAUL ______________________________

______________________________

______________________________

______________________________

TIMOTHY'S FAMILY ______________________________

______________________________

______________________________

TIMOTHY ______________________________

______________________________

______________________________

______________________________

*1:6-10* What is revealed about:

GOD ______________________________

______________________________

______________________________

CHRIST ______________________________

______________________________

______________________________

*1:11-14* What is the main point of the paragraph?

______________________________

______________________________

What are the commands? ______________________________

______________________________

______________________________

*1:15-18* Compare verse 15 with verses 16-18.

______________________________

______________________________

______________________________

NEW INTERNATIONAL VERSION

Write a list of descriptions of a loyal soldier of Jesus Christ, based on this passage.

2 You then, my son, be strong in the
grace that is in Christ Jesus. 2And the
things you have heard me say in the presence of many witnesses entrust to reliable
men who will also be qualified to teach
others. 3Endure hardship with us like a
good soldier of Christ Jesus. 4No one serving as a soldier gets involved in civilian
affairs—he wants to please his commanding officer. 5Similarly, if anyone competes
as an athlete, he does not receive the vic-
tor's crown unless he competes according
to the rules. 6The hardworking farmer
should be the first to receive a share of the
crops. 7Reflect on what I am saying, for the
Lord will give you insight into all this.●
8Remember Jesus Christ, raised from the
dead, descended from David. This is my
gospel, 9for which I am suffering even to
the point of being chained like a criminal.
But God's word is not chained. 10Therefore
I endure everything for the sake of the
elect, that they too may obtain the salvation that is in Christ Jesus, with eternal
glory.
11Here is a trustworthy saying:

If we died with him,
  we will also live with him;
12if we endure,
  we will also reign with him.
If we disown him,
  he will also disown us;
13if we are faithless,
  he will remain faithful,
  for he cannot disown himself.●

*A Workman Approved by God*

14Keep reminding them of these things.
Warn them before God against quarreling
about words; it is of no value, and only
ruins those who listen. 15Do your best to
present yourself to God as one approved,
a workman who does not need to be
ashamed and who correctly handles the
word of truth. 16Avoid godless chatter, because those who indulge in it will become
more and more ungodly. 17Their teaching
will spread like gangrene. Among them are
Hymenaeus and Philetus, 18who have
wandered away from the truth. They say
that the resurrection has already taken
place, and they destroy the faith of some.
19Nevertheless, God's solid foundation
stands firm, sealed with this inscription:
"The Lord knows those who are his,"[a]
and, "Everyone who confesses the name
of the Lord must turn away from wickedness."●
20In a large house there are articles not
only of gold and silver, but also of wood
and clay; some are for noble purposes and
some for ignoble. 21If a man cleanses himself from the latter, he will be an instrument for noble purposes, made holy, useful to the Master and prepared to do any
good work.
22Flee the evil desires of youth, and pursue righteousness, faith, love and peace,
along with those who call on the Lord out
of a pure heart. 23Don't have anything to do
with foolish and stupid arguments, because
you know they produce quarrels. 24And the
Lord's servant must not quarrel; instead,
he must be kind to everyone, able to teach,
not resentful. 25Those who oppose him he
must gently instruct, in the hope that God
will grant them repentance leading them to
a knowledge of the truth, 26and that they
will come to their senses and escape from
the trap of the devil, who has taken them
captive to do his will.●

[a]19 Num. 16:5 (see Septuagint)

KING JAMES

1. SERVICE

BE STRONG

2 Thou therefore, my son, be strong in
the grace that is in Christ Jesus.
2 And the things that thou hast heard of
me among many witnesses, the same commit thou to faithful men, who shall be
able to teach others also. 3 Thou therefore endure hardness, as a good soldier of
Jesus Christ. 4 No man that warreth en-
tangleth himself with the affairs of *this*
life; that he may please him who hath
chosen him to be a soldier. 5 And if a
man also strive for masteries, *yet* is he not
crowned, except he strive lawfully. 6 The
husbandman that laboreth must be first
partaker of the fruits. 7 Consider what I
say; and the Lord give thee understanding
in all things.●

2. FUTURE HOPE

8 Remember that Jesus Christ of the
seed of David was raised from the dead,
according to my gospel: 9 wherein I suffer trouble, as an evildoer, *even* unto
bonds; but the word of God is not bound.
10 Therefore I endure all things for the
elect's sake, that they may also obtain the
salvation which is in Christ Jesus with
eternal glory. 11 *It is* a faithful saying:
For if we be dead with *him*, we shall
also live with *him*:
12 if we suffer, we shall also reign with
*him*:
if we deny *him*, he also will deny us:
13 if we believe not, *yet* he abideth
faithful:
he cannot deny himself.●

3. FOES

14 Of these things put *them* in remembrance, charging *them* before the Lord
that they strive not about words to no
profit, *but* to the subverting of the hearers.
15 Study to show thyself approved unto
God, a workman that needeth not to be
ashamed, rightly dividing the word of
truth. 16 But shun profane *and* vain babblings: for they will increase unto more
ungodliness. 17 And their word will eat
as doth a canker: of whom is Hymene'us
and Phile'tus; 18 who concerning the
truth have erred, saying that the resurrection is past already; and overthrow the
faith of some. 19 Nevertheless the foundation of God standeth sure, having this
seal, The Lord knoweth them that are his.
And, Let every one that nameth the name
of Christ depart from iniquity.●

4. CHARACTER

20 But in a great house there are not
only vessels of gold and of silver, but also
of wood and of earth; and some to honor,
and some to dishonor. 21 If a man therefore purge himself from these, he shall be
a vessel unto honor, sanctified, and meet
for the master's use, *and* prepared unto
every good work. 22 Flee also youthful
lusts: but follow righteousness, faith,
charity, peace, with them that call on the
Lord out of a pure heart. 23 But foolish
and unlearned questions avoid, knowing
that they do gender strifes. 24 And the
servant of the Lord must not strive; but
be gentle unto all *men*, apt to teach,
patient; 25 in meekness instructing those
that oppose themselves; if God peradventure will give them repentance to the
acknowledging of the truth; 26 and *that*
they may recover themselves out of the
snare of the devil, who are taken captive
by him at his will.●

BE GENTLE

*2:1-7* Record the commands: ____________

What is revealed about Christ? ____________

*2:8-13* What truth about Christ is taught in verse 8?

Does this reappear in the paragraph? ____________

*2:14-19* What comparisons are made of falsehood and truth?

*2:20-26* Record the commands: ____________

NEW INTERNATIONAL VERSION

What does this passage teach about:

LAST DAYS

UNGODLINESS

GODLINESS

TRUTH

PERSECUTION

THE WORD OF GOD

OTHER

*Godlessness in the Last Days*

3 But mark this: There will be terrible
times in the last days. 2People will be
lovers of themselves, lovers of money,
boastful, proud, abusive, disobedient to
their parents, ungrateful, unholy, 3without
love, unforgiving, slanderous, without
self-control, brutal, not lovers of the good,
4treacherous, rash, conceited, lovers of
pleasure rather than lovers of God— 5hav-
ing a form of godliness but denying its
power. Have nothing to do with them.
6They are the kind who worm their way
into homes and gain control over weak-
willed women, who are loaded down with
sins and are swayed by all kinds of evil
desires, 7always learning but never able to
acknowledge the truth. 8Just as Jannes and
Jambres opposed Moses, so also these
men oppose the truth—men of depraved
minds, who, as far as the faith is concerned, are rejected. 9But they will not get
very far because, as in the case of those
men, their folly will be clear to everyone.●

*Paul's Charge to Timothy*

10You, however, know all about my
teaching, my way of life, my purpose,
faith, patience, love, endurance, 11perse-
cutions, sufferings—what kinds of things
happened to me in Antioch, Iconium and
Lystra, the persecutions I endured. Yet
the Lord rescued me from all of them. 12In
fact, everyone who wants to live a godly
life in Christ Jesus will be persecuted,
13while evil men and impostors will go from
bad to worse, deceiving and being deceived.● 14But as for you, continue in what
you have learned and have become convinced of, because you know those from
whom you learned it, 15and how from in-
fancy you have known the holy Scriptures,
which are able to make you wise for salvation through faith in Christ Jesus. 16All
Scripture is God-breathed and is useful for
teaching, rebuking, correcting and training
in righteousness, 17so that the man of God
may be thoroughly equipped for every
good work.●

KING JAMES

1.UNGODLY MEN

EVIL WORKS

3 This know also, that in the last days
perilous times shall come. 2 For men
shall be lovers of their own selves, covetous, boasters, proud, blasphemers, disobedient to parents, unthankful, unholy,
3 without natural affection, trucebreakers,
false accusers, incontinent, fierce, despisers of those that are good, 4 traitors,
heady, high-minded, lovers of pleasures
more than lovers of God; 5 having a
form of godliness, but denying the power
thereof: from such turn away. 6 For of
this sort are they which creep into houses,
and lead captive silly women laden with
sins, led away with divers lusts, 7 ever
learning, and never able to come to the
knowledge of the truth. 8 Now as Jannes
and Jambres withstood Moses, so do
these also resist the truth: men of corrupt
minds, reprobate concerning the faith.
9 But they shall proceed no further: for
their folly shall be manifest unto all *men*,
as theirs also was.●

2.PERSECUTED PAUL

10 But thou hast fully known my doctrine, manner of life, purpose, faith, long-
suffering, charity, patience, 11 persecutions, afflictions, which came unto me at
An'ti-och, at Ico'ni-um, at Lystra;
what persecutions I endured: but out of
*them* all the Lord delivered me. 12 Yea,
and all that will live godly in Christ Jesus
shall suffer persecution. 13 But evil men
and seducers shall wax worse and worse,
deceiving, and being deceived.● 14 But

3.INSTRUCTED TIMOTHY

continue thou in the things which thou
hast learned and hast been assured of,
knowing of whom thou hast learned
*them*; 15 and that from a child thou hast
known the holy Scriptures, which are able
to make thee wise unto salvation through
faith which is in Christ Jesus. 16 All
Scripture *is* given by inspiration of God,
and *is* profitable for doctrine, for reproof,
for correction, for instruction in righteousness: 17 that the man of God may be
perfect, thoroughly furnished unto all
good works.●

GOOD WORKS

*3:1-9* Record different evils mentioned here.

How is the paragraph introduced (v.1) and concluded (v.9)?

*3:10-13* What does Paul write about persecution?

*3:14-17* What is the main point of the paragraph?

List the ministries and values of Scripture:

NEW INTERNATIONAL VERSION

Write a list of practical applications of this passage to Christian living today.

4 In the presence of God and of Christ Jesus, who will judge the living and the dead, and in view of his appearing and his kingdom, I give you this charge: [2]Preach the Word; be prepared in season and out of season; correct, rebuke and encourage—with great patience and careful instruction. [3]For the time will come when men will not put up with sound doctrine. Instead, to suit their own desires, they will gather around them a great number of teachers to say what their itching ears want to hear. [4]They will turn their ears away from the truth and turn aside to myths. [5]But you, keep your head in all situations, endure hardship, do the work of an evangelist, discharge all the duties of your ministry.●

[6]For I am already being poured out like a drink offering, and the time has come for my departure. [7]I have fought the good fight, I have finished the race, I have kept the faith. [8]Now there is in store for me the crown of righteousness, which the Lord, the righteous Judge, will award to me on that day—and not only to me, but also to all who have longed for his appearing.●

*Personal Remarks*

[9]Do your best to come to me quickly, [10]for Demas, because he loved this world, has deserted me and has gone to Thessalonica. Crescens has gone to Galatia, and Titus to Dalmatia. [11]Only Luke is with me. Get Mark and bring him with you, because he is helpful to me in my ministry. [12]I sent Tychicus to Ephesus. [13]When you come, bring the cloak that I left with Carpus at Troas, and my scrolls, especially the parchments.

[14]Alexander the metalworker did me a great deal of harm. The Lord will repay him for what he has done. [15]You too should be on your guard against him, because he strongly opposed our message.

[16]At my first defense, no one came to my support, but everyone deserted me. May it not be held against them. [17]But the Lord stood at my side and gave me strength, so that through me the message might be fully proclaimed and all the Gentiles might hear it. And I was delivered from the lion's mouth. [18]The Lord will rescue me from every evil attack and will bring me safely to his heavenly kingdom. To him be glory for ever and ever. Amen.●

*Final Greetings*

[19]Greet Priscilla[a] and Aquila and the household of Onesiphorus. [20]Erastus stayed in Corinth, and I left Trophimus sick in Miletus. [21]Do your best to get here before winter. Eubulus greets you, and so do Pudens, Linus, Claudia and all the brothers.●

[22]The Lord be with your spirit. Grace be with you.●

[a]*19* Greek *Prisca*, a variant of *Priscilla*

KING JAMES

1.CHARGE

JUDGMENT

4 I charge *thee* therefore before God,
and the Lord Jesus Christ, who shall
judge the quick and the dead at his appearing and his kingdom; 2 preach the
word; be instant in season, out of season;
reprove, rebuke, exhort with all long-
suffering and doctrine. 3 For the time
will come when they will not endure sound
doctrine; but after their own lusts shall
they heap to themselves teachers, having
itching ears; 4 and they shall turn away
*their* ears from the truth, and shall be
turned unto fables. 5 But watch thou in
all things, endure afflictions, do the work
of an evangelist, make full proof of thy
ministry.●

2.TESTIMONY

6 For I am now ready to be offered, and
the time of my departure is at hand. 7 I
have fought a good fight, I have finished
*my* course, I have kept the faith: 8 henceforth there is laid up for me a crown of
righteousness, which the Lord, the righteous judge, shall give me at that day: and
not to me only, but unto all them also
that love his appearing.●

3.PERSONAL NOTES

9 Do thy diligence to come shortly unto
me: 10 for Demas hath forsaken me,
having loved this present world, and is
departed unto Thessaloni'ca; Crescens to
Galatia, Titus unto Dalma'tia. 11 Only
Luke is with me. Take Mark, and bring
him with thee: for he is profitable to me
for the ministry. 12 And Tych'icus have
I sent to Ephesus. 13 The cloak that I
left at Tro'as with Carpus, when thou
comest, bring *with thee*, and the books,
*but* especially the parchments. 14 Alexander the coppersmith did me much evil:
the Lord reward him according to his
works: 15 of whom be thou ware also;
for he hath greatly withstood our words.
16 At my first answer no man stood with
me, but all *men* forsook me: *I pray God*
that it may not be laid to their charge.
17 Notwithstanding the Lord stood with
me, and strengthened me; that by me the
preaching might be fully known, and *that*
all the Gentiles might hear: and I was delivered out of the mouth of the lion.
18 And the Lord shall deliver me from
every evil work, and will preserve *me* unto
his heavenly kingdom: to whom *be* glory
for ever and ever. Amen.●

19 Salute Prisca and Aquila, and the
household of Onesiph'orus. 20 Eras'tus
abode at Corinth: but Troph'imus have
I left at Mile'tus sick. 21 Do thy diligence to come before winter. Eubu'lus
greeteth thee, and Pudens, and Linus, and
Claudia, and all the brethren.●

—benediction

GRACE

22 The Lord Jesus Christ *be* with thy
spirit. Grace *be* with you. Amen.●

*4:1-5* Record the appeals of Paul to Timothy.

*4:6-8* Compare verse 6 with verse 7.

*4:9-18* Record the names of people, and what is said about each.

What is Paul's testimony in verses 16-18?

*4:19-21* What are your impressions here?

*4:22* These are Paul's last recorded words. What are your impressions?

# TITUS

## AUTHORSHIP

The text identifies the writer and addressee: "Paul...to Titus" (1:1,4).

## DATE

Paul wrote this letter soon after writing 1 Timothy, probably while the apostle was in Macedonia, enroute to Nicopolis (3:12). Date was A.D. 62.

## OCCASION

Paul wrote the letter to Titus for many of the same reasons he wrote to Timothy. Titus was ministering to churches on the island of Crete just as Timothy was ministering to the saints at Ephesus. The situation at the churches of Crete was:

1) disorder and false teaching threatening the local churches
2) inconsistent living by church members
3) need for instruction about church organization.

## PURPOSES

The main purposes of the Epistle, in the immediate setting, included

1) to advise Titus in superintending the circuit of Cretan churches as Paul's representative (1:5)
2) to instruct and exhort both Titus and the churches regarding Christian behavior consistent with Christian doctrine (chapters 1-3)
3) to instruct Titus concerning personal matters (3:12-13).

A theme reflecting the second purpose is "adorning the doctrine of God" (2:10).

## TITUS: Adorning the Doctrine of God

| | |
|---|---|
| Salutation and Introduction | 1:1-4 |
| CHURCH LEADERS DEALING WITH FALSE TEACHERS | 1:1-16 |
| MAKING CHRISTIAN DOCTRINE ATTRACTIVE BY EXAMPLE | 2:1-15 |
| THE GOOD WORKS OF A BELIEVER | 3:1-11 |
| Conclusion and Benediction | 3:12-15 |

# TITUS

NEW INTERNATIONAL VERSION

What do you learn here about:

CHRISTIAN SERVICE

PREACHING AND TEACHING THE WORD

SALVATION

PASTORS AND LEADERS OF THE CHURCH

FALSE TEACHERS

OTHER

1 Paul, a servant of God and an apostle
of Jesus Christ for the faith of God's
elect and the knowledge of the truth that
leads to godliness— [2]a faith and knowledge
resting on the hope of eternal life, which
God, who does not lie, promised before the
beginning of time, [3]and at his appointed
season he brought his word to light through
the preaching entrusted to me by the command of God our Savior,

[4]To Titus, my true son in our common
faith:

Grace and peace from God the Father
and Christ Jesus our Savior.●

### *Titus' Task on Crete*

[5]The reason I left you in Crete was that
you might straighten out what was left unfinished and appoint[a] elders in every town,
as I directed you. [6]An elder must be blameless, the husband of but one wife, a man
whose children believe and are not open to
the charge of being wild and disobedient.
[7]Since an overseer[b] is entrusted with
God's work, he must be blameless—not
overbearing, not quick-tempered, not giv-
en to much wine, not violent, not pursuing
dishonest gain. [8]Rather he must be hospitable, one who loves what is good, who is
self-controlled, upright, holy and disciplined. [9]He must hold firmly to the trustworthy message as it has been taught, so
that he can encourage others by sound doctrine and refute those who oppose it.●
[10]For there are many rebellious people,
mere talkers and deceivers, especially
those of the circumcision group. [11]They
must be silenced, because they are ruining
whole households by teaching things they
ought not to teach—and that for the sake of
dishonest gain. [12]Even one of their own
prophets has said, "Cretans are always liars, evil brutes, lazy gluttons." [13]This testimony is true. Therefore, rebuke them
sharply, so that they will be sound in the
faith [14]and will pay no attention to Jewish
myths or to the commands of those who
reject the truth. [15]To the pure, all things are
pure, but to those who are corrupted and
do not believe, nothing is pure. In fact,
both their minds and consciences are corrupted. [16]They claim to know God, but by
their actions they deny him. They are detestable, disobedient and unfit for doing
anything good.●

[a]5 Or *ordain* [b]7 Traditionally *bishop*

KING JAMES

# TITUS

1. INTRODUCTION

1 Paul, a servant of God, and an apostle
of Jesus Christ, according to the faith
of God's elect, and the acknowledging of
the truth which is after godliness; 2 in
hope of eternal life, which God, that cannot lie, promised before the world began;
3 but hath in due times manifested his
word through preaching, which is committed unto me according to the commandment of God our Saviour;
4 To Titus, *mine* own son after the
common faith:
Grace, mercy, *and* peace, from God the
Father and the Lord Jesus Christ our
Saviour.●

FAITH

2. LEADERSHIP

5 For this cause left I thee in Crete, that
thou shouldest set in order the things that
are wanting, and ordain elders in every
city, as I had appointed thee: 6 if any be
blameless, the husband of one wife, having faithful children not accused of riot or
unruly. 7 For a bishop must be blameless,
as the steward of God; not self-willed, not
soon angry, not given to wine, no striker,
not given to filthy lucre; 8 but a lover of
hospitality, a lover of good men, sober,
just, holy, temperate; 9 holding fast the
faithful word as he hath been taught, that
he may be able by sound doctrine both to
exhort and to convince the gainsayers.●

3. FALSE TEACHING

10 For there are many unruly and vain
talkers and deceivers, specially they of the
circumcision: 11 whose mouths must be
stopped, who subvert whole houses,
teaching things which they ought not, for
filthy lucre's sake. 12 One of themselves,
*even* a prophet of their own, said, The
Cretians *are* always liars, evil beasts, slow
bellies. 13 This witness is true. Wherefore rebuke them sharply, that they may
be sound in the faith; 14 not giving heed
to Jewish fables, and commandments of
men, that turn from the truth. 15 Unto
the pure all things *are* pure: but unto them
that are defiled and unbelieving *is* nothing
pure; but even their mind and conscience
is defiled. 16 They profess that they know
God; but in works they deny *him*, being
abominable, and disobedient, and unto
every good work reprobate.●

DENIAL

*1:1-4* Record the doctrines taught here.

*1:5-9* Record the qualifications of pastors (elders, bishops).

*1:10-16* What is said here about false teachers?

NEW INTERNATIONAL VERSION

Make two lists based on this passage on the following:

DOCTRINES

PRACTICING THE CHRISTIAN LIFE

*What Must Be Taught to Various Groups*

2 You must teach what is in accord with
sound doctrine. 2Teach the older men
to be temperate, worthy of respect, self-
controlled, and sound in faith, in love and
in endurance.
3Likewise, teach the older women to be
reverent in the way they live, not to be
slanderers or addicted to much wine, but to
teach what is good. 4Then they can train
the younger women to love their husbands
and children, 5to be self-controlled and
pure, to be busy at home, to be kind, and
to be subject to their husbands, so that no
one will malign the word of God.
6Similarly, encourage the young men to
be self-controlled. 7In everything set them
an example by doing what is good. In your
teaching show integrity, seriousness 8and
soundness of speech that cannot be condemned, so that those who oppose you
may be ashamed because they have nothing bad to say about us.
9Teach slaves to be subject to their masters in everything, to try to please them,
not to talk back to them, 10and not to steal
from them, but to show that they can be
fully trusted, so that in every way they will
make the teaching about God our Savior
attractive.●
11For the grace of God that brings salvation has appeared to all men. 12It teaches us
to say "No" to ungodliness and worldly
passions, and to live self-controlled, upright and godly lives in this present age,
13while we wait for the blessed hope—the
glorious appearing of our great God and
Savior, Jesus Christ, 14who gave himself
for us to redeem us from all wickedness
and to purify for himself a people that are
his very own, eager to do what is good.
15These, then, are the things you should
teach. Encourage and rebuke with all authority. Do not let anyone despise you.●

## KING JAMES

1.THE PRACTICE

SOUND DOCTRINE

**2** But speak thou the things which become sound doctrine: 2 that the
aged men be sober, grave, temperate,
sound in faith, in charity, in patience.
3 The aged women likewise, that *they be*
in behavior as becometh holiness, not
false accusers, not given to much wine,
teachers of good things; 4 that they may
teach the young women to be sober, to
love their husbands, to love their children,
5 *to be* discreet, chaste, keepers at home,
good, obedient to their own husbands,
that the word of God be not blasphemed.
6 Young men likewise exhort to be sober-
minded. 7 In all things showing thyself a
pattern of good works: in doctrine *show-*
*ing* uncorruptness, gravity, sincerity,
8 sound speech, that cannot be condemned; that he that is of the contrary
part may be ashamed, having no evil thing
to say of you. 9 *Exhort* servants to be
obedient unto their own masters, *and* to
please *them* well in all things; not answering again; 10 not purloining, but showing
all good fidelity; that they may adorn the
doctrine of God our Saviour in all things.●

2.THE DOCTRINE

11 For the grace of God that bringeth
salvation hath appeared to all men,
12 teaching us that, denying ungodliness
and worldly lusts, we should live soberly,
righteously, and godly, in this present
world; 13 looking for that blessed hope,
and the glorious appearing of the great
God and our Saviour Jesus Christ;
14 who gave himself for us, that he might
redeem us from all iniquity, and purify
unto himself a peculiar people, zealous
of good works.

ALL AUTHORITY

15 These things speak, and exhort, and
rebuke with all authority. Let no man
despise thee.●

*2:1-10* Record the different groups, and the appeals to each.

v.2

v.3

vv.4-5

vv.6-8

vv.9-10

*2:11-15* Record all the doctrines taught in the paragraph.

Record the commands.

NEW INTERNATIONAL VERSION

What do you learn here about:

SALVATION

FAITH

WORKS

EVERYDAY CHRISTIAN LIVING

DIVISIVE ACTIVITIES

CHRISTIAN LOVE

OTHER

### *Doing What Is Good*

3 Remind the people to be subject to rulers and authorities, to be obedient, to
be ready to do whatever is good, [2]to slander no one, to be peaceable and considerate, and to show true humility toward all
men.
[3]At one time we too were foolish,
disobedient, deceived and enslaved by all
kinds of passions and pleasures. We lived
in malice and envy, being hated and hating
one another. [4]But when the kindness and
love of God our Savior appeared, [5]he saved
us, not because of righteous things we had
done, but because of his mercy. He saved
us through the washing of rebirth and
renewal by the Holy Spirit, [6]whom he
poured out on us generously through Jesus
Christ our Savior, [7]so that, having been
justified by his grace, we might become
heirs having the hope of eternal life. [8]This
is a trustworthy saying. And I want you to
stress these things, so that those who have
trusted in God may be careful to devote
themselves to doing what is good. These
things are excellent and profitable for
everyone.
[9]But avoid foolish controversies and
genealogies and arguments and quarrels
about the law, because these are unprofitable and useless. [10]Warn a divisive person
once, and then warn him a second time.
After that, have nothing to do with him.
[11]You may be sure that such a man is
warped and sinful; he is self-condemned.

### *Final Remarks*

[12]As soon as I send Artemas or Tychicus
to you, do your best to come to me at
Nicopolis, because I have decided to winter there. [13]Do everything you can to help
Zenas the lawyer and Apollos on their way
and see that they have everything they
need. [14]Our people must learn to devote
themselves to doing what is good, in order
that they may provide for daily necessities
and not live unproductive lives.
[15]Everyone with me sends you greetings.
Greet those who love us in the faith.
Grace be with you all.

KING JAMES

1.READINESS

CIVIL OBEDIENCE

**3** Put them in mind to be subject to
principalities and powers, to obey
magistrates, to be ready to every good
work, 2 to speak evil of no man, to be no
brawlers, *but* gentle, showing all meekness
unto all men. 3 For we ourselves also
were sometime foolish, disobedient, deceived, serving divers lusts and pleasures,
living in malice and envy, hateful, *and* hating one another. 4 But after that the
kindness and love of God our Saviour toward man appeared, 5 not by works of
righteousness which we have done, but
according to his mercy he saved us, by the
washing of regeneration, and renewing of
the Holy Ghost; 6 which he shed on us
abundantly through Jesus Christ our
Saviour; 7 that being justified by his
grace, we should be made heirs according
to the hope of eternal life.●

2.CAREFULNESS

8 *This is* a faithful saying, and these
things I will that thou affirm constantly,
that they which have believed in God
might be careful to maintain good works.
These things are good and profitable unto
men. 9 But avoid foolish questions, and
genealogies, and contentions, and striv-
ings about the law; for they are unprofitable and vain. 10 A man that is a
heretic, after the first and second admonition, reject; 11 knowing that he that is
such is subverted, and sinneth, being condemned of himself.●

3.FRUITFULNESS

12 When I shall send Ar'temas unto
thee, or Tych'icus, be diligent to come
unto me to Nicop'olis: for I have determined there to winter. 13 Bring Zenas the
lawyer and Apol'los on their journey diligently, that nothing be wanting unto them.
14 And let ours also learn to maintain
good works for necessary uses, that they
be not unfruitful.

BROTHERLY LOVE

—benediction

15 All that are with me salute thee.
Greet them that love us in the faith.●
Grace *be* with you all. Amen.●

*3:1-7* What two kinds of works are contrasted in verses 1-3?

______

______

______

What are works compared with in verses 4-7?

______

______

______

Record the strong *doctrine* words of verses 4-7.

______

______

______

______

*3:8-11* What is the appeal of verse 8? ______

______

______

______

______

What evils are mentioned in verses 9-11?

______

______

______

______

______

*3:12-15* What verse makes an appeal? ______

______

______

______

______

What is meant by this verse? ______

______

______

______

______

# PHILEMON

## AUTHORSHIP

Paul was the author of the letter to Philemon. It is the most personal of all his letters, as well as the shortest.

## DATE

Around A.D. 61.

## OCCASION AND PURPOSE

Onesimus, a household servant of Philemon, friend of Paul, had apparently stolen money or goods from his master (v.18), and had fled to Rome. Through circumstances unknown to us, he came in contact with Paul, who led him to the Lord (v.10). Paul's immediate concern was for Onesimus's restoration and reconciliation with Philemon. Hence this tender letter, a classic plea for forgiveness.

## PHILEMON: Appeal for a Runaway Slave

| | |
|---|---|
| Salutation and Benediction | 1-3 |
| PRAISE OF PHILEMON | 4-7 |
| PLEA FOR ONESIMUS | 8-16 |
| PROMISE OF PAUL | 17-21 |
| Conclusion and Benediction | 22-25 |

# PHILEMON

NEW INTERNATIONAL VERSION

What does this letter reveal about:

FORGIVENESS ______________________________

LOVE ______________________________

TACTFULNESS ______________________________

OTHER ______________________________

1 Paul, a prisoner of Christ Jesus, and
Timothy our brother,

To Philemon our dear friend and fellow
worker, 2 to Apphia our sister, to Archippus our fellow soldier and to the church
that meets in your home:

3 Grace to you and peace from God our
Father and the Lord Jesus Christ.

*Thanksgiving and Prayer*

4 I always thank my God as I remember
you in my prayers, 5 because I hear about
your faith in the Lord Jesus and your love
for all the saints. 6 I pray that you may be
active in sharing your faith, so that you will
have a full understanding of every good
thing we have in Christ. 7 Your love has
given me great joy and encouragement, because you, brother, have refreshed the
hearts of the saints.

*Paul's Plea for Onesimus*

8 Therefore, although in Christ I could be
bold and order you to do what you ought
to do, 9 yet I appeal to you on the basis of
love. I then, as Paul—an old man and now
also a prisoner of Christ Jesus— 10 I appeal
to you for my son Onesimus,[a] who became
my son while I was in chains. 11 Formerly
he was useless to you, but now he has
become useful both to you and to me.
12 I am sending him—who is my very
heart—back to you. 13 I would have liked to
keep him with me so that he could take
your place in helping me while I am in
chains for the gospel. 14 But I did not want
to do anything without your consent, so
that any favor you do will be spontaneous
and not forced. 15 Perhaps the reason he
was separated from you for a little while
was that you might have him back for
good— 16 no longer as a slave, but better
than a slave, as a dear brother. He is very
dear to me but even dearer to you, both as
a man and as a brother in the Lord.
17 So if you consider me a partner, welcome him as you would welcome me. 18 If
he has done you any wrong or owes you
anything, charge it to me. 19 I, Paul, am
writing this with my own hand. I will pay
it back—not to mention that you owe me
your very self. 20 I do wish, brother, that I
may have some benefit from you in the
Lord; refresh my heart in Christ. 21 Confident of your obedience, I write to you,
knowing that you will do even more than I
ask.
22 And one thing more: Prepare a guest
room for me, because I hope to be restored
to you in answer to your prayers.

23 Epaphras, my fellow prisoner for
Christ Jesus, sends you greetings. 24 And so
do Mark, Aristarchus, Demas and Luke,
my fellow workers.
25 The grace of the Lord Jesus Christ be
with your spirit.

[a] 10 *Onesimus* means *useful.*

KING JAMES

# PHILEMON

—salutation

PAUL, a prisoner of Jesus Christ, and
Timothy *our* brother,
Unto Phile'mon our dearly beloved,
and fellow laborer, 2 and to *our* beloved Ap'phi-a, and Archip'pus our
fellow soldier, and to the church in thy
house:
3 Grace to you, and peace, from God
our Father and the Lord Jesus Christ.●

1.OBJECT OF THE APPEAL

LOVE

4 I thank my God, making mention of
thee always in my prayers, 5 hearing of
thy love and faith, which thou hast toward the Lord Jesus, and toward all
saints; 6 that the communication of thy
faith may become effectual by the acknowledging of every good thing which is
in you in Christ Jesus. 7 For we have
great joy and consolation in thy love, because the bowels of the saints are refreshed by thee, brother.●

2.THE APPEAL

8 Wherefore, though I might be much
bold in Christ to enjoin thee that which is
convenient, 9 yet for love's sake I rather
beseech *thee*, being such a one as Paul the
aged, and now also a prisoner of Jesus
Christ. 10 I beseech thee for my son
Ones'imus, whom I have begotten in my
bonds: 11 which in time past was to thee
unprofitable, but now profitable to thee
and to me: 12 whom I have sent again:
thou therefore receive him, that is, mine
own bowels: 13 whom I would have retained with me, that in thy stead he might
have ministered unto me in the bonds of
the gospel: 14 but without thy mind
would I do nothing; that thy benefit
should not be as it were of necessity, but
willingly.
15 For perhaps he therefore departed
for a season, that thou shouldest receive
him for ever; 16 not now as a servant,
but above a servant, a brother beloved,
specially to me, but how much more unto
thee, both in the flesh, and in the Lord?●

3.SOURCE OF THE APPEAL

17 If thou count me therefore a partner,
receive him as myself. 18 If he hath
wronged thee, or oweth *thee* aught, put
that on mine account; 19 I Paul have
written *it* with mine own hand, I will repay *it*: albeit I do not say to thee how
thou owest unto me even thine own self
besides. 20 Yea, brother, let me have joy
of thee in the Lord: refresh my bowels in
the Lord.

OBEDIENCE

21 Having confidence in thy obedience
I wrote unto thee, knowing that thou wilt
also do more than I say.●

—personal notes

22 But withal
prepare me also a lodging: for I trust that
through your prayers I shall be given unto
you.
23 There salute thee Ep'aphras, my
fellow prisoner in Christ Jesus; 24 Mark,
Aristar'chus, Demas, Luke, my fellow
laborers.●

—benediction

25 The grace of our Lord Jesus Christ
*be* with your spirit. Amen.●

*1-3* What are the main words and phrases of the salutation?

*4-7* What does this paragraph reveal about Onesimus?

*8-16* What appeal does Paul make?

What does he base the appeal on (vv.8-11)?

What new relationship (vv.15-16) did Paul have in mind between Onesimus and Philemon?

*17-21* How does Paul identify himself as the one interceding?

*22-25* What are your impressions?

# HEBREWS

## AUTHORSHIP

The author is anonymous. Many suggestions have been made as to who he was, such as: Paul, Apollos, Luke, Barnabas, Silas, and Clement of Rome. The view that the author was a co-worker of Paul accounts for both Pauline and non-Pauline traits of the Epistle.

The interval between A.D. 65 and 70 is a likely time

## DATE

The interval between A.D. 65 and 70 is a likely time for the letter's writing. The lack of any reference to the Fall of Jerusalem in A.D. 70 is strong argument for a date before A.D. 70, since the very argument of the letter would use that event for its support.

## PURPOSES AND THEME

Hebrews was written to Jewish Christians to rekindle a dampened spiritual fire. It teaches the superiority of the finished sacrificial work of God's Son Jesus; warns concerning just recompense for sinning against God; and exhorts the believer to appropriate the power and privileges of God's children and to press on to fuller stature as Christians. The theme of the book is: The antidote for backsliding is a growing personal knowledge of Jesus our great High Priest.

## HEBREWS: Jesus, Our Great High Priest

| | |
|---|---|
| SUPERIOR PERSON | 1:1-7:28 |
| Son Superior to Angels | 1:1-2:4 |
| Jesus as Redeemer | 2:5-18 |
| Christ Superior to Moses and Joshua | 3:1-4:13 |
| Jesus Superior to Aaron | 4:14-5:10 |
| Warning of Sloth and Apostasy | 5:11-6:20 |
| Jesus, Priest Forever | 7:1-28 |
| SUPERIOR INSTITUTIONS | 8:1-10:18 |
| Better Covenant and Tabernacle | 8:1-9:12 |
| Better Sacrifice | 9:13-10:18 |
| SUPERIOR LIFE | 10:19-13:25 |
| Confidence of Faith | 10:19-39 |
| Examples of Faith | 11:1-12:2 |
| Endurance of Faith | 12:3-29 |
| Workings of Faith | 13:1-25 |

# HEBREWS

NEW INTERNATIONAL VERSION

What does this passage teach about:

DIVINE REVELATION

SON OF GOD

MINISTRY OF JESUS

ANGELS

GOSPEL OF SALVATION

MAN'S ACCOUNTABILITY

OTHER

### *The Son Superior to Angels*

1 In the past God spoke to our forefathers through the prophets at many
times and in various ways, 2 but in these
last days he has spoken to us by his Son,
whom he appointed heir of all things, and
through whom he made the universe. 3 The
Son is the radiance of God's glory and the
exact representation of his being, sustain-
ing all things by his powerful word. After
he had provided purification for sins, he sat
down at the right hand of the Majesty in
heaven. 4 So he became as much superior to
the angels as the name he has inherited is
superior to theirs.
5 For to which of the angels did God ever
say,

> "You are my Son;
> today I have become your
> Father[a]"[b]?

Or again,

> "I will be his Father,
> and he will be my Son"[c]?

6 And again, when God brings his firstborn
into the world, he says,

> "Let all God's angels worship
> him."[d]

7 In speaking of the angels he says,

> "He makes his angels winds,
> his servants flames of fire."[e]

8 But about the Son he says,

> "Your throne, O God, will last for
> ever and ever,
> and righteousness will be the
> scepter of your kingdom.
> 9 You have loved righteousness and
> hated wickedness;
> therefore God, your God, has set
> you above your companions
> by anointing you with the oil of
> joy."[f]

10 He also says,

> "In the beginning, O Lord, you laid
> the foundations of the earth,
> and the heavens are the work of
> your hands.
> 11 They will perish, but you remain;
> they will all wear out like a
> garment.
> 12 You will roll them up like a robe;
> like a garment they will be
> changed.
> But you remain the same,
> and your years will never end."[g]

13 To which of the angels did God ever say,

> "Sit at my right hand
> until I make your enemies
> a footstool for your feet"[h]?

14 Are not all angels ministering spirits sent
to serve those who will inherit salvation?

### *Warning to Pay Attention*

2 We must pay more careful attention,
therefore, to what we have heard, so
that we do not drift away. 2 For if the message spoken by angels was binding, and
every violation and disobedience received
its just punishment, 3 how shall we escape
if we ignore such a great salvation? This
salvation, which was first announced by
the Lord, was confirmed to us by those
who heard him. 4 God also testified to it by
signs, wonders and various miracles, and
gifts of the Holy Spirit distributed according to his will.

[a]5 Or *have begotten you* [b]5 Psalm 2:7 [c]5 2 Samuel 7:14
[d]6 Deut. 32:43 (see Dead Sea Scrolls and Septuagint)
[e]7 Psalm 104:4 [f]9 Psalm 45:6,7
[g]12 Psalm 102:25-27 [h]13 Psalm 110:1

KING JAMES

# HEBREWS

1.GREAT SALVATION

GOD HATH SPOKEN

1 God, who at sundry times and in
divers manners spake in time past unto the fathers by the prophets, 2 hath in
these last days spoken unto us by *his* Son,
whom he hath appointed heir of all things,
by whom also he made the worlds;
3 who being the brightness of *his* glory,
and the express image of his person, and
upholding all things by the word of his
power, when he had by himself purged
our sins, sat down on the right hand of the
Majesty on high;● 4 being made so much
better than the angels, as he hath by inheritance obtained a more excellent name
than they.

2.SUPERIOR MESSENGER

5 For unto which of the angels said he
at any time,

Thou art my Son,
this day have I begotten thee ? (Ps. 2:7)

And again,

I will be to him a Father,
and he shall be to me a Son ? (2 Sa. 7:14)

6 And again, when he bringeth in the
first-begotten into the world, he saith,

And let all the angels of God worship him. (Deu. 32:43)

7 And of the angels he saith,

Who maketh his angels spirits,
and his ministers a flame of fire. (Ps. 104:4)

8 But unto the Son *he saith*,

Thy throne, O God, *is* for ever and ever: (Ps. 45:6-7)
a sceptre of righteousness *is* the sceptre of thy kingdom.
9 Thou hast loved righteousness, and hated iniquity;
therefore God, *even* thy God, hath anointed thee
with the oil of gladness above thy fellows.

10 And, (Ps. 102:25-27)

Thou, Lord, in the beginning hast laid the foundation of the earth;
and the heavens are the works of thine hands.
11 They shall perish, but thou remainest:
and they all shall wax old as doth a garment;
12 and as a vesture shalt thou fold them up,
and they shall be changed:
but thou art the same,
and thy years shall not fail.

13 But to which of the angels said he at
any time,

Sit on my right hand, (Ps. 110:1)
until I make thine enemies thy footstool ? (Josh. 10:24)

14 Are they not all ministering spirits,
sent forth to minister for them who shall
be heirs of salvation ?●

3.NECESSARY RESPONSE

WE MUST HEED

2 Therefore we ought to give the more
earnest heed to the things which we
have heard, lest at any time we should let
*them* slip. 2 For if the word spoken by
angels was steadfast, and every transgression and disobedience received a just
recompense of reward; 3 how shall we
escape, if we neglect so great salvation;
which at the first began to be spoken by
the Lord, and was confirmed unto us by
them that heard *him*; 4 God also bearing
*them* witness, both with signs and wonders,
and with divers miracles, and gifts of
the Holy Ghost, according to his own
will ?●

*1:1-3* Compare what is written about:

PAST ______

PRESENT ______

*1:4-14* With whom is Jesus compared? ______

Record the comparisons:

NAME (4-5) ______

WORSHIP (6) ______

REIGN (7-9) ______

CREATION (10) ______

DURATION (11-12) ______

REIGN (13-14) ______

*2:1-4* What does the first word refer to? ______

What is the point of the paragraph? ______

NEW INTERNATIONAL VERSION

What does this passage teach about:

GRACE OF GOD ______

DEATH OF CHRIST ______

SANCTIFICATION ______

THE DEVIL ______

DEATH ______

JESUS AS OUR HIGH PRIEST ______

JESUS THE PERFECT MAN ______

### *Jesus Made Like His Brothers*

5 It is not to angels that he has subjected
the world to come, about which we are
speaking. 6 But there is a place where someone has testified:

> "What is man that you are mindful
> of him,
> the son of man that you care for
> him?
> 7 You made him a little[a] lower than
> the angels;
> you crowned him with glory and
> honor
> 8 and put everything under his
> feet."[b]

In putting everything under him, God left
nothing that is not subject to him. Yet at
present we do not see everything subject to
him. 9 But we see Jesus, who was made a
little lower than the angels, now crowned
with glory and honor because he suffered
death, so that by the grace of God he might
taste death for everyone.●
10 In bringing many sons to glory, it was
fitting that God, for whom and through
whom everything exists, should make the
author of their salvation perfect through
suffering. 11 Both the one who makes men
holy and those who are made holy are of
the same family. So Jesus is not ashamed
to call them brothers. 12 He says,

> "I will declare your name to my
> brothers;
> in the presence of the congregation
> I will sing your praises."[c]

13 And again,

> "I will put my trust in him."[d]

And again he says,

> "Here am I, and the children God
> has given me."[e]●

14 Since the children have flesh and
blood, he too shared in their humanity so
that by his death he might destroy him who
holds the power of death—that is, the
devil— 15 and free those who all their lives
were held in slavery by their fear of death.
16 For surely it is not angels he helps, but
Abraham's descendants. 17 For this reason
he had to be made like his brothers in every
way, in order that he might become a merciful and faithful high priest in service to
God, and that he might make atonement
for[f] the sins of the people. 18 Because he
himself suffered when he was tempted,
he is able to help those who are being
tempted.●

[a]7 Or *him for a little while;* also in verse 9
[b]8 Psalm 8:4-6 [c]12 Psalm 22:22
[d]13 Isaiah 8:17 [e]13 Isaiah 8:18
[f]17 Or *and that he might turn aside God's wrath, taking away*

KING JAMES

1.OUR SACRIFICE

DOMINION

**5 For unto the angels hath he not put
in subjection the world to come, whereof
we speak. 6 But one in a certain place
testified, saying,**

Ps. 8:4-6

**What is man, that thou art mindful
of him?
or the son of man, that thou visitest
him?
7 Thou madest him a little lower than
the angels;
thou crownedst him with glory and
honor,
and didst set him over the works of
thy hands:
8 thou hast put all things in subjection
under his feet.
For in that he put all in subjection under
him, he left nothing *that is* not put under
him. But now we see not yet all things put
under him. 9 But we see Jesus, who was
made a little lower than the angels for the
suffering of death, crowned with glory and
honor; that he by the grace of God should
taste death for every man.●**

2.OUR BROTHER

**10 For it became him, for whom *are* all
things, and by whom *are* all things, in
bringing many sons unto glory, to make
the captain of their salvation perfect
through sufferings. 11 For both he that
sanctifieth and they who are sanctified *are*
all of one: for which cause he is not
ashamed to call them brethren, 12 saying,**

Ps. 22:22

**I will declare thy name unto my
brethren,
in the midst of the church will I sing
praise unto thee.
13 And again,**

Isa. 8:17-18

**I will put my trust in him.
And again,
Behold I and the children which God
hath given me.●**

3.OUR HIGH PRIEST

**14 Forasmuch then as the children are
partakers of flesh and blood, he also himself likewise took part of the same; that
through death he might destroy him that
had the power of death, that is, the devil;
15 and deliver them, who through fear of
death were all their lifetime subject to
bondage. 16 For verily he took not on
*him the nature of* angels; but he took on
*him* the seed of Abraham. 17 Wherefore
in all things it behooved him to be made
like unto *his* brethren, that he might be a
merciful and faithful high priest in things
*pertaining* to God, to make reconciliation
for the sins of the people. 18 For in that
he himself hath suffered being tempted, he
is able to succor them that are tempted.●**

SUFFERING

The first segment of this epistle showed Jesus as Son of God. Observe how this segment shows Him as Son of Man.

*2:5-9* What is the main point of verses 5-8a?

What is the first word of verse 8b?

How does verse 9 expand on the fact of verse 8b?

*2:10-13* In what different ways is Jesus' intimate relationship to believers shown here?

*2:14-18* Record the different references to death and suffering.

What qualifies Jesus as high priest?

NEW INTERNATIONAL VERSION

Record what this short passage reveals about Moses. Add to your observations other facts and truths about Moses' life and ministry known from the Old Testament. (Refer to outside helps for this, such as a Bible dictionary.)

In your own words write what this passage reveals about Christ.

*Jesus Greater Than Moses*

3 Therefore, holy brothers, who share in
the heavenly calling, fix your thoughts
on Jesus, the apostle and high priest whom
we confess. 2He was faithful to the one
who appointed him, just as Moses was
faithful in all God's house. 3Jesus has been
found worthy of greater honor than Moses,
just as the builder of a house has greater
honor than the house itself. 4For every
house is built by someone, but God is the
builder of everything. 5Moses was faithful
as a servant in all God's house, testifying
to what would be said in the future. 6But
Christ is faithful as a son over God's house.
And we are his house, if we hold on to our
courage and the hope of which we boast.

KING JAMES

1.OUR HIGH PRIEST

2.CREATOR

3.SON OVER US

3 Wherefore, holy brethren, partakers
of the heavenly calling, consider the
Apostle and High Priest of our profession,
Christ Jesus;● 2 who was faithful to him
that appointed him, as also Moses *was*
*faithful* in all his house.[e] 3 For this *man*
was counted worthy of more glory than
Moses, inasmuch as he who hath builded
the house hath more honor than the house.
4 For every house is builded by some *man*;
but he that built all things *is* God.● 5 And
Moses verily *was* faithful in all his house
as a servant, for a testimony of those
things which were to be spoken after;
6 but Christ as a son over his own house;
whose house are we, if we hold fast the
confidence and the rejoicing of the hope
firm unto the end.●

HEAVENLY CALLING

THE END

Read the segment. With whom is Jesus compared?

Why would such a comparison be especially effective in moving the hearts of Jewish readers of the epistle?

*3:1* Record the references to:

THE BELIEVER

CHRIST

*3:2-4* What comparisons are made:

MOSES

CHRIST

*3:5-6*

MOSES

CHRIST

What is the appeal of verse 6b?

NEW INTERNATIONAL VERSION

After you have studied this passage about God's rest, reach conclusions about the following:

WHAT GOD'S REST IS (For example, is it salvation, victorious Christian living, or heaven?)

FOR WHOM GOD'S REST IS

HOW TO ENTER GOD'S REST

### *Warning Against Unbelief*

[7]So, as the Holy Spirit says:

"Today, if you hear his voice,
[8] do not harden your hearts
as you did in the rebellion,
during the time of testing in the desert,
[9]where your fathers tested and tried me
and for forty years saw what I did.
[10]That is why I was angry with that generation,
and I said, 'Their hearts are always going astray,
and they have not known my ways.'
[11]So I declared on oath in my anger,
'They shall never enter my rest.' "[g]

[12]See to it, brothers, that none of you has
a sinful, unbelieving heart that turns away
from the living God. [13]But encourage one
another daily, as long as it is called Today,
so that none of you may be hardened by
sin's deceitfulness. [14]We have come to
share in Christ if we hold firmly till the end
the confidence we had at first. [15]As has just
been said:

"Today, if you hear his voice,
do not harden your hearts
as you did in the rebellion."[h]

[16]Who were they who heard and re-
belled? Were they not all those Moses led
out of Egypt? [17]And with whom was he
angry for forty years? Was it not with those
who sinned, whose bodies fell in the
desert? [18]And to whom did God swear that
they would never enter his rest if not to
those who disobeyed[a]? [19]So we see that
they were not able to enter, because of
their unbelief.●

### *A Sabbath-Rest for the People of God*

4 Therefore, since the promise of entering his rest still stands, let us be careful
that none of you be found to have fallen
short of it. [2]For we also have had the gospel preached to us, just as they did; but the
message they heard was of no value to
them, because those who heard did not
combine it with faith.[b] [3]Now we who have
believed enter that rest, just as God has
said,

"So I declared on oath in my anger,
'They shall never enter my rest.' "[c]

And yet his work has been finished since
the creation of the world. [4]For somewhere
he has spoken about the seventh day in
these words: "And on the seventh day God
rested from all his work."[d] [5]And again in
the passage above he says, "They shall
never enter my rest."
[6]It still remains that some will enter that
rest, and those who formerly had the gospel preached to them did not go in, because
of their disobedience. [7]Therefore God
again set a certain day, calling it Today,
when a long time later he spoke through
David, as was said before:

"Today, if you hear his voice,
do not harden your hearts."[e]●

[g] *11* Psalm 95:7-11
[h] *15* Psalm 95:7,8
[a] *18* Or *disbelieved* [b] *2* Many manuscripts *because they did not share in the faith of those who obeyed*
[c] *3* Psalm 95:11; also in verse 5
[d] *4* Gen. 2:2 [e] *7* Psalm 95:7,8

KING JAMES

1. EXHORTATION

7 Wherefore as the Holy Ghost saith,
Today if ye will hear his voice,
8 harden not your hearts, as in the
provocation,
in the day of temptation in the
wilderness:
9 when your fathers tempted me,
proved me,
and saw my works forty years.
10 Wherefore I was grieved with that
generation,
and said, They do always err in *their*
heart;
and they have not known my ways.
11 So I sware in my wrath,
They shall not enter into my rest.
12 Take heed, brethren, lest there be in
any of you an evil heart of unbelief, in departing from the living God. 13 But exhort one another daily, while it is called
Today; lest any of you be hardened
through the deceitfulness of sin. 14 For
we are made partakers of Christ, if we
hold the beginning of our confidence
steadfast unto the end; 15 while it is said,
Today if ye will hear his voice,
harden not your hearts, as in the
provocation.
16 For some, when they had heard, did
provoke: howbeit not all that came out of
Egypt by Moses. 17 But with whom was
he grieved forty years? *was it* not with
them that had sinned, whose carcasses fell
in the wilderness? 18 And to whom
sware he that they should not enter into
his rest, but to them that believed not?
19 So we see that they could not enter in
because of unbelief.●

HARDEN NOT

Ps. 95:7-11

Ps. 95:7f.

2. DESCRIPTION

4 Let us therefore fear, lest, a promise
being left *us* of entering into his rest,
any of you should seem to come short of
it. 2 For unto us was the gospel preached,
as well as unto them: but the word
preached did not profit them, not being
mixed with faith in them that heard *it*.
3 For we which have believed do enter
into rest, as he said,
As I have sworn in my wrath,
if they shall enter into my rest:
although the works were finished from the
foundation of the world. 4 For he spake
in a certain place of the seventh *day* on
this wise,
And God did rest the seventh day
from all his works.
5 And in this *place* again,
If they shall enter into my rest.
6 Seeing therefore it remaineth that some
must enter therein, and they to whom it
was first preached entered not in because
of unbelief: 7 again, he limiteth a certain
day, saying in David, Today, after so long
a time; as it is said,
Today if ye will hear his voice,
harden not your hearts.●

Ps. 95:11

Gen. 2:2

Ps. 95:11

Ps. 95:7f.
HARDEN NOT

Compare the beginning and end of the segment.
Read the whole segment, underlining the word "rest" each time it appears.

*3:7-19* Record the exhortations and commands:

What keeps a person from entering God's rest?

*4:1-7* Record the different ways that God's rest is described here.

Record also the commands and exhortations.

NEW INTERNATIONAL VERSION

[8]For if Joshua had given them rest, God
would not have spoken later about another
day. [9]There remains, then, a Sabbath-rest
for the people of God; [10]for anyone who
enters God's rest also rests from his own
work, just as God did from his. [11]Let us,
therefore, make every effort to enter that
rest, so that no one will fall by following
their example of disobedience.●
[12]For the word of God is living and active. Sharper than any double-edged
sword, it penetrates even to dividing soul
and spirit, joints and marrow; it judges the
thoughts and attitudes of the heart. [13]Noth-
ing in all creation is hidden from God's
sight. Everything is uncovered and laid
bare before the eyes of him to whom we
must give account.●

Record practical applications of this passage, concerning the rest for God's people.

Make a list of spiritual applications of 4:12-13 concerning the Word of God. Include each word and phrase involved in the text's description.

KING JAMES

1. OUR LABORING

[8] For if Jesus had given them rest, then
would he not afterward have spoken of
another day. [9] There remaineth therefore
a rest to the people of God. [10] For he
that is entered into his rest, he also hath
ceased from his own works, as God *did*
from his.
11 Let us labor therefore to enter into
that rest, lest any man fall after the same
example of unbelief.● [12] For the word of
God *is* quick, and powerful, and sharper
than any two-edged sword, piercing even
to the dividing asunder of soul and spirit,
and of the joints and marrow, and *is* a dis-
cerner of the thoughts and intents of the
heart. [13] Neither is there any creature
that is not manifest in his sight: but all
things *are* naked and opened unto the eyes
of him with whom we have to do.●

2. THE WORD'S WORK

JOSHUA

GOD

Read the name "Jesus" as "Joshua" (The Living Bible).

*4:8-11* Was Israel's conquest of Canaan, under Joshua, the obtaining of God's rest (v.8)?

What do these verses teach about God's rest:

v.9

v.10

v.11

*4:12-13* List the different words and phrases referring to the word of God.

How are these verses related to the subject of God's rest?

NEW INTERNATIONAL VERSION

Make a list of the various things taught in this passage about Jesus the High Priest.

List spiritual applications of the passage to the everyday life of the believer.

*Jesus the Great High Priest*

14Therefore, since we have a great high
priest who has gone through the heavens,[f]
Jesus the Son of God, let us hold firmly to
the faith we profess. 15For we do not have
a high priest who is unable to sympathize
with our weaknesses, but we have one who
has been tempted in every way, just as we
are—yet was without sin. 16Let us then
approach the throne of grace with confidence, so that we may receive mercy and
find grace to help us in our time of need.●

5 Every high priest is selected from
among men and is appointed to represent them in matters related to God, to
offer gifts and sacrifices for sins. 2He is
able to deal gently with those who are ignorant and are going astray, since he himself
is subject to weakness. 3This is why he has
to offer sacrifices for his own sins, as well
as for the sins of the people.●

4No one takes this honor upon himself;
he must be called by God, just as Aaron
was. 5So Christ also did not take upon himself the glory of becoming a high priest. But
God said to him,

> "You are my Son;
> today I have become your
> Father.[g]"[h]

6And he says in another place,

> "You are a priest forever,
> in the order of Melchizedek."[i]●

7During the days of Jesus' life on earth,
he offered up prayers and petitions with
loud cries and tears to the one who could
save him from death, and he was heard
because of his reverent submission. 8Al-
though he was a son, he learned obedience
from what he suffered 9and, once made
perfect, he became the source of eternal
salvation for all who obey him 10and was
designated by God to be high priest in the
order of Melchizedek.●

f14 Or *gone into heaven* g5 Or *have begotten you*
h5 Psalm 2:7 i6 Psalm 110:4

KING JAMES

1. CREDENTIALS

SON OF GOD

**14 Seeing then that we have a great high**
**priest, that is passed into the heavens,**
**Jesus the Son of God, let us hold fast *our***
**profession. 15 For we have not a high**
**priest which cannot be touched with the**
**feeling of our infirmities; but was in all**
**points tempted like as *we are*, *yet* without**
**sin. 16 Let us therefore come boldly unto**
**the throne of grace, that we may obtain**
**mercy, and find grace to help in time of**
**need.●**

**5 For every high priest taken from**
**among men is ordained for men in**
**things *pertaining* to God, that he may offer**
**both gifts and sacrifices for sins: 2 who**
**can have compassion on the ignorant, and**
**on them that are out of the way; for that**
**he himself also is compassed with infir-**
**mity. 3 And by reason hereof he ought, as**
**for the people, so also for himself, to offer**
**for sins.● 4 And no man taketh this honor**
**unto himself, but he that is called of God,**
**as *was* Aaron.**

2. CALLING

**5 So also Christ glorified not himself to**
**be made a high priest; but he that said un-**
**to him,**
**Thou art my Son,**
**today have I begotten thee.**
**6 As he saith also in another *place*,**
**Thou *art* a priest for ever**
**after the order of Melchiz'edek.●**

Ps. 2:7

Ps. 110:4

3. OBEDIENCE

**7 Who in the days of his flesh, when he**
**had offered up prayers and supplications**
**with strong crying and tears unto him that**
**was able to save him from death, and was**
**heard in that he feared; 8 though he were**
**a Son, yet learned he obedience by the**
**things which he suffered; 9 and being**
**made perfect, he became the author of**
**eternal salvation unto all them that obey**
**him; 10 called of God a high priest after**
**the order of Melchiz'edek.●**

CALLED OF GOD

*4:14—5:3* Record the credentials of Jesus as High Priest.

What are the references to Jesus being a *unique* High Priest?

Record the exhortations.

*5:4-6* What is the point of this paragraph?

With whom is Christ compared?

*5:7-10* Record key words and phrases of the paragraph.

NEW INTERNATIONAL VERSION

What does this passage teach about:

STUDYING THE BIBLE

MATURING IN THE CHRISTIAN LIFE

WARNINGS OF SPIRITUAL FALLING AWAY

LOVE OF THE BRETHREN

OTHER

*Warning Against Falling Away*

[11]We have much to say about this, but it is hard to explain because you are slow to learn. [12]In fact, though by this time you ought to be teachers, you need someone to teach you the elementary truths of God's word all over again. You need milk, not solid food! [13]Anyone who lives on milk, being still an infant, is not acquainted with the teaching about righteousness. [14]But solid food is for the mature, who by constant use have trained themselves to distinguish good from evil.●

6 Therefore let us leave the elementary teachings about Christ and go on to maturity, not laying again the foundation of repentance from acts that lead to death, and of faith in God, [2]instruction about baptisms, the laying on of hands, the resurrection of the dead, and eternal judgment. [3]And God permitting, we will do so.●

[4]It is impossible for those who have once been enlightened, who have tasted the heavenly gift, who have shared in the Holy Spirit, [5]who have tasted the goodness of the word of God and the powers of the coming age, [6]if they fall away, to be brought back to repentance, because[a] to their loss they are crucifying the Son of God all over again and subjecting him to public disgrace.

[7]Land that drinks in the rain often falling on it and that produces a crop useful to those for whom it is farmed receives the blessing of God. [8]But land that produces thorns and thistles is worthless and is in danger of being cursed. In the end it will be burned.●

[9]Even though we speak like this, dear friends, we are confident of better things in your case—things that accompany salvation. [10]God is not unjust; he will not forget your work and the love you have shown him as you have helped his people and continue to help them.●

[a]6 Or *repentance while*

KING JAMES

1. DULL OF HEARING

11 Of whom we have many things to
say, and hard to be uttered, seeing ye are
dull of hearing. 12 For when for the time
ye ought to be teachers, ye have need that
one teach you again which *be* the first
principles of the oracles of God; and are
become such as have need of milk, and
not of strong meat. 13 For every one that
useth milk *is* unskilful in the word of
righteousness: for he is a babe. 14 But
strong meat belongeth to them that are of
full age, *even* those who by reason of use
have their senses exercised to discern both
good and evil.●

Ye

—application

6 Therefore leaving the principles of the
doctrine of Christ, let us go on unto
perfection; not laying again the foundation of repentance from dead works, and
of faith toward God, 2 of the doctrine of
baptisms, and of laying on of hands, and
of resurrection of the dead, and of eternal
judgment. 3 And this will we do, if God
permit.●

We

2. FALLING AWAY

4 For *it is* impossible for those
who were once enlightened, and have
tasted of the heavenly gift, and were made
partakers of the Holy Ghost, 5 and have
tasted the good word of God, and the
powers of the world to come, 6 if they
shall fall away, to renew them again unto
repentance; seeing they crucify to themselves the Son of God afresh, and put *him*
to an open shame. 7 For the earth which
drinketh in the rain that cometh oft upon
it, and bringeth forth herbs meet for them
by whom it is dressed, receiveth blessing
from God: 8 but that which beareth
thorns and briers *is* rejected, and *is* nigh
unto cursing; whose end *is* to be burned.●

They

—encouragement

9 But, beloved, we are persuaded better
things of you, and things that accompany
salvation, though we thus speak. 10 For
God *is* not unrighteous to forget your
work and labor of love, which ye have
showed toward his name, in that ye have
ministered to the saints, and do minister.●

Ye

What are the prominent pronouns of each paragraph?

Use that observation as a clue to the interpretation and application of the passage.

*5:11-14* What spiritual deficiencies are mentioned here?

*6:1-3* What is the exhortation?

How is the exhortation applied?

*6:4-8* Record:

THE SIN

THE RECOMPENSE

*6:9-10* What is the point of this paragraph?

How is it related to the previous paragraph?

NEW INTERNATIONAL VERSION

What is taught here about:

ASSURANCE IN THE CHRISTIAN LIFE

PROMISES OF GOD

FAITH

PATIENCE

HOPE

JESUS OUR HIGH PRIEST

OTHER

[11]We want each of you
to show this same diligence to the very
end, in order to make your hope sure. [12]We
do not want you to become lazy, but to
imitate those who through faith and patience inherit what has been promised.●

*The Certainty of God's Promise*

[13]When God made his promise to Abraham, since there was no one greater for
him to swear by, he swore by himself,
[14]saying, "I will surely bless you and give
you many descendants."[b] [15]And so after
waiting patiently, Abraham received what
was promised.
[16]Men swear by someone greater than
themselves, and the oath confirms what is
said and puts an end to all argument. [17]Be-
cause God wanted to make the unchanging
nature of his purpose very clear to the heirs
of what was promised, he confirmed it with
an oath. [18]God did this so that, by two
unchangeable things in which it is impossible for God to lie, we who have fled to
take hold of the hope offered to us may be
greatly encouraged.● [19]We have this hope as
an anchor for the soul, firm and secure. It
enters the inner sanctuary behind the curtain, [20]where Jesus, who went before us,
has entered on our behalf. He has become
a high priest forever, in the order of Melchizedek.●

[b]14 Gen. 22:17

KING JAMES

1. OUR FAITH

11 And we desire that every one of you do
show the same diligence to the full assurance of hope unto the end: 12 that ye be
not slothful, but followers of them who
through faith and patience inherit the
promises.●

2. GOD'S PROMISE

13 For when God made promise to
Abraham, because he could swear by no
greater, he sware by himself, 14 saying,
Surely blessing I will bless thee, and multiplying I will multiply thee. 15 And so,
after he had patiently endured, he obtained the promise. 16 For men verily
swear by the greater: and an oath for confirmation *is* to them an end of all strife.
17 Wherein God, willing more abundantly
to show unto the heirs of promise the im-
mutability of his counsel, confirmed *it* by
an oath: 18 that by two immutable things,
in which *it was* impossible for God to lie,
we might have a strong consolation, who
have fled for refuge to lay hold upon the
hope set before us:●

3. JESUS' WORK

19 which *hope* we
have as an anchor of the soul, both sure
and steadfast, and which entereth into
that within the veil; 20 whither the fore-
runner is for us entered, *even* Jesus, made
a high priest for ever after the order of
Melchiz'edek. ●

FOL-LOWERS

FORE-RUNNER

This segment is a continuation of the over-all theme of the preceding segment.

*6:11-12* Record the appeals: ____________

*6:13-18* Record what is written about:

PROMISE ____________

OATH ____________

*6:19-20* Record:

BELIEVER'S HOPE ____________

JESUS' MINISTRY ____________

NEW INTERNATIONAL VERSION

Relate this entire passage to Christ:

1. List ways Christ's priesthood resembled that of Melchizedek. ______

2. Show how Christ's priesthood surpassed that of Melchizedek. ______

### *Melchizedek the Priest*

**7** This Melchizedek was king of Salem and priest of God Most High. He met Abraham returning from the defeat of the kings and blessed him, 2and Abraham gave him a tenth of everything. First, his name means "king of righteousness"; then also, "king of Salem" means "king of peace." 3Without father or mother, without genealogy, without beginning of days or end of life, like the Son of God he remains a priest forever.●

4Just think how great he was: Even the patriarch Abraham gave him a tenth of the plunder! 5Now the law requires the descendants of Levi who become priests to collect a tenth from the people—that is, their brothers—even though their brothers are descended from Abraham. 6This man, however, did not trace his descent from Levi, yet he collected a tenth from Abraham and blessed him who had the promises. 7And without doubt the lesser person is blessed by the greater. 8In the one case, the tenth is collected by men who die; but in the other case, by him who is declared to be living. 9One might even say that Levi, who collects the tenth, paid the tenth through Abraham, 10because when Melchizedek met Abraham, Levi was still in the body of his ancestor.●

### *Jesus Like Melchizedek*

11If perfection could have been attained through the Levitical priesthood (for on the basis of it the law was given to the people), why was there still need for another priest to come—one in the order of Melchizedek, not in the order of Aaron? 12For when there is a change of the priesthood, there must also be a change of the law. 13He of whom these things are said belonged to a different tribe, and no one from that tribe has ever served at the altar. 14For it is clear that our Lord descended from Judah, and in regard to that tribe Moses said nothing about priests.●

KING JAMES

1. IDENTITY

7 For this Melchiz'edek, king of Salem,
priest of the most high God, who met
Abraham returning from the slaughter of
the kings, and blessed him; 2 to whom
also Abraham gave a tenth part of all;
first being by interpretation King of righteousness, and after that also King of
Salem, which is, King of peace; 3 without
father, without mother, without descent, having neither beginning of days,
nor end of life; but made like unto
the Son of God; abideth a priest continually.●

2. GREATNESS

4 Now consider how great this man
*was*, unto whom even the patriarch Abraham gave the tenth of the spoils. 5 And
verily they that are of the sons of Levi,
who receive the office of the priesthood,
have a commandment to take tithes of the
people according to the law, that is, of
their brethren, though they come out of
the loins of Abraham: 6 but he whose
descent is not counted from them received
tithes of Abraham, and blessed him that
had the promises. 7 And without all contradiction the less is blessed of the better.
8 And here men that die receive tithes;
but there he *receiveth them*, of whom it is
witnessed that he liveth. 9 And as I may
so say, Levi also, who receiveth tithes,
paid tithes in Abraham. 10 For he was
yet in the loins of his father, when Melchiz'edek met him.●

3. LIMITATIONS

11 If therefore perfection were by the
Levitical priesthood, (for under it the people received the law,) what further need
*was there* that another priest should rise
after the order of Melchiz'edek, and not
be called after the order of Aaron? 12 For
the priesthood being changed, there is
made of necessity a change also of the law.
13 For he of whom these things are spoken
pertaineth to another tribe, of which no
man gave attendance at the altar. 14 For
*it is* evident that our Lord sprang out of
Judah; of which tribe Moses spake nothing concerning priesthood.●

MELCHIZEDEK

MOSES

The theme of this segment is continued in the segment that follows.

*7:1-3* Record the descriptions of Melchizedek.

*7:4-10* Record the points of greatness. (Compare the Living Bible list.)

*7:11-14* What did the Levitical priesthood fail to accomplish?

NEW INTERNATIONAL VERSION

Keeping in mind the ministries of a high priest, make a list of applications of this passage, showing how Christ serves believers today.

[15]And
what we have said is even more clear if
another priest like Melchizedek appears,
[16]one who has become a priest not on the
basis of a regulation as to his ancestry but
on the basis of the power of an indestructible life. [17]For it is declared:

"You are a priest forever,
in the order of Melchizedek."[c]

[18]The former regulation is set aside because it was weak and useless [19](for the law
made nothing perfect), and a better hope is
introduced, by which we draw near to
God.●

[20]And it was not without an oath! Others
became priests without any oath, [21]but he
became a priest with an oath when God
said to him:

"The Lord has sworn
and will not change his mind:
'You are a priest forever.' "[a]

[22]Because of this oath, Jesus has become
the guarantee of a better covenant.●

[23]Now there were many of those priests,
since death prevented them from continuing in office; [24]but because Jesus lives forever, he has a permanent priesthood.
[25]Therefore he is able to save completely[b]
those who come to God through him, because he always lives to intercede for
them.●

[26]Such a high priest meets our need—one
who is holy, blameless, pure, set apart
from sinners, exalted above the heavens.
[27]Unlike the other high priests, he does not
need to offer sacrifices day after day, first
for his own sins, and then for the sins of the
people. He sacrificed for their sins once for
all when he offered himself. [28]For the law
appoints as high priests men who are weak;
but the oath, which came after the law,
appointed the Son, who has been made
perfect forever.●

[a]21 Psalm 110:4 [b]25 Or *forever* [c]17 Psalm 110:4

KING JAMES

1.BETTER HOPE

15 And it is yet far more evident: for
that after the similitude of Melchiz'edek
there ariseth another priest, 16 who is
made, not after the law of a carnal commandment, but after the power of an
endless life. 17 For he testifieth,
Thou *art* a priest for ever
after the order of Melchiz'edek.
18 For there is verily a disannulling of the
commandment going before for the weakness and unprofitableness thereof. 19 For
the law made nothing perfect, but the
bringing in of a better hope *did;* by the
which we draw nigh unto God.●

IM-MORTAL

2.BETTER COVENANT

20 And inasmuch as not without an
oath *he was made priest:* 21 (for those
priests were made without an oath; but
this with an oath by him that said unto
him,
The Lord sware and will not repent,
Thou *art* a priest for ever
after the order of Melchiz'edek: )
22 by so much was Jesus made a surety of
a better testament.●

Ps. 110:4

3.ENDLESS MINISTRY

23 And they truly were many priests,
because they were not suffered to continue
by reason of death: 24 but this *man*, because he continueth ever, hath an unchangeable priesthood. 25 Wherefore he
is able also to save them to the uttermost
that come unto God by him, seeing he
ever liveth to make intercession for them.●

4.ETERNAL PERFEC-TION

26 For such a high priest became us,
*who is* holy, harmless, undefiled, separate
from sinners, and made higher than the
heavens; 27 who needeth not daily, as
those high priests, to offer up sacrifice,
first for his own sins, and then for the people's: for this he did once, when he offered
up himself. 28 For the law maketh men
high priests which have infirmity; but the
word of the oath, which was since the law,
*maketh* the Son, who is consecrated
for evermore.●

CONSE-CRATED

For each of the paragraphs record words and phrases which show Jesus either to be like Melchizedek or to surpass his life and ministry.

*7:15-19* ______

*7:20-22* ______

*7:23-25* ______

*7:26-28* ______

NEW INTERNATIONAL VERSION

What does this passage teach about:

COVENANTS OF GOD

GRACE OF GOD

MINISTRIES OF CHRIST

TRUE WORSHIP

CHRIST AS HIGH PRIEST

OTHER

### *The High Priest of a New Covenant*

8 The point of what we are saying is this:
We do have such a high priest, who sat
down at the right hand of the throne of the
Majesty in heaven, 2and who serves in the
sanctuary, the true tabernacle set up by the
Lord, not by man.●
3Every high priest is appointed to offer
both gifts and sacrifices, and so it was
necessary for this one also to have something to offer. 4If he were on earth, he
would not be a priest, for there are already
men who offer the gifts prescribed by the
law. 5They serve at a sanctuary that is a
copy and shadow of what is in heaven. This
is why Moses was warned when he was
about to build the tabernacle: "See to it
that you make everything according to the
pattern shown you on the mountain."[c]
6But the ministry Jesus has received is as
superior to theirs as the covenant of which
he is mediator is superior to the old one,
and it is founded on better promises.●
7For if there had been nothing wrong
with that first covenant, no place would
have been sought for another. 8But God
found fault with the people and said[d]:

"The time is coming, declares the
Lord,
when I will make a new covenant
with the house of Israel
and with the house of Judah.
9It will not be like the covenant
I made with their forefathers
when I took them by the hand
to lead them out of Egypt,
because they did not remain faithful
to my covenant,
and I turned away from them,
declares the Lord.
10This is the covenant I will make
with the house of Israel
after that time, declares the Lord.
I will put my laws in their minds
and write them on their hearts.
I will be their God,
and they will be my people.
11No longer will a man teach his
neighbor,
or a man his brother, saying,
'Know the Lord,'
because they will all know me,
from the least of them to the
greatest.
12For I will forgive their wickedness
and will remember their sins no
more."[e]

13By calling this covenant "new," he has
made the first one obsolete; and what is
obsolete and aging will soon disappear.●

[c]5 Exodus 25:40 [d]8 Some manuscripts may be translated *fault and said to the people.* [e]12 Jer. 31:31-34

KING JAMES

—introduction

**8** Now of the things which we have
spoken *this is* the sum: We have such
a high priest, who is set on the right hand
of the throne of the Majesty in the
heavens; 2 a minister of the sanctuary,
and of the true tabernacle, which the
Lord pitched, and not man. ● 3 For every
high priest is ordained to offer gifts and
sacrifices: wherefore *it is* of necessity that
this man have somewhat also to offer.
4 For if he were on earth, he should not
be a priest, seeing that there are priests
that offer gifts according to the law:
5 who serve unto the example and shadow
of heavenly things, as Moses was admonished of God when he was about to
make the tabernacle: for, See, saith he,
*that* thou make all things according to the
pattern showed to thee in the mount.
6 But now hath he obtained a more excellent ministry, by how much also he is
the mediator of a better covenant, which
was established upon better promises. ●

PRIEST

1. BETTER MINISTRY

2. NEW COVENANT

7 For if that first *covenant* had been faultless, then should no place have been
sought for the second.

8 For finding fault with them, he saith,
Behold, the days come, saith the Lord,
when I will make a new covenant with the house of Israel and with the house of Judah:
9 not according to the covenant that I made with their fathers,
in the day when I took them by the hand to lead them out of the land of Egypt;
because they continued not in my covenant,
and I regarded them not, saith the Lord.
10 For this *is* the covenant that I will make with the house of Israel
after those days, saith the Lord;
I will put my laws into their mind,
and write them in their hearts:
and I will be to them a God,
and they shall be to me a people:
11 and they shall not teach every man his neighbor,
and every man his brother, saying, Know the Lord:
for all shall know me,
from the least to the greatest.
12 For I will be merciful to their unrighteousness,
and their sins and their iniquities will I remember no more.

Jer. 31:31-34

13 In that he saith, A new *covenant*, he
hath made the first old. Now that which
decayeth and waxeth old *is* ready to
vanish away. ●

COVENANT

*8:1-2* How does the first phrase relate to all that has been written before this?

What is "the sum"?

(Note: the section 8:3—10:18 expands on the statement of 8:1-2.)

*8:3-6* Note the repetition of the word "better." What does verse 3 suggest as an important part of Christ's better ministry?

*8:7-13* What is written here about:

THE OLD COVENANT

THE NEW COVENANT

Why are the two covenants called "new" and "old"?

NEW INTERNATIONAL VERSION

What do you learn here about the ministries of Christ for the believer today? (With outside help you may want to include what the tabernacle items prefigured.)

### *Worship in the Earthly Tabernacle*

9 Now the first covenant had regulations
for worship and also an earthly sanctuary. 2A tabernacle was set up. In its first
room were the lampstand, the table and the
consecrated bread; this was called the
Holy Place. 3Behind the second curtain
was a room called the Most Holy Place,
4which had the golden altar of incense and
the gold-covered ark of the covenant. This
ark contained the gold jar of manna,
Aaron's rod that had budded, and the stone
tablets of the covenant. 5Above the ark
were the cherubim of the Glory, overshad-
owing the place of atonement. But we cannot discuss these things in detail now.●
6When everything had been arranged
like this, the priests entered regularly into
the outer room to carry on their ministry.
7But only the high priest entered the inner
room, and that only once a year, and never
without blood, which he offered for himself and for the sins the people had committed in ignorance. 8The Holy Spirit was
showing by this that the way into the Most
Holy Place had not yet been disclosed as
long as the first tabernacle was still standing. 9This is an illustration for the present
time, indicating that the gifts and sacrifices
being offered were not able to clear the
conscience of the worshiper. 10They are
only a matter of food and drink and various
ceremonial washings—external regulations applying until the time of the new
order.●

### *The Blood of Christ*

11When Christ came as high priest of the
good things that are already here,[a] he went
through the greater and more perfect tabernacle that is not man-made, that is to say,
not a part of this creation. 12He did not
enter by means of the blood of goats and
calves; but he entered the Most Holy Place
once for all by his own blood, having obtained eternal redemption.●

[a]11 Some early manuscripts *are to come*

KING JAMES

1. TABERNACLE

OLD COVENANT

9 Then verily the first *covenant* had also
ordinances of divine service, and a
worldly sanctuary. 2 For there was a
tabernacle made; the first, wherein *was*
the candlestick, and the table, and the
showbread; which is called the sanctuary.
3 And after the second veil, the tabernacle which is called the holiest of all;
4 which had the golden censer, and the
ark of the covenant overlaid round about
with gold, wherein *was* the golden pot
that had manna, and Aaron's rod that
budded, and the tables of the covenant;
5 and over it the cherubim of glory shad-
owing the mercy seat; of which we cannot now speak particularly.●

2. SERVICES

6 Now when these things were thus ordained, the priests went always into the
first tabernacle, accomplishing the service
*of God*. 7 But into the second *went* the
high priest alone once every year, not
without blood, which he offered for himself, and *for* the errors of the people:
8 the Holy Ghost this signifying, that the
way into the holiest of all was not yet
made manifest, while as the first tabernacle was yet standing: 9 which *was* a
figure for the time then present, in which
were offered both gifts and sacrifices, that
could not make him that did the service
perfect, as pertaining to the conscience;
10 *which stood* only in meats and drinks,
and divers washings, and carnal ordinances, imposed *on them* until the time of
reformation.●

3. CHRIST THE HIGH PRIEST

11 But Christ being come a high priest
of good things to come, by a greater and
more perfect tabernacle, not made with
hands, that is to say, not of this building;
12 neither by the blood of goats and
calves, but by his own blood he entered in
once into the holy place, having obtained
eternal redemption *for us*.●

ETERNAL REDEMPTION

*9:1-5* List the areas and pieces of furniture of the tabernacle.

What names of the list suggest theological or spiritual meaning?

*9:6-10* Record:

THE SERVICES

WHAT THE SERVICES PRE-FIGURED

*9:11-12* Record the strong words and phrases of the paragraph.

NEW INTERNATIONAL VERSION

What does this passage teach about:

THE DEATH OF CHRIST

REDEMPTION

FORGIVENESS OF SINS

SECOND COMING OF CHRIST

FUTURE JUDGMENT

OTHER

[13]The blood of goats and bulls and the ashes of a heifer sprinkled on those who are ceremonially unclean sanctify them so that they are outwardly clean. [14]How much more, then, will the blood of Christ, who through the eternal Spirit offered himself unblemished to God, cleanse our consciences from acts that lead to death, so that we may serve the living God!●

[15]For this reason Christ is the mediator of a new covenant, that those who are called may receive the promised eternal inheritance—now that he has died as a ransom to set them free from the sins committed under the first covenant.

[16]In the case of a will,[b] it is necessary to prove the death of the one who made it, [17]because a will is in force only when somebody has died; it never takes effect while the one who made it is living. [18]This is why even the first covenant was not put into effect without blood. [19]When Moses had proclaimed every commandment of the law to all the people, he took the blood of calves, together with water, scarlet wool and branches of hyssop, and sprinkled the scroll and all the people. [20]He said, "This is the blood of the covenant, which God has commanded you to keep."[c] [21]In the same way, he sprinkled with the blood both the tabernacle and everything used in its ceremonies. [22]In fact, the law requires that nearly everything be cleansed with blood, and without the shedding of blood there is no forgiveness.●

[23]It was necessary, then, for the copies of the heavenly things to be purified with these sacrifices, but the heavenly things themselves with better sacrifices than these. [24]For Christ did not enter a man-made sanctuary that was only a copy of the true one; he entered heaven itself, now to appear for us in God's presence. [25]Nor did he enter heaven to offer himself again and again, the way the high priest enters the Most Holy Place every year with blood that is not his own. [26]Then Christ would have had to suffer many times since the creation of the world. But now he has appeared once for all at the end of the ages to do away with sin by the sacrifice of himself. [27]Just as man is destined to die once, and after that to face judgment, [28]so Christ was sacrificed once to take away the sins of many people; and he will appear a second time, not to bear sin, but to bring salvation to those who are waiting for him.●

[b]*16* Same Greek word as *covenant*; also in verse 17
[c]*20* Exodus 24:8

KING JAMES

—theme

13 For if the
blood of bulls and of goats, and the
ashes of a heifer sprinkling the unclean,
sanctifieth to the purifying of the flesh;
14 how much more shall the blood of
Christ, who through the eternal Spirit
offered himself without spot to God,
purge your conscience from dead works
to serve the living God?●

BLOOD OF ANIMALS

1. PRICE OF THE SACRIFICE

15 And for this cause he is the mediator
of the new testament, that by means of
death, for the redemption of the transgressions *that were* under the first testament, they which are called might receive
the promise of eternal inheritance. 16 For
where a testament *is*, there must also of
necessity be the death of the testator.
17 For a testament *is* of force after men
are dead: otherwise it is of no strength at
all while the testator liveth. 18 Whereupon neither the first *testament* was dedicated without blood. 19 For when Moses
had spoken every precept to all the people
according to the law, he took the blood of
calves and of goats, with water, and scarlet wool, and hyssop, and sprinkled both
the book and all the people, 20 saying,
This *is* the blood of the testament which
God hath enjoined unto you. 21 Moreover he sprinkled likewise with blood both
the tabernacle, and all the vessels of the
ministry. 22 And almost all things are
by the law purged with blood; and without shedding of blood is no remission.●

2. FINALITY OF THE SACRIFICE

23 *It was* therefore necessary that the
patterns of things in the heavens should be
purified with these; but the heavenly
things themselves with better sacrifices
than these. 24 For Christ is not entered
into the holy places made with hands,
*which are* the figures of the true; but into
heaven itself, now to appear in the presence of God for us: 25 nor yet that he
should offer himself often, as the high
priest entereth into the holy place every
year with blood of others; 26 for then
must he often have suffered since the
foundation of the world: but now once in
the end of the world hath he appeared to
put away sin by the sacrifice of himself.
27 And as it is appointed unto men once
to die, but after this the judgment: 28 so
Christ was once offered to bear the sins of
many; and unto them that look for him
shall he appear the second time without
sin unto salvation.●

BLOOD OF CHRIST

*9:13-14* How do the first three words of verse 14 bind together the two surrounding parts of the paragraph?

*9:15-22* What are the key repeated words of the paragraph?

What is the price of Christ's sacrifice?

Observe how often the words "blood" and "death" are repeated here.

*9:23-28* Record the different references that show the *finality* of Christ's sacrifice.

NEW INTERNATIONAL VERSION

Write a list of all the words and phrases of this passage which describe the person and work of Christ.

*Christ's Sacrifice Once for All*

10 The law is only a shadow of the good
things that are coming—not the
realities themselves. For this reason it can
never, by the same sacrifices repeated end-
lessly year after year, make perfect those
who draw near to worship. 2If it could,
would they not have stopped being offered? For the worshipers would have been
cleansed once for all, and would no longer
have felt guilty for their sins. 3But those
sacrifices are an annual reminder of sins,
4because it is impossible for the blood of
bulls and goats to take away sins.●
5Therefore, when Christ came into the
world, he said:

"Sacrifice and offering you did not
desire,
but a body you prepared for me;
6with burnt offerings and sin
offerings
you were not pleased.
7Then I said, 'Here I am—it is
written about me in the
scroll—
I have come to do your will,
O God.' "[d]

8First he said, "Sacrifices and offerings,
burnt offerings and sin offerings you did
not desire, nor were you pleased with
them" (although the law required them to
be made). 9Then he said, "Here I am, I
have come to do your will." He sets aside
the first to establish the second. 10And by
that will, we have been made holy through
the sacrifice of the body of Jesus Christ
once for all.●
11Day after day every priest stands and
performs his religious duties; again and
again he offers the same sacrifices, which
can never take away sins. 12But when this
priest had offered for all time one sacrifice
for sins, he sat down at the right hand of
God. 13Since that time he waits for his enemies to be made his footstool, 14because by
one sacrifice he has made perfect forever
those who are being made holy.●
15The Holy Spirit also testifies to us
about this. First he says:

16"This is the covenant I will make
with them
after that time, says the Lord.
I will put my laws in their hearts,
and I will write them on their
minds."[a]

17Then he adds:

"Their sins and lawless acts
I will remember no more."[b]

18And where these have been forgiven,
there is no longer any sacrifice for sin.●

[d]7 Psalm 40:6-8 (see Septuagint)
[a]16 Jer. 31:33 [b]17 Jer. 31:34

KING JAMES

1. EXTERNAL LAW

SHADOW

**10** For the law having a shadow of
good things to come, *and* not the
very image of the things, can never with
those sacrifices, which they offered year by
year continually, make the comers thereunto perfect. 2 For then would they not
have ceased to be offered? because that
the worshippers once purged should have
had no more conscience of sins. 3 But in
those *sacrifices there is* a remembrance
again *made* of sins every year. 4 For *it is*
not possible that the blood of bulls and of
goats should take away sins.●

2. WILLING OFFERING

Ps. 40:6-7

5 Wherefore, when he cometh into the
world, he saith,
Sacrifice and offering thou wouldest
not,
but a body hast thou prepared me:
6 in burnt offerings and *sacrifices* for
sin thou hast had no pleasure.
7 Then said I, Lo, I come
(in the volume of the book it is
written of me)
to do thy will, O God.
8 Above when he said, Sacrifice and offering and burnt offerings and *offering* for sin
thou wouldest not, neither hadst pleasure
*therein;* which are offered by the law;
9 then said he, Lo, I come to do thy will,
O God. He taketh away the first, that he
may establish the second. 10 By the
which will we are sanctified through the
offering of the body of Jesus Christ once
*for all.*●

3. FINISHED WORK

11 And every priest standeth daily ministering and offering oftentimes the same
sacrifices, which can never take away sins:
12 but this man, after he had offered one
sacrifice for sins for ever, sat down on the
right hand of God; 13 from henceforth
expecting till his enemies be made his
footstool. 14 For by one offering he hath
perfected for ever them that are sanctified.●

4. INTERNAL LAW

Jer. 31:33-34

15 *Whereof* the Holy Ghost also is a witness to us: for after that he had said before,
16 This *is* the covenant that I will make
with them
after those days, saith the Lord;
I will put my laws into their hearts,
and in their minds will I write them;
17 and their sins and iniquities will I
remember no more.
18 Now where remission of these *is, there*
*is* no more offering for sin.●

REMISSION

*10:1-4* What was the shortcoming of the law, according to verse 1? __________

How is this shortcoming confirmed in verses 2-4?

*10:5-10* What is revealed here about Jesus' offering?

*10:11-14* Compare:

OLD TESTAMENT PRIESTS __________

JESUS __________

*10:15-18* What does this paragraph teach?

Compare this paragraph with the first paragraph. __________

NEW INTERNATIONAL VERSION

What does this passage teach about:

FAITH

CONFIDENCE

PRAYER

REJECTION OF CHRIST

JUDGMENT

PATIENCE AND ENDURANCE

*A Call to Persevere*

[19]Therefore, brothers, since we have
confidence to enter the Most Holy Place by
the blood of Jesus, [20]by a new and living
way opened for us through the curtain, that
is, his body, [21]and since we have a great
priest over the house of God, [22]let us draw
near to God with a sincere heart in full
assurance of faith, having our hearts sprinkled to cleanse us from a guilty conscience
and having our bodies washed with pure
water. [23]Let us hold unswervingly to the
hope we profess, for he who promised is
faithful. [24]And let us consider how we may
spur one another on toward love and good
deeds. [25]Let us not give up meeting together, as some are in the habit of doing,
but let us encourage one another—and all
the more as you see the Day approaching.●
[26]If we deliberately keep on sinning after
we have received the knowledge of the
truth, no sacrifice for sins is left, [27]but only
a fearful expectation of judgment and of
raging fire that will consume the enemies of
God. [28]Anyone who rejected the law of
Moses died without mercy on the testimony of two or three witnesses. [29]How
much more severely do you think a man
deserves to be punished who has trampled
the Son of God under foot, who has treated
as an unholy thing the blood of the covenant that sanctified him, and who has insulted the Spirit of grace? [30]For we know
him who said, "It is mine to avenge; I will
repay,"[c] and again, "The Lord will judge
his people."[d] [31]It is a dreadful thing to fall
into the hands of the living God.●
[32]Remember those earlier days after you
had received the light, when you stood
your ground in a great contest in the face
of suffering. [33]Sometimes you were publicly exposed to insult and persecution; at
other times you stood side by side with
those who were so treated. [34]You sympa-
thized with those in prison and joyfully accepted the confiscation of your property,
because you knew that you yourselves had
better and lasting possessions.
[35]So do not throw away your confidence;
it will be richly rewarded. [36]You need to
persevere so that when you have done the
will of God, you will receive what he has
promised. [37]For in just a very little while,

"He who is coming will come and
will not delay.
38 But my righteous one[e] will live by
faith.
And if he shrinks back,
I will not be pleased with him."[f]

[39]But we are not of those who shrink back
and are destroyed, but of those who believe and are saved.●

[c]30 Deut. 32:35 [d]30 Deut. 32:36; Psalm 135:14
[e]38 One early manuscript *But the righteous* [f]38 Hab. 2:3,4

KING JAMES

**1. FAITH'S EXHORTATION**

BLOOD OF JESUS

19 Having therefore, brethren, boldness to enter into the holiest by the blood
of Jesus, 20 by a new and living way,
which he hath consecrated for us, through
the veil, that is to say, his flesh; 21 and
*having* a high priest over the house of God;
22 let us draw near with a true heart in
full assurance of faith, having our hearts
sprinkled from an evil conscience, and
our bodies washed with pure water.
23 Let us hold fast the profession of *our*
faith without wavering; for he *is* faithful
that promised; 24 and let us consider one
another to provoke unto love and to good
works: 25 not forsaking the assembling
of ourselves together, as the manner of
some *is;* but exhorting *one another:* and
so much the more, as ye see the day approaching.●

**2. FAITH'S WARNING**

26 For if we sin wilfully after that we
have received the knowledge of the truth,
there remaineth no more sacrifice for sins,
27 but a certain fearful looking for of
judgment and fiery indignation, which
shall devour the adversaries. 28 He that
despised Moses' law died without mercy
under two or three witnesses: 29 of how
much sorer punishment, suppose ye, shall
he be thought worthy, who hath trodden
under foot the Son of God, and hath
counted the blood of the covenant, wherewith he was sanctified, an unholy thing,
and hath done despite unto the Spirit of
grace? 30 For we know him that hath
said,

Vengeance *belongeth* unto me,
I will recompense, saith the Lord.

And again,

The Lord shall judge his people.

Deu. 32:35-36

31 *It is* a fearful thing to fall into the
hands of the living God.●

**3. FAITH'S APPEAL**

32 But call to remembrance the former
days, in which, after ye were illuminated,
ye endured a great fight of afflictions;
33 partly, whilst ye were made a gazing-
stock both by reproaches and afflictions;
and partly, whilst ye became companions
of them that were so used. 34 For ye had
compassion of me in my bonds, and took
joyfully the spoiling of your goods, knowing in yourselves that ye have in heaven a
better and an enduring substance. 35 Cast
not away therefore your confidence,
which hath great recompense of reward.
36 For ye have need of patience, that,
after ye have done the will of God, ye
might receive the promise.

37 For yet a little while,
and he that shall come will come, and
will not tarry.
38 Now the just shall live by faith:
but if *any man* draw back,
my soul shall have no pleasure in
him.

Hab. 2:3-4

39 But we are not of them who draw back
unto perdition; but of them that believe
to the saving of the soul.●

SALVATION

---

This segment begins the practical *exhortation* section of the epistle. Observe how the previous doctrinal section leads into the opening verse (v.19).

*10:19-25* Record the exhortation introduced by the words "let us."

______________________________

______________________________

______________________________

______________________________

______________________________

______________________________

*10:26-31* Record words and phrases identifying:

THE SIN ______________________________

______________________________

______________________________

______________________________

______________________________

THE JUDGMENT ______________________________

______________________________

______________________________

______________________________

______________________________

*10:32-39* Record:

ENCOURAGEMENT ______________________________

______________________________

______________________________

______________________________

PROMISE ______________________________

______________________________

______________________________

______________________________

EXHORTATION ______________________________

______________________________

______________________________

______________________________

NEW INTERNATIONAL VERSION

Write a list of truths taught here about:

FAITH

VISION

HEAVEN

*By Faith*

11 Now faith is being sure of what we hope for and certain of what we do not see. [2]This is what the ancients were commended for.

[3]By faith we understand that the universe was formed at God's command, so that what is seen was not made out of what was visible.●

[4]By faith Abel offered God a better sacrifice than Cain did. By faith he was commended as a righteous man, when God spoke well of his offerings. And by faith he still speaks, even though he is dead.

[5]By faith Enoch was taken from this life, so that he did not experience death; he could not be found, because God had taken him away. For before he was taken, he was commended as one who pleased God.
[6]And without faith it is impossible to please God, because anyone who comes to him must believe that he exists and that he rewards those who earnestly seek him.

[7]By faith Noah, when warned about things not yet seen, in holy fear built an ark to save his family. By his faith he condemned the world and became heir of the righteousness that comes by faith.●

[8]By faith Abraham, when called to go to a place he would later receive as his inheritance, obeyed and went, even though he did not know where he was going. [9]By faith he made his home in the promised land like a stranger in a foreign country; he lived in tents, as did Isaac and Jacob, who were heirs with him of the same promise. [10]For he was looking forward to the city with foundations, whose architect and builder is God.

[11]By faith Abraham, even though he was past age—and Sarah herself was barren—was enabled to become a father because he[a] considered him faithful who had made the promise. [12]And so from this one man, and he as good as dead, came descendants as numerous as the stars in the sky and as countless as the sand on the seashore.●

[13]All these people were still living by faith when they died. They did not receive the things promised; they only saw them and welcomed them from a distance. And they admitted that they were aliens and strangers on earth. [14]People who say such things show that they are looking for a country of their own. [15]If they had been thinking of the country they had left, they would have had opportunity to return. [16]Instead, they were longing for a better country—a heavenly one. Therefore God is not ashamed to be called their God, for he has prepared a city for them.●

[a]*11* Or *By faith even Sarah, who was past age, was enabled to bear children because she*

KING JAMES

1.FAITH DESCRIBED

HOPE

**11** Now faith is the substance of things
hoped for, the evidence of things
not seen. 2 For by it the elders obtained a
good report. 3 Through faith we understand that the worlds were framed by the
word of God, so that things which are
seen were not made of things which do
appear.●

2.FAITH ILLUSTRATED

4 By faith Abel offered unto God a more
excellent sacrifice than Cain, by which he
obtained witness that he was righteous,
God testifying of his gifts: and by it he
being dead yet speaketh. 5 By faith
Enoch was translated that he should not
see death; and was not found, because
God had translated him: for before his
translation he had this testimony, that he
pleased God. 6 But without faith *it is*
impossible to please *him:* for he that
cometh to God must believe that he is,
and *that* he is a rewarder of them that
diligently seek him. 7 By faith Noah, being warned of God of things not seen as
yet, moved with fear, prepared an ark to
the saving of his house; by the which he
condemned the world, and became heir of
the righteousness which is by faith.●
8 By faith Abraham, when he was called
to go out into a place which he should
after receive for an inheritance, obeyed;
and he went out, not knowing whither he
went. 9 By faith he sojourned in the land
of promise, as *in* a strange country, dwelling in tabernacles with Isaac and Jacob,
the heirs with him of the same promise:
10 for he looked for a city which hath
foundations, whose builder and maker *is*
God. 11 Through faith also Sarah herself
received strength to conceive seed, and
was delivered of a child when she was past
age, because she judged him faithful who
had promised. 12 Therefore sprang there
even of one, and him as good as dead, *so*
*many* as the stars of the sky in multitude,
and as the sand which is by the seashore
innumerable.●

3.FAITH'S VISION

13 These all died in faith, not having
received the promises, but having seen
them afar off, and were persuaded of
*them,* and embraced *them,* and confessed that they were strangers and pilgrims on the earth. 14 For they that say
such things declare plainly that they seek a
country. 15 And truly, if they had been
mindful of that *country* from whence they
came out, they might have had opportunity to have returned. 16 But now they
desire a better *country,* that is, a heavenly:
wherefore God is not ashamed to be called
their God: for he hath prepared for them
a city.●

DESIRE

Read 10:39b for an introduction to this segment about faith. (Note: the next two segments on faith continue the theme of this passage.)

*11:1-3* What words are used here to describe faith?

*11:4-12* What five persons are cited as examples of faith, and what is said about each?

(1)

(2)

(3)

(4)

(5)

*11:13-16* What are the different references to the future?

## NEW INTERNATIONAL VERSION

Write a list of practical applications of this passage to everyday living in the present time.

17By faith Abraham, when God tested
him, offered Isaac as a sacrifice. He who
had received the promises was about to
sacrifice his one and only son, 18even
though God had said to him, "It is through
Isaac that your offspring[b] will be reckoned."[c] 19Abraham reasoned that God
could raise the dead, and figuratively
speaking, he did receive Isaac back from
death.
20By faith Isaac blessed Jacob and Esau
in regard to their future.
21By faith Jacob, when he was dying,
blessed each of Joseph's sons, and worshiped as he leaned on the top of his staff.
22By faith Joseph, when his end was
near, spoke about the exodus of the Israelites from Egypt and gave instructions
about his bones.●
23By faith Moses' parents hid him for
three months after he was born, because
they saw he was no ordinary child, and
they were not afraid of the king's edict.
24By faith Moses, when he had grown
up, refused to be known as the son of Pharaoh's daughter. 25He chose to be mistreated along with the people of God rather than
to enjoy the pleasures of sin for a short
time. 26He regarded disgrace for the sake
of Christ as of greater value than the treasures of Egypt, because he was looking
ahead to his reward. 27By faith he left
Egypt, not fearing the king's anger; he persevered because he saw him who is invisible. 28By faith he kept the Passover and the
sprinkling of blood, so that the destroyer of
the firstborn would not touch the firstborn
of Israel.●
29By faith the people passed through the
Red Sea[d] as on dry land; but when the
Egyptians tried to do so, they were
drowned.
30By faith the walls of Jericho fell, after
the people had marched around them for
seven days.
31By faith the prostitute Rahab, because
she welcomed the spies, was not killed
with those who were disobedient.[e]●

[b]18 Greek *seed* [c]18 Gen. 21:12
[d]29 That is, Sea of Reeds [e]31 Or *unbelieving*

## KING JAMES

1.FROM UR TO EGYPT

RIGHTEOUS ABRAHAM

17 By faith Abraham, when he was
tried, offered up Isaac: and he that had
received the promises offered up his only
begotten *son*, 18 of whom it was said,
That in Isaac shall thy seed be called:
19 accounting that God *was* able to raise
*him* up, even from the dead; from whence
also he received him in a figure. 20 By
faith Isaac blessed Jacob and Esau concerning things to come. 21 By faith
Jacob, when he was a dying, blessed both
the sons of Joseph; and worshipped,
*leaning* upon the top of his staff. 22 By
faith Joseph, when he died, made mention
of the departing of the children of Israel;
and gave commandment concerning his
bones.●

2.EGYPT

23 By faith Moses, when he was born,
was hid three months of his parents, because they saw *he was* a proper child; and
they were not afraid of the king's commandment. 24 By faith Moses, when he
was come to years, refused to be called the
son of Pharaoh's daughter; 25 choosing
rather to suffer affliction with the people
of God, than to enjoy the pleasures of sin
for a season; 26 esteeming the reproach
of Christ greater riches than the treasures
in Egypt: for he had respect unto the recompense of the reward. 27 By faith he
forsook Egypt, not fearing the wrath of
the king: for he endured, as seeing him
who is invisible. 28 Through faith he kept
the passover, and the sprinkling of blood,
lest he that destroyed the firstborn should
touch them.●

3.FROM EGYPT TO CANAAN

29 By faith they passed through the Red
sea as by dry *land:* which the Egyptians
assaying to do were drowned. 30 By faith
the walls of Jericho fell down, after
they were compassed about seven days.
31 By faith the harlot Rahab perished not
with them that believed not, when she
had received the spies with peace.●

HARLOT RAHAB

Record what is written about each Old Testament person or group.

ABRAHAM ____________________

ISAAC ____________________

JACOB ____________________

JOSEPH ____________________

MOSES ____________________

ISRAELITES ____________________

RAHAB ____________________

NEW INTERNATIONAL VERSION

What does this passage teach about:

VICTORY THROUGH FAITH

ENDURANCE IN TRIALS

PATIENCE

THE CHRISTIAN RACE

JESUS

32And what more shall I say? I do not
have time to tell about Gideon, Barak,
Samson, Jephthah, David, Samuel and the
prophets, 33who through faith conquered
kingdoms, administered justice, and
gained what was promised; who shut the
mouths of lions, 34quenched the fury of the
flames, and escaped the edge of the sword;
whose weakness was turned to strength;
and who became powerful in battle and
routed foreign armies. 35Women received
back their dead, raised to life again. Others
were tortured and refused to be released,
so that they might gain a better resurrection. 36Some faced jeers and flogging, while
still others were chained and put in prison.
37They were stoned[f]; they were sawed in
two; they were put to death by the sword.
They went about in sheepskins and goatskins, destitute, persecuted and mistreated— 38the world was not worthy of them.
They wandered in deserts and mountains,
and in caves and holes in the ground.
39These were all commended for their
faith, yet none of them received what had
been promised. 40God had planned something better for us so that only together
with us would they be made perfect.

*God Disciplines His Sons*

12 Therefore, since we are surrounded
by such a great cloud of witnesses,
let us throw off everything that hinders and
the sin that so easily entangles, and let us
run with perseverance the race marked out
for us. 2Let us fix our eyes on Jesus, the
author and perfecter of our faith, who for
the joy set before him endured the cross,
scorning its shame, and sat down at the
right hand of the throne of God.

f37 Some early manuscripts *stoned; they were put to the test;*

## KING JAMES

1. DELIVERANCE

PEOPLE OF FAITH

32 And what shall I more say? for the
time would fail me to tell of Gideon, and
*of* Barak, and *of* Samson, and *of* Jephthah; *of* David also, and Samuel, and
*of* the prophets: 33 who through faith
subdued kingdoms, wrought righteousness, obtained promises, stopped the
mouths of lions, 34 quenched the violence of fire, escaped the edge of the
sword, out of weakness were made strong,
waxed valiant in fight, turned to flight the
armies of the aliens. 35 Women received
their dead raised to life again:●

2. ENDURANCE

and others
were tortured, not accepting deliverance;
that they might obtain a better resurrection: 36 and others had trial of *cruel*
mockings and scourgings, yea, moreover
of bonds and imprisonment: 37 they
were stoned, they were sawn asunder,
were tempted, were slain with the sword:
they wandered about in sheepskins and
goatskins; being destitute, afflicted, tormented; 38 of whom the world was not
worthy: they wandered in deserts, and *in*
mountains, and *in* dens and caves of the
earth.●

3. REWARDS DELAYED

39 And these all, having obtained a
good report through faith, received not
the promise: 40 God having provided
some better thing for us, that they without
us should not be made perfect.●

4. APPLICATION TODAY

12 Wherefore, seeing we also are compassed about with so great a cloud
of witnesses, let us lay aside every weight,
and the sin which doth so easily beset *us*,
and let us run with patience the race that
is set before us, 2 looking unto Jesus the
author and finisher of *our* faith; who for
the joy that was set before him endured
the cross, despising the shame, and is set
down at the right hand of the throne of
God.●

AUTHOR OF FAITH

This is the third segment of the passage on faith (11:1—2:2).

*11:32-35a* Record the different kinds of deliverances below. How is the word "faith" related to these deliverances?

*11:35b-38* How is this paragraph different from the preceding one?

What is common to both paragraphs?

Record the list of experiences.

*11:39-40* What point is made here?

*12:1-2* Record:

THE EXHORTATIONS

REFERENCES TO JESUS

NEW INTERNATIONAL VERSION

What do you learn here about:

SUFFERING

CHASTISEMENT

DISCIPLINE

HOLINESS

REWARDS

CHRISTIAN WALK

3Consider him who endured such opposition from sinful men, so that you will not grow weary and lose heart.

4In your struggle against sin, you have not yet resisted to the point of shedding your blood. 5And you have forgotten that word of encouragement that addresses you as sons:

"My son, do not make light of the Lord's discipline,
and do not lose heart when he rebukes you,
6because the Lord disciplines those he loves,
and he punishes everyone he accepts as a son."[a]

7Endure hardship as discipline; God is treating you as sons. For what son is not disciplined by his father? 8If you are not disciplined (and everyone undergoes discipline), then you are illegitimate children and not true sons. 9Moreover, we have all had human fathers who disciplined us and we respected them for it. How much more should we submit to the Father of our spirits and live! 10Our fathers disciplined us for a little while as they thought best; but God disciplines us for our good, that we may share in his holiness. 11No discipline seems pleasant at the time, but painful. Later on, however, it produces a harvest of righteousness and peace for those who have been trained by it.

12Therefore, strengthen your feeble arms and weak knees. 13"Make level paths for your feet,"[b] so that the lame may not be disabled, but rather healed.

*Warning Against Refusing God*

14Make every effort to live in peace with all men and to be holy; without holiness no one will see the Lord. 15See to it that no one misses the grace of God and that no bitter root grows up to cause trouble and defile many. 16See that no one is sexually immoral, or is godless like Esau, who for a single meal sold his inheritance rights as the oldest son. 17Afterward, as you know, when he wanted to inherit this blessing, he was rejected. He could bring about no change of mind, though he sought the blessing with tears.

[a]6 Prov. 3:11,12 [b]13 Prov. 4:26

KING JAMES

—introduction

3 For consider him that endured such
contradiction of sinners against himself,
lest ye be wearied and faint in your minds.
4 Ye have not yet resisted unto blood,
striving against sin.● 5 And ye have forgotten the exhortation which speaketh
unto you as unto children,
My son, despise not thou the chastening of the Lord,
nor faint when thou art rebuked of
him:
6 for whom the Lord loveth he chasteneth,
and scourgeth every son whom he
receiveth.
7 If ye endure chastening, God dealeth
with you as with sons; for what son is he
whom the father chasteneth not? 8 But if
ye be without chastisement, whereof all
are partakers, then are ye bastards, and
not sons. 9 Furthermore, we have had
fathers of our flesh which corrected *us*,
and we gave *them* reverence: shall we not
much rather be in subjection unto the
Father of spirits, and live? 10 For they
verily for a few days chastened *us* after
their own pleasure; but he for *our* profit,
that *we* might be partakers of his holiness.
11 Now no chastening for the present
seemeth to be joyous, but grievous: nevertheless, afterward it yieldeth the peaceable fruit of righteousness unto them
which are exercised thereby.●

JESUS

1. BLESSINGS OF DISCIPLINE

Prov. 3:11-12

2. DEMANDS OF DISCIPLINE

12 Wherefore lift up the hands which
hang down, and the feeble knees;
13 and make straight paths for your feet,
lest that which is lame be turned out of the
way; but let it rather be healed. 14 Follow
peace with all *men*, and holiness, without
which no man shall see the Lord: 15 looking diligently lest any man fail of the grace
of God; lest any root of bitterness
springing up trouble *you*, and thereby
many be defiled; 16 lest there *be* any for-
nicator, or profane person, as Esau, who
for one morsel of meat sold his birth-
right. 17 For ye know how that afterward, when he would have inherited the
blessing, he was rejected: for he found no
place of repentance, though he sought it
carefully with tears.●

ESAU

Read the passage. How is it related to the preceding segment (11:32—12:2)?

*12:3-4* Who is referred to by "him" (v.3)?

What is the point of verse 4?

*12:5-11* What is the key repeated word and phrase?

What is the main point of the paragraph?

What comparison, involving time, is made in verse 11?

*12:12-17* Record the commands:

Also record what follows the word "lest" (vv.13,15,16).

NEW INTERNATIONAL VERSION

What does this passage teach about:

SALVATION

GRATITUDE

JESUS

OBEDIENCE

CHRISTIAN SERVICE

GODLY FEAR

OTHER

18You have not come to a mountain that
can be touched and that is burning with
fire; to darkness, gloom and storm; 19to a
trumpet blast or to such a voice speaking
words, so that those who heard it begged
that no further word be spoken to them,
20because they could not bear what was
commanded: "If even an animal touches
the mountain, it must be stoned."[c] 21The
sight was so terrifying that Moses said, "I
am trembling with fear."[d]
22But you have come to Mount Zion, to
the heavenly Jerusalem, the city of the living God. You have come to thousands
upon thousands of angels in joyful assembly, 23to the church of the firstborn, whose
names are written in heaven. You have
come to God, the judge of all men, to the
spirits of righteous men made perfect, 24to
Jesus the mediator of a new covenant, and
to the sprinkled blood that speaks a better
word than the blood of Abel.●
25See to it that you do not refuse him who
speaks. If they did not escape when they
refused him who warned them on earth,
how much less will we, if we turn away
from him who warns us from heaven? 26At
that time his voice shook the earth, but
now he has promised, "Once more I will
shake not only the earth but also the heavens."[e] 27The words "once more" indicate
the removing of what can be shaken—that
is, created things—so that what cannot be
shaken may remain.
28Therefore, since we are receiving a
kingdom that cannot be shaken, let us be
thankful, and so worship God acceptably
with reverence and awe, 29for our God is a
consuming fire.●

[c]*20* Exodus 19:12,13 [d]*21* Deut. 9:19 [e]*26* Haggai 2:6

KING JAMES

1. BLESSINGS

MOUNT OF FIRE

18 For ye are not come unto the mount
that might be touched, and that burned
with fire, nor unto blackness, and darkness, and tempest, 19 and the sound of a
trumpet, and the voice of words; which
*voice* they that heard entreated that the
word should not be spoken to them any
more: 20 (for they could not endure that
which was commanded, And if so much as
a beast touch the mountain, it shall be
stoned, or thrust through with a dart:
21 and so terrible was the sight, *that*
Moses said, I exceedingly fear and quake:)
22 but ye are come unto mount Zion, and
unto the city of the living God, the
heavenly Jerusalem, and to an innumerable company of angels, 23 to the general
assembly and church of the firstborn,
which are written in heaven, and to God
the Judge of all, and to the spirits of just
men made perfect, 24 and to Jesus the
mediator of the new covenant, and to the
blood of sprinkling, that speaketh better
things than *that of* Abel.●

2. DEMANDS

25 See that ye refuse not him that
speaketh: for if they escaped not who refused him that spake on earth, much
more *shall not* we *escape*, if we turn away
from him that *speaketh* from heaven:
26 whose voice then shook the earth: but
now he hath promised, saying, Yet once
more I shake not the earth only, but also
heaven. 27 And this *word*, Yet once more,
signifieth the removing of those things
that are shaken, as of things that are made,
that those things which cannot be shaken
may remain. 28 Wherefore we receiving
a kingdom which cannot be moved, let
us have grace, whereby we may serve
God acceptably with reverence and godly
fear: 29 for our God *is* a consuming
fire.●

SOURCE OF FIRE

*12:18-24* What is the theme of this paragraph?

____________________

Record the comparisons of the two parts:

vv.18-21 ____________________

vv.22-24 ____________________

*12:25-29* What is the command of verse 25?

____________________

How is this supported with the words following "for" (v.25)?

____________________

What is the exhortation of verse 28? ____________________

How is this supported with the words following "for" (v.29)?

____________________

NEW INTERNATIONAL VERSION

What is taught here about:

SHOWING LOVE TO OTHERS

RULERS

WORD OF GOD

SUFFERING FOR CHRIST

JESUS

PRAISE

OTHER

*Concluding Exhortations*

13 Keep on loving each other as brothers. [2]Do not forget to entertain
strangers, for by so doing some people
have entertained angels without knowing
it. [3]Remember those in prison as if you
were their fellow prisoners, and those who
are mistreated as if you yourselves were
suffering.
[4]Marriage should be honored by all, and
the marriage bed kept pure, for God will
judge the adulterer and all the sexually immoral. [5]Keep your lives free from the love
of money and be content with what you
have, because God has said,

> "Never will I leave you;
> never will I forsake you."[f]

[6]So we say with confidence,

> "The Lord is my helper; I will not
> be afraid.
> What can man do to me?"[g] ●

[7]Remember your leaders, who spoke the
word of God to you. Consider the outcome
of their way of life and imitate their faith.
[8]Jesus Christ is the same yesterday and
today and forever.
[9]Do not be carried away by all kinds of
strange teachings. It is good for our hearts
to be strengthened by grace, not by
ceremonial foods, which are of no value to
those who eat them. ● [10]We have an altar
from which those who minister at the tabernacle have no right to eat.
[11]The high priest carries the blood of animals into the Most Holy Place as a sin
offering, but the bodies are burned outside
the camp. [12]And so Jesus also suffered outside the city gate to make the people holy
through his own blood. [13]Let us, then, go
to him outside the camp, bearing the disgrace he bore. [14]For here we do not have
an enduring city, but we are looking for the
city that is to come.
[15]Through Jesus, therefore, let us continually offer to God a sacrifice of praise—
the fruit of lips that confess his name.
[16]And do not forget to do good and to share
with others, for with such sacrifices God is
pleased. ●

f5 Deut. 31:6 g6 Psalm 118:6,7

## KING JAMES

1.LOVE **13** Let brotherly love continue. 2 Be LOVE
not forgetful to entertain strangers:
for thereby some have entertained angels
unawares. 3 Remember them that are
in bonds, as bound with them; *and* them
which suffer adversity, as being yourselves also in the body. 4 Marriage *is*
honorable in all, and the bed undefiled:
but whoremongers and adulterers God
will judge. 5 *Let your* conversation *be*
without covetousness; *and be* content with
such things as ye have: for he hath said,
I will never leave thee, nor forsake Deu. 31:6
thee.
6 So that we may boldly say,
The Lord *is* my helper,
and I will not fear what man shall do Ps. 118:6
unto me.●
2.FAITH 7 Remember them which have the rule
over you, who have spoken unto you the
word of God: whose faith follow, con-
sidering the end of *their* conversation.
8 Jesus Christ the same yesterday, and today, and for ever. 9 Be not carried about
with divers and strange doctrines: for *it is*
a good thing that the heart be established
with grace; not with meats, which have
not profited them that have been occupied
3.SAC- therein.● 10 We have an altar, whereof
RIFICE they have no right to eat which serve the
tabernacle. 11 For the bodies of those
beasts, whose blood is brought into the
sanctuary by the high priest for sin, are
burned without the camp. 12 Wherefore
Jesus also, that he might sanctify the people with his own blood, suffered without
the gate. 13 Let us go forth therefore unto
him without the camp, bearing his reproach. 14 For here have we no continuing city, but we seek one to come.
15 By him therefore let us offer the sacrifice of praise to God continually, that is,
the fruit of *our* lips, giving thanks to his
name. 16 But to do good and to communicate forget not: for with such sac- SHARE
rifices God is well pleased.●

*13:1-6* Record the commands. Then try to discover any groupings of the commands.

*13:7-9* Record the commands.

How is verse 8 related to either of the surrounding verses?

*13:10-16* What is the main theme of this paragraph?

Relate verse 15 to verse 13.

NEW INTERNATIONAL VERSION

Write a list of practical applications of this passage to Christian living today.

17Obey your leaders and submit to their
authority. They keep watch over you as
men who must give an account. Obey them
so that their work will be a joy, not a burden, for that would be of no advantage to
you.
18Pray for us. We are sure that we have
a clear conscience and desire to live honor-
ably in every way. 19I particularly urge you
to pray so that I may be restored to you
soon.●
20May the God of peace, who through
the blood of the eternal covenant brought
back from the dead our Lord Jesus, that
great Shepherd of the sheep, 21equip you
with everything good for doing his will, and
may he work in us what is pleasing to him,
through Jesus Christ, to whom be glory for
ever and ever. Amen.●

22Brothers, I urge you to bear with my
word of exhortation, for I have written you
only a short letter.
23I want you to know that our brother
Timothy has been released. If he arrives
soon, I will come with him to see you.
24Greet all your leaders and all God's
people. Those from Italy send you their
greetings.
25Grace be with you all.●

KING JAMES

1. LAST APPEALS

17 Obey them that have the rule over you, and submit yourselves: for they watch for your souls, as they that must give account, that they may do it with joy, and not with grief: for that *is* unprofitable for you.

JOY

18 Pray for us: for we trust we have a
good conscience, in all things willing to
live honestly. 19 But I beseech *you* the
rather to do this, that I may be restored to
you the sooner.●

2. BENEDICTION

20 Now the God of peace, that brought
again from the dead our Lord Jesus, that
great shepherd of the sheep, through the
blood of the everlasting covenant, 21 make
you perfect in every good work to do his
will, working in you that which is well-pleasing in his sight, through Jesus Christ; to whom *be* glory for ever and ever. Amen.●

3. PERSONAL NOTES

22 And I beseech you, brethren, suffer
the word of exhortation: for I have written
a letter unto you in few words. 23 Know
ye that *our* brother Timothy is set at
liberty; with whom, if he come shortly, I
will see you. 24 Salute all them that have
the rule over you, and all the saints. They
of Italy salute you. 25 Grace *be* with
you all. Amen.●

GRACE

*13:17-19* Record what is written about:

CHURCH LEADERS

PAUL

*13:20-21* List the different parts of this benediction.

*13:22-25* Record your observations and impressions.

# JAMES

## AUTHORSHIP

The author was James, half brother of Jesus. This was the James of the New Testament who succeeded Peter as leader of the Jerusalem church during the years of Acts.

## DATE

This letter was either the earliest or one of the earliest New Testament books to be written. Date: around A.D. 45-50.

## OCCASION AND PURPOSE

Persecution of the Christians, unchristian conduct (e.g. in speech) by many believers, and erroneous views on such doctrines as faith and sin were some of the circumstances which called for this epistle. Most of the letter was written to correct evils, to teach right Christian behavior, and to encourage the persecuted believers regarding the Lord's return. The epistle shows the correct relation of works to faith. It has been called "A Practical Guide to Christian Life and Conduct."

## JAMES: Faith for Living

| | |
|---|---|
| FAITH IN TESTINGS | 1:1-18 |
| FAITH AT WORK | 1:19-4:12 |
| Doers of the Word | 1:19-27 |
| The Case Against Discrimination | 2:1-13 |
| The Faith that Saves | 2:14-26 |
| The Christian and His Tongue | 3:1-12 |
| Evils of Faction Among Christians | 3:13-4:12 |
| FAITH AND THE FUTURE | 4:13-5:12 |
| FAITH AND CHRISTIAN FELLOWSHIP | 5:13-20 |

# JAMES

NEW INTERNATIONAL VERSION

What does this passage teach about:

TRIAL

TEMPTATION

PRAYER

FAITH

WORKS

REWARDS

BRIGHT OUTLOOK ON LIFE

RESPONSIBILITIES OF CHRISTIANS

1 James, a servant of God and of the
Lord Jesus Christ,

To the twelve tribes scattered among the
nations:

Greetings.●

*Trials and Temptations*

2 Consider it pure joy, my brothers,
whenever you face trials of many kinds,
3 because you know that the testing of your
faith develops perseverance. 4 Perseverance must finish its work so that you may
be mature and complete, not lacking anything.● 5 If any of you lacks wisdom, he
should ask God, who gives generously to
all without finding fault, and it will be given
to him. 6 But when he asks, he must believe
and not doubt, because he who doubts is
like a wave of the sea, blown and tossed by
the wind. 7 That man should not think he
will receive anything from the Lord; 8 he is
a double-minded man, unstable in all he
does.●
9 The brother in humble circumstances
ought to take pride in his high position.
10 But the one who is rich should take pride
in his low position, because he will pass
away like a wild flower. 11 For the sun rises
with scorching heat and withers the plant;
its blossom falls and its beauty is destroyed. In the same way, the rich man will
fade away even while he goes about his
business.
12 Blessed is the man who perseveres under trial, because when he has stood the
test, he will receive the crown of life that
God has promised to those who love him.●
13 When tempted, no one should say,
"God is tempting me." For God cannot be
tempted by evil, nor does he tempt anyone;
14 but each one is tempted when, by his own
evil desire, he is dragged away and enticed.
15 Then, after desire has conceived, it gives
birth to sin; and sin, when it is full-grown,
gives birth to death.●
16 Don't be deceived, my dear brothers.
17 Every good and perfect gift is from
above, coming down from the Father of the
heavenly lights, who does not change like
shifting shadows. 18 He chose to give us
birth through the word of truth, that we
might be a kind of firstfruits of all he
created.●

KING JAMES

# JAMES

—salutation

TRIED

1 James, a servant of God and of the
Lord Jesus Christ,
To the twelve tribes which are scattered
abroad,
Greeting.●

1.SUFFICIENCY

2 My brethren, count it all joy when ye
fall into divers temptations; 3 knowing
*this*, that the trying of your faith worketh
patience. 4 But let patience have *her* perfect work, that ye may be perfect and
entire, wanting nothing.●

2.ANSWERS TO PRAYER

5 If any of you lack wisdom, let him ask
of God, that giveth to all *men* liberally,
and upbraideth not; and it shall be given
him. 6 But let him ask in faith, nothing
wavering: for he that wavereth is like a
wave of the sea driven with the wind and
tossed. 7 For let not that man think that
he shall receive any thing of the Lord.
8 A double-minded man *is* unstable in all
his ways.●

3.CROWN OF LIFE

9 Let the brother of low degree rejoice
in that he is exalted: 10 but the rich, in
that he is made low: because as the flower
of the grass he shall pass away. 11 For the
sun is no sooner risen with a burning heat,
but it withereth the grass, and the flower
thereof falleth, and the grace of the
fashion of it perisheth: so also shall the
rich man fade away in his ways.

12 Blessed *is* the man that endureth
temptation: for when he is tried, he shall
receive the crown of life, which the Lord
hath promised to them that love him.●

4.DIVINE CARE

13 Let no man say when he is tempted, I
am tempted of God: for God cannot be
tempted with evil, neither tempteth he any
man: 14 but every man is tempted, when
he is drawn away of his own lust, and
enticed. 15 Then when lust hath conceived, it bringeth forth sin; and sin,
when it is finished, bringeth forth death.●

5.LIGHT AND TRUTH

16 Do not err, my beloved brethren.
17 Every good gift and every perfect gift
is from above, and cometh down from the
Father of lights, with whom is no vari-
ableness, neither shadow of turning.
18 Of his own will begat he us with the
word of truth, that we should be a kind of
firstfruits of his creatures.●

BEGOTTEN

*1:1* What does the salutation suggest about the epistle's original readers?

*1:2-4* Record the strong words (e.g. "joy") of the paragraph. How are they related to each other?

*1:5-8* Record the truths taught here.

*1:9-12* What is the point of verses 9-11?

Relate verse 12 to verses 9-11.

*1:13-15* According to the context of this paragraph, what does the word "tempted" mean here?

*1:16-18* Record the different bright words and phrases.

NEW INTERNATIONAL VERSION

*Listening and Doing*

[19]My dear brothers, take note of this:
Everyone should be quick to listen, slow to
speak and slow to become angry, [20]for
man's anger does not bring about the righteous life that God desires. [21]Therefore, get
rid of all moral filth and the evil that is so
prevalent, and humbly accept the word
planted in you, which can save you.●
[22]Do not merely listen to the word, and
so deceive yourselves. Do what it says.
[23]Anyone who listens to the word but does
not do what it says is like a man who looks
at his face in a mirror [24]and, after looking
at himself, goes away and immediately forgets what he looks like. [25]But the man who
looks intently into the perfect law that
gives freedom, and continues to do this,
not forgetting what he has heard, but doing
it—he will be blessed in what he does.●
[26]If anyone considers himself religious
and yet does not keep a tight rein on his
tongue, he deceives himself and his religion is worthless. [27]Religion that God our
Father accepts as pure and faultless is this:
to look after orphans and widows in their
distress and to keep oneself from being polluted by the world.●

What do you learn here about:

SPEECH ______

THE WORD OF GOD ______

RELIGION ______

List practical applications of the passage. ______

KING JAMES

1. RECEIVE THE WORD

19 Wherefore, my beloved brethren, let
every man be swift to hear, slow to speak,
slow to wrath: 20 for the wrath of man
worketh not the righteousness of God.
21 Wherefore lay apart all filthiness and
superfluity of naughtiness, and receive
with meekness the engrafted word, which
is able to save your souls.●

EN-GRAFTED WORD

2. REMEMBER THE WORD

22 But be ye doers of the word, and not
hearers only, deceiving your own selves.
23 For if any be a hearer of the word, and
not a doer, he is like unto a man beholding
his natural face in a glass: 24 for he be-
holdeth himself, and goeth his way, and
straightway forgetteth what manner of
man he was. 25 But whoso looketh into
the perfect law of liberty, and continueth
*therein*, he being not a forgetful hearer,
but a doer of the work, this man shall be
blessed in his deed.●

3. PRACTICE THE WORD

26 If any man among you seem to be
religious, and bridleth not his tongue, but
deceiveth his own heart, this man's religion
*is* vain. 27 Pure religion and undefiled before God and the Father is this, To visit
the fatherless and widows in their affliction, *and* to keep himself unspotted from
the world.●

SPOTTED WORLD

This segment begins the main section of the epistle, FAITH AT WORK (1:19—4:12). One key verse of the epistle is 1:22, of this segment.

*1:19-21* Record the different attitudes appealed to here.

*1:22-25* Record:

THE COMMAND

ILLUSTRATION

APPLICATION

*1:26-27* What is compared here? Record the comparisons.

NEW INTERNATIONAL VERSION

What does this passage teach about:

DISCRIMINATION

LOVE

TRUE WEALTH

LAW OF GOD

MERCY

JUDGMENT OF GOD

*Favoritism Forbidden*

2 My brothers, as believers in our glorious Lord Jesus Christ, don't show favoritism. [2]Suppose a man comes into your
meeting wearing a gold ring and fine
clothes, and a poor man in shabby clothes
also comes in. [3]If you show special attention to the man wearing fine clothes and
say, "Here's a good seat for you," but say
to the poor man, "You stand there" or
"Sit on the floor by my feet," [4]have you
not discriminated among yourselves and
become judges with evil thoughts?●
[5]Listen, my dear brothers: Has not God
chosen those who are poor in the eyes of
the world to be rich in faith and to inherit
the kingdom he promised those who love
him? [6]But you have insulted the poor. Is it
not the rich who are exploiting you? Are
they not the ones who are dragging you
into court? [7]Are they not the ones who are
slandering the noble name of him to whom
you belong?●
[8]If you really keep the royal law found in
Scripture, "Love your neighbor as yourself,"[a] you are doing right. [9]But if you
show favoritism, you sin and are convicted
by the law as lawbreakers. [10]For whoever
keeps the whole law and yet stumbles at
just one point is guilty of breaking all of it.
[11]For he who said, "Do not commit adultery,"[b] also said, "Do not murder."[c] If
you do not commit adultery but do commit
murder, you have become a lawbreaker.
[12]Speak and act as those who are going
to be judged by the law that gives freedom,
[13]because judgment without mercy will be
shown to anyone who has not been merciful. Mercy triumphs over judgment!●

[a]*8* Lev. 19:18 [b]*11* Exodus 20:14; Deut. 5:18
[c]*11* Exodus 20:13; Deut. 5:17

## KING JAMES

1.APPEAL

DISCRIMINATION

2 My brethren, have not the faith of our
Lord Jesus Christ, *the Lord* of glory,
with respect of persons. 2 For if there
come unto your assembly a man with a
gold ring, in goodly apparel, and there
come in also a poor man in vile raiment;
3 and ye have respect to him that weareth
the gay clothing, and say unto him, Sit
thou here in a good place; and say to the
poor, Stand thou there, or sit here under
my footstool: 4 are ye not then partial in
yourselves, and are become judges of evil
thoughts? ● 5 Hearken, my beloved brethren, Hath not God chosen the poor of
this world rich in faith, and heirs of the
kingdom which he hath promised to them
that love him? 6 But ye have despised the
poor. Do not rich men oppress you, and
draw you before the judgment seats?
7 Do not they blaspheme that worthy
name by the which ye are called?
8 If ye fulfil the royal law according to
the Scripture, Thou shalt love thy neighbor as thyself, ye do well: 9 but if ye
have respect to persons, ye commit sin,
and are convinced of the law as transgressors. 10 For whosoever shall keep the
whole law, and yet offend in one *point*, he
is guilty of all. 11 For he that said, Do
not commit adultery, said also, Do not
kill. Now if thou commit no adultery,
yet if thou kill, thou art become a transgressor of the law. 12 So speak ye, and so
do, as they that shall be judged by the law
of liberty. 13 For he shall have judgment
without mercy, that hath showed no
mercy; and mercy rejoiceth against
judgment. ●

2.GOD'S WAYS

3.GOD'S LAW

MERCY

*2:1-4* What is the meaning of verse 1?

What is the indictment of verse 4?

*2:5-7* Record what is written here about:

GOD

READERS OF THE EPISTLE

RICH PEOPLE

*2:8-13* Compare verse 8 with verse 9.

What is the theme of:

verses 10-11:

verses 12-13:

NEW INTERNATIONAL VERSION

Write lists of truths taught here about:

FAITH

WORKS

HEART

GOD

List practical applications of the passage.

### *Faith and Deeds*

[14]What good is it, my brothers, if a man
claims to have faith but has no deeds? Can
such faith save him? [15]Suppose a brother or
sister is without clothes and daily food. [16]If
one of you says to him, "Go, I wish you
well; keep warm and well fed," but does
nothing about his physical needs, what
good is it? [17]In the same way, faith by itself,
if it is not accompanied by action, is dead.
[18]But someone will say, "You have faith;
I have deeds."
Show me your faith without deeds, and
I will show you my faith by what I do.●
[19]You believe that there is one God. Good!
Even the demons believe that—and shud-
der.
[20]You foolish man, do you want evidence that faith without deeds is useless[d]?
[21]Was not our ancestor Abraham considered righteous for what he did when he
offered his son Isaac on the altar? [22]You
see that his faith and his actions were
working together, and his faith was made
complete by what he did. [23]And the scripture was fulfilled that says, "Abraham believed God, and it was credited to him as
righteousness,"[e] and he was called God's
friend. [24]You see that a person is justified
by what he does and not by faith alone.
[25]In the same way, was not even Rahab
the prostitute considered righteous for
what she did when she gave lodging to the
spies and sent them off in a different direction? [26]As the body without the spirit is
dead, so faith without deeds is dead.●

[d]*20* Some early manuscripts *dead* [e]*23* Gen. 15:6

## KING JAMES

1.FAITH PRODUCING WORKS

NO PROFIT

14 What *doth it* profit, my brethren,
though a man say he hath faith, and have
not works? can faith save him? 15 If a
brother or sister be naked, and destitute
of daily food, 16 and one of you say unto
them, Depart in peace, be *ye* warmed and
filled; notwithstanding ye give them not
those things which are needful to the body;
what *doth it* profit? 17 Even so faith, if it
hath not works, is dead, being alone.
18 Yea, a man may say, Thou hast
faith, and I have works: show me thy faith
without thy works, and I will show thee
my faith by my works.●

2.FAITH FROM THE HEART

19Thou believest
that there is one God; thou doest well: the
devils also believe, and tremble. 20 But
wilt thou know, O vain man, that faith
without works is dead? 21 Was not
Abraham our father justified by works,
when he had offered Isaac his son upon
the altar? 22 Seest thou how faith
wrought with his works, and by works
was faith made perfect? 23 And the
Scripture was fulfilled which saith,

> Abraham believed God,
> and it was imputed unto him for
> righteousness:

and he was called the Friend of God. (Gen. 15:6)
24 Ye see then how that by works a man
is justified, and not by faith only. 25 Likewise also was not Rahab the harlot justified by works, when she had received the
messengers, and had sent *them* out another way? 26 For as the body without
the spirit[1] is dead, so faith without works
is dead also.●

DEAD

James shows that only *genuine* faith saves. That kind of faith produces works. So faith and works are inseparable.

*2:14-18* How does verse 14a refer to a professing faith?

______________________________

______________________________

______________________________

______________________________

What is the last question of verse 14?

______________________________

______________________________

______________________________

Use the correct Living Bible translation of that question, for your study.
How does the paragraph teach that:
(1) Works are faith's partner

______________________________

______________________________

______________________________

(2) Works are faith's demonstrators

______________________________

______________________________

______________________________

*2:19-26* What two Old Testament characters are mentioned here?

______________________________

______________________________

What is the teaching of each illustration?

______________________________

______________________________

______________________________

______________________________

How does verse 26 conclude the paragraph?

______________________________

______________________________

______________________________

______________________________

NEW INTERNATIONAL VERSION

Write a list of practical applications of the passage to the Christian and his tongue, in the present time.

*Taming the Tongue*

3 Not many of you should presume to be
teachers, my brothers, because you
know that we who teach will be judged
more strictly. 2We all stumble in many
ways. If anyone is never at fault in what he
says, he is a perfect man, able to keep his
whole body in check.●
3When we put bits into the mouths of
horses to make them obey us, we can turn
the whole animal. 4Or take ships as an example. Although they are so large and are
driven by strong winds, they are steered by
a very small rudder wherever the pilot
wants to go. 5Likewise the tongue is a
small part of the body, but it makes great
boasts.● Consider what a great forest is set
on fire by a small spark. 6The tongue also
is a fire, a world of evil among the parts of
the body. It corrupts the whole person,
sets the whole course of his life on fire, and
is itself set on fire by hell.●
7All kinds of animals, birds, reptiles and
creatures of the sea are being tamed and
have been tamed by man, 8but no man can
tame the tongue. It is a restless evil, full of
deadly poison.●
9With the tongue we praise our Lord and
Father, and with it we curse men, who
have been made in God's likeness. 10Out of
the same mouth come praise and cursing.
My brothers, this should not be. 11Can
both fresh water and salt water flow from
the same spring? 12My brothers, can a fig
tree bear olives, or a grapevine bear figs?
Neither can a salt spring produce fresh
water.●

KING JAMES

—introduction

**3** My brethren, be not many masters, knowing that we shall receive the greater condemnation. 2 For in many things we offend all. If any man offend not in word, the same *is* a perfect man, *and* able also to bridle the whole body. ●

KINDNESS

1. INFLUENTIAL

3 Behold, we put bits in the horses' mouths, that they may obey us; and we turn about their whole body. 4 Behold also the ships, which though *they be* so great, and *are* driven of fierce winds, yet are they turned about with a very small helm, whithersoever the governor listeth. 5 Even so the tongue is a little member, and boasteth great things. ●

2. DESTRUCTIVE

Behold, how great a matter a little fire kindleth!

6 And the tongue *is* a fire, a world of iniquity: so is the tongue among our members, that it defileth the whole body, and setteth on fire the course of nature; and it is set on fire of hell. ●

3. UNTAMEABLE

7 For every kind of beasts, and of birds, and of serpents, and of things in the sea, is tamed, and hath been tamed of mankind: 8 but the tongue can no man tame; *it is* an unruly evil, full of deadly poison. ●

4. INCONSISTENT

9 Therewith bless we God, even the Father; and therewith curse we men, which are made after the similitude of God. 10 Out of the same mouth proceedeth blessing and cursing. My brethren, these things ought not so to be. 11 Doth a fountain send forth at the same place sweet *water* and bitter? 12 Can the fig tree, my brethren, bear olive berries? either a vine, figs? so *can* no fountain both yield salt water and fresh. ●

CONSISTENCY

*3:1-2* How does this paragraph introduce the segment?

*3:3-5a* What are the two illustrations?

What is the point?

*3:5b-6* What is a key repeated word here?

Why is verse 5b included in this paragraph?

Could it also be studied as part of the preceding paragraph?

*3:7-8* What are the strong words and phrases of this paragraph?

*3:9-12* List the different contrasts of the paragraph.

NEW INTERNATIONAL VERSION

What does this passage teach about:

HUMILITY

STRIFE

LUST

DEVIL

LOVE

LAWS OF GOD

OTHER

*Two Kinds of Wisdom*

13Who is wise and understanding among
you? Let him show it by his good life, by
deeds done in the humility that comes from
wisdom. 14But if you harbor bitter envy
and selfish ambition in your hearts, do not
boast about it or deny the truth. 15Such
"wisdom" does not come down from
heaven but is earthly, unspiritual, of the
devil. 16For where you have envy and selfish ambition, there you find disorder and
every evil practice.

17But the wisdom that comes from
heaven is first of all pure; then peace loving, considerate, submissive, full of mercy
and good fruit, impartial and sincere.
18Peacemakers who sow in peace raise a
harvest of righteousness.●

*Submit Yourselves to God*

4 What causes fights and quarrels among
you? Don't they come from your desires that battle within you? 2You want
something but don't get it. You kill and
covet, but you cannot have what you want.
You quarrel and fight. You do not have,
because you do not ask God. 3When you
ask, you do not receive, because you ask
with wrong motives, that you may spend
what you get on your pleasures.●

4You adulterous people, don't you know
that friendship with the world is hatred
toward God? Anyone who chooses to be a
friend of the world becomes an enemy of
God. 5Or do you think Scripture says without reason that the spirit he caused to live
in us tends toward envy,[a] 6but he gives us
more grace? That is why Scripture says:

"God opposes the proud
but gives grace to the humble."[b]

7Submit yourselves, then, to God. Resist
the devil, and he will flee from you. 8Come
near to God and he will come near to you.
Wash your hands, you sinners, and purify
your hearts, you double-minded. 9Grieve,
mourn and wail. Change your laughter to
mourning and your joy to gloom. 10Humble
yourselves before the Lord, and he will lift
you up.●

11Brothers, do not slander one another.
Anyone who speaks against his brother or
judges him speaks against the law and
judges it. When you judge the law, you are
not keeping it, but sitting in judgment on it.
12There is only one Lawgiver and Judge,
the one who is able to save and destroy.
But you—who are you to judge your neighbor?●

[a]5 Or *that God jealously longs for the spirit that he made to live in us;* or *that the Spirit he caused to live in us longs jealously*
[b]6 Prov. 3:34

## KING JAMES

1. DEVILISH 13 Who *is* a wise man and endued with HUMILITY
knowledge among you? let him show out
of a good conversation his works with
meekness of wisdom. 14 But if ye have
bitter envying and strife in your hearts,
glory not, and lie not against the truth.
15 This wisdom descendeth not from
above, but *is* earthly, sensual, devilish.
16 For where envying and strife *is*, there
*is* confusion and every evil work. 17 But
the wisdom that is from above is first
pure, then peaceable, gentle, *and* easy to
be entreated, full of mercy and good fruits,
without partiality, and without hypocrisy.
18 And the fruit of righteousness is sown
in peace of them that make peace.●
2. LUSTFUL 4 From whence *come* wars and fightings
among you? *come they* not hence,
*even* of your lusts that war in your members? 2 Ye lust, and have not: ye kill, and
desire to have, and cannot obtain: ye fight
and war, yet ye have not, because ye ask
not. 3 Ye ask, and receive not, because ye
ask amiss, that ye may consume *it* upon
3. ANTI-GOD your lusts. ● 4 Ye adulterers and adulter-
esses, know ye not that the friendship of
the world is enmity with God? whosoever
therefore will be a friend of the world is
the enemy of God. 5 Do ye think that the
Scripture saith in vain, The spirit that
dwelleth in us lusteth to envy? 6 But
he giveth more grace. Wherefore he saith,
God resisteth the proud,
but giveth grace unto the humble. Ps. 138:6
7 Submit yourselves therefore to God.
Resist the devil, and he will flee from you.
8 Draw nigh to God, and he will draw
nigh to you. Cleanse *your* hands, *ye* sinners; and purify *your* hearts, *ye* double-
minded. 9 Be afflicted, and mourn, and
weep: let your laughter be turned to
mourning, and *your* joy to heaviness.
10 Humble yourselves in the sight of the
Lord, and he shall lift you up.●
4. PRESUMPTUOUS 11 Speak not evil one of another, brethren. He that speaketh evil of *his* brother,
and judgeth his brother, speaketh evil of
the law, and judgeth the law: but if thou
judge the law, thou art not a doer of the
law, but a judge. 12 There is one lawgiver, who is able to save and to destroy: LOVE
who art thou that judgest another?●

*3:13-18* What is the point of verse 13? _____

What sins are described in verses 14-16? _____

Compare verses 17-18 with verses 14-16. _____

*4:1-3* Where does war originate? _____

Why does James include verse 3 here? _____

*4:4-10* List the commands: _____

*4:11-12* What is written here about:

GOD'S LAW _____

JUDGING _____

NEW INTERNATIONAL VERSION

What do you learn here about:

PLANS FOR THE FUTURE

FAITH

MATERIALISM

JUDGMENT

PATIENCE

OTHER

### *Boasting About Tomorrow*

13Now listen, you who say, "Today or
tomorrow we will go to this or that city,
spend a year there, carry on business and
make money." 14Why, you do not even
know what will happen tomorrow. What is
your life? You are a mist that appears for
a little while and then vanishes. 15Instead,
you ought to say, "If it is the Lord's will,
we will live and do this or that." 16As it is,
you boast and brag. All such boasting is
evil. 17Anyone, then, who knows the good
he ought to do and doesn't do it, sins.●

### *Warning to Rich Oppressors*

5 Now listen, you rich people, weep and
wail because of the misery that is coming upon you. 2Your wealth has rotted, and
moths have eaten your clothes. 3Your gold
and silver are corroded. Their corrosion
will testify against you and eat your flesh
like fire. You have hoarded wealth in the
last days. 4Look! The wages you failed to
pay the workmen who mowed your fields
are crying out against you. The cries of the
harvesters have reached the ears of the
Lord Almighty. 5You have lived on earth in
luxury and self-indulgence. You have fattened yourselves in the day of slaughter.
6You have condemned and murdered innocent men, who were not opposing you.●

### *Patience in Suffering*

7Be patient, then, brothers, until the
Lord's coming. See how the farmer waits
for the land to yield its valuable crop and
how patient he is for the autumn and spring
rains. 8You too, be patient and stand firm,
because the Lord's coming is near. 9Don't
grumble against each other, brothers, or
you will be judged. The Judge is standing
at the door!
10Brothers, as an example of patience in
the face of suffering, take the prophets who
spoke in the name of the Lord. 11As you
know, we consider blessed those who have
persevered. You have heard of Job's
perseverance and have seen what the Lord
finally brought about. The Lord is full of
compassion and mercy.
12Above all, my brothers, do not swear—
not by heaven or by earth or by anything
else. Let your "Yes" be yes, and your
"No," no, or you will be condemned.●

## KING JAMES

1. THIS LIFE

—unknown

13 Go to now, ye that say, Today or tomorrow we will go into such a city, and
continue there a year, and buy and sell,
and get gain: 14 whereas ye know not
what *shall be* on the morrow. For what
*is* your life? It is even a vapor, that appeareth for a little time, and then vanish-
eth away. 15 For that ye *ought* to say, If
the Lord will, we shall live, and do this, or
that. 16 But now ye rejoice in your boast-
ings: all such rejoicing is evil. 17 Therefore to him that knoweth to do good, and
doeth *it* not, to him it is sin. ●

2. NEXT LIFE

—misery

5 Go to now, *ye* rich men, weep and
howl for your miseries that shall come
upon *you*. 2 Your riches are corrupted,
and your garments are moth-eaten.
3 Your gold and silver is cankered; and
the rust of them shall be a witness against
you, and shall eat your flesh as it were fire.
Ye have heaped treasure together for the
last days. 4 Behold, the hire of the
laborers who have reaped down your
fields, which is of you kept back by fraud,
crieth: and the cries of them which have
reaped are entered into the ears of the
Lord of Sab'a-oth. 5 Ye have lived in
pleasure on the earth, and been wanton;
ye have nourished your hearts, as in a day
of slaughter. 6 Ye have condemned *and*
killed the just; *and* he doth not resist
you. ●

—happiness

7 Be patient therefore, brethren, unto
the coming of the Lord. Behold, the husbandman waiteth for the precious fruit of
the earth, and hath long patience for it,
until he receive the early and latter rain.
8 Be ye also patient; stablish your hearts:
for the coming of the Lord draweth nigh.
9 Grudge not one against another, brethren, lest ye be condemned: behold, the
judge standeth before the door. 10 Take,
my brethren, the prophets, who have
spoken in the name of the Lord, for an
example of suffering affliction, and of patience. 11 Behold, we count them happy
which endure. Ye have heard of the patience of Job, and have seen the end of
the Lord; that the Lord is very pitiful, and
of tender mercy.
12 But above all things, my brethren,
swear not, neither by heaven, neither by
the earth, neither by any other oath: but
let your yea be yea; and *your* nay, nay;
lest ye fall into condemnation. ●

PLANNING

*4:13-17* Record:

FACTS __________

APPEAL __________

*5:1-6*

SINS __________

JUDGMENTS __________

*5:7-12* Note the repetition of "the coming of the Lord." What appeal is made in each reference?

SPEAKING

Underline the repeated word "patient" in the paragraph.

How is verse 12 related to the preceding verses?

NEW INTERNATIONAL VERSION

What does this concluding passage of James teach about:

PRAYER

PRAISE

INTERCESSION

COMPASSION

FAITH

MIRACLES

LOVE OF THE BRETHREN

OTHER

### *The Prayer of Faith*

[13]Is any one of you in trouble? He should
pray. Is anyone happy? Let him sing songs
of praise. [14]Is any one of you sick? He
should call the elders of the church to pray
over him and anoint him with oil in the
name of the Lord. [15]And the prayer offered
in faith will make the sick person well; the
Lord will raise him up. If he has sinned, he
will be forgiven. [16]Therefore confess your
sins to each other and pray for each other
so that you may be healed. The prayer of
a righteous man is powerful and effective.
[17]Elijah was a man just like us. He
prayed earnestly that it would not rain, and
it did not rain on the land for three and a
half years. [18]Again he prayed, and the
heavens gave rain, and the earth produced
its crops.●
[19]My brothers, if one of you should wander from the truth and someone should
bring him back, [20]remember this: Whoever
turns a sinner from the error of his way will
save him from death and cover over a multitude of sins.●

KING JAMES

1.PRAYING

13 Is any among you afflicted? let him
pray. Is any merry? let him sing psalms.
14 Is any sick among you? let him call for
the elders of the church; and let them
pray over him, anointing him with oil in
the name of the Lord: 15 and the prayer
of faith shall save the sick, and the Lord
shall raise him up; and if he have committed sins, they shall be forgiven him.
16 Confess *your* faults one to another, and
pray one for another, that ye may be
healed. The effectual fervent prayer of a
righteous man availeth much. 17 Eli'jah
was a man subject to like passions as we
are, and he prayed earnestly that it might
not rain: and it rained not on the earth by
the space of three years and six months.
18 And he prayed again, and the heaven
gave rain, and the earth brought forth
her fruit. ●

PHYSICAL SICKNESS

2.RESTORING

19 Brethren, if any of you do err from
the truth, and one convert him; 20 let
him know, that he which converteth the
sinner from the error of his way shall save
a soul from death, and shall hide a multitude of sins. ●

SPIRITUAL DEATH

*5:13-18* What is the key repeated word of the paragraph?

What two activities of praying are mentioned in verse 13?

Record the different references to prayer in the paragraph:

*5:19-20* To whom does the phrase "any of you" (v.19) refer?

What is the sad situation of verse 19?

Compare this with the need of verse 13a.

# 1 PETER

## AUTHORSHIP

The opening verse identifies the writer as the apostle Peter (1:1). Peter is writing to exiles who are being persecuted for their Christian faith (cf. 1:1,6,7).

## DATE

The letter was written probably around the time of the outbreak of the Neronian persecution, or A.D. 64.

## PURPOSE AND THEME

Peter wrote this letter to encourage the Christian readers concerning the times of persecution. He urges them to stand true and endure suffering for Christ's sake and with His strength, even as the persecution grows more intense. The theme of the letter is that of trials, holy living and the Lord's coming.

## 1 PETER: God's Chosen People

| | |
|---|---|
| Salutation and Benediction | 1:1-2 |
| THEIR SUFFERING AND SALVATION | 1:3-12 |
| THEIR PILGRIMAGE | 1:13-25 |
| THEIR UNIQUE POSITION | 2:1-10 |
| HOW THEY SHOULD LIVE | 2:11-3:12 |
| THEIR SUFFERING AND GLORY | 3:13-5:11 |
| Greetings and Benediction | 5:12-14 |

# 1 PETER

NEW INTERNATIONAL VERSION

What do you learn from this passage about:

PERSECUTION

TRIAL

SALVATION

ASSURANCE

SECOND COMING OF CHRIST

OLD TESTAMENT PROPHETS

WORD OF GOD

OTHER

1 Peter, an apostle of Jesus Christ,
To God's elect, strangers in the world,
scattered throughout Pontus, Galatia, Cap-
padocia, Asia and Bithynia, 2who have
been chosen according to the foreknowledge of God the Father, through the sanctifying work of the Spirit, for obedience to
Jesus Christ and sprinkling by his blood:
Grace and peace be yours in abundance.●

*Praise to God for a Living Hope*

3Praise be to the God and Father of our
Lord Jesus Christ! In his great mercy he
has given us new birth into a living hope
through the resurrection of Jesus Christ
from the dead, 4and into an inheritance that
can never perish, spoil or fade—kept in
heaven for you, 5who through faith are
shielded by God's power until the coming
of the salvation that is ready to be revealed
in the last time.● 6In this you greatly rejoice,
though now for a little while you may have
had to suffer grief in all kinds of trials.
7These have come so that your faith—of
greater worth than gold, which perishes
even though refined by fire—may be
proved genuine and may result in praise,
glory and honor when Jesus Christ is revealed. 8Though you have not seen him,
you love him; and even though you do not
see him now, you believe in him and are
filled with an inexpressible and glorious
joy, 9for you are receiving the goal of your
faith, the salvation of your souls.●
10Concerning this salvation, the prophets, who spoke of the grace that was to
come to you, searched intently and with
the greatest care, 11trying to find out the
time and circumstances to which the Spirit
of Christ in them was pointing when he
predicted the sufferings of Christ and the
glories that would follow. 12It was revealed
to them that they were not serving themselves but you, when they spoke of the
things that have now been told you by
those who have preached the gospel to you
by the Holy Spirit sent from heaven. Even
angels long to look into these things.●

KING JAMES

# 1 PETER

—salutation

EARTH

1 Peter, an apostle of Jesus Christ,
To the strangers scattered throughout Pontus, Galatia, Cappado′cia, Asia,
and Bithyn′i-a, 2 elect according to the
foreknowledge of God the Father, through
sanctification of the Spirit, unto obedience
and sprinkling of the blood of Jesus Christ:
Grace unto you, and peace, be multiplied.●

1. GUARDED FAITH

3 Blessed *be* the God and Father of our
Lord Jesus Christ, which according to his
abundant mercy hath begotten us again
unto a lively hope by the resurrection of
Jesus Christ from the dead, 4 to an inheritance incorruptible, and undefiled,
and that fadeth not away, reserved in
heaven for you, 5 who are kept by the
power of God through faith unto salvation ready to be revealed in the last time.●

2. TRIED FAITH

6 Wherein ye greatly rejoice, though now
for a season, if need be, ye are in heaviness
through manifold temptations: 7 that the
trial of your faith, being much more precious than of gold that perisheth, though
it be tried with fire, might be found unto
praise and honor and glory at the appearing of Jesus Christ: 8 whom having not
seen, ye love; in whom, though now ye see
*him* not, yet believing, ye rejoice with joy
unspeakable and full of glory: 9 receiving
the end of your faith, *even* the salvation of
*your* souls.●

3. FORE-TOLD FAITH

10 Of which salvation the prophets
have inquired and searched diligently,
who prophesied of the grace *that should*
*come* unto you: 11 searching what, or
what manner of time the Spirit of Christ
which was in them did signify, when it
testified beforehand the sufferings of
Christ, and the glory that should follow.
12 Unto whom it was revealed, that not
unto themselves, but unto us they did
minister the things, which are now reported unto you by them that have
preached the gospel unto you with the
Holy Ghost sent down from heaven;
which things the angels desire to look into.●

HEAVEN

*1:1-2* Record the references to the three persons of the Trinity.

How are the readers identified?

*1:3-5* Record all the words and phrases that suggest the fact of a *guarded* and sure faith.

*1:6-9* Compare verses 6-7 with verses 8-9.

*1:10-12* Who are the groups referred to in the paragraph?

What is the point of this paragraph?

NEW INTERNATIONAL VERSION

What do you learn here about:

HOLY LIVING

FEAR OF GOD

REDEMPTION

RESURRECTION HOPE

LOVE OF BRETHREN

WORD OF GOD

List practical applications of the passage.

*Be Holy*

[13]Therefore, prepare your minds for action; be self-controlled; set your hope fully
on the grace to be given you when Jesus
Christ is revealed. [14]As obedient children,
do not conform to the evil desires you had
when you lived in ignorance. [15]But just as
he who called you is holy, so be holy in all
you do; [16]for it is written: "Be holy, because I am holy."[a]
[17]Since you call on a Father who judges
each man's work impartially, live your
lives as strangers here in reverent fear.
[18]For you know that it was not with perishable things such as silver or gold that you
were redeemed from the empty way of life
handed down to you from your forefathers,
[19]but with the precious blood of Christ, a
lamb without blemish or defect. [20]He was
chosen before the creation of the world,
but was revealed in these last times for
your sake. [21]Through him you believe in
God, who raised him from the dead and
glorified him, and so your faith and hope
are in God.
[22]Now that you have purified yourselves
by obeying the truth so that you have sincere love for your brothers, love one another deeply, from the heart.[b] [23]For you
have been born again, not of perishable
seed, but of imperishable, through the living and enduring word of God. [24]For,

"All men are like grass,
and all their glory is like the
flowers of the field;
the grass withers and the flowers
fall,
[25] but the word of the Lord stands
forever."[c]

And this is the word that was preached to
you.

[a]16 Lev. 11:44,45; 19:2; 20:7
[b]22 Some early manuscripts *from a pure heart*
[c]25 Isaiah 40:6-8

## KING JAMES

**1. BE HOLY**

13 Wherefore gird up the loins of your
mind, be sober, and hope to the end for
the grace that is to be brought unto you at
the revelation of Jesus Christ; 14 as
obedient children, not fashioning yourselves according to the former lusts in
your ignorance: 15 but as he which hath
called you is holy, so be ye holy in all manner of conversation; 16 because it is
written, Be ye holy; for I am holy. ●

COMING OF JESUS

Lev. 11:44

**2. FEAR GOD**

17 And if ye call on the Father, who without respect of persons judgeth according
to every man's work, pass the time of your
sojourning *here* in fear: 18 forasmuch as
ye know that ye were not redeemed with
corruptible things, *as* silver and gold,
from your vain conversation *received* by
tradition from your fathers; 19 but with
the precious blood of Christ, as of a lamb
without blemish and without spot:
20 who verily was foreordained before the
foundation of the world, but was manifest
in these last times for you, 21 who by him
do believe in God, that raised him up
from the dead, and gave him glory; that
your faith and hope might be in God.●

**3. LOVE ONE ANOTHER**

22 Seeing ye have purified your souls in
obeying the truth through the Spirit unto
unfeigned love of the brethren, *see that ye*
love one another with a pure heart fervently: 23 being born again, not of corruptible seed, but of incorruptible, by the
word of God, which liveth and abideth for
ever.
24 For all flesh *is* as grass,
and all the glory of man as the flower
of grass.
The grass withereth,
and the flower thereof falleth away:
25 but the word of the Lord endureth
for ever.
And this is the word which by the gospel
is preached unto you.●

Isa. 40:6-8

WORD OF LORD

*1:13-16* Record:

THE COMMANDS ____________

THE MOTIVES ____________

*1:17-21* What is the command here? ____________

What reason is given for fearing God? ____________

What is written about Christ? ____________

*1:22-25* What is the command? ____________

What is the subject of verses 23-25? ____________

How is this related to the command of verse 22? ____________

NEW INTERNATIONAL VERSION

What does this passage teach about:

HATRED

WORD OF GOD

JESUS CHRIST

FAITH

UNBELIEVERS

CHOSEN IN CHRIST

MERCY OF GOD

OTHER

2 Therefore, rid yourselves of all malice
and all deceit, hypocrisy, envy, and
slander of every kind. 2 Like newborn babies, crave pure spiritual milk, so that by
it you may grow up in your salvation, 3 now
that you have tasted that the Lord is good.●

*The Living Stone and a Chosen People*

4 As you come to him, the living Stone—
rejected by men but chosen by God and
precious to him— 5 you also, like living
stones, are being built into a spiritual house
to be a holy priesthood, offering spiritual
sacrifices acceptable to God through Jesus
Christ. 6 For in Scripture it says:

"See, I lay a stone in Zion,
a chosen and precious
cornerstone,
and the one who trusts in him
will never be put to shame."[d]

7 Now to you who believe, this stone is precious. But to those who do not believe,

"The stone the builders rejected
has become the capstone,[e]"[f]

8 and,

"A stone that causes men to
stumble
and a rock that makes them
fall."[g]

They stumble because they disobey the
message—which is also what they were
destined for.●
9 But you are a chosen people, a royal
priesthood, a holy nation, a people belonging to God, that you may declare the
praises of him who called you out of darkness into his wonderful light. 10 Once you
were not a people, but now you are the
people of God; once you had not received
mercy, but now you have received mercy.●

[d]6 Isaiah 28:16 [e]7 Or *cornerstone*
[f]7 Psalm 118:22 [g]8 Isaiah 8:14

KING JAMES

1. APPEAL

2 Wherefore laying aside all malice, and
all guile, and hypocrisies, and envies,
and all evil speakings, 2 as newborn
babes, desire the sincere milk of the word,
that ye may grow thereby: 3 if so be ye
have tasted that the Lord *is* gracious. ●

GROW

2. A CHOSEN REDEEMER

4 To whom coming, *as unto* a living
stone, disallowed indeed of men, but
chosen of God, *and* precious, 5 ye also, as
lively stones, are built up a spiritual house,
a holy priesthood, to offer up spiritual
sacrifices, acceptable to God by Jesus
Christ. 6 Wherefore also it is contained
in the Scripture,

Behold, I lay in Zion a chief corner stone, elect, precious:
and he that believeth on him shall not be confounded.

Isa. 28:16

7 Unto you therefore which believe *he is*
precious: but unto them which be disobedient,

the stone which the builders disallowed,
the same is made the head of the corner,

Ps. 118:22

8 and a stone of stumbling,
and a rock of offense,

Isa. 8:14

*even to them* which stumble at the word,
being disobedient: whereunto also they
were appointed. ●

3. A CHOSEN PEOPLE

9 But ye *are* a chosen generation, a
royal priesthood, a holy nation, a peculiar people; that ye should show forth the
praises of him who hath called you out
of darkness into his marvelous light:
10 which in time past *were* not a people,
but *are* now the people of God: which had
not obtained mercy, but now have obtained mercy. ●

SHOW FORTH

This is the central passage of 1 Peter. (See Outline.)

*2:1-3* Relate this paragraph to the last paragraph of chapter 1 (1:22-25).

What is the command here?

*2:4-8* Record what Peter writes about:

CHRIST

BELIEVERS

UNBELIEVERS

*2:9-10* Record what is written about:

CHRISTIANS

HOW CHRISTIANS SHOULD LIVE

NEW INTERNATIONAL VERSION

Record what this passage teaches about:

PERSECUTION

GODLY LIVING

CITIZENS

RULERS

SUBMISSION TO THOSE IN AUTHORITY

Write a list of practical applications of this passage.

11Dear friends, I urge you, as aliens and
strangers in the world, to abstain from sinful desires, which war against your soul.
12Live such good lives among the pagans
that, though they accuse you of doing
wrong, they may see your good deeds and
glorify God on the day he visits us.●

*Submission to Rulers and Masters*

13Submit yourselves for the Lord's sake
to every authority instituted among men:
whether to the king, as the supreme authority, 14or to governors, who are sent by
him to punish those who do wrong and to
commend those who do right. 15For it is
God's will that by doing good you should
silence the ignorant talk of foolish men.
16Live as free men, but do not use your
freedom as a cover-up for evil; live as servants of God. 17Show proper respect to
everyone: Love the brotherhood of believers, fear God, honor the king.●
18Slaves, submit yourselves to your masters with all respect, not only to those who
are good and considerate, but also to those
who are harsh. 19For it is commendable if
a man bears up under the pain of unjust
suffering because he is conscious of God.
20But how is it to your credit if you receive
a beating for doing wrong and endure it?
But if you suffer for doing good and you
endure it, this is commendable before God.
21To this you were called, because Christ
suffered for you, leaving you an example,
that you should follow in his steps.

22"He committed no sin,
and no deceit was found in his
mouth."[a]

23When they hurled their insults at him, he
did not retaliate; when he suffered, he
made no threats. Instead, he entrusted
himself to him who judges justly. 24He himself bore our sins in his body on the tree,
so that we might die to sins and live for
righteousness; by his wounds you have
been healed. 25For you were like sheep going astray, but now you have returned to
the Shepherd and Overseer of your souls.●

[a]22 Isaiah 53:9

## KING JAMES

1. PILGRIMS

REFUGEES

11 Dearly beloved, I beseech *you* as
strangers and pilgrims, abstain from
fleshly lusts, which war against the soul;
12 having your conversation honest
among the Gentiles: that, whereas they
speak against you as evildoers, they may
by *your* good works, which they shall behold, glorify God in the day of visitation.●

2. CITIZENS

13 Submit yourselves to every ordinance of man for the Lord's sake: whether
it be to the king, as supreme; 14 or unto
governors, as unto them that are sent by
him for the punishment of evildoers, and
for the praise of them that do well. 15 For
so is the will of God, that with well doing
ye may put to silence the ignorance of
foolish men: 16 as free, and not using
*your* liberty for a cloak of maliciousness,
but as the servants of God. 17 Honor all
*men.* Love the brotherhood. Fear God.
Honor the king.●

3. SERVANTS

18 Servants, *be* subject to *your* masters
with all fear; not only to the good and
gentle, but also to the froward. 19 For
this *is* thankworthy, if a man for conscience toward God endure grief, suffering
wrongfully. 20 For what glory *is it*, if,
when ye be buffeted for your faults, ye
shall take it patiently? but if, when ye do
well, and suffer *for it*, ye take it patiently,
this *is* acceptable with God. 21 For even
hereunto were ye called: because Christ
also suffered for us, leaving us an example,
that ye should follow his steps: 22 who
did no sin, neither was guile found in his
mouth: 23 who, when he was reviled,
reviled not again; when he suffered, he
threatened not; but committed *himself* to
him that judgeth righteously: 24 who his
own self bare our sins in his own body on
the tree, that we, being dead to sins,
should live unto righteousness: by whose
stripes ye were healed. 25 For ye were as
sheep going astray; but are now returned unto the Shepherd and Bishop of
your souls.●

SHEEP ASTRAY

The theme of this segment (counsel to groups of Christians) carries over into the next segment (3:1-12).

*2:11-12* What is recorded here about the epistle's readers?

What appeal is made?

Who are the Gentiles?

*2:13-17* What group does Peter counsel with here?

List the commands.

*2:18-25* Record what Peter writes about:

SERVANTS

CHRIST

NEW INTERNATIONAL VERSION

Write three lists of practical Christian living, based on this passage.

A GOOD WIFE

A GOOD HUSBAND

ALL CHRISTIANS

*Wives and Husbands*

3 Wives, in the same way be submissive
to your husbands so that, if any of them
do not believe the word, they may be won
over without talk by the behavior of their
wives, 2when they see the purity and reverence of your lives. 3Your beauty should not
come from outward adornment, such as
braided hair and the wearing of gold jewel-
ry and fine clothes. 4Instead, it should be
that of your inner self, the unfading beauty
of a gentle and quiet spirit, which is of great
worth in God's sight. 5For this is the way
the holy women of the past who put their
hope in God used to make themselves
beautiful. They were submissive to their
own husbands, 6like Sarah, who obeyed
Abraham and called him her master. You
are her daughters if you do what is right
and do not give way to fear.●
7Husbands, in the same way be considerate as you live with your wives, and treat
them with respect as the weaker partner
and as heirs with you of the gracious gift of
life, so that nothing will hinder your
prayers.●

*Suffering for Doing Good*

8Finally, all of you, live in harmony with
one another; be sympathetic, love as
brothers, be compassionate and humble.
9Do not repay evil with evil or insult with
insult, but with blessing, because to this
you were called so that you may inherit a
blessing. 10For,

"Whoever would love life
and see good days
must keep his tongue from evil
and his lips from deceitful speech.
11He must turn from evil and do
good;
he must seek peace and pursue it.
12For the eyes of the Lord are on the
righteous
and his ears are attentive to their
prayer,
but the face of the Lord is against
those who do evil."[b]●

[b]12 Psalm 34:12-16

KING JAMES

1. WIVES

LIFE SEEN BY HUSBANDS

**3** Likewise, ye wives, *be* in subjection to
your own husbands; that, if any
obey not the word, they also may without
the word be won by the conversation of
the wives; 2 while they behold your chaste
conversation *coupled* with fear. 3 Whose
adorning, let it not be that outward
*adorning* of plaiting the hair, and of wearing of gold, or of putting on of apparel;
4 but *let it be* the hidden man of the heart,
in that which is not corruptible, *even the*
*ornament* of a meek and quiet spirit, which
is in the sight of God of great price. 5 For
after this manner in the old time the holy
women also, who trusted in God, adorned
themselves, being in subjection unto their
own husbands: 6 even as Sarah obeyed
Abraham, calling him lord: whose daughters ye are, as long as ye do well, and are
not afraid with any amazement.●

2. HUSBANDS

7 Likewise, ye husbands, dwell with
*them* according to knowledge, giving
honor unto the wife, as unto the weaker
vessel, and as being heirs together of the
grace of life; that your prayers be not
hindered.●

3. ALL CHRISTIANS

8 Finally, *be ye* all of one mind, having
compassion one of another; love as brethren, *be* pitiful, *be* courteous: 9 not rendering evil for evil, or railing for railing:
but contrariwise blessing; knowing that
ye are thereunto called, that ye should inherit a blessing.

10 For he that will love life,
and see good days,
let him refrain his tongue from evil,
and his lips that they speak no guile:
11 let him eschew evil, and do good;
let him seek peace, and ensue it.
12 For the eyes of the Lord *are* over the righteous,
and his ears *are open* unto their prayers:
but the face of the Lord *is* against them that do evil. ●

Ps. 34:12-16

LIFE SEEN BY THE LORD

This segment continues the theme of the previous one.

*3:1-6* List all the adjectives of the paragraph (e.g. "chaste").

What is intended by the phrase "without the word be won by the conversation" (v.1)? See The Living Bible.

*3:7* Record the strong words of this paragraph.

*3:8-12* Record the commands.

What are these three parts of the Psalms quotation about:

v.10a

v.10b-11

v.12

NEW INTERNATIONAL VERSION

What does this passage teach about:

PERSECUTION

SUFFERING

GODLY LIVING

SEPARATED LIFE

SERVING OTHERS

JESUS CHRIST

13 Who is going to harm you if you are
eager to do good? 14 But even if you should
suffer for what is right, you are blessed.
"Do not fear what they fear[c]; do not be
frightened."[d] 15 But in your hearts set apart
Christ as Lord. Always be prepared to give
an answer to everyone who asks you to
give the reason for the hope that you have.
But do this with gentleness and respect,
16 keeping a clear conscience, so that those
who speak maliciously against your good
behavior in Christ may be ashamed of their
slander. 17 It is better, if it is God's will, to
suffer for doing good than for doing evil.●
18 For Christ died for sins once for all, the
righteous for the unrighteous, to bring you
to God. He was put to death in the body but
made alive by the Spirit, 19 through whom[e]
also he went and preached to the spirits in
prison 20 who disobeyed long ago when God
waited patiently in the days of Noah while
the ark was being built. In it only a few
people, eight in all, were saved through
water, 21 and this water symbolizes baptism
that now saves you also—not the removal
of dirt from the body but the pledge of a
good conscience toward God. It saves you
by the resurrection of Jesus Christ, 22 who
has gone into heaven and is at God's right
hand—with angels, authorities and powers
in submission to him.●

*Living for God*

4 Therefore, since Christ suffered in his
body, arm yourselves also with the
same attitude, because he who has suffered in his body is done with sin. 2 As a
result, he does not live the rest of his earthly life for evil human desires, but rather for
the will of God. 3 For you have spent
enough time in the past doing what pagans
choose to do—living in debauchery, lust,
drunkenness, orgies, carousing and detestable idolatry. 4 They think it strange that
you do not plunge with them into the same
flood of dissipation, and they heap abuse
on you. 5 But they will have to give account
to him who is ready to judge the living and
the dead. 6 For this is the reason the gospel
was preached even to those who are now
dead, so that they might be judged according to men in regard to the body, but live
according to God in regard to the spirit.●
7 The end of all things is near. Therefore
be clear minded and self-controlled so that
you can pray. 8 Above all, love each other
deeply, because love covers over a multitude of sins. 9 Offer hospitality to one another without grumbling. 10 Each one
should use whatever gift he has received to
serve others, faithfully administering
God's grace in its various forms. 11 If anyone speaks, he should do it as one speaking
the very words of God. If anyone serves,
he should do it with the strength God provides, so that in all things God may be
praised through Jesus Christ. To him be
the glory and the power for ever and ever.
Amen.●

[c]14 Or *not fear their threats* [d]14 Isaiah 8:12
[e]18,19 Or *the spirit* [19]*through which*

KING JAMES

1.GOODNESS — PERSECUTION

13 And who *is* he that will harm you, if
ye be followers of that which is good?
14 But and if ye suffer for righteousness'
sake, happy *are ye:* and be not afraid of
their terror, neither be troubled; 15 but
sanctify the Lord God in your hearts:
and *be* ready always to *give* an answer to
every man that asketh you a reason of the
hope that is in you, with meekness and
fear: 16 having a good conscience; that,
whereas they speak evil of you, as of evildoers, they may be ashamed that falsely
accuse your good conversation in Christ.
17 For *it is* better, if the will of God be so,
that ye suffer for well doing, than for evildoing. ● 18 For Christ also hath once

2.NEWNESS OF LIFE

suffered for sins, the just for the unjust,
that he might bring us to God, being put
to death in the flesh, but quickened by the
Spirit: 19 by which also he went and
preached unto the spirits in prison;
20 which sometime were disobedient,
when once the long-suffering of God waited
in the days of Noah, while the ark was a
preparing, wherein few, that is, eight souls
were saved by water. 21 The like figure
whereunto *even* baptism doth also now
save us, (not the putting away of the filth
of the flesh, but the answer of a good conscience toward God,) by the resurrection
of Jesus Christ: 22 who is gone into
heaven, and is on the right hand of God;
angels and authorities and powers being
made subject unto him.●

3.SEPARATION IN LIVING

4 Forasmuch then as Christ hath suffered for us in the flesh, arm yourselves likewise with the same mind: for he
that hath suffered in the flesh hath ceased
from sin; 2 that he no longer should live
the rest of *his* time in the flesh to the lusts
of men, but to the will of God. 3 For the
time past of *our* life may suffice us to have
wrought the will of the Gentiles, when we
walked in lasciviousness, lusts, excess of
wine, revelings, banquetings, and abominable idolatries: 4 wherein they think it
strange that ye run not with *them* to the
same excess of riot, speaking evil of *you:*
5 who shall give account to him that is
ready to judge the quick and the dead.
6 For, for this cause was the gospel
preached also to them that are dead, that
they might be judged according to men in
the flesh, but live according to God in the
spirit.●

4.SERVICE TO OTHERS

7 But the end of all things is at hand: be
ye therefore sober, and watch unto prayer.
8 And above all things have fervent
charity among yourselves: for charity
shall cover the multitude of sins. 9 Use
hospitality one to another without grudg-
ing. 10 As every man hath received the
gift, *even so* minister the same one to another, as good stewards of the manifold
grace of God. 11 If any man speak, *let
him speak* as the oracles of God; if any
man minister, *let him do it* as of the ability
which God giveth; that God in all things
may be glorified through Jesus Christ: to
whom be praise and dominion for ever
and ever. Amen.●

PRAISE

*3:13-17* Observe the repetition of the word "good." Record the different appeals here.

*3:18-22* Who is this paragraph mainly about?

Record the different activities and ministries of Jesus:

*4:1-6* What is the main appeal of this paragraph?

How are believers and unbelievers compared here?

*4:7-11* Record the different references to serving others.

How does verse 11 conclude this segment?

NEW INTERNATIONAL VERSION

What do you learn here about:

TRIALS ______________________

GODLY LIVING ______________________

MINISTERING IN THE CHURCH ______________________

SUBMISSION TO OTHERS ______________________

SATAN ______________________

### *Suffering for Being a Christian*

12 Dear friends, do not be surprised at the
painful trial you are suffering, as though
something strange were happening to you.
13 But rejoice that you participate in the sufferings of Christ, so that you may be overjoyed when his glory is revealed. 14 If you
are insulted because of the name of Christ,
you are blessed, for the Spirit of glory and
of God rests on you. 15 If you suffer, it
should not be as a murderer or thief or any
other kind of criminal, or even as a med-
dler. 16 However, if you suffer as a Christian, do not be ashamed, but praise God
that you bear that name. 17 For it is time for
judgment to begin with the family of God;
and if it begins with us, what will the outcome be for those who do not obey the
gospel of God? 18 And,

> "If it is hard for the righteous to be
> saved,
> what will become of the ungodly
> and the sinner?"[a]

19 So then, those who suffer according to
God's will should commit themselves to
their faithful Creator and continue to do
good.●

### *To Elders and Young Men*

5 To the elders among you, I appeal as a
fellow elder, a witness of Christ's sufferings and one who also will share in the
glory to be revealed: 2 Be shepherds of
God's flock that is under your care, serving
as overseers—not because you must, but
because you are willing, as God wants you
to be; not greedy for money, but eager to
serve; 3 not lording it over those entrusted
to you, but being examples to the flock.
4 And when the Chief Shepherd appears,
you will receive the crown of glory that will
never fade away.●
5 Young men, in the same way be submissive to those who are older. Clothe yourselves with humility toward one another,
because,

> "God opposes the proud
> but gives grace to the
> humble."[b]

6 Humble yourselves, therefore, under
God's mighty hand, that he may lift you up
in due time. 7 Cast all your anxiety on him
because he cares for you.
8 Be self-controlled and alert. Your enemy the devil prowls around like a roaring
lion looking for someone to devour. 9 Resist
him, standing firm in the faith, because you
know that your brothers throughout the
world are undergoing the same kind of sufferings.
10 And the God of all grace, who called
you to his eternal glory in Christ, after you
have suffered a little while, will himself
restore you and make you strong, firm and
steadfast. 11 To him be the power for ever
and ever. Amen.●

### *Final Greetings*

12 With the help of Silas,[c] whom I regard
as a faithful brother, I have written to you
briefly, encouraging you and testifying that
this is the true grace of God. Stand fast
in it.
13 She who is in Babylon, chosen together
with you, sends you her greetings, and so
does my son Mark. 14 Greet one another
with a kiss of love.
Peace to all of you who are in Christ.●

[a] 18 Prov. 11:31 [b] 5 Prov. 3:34
[c] 12 Greek *Silvanus*, a variant of *Silas*

KING JAMES

1.JUDG-
MENT

TRIAL

12 Beloved, think it not strange concerning the fiery trial which is to try you,
as though some strange thing happened
unto you: 13 but rejoice, inasmuch as ye
are partakers of Christ's sufferings; that,
when his glory shall be revealed, ye may
be glad also with exceeding joy. 14 If ye
be reproached for the name of Christ,
happy *are ye;* for the Spirit of glory and
of God resteth upon you: on their part he
is evil spoken of, but on your part he is
glorified. 15 But let none of you suffer as
a murderer, or *as* a thief, or *as* an evildoer,
or as a busybody in other men's matters.
16 Yet if *any man suffer* as a Christian, let
him not be ashamed; but let him glorify
God on this behalf. 17 For the time *is*
*come* that judgment must begin at the
house of God: and if *it* first *begin* at us,
what shall the end *be* of them that obey
not the gospel of God? 18 And if the
righteous scarcely be saved, where shall
the ungodly and the sinner appear?
19 Wherefore, let them that suffer according to the will of God commit the keeping
of their souls *to him* in well doing, as unto
a faithful Creator. ●

2.SERVICE

5 The elders which are among you I exhort, who am also an elder, and a witness of the sufferings of Christ, and also a
partaker of the glory that shall be revealed: 2 Feed the flock of God which
is among you, taking the oversight *there-*
*of,* not by constraint, but willingly; not
for filthy lucre, but of a ready mind;
3 neither as being lords over *God's* heritage, but being ensamples to the flock.
4 And when the chief Shepherd shall appear, ye shall receive a crown of glory that
fadeth not away.● 5 Likewise, ye younger,

3.SUB-
MISSION

submit yourselves unto the elder. Yea,
all *of you* be subject one to another, and
be clothed with humility: for God resisteth the proud, and giveth grace to the
humble.
6 Humble yourselves therefore under
the mighty hand of God, that he may
exalt you in due time: 7 casting all your
care upon him; for he careth for you.
8 Be sober, be vigilant; because your adversary the devil, as a roaring lion, walketh about, seeking whom he may devour:
9 whom resist steadfast in the faith,
knowing that the same afflictions are accomplished in your brethren that are in
the world. 10 But the God of all grace,
who hath called us unto his eternal glory
by Christ Jesus, after that ye have suffered
a while, make you perfect, stablish,
strengthen, settle *you.* 11 To him *be* glory
and dominion for ever and ever. Amen.●

—final
greetings

12 By Silva'nus, a faithful brother unto you, as I suppose, I have written briefly,
exhorting, and testifying that this is the
true grace of God wherein ye stand.
13 The *church that is* at Babylon, elected
together with *you,* saluteth you; and *so*
*doth* Mark my son. 14 Greet ye one
another with a kiss of charity.
Peace *be* with you all that are in Christ
Jesus. Amen.●

PEACE

*4:12-19* What kind of trials does Peter refer to here?

What different encouragements does he give to those experiencing such trials?

*5:1-4* What kinds of burdens rest on elders?

*5:5-11* Record references to submission and humility.

What does the benediction of verses 10-11 teach?

*5:12-14* Record the strong words and phrases of this conclusion to the epistle.

# 2 PETER

## AUTHORSHIP

The apostle Peter wrote this letter, probably to the same groups to whom he wrote 1 Peter.

## DATE

Peter wrote from Rome around A.D. 67, when his death was imminent (1:14; cf. 2 Tim. 4:6).

## OCCASION AND PURPOSE

In his first letter Peter had much to say about opposition to Christians originating outside the group, in the form of persecution. In this letter he refers mostly to the more serious danger originating inside the group, namely apostasy and false teaching. Thus his purpose in writing the letter is to expose the false teachers and instruct the Christians as to what they should do to combat the ugly threat of apostasy. A theme of the book is true and false prophecy.

## 2 PETER: True and False Prophecy

| | |
|---|---|
| Salutation and Benediction | 1:1-2 |
| THE MAN WHO KNOWS GOD | 1:3-15 |
| TRUE PROPHECY: SURETY OF CHRIST'S SECOND COMING | 1:16-21 |
| FALSE PROPHECY | 2:1-22 |
| General Statement | 2:1-3 |
| Law of Recompense | 2:4-10a |
| Description of the Unrighteous | 2:10b-16 |
| Destiny of the Unrighteous | 2:17-22 |
| TRUE PROPHECY: FACT AND DELAY OF CHRIST'S SECOND COMING | 3:1-18a |
| Doxology | 3:18b |

# 2 PETER

NEW INTERNATIONAL VERSION

Write a list of practical applications of this passage to present-day living.

1 Simon Peter, a servant and apostle of
Jesus Christ,

To those who through the righteousness
of our God and Savior Jesus Christ have
received a faith as precious as ours:

[2]Grace and peace be yours in abundance
through the knowledge of God and of Jesus
our Lord.●

*Making One's Calling and Election Sure*

[3]His divine power has given us everything we need for life and godliness
through our knowledge of him who called
us by his own glory and goodness.
[4]Through these he has given us his very
great and precious promises, so that
through them you may participate in the
divine nature and escape the corruption in
the world caused by evil desires.
[5]For this very reason, make every effort
to add to your faith goodness; and to goodness, knowledge; [6]and to knowledge, self-
control; and to self-control, perseverance;
and to perseverance, godliness; [7]and to
godliness, brotherly kindness; and to
brotherly kindness, love. [8]For if you possess these qualities in increasing measure,
they will keep you from being ineffective
and unproductive in your knowledge of our
Lord Jesus Christ. [9]But if anyone does not
have them, he is nearsighted and blind, and
has forgotten that he has been cleansed
from his past sins.
[10]Therefore, my brothers, be all the more
eager to make your calling and election
sure. For if you do these things, you will
never fall, [11]and you will receive a rich
welcome into the eternal kingdom of our
Lord and Savior Jesus Christ.●

*Prophecy of Scripture*

[12]So I will always remind you of these
things, even though you know them and
are firmly established in the truth you now
have. [13]I think it is right to refresh your
memory as long as I live in the tent of this
body, [14]because I know that I will soon put
it aside, as our Lord Jesus Christ has made
clear to me. [15]And I will make every effort
to see that after my departure you will always be able to remember these things.●

KING JAMES

# 2 PETER

—salutation

SERVANT OF CHRIST

**1** Simon Peter, a servant and an apostle
of Jesus Christ,
To them that have obtained like precious
faith with us through the righteousness of
God and our Saviour Jesus Christ:
2 Grace and peace be multiplied unto
you through the knowledge of God, and
of Jesus our Lord.●

1. APPLYING THE TRUTH

3 According as his divine power hath
given unto us all things that *pertain* unto
life and godliness, through the knowledge
of him that hath called us to glory and
virtue: 4 whereby are given unto us exceeding great and precious promises; that
by these ye might be partakers of the
divine nature, having escaped the corruption that is in the world through lust.
5 And besides this, giving all diligence,
add to your faith virtue; and to virtue,
knowledge; 6 and to knowledge, temperance; and to temperance, patience;
and to patience, godliness; 7 and to godliness, brotherly kindness; and to brotherly kindness, charity. 8 For if these
things be in you, and abound, they make
*you that ye shall* neither *be* barren nor unfruitful in the knowledge of our Lord
Jesus Christ. 9 But he that lacketh these
things is blind, and cannot see afar off,
and hath forgotten that he was purged
from his old sins. 10 Wherefore the
rather, brethren, give diligence to make
your calling and election sure: for if ye do
these things, ye shall never fall: 11 for so
an entrance shall be ministered unto you
abundantly into the everlasting kingdom
of our Lord and Saviour Jesus Christ.●

2. REMEMBERING THE TRUTH

12 Wherefore I will not be negligent to
put you always in remembrance of these
things, though ye know *them*, and be established in the present truth. 13 Yea, I
think it meet, as long as I am in this tabernacle, to stir you up by putting *you* in remembrance; 14 knowing that shortly I
must put off *this* my tabernacle, even as
our Lord Jesus Christ hath showed me.
15 Moreover I will endeavor that ye may
be able after my decease to have these
things always in remembrance.●

SERVANT OF BRETHREN

*1:1-2* What are the strong words and phrases of the salutation?

What does Peter write about "knowledge" in verse 2?

*1:3-11* Underline the repeated word "knowledge". Record:

What has been given to the believer (vv.3-4):

What the believer must do (vv.5-10):

*1:12-15* What does Peter write about "remembrance"?

NEW INTERNATIONAL VERSION

What does Peter teach here about:

THE SECOND COMING OF CHRIST

TRUE PROPHECY

INSPIRATION OF SCRIPTURE

FALSE TEACHING

JUDGMENT FOR SIN

DELIVERANCE OF THE RIGHTEOUS

16We did not follow cleverly invented
stories when we told you about the power
and coming of our Lord Jesus Christ, but
we were eyewitnesses of his majesty. 17For
he received honor and glory from God the
Father when the voice came to him from
the Majestic Glory, saying, "This is my
Son, whom I love; with him I am well
pleased."[a] 18We ourselves heard this voice
that came from heaven when we were with
him on the sacred mountain.
19And we have the word of the prophets
made more certain, and you will do well to
pay attention to it, as to a light shining in
a dark place, until the day dawns and the
morning star rises in your hearts. 20Above
all, you must understand that no prophecy
of Scripture came about by the prophet's
own interpretation. 21For prophecy never
had its origin in the will of man, but men
spoke from God as they were carried along
by the Holy Spirit.●

*False Teachers and Their Destruction*

2 But there were also false prophets
among the people, just as there will be
false teachers among you. They will secretly introduce destructive heresies, even
denying the sovereign Lord who bought
them—bringing swift destruction on themselves. 2Many will follow their shameful
ways and will bring the way of truth into
disrepute. 3In their greed these teachers
will exploit you with stories they have
made up. Their condemnation has long
been hanging over them, and their destruction has not been sleeping.●
4For if God did not spare angels when
they sinned, but sent them to hell,[b] putting
them into gloomy dungeons[c] to be held for
judgment; 5if he did not spare the ancient
world when he brought the flood on its
ungodly people, but protected Noah, a
preacher of righteousness, and seven
others; 6if he condemned the cities of
Sodom and Gomorrah by burning them to
ashes, and made them an example of what
is going to happen to the ungodly; 7and if
he rescued Lot, a righteous man, who was
distressed by the filthy lives of lawless men
8(for that righteous man, living among
them day after day, was tormented in his
righteous soul by the lawless deeds he saw
and heard)— 9if this is so, then the Lord
knows how to rescue godly men from trials
and to hold the unrighteous for the day of
judgment, while continuing their punishment.[a] 10This is especially true of those
who follow the corrupt desire of the sinful
nature[b] and despise authority.●

[a]*17* Matt. 17:5; Mark 9:7; Luke 9:35 [b]*4* Greek *Tartarus*
[c]*4* Some manuscripts *into chains of darkness*
[a]*9* Or *unrighteous for punishment until the day of judgment*
[b]*10* Or *the flesh*

## KING JAMES

### 1. TRUE PROPHECY

COMING OF CHRIST

16 For we have not followed cunningly
devised fables, when we made known unto
you the power and coming of our Lord
Jesus Christ, but were eyewitnesses of his
majesty. 17 For he received from God the
Father honor and glory, when there came
such a voice to him from the excellent
glory, This is my beloved Son, in whom I
am well pleased. 18 And this voice which
came from heaven we heard, when we
were with him in the holy mount. 19 We
have also a more sure word of prophecy;
whereunto ye do well that ye take heed, as
unto a light that shineth in a dark place,
until the day dawn, and the day-star arise
in your hearts: 20 knowing this first, that
no prophecy of the Scripture is of any
private interpretation. 21 For the prophecy came not in old time by the will of
man: but holy men of God spake *as they
were* moved by the Holy Ghost.●

### 2. FALSE PROPHECY

2 But there were false prophets also
among the people, even as there shall
be false teachers among you, who privily
shall bring in damnable heresies, even
denying the Lord that bought them, and
bring upon themselves swift destruction.
2 And many shall follow their pernicious
ways; by reason of whom the way of truth
shall be evil spoken of. 3 And through
covetousness shall they with feigned
words make merchandise of you: whose
judgment now of a long time lingereth
not, and their damnation slumbereth not.●

### 3. LAW OF RECOMPENSE

4 For if God spared not the angels that
sinned, but cast *them* down to hell, and
delivered *them* into chains of darkness, to
be reserved unto judgment; 5 and spared
not the old world, but saved Noah the
eighth *person*, a preacher of righteousness, bringing in the flood upon the world
of the ungodly; 6 and turning the cities
of Sodom and Gomor'rah into ashes
condemned *them* with an overthrow, making *them* an ensample unto those that after
should live ungodly; 7 and delivered just
Lot, vexed with the filthy conversation of
the wicked: 8 (for that righteous man
dwelling among them, in seeing and hearing, vexed *his* righteous soul from day to
day with *their* unlawful deeds:) 9 the
Lord knoweth how to deliver the godly
out of temptation, and to reserve the unjust unto the day of judgment to be
punished: 10 but chiefly them that walk
after the flesh in the lust of uncleanness,
and despise government.●

DAY OF JUDGMENT

*1:16-21* What coming of Christ to earth is verse 16 about?

What truth do verses 17-18 establish?

How do verses 19-21 reinforce the truth of verse 16?

*2:1-3* Record the different descriptions and activities of false prophets and teachers.

*2:4-10a* What is the law of recompense, according to verse 9?

List the various illustrations of this law:

v.4

v.5

v.6

v.7

In your own words list the various descriptions of unrighteous people, and the destiny reserved for them.

DESCRIPTIONS

DESTINY

What do verses 20-22 teach about apostasy?

## NEW INTERNATIONAL VERSION

Bold and arrogant, these men are not
afraid to slander celestial beings; [11]yet even
angels, although they are stronger and
more powerful, do not bring slanderous accusations against such beings in the presence of the Lord. [12]But these men blaspheme in matters they do not understand.
They are like brute beasts, creatures of
instinct, born only to be caught and destroyed, and like beasts they too will perish.
[13]They will be paid back with harm for
the harm they have done. Their idea of
pleasure is to carouse in broad daylight.
They are blots and blemishes, reveling in
their pleasures while they feast with you.[c]
[14]With eyes full of adultery, they never
stop sinning; they seduce the unstable;
they are experts in greed—an accursed
brood! [15]They have left the straight way
and wandered off to follow the way of Balaam son of Beor, who loved the wages of
wickedness. [16]But he was rebuked for his
wrongdoing by a donkey—a beast without
speech—who spoke with a man's voice
and restrained the prophet's madness.●
[17]These men are springs without water
and mists driven by a storm. Blackest
darkness is reserved for them. [18]For they
mouth empty, boastful words and, by appealing to the lustful desires of sinful human nature, they entice people who are
just escaping from those who live in error.
[19]They promise them freedom, while they
themselves are slaves of depravity—for a
man is a slave to whatever has mastered
him. [20]If they have escaped the corruption
of the world by knowing our Lord and Savior Jesus Christ and are again entangled in
it and overcome, they are worse off at the
end than they were at the beginning. [21]It
would have been better for them not to
have known the way of righteousness, than
to have known it and then to turn their
backs on the sacred commandment that
was passed on to them. [22]Of them the proverbs are true: "A dog returns to its vomit,"[d] and, "A sow that is washed goes back
to her wallowing in the mud."●

[c]*13* Some manuscripts *in their love feasts*
[d]*22* Prov. 26:11

KING JAMES

1. DESCRIPTION

ANGELS

Presumptuous *are they*, self-willed, they
are not afraid to speak evil of dignities.
11 Whereas angels, which are greater in
power and might, bring not railing accusation against them before the Lord. 12 But
these, as natural brute beasts made to be
taken and destroyed, speak evil of the
things that they understand not; and
shall utterly perish in their own corruption; 13 and shall receive the reward of
unrighteousness, *as* they that count it
pleasure to riot in the daytime. Spots *they
are* and blemishes, sporting themselves
with their own deceivings while they feast
with you; 14 having eyes full of adultery,
and that cannot cease from sin; beguiling
unstable souls: a heart they have exercised
with covetous practices; cursed children:
15 which have forsaken the right way, and
are gone astray, following the way of
Ba'laam *the son* of Beor, who loved the
wages of unrighteousness; 16 but was rebuked for his iniquity: the dumb ass
speaking with man's voice forbade the
madness of the prophet. ●

2. DESTINY

17 These are wells without water,
clouds that are carried with a tempest;
to whom the mist of darkness is reserved
for ever. 18 For when they speak great
swelling *words* of vanity, they allure
through the lusts of the flesh, *through
much* wantonness, those that were clean
escaped from them who live in error.
19 While they promise them liberty, they
themselves are the servants of corruption:
for of whom a man is overcome, of the
same is he brought in bondage. 20 For if
after they have escaped the pollutions of
the world through the knowledge of the
Lord and Saviour Jesus Christ, they are
again entangled therein, and overcome,
the latter end is worse with them than the
beginning. 21 For it had been better for
them not to have known the way of righteousness, than, after they have known *it*,
to turn from the holy commandment delivered unto them. 22 But it is happened
unto them according to the true proverb,
The dog *is* turned to his own vomit again;
and the sow that was washed to her wallowing in the mire. ●

DOGS AND PIGS

This segment continues the general subject of the preceding two paragraphs (2:1-10a).

*2:10b-16* Most of the paragraph is *description* of the unrighteous. Do you see any reference to the law of recompense?

Record the words or phrases that describe unrighteous people.

*2:17-22* Record the *descriptions* of the unrighteous:

Record the references to the *destiny* of the unrighteous:

NEW INTERNATIONAL VERSION

What is Peter's answer to the scoffers who maintain that there is a status quo about history, that is, that "everything has remained exactly as it was" (v.4)?

Record the different truths taught by this passage about Christ's second coming.

List some practical applications of the passage.

*The Day of the Lord*

3 Dear friends, this is now my second
letter to you. I have written both of
them as reminders to stimulate you to
wholesome thinking. 2I want you to recall
the words spoken in the past by the holy
prophets and the command given by our
Lord and Savior through your apostles.
3First of all, you must understand that in
the last days scoffers will come, scoffing
and following their own evil desires. 4They
will say, "Where is this 'coming' he promised? Ever since our fathers died, everything goes on as it has since the beginning
of creation." 5But they deliberately forget
that long ago by God's word the heavens
existed and the earth was formed out of
water and with water. 6By water also the
world of that time was deluged and destroyed. 7By the same word the present
heavens and earth are reserved for fire,
being kept for the day of judgment and
destruction of ungodly men.●
8But do not forget this one thing, dear
friends: With the Lord a day is like a thousand years, and a thousand years are like
a day. 9The Lord is not slow in keeping his
promise, as some understand slowness. He
is patient with you, not wanting anyone to
perish, but everyone to come to repentance.
10But the day of the Lord will come like
a thief. The heavens will disappear with a
roar; the elements will be destroyed by
fire, and the earth and everything in it will
be laid bare.[e]●

[e]10 Some manuscripts *be burned up*

KING JAMES

1.COMING CHALLENGED

**3** This second epistle, beloved, I now
write unto you; in *both* which I stir up
your pure minds by way of remembrance:
2 that ye may be mindful of the words
which were spoken before by the holy
prophets, and of the commandment of us
the apostles of the Lord and Saviour:
3 knowing this first, that there shall come
in the last days scoffers, walking after their
own lusts, 4 and saying, Where is the
promise of his coming? for since the
fathers fell asleep, all things continue as
*they were* from the beginning of the creation.
5 For this they willingly are ignorant of, that by the word of God the
heavens were of old, and the earth standing out of the water and in the water:
6 whereby the world that then was, being
overflowed with water, perished: 7 but
the heavens and the earth, which are now,
by the same word are kept in store,
reserved unto fire against the day of
judgment and perdition of ungodly
men.●

REMEMBER

2.DELAY EXPLAINED

8 But, beloved, be not ignorant of this
one thing, that one day *is* with the Lord as
a thousand years, and a thousand years as
one day. 9 The Lord is not slack concerning his promise, as some men count
slackness; but is long-suffering to us-ward,
not willing that any should perish, but
that all should come to repentance.
10 But the day of the Lord will come as a
thief in the night; in the which the
heavens shall pass away with a great noise,
and the elements shall melt with fervent
heat, the earth also and the works that are
therein shall be burned up. ●

DON'T BE IGNORANT

*3:1-7* What is the challenge made by scoffers (v.4)?

What three supernatural events originating with the decree of God ("word of God") does Peter cite?

v.5

v.6

v.7

*3:8-10* What in the paragraph suggests that the question had been raised as to what was delaying the Lord's second coming?

What is Peter's answer to that question?

Compare "day of the Lord" (v.10) with "day of judgment" (v.7).

NEW INTERNATIONAL VERSION

What does this passage teach about:

GODLY LIVING

SECOND COMING OF CHRIST

FINAL JUDGMENTS

LONGSUFFERING OF CHRIST

CHRISTIAN GROWTH

OTHER

11 Since everything will be destroyed in
this way, what kind of people ought you to
be? You ought to live holy and godly lives
12 as you look forward to the day of God and
speed its coming.[f] That day will bring
about the destruction of the heavens by
fire, and the elements will melt in the heat.
13 But in keeping with his promise we are
looking forward to a new heaven and a new
earth, the home of righteousness.●
14 So then, dear friends, since you are
looking forward to this, make every effort
to be found spotless, blameless and at
peace with him. 15 Bear in mind that our
Lord's patience means salvation, just as
our dear brother Paul also wrote you with
the wisdom that God gave him. 16 He writes
the same way in all his letters, speaking in
them of these matters. His letters contain
some things that are hard to understand,
which ignorant and unstable people distort, as they do the other Scriptures, to
their own destruction.●
17 Therefore, dear friends, since you already know this, be on your guard so that
you may not be carried away by the error
of lawless men and fall from your secure
position. 18 But grow in the grace and
knowledge of our Lord and Savior Jesus
Christ. To him be glory both now and forever! Amen.●

f12 *Or as you wait eagerly for the day of God to come*

## KING JAMES

1. LOOK FORWARD TO

2. BE DILIGENT

3. BEWARE

11 *Seeing* then *that* all these things shall
be dissolved, what manner *of persons*
ought ye to be in *all* holy conversation
and godliness, 12 looking for and hasting
unto the coming of the day of God,
wherein the heavens being on fire shall be
dissolved, and the elements shall melt with
fervent heat? 13 Nevertheless we, according to his promise, look for new
heavens and a new earth, wherein dwelleth righteousness. ●
14 Wherefore, beloved, seeing that ye
look for such things, be diligent that ye
may be found of him in peace, without
spot, and blameless. 15 And account *that*
the long-suffering of our Lord *is* salvation;
even as our beloved brother Paul also
according to the wisdom given unto him
hath written unto you; 16 as also in all
*his* epistles, speaking in them of these
things; in which are some things hard to
be understood, which they that are unlearned and unstable wrest, as *they do* also
the other Scriptures, unto their own destruction. ● 17 Ye therefore, beloved, seeing ye know *these things* before, beware
lest ye also, being led away with the error
of the wicked, fall from your own stead-
fastness. 18 But grow in grace, and *in* the
knowledge of our Lord and Saviour Jesus
Christ. To him *be* glory both now and
for ever. Amen. ●

GODLINESS

GLORY OF CHRIST

*3:11-13* What words refer to end-time cataclysm?

What words describe the kind of heart and life which Peter is here appealing for?

Compare the two things which believers are to "look for" (vv.12,13).

*3:14-16* What is the exhortation of this paragraph?

How is the exhortation related to the preceding paragraph?

*3:17-18* Compare the positive command of verse 18 with the negative warning of verse 17.

# 1 JOHN

## AUTHORSHIP

The author was John, son of Zebedee (Matt. 4:21), an apostle of Jesus (Matt. 10:2), who called himself "the elder" in 2 John 1 and 3 John 1. This John also wrote one of the four Gospels and the book of Revelation.

## DATE

John wrote the letter approximately A.D. 85-90. He probably wrote from Ephesus, where he spent his last years.

## OCCASION AND PURPOSE

John wrote this letter to Christians who were falling prey to the deceptive devices of Satan. Christians were fighting each other, and were beginning to love the evil things of the world. They were being drawn away from Christ by false teachers, and were doubting their own salvation. A theme of the letter is fellowship with God and with God's children.

## 1 JOHN: Fellowship with God and His Children

| | |
|---|---|
| PERSONS OF THE FELLOWSHIP | 1:1-4 |
| LIGHT OF FELLOWSHIP | 1:5-2:29 |
| Conditions —for Fellowship with God | 1:5-2:2 |
| Abiding in Christ | 2:3-17 |
| Antichrists and Christians | 2:18-29 |
| LOVE OF FELLOWSHIP | 3:1-4:21 |
| Beloved Sons of God | 3:1-24 |
| Truth and Love | 4:1-21 |
| WAY TO FELLOWSHIP | 5:1-12 |
| CERTAINTY OF FELLOWSHIP | 5:13-21 |

# 1 JOHN

NEW INTERNATIONAL VERSION

What does this passage teach about:

ETERNAL LIFE

SIN

FELLOWSHIP WITH GOD

FELLOWSHIP OF CHRISTIANS

HOLINESS

CONFESSION

MINISTRIES OF JESUS

### *The Word of Life*

1 That which was from the beginning,
which we have heard, which we have
seen with our eyes, which we have looked
at and our hands have touched—this we
proclaim concerning the Word of life. 2The
life appeared; we have seen it and testify to
it, and we proclaim to you the eternal life,
which was with the Father and has appeared to us. 3We proclaim to you what we
have seen and heard, so that you also may
have fellowship with us. And our fellowship is with the Father and with his Son,
Jesus Christ. 4We write this to make our[a]
joy complete.●

### *Walking in the Light*

5This is the message we have heard from
him and declare to you: God is light; in him
there is no darkness at all. 6If we claim to
have fellowship with him yet walk in the
darkness, we lie and do not live by the
truth. 7But if we walk in the light, as he is
in the light, we have fellowship with one
another, and the blood of Jesus, his Son,
purifies us from all[b] sin.●
8If we claim to be without sin, we deceive ourselves and the truth is not in us.
9If we confess our sins, he is faithful and
just and will forgive us our sins and purify
us from all unrighteousness. 10If we claim
we have not sinned, we make him out to be
a liar and his word has no place in our lives.●
2 My dear children, I write this to you so
that you will not sin. But if anybody
does sin, we have one who speaks to the
Father in our defense—Jesus Christ, the
Righteous One. 2He is the atoning sacrifice
for our sins, and not only for ours but also
for[c] the sins of the whole world.●

[a]4 Some manuscripts *your* [b]7 Or *every*
[c]2 Or *He is the one who turns aside God's wrath, taking away our sins, and not only ours but also*

KING JAMES

# 1 JOHN

1.WORD OF LIFE

**1** That which was from the beginning,
which we have heard, which we have
seen with our eyes, which we have looked
upon, and our hands have handled, of the
Word of life; 2 (for the life was manifested, and we have seen *it*, and bear witness, and show unto you that eternal life,
which was with the Father, and was manifested unto us;) 3 that which we have
seen and heard declare we unto you, that
ye also may have fellowship with us: and
truly our fellowship *is* with the Father,
and with his Son Jesus Christ. 4 And
these things write we unto you, that your
joy may be full.●

BEGIN-NING OF TIME

2.GOD

5 This then is the message which we
have heard of him, and declare unto you,
that God is light, and in him is no darkness at all. 6 If we say that we have fellowship with him, and walk in darkness, we
lie, and do not the truth: 7 but if we walk
in the light, as he is in the light, we have
fellowship one with another, and the
blood of Jesus Christ his Son cleanseth
us from all sin.●

3.SINNERS

8 If we say that we have no sin, we deceive ourselves, and the truth is not in us.
9 If we confess our sins, he is faithful and
just to forgive us *our* sins, and to cleanse
us from all unrighteousness. 10 If we say
that we have not sinned, we make him a
liar, and his word is not in us.●

4.ADVO-CATE

**2** My little children, these things write
I unto you, that ye sin not. And if any
man sin, we have an advocate with the
Father, Jesus Christ the righteous: 2 and
he is the propitiation for our sins: and not
for ours only, but also for *the sins of* the
whole world.●

WHOLE WORLD

*1:1-4* What are the first two words of the paragraph? ______

Where is the phrase repeated? ______

How are the words "declare we" (v.3) related to the phrase? ______

What is the purpose of the declaration (v.3)? ______

Why does John write the epistle (v.4)? ______

*1:5-7* How is God identified here? ______

What are the strong words of verses 6-7? ______

*1:8-10* What word begins each verse? ______

What point is made in each case? ______

*2:1-2* What is the central truth here? ______

NEW INTERNATIONAL VERSION

Record what is taught here about:

ABIDING IN CHRIST

OBEDIENCE

WORD OF GOD

LOVE

HATE

PERSONAL KNOWLEDGE OF GOD

SATAN

LUST

THE WORLD

3We know that we have come to know
him if we obey his commands. 4The man
who says, "I know him," but does not do
what he commands is a liar, and the truth
is not in him. 5But if anyone obeys his
word, God's love is truly made complete in
him. This is how we know we are in him:
6Whoever claims to live in him must walk
as Jesus did.●

7Dear friends, I am not writing you a new
command but an old one, which you have
had since the beginning. This old command
is the message you have heard. 8Yet I am
writing you a new command; its truth is
seen in him and you, because the darkness
is passing and the true light is already shining.

9Anyone who claims to be in the light but
hates his brother is still in the darkness.
10Whoever loves his brother lives in the
light, and there is nothing in him[d] to make
him stumble. 11But whoever hates his
brother is in the darkness and walks
around in the darkness; he does not know
where he is going, because the darkness
has blinded him.●

12I write to you, dear children,
because your sins have been
forgiven on account of his
name.
13I write to you, fathers,
because you have known him
who is from the beginning.
I write to you, young men,
because you have overcome the
evil one.
I write to you, dear children,
because you have known the
Father.
14I write to you, fathers,
because you have known him
who is from the beginning.
I write to you, young men,
because you are strong,
and the word of God lives in you,
and you have overcome the evil
one.●

*Do Not Love the World*

15Do not love the world or anything in
the world. If anyone loves the world, the
love of the Father is not in him. 16For
everything in the world—the cravings of
sinful man, the lust of his eyes and the
boasting of what he has and does—comes
not from the Father but from the world.
17The world and its desires pass away, but
the man who does the will of God lives
forever.●

[d]10 Or *it*

KING JAMES

1.COM-
MAND-
MENTS

3 And hereby we do know that we know
him, if we keep his commandments. 4 He
that saith, I know him, and keepeth not
his commandments, is a liar, and the
truth is not in him. 5 But whoso keepeth
his word, in him verily is the love of God
perfected: hereby know we that we are in
him. 6 He that saith he abideth in him
ought himself also so to walk, even as he
walked.●

KEEP

2.LIGHT

7 Brethren, I write no new commandment unto you, but an old commandment
which ye had from the beginning. The
old commandment is the word which ye
have heard from the beginning. 8 Again,
a new commandment I write unto you,
which thing is true in him and in you:
because the darkness is past, and the true
light now shineth. 9 He that saith he is in
the light, and hateth his brother, is in
darkness even until now. 10 He that
loveth his brother abideth in the light, and
there is none occasion of stumbling in
him. 11 But he that hateth his brother is
in darkness, and walketh in darkness, and
knoweth not whither he goeth, because
that darkness hath blinded his eyes.●

3.PERSONAL
KNOWL-
EDGE

12 I write unto you, little children, because your sins are forgiven you for his
name's sake. 13 I write unto you, fathers,
because ye have known him *that is* from
the beginning. I write unto you, young
men, because ye have overcome the
wicked one. I write unto you, little children, because ye have known the Father.
14 I have written unto you, fathers, because ye have known him *that is* from the
beginning. I have written unto you, young
men, because ye are strong, and the word
of God abideth in you, and ye have overcome the wicked one.●

4.WORLD

15 Love not the world, neither the
things *that are* in the world. If any man
love the world, the love of the Father is
not in him. 16 For all that *is* in the world,
the lust of the flesh, and the lust of the
eyes, and the pride of life, is not of the
Father, but is of the world. 17 And
the world passeth away, and the lust
thereof: but he that doeth the will of God
abideth for ever.●

DO

*2:3-6* Record repeated key words. ______

What is the main point of the paragraph?

*2:7-11* What things are contrasted here?

*2:12-14* List the things written about the readers.

*2:15-17* What key word appears in each
verse?

What is the last truth of the paragraph?

NEW INTERNATIONAL VERSION

What do you learn here about:

ANTICHRIST

LAST TIMES

HOLY SPIRIT

TRUTH

ABIDING IN CHRIST

OTHER

### *Warning Against Antichrists*

18 Dear children, this is the last hour; and
as you have heard that the antichrist is
coming, even now many antichrists have
come. This is how we know it is the last
hour. 19 They went out from us, but they did
not really belong to us. For if they had
belonged to us, they would have remained
with us; but their going showed that none
of them belonged to us.●
20 But you have an anointing from the
Holy One, and all of you know the truth.[a]
21 I do not write to you because you do not
know the truth, but because you do know
it and because no lie comes from the truth.●
22 Who is the liar? It is the man who denies
that Jesus is the Christ. Such a man is the
antichrist—he denies the Father and the
Son. 23 No one who denies the Son has the
Father; whoever acknowledges the Son
has the Father also.●
24 See that what you have heard from the
beginning remains in you. If it does, you
also will remain in the Son and in the Father. 25 And this is what he promised us—
even eternal life.●
26 I am writing these things to you about
those who are trying to lead you astray.
27 As for you, the anointing you received
from him remains in you, and you do not
need anyone to teach you. But as his
anointing teaches you about all things and
as that anointing is real, not counterfeit—
just as it has taught you, remain in him.●

### *Children of God*

28 And now, dear children, continue in
him, so that when he appears we may be
confident and unashamed before him at his
coming.
29 If you know that he is righteous, you
know that everyone who does what is right
has been born of him.●

[a]20 Some manuscripts *and you know all things*

KING JAMES

—enemies of Christ

ANTICHRIST'S COMING

18 Little children, it is the last time: and
as ye have heard that antichrist shall
come, even now are there many antichrists; whereby we know that it is the
last time. 19 They went out from us, but
they were not of us; for if they had been
of us, they would *no doubt* have continued
with us: but *they went out*, that they
might be made manifest that they were
not all of us. ●

—believers

20 But ye have an unction
from the Holy One, and ye know all
things. 21 I have not written unto you
because ye know not the truth, but because ye know it, and that no lie is of the
truth. ●

—enemies

22 Who is a liar but he that denieth
that Jesus is the Christ? He is antichrist,
that denieth the Father and the Son.
23 Whosoever denieth the Son, the same
hath not the Father: [*but*] *he that ac-*
*knowledgeth the Son hath the Father also.* ●

—believers

24 Let that therefore abide in you, which
ye have heard from the beginning. If that
which ye have heard from the beginning
shall remain in you, ye also shall continue
in the Son, and in the Father. 25 And
this is the promise that he hath promised
us, *even* eternal life. ●

—enemies

26 These things have I written unto you
concerning them that seduce you. 27 But
the anointing which ye have received of
him abideth in you, and ye need not that
any man teach you: but as the same anointing teacheth you of all things, and is truth,
and is no lie, and even as it hath taught
you, ye shall abide in him. ●

—believers

CHRIST'S COMING

28 And now, little children, abide in
him; that, when he shall appear, we may
have confidence, and not be ashamed before him at his coming. 29 If ye know
that he is righteous, ye know that every
one that doeth righteousness is born of
him. ●

*2:18-19* What does John write about antichrists?

______________________________

______________________________

______________________________

*2:20-21* What are the first two words of the paragraph?

______________________________

What is written about these readers? ______________________________

______________________________

______________________________

______________________________

*2:22-23* What is revealed about antichrists here?

______________________________

______________________________

______________________________

*2:24-25* Record the truths of the paragraph.

______________________________

______________________________

______________________________

*2:26-27* How does verse 26 introduce the paragraph?

______________________________

______________________________

Then what does verse 27 say? ______________________________

______________________________

______________________________

*2:28-29* Record:

COMMAND: ______________________________

______________________________

______________________________

PROMISES: ______________________________

______________________________

______________________________

______________________________

NEW INTERNATIONAL VERSION

What does this passage teach about:

LOVE OF GOD ______

GOD'S FAMILY ______

SECOND COMING OF CHRIST ______

SIN ______

THE DEVIL ______

Record some practical applications of the passage. ______

3 How great is the love the Father has
lavished on us, that we should be
called children of God! And that is what we
are! The reason the world does not know
us is that it did not know him. [2]Dear
friends, now we are children of God, and
what we will be has not yet been made
known. But we know that when he appears,[b] we shall be like him, for we shall
see him as he is. [3]Everyone who has this
hope in him purifies himself, just as he is
pure.●

[4]Everyone who sins breaks the law; in
fact, sin is lawlessness. [5]But you know that
he appeared so that he might take away our
sins. And in him is no sin. [6]No one who
lives in him keeps on sinning. No one who
continues to sin has either seen him or
known him.

[7]Dear children, do not let anyone lead
you astray. He who does what is right is
righteous, just as he is righteous. [8]He who
does what is sinful is of the devil, because
the devil has been sinning from the beginning. The reason the Son of God appeared
was to destroy the devil's work. [9]No one
who is born of God will continue to sin,
because God's seed remains in him; he
cannot go on sinning, because he has been
born of God. [10]This is how we know who
the children of God are and who the children of the devil are: Anyone who does not
do what is right is not a child of God;
neither is anyone who does not love his
brother.●

[b]2 Or *when it is made known*

KING JAMES

1.PURIFYING HOPE

SONS OF GOD

3 Behold, what manner of love the
Father hath bestowed upon us, that
we should be called the sons of God:
therefore the world knoweth us not, because it knew him not. 2 Beloved, now
are we the sons of God, and it doth not
yet appear what we shall be: but we know
that, when he shall appear, we shall be
like him; for we shall see him as he is.
3 And every man that hath this hope
in him purifieth himself, even as he is
pure.●

2.RIGHTEOUS WALK

4 Whosoever committeth sin transgresseth also the law: for sin is the transgression of the law. 5 And ye know that
he was manifested to take away our sins;
and in him is no sin. 6 Whosoever abideth in him sinneth not: whosoever sinneth
hath not seen him, neither known him.
7 Little children, let no man deceive you:
he that doeth righteousness is righteous,
even as he is righteous. 8 He that committeth sin is of the devil; for the devil
sinneth from the beginning. For this purpose the Son of God was manifested, that
he might destroy the works of the devil.
9 Whosoever is born of God doth not
commit sin; for his seed remaineth in him:
and he cannot sin, because he is born of
God. 10 In this the children of God are
manifest, and the children of the devil:
whosoever doeth not righteousness is not
of God, neither he that loveth not his
brother.●

CHILDREN OF THE DEVIL

The main theme of this segment carries over into the segment that follows (3:11-24).

*3:1-3* Compare "love...upon us" (v.1) with "hope in him" (v.3).

What is written here about "sons of God"?

Relate verse 3 to verse 2.

*3:4-10* Record what John writes about:

CHILDREN OF GOD

CHILDREN OF THE DEVIL

NEW INTERNATIONAL VERSION

What is taught here about:

CHRISTIANS LOVING ONE ANOTHER

GOD'S LOVE

OBEDIENCE

FAITH

ASSURANCE

HOLY SPIRIT

Write some spiritual applications of the passage.

*Love One Another*

11This is the message you heard from the
beginning: We should love one another.
12Do not be like Cain, who belonged to the
evil one and murdered his brother. And
why did he murder him? Because his own
actions were evil and his brother's were
righteous. 13Do not be surprised, my brothers, if the world hates you. 14We know that
we have passed from death to life, because
we love our brothers. Anyone who does
not love remains in death. 15Anyone who
hates his brother is a murderer, and you
know that no murderer has eternal life in
him.
16This is how we know what love is:
Jesus Christ laid down his life for us. And
we ought to lay down our lives for our
brothers. 17If anyone has material possessions and sees his brother in need but has
no pity on him, how can the love of God be
in him? 18Dear children, let us not love with
words or tongue but with actions and in
truth. 19This then is how we know that we
belong to the truth, and how we set our
hearts at rest in his presence 20whenever
our hearts condemn us. For God is greater
than our hearts, and he knows everything.
21Dear friends, if our hearts do not condemn us, we have confidence before God
22and receive from him anything we ask,
because we obey his commands and do
what pleases him. 23And this is his command: to believe in the name of his Son,
Jesus Christ, and to love one another as he
commanded us. 24Those who obey his
commands live in him, and he in them. And
this is how we know that he lives in us: We
know it by the Spirit he gave us.

KING JAMES

1. LOVE

11 For this is the message that ye heard
from the beginning, that we should love
one another. 12 Not as Cain, *who* was of
that wicked one, and slew his brother.
And wherefore slew he him? Because his
own works were evil, and his brother's
righteous. 13 Marvel not, my brethren, if
the world hate you. 14 We know that we
have passed from death unto life, because we love the brethren. He that loveth
not *his* brother abideth in death. 15 Whosoever hateth his brother is a murderer:
and ye know that no murderer hath eternal life abiding in him. 16 Hereby perceive we the love *of God*, because he laid
down his life for us: and we ought to lay
down *our* lives for the brethren. 17 But
whoso hath this world's good, and seeth
his brother have need, and shutteth up his
bowels *of compassion* from him, how
dwelleth the love of God in him? 18 My
little children, let us not love in word,
neither in tongue; but in deed and in
truth.●

2. ASSURANCE

19 And hereby we know that we are of
the truth, and shall assure our hearts before him. 20 For if our heart condemn us,
God is greater than our heart, and knoweth all things. 21 Beloved, if our heart
condemn us not, *then* have we confidence
toward God. 22 And whatsoever we ask,
we receive of him, because we keep his
commandments, and do those things that
are pleasing in his sight. 23 And this is
his commandment, That we should believe on the name of his Son Jesus Christ,
and love one another, as he gave us commandment. 24 And he that keepeth his
commandments dwelleth in him, and he
in him. And hereby we know that he
abideth in us, by the Spirit which he hath
given us.●

LOVE

KNOW

This segment continues the main theme of the preceding segment.

*3:11-18* What is the appeal of the opening verse?

Underline the word "love" whenever it appears in the text.

Record what John writes about these two aspects of love of the brethren:

DESCRIPTIONS

MOTIVES

*3:19-24* A key word is "know." Underline the word in the places where it appears.
Record other key repeated words in the paragraph.

NEW INTERNATIONAL VERSION

Write a list of truths and appeals about love which this passage teaches.

TRUTHS ABOUT LOVE

APPEALS TO LOVE

*Test the Spirits*

4 Dear friends, do not believe every
spirit, but test the spirits to see
whether they are from God, because many
false prophets have gone out into the
world. [2]This is how you can recognize the
Spirit of God: Every spirit that acknowledges that Jesus Christ has come in the
flesh is from God, [3]but every spirit that
does not acknowledge Jesus is not from
God. This is the spirit of the antichrist,
which you have heard is coming and even
now is already in the world.
[4]You, dear children, are from God and
have overcome them, because the one who
is in you is greater than the one who is in
the world. [5]They are from the world and
therefore speak from the viewpoint of the
world, and the world listens to them. [6]We
are from God, and whoever knows God
listens to us; but whoever is not from God
does not listen to us. This is how we recognize the Spirit[a] of truth and the spirit of
falsehood.●

*God's Love and Ours*

[7]Dear friends, let us love one another,
for love comes from God. Everyone who
loves has been born of God and knows
God. [8]Whoever does not love does not
know God, because God is love. [9]This is
how God showed his love among us: He
sent his one and only Son[b] into the world
that we might live through him. [10]This is
love: not that we loved God, but that he
loved us and sent his Son as an atoning
sacrifice for[c] our sins. [11]Dear friends, since
God so loved us, we also ought to love one
another. [12]No one has ever seen God; but
if we love each other, God lives in us and
his love is made complete in us.●
[13]We know that we live in him and he in
us, because he has given us of his Spirit.
[14]And we have seen and testify that the
Father has sent his Son to be the Savior of
the world. [15]If anyone acknowledges that
Jesus is the Son of God, God lives in him
and he in God. [16]And so we know and rely
on the love God has for us.●
God is love. Whoever lives in love lives
in God, and God in him. [17]Love is made
complete among us so that we will have
confidence on the day of judgment, because in this world we are like him. [18]There
is no fear in love. But perfect love drives
out fear, because fear has to do with punishment. The man who fears is not made
perfect in love.
[19]We love because he first loved us. [20]If
anyone says, "I love God," yet hates his
brother, he is a liar. For anyone who does
not love his brother, whom he has seen,
cannot love God, whom he has not seen.
[21]And he has given us this command: Whoever loves God must also love his brother.●

[a]6 Or *spirit* [b]9 Or *his only begotten Son*
[c]10 Or *as the one who would turn aside his wrath, taking away*

KING JAMES

1.TRUTH IN DOCTRINE

FALSEHOOD

4 Beloved, believe not every spirit, but
try the spirits whether they are of
God: because many false prophets are
gone out into the world. 2 Hereby know
ye the Spirit of God: Every spirit that
confesseth that Jesus Christ is come in the
flesh is of God: 3 and every spirit that
confesseth not that Jesus Christ is come
in the flesh is not of God: and this is that
*spirit* of antichrist, whereof ye have heard
that it should come; and even now already is it in the world. 4 Ye are of God,
little children, and have overcome them:
because greater is he that is in you, than
he that is in the world. 5 They are of the
world: therefore speak they of the world,
and the world heareth them. 6 We are of
God: he that knoweth God heareth us;
he that is not of God heareth not us.
Hereby know we the spirit of truth, and
the spirit of error.●

2.LOVE IN ACTION

7 Beloved, let us love one another: for
love is of God; and every one that loveth
is born of God, and knoweth God. 8 He
that loveth not, knoweth not God; for
God is love. 9 In this was manifested the
love of God toward us, because that God
sent his only begotten Son into the world,
that we might live through him. 10 Herein
is love, not that we loved God, but that he
loved us, and sent his Son *to be* the propitiation for our sins. 11 Beloved, if God
so loved us, we ought also to love one
another. 12 No man hath seen God at any
time. If we love one another, God dwelleth in us, and his love is perfected in us.●
13 Hereby know we that we dwell in
him, and he in us, because he hath given
us of his Spirit. 14 And we have seen and
do testify that the Father sent the Son *to*
*be* the Saviour of the world. 15 Whosoever shall confess that Jesus is the Son of
God, God dwelleth in him, and he in God.
16 And we have known and believed the
love that God hath to us. God is love;
and he that dwelleth in love dwelleth in
God, and God in him.● 17 Herein is our
love made perfect, that we may have boldness in the day of judgment: because as he
is, so are we in this world. 18 There is no
fear in love; but perfect love casteth out
fear: because fear hath torment. He
that feareth is not made perfect in love.
19 We love him, because he first loved us.
20 If a man say, I love God, and hateth
his brother, he is a liar: for he that loveth
not his brother whom he hath seen, how
can he love God whom he hath not seen?
21 And this commandment have we from
him, That he who loveth God love his
brother also.●

LOVE

*4:1-6* What are the two contrasting spirits (v.6)?

Underline the word "spirit" in the text wherever it appears.
List the contrasts of the paragraph.

*4:7-21* Underline every appearance of the word "love" in the three paragraphs.
Record a main theme about love which identifies each paragraph.

What reference does John make to:

GOD

JESUS

HOLY SPIRIT

NEW INTERNATIONAL VERSION

What does this passage teach about:

LOVE

OBEDIENCE

FAITH

DEATH OF CHRIST

ASSURANCE OF SALVATION

ETERNAL LIFE

OTHER

*Faith in the Son of God*

5 Everyone who believes that Jesus is
the Christ is born of God, and everyone who loves the father loves his child as
well. 2This is how we know that we love
the children of God: by loving God and
carrying out his commands. 3This is love
for God: to obey his commands. And his
commands are not burdensome, ● 4for
everyone born of God overcomes the
world. This is the victory that has overcome the world, even our faith. 5Who is it
that overcomes the world? Only he who
believes that Jesus is the Son of God. ●
6This is the one who came by water and
blood—Jesus Christ. He did not come by
water only, but by water and blood. And it
is the Spirit who testifies, because the
Spirit is the truth. 7For there are three that
testify: 8the[d] Spirit, the water and the
blood; and the three are in agreement. ● 9We
accept man's testimony, but God's testimony is greater because it is the testimony
of God, which he has given about his Son.
10Anyone who believes in the Son of God
has this testimony in his heart. Anyone
who does not believe God has made him
out to be a liar, because he has not believed
the testimony God has given about his Son.
11And this is the testimony: God has given
us eternal life, and this life is in his Son.
12He who has the Son has life; he who does
not have the Son of God does not have life. ●

[d]7,8 Late manuscripts of the Vulgate *testify in heaven: the Father, the Word and the Holy Spirit, and these three are one. 8And there are three that testify on earth: the*

KING JAMES

1.LOVE

5 Whosoever believeth that Jesus is the
Christ is born of God: and every one
that loveth him that begat loveth him also
that is begotten of him. 2 By this we
know that we love the children of God,
when we love God, and keep his commandments. 3 For this is the love of God,
that we keep his commandments: and
his commandments are not grievous.●

2.VICTORY

4 For whatsoever is born of God overcometh the world: and this is the victory
that overcometh the world, *even* our faith.
5 Who is he that overcometh the world,
but he that believeth that Jesus is the Son
of God?●

3.BLOOD

6 This is he that came by water and
blood, *even* Jesus Christ; not by water
only, but by water and blood. And it is
the Spirit that beareth witness, because
the Spirit is truth. 7 For there are three
that bear record in heaven, the Father, the
Word, and the Holy Ghost: and these
three are one. 8 And there are three that
bear witness in earth, the spirit, and the
water, and the blood: and these three

4.WITNESS

agree in one.● 9 If we receive the witness
of men, the witness of God is greater: for
this is the witness of God which he hath
testified of his Son. 10 He that believeth
on the Son of God hath the witness in
himself: he that believeth not God hath
made him a liar; because he believeth not
the record that God gave of his Son.
11 And this is the record, that God hath
given to us eternal life, and this life is in
his Son. 12 He that hath the Son hath
life; *and* he that hath not the Son of God
hath not life.●

CHRIST

SON OF GOD

*5:1-3* How is a child of God identified here?

*5:4-5* What three statements are made concerning overcoming the world?

*5:6-8* What fact of Christ's ministry does "blood" represent?

What does "water" signify, in Jesus' ministry?

*5:9-12* What witnesses are compared here?

What witness has God given to each believer?

NEW INTERNATIONAL VERSION

What do you learn here about:

ETERNAL LIFE

ASSURANCE

PRAYER

SIN

SON OF GOD

List spiritual applications of the passage.

*Concluding Remarks*

[13]I write these things to you who believe
in the name of the Son of God so that you
may know that you have eternal life. [14]This
is the assurance we have in approaching
God: that if we ask anything according to
his will, he hears us. [15]And if we know that
he hears us—whatever we ask—we know
that we have what we asked of him.
[16]If anyone sees his brother commit a sin
that does not lead to death, he should pray
and God will give him life. I refer to those
whose sin does not lead to death. There is
a sin that leads to death. I am not saying
that he should pray about that. [17]All
wrongdoing is sin, and there is sin that does
not lead to death.
[18]We know that anyone born of God
does not continue to sin; the one who was
born of God keeps him safe, and the evil
one does not touch him. [19]We know that
we are children of God, and that the whole
world is under the control of the evil one.
[20]We know also that the Son of God has
come and has given us understanding, so
that we may know him who is true. And we
are in him who is true—even in his Son
Jesus Christ. He is the true God and eternal
life.
[21]Dear children, keep yourselves from
idols.

KING JAMES

1. ASSURANCE IN PRAYER

**13 These things have I written unto you
that believe on the name of the Son of
God; that ye may know that ye have
eternal life, and that ye may believe on the
name of the Son of God. ● 14 And this is
the confidence that we have in him, that,
if we ask any thing according to his will,
he heareth us: 15 and if we know that he
hear us, whatsoever we ask, we know that
we have the petitions that we desired of
him. 16 If any man see his brother sin a
sin *which is* not unto death, he shall ask,
and he shall give him life for them that sin
not unto death. There is a sin unto death:
I do not say that he shall pray for it. 17 All
unrighteousness is sin: and there is a sin
not unto death.●**

SON OF GOD

2. KNOWLEDGE OF TRUTH

**18 We know that whosoever is born of
God sinneth not; but he that is begotten
of God keepeth himself, and that wicked
one toucheth him not.
19 *And* we know that we are of God,
and the whole world lieth in wickedness.
20 And we know that the Son of God is
come, and hath given us an understanding,
that we may know him that is true;
and we are in him that is true, *even* in his
Son Jesus Christ. This is the true God,
and eternal life. 21 Little children, keep
yourselves from idols. Amen.●**

IDOLS

*5:13* What were John's purposes in writing the letter?

*5:14-17* Record the different references to prayer.

*5:18-21* Record the different words and phrases which are the object of the phrase "we know."

# 2 JOHN

## AUTHORSHIP

The writer identifies himself only as "the elder" (1:1). Internal evidence and tradition point to the apostle John as the author.

## DATE

This letter was written around A.D. 90 from the city of Ephesus.

## ADDRESSEE

The letter was written "to the chosen lady and her children" (1:1). If the phrase "chosen lady" is taken figuratively, it probably refers to a local church or the church as a whole; and "her children" refers to members of the church. If the phrase is literal designation, a particular lady is meant, who was a friend of John, mother of children, and well known in her community.

## PURPOSE

John wrote this letter 1) to encourage the readers to walk according to the commandments of God; and 2) to caution them about false teachers. A theme is truth and the Christian's walk.

## 2 JOHN: Truth and the Christian

# 2 JOHN

NEW INTERNATIONAL VERSION

Write a list of practical applications of this letter to present-day living.

[1]The elder,

To the chosen lady and her children,
whom I love in the truth—and not I only,
but also all who know the truth— [2]because
of the truth, which lives in us and will be
with us forever:

[3]Grace, mercy and peace from God the
Father and from Jesus Christ, the Father's
Son, will be with us in truth and love.●

[4]It has given me great joy to find some of
your children walking in the truth, just as
the Father commanded us. [5]And now, dear
lady, I am not writing you a new command
but one we have had from the beginning. I
ask that we love one another. [6]And this is
love: that we walk in obedience to his commands. As you have heard from the beginning, his command is that you walk in love.●
[7]Many deceivers, who do not acknowledge Jesus Christ as coming in the flesh,
have gone out into the world. Any such
person is the deceiver and the antichrist.
[8]Watch out that you do not lose what you
have worked for, but that you may be rewarded fully. [9]Anyone who runs ahead and
does not continue in the teaching of Christ
does not have God; whoever continues in
the teaching has both the Father and the
Son. [10]If anyone comes to you and does not
bring this teaching, do not take him into
your house or welcome him. [11]Anyone
who welcomes him shares in his wicked
work.●
[12]I have much to write to you, but I do
not want to use paper and ink. Instead, I
hope to visit you and talk with you face to
face, so that our joy may be complete.

[13]The children of your chosen sister send
their greetings.●

KING JAMES

# 2 JOHN

1. LOVING IN TRUTH

LOVE

THE elder unto the elect lady and her
children, whom I love in the truth;
and not I only, but also all they that have
known the truth; 2 for the truth's sake,
which dwelleth in us, and shall be with us
for ever.
3 Grace be with you, mercy, *and* peace,
from God the Father, and from the Lord
Jesus Christ, the Son of the Father, in
truth and love.●

2. WALKING IN TRUTH

4 I rejoiced greatly that I found of thy
children walking in truth, as we have received a commandment from the Father.
5 And now I beseech thee, lady, not as
though I wrote a new commandment unto
thee, but that which we had from the beginning, that we love one another. 6 And
this is love, that we walk after his commandments. This is the commandment,
That, as ye have heard from the beginning,
ye should walk in it.●

3. ABIDING IN TRUTH

7 For many deceiv-
ers are entered into the world, who confess not that Jesus Christ is come in the
flesh. This is a deceiver and an antichrist.
8 Look to yourselves, that we lose not
those things which we have wrought, but
that we receive a full reward. 9 Whosoever transgresseth, and abideth not in the
doctrine of Christ, hath not God. He that
abideth in the doctrine of Christ, he hath
both the Father and the Son. 10 If there
come any unto you, and bring not this
doctrine, receive him not into *your* house,
neither bid him God-speed: 11 for he that
biddeth him God-speed is partaker of his
evil deeds.●

—final greetings

12 Having many things to write unto
you, I would not *write* with paper and ink:
but I trust to come unto you, and speak
face to face, that our joy may be full.
13 The children of thy elect sister greet
thee. Amen.●

JOY

*1-3* Record the different phrases which include the word "truth."

*4-6* What is a key repeated word?

What is the central exhortation?

*7-11* Does the word "truth" appear in this paragraph?

Does a similar word appear here?

What does John write about *abiding*?

*12-13* What is the key "feeling" word?

# 3 JOHN

## AUTHORSHIP

John the apostle wrote this letter.

## DATE

The letter was written around A.D. 90.

## ADDRESSEE

Third John is addressed to a man—Gaius (1:1), whereas 2 John is addressed to a woman. There is no way to identify who this Gaius was. He was a personal friend of John, and may have been an active lay member of a local church.

## OCCASION

An immediate occasion for writing this letter was Diotrephes' rejection of messengers of the gospel whom John had sent to the church, of which Gaius and Diotrephes were members (vv.9-10).

## PURPOSE

John wrote this letter to commend Gaius and Demetrius for their Christian testimony and walk, and to reprove the unchristian behavior of Diotrephes. A practical theme of the letter is spiritual health and prosperity.

## 3 JOHN: Spiritual Health and Prosperity

| | |
|---|---|
| Salutation | v.1 |
| CHRISTIAN'S RELATION TO TRUTH | 2-4 |
| CHRISTIAN'S RELATION | 5-8 |
| TO OTHER FELLOW WORKERS | 9-12 |
| CHRISTIAN'S RELATION | |
| TO GOOD AND EVIL | |
| Greetings | 13-14 |

# 3 JOHN

NEW INTERNATIONAL VERSION

What does this short epistle teach about:

TRUTH

JOY

HOSPITALITY

EVIL

Write a list of spiritual applications of the text.

1The elder,

To my dear friend Gaius, whom I love in
the truth.●

2Dear friend, I pray that you may enjoy
good health and that all may go well with
you, even as your soul is getting along well.
3It gave me great joy to have some brothers
come and tell about your faithfulness to the
truth and how you continue to walk in the
truth. 4I have no greater joy than to hear
that my children are walking in the truth.●
5Dear friend, you are faithful in what you
are doing for the brothers, even though
they are strangers to you. 6They have told
the church about your love. You will do
well to send them on their way in a manner
worthy of God. 7It was for the sake of the
Name that they went out, receiving no help
from the pagans. 8We ought therefore to
show hospitality to such men so that we
may work together for the truth.●
9I wrote to the church, but Diotrephes,
who loves to be first, will have nothing to
do with us. 10So if I come, I will call attention to what he is doing, gossiping maliciously about us. Not satisfied with that,
he refuses to welcome the brothers. He
also stops those who want to do so and
puts them out of the church.●
11Dear friend, do not imitate what is evil
but what is good. Anyone who does what
is good is from God. Anyone who does
what is evil has not seen God. 12Demetrius
is well spoken of by everyone—and even
by the truth itself. We also speak well of
him, and you know that our testimony is
true.●
13I have much to write you, but I do not
want to do so with pen and ink. 14I hope to
see you soon, and we will talk face to face.

Peace to you. The friends here send their greetings. Greet the friends there by name.●

KING JAMES

# 3 JOHN

1.WALK

PROS-PERITY

THE elder unto the well-beloved Gai'us,
whom I love in the truth.●
2 Beloved, I wish above all things that
thou mayest prosper and be in health,
even as thy soul prospereth. 3 For I rejoiced greatly, when the brethren came
and testified of the truth that is in thee,
even as thou walkest in the truth. 4 I have
no greater joy than to hear that my children walk in truth.●

2.FEL-LOWSHIP

5 Beloved, thou doest faithfully whatsoever thou doest to the brethren, and to
strangers; 6 which have borne witness of
thy charity before the church: whom if
thou bring forward on their journey after
a godly sort, thou shalt do well: 7 because
that for his name's sake they went forth,
taking nothing of the Gentiles. 8 We
therefore ought to receive such, that we
might be fellow helpers to the truth.●

3.GOD-LINESS

9 I wrote unto the church: but Diot're-
phes, who loveth to have the preeminence
among them, receiveth us not. 10 Wherefore, if I come, I will remember his deeds
which he doeth, prating against us with
malicious words: and not content therewith, neither doth he himself receive
the brethren, and forbiddeth them that
would, and casteth *them* out of the
church.●
11 Beloved, follow not that which is
evil, but that which is good. He that doeth
good is of God: but he that doeth evil
hath not seen God. 12 Deme'tri-us
hath good report of all *men*, and of
the truth itself: yea, and we *also* bear
record; and ye know that our record is
true.

—concluding words

13 I had many things to write, but I
will not with ink and pen write unto
thee: 14 but I trust I shall shortly
see thee, and we shall speak face to
face.●
Peace *be* to thee. *Our* friends salute
thee. Greet the friends by name.●

PEACE

*1-4* What do you learn here about:

GAIUS ______

______

______

JOHN ______

______

______

*5-8* Record key words and phrases.

______

______

______

______

What is the main point of the paragraph?

______

______

______

______

______

*9-12* What does John write here about:

EVIL ______

______

______

______

GOOD ______

______

______

______

______

*13-14* Record the strong words of these verses.

______

______

______

______

______

______

# JUDE

## AUTHORSHIP

The author is Jude, brother of James. This James was the half brother of Jesus, which relates Jude to Jesus in the same way. From verse 17 we gather that Jude did not class himself as an apostle.

## DATE

The letter was probably written around A.D. 67-68, shortly before the fall of Jerusalem (A.D. 70).

## ADDRESSEE

The salutation of 1:1 is very general. The readers may have been members of Jewish churches of Palestine or Asia Minor, where Jude was probably ministering at this time.

## OCCASION AND PURPOSE

The leaven of such evils as gross immorality, antinomianism, rejection of the lordship of Christ, and mockery, was beginning to spread in the churches through the influences of "certain persons" (v.4). This stirred Jude to write this exposure and indictment of the false teachers. Jude also used the letter to exhort the faithful believers to keep building their lives on their "most holy faith" (v.20). A theme of the book is that of contending earnestly for the faith.

## JUDE: Keeping Oneself in the Love of God

| | |
|---|---|
| Salutation | 1-2 |
| WARNINGS ABOUT UNGODLY MEN | 3-16 |
| EXHORTATIONS TO BELIEVERS | 17-23 |
| Doxology | 24-25 |

# JUDE

NEW INTERNATIONAL VERSION

Write lists of what this passage teaches about sin and its judgment.

SIN

JUDGMENT OF SIN

1 Jude, a servant of Jesus Christ and a
brother of James,

To those who have been called, who are
loved by God the Father and kept by[a]
Jesus Christ:

2 Mercy, peace and love be yours in
abundance.●

*The Sin and Doom of Godless Men*

3 Dear friends, although I was very eager
to write to you about the salvation we
share, I felt I had to write and urge you to
contend for the faith that was once for all
entrusted to the saints. 4 For certain men
whose condemnation was written about[b]
long ago have secretly slipped in among
you. They are godless men, who change
the grace of our God into a license for immorality and deny Jesus Christ our only
Sovereign and Lord.●
5 Though you already know all this, I
want to remind you that the Lord[c] delivered his people out of Egypt, but later
destroyed those who did not believe. 6 And
the angels who did not keep their positions
of authority but abandoned their own
home—these he has kept in darkness,
bound with everlasting chains for judgment
on the great Day. 7 In a similar way, Sodom
and Gomorrah and the surrounding towns
gave themselves up to sexual immorality
and perversion. They serve as an example
of those who suffer the punishment of eternal fire.●
8 In the very same way, these dreamers
pollute their own bodies, reject authority
and slander celestial beings. 9 But even the
archangel Michael, when he was disputing
with the devil about the body of Moses, did
not dare to bring a slanderous accusation
against him, but said, "The Lord rebuke
you!" 10 Yet these men speak abusively
against whatever they do not understand;
and what things they do understand by instinct, like unreasoning animals—these are
the very things that destroy them.
11 Woe to them! They have taken the way
of Cain; they have rushed for profit into
Balaam's error; they have been destroyed
in Korah's rebellion.
12 These men are blemishes at your love
feasts, eating with you without the slight-
est qualm—shepherds who feed only themselves. They are clouds without rain,
blown along by the wind; autumn trees,
without fruit and uprooted—twice dead.
13 They are wild waves of the sea, foaming
up their shame; wandering stars, for whom
blackest darkness has been reserved forever.●
14 Enoch, the seventh from Adam, prophesied about these men: "See, the Lord is
coming with thousands upon thousands of
his holy ones 15 to judge everyone, and to
convict all the ungodly of all the ungodly
acts they have done in the ungodly way,
and of all the harsh words ungodly sinners
have spoken against him." 16 These men
are grumblers and faultfinders; they follow
their own evil desires; they boast about
themselves and flatter others for their own
advantage.●

[a]*1* Or *for;* or *in*
[b]*4* Or *men who were marked out for condemnation*
[c]*5* Some early manuscripts *Jesus*

KING JAMES

# JUDE

—salutation

SAINTS

JUDE, the servant of Jesus Christ, and
brother of James,
To them that are sanctified by God the
Father, and preserved in Jesus Christ, *and*
called:
2 Mercy unto you, and peace, and love,
be multiplied.●

1.EXHORTATION

3 Beloved, when I gave all diligence to
write unto you of the common salvation,
it was needful for me to write unto you,
and exhort *you* that ye should earnestly
contend for the faith which was once delivered unto the saints. 4 For there are
certain men crept in unawares, who were
before of old ordained to this condemnation, ungodly men, turning the grace of
our God into lasciviousness, and denying
the only Lord God, and our Lord Jesus
Christ.●

2.WARNING

—past judgment

5 I will therefore put you in remembrance, though ye once knew this, how
that the Lord, having saved the people out
of the land of Egypt, afterward destroyed
them that believed not. 6 And the angels
which kept not their first estate, but left
their own habitation, he hath reserved in
everlasting chains under darkness unto
the judgment of the great day. 7 Even as
Sodom and Gomor'rah, and the cities
about them in like manner, giving themselves over to fornication, and going after
strange flesh, are set forth for an example, suffering the vengeance of eternal
fire. ●

—description

8 Likewise also these *filthy* dreamers
defile the flesh, despise dominion, and
speak evil of dignities. 9 Yet Michael the
archangel, when contending with the
devil he disputed about the body of
Moses, durst not bring against him a
railing accusation, but said, The Lord
rebuke thee. 10 But these speak evil of
those things which they know not: but
what they know naturally, as brute beasts,
in those things they corrupt themselves.
11 Woe unto them! for they have gone in
the way of Cain, and ran greedily after
the error of Ba'laam for reward, and
perished in the gainsaying of Korah.
12 These are spots in your feasts of charity, when they feast with you, feeding
themselves without fear: clouds *they are*
without water, carried about of winds;
trees whose fruit withereth, without fruit,
twice dead, plucked up by the roots;
13 raging waves of the sea, foaming out
their own shame; wandering stars, to
whom is reserved the blackness of darkness for ever.●

—future judgment

14 And Enoch also, the seventh from
Adam, prophesied of these, saying, Behold, the Lord cometh with ten thousands
of his saints, 15 to execute judgment upon
all, and to convince all that are ungodly
among them of all their ungodly deeds
which they have ungodly committed, and
of all their hard *speeches* which ungodly
sinners have spoken against him. 16 These
are murmurers, complainers, walking
after their own lusts; and their mouth
speaketh great swelling *words*, having
men's persons in admiration because of
advantage.●

UNGODLY MEN

*1-2* How are these described:

JUDE ______________________

______________________

______________________

READERS ______________________

______________________

______________________

*3-4* What is the key exhortation of the paragraph?

______________________

______________________

What reason is given for contending for the faith?

______________________

______________________

*5-7* Does the word "remember" express the purpose of this paragraph?

______________________

What three historical situations does Jude cite?

v.5 ______________________

______________________

v.6 ______________________

______________________

v.7 ______________________

______________________

*8-13* Record some of the descriptions of evil men:

______________________

______________________

______________________

______________________

*14-16* What is the main teaching of verses 14-15?

______________________

______________________

NEW INTERNATIONAL VERSION

What does this passage teach about:

EVIL MEN

CHRISTIAN GROWTH

ATTRIBUTES AND MINISTRIES OF GOD

Write a list of spiritual applications of the passage.

*A Call to Persevere*

17But, dear friends, remember what the
apostles of our Lord Jesus Christ foretold.
18They said to you, "In the last times there
will be scoffers who will follow their own
ungodly desires." 19These are the men who
divide you, who follow mere natural in-
stincts and do not have the Spirit.
20But you, dear friends, build yourselves
up in your most holy faith and pray in the
Holy Spirit. 21Keep yourselves in God's
love as you wait for the mercy of our Lord
Jesus Christ to bring you to eternal life.
22Be merciful to those who doubt; 23snatch
others from the fire and save them; to
others show mercy, mixed with
fear — hating even the clothing stained by
corrupted flesh.●

*Doxology*

24To him who is able to keep you from
falling and to present you before his glorious presence without fault and with great
joy— 25to the only God our Savior be glory, majesty, power and authority, through
Jesus Christ our Lord, before all ages, now
and forevermore! Amen.●

KING JAMES

1. EXHORTATION

**17 But, beloved, remember ye the words
which were spoken before of the apostles
of our Lord Jesus Christ; 18 how that
they told you there should be mockers in
the last time, who should walk after their
own ungodly lusts. 19 These be they who
separate themselves, sensual, having not
the Spirit. 20 But ye, beloved, building
up yourselves on your most holy faith,
praying in the Holy Ghost, 21 keep yourselves in the love of God, looking for the
mercy of our Lord Jesus Christ unto eternal life. 22 And of some have compassion,
making a difference: 23 and others save
with fear, pulling *them* out of the fire;
hating even the garment spotted by the
flesh.●**

2. DOXOLOGY

**24 Now unto him that is able to keep
you from falling, and to present *you* faultless before the presence of his glory with
exceeding joy, 25 to the only wise God
our Saviour, *be* glory and majesty,
dominion and power, both now and ever.
Amen.**

EVIL

FAULTLESS

*17-23* How do the words "But...ye" introduce this segment?

Record the commands of the paragraph:

v.17

v.21

v.22

v.23

Note the various "ing" words, qualifying the commands.
Record these:

v.20

v.20

v.21

v.22

v.23

v.23

*24-25* What ministries of the Lord to the believer are mentioned in verse 24?

# REVELATION

## AUTHORSHIP

Four times in the text the author is identified as John (1:1,4,9; 22:8). This is the apostle John, author of a Gospel and the three Epistles.

## DATE

John wrote this book of visions around A.D. 96, at the end of the reign of the Roman emperor Domitian (A.D. 81-96). He was an exile on the island of Patmos at the time.

## PURPOSES AND THEME

God inspired John to record the visions as 1) a revelation of the person Jesus Christ; and 2) a revelation of instruction of prophecy, doctrine and spiritual application. Most of the prophecies are about events of end times, culminating in Christ's thousand-year reign (20:1-6) and in eternal heaven (chaps. 21-22). The book encourages believers to persevere under the stress of persecution and to beware the treacherous pitfalls of apostasy. Two chapters (2-3) are especially directed to the spiritual condition of seven local churches of John's time. The opening words of the book identify its theme: the revelation of Jesus Christ.

## REVELATION

| | |
|---|---|
| Introduction | 1:1-8 |
| VISIONS, MESSAGES AND SONGS | 1:9-5:14 |
| John's Vision of Christ | 1:9-20 |
| Letters to the Seven Churches | 2:1-3:22 |
| Visions of God and the Lamb | 4:1-5:14 |
| JUDGMENTS | 6:1-20:15 |
| Seals of Judgment | 6:1-7:17 |
| Trumpets of Judgment | 8:1-9:21 |
| Little Book, Two Witnesses and Seventh Trumpet | 10:1-11:19 |
| The Woman, Dragon and Two Beasts | 12:1-14:20 |
| Bowls of Judgment | 15:1-16:21 |
| Fall of Babylon | 17:1-18:24 |
| Final Judgment | 19:1-20:15 |
| GLORY | 21:1-22:20 |
| Eternal Home of the Saints | 21:1-22:5 |
| "I am Coming Soon" | 22:6-20 |
| Benediction | 22:21 |

# REVELATION

NEW INTERNATIONAL VERSION

What does this opening segment of the book of Revelation reveal about:

THE PERSON OF JESUS ____________________

THE WORKS OF JESUS ____________________

THE PERSON AND WORKS OF GOD THE FATHER ____________________

THE WORD OF GOD ____________________

PROPHECY ____________________

END TIMES ____________________

OTHER ____________________

*Prologue*

1 The revelation of Jesus Christ, which
God gave him to show his servants
what must soon take place. He made it
known by sending his angel to his servant
John, 2who testifies to everything he saw—
that is, the word of God and the testimony
of Jesus Christ. 3Blessed is the one who
reads the words of this prophecy, and
blessed are those who hear it and take to
heart what is written in it, because the time
is near.●

*Greetings and Doxology*

4John,

To the seven churches in the province of Asia:

Grace and peace to you from him who is, and who was, and who is to come, and from the seven spirits[a] before his throne,
5and from Jesus Christ, who is the faithful witness, the firstborn from the dead, and the ruler of the kings of the earth.●

To him who loves us and has freed us from our sins by his blood,
6and has made us to be a kingdom and priests to serve his God and Father—to him be glory and power for ever and ever! Amen.●

7Look, he is coming with the clouds,
and every eye will see him,
even those who pierced him;
and all the peoples of the earth
will mourn because of him.
So shall it be! Amen.●

8"I am the Alpha and the Omega," says the Lord God, "who is, and who was, and who is to come, the Almighty."●

[a]4 Or *the sevenfold Spirit*

KING JAMES

# REVELATION

1. INTRODUCTION

1 The Revelation of Jesus Christ, which God gave unto him, to show unto his servants things which must shortly come to pass; and he sent and signified *it* by his angel unto his servant John: 2 who bare record of the word of God, and of the testimony of Jesus Christ, and of all things that he saw. 3 Blessed *is* he that readeth, and they that hear the words of this prophecy, and keep those things which are written therein: for the time *is* at hand. ●

THE CHRIST

2. BENEDICTION

4 John to the seven churches which are in Asia:

Grace *be* unto you, and peace, from him which is, and which was, and which is to come; and from the seven Spirits which are before his throne; 5 and from Jesus Christ, *who is* the faithful witness, *and* the first-begotten of the dead, and the prince of the kings of the earth. ●

3. DOXOLOGY

Unto him that loved us, and washed us from our sins in his own blood, 6 and hath made us kings and priests unto God and his Father; to him *be* glory and dominion for ever and ever. Amen. ●

4. PROPHECY

7 Behold, he cometh with clouds; and every eye shall see him, and they *also* which pierced him: and all kindreds of the earth shall wail because of him. Even so, Amen. ●

5. TESTIMONY

8 I am Alpha and Ome'ga, the beginning and the ending, saith the Lord, which is, and which was, and which is to come, the Almighty. ●

THE ALMIGHTY

*1:1-3* About whom is the revelation?

______________________

Where did this revelation originate?

______________________

List the ones to whom it was given, in the correct order.

______________________

______________________

What is the time reference of verse 3?

______________________

______________________

*1:4-5a* Record concerning the benediction:

THE WHAT ______________________

______________________

TO WHOM ______________________

______________________

FROM WHOM ______________________

______________________

*1:5b-6* Record the works of Christ: ______________________

______________________

______________________

______________________

______________________

______________________

*1:7* What is the tone here? ______________________

______________________

______________________

*1:8* Relate this verse to verse 7. ______________________

______________________

______________________

______________________

______________________

______________________

______________________

______________________

NEW INTERNATIONAL VERSION

What is taught here about:

TRIBULATION

JESUS CHRIST

LOCAL CHURCHES

ETERNAL LIFE

OTHER

*One Like a Son of Man*

9I, John, your brother and companion in
the suffering and kingdom and patient endurance that are ours in Jesus, was on the
island of Patmos because of the word of
God and the testimony of Jesus. 10On the
Lord's Day I was in the Spirit, and I heard
behind me a loud voice like a trumpet,
11which said: "Write on a scroll what you
see and send it to the seven churches: to
Ephesus, Smyrna, Pergamum, Thyatira,
Sardis, Philadelphia and Laodicea."●

12I turned around to see the voice that
was speaking to me. And when I turned I
saw seven golden lampstands, 13and
among the lampstands was someone "like
a son of man,"[a] dressed in a robe reaching
down to his feet and with a golden sash
around his chest. 14His head and hair were
white like wool, as white as snow, and his
eyes were like blazing fire. 15His feet were
like bronze glowing in a furnace, and his
voice was like the sound of rushing waters.
16In his right hand he held seven stars, and
out of his mouth came a sharp double-
edged sword. His face was like the sun
shining in all its brilliance.●

17When I saw him, I fell at his feet as
though dead. Then he placed his right hand
on me and said: "Do not be afraid. I am the
First and the Last. 18I am the Living One;
I was dead, and behold I am alive for ever
and ever! And I hold the keys of death and
Hades.

19"Write, therefore, what you have
seen, what is now and what will take place
later. 20The mystery of the seven stars that
you saw in my right hand and of the seven
golden lampstands is this: The seven stars
are the angels[b] of the seven churches, and
the seven lampstands are the seven
churches.●

[a]13 Daniel 7:13 [b]20 Or *messengers*

KING JAMES

1. JESUS' SERVANT JOHN

9 I John, who also am your brother,
and companion in tribulation, and in the
kingdom and patience of Jesus Christ,
was in the isle that is called Patmos, for
the word of God, and for the testimony of
Jesus Christ. 10 I was in the Spirit on the
Lord's day, and heard behind me a great
voice, as of a trumpet, 11 saying, I am
Alpha and Ome′ga, the first and the last:
and, What thou seest, write in a book, and
send *it* unto the seven churches which are
in Asia; unto Ephesus, and unto Smyrna,
and unto Per′gamos, and unto Thy-ati′ra,
and unto Sardis, and unto Philadelphia,
and unto La-odice′a.●

2. JESUS' APPEARANCE IN VISION

12 And I turned to see the voice that
spake with me. And being turned, I saw
seven golden candlesticks; 13 and in the
midst of the seven candlesticks *one* like
unto the Son of man, clothed with a garment down to the foot, and girt about the
paps with a golden girdle. 14 His head
and *his* hairs *were* white like wool, as
white as snow; and his eyes *were* as a
flame of fire; 15 and his feet like unto
fine brass, as if they burned in a furnace;
and his voice as the sound of many
waters. 16 And he had in his right hand
seven stars: and out of his mouth went a
sharp two-edged sword: and his countenance *was* as the sun shineth in his
strength.●

3. JESUS' INSTRUCTIONS

17 And when I saw him, I fell at his
feet as dead. And he laid his right hand
upon me, saying unto me, Fear not; I am
the first and the last: 18 *I am* he that
liveth, and was dead; and, behold, I am
alive for evermore, Amen; and have the
keys of hell and of death. 19 Write the
things which thou hast seen, and the things
which are, and the things which shall be
hereafter; 20 the mystery of the seven
stars which thou sawest in my right
hand, and the seven golden candlesticks.
The seven stars are the angels of the
seven churches: and the seven candlesticks which thou sawest are the seven
churches.●

TRIBULATION

PROTECTION

*1:9-11* How does John relate himself to his readers?

Why was he on Patmos?

What is meant by, "I was in the Spirit" (v.10)?

*1:12-16* Who is the "Son of man"? (Cf. Luke 7:34 and John 5:27.)

Record the main parts of the vision:

*1:17-20* Account for John's fear (v.17).

How did the Lord console John (vv.17b-20)?

NEW INTERNATIONAL VERSION

What do you learn here about:

JESUS CHRIST

THE BELIEVER'S LOVE FOR CHRIST

SPIRITUAL RICHES

FALSE DOCTRINE

JUDGMENT FOR SIN

*To the Church in Ephesus*

2 "To the angel[c] of the church in Ephesus write:

These are the words of him who
holds the seven stars in his right hand
and walks among the seven golden
lampstands: 2I know your deeds, your
hard work and your perseverance. I
know that you cannot tolerate wicked
men, that you have tested those who
claim to be apostles but are not, and
have found them false. 3You have persevered and have endured hardships
for my name, and have not grown
weary.
4Yet I hold this against you: You
have forsaken your first love.
5Remember the height from which you
have fallen! Repent and do the things
you did at first. If you do not repent,
I will come to you and remove your
lampstand from its place. 6But you
have this in your favor: You hate the
practices of the Nicolaitans, which I
also hate.
7He who has an ear, let him hear
what the Spirit says to the churches.
To him who overcomes, I will give the
right to eat from the tree of life, which
is in the paradise of God.●

*To the Church in Smyrna*

8"To the angel of the church in Smyrna
write:

These are the words of him who is
the First and the Last, who died and
came to life again. 9I know your afflictions and your poverty—yet you are
rich! I know the slander of those who
say they are Jews and are not, but are
a synagogue of Satan. 10Do not be
afraid of what you are about to suffer.
I tell you, the devil will put some of
you in prison to test you, and you will
suffer persecution for ten days. Be
faithful, even to the point of death, and
I will give you the crown of life.
11He who has an ear, let him hear
what the Spirit says to the churches.
He who overcomes will not be hurt at
all by the second death.●

*To the Church in Pergamum*

12"To the angel of the church in Pergamum
write:

These are the words of him who has
the sharp, double-edged sword. 13I
know where you live—where Satan
has his throne. Yet you remain true to
my name. You did not renounce your
faith in me, even in the days of An-
tipas, my faithful witness, who was
put to death in your city—where Satan
lives.
14Nevertheless, I have a few things
against you: You have people there
who hold to the teaching of Balaam,
who taught Balak to entice the Israelites to sin by eating food sacrificed to
idols and by committing sexual immorality. 15Likewise you also have those
who hold to the teaching of the
Nicolaitans. 16Repent therefore! Otherwise, I will soon come to you and
will fight against them with the sword
of my mouth.
17He who has an ear, let him hear
what the Spirit says to the churches.
To him who overcomes, I will give
some of the hidden manna. I will also
give him a white stone with a new
name written on it, known only to him
who receives it.●

c1 Or *messenger*; also in verses 8, 12 and 18

KING JAMES

1.EPHESUS

SEVEN STARS

2 Unto the angel of the church of Ephesus write; These things saith he that
holdeth the seven stars in his right hand,
who walketh in the midst of the seven
golden candlesticks.
2 I know thy works, and thy labor, and
thy patience, and how thou canst not bear
them which are evil: and thou hast tried
them which say they are apostles, and are
not, and hast found them liars: 3 and hast
borne, and hast patience, and for my
name's sake hast labored, and hast not
fainted. 4 Nevertheless I have *somewhat*
against thee, because thou hast left thy
first love. 5 Remember therefore from
whence thou art fallen, and repent, and
do the first works; or else I will come unto
thee quickly, and will remove thy candlestick out of his place, except thou repent.
6 But this thou hast, that thou hatest the
deeds of the Nicola'itans, which I also
hate. 7 He that hath an ear, let him hear
what the Spirit saith unto the churches;
To him that overcometh will I give to eat
of the tree of life, which is in the midst
of the paradise of God.●

2.SMYRNA

8 And unto the angel of the church in
Smyrna write; These things saith the first
and the last, which was dead, and is
alive.
9 I know thy works, and tribulation,
and poverty, (but thou art rich) and *I
know* the blasphemy of them which say
they are Jews, and are not, but *are* the
synagogue of Satan. 10 Fear none of
those things which thou shalt suffer: behold, the devil shall cast *some* of you into
prison, that ye may be tried; and ye shall
have tribulation ten days: be thou faithful unto death, and I will give thee a
crown of life. 11 He that hath an ear, let
him hear what the Spirit saith unto the
churches; He that overcometh shall not
be hurt of the second death.●

3.PER-GAMOS

SHARP SWORD

12 And to the angel of the church in
Per'gamos write; These things saith he
which hath the sharp sword with two
edges.
13 I know thy works, and where thou
dwellest, *even* where Satan's seat *is:* and
thou holdest fast my name, and hast not
denied my faith, even in those days wherein An'tipas *was* my faithful martyr, who
was slain among you, where Satan dwelleth. 14 But I have a few things against
thee, because thou hast there them that
hold the doctrine of Ba'laam, who taught
Balak to cast a stumblingblock before the
children of Israel, to eat things sacrificed
unto idols, and to commit fornication.
15 So hast thou also them that hold the
doctrine of the Nicola'itans, which thing
I hate. 16 Repent; or else I will come unto thee quickly, and will fight against them
with the sword of my mouth. 17 He that
hath an ear, let him hear what the Spirit
saith unto the churches; To him that overcometh will I give to eat of the hidden
manna, and will give him a white stone,
and in the stone a new name written,
which no man knoweth saving he that
receiveth *it.*●

For each of the seven churches (2:1—3:22), record observations on the different subjects shown.

*2:1-7* Ephesus:

*Commendation* ____________________

____________________

____________________

*Condemnation* ____________________

____________________

____________________

*Warning* ____________________

____________________

____________________

*2:8-11* Smyrna:

*Commendation* ____________________

____________________

____________________

*Condemnation* ____________________

____________________

____________________

*Warning* ____________________

____________________

____________________

*2:12-17* Pergamos

*Commendation* ____________________

____________________

____________________

____________________

*Condemnation* ____________________

____________________

____________________

____________________

*Warning* ____________________

____________________

____________________

____________________

____________________

NEW INTERNATIONAL VERSION

What do these messages teach about:

SON OF GOD ______________________________

IMMORALITY ______________________________

WATCHFULNESS ______________________________

HYPOCRISY ______________________________

REPENTANCE ______________________________

*To the Church in Thyatira*

18"To the angel of the church in Thyatira
write:

These are the words of the Son of
God, whose eyes are like blazing fire
and whose feet are like burnished
bronze. 19I know your deeds, your
love and faith, your service and perseverance, and that you are now doing
more than you did at first.
20Nevertheless, I have this against
you: You tolerate that woman Jezebel,
who calls herself a prophetess. By her
teaching she misleads my servants into
sexual immorality and the eating of
food sacrificed to idols. 21I have given
her time to repent of her immorality,
but she is unwilling. 22So I will cast her
on a bed of suffering, and I will make
those who commit adultery with her
suffer intensely, unless they repent of
her ways. 23I will strike her children
dead. Then all the churches will know
that I am he who searches hearts and
minds, and I will repay each of you
according to your deeds. 24Now I say
to the rest of you in Thyatira, to you
who do not hold to her teaching and
have not learned Satan's so-called
deep secrets (I will not impose any
other burden on you): 25Only hold on
to what you have until I come.
26To him who overcomes and does
my will to the end, I will give authority
over the nations—

27'He will rule them with an iron
scepter;
he will dash them to pieces
like pottery'[a]—

just as I have received authority from
my Father. 28I will also give him the
morning star. 29He who has an ear, let
him hear what the Spirit says to the
churches.●

*To the Church in Sardis*

3 "To the angel[b] of the church in Sardis
write:

These are the words of him who
holds the seven spirits[c] of God and the
seven stars. I know your deeds; you
have a reputation of being alive, but
you are dead. 2Wake up! Strengthen
what remains and is about to die, for I
have not found your deeds complete in
the sight of my God. 3Remember,
therefore, what you have received and
heard; obey it, and repent. But if you
do not wake up, I will come like a
thief, and you will not know at what
time I will come to you.●
4Yet you have a few people in Sardis
who have not soiled their clothes.
They will walk with me, dressed in
white, for they are worthy. 5He who
overcomes will, like them, be dressed
in white. I will never erase his name
from the book of life, but will acknowledge his name before my Father and
his angels. 6He who has an ear, let him
hear what the Spirit says to the
churches.●

[a]27 Psalm 2:9
[b]1 Or *messenger;* also in verses 7 and 14
[c]1 Or *the sevenfold Spirit*

KING JAMES

1. THYATIRA

18 And unto the angel of the church in
Thy-ati'ra write; These things saith the
Son of God, who hath his eyes like unto a
flame of fire, and his feet *are* like fine
brass.
19 I know thy works, and charity, and
service, and faith, and thy patience, and
thy works; and the last *to be* more than
the first. 20 Notwithstanding I have a few
things against thee, because thou sufferest
that woman Jez'ebel, which calleth herself a prophetess, to teach and to seduce
my servants to commit fornication, and to
eat things sacrificed unto idols. 21 And I
gave her space to repent of her fornication; and she repented not. 22 Behold, I
will cast her into a bed, and them that
commit adultery with her into great tribulation, except they repent of their deeds.
23 And I will kill her children with death;
and all the churches shall know that I am
he which searcheth the reins and hearts:
and I will give unto every one of you according to your works. 24 But unto you
I say, and unto the rest in Thy-ati'ra, as
many as have not this doctrine, and which
have not known the depths of Satan, as
they speak; I will put upon you none
other burden. 25 But that which ye have
*already*, hold fast till I come. 26 And he
that overcometh, and keepeth my works
unto the end, to him will I give power over
the nations: 27 and he shall rule them
with a rod of iron; as the vessels of a
potter shall they be broken to shivers:
even as I received of my Father. 28 And
I will give him the morning star. 29 He
that hath an ear, let him hear what the
Spirit saith unto the churches.●

SON OF GOD

SARDIS

3 And unto the angel of the church in
Sardis write; These things saith he
that hath the seven Spirits of God, and the
seven stars.
I know thy works, that thou hast a
name that thou livest, and art dead.
2 Be watchful, and strengthen the things
which remain, that are ready to die: for I
have not found thy works perfect before
God. 3 Remember therefore how thou
hast received and heard, and hold fast,
and repent. If therefore thou shalt not
watch, I will come on thee as a thief, and
thou shalt not know what hour I will
come upon thee. 4 Thou hast a few
names even in Sardis which have not defiled their garments; and they shall walk
with me in white: for they are worthy.
5 He that overcometh, the same shall be
clothed in white raiment; and I will not
blot out his name out of the book of life,[c]
but I will confess his name before my
Father, and before his angels.[d] 6 He that
hath an ear, let him hear what the Spirit
saith unto the churches.●

FATHER

*2:18-29* Thyatira:

*Commendation* ____________________

*Condemnation* ____________________

*Warning* ____________________

*Promise* ____________________

*3:1-6* Sardis:

*Commendation* ____________________

*Condemnation* ____________________

*Warning* ____________________

*Promise* ____________________

NEW INTERNATIONAL VERSION

What do these messages teach about:

JESUS CHRIST

TRIALS

HEAVEN

LUKEWARM CHRISTIANS

CHASTENING

*To the Church in Philadelphia*

7"To the angel of the church in Philadelphia write:

These are the words of him who is
holy and true, who holds the key of
David. What he opens, no one can
shut; and what he shuts, no one can
open. 8I know your deeds. See, I have
placed before you an open door that no
one can shut. I know that you have
little strength, yet you have kept my
word and have not denied my name. 9I
will make those who are of the synagogue of Satan, who claim to be Jews
though they are not, but are liars—I
will make them come and fall down at
your feet and acknowledge that I have
loved you. 10Since you have kept my
command to endure patiently, I will
also keep you from the hour of trial
that is going to come upon the whole
world to test those who live on the
earth.

11I am coming soon. Hold on to what
you have, so that no one will take your
crown. 12Him who overcomes I will
make a pillar in the temple of my God.
Never again will he leave it. I will write
on him the name of my God and the
name of the city of my God, the new
Jerusalem, which is coming down out
of heaven from my God; and I will also
write on him my new name. 13He who
has an ear, let him hear what the Spirit
says to the churches.●

*To the Church in Laodicea*

14"To the angel of the church in Laodicea
write:

These are the words of the Amen,
the faithful and true witness, the ruler
of God's creation. 15I know your
deeds, that you are neither cold nor
hot. I wish you were either one or the
other! 16So, because you are lukewarm—neither hot nor cold—I am
about to spit you out of my mouth.
17You say, 'I am rich; I have acquired
wealth and do not need a thing.' But
you do not realize that you are
wretched, pitiful, poor, blind and
naked. 18I counsel you to buy from me
gold refined in the fire, so you can
become rich; and white clothes to
wear, so you can cover your shameful
nakedness; and salve to put on your
eyes, so you can see.

19Those whom I love I rebuke and
discipline. So be earnest, and repent.
20Here I am! I stand at the door and
knock. If anyone hears my voice and
opens the door, I will come in and eat
with him, and he with me.

21To him who overcomes, I will give
the right to sit with me on my throne,
just as I overcame and sat down with
my Father on his throne. 22He who has
an ear, let him hear what the Spirit
says to the churches."●

KING JAMES

1.PHILA-DELPHIA — OPEN DOOR

**7 And to the angel of the church in
Philadelphia write; These things saith he
that is holy, he that is true, he that hath
the key of David, he that openeth, and no
man shutteth; and shutteth, and no man
openeth.
8 I know thy works: behold, I have set
before thee an open door, and no man can
shut it: for thou hast a little strength, and
hast kept my word, and hast not denied
my name. 9 Behold, I will make them of
the synagogue of Satan, which say they
are Jews, and are not, but do lie; behold,
I will make them to come and worship
before thy feet, and to know that I have
loved thee. 10 Because thou hast kept the
word of my patience, I also will keep thee
from the hour of temptation, which shall
come upon all the world, to try them that
dwell upon the earth. 11 Behold, I come
quickly: hold that fast which thou hast,
that no man take thy crown. 12 Him that
overcometh will I make a pillar in the
temple of my God, and he shall go no
more out: and I will write upon him the
name of my God, and the name of the city
of my God, *which is* new Jerusalem, which
cometh down out of heaven from my
God: and *I will write upon him* my new
name. 13 He that hath an ear, let him
hear what the Spirit saith unto the
churches.** ●

2.LAODI-CEA

**14 And unto the angel of the church of
the La-odice'ans write; These things saith
the Amen, the faithful and true witness,
the beginning of the creation of God.
15 I know thy works, that thou art
neither cold nor hot: I would thou wert
cold or hot. 16 So then because thou art
lukewarm, and neither cold nor hot, I will
spew thee out of my mouth. 17 Because
thou sayest, I am rich, and increased with
goods, and have need of nothing; and
knowest not that thou art wretched, and
miserable, and poor, and blind, and naked:
18 I counsel thee to buy of me gold tried
in the fire, that thou mayest be rich; and
white raiment, that thou mayest be
clothed, and *that* the shame of thy nakedness do not appear; and anoint thine eyes
with eyesalve, that thou mayest see.
19 As many as I love, I rebuke and
chasten: be zealous therefore, and repent. 20 Behold, I stand at the door, and
knock: if any man hear my voice, and open
the door, I will come in to him, and will
sup with him, and he with me. 21 To him
that overcometh will I grant to sit with
me in my throne, even as I also overcame,
and am set down with my Father in his
throne. 22 He that hath an ear, let him
hear what the Spirit saith unto the
churches.** ●

SEAT

*3:7-13* Philadelphia

*Commendation* ______

*Promise* ______

*3:14-22* Laodicea:

Is anything good said of this church?

*Condemnation* ______

*Warning* ______

*Invitation* ______

NEW INTERNATIONAL VERSION

What does this passage teach about:

GOD THE FATHER

CREATION

WORSHIP

Does the passage suggest any practical applications for today? If so list them.

### *The Throne in Heaven*

4 After this I looked, and there before
me was a door standing open in
heaven. And the voice I had first heard
speaking to me like a trumpet said, "Come
up here, and I will show you what must
take place after this." 2At once I was in the
Spirit, and there before me was a throne in
heaven with someone sitting on it. 3And
the one who sat there had the appearance
of jasper and carnelian. A rainbow, resem-
bling an emerald, encircled the throne.
4Surrounding the throne were twenty-four
other thrones, and seated on them were
twenty-four elders. They were dressed in
white and had crowns of gold on their
heads. 5From the throne came flashes of
lightning, rumblings and peals of thunder.
Before the throne, seven lamps were blazing. These are the seven spirits[a] of God.
6Also before the throne there was what
looked like a sea of glass, clear as crystal.●

In the center, around the throne, were
four living creatures, and they were
covered with eyes, in front and in back.
7The first living creature was like a lion, the
second was like an ox, the third had a face
like a man, the fourth was like a flying
eagle. 8Each of the four living creatures
had six wings and was covered with eyes
all around, even under his wings. Day and
night they never stop saying:

"Holy, holy, holy
is the Lord God Almighty,
who was, and is, and is to come."●

9Whenever the living creatures give glory,
honor and thanks to him who sits on the
throne and who lives for ever and ever,
10the twenty-four elders fall down before
him who sits on the throne, and worship
him who lives for ever and ever. They lay
their crowns before the throne and say:

11"You are worthy, our Lord and
God,
to receive glory and honor and
power,
for you created all things,
and by your will they were
created
and have their being."●

[a]5,6 Or *the sevenfold Spirit*

KING JAMES

1. GOD'S THRONE

INVITATION

4 After this I looked, and, behold, a
door *was* opened in heaven: and the
first voice which I heard *was* as it were of
a trumpet talking with me; which said,
Come up hither, and I will show thee
things which must be hereafter. 2 And
immediately I was in the Spirit: and, behold, a throne was set in heaven, and *one*
sat on the throne. 3 And he that sat was
to look upon like a jasper and a sardine
stone: and *there was* a rainbow round
about the throne, in sight like unto an
emerald. 4 And round about the throne
*were* four and twenty seats: and upon the
seats I saw four and twenty elders sitting,
clothed in white raiment; and they had
on their heads crowns of gold. 5 And out
of the throne proceeded lightnings and
thunderings and voices: and *there were*
seven lamps of fire burning before the
throne, which are the seven Spirits of
God. 6 And before the throne *there was*
a sea of glass like unto crystal.●

2. GOD'S CHARACTER

And in the midst of the throne, and
round about the throne, *were* four beasts
full of eyes before and behind. 7 And the
first beast *was* like a lion, and the second
beast like a calf, and the third beast had a
face as a man, and the fourth beast *was*
like a flying eagle. 8 And the four beasts
had each of them six wings about *him;*
and *they were* full of eyes within: and
they rest not day and night, saying,

Holy, holy, holy, Lord God Almighty,
which was, and is, and is to come.●

3. GOD'S WORK

WORSHIP

9 And when those beasts give glory and
honor and thanks to him that sat on the
throne, who liveth for ever and ever,
10 the four and twenty elders fall down
before him that sat on the throne, and
worship him that liveth for ever and ever,
and cast their crowns before the throne,
saying,

11 Thou art worthy, O Lord,
to receive glory and honor and power:
for thou hast created all things,
and for thy pleasure they are and
were created.●

*4:1-6a* What invitation did John receive? _____

Record the main parts of the vision: _____

Is there any suggestion here as to who is sitting on this throne?

*4:6b-8* Does this paragraph identify the one sitting on the throne?

What is His character? _____

*4:9-11* Who sings the song of verse 11? _____

What reason is given for the worthiness of the Lord?

NEW INTERNATIONAL VERSION

What is taught here about:

JUDGMENT OF MAN

REDEMPTION

BLOOD OF CHRIST

PRAISE

FIGURATIVE TITLES OF JESUS

OTHER

*The Scroll and the Lamb*

5 Then I saw in the right hand of him who
sat on the throne a scroll with writing
on both sides and sealed with seven seals.
2And I saw a mighty angel proclaiming in
a loud voice, "Who is worthy to break the
seals and open the scroll?" 3But no one in
heaven or on earth or under the earth could
open the scroll or even look inside it. 4I
wept and wept because no one was found
who was worthy to open the scroll or look
inside. 5Then one of the elders said to me,
"Do not weep! See, the Lion of the tribe of
Judah, the Root of David, has triumphed.
He is able to open the scroll and its seven
seals."●

6Then I saw a Lamb, looking as if it had
been slain, standing in the center of the
throne, encircled by the four living creatures and the elders. He had seven horns
and seven eyes, which are the seven
spirits[a] of God sent out into all the earth.
7He came and took the scroll from the right
hand of him who sat on the throne. 8And
when he had taken it, the four living creatures and the twenty-four elders fell down
before the Lamb. Each one had a harp and
they were holding golden bowls full of incense, which are the prayers of the saints.
9And they sang a new song:

"You are worthy to take the scroll
and to open its seals,
because you were slain,
and with your blood you
purchased men for God
from every tribe and language and
people and nation.
10You have made them to be a
kingdom and priests to
serve our God,
and they will reign on the earth."●

11Then I looked and heard the voice of
many angels, numbering thousands upon
thousands, and ten thousand times ten
thousand. They encircled the throne and
the living creatures and the elders. 12In a
loud voice they sang:

"Worthy is the Lamb, who was
slain,
to receive power and wealth and
wisdom and strength
and honor and glory and praise!"●

13Then I heard every creature in heaven
and on earth and under the earth and on the
sea, and all that is in them, singing:

"To him who sits on the throne and
to the Lamb
be praise and honor and glory and
power,
for ever and ever!"

14The four living creatures said, "Amen,"
and the elders fell down and worshiped.●

KING JAMES

1.PREVAILS WITH POWER

5 And I saw in the right hand of him
that sat on the throne a book written
within and on the back side, sealed with
seven seals. 2 And I saw a strong angel
proclaiming with a loud voice, Who is
worthy to open the book, and to loose the
seals thereof? 3 And no man in heaven,
nor in earth, neither under the earth, was
able to open the book, neither to look
thereon. 4 And I wept much, because no
man was found worthy to open and to
read the book, neither to look thereon.
5 And one of the elders saith unto me,
Weep not: behold, the Lion of the tribe
of Judah, the Root of David, hath prevailed to open the book, and to loose
the seven seals thereof. ●

WHO IS WORTHY?

2.REDEEMS WITH BLOOD

6 And I beheld, and, lo, in the midst of
the throne and of the four beasts, and in
the midst of the elders, stood a Lamb as it
had been slain, having seven horns and
seven eyes, which are the seven Spirits of
God sent forth into all the earth. 7 And
he came and took the book out of the
right hand of him that sat upon the
throne. 8 And when he had taken the
book, the four beasts and four *and* twenty
elders fell down before the Lamb, having
every one of them harps, and golden vials
full of odors, which are the prayers of
saints. 9 And they sung a new song,
saying,

Thou art worthy to take the book,
and to open the seals thereof:
for thou wast slain,
and hast redeemed us to God by thy blood
out of every kindred, and tongue, and people, and nation;
10 and hast made us unto our God kings and priests:
and we shall reign on the earth. ●

3.DESERVES ALL PRAISE

11 And I beheld, and I heard the voice of
many angels round about the throne, and
the beasts, and the elders: and the number of them was ten thousand times ten
thousand, and thousands of thousands;
12 saying with a loud voice,

Worthy is the Lamb that was slain to
receive power, and riches, and wisdom, and strength, and honor, and
glory, and blessing. ●

WORTHY IS THE LAMB

—universal praise

13 And every creature which is in heaven,
and on the earth, and under the earth, and
such as are in the sea, and all that are in
them, heard I saying,

Blessing, and honor, and glory, and
power, *be* unto him that sitteth upon
the throne, and unto the Lamb for
ever and ever.

14 And the four beasts said, Amen. And
the four *and* twenty elders fell down and
worshipped him that liveth for ever
and ever. ●

*5:1-5* How is the "book" identified by this paragraph? ______

What was the angel's question (v.2)? ______

Account for John's reaction (v.4). ______

How is Christ identified in verse 5? ______

*5:6-10* Record references to:

LAMB (Who is this?) ______

DEATH OF CHRIST ______

*5:11-12* What is the Lamb worthy to receive? ______

*5:13-14* Who sings the song of verse 13? ______

About whom is this song? ______

NEW INTERNATIONAL VERSION

Do the judgments of the seals grow in intensity with each new seal? If so give examples.

Is famine suggested in the third seal?

How many inhabitants of the world die as a result of the fourth seal?

How is the fifth seal different from the first four? For example, who are the objects of the tribulation here?

What is the main characteristic of the sixth seal?

What is the effect of this seal upon people?

*The Seals*

6 I watched as the Lamb opened the first
of the seven seals. Then I heard one of
the four living creatures say in a voice like
thunder, "Come!" 2 I looked, and there before me was a white horse! Its rider held a
bow, and he was given a crown, and he
rode out as a conqueror bent on conquest.●
3 When the Lamb opened the second
seal, I heard the second living creature say,
"Come!" 4 Then another horse came out, a
fiery red one. Its rider was given power to
take peace from the earth and to make men
slay each other. To him was given a large
sword.●
5 When the Lamb opened the third seal,
I heard the third living creature say,
"Come!" I looked, and there before me
was a black horse! Its rider was holding a
pair of scales in his hand. 6 Then I heard
what sounded like a voice among the four
living creatures, saying, "A quart[a] of
wheat for a day's wages,[b] and three quarts
of barley for a day's wages,[b] and do not
damage the oil and the wine!"●
7 When the Lamb opened the fourth seal,
I heard the voice of the fourth living creature say, "Come!" 8 I looked, and there
before me was a pale horse! Its rider was
named Death, and Hades was following
close behind him. They were given power
over a fourth of the earth to kill by sword,
famine and plague, and by the wild beasts
of the earth.●
9 When he opened the fifth seal, I saw
under the altar the souls of those who had
been slain because of the word of God and
the testimony they had maintained. 10 They
called out in a loud voice, "How long, Sovereign Lord, holy and true, until you judge
the inhabitants of the earth and avenge our
blood?" 11 Then each of them was given a
white robe, and they were told to wait a
little longer, until the number of their fellow servants and brothers who were to be
killed as they had been was completed.●
12 I watched as he opened the sixth seal.
There was a great earthquake. The sun
turned black like sackcloth made of goat
hair, the whole moon turned blood red,
13 and the stars in the sky fell to earth, as
late figs drop from a fig tree when shaken
by a strong wind. 14 The sky receded like a
scroll, rolling up, and every mountain and
island was removed from its place.
15 Then the kings of the earth, the
princes, the generals, the rich, the mighty,
and every slave and every free man hid in
caves and among the rocks of the mountains. 16 They called to the mountains and
the rocks, "Fall on us and hide us from the
face of him who sits on the throne and from
the wrath of the Lamb! 17 For the great day
of their wrath has come, and who can
stand?"●

[a]6 Greek *a choinix* (probably about a liter)
[b]6 Greek *a denarius*

KING JAMES

FIRST SEAL

6 And I saw when the Lamb opened one
of the seals, and I heard, as it were the
noise of thunder, one of the four beasts
saying, Come and see. 2 And I saw, and
behold a white horse: and he that sat on
him had a bow; and a crown was given
unto him: and he went forth conquering,
and to conquer.

THUNDER

SECOND SEAL

3 And when he had opened the second
seal, I heard the second beast say, Come
and see. 4 And there went out another
horse *that was* red: and *power* was given
to him that sat thereon to take peace from
the earth, and that they should kill one
another: and there was given unto him a
great sword.●

THIRD SEAL

5 And when he had opened the third
seal, I heard the third beast say, Come and
see. And I beheld, and lo a black horse;
and he that sat on him had a pair of
balances in his hand. 6 And I heard a
voice in the midst of the four beasts say,
A measure of wheat for a penny, and
three measures of barley for a penny; and
*see* thou hurt not the oil and the wine.●

FOURTH SEAL

7 And when he had opened the fourth
seal, I heard the voice of the fourth beast
say, Come and see. 8 And I looked, and
behold a pale horse: and his name that sat
on him was Death, and Hell followed
with him. And power was given unto
them over the fourth part of the earth, to
kill with sword, and with hunger, and
with death, and with the beasts of the
earth.●

FIFTH SEAL

9 And when he had opened the fifth
seal, I saw under the altar the souls of
them that were slain for the word of God,
and for the testimony which they held:
10 and they cried with a loud voice, saying, How long, O Lord, holy and true,
dost thou not judge and avenge our blood
on them that dwell on the earth? 11 And
white robes were given unto every one of
them; and it was said unto them, that
they should rest yet for a little season,
until their fellow servants also and their
brethren, that should be killed as they
*were*, should be fulfilled.●

SIXTH SEAL

12 And I beheld when he had opened
the sixth seal, and, lo, there was a great
earthquake; and the sun became black as
sackcloth of hair, and the moon became
as blood; 13 and the stars of heaven fell
unto the earth, even as a fig tree casteth
her untimely figs, when she is shaken of a
mighty wind. 14 And the heaven departed as a scroll when it is rolled together; and every mountain and island
were moved out of their places. 15 And
the kings of the earth, and the great men,
and the rich men, and the chief captains,
and the mighty men, and every bond-
man, and every free man, hid themselves
in the dens and in the rocks of the mountains; 16 and said to the mountains and
rocks, Fall on us, and hide us from the
face of him that sitteth on the throne, and
from the wrath of the Lamb: 17 for the
great day of his wrath is come; and who
shall be able to stand?●

WRATH

The seals are the first series of judgments predicted in Revelation.
Record the main parts of each of the judgments:

____________________

*6:5-6* (3) ____________________

*6:7-8* (4) ____________________

*6:9-11* (5) ____________________

*6:12-17* (6) ____________________

NEW INTERNATIONAL VERSION

What do you learn here about:

ISRAEL

GREAT TRIBULATION

SOVEREIGN PROTECTION BY GOD

PRAISING GOD

SERVING GOD

HEAVEN

OTHER

*144,000 Sealed*

7 After this I saw four angels standing at
the four corners of the earth, holding
back the four winds of the earth to prevent
any wind from blowing on the land or on
the sea or on any tree. 2Then I saw another
angel coming up from the east, having the
seal of the living God. He called out in a
loud voice to the four angels who had been
given power to harm the land and the sea:
3"Do not harm the land or the sea or the
trees until we put a seal on the foreheads
of the servants of our God." 4Then I heard
the number of those who were sealed:
144,000 from all the tribes of Israel.

5From the tribe of Judah 12,000 were sealed,
from the tribe of Reuben 12,000,
from the tribe of Gad 12,000,
6from the tribe of Asher 12,000,
from the tribe of Naphtali 12,000,
from the tribe of Manasseh 12,000,
7from the tribe of Simeon 12,000,
from the tribe of Levi 12,000,
from the tribe of Issachar 12,000,
8from the tribe of Zebulun 12,000,
from the tribe of Joseph 12,000,
from the tribe of Benjamin 12,000.●

*The Great Multitude in White Robes*

9After this I looked and there before me
was a great multitude that no one could
count, from every nation, tribe, people and
language, standing before the throne and in
front of the Lamb. They were wearing
white robes and were holding palm
branches in their hands. 10And they cried
out in a loud voice:

"Salvation belongs to our God,
who sits on the throne,
and to the Lamb."

11All the angels were standing around the
throne and around the elders and the four
living creatures. They fell down on their
faces before the throne and worshiped
God, 12saying:

"Amen!
Praise and glory
and wisdom and thanks and honor
and power and strength
be to our God for ever and ever.
Amen!"●

13Then one of the elders asked me,
"These in white robes—who are they, and
where did they come from?"
14I answered, "Sir, you know."
And he said, "These are they who have
come out of the great tribulation; they have
washed their robes and made them white in
the blood of the Lamb. 15Therefore,

"they are before the throne of God
and serve him day and night in his temple;
and he who sits on the throne will
spread his tent over them.
16Never again will they hunger;
never again will they thirst.
The sun will not beat upon them,
nor any scorching heat.
17For the Lamb at the center of the
throne will be their shepherd;
he will lead them to springs of
living water.
And God will wipe away every tear
from their eyes."●

KING JAMES

1.PROTECTED BY GOD

7 And after these things I saw four
angels standing on the four corners of
the earth, holding the four winds of the
earth, that the wind should not blow on
the earth, nor on the sea, nor on any tree.
2 And I saw another angel ascending from
the east, having the seal of the living God:
and he cried with a loud voice to the four
angels, to whom it was given to hurt the
earth and the sea, 3 saying, Hurt not the
earth, neither the sea, nor the trees, till we
have sealed the servants of our God in
their foreheads. 4 And I heard the number of them which were sealed: *and there
were* sealed a hundred *and* forty *and* four
thousand of all the tribes of the children
of Israel.

NO HURT

5 Of the tribe of Judah *were* sealed twelve thousand.
Of the tribe of Reuben *were* sealed twelve thousand.
Of the tribe of Gad *were* sealed twelve thousand.
6 Of the tribe of Asher *were* sealed twelve thousand.
Of the tribe of Naph'tali *were* sealed twelve thousand.
Of the tribe of Manas'seh *were* sealed twelve thousand.
7 Of the tribe of Simeon *were* sealed twelve thousand.
Of the tribe of Levi *were* sealed twelve thousand.
Of the tribe of Is'sachar *were* sealed twelve thousand.
8 Of the tribe of Zeb'ulun *were* sealed twelve thousand.
Of the tribe of Joseph *were* sealed twelve thousand.
Of the tribe of Benjamin *were* sealed twelve thousand.●

2.PRAISING GOD

9 After this I beheld, and, lo, a great
multitude, which no man could number,
of all nations, and kindreds, and people,
and tongues, stood before the throne, and
before the Lamb, clothed with white robes,
and palms in their hands; 10 and cried
with a loud voice, saying,
Salvation to our God which sitteth
upon the throne, and unto the Lamb.
11 And all the angels stood round about
the throne, and *about* the elders and the
four beasts, and fell before the throne on
their faces, and worshipped God, 12 saying,

Amen: Blessing, and glory, and wisdom, and thanksgiving, and honor,
and power, and might, *be* unto our
God for ever and ever. Amen.●

3.SERVING GOD

13 And one of the elders answered, saying unto me, What are these which are
arrayed in white robes? and whence
came they? 14 And I said unto him, Sir,
thou knowest. And he said to me, These
are they which came out of great tribulation, and have washed their robes, and
made them white in the blood of the
Lamb. 15 Therefore are they before the
throne of God, and serve him day and
night in his temple: and he that sitteth on
the throne shall dwell among them.
16 They shall hunger no more, neither
thirst any more; neither shall the sun
light on them, nor any heat. 17 For the
Lamb which is in the midst of the throne
shall feed them, and shall lead them unto
living fountains of waters: and God shall
wipe away all tears from their eyes.●

NO MORE TEARS

*7:1-8* Where is the setting of this vision? ____

What was the mission of the four angels (v.1)?

What was the mission of the angel of verse 2?

What was the purpose of the sealing? ____

How are the sealed ones identified in verse 3?

How are they identified in verses 4-8? ____

*7:9-12* Where is the setting of this vision? ____

Are the multitudes of verses 9-10 believers?

*7:13-17* How are the multitudes of 7:9-10 identified here?

What do verses 15-17 give a picture of? ____

NEW INTERNATIONAL VERSION

What does this passage teach about:

HOLINESS OF GOD

PRAYER

OMNIPOTENCE OF GOD

JUDGMENT

OTHER

*The Seventh Seal and the Golden Censer*

8 When he opened the seventh seal,
there was silence in heaven for about
half an hour.
2And I saw the seven angels who stand
before God, and to them were given seven
trumpets.●
3Another angel, who had a golden censer, came and stood at the altar. He was
given much incense to offer, with the
prayers of all the saints, on the golden altar
before the throne. 4The smoke of the incense, together with the prayers of the
saints, went up before God from the angel's hand. 5Then the angel took the censer, filled it with fire from the altar, and
hurled it on the earth; and there came peals
of thunder, rumblings, flashes of lightning
and an earthquake.

*The Trumpets*

6Then the seven angels who had the
seven trumpets prepared to sound them.●
7The first angel sounded his trumpet, and
there came hail and fire mixed with blood,
and it was hurled down upon the earth. A
third of the earth was burned up, a third of
the trees were burned up, and all the green
grass was burned up.●
8The second angel sounded his trumpet,
and something like a huge mountain, all
ablaze, was thrown into the sea. A third of
the sea turned into blood, 9a third of the
living creatures in the sea died, and a third
of the ships were destroyed.●
10The third angel sounded his trumpet,
and a great star, blazing like a torch, fell
from the sky on a third of the rivers and on
the springs of water— 11the name of the
star is Wormwood.[a] A third of the waters
turned bitter, and many people died from
the waters that had become bitter.●
12The fourth angel sounded his trumpet,
and a third of the sun was struck, a third of
the moon, and a third of the stars, so that
a third of them turned dark. A third of the
day was without light, and also a third of
the night.●

[a] *11* That is, Bitterness

KING JAMES

—silence—

**8** And when he had opened the seventh
seal, there was silence in heaven about
the space of half an hour. 2 And I saw the
seven angels which stood before God; and
to them were given seven trumpets.● 3 And
another angel came and stood at the
altar, having a golden censer; and there
was given unto him much incense, that he
should offer *it* with the prayers of all saints
upon the golden altar which was before
the throne. 4 And the smoke of the incense, *which came* with the prayers of the
saints, ascended up before God out of the
angel's hand. 5 And the angel took
the censer, and filled it with fire of the
altar, and cast *it* into the earth: and
there were voices, and thunderings, and
lightnings, and an earthquake.

NO SOUND

—prayer—

6 And the seven angels which had the
seven trumpets prepared themselves to
sound.●

FIRST TRUMPET

7 The first angel sounded, and there
followed hail and fire mingled with blood,
and they were cast upon the earth: and the
third part of trees was burnt up, and all
green grass was burnt up.●

SECOND TRUMPET

8 And the second angel sounded, and as
it were a great mountain burning with fire
was cast into the sea: and the third part of
the sea became blood; 9 and the third
part of the creatures which were in the
sea, and had life, died; and the third part
of the ships were destroyed.

THIRD TRUMPET

10 And the third angel sounded, and
there fell a great star from heaven, burning as it were a lamp, and it fell upon the
third part of the rivers, and upon the
fountains of waters; 11 and the name of
the star is called Wormwood: and the
third part of the waters became wormwood; and many men died of the waters,
because they were made bitter.●

FOURTH TRUMPET

12 And the fourth angel sounded, and
the third part of the sun was smitten, and
the third part of the moon, and the third
part of the stars; so as the third part of
them was darkened, and the day shone
not for a third part of it, and the night
likewise.●

NO LIGHT

The trumpets are the second series of judgments in Revelation, more intense than the seals. There are seven trumpets in all. The fifth and sixth appear in the two segments that follow. For the seventh trumpet, see 11:15.

*8:1-2* What is the source of the trumpet judgments?

______

______

______

______

*8:3-6* What is the repeated activity in this paragraph?

______

______

Who prays? ______

______

How does this paragraph introduce the series of judgments?

______

______

______

Record the main parts of each trumpet judgment:

*8:7* (1) ______

______

______

*8:8-9* (2) ______

______

______

*8:10-11* (3) ______

______

______

*8:12* (4) ______

______

______

______

______

What does this passage teach about:

GOD'S PROTECTION OF HIS PEOPLE

TORMENT OF SIN'S JUDGMENT

SATANIC POWER

If the judgment by locusts is to be interpreted *literally*, what kind of locust are these?

If the judgment is to be interpreted *figuratively*, what may the locust represent?

NEW INTERNATIONAL VERSION

13As I watched, I heard an eagle that was
flying in midair call out in a loud voice:
"Woe! Woe! Woe to the inhabitants of the
earth, because of the trumpet blasts about
to be sounded by the other three angels!" ●
9 The fifth angel sounded his trumpet,
and I saw a star that had fallen from the
sky to the earth. The star was given the key
to the shaft of the Abyss. 2When he opened
the Abyss, smoke rose from it like the
smoke from a gigantic furnace. The sun
and sky were darkened by the smoke from
the Abyss. 3And out of the smoke locusts
came down upon the earth and were given
power like that of scorpions of the earth.
4They were told not to harm the grass of
the earth or any plant or tree, but only
those people who did not have the seal of
God on their foreheads. 5They were not
given power to kill them, but only to torture
them for five months. And the agony
they suffered was like that of the sting of a
scorpion when it strikes a man. 6During
those days men will seek death, but will not
find it; they will long to die, but death will
elude them. ●
7The locusts looked like horses prepared
for battle. On their heads they wore something
like crowns of gold, and their faces
resembled human faces. 8Their hair was
like women's hair, and their teeth were like
lions' teeth. 9They had breastplates like
breastplates of iron, and the sound of their
wings was like the thundering of many
horses and chariots rushing into battle.
10They had tails and stings like scorpions,
and in their tails they had power to torment
people for five months. 11They had as king
over them the angel of the Abyss, whose
name in Hebrew is Abaddon, and in Greek,
Apollyon.[a] ●
12The first woe is past; two other woes
are yet to come. ●

[a]11 *Abaddon* and *Apollyon* mean *Destroyer*.

KING JAMES

—introduction

13 And I beheld, and heard an angel flying through the midst of heaven, saying with a loud voice, Woe, woe, woe, to the inhabiters of the earth by reason of the other voices of the trumpet of the three angels, which are yet to sound! ●

3 WOES TO COME

FIFTH TRUMPET —power of locusts

9 And the fifth angel sounded, and I saw a star fall from heaven unto the earth: and to him was given the key of the bottomless pit. 2 And he opened the bottomless pit; and there arose a smoke out of the pit, as the smoke of a great furnace; and the sun and the air were darkened by reason of the smoke of the pit. 3 And there came out of the smoke locusts upon the earth: and unto them was given power, as the scorpions of the earth have power. 4 And it was commanded them that they should not hurt the grass of the earth, neither any green thing, neither any tree; but only those men which have not the seal of God in their foreheads. 5 And to them it was given that they should not kill them, but that they should be tormented five months: and their torment *was* as the torment of a scorpion, when he striketh a man. 6 And in those days shall men seek death, and shall not find it; and shall desire to die, and death shall flee from them. ●

—description of locusts

7 And the shapes of the locusts *were* like unto horses prepared unto battle; and on their heads *were* as it were crowns like gold, and their faces *were* as the faces of men. 8 And they had hair as the hair of women, and their teeth were as *the teeth* of lions. 9 And they had breastplates, as it were breastplates of iron; and the sound of their wings *was* as the sound of chariots of many horses running to battle. 10 And they had tails like unto scorpions, and there were stings in their tails: and their power *was* to hurt men five months. 11 And they had a king over them, *which is* the angel of the bottomless pit, whose name in the Hebrew tongue *is* Abad'don, but in the Greek tongue hath *his* name Apol'ly-on. ●

12 One woe is past; *and*, behold, there come two woes more hereafter. ●

ONE WOE PAST

First, compare the first paragraph with the last. Then read the two paragraphs on the fifth trumpet judgment. How do these two paragraphs differ?

*8:13* What did John hear about the geographical extent of the last three trumpet judgments?

*9:1-6* Record:

POWER OF THE LOCUSTS:

EFFECT OF THE JUDGMENT:

*9:7-11* What are your impressions of verses 7-10?

What does verse 11 teach?

*9:12* What does the word "woe" suggest?

NEW INTERNATIONAL VERSION

What do you learn here about:

SIN ______

UNREPENTANT HEART ______

JUDGMENT FOR SIN ______

SOVEREIGNTY OF GOD ______

Some unbelievers say they are putting off becoming Christians until the day they are up against a wall of trouble, as a last resort. How do verses 20-21 expose the folly of such plans?

______

13The sixth angel blew his trumpet, and
I heard a voice coming from the horns[b] of
the golden altar that is before God. 14It said
to the sixth angel who had the trumpet,
"Release the four angels who are bound at
the great river Euphrates." 15And the four
angels who had been kept ready for this
very hour and day and month and year
were released to kill a third of mankind.
16The number of the mounted troops was
two hundred million. I heard their number.●
17The horses and riders I saw in my vision looked like this: Their breastplates
were fiery red, dark blue, and yellow as
sulfur. The heads of the horses resembled
the heads of lions, and out of their mouths
came fire, smoke and sulfur. 18A third of
mankind was killed by the three plagues of
fire, smoke and sulfur that came out of
their mouths. 19The power of the horses
was in their mouths and in their tails; for
their tails were like snakes, having heads
with which they inflict injury.●
20The rest of mankind that were not
killed by these plagues still did not repent
of the work of their hands; they did not
stop worshiping demons, and idols of gold,
silver, bronze, stone and wood—idols that
cannot see or hear or walk. 21Nor did they
repent of their murders, their magic arts,
their sexual immorality or their thefts.●

*b13* That is, projections

KING JAMES

SIXTH TRUMPET

1.THE ARMY

13 And the sixth angel sounded, and I
heard a voice from the four horns of the
golden altar[f] which is before God, 14 saying to the sixth angel which had the trumpet, Loose the four angels which are
bound in the great river Euphra'tes.
15 And the four angels were loosed, which
were prepared for an hour, and a day, and
a month, and a year, for to slay the third
part of men. 16 And the number of the
army of the horsemen *were* two hundred
thousand thousand: and I heard the number of them.● 17 And thus I saw the horses

GOLDEN ALTAR

2.THE SLAUGHTER

in the vision, and them that sat on them,
having breastplates of fire, and of jacinth,
and brimstone: and the heads of the horses
*were* as the heads of lions; and out of their
mouths issued fire and smoke and brimstone. 18 By these three was the third part
of men killed, by the fire, and by the
smoke, and by the brimstone, which
issued out of their mouths. 19 For their
power is in their mouth, and in their tails:
for their tails *were* like unto serpents,
and had heads, and with them they do
hurt.●

3.EFFECT ON SURVIVORS

20 And the rest of the men which were
not killed by these plagues yet repented
not of the works of their hands, that they
should not worship devils, and idols of
gold, and silver, and brass, and stone, and
of wood; which neither can see, nor hear,
nor walk: 21 neither repented they of
their murders, nor of their sorceries, nor
of their fornication, nor of their thefts.●

NO REPENTANCE

*9:13-16* Does the text show that God sends this judgment?

From what direction does this judgment come, with relation to the location of Palestine?

How many horsemen are involved?

*9:17-19* How are the horses and riders described?

How many people are killed in this judgment?

*9:20-21* What was the effect of this judgment on those that survived?

For what sins was there no repentance?

NEW INTERNATIONAL VERSION

What does this passage teach about:

SUSPENSE OF COMING JUDGMENT

AUTHORITATIVE WORD OF GOD

MYSTERY OF GOD

MESSAGE FROM GOD

UNIVERSALITY OF JUDGMENT

SERVANT OF GOD

*The Angel and the Little Scroll*

10 Then I saw another mighty angel
coming down from heaven. He was
robed in a cloud, with a rainbow above his
head; his face was like the sun, and his legs
were like fiery pillars. 2He was holding a
little scroll, which lay open in his hand. He
planted his right foot on the sea and his left
foot on the land, 3and he gave a loud shout
like the roar of a lion. When he shouted,
the voices of the seven thunders spoke.
4And when the seven thunders spoke, I
was about to write; but I heard a voice from
heaven say, "Seal up what the seven thunders have said and do not write it down."●
5Then the angel I had seen standing on
the sea and on the land raised his right hand
to heaven. 6And he swore by him who lives
for ever and ever, who created the heavens
and all that is in them, the earth and all that
is in it, and the sea and all that is in it, and
said, "There will be no more delay! 7But in
the days when the seventh angel is about to
sound his trumpet, the mystery of God will
be accomplished, just as he announced to
his servants the prophets."●
8Then the voice that I had heard from
heaven spoke to me once more: "Go, take
the scroll that lies open in the hand of the
angel who is standing on the sea and on the
land."
9So I went to the angel and asked him to
give me the little scroll. He said to me,
"Take it and eat it. It will turn your stomach sour, but in your mouth it will be as
sweet as honey." 10I took the little scroll
from the angel's hand and ate it. It tasted
as sweet as honey in my mouth, but when
I had eaten it, my stomach turned sour.
11Then I was told, "You must prophesy
again about many peoples, nations, languages and kings."●

KING JAMES

1.ANGEL AND THE LITTLE BOOK

**10** And I saw another mighty angel
come down from heaven, clothed
with a cloud: and a rainbow *was* upon his
head, and his face *was* as it were the sun,
and his feet as pillars of fire: 2 and he had
in his hand a little book open: and he set
his right foot upon the sea, and *his* left
*foot* on the earth, 3 and cried with a loud
voice, as *when* a lion roareth: and when
he had cried, seven thunders uttered their
voices. 4 And when the seven thunders
had uttered their voices, I was about to
write: and I heard a voice from heaven
saying unto me, Seal up those things
which the seven thunders uttered, and
write them not.●

2.ANGEL SPEAKS

5 And the angel which I
saw stand upon the sea and upon the
earth lifted up his hand to heaven, 6 and
sware by him that liveth for ever and ever,
who created heaven, and the things that
therein are, and the earth, and the things
that therein are, and the sea, and the
things which are therein, that there should
be time no longer: 7 but in the days of
the voice of the seventh angel, when he
shall begin to sound, the mystery of God
should be finished, as he hath declared to
his servants the prophets.●

3.JOHN EATS THE BOOK

8 And the voice which I heard from
heaven spake unto me again, and said, Go
*and* take the little book which is open in
the hand of the angel which standeth upon
the sea and upon the earth. 9 And I went
unto the angel, and said unto him, Give
me the little book. And he said unto me,
Take *it*, and eat it up; and it shall make
thy belly bitter, but it shall be in thy
mouth sweet as honey. 10 And I took the
little book out of the angel's hand, and
ate it up; and it was in my mouth sweet as
honey: and as soon as I had eaten it, my
belly was bitter. 11 And he said unto me,
Thou must prophesy again before many
peoples, and nations, and tongues, and
kings.●

HOLDING THE BOOK

EATING THE BOOK

Chapter 10 begins a long parenthesis or interlude (10:1—15:4) in the series of judgments. In world history of the last days it will be a time of preparation for God's final judgment. The third group of judgments (BOWLS) begins at 15:5.

*10:1-4* List the main symbols of this paragraph:

*10:5-7* What is the message of this angel?

See 11:15, where the seventh angel blows his trumpet.

*10:8-11* Are the contents of the little book revealed?

Compare Jeremiah 15:16-18 and Ezekiel 2:9—3:4-14 for experience similar to that of verses 9-11. Why does a prophet of God have this experience?

What is the scope of John's ministry, according to verse 11?

NEW INTERNATIONAL VERSION

What do you learn from this passage about:

ISRAEL AND GENTILES IN LAST DAYS

WORSHIP

THE TEMPLE IN JERUSALEM

WITNESSES FOR GOD

PERSECUTION

REJECTORS OF GOD'S MESSAGE

RESURRECTION POWER OF GOD

OTHER

*The Two Witnesses*

11 I was given a reed like a measuring
rod and was told, "Go and measure
the temple of God and the altar, and count
the worshipers there. 2But exclude the outer court; do not measure it, because it has
been given to the Gentiles. They will trample on the holy city for 42 months.● 3And I
will give power to my two witnesses, and
they will prophesy for 1,260 days, clothed
in sackcloth." 4These are the two olive
trees and the two lampstands that stand
before the Lord of the earth. 5If anyone
tries to harm them, fire comes from their
mouths and devours their enemies. This is
how anyone who wants to harm them must
die. 6These men have power to shut up the
sky so that it will not rain during the time
they are prophesying; and they have power
to turn the waters into blood and to strike
the earth with every kind of plague as often
as they want.●
7Now when they have finished their testimony, the beast that comes up from the
Abyss will attack them, and overpower
and kill them. 8Their bodies will lie in the
street of the great city, which is figuratively called Sodom and Egypt, where also
their Lord was crucified. 9For three and a
half days men from every people, tribe,
language and nation will gaze on their bodies and refuse them burial. 10The inhabitants of the earth will gloat over them and
will celebrate by sending each other gifts,
because these two prophets had tormented
those who live on the earth.●
11But after the three and a half days a
breath of life from God entered them, and
they stood on their feet, and terror struck
those who saw them. 12Then they heard a
loud voice from heaven saying to them,
"Come up here." And they went up to
heaven in a cloud, while their enemies
looked on.
13At that very hour there was a severe
earthquake and a tenth of the city collapsed. Seven thousand people were killed
in the earthquake, and the survivors were
terrified and gave glory to the God of
heaven.●

KING JAMES

1.HOLY CITY

TEMPLE IN THE CITY

**11** And there was given me a reed like
unto a rod: and the angel stood,
saying, Rise, and measure the temple of
God, and the altar, and them that worship therein. 2 But the court which is
without the temple leave out, and measure it not; for it is given unto the Gentiles: and the holy city shall they tread
under foot forty *and* two months.● 3 And
I will give *power* unto my two witnesses,
and they shall prophesy a thousand two
hundred *and* threescore days, clothed in
sackcloth.

2.TWO WITNESSES

4 These are the two olive trees, and the
two candlesticks standing before the God
of the earth. 5 And if any man will hurt
them, fire proceedeth out of their mouth,
and devoureth their enemies: and if any
man will hurt them, he must in this manner be killed. 6 These have power to shut
heaven, that it rain not in the days of their
prophecy: and have power over waters
to turn them to blood, and to smite the
earth with all plagues, as often as they
will.● 7 And when they shall have finished

3.BEAST KILLS THE WITNESSES

their testimony, the beast that ascendeth
out of the bottomless pit shall make war
against them, and shall overcome them,
and kill them. 8 And their dead bodies
*shall lie* in the street of the great city,
which spiritually is called Sodom and
Egypt, where also our Lord was crucified.
9 And they of the people and kindreds
and tongues and nations shall see their
dead bodies three days and a half, and
shall not suffer their dead bodies to be put
in graves. 10 And they that dwell upon
the earth shall rejoice over them, and
make merry, and shall send gifts one to
another; because these two prophets tormented them that dwelt on the earth.●

4.WITNESSES ARE RESURRECTED

11 And after three days and a half the
Spirit of life from God entered into them,
and they stood upon their feet; and great
fear fell upon them which saw them.
12 And they heard a great voice from
heaven saying unto them, Come up hither.
And they ascended up to heaven in a
cloud; and their enemies beheld them.
13 And the same hour was there a great
earthquake, and the tenth part of the city
fell, and in the earthquake were slain of
men seven thousand: and the remnant
were affrighted, and gave glory to the God
of heaven.

EARTHQUAKE HURTS THE CITY

*11:1-2* What is the "holy city" (see v.8)? ______

What part of the city is singled out here? ______

What two groups are referred to in the paragraph?

*11:3-6* Are the two witnesses persons? ______

What is said about them? ______

*11:7-10* When does the beast begin to war against the witnesses?

What is the outcome? ______

What is the people's reaction? ______

*11:11-13* Record the events: ______

NEW INTERNATIONAL VERSION

What spiritual truths are taught by this passage in these areas:

KINGDOM OF GOD

WORSHIP OF GOD

POWER OF GOD

WRATH OF GOD

RECOMPENSE AND REWARD

TEMPLE OF GOD

OTHER

[14]The second woe has passed; the third
woe is coming soon.●

*The Seventh Trumpet*

[15]The seventh angel sounded his trumpet, and there were loud voices in heaven,
which said:

"The kingdom of the world has
become the kingdom of our
Lord and of his Christ,
and he will reign for ever and
ever."

[16]And the twenty-four elders, who were
seated on their thrones before God, fell on
their faces and worshiped God, [17]saying:

"We give thanks to you, Lord God
Almighty,
who is and who was,
because you have taken your great
power
and have begun to reign.
[18]The nations were angry;
and your wrath has come.

The time has come for judging the
dead,
and for rewarding your servants
the prophets
and your saints and those who
reverence your name,
both small and great—
and for destroying those who
destroy the earth."●

[19]Then God's temple in heaven was
opened, and within his temple was seen the
ark of his covenant. And there came
flashes of lightning, rumblings, peals of
thunder, an earthquake and a great hail-
storm.●

## KING JAMES

1.THIRD WOE

2.SEVENTH ANGEL

3.TEMPLE IN HEAVEN

14 The second woe is past; *and*, behold,
the third woe cometh quickly.●
15 And the seventh angel sounded; and
there were great voices in heaven, saying,
The kingdoms of this world are become *the kingdoms* of our Lord, and
of his Christ; and he shall reign for
ever and ever.
16 And the four and twenty elders, which
sat before God on their seats, fell upon
their faces, and worshipped God, 17 saying,
We give thee thanks, O Lord God
Almighty, which art, and wast, and
art to come; because thou hast taken
to thee thy great power, and hast
reigned. 18 And the nations were
angry, and thy wrath is come, and the
time of the dead, that they should be
judged, and that thou shouldest give
reward unto thy servants the prophets, and to the saints, and them that
fear thy name, small and great; and
shouldest destroy them which destroy
the earth.●
19 And the temple of God was opened
in heaven, and there was seen in his temple
the ark of his testament: and there were
lightnings, and voices, and thunderings,
and an earthquake, and great hail.●

GREAT VOICES

GREAT HAIL

First review these parts of earlier chapters:

8:13—How many woes were predicted? ____

9:1—What trumpet was blown? ____

9:12—Which trumpet judgment was this first woe?

9:13—What trumpet was blown? ____

*11:14* Now read 11:14 of this segment. Which trumpet is "the second woe"?

Which is the "third woe"? ____

*11:15-18* What trumpet is sounded at 11:15?

What is the theme of the song of verse 15? ____

What are the main truths of the song of verses 17-18?

*11:19* Where is the temple located? ____

May the natural phenomena of v.19b suggest judgments to come?

NEW INTERNATIONAL VERSION

Read Isaiah 26:17-18; 66:7ff. and Micah 4:10;5:3 for support of the interpretation that the woman of this Revelation passage is Israel, and the man-child is Jesus. Then apply this interpretation to this passage, listing the prophesied events:

ISRAEL (woman)

JESUS (man-child)

Is Israel protected from the onslaughts of Satan?

*The Woman and the Dragon*

12 A great and wondrous sign appeared
in heaven: a woman clothed with the
sun, with the moon under her feet and a
crown of twelve stars on her head. 2She
was pregnant and cried out in pain as she
was about to give birth. 3Then another sign
appeared in heaven: an enormous red
dragon with seven heads and ten horns and
seven crowns on his heads. 4His tail swept
a third of the stars out of the sky and flung
them to the earth. The dragon stood in
front of the woman who was about to give
birth, so that he might devour her child the
moment it was born. 5She gave birth to a
son, a male child, who will rule all the nations with an iron scepter. And her child
was snatched up to God and to his throne.
6The woman fled into the desert to a place
prepared for her by God, where she might
be taken care of for 1,260 days.●

7And there was war in heaven. Michael
and his angels fought against the dragon,
and the dragon and his angels fought back.
8But he was not strong enough, and they
lost their place in heaven. 9The great
dragon was hurled down—that ancient serpent called the devil or Satan, who leads
the whole world astray. He was hurled to
the earth, and his angels with him.

10Then I heard a loud voice in heaven
say:

"Now have come the salvation and
the power and the kingdom
of our God,
and the authority of his Christ.
For the accuser of our brothers,
who accuses them before our God
day and night,
has been hurled down.
11They overcame him
by the blood of the Lamb
and by the word of their
testimony;
they did not love their lives so
much
as to shrink from death.
12Therefore rejoice, you heavens
and you who dwell in them!
But woe to the earth and the sea,
because the devil has gone down
to you!
He is filled with fury,
because he knows that his time is
short."●

13When the dragon saw that he had been
hurled to the earth, he pursued the woman
who had given birth to the male child.
14The woman was given the two wings of
a great eagle, so that she might fly to the
place prepared for her in the desert, where
she would be taken care of for a time, times
and half a time, out of the serpent's reach.
15Then from his mouth the serpent spewed
water like a river, to overtake the woman
and sweep her away with the torrent. 16But
the earth helped the woman by opening its
mouth and swallowing the river that the
dragon had spewed out of his mouth.
17Then the dragon was enraged at the
woman and went off to make war against
the rest of her offspring—those who obey
God's commandments and hold to the testimony of Jesus.●

KING JAMES

1.WOMAN BRINGS FORTH CHILD

THE WOMAN IN HEAVEN

**12** And there appeared a great wonder
in heaven; a woman clothed with
the sun, and the moon under her feet, and
upon her head a crown of twelve stars:
2 and she being with child cried, travailing
in birth, and pained to be delivered.
3 And there appeared another wonder in
heaven; and behold a great red dragon,
having seven heads and ten horns, and
seven crowns upon his heads. 4 And his
tail drew the third part of the stars of
heaven, and did cast them to the earth:
and the dragon stood before the woman
which was ready to be delivered, for to
devour her child as soon as it was born.
5 And she brought forth a man child,
who was to rule all nations with a rod of
iron: and her child was caught up unto
God, and *to* his throne. 6 And the woman
fled into the wilderness, where she hath a
place prepared of God, that they should
feed her there a thousand two hundred
*and* threescore days.●

2.WAR IN HEAVEN

7 And there was war in heaven: Michael and his angels fought against the
dragon; and the dragon fought and his
angels, 8 and prevailed not; neither was
their place found any more in heaven.
9 And the great dragon was cast out, that
old serpent, called the Devil, and Satan,
which deceiveth the whole world: he was
cast out into the earth, and his angels
were cast out with him. 10 And I heard a
loud voice saying in heaven,

Now is come salvation, and strength,
and the kingdom of our God, and the
power of his Christ: for the accuser
of our brethren is cast down, which
accused them before our God day
and night. 11 And they overcame
him by the blood of the Lamb, and
by the word of their testimony; and
they loved not their lives unto the
death. 12 Therefore rejoice, *ye* heavens, and ye that dwell in them. Woe
to the inhabiters of the earth and of
the sea! for the devil is come down
unto you, having great wrath, because he knoweth that he hath but a
short time.●

3.DRAGON PERSE-CUTES WOMAN

13 And when the dragon saw that he
was cast unto the earth, he persecuted the
woman which brought forth the man *child*.
14 And to the woman were given two
wings of a great eagle, that she might fly
into the wilderness, into her place, where
she is nourished for a time, and times, and
half a time, from the face of the serpent.
15 And the serpent cast out of his mouth
water as a flood after the woman, that he
might cause her to be carried away of the
flood. 16 And the earth helped the woman; and the earth opened her mouth, and
swallowed up the flood which the dragon
cast out of his mouth. 17 And the dragon
was wroth with the woman, and went to
make war with the remnant of her seed,
which keep the commandments of God,
and have the testimony of Jesus Christ.●

THE WOMAN ON EARTH

*12:1-6* Who are the three main characters of the paragraph?

v.1 ____________________

v.3 ____________________

v.5 ____________________

Who is the red dragon, according to verse 9?

____________________

____________________

What ministry was the man-child to have (v.5)?

____________________

____________________

*12:7-12* Record the events of verses 7-9: ____

____________________

____________________

____________________

____________________

Record the main parts of the song of verses 10-12:

____________________

____________________

____________________

____________________

____________________

____________________

*12:13-17* Underline every reference to the woman. Record the things happening to her at this time.

____________________

____________________

____________________

____________________

____________________

____________________

____________________

____________________

____________________

What does this passage teach about:

BLASPHEMY

WORSHIP OF SATANIC POWERS

FALSE SIGNS

THE ORIGIN OF SATANIC WORKS

PATIENCE AND FAITH OF SAINTS

OTHER

**13** 1And the dragon[a]
stood on the shore of the sea.

### *The Beast out of the Sea*

And I saw a beast coming out of the sea.
He had ten horns and seven heads, with ten
crowns on his horns, and on each head a
blasphemous name. 2The beast I saw
resembled a leopard, but had feet like
those of a bear and a mouth like that of a
lion. The dragon gave the beast his power
and his throne and great authority. 3One of
the heads of the beast seemed to have had
a fatal wound, but the fatal wound had
been healed. The whole world was astonished and followed the beast. 4Men worshiped the dragon because he had given
authority to the beast, and they also worshiped the beast and asked, "Who is like
the beast? Who can make war against
him?" ●

5The beast was given a mouth to utter
proud words and blasphemies and to exercise his authority for forty-two months.
6He opened his mouth to blaspheme God,
and to slander his name and his dwelling
place and those who live in heaven. 7He
was given power to make war against the
saints and to conquer them. And he was
given authority over every tribe, people,
language and nation. 8All inhabitants of the
earth will worship the beast—all whose
names have not been written in the book of
life belonging to the Lamb that was slain
from the creation of the world.[b] ●

9He who has an ear, let him hear.

10If anyone is to go into captivity,
into captivity he will go.
If anyone is to be killed with the
sword,
with the sword he will be killed.

This calls for patient endurance and faithfulness on the part of the saints. ●

### *The Beast out of the Earth*

11Then I saw another beast, coming out
of the earth. He had two horns like a lamb,
but he spoke like a dragon. 12He exercised
all the authority of the first beast on his
behalf, and made the earth and its inhabitants worship the first beast, whose fatal
wound had been healed. 13And he performed great and miraculous signs, even
causing fire to come down from heaven to
earth in full view of men. 14Because of the
signs he was given power to do on behalf
of the first beast, he deceived the inhabitants of the earth. He ordered them to set up
an image in honor of the beast who was
wounded by the sword and yet lived. 15He
was given power to give breath to the image of the first beast, so that it could speak
and cause all who refused to worship the
image to be killed. 16He also forced everyone, small and great, rich and poor, free
and slave, to receive a mark on his right
hand or on his forehead, 17so that no one
could buy or sell unless he had the mark,
which is the name of the beast or the number of his name.

18This calls for wisdom. If anyone has
insight, let him calculate the number of the
beast, for it is man's number. His number
is 666. ●

[a]1 Some late manuscripts *And I*
[b]8 Or *written from the creation of the world in the book of life belonging to the Lamb that was slain*

KING JAMES

1.SEA BEAST

OUT OF THE SEA

**13** And I stood upon the sand of the
sea, and saw a beast rise up out of
the sea, having seven heads and ten
horns, and upon his horns ten crowns,
and upon his heads the name of blasphemy. 2 And the beast which I saw was
like unto a leopard, and his feet were as
*the feet* of a bear, and his mouth as the
mouth of a lion: and the dragon gave him
his power, and his seat, and great authority. 3 And I saw one of his heads as
it were wounded to death; and his deadly
wound was healed: and all the world wondered after the beast. 4 And they worshipped the dragon which gave power
unto the beast: and they worshipped the
beast, saying, Who *is* like unto the beast?
who is able to make war with him? ●

2.HIS POWER AND WORKS

5 And there was given unto him a
mouth speaking great things and blasphemies; and power was given unto him
to continue forty *and* two months. 6 And
he opened his mouth in blasphemy against
God, to blaspheme his name, and his
tabernacle, and them that dwell in heaven.
7 And it was given unto him to make war
with the saints, and to overcome them:
and power was given him over all kindreds,
and tongues, and nations. 8 And all that
dwell upon the earth shall worship him,
whose names are not written in the book
of life of the Lamb slain from the foundation of the world.● 9 If any man have an
ear, let him hear. 10 He that leadeth into
captivity shall go into captivity: he that
killeth with the sword must be killed with
the sword. Here is the patience and the
faith of the saints. ●

—exhortation

3.EARTH BEAST

11 And I beheld another beast coming
up out of the earth; and he had two horns
like a lamb, and he spake as a dragon.
12 And he exerciseth all the power of the
first beast before him, and causeth the
earth and them which dwell therein to
worship the first beast, whose deadly
wound was healed. 13 And he doeth great
wonders, so that he maketh fire come
down from heaven on the earth in the
sight of men, 14 and deceiveth them that
dwell on the earth by *the means of* those
miracles which he had power to do in the
sight of the beast; saying to them that
dwell on the earth, that they should make
an image to the beast, which had the
wound by a sword, and did live. 15 And
he had power to give life unto the image
of the beast, that the image of the beast
should both speak, and cause that as
many as would not worship the image of
the beast should be killed. 16 And he
causeth all, both small and great, rich and
poor, free and bond, to receive a mark in
their right hand, or in their foreheads:
17 and that no man might buy or sell,
save he that had the mark, or the name of
the beast, or the number of his name.
18 Here is wisdom. Let him that hath understanding count the number of the
beast: for it is the number of a man; and
his number *is* Six hundred threescore *and*
six. ●

ON LAND

*13:1-4* What things are written here about the sea beast?

*13:5-8* Underline the repeated word "blasphemy." Record what is written about the sea beast's power and works.

*13:9-10* What is the function of this short paragraph in the segment?

*13:11-18* Record the power and works of the earth beast:

NEW INTERNATIONAL VERSION

What do you learn here about:

THE LAMB OF GOD

PRESERVATION OF THE SAINTS

GOSPEL

JUDGMENT

PATIENCE AND FAITH

OTHER

*The Lamb and the 144,000*

14 Then I looked, and there before me
was the Lamb, standing on Mount
Zion, and with him 144,000 who had his
name and his Father's name written on
their foreheads. 2And I heard a sound from
heaven like the roar of rushing waters and
like a loud peal of thunder. The sound I
heard was like that of harpists playing their
harps. 3And they sang a new song before
the throne and before the four living creatures and the elders. No one could learn
the song except the 144,000 who had been
redeemed from the earth. 4These are those
who did not defile themselves with
women, for they kept themselves pure.
They follow the Lamb wherever he goes.
They were purchased from among men and
offered as firstfruits to God and the Lamb.
5No lie was found in their mouths; they are
blameless.●

*The Three Angels*

6Then I saw another angel flying in midair, and he had the eternal gospel to proclaim to those who live on the earth—to
every nation, tribe, language and people.
7He said in a loud voice, "Fear God and
give him glory, because the hour of his
judgment has come. Worship him who
made the heavens, the earth, the sea and
the springs of water."●
8A second angel followed and said,
"Fallen! Fallen is Babylon the Great,
which made all the nations drink the maddening wine of her adulteries."●
9A third angel followed them and said in
a loud voice: "If anyone worships the
beast and his image and receives his mark
on the forehead or on the hand, 10he, too,
will drink of the wine of God's fury, which
has been poured full strength into the cup
of his wrath. He will be tormented with
burning sulfur in the presence of the holy
angels and of the Lamb. 11And the smoke
of their torment rises for ever and ever.
There is no rest day or night for those who
worship the beast and his image, or for
anyone who receives the mark of his
name."● 12This calls for patient endurance
on the part of the saints who obey God's
commandments and remain faithful to
Jesus.●

KING JAMES

1.NEW SONG

**14** And I looked, and, lo, a Lamb
stood on the mount Zion, and with
him a hundred forty *and* four thousand,
having his Father's name written in their
foreheads. 2 And I heard a voice from
heaven, as the voice of many waters, and
as the voice of a great thunder: and I
heard the voice of harpers harping with
their harps: 3 and they sung as it were a
new song before the throne, and before
the four beasts, and the elders: and no
man could learn that song but the hundred *and* forty *and* four thousand, which
were redeemed from the earth. 4 These
are they which were not defiled with
women; for they are virgins. These are
they which follow the Lamb whithersoever he goeth. These were redeemed from
among men, *being* the firstfruits unto God
and to the Lamb. 5 And in their mouth
was found no guile: for they are without
fault before the throne of God.●

SONG

2.EVERLASTING GOSPEL

6 And I saw another angel fly in the
midst of heaven, having the everlasting
gospel to preach unto them that dwell on
the earth, and to every nation, and kindred, and tongue, and people, 7 saying
with a loud voice, Fear God, and give
glory to him; for the hour of his judgment is come: and worship him that made
heaven, and earth, and the sea, and the
fountains of waters.●

first angel

3.FALLEN BABYLON

8 And there followed another angel,
saying, Babylon is fallen, is fallen, that
great city, because she made all nations
drink of the wine of the wrath of her fornication.●

second angel

3.TORMENT

9 And the third angel followed them,
saying with a loud voice, If any man worship the beast and his image, and receive
*his* mark in his forehead, or in his hand,
10 the same shall drink of the wine of the
wrath of God, which is poured out without mixture into the cup of his indignation; and he shall be tormented with fire
and brimstone in the presence of the holy
angels, and in the presence of the Lamb:
11 and the smoke of their torment ascendeth up for ever and ever: and they
have no rest day nor night, who worship
the beast and his image, and whosoever
receiveth the mark of his name.●

third angel

4.SAINTS' PATIENCE

12 Here is the patience of the saints:
here *are* they that keep the commandments of God, and the faith of Jesus.●

FAITH

*14:1-5* Recall chapter 7, about the sealing of the 144,000 saints to preserve them from harm. What is written here about the 144,000?

________________________________________

________________________________________

________________________________________

________________________________________

________________________________________

________________________________________

________________________________________

*14:6-7* What is the invitation of this gospel?

________________________________________

________________________________________

To whom is it given? ____________________

________________________________________

*14:8* What is "that great city"? ____________

________________________________________

*14:9-11* Record the third angel's message:

SIN ______________________________________

________________________________________

________________________________________

JUDGMENT ________________________________

________________________________________

________________________________________

*14:12* Relate this paragraph to the first paragraph.

________________________________________

________________________________________

________________________________________

________________________________________

________________________________________

________________________________________

________________________________________

________________________________________

________________________________________

NEW INTERNATIONAL VERSION

What do these visions of John teach about:

DEATH OF MARTYRS

SON OF MAN

HARVEST OF SOULS

WRATH OF GOD

What practical lessons do you learn here?

[13]Then I heard a voice from heaven say,
"Write: Blessed are the dead who die in the
Lord from now on."
"Yes," says the Spirit, "they will rest
from their labor, for their deeds will follow
them."●

*The Harvest of the Earth*

[14]I looked, and there before me was a
white cloud, and seated on the cloud was
one "like a son of man"[a] with a crown of
gold on his head and a sharp sickle in his
hand. [15]Then another angel came out of the
temple and called in a loud voice to him
who was sitting on the cloud, "Take your
sickle and reap, because the time to reap
has come, for the harvest of the earth is
ripe." [16]So he that was seated on the cloud
swung his sickle over the earth, and the
earth was harvested.●
[17]Another angel came out of the temple
in heaven, and he too had a sharp sickle.
[18]Still another angel, who had charge of the
fire, came from the altar and called in a
loud voice to him who had the sharp sickle,
"Take your sharp sickle and gather the
clusters of grapes from the earth's vine,
because its grapes are ripe." [19]The angel
swung his sickle on the earth, gathered its
grapes and threw them into the great winepress of God's wrath. [20]They were trampled in the winepress outside the city, and
blood flowed out of the press, rising as high
as the horses' bridles for a distance of 1,600
stadia.[b]●

[a]*14* Daniel 7:13
[b]*20* That is, about 180 miles (about 300 kilometers)

KING JAMES

—beatitude

BLESS-ING

**13 And I heard a voice from heaven**
**saying unto me, Write, Blessed *are* the**
**dead which die in the Lord from hence-**
**forth: Yea, saith the Spirit, that they may**
**rest from their labors; and their works do**
**follow them.●**

1.SON OF MAN WITH SICKLE

**14 And I looked, and behold a white**
**cloud, and upon the cloud *one* sat like un-**
**to the Son of man, having on his head a**
**golden crown, and in his hand a sharp**
**sickle. 15 And another angel came out of**
**the temple, crying with a loud voice to**
**him that sat on the cloud, Thrust in thy**
**sickle, and reap: for the time is come for**
**thee to reap; for the harvest of the earth**
**is ripe. 16 And he that sat on the cloud**
**thrust in his sickle on the earth; and the**
**earth was reaped.●**

2.ANGEL WITH SICKLE

**17 And another angel came out of the**
**temple which is in heaven, he also having**
**a sharp sickle. 18 And another angel**
**came out from the altar, which had power**
**over fire; and cried with a loud cry to him**
**that had the sharp sickle, saying, Thrust**
**in thy sharp sickle, and gather the clusters**
**of the vine of the earth; for her grapes are**
**fully ripe. 19 And the angel thrust in his**
**sickle into the earth, and gathered the**
**vine of the earth, and cast *it* into the great**
**winepress of the wrath of God. 20 And**
**the winepress was trodden without the**
**city, and blood came out of the winepress,**
**even unto the horse bridles, by the space**
**of a thousand *and* six hundred furlongs.**

WRATH

First read 14:12 and relate that verse to the opening verse of this segment (v.13).

*14:13* Record the different bright words and phrases of this verse.

____________________

____________________

Contrast the verse with the remainder of the segment.

____________________

____________________

*14:14-16* Who is the Son of man? __________

____________________

____________________

What does the angel say to him? __________

____________________

____________________

What does he do? __________

____________________

____________________

*14:17-20* Record the action of the verses: _____

v.17 ____________________

____________________

____________________

____________________

____________________

v.18 ____________________

____________________

____________________

____________________

vv.19-20 ____________________

____________________

____________________

____________________

____________________

____________________

____________________

____________________

NEW INTERNATIONAL VERSION

What do you learn here about:

HOLINESS OF GOD

SONG OF REDEMPTION

GLORY OF GOD

WORSHIP OF GOD

TEMPLE

WRATH OF GOD

JUDGMENT FOR SIN

*Seven Angels With Seven Plagues*

15 I saw in heaven another great and
marvelous sign: seven angels with
the seven last plagues—last, because with
them God's wrath is completed. ²And I
saw what looked like a sea of glass mixed
with fire and, standing beside the sea,
those who had been victorious over the
beast and his image and over the number of
his name. They held harps given them by
God ³and sang the song of Moses the servant of God and the song of the Lamb:

"Great and marvelous are your
deeds,
Lord God Almighty.
Just and true are your ways,
King of the ages.
⁴Who will not fear you, O Lord,
and bring glory to your name?
For you alone are holy.
All nations will come
and worship before you,
for your righteous acts have been
revealed."

⁵After this I looked and in heaven the
temple, that is, the tabernacle of Testimony, was opened. ⁶Out of the temple
came the seven angels with the seven
plagues. They were dressed in clean, shining linen and wore golden sashes around
their chests. ⁷Then one of the four living
creatures gave to the seven angels seven
golden bowls filled with the wrath of God,
who lives for ever and ever. ⁸And the temple was filled with smoke from the glory of
God and from his power, and no one could
enter the temple until the seven plagues of
the seven angels were completed.

KING JAMES

1.SEVEN ANGELS

**15** And I saw another sign in heaven,
great and marvelous, seven angels
having the seven last plagues; for in them
is filled up the wrath of God.●

2.SONG

2 And I saw as it were a sea of glass
mingled with fire: and them that had
gotten the victory over the beast, and over
his image, and over his mark, *and* over the
number of his name, stand on the sea of
glass, having the harps of God. 3 And
they sing the song of Moses the servant
of God, and the song of the Lamb, saying,
Great and marvelous *are* thy works,
Lord God Almighty;
just and true *are* thy ways,
thou King of saints.
4 Who shall not fear thee, O Lord, and
glorify thy name?
For *thou* only *art* holy:
for all nations shall come and worship before thee;
for thy judgments are made manifest.●

3.TEMPLE OPENED

5 And after that I looked, and, behold,
the temple of the tabernacle of the testimony in heaven was opened: 6 and the
seven angels came out of the temple,
having the seven plagues, clothed in pure
and white linen, and having their breasts
girded with golden girdles. 7 And one of
the four beasts gave unto the seven angels
seven golden vials full of the wrath of
God, who liveth for ever and ever. 8 And
the temple was filled with smoke from the
glory of God, and from his power; and
no man was able to enter into the temple,
till the seven plagues of the seven angels
were fulfilled.●

HEAVEN

TEMPLE

The last and worst judgments in the vision to John begin with this chapter. They are known as the BOWLS.

There was no actual judgment associated with the seventh trumpet (11:15). This is because the seventh trumpet constitutes the *whole series* of BOWLS, just as the seventh seal constitutes the *whole series* of TRUMPETS.

*15:1* What words reveal the *finality* of the judgments now coming up?

*15:2-4* How are the singers identified?

What are the main parts of the song?

*15:5-8* What is the setting of this paragraph (v.5)?

Underline the repeated word "temple". How is this setting a sharp introduction to the final judgments that follow?

NEW INTERNATIONAL VERSION

Do you see a progression in the judgments of the bowls? If so, record this. (Recall that there was a progression of intensity in the seals and trumpets.)

How will people react to the bowl judgments (vv. 9,11)?

How do you account for such a reaction?

What are the words of the two angels of verses 5-7?

What do such words contribute to a prophecy about awful judgment?

*The Seven Bowls of God's Wrath*

16 Then I heard a loud voice from the
temple saying to the seven angels,
"Go, pour out the seven bowls of God's
wrath on the earth."●
2The first angel went and poured out his
bowl on the land, and ugly and painful
sores broke out on the people who had the
mark of the beast and worshiped his image.●
3The second angel poured out his bowl
on the sea, and it turned into blood like that
of a dead man, and every living thing in the
sea died.●
4The third angel poured out his bowl on
the rivers and springs of water, and they
became blood. 5Then I heard the angel in
charge of the waters say:

"You are just in these judgments,
you who are and who were, the
Holy One,
because you have so judged;
6for they have shed the blood of
your saints and prophets,
and you have given them blood to
drink as they deserve."

7And I heard the altar respond:

"Yes, Lord God Almighty,
true and just are your
judgments."●

8The fourth angel poured out his bowl on
the sun, and the sun was given power to
scorch people with fire. 9They were seared
by the intense heat and they cursed the
name of God, who had control over these
plagues, but they refused to repent and
glorify him.●
10The fifth angel poured out his bowl on
the throne of the beast, and his kingdom
was plunged into darkness. Men gnawed
their tongues in agony 11and cursed the
God of heaven because of their pains and
their sores, but they refused to repent of
what they had done.●

KING JAMES

—introduction

16 And I heard a great voice out of the
temple saying to the seven angels,
Go your ways, and pour out the vials of
the wrath of God upon the earth.●

FIRST BOWL

2 And the first went, and poured out his
vial upon the earth; and there fell a noi-
some and grievous sore upon the men
which had the mark of the beast, and *upon*
them which worshipped his image.●

SECOND BOWL

3 And the second angel poured out his
vial upon the sea; and it became as the
blood of a dead *man*: and every living soul
died in the sea.●

THIRD BOWL

4 And the third angel poured out his
vial upon the rivers and fountains of
waters; and they became blood. 5 And I
heard the angel of the waters say, Thou
art righteous, O Lord, which art, and
wast, and shalt be, because thou hast
judged thus. 6 For they have shed the
blood of saints and prophets, and thou
hast given them blood to drink; for they
are worthy. 7 And I heard another out of
the altar say, Even so, Lord God Almighty, true and righteous *are* thy judgments.●

FOURTH BOWL

8 And the fourth angel poured out his
vial upon the sun; and power was given
unto him to scorch men with fire. 9 And
men were scorched with great heat, and
blasphemed the name of God, which hath
power over these plagues: and they repented not to give him glory.●

FIFTH BOWL

10 And the fifth angel poured out his
vial upon the seat of the beast; and his
kingdom was full of darkness; and they
gnawed their tongues for pain, 11 and
blasphemed the God of heaven because
of their pains and their sores, and repented not of their deeds.●

UPON THE BEAST'S THRONE

UPON THE EARTH

The vision begun in this segment carries over into the next (16:12-21). Both should be studied together, as a series of *seven* judgments.

Record the following for each of the bowls of this segment:

UPON WHAT THE BOWL IS POURED

WHO REAPS THE JUDGMENT

WHAT THE JUDGMENT IS

REACTIONS OF THE PEOPLE

*16:2*

*16:3*

*16:4-7*

*16:8-9*

*16:10-11*

NEW INTERNATIONAL VERSION

The outpouring of God's wrath by the bowls concludes the series of many ever-intensifying judgments upon the world. Why do you think God chooses to send *many partial* judgments before *the* final judgment (of chapter 20)?

Observe that the armies attacking the land of Israel will come from the east (v.12). From what country do you think those armies will come, if the present location and relative size of nations remain up until end-times?

List some practical applications of this passage.

12The sixth angel poured out his bowl on
the great river Euphrates, and its water
was dried up to prepare the way for the
kings from the East. 13Then I saw three
evil[a] spirits that looked like frogs; they
came out of the mouth of the dragon, out
of the mouth of the beast and out of the
mouth of the false prophet. 14They are
spirits of demons performing miraculous
signs, and they go out to the kings of the
whole world, to gather them for the battle
on the great day of God Almighty.
15"Behold, I come like a thief! Blessed is
he who stays awake and keeps his clothes
with him, so that he may not go naked and
be shamefully exposed."
16Then they gathered the kings together
to the place that in Hebrew is called Armageddon.●
17The seventh angel poured out his bowl
into the air, and out of the temple came a
loud voice from the throne, saying, "It is
done!" 18Then there came flashes of lightning, rumblings, peals of thunder and a
severe earthquake. No earthquake like it
has ever occurred since man has been on
earth, so tremendous was the quake. 19The
great city split into three parts, and the
cities of the nations collapsed. God
remembered Babylon the Great and gave
her the cup filled with the wine of the fury
of his wrath. 20Every island fled away and
the mountains could not be found. 21From
the sky huge hailstones of about a hundred
pounds each fell upon men. And they
cursed God on account of the plague of
hail, because the plague was so terrible.●

[a]13 Greek *unclean*

KING JAMES

SIXTH BOWL

12 And the sixth angel poured out his
vial upon the great river Euphra'tes; and
the water thereof was dried up, that the
way of the kings of the east might be prepared. 13 And I saw three unclean
spirits like frogs *come* out of the mouth of
the dragon, and out of the mouth of the
beast, and out of the mouth of the false
prophet. 14 For they are the spirits of
devils, working miracles, *which* go forth
unto the kings of the earth and of the
whole world, to gather them to the battle
of that great day of God Almighty.
15 Behold, I come as a thief. Blessed *is*
he that watcheth, and keepeth his garments, lest he walk naked, and they see his
shame. 16 And he gathered them together into a place called in the Hebrew
tongue Armaged'don.●

BATTLE

SEVENTH BOWL

17 And the seventh angel poured out his
vial into the air; and there came a great
voice out of the temple of heaven, from
the throne, saying, It is done. 18 And
there were voices, and thunders, and lightnings; and there was a great earthquake,
such as was not since men were upon the
earth, so mighty an earthquake, *and* so
great. 19 And the great city was divided
into three parts, and the cities of the nations fell: and great Babylon came in
remembrance before God, to give unto
her the cup of the wine of the fierceness of
his wrath. 20 And every island fled
away, and the mountains were not found.
21 And there fell upon men a great hail
out of heaven, *every stone* about the
weight of a talent: and men blasphemed
God because of the plague of the hail;
for the plague thereof was exceeding
great.●

PLAGUE

This segment continues the judgments of the preceding segment.

*16:12-16* List the main parts of this judgment.

How is the battle of verse 14 identified?

Where will that battle take place (v.16)?

Where will the armies come from?

*16:17-21* List the main parts of this judgment:

What will the effect of this judgment be upon mankind?

NEW INTERNATIONAL VERSION

Try to compose a picture in your mind of the things revealed in this vision of end-times. In later studies you may want to identify the *specific* details (e.g. identification of who the seven kings are). Record below the *general* picture of these things:

POWER OF NATIONS AND WORLD-RULERS IN END-TIMES

POLITICAL ALIGNMENTS AND WARS

PERSECUTION OF THE SAINTS

DESTINIES OF NATIONS CONTROLLED BY THE SOVEREIGN GOD

### *The Woman on the Beast*

17 One of the seven angels who had the
seven bowls came and said to me,
"Come, I will show you the punishment of
the great prostitute, who sits on many waters. 2With her the kings of the earth committed adultery and the inhabitants of the
earth were intoxicated with the wine of her
adulteries."●
3Then the angel carried me away in the
Spirit into a desert. There I saw a woman
sitting on a scarlet beast that was covered
with blasphemous names and had seven
heads and ten horns. 4The woman was
dressed in purple and scarlet, and was glittering with gold, precious stones and
pearls. She held a golden cup in her hand,
filled with abominable things and the filth
of her adulteries. 5This title was written on
her forehead:

MYSTERY
BABYLON THE GREAT
THE MOTHER OF PROSTITUTES
AND OF THE ABOMINATIONS OF THE EARTH.

6I saw that the woman was drunk with the
blood of the saints, the blood of those who
bore testimony to Jesus.●
When I saw her, I was greatly astonished. 7Then the angel said to me: "Why
are you astonished? I will explain to you
the mystery of the woman and of the beast
she rides, which has the seven heads and
ten horns. 8The beast, which you saw,
once was, now is not, and will come up out
of the Abyss and go to his destruction. The
inhabitants of the earth whose names have
not been written in the book of life from the
creation of the world will be astonished
when they see the beast, because he once
was, now is not, and yet will come.
9"This calls for a mind with wisdom. The
seven heads are seven hills on which the
woman sits. They are also seven kings.
10Five have fallen, one is, the other has not
yet come; but when he does come, he must
remain for a little while. 11The beast who
once was, and now is not, is an eighth king.
He belongs to the seven and is going to his
destruction.
12"The ten horns you saw are ten kings
who have not yet received a kingdom, but
who for one hour will receive authority as
kings along with the beast. 13They have
one purpose and will give their power and
authority to the beast. 14They will make
war against the Lamb, but the Lamb will
overcome them because he is Lord of lords
and King of kings—and with him will be his
called, chosen and faithful followers."●
15Then the angel said to me, "The waters
you saw, where the prostitute sits, are peoples, multitudes, nations and languages.
16The beast and the ten horns you saw will
hate the prostitute. They will bring her to
ruin and leave her naked; they will eat her
flesh and burn her with fire. 17For God has
put it into their hearts to accomplish his
purpose by agreeing to give the beast their
power to rule, until God's words are fulfilled. 18The woman you saw is the great
city that rules over the kings of the earth."●

KING JAMES

1. INVITATION

SINNING WITH THE KINGS

17 And there came one of the seven
angels which had the seven vials,
and talked with me, saying unto me,
Come hither; I will show unto thee the
judgment of the great whore that sitteth
upon many waters;[a] 2 with whom the
kings of the earth have committed fornication, and the inhabitants of the earth
have been made drunk with the wine of
her fornication.[b] 3 So he carried me

2. VISION

away in the spirit into the wilderness: and
I saw a woman sit upon a scarlet-colored
beast, full of names of blasphemy, having
seven heads and ten horns.[c] 4 And the
woman was arrayed in purple and scarlet
color, and decked with gold and precious
stones and pearls, having a golden cup[d] in
her hand full of abominations and filthiness of her fornication: 5 and upon her
forehead *was* a name written, MYSTERY,
BABYLON THE GREAT, THE MOTHER OF
HARLOTS AND ABOMINATIONS OF THE
EARTH. 6 And I saw the woman drunken
with the blood of the saints, and with the
blood of the martyrs of Jesus.●

3. INTERPRETATION

And when I saw her, I wondered with
great admiration. 7 And the angel said
unto me, Wherefore didst thou marvel?
I will tell thee the mystery of the woman,
and of the beast that carrieth her, which
hath the seven heads and ten horns.
8 The beast that thou sawest was, and is
not; and shall ascend out of the bottomless pit,[e] and go into perdition: and they
that dwell on the earth shall wonder,
whose names were not written in the book
of life[f] from the foundation of the world,
when they behold the beast that was, and
is not, and yet is. 9 And here *is* the mind
which hath wisdom. The seven heads are
seven mountains, on which the woman
sitteth. 10 And there are seven kings: five
are fallen, and one is, *and* the other is not
yet come; and when he cometh, he must
continue a short space. 11 And the beast
that was, and is not, even he is the eighth,
and is of the seven, and goeth into perdition. 12 And the ten horns which thou
sawest are ten kings,[g] which have received
no kingdom as yet; but receive power as
kings one hour with the beast. 13 These
have one mind, and shall give their power
and strength unto the beast. 14 These
shall make war with the Lamb, and the
Lamb shall overcome them: for he is
Lord of lords, and King of kings: and
they that are with him *are* called, and
chosen, and faithful.●

15 And he saith unto me, The waters
which thou sawest, where the whore sitteth, are peoples, and multitudes, and
nations, and tongues. 16 And the ten
horns which thou sawest upon the beast,
these shall hate the whore, and shall make
her desolate and naked, and shall eat her
flesh, and burn her with fire. 17 For God
hath put in their hearts to fulfil his will,
and to agree, and give their kingdom unto
the beast, until the words of God shall be
fulfilled. 18 And the woman which thou
sawest is that great city, which reigneth
over the kings of the earth.●

REIGNING OVER THE KINGS

Chapters 17-18 are about the sins and judgments of Babylon. The name Babylon is symbolic of a real city of the end-times and also symbolic of a world system: religious, political and commercial.

*17:1-2* Is the woman of this passage good or evil?

Who is the woman, according to verses 5 and 18?

*17:3-6a* How is the woman identified with:

THE BEAST (v.3)

SAINTS AND MARTYRS (v.6)

*17:6b-14* For the remainder of this segment the angel interprets the vision for John.
The beast has how many heads and horns?

What are these?

*7 HEADS*

*10 HORNS*

What does verse 14 reveal?

*17:15-18* What are the waters?

What do verses 16-17 predict?

NEW INTERNATIONAL VERSION

Record the different things taught here about:

SPITITUAL CORRUPTION

PHYSICAL CORRUPTION

MATERIALISTIC CORRUPTION

JUDGMENT FOR SIN

GOD

*The Fall of Babylon*

18 After this I saw another angel coming down from heaven. He had great
authority, and the earth was illuminated by
his splendor. 2With a mighty voice he
shouted:

"Fallen! Fallen is Babylon the
Great!
She has become a home for
demons
and a haunt for every evil[a] spirit,
a haunt for every unclean and
detestable bird.
3For all the nations have drunk
the maddening wine of her
adulteries.
The kings of the earth committed
adultery with her,
and the merchants of the earth
grew rich from her excessive
luxuries."●

4Then I heard another voice from heaven
say:

"Come out of her, my people,
so that you will not share in her
sins,
so that you will not receive any of
her plagues;
5for her sins are piled up to heaven,
and God has remembered her
crimes.
6Give back to her as she has given;
pay her back double for what she
has done.
Mix her a double portion from her
own cup.
7Give her as much torture and grief
as the glory and luxury she gave
herself.
In her heart she boasts,
'I sit as queen; I am not a widow,
and I will never mourn.'
8Therefore in one day her plagues
will overtake her:
death, mourning and famine.
She will be consumed by fire,
for mighty is the Lord God who
judges her.●

9"When the kings of the earth who committed adultery with her and shared her
luxury see the smoke of her burning, they
will weep and mourn over her. 10Terrified
at her torment, they will stand far off and
cry:

" 'Woe! Woe, O great city,
O Babylon, city of power!
In one hour your doom has come!'●

[a]2 Greek *unclean*

KING JAMES

1. BABYLON

**18** And after these things I saw another
angel come down from heaven, having great power; and the earth was lightened with his glory. 2 And he cried
mightily with a strong voice, saying,
Babylon the great is fallen, is fallen, and
is become the habitation of devils, and the
hold of every foul spirit, and a cage of
every unclean and hateful bird. 3 For all
nations have drunk of the wine of the
wrath of her fornication, and the kings of
the earth have committed fornication with
her, and the merchants of the earth are
waxed rich through the abundance of her
delicacies.● 4 And I heard another voice
from heaven, saying, Come out of her, my
people, that ye be not partakers of her
sins, and that ye receive not of her plagues.
5 For her sins have reached unto heaven,
and God hath remembered her iniquities.
6 Reward her even as she rewarded you,
and double unto her double according to
her works: in the cup which she hath filled,
fill to her double. 7 How much she hath
glorified herself, and lived deliciously, so
much torment and sorrow give her: for
she saith in her heart, I sit a queen, and
am no widow, and shall see no sorrow.
8 Therefore shall her plagues come in one
day, death, and mourning, and famine;
and she shall be utterly burned with fire:
for strong *is* the Lord God who judgeth
her.●
9 And the kings of the earth, who have
committed fornication and lived deliciously with her, shall bewail her, and
lament for her, when they shall see the
smoke of her burning, 10 standing afar
off for the fear of her torment, saying,
Alas, alas, that great city Babylon, that
mighty city! for in one hour is thy judgment come.●

ANGEL IN SPLENDOR

2. SAINTS

3. KINGS

CITY IN JUDGMENT

This vision continues that of chapter 17, concerning the "great" city Babylon. The theme of this segment continues into the next segment (18:11-24).

*18:1-3* Record the main parts of the paragraph.

*18:4-8* Record:

INSTRUCTION TO SAINTS

SINS AND JUDGMENTS OF BABYLON

*18:9-10* Record the lamentations:

NEW INTERNATIONAL VERSION

How much of this passage is about the *commercialism* of Babylon?

Does the vision teach that material goods, of themselves, are evil? If not, what is being taught about materialism, directly or indirectly?

What do verses 23 and 24 teach about the sins of Babylon?

Record practical lessons taught by chapters 17-18:

11"The merchants of the earth will weep
and mourn over her because no one buys
their cargoes any more— 12cargoes of gold,
silver, precious stones and pearls; fine lin-
en, purple, silk and scarlet cloth; every sort
of citron wood, and articles of every kind
made of ivory, costly wood, bronze, iron
and marble; 13cargoes of cinnamon and
spice, of incense, myrrh and frankincense,
of wine and olive oil, of fine flour and
wheat; cattle and sheep; horses and carriages; and bodies and souls of men.
14"They will say, 'The fruit you longed
for is gone from you. All your riches and
splendor have vanished, never to be recov-
ered.' 15The merchants who sold these
things and gained their wealth from her will
stand far off, terrified at her torment. They
will weep and mourn 16and cry out:

" 'Woe! Woe, O great city,
dressed in fine linen, purple and
scarlet,
and glittering with gold, precious
stones and pearls!
17In one hour such great wealth has
been brought to ruin!'

"Every sea captain, and all who travel
by ship, the sailors, and all who earn their
living from the sea, will stand far off.
18When they see the smoke of her burning,
they will exclaim, 'Was there ever a city
like this great city?' 19They will throw dust
on their heads, and with weeping and
mourning cry out:

" 'Woe! Woe, O great city,
where all who had ships on the
sea
became rich through her wealth!
In one hour she has been brought to
ruin! ●
20Rejoice over her, O heaven!
Rejoice, saints and apostles and
prophets!
God has judged her for the way she
treated you.' "●

21Then a mighty angel picked up a boul-
der the size of a large millstone and threw
it into the sea, and said:

"With such violence
the great city of Babylon will be
thrown down,
never to be found again.
22The music of harpists and musicians,
flute players and trumpeters,
will never be heard in you again.
No workman of any trade
will ever be found in you again.
The sound of a millstone
will never be heard in you again.
23The light of a lamp
will never shine in you again.
The voice of bridegroom and bride
will never be heard in you again.
Your merchants were the world's
great men.
By your magic spell all the
nations were led astray.
24In her was found the blood of
prophets and of the saints,
and of all who have been killed
on the earth."●

KING JAMES

1.LAMENTATION

MERCHANDISE

11 And the merchants of the earth shall
weep and mourn over her; for no man
buyeth their merchandise any more:
12 the merchandise of gold, and silver,
and precious stones, and of pearls, and
fine linen, and purple, and silk, and scarlet, and all thyine wood, and all manner
vessels of ivory, and all manner vessels of
most precious wood, and of brass, and
iron, and marble, 13 and cinnamon, and
odors, and ointments, and frankincense,
and wine, and oil, and fine flour, and
wheat, and beasts, and sheep, and horses,
and chariots, and slaves, and souls of men.
14 And the fruits that thy soul lusted after
are departed from thee, and all things
which were dainty and goodly are departed from thee, and thou shalt find
them no more at all. 15 The merchants of
these things, which were made rich by her,
shall stand afar off for the fear of her torment, weeping and wailing, 16 and saying, Alas, alas, that great city, that was
clothed in fine linen, and purple, and scarlet, and decked with gold, and precious
stones, and pearls! 17 For in one hour so
great riches is come to nought. And every
shipmaster, and all the company in ships,
and sailors, and as many as trade by sea,
stood afar off, 18 and cried when they
saw the smoke of her burning, saying,
What *city is* like unto this great city!
19 And they cast dust on their heads, and
cried, weeping and wailing, saying, Alas,
alas, that great city, wherein were made
rich all that had ships in the sea by reason
of her costliness! for in one hour is she
made desolate.● 20 Rejoice over her, *thou*
heaven, and *ye* holy apostles and prophets; for God hath avenged you on her.●

2.REJOICING

3.DECREE

21 And a mighty angel took up a stone
like a great millstone, and cast *it* into the
sea, saying, Thus with violence shall that
great city Babylon be thrown down, and
shall be found no more at all. 22 And the
voice of harpers, and musicians, and of
pipers, and trumpeters, shall be heard no
more at all in thee; and no craftsman, of
whatsoever craft *he be*, shall be found any
more in thee; and the sound of a millstone
shall be heard no more at all in thee;
23 and the light of a candle shall shine no
more at all in thee; and the voice of the
bridegroom and of the bride shall be
heard no more at all in thee: for thy
merchants were the great men of the
earth; for by thy sorceries were all nations
deceived. 24 And in her was found the
blood of prophets, and of saints, and of
all that were slain upon the earth.●

LIVES

This segment continues the theme of the preceding one (18:1-10).

*18:11-19* Who are the ones bewailing the fall of Babylon?

Record the different things bewailed:

What is the point of the phrase "in one hour" (vv.17,19)?

*18:20* Record the truths:

*18:21-24* Record the various decrees (vv.21-23):

How does the vision conclude (v.24)?

NEW INTERNATIONAL VERSION

What do you learn from this passage about:

PRAISE

GOD'S VENGEANCE

WORSHIP OF GOD

MARRIAGE OF THE LAMB

Record practical lessons taught here.

*Hallelujah!*

19 After this I heard what sounded like
the roar of a great multitude in
heaven shouting:

"Hallelujah!
Salvation and glory and power
belong to our God,
2 for true and just are his
judgments.
He has condemned the great
prostitute
who corrupted the earth by her
adulteries.
He has avenged on her the blood of
his servants."

3 And again they shouted:

"Hallelujah!
The smoke from her goes up for
ever and ever."

4 The twenty-four elders and the four living creatures fell down and worshiped
God, who was seated on the throne. And
they cried:

"Amen, Hallelujah!" ●

5 Then a voice came from the throne, saying:

"Praise our God,
all you his servants,
you who fear him,
both small and great!"

6 Then I heard what sounded like a great
multitude, like the roar of rushing waters
and like loud peals of thunder, shouting:

"Hallelujah!
For our Lord God Almighty
reigns.
7 Let us rejoice and be glad
and give him glory!
For the wedding of the Lamb has
come,
and his bride has made herself
ready.
8 Fine linen, bright and clean,
was given her to wear."
(Fine linen stands for the righteous acts of
the saints.) ●

9 Then the angel said to me, "Write:
'Blessed are those who are invited to the
wedding supper of the Lamb!'" And he
added, "These are the true words of God."
10 At this I fell at his feet to worship him.
But he said to me, "Do not do it! I am a
fellow servant with you and with your
brothers who hold to the testimony of
Jesus. Worship God! For the testimony of
Jesus is the spirit of prophecy." ●

KING JAMES

1. JUDGMENT SONG

PRAISE GOD

**19** And after these things I heard a
great voice of much people in
heaven, saying,
Alleluia; Salvation, and glory, and
honor, and power, unto the Lord our
God: 2 for true and righteous *are* his
judgments; for he hath judged the
great whore, which did corrupt the
earth with her fornication, and hath
avenged the blood of his servants at
her hand.
3 And again they said, Alleluia. And her
smoke rose up for ever and ever. 4 And
the four and twenty elders and the four
beasts fell down and worshipped God
that sat on the throne, saying, Amen;
Alleluia.●

2. MARRIAGE SONG

5 And a voice came out of the
throne, saying,
Praise our God, all ye his servants,
and ye that fear him, both small and
great.
6 And I heard as it were the voice of a
great multitude, and as the voice of many
waters, and as the voice of mighty
thunderings, saying,
Alleluia: for the Lord God omnipotent reigneth. 7 Let us be glad and
rejoice, and give honor to him: for
the marriage of the Lamb is come,
and his wife hath made herself ready.
8 And to her was granted that she
should be arrayed in fine linen, clean
and white: for the fine linen is the
righteousness of saints.●

—conclusion

9 And he saith unto me, Write, Blessed
*are* they which are called unto the marriage supper of the Lamb. And he saith
unto me, These are the true sayings of
God. 10 And I fell at his feet to worship
him. And he said unto me, See *thou do it*
not: I am thy fellow servant, and of thy
brethren that have the testimony of Jesus:
worship God: for the testimony of Jesus
is the spirit of prophecy.●

WORSHIP GOD

Chapters 19 and 20 conclude the judgment section of the book of Revelation (chapters 6-20). A pattern of the visions is that *songs* precede each new situation of judgment. Hence the songs of this segment.

*19:1-4* Record:

*The singers* (v.1) ______________

*The song* (vv.1-3) ______________

*The singers* (v.4) ______________

*The song* (v.4) ______________

*19:5-8*

*The singer* (v.5) ______________

*The song* (v.5) ______________

*The singers* (v.6) ______________

*The song* (vv.6-8) ______________

*19:9-10* Record the main points of this paragraph:

______________

NEW INTERNATIONAL VERSION

What is revealed here about:

SECOND COMING OF CHRIST TO THIS EARTH

ENEMIES OF CHRIST

BATTLE OF ARMAGEDDON

CHRIST AS CONQUEROR

BEAST AND FALSE PROPHET

HELL

OTHER

*The Rider on the White Horse*

11I saw heaven standing open and there
before me was a white horse, whose rider
is called Faithful and True. With justice he
judges and makes war. 12His eyes are like
blazing fire, and on his head are many
crowns. He has a name written on him that
no one but he himself knows. 13He is
dressed in a robe dipped in blood, and his
name is the Word of God. 14The armies of
heaven were following him, riding on white
horses and dressed in fine linen, white and
clean. 15Out of his mouth comes a sharp
sword with which to strike down the nations. "He will rule them with an iron scepter."[a] He treads the winepress of the fury
of the wrath of God Almighty. 16On his
robe and on his thigh he has this name
written:●

KING OF KINGS AND LORD OF LORDS.

17And I saw an angel standing in the sun,
who cried in a loud voice to all the birds
flying in midair, "Come, gather together
for the great supper of God, 18so that you
may eat the flesh of kings, generals, and
mighty men, of horses and their riders, and
the flesh of all people, free and slave, small
and great."●
19Then I saw the beast and the kings of
the earth and their armies gathered together to make war against the rider on the
horse and his army. 20But the beast was
captured, and with him the false prophet
who had performed the miraculous signs
on his behalf. With these signs he had
deluded those who had received the mark
of the beast and worshiped his image. The
two of them were thrown alive into the
fiery lake of burning sulfur. 21The rest of
them were killed with the sword that came
out of the mouth of the rider on the horse,
and all the birds gorged themselves on their
flesh.●

*a15* Psalm 2:9

KING JAMES

1. CHRIST AND HIS ARMIES

GOING TO WAR

11 And I saw heaven opened, and behold a white horse; and he that sat upon
him *was* called Faithful and True, and in
righteousness he doth judge and make
war. 12 His eyes *were* as a flame of fire,
and on his head *were* many crowns; and
he had a name written, that no man knew,
but he himself. 13 And he *was* clothed
with a vesture dipped in blood: and his
name is called The Word of God. 14 And
the armies *which were* in heaven followed
him upon white horses, clothed in fine
linen, white and clean. 15 And out of his
mouth goeth a sharp sword, that with it
he should smite the nations; and he shall
rule them with a rod of iron: and he
treadeth the winepress of the fierceness
and wrath of Almighty God. 16 And he
hath on *his* vesture and on his thigh a
name written, KING OF KINGS, AND LORD
OF LORDS.●

2. OUTCOME PREDICTED

17 And I saw an angel standing in the
sun; and he cried with a loud voice, saying
to all the fowls that fly in the midst of
heaven, Come and gather yourselves together unto the supper of the great God;
18 that ye may eat the flesh of kings, and
the flesh of captains, and the flesh of
mighty men, and the flesh of horses, and
of them that sit on them, and the flesh of
all *men, both* free and bond, both small
and great.●

3. THE BATTLE

19 And I saw the beast, and
the kings of the earth, and their armies,
gathered together to make war against
him that sat on the horse, and against his
army. 20 And the beast was taken, and
with him the false prophet that wrought
miracles before him, with which he deceived them that had received the mark of
the beast, and them that worshipped his
image. These both were cast alive into a
lake of fire burning with brimstone.
21 And the remnant were slain with the
sword of him that sat upon the horse,
which *sword* proceeded out of his mouth:
and all the fowls were filled with their
flesh.●

WAR IS OVER

*19:11-16* This is a key paragraph in Revelation, because it records the second coming of Christ *to the earth.* (In the rapture, 1 Thess. 4:14-17, Christ comes not to the earth but to the air, to "catch up" the saints.)
What phrases identify the rider on the white horse as Christ?

Record the descriptions of Him:

*19:17-18* What outcome of the battle is predicted by the angel?

*19:19-21* Who wars against Christ?

Record the dispositions of the opponents:

NEW INTERNATIONAL VERSION

Record the many important truths revealed in these visions about:

SATAN DURING AND AFTER THE MILLENNIUM

THE MILLENNIUM

THE WORLD'S LAST BATTLE (20:7-10)

THE GREAT WHITE THRONE JUDGMENT

### *The Thousand Years*

20 And I saw an angel coming down
out of heaven, having the key to the
Abyss and holding in his hand a great
chain. 2He seized the dragon, that ancient
serpent, who is the devil, or Satan, and
bound him for a thousand years. 3He threw
him into the Abyss, and locked and sealed
it over him, to keep him from deceiving the
nations any more until the thousand years
were ended. After that, he must be set free
for a short time.●
4I saw thrones on which were seated
those who had been given authority to
judge. And I saw the souls of those who
had been beheaded because of their testimony for Jesus and because of the word of
God. They had not worshiped the beast or
his image and had not received his mark on
their foreheads or their hands. They came
to life and reigned with Christ a thousand
years. 5(The rest of the dead did not come
to life until the thousand years were
ended.) This is the first resurrection.
6Blessed and holy are those who have part
in the first resurrection. The second death
has no power over them, but they will be
priests of God and of Christ and will reign
with him for a thousand years.●

### *Satan's Doom*

7When the thousand years are over, Satan will be released from his prison 8and
will go out to deceive the nations in the
four corners of the earth—Gog and
Magog—to gather them for battle. In number they are like the sand on the seashore.
9They marched across the breadth of the
earth and surrounded the camp of God's
people, the city he loves. But fire came
down from heaven and devoured them.
10And the devil, who deceived them, was
thrown into the lake of burning sulfur,
where the beast and the false prophet had
been thrown. They will be tormented day
and night for ever and ever.●

### *The Dead Are Judged*

11Then I saw a great white throne and
him who was seated on it. Earth and sky
fled from his presence, and there was no
place for them. 12And I saw the dead, great
and small, standing before the throne, and
books were opened. Another book was
opened, which is the book of life. The dead
were judged according to what they had
done as recorded in the books. 13The sea
gave up the dead that were in it, and death
and Hades gave up the dead that were in
them, and each person was judged according to what he had done. 14Then death and
Hades were thrown into the lake of fire.
The lake of fire is the second death. 15If
anyone's name was not found written in
the book of life, he was thrown into the
lake of fire.●

KING JAMES

**1.MILLENNIUM**

**20** And I saw an angel come down
from heaven, having the key of the
bottomless pit and a great chain in his
hand. 2 And he laid hold on the dragon,
that old serpent, which is the Devil, and
Satan, and bound him a thousand years,
3 and cast him into the bottomless pit,
and shut him up, and set a seal upon him,
that he should deceive the nations no
more, till the thousand years should be
fulfilled: and after that he must be loosed
a little season.●

BOTTOMLESS PIT

**2.SAINTS ON THRONES**

4 And I saw thrones, and they sat upon
them, and judgment was given unto
them: and *I saw* the souls of them that
were beheaded for the witness of Jesus,
and for the word of God, and which had
not worshipped the beast, neither his
image, neither had received *his* mark upon
their foreheads, or in their hands; and
they lived and reigned with Christ a thousand years. 5 But the rest of the dead
lived not again until the thousand years
were finished. This *is* the first resurrection. 6 Blessed and holy *is* he that hath
part in the first resurrection: on such the
second death hath no power, but they
shall be priests of God and of Christ,
and shall reign with him a thousand
years.●

**3.SATAN'S DOOM**

7 And when the thousand years are expired, Satan shall be loosed out of his
prison, 8 and shall go out to deceive the
nations which are in the four quarters of
the earth, Gog and Magog, to gather
them together to battle: the number of
whom *is* as the sand of the sea. 9 And
they went up on the breadth of the earth,
and compassed the camp of the saints
about, and the beloved city: and fire came
down from God out of heaven, and devoured them. 10 And the devil that deceived them was cast into the lake of fire
and brimstone, where the beast and the
false prophet *are*, and shall be tormented
day and night for ever and ever.●

**4.THE DEAD ARE JUDGED**

11 And I saw a great white throne, and
him that sat on it, from whose face the
earth and the heaven fled away; and there
was found no place for them. 12 And I
saw the dead, small and great, stand before God; and the books were opened:
and another book was opened, which is
*the book* of life: and the dead were judged
out of those things which were written in
the books, according to their works.
13 And the sea gave up the dead which
were in it; and death and hell delivered
up the dead which were in them: and they
were judged every man according to their
works. 14 And death and hell were cast
into the lake of fire. This is the second
death. 15 And whosoever was not found
written in the book of life was cast into the
lake of fire.●

LAKE OF FIRE

*20:1-3* How is Satan identified here? ______________

______________

______________

What is revealed about him in connection with the thousand years (millennium)?

______________

______________

*20:4-6* Who are the main persons of this description of the millennium?

______________

______________

______________

What is taught about the millennium here? ______________

______________

______________

______________

*20:7-10* This vision concerns the battle of Gog and Magog. Who instigates the battle?

______________

Whom does he and his armies fight against?

______________

______________

What is the outcome? ______________

______________

______________

What does verse 10 teach? ______________

______________

______________

*20:11-15* This is the world's final judgment. Who are judged?

______________

By what are they judged? ______________

______________

What are the outcomes (vv.13-15)? ______________

______________

______________

NEW INTERNATIONAL VERSION

What do you learn here about:

HEAVEN

TEARS

SALVATION

INHERITANCE OF THE SAINTS

ETERNAL JUDGMENT OF UNBELIEVERS

GOD

*The New Jerusalem*

21 Then I saw a new heaven and a new
earth, for the first heaven and the
first earth had passed away, and there was
no longer any sea. 2I saw the Holy City, the
new Jerusalem, coming down out of
heaven from God, prepared as a bride
beautifully dressed for her husband. 3And
I heard a loud voice from the throne saying, "Now the dwelling of God is with
men, and he will live with them. They will
be his people, and God himself will be with
them and be their God. 4He will wipe every
tear from their eyes. There will be no more
death or mourning or crying or pain, for the
old order of things has passed away."●
5He who was seated on the throne said,
"I am making everything new!" Then he
said, "Write this down, for these words are
trustworthy and true."
6He said to me: "It is done. I am the
Alpha and the Omega, the Beginning and
the End. To him who is thirsty I will give
to drink without cost from the spring of the
water of life. 7He who overcomes will inherit all this, and I will be his God and he
will be my son. 8But the cowardly, the unbelieving, the vile, the murderers, the sexually immoral, those who practice magic
arts, the idolaters and all liars—their place
will be in the fiery lake of burning sulfur.
This is the second death."●

KING JAMES

1.NEW JERUSALEM

NEW HEAVEN

**21** And I saw a new heaven and a new
earth: for the first heaven and the
first earth were passed away; and there
was no more sea. 2 And I John saw the
holy city, new Jerusalem, coming down
from God out of heaven, prepared as a
bride adorned for her husband. 3 And I
heard a great voice out of heaven saying,
Behold, the tabernacle of God *is* with
men, and he will dwell with them, and
they shall be his people, and God himself
shall be with them, *and be* their God.
4 And God shall wipe away all tears from
their eyes; and there shall be no more
death, neither sorrow, nor crying, neither
shall there be any more pain: for the former things are passed away.●

2.ALL THINGS NEW

5 And he that sat upon the throne said,
Behold, I make all things new. And he
said unto me, Write: for these words are
true and faithful. 6 And he said unto me,
It is done. I am Alpha and Ome'ga, the
beginning and the end. I will give unto
him that is athirst of the fountain of the
water of life freely. 7 He that overcometh
shall inherit all things; and I will be his
God, and he shall be my son. 8 But the
fearful, and unbelieving, and the abominable, and murderers, and whoremongers,
and sorcerers, and idolaters, and all liars,
shall have their part in the lake which
burneth with fire and brimstone: which is
the second death.●

LAKE OF FIRE

This and the two segments that follow may be studied together under the one subject, *The New Jerusalem*.
Read the whole segment and underline the repeated word "new."

*21:1-4* Record what the verses reveal:

v.1 ______________________________

______________________________

______________________________

______________________________

v.2 ______________________________

______________________________

______________________________

______________________________

v.3 ______________________________

______________________________

______________________________

______________________________

v.4 ______________________________

______________________________

______________________________

______________________________

*21:5-8* Record the truths:

v.5 ______________________________

______________________________

______________________________

______________________________

v.6 ______________________________

______________________________

______________________________

______________________________

v.7 ______________________________

______________________________

______________________________

v.8 ______________________________

______________________________

______________________________

______________________________

NEW INTERNATIONAL VERSION

This is one of Scriptures' few descriptions of heaven. The picture is that of a city. What does a *city* reveal about heaven?

Some Bible students interpret the descriptions symbolically; others interpret the descriptions literally. In either case, the descriptions, because only human words can be used, can never fully reveal all the beauties, joys and glories of heaven. Record what you learn about heaven from this vision of Revelation.

What do these verses reveal?

verse 10b:

verse 12b:

9 One of the seven angels who had the
seven bowls full of the seven last plagues
came and said to me, "Come, I will show
you the bride, the wife of the Lamb."
10 And he carried me away in the Spirit to
a mountain great and high, and showed me
the Holy City, Jerusalem, coming down
out of heaven from God. 11 It shone with the
glory of God, and its brilliance was like that
of a very precious jewel, like a jasper, clear
as crystal. 12 It had a great, high wall with
twelve gates, and with twelve angels at the
gates. On the gates were written the names
of the twelve tribes of Israel. 13 There were
three gates on the east, three on the north,
three on the south and three on the west.
14 The wall of the city had twelve foundations, and on them were the names of the
twelve apostles of the Lamb.●

15 The angel who talked with me had a
measuring rod of gold to measure the city,
its gates and its wall. 16 The city was laid out
like a square, as long as it was wide. He
measured the city with the rod and found
it to be 12,000 stadia[a] in length, and as wide
and high as it is long.● 17 He measured its
wall and it was 144 cubits[b] thick,[c] by man's
measurement, which the angel was using.
18 The wall was made of jasper, and the city
of pure gold, as pure as glass. 19 The foundations of the city walls were decorated
with every kind of precious stone. The first
foundation was jasper, the second sapphire, the third chalcedony, the fourth emerald, 20 the fifth sardonyx, the sixth carnelian, the seventh chrysolite, the eighth
beryl, the ninth topaz, the tenth chrysoprase, the eleventh jacinth, and the twelfth
amethyst.[d] 21 The twelve gates were twelve
pearls, each gate made of a single pearl.
The street of the city was of pure gold, like
transparent glass.●

[a] *16* That is, about 1,400 miles (about 2,200 kilometers)
[b] *17* That is, about 200 feet (about 65 meters)
[c] *17* Or *high*
[d] *20* The precise identification of some of these precious stones is uncertain.

## KING JAMES

1.STRUCTURES

PLAGUES

9 And there came unto me one of the
seven angels which had the seven vials full
of the seven last plagues, and talked with
me, saying, Come hither, I will show thee
the bride, the Lamb's wife. 10 And he
carried me away in the spirit to a great
and high mountain, and showed me that
great city, the holy Jerusalem,[k] descending
out of heaven from God, 11 having the
glory of God: and her light *was* like unto
a stone most precious, even like a jasper
stone, clear as crystal; 12 and had a wall
great and high, *and* had twelve gates, and
at the gates twelve angels, and names
written thereon, which are *the names* of
the twelve tribes of the children of Israel:
13 on the east three gates; on the north
three gates; on the south three gates; and
on the west three gates.[l] 14 And the wall
of the city had twelve foundations, and in
them the names of the twelve apostles of
the Lamb.●

2.DIMENSIONS

15 And he that talked with me had a
golden reed to measure the city, and the
gates thereof, and the wall thereof.[m]
16 And the city lieth foursquare, and the
length is as large as the breadth: and he
measured the city with the reed, twelve
thousand furlongs. The length and the
breadth and the height of it are equal.
17 And he measured the wall thereof, a
hundred *and* forty *and* four cubits, *according to*
the measure of a man, that is, of the

3.ADORNMENTS

angel.● 18 And the building of the wall of
it was *of* jasper: and the city *was* pure gold,
like unto clear glass. 19 And the foundations
of the wall of the city *were* garnished
with all manner of precious stones. The
first foundation *was* jasper; the second,
sapphire; the third, a chalcedony; the
fourth, an emerald; 20 the fifth, sardonyx;
the sixth, sardius; the seventh,
chrysolite; the eighth, beryl; the ninth, a
topaz; the tenth, a chrysoprasus; the
eleventh, a jacinth; the twelfth, an amethyst.
21 And the twelve gates *were*
twelve pearls;[n] every several gate was of
one pearl: and the street of the city *was*
pure gold, as it were transparent glass.●

PEARLS

This part of the vision gave John a description of the new city of Jerusalem.
Record the descriptions of each paragraph.

*21:9-14* What do verses 9-10 teach? ______

STRUCTURES (vv.11-14) ______

*21:15-17*

DIMENSIONS ______

*21:18-21*

ADORNMENTS ______

NEW INTERNATIONAL VERSION

This brief description of New Jerusalem reveals many important truths about heaven. Record these.

What is significant about these things not being found in the city:

NO TEMPLE

NO SUNLIGHT

22I did not see a temple in the city, because the Lord God Almighty and the
Lamb are its temple. 23The city does not
need the sun or the moon to shine on it, for
the glory of God gives it light, and the
Lamb is its lamp. 24The nations will walk
by its light, and the kings of the earth will
bring their splendor into it. 25On no day will
its gates ever be shut, for there will be no
night there. 26The glory and honor of the
nations will be brought into it. 27Nothing
impure will ever enter it, nor will anyone
who does what is shameful or deceitful, but
only those whose names are written in the
Lamb's book of life.●

*The River of Life*

22 Then the angel showed me the river
of the water of life, as clear as crystal, flowing from the throne of God and of
the Lamb 2down the middle of the great
street of the city. On each side of the river
stood the tree of life, bearing twelve crops
of fruit, yielding its fruit every month. And
the leaves of the tree are for the healing of
the nations. 3No longer will there be any
curse. The throne of God and of the Lamb
will be in the city, and his servants will
serve him. 4They will see his face, and his
name will be on their foreheads. 5There
will be no more night. They will not need
the light of a lamp or the light of the sun,
for the Lord God will give them light. And
they will reign for ever and ever.●

KING JAMES

1.EXCLUSIONS

NO TEMPLE

22 And I saw no temple therein: for the
Lord God Almighty and the Lamb are the
temple of it. 23 And the city had no need
of the sun, neither of the moon, to shine in
it: for the glory of God did lighten it, and
the Lamb *is* the light thereof. 24 And the
nations of them which are saved shall
walk in the light of it: and the kings of the
earth do bring their glory and honor into
it. 25 And the gates of it shall not be shut
at all by day: for there shall be no night
there. 26 And they shall bring the glory
and honor of the nations into it. 27 And
there shall in no wise enter into it any
thing that defileth, neither *whatsoever*
worketh abomination, or *maketh* a lie:
but they which are written in the Lamb's
book of life. ●

2.LIFE

22 And he showed me a pure river of
water of life, clear as crystal, pro-
ceeding out of the throne of God and of
the Lamb. 2 In the midst of the street of
it, and on either side of the river, *was there*
the tree of life, which bare twelve *manner*
*of* fruits, *and* yielded her fruit every
month: and the leaves of the tree *were* for
the healing of the nations. 3 And there
shall be no more curse: but the throne
of God and of the Lamb shall be in it;
and his servants shall serve him: 4 and
they shall see his face; and his name *shall*
*be* in their foreheads. 5 And there shall be
no night there; and they need no candle,
neither light of the sun; for the Lord God
giveth them light: and they shall reign
for ever and ever.●

NO SUN-LIGHT

This segment continues the vision of the preceding segment.

*21:22-27* List what are excluded from the city, and what are included.

EXCLUSIONS (underline the repeated word "no")

INCLUSIONS

*22:1-5* Record references to:

LIFE (vv.1-2)

ACTIVITIES (vv.3-5)

NEW INTERNATIONAL VERSION

Record practical lessons taught here about the second coming of Christ.

List things revealed here about:

HEAVEN

GOD

CHRIST

How appropriate is this passage as a conclusion to the New Testament?

6The angel said to me, "These words are
trustworthy and true. The Lord, the God of
the spirits of the prophets, sent his angel to
show his servants the things that must soon
take place."

### *Jesus Is Coming*

7"Behold, I am coming soon! Blessed is
he who keeps the words of the prophecy in
this book."●

8I, John, am the one who heard and saw
these things. And when I had heard and
seen them, I fell down to worship at the
feet of the angel who had been showing
them to me. 9But he said to me, "Do not
do it! I am a fellow servant with you and
with your brothers the prophets and of all
who keep the words of this book. Worship
God!"
10Then he told me, "Do not seal up the
words of the prophecy of this book, because the time is near. 11Let him who does
wrong continue to do wrong; let him who
is vile continue to be vile; let him who does
right continue to do right; and let him who
is holy continue to be holy."●

12"Behold, I am coming soon! My reward is with me, and I will give to everyone
according to what he has done. 13I am the
Alpha and the Omega, the First and the
Last, the Beginning and the End.●
14"Blessed are those who wash their
robes, that they may have the right to the
tree of life and may go through the gates
into the city. 15Outside are the dogs, those
who practice magic arts, the sexually immoral, the murderers, the idolaters and
everyone who loves and practices falsehood.●
16"I, Jesus, have sent my angel to give
you[a] this testimony for the churches. I am
the Root and the Offspring of David, and
the bright Morning Star."

17The Spirit and the bride say, "Come!"
And let him who hears say, "Come!"
Whoever is thirsty, let him come; and whoever wishes, let him take the free gift of the
water of life.●

18I warn everyone who hears the words
of the prophecy of this book: If anyone
adds anything to them, God will add to him
the plagues described in this book. 19And if
anyone takes words away from this book
of prophecy, God will take away from him
his share in the tree of life and in the holy
city, which are described in this book.●
20He who testifies to these things says,
"Yes, I am coming soon."
Amen. Come, Lord Jesus.
21The grace of the Lord Jesus be with
God's people. Amen.●

[a] *16* The Greek is plural.

KING JAMES

1.BOOK
6 And he said unto me, These sayings
*are* faithful and true: and the Lord God
of the holy prophets sent his angel to show
unto his servants the things which must
shortly be done. 7 Behold, I come quickly.
Blessed *is* he that keepeth the sayings of
the prophecy of this book.●

BLESSING

2.WRITER
8 And I John saw these things, and
heard *them*. And when I had heard and
seen, I fell down to worship before the
feet of the angel which showed me these
things. 9 Then saith he unto me, See *thou*
*do it* not: for I am thy fellow servant, and
of thy brethren the prophets, and of them
which keep the sayings of this book:
worship God.
10 And he saith unto me, Seal not the
sayings of the prophecy of this book: for
the time is at hand. 11 He that is unjust,
let him be unjust still: and he which is
filthy, let him be filthy still: and he that is
righteous, let him be righteous still: and
he that is holy, let him be holy still.●

3.SUBJECT
12 And, behold, I come quickly; and
my reward *is* with me, to give every man
according as his work shall be. 13 I am
Alpha and Ome′ga, the beginning and the
end, the first and the last.●

4.READER
14 Blessed *are* they that do his commandments, that they may have right to
the tree of life, and may enter in through
the gates into the city. 15 For without *are*
dogs, and sorcerers, and whoremongers,
and murderers, and idolaters, and whosoever loveth and maketh a lie.●

5.INVITATION
16 I Jesus have sent mine angel to tes-
tify unto you these things in the churches.
I am the root and the offspring of
David, *and* the bright and morning star.
17 And the Spirit and the bride say,
Come. And let him that heareth say,
Come. And let him that is athirst come.
And whosoever will, let him take the
water of life freely.●

6.WARNING
18 For I testify unto every man that
heareth the words of the prophecy of this
book, If any man shall add unto these
things, God shall add unto him the plagues
that are written in this book: 19 and if
any man shall take away from the words
of the book of this prophecy, God shall
take away his part out of the book of
life, and out of the holy city, and *from* the
things which are written in this book.●

7.LAST WORDS
20 He which testifieth these things saith,
Surely I come quickly: Amen. Even so,
come, Lord Jesus.

GRACE

21 The grace of our Lord Jesus Christ
*be* with you all. Amen.●

This concluding segment of Revelation has a variety of paragraphs. Read through the entire segment, and note how the words of Jesus are interspersed throughout.
What key statement of Jesus is repeated in the segment?

_______________

Record the main truths of each paragraph.

*22:6-7* _______________

*22:8-11* _______________

*22:12-13* _______________

*22:14-15* _______________

*22:16-17* _______________

*22:18-19* _______________

*22:20-21* _______________

# FOOTNOTES

NEW INTERNATIONAL VERSION

**MATTHEW**

**ch. 1:**

a Literally, "So all the generation from Abraham unto David are fourteen."
b Literally, "her husband."
c Literally, "a just man."
d Implied in remainder of verse.

**ch. 2:**

a Literally, "and all Jerusalem with him."
b Implied. Micah 5:2.
c Literally, "went before them until it came and stood over where the baby was."
d Implied.
e Hosea 11:1.
f Jeremiah 31:15.
g Or, "the region of Ramah."

**ch. 3:**

a Literally, "in those days."
b Or, "has arrived." Literally, "is at hand."
c Implied. Isaiah 40:3.
d Jewish religious leaders who strictly followed the letter of the law but often violated its intent.
e Jewish political leaders.
f Literally, "God is able of these stones to raise up children unto Abraham."
g Or, "in water."
h Or, "in the Holy Spirit and in fire."
i Literally, "to fulfill all righteousness."

**ch. 4:**

a Implied.
b Isaiah 9:1,2.
c Or, "is at hand," or, "has arrived."
d Implied.

**ch. 5:**

a Literally, "until all things be accomplished."
b Literally, "righteousness."
c Literally, "But I say."
d Literally, "with your brother."
e Literally, "the hell of fire."
f Literally, "your right eye."
g Literally, "an eye for an eye and a tooth for a tooth."

**ch. 6:**

a Or, "from evil." Some manuscripts add here, "For yours is the kingdom and the power and the glory forever. Amen."
b Literally, "sufficient unto the day is the evil thereof."

**ch. 7:**

a Literally, "this is the law and the prophets."
b Literally, "the way that leads to destruction."
c Implied.
d Literally, "in that day."
e Literally, "I never knew you."
f Literally, "not as the scribes." These leaders only quoted others, and did not presume to present any fresh revelation.

**ch. 8:**

a Literally, "See you tell no man."
b Implied.
c Literally, "ministered unto them."
d Isaiah 53:4.
e Implied.
f Literally, "a scribe."
g Literally, "the Son of Man."
h Or, "Let me first go and bury my father."
i Literally, "Have you come here to torment us before the time?"

**ch. 9:**

a Literally, "his own city."
b Literally, "the Son of Man."
c The Matthew who wrote this book.
d Implied.
e Hosea 6:6.
f Literally, "the Bridegroom."
g These were leather bags for storing wine.
h Literally, "in all that land."

**ch. 10:**

a Or, "at hand," or, "has arrived."
b Literally, "the Son of Man."
c See Matthew 9:34, where they called him this.

**ch. 11:**

a Literally, "to teach and preach in their cities." Luke 10:1 remarks, "The Lord appointed seventy others and sent them two and two before his face, into every city and place where he himself was about to come."
b Literally, "prepare your way before you."
c Literally, "the Kingdom of Heaven suffers violence and men of violence take it by force."
d Implied.
e Literally, "he has a demon."
f Literally, "the Son of Man."
g Literally, "wisdom is justified by her children."
h Cities destroyed by God for their wickedness.
i Highly honored by Christ's being there.

**ch. 12:**

a Literally, "the Son of Man."
b Implied.
c Literally, "accuse."
d Isaiah 42:1-4.
e Literally, "the Son of David."
f Literally, "Beelzebub."
g Literally, "the strong."
h Literally, "then will he spoil his house."
i Literally, "the Son of Man."
j Implied.
k Literally, "passes through waterless places."
l Implied in Mark 3:32.

**ch. 13:**

a Implied.
b Those who were receptive to spiritual truth understood the illustrations. To others they were only stories without meaning.
c Literally, "the evil."
d Literally, "produces a crop many times greater than the amount planted—thirty, sixty, or even a hundred times as much."
e Psalm 78:2.
f Literally, "the Son of Man."
g Or, "age."
h Or, "age."
i Literally, "brings back out of his treasure things both new and old." The paraphrase is of course highly anachronistic!
j Implied.

**ch. 14:**

a Literally, "the Tetrarch"—he was one of four "kings" over the area, his sovereignty being Galilee and Peraea.
b Literally, "on account of."

**ch. 15:**

a Literally, "to God."
b Isaiah 29:13.
c Implied. Literally, "what comes out of a man defiles a man."
d Implied. Literally, "withdrew into the parts of Tyre and Sidon."

**ch. 16:**

a Jewish politico-religious leaders of two different parties.
b Literally, "the Son of Man."
c Literally, "of the elders, and chief priests, and scribes."

**ch. 17:**

a Literally, "three tabernacles" or "tents." What was in Peter's mind is not explained.
b Literally, "hear him."
c Implied. Literally, "that Elijah must come first."
d Literally, "the Son of Man."
e This verse is omitted in many of the ancient manuscripts.

**ch. 18:**

a Literally, "cause to stumble."
b Literally, "because of occasions of stumbling."
c "Do always behold..."
d Literally, "the Son of Man."
e This verse is omitted in many manuscripts, some ancient.
f Literally, "let him be to you as the Gentile and the publican."
g Literally, "10,000 talents." Approximately £3,000,000.
h Approximately £700.

**ch. 19:**

a "And the man who marries a divorced woman commits adultery." This sentence is added in some ancient manuscripts.
b Literally, "born eunuchs," or "born emasculated."
c Implied from Luke 18:19.
d Literally, "the Son of Man."
e Literally, "in the regeneration."
f Omitted here in many manuscripts, but included in Luke 18:29.

**ch. 20:**

a Literally, "a denarius," the payment for a day's labor; equivalent to $20 in modern times, or £7.
b Literally, "the Son of man."
c Implied.
d Implied.
e Literally, "the Son of Man."

**ch. 21:**

a Implied.
b Literally, "Blessed is he who comes in the name of the Lord."
c Or, "immediately."
d Literally, "By what authority do you do these things?"
e Literally, "the head of the corner."
f Literally, "bringing forth the fruits."
g Literally, "on this stone."

**ch. 22:**

a Implied.
b The Herodians were a Jewish political party.
c i.e., if Abraham, Isaac, and Jacob, long dead, were not alive in the presence of God, then God would have said, "I *was* the God of Abraham, etc."

**ch. 23:**

a Literally, "sit on Moses' seat."
b Implied.
c Literally, "enlarge their phylacteries."
d Literally, "in the name of the Lord."

**ch. 24:**

a Literally, "age."
b Literally, "the abomination of desolation."

c Daniel 9:27, 11:31, 12:11.
d Literally, "Let the reader take note."
e Literally, "roof tops" which, being flat, were used as porches at that time. See Acts 10:9.
f The city gates were closed on the Sabbath.
g Literally, "the elect."
h Literally, "the Son of Man."
i Literally, "the stars shall fall from heaven."
j Literally, "the powers of the heavens shall be shaken." See Ephesians 6:12.
k Literally, "of the coming of the Son of Man."
l "From the four winds, from one end of heaven to the other."
m Literally, "He is nigh."
n Or, "after all these things take place, this generation shall pass away."
o Literally, "neither the Son." Many ancient manuscripts omit this phrase.
p Implied.
q Literally, "knew not."

**ch. 25:**

a Literally, "virgins."
b Literally, "I know you not!"
c Implied.
d Literally, "reaping where you didn't sow, and gathering where you didn't scatter, and I was afraid..."
e Literally, "the Son of Man."
f Or, "separate the nations."

**ch. 26:**

a Literally, "the Son of Man."
b Literally, "he that dipped his hand with me in the dish."
c Literally, "the Son of Man goes."
d Zechariah 13:7.
e Literally, "the Son of Man."
f Literally, "kissed," the greeting still used among men in Eastern lands.
g Literally, "with Jesus the Galilean."
h Implied.

**ch. 27:**

a Literally, "took counsel against Jesus to put him to death." They did not have the authority themselves.
b Literally, "repented himself."
c Literally, "'King' of the Jews."
d Literally, "Jesus who is called Christ."
e Implied.
f Or, "land."
g Implied.
h Or, "a godly man."
i Implied; literally, "on the morrow, which is after the Preparation."
j This was done by stringing a cord across the rock, the cord being sealed at each end with clay.

**ch. 28:**

a Literally, "All hail!"
b Literally, "of."
c Or, "age."

## MARK

**ch. 1:**

a Implied.
b Some ancient manuscripts read, "the prophets said." This quotation, unrecorded in the book of Isaiah, appears in Malachi 3:1.
c Literally, "make ready the way of the Lord; make his paths straight."
d Literally, "preaching a baptism of repentance for the forgiveness of sins."
e Literally, "Whose shoes I am not worthy to unloose."
f Or, "in." The Greek word is not clear on this controversial point.
g Implied in parallel passages.
h Implied.
i Literally, "not as the scribes."

**ch. 2:**

a Implied.
b Literally, "scribes."
c Literally, "Son of Man."
d Literally, "the scribes of the Pharisees."
e Implied.
f Literally, "shewbread."
g Literally, "the Son of Man."

**ch. 3:**

a The Pharisees were a religious sect of the Jews.
b A pro-Roman political party.
c Implied.

**ch. 4:**

a Literally, "as they were able to hear."

**ch. 5:**

a Or, "to visit Decapolis."

**ch. 6:**

a Literally, "200 denarii," a year's wage.
b Literally, "for their hearts were hardened," perhaps implying jealousy, as in Mark 6:2-6.

**ch. 7:**

a Literally, "to wash with the fist."
b Verse 16 is omitted in many of the ancient manuscripts. "If any man has ears to hear, let him hear."
c Literally, "what proceeds out of the man defiles the man."
d About fifty miles away.
e Literally, "Let the children eat first."

**ch. 8:**

a Literally, "to test him."
b Literally, "Why does this generation seek a sign?"
c Literally, "Do you not yet understand?"
d Literally, "the Son of Man."
e Literally, "Peter began to rebuke him."

**ch. 9:**

a Literally, "the Son of Man."
b Implied.
c Or, "is growing weaker day by day."
d Literally, "O unbelieving generation."
e "And fasting" is added in some manuscripts, but not the most ancient.
f Literally, "will be able to speak evil of me."
g Verses 44 and 46 (which are identical with verse 48) are omitted in some of the ancient manuscripts.
h Literally, "For everyone shall be salted with fire."

**ch. 10:**

a Literally, "and rising up, he went from there." Mentioned here so quietly, this was his final farewell to Galilee. He never returned until after his death and resurrection.
b Implied.
c Literally, "from my youth."
d Some of the ancient manuscripts do not contain the words, "for those who trust in riches."
e Literally, "the Son of Man."
f Literally, "came up to him."
g Literally, "the Son of Man."
h Literally, "Be of good cheer."
i Literally, "Go your way."

**ch. 11:**

a Many ancient authorities add verse 26, "but if you do not forgive, neither will your Father who is in heaven forgive your trespasses." All include this in Matthew 6:15.
b Literally, "scribes and elders."

**ch. 12:**

a Literally, "Pharisees and Herodians."
b Implied.
c Literally, "out of their surplus."

**ch. 13:**

a Implied.
b Literally, "standing where he ought not."
c Literally, "elect of God."
d Literally, "the Son of Man."
e Literally, "of this generation."
f Literally, "the Son."
g Literally, "You do not know when the master of the house will come."
h Implied.

**ch. 14:**

a Literally, "the Son of Man."
b Literally, "This is my blood of the covenant." Some ancient manuscripts read, "new covenant."
c Literally, "drink it new."
d Literally, "that the hour might pass away from him."
e Literally, "the Son of Man."
f Literally, "kiss"—the usual oriental greeting, even to this day.
g It was Peter. John 18:10.
h Implied. Literally, "wearing only a linen cloth."
i This statement is found in only some of the manuscripts.

**ch. 15:**

a Implied.
b Verse 28 is omitted in some of the ancient manuscripts. The quotation is from Isaiah 53:12.
c Or, "over the entire world."
d He spoke here in Aramaic. The onlookers, who spoke Greek and Latin, misunderstood his first two words ("Eloi, Eloi") and thought he was calling for the prophet Elijah.
e A heavy veil hung in front of the room in the Temple called "The Holy of Holies," a place reserved by God for himself; the veil separated him from sinful mankind. Now this veil was split from above, showing that Christ's death, for man's sin, had opened up access to the holy God.

**ch. 16:**

a Verses 9 through 20 are not found in the most ancient manuscripts, but may be considered an appendix giving additional facts.
b Literally, "after these things."
c Literally, "they will speak in new tongues." Some ancient manuscripts omit "new."

## LUKE

**ch. 1:**

a From verse 3. Literally, "most excellent Theophilus." The name means "one who loves God."
b Literally, "an account of the things accomplished among us."
c Probably by throwing dice or something similar—"drawing straws" would be a modern equivalent.
d Implied.
e Literally, "to turn the hearts of the fathers to the children, and the disobedient to the wisdom of the just."
f Some ancient versions add, "Blessed are you among women," as in verse 42 which appears in all the manuscripts.
g Literally, "relative."
h Zacharias was apparently stone deaf as well as speechless, and had not heard what his wife had said.
i Literally, "became strong in spirit."

**ch. 2:**

a Literally, "swaddling clothes."
b Literally, "in the City of David."
c Literally, "swaddling clothes."
d Literally, "said."
e Literally, "the Consolation of Israel."
f Literally, "looking for the redemption of Jerusalem."

**ch. 3:**

a Or, "preaching the baptism of repentance for remission of sins."
b Implied.

c Literally, "of loosing (the sandal strap of) his shoe."
d "Sala."

**ch. 4:**

a Literally, "Man shall not live by bread alone." Deuteronomy 8:3.
b Literally, "to proclaim the acceptable year of the Lord."
c Literally, "ministered unto them."

**ch. 5:**

a Literally, "Pharisees."
b Literally, "the Son of Man."
c Literally, "taken away from them."

**ch. 6:**

a Literally, "the Son of Man."
b Literally, "on account of the Son of Man."
c Literally, "release, and you shall be released."
d Implied.

**ch. 7:**

a Implied.
b Literally, "the one who is coming."
c Literally, "Blessed is he who keeps from stumbling over me."
d Literally, "even the tax collectors"; i.e., the publicans.
e Literally, "We played the flute for you and you didn't dance; we sang a dirge and you didn't weep."
f Literally, "He has a demon."
g Literally, "is a friend of tax gatherers and sinners."
h Literally, "but wisdom is justified of all her children."

**ch. 8:**

a Implied.
b Implied. See Matthew 5:16.
c Implied; a legion consisted of 6,000 troops. Whether the demons were speaking literally is, of course, unknown.
d This clause is not included in some of the ancient manuscripts.

**ch. 9:**

a Literally, "as a testimony against them."
b Literally, "Herod the Tetrarch."
c Literally, "the Son of Man."
d Literally, "the Son of Man."
e Literally, "the appearance of his face changed."
f Implied.
g A typical case of discrimination (cf. John 4:9). The Jews called the Samaritans "half-breeds," so the Samaritans naturally hated the Jews.
h Later manuscripts add to verses 55 and 56, "And Jesus said, You don't realize what your hearts are like. For the Son of Man has not come to destroy men's lives, but to save them."
i Literally, "the Son of Man."
j Literally, "But he said, 'Lord, suffer me first to go and bury my father.'"—perhaps meaning that the man could, when his father died, collect the inheritance and have some security.
k Or, "Let those who are spiritually dead care for their own dead."
l Literally, "bid them farewell at home."

**ch. 10:**

a Literally, "Salute no one in the way."
b Cities destroyed by God in judgment for their wickedness. For a description of this event, see Ezekiel, chapters 26-28.
c Literally, "babies."
d Literally, "wanting to justify himself."
e Literally, "Levite."
f Literally, "a Samaritan." All Samaritans were despised by Jews, and the feeling was mutual due to historic reasons.
g Literally, "took care of him."
h Literally, "two denarii," each the equivalent of a modern day's wage.
i Implied.
j Literally, "Martha, Martha."

**ch 11:**

a Implied.
b Some ancient manuscripts add at this point additional portions of the Lord's Prayer as recorded in Matthew 6:9-13.
c Implied.
d Literally, "from Beelzebub."
e Implied; literally, "Others, tempting, sought of him a sign from heaven."
f Literally, "the Strong."
g But empty, since the person is neutral about Christ.
h Literally, "Queen of the South." See 1 Kings, chapter 10.

**ch. 12:**

a Literally, "you."
b Literally, "the Son of Man."
c Literally, "Eat, drink, and be merry."
d Literally, "the Son of Man."
e Implied by ancient custom.

**ch. 14:**

a Literally, "If anyone comes to me and does not hate his father and mother...."
b Implied in verse 33.
c Perhaps the reference is to impure salt; when wet, the salt dissolves and drains out, leaving a tasteless residue. Matthew 5:13.

**ch. 16:**

a Or, "Do you think the rich man commended the scoundrel for being so shrewd?"
b Implied.
c Literally, "sons of the light."
d Literally, and probably ironically, "Make to yourselves friends by means of the mammon of unrighteousness; that when it shall fail you, they may receive you into the eternal tabernacles!" Some commentators would interpret this to mean: "Use your money for good, so that it will be waiting to befriend you when you get to heaven." But this would imply the end justifies the means, an unbiblical idea.
e Literally, "into Abraham's bosom."
f Literally, "into Hades."
g Even Christ's resurrection failed to convince the Pharisees, to whom he gave this illustration.

**ch. 17:**

a Implied. Samaritans were despised by Jews as being only "half-breed" Hebrews.
b Or, "among you."
c Or, "long for the Son of Man."
d Implied.
e Or, "the hour I am revealed."
f This may mean that God's people will be taken out to the execution grounds and their bodies left to the vultures.

**ch. 18:**

a Literally, "the Son of Man."
b Implied.

**ch. 19:**

a Implied.
b Literally, "the Son of Man."
c Literally, "the leading men among the people."

**ch. 20:**

a Otherwise the statement would be, "He *had been* that person's God."

**ch. 21:**

a Literally, "will come in my Name."
b Literally, "It shall turn out unto you for a testimony."
c Literally, "days of vengeance."
d Literally, "upon the land," or, "upon the earth."
e Literally, "the Son of Man."
f Or, "this generation."
g Or, "Pray for strength to pass safely through these coming horrors."

**ch. 22:**

a Literally, "the city."
b Literally, "This cup is the new covenant in my blood, poured out for you."
c Literally, "the Son of Man."
d Implied.
e Literally, "they (the kings and great men) are called 'benefactors.'"
f Literally, "you have continued with me in my temptation."
g Literally, "fail not."
h Literally, "that you enter not into temptation."
i Literally, "approached Jesus to kiss him." This is still the traditional greeting among men in eastern lands.
j Literally, "the Son of Man."

**ch. 23:**

a Implied.
b Literally, "Are you the King of the Jews?"
c Literally, "as one who perverts the people."
d Some ancient authorities add verse 17, "For it was necessary for him to release unto them at the feast one (prisoner)."
e Literally, "For if they do this when the tree is green, what will happen when it is dry?"
f Or, "the whole world."
g Implied.
h Literally, "yielded up the spirit."
j Literally, "righteous."

**ch. 24:**

a Literally, "the Son of Man."
b Literally, "returned from the tomb."
c Literally, "in these days."
d Implied.
e Implied. Literally, "the promise of my Father."
f Literally, "but wait here in the city until...." The paraphrase relates this to verse 47.
g Implied. Bethany was a mile or so away, across the valley on the Mount of Olives.

**JOHN**

**ch. 1:**

a Literally, "In the beginning."
b Literally, "the Word," meaning Christ, the wisdom and power of God and the first cause of all things; God's personal expression of himself to men.
c Literally, "to believe on his name."
d Literally, "not of blood."
e Literally, "grace."
f See Matthew 17:2.
g Or, "his unique Son."
h Literally, "the Jews."
i See Deuteronomy 18:15.
j Or, "in."
k Literally, "the Son of Man."

**ch. 2:**

a Literally, "Woman, what have I to do with you?"
b Literally, "His disciples believed on him."
c Literally, "the Jews."

**ch. 3:**

a Or, "Physical birth is not enough. You must also be born spiritually...." This alternate paraphrase interprets "born of water" as meaning the normal process observed during every human birth. Some think this means water baptism.
b Literally, "the Son of Man."
c Or, "the unique Son of God."
d Literally, "about purification."

e Implied.

**ch. 4:**

a Implied.
b See John 2:23.

**ch. 5:**

a Many of the ancient manuscripts omit the material within the parentheses.
b Implied. Literally, "sin no more."
c Implied. Literally, "My Father works even until now, and I work."
d Implied. However, most commentators believe the reference is to the witness of his Father. See verse 37.

**ch. 6:**

a Literally, "Now the Passover, the feast of the Jews, was at hand."
b Literally, 200 denarii, a denarius being a full day's wage.
c Literally, "and straightway the boat was at the land...."
d Implied.
e Literally, "the Son of Man."
f Implied. Literally, "Son of Man."
g Literally, "the Son of Man."
h Literally, "It is the Spirit who quickens."
i See John 1:13. Literally, "the flesh profits nothing."

**ch. 7:**

a Literally, "I go not up (yet) unto this feast." The word "yet" is included in the text of many ancient manuscripts.
b Implied.
c Literally, "This multitude is accursed."
d Most ancient manuscripts omit John 7:53—8:11.

**ch. 8:**

a Literally, "the Father."
b Literally, "when you have lifted up the Son of Man."
c Implied.
d Implied. Literally, "There is one who seeks and judges."

**ch. 9:**

a i.e., on Saturday, the weekly Jewish holy day when all work was forbidden.
b Literally, "You were altogether born in sin."
c Literally, "the Son of Man."

**ch. 10:**

a December 25 was the usual date for this celebration of the cleansing of the Temple.
b Chapter 5:19; 8:36,56,58,etc.
c Literally, "Many believed on him there."

**ch. 11:**

a See John 12:3.

**ch. 12:**

a Philip's name was Greek, though he was a Jew.
b Literally, "if any man."
c Literally, "prince of this world." See 2 Corinthians 4:4, and Ephesians 2:2 and 6:12.
d Implied.
e Literally, "sons of light."
f Literally, "To whom has the arm of the Lord been revealed?" Isaiah 53:1.
g Literally, "He." The Greek here is a very free rendering, or paraphrase, of Isaiah 6:10.

**ch. 13:**

a As the lowliest of slaves would dress.
b Literally, "There was one at the table." All commentators believe him to be John, the writer of this book.
c Literally, "reclining on Jesus' bosom." The custom of the period was to recline around the table, leaning on the left elbow. John, next to Jesus, was at his side.
d Literally, "leaning back against Jesus' chest," to whisper his inquiry.
e Literally, "He it is for whom I shall dip the sop and give it him." The honored guest was thus singled out in the custom of that time.

**ch. 14:**

a Or, "Helper."
b Literally, "in my name."
c Implied.

**ch. 16:**

a Implied.
b Literally, "none of you is asking me whither I am going." The question had been asked before (John 13:36, 14:5), but apparently not in this deeper sense.
c Literally, "he will convict the world of sin and righteousness and judgment."
d Implied.
e Literally, "you shall ask *in my name*." The above paraphrase is the modern equivalent of this idea, otherwise obscure.
f Literally, "and need not that anyone should ask you," i.e., discuss what is true.

**ch. 17:**

a Literally, "kept in your name those whom you have given me."

**ch. 18:**

a By Jewish law, entering the house of a Gentile was a serious offense.
b Literally, "It is not lawful for us to put any man to death."
c This prophecy is recorded in Matthew 20:19, which indicates his death by crucifixion, a practice under Roman law.
d A paraphrase of this verse—that goes beyond the limits of this book's paraphrasing would be, "Do you mean their King, or their Messiah?" If Pilate was asking as the Roman governor, he would be inquiring whether Jesus was setting up a rebel government. But the Jews were using the word "King" to mean their religious ruler, the Messiah. Literally this verse reads, "Are you saying this of yourself, or did someone else say it about me?"

**ch. 19:**

a Literally, "he."
b Literally, "the judgment seat in a place that is called The Pavement, but in Hebrew, Gabbatha."
c Psalm 22:18.
d Literally, "standing by the disciple whom he loved."
e Literally, "to the disciple."
f Literally, "had received."
g Literally, "And he who has seen has borne witness, and his witness is true, and he knows what he says is true, that you also may believe."
h See chapter 3.
i Literally "a garden."

**ch. 20:**

a Literally, "on the first day of the week."
b Literally, "the other disciple whom Jesus loved."
c Literally, "Peter and the other disciple."
d Literally, "the other disciple also, who came first."
e Implied.
f Literally, "the disciples."

**ch. 21:**

a Literally, "the sons of Zebedee."
b Literally, "children."
c Literally, "that disciple therefore whom Jesus loved."
d Implied.
e Literally, "more than these." See Mark 14:29.
f Literally, "all things."
g Implied. Literally, "and this man, what?"
h Literally, "tarry."

## ACTS

**ch. 1:**

a i.e., the book of Luke; see footnote chapter 1, verse 1.
b Or, "in."
c Implied.
d Psalm 69:25.
e Psalm 109:8.
f Literally, "cast lots," or, "threw dice."

**ch. 2:**

a This annual celebration came fifty days after the Passover ceremonies, when Christ was crucified. See Leviticus 23:16.
b Literally, "in other tongues."
c Literally, "Asia," a province of what is now Turkey.
d Literally, "men without the Law." See Romans 2:12.
e Implied in verse 31.
f Literally, "the breaking of bread," i.e., "the Lord's Supper."

**ch. 3:**

a Literally, "like unto me."
b Literally, "destroyed from among the people."

**ch. 4:**

a The Sadducees were members of a Jewish religious sect that denied the resurrection of the dead.
b Implied. Literally, "became the head of the corner."
c Literally, "great grace was upon them all."

**ch. 5:**

a Literally, "to try the Spirit of the Lord."
b Implied.
c Literally, "the captain of the Temple."

**ch. 6:**

a Literally, "full of grace and power." See verse 5.
b Literally, "the elders and the Scribes."

**ch. 7:**

a Literally, "Mesopotamia."
b Literally, "Haran," a city in the area we now know as Syria.
c Literally, "our fathers."
d Literally, "like unto me."
e Literally, "the Law as it was ordained by angels."
f Literally, "the Son of Man."
g Paul is also known as Saul.

**ch. 8:**

a Literally, "devout men." It is not clear whether these were Christians who braved the persecution, or whether they were godly and sympathetic Jews.
b Literally, "the church."
c Literally, "this man is that Power of God which is called great."
d Literally, "the gall of bitterness."
e Implied. Literally, "Who can declare his generation." Alternatively, "Who will be able to speak of his posterity? For..."
f Many ancient manuscripts omit verse 37 wholly or in part.

**ch. 9:**

a Implied.
b Literally, "Tabitha," her name in Hebrew.

**ch. 10:**

a Implied.
b Implied; see Leviticus 11 for the forbidden list.
c Implied.

**ch. 11:**

a Implied.
b Or, "in."
c Literally, "upon the earth."

**ch. 12:**
a Implied.
b Implied.

**ch. 13:**
a Literally, "Pamphylia."
b Literally, "departed from them." See chapter 15, verse 38.
c Literally, "beckoning with the hand."
d Implied.
e Literally, "This day have I begotten you."
f Implied.
g Literally, "saw no corruption."
h Literally, "the Jews."
i Or, "blasphemed."
j Or, "were disposed to," or, "ordained to." Literally, "the disciples."

**ch. 15:**
a Implied. See Amos 9:11-12.
b Literally, " rebuild the tabernacle of David which is fallen."
c Literally, "subverted your souls."
d Literally, "and from blood."
e Or, "prophets."
f Literally, "spent some time."
g Implied. Literally, "return now and visit every city wherein we proclaimed the word of the Lord."

**ch. 16:**
a Implied.
b Literally, "in the night."
c Luke, the writer of this book, now joined Paul and accompanied him on his journey.
d Implied.

**ch. 17:**
a Some manuscripts read, "many of the wives of the leading men."
b Implied.
c Implied.

**ch. 18:**
a Implied.
b Probably a vow to offer a sacrifice in Jerusalem in thanksgiving for answered prayer. The head was shaved thirty days before such gifts and sacrifices were given to God at the Temple.
c Possibly in order to arrive in Jerusalem within the prescribed thirty days.
d Literally, "feast." This entire sentence is omitted in many of the ancient manuscripts.
e Implied.
f Literally, "explained to him the way of God more accurately."

**ch. 19:**
a Or, "into."
b Implied.
c Literally, "concerning the Kingdom of God."
d Approximately £3,500.
e Literally, "purposed in the spirit."
f Literally, "is the templekeeper."

**ch. 20:**
a Literally, "Asia."
b Or, "on Saturday night." Literally, "the first day of the week," by Jewish reckoning, from sundown to sundown.
c Or, "by an inner compulsion."

**ch. 21:**
a See Acts 6:5; 8:1-13.
b Literally, "virgins."
c Literally, "they are all zealous for the law."
d Literally, "the days of purification."
e Implied.
f Literally, "castle," or "fort."
g Literally, "before these days."

**ch. 22:**
a Literally, "Righteous One."

**ch. 23:**
a Literally, "you whitewashed wall."
b Literally, "nor spirit."
c Literally, "scribes."
d Implied.

**ch. 24:**
a Literally, "elders."
b Literally, "orator."
c Implied.
d Literally, "except it be for this one voice."
e Literally, "having more accurate knowledge."
f Literally, "his own wife."

**ch. 25:**
a She was his sister.

**ch. 26:**
a Literally, "stretched forth his hand."
b Literally, "my own nation."
c Literally, "the name."
d Literally, "It is hard for you to kick against the oxgoad!"
e Literally, "with little (persuasion)."

**ch. 27:**
a Literally, "a ship of Adramyttium."
b Literally, "the coast of Asia."
c See Acts 19:29,20:4,Philemon 24.
d Implied. Literally, "we sailed under the lee of Cyprus." Narratives from that period interpret this as meaning what is indicated in the paraphrase above.
e Cnidus was a port on the southeast coast of Turkey.
f Literally, "because the Fast was now already gone by." It came at about the time of the autumn equinox.
g Implied.
h Literally, "fearing lest they should be cast upon the Syrtis."
i Literally, "neither sun nor stars shone upon us."
j Literally, "a place where two seas met."
k Implied.

**ch. 28:**
a Literally, "honors."
b About forty-three miles from Rome.
c About thirty-five miles from Rome.
d Literally, "the hope of Israel." But perhaps he is referring here, as in his other defenses, to his belief in the resurrection of the dead.
e Implied.
f Isaiah 6:9,10.
g Some of the ancient manuscripts add, "And when he had said these words, the Jews departed, having much dissenting among themselves."
h Or, "at his own expense."

## ROMANS

**ch. 1:**
a Literally, "in the will of God."
b Or, "that I will finally succeed in coming."
c Literally, "some spiritual gift...that is,...faith."
d Literally, "among the Gentiles."
e Literally: "(this) righteousness of God is *revealed* from faith to faith."
f Habakkuk 2:4
g Literally, "is manifest in them."
h Implied. Or, "They have no excuse for saying there is no God."
i Literally, "mortal."
j Or, "were confused fools."

**ch.2:**
a Literally, "who patiently do good."
b Implied.
c Literally, "all who do good."
d Or, "you rely upon the law for your salvation."
e Literally, "do you rob temples?"
f Literally, "will condemn" you.

**ch. 3:**
a Implied.
b Psalm 51:4.
c Psalm 14:3.
d Literally, "Their throat is an open grave." Perhaps the meaning is "Their speech injures others."
e Implied.
f Implied. Literally, "A righteousness of God has been manifested."
g Literally, "to be a propitiation."
h Literally, "justified."

**ch. 4:**
a Literally, "faith is reckoned for righteousness."
b Literally, "righteous."
c Psalm 32:1-2.
d Genesis 17:17.
e Literally, "raised for our justification."

**ch. 5**
a Literally, "Sin entered into the world, and death through sin."
b Implied.
c Literally, "reign in life."

**ch. 6**
a Literally, "united with him in the likeness of his death."
b Literally, "Sin will never again be your master."

**ch. 7:**
a Implied. Literally, "men who know (the) law."
b Literally, "Now we are delivered from the law."
c Implied.
d Or, "It will be done." Literally, "I thank God through Jesus Christ our Lord."

**ch. 8:**
a Or possibly, "but the Holy Spirit who lives in you will give you life, for he has already given you righteousness." Literally, "but the spirit is life because of righteousness."
b Literally, "waiting for the revelation of the sons of God."
c Implied.
d Literally, "The whole creation has been groaning in travail together until now."
e Implied. Literally, "in like manner."

**ch. 9:**
a Implied.
b Literally, "that my name might be published abroad in all the earth."
c Hosea 2:23.
d Literally, "as the sand of the sea,"i.e., numberless.
e Isaiah 10:22, 28:22.
f Isaiah 1:9.
g Isaiah 28:16.

**ch. 10:**
a Literally, "Confession is made unto salvation."
b Isaiah 52:7
c Isaiah 53:l.
d Implied.
e Isaiah 65:1.
f Literally, "disobedient, obstinate."

**ch. 11:**
a 1Kings 19:18.
b Literally, "shut up all unto disobedience."

**ch. 12:**
a Implied.

**ch. 13:**
a Literally, "our salvation."

**ch. 14:**
a Literally, "Receive him that is weak in faith, not for decisions of scruples." Perhaps the meaning is, "Receive those whose

consciences hurt them when they do things others have no doubts about." Accepting them might cause discord in the church, but Paul says to welcome them anyway.

**ch. 15:**

a Or, "I have fully accomplished my Gospel ministry."
b Literally, "For if the Gentiles have come to share in their spiritual blessings, they ought also to be of service to them in material blessings."

**1 CORINTHIANS**

**ch. 1:**

a Or, "chosen by Christ Jesus." Literally, "sanctified in Christ Jesus."
b Or, "are being..."
c Or, "he brought us near to God."
d Or, "to free us from slavery to sin."

**ch. 2:**

a Or, "interpreting spiritual truth in spiritual language."
b Or, "who can advise him?"

**ch. 3:**

a Literally, "Are you not (mere) men?"
b Literally, "Let no one glory in men."

**ch. 5:**

a Possibly his stepmother.
b Literally, "for the destruction of the flesh."

**ch. 6:**

a Or, "Even the least capable people in the church should be able to decide these things for you." Both interpretations are possible.
b Literally, "All things are lawful for me." Obviously, Paul is not here permitting sins such as have just been expressly prohibited in verses 8 and 9. He is apparently quoting some in the church of lustful Corinth who were excusing their sins.

**ch. 7:**

a Literally, "Become not bondservants of men."
b Implied.
c Literally, "(that) those who have wives may be as though they didn't."
d Literally, "pure in body and in spirit."

**ch. 8:**

a Literally, "of whom are all things."
b Implied. Literally, "faith."

**ch. 9:**

a Implied. Literally, "Have we no right to lead about a wife that is a believer?"
b Implied.
c Literally, "a wreath that quickly fades," given to the winners of the original Olympic races of Paul's time.

**ch. 10:**

a Implied. Literally, "all ate the same supernatural food and drink."
b Literally, "For they drank of a spiritual Rock that followed them, and the Rock was Christ."

**ch. 11:**

a Implied in verses 7, 10.
b Implied.
c Genesis 2:21-22.
d Literally, "For this cause ought the woman to have power on (her) head."
e Literally, "because of the angels."
f Some ancient manuscripts read, "broken."

**ch. 14:**

a The local language, whatever it is.
b Implied. See verses 19 and 28.
c Implied.
d Literally, "The spirits of the prophets are subject to the prophets."
e Literally, "They are not authorized to speak." They are permitted to pray and prophesy (1 Cor. 11:5), apparently in public meetings, but not to teach men (1 Tim 2:12).
f Or, "If he disagrees, ignore his opinion."

**ch. 15:**

a The name given to Jesus' twelve disciples, and still used after Judas was gone from among them.
b Literally, "the first-fruits of them that are asleep."
c Or, "there are some who know nothing of God."
d Literally, "There are celestial bodies." But perhaps this may refer to the sun, moon, planets, and stars.
e Literally, "was made a living soul."
f Literally, "the last Adam."
g Implied.
h Implied.

**ch. 16:**

a Implied.
b Implied in 1 Timothy 4:12.

**2 CORINTHIANS**

**ch. 1:**

a Or, "throughout Achaia."

**ch. 2:**

a Implied.

**ch. 3:**

a Implied.

**ch. 4:**

a Implied.
b Literally, "who is the image of God."
c Implied.

**ch. 5:**

a Implied.
b Literally, "Him who knew no sin, he made sin on our behalf, that we might become the righteousness of God in him."

**ch. 7:**

a Implied.

**ch. 11:**

a Implied.
b Implied.

**ch. 12:**

a Literally, "A man in Christ."
b Literally, "the third heaven."

**ch. 13:**

a Implied.
b Literally, "not that we may appear approved."
c Literally, "For we can do nothing against the truth, but for the truth."

**GALATIANS**

**ch. 1:**

a Galatia was a province in what is now called Turkey.

**ch. 2:**

a Implied.
b Literally, "For I through the law died unto the law, that I might live unto God."

**ch. 3:**

a Implied.

**ch. 4:**

a It is traditional to suppose that Paul was handicapped by a disease of the eyes.

**ch. 5:**

a Or, "Would that those disturbing you would go and castrate themselves."

**EPHESIANS**

**ch. 2**

a Literally, "he made us alive."
b Or, "Salvation is not of yourselves."
c Literally, "by making us one."
d Implied.

**ch. 4:**

a Literally, "that he might fill all things."
b Amplified New Testament.
c Literally, "in whom you were sealed unto the day of redemption."

**ch. 5:**

a Or, "your lives should be an example."
b Literally, "having cleansed it by washing of water with the word."

**PHILIPPIANS**

**ch. 2:**

a Literally, "was made in the likeness of men."
b Literally, "became obedient unto death, even the death of the cross."

**COLOSSIANS**

**ch. 1:**

a Literally, "he is the firstborn of all creation."
b Literally, "he is the Beginning, the firstborn from the dead."

**ch. 2:**

a Literally, "by the rudiments of the world."

**1 THESSALONIANS**

**ch. 1:**

a Literally, "receive him."

**ch. 3:**

a Literally, "with all his saints. Amen."

**2 THESSALONIANS**

**ch. 2:**

a Literally, "the mystery of lawlessness is already at work."
b Or, "because God chose you to be among the first to believe."

**1 TIMOTHY**

**ch. 2:**

a Literally, "in gravity."

**ch. 3:**

a More literally, "church leader" or "presiding elder."

**ch. 4:**

a Literally, "enrolled as a widow."

**2 TIMOTHY**

**ch. 1:**

a Implied. Literally, "stir up the gift of God."
b Literally, "and love that is in Christ Jesus."

**ch. 3:**

a Literally, "having a form of godliness."
b Literally, "Every Scripture."

**ch. 4:**

a Literally, "I was delivered out of the mouth of the lion."

**TITUS**

**ch. I:**

a More literally, "elders."

**HEBREWS**

**ch. I:**

a Implied.
b Literally, "this day I have begotten you."

**ch. 3:**

a Literally, "deceitfulness."

**ch. 5:**

a Literally, "begotten you." Probably the reference is to the day of Christ's resurrection.
b Implied. Christ's longing was to live until he could die on the cross for all mankind. There is a strong case to be made that Satan's great desire was that Christ should die prematurely, before the mighty work at the cross could be performed. Christ's body, being human, was frail and weak like ours (except that his was sinless). He had said

just a few moments before, "My soul is exceeding sorrowful *unto death*." And can a human body live long under such pressure of spirit as he underwent in the Garden, that caused sweating of great drops of blood? But God graciously heard and answered his anguished cry in Gethsemane ("Let this cup cup pass from me") and preserved him from seemingly imminent and premature death: for an angel was sent to strengthen him so that he could live to accomplish God's perfect will at the cross.... But some readers may prefer the explanation that Christ's plea was that he be saved *out from* death, at the Resurrection.

**ch. 6:**

a Literally, "the laying on of hands."
b Literally, "having become our High Priest."

**ch. 7:**

a No one can be sure whether this means that Melchizedek was Christ appearing to Abraham in human form, or simply that there is no *record* of who Melchizedek's father or mother were, no *record* of his birth or death.

**ch. 9:**

a Implied.

**ch. 10:**

a The blood of bulls and goats merely covered over the sins, taking them out of sight for hundreds of years until Jesus Christ came to die on the cross. There he gave his own blood which forever took those sins away.

**ch. 11:**

a Perhaps the reference is to atoms, electrons, etc.
b Implied.

**JAMES**

**ch. 1:**

a Implied.

**ch. 2:**

a Literally, "Of his own free will he gave us, etc."

**ch. 3:**

a Literally, "Not many (of you) should become masters (teachers)."

**ch. 5:**

a Implied.

**1 PETER**

**ch. 2**

a An alternative paraphrase of these verses could read: "If you have tasted the Lord's goodness and kindness, cry for more, as a baby cries for milk. Eat God's Word—read it, think about it—and grow strong in the Lord and be saved."
b Implied.

**ch. 3**

a Implied.
b Or, "Baptism, which corresponds to this, now saves you through the Resurrection."

**ch. 4:**

a Literally, "lawless idolatries."
b Implied. See 1 Peter 3:19,20.
c Or, "love overlooks each other's many faults."
d Or, "the glory of the Spirit of God is being seen in you."

**2 PETER**

**ch. 1:**

a Literally, "She who is at Babylon is likewise chosen"; but Babylon was the Christian nickname for Rome, and the "she" is thought by many to be Peter's wife to whom reference is made in Matthew 8:14, 1 Corinthians 9:5, etc. Others believe this should read: "Your sister church here in Babyon salutes you, and so does my son Mark."

**ch. 2:**

a Or, "the glories of the unseen world."
b Literally, "the things they do not understand."
c Implied. Literally, "will be destroyed in the same destruction with them."

**ch. 3:**

a Literally, "wherein righteousness dwells."

**1 JOHN**

**ch. 1:**

a Implied. Literally, "if we confess our sins."
b Literally, "he is...just."

**ch. 2:**

a Or, "atoning sacrifice."

**ch. 3:**

a Or, perhaps, "the Lord will be merciful anyway." Literally, "If our heart condemns us, God is greater than our heart."

**ch. 5:**

a Literally, "This is he who came by water and blood." See Matthew 3:16,17; Luke 9:31,35; John 12:27,28,32,33. Other interpretations of this verse are equally possible.
b Literally, "not by water only, but by water and blood."
c Literally, "the Spirit, and the water, and the blood."
d Implied.
e Commentators differ widely in their thought about what sin this is, and whether it causes physical death or spiritual death. Blasphemy against the Holy Spirit results in spiritual death (Mark 3:29) but can a Christian ever sin in such a way? Impenitence at the Communion Table sometimes ends in physical death (1 Cor. 11:30). And Hebrews 6:4-8 speaks of the terrible end of those who fall away.

**JUDE**

**ch. 1:**

a Or, "who abandoned their original rank and left their proper home."

**THE REVELATION**

**ch. 1:**

a Literally, "the revelation of (*concerning*, or, *from*) Jesus Christ."
b Literally, "in Asia."
c Literally, "the seven spirits." But see Isaiah 11:2, where various aspects of the Holy Spirit are described, and Zechariah 4:2-6, giving probability to the paraphrase; also see Revelation 2:7.
d Literally, "the First-born from the dead." Others (Lazarus, etc.) rose to die again. As used here the expression therefore implies "to die no more."
e John saw this happen with his own eyes—the piercing of Jesus—and never forgot the horror of it.
f Literally, "I am Alpha and Omega"; these are the first and last letters of the Greek alphabet.
g Literally, "who comes" or "who is to come."
h "The seven churches in Asia."
i Literally, "like unto a Son of Man"; John recognizes him from having lived with him for three years, and from seeing him in glory at the Transfiguration.
j Literally, "His head—the hair—was white like wool."
k Literally, "coming out from his mouth."
l Literally, "angels." Some expositors (Origen, Jerome, etc.) believe from this that an angelic being is appointed by God to oversee each local church.

**ch. 2:**

a Literally, "angel," as in 1:20.
b Literally, "from him who holds the seven stars in his right hand and walks aong the golden candlesticks."
c Nicolaitans, when translated from Greek to Hebrew, becomes Balaamites; followers of the man who induced the Israelites to fall by lust. (See Revelation 2:14 and Numbers 31:15,16.)
d Literally, "angel" See note on 1:20.
e Implied.
f Literally, "Nicolaitans," Greek form of "Balaamites."
g Literally, "together with all those who commit adultery with her."

**ch. 3:**

a Literally, "angel." See note on 1:20.
b Literally, "the seven spirits of God." See note on 1:4.
c Literally, "you have kept my word."
d Literally, "say they are Jews but are not."
e Or, "I will keep you from failing in the hour of testing..." The inference is not clear in the Greek as to whether this means "kept from" or "kept through" the coming horror.
f Or, "suddenly," "unexpectedly."
g Literally, "from the Amen."
h Implied.

**ch. 4:**

a Literally, "the seven spirits of God." But see Zechariah 4:2-6, where the lamps are equated with the one Spirit.

**ch. 5:**

a Implied.
b Literally, "the seven spirits of God"; but see Zechariah 4:2-6,10, where the seven eyes are equated with the seven lamps and the one Spirit.
c Literally, "saying" or "said."
d Literally, "saying" or "said."

**ch. 6:**

a Literally, "A choenix of wheat for a denarius, and three choenix of barley for a denarius...."
b Literally, "do not damage the oil and wine."
c Literally, "the stars of heaven fell to the earth."
d Literally, "the sky departed."

**ch. 7:**

a Literally, "in the center of the throne"; i.e., directly in front, not to one side. An alternate rendering might be, "at the heart of the throne."

**ch. 8:**

a Literally, "became blood."
b Literally, "Wormwood."

**ch. 9:**

a Literally, "a star fallen from heaven"; it is unclear whether this person is of satanic origin, as most commentators believe, or whether the reference is to Christ.
b Implied.
c Literally, "(fallen) angels."
d If this is a literal figure, it is no longer incredible, in view of a world population of 6,000,000,000 in the near future. In China alone, in 1961, there were an "estimated 200,000,000 armed and organized militiamen" (Associated Press Release, April 24, 1964).
e Literally, "horsemen."

**ch. 11:**

a Literally, "Rise and measure the temple of God, and the altar, and them that worship therein."

b 3½ years, as in Daniel 12:7.
c Zechariah 4:3,4,11.
d Revelation 9:11.
e Or, "The Lord and his Anointed shall now rule the world *from* this day to eternity."

**ch. 12:**

a Literally, "a time and times and half a time."

**ch. 13:**

a Literally, "It was permitted to fight against God's people."
b Or. "those whose names were not written in the Book of Life of the Lamb slain before the founding of the world." That is, regarded as slain in the eternal plan and knowledge of God.
c Or, "If anyone imprisons you, he will be imprisoned! If anyone kills you, he will be killed!"
d Some manuscripts read "616."

**ch. 14:**

a Literally, "They have not defiled themselves with women, for they are virgins."
b Implied.
c Literally, "those who die in the faith of Jesus." Verse 12 implies death from persecution for Christ's sake.
d Literally, "one like a Son of Man."
e Literally, "who has power over fire."

**ch. 15:**

a Some manuscripts read, "King of the Nations."

**ch. 16:**

a Literally, "I heard the altar cry...."
b Implied.
c Described in 13:11-15 and 19:20.
d Literally, "It has happened." An epoch of human history has come to an end.

**ch. 17**

a The Dragon—Satan—and the Creature from the sea are also described in 12:3,9 and 13:l.
b Literally, "go to perdition."
c Literally, "dumbfounded at the ruler who was, and is not, and will be present."
d Implied in verse 18.

**ch. 18:**

a Literally, "of every foul and hateful bird."
b Literally, "have committed fornication with her."
c Literally, "harpers...pipers...and trumpeters."

**ch. 19:**

a Literally, "fornication," the word used symbolically through the prophets for the worship of false gods.
b Literally, "he"; the exact antecedent is unclear.
c Literally, "These are the true words of God."
d Literally, "The testimony of Jesus is the spirit of prophecy."
e Implied.
f Literally, "The Logos," as in John 1:1—the ultimate method of God's revealing himself to man.
g See chapter 13, verses 11-16.

**ch. 20:**

a Implied.
b Implied: Revelation 20:3.
c Literally, "There was no longer any place for them."

**ch. 21:**

a Some manuscripts add, "and be their God."
b Literally, "144 cubits by human measurements." A cubit was the average length of a man's arm—not an angel's! The angel used normal units of measurement that John could understand.
c Implied.
d Literally, "are its temple."

**ch. 22:**

a Literally, "the tree of life"—used here as a collective noun, implying plurality.
b Or, "suddenly," "unexpectedly."